W9-BTM-773

Economic
Development

The Addison-Wesley Series in Economics

Abel/Bernanke
Macroeconomics

Bade/Parkin
Foundations of Economics

Bierman/Fernandez
Game Theory with Economic Applications

Binger/Hoffman
Microeconomics with Calculus

Boyer
Principles of Transportation Economics

Branson
Macroeconomic Theory and Policy

Bruce
Public Finance and the American Economy

Byrns/Stone
Economics

Carlton/Perloff
Modern Industrial Organization

Caves/Frankel/Jones
World Trade and Payments

Chapman
Environmental Economics: Theory, Application, and Policy

Cooter/Ulen
Law and Economics

Downs
An Economic Theory of Democracy

Ehrenberg/Smith
Modern Labor Economics

Ekelund/Ressler/Tollison
Economics

Fusfeld
The Age of the Economist

Gerber
International Economics

Ghiara
Learning Economics

Gordon
Macroeconomics

Gregory
Essentials of Economics

Gregory/Stuart
Russian and Soviet Economic Performance and Structure

Hartwick/Olewiler
The Economics of Natural Resource Use

Hoffman/Averett
Women and the Economy

Hubbard
Money, the Financial System, and the Economy

Hughes/Cain
American Economic History

Husted/Melvin
International Economics

Jehle/Reny
Advanced Microeconomic Theory

Johnson-Lans
A Health Care Economics Primer

Klein
Mathematical Methods for Economics

Krugman/Obstfeld
International Economics

Laidler
The Demand for Money

Leeds/von Allmen
The Economics of Sports

Leeds/von Allmen/Schiming
Economics

Lipsey/Courant/Ragan
Economics

Melvin
International Money and Finance

Miller
Economics Today

Miller/Benjamin/North
The Economics of Public Issues

Miller/Benjamin
The Economics of Macro Issues

Mills/Hamilton
Urban Economics

Mishkin
The Economics of Money, Banking, and Financial Markets

Murray
Econometrics

Parkin
Economics

Perloff
Microeconomics

Phelps
Health Economics

Riddell/Shackelford/Stamos/Schneider
Economics: A Tool for Critically Understanding Society

Ritter/Silber/Udell
Principles of Money, Banking, and Financial Markets

Rohlf
Introduction to Economic Reasoning

Ruffin/Gregory
Principles of Economics

Sargent
Rational Expectations and Inflation

Scherer
Industry Structure, Strategy, and Public Policy

Stock/Watson
Introduction to Econometrics

Studenmund
Using Econometrics

Tietenberg
Environmental and Natural Resource Economics

Tietenberg
Environmental Economics and Policy

Todaro/Smith
Economic Development

Waldman
Microeconomics

Waldman/Jensen
Industrial Organization

Weil
Economic Growth

Williamson
Macroeconomics

Economic Development

NINTH EDITION

Michael P. Todaro

New York University and the Population Council

Stephen C. Smith

The George Washington University

PEARSON
Addison
Wesley

Boston San Francisco New York
London Toronto Sydney Tokyo Singapore Madrid
Mexico City Munich Paris Cape Town Hong Kong Montreal

Vice President and Editorial Director: Daryl Fox
Editor in Chief: Denise Clinton
Acquisitions Editor: Roxanne Hoch
Director of Development: Sylvia Mallory
Assistant Development Editor: Amy Fleischer
Senior Production Supervisor: Meredith Gertz
Supplements Editor: Kirsten Dickerson
Executive Marketing Manager: Stephen Frail
Design Manager: Regina Hagen Kolenda
Associate Media Producer: Bridget Page
Senior Manufacturing Buyer: Carol Melville
Project Coordination, Text Design, and Electronic Page Makeup: Nesbitt Graphics, Inc.
Cover Designer: Rebecca Light

Cover Images: © The World Bank Group, age fotostock, Index Stock Imagery, SuperStock, Inc., and NASA
About the Cover: The image on the back cover is a composite of hundreds of photos of the Earth at night taken by satellite. Human-made lights show highly developed or populated regions, particularly the seacoasts of Europe, the eastern United States, and Japan. Despite its middle-income status, Eastern China also shows up clearly, because of its high-population density. The same may be said for India, which is a low-income country, but with high-population density. Africa, the poorest region, is relatively dark. Middle-income areas of very low-population density such as the central parts of South America and Asia are also dark. As the map suggests much economic activity is located on rivers or seacoasts so that economies can exchange goods utilizing low-cost shipping. Note that the per capita use of lighting parallels the overall use of electric power and other resources. Thus, the image also provides a vivid picture of the extraordinarily unequal distribution of resource use among high-, middle-, and low-income countries.

Library of Congress Cataloging-in-Publication Data

Todaro, Michael P.
  Economic development / Michael P. Todaro, Stephen C. Smith.— 9th ed.
     p. cm. — (The Addison-Wesley series in economics)
  Includes bibliographical references and index.
  ISBN 0-321-27888-7
     1. Economic development. 2. Developing countries—Economic policy. I. Smith, Stephen C., 1955- II. Title. III. Series.

HD82.T552 2006
338.9'009172'4—dc22

2005011342

Copyright © 2006 by Michael P. Todaro and Stephen C. Smith

All rights reserved. No part of this publication may be reproduced, stored in a retrieval system, or transmitted, in any form or by any means, without the prior written permission of the publisher. Printed in the United States of America.

2 3 4 5 6 7 8 9 10—CRW—09 08 07 06 05

For Donna Renée

and

For Renee, Martin, and Helena

Preface

Economic Development, Ninth Edition, marries the latest thinking in development economics with the clear and comprehensive approach that has been so well received in previous editions. The text places the established themes of early editions into today's global setting, and introduces current topics such as the Millennium Development Goals, complementarities and coordination failure, industrialization strategy, new strategies for poverty reduction, the capabilities approach to well-being, the central role of health, new thinking on the role of cities, and the economic character and comparative advantage of nongovernmental organizations in economic development. This book also emphasizes the international context for development, including the implications of the rapid pace of globalization and the rise of China, the continuing crisis of sub-Saharan Africa, and the conflict over funding for debt relief and poverty reduction. We have entirely rewritten the end-of-chapter analytical case studies for this edition; most cover new topics and each case builds on and illustrates the central topics of the chapter. While there is legitimate disagreement about which topics in economic development deserve the greatest emphasis, we have structured the presentation of the text so as to provide instructors with considerable leeway in selecting lecture topics.

Audience

This book is designed for use in courses that focus on the economics of development in Africa, Asia, and Latin America, as well as the "transition" countries of Eastern Europe and the former Soviet Union now classified as developing countries. It is written for students who have had some basic training in economics and for those with little or no formal economics background. Essential principles of economics that are relevant to understanding development problems are highlighted in boldface and explained at appropriate points throughout the text. They are also defined in a detailed glossary. Thus the book should be of special value in undergraduate development courses that attract students from a variety of disciplines. Yet the material is sufficiently broad in scope and rigorous in coverage to satisfy any undergraduate and some graduate economics requirements in the field of development.

Approach

Economic Development originally resulted from Professor Todaro's five years of living and teaching in Africa as well as two decades of extensive travel throughout Latin America and Asia, first as a director of the Rockefeller Foundation and then as a professor of economics at New York University. These experiences have helped shape and refine a book that is unique among development texts in approach, organization, and pedagogy. Among its most significant innovations are the following:

1. It teaches economic development within the context of a *major set of problems,* such as poverty, inequality, population growth, environmental decay, and rural stagnation. Formal abstract models and concepts are used to elucidate real-world development problems rather than being presented in isolation from these problems.

2. It adopts a *problem- and policy-oriented approach* because a central objective of the development economics course is to foster a student's ability to understand contemporary economic problems of developing countries and to reach independent and informed judgments and policy conclusions about their possible resolution.

3. It simultaneously uses the *best available cross-sectional data* from Africa, Asia, and Latin America and *appropriate theoretical tools* to illuminate common developing country problems. Although these problems will differ in both scope and magnitude when we deal with such diverse countries as India, Bangladesh, Kenya, Egypt, Nigeria, Brazil, Mexico, and Guatemala, the fact remains that most face similar development problems: widespread poverty and large income and asset inequalities, rapid population growth, low levels of literacy and health, high levels of urban unemployment and underemployment, and chronic balance of payments and foreign-debt burdens, to name a few.

4. It focuses on a wide range of developing countries not only as *independent nation-states* but also in relation to one another and in their *interactions with rich nations in a global economy.*

5. It recognizes the necessity of treating the problems of development and underdevelopment from an *institutional* and *structural* as well as a market perspective, with appropriate modifications of received general economic principles, theories, and policies. It thus attempts to combine relevant theory with realistic institutional analyses.

6. It views development and underdevelopment in both domestic and international contexts, stressing the *increasing interdependence of the world economy* in areas such as food, energy, natural resources, technology, information, and financial flows.

7. It considers the economic, social, and institutional problems of underdevelopment as closely interrelated and requiring *coordinated approaches* to their solution at local, national, and international levels.

Organization and Orientation

The book is organized into three parts. Part One focuses on the nature and meaning of development and underdevelopment and its various manifestations in developing nations. After examining the historical growth experience of now developed countries, and ascertaining the degree to which this experience is relevant to contemporary developing nations, we review four classic theories of development and examine recent development models.

Parts Two and Three focus on major development problems and policies, both domestic and international. Topics of analysis include economic growth, poverty and income distribution, population, migration, urbanization, technology, agricultural and rural development, the environment, education, health, international trade and finance, problems of high debt burdens, foreign aid, private foreign investment, and the roles of market, state, and nongovernmental organizations in economic development. The book concludes with a look ahead at key emerging issues in economic development.

All three parts of the book ask fundamental questions: What kind of development is most desirable? How can developing nations best achieve these economic and social objectives either individually or, better, in cooperation with one another and, it is to be hoped, with appropriate and meaningful assistance from the more developed countries of the world?

Case Studies

In order to provide students with up-to-date case study materials, there are 16 in-depth *case studies*, which appear at the ends of chapters. Each chapter's case study reflects and illustrates the specific problem analyzed in that chapter.

We have completely redesigned the format of the case studies for this edition. We have removed the general country cases because such background material is now readily available from the Internet and other sources. Instead, each case spotlights one or more of the issues raised in the foregoing chapter. Two of the comparative case studies from the previous edition, "Schools of Thought in Context: Argentina and South Korea" and "Privatization and Financial Reform: China and Poland," have been retained and updated for Chapters 3 and 16, respectively. Six case studies were adapted and updated from an earlier companion volume, *Case Studies in Economic Development*. The remainder of the case studies are new to the text. Overall, six of the cases compare key features of two countries, while ten focus on a key development issue in one country.

New to the Ninth Edition

The book is now divided into three parts, instead of four: Part One, "Principles and Concepts"; Part Two, "Problems and Policies: Domestic"; and Part Three, "Problems and Policies: International and Macro." Chapters 2 and 3 from the Eighth

Edition have been combined into a new Chapter 2, "Comparative Development: Differences and Commonalities among Developing Countries." The most recent data and information have been incorporated in the tables and text.

In Chapter 1, we have added coverage of the Millennium Development Goals, which have become the benchmark for the work of all major development organizations. We have retained the material on Amartya Sen's capabilities approach that we introduced in the Eighth Edition. Chapter 1 concludes with a case study on Brazil, which we have rewritten to explore more directly the chapter's theme of the meaning of development.

The new title of Chapter 2, "Comparative Development: Differences and Commonalities among Developing Countries," reflects that this chapter is a combination of Chapters 2 and 3 from the previous edition. A new case study, "Divergent Development: Pakistan and Bangladesh," further probes into the meaning of development and offers perspectives on comparative development. Chapter 3, "Classic Theories of Economic Development," appeared as Chapter 4 in the previous edition. The popular comparative case study on South Korea and Argentina from previous editions has been retained and placed at the end of this chapter.

Chapter 4 is "Contemporary Models of Development and Underdevelopment." This chapter was entirely new to the Eighth Edition (where it appeared as Chapter 5), and it has proved very popular with instructors. However, it is possible to omit this chapter from a course syllabus. We have added an entirely new case study, "Understanding a Development Miracle: China."

Part Two addresses "Problems and Policies: Domestic." Chapter 5, "Poverty, Inequality, and Development" (formerly Chapter 6), features the case study "Making Microfinance Work for the Poor: The Grameen Bank of Bangladesh," which considers the role of microfinance in poverty alleviation and examines in depth the well-known case of Grameen.

At the end of Chapter 6, "Population Growth and Economic Development: Causes, Consequences, and Controversies," a new case study, "Population, Poverty, and Development: China and India," surveys alternative family planning policies and their potential links to development outcomes. The Indian state of Kerala is featured.

In Chapter 7, "Urbanization and Rural-Urban Migration: Theory and Policy," the case study "Rural-Urban Migration and Urbanization in Developing Countries: India and Botswana" was adapted and updated from *Case Studies in Economic Development*. The expanded coverage of the role of cities in economic development, introduced in the Eighth Edition, has been updated.

Chapter 8, "Human Capital: Education and Health in Economic Development," was largely new to the Eighth Edition. The chapter retains its integrated presentation of human capital by stressing the relationships between investments in health and education. The case study "AIDS—Economic Development Impact and the Needed Response: Uganda and South Africa" adapts and updates some material on AIDS in Uganda from *Case Studies in Economic Development* and also introduces new comparative material on AIDS in South Africa.

In Chapter 9, "Agricultural Transformation and Rural Development," we have expanded the coverage of new research on rural development economics and the green revolution. The case study "Improving Agricultural Extension for Women Farmers: Kenya" was adapted and updated from *Case Studies in Economic Development.*

Chapter 10, "The Environment and Development," features a special case study, "Economic Growth and Environmental Sustainability: The Philippines." It is guest-authored by a scholar and practitioner on the subject, Professor Elizabeth Remedio of the University of San Carlos, the Philippines.

Chapter 11, formerly Chapter 16, is now called "Development Policymaking and the Roles of Market, State, and Civil Society." As the modified title suggests, we now give extended coverage of the nature of nongovernmental organizations and their role in development in relation to government and private sectors. This material is entirely new to this edition.

Part Three addresses "Problems and Policies: International and Macro." New case studies for Chapters 12 and 13 look at two countries, Taiwan and South Korea, that experienced growth and development as a result of taking advantage of opportunities offered by international trade. These two countries were the subjects of the case studies for these chapters in the Eighth Edition, but for this edition the cases were adapted and updated from two chapters in *Case Studies in Economic Development.*

In Chapter 14, "Balance of Payments, Developing-Country Debt, and the Macroeconomic Stabilization Controversy," there is expanded coverage of debt problems of low-income countries, especially in Africa. The case study examines the historical origins and subsequent approaches to resolution of the 1980s debt crisis in Mexico.

In Chapter 15, an entirely new case study examines the sources of Botswana's success. Chapter 16, "Finance and Fiscal Policy for Development," concludes with a case study, "Chile and Poland: Privatization: What, When, and to Whom?" based on the last comparative case study from the Eighth Edition.

Finally, in Chapter 17, we take a further look ahead at three key emerging issues in economic development: looming environmental problems, the crisis in sub-Saharan Africa, and globalization and issues in financial market reform.

Supplementary Materials

The Ninth Edition comes with a comprehensive companion website with content by Abbas Grammy of California State University, Bakersfield. Available at http://www.aw-bc.com/todaro_smith, this site offers an online Student Study Guide for each chapter that includes multiple-choice quizzes and sets of graphing and quantitative exercises. In addition, Internet exercises allow students to explore the countries highlighted in the country case studies in more depth. A Recommended Readings section provides links to and questions about additional development resources.

The Web site also links to material for the instructor, including PowerPoint slides for each chapter, which have been updated for this edition by Meenakshi Rishi of Ohio Northern University.

The text is further supplemented with an Instructor's Manual by Andreas Savvides of Oklahoma State University. It has been thoroughly revised and updated to reflect changes to the Ninth Edition.

Acknowledgments

Our indebtedness and gratitude to the many individuals who have helped shape this new edition cannot adequately be conveyed in a few sentences. However, we must record our immense indebtedness to the hundreds of former students and contemporary colleagues who took the time and trouble during the past three years to write or speak to us about the ways in which this text could be further improved. We are indebted to a great number of friends (far too many to mention individually) in both the developing world and the developed world who have directly and indirectly helped shape our ideas about development economics and how an economic development text should be structured. Professor Todaro would like to thank his former students in Africa and the United States and colleagues in Latin America and Asia, for their probing and challenging questions; two good friends and colleagues, Edgar O. Edwards and Lloyd G. Reynolds, who were particularly helpful at an earlier stage; and Kenneth W. Thompson, a close friend and in many ways a mentor in the field on international relations, who indirectly provided much of the inspiration for this book. The Compton Foundation once again supported Professor Todaro's research in the fields of population, human resources, and the environment, which is gratefully acknowledged.

We are also very appreciative of the advice, criticisms, and suggestions of the many reviewers, both in the United States and abroad, who provided detailed and insightful comments for the Eighth and Ninth Editions:

U.S. Reviewers

Valerie R. Bencivenga, UNIVERSITY OF TEXAS, AUSTIN

Sylvain H. Boko, WAKE FOREST UNIVERSITY

Milica Z. Bookman, ST. JOSEPH'S UNIVERSITY

Fernando De Paolis, MONTEREY INSTITUTE

Luc D'Haese, UNIVERSITY OF GHENT

Abbas P. Grammy, CALIFORNIA STATE UNIVERSITY, BAKERSFIELD

Bradley Hansen, MARY WASHINGTON COLLEGE

Seid Hassan, MURRAY STATE UNIVERSITY

Jeffrey James, TILBURG UNIVERSITY

Barbara John, UNIVERSITY OF DAYTON

John McPeak, SYRACUSE UNIVERSITY

Michael A. McPherson, UNIVERSITY OF NORTH TEXAS

Daniel L. Millimet, SOUTHERN METHODIST UNIVERSITY

Elliott Parker, UNIVERSITY OF NEVADA, RENO

Julia Paxton, OHIO UNIVERSITY
Meenakshi Rishi, OHIO NORTHERN UNIVERSITY
James Robinson, UNIVERSITY OF CALIFORNIA, BERKELEY
Andreas Savvides, OKLAHOMA STATE UNIVERSITY
Rodrigo R. Soares, UNIVERSITY OF MARYLAND
Michael Twomey, UNIVERSITY OF MICHIGAN, DEARBORN
Nora Underwood, UNIVERSITY OF CALIFORNIA, DAVIS
Adel Varghese, ST. LOUIS UNIVERSITY
Jonathan B. Wight, UNIVERSITY OF RICHMOND
Lester A. Zeager, EAST CAROLINA UNIVERSITY

U.K. Reviewers

Arild Angelsen, AGRICULTURAL UNIVERSITY OF NORWAY
Bernard Carolan, UNIVERSITY OF STAFFORDSHIRE
Alex Cunliffe, UNIVERSITY OF PLYMOUTH
Chris Dent, UNIVERSITY OF HULL
Sanjit Dhami, UNIVERSITY OF NEWCASTLE
Diana Hunt, SUSSEX UNIVERSITY
Colin Simmons, UNIVERSITY OF SALFORD
Pritam Singh, OXFORD BROOKES UNIVERSITY
Shinder Thandi, UNIVERSITY OF COVENTRY
Paul Vandenberg, UNIVERSITY OF BRISTOL

Their input has strengthened the book in many ways and has been much appreciated. Our thanks also go to the staff at Addison-Wesley in both the United States and the United Kingdom, particularly Amy Fleischer, Sylvia Mallory, Meredith Gertz, Denise Clinton, Paula Harris, and Claire Brewer.

Finally, to his lovely wife, Donna Renée, Michael Todaro wishes to express great thanks for typing the entire first-edition manuscript and for providing the spiritual and intellectual inspiration to persevere under difficult circumstances. He reaffirms here his eternal devotion to her for always being there to help him maintain a proper perspective on life and living, and through her own creative and artistic talents, to inspire him to think in original and sometimes unconventional ways about the global problems of human development.

Stephen Smith would like to thank his wonderful wife, Renee, and his children, Martin and Helena, for putting up with the many working Saturdays that went into the revision of this text.

Michael P. Todaro
Stephen C. Smith

Contents

Part One   Principles and Concepts

Part Three Problems and Policies: International and Macro

12 Trade Theory and Development Experience   577

Case Studies

Principles and Concepts

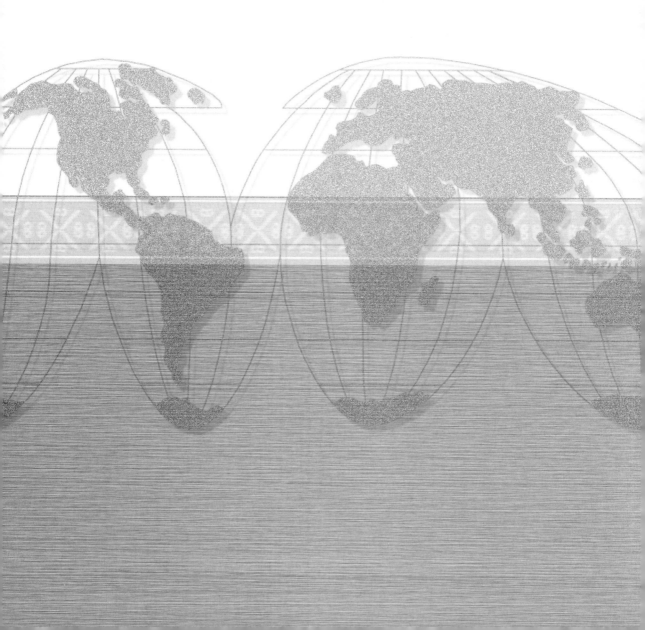

CHAPTER ONE

Economics, Institutions, and Development: A Global Perspective

We have a collective responsibility to uphold the principles of human dignity, equality and equity at the global level. As leaders we have a duty therefore to all the world's people, especially the most vulnerable and, in particular, the children of the world, to whom the future belongs.

—UNITED NATIONS, *Millennium Declaration*, September 8, 2000, signed by the 189 UN member countries

What is the meaning of growth if it is not translated into the lives of people?
—UNITED NATIONS Development Program, *Human Development Report, 1995*

Our primary goal in development must be to reduce the disparities across and within countries . . . . The key development challenge of our time is the challenge of inclusion.
—JAMES D. WOLFENSOHN, President, World Bank

How the Other Half Live

As people throughout the world awake each morning to face a new day, they do so under very different circumstances. Some live in comfortable homes with many rooms. They have more than enough to eat, are well clothed and healthy, and have a reasonable degree of financial security. Others, and these constitute a majority of the earth's 6.4 billion people, are much less fortunate. They may have little or no shelter and an inadequate food supply, especially if they are among the poorest third. Their health is poor, they may not know how to read or write, they may be unemployed, and their prospects for a better life are uncertain at best. Nearly half the world's population lives on less than $2 per day. An examination of these global differences in living standards is revealing.

If, for example, we looked first at an average family in North America, we would probably find a "nuclear" family of four with an annual income of approximately $50,000. They would live in a comfortable suburban house with a small garden and two cars. The dwelling would have many comfortable features, including a separate bedroom for each of the two children. It would be filled with numerous

3

consumer goods and electrical appliances, many of which were manufactured outside North America in countries as far away as South Korea, Argentina, and China. Examples might include computer hard disks made in Malaysia, DVD players manufactured in Thailand, garments assembled in Guatemala, and mountain bikes made in China. There would always be three meals a day and plenty of processed snack foods, and many of the food products would also be imported from overseas: coffee from Brazil, Kenya, or Colombia; canned fish and fruit from Peru and Australia; and bananas and other tropical fruits from Central America. Both children would be healthy and attending school. They could expect to complete their secondary education and probably go to a university, choose from a variety of careers to which they are attracted, and live to an average age of 78 years.

This family, which is typical of families in many rich nations, appears to have a reasonably good life. The parents have the opportunity and the necessary education or training to secure regular employment; to shelter, clothe, feed, and educate their children; and to save some money for later life. Against these "economic" benefits, there are always "noneconomic" costs. The competitive pressures to "succeed" financially are very strong, and during inflationary or recessionary times, the mental strain and physical pressure of trying to provide for a family at levels that the community regards as desirable can take its toll on the health of both parents. Their ability to relax, to enjoy the simple pleasures of a country stroll, to breathe clean air and drink pure water, and to see a crimson sunset is constantly at risk with the onslaught of economic progress and environmental decay. But on the whole, theirs is an economic status and lifestyle toward which many millions of less fortunate people throughout the world seem to be aspiring.

Now let us examine a typical "extended" family in a poor rural area of Asia. The household is likely to comprise eight or more people, including parents, several children, two grandparents, and some aunts and uncles. They have a combined per capita annual income, in money and in "kind" (meaning that they consume a share of the food they grow), of $250 to $300. Together they live in a poorly constructed one- or two-room house as tenant farmers on a large agricultural estate owned by an absentee landlord who lives in the nearby city. The father, mother, uncle, and older children must work all day on the land. None of the adults can read or write; the younger children attend school irregularly and cannot expect to proceed beyond a basic primary education. All too often, when they do get to school, the teacher is absent. There is often only one meal a day; it rarely changes, and it is rarely sufficient to alleviate the children's persistent hunger pains. The house has no electricity, sanitation, or fresh water supply. There is much sickness, but qualified doctors and medical practitioners are far away in the cities, attending to the needs of wealthier families. The work is hard, the sun is hot, and aspirations for a better life are continually being snuffed out. In this part of the world, the only relief from the daily struggle for physical survival lies in the spiritual traditions of the people.

Shifting to another part of the world, suppose we were to visit a large city situated along the coast of South America. We would immediately be struck by the sharp contrasts in living conditions from one section of this sprawling metropolis to another. There is a modern stretch of tall buildings and wide, tree-lined boulevards along the edge of a gleaming white beach; just a few hundred meters back and up the side of a steep hill, squalid shanties are pressed together in precarious balance.

If we were to examine two representative families—one a wealthy family from the local ruling class and the other of peasant background—we would no doubt also be struck by the wide disparities in their individual living conditions. The wealthy family lives in a multiroom complex on the top floor of a modern building overlooking the sea, while the peasant family is cramped tightly into a small makeshift shack in a shantytown, or *favela* (a squatters' slum) on the hill behind that seafront building.

For illustrative purposes, let us assume that it is a typical Saturday evening at an hour when the families should be preparing for dinner. In the penthouse apartment of the wealthy family, a servant is setting the table with expensive imported china, high-quality silverware, and fine linen. Russian caviar, French hors d'oeuvres, and Italian wine will constitute the first of several courses. The family's eldest son is home from his university in North America, and the other two children are on vacation from their boarding schools in France and Switzerland. The father is a prominent surgeon trained in the United States. His clientele consists of wealthy local and foreign dignitaries and businesspeople. In addition to his practice, he owns a considerable amount of land in the countryside. Annual vacations abroad, imported luxury automobiles, and the finest food and clothing are commonplace amenities for this fortunate family in the penthouse apartment.

And what about the poor family living in the dirt-floored shack on the side of the hill? They too can view the sea, but somehow it seems neither scenic nor relaxing. The stench of open sewers makes such enjoyment rather remote. There is no dinner table being set; in fact, there is no dinner—only a few scraps of stale bread. Most of the four children spend their time out on the streets begging for money, shining shoes, or occasionally even trying to steal purses from unsuspecting people who stroll along the boulevard. Violence from drug gang warfare is a constant threat. The father migrated to the city from the rural hinterland a few years ago, and the rest of the family recently followed. He has had part-time jobs over the years, but nothing permanent. The family income is less than $800 per year. The children have been in and out of school many times, as they have to help out financially in any way they can. Occasionally the eldest teenage daughter, who lives with friends across town, seems to have some extra money—but no one ever asks where it comes from or how it is obtained.

One could easily be disturbed by the sharp contrast between these two ways of life. However, had we looked at almost any other major city in Latin America, Asia, and Africa, we would have seen much the same contrast (although the extent of inequality might have been less pronounced).

As a final aspect of this brief view of living conditions around the world, imagine that you are in a remote rural area in the eastern part of Africa, where many small clusters of tiny huts dot a dry and barren land. Each cluster contains a group of extended families, all participating in and sharing the work. There is little money income here because most food, clothing, shelter, and worldly goods are made and consumed by the people themselves—theirs is a **subsistence economy**. There are few passable roads and no schools, hospitals, electric wires, or water supplies; life here seems to be much as it has been for thousands of years. In many respects it is as stark and difficult an existence as that of the people in that Latin American *favela* across the ocean. Yet perhaps it is not as psychologically troubling because there is no luxurious penthouse by the sea to emphasize the relative deprivation of the very poor. Life here seems to be eternal and unchanging—but not for much longer.

One hundred kilometers away, a new road is being built that will pass near this village. No doubt it will bring with it the means for prolonging life through improved medical care. But it will also bring information about the world outside, along with the gadgets of modern civilization. The possibilities of a "better" life will be promoted, and the opportunities for such a life will become feasible. Aspirations will be raised, but so will frustrations. In short, the **development** process will have been set in motion.

Before long, exportable fruits and vegetables will probably be grown in this now sparsely settled region. They may even end up on the dinner table of the rich South American family in the seaside penthouse. Meanwhile, transistor radios made in Southeast Asia and playing music recorded in northern Europe have become prized possessions in this African village. Throughout the world, remote subsistence villages such as this one are inexorably being linked up with modern civilization in an increasing number of ways. The process is now well under way and will become even more intensified in the coming years.

Listening to the poor explain what poverty is like in their own words is more vivid than reading descriptions of it. Listen to some of the voices of the poor about the experience of poverty in Box 1.1.[1]

This first fleeting glimpse at life in different parts of our planet is sufficient to raise various questions. Why does affluence coexist with dire poverty not only across different continents but also within the same country or even the same city? Can traditional, low-productivity, subsistence societies be transformed into modern, high-productivity, high-income nations? To what extent are the development aspirations of poor nations helped or hindered by the economic activities of rich nations? By what process and under what conditions do rural subsistence farmers in the remote regions of Nigeria, Brazil, or the Philippines evolve into successful commercial farmers? These and many other questions concerning international and national differences in standards of living, in areas including health and nutrition, education, employment, population growth, and life expectancies, might be posed on the basis of even this very superficial look at life around the world.

This book is designed to help students obtain a better understanding of the major problems and prospects for economic development by focusing specifically on the plight of the half or more of the world's population for whom low levels of living are a fact of life. However, as we shall soon discover, the process in **developing countries** cannot be analyzed realistically without also considering the role of economically developed nations in directly or indirectly promoting or retarding

---

BOX 1.1   **The Experience of Poverty: Voices of the Poor**

When one is poor, she has no say in public, she feels inferior. She has no food, so there is famine in her house; no clothing, and no progress in her family.

—A poor woman from Uganda

For a poor person everything is terrible—illness, humiliation, shame. We are cripples; we are afraid of everything; we depend on everyone. No one needs us. We are like garbage that everyone wants to get rid of.

—A blind woman from Tiraspol, Moldova

Life in the area is so precarious that the youth and every able person have to migrate to the towns or join the army at the war front in order to escape the hazards of hunger escalating over here.

—Participant in a discussion group in rural Ethiopia

When food was in abundance, relatives used to share it. These days of hunger, however, not even relatives would help you by giving you some food.

—Young man in Nichimishi, Zambia

We have to line up for hours before it is our turn to draw water.

—Participant in a discussion group from Mbwadzulu Village (Mangochi), Malawi

[Poverty is] . . . low salaries and lack of jobs. And it's also not having medicine, food, and clothes.

—Participant in a discussion group in Brazil

Don't ask me what poverty is because you have met it outside my house. Look at the house and count the number of holes. Look at the utensils and the clothes I am wearing. Look at everything and write what you see. What you see is poverty.

—Poor man in Kenya

---

that development.[2] Perhaps even more important to students in the developed nations is that as our earth shrinks with the spread of modern transport and communications, the futures of *all* peoples on this small planet are becoming increasingly interdependent. What happens to the health and economic welfare of the poor rural family and many others in Southeast Asia, Africa, the Middle East, or Latin America will in one way or another, directly or indirectly, affect the health and economic welfare of families in Europe and North America, and vice versa.

The steady loss of tropical forests contributes to global warming; new diseases spread much more rapidly; economic interdependence steadily grows. The hows and whys of this global economic interdependence will unfold in the remaining chapters. But it is within this context of a common future for all humankind in the rapidly shrinking world of the twenty-first century that we now commence our study of economic development.

Economics and Development Studies

The study of economic development is one of the newest, most exciting, and most challenging branches of the broader disciplines of economics and political economy. Although one could claim that Adam Smith was the first "development economist" and that his *Wealth of Nations*, published in 1776, was the first treatise on economic development, the systematic study of the problems and processes of economic development in Africa, Asia, and Latin America has emerged only over the past five decades. Yet there are some people who would still claim that development economics is not really a distinct branch of economics in the same sense as, say, macroeconomics, labor economics, public finance, or monetary economics. Rather, they would assert, it is simply an amalgamation and basically an unaltered application of all these traditional fields, but with a specific focus on the individual economies of Africa, Asia, and Latin America.[3]

We disagree with this viewpoint. Although development economics often draws on relevant principles and concepts from other branches of economics in either a standard or modified form, for the most part it is a field of study that is rapidly evolving its own distinctive analytical and methodological identity. Development economics is not the same as the economics of advanced capitalist nations (modern "neoclassical" economics). Nor is it similar to the economics of the formerly centralized socialist societies. It is nothing more or less than the economics of contemporary poor, underdeveloped nations with varying ideological orientations, diverse cultural backgrounds, and very complex yet similar economic problems that usually demand new ideas and novel approaches. Recent developments in theories of poverty traps and the role of institutions confirm this. The awarding of the 1979 Nobel Prize in economics to two eminent development economists, W. Arthur Lewis of Princeton University and Theodore Schultz of the University of Chicago, for their pioneering studies of the development process, provided dramatic confirmation of the status of economic development as a separate field within the economics discipline. Other Nobel laureates have also made major contributions to development economics, notably Amartya Sen, who won the prize in 1998, and Joseph Stiglitz, who won it in 2001. We begin, therefore, by contrasting modern development economics with "traditional" neoclassical economics. We then devote the bulk of this initial chapter to an analysis of the meaning of development. In Chapter 2 we look at the diverse structure and common characteristics in the historic growth and contemporary development of developing countries.

The Nature of Development Economics

Traditional economics is concerned primarily with the efficient, least-cost allocation of scarce productive resources and with the optimal growth of these resources over time so as to produce an ever-expanding range of goods and services. By traditional economics we simply mean the neoclassical economics taught in introductory textbooks. Traditional neoclassical economics deals with an advanced capitalist world of perfect markets; consumer sovereignty; automatic price adjustments; decisions made on the basis of marginal, private-profit, and utility calculations; and equilibrium outcomes in all product and resource markets. It assumes economic "rationality" and a purely materialistic, individualistic, self-interested orientation toward economic decision making.

Political economy goes beyond traditional economics to study, among other things, the social and institutional processes through which certain groups of economic and political elites influence the allocation of scarce productive resources now and in the future, either for their own benefit exclusively or for that of the larger population as well. Political economy is therefore concerned with the relationship between politics and economics, with a special emphasis on the role of power in economic decision making.

Development economics has an even greater scope. In addition to being concerned with the efficient allocation of existing scarce (or idle) productive resources and with their sustained growth over time, it must also deal with the *economic, social, political*, and *institutional* mechanisms, both public and private, necessary to bring about *rapid* (at least by historical standards) and *large-scale improvements* in levels of living for the peoples of Africa, Asia, Latin America, and the formerly socialist transition economies. Unlike the **more developed countries (MDCs)**, in the **less developed countries (LDCs)**, most commodity and resource markets are highly imperfect, consumers and producers have limited information, major structural changes are taking place in both the society and the economy, the potential for multiple equilibria rather than a single equilibrium are common, and disequilibrium situations often prevail (prices do not equate supply and demand). In many cases, economic calculations are dominated by political and social priorities such as unifying the nation, replacing foreign advisers with local decision makers, resolving tribal or ethnic conflicts, or preserving religious and cultural traditions. At the individual level, family, clan, religious, or tribal considerations may take precedence over private, self-interested utility or profit-maximizing calculations.

Thus development economics, to a greater extent than traditional neoclassical economics or even political economy, must be concerned with the economic, cultural, and political requirements for effecting rapid structural and institutional transformations of entire societies in a manner that will most efficiently bring the fruits of economic progress to the broadest segments of their populations. It must focus on the mechanisms that keep families, regions, and entire nations in poverty traps and on the most effective strategies for breaking out of these traps. Consequently, a larger government role and some degree of coordinated economic decision making directed toward transforming the economy are usually viewed as essential components of development economics. In recent years, activities of nongovernmental organizations, both national and international, have grown rapidly and are receiving increasing attention (see Chapter 11).

Because of the heterogeneity of the developing world and the complexity of the development process, development economics must be eclectic, attempting to combine relevant concepts and theories from traditional economic analysis along with new models and broader multidisciplinary approaches derived from studying the historical and contemporary development experience of Africa, Asia, and Latin America. Development economics is a field on the crest of a breaking wave, with new theories and new data constantly emerging. These theories and statistics sometimes confirm and sometimes challenge traditional ways of viewing the world. The ultimate purpose of development economics, however, remains unchanged: to help us better understand developing economies in order to help improve the material lives of the majority of the global population.

Why Study Development Economics? Some Critical Questions

An introductory course in development economics should help students gain a better understanding of a number of critical questions about the economies of developing nations. The following is a sample list of 24 such questions followed by the chapters (in parentheses) in which they are discussed. They illustrate the kinds of issues faced by almost every developing nation and, indeed, every development economist.

1. What is the real meaning of *development*, and how can different economic concepts and theories contribute to a better understanding of the development process? (Chapters 1, 3, and 4)

2. What can be learned from the historical record of economic progress in the now developed world? Are the initial conditions similar or different for contemporary LDCs from what the developed countries faced on the eve of their industrialization? (Chapter 2)

3. How can the extremes between rich and poor countries be so very great? Figure 1.1 illustrates this disparity. (Chapters 2, 3, 4, and 6)

4. What are the sources of national and international economic growth? Who benefits from such growth and why? Why do some countries make rapid progress toward development while many others remain poor? (Chapters 2, 3, and 4)

5. Which are the most influential theories of development, and are they compatible? Is underdevelopment an internally (domestically) or externally (internationally) induced phenomenon? (Chapters 3 and 4)

6. How can improvement in the role and status of women have an especially beneficial impact on development prospects? (Chapters 5, 6, 7, 8, 9, and 10)

FIGURE 1.1   The Rich and the Poor

The countries in black contain 15% of the world population but produce 50% of world gross domestic product (GDP). The countries in dark gray contain 50% of the world population but produce less than 15% of world GDP.

Source: William Easterly and Ross Levine, "It's not factor accumulation: Stylized facts and growth models," *World Bank Economic Review* 15 (2001): 177–219, page 199. Reprinted with permission.

7. What are the causes of extreme poverty, and what policies have been most effective for improving the lives of the poorest of the poor? (Chapters 5, 6, 7, 8, 9, 10, and 11)

8. Is rapid population growth threatening the economic progress of developing nations? Do large families make economic sense in an environment of widespread poverty and financial insecurity? (Chapter 6)

9. Why is there so much unemployment in the developing world, especially in the cities, and why do people continue to migrate to the cities from rural areas even though their chances of finding a job are very slim? (Chapter 7)

10. Wealthier societies are also healthier ones because they have more resources for improving nutrition and health care. But does better health also help spur successful development? (Chapter 8)

11. What is the impact of poor public health on the propects for development, and what is needed to address these problems? (Chapter 8)

12. Do educational systems in LDCs really promote economic development, or are they simply a mechanism to enable certain select groups or classes of people to maintain positions of wealth, power, and influence? (Chapter 8)

13. As 60% to 70% of many LDC populations still reside in rural areas, how can agricultural and rural development best be promoted? Are higher agricultural prices sufficient to stimulate food production, or are rural institutional changes (land redistribution, roads, transport, education, credit, etc.) also needed? (Chapter 9)

14. What do we mean by "environmentally sustainable development"? Are there serious economic costs of pursuing sustainable development as opposed to simple output growth, and who bears the major responsibility for global environmental damage—the rich North or the poor South? (Chapter 10)

15. Are free markets and economic privatization the answer to development problems, or do developing governments still have major roles to play in their economies? (Chapter 11)

16. Why do so many developing countries select such poor development policies, and what can be done to improve these choices? (Chapter 11)

17. Is expanded international trade desirable from the point of view of the development of poor nations? Who really gains from trade, and how are the advantages distributed among nations? (Chapter 12)

18. What is meant by **globalization**, and how is it affecting the developing countries? (Chapters 12 and 13)

19. Should exports of primary products such as agricultural commodities be promoted, or should all LDCs attempt to industrialize by developing their own manufacturing industries as rapidly as possible? (Chapter 13)

20. When and under what conditions should LDC governments adopt a policy of foreign-exchange control, raise tariffs, or set quotas on the importation of certain "nonessential" goods in order to promote their own industrialization or to ameliorate chronic balance of payments problems? What has been the impact of International Monetary Fund "stabilization programs" and World Bank "structural adjustment" lending on the balance of payments and growth prospects of heavily indebted LDCs? (Chapters 13 and 14)

21. How did developing nations get into such serious foreign-debt problems, and what are the implications of this debt for the economies of both less developed and more developed nations? (Chapter 14)

22. What is the impact of foreign economic aid from rich countries? Should developing countries continue to seek such aid, and if so, under what conditions and for what purposes? Should developed countries continue to offer such aid, and if so, under what conditions and for what purposes? (Chapter 15)

23. Should large and powerful multinational corporations be encouraged to invest in the economies of poor nations, and if so, under what conditions? How have the emergence of the "global factory" and the globalization of trade and finance influenced international economic relations? (Chapter 15)

24. What is the role of financial and fiscal policy in promoting development? Do large military expenditures stimulate or retard economic growth? (Chapter 16)

The following chapters analyze and explore these and many related questions. The answers are often more complex than one might think. Remember that the ultimate purpose of any course in economics, including development economics, is to help students think *systematically* about economic problems and issues and formulate judgments and conclusions on the basis of relevant analytical principles and reliable statistical information. Because the problems of development are in many cases unique in the modern world and not often easily understood through the use of traditional economic theories, we may often need unconventional approaches to what may appear to be conventional economic problems. Traditional economic principles can play a useful role in enabling us to improve our understanding of development problems, but they should not blind us to the realities of local conditions in less developed countries.

The Important Role of Values in Development Economics

Economics is a social science. It is concerned with human beings and the social systems by which they organize their activities to satisfy basic material needs (e.g., food, shelter, clothing) and nonmaterial wants (e.g., education, knowledge, spiritual fulfillment). Many economic models are based on a set of implicit assumptions about human behavior and economic relationships that may have little connection to the realities of developing economies. Economic investigations and analyses cannot simply be lifted out of their institutional, social, and political context, especially when one must deal with the human dilemmas of hunger, poverty, and ill health that plague so much of the world's population.

It is necessary to recognize from the outset that ethical or normative **value premises** about what is or is not desirable are central features of the economic discipline in general and of development economics in particular. The very concepts of economic development and modernization represent implicit as well as explicit value premises about desirable goals for achieving what Mahatma Gandhi once called the "realization of the human potential." Concepts or goals such as economic and social equality, the elimination of poverty, universal education, rising levels of living, national independence, modernization of institutions, political and economic participation, grassroots democracy, self-reliance, and personal fulfillment all derive from subjective value judgments about what is good and desirable and what is not. So too, for that matter, do other values—for example, the sanctity of private property, however acquired, and the right of individuals to accumulate unlimited personal wealth; the preservation of traditional hierarchical social institutions and rigid, inegalitarian class structures; and the supposed "natural right" of some to lead while others follow.

When we deal in Part Two with such major issues of development as poverty, inequality, unemployment, population growth, rural stagnation, and environmental decay, the mere identification of these topics as problems conveys the value judgment that their improvement or elimination is desirable and therefore good. That

increases. Development strategies have therefore usually focused on rapid indus-trialization, often at the expense of agriculture and rural development.

With few exceptions, such as in development policy circles in the 1970s, devel-opment was until recently nearly always seen as an economic phenomenon in which rapid gains in overall and per capita GNI growth would either "trickle down" to the masses in the form of jobs and other economic opportunities or create the necessary conditions for the wider distribution of the economic and social bene-fits of growth. Problems of poverty, discrimination, unemployment, and income distribution were of secondary importance to "getting the growth job done."

The New Economic View of Development

The experience of the 1950s and 1960s, when many developing nations did reach their economic growth targets but the levels of living of the masses of people re-mained for the most part unchanged, signaled that something was very wrong with this narrow definition of development. An increasing number of economists and policymakers clamored for more direct attacks on widespread absolute poverty, in-creasingly inequitable income distributions, and rising unemployment. In short, during the 1970s, economic development came to be redefined in terms of the re-duction or elimination of poverty, inequality, and unemployment within the con-text of a growing economy. "Redistribution from growth" became a common slo-gan. Dudley Seers posed the basic question about the meaning of development succinctly when he asserted:

> The questions to ask about a country's development are therefore: What has been hap-pening to poverty? What has been happening to unemployment? What has been happen-ing to inequality? If all three of these have declined from high levels, then beyond doubt this has been a period of development for the country concerned. If one or two of these central problems have been growing worse, especially if all three have, it would be strange to call the result "development" even if per capita income doubled.[6]

This assertion was neither idle speculation nor the description of a hypotheti-cal situation. A number of developing countries experienced relatively high rates of growth of per capita income during the 1960s and 1970s but showed little or no improvement or even an actual decline in employment, equality, and the real in-comes of the bottom 40% of their populations. By the earlier growth definition, these countries were developing; by the newer poverty, equality, and employment criteria, they were not. The situation in the 1980s and 1990s worsened further as GNI growth rates turned negative for many LDCs, and governments, facing mounting foreign-debt problems, were forced to cut back on their already limited social and economic programs. Nor can we count on high rates of growth in the developed world to trickle down to the poor in developing countries. In the 1990s, while the United States, the United Kingdom, and other high-income countries enjoyed a strong economic boom, average incomes declined in sub-Saharan Africa, and the number of people in the region living in extreme poverty (on less than $1 per day) rose by some 50 million.

But the phenomenon of development or the existence of a chronic state of un-derdevelopment is not merely a question of economics or even one of quantitative measurement of incomes, employment, and inequality. Underdevelopment is a real fact of life for more than 3 billion people in the world—a state of mind as much as a state of national poverty. As Denis Goulet has forcefully portrayed it:

> Underdevelopment is shocking: the squalor, disease, unnecessary deaths, and hopeless-ness of it all! No man understands if underdevelopment remains for him a mere statistic reflecting low income, poor housing, premature mortality or underemployment. The most empathetic observer can speak objectively about underdevelopment only after un-dergoing, personally or vicariously, the "shock of underdevelopment." This unique cul-ture shock comes to one as he is initiated to the emotions which prevail in the "culture of poverty." The reverse shock is felt by those living in destitution when a new self-under-standing reveals to them that their life is neither human nor inevitable. . . . The prevalent emotion of underdevelopment is a sense of personal and societal impotence in the face of disease and death, of confusion and ignorance as one gropes to understand change, of servility toward men whose decisions govern the course of events, of hopelessness before hunger and natural catastrophe. Chronic poverty is a cruel kind of hell, and one cannot understand how cruel that hell is merely by gazing upon poverty as an object.[7]

The World Bank, which during the 1980s championed economic growth as the goal of development, joined the chorus of observers taking a broader perspective when, in its 1991 *World Development Report*, it asserted:

> The challenge of development . . . is to improve the quality of life. Especially in the world's poor countries, a better quality of life generally calls for higher incomes—but it involves much more. It encompasses as ends in themselves better education, higher standards of health and nutrition, less poverty, a cleaner environment, more equality of opportunity, greater individual freedom, and a richer cultural life.[8]

Development must therefore be conceived of as a multidimensional process in-volving major changes in social structures, popular attitudes, and national institu-tions, as well as the acceleration of economic growth, the reduction of inequality, and the eradication of poverty. Development, in its essence, must represent the whole gamut of change by which an entire social system, tuned to the diverse ba-sic needs and desires of individuals and social groups within that system, moves away from a condition of life widely perceived as unsatisfactory toward a situation or condition of life regarded as materially and spiritually better. No one has identi-fied the human goals of economic development as well as Amartya Sen, perhaps the leading thinker on the meaning of development.

Sen's "Capabilities" Approach

The view that income and wealth are not ends in themselves but instruments for other purposes goes back at least as far as Aristotle. Amartya Sen, the 1998 Nobel laureate in economics, argues that the "capability to function" is what really mat-ters for status as a poor or nonpoor person.[9] As Sen put it, "Economic growth can-not be sensibly treated as an end in itself. Development has to be more concerned with enhancing the lives we lead and the freedoms we enjoy."[10]

In effect, Sen argues that poverty cannot be properly measured by income or even by utility as conventionally understood; what matters is not the things a per-son has—or the feelings these provide—but what a person *is,* or can be, and does, or *can do*. What matters for well-being is not just the characteristics of commodities consumed, as in the utility approach, but what use the consumer can and does make of commodities. For example, a book is of little value to an illiterate person (except perhaps as cooking fuel or as a status symbol). Or as Sen noted, a person with parasitic diseases will be less able to extract nourishment from a given quantity of food than someone without parasites. Sen's approach is valid for more developed countries as well. For example, most of the things one could do with the personal computer one buys are never understood or even known, let alone ever used, by anyone other than specialists. Of course, sometimes people want more "features" just in case they might want to use them. But if we exclude items of this kind, a computer with unused characteristics is no better than one without these characteristics.

The point is that to make any sense of the concept of human well-being in general, and poverty in particular, we need to think beyond the availability of commodities and consider their use: to address what Sen calls **functionings**, that is, what a person does (or can do) with the commodities of given characteristics that they come to possess or control. Freedom of choice, or control of one's own life, is itself a central aspect of most understandings of well-being. As Sen explains,

> The concept of "functionings" . . . reflects the various things a person may value doing or being. The valued functionings may vary from elementary ones, such as being adequately nourished and being free from avoidable disease, to very complex activities or personal states, such as being able to take part in the life of the community and having self-respect.[11]

Sen identifies five sources of disparity between (measured) real incomes and actual advantages:[12] first, personal heterogeneities, such as those connected with disability, illness, age, or gender; second, environmental diversities, such as heating and clothing requirements in the cold, infectious diseases in the tropics, or the impact of pollution; third, variations in social climate, such as the prevalence of crime and violence, and "social capital"; fourth, differences in relational perspectives, meaning that

> the commodity requirements of established patterns of behavior may vary between communities, depending on conventions and customs. For example, being relatively poor in a rich community can prevent a person from achieving some elementary "functionings" (such as taking part in the life of the community) even though her income, in absolute terms, may be much higher than the level of income at which members of poorer communities can function with great ease and success. For example, to be able to "appear in public without shame" may require higher standards of clothing and other visible consumption in a richer society than in a poorer one

In a richer society, the ability to partake in community life would be extremely difficult without certain commodities, such as a telephone, a television, or an automobile; it is increasingly difficult to function socially in Singapore or South Korea without an e-mail address. Fifth, distribution within the family: Economic statistics measure incomes received in a family, because it is the basic unit of shared consumption, but family resources may be distributed unevenly, for example, when girls get less medical attention or education than boys do.

Thus, looking at even real income levels, or even the levels of consumption of specific commodities, cannot suffice as a measure of well-being. One may have a lot of commodities, but these are of little value if they are not what consumers desire (as in the former Soviet Union). One may have income, but certain commodities essential for well-being, such as nutritious foods, may be unavailable. Even when providing an equal number of calories, the available staple foods in one country (cassava, bread, rice, cornmeal, potatoes, etc.) will differ in nutritional content from staple foods in other countries. Moreover, even some subvarieties of, for example, rice, are much more nutritious than others. Finally, even when comparing absolutely identical commodities, one has to frame their consumption in a personal and social context. Sen provides an excellent example:

> Consider a commodity such as bread. It has many characteristics, of which yielding nutrition is one. This can—often with advantage—be split into different *types* of nutrition, related to calories, protein, etc. In addition to nutrition-giving characteristics, bread possesses other characteristics as well, e.g., helping get-togethers over food and drinks, meeting the demands of social conventions or festivities. For a given person at a particular point in time, having more bread increases, up to a point, the person's ability to function in these ways. . . . But in comparing the functionings of two different persons, we do not get enough information by looking merely at the amounts of bread (and similar goods) enjoyed by the two persons respectively. The conversion of commodity-characteristics into personal achievements of functionings depends on a variety of factors—personal and social. In the case of nutritional achievements it depends on such factors as (1) metabolic rates, (2) body size, (3) age, (4) sex (and, if a woman, whether pregnant or lactating), (5) activity levels, (6) medical conditions (including the absence or presence of parasites), (7) access to medical services and the ability to use them, (8) nutritional knowledge and education, and (9) climactic conditions.[13]

In part because such factors, even on so basic a matter as nutrition, can vary so widely across individuals, measuring individual well-being across people by levels of consumption of goods and services obtained confuses the role of commodities by regarding them as ends in themselves rather than as means to an end. In the case of nutrition, the end is health and what one can do with good health, as well as personal enjoyment and social functioning. But measuring well-being using the concept of utility, in any of its standard definitions, does not offer enough of an improvement over measuring consumption to capture the meaning of development.[14]

As Sen stresses, a person's own valuation of what kind of life would be worthwhile is not necessarily the same as what gives pleasure to that person. If we identify utility with happiness, then very poor people can have very high utility. Sometimes even malnourished people either have a disposition that keeps them feeling very happy and satisfied or have learned to appreciate greatly any small comforts they can find in life, such as a single breeze on a very hot day, and to avoid disappointment by striving only for what seems attainable. (Indeed, it is only too human to tell yourself that you do not want the things you cannot have.) If there is really nothing to be done about a person's deprivation, this attitude of subjective bliss would have undoubted advantages in a spiritual sense, but it does not change the objective reality of deprivation. In particular, such an attitude would not prevent the happy but homeless poor person from greatly valuing an opportunity to become freed of parasites or provided with basic shelter. Rather than a *feeling*, as Sen defines it, the functioning of a person is an *achievement;* it is

> what the person succeeds in doing with the commodities and characteristics at his or her command. . . . For example, bicycling has to be distinguished from possessing a bike. It has to be distinguished also from the happiness generated by [bicycling]. . . . A functioning is thus different both from (1) having goods (and the corresponding characteristics), to which it is posterior, and (2) having utility (in the form of happiness resulting from that functioning), to which it is, in an important way, prior.[15]

Sen then defines **capabilities** as "the freedom that a person has in terms of the choice of functionings, given his personal features (conversion of characteristics into functionings) and his command over commodities." Just as in basic microeconomics, where income matters to the extent that it affects utility, utility is important here to the extent that it exhibits a person's capabilities. And clearly, capabilities are determined in part by income. Even so, many important problems of developing countries, such as social deprivation of girls (see Chapter 8), simply cannot be adequately addressed by a focus on income. Sen's perspective helps explain why development economists have placed so much emphasis on health and education and have referred to countries with high levels of income but poor health and education standards as cases of "growth without development."[16] Real income is essential, but to convert the characteristics of commodities into functionings, in most important cases, surely requires health and education as well as income. The role of health and education ranges from something so basic as the nutritional advantages and greater personal energy that are possible when one lives free of certain parasites to the expanded ability to appreciate the richness of human life that comes with a broad and deep education.

Over the past two decades, Sen's view has become extremely popular among development economists and social science methodologists. Sometimes students seem less impressed, arguing that fulfillment is more about the quality of social relationships or following religious values than about capabilities. But however the matter is framed, it is clear that income or consumption, or purely subjective pleasure or desire fulfillment, cannot define *well-being* in any adequate sense. Sen's analysis is part of what has given the United Nations' *Human Development Index,* which accounts for health and education as well as income, its wide respect and following (see Chapter 2).

Three Core Values of Development

Is it possible, then, to define or broadly conceptualize what we mean when we talk about development as the sustained elevation of an entire society and social system toward a "better" or "more humane" life? What constitutes the good life is a question as old as philosophy, one that must be periodically reevaluated and answered afresh in the changing environment of world society. The appropriate answer for developing nations today is not necessarily the same as it would have been in previous decades. But at least three basic components or core values serve as a conceptual basis and practical guideline for understanding the inner meaning of development. These core values—**sustenance**, **self-esteem**, and **freedom**—represent common goals sought by all individuals and societies.[17] They relate to fundamental human needs that find their expression in almost all societies and cultures at all times. Let us therefore examine each in turn.

Sustenance: The Ability to Meet Basic Needs   All people have certain basic needs without which life would be impossible. These life-sustaining basic human needs include food, shelter, health, and protection.[18] When any of these is absent or in critically short supply, a condition of "absolute underdevelopment" exists. A basic function of all economic activity, therefore, is to provide as many people as possible with the means of overcoming the helplessness and misery arising from a lack of food, shelter, health, and protection. To this extent, we may claim that economic development is a necessary condition for the improvement in the quality of life that is development. Without sustained and continuous economic progress at the individual as well as the societal level, the realization of the human potential would not be possible. One clearly has to "have enough in order to be more."[19] Rising per capita incomes, the elimination of absolute poverty, greater employment opportunities, and lessening income inequalities therefore constitute the *necessary* but not the *sufficient* conditions for development.[20]

Self-Esteem: To Be a Person   A second universal component of the good life is self-esteem—a sense of worth and self-respect, of not being used as a tool by others for their own ends. All peoples and societies seek some basic form of self-esteem, although they may call it authenticity, identity, dignity, respect, honor, or recognition. The nature and form of this self-esteem may vary from society to society and from culture to culture. However, with the proliferation of the "modernizing values" of developed nations, many societies in developing countries that have had a profound sense of their own worth suffer from serious cultural confusion when they come in contact with economically and technologically advanced societies. This is because national prosperity has become an almost universal measure of worth. Due to the significance attached to material values in developed nations, worthiness and esteem are nowadays increasingly conferred only on countries that possess economic wealth and technological power—those that have "developed."

As Denis Goulet put it, "Development is legitimized as a goal because it is an important, perhaps even an indispensable, way of gaining esteem."[21]

Freedom from Servitude: To Be Able to Choose   A third and final universal value that we suggest should constitute the meaning of development is the concept of human freedom. Freedom here is to be understood in the sense of emancipation from alienating material conditions of life and from social servitude to nature, ignorance, other people, misery, institutions, and dogmatic beliefs, especially that poverty is predestination. Freedom involves an expanded range of choices for societies and their members together with a minimization of external constraints in the pursuit of some social goal we call development. W. Arthur Lewis stressed the relationship between economic growth and freedom from servitude when he concluded that "the advantage of economic growth is not that wealth increases happiness, but that it increases the range of human choice."[22] Wealth can enable people to gain greater control over nature and the physical environment (e.g., through the production of food, clothing, and shelter) than they would have if they remained poor. It also gives them the freedom to choose greater leisure, to have more goods and services, or to deny the importance of these material wants and choose to live a life of spiritual contemplation. The concept of human freedom should also encompass various components of political freedom including, but not limited to, personal security, the rule of law, freedom of expression, political participation, and equality of opportunity.[23] Some of the most notable economic success stories of the 1970s and 1980s (Saudi Arabia, Singapore, Malaysia, Thailand, Indonesia, Turkey, and China, among others) did not score high on the 1991 Human Freedom Index compiled by the United Nations Development Program (UNDP).[24]

The Three Objectives of Development

We may conclude that development is both a physical reality and a state of mind in which society has, through some combination of social, economic, and institutional processes, secured the means for obtaining a better life. Whatever the specific components of this better life, development in all societies must have at least the following three objectives:

1. *To increase the availability and widen the distribution of basic life-sustaining goods* such as food, shelter, health, and protection

2. *To raise levels of living*, including, in addition to higher incomes, the provision of more jobs, better education, and greater attention to cultural and human values, all of which will serve not only to enhance material well-being but also to generate greater individual and national self-esteem

3. *To expand the range of economic and social choices* available to individuals and nations by freeing them from servitude and dependence not only in relation to other people and nation-states but also to the forces of ignorance and human misery

The Millennium Development Goals

In September 2000, the 189 member countries of the United Nations adopted eight Millennium Development Goals (MDGs), committing themselves to making substantial progress toward the eradication of poverty and achieving other human development goals by the year 2015. The MDGs are the strongest statement yet of the international commitment to ending global poverty. They acknowledge the multidimensional nature of development and poverty alleviation; an end to poverty requires more than just increasing incomes of the poor. Although some observers still suspect that the MDGs will amount to no more than just another UN proclamation of worthy goals, by the first five-year review in 2005, these goals had become central to the way governments, international development agencies, and nongovernmental organizations carry out their development efforts. Although if current trends continue, few of the goals will be achieved by 2015, the MDGs have provided a unified focus in the development community unlike anything that preceded them.[25]

The eight goals are ambitious: to eradicate extreme poverty and hunger; achieve universal primary education; promote gender equality and empower women; reduce child mortality; improve maternal health; combat HIV/AIDS, malaria, and other diseases; ensure environmental sustainability; and develop a global partnership for development. The goals are then assigned specific targets deemed achievable by 2015 based on the pace of past international development achievements.

Appropriately, the first MDG addresses the problem of extreme poverty and hunger. The two targets for this goal are more modest: to reduce by half the proportion of people living on less than $1 a day and to reduce by half the proportion of people who suffer from hunger. "Halving poverty" has come to serve as a touchstone for the MDGs as a whole. To achieve this target requires that progress be made on the other goals as well.

Unfortunately, according to the UNDP's 2003 *Human Development Report*, in the 1990s, income poverty increased in 37 countries, and hunger increased in 21 countries. Sub-Saharan Africa is not only off track, but income poverty is actually *increasing* in this the poorest region of the world. And while South Asia is on track to halve income poverty, current trends indicate that hunger will not be halved in that part of the world until at least a century from now. Very little progress is being made in Latin America. In contrast, East Asia has already nearly met these two targets, although some observers fear that the region remains vulnerable to a potential economic crisis in China.

Other targets include reducing by two-thirds the mortality rate among children under 5, reducing by three-quarters the incidence of women dying in childbirth, and eliminating gender disparities in school enrollment. The goal of ensuring environmental sustainability is also essential for securing an escape from poverty. This is immediately seen by looking at two of the targets: reduce by half the proportion of people without access to safe drinking water and achieve significant improvement in the lives of at least 100 million slum dwellers. But more generally, without protecting the environment of the poor, there is little chance that their escape from poverty can be permanent. Finally, the governments and citizens of the rich countries need to play their part in pursuit of the goal of "global partnership for development."

The MDGs were developed in consultation with the developing countries, to ensure that they addressed their most pressing problems. In addition, key international agencies, including the United Nations, the World Bank, the International Monetary Fund (IMF), the Organization for Economic Cooperation and Development (OECD), and the World Trade Organization (WTO) all helped to develop the *Millennium Declaration* and so have a collective policy commitment to attacking poverty directly. The MDGs assign specific responsibilities to rich countries, including increased aid, removal of trade and investment barriers, and eliminating unsustainable debts of the poorest nations. The goals and targets are found in Box 1.2.

BOX 1.2   **Millennium Development Goals: Themes and Targets**

1. **Eradicate extreme poverty and hunger**

   Target for 2015:   Halve the proportion of people living on less than $1 a day and those who suffer from hunger.

2. **Achieve universal primary education**

   Target for 2015:   Ensure that all boys and girls complete primary school.

3. **Promote gender equality and empower women**

   Targets for 2005: Eliminate gender disparities in primary and secondary education (preferred).

   Targets for 2015: Eliminate gender disparities at all levels.

4. **Reduce child mortality**

   Target for 2015:   Reduce by two-thirds the mortality rate among children under 5.

5. **Improve maternal health**

   Target for 2015:   Reduce by three-quarters the ratio of women dying in childbirth.

6. **Combat HIV/AIDS, malaria, and other diseases**

   Target for 2015:   Halt and begin to reverse the spread of HIV/AIDS and the incidence of malaria and other major diseases.

7. **Ensure environmental sustainability**

   General target: Integrate the principles of sustainable development into country policies and programs and reverse the loss of environmental resources.

   Target for 2015:   Reduce by half the proportion of people without access to safe drinking water.

   Target for 2020: Achieve significant improvement in the lives of at least 100 million slum dwellers.

8. **Develop a global partnership for development**

   Targets:
   - Develop further an open trading and financial system that includes a commitment to good governance, development, and poverty reduction, nationally and internationally.
   - Address the least developed countries' special needs and the special needs of landlocked and small-island developing states.
   - Deal comprehensively with developing countries' debt problems.
   - Develop decent and productive work for youth.
   - In cooperation with pharmaceutical companies, provide access to affordable essential drugs in developing countries.
   - In cooperation with the private sector, make available the benefits of new technologies—especially information and communications technologies.

Source: United Nations Development Program (UNDP), http://www.undp.org/mdg.

Conclusions

Development economics is a distinct yet very important extension of both traditional economics and political economy. While necessarily also concerned with efficient resource allocation and the steady growth of aggregate output over time, development economics focuses primarily on the economic, social, and institutional mechanisms needed to bring about rapid and large-scale improvements in standards of living for the masses of poor people in developing nations. As such, development economics must be concerned with the formulation of appropriate public policies designed to effect major economic, institutional, and social transformations of entire societies in a very short time. Otherwise, the gap between aspiration and reality will continue to widen with each passing year. It is for this reason that the public sector has assumed a much broader and more determining role in development economics than it has in traditional neoclassical economic analysis.

As a social science, economics is concerned with people and how best to provide them with the material means to help them realize their full human potential. But what constitutes the good life is a perennial question, and hence economics necessarily involves values and value judgments. Our very concern with promoting development represents an implicit value judgment about good (development) and evil (underdevelopment). But development may mean different things to different people. Therefore, the nature and character of development and the meaning we attach to it must be carefully spelled out. We did this at the end of the chapter and will continue to explore these definitions throughout the book.

The central economic problems of all societies include traditional questions such as what, where, how, how much, and for whom goods and services should be produced. But they should also include the fundamental question at the national level about who actually makes or influences economic decisions and for whose principal benefit these decisions are made. Finally, at the international level, it is necessary to consider the question of which nations and which powerful groups within nations exert the most influence with regard to the control, transmission, and use of technology, information, and finance. Moreover, for whom do they exercise this power?

Any realistic analysis of development problems necessitates the supplementation of strictly economic variables such as incomes, prices, and savings rates with equally relevant noneconomic institutional factors, including the nature of land tenure arrangements; the influence of social and class stratifications; the structure of credit, education, and health systems; the organization and motivation of government bureaucracies; the machinery of public administrations; the nature of popular attitudes toward work, leisure, and self-improvement; and the values, roles, and attitudes of political and economic elites. Economic development strategies that seek to raise agricultural output, create employment, and eradicate poverty have often failed in the past because economists and other policy advisers neglected to view the economy as an interdependent social system in which economic and noneconomic forces are continually interacting in ways that are at times self-reinforcing and at other times contradictory. As we will discover, underdevelopment reflects many individual market failures, but these failures often add up to more than the sum of their parts, combining to keep a country in a poverty trap. Government can play a key role in moving the economy to a better equilibrium, and in many countries, notably in East Asia, government has done so; but all too often government itself is part and parcel of the bad equilibrium.

Despite the great diversity of developing nations—some large, others small; some resource-rich, others resource-barren; some subsistence economies, others modern manufactured-good exporters; some private-sector-oriented, others largely run by the government—most share common problems that define their underdevelopment. We will discuss these diverse structures and common characteristics of LDCs in Chapter 2.

The oil price shocks of the 1970s, the foreign-debt crisis of the 1980s, the economic globalization and environmental concerns of the 1990s, and the tragedy and aftermath of September 11, 2001, have underlined the growing interdependence of all nations and peoples in the international social system. What happens to life in Caracas, Cairo, and Calcutta will in one way or another have important implications for life in New York, London, and Tokyo. It was once said that "when the United States sneezes, the world catches pneumonia." A more fitting expression for the twenty-first century would perhaps be that "the world is like the human body: If one part aches, the rest will feel it; if many parts hurt, the whole will suffer."

Developing nations constitute these "many parts" of the global organism. The nature and character of their future development should therefore be a major concern of *all* nations irrespective of political, ideological, or economic orientation. There can no longer be two futures, one for the few rich and the other for the very many poor. In the words of a poet, "There will be only one future—or none at all."

Progress in the Struggle for More Meaningful Development: Brazil

There are two faces of development in Brazil. World-competitive industry coexists with stagnant, protected sectors. Modern agriculture coexists with low productivity, traditional practices. Many Brazilians have been frustrated with the uneven pace of development and tell self-deprecating jokes such as "Brazil is the country of the future—and always will be." Brazil has even been cited as an example of a country that has experienced "growth without development." But a close examination reveals the great complexity of these issues. Despite huge inequities, Brazil has made economic and social progress and probably should not be tarred with the same brush as countries such as Pakistan or Saudi Arabia that have had less social development for their levels of growth and investment. Extremely high economic inequality and social divisions do pose a serious threat to further progress in Brazil. But there are reasons to hope that Brazil may overcome its legacy of inequality so that the country may yet join the ranks of the developed countries.

Brazil is of special interest in part because its growth performance from the 1960s through the 1980s was the best in Latin America, with at least some parallels with East Asian policy and performance—although Brazil had a larger role for state-owned enterprises, much lower education and other social expenditures, and much higher inflation.

Brazil's performance is followed widely in the developing world, as it is the largest and most populous country in Latin America; and with 175 million people in 2003, it is the world's fifth-largest country in both area and population. Brazil is traditionally considered a leader of the developing world, and it is a key member of the Group of 20 developing countries pushing for fairer international trade rules.

But despite its growth, other indicators of development in Brazil lagged, eventually undermining growth prospects. Without being torn apart by civil war, and benefiting from much higher incomes than Central American countries, Brazil, it would seem, should have been in a much better position to fight extreme poverty and improve economic equity and social indicators. Instead, the country has continued to see a higher percentage of its population in poverty than would be expected for an upper-middle-income country, and despite some modest recent improvement, Brazil remains one of the countries with the highest levels of inequality in the world. So how should Brazil's development performance be evaluated and future priorities chosen?

Income and Growth

Growth is generally necessary, though not sufficient, for achieving development. In 2002, Brazil's per capita income was $2,830.

Using purchasing power parity (see Chapter 2), its average income was still only $7,450, about one-fifth of that of the United States, but five times that of Haiti.

Growth has been erratic, with substantial swings over time. Data for growth of gross domestic product (GDP) per capita are sometimes presented for the periods 1965–1990, when for Brazil it was 1.4%, and for 1990-2000, when it was 1.5%. This appears to suggest a remarkable stability. But the former figures combine the booming years from 1967 to 1980 and Brazil's "lost decade of development" of the 1980s. Nevertheless, this performance was still better than most other countries of Latin America.

Brazil has had an export policy stressing incentives for manufacturing exports, as well as protections for domestic industry, with numerous parallels with Taiwan and South Korea (see Chapters 12 and 13). Its percentage share of manufactured exports in total exports grew dramatically, reaching 57% in 1980, although it dropped dramatically during the lost decade of the 1980s. Although the share of exports increased again to reach 54% by 2000, these largely represented processed foods and ores. Brazil's chronic status as a highly indebted country (see chapter 14) has been a substantial drag on growth performance, as have continued problems with infrastructure.

High and growing taxes have also slowed formal sector employment growth. Overall tax burden has increased from about 25% of gross national income to nearly 40% in the decade from 1993 to 2004. Payroll taxes are so high that as many as half of Brazil's labor force now works in the informal sector, where taxes may be avoided (as well as labor rights and regulation circumvented).

Technology transfer is critical to more rapid growth, competing internationally, and beginning to catch up with advanced countries. Brazil has made notable progress. The country is viewed as being at the cutting edge of agricultural research and extension in commercially successful export crops such as citrus and soybeans. After a disastrous attempt to protect the computer industry in the 1980s was abandoned, Brazil has begun to see the expansion of a software industry, as also seen in India. But Brazil has not absorbed technology to the degree that East Asian countries have.

Social Indicators

Brazil's human development statistics compare unfavorably with many other middle-income countries such as Costa Rica and quite a few low-income countries, let alone with the advanced industrialized countries. As of 2004, Brazil ranked seventy-second on the United Nations Development Program's Human Development Index (explained in Chapter 2), 9 positions lower than would be predicted by its income.

In Brazil, life expectancy at birth in 2000 was 68 years, compared with 75 in some other upper-middle-income countries such as South Korea. Similarly, Brazil's under-5 mortality rate is 36 per thousand, compared with 11 in similar-income Costa Rica and just 5 in Korea. Although the child mortality rate is quite poor by the standards of comparable countries today, Brazil, like most developing countries, has made great progress from 1960, when its rate was 159 per thousand. But over 10 percent of all children under the age of 5 still suffer from malnutrition in Brazil. The UNDP noted that "for health care the poor have to resort to lower-quality public hospitals and clinics, while the better-off tend to go to private facilities—many funded with public resources."

The primary school completion rate is only 71%, very low for an upper-middle-income country. Relatedly, Brazil also suffers from a very high incidence of child labor for its income level, as a December 2001 World Bank study and reports by the International Labor Office have underlined. As many as 7 million children still work in Brazil, despite the country's having officially made the eradication of child labor a priority. (For an analysis of the problems of child labor and appropriate child labor policies, see Chapter 8.) In the education sphere, Brazil's adult literacy rate is 85% (independant observers have concluded that Brazil's effective literacy is under 50%), while that of similar-income Costa Rica is 95%. Helping to explain this difference, in Costa Rica, six years of school attendance are mandatory and 99% attendance is reported.

The UNDP concluded that

> the unequal distribution of social spending is no doubt a major factor in maintaining inequality and thus poverty.... The bulk of the benefits go to the middle classes and the rich. Close to a third of the poorest fifth of the population does not attend primary school. But the sharpest differences show up in secondary and tertiary education. More than 90% of the poorest four-fifths of the population do not attend secondary school, and practically none make it to universities. Only primary schools end up being relatively targeted to the poor, not because the government succeeds in targeting resources, but because richer households send their children to private schools. Public expenditures on secondary and tertiary education are very badly targeted to the poor. For scholarships—chiefly to graduate students—four-fifths of the money goes to the richest fifth of the population.

In fact, with public universities offering free tuition to mostly high-income undergrads as well as grad students, the distortion is even greater.

So while the persistence of poverty in Brazil over the past 20 years is undoubtedly due in part to mediocre growth relative to East Asia or to Brazil's potential, the most important explanation is the highly concentrated distribution of income, worsened by inequitable social spending.

Development depends on a healthy, skilled, and secure workforce. Ultimately, a slower improvement in health, education, and community development can feed back to a slower rate of growth, a process that has plagued Brazilian development.

Poverty

Perhaps the most important social indicator is the extent of extreme poverty among a country's people. Poverty has been high in Brazil for an upper-middle-income country. There has been progress; a World Bank study found that Brazil's average per capita income grew by 220% in the high-growth years from 1960 to 1980, with a 34% decline in the share of the poor in the population. On the other hand, similarly sized Indonesia grew 108% from 1971 to 1987, with a 42% decline in poverty incidence. And some of the ground gained on poverty was subsequently lost in Brazil in the 1980s and 1990s. According to World Bank estimates, in 2000, 25.4% of the population of Brazil lived on less than $2 per day. And 9 percent actually lived in extreme poverty, with incomes below $1 per day, worse than some low-income countries such as Sri Lanka. But this may actually be an underestimate. According to a Brazilian government research institute cited by the United Nations Development Program, an even more shocking 15% of Brazilians have incomes of less than $1 a day. Although poverty is believed to have fallen since the mid-1990s, that put the incidence of poverty at little less than it was in the late 1970s.

Inequality

For decades, Brazil's inequality in income (as well as in land and other assets) has ranked among the worst in the world. High inequality not only produces social strains but can also ultimately retard growth, as examined in detail in Chapter 5. The degree of income inequality in Brazil is reflected in the low share of income going to the bottom 60 percent and the high share to the top 10% of the population, as seen in the following income distribution data for Brazil:

Fraction of Population	Share Received
Lowest quintile	2.1%
Second quintile	4.9%
Third quintile	8.9%
Fourth quintile	16.8%
Highest quintile	67.5%
Highest 10%	51.3%

As these figures show, the top 10% of income earners receive over half of national income, while the bottom 40% receive just 7%. These figures make inequality in Brazil among the highest in the world, probably the highest in Latin America, the region with the world's highest average inequality. The dramatic contrasts of Brazil are often expressed with the saying that it is "a Belgium inside an India," which is a substantial exaggeration but a telling one. Inequality, which started at a high level, actually increased in Brazil in the 1950–1990 period. In recent years, inequality in Brazil has moderated but seems to have leveled off at a high rate, comparable to that of 1980. The UNDP concludes that high inequality is the reason for the high level of extreme poverty and the very slow rate of poverty reduction. Inequality in assets is also high. It has been estimated that the top 5% of farms comprise 69.3% of the farmland in Brazil.

Land Reform

Land is very unequally distributed in Brazil, and there is both an efficiency and a social equity case for land reform (a subject discussed in Chapter 9). But land reform has been repeatedly blocked in Brazil by the political power of large plantation (*latifundia*) owners. In response, in the past decade, impoverished farmers in the "landless movement," or MST, have increasingly seized land, often arable but unused land within large

plantations. Hundreds of thousands of families have taken part. Farmers have also settled in fragile rain forest areas, finding themselves unable to acquire land in areas that are more agriculturally suitable—and less ecologically sensitive. In response, the government has initiated a land reform program, but the results to date have been modest in relation to the scope of the problem.

Sustainability of Development

As described in Chapter 10, growth that relies on running down the natural environment is contrasted with sustainable development, which preserves the ecology on which future income and people's health vitally depend. Deforestation of the Brazilian Amazon rain forest displays conflicts between short- and long-term development goals and the consequences of huge inequality and state intervention on behalf of the rich. Despite their destructiveness, economic activities in the Amazon often benefited from ill-conceived subsidies that operated until the end of the 1980s, now curtailed. Grandiose showcase development projects and schemes, such as subsidized ore mining, charcoal-consuming industries, and cattle ranching, were carried out on a large scale. In many cases where there is a highly unequal distribution of land, sustainable development requires serious attention to land reform.

The encouragement of rain forest settlement seemed to be a politically inexpensive alternative to land reform. In the end, the best lands became concentrated in the hands of large, powerful farmers. Rights of indigenous peoples were flagrantly violated, with some terrible atrocities committed by settlers. Ecological campaigners and activists among rubber-tappers whose livelihoods were threatened were attacked and sometimes murdered. In the meantime, much of these fragile lands appears to have become irreversibly degraded. Many of the subsidies have now been withdrawn, and at least some protections and "extractive reserves" have been put in place, but rain forest destruction is hard to reverse. Forest management in other tropical rain forests has led to a rapid growth in ecotourism and very high, profitable, and sustainable fruit yields. Products that can be harvested without serious ecological disruption include fibers, latex, resins, gums, medicines, and game. However, it is clear that this cannot protect land on the vast scale at risk. Because the rest of the world benefits from Brazil's rain forests through prevention of global warming, ecological cleansing, and the irreplaceable biodiversity needed for future antibiotics and other medicines and goods, the international community should be prepared to pay something to ensure its continuation, such as paying forest dwellers to preserve and protect natural resources. Financial support for land reform outside sensitive areas is one clear direction.

Problems of Social Inclusion

Few discussions about poverty in Brazil pay much attention to race. But about half of the population of Brazil is African or mulatto in origin. As a result, it is sometimes noted that Brazil is the world's second largest black nation, after Nigeria. And most of the poor in Brazil are black or mulatto. Although racism is a crime in Brazil, no one has ever been sent to jail for it. According to one estimate, the average black worker receives only 41% of the salary of the average white worker. Most of the more than one million Brazilians living in the worst *favelas*, or shantytown slums, are black. The endemic extreme poverty of the Northeast afflicts indigenous and mulatto populations. Although the Northeast has only about 30% of Brazil's population, 62% of the country's poor live in the region. Black representation in government is shockingly rare, even in the states where nonwhites make up a majority of the population. University

places are overwhelmingly claimed by whites. Brazil probably needs a movement comparable to the U.S. civil rights struggle of the 1960s, but in the absence of overt Jim Crow laws, it is sometimes hard to identify the appropriate target. Some form of meaningful affirmative action may be the only way to begin to overcome the problem.

Conclusion

In Brazil, it might be most accurate to say that there has been some economic growth without as much social development, rather than the more blanketing "growth without development," which applies better to a few Middle Eastern and other energy-exporting countries as well as some lower-income countries such as Pakistan. But continuing racial disparities, unjust treatment of indigenous peoples, lack of access of the poor to fertile land, extremely high inequality and surprisingly high poverty for its income level, and the danger that growth will prove ecologically unsustainable all mean that Brazil will have to make social inclusion and human development, as well as environmental sustainability, top priorities if it is to resume rapid economic growth, let alone achieve true multidimensional development.

Part of the explanation for high rates of income poverty and poor social indicators in Brazil is the relatively slower growth that has prevailed since the early 1980s. But a major explanation is that government social spending on health, education, pensions, unemployment benefits, and other transfers are going to the well-off, frequently to those in the top 20% of income distribution. Government has been worsening inequality rather than softening it. The Bolsa-Escola program, which is similar to Mexico's Progresa program described in Chapter 8, is an important recent exception that may herald a broader change in Brazil. Bolsa-Escola transfers income to poor families on the condition that their children stay in school, thus providing current consumption as well as the potential of future higher earnings for families trapped in chronic poverty.

In November 2002, the left-leaning labor leader Luiz Inacio Lula da Silva, known universally as Lula, was elected president of Brazil on a platform promising greater equity. This generated a lot of excitement in the country, with renewed hopes for greater social inclusion. Whether this will result remains in question; the first two years have seen some renewal of growth and a greater public policy focus on poverty, though the slow rate of progress on social inclusion has been disappointing to many Brazilians. But for many Brazilians, hopes have been high that the future may have finally arrived. ∎

Sources

Anderson, Anthony B. "Smokestacks in the rainforest: Industrial development and deforestation in the Amazon basin." *World Development* 18, (1990): 1191–1205.

Anderson, Anthony B., ed. *Alternatives to Deforestation.* New York: Columbia University Press, 1990.

Bank Information Center. *Funding Ecological and Social Destruction: The World Bank and the IMF.* Washington, D.C.: Bank Information Center, 1990.

Bauman, Renato, and Helson C. Braga. "Export financing in the LDCs: The role of subsidies for export performance in Brazil." *World Development* 16 (1988): 821–833.

Hans P. Binswanger. "Brazilian policies that encourage deforestation in the Amazon." *World Development* 19 (1991): 821–829.

Downing, Theodore E., Susanna B. Hecht, and Henry A. Pearson (eds.). *Development or Destruction: The Conversion of Tropical Forest to Pasture in Latin America.* Boulder, Colo: Westview Press, 1992.

Dinsmoor, James. *Brazil: Responses to the Debt Crisis.* Washington, D.C.: Inter-American Development Bank, 1990.

Erber, Fabio Stefano. "The development of the electronics complex and government policies in Brazil." *World Development* 13 (1985): 293–310.

Fields, Gary. *Poverty Inequality and Development.* New York: Cambridge University Press, 1980.

INCRA (the Brazilian agency for land reform), http://www.incra.gov.br. See, for example, http://www.incra.gov.br/_htm/serveinf/_htm/pubs/_down/gini.pdf.

Sercovich, Francisco Colman. "Brazil." (special issue: "Exports of technology by newly industrializing economies"). *World Development* 12 (1984): 575–600.

Siddiqi, Faraaz, and Harry Anthony Patrinos. *Child Labor: Issues, Causes, and Interventions.* World Bank, n.d. http://www.worldbank.org/html/extdr/hnp/hddflash/workp /wp_00056.html.

Smith, Stephen C. *Case Studies in Economic Development,* 2nd ed. Reading, Mass.: Addison-Wesley, 1997

United Nations Development Program. *Human Poverty Report, 2000.* New York: United Nations, 2000.

World Bank. *World Development Report.* 1990, 1992, 2000–2001, 2002. New York: Oxford University Press, 1990, 1992, 2000, 2002.

World Bank. *Eradicating Child Labor in Brazil.* Washington, D.C.: World Bank, 2001.

Yusuf, Shahid. *Globalization and the Challenge for Developing Countries.* New York: World Bank, 2001.

Concepts for Review*

Attitudes	Gross national income (GNI)	Political economy
Capabilities	Income per capita	Self-esteem
Developing countries	Institutions	Social system
Development	Less developed countries	Subsistence economy
Development economics	(LDCs)	Sustenance
Freedom	More developed countries	Traditional economics
Functionings	(MDCs)	Value premises
Globalization	Noneconomic variables	Values

*All boldfaced terms that appear in the text are listed in Concepts for Review. A glossary at the back of the book provides quick-reference definitions for these and other, more general economic concepts.

Questions for Discussion

1. Why is economics central to an understanding of the problems of development?

2. Is the concept of the developing world a useful one? Why or why not?

3. What do you hope to gain from this course on development economics (besides a passing grade)?

4. Briefly describe the various definitions of the term *development* encountered in the text. What are the strengths and weaknesses of each approach? Do you think that there are other dimensions of development not mentioned in the text? If so, describe them. If not, explain why you believe that the text description of development is adequate.

5. Why is an understanding of development crucial to policy formulation in developing nations? Do you think it is possible for a nation to agree on a rough definition of development and orient its strategies accordingly?

6. Why is a strictly economic definition of development inadequate? What do you understand *economic development* to mean? Can you give hypothetical or real examples of situations in which a country may be developing economically but still be underdeveloped?

7. How does the concept of "capabilities to function" help us gain insight into development goals and achievements?

8. What forces may be at work in giving the Millennium Development Goals such a high profile in international economic relations?

Notes

1. "Voices of the Poor" boxed quotations (see Box 1.1 and boxes later in the text) are for the most part drawn from the World Bank Voices of the Poor Web site, http://www.worldbank.org/poverty/voices/overview.htm. The voices project was undertaken as

background for the World Development Report *Attacking Poverty*. The results were published for the World Bank by Oxford University Press in a three-volume series titled *Can Anyone Hear Us?*, *Crying Out for Change*, and *From Many Lands*.

2. The 157 developing African, Asian, and Latin American member countries of the United Nations often collectively refer to themselves as the *Third World*. They do this primarily to distinguish themselves from the economically advanced capitalist (*First World*) and the formerly socialist (*Second World*) countries of Eastern Europe and the Soviet Union—some of which could now justifiably be considered part of the Third World. It is unfortunate that the terms *first*, *second*, and *third* may sometimes be taken to connote superiority or inferiority when in fact they merely reflect the historical sequence of industrialization.

3. For a critique of this argument, see Paul Krugman, "Toward a counter-counterrevolution in development theory," *Proceedings of the World Bank Annual Conference on Development Economics, 1992* (Washington, D.C.: World Bank, 1993), p. 15. See also Syed Nawab Haider Naqvi, "The significance of development economics," *World Development* 24 (1996): 975–987.

4. For a provocative dissection of the role of values in development economics, see Gunnar Myrdal, *The Challenge of World Poverty* (New York: Pantheon, 1970), ch. 1. A more general critique of the idea that economics can be "value-free" is to be found in Robert Heilbroner's "Economics as a 'value-free' science," *Social Research* 40 (1973): 129–143, and his *Behind the Veil of Economics* (New York: Norton, 1988). See also Dwight Perkins, "Economic development: The role of values," in *International Ethics in the Nuclear Age*, ed. Robert J. Myers (Baton Rouge: Louisiana State University Press, 1987), ch. 8; Barbara Ingham, "The meaning of development: Interactions between 'new' and 'old' ideas," *World Development* 21 (1993): 1816–1818; Paul P. Streeten, *Strategies for Human Development* (Copenhagen: Handelshøjskolens Forlag, 1994), pt. 1; Selo Soemardjan and Kenneth W. Thompson (eds.), *Culture, Development, and Democracy* (New York: United Nations University Press, 1994); and Mozaffar Qizilbash, "Ethical development," *World Development* 24 (1996): 1209–1221.

5. Soedjatmoko, *The Primacy of Freedom in Development* (Lanham, Md.: University Press of America, 1985), p. 11.

6. Dudley Seers, "The meaning of development," paper presented at the Eleventh World Conference of the Society for International Development, New Delhi (1969), p. 3. See also Richard Brinkman, "Economic growth versus economic development: Toward a conceptual clarification," *Journal of Economic Issues* 29 (1995): 1171–1188; and P. Jegadish Gandhi, "The concept of development: Its dialectics and dynamics," *Indian Journal of Applied Economics* 5 (1996): 283–311.

7. Denis Goulet, *The Cruel Choice: A New Concept in the Theory of Development* (New York: Atheneum, 1971), p. 23. Reprinted with permission of the author.

8. World Bank, *World Development Report, 1991* (New York: Oxford University Press, 1991), p. 4.

9. Amartya Sen, *Commodities and Capabilities* (Amsterdam: Elsevier, 1985) and *Development as Freedom* (New York: Knopf, 1999).

10. Sen, *Development as Freedom*, p. 14.

11. Ibid., p. 75.

12. Ibid., pp. 70–71.

13. Sen, *Commodities and Capabilities*, pp. 25–26.

14. Ibid., p. 21. Sen points out that even if we identify utility with "desire fulfillment," we still suffer from twin defects of "physical-condition neglect" and "valuation neglect." He notes that "valuing is not the same thing as desiring." Note that ignoring a person's objectively deprived physical condition just because the person considers this subjectively unimportant yields an obviously defective measure of well-being.

15. Ibid., pp. 10–11.

16. See, for example, William Easterly, "The political economy of growth without development: A case study of Pakistan," in *In Search of Prosperity: Analytic Narratives on Economic Growth*, ed. Dani Rodrik (Princeton, N.J.: Princeton University Press, 2003).

17. See Goulet, *Cruel Choice*, pp. 87–94.

18. For a description of the "basic needs" approach, see Pradip K. Ghosh (ed.), *Third World Development: A Basic Needs Approach* (Westport, Conn.: Greenwood Press, 1984).

19. Goulet, *Cruel Choice*, p. 124.

20. For an attempt to specify and quantify the concept of basic needs, see International Labor Organization, *Employment, Growth, and Basic Needs* (Geneva: International Labor Organization, 1976). A similar view with a focus on the notion of entitlements and capabilities can be found in Amartya Sen, "Development: Which way now?" *Economic Journal* 93 (1983): 754–757. See also United Nations Development Program, *Human Development Report, 1994* (New York: Oxford University Press, 1994).

21. Goulet, *Cruel Choice*, p. 90. For an even more provocative discussion of the meaning of individual self-esteem and respect in the context of Latin American development, see Paulo Freire, *Pedagogy of the Oppressed* (New York: Continuum, 1990).

22. W. Arthur Lewis, "Is economic growth desirable?" in *The Theory of Economic Growth* (London: Allen & Unwin, 1963), p. 420. For an outstanding and thoughtful analysis of the importance of freedom in development by a leading Third World intellectual, see Soedjatmoko, *Primacy of Freedom*. See also Owens, *Future of Freedom*, and Sen, *Development as Freedom*.

23. For an interesting attempt to measure political freedom quantitatively and to rank groups of nations according to a "political freedom index," see United Nations Development Program, *Human Development Report, 1992* (New York: Oxford University Press, 1992), pp. 26–33. The Heritage Foundation and the *Wall Street Journal* produce an annual "Index of Economic Freedom." For 1998 rankings of 154 countries from "free" to "repressed," see the *Wall Street Journal*, December 1, 1997.

24. United Nations Development Program, *Human Development Report, 1992*, p. 20.

25. United Nations Development Program, *Human Development Report, 2003–Millennium Development Goals: A Compact among Nations to End Human Poverty* (New York: Oxford University Press, 2003), also available at http://hdr.undp.org/reports/global/2003.

Further Reading

On the complex question of the meaning of development and underdevelopment, see Amartya Sen, *Development as Freedom* (New York: Knopf, 1999). Also see Barbara Ingham, "The meaning of development: Interactions between 'new' and 'old' ideas," *World Development* 21 (1993): 1803–1821; Dudley Seers, "The meaning of development," in *Measuring Development: The Role and Adequacy of Development Indicators,* ed. Nancy Bastor (London: Cass, 1972); Denis Goulet, *The Cruel Choice: A New Concept in the Theory of Development* (New York: Atheneum, 1971), ch. 2; Norman L. Hicks and Paul P. Streeten, "Indicators of development: The search for a basic needs yardstick," *World Development* 7 (1979); Howard J. Wiarda, "Towards a nonethnocentric theory of development: Alternative conceptions from the Third World," *Journal of Developing Areas* 17 (1983); United Nations Development Program, *Human Development Report, 1994* (New York: Oxford University Press, 1994), ch. 1 and 2; and Syed Nawab Haider Naqvi, "The nature of economic development," *World Development* 23 (1995): 543–556, and "The significance of development economics," *World Development* 24 (1996): 975–987. For an excellent discussion of the Millennium Development Goals, see United Nations Development Program, *Human Development Report, 2003* (New York: Oxford University Press, 2003). See also Timothy Besley and Robin Burgess, "Halving Global Poverty," *Journal of Economic Perspectives* 17, issue 3 (2003): 3–22.

CHAPTER TWO

Comparative Development: Differences and Commonalities among Developing Countries

The range of human development in the world is vast and uneven, with astounding progress in some areas amidst stagnation and dismal decline in others.

—United Nations Development Program, *Human Development Report, 2003*

Of course there must be differences between developing countries . . . [but] to maintain that no common ground exists is to make any discussion outside or across the frontiers of a single country meaningless.

—Julian West, Oxford University

Rates of growth of real per capita GNP are diverse, even over sustained periods. . . . Is there some action a government of India could take that would lead the Indian economy to grow like Indonesia's? If so, what, exactly? The consequences for human welfare involved in questions like these are simply staggering: Once one starts to think about them, it is hard to think about anything else.

—Robert Lucas, Nobel Laureate in Economics

The growth position of the less developed countries today is significantly different in many respects from that of the presently developed countries on the eve of their entry into modern economic growth.

—Simon Kuznets, Nobel Laureate in Economics

It is hazardous to try to generalize too much about the 160 member countries of the United Nations (UN) that constitute the developing world. The gaps between the poorest and richest developing countries are greater than those between the rich economies and upper-middle-income developing nations. And while almost all of these countries are relatively poor in money terms, they are diverse in culture, economic conditions, and social and political structures. Thus, for example, developing countries include India, with over 1 billion people and 26 states, as well as Grenada, with less than 100,000 people, fewer than most cities in the United States. Large size entails complex problems of national cohesion and administration while offering the benefits of relatively large markets, a wide range of resources, and the potential for self-sufficiency and economic diversity. In contrast, for many small countries, the situation is reversed, with problems including limited markets, shortages of skills, scarce physical resources, weak bargaining power, and little prospect of significant economic self-reliance but strong incentives for exports of manufactured goods.

In this chapter, we provide an overview of the great diversity of developing countries. Despite these variations, however, developing nations share a common set of problems, both domestic and international—problems that in fact define their state of underdevelopment. We then put these problems and the shared objectives and underlying requirements for growth in comparative historical, geographic, international economic relations, and institutional context.

Defining the Developing World

The most common way to define the developing world is by per capita income. Several international agencies, including the Organization for Economic Cooperation and Development (OECD) and the United Nations, offer classifications of countries by their economic status, but the best-known system is that of the International Bank for Reconstruction and Development (IBRD), more commonly known as the **World Bank.** In the World Bank's classification system, 208 economies with a population of at least 30,000 are ranked by their levels of gross national income (GNI) per capita. These economies are then classified as **low-income countries (LICs)**, lower-middle-income countries (LMCs), upper-middle-income countries (UMCs), high-income OECD countries, and other high-income countries.

Generally speaking, the developing countries are those with low-, lower-middle, or upper-middle incomes. These countries are grouped by their geographic region in Table 2.1, making them easier to identify on the map in Figure 2.1. Low-income countries are defined by the World Bank as having a per capita gross national income in 2003 of $765 or less; lower-middle-income countries have incomes between $766 and $3,035; upper-middle-income countries have incomes between $3,036 and $9,385; and high-income countries have incomes of $9,386 or more.

Note, however, that a few of the countries grouped as "other high income" economies in Table 2.1 are sometimes classified by the UN as developing countries. For example, high-income countries that have one or two highly developed export sectors but in which significant parts of the population remain relatively uneducated or in poor health for the country's income level may be viewed as still developing. Examples may include oil exporters such as Kuwait, Qatar, and the United Arab Emirates. Upper-income economies also include some tourism-dependent islands with lingering development problems. Even a few of the high-income OECD member countries, notably Portugal and Greece, have been viewed as developing countries at least until very recently. Nevertheless, the characterization of the developing world as sub-Saharan Africa, North Africa and the Middle East, Asia except for Japan, Latin America and the Carribean, and the "transition" countries of Eastern Europe and Central Asia including the former Soviet Union,

TABLE 2.1   Classification of Economies by Region and Income, 2003

East Asia and the Pacific		Latin America and the Caribbean		South Asia	
American Samoa	UMC	Antigua and Barbuda	UMC	Afghanistan	LIC
Cambodia	LIC	Argentina	UMC	Bangladesh	LIC
China	LMC	Belize	UMC	Bhutan	LIC
Fiji	LMC	Bolivia	LMC	India	LIC
Indonesia	LMC	Brazil	LMC	Maldives	LMC
Kiribati	LMC	Chile	UMC	Nepal	LIC
Korea, Dem. Rep.	LIC	Colombia	LMC	Pakistan	LIC
Laos	LIC	Costa Rica	UMC	Sri Lanka	LMC
Malaysia	UMC	Cuba	LMC		
Marshall Islands	LMC	Dominica	UMC	**Sub-Saharan Africa**	
Micronesia	LMC	Dominican Republic	LMC	Angola	LIC
Mongolia	LIC	Ecuador	LMC	Benin	LIC
Myanmar	LIC	El Salvador	LMC	Botswana	UMC
Palau	UMC	Grenada	UMC	Burkina Faso	LIC
Papua New Guinea	LMC	Guatemala	LMC	Burundi	LIC
Philippines	LMC	Guyana	LMC	Cameroon	LIC
Samoa	LMC	Haiti	LIC	Cape Verde	LMC
Solomon Islands	LIC	Honduras	LMC	Central African Republic	LIC
Thailand	LMC	Jamaica	LMC	Chad	LIC
Tonga	LMC	Mexico	UMC	Comoros	LIC
Vanuatu	LMC	Nicaragua	LIC	Congo, Dem. Rep.	LIC
Vietnam	LIC	Panama	UMC	Congo, Rep.	LIC
		Paraguay	LMC	Côte d'Ivoire	LIC
Europe and Central Asia		Peru	LMC	Equatorial Guinea	LIC
Albania	LMC	St. Kitts and Nevis	UMC	Eritrea	LIC
Armenia	LMC	St. Lucia	UMC	Ethiopia	LIC
Azerbaijan	LMC	St. Vincent and the		Gabon	UMC
Belarus	LMC	Grenadines	UMC	Gambia	LIC
Bosnia and Herzegovina	LMC	Suriname	LMC	Ghana	LIC
Bulgaria	LMC	Trinidad and Tobago	UMC	Guinea	LIC
Croatia	UMC	Uruguay	UMC	Guinea-Bissau	LIC
Czech Republic	UMC	Venezuela	UMC	Kenya	LIC
Estonia	UMC			Lesotho	LIC
Georgia	LMC			Liberia	LIC
Hungary	UMC			Madagascar	LIC
Kazakhstan	LMC	**Middle East and North Africa**		Malawi	LIC
Kyrgyz Republic	LIC	Algeria	LMC	Mali	LIC
Latvia	UMC	Djibouti	LMC	Mauritania	LIC
Lithuania	UMC	Egypt	LMC	Mauritius	UMC
Macedonia	LMC	Iran	LMC	Mayotte	UMC
Moldova	LIC	Iraq	LMC	Mozambique	LIC
Poland	UMC	Jordan	LMC	Namibia	LMC
Romania	LMC	Lebanon	UMC	Niger	LIC
Russian Federation	LMC	Libya	UMC	Nigeria	LIC
Serbia and Montenegro	LMC	Morocco	LMC	Rwanda	LIC
Slovak Republic	UMC	Oman	UMC	São Tomé and Principe	LIC
Tajikistan	LIC	Saudi Arabia	UMC	Senegal	LIC
Turkey	LMC	Syria	LMC	Seychelles	UMC
Turkmenistan	LMC	Tunisia	LMC	Sierra Leone	LIC
Ukraine	LMC	West Bank and Gaza	LMC	Somalia	LIC
Uzbekistan	LIC	Yemen	LIC	South Africa	LMC

(continued)

TABLE 2.1 *(continued)*

Sudan	LIC	Korea, Rep.	Cyprus

Sudan	LIC	Korea, Rep.	Cyprus
Swaziland	LMC	Luxembourg	Faeroe Islands
Tanzania	LIC	Netherlands	French Polynesia
Togo	LIC	New Zealand	Greenland
Uganda	LIC	Norway	Guam
Zambia	LIC	Portugal	Hong Kong (China)
Zimbabwe	LIC	Spain	Israel
		Sweden	Kuwait
High-Income OECD Countries		Switzerland	Liechtenstein
Australia		United Kingdom	Macao (China)
Austria		United States	Malta
Belgium			Monaco
Canada		**Other High-Income Countries**	Netherlands Antilles
Denmark		Andorra	New Caledonia
Finland		Aruba	Northern Mariana Islands
France		Bahamas	Qatar
Germany		Bahrain	San Marino
Greece		Barbados	Singapore
Iceland		Bermuda	Slovenia
Ireland		Brunei	Taiwan (China)
Italy		Cayman Islands	United Arab Emirates
Japan		Channel Islands	Virgin Islands (U.S.)

This table classifies all World Bank member economies and all other economies with populations of more than 30,000. Economies are divided among income groups according to 2003 GNI per capita, calculated using the World Bank Atlas method. The groups are low-income countries (LICs), $765 or less; lower-middle-income countries (LMCs), $766–$3,035; upper-middle-income countries (UMCs), $3,036–$9,385; and high-income countries, $9,386 or more.

Source: World Bank, August 2004, http://www.worldbank.org/data.

remains a useful generalization. In contrast, the developed world constituting the core of the OECD is comprised of the countries of Western Europe, North America, Japan, Australia, and New Zealand.

Sometimes a special distinction is made among upper-middle-income economies, designating some that have achieved relatively advanced manufacturing sectors as **newly industrializing countries (NICs)**. Yet another way to classify the nations of the developing world is through their degree of international indebtedness; the World Bank classifies countries as severely indebted, moderately indebted, and less indebted. Finally, the United Nations Development Program (UNDP) classifies countries according to their level of human development, including health and education attainments. Because of its great importance, we consider the UNDP Human Development Index (HDI) in detail later in the chapter, after providing some vital background.[1]

The simple division of the world into developed and developing countries is often useful for analytical and policy purposes. However, the wide income range of the latter serves as an early warning for us not to overgeneralize. Indeed, the economic differences between low-income countries in sub-Saharan Africa and South Asia and between upper-middle-income countries in East Asia and Latin

America can be every bit as profound as those between high-income OECD and upper-middle-income developing countries.

Nevertheless, despite the obvious diversity of these countries, most developing nations share a set of common and well-defined goals. These include a reduction in poverty, inequality, and unemployment; the provision of minimum levels of education, health, housing, and food to every citizen; the broadening of economic and social opportunities; and the forging of a cohesive nation-state. Related to these economic, social, and political goals are the common problems shared in varying degrees by most developing countries: widespread and chronic absolute poverty, high levels of unemployment and underemployment, wide and growing disparities in the distribution of income, low levels of agricultural productivity, sizable and growing imbalances between urban and rural levels of living and economic opportunities, serious and worsening environmental decay, antiquated and inappropriate educational and health systems, severe balance of payments and international debt problems, and substantial and increasing dependence on foreign technologies, institutions, and value systems. It is therefore possible and useful to talk about the similarities of critical development problems and to analyze these problems in a broad developing world perspective.

First we will attempt to identify some of the most important structural differences among developing countries and then provide relevant data to delineate some of their most common characteristic features. In spite of obvious physical, demographic, historical, cultural, and structural differences, most developing nations face very similar economic and social dilemmas. We then consider how developing countries today differ from developed countries in their earlier stages of development, and examine whether developing and developed countries are converging in their levels of development. The chapter concludes with a comparative case study of Bangladesh and Pakistan. An appendix to the chapter provides an overview of the components of economic growth—factor accumulation and technological progress.

The Structural Diversity of Developing Economies

Any portrayal of the structural diversity of developing nations requires an examination of eight critical components:

1. The size of the country (geographic area, population, and income)

2. Its historical and colonial background

3. Its endowments of physical and human resources

4. Its ethnic and religious composition

5. The relative importance of its public and private sectors and civil society

6. The nature of its industrial structure

FIGURE 2.1   The Developed and Developing World, 2005

Low-income countries
($765 or less)

Lower-middle-income
countries
($766–3,035)

Upper-middle-income
countries
($3,036–9,385)

High-income countries
($9,386 or more)

No data

Source: World Bank, http://www.worldbank.org/data/maps/images/gni-capita.gif. Reprinted with permission.

7. Its degree of dependence on external economic and political forces

8. The distribution of power in the nation, its social and political structures, and the underlying institutions or economic "rules of the game."

Size and Income Level

Obviously, the sheer physical size of a country, the size of its population, and its level of national income per capita are important determinants of its economic potential and major factors differentiating one developing nation from another. Of the 160 developing countries that were full members of the United Nations in 2000, 87 had fewer than 5 million people, 58 had fewer than 2.5 million, and 38 had fewer than 500,000. Large and populated nations like Brazil, India, Egypt, and Nigeria ex-

ist side-by-side with small countries like Paraguay, Nepal, Jordan, and Chad. Large size usually presents advantages of diverse resource endowment, large potential markets, and more local sources of materials and products. But it also creates problems of administrative control, national cohesion, and regional imbalances. As we shall see in Chapter 5, there is no necessary relationship among a country's size, its level of per capita national income, and the degree of equality or inequality in its distribution of that income. For example, India, with a 2002 population of 1,049 million, had a 2002 per capita income level of $470, while nearby Singapore, with only 4 million people, had a 2002 per capita income of $20,690.

Table 2.2 illustrates the point by listing the ten most and least populated countries in 2002 and their respective per capita income levels.[2] Only two of these are developed countries (the United States and Japan).

TABLE 2.2	The Ten Most and Least Populated Countries and Their Per Capita Income, 2002				
Most Populous	Population (millions)	GNI Per Capita (U.S. $)	Least Populous	Population (thousands)	GNI Per Capita (U.S. $)
1. China	1,280	960	1. St. Kitts and Nevis	47	6,540
2. India	1,049	470	2. Antigua and Barbuda	76	9,720
3. United States	288	35,400	3. Dominica	71	3,000
4. Indonesia	212	710	4. Seychelles	82	6,780
5. Brazil	174	2,830	5. Kiribati	95	960
6. Pakistan	145	420	6. Tonga	101	1,440
7. Russian Federation	144	2,130	7. Grenada	104	3,530
8. Bangladesh	136	380	8. St. Vincent and the Grenadines	109	2,820
9. Nigeria	133	300	9. Micronesia	122	1,970
10. Japan	127	34,010	10. São Tomé and Principe	154	300

Source: World Bank, August 2004, http://www.worldbank.org/data.

Historical Background

Most African and Asian nations were at one time or another colonies of Western European countries, primarily Britain and France but also Belgium, the Netherlands, Germany, Portugal, and Spain. The economic structures of these nations, as well as their educational and social institutions, have typically been modeled on those of their former colonial rulers. Countries like those in Africa that more recently gained their independence are therefore likely to be more concerned with consolidating and evolving their own national economic and political structures than with simply promoting rapid economic development.

Perhaps more important, the European colonial powers had a dramatic and long-lasting impact on the economies and political and institutional structures of their African and Asian colonies by their introduction of three powerful and tradition-shattering ideas: private property, personal taxation, and the requirement that taxes be paid in money rather than in kind. As we will discover later, these ideas combined to erode the autonomy of local communities and to expose their people to many new forms of potential exploitation. The worst impact of colonization was probably felt in Africa, especially if one also considers the earlier slave trade. Whereas in former colonies such as India local people played a role in colonial governance, in Africa most governance was administered by expatriates.

In Latin America, a longer history of political independence plus a more shared colonial heritage (Spanish and Portuguese) has meant that in spite of geographic and demographic diversity, the countries possess relatively similar economic, social, and cultural institutions and face similar problems. In Asia, different colonial heritages and the diverse cultural traditions of the indigenous peoples have combined to create different institutional and social patterns in countries such as India (British), the Philippines (Spanish and American), Vietnam (French), Indonesia (Dutch), and Korea (Japanese).

Physical and Human Resources

A country's potential for economic growth is greatly influenced by its endowments of **physical resources** (land, minerals, and other raw materials) and **human resources** (numbers of people and their level of skills). The extreme case of favorable physical **resource endowment** is the Persian Gulf oil states. At the other extreme are countries like Chad, Yemen, Haiti, and Bangladesh, where endowments of raw materials and minerals and even fertile land are relatively minimal. However, as the case of the Congo shows vividly, high mineral wealth is no guarantee of development success. Conflict over the profits from these industries often leads to a focus on the distribution of wealth rather than its creation and to social strife, undemocratic governance, and high inequality, in what is called the "curse of natural resources." Geography and climate can also play an important role in the success or failure of development efforts. Coastal economies seem to do better than land-locked economies, and temperate zone countries do better than tropical zone nations, all other things being equal.[3]

In the realm of human resource endowments, not only are sheer numbers of people and their skill levels important, but so are their cultural outlooks, attitudes toward work, access to information, willingness to innovate, and desire for self-improvement. The quality of public administration is also of particular importance. The role of human capital in economic development is examined in Chapter 8.

Ethnic and Religious Composition

One of the direct benefits of the end of the 45-year cold war between the United States and the former Soviet Union has been a substantial decline in foreign military and political presence in the developing world. An indirect cost of this withdrawal, however, has been the acceleration of ethnic, tribal, and religious conflict, such as in the violent disintegration of Yugoslavia. Although ethnic and religious tensions and occasional violence have always existed in LDCs, the waning of superpower influence triggered a revival of these internal conflicts and may even have accelerated the incidence of political and economic discrimination. Ethnicity and religion often play a major role in the success or failure of development efforts. Clearly, the greater the ethnic and religious diversity of a country, the more likely it is that there will be internal strife and political instability. It is not surprising, therefore, that some of the most successful recent development experiences—South Korea, Taiwan, Singapore, and Hong Kong—have occurred in culturally homogeneous societies.

Today, more than 40% of the world's nations have more than five significant ethnic populations. In most cases, one or more of these groups face serious problems of discrimination. Over half of the world's LDCs have recently experienced some form of interethnic conflict. Just in the 1990s, ethnic and religious conflicts leading to widespread death and destruction took place in Afghanistan, Rwanda, Mozambique, Sri Lanka, Iraq, India, Somalia, Ethiopia, Liberia, Angola, Myanmar, Sudan, Yugoslavia, Haiti, Indonesia, and the Democratic Republic of Congo.[4]

Moreover, descendents of African slaves brought forcefully to the western hemisphere continue to suffer discrimination in countries such as Brazil.

But neither overt physical conflict nor widespread violence is necessary to disrupt an economy or cause political instability. If development is about improving human lives and providing a widening range of choice to all peoples, racial, ethnic, caste, or religious discrimination can be equally pernicious. For example, throughout Latin America, indigenous populations have significantly lagged behind other groups on almost every measure of economic and social progress. Whether in Bolivia, Brazil, Peru, Mexico, Guatemala, or Venezuela, indigenous groups have benefited little from overall economic growth. To give just one illustration, almost 90% of Guatemala's native population is poor, compared to 50% of the rest of the population. Being indigenous makes it much more likely that an individual will be less educated, in poorer health, and in a lower socioeconomic stratum than other citizens.[5] This is particularly true for indigenous women.

Ethnic and religious diversity need not necessarily lead to inequality, turmoil, or instability, and unqualified statements about its impact cannot be made. There have been numerous instances of successful economic and social integration of minority or indigenous ethnic populations in countries as diverse as Malaysia and Mauritius. And in the United States, diversity is often cited as a source of creativity and innovation. The broader point is that the ethnic and religious composition of a developing nation and whether or not that diversity leads to conflict or cooperation can be important determinants of the success or failure of development efforts.[6]

Relative Importance of the Public and Private Sectors and Civil Society

Most developing countries have **mixed economic systems**, featuring both public and private ownership and use of resources. The division between the two and their relative importance are mostly a function of historical and political circumstances. Thus, in general, Latin American and Southeast Asian nations have larger private sectors than South Asian and African nations. The degree of foreign ownership in the private sector is another important variable to consider when differentiating among LDCs. A large foreign-owned private sector usually creates economic and political opportunities as well as potential problems not found in countries where foreign investors are less prevalent. Often countries like those in Africa with severe shortages of skilled human resources have tended to put greater emphasis on public-sector activities and state-run enterprises on the assumption that limited skilled manpower can be best used by coordinating rather than fragmenting administrative and entrepreneurial activities. The widespread economic failures and financial difficulties of many of these public concerns in countries such as Ghana, Senegal, Kenya, and Tanzania raise questions, however, about the validity of this assumption. As a result, these and other nations have moved in recent years toward less public and more private enterprise. The most dramatic examples are found in the 15 countries of the former Soviet Union and other once centrally planned economies, which have privatized a majority of their once mostly state-owned economies.

Economic policies, such as those designed to promote more employment, will naturally be different for countries with large public sectors and ones with sizable private sectors. In economies dominated by the public sector, direct government investment projects and large rural works programs will take precedence, whereas in private-oriented economies, special tax allowances designed to induce private businesses to employ more workers might be more common. Finally, note that the degree of corruption differs widely across developing countries and may influence both the size of the public sector and the design of privatization programs.

In recent years, there has been an increasing appreciation of the role played by the citizen sector, or "civil society"—voluntary action, including that of **nongovernmental organizations (NGOs)**, outside of government and for-profit activities of the private sector. Developed societies have vibrant civil societies, and NGOs and other nonprofit organizations play key and unique roles in social innovation and development through their capacities in social problem solving and program flexibility, specialized knowledge, targeted public goods provision, common property management, trust and credibility, and advocacy activities. Developing nations that have strong NGO sectors have often been able to make better progress in addressing problems of development such as poverty alleviation and expanding social inclusion.[7]

Industrial Structure

Though rapidly urbanizing, the majority of developing countries are agrarian in economic, social, and cultural outlook. Agriculture, both subsistence and commercial, is a principal economic activity in terms of the occupational distribution of the labor force, if not in terms of proportionate contributions to national income. As we shall see in Chapter 9, farming is not merely an occupation but a way of life for a majority of people in Asia, Africa, and Latin America. Nevertheless, there are great differences between the structure of agrarian systems and patterns of land ownership in Latin America and Africa. Asian agrarian systems are somewhat closer to those of Latin America in terms of patterns of land ownership, but the similarities are lessened by substantial cultural differences.

It is in the relative importance of the agricultural, manufacturing, and service sectors that we find the widest variation among developing nations. Most Latin American countries, having a longer history of independence and generally higher levels of national income than African or South Asian nations, possess more advanced industrial sectors. But in the 1970s and 1980s, economies like those of Taiwan, South Korea, and Singapore greatly accelerated the growth of their manufacturing output, and by 2002 these countries were classified as industrialized states. In terms of sheer size, India has one of the largest manufacturing sectors in the developing world, but this sector is nevertheless small in relation to the nation's enormous rural population. Table 2.3 provides information on the distribution of labor force and gross domestic product (GDP) between agriculture and industry in 15 developing countries, the United States, and the United Kingdom. The contrasts among the industrial structures of these countries is striking, especially in terms of the relative importance of agriculture. Note that in recent years, the role

TABLE 2.3 Industrial Structure in Seventeen Developing Countries, United States, and the United Kingdom, 1996

Country	Percentage of Labor Force[a]		Percentage of GDP	
	Agriculture	Industry	Agriculture	Industry
Africa				
Congo, Dem. Rep	75	12	64	13
Kenya	81	7	29	16
Nigeria	54	5	43	25
Tanzania	90	5	48	21
Uganda	86	4	46	16
Asia				
Bangladesh	64	14	30	18
India	65	13	28	29
Indonesia	55	10	16	43
Philippines	46	16	21	32
South Korea	21	27	6	43
Sri Lanka	46	13	22	25
Latin America				
Brazil	31	27	14	36
Colombia	30	24	16	20
Guatemala	60	12	24	20
Mexico	28	19	5	26
Peru	37	19	7	37
Venezuela	16	28	4	47
All developing countries	60	17	20	38
United States	2	25	2	29
United Kingdom	1	24	2	37

Sources: United Nations Development Program, *Human Development Report, 1996* (New York: Oxford University Press, 1996), tab. 31; Central Intelligence Agency, *The World Factbook, 1994* (Washington, D.C.: Central Intelligence Agency, 1994); and World Bank, *1998 World Development Indicators* (Washington, D.C.: World Bank, 1998), tabs. 2.5 and 4.2.

[a]Data are for 1994.

of industry in the most advanced countries has been shrinking as the economy increases in productivity and education and shifts to advanced services.

In spite of common problems, therefore, development strategies may vary from one country to the next, depending on the current nature, structure, and degree of interdependence among its **primary**, **secondary**, and **tertiary industrial sectors**. The primary sector consists of agriculture, forestry, and fishing; the secondary, mostly of manufacturing; and the tertiary, of commerce, finance, transport, and services.

External Dependence: Economic, Political, and Cultural

The degree to which a country is dependent on foreign economic, social, and political forces is related to its size, resource endowment, and political history. For most developing countries, this dependence is substantial. In some cases, it touches almost every facet of life. Most small nations are highly dependent on foreign investment and trade with the developed world (see Chapter 12). Almost all small nations are dependent on the importation of foreign and often excessively capital-intensive technologies of production. This fact alone exerts an extraordinary influence on the character of the growth process in these dependent nations.

But even beyond the strictly economic manifestations of dependence in the form of the international transfer of goods and technologies is the international transmission of systems of education and governance values, patterns of consumption, and attitudes toward life, work, and self. A country's ability to chart its own economic and social destiny is significantly affected by its degree of dependence on these and other external forces.

Political Structure, Power, and Interest Groups

In the final analysis, it is often not the correctness of economic policies alone that determines the outcome of national approaches to critical development problems. The political structure and the vested interests and allegiances of ruling elites (e.g., large landowners, urban industrialists, bankers, foreign manufacturers, the military, trade unionists) will typically determine what strategies are possible and where the main roadblocks to effective economic and social change may lie.

The constellation of interests and power among different segments of the populations of most developing countries is itself the result of their economic, social, and political histories and is likely to differ from one country to the next. Nevertheless, whatever the specific distribution of power among the military, the industrialists, and the large landowners of Latin America; the politicians and high-level civil servants in Africa; the oil sheiks and financial moguls of the Middle East; or the landlords, moneylenders, and wealthy industrialists of Asia, most developing countries are ruled directly or indirectly by small and powerful elites to a greater extent than the developed nations are.

Effective social and economic change thus requires either that the support of elite groups be enlisted or that the power of the elites be offset by more powerful democratic forces. Either way, and this point will be applied often throughout this book, economic and social development will often be impossible without corresponding changes in the social, political, legal, and economic institutions of a nation (e.g., land tenure systems, forms of governance, educational structures, labor market relationships, property rights, contract law, civic freedoms, the distribution and control of physical and financial assets, laws of taxation and inheritance, and provision of credit).

Common Characteristics of Developing Nations

The foregoing discussion should have demonstrated why it is sometimes risky to generalize too much about such a diverse set of nations as those in Africa, Asia, and Latin America. Nevertheless, common economic features of developing countries permit us to view them in a broadly similar framework. We will attempt to identify these similarities and provide illustrative data to demonstrate their importance. For convenience, we can classify these common characteristics into six broad categories:

1. Low levels of living, characterized by low incomes, inequality, poor health, and inadequate education

2. Low levels of productivity

3. High rates of population growth and dependency burdens

4. Substantial dependence on agricultural production and primary-product exports

5. Prevalence of imperfect markets and limited information

6. Dominance, dependence, and vulnerability in international relations

Low Levels of Living

In developing nations, general **levels of living** tend to be very low for the vast majority of people. This is true not only in relation to their counterparts in rich nations but often also in relation to small elite groups within their own societies. These low levels of living are manifested quantitatively and qualitatively in the form of low incomes (poverty), inadequate housing, poor health, limited education, high infant mortality, low life and work expectancies, and in many cases a general sense of malaise and hopelessness. Let us look at some recent statistics comparing certain aspects of life in the underdeveloped countries and in the more economically advanced nations. Although these statistics are national aggregates, often incorporate substantial errors of measurement, and in some cases are not strictly comparable due to exchange-rate variations, they do provide at least a summary indication of relative levels of living in different nations.

Per Capita National Income The **gross national income (GNI)** per capita, the most commonly used measure of the overall level of economic activity, is often used as a summary index of the relative economic well-being of people in different nations. It is calculated as the total domestic and foreign value added claimed by a country's residents without making deductions for depreciation of the domestic capital stock. The **gross domestic product (GDP)** measures the total value for final use of output produced by an economy, by both residents and nonresidents. Thus GNI comprises GDP plus the difference between the income residents receive from abroad for factor services (labor and capital) less payments made to nonresidents who contribute to the domestic economy. Where there is a large nonresident population playing a major role in the domestic economy (such as foreign corporations), these differences can be significant (see Chapter 12). In 2002, the total national income of all the nations of the world was valued at more than U.S. $32 trillion, of which almost $26 trillion originated in the economically developed regions and less than $7 trillion was generated in the less developed nations. When one takes account of the distribution of world population, this means that over 80% of the world's income is produced in the economically developed regions by 15% of the world's people. Thus the remaining 85% of the world's population is living on only one-fifth of total world income. The collective per capita incomes of the low- and middle-income countries average less than one-twentieth the per capita incomes of rich nations.

As an illustration of the per capita income gap between rich and poor nations, look at Figure 2.2. Notice that in 2002, the country with the highest per capita income, Switzerland, had 362 times the per capita income of one of the world's

FIGURE 2.2   **Per Capita Gross National Income in Selected Countries, 2002 (in U.S. $ at official exchange rates)**

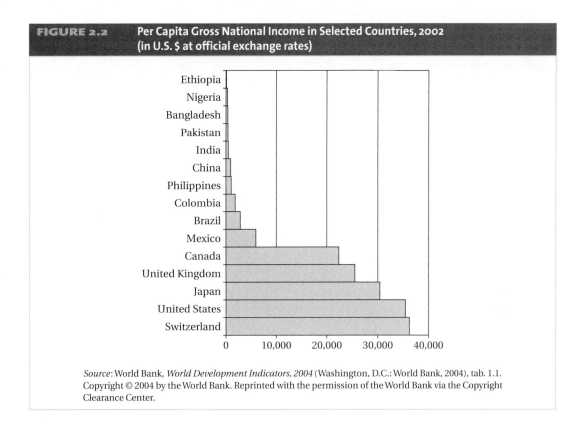

Source: World Bank, *World Development Indicators, 2004* (Washington, D.C.: World Bank, 2004), tab. 1.1. Copyright © 2004 by the World Bank. Reprinted with the permission of the World Bank via the Copyright Clearance Center.

poorest countries, Ethiopia, and 77 times that of one of the world's largest nations, India.

Per capita GNI comparisons between developed and less developed countries like those shown in Figure 2.2 are, however, exaggerated by the use of official foreign-exchange rates to convert the LDC national currency figures into U.S. dollars. This conversion does not measure the relative domestic purchasing power of different currencies. In an attempt to rectify this problem, researchers have tried to compare relative GNIs and GDPs by using **purchasing power parity (PPP)** instead of exchange rates as conversion factors. PPP is calculated using a common set of international prices for all goods and services produced, valuing goods in all countries at U.S. prices. In a simple version, purchasing power parity is defined as the number of units of a foreign country's currency required to purchase the identical quantity of goods and services in the local (LDC) market as $1 would buy in the United States. Generally, prices of nontraded services are much lower in developing countries because wages are so much lower. Clearly, if LDC domestic prices are lower, PPP measures of GNI per capita will be higher than estimates using foreign-exchange rates as the conversion factor. For example, China's 1997 GNI per capita was only 2.7% of that of the United States using the exchange-rate conversion but rises to 12.5% when estimated by the PPP method of conversion. Income gaps between rich and poor nations thus tend to be less when PPP is used.

TABLE 2.4   A Comparison of Per Capita GNI in Selected Developing Countries, plus the United Kingdom and United States, Using Official Exchange-Rate and Purchasing Power Parity Conversions, 2002

Country	GNI Per Capita (U.S. $)	
	Exchange Rate	Purchasing Power Parity
Argentina	4,220	10,190
Bangladesh	380	1,770
Brazil	2,830	7,450
Burundi	100	630
Cameroon	550	1,910
Chile	4,250	9,420
China	960	4,520
Costa Rica	4,070	8,560
Ghana	270	2,080
Guatemala	1,760	4,030
India	470	2,650
Indonesia	710	3,070
Kenya	360	1,010
Malawi	160	570
Malaysia	3,540	8,500
Mexico	5,920	8,800
Nicaragua	710	2,350
Sierra Leone	140	500
South Korea	9,930	16,960
Sri Lanka	850	3,510
Thailand	2,000	6,890
Uganda	240	1,360
United Kingdom	25,510	26,580
United States	35,400	36,110
Venezuela	4,080	5,220
Zambia	340	800

Source: World Bank, *World Development Indicators, 2004* (Washington, D.C.: World Bank, 2004) tab. 1.1. Copyright © 2004 by the World Bank. Reprinted with the permission of the World Bank via the Copyright Clearance Center.

Table 2.4 provides a comparison of exchange-rate and PPP GNI per capita for various developing countries. Measured in PPP dollars, the gap between the United States and Burundi would be 57 to 1 instead of the 354 to 1 gap using official foreign-exchange rates.[8]

Relative Growth Rates of National and Per Capita Income In addition to having much lower levels of per capita income, many developing countries and regions have experienced slower GNI growth than the developed nations and others have grown much more quickly. In the case of both per capita output and population growth, all contemporary developed countries have experienced large multiples of their previous historical rates during the epoch of modern economic growth, roughly from around 1770 to the present. For the now industrialized countries, annual growth rates over this period averaged almost 2% for per capita output and 1% for population, or 3% for total output (real GNI). These rates imply a doubling time of roughly 35 years for per capita output, 70 years for population, and 23 years for real GNI. These doubling times are calculated in a straightforward manner.[9]

TABLE 2.5	Growth Rates of Real Gross National Income Per Capita: Percentage Average Annual Growth, 1980–1990 and 1990–2000	
Country	1980–1990	1990–2000
Africa		
Kenya	0.3	−0.3
Nigeria	−3.0	−0.4
Tanzania	−0.7	0.3
Uganda	0.8	4.1
Congo, Dem. Rep.	1.5	−8.3
Asia		
Bangladesh	1.0	3.2
India	3.2	4.2
Indonesia	4.1	2.5
Philippines	−1.5	1.0
South Korea	8.9	4.7
Sri Lanka	2.4	4.0
Latin America		
Brazil	0.6	1.5
Colombia	1.1	1.1
Guatemala	−2.1	1.5
Mexico	−0.9	1.5
Peru	−2.0	3.0
Venezuela	−2.0	−0.5

Sources: World Bank, *World Bank Atlas, 1991* (Washington, D.C.: World Bank, 1991), pp 6–9; World Bank, *World Bank Atlas, 1996* (Washington, D.C.: World Bank, 1996), pp. 18–19; World Bank, *World Development Report, 2002* (New York: Oxford University Press, 2002), pp. 234–237.

Table 2.5 provides figures on recent growth rates of real GNI per capita for some representative countries. For many of them, the 1980s was a lost decade for development. In fact, during the 1980s and early 1990s, the **income gap** between rich and poor nations widened at the fastest pace in more than three decades. The impact of this widening gap is striking. If, for example, we look at the income levels of the richest 20% of the world's population in comparison with the poorest 20%, we find that whereas in 1960 the income ratio was 30 to 1, by 2000 the rich were receiving over 70 times the income of the poor. The richest 1% of people in the world receive as much income as the bottom 57%; this means that less than 50 million people receive as much income as 2.7 billion do.[10]

Table 2.5 provides data on comparative trends in the growth of real GNI per capita between 1980 and 1990 and 1990 and 2000 for a group of developing countries. Table 2.6 gives the details of the ever-growing income disparity between the richest and poorest 20% of the world's population.

Distribution of National Income The enormous gap in per capita incomes between rich and poor nations is not the only manifestation of the widening economic disparity between the world's rich and poor. To appreciate the breadth and depth of poverty in developing countries, it is also necessary to look at the gap between rich and poor *within* individual LDCs. We discuss the question of income distribution and equity more fully in Chapter 5, but a few remarks at this point seem appropriate.

	Ratio of Income Shares
TABLE 2.6 Global Income Disparity between the Richest and Poorest 20 % of the World's Population, 1960–2000	
Year	Richest to Poorest
1960	30 to 1
1970	32 to 1
1980	45 to 1
1991	61 to 1
2000	70 to 1

Sources: United Nations Development Program, *Human Development Report, 1992, 1994, 2001* (New York: Oxford University Press, 1992, 1994, 2001). Reprinted with permission.

First, all nations of the world show some degree of **income inequality.** There are large disparities between the income of the rich and of the poor in both developed and underdeveloped countries. Nevertheless, the gap between rich and poor is generally greater in less developed nations than in developed nations. For example, if we compare the share of national income that accrues to the poorest 40% of a country's population with that of the richest 20% as an arbitrary measure of the degree of inequality, we discover that countries like Brazil, Ecuador, Colombia, Nicaragua, Jamaica, Mexico, Venezuela, Kenya, Sierra Leone, South Africa, and Guatemala have substantial income inequality; others like India, Tanzania, Chile, Malaysia, China, Costa Rica, and Libya have moderate inequality; and others like Taiwan, Slovakia, Hungary, Indonesia, Canada, Japan, Sweden, and South Korea have relatively lesser inequalities in overall income distribution. Moreover, there is no obvious relationship or correlation between levels of per capita income and degree of income inequality. Nicaragua, with a similar low per capita income as India, has a much wider income disparity between the top 20% and bottom 40% of the population. Similarly, Kuwait, with almost the same high per capita income as Portugal, has a much lower percentage of its income distributed to the bottom 40% of its population. This phenomenon underlines the important point that economic development cannot be measured solely in terms of the level and growth of overall income or income per capita; one must also look at how that income is distributed among the population—at who benefits from development and why.

Extent of Poverty The magnitude and extent of poverty in any country depend on two factors: the average level of national income and the degree of inequality in its distribution. Clearly, for any given level of national per capita income, the more unequal the distribution, the greater the incidence of poverty. Similarly, for any given distribution, the lower the average income level, the greater the incidence of poverty. But how is one to measure poverty in any meaningful quantitative sense?

Development economists use the concept of **absolute poverty** to represent a specific minimum level of income needed to satisfy the basic physical needs of food, clothing, and shelter in order to ensure continued survival. A problem, however, arises when one recognizes that these minimum subsistence levels will vary from country to country and region to region, reflecting different physiological as well as social and economic requirements. Economists have therefore tended to make conservative estimates of world poverty in order to avoid unsubstantiated exaggerations of the problem. One common methodology has been to establish an **international poverty line** at, say, a constant U.S. $370 (based, e.g., on the value of the 1993 dollar) and then attempt to estimate the **purchasing power equivalent** of that sum of money in terms of a developing country's own currency.

Table 2.7 shows trends in the extent of absolute poverty in the developing world at selected intervals between 1987 and 1998, based on survey data. In Table 2.7, the poverty line is referred to as $1 per day, but in 1993 purchasing power parity dollars, the actual poverty line is drawn at $1.08. This is extreme poverty by any standard, and looking at the table, we see that a staggering 1.2 billion people still live below this daily income level. Table 2.7 also indicates that the estimated number of absolutely poor people remained little changed (and in fact increased somewhat) over the 11-year period of study. However, the conclusion that no progress had been made during this period would be misleading, because population growth was also substantial. In fact, the proportion of the population in developing countries that live in absolute poverty declined significantly, from 28.3% in 1987 to an estimated 24% in 1998. Note also that regional performance varied widely. While the percentage of the population in absolute poverty plummeted in East Asia, from 26.5% to 15.3%, the share was virtually unchanged in sub-Saharan Africa, the region with the fastest population growth. In practice, this meant that the number of poor people increased in sub-Saharan Africa from 217 million to 290 million. In Eastern Europe and Central Asia, the number in poverty increased from just 1.1 million to some 24 million persons, the result of the catastrophic drop in economic activity in the "transition" countries. As a result, the regional distribution of the poor is shifting from East Asia and South Asia to the "transition" countries, and sub-Saharan Africa. By 1998, the latter two regions accounted for more than two-thirds of all the poor people in the world. In sum, developing countries vary significantly in the amount of absolute poverty they face and in the extent of their progress, or lack of progress, in reducing poverty. (We cover problems of absolute poverty and policies to address it in detail in Chapter 5).

Health   In addition to struggling on low income, many people in developing nations fight a constant battle against malnutrition, disease, and ill health. Although there have been significant improvements since the 1960s, in the least developed countries of the world, life expectancy in 2002 still averaged only 50 years, compared to 64 years among all developing countries and 78 years in developed nations. **Infant mortality rates** (the number of children who die before their first birthday out of every 1,000 live births) average about 96 in the least developed countries, compared with approximately 64 in other less developed countries and 8 in developed countries. The rates for some specific countries are shown in Figure 2.3.

In the 1990s and early 2000s, the situation continued to deteriorate in sub-Saharan Africa, with deep declines in food consumption and widespread famine. In both Asia and Africa, over 60% of the population barely met minimum caloric requirements necessary to maintain adequate health. Moreover, it has been estimated that this caloric deficit amounted to less than 2% of the world cereal production. This contradicts the widely held view that malnutrition is the inevitable result of an imbalance between world population and world food supplies. The

this at $40,000 PPP. So we then divide by the difference between the log of $40,000 and the log of $100 to find the country's relative income achievement. This gives each country an index number that ranges between 0 and 1. For example, for the case of Armenia, whose 1999 PPP income per capita was $2,215, the income index is calculated as follows:

$$\text{Income index} = \frac{[\log(2{,}215) - \log(100)]}{[\log(40{,}000) - \log(100)]} = 0.517 \qquad (2.1)$$

With a value of the income index about midway through the maximum and minimum points (0.517 is close to 0.5), for the case of Armenia, it is easy to see the effect of diminishing marginal utility at work. An income of $2,215, which is less than 6% of the maximum goalpost of $40,000, is already enough to reach more than halfway to the maximum value that the index can take. Note that one (small) country, Luxembourg, has already exceeded the $40,000 PPP income target; for this case, the UNDP assigns Luxembourg the maximum value of $40,000 PPP income, and so the country gets the maximum income index of 1.[15]

To find the life expectancy (health proxy) index, the UNDP starts with a country's current life expectancy at birth and subtracts 25 years. The latter is the lower goalpost, the lowest that life expectancy could have been in any country over the last generation. Then the UNDP divides the result by 85 years minus 25 years, or 60 years, which represents the range of life expectancies expected over the previous and next generations. That is, it is anticipated that 85 years is a maximum reasonable life expectancy for a country to try to achieve over the coming generation. For example, for the case of Armenia, whose population life expectancy in 1999 was 72.7 years, the life expectancy index is calculated as follows:

$$\text{Life expectancy index} = \frac{(72.7 - 25)}{(85 - 25)} = 0.795 \qquad (2.2)$$

Notice that no diminishing marginal utility of years of life are assumed; the same holds for the education index. The education index is made up of two parts, with two-thirds weight on literacy and one-third weight on school enrollment. Because gross school enrollments can exceed 100% (because of older students going back to school), this index is also capped at 100%. For the case of Armenia, adult literacy is estimated at 98.3%, so

$$\text{Adult literacy index} = \frac{(98.3 - 0)}{(100 - 0)} = 0.983 \qquad (2.3)$$

For the gross enrollment index, Armenia estimates that 79.9% of its primary, secondary, and tertiary age population are enrolled in school, so the country receives the following value:

$$\text{Gross enrollment index} = \frac{(79.9 - 0)}{(100 - 0)} = 0.799 \qquad (2.4)$$

Then, to get the overall education index, the adult literacy index is multiplied by two-thirds and the gross enrollment index is multiplied by one-third. This choice reflects the view that literacy is the fundamental characteristic of an educated person. In the case of Armenia, this gives us

$$\text{Education index} = \frac{2}{3} \text{ (adult literacy index)} + \frac{1}{3} \text{ (gross enrollment index)}$$

$$= \frac{2}{3} (0.983) + \frac{1}{3} (0.799) = 0.922 \tag{2.5}$$

In the final index, each of the three components receives equal, or one-third, weight. Thus

$$\text{HDI} = \frac{1}{3} \text{ (income index)} + \frac{1}{3} \text{ (life expectancy index)} + \frac{1}{3} \text{ (education index)} \tag{2.6}$$

For the case of Armenia,

$$\text{HDI} = \frac{1}{3} (0.517) + \frac{1}{3} (0.795) + \frac{1}{3} (0.922) = 0.745 \tag{2.7}$$

One major advantage of the HDI is that it does reveal that a country can do much better than might be expected at a low level of income and that substantial income gains can still accomplish relatively little in human development.

Further, the HDI points up clearly that disparities in income are greater than disparities in other indicators of development, at least health and education measures. Moreover, the HDI reminds us that by *development,* we clearly mean broad human development, not just higher income. Many countries, such as some of the higher-income oil producers, have been said to have experienced "growth without development." Health and education are not just inputs into a production function (as in their role as components of human capital) but are fundamental development goals in their own right (see Chapter 8). We cannot easily argue that a nation of high-income individuals who are not well educated and suffer from significant health problems that lead to their living much shorter lives than others around the globe has achieved a higher level of development than a low-income country with high life expectancy and literacy. A better indicator of development disparities and rankings might be found by including health and education variables in a weighted welfare measure rather than by simply looking at income levels, and the HDI offers one very useful way to get at this.

There are other criticisms and possible drawbacks of the HDI. One is that gross enrollment in many cases overstates the amount of schooling, because in many countries a student who begins primary school is counted as enrolled without considering whether the student drops out at some stage. Equal (one-third) weight is given to each of the three components, which clearly has some value judgment behind it, but it is difficult to determine what this is. Note that because the variables are measured in very different types of units, it is difficult even to say precisely what equal weights mean. Finally, there is no attention to the role of quality. For example, there is a big difference between an extra year of life as a healthy, well-functioning individual and an extra year with a sharply limited range of capabilities (such as being confined to bed). Moreover, the quality of schooling counts, not just the number of years of enrollment. Finally, it should be noted that while one could imagine better proxies for health and education, measures for these variables were chosen partly on the criterion that sufficient data must be available to include as many countries as possible.

TABLE 2.9	Human Development Index for Twenty-Two Selected Countries, 2002			
Country	Relative Ranking (lowest to highest)	Human Development Index (HDI)	Real 2002 GDP Per Capital (PPP$)	GDP Rank minus HDI Rank[a]
Low human development				
Sierra Leone	177	0.273	520	−1
Ethiopia	170	0.359	780	−1
Angola	166	0.381	2,130	−38
Malawi	165	0.388	580	+9
Tanzania	162	0.407	580	+12
Guinea	160	0.425	2,100	−30
Medium human development				
Bangladesh	138	0.509	1,700	+1
India	127	0.595	2,670	−10
South Africa	119	0.666	10,070	−66
Nicaragua	118	0.667	2,470	+1
China	94	0.745	4,580	+5
Turkey	88	0.751	6,390	−12
Peru	85	0.752	5,010	+7
Thailand	76	0.768	7,010	−9
Oman	74	0.770	13,340	−32
Malaysia	59	0.793	9,120	−2
High human development				
Costa Rica	45	0.834	8,840	+14
Kuwait	44	0.838	16,240	−6
United Kingdom	12	0.936	26,150	+8
United States	8	0.939	35,750	−4
Canada	4	0.943	29,480	+5
Norway	1	0.956	36,600	+1

Source: United Nations Development Program, *Human Development Report, 2004* (New York: Oxford University Press, 2004), annex tab. 1. Reprinted with permission.

[a]A positive figure indicates that the HDI rank is better than the real GDP per capita (PPP$) rank; a negative indicates the opposite.

Table 2.9 shows the 2002 Human Development Index for a sample of 22 developed and developing nations ranked from low to high human development (column 3) along with their respective real GDP per capita (column 4) and a measure of the differential between the GDP per capita rank and the HDI rank (column 5). A positive number shows by how much a country's relative ranking rises when HDI is used instead of GDP per capita, and a negative number shows the opposite. Clearly, this is one of the critical issues for the HDI. If country rankings did not vary much when the HDI is used instead of GDP per capita, the latter would (as some economists claim) serve as a reliable proxy for socioeconomic development, and there would be no need to worry about such things as health and education indicators.

We see from Table 2.9 that the country with the lowest HDI (0.273) in 2002 was Sierra Leone, and the one with the highest (0.956) was Norway. What is more interesting for our purposes is that even though countries with high HDIs tend to have higher per capita incomes, within and across the three subgroups we find some

TABLE 2.10	Human Development Index Variations for Similar Incomes, 2002				
Country	GDP Per Capita (U.S. $ PPP)	HDI	HDI Rank	Life Expectancy (years)	Adult Literacy (%)
GDP per capita around PPP $1,000					
Tajikistan	980	0.671	116	68.6	99.5
Kenya	1,020	0.488	148	45.2	84.3
Central African Republic	1,170	0.361	169	39.8	48.6
Burkina Faso	1,100	0.302	175	45.8	12.8
GDP per capita around PPP $2,000					
Vietnam	2,300	0.691	112	69.0	90.3
Pakistan	1,940	0.497	142	60.8	41.5
Guinea	2,100	0.425	160	48.9	41.0
Angola	2,130	0.381	166	40.1	42.0
GDP per capita around PPP $3,500					
Jamaica	3,980	0.764	79	75.6	87.6
Sri Lanka	3,570	0.740	96	72.5	92.1
Indonesia	3,230	0.692	111	66.6	87.9
Morocco	3,810	0.620	125	68.5	50.7

Source: United Nations Development Program, *Human Development Report, 2002* (New York: Oxford University Press, 2002, 139–142). Reprinted with permission.

countries whose HDI is considerably higher than others even though the latter have substantially higher per capita incomes. Thus, for example, we see that Tanzania's HDI is 50% higher than that of Sierra Leone even though Sierra Leone's real GDP per capita is roughly the same as Tanzania's. Similarly, Malawi's HDI is very close to Angola's even though the latter's per capita GDP is nearly four times the former's. In the medium HDI group, China's per capita GDP is less than half of South Africa's even though its HDI is nearly a fifth higher. Thailand versus Oman and Costa Rica versus Kuwait also pose interesting contrasts.

To emphasize the point that countries at similar levels of GDP per capita can have significantly different human development indicators, depending on how that income is used, let us look briefly at Table 2.10. We see, for example, that Vietnam and Guinea have about the same income level, but Vietnam's HDI is 163% higher than Guinea's. Similar results are shown for Sri Lanka and Morocco, and for Kenya and the Central African Republic.

One of the major innovations of the HDI over the past few years has occurred through the disaggregation of a country's overall HDI into separate components to distinguish between men and women, different social classes reflecting skewed income distributions, and different regions and ethnic groups. The results show, not surprisingly, that men generally fare better than women for almost every socioeconomic indicator. For example, in the 43 countries for which gender-based income data were available in a recent year, women's income averaged less than 40% of men's in 14 countries (mostly developing countries, although the figure was 35% in Japan and 33% in Ireland) and above 60% in only 11, all of which were developed nations like Sweden and Norway.

When the aggregate HDI for various countries was adjusted for income distribution, the relative rankings of many developing nations also changed significantly.[16] For example, Brazil and Botswana have highly unequal distributions so that their rankings slip by seven and eight places, respectively, while China and Sri Lanka see their HDI rankings rise by a similar factor due to their more egalitarian distributions. When HDIs were then adjusted for race, region, and ethnicity, we find, for example, that even though South Africa's overall HDI was 0.666 (medium), the HDI for whites was 0.876 (high), while for blacks it was 0.462 (low); even though Brazil's HDI was 0.775, its wealthy southern regions (Rio de Janeiro and São Paulo) had an HDI of 0.838, while its poor northeast regions had an HDI of 0.549; and even though Nigeria had an HDI of 0.466, its richest state, Bendel, had an HDI of 0.666, while the poorest, Borno, had a value of only 0.156 (lower than any country).

The United Nations Human Development Index has thus made a major contribution to improving our understanding of what constitutes development, which countries are succeeding (as reflected by rises in their HDI over time), and how different groups and regions within countries are faring. By combining social and economic data, the HDI allows nations to take a broader measure of their development performance, both relatively and absolutely, and thus to focus their economic and social policies more directly on areas in need of improvement.

Although there are somewhat valid criticisms, the fact remains that the HDI, when used in conjunction with traditional economic measures of development, greatly increases our understanding of which countries are experiencing development and which are not. More important, by examining each of the three major components of the HDI-adjusted real per capita income, life expectancy, and literacy and schooling measures and by disaggregating a country's overall HDI to reflect income distribution, gender, regional, and ethnic differentials, we are now able to identify not only whether a country is developing but also whether various significant groups within that country are participating in that development.

Low Levels of Productivity

In addition to low levels of living and deprivations in human development, developing countries are characterized by relatively low levels of **labor productivity**. The concept of a **production function** systematically relating outputs to different combinations of factor inputs for a given technology is often used to describe the way in which societies go about providing for their material needs. But the technical engineering concept of a production function must be supplemented by a broader conceptualization that includes among its other inputs managerial competence, access to information, worker motivation, and institutional flexibility. Throughout the developing world, levels of labor productivity (output per worker) are extremely low compared with those in developed countries. This can be explained by a number of basic economic concepts.

For example, the principle of *diminishing marginal productivity* states that if increasing amounts of a variable factor (labor) are applied to fixed amounts of other factors (e.g., capital, land, materials), the extra or marginal product of the variable factor declines beyond a certain number. Low levels of labor productivity can therefore be explained by the absence or severe lack of "complementary" factor inputs such as physical capital or experienced management.

To raise productivity, according to this argument, domestic *savings* and foreign *finance* must be mobilized to generate new investment in physical capital goods and build up the stock of human capital (e.g., managerial skills) through investment in education and training. Institutional changes are also necessary to maximize the potential of this new physical and human investment. These changes might include such diverse activities as the reform of land tenure, corporate tax, credit, and banking structures; the creation or strengthening of an independent, honest, and efficient administrative service; and the restructuring of educational and training programs to make them more appropriate to the needs of the developing societies. These and other noneconomic inputs into the social production function must be taken into account if strategies to raise productivity are to succeed. In the absence of the proper institutional and structural arrangements, development may not succeed.

One must also take into account the impact of worker and management *attitudes* toward self-improvement; people's degree of alertness, adaptability, ambition, and general willingness to innovate and experiment; and their attitudes toward manual work, discipline, authority, and exploitation. Added to all these must be the physical and mental capacity of the individual to do the job satisfactorily. The economic success stories of the "Four Asian Tigers"—South Korea, Singapore, Hong Kong, and Taiwan—are often attributed in part to the quality of their human resources, the organization of their production systems, and the institutional arrangements undertaken to accelerate their productivity growth.

The area of physical health most clearly reveals the close linkage that exists between low levels of income and low levels of productivity in developing nations. It is well known, for example, that poor nutrition in childhood can severely restrict the mental and physical growth of individuals. Poor dietary habits, inadequate food, and low standards of personal hygiene in later years can cause further deterioration in a worker's health and can therefore adversely influence attitudes toward the job and the other people at work. The worker's low productivity may be due in large part to physical lethargy and the inability, both physical and emotional, to withstand the daily pressures of competitive work.[17] Low productivity leads to low income, which leads to low ability to purchase nutritious foods, which can lead to low capacity for work, and hence to low productivity.[18]

We may conclude, therefore, that low levels of living and low productivity are self-reinforcing social and economic phenomena in poor countries and as such are the principal manifestations of and contributors to their underdevelopment. Gunnar Myrdal's well-known theory of "circular and cumulative causation" in underdeveloped countries is based on these mutually reinforcing interactions between low living levels and low productivity.[19]

High Rates of Population Growth and Dependency Burdens

Of the world's population of just over 6.4 billion people in 2004, more than five-sixths live in the less developed countries and less than one-sixth in the developed nations. Both birth and death rates are strikingly different between the two groups

TABLE 2.11	Crude Birthrates throughout the World, 2002
Crude Birthrate[a]	**Countries**
50	Niger, Mali, Somalia, Afghanistan, Angola
45	Malawi, Liberia, Chad, Rwanda, Sierra Leone, Congo (Dem. Rep.), Uganda, Burkina Faso, Gambia
40	Burundi, Guinea, Senegal, Ethiopia, Tanzania, Mozambique, Zambia, Benin, Nigeria, Yemen
35	Central African Republic, Laos, Pakistan, Gabon, Swaziland, Namibia, Kenya, Togo, Sudan
30	Honduras, Paraguay, Bolivia, Botswana, Jordan, Haiti, Nepal, Iraq, Bangladesh, Syria, Paraguay, Zimbabwe
25	Egypt, India, Cameroon, Libya, Cambodia, Myanmar, Philippines, El Salvador, South Africa, Venezuela
20	Algeria, Costa Rica, Mexico, Vietnam, Peru, Turkey, Colombia, Lebanon, Malyasia, Kuwait, Indonesia, Panama, Sri Lanka, Argentina, Jamaica, Brazil, Iran
15	United States, Australia, Ireland, South Korea, China, Thailand, Chile
10	Canada, Cuba, Switzerland, Austria, Germany, Japan, Russia, Singapore

Source: World Bank, *World Development Indicators, 2004* (Washington, D.C.: World Bank, 2004), tab. 2.1. Copyright © 2004 by the World Bank. Reprinted with the permission of the World Bank via the Copyright Clearance Center.

[a]Yearly number of live births per 1,000 population.

of countries. Birthrates in less developed countries are generally high, on the order of 30 to 40 per 1,000, whereas those in the developed countries are less than half that figure. Indeed, as shown in Table 2.11, the **crude birthrate** (the yearly number of live births per 1,000 population) is probably one of the most efficient ways of distinguishing the less developed from the developed countries. There are few less developed countries with a birthrate below 20 per 1,000 and no developed nations with a birthrate above it.

Death rates (the yearly number of deaths per 1,000 population) in developing countries are also high relative to the developed nations, but thanks to improved health conditions and the control of major infectious diseases, the differences are substantially smaller than the corresponding differences in birthrates. As a result, the average rate of population growth is now about 1.6% per year in developing countries, compared to population growth of 0.7% per year in the high-income countries.

A major implication of high LDC birthrates is that children under age 15 make up almost 40% of the total population in these countries, as opposed to less than 20% of the total population in the developed countries. Thus in most developing countries, the active labor force has to support proportionally almost twice as many children as it does in richer countries. By contrast, the proportion of people over the age of 65 is much greater in the developed nations. Both older people and children are often referred to as an economic **dependency burden** in the sense that they are nonproductive members of society and therefore must be supported financially by a country's labor force (usually defined as citizens between the ages of 15 and 64). The overall dependency burden (i.e., both young and old) represents only about one-third of the populations of developed countries but almost 45% of the populations of the less developed nations. Moreover, in the latter countries, almost 90% of the dependents are children, whereas only 66% are children in the richer nations.

We may conclude, therefore, that not only are developing countries character-ized by higher rates of population growth, but they must also contend with greater dependency burdens than rich nations. The circumstances and conditions under which population growth becomes a deterrent to economic development is a crit-ical issue and is examined in Chapter 6.

Substantial Dependence on Agricultural Production and Primary-Product Exports

The vast majority of people in LDCs live and work in rural areas. Over 65% are ru-rally based, compared to less than 27% in economically developed countries. Simi-larly, 58% of the labor force is engaged in agriculture, compared to only 5% in de-veloped nations. Agriculture contributes about 14% of the GNI of developing nations but only 3% of the GNI of developed nations.

Small-Scale Agriculture Table 2.12 provides a breakdown of population, labor force, and agricultural production by regions of the developed and the less devel-oped world. Note in particular the striking difference between the proportionate size of the agricultural population in Africa (68%) and South Asia (64%) versus North America (3%). In terms of actual numbers, there were almost 685 million agricultural labor force members in Asia and Africa producing an annual volume of output valued at U.S. $195 million.[20] By contrast, in North America, less than 1% of this total number of agricultural workers (4.5 million) produced almost one-third as much total output ($60 million). This means that the average productivity of agricultural labor expressed in U.S. dollars is almost 35 times greater in North America than in Asia and Africa combined. Although international comparative figures such as these are often of dubious quality regarding both precision and methods of measurements, they nevertheless give us rough orders of magnitude. Even adjusting them for, say, undervaluing nonmarketed agricultural output, the differences in agricultural labor productivity would still be very sizable.

The basic reason for the concentration of people and production in agricultural and other primary production activities in developing countries is the simple fact that at low income levels, the first priorities of any person are food, clothing, and shelter. Agricultural productivity is low not only because of the large numbers of people in relation to available land but also because LDC agriculture is often char-acterized by primitive technologies, poor organization, and limited physical and human capital inputs. Technological backwardness persists because developing country agriculture is predominantly noncommercial peasant farming. In many parts of the world, especially in Asia and Latin America, it is characterized further by land tenure arrangements in which peasants rent rather than own their small plots of land. As we shall see in Chapter 9, such land tenure arrangements take away much of the economic incentive for output expansion and productivity im-provement. Even where land is abundant, primitive techniques and the use of hand plows, drag harrows, and animal (oxen, buffaloes, donkeys) or raw human power necessitate that typical family holdings be not more than 5 to 8 hectares (12

TABLE 2.12	Population, Labor Force, and Production in Developed and Less Developed Regions, 2002–2003				
Region	Population (millions)	Urban (%)	Rural (%)	Labor Force in Agriculture (%)	Agricultural Share of GDP (%)
World	6,314	47	53	49	5
Developed countries	1,202	75	25	5	3
Europe	727	73	27	7	3
North America	323	79	21	3	2
Japan	127	78	22	7	2
Less developed countries	5,112	40	60	58	14
Africa	861	33	67	68	20
South Asia	1,480	30	70	64	30
East Asia	1,918	40	60	70	18
Latin America	540	75	25	25	10

Sources: Population Reference Bureau, *2003 World Population Data Sheet* (Washington, D.C.: Population Reference Bureau, 2003); *World Bank, World Development indicators, 2004* (New York: Oxford University Press, 2004), tabs. 4 and 12, Agriculture labor force figures are based on 1997 World Bank estimates.

to 20 acres). In fact, in many countries, average holdings can be as low as 1 to 3 hectares. The number of people that this land must support both directly (through on-the-farm consumption) and indirectly (through production for urban and nonfarm rural food consumption) often runs as high as 10 to 15 people per hectare. It is no wonder that efforts to improve the efficiency of agricultural production and increase the average yields of rice, wheat, maize (corn), soybeans, and millet are now and will continue to be top-priority development objectives.

Comparative Dependence on Primary Exports Many economies of less developed countries are still oriented toward the production of primary products (agriculture, fuel, forestry, and raw materials) as opposed to secondary (manufacturing) and tertiary (service) activities. These primary commodities form their main exports to other nations (both developed and less developed). For example, as shown by Figure 2.4, manufactures represented less than half of merchandise exports developing regions outside of East and South Asia.

As we shall see in Chapter 14, most poor countries need to obtain **foreign exchange** in addition to domestic savings in order to finance priority development projects. Although private foreign investment and foreign aid are a significant but declining source of foreign exchange, exports of primary products typically account for a substantial fraction of the annual flow of foreign currency into the developing world. Unfortunately for many debt-ridden LDCs, much of the foreign exchange earned through exports in the 1980s and 1990s went to pay the interest on earlier borrowing. In fact, some years, these countries witnessed a negative international flow of capital, with more foreign currency flowing out of the LDCs than they actually received.

Even though exports are so important to many developing nations, LDC export growth (excluding oil exports) has barely kept pace with that of developed countries. Consequently, even in their best years, most non-oil-exporting developing

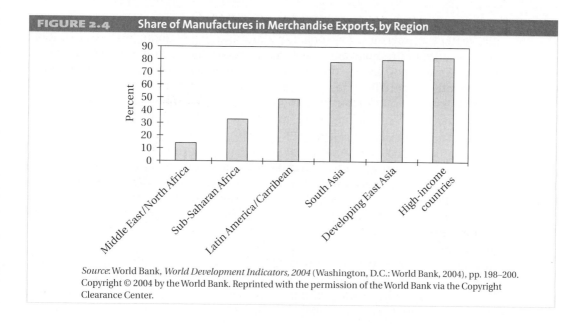

FIGURE 2.4   Share of Manufactures in Merchandise Exports, by Region

Source: World Bank, *World Development Indicators, 2004* (Washington, D.C.: World Bank, 2004), pp. 198–200. Copyright © 2004 by the World Bank. Reprinted with the permission of the World Bank via the Copyright Clearance Center.

nations have been losing ground to the more developed countries in terms of their share of total world merchandise trade. In 1950, for example, the LDCs' share was nearly 33%. It has fallen in almost every year since and by 2000 stood at around 25%. The share of the low-income countries is a mere 3%.[21] Most of the success in export promotion was captured by the Four Asian Tigers, along with a few other NICs in the 1980s and 1990s. The majority of LDCs have experienced a continuing decline in their share of world trade (see Chapter 12). Finally, many developing countries outside East Asia and India are producing simple manufactures whose prices are declining in world markets.

Prevalence of Imperfect Markets and Incomplete Information

In the 1990s, almost every developing country was moving, at its own pace, toward the establishment of a market economy. There seemed to be a growing consensus that there had been too much government intervention in the workings of developing economies and that free markets and unfettered competition held the key to rapid economic growth. But as we shall discover in greater detail in later chapters, the presumed benefits of market economies and market-friendly policies depend heavily on the existence of institutional, cultural, and legal prerequisites that most of us in industrial societies take for granted.

In many LDCs, these legal and institutional foundations are either absent or extremely weak. They include the existence of a legal system that enforces contracts and validates property rights; a stable and trustworthy currency; an infrastructure of roads and utilities that results in low transport and communication costs so as to facilitate interregional trade; a well-developed system of banking and insurance; formal credit markets that select projects and allocate loanable funds on the basis of relative economic profitability and enforce rules of repayment; substantial market information for consumers and producers about prices, quantities, and qualities of products and resources as well as the creditworthiness of potential borrowers; and norms of behavior that facilitate successful long-term business relationships. These seven factors, along with the existence of economies of scale in major sectors of the economy, thin markets for many products due to limited demand and few sellers, widespread externalities (costs or benefits that accrue to companies or individuals not doing the producing or consuming) in production and consumption, and the prevalence of common property resources (e.g., fisheries, grazing lands, waterholes) mean that markets are often highly imperfect. Moreover, information is limited and costly to obtain, thereby often causing goods, finances, and resources to be misallocated. We have come to understand that small externalities can interact in ways that add up to very large distortions in an economy and present the real possibility of an underdevelopment trap (see Chapter 4). Whether or not these **imperfect markets** and **incomplete information** systems justify a more active role for government (which is also subject to similar problems of incomplete and imperfect information) is an issue that we will be dealing with in later chapters. But their existence remains a common characteristic of developing nations and an important contributing factor to their state of underdevelopment.[22]

Dependence and Vulnerability in International Relations

For many less developed countries, a final significant factor contributing to the persistence of low levels of living, rising unemployment, and growing income inequality is the highly unequal distribution of economic and political power between rich and poor nations. As we shall see later, these unequal strengths are manifested not only in the dominant power of rich nations to control the pattern of international trade and agreements regulating it but also in their ability often to dictate the terms whereby technology, foreign aid, and private capital are transferred to developing countries.

Other equally important aspects of the international transfer process can serve to inhibit the development of poor nations. One subtle but nonetheless significant factor has been the transfer of developed world values, attitudes, institutions, and standards of behavior to developing world nations. Examples include the colonial transfer of often inappropriate educational structures, curricula, and school systems; the formation of Western-style trade unions; the organization and orientation of health services in accordance with the curative rather than the preventive model; and the importation of inappropriate structures and procedures for public bureaucratic and administrative systems. Of even greater potential significance may be the influence of rich-country social and economic standards on developing-country salary scales, elite lifestyles, and general attitudes toward the private accumulation of wealth. Whether there are market-friendly policies or extensive government intervention, such attitudes can often lead to corruption and economic plunder by a privileged minority. Finally, the penetration of rich-country attitudes, values, and standards also contributes to the international **brain drain**—

the migration of professional and skilled personnel, who were often educated in the developing country at great expense, to the various developed nations. Examples include doctors, nurses, scientists, engineers, and computer programmers.

The net effect of all these factors is to create a situation of vulnerability among developing nations in which forces largely outside their control can have decisive and dominating influences on their economic and social well-being. Many countries—most of the least developed—are small, and their economies are dependent, with very little prospect for self-reliance. But they can often join forces economically to strengthen their joint bargaining power and enable them to scrutinize more carefully and be more selective about foreign investment and technical assistance.

For developing nations that possess greater resources and relatively more bargaining power, the phenomenon of dominance becomes manifested more in the general tendency of the rich to get richer, often at the expense of the poor. But as mentioned, this is not simply a matter of rich nations growing at a faster pace than poorer nations. It is also a matter of rich and dominating sectors or groups *within* the LDC economy (e.g., the modern industrial or agricultural sector; landlords, trade union leaders, industrialists, politicians, bureaucrats, and civil servants in positions of power) growing richer, often at the expense of the much larger but politically and economically less powerful masses of poor people. This dual process of rich nations and powerful groups within poor nations prospering while others stagnate is in fact a widespread phenomenon.

One does not have to accept the thesis of some in the dependency school, described in the next chapter, that governments of rich countries today act systematically and intentionally against the interests of the developing countries, to perceive that colonialism and slavery produced deep distortions that in all too many cases persist to the present day. And it is not adequate to complain that developing countries have had several decades of independence to break out of the underdevelopment traps set in the colonial era. This is because, as we will see in Chapters 4 and 11, government itself can become part of a bad equilibrium that is profoundly difficult to escape. Recently, scholarship has more clearly demonstrated that institutions put in place by colonial powers centuries ago and still persisting today can explain much of the gulf between the performance of developed and developing countries. In many cases, the once-richest of the former colonies have been the ones most impoverished by the predations of the colonial experience.[23]

How Developing Countries Today Differ from Developed Countries in Their Earlier Stages

The position of developing countries today is in many important ways significantly different from that of the currently developed countries when they embarked on their era of modern economic growth. We can identify nine significant differences in initial conditions that require a special analysis of the growth prospects and requirements of modern economic development:

1. Physical and human resource endowments

2. Per capita incomes and levels of GDP in relation to the rest of the world

3. Climate

4. Population size, distribution, and growth

5. Historical role of international migration

6. International trade benefits

7. Basic scientific and technological research and development capabilities

8. Stability and flexibility of political and social institutions

9. Efficacy of domestic economic institutions

We will discuss each of these conditions with a view to formulating requirements and priorities for generating and sustaining economic growth in the contemporary world.

Physical and Human Resource Endowments

Contemporary developing countries are often less well endowed with natural resources than the currently developed nations were at the time when the latter nations began their modern growth. A few developing nations are blessed with abundant supplies of petroleum, other minerals, and raw materials for which world demand is growing; most less developed countries, however—especially in Asia, where more than half of the world's population resides—are poorly endowed with natural resources. Moreover, in parts of Latin America and Africa, where natural resources are more plentiful, heavy investments of capital are needed to exploit them. Such financing is not easy to come by without sacrificing substantial control to powerful developed-country multinational corporations that alone are currently capable of large-scale, efficient resource exploitation.

The difference in skilled human resource endowments is even more pronounced. The ability of a country to exploit its natural resources and to initiate and sustain long-term economic growth is dependent on, among other things, the ingenuity and the managerial and technical skills of its people and its access to critical market and product information at minimal cost.[24] The populations of today's low-income developing nations are generally less educated, less informed, less experienced, and less skilled than their counterparts were in the early days of economic growth in the West. Paul Romer argues that today's developing nations "are poor because their citizens do not have access to the ideas that are used in industrial nations to generate economic value.[25] For Romer, the technology gap between rich and poor nations can be divided into two components, a physical object gap, involving factories, roads, and modern machinery, and an idea gap, including knowledge about marketing, distribution, inventory control, transactions processing, and worker motivation. It is this idea gap, or what Thomas Homer-Dixon calls the ingenuity gap (the ability to apply innovative ideas to solve practical social and technical problems), between rich and poor nations that lies at the core of the development divide. No such human resource gaps existed for the now developed countries on the eve of their industrialization.

Relative Levels of Per Capita Income and GDP

The four-fifths of the world's population at present living in developing countries have on the average a lower level of real per capita income than their developed-country counterparts had in the nineteenth century. First of all, about half of the population of developing countries is attempting to subsist at bare minimum levels. Obviously, the average standard of living in, say, early-nineteenth-century England was nothing to envy or boast about, but it was not as economically debilitating or precarious as it is today for a large fraction of people in the 40 or so least developed countries.

Second, at the beginning of their modern growth era, today's developed nations were economically in advance of the rest of the world. They could therefore take advantage of their relatively strong financial position to widen the income gaps between themselves and less fortunate countries. By contrast, today's LDCs begin their growth process at the low end of the international per capita income scale.

The relatively weak position of the poorest countries in the world economy is analogous to that of a 1,500-meter race between a young athlete and an old man in which the former is given a 1,000-meter head start. Not only is such backwardness economically difficult to overcome or even reduce, but psychologically it creates a sense of frustration and a desire to grow at any cost. This can in fact inhibit the long-run improvement in national levels of living.

Climatic Differences

Almost all developing countries are situated in tropical or subtropical climatic zones. It has been observed that the economically most successful countries are located in the temperate zone. The dichotomy cannot simply be attributed to coincidence; it must bear some relation to the special difficulties caused directly or indirectly by differing climatic conditions.

It is undeniable that the extremes of heat and humidity in most poor countries contribute to deteriorating soil quality and the rapid depreciation of many natural goods. They also contribute to the low productivity of certain crops, the weakened regenerative growth of forests, and the poor health of animals. Extremes of heat and humidity not only cause discomfort to workers but can also weaken their health, reduce their desire to engage in strenuous physical work, and generally lower their levels of productivity and efficiency. As we will see in Chapter 8, malaria and other serious parasitic diseases are often concentrated in tropical areas. There is growing evidence that tropical geography does pose serious problems for economic development and that special attention in development assistance must be given to these problems, such as a concerted international effort to develop a malaria vaccine.[26]

Population Size, Distribution, and Growth

In Chapter 6, we will examine in detail some of the development problems and is-sues associated with rapid population growth. At this point, it is sufficient to note that population size, density, and growth constitute another important difference between less developed and developed countries. Before and during their early growth years, Western nations experienced a very slow rise in population growth. As industrialization proceeded, population growth rates increased primarily as a result of falling death rates but also because of slowly rising birthrates. However, at no time during their modern growth epoch did European and North American countries have natural population growth rates in excess of 2% per annum, and they generally averaged much less.

By contrast, the populations of many developing countries have been increas-ing at annual rates in excess of 2.5% over the past few decades, and some are rising even faster today. Moreover, the concentration of these large and growing popula-tions in a few areas means that most LDCs today start with considerably higher person-to-land ratios than the European countries did in their early growth years. Finally, in terms of comparative absolute size, with the exception of the former So-viet Union, no country that embarked on a long-term period of economic growth approached the present-day population size of India, Egypt, Pakistan, Indonesia, Nigeria, or Brazil. Nor, as we have just seen, were their rates of natural increase anything like that of present-day Kenya, the Philippines, Bangladesh, Malawi, or Guatemala. In fact, many observers doubt whether the industrial revolution and the high long-term growth rates of contemporary developed countries could have been achieved or proceeded so fast and with so few setbacks and disturbances, es-pecially for the very poor, had their populations been expanding so rapidly.

The Historical Role of International Migration

Of perhaps equal historical importance to the differing rates of natural population increase is the fact that in the nineteenth and early twentieth centuries, there was a major outlet for excess rural populations in international migration, which was both widespread and large-scale. Over 60 million people migrated to the Americas between 1850 and 1914, a time when world population averaged less than a quarter of its current levels. In countries such as Italy, Germany, and Ireland, periods of se-vere famine or pressure on the land often combined with limited economic oppor-tunities in urban industry to push unskilled rural workers toward the labor-scarce nations of North America and Australia. Thus, as Brinley Thomas argues, the "three outstanding contributions of European labor to the American economy— 1,187,000 Irish and 919,000 Germans between 1847 and 1855, 418,000 Scandina-vians and 1,045,000 Germans between 1880 and 1885, and 1,754,000 Italians be-tween 1898 and 1907—had the character of evacuations."[27]

Whereas the main thrust of international emigration up to the First World War was both distant and permanent, the period since the Second World War has wit-nessed a resurgence of international migration within Europe itself, which is es-sentially over short distances and to a large degree temporary. However, the eco-nomic forces giving rise to this migration are basically the same; that is, during the

1950s and especially the 1960s, surplus rural workers from southern Italy, Greece, and Turkey flocked into areas of labor shortages, most notably western Germany and Switzerland. The fact that this more contemporary migration from regions of surplus labor in southern and southeastern Europe was initially of both a permanent and a nonpermanent nature provided a valuable dual benefit to the relatively poor areas from which these unskilled workers migrated. The home governments were relieved of the costs of providing for people who in all probability would remain unemployed, and because a large percentage of the workers' earnings were sent home, these governments received a valuable and not insignificant source of foreign exchange.[28] In the early years of the twenty-first century, these international remittances have been topping $100 billion annually.

In view of the foregoing discussion, you might reasonably ask why the large numbers of impoverished peoples in Africa, Asia, and Latin America do not follow the example of workers from southeastern Europe and seek temporary or permanent jobs in areas of labor shortage. Historically, at least in the case of Africa, migrant labor both within and between countries was rather common and did provide some relief for locally depressed areas. Even today, considerable benefits accrue and numerous potential problems are avoided by the fact that thousands of unskilled laborers in Burkina Faso are able to find temporary work in neighboring Côte d'Ivoire. The same is true for Egyptians, Pakistanis, and Indians in Kuwait and Saudi Arabia; Tunisians, Moroccans, and Algerians in southern Europe; Colombians in Venezuela; and Haitians in the Dominican Republic. The fact remains, however, that there is very little scope for reducing the pressures of overpopulation in developing countries today through massive international emigration. The reasons for this relate not so much to a lack of local knowledge about opportunities in other countries as to the combined effects of distance and, more important, the very restrictive nature of immigration laws in modern developed countries.

Despite these restrictions, at least 50 million people from the developing world have managed to migrate to the developed world since 1960. The pace of migration from developing to developed countries—particularly to the United States, Canada, and Australia—has picked up since the mid-1980s to between 2 and 3 million people per year. And the numbers of undocumented or illegal migrants have increased dramatically since 1980. Some people in recipient industrialized nations feel that these migrants are taking jobs away from poor, unskilled citizen workers. Moreover, illegal migrants and their families are often believed to be taking unfair advantage of free local health, educational, and social services, causing upward pressure on local taxes to support these services. As a result, major debates are now under way in both the United States and Europe regarding the treatment of illegal migrants. Many citizens want severe restrictions, even total bans, on the number of immigrants that are permitted to enter or reside in developed countries. Others call for legislation to bar illegal workers and their families from the generous benefits that states and localities offer to their citizens. In the United States, the backlash against illegal migrants was most vividly evident in 1994, when voters in the state of California overwhelmingly passed Proposition 187, denying economic and social benefits to all illegal workers and their families. Although this trend has moderated in recent years, few people expect the historical safety valve of international migration to be as open as it has historically been for the vast numbers of contemporary unskilled LDC workers.[29]

The irony of international migration today, however, is not merely that this traditional outlet for surplus people has effectively been closed off but that many of the people who migrate from poor to richer lands are the very ones that developing countries can least afford to lose: the highly educated and skilled. Since the great majority of these migrants move on a permanent basis, this perverse brain drain not only represents a loss of valuable human resources but could prove to be a serious constraint on the future economic progress of developing nations. For example, between 1960 and 1990, more than a million high-level professional and technical workers from the developing countries migrated to the United States, Canada, and the United Kingdom alone. By the late 1980s, Africa had lost nearly one-third of its skilled workers, with up to 60,000 middle and high-level managers migrating to Europe and North America between 1985 and 1990. Sudan, for example, lost 17% of its doctors and dentists, 20% of its university teachers, 30% of its engineers, and 45% of its surveyors. The Philippines lost 12% of its professional workers to the United States, and 60% of Ghanaian doctors now practice abroad.[30] In the early 2000s, India has been concerned that it may be unable to meet its burgeoning requirements for information technology workers in its growing high-tech enclaves if emigration to the United States, Canada, and the United Kingdom continues at its current pace. The fundamental point remains, however, that the possibility of international migration of unskilled workers on a scale proportional to that of the nineteenth and early twentieth centuries no longer exists to provide an effective safety valve for the contemporary populations of Africa, Asia, and Latin America.[31]

The Growth Stimulus of International Trade

International **free trade** has been called the "engine of growth" that propelled the development of today's economically advanced nations during the nineteenth and early twentieth centuries. Rapidly expanding export markets provided an additional stimulus to growing local demands that led to the establishment of large-scale manufacturing industries. Together with a relatively stable political structure and flexible social institutions, these increased export earnings enabled the developing country of the nineteenth century to borrow funds in the international capital market at very low interest rates. This capital accumulation in turn stimulated further production, made possible increased imports, and led to a more diversified industrial structure. In the nineteenth century, European and North American countries were able to participate in this dynamic growth of international exchange largely on the basis of relatively free trade, free capital movements, and the unfettered international migration of unskilled surplus labor.

Today, the situation for many LDCs is very different. With the exception of a few very successful East Asian countries, the non-oil-exporting (and, indeed, some oil-exporting) developing countries face formidable difficulties in trying to generate rapid economic growth on the basis of world trade. Ever since the First World War, many developing countries have experienced a deteriorating trade position.

Their exports have expanded, but usually not as fast as the exports of developed nations. Their **terms of trade** (the price they receive for their exports relative to the price they have to pay for imports) have declined steadily. Export volume has therefore had to grow faster just to earn the same amount of foreign currencies as in previous years. Moreover, the developed countries are so far ahead of the LDCs economically that they can afford through their advanced science and technology to remain more competitive, develop more new products (often synthetic substitutes for traditional LDC primary commodity exports), and obtain international financing on much better terms. Finally, where developing countries are successful at becoming lower-cost producers of competitive products with the developed countries (e.g., textiles, clothing, shoes, some light manufactures), the latter have typically resorted to various forms of tariff and nontariff barriers to trade, including import quotas, sanitary requirements, and special licensing arrangements. We will discuss the economics of international trade and finance in detail in Part Three. For now, note that the international engine of growth that roared across the northern hemisphere in the nineteenth century for the most part struggled for most newcomers to growth outside of East Asia in the southern hemisphere in the twentieth century.

Basic Scientific and Technological Research and Development Capabilities

A recurrent theme throughout this chapter has been the crucial role played by basic scientific research and technological development in the modern economic growth experience of contemporary developed countries. Their high rates of growth have been sustained by the interplay between mass applications of many new technological innovations based on a rapid advancement in the stock of scientific knowledge and further additions to that stock of knowledge made possible by growing surplus wealth. And even today, the process of scientific and technological advance in all its stages, from basic research to product development, is heavily concentrated in the rich nations. Over 90% of all world **research and development (R&D)** expenditures originate in these countries. Moreover, research funds are spent on solving the economic and technological problems of concern to rich countries in accordance with their own economic priorities and resource endowments. Rich countries are interested mainly in the development of sophisticated products, large markets, and technologically advanced production methods using large inputs of capital and high levels of skills and management while economizing on their relatively scarce supplies of labor and raw materials. The poor countries, by contrast, are much more interested in simple products, simple designs, saving of capital, use of abundant labor, and production for smaller markets. But they have neither the financial resources nor the scientific and technological know-how to undertake the kind of research and development that would be in their best long-term economic interests. Their dependence on foreign technologies can create and perpetuate internal economic dualism (see Chapter 3).

We may conclude, therefore, that in the important area of scientific and technological research, contemporary developing nations are in an extremely disadvantageous competitive position vis-à-vis the developed nations. In contrast, when the latter countries were embarking on their early growth process, they were scientifically and technologically greatly in advance of the rest of the world. They could consequently focus on staying ahead by designing and developing new technology at a pace dictated by their long-term economic growth requirements.

Stability and Flexibility of Political and Social Institutions

Yet another distinction between the historical experience of developed countries and the situation faced by contemporary developing nations relates to the nature of social and political institutions. One very obvious difference between the now developed and the underdeveloped nations is that well before their industrial revolutions, the former were independent consolidated nation-states able to pursue national policies on the basis of consensus toward modernization. As Nobel laureate Gunnar Myrdal pointed out, the now developed countries

> formed a small world of broadly similar cultures, within which people and ideas circulated rather freely. . . . Modern scientific thought developed in these countries (long before their industrial revolutions) and a modernized technology began early to be introduced in their agriculture and their industries, which at that time were all small-scale.[32]

In contrast to those preindustrial, culturally homogeneous, materially oriented, and politically unified societies, with their emphasis on rationalism and modern scientific thought, many developing countries of today gained political independence relatively recently and have yet to become consolidated nation-states with an effective ability to formulate and pursue national development strategies. Moreover, the modernization ideals embodied in the notions of rationalism, scientific thought, individualism, social and economic mobility, the work ethic, and dedication to national material and cultural values are concepts largely alien to many contemporary developing societies, except perhaps among their educated ruling elites. Until stable and flexible political institutions can be consolidated with broad public support, the present social and cultural fragmentation of many developing countries is likely to inhibit their ability to accelerate national economic progress.[33]

With the end of the cold war and the rapid globalization of trade, finance, and technology, social and political stability has assumed even greater importance for economic development. For example, given modern technology and the ability to move money around the world in a matter of seconds, international financial flows can respond quickly to changes in the political and economic climate of LDCs. The advent of these "hot money" flows was never more evident than after the surprise devaluation of the Mexican peso in December 1994. Huge sums of money were withdrawn by foreign investors not only from Mexico but throughout Latin America in a process known as financial market contagion. This turned a serious foreign-exchange situation into a crisis for many countries. A similar scenario presented itself during the Asian Crisis of 1997–1998, when Thailand, Indonesia, Malaysia, and South Korea were drawn into a vortex of speculative hot-money currency outflows, competitive devaluations, and widespread economic panic. We will return to this theme in Part Three.

The critical importance of political stability for economic growth is further underlined by a number of recent quantitative studies.[34] Researchers have found that growth is more influenced by the stability of the political regime than by its type (democracy or dictatorship). They also found that in the transition from dictatorship to democracy, the tremendous pressures from competing interest groups tend to slow down economic growth, but in the longer run, stable democracies experience higher growth than dictatorships.[35]

Efficacy of Domestic Economic Institutions

At several places in this book, we will consider the role of economic institutions in shaping the prospects for successful development. The World Bank broadly defines *institutions* as "rules, enforcement mechanisms, and organizations," the sense in which it is used in this chapter, though the term is sometimes used more narrowly following Douglass North as the "formal and informal rules of the economic game." The quality of institutions varies greatly across countries both generally and, in particular, specifically in the incentives they create for people to take actions that spur growth and provide access to economic opportunities for a broad range of citizens. Institutions differ across the developing countries as well as, on average, from those in the developed world. But generally, more developed countries generally have institutions that provide property rights to more individuals and that provide low-cost, effective, and rapid access to dispute resolution mechanisms, such as contract enforcement through courts and other venues. Institutions are generally more transparent in developed countries: The degree to which systems such as corporate governance, regulatory agency procedures, and taxation are efficiently and impartially implemented can be seen more clearly, and the actions of those who govern is less arbitrary.[36] Unfortunately, prospects for rapid change of institutions are limited, and North points out that "institutions are not necessarily or even usually created to be socially effective; rather they or at least the formal rules are created to serve the interests of those with the bargaining power to create new rules." He also stresses that although the formal rules "may be changed overnight, the informal rules usually change only ever so gradually."[37]

It is difficult to identify the specific effects of bad institutions. But recent scholarship has made significant strides in demonstrating that institutions put in place by colonial powers centuries ago explain much of the gulf between the performance of developed and developing countries. The systems the colonizers put in place to extract resources while maintaining their own dominance, rather than to encourage economic development, in all too many cases still remain in place and have proved tragically difficult to reform (see Chapters 4 and 11).[38]

Are Living Standards of Developing and Developed Countries Converging?

The implications of differing conditions for growth in developed and developing countries can perhaps be most vividly seen in tests for economic "convergence" across countries. If the growth experience of developing and developed countries were similar, there are two important reasons to expect that developing countries would be "catching up" by growing faster on average than developed countries. The first reason is due to technology transfer. Today's developing countries do not have to "reinvent the wheel"; for example, they do not have to use vacuum tubes before they can use modern miniaturized transistors. Even if royalties must be paid, it is cheaper to replicate technology than to undertake original R&D, partly because one does not have to pay for the mistakes and dead ends encountered along the way. This should enable developing countries to "leapfrog" over some of the earlier stages of technological development, moving immediately to high-productivity techniques of production. As a result, they should be able to grow much faster than today's developed countries are growing now, or were able to grow in the past, when they had to invent the technology as they went along, and proceed step by step through the historical stages of innovation. In fact, if we confine our attention to cases of successful development, the later a country begins its modern economic growth, the shorter the time needed to double output per worker. For example, Britain doubled its output per person in the first 60 years of its industrial revolution, America did so in 45 years, and South Korea in just 11.

The second reason to expect convergence if conditions are similar is based on factor accumulation. Today's developed countries have high levels of physical and human capital; in a production function analysis, this would explain their high levels of output per person. But the marginal product of capital and the profitability of investments would be lower in developed countries where capital intensity is higher, due to the law of diminishing returns. That is, the impact of additional capital on output would be expected to be smaller in a developed country that already has a lot of capital in relation to the size of its workforce than in a developing country where capital is scarce. As a result, we would expect higher investment rates in developing countries, either through domestic sources or through attracting foreign investment (see Chapter 15). With higher investment rates, output would grow more quickly in developing countries until approximately equal levels of capital per worker were achieved.[39]

Given one or both of these two conditions, technology transfer and more rapid capital accumulation, incomes would tend to converge in the long run as the faster-growing developing countries would be catching up with the slower-growing developed countries. Even if incomes did not eventually turn out to be identical, they would at least tend to be equalized *conditional on* (i.e., after also taking account of any systematic differences in) key variables such as population growth rates and savings rates (this argument is formalized in the neoclassical growth model examined in Chapter 3). Given the huge differences in capital and technology across countries, if growth conditions are similar, we should see at least some tendencies for convergence in the data.

However, as it turns out, evidence of (unconditional) convergence at least is very hard to find in the data. Figure 2.5a is illustrative of the findings. On the *x*-axis, income data is plotted from the initial year (in this case, 1960), while on the *y*-axis, the growth rate of real income is plotted (in this case, over the following 25 years). If there were convergence, there would be a tendency for the points plotted to show a clear negative relationships, with the lower income countries growing faster in the subsequent period. But as Figure 2.5a makes clear enough, there is no tendency

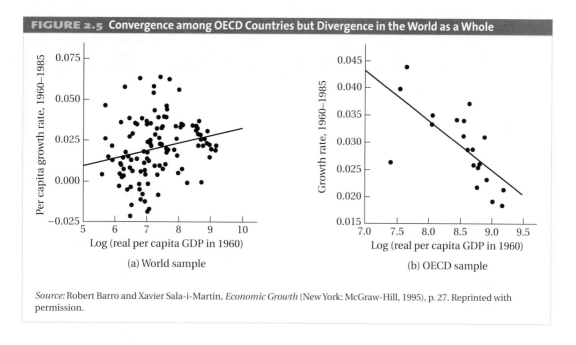

FIGURE 2.5 Convergence among OECD Countries but Divergence in the World as a Whole

(a) World sample

(b) OECD sample

Source: Robert Barro and Xavier Sala-i-Martin, *Economic Growth* (New York: McGraw-Hill, 1995), p. 27. Reprinted with permission.

for convergence. In fact, if anything, there is a slight tendency for the poorer countries to grow more slowly than the rich countries. This is reflected in the regression line in the diagram, which is a statistician's choice of the line that best fits these data.[40]

However, in Figure 2.5b, the 20 high-income OECD countries are removed from Figure 2.5a and plotted separately. Here we clearly see convergence. One explanation is that all of these countries have similar features, including a relatively early start at modern economic growth. This makes the countries more able to borrow technology from each other, as well as trade with and invest in each other's economies. We might conclude that if developing countries closely followed the institutions and policies of these OECD economies, they might converge as well. However, as we have seen, there are many differences between low- and high-income countries today that may be very difficult to change, including climate and the incidence of diseases such as malaria. Institutions may prove very difficult to change as well (see Chapter 11). Moreover, a poor country cannot force a rich country to lower its trade barriers. In any case, one must draw conclusions from the results with great caution because of *selection bias*. That is, among today's rich countries, some were relatively rich in the past and some were relatively poor; in order for them all to be rich countries today, the poor countries *had* to have grown faster than the rich ones, simply as a matter of logic. Thus, confining attention just to the rich countries commits the statistical error of selection bias.[41] Nevertheless, the strong evidence for convergence among the OECD countries, together with the failure to find convergence for the world as a whole, is likely one reflection of the difference in growth conditions between now developed and developing countries.

Finally, we note that although the evidence indicates that there is no unconditional income convergence across developed and developing countries, the picture is more clouded regarding conditional convergence; that is, there is at least some evidence, though controversial, that if developing countries raised investment rates and lowered population growth rates to those seen in developed countries, they might grow faster and even eventually catch up. We return to this question in the next chapter.

Conclusion

The phenomenon of underdevelopment must be viewed in both a national and an international context. Problems of poverty, low productivity, population growth, unemployment, primary-product export dependence, and international vulnerability have both domestic and global origins and potential solutions. Economic and social forces, both internal and external, are therefore responsible for the poverty, inequality, and low productivity that characterize most developing nations. The successful pursuit of economic and social development will require not only the formulation of appropriate strategies within the developing world but also a modification of the present international economic order to make it more responsive to the development needs of poor nations.

Although the picture of life in much of the developing world painted throughout our review may seem bleak, it should be remembered that many countries have succeeded in raising incomes, lowering infant mortality, improving educational access, narrowing gender disparities, and increasing life expectancy.[42] By pursuing appropriate economic and social policies both at home and abroad and with effective assistance from developed nations, poor countries do indeed have the means to realize their development aspirations. Parts Two and Three will discuss the ways in which these hopes and objectives can be attained.

But concomitant and complementary technological, social, and institutional changes must take place if long-term economic growth is to be realized. Such transformations must occur not only within individual developing countries but in the international economy as well. In other words, unless there is some major structural, attitudinal, and institutional reform in the world economy, one that accommodates the rising aspirations and rewards the outstanding performances of individual developing nations, internal economic and social transformation within the developing world may be insufficient.[43]

There may be some "advantages of backwardness" in development, such as the ability to use existing, proven technologies rather than having to reinvent the wheel and even leapfrogging over older technology standards that developed countries have become locked into, such as old-fashioned television broadcasting signals. One can also learn valuable lessons from economic policies that have been tried in various countries around the world. These advantages are especially helpful if an economy can successfully manage to get sustained modern economic growth under way, as, for example, the cases of Taiwan, South Korea, China, and a few other nations. However, for most very poor countries, backwardness comes with severe disadvantages, many of which have been compounded by legacies of colonialism, slavery, and cold war dictatorships. In either case, countries will generally have to do more than simply emulate polices followed by today's developed countries while they were in their early stages of development.

Moreover, every developing country confronts its own constraints on feasible policy options and other special circumstances; and each will have to find its own path to effective economic and social institutions. Examples offered by developed countries' earlier experiences and current institutions, as well as those of other countries in the developing world, provide important insights for policy formulation. Economic institutions of Europe and North America are in most cases closer to optimal than those of many developing countries, although all countries have room for further institutional innovations. But developing countries cannot assume without additional investigation that patterning their policies and institutions on those of developed countries will always provide the fastest route to successful economic development.

So far, there is little evidence of income convergence for the world as a whole. Still, the experience of the past 50 years shows that while development is not inevitable and poverty traps are quite real, it is possible to escape from poverty and initiate sustainable development. Before examining specific policies for doing so, in the next chapters we will set the context further by examining important theories and models of development and underdevelopment. In Chapter 3, we examine classic theories that remain influential and useful in many respects, and in Chapter 4, we consider recent models of poverty traps and conceptual strategies for escaping from them.

Concepts for Review

Absolute poverty	Human resources	Newly industrializing coun-
Brain drain	Imperfect markets	tries (NICs)
Capital accumulation	Income gap	Nongovernmental organiza-
Capital-augmenting techno-	Income inequality	tions (NGOs)
logical progress	Incomplete information	Physical resources
Capital-saving technological	Infant mortality rate	Primary industrial sector
progress	Infrastructure	Production function
Capital stock	International poverty line	Production possibility curve
Crude birthrate	Labor-augmenting techno-	Purchasing power equivalent
Death rate	logical progress	Purchasing power parity
Dependency burden	Labor productivity	(PPP)
Foreign exchange	Laborsaving technological	Research and development
Free trade	progress	(R&D)
Gross domestic product	Levels of living	Resource endowment
(GDP)	Low-income countries (LICs)	Secondary industrial sector
Gross national income (GNI)	Malnutrition	Technological progress
Human capital	Mixed economic systems	Terms of trade
Human Development Index	Neutral technological	Tertiary industrial sector
(HDI)	progress	World Bank

Questions for Discussion

1. For all of their diversity, less developed countries are linked by a range of common problems. What are these problems? Which do you think are the most important? Why?

2. Explain the distinction between low levels of living and low per capita incomes. Can low levels of living exist simultaneously with high levels of per capita income? Explain and give some examples.

3. Can you think of other common characteristics of less developed countries not mentioned in the text? See if you can list four or five and briefly justify them.

4. What are the advantages and disadvantages of using a concept such as the international poverty line? Do you think that a real annual income of $370 in, say, Mexico has the same meaning as in, say, Nigeria or Thailand? Explain your answer.

5. Do you think that there is a strong relationship among health, labor productivity, and income levels? Explain your answer.

6. What is meant by the statement that many developing nations are subject to "dominance, dependence, and vulnerability" in their relations with rich nations? Can you give some examples?

7. Explain the many ways in which developing countries may differ in their economic, social, and political structures.

8. What are some additional strengths and weaknesses of the HDI as a comparative measure of human welfare? If you were designing the HDI, what might you do differently, and why? (You may wish to refer to the appendix to this chapter.)

9. How would you describe the economic growth process in terms of production possibility analysis? What are the principal sources of economic growth, and how can they be illustrated using production possibility frontier diagrams? (Again, you may wish to refer to the appendix to this chapter.)

10. "Social and institutional innovations are as important for economic growth as technological and scientific inventions and innovations." What is meant by this statement? Explain your answer.

11. Why do many economists expect income convergence between developed and developing countries, and what factors would you look to for an explanation of why this has not occurred?

Notes

1. For more information on country classification systems and other key comparative data, go to the World Bank Web site at http://www.worldbank.org/data, the OECD Web site at http://www.oecd.org/oecd, and the United Nations Development Program Web site at http://www.undp.org.

2. For an interesting discussion of the relative benefits and costs of country size, see Alberto Alesina and Enrico Spolaore, "On the number and size of nations," *Quarterly Journal of Economics* 112 (1997): 1027–1056.

3. An analysis of the role of geography and climate can be found in John Luke Gallup and Jeffrey Sachs, "Geography and economic growth," *Annual World Bank Conference on Development Economics, 1998* (Washington D.C.: World Bank, 1999). For a provocative perspective on the historical impact of geography, see Jared Diamond, *Guns, Germs, and Steel: The Fates of Human Societies* (New York: Norton, 1997). The June 2003 issue of *Finance and Development* contains several good articles offering competing views on the role of geography and institutions; they can be accessed at http://www.imf.org/external/pubs/ft/fandd/2003/06.

4. For a more detailed account of these conflicts, with data on casualties and refugees, see United Nations Development Program, *Human Development Report, 1994* (New York: Oxford University Press, 1994), pp. 32–46, and United Nations, *World Social Situation in the 1990s* (New York: United Nations, 1994), ch. 13.

5. For a discussion of these issues, see Haeduck Lee, *The Ethnic Dimension of Poverty and Income Distribution in Latin America* (Washington, D.C.: World Bank, 1993), and Paul Collier, "The political economy of ethnicity," *Annual World Bank Conference on Development Economics, 1998* (Washington, D.C.: World Bank, 1999).

6. For a review of the complex statistical issues in sorting out the possible impact of ethnic, religious, and linguistic fractionalization, see Alberto Alesina et al., "Fractionalization," *Journal of Economic Growth* 8 (2003): 155–194. An earlier paper drawing somewhat different conclusions using less comprehensive measures is William Easterly and

Ross Levine, "Africa's growth tragedy: Policies and ethnic divisions," *Quarterly Journal of Economics* 112 (1997): 1203–1250.

7. These issues are examined further in Chapter 11. See also the collection of articles on the role of NGOs in attaining the Millennium Development Goals, including Jennifer Brinkerhoff, Stephen C. Smith and Hildy Teegen, "Beyond the 'Non': The Strategic Space for NGOs in Development," George Washington, Center for Economic Research Discussion Paper D-0501, 2004. For a detailed look at the role of NGO programs, see Stephen C. Smith, *Ending Global Poverty* (New York: Palgrave/Macmillan, 2005).

8. For a description of the use of PPPs for international GNI comparisons, see Robert Summers and Alan Heston, "A new set of international comparisons of real product and price level estimates for 130 countries, 1950–1985," *Review of Income and Wealth* 34 (1988): 1–24, and "The Penn World Table (Mark 5): An expanded set of international comparisons, 1950–88," *Quarterly Journal of Economics* 56 (1991): 327–368. Clearly, where currencies are weak, PPP estimates of GDP and GNI will be much higher than exchange-rate conversion estimates. Unfortunately, the reliability of PPP estimates for developing world GNIs is much lower than for OECD countries because the former are typically only rough approximations, whereas the latter are quite accurate. Note that in these estimates an adjustment for preference differences means that U.S. PPP income will differ slightly from U.S. GNI.

There are also many other limitations of GNI (or, for that matter, PPP) calculations as measures of economic performance and welfare. For example, GNI does not take account of the depletion or degradation of natural resources. It assigns positive values to natural disasters (e.g., earthquakes, hurricanes, floods), to polluting activities, and to the costs of environmental cleanups (see Chapter 10). It ignores nonmonetary transactions, household unpaid labor, and subsistence consumption, each significant activities in LDCs (see Chapter 9). Finally, GNI figures take no account of income distribution (Chapter 5).

9. You may recall from algebra that the doubling time of a value (such as the real GNI of an economy) growing at rate $p\%$ per year may be found with the formula $[1 + p/100]^T = 2$. Taking natural logs of each side, T $ln[1 + p/100] = ln 2$. The natural log of 2 is approximately 0.7. On the left hand side, for small p, $ln[1 + p/100]$ is approximately equal to $p/100$. Substituting, $Tp/100 = 0.7$, or $T = 70/p$. For example, for reasonably small values of growth such as 4%, simply divide 70 by the percentage growth: After about $70/4 = 17.5$ years, national income would double. As a further approximation, to find the growth of income per capita, simply subtract off the rate of growth of population. Thus if population is growing at 2% per year, in this example income per capita would be growing at $4\% - 2\% = 2\%$ per year, and income per capita would double in approximately $70/2 = 35$ years.

10. United Nations Development Program, *Human Development Report, 1994*, p. 35. For world income distribution calculations, see Branko Milanovic, "True world income distribution, 1988 and 1993: First calculations based on household surveys alone," *Economic Journal* 112 (2002): 51–92.

11. World Bank, *World Bank Atlas, 1995* (Washington, D.C.: World Bank, 1994), pp. 8–9.

12. United Nations Children's Fund, *The State of the World's Children, 1990* (New York: Oxford University Press, 1990), pp. 42–44.

13. World Bank, *Confronting AIDS: Public Priorities in a Global Epidemic* (New York: Oxford University Press, 1997); UNAIDS, *2004 Report on the Global AIDS Epidemic* (New York: United Nations, 2004).

14. United Nations Development Program, *Human Development Report, 2001* (New York: Oxford University Press, 2001), tab. 1.1.

15. These examples are adapted from ibid., p. 240.

16. United Nations Development Program, *Human Development Report, 1994*.

17. For an excellent review of evidence of these linkages, see John Strauss and Duncan Thomas, "Health, nutrition, and economic development," *Journal of Economic Literature 36* (1998): 766–817.

18. For an analysis of such "undernutrition traps," see Partha Dasgupta and Debraj Ray, "Inequality as a determinant of malnutrition and unemployment: Theory," *Economic Journal 96* (1986): 1011–1134, and "Inequality as a determinant of malnutrition and unemployment: Policy," *Economic Journal 97* (1987): 177–188.

19. See Gunnar Myrdal, *Asian Drama* (New York: Pantheon, 1968), app. 2.

20. The total value of actual agricultural output was probably somewhat higher than this figure, for much of the food output in LDCs is consumed directly by farm families and is therefore not always estimated in aggregate production figures.

21. United Nations Development Program, *Human Development Report, 1994*, p. 35; World Bank, *World Development Indicators, 2001.* (Washington, D.C.: World Bank, 2001), tab. 4.5.

22. For a detailed analysis of the importance of information acquisition, its absence in many LDCs, and the consequent role of governments in promoting knowledge and information in the context of limited markets, see World Bank, *World Development Report, 1998/99: Knowledge for Development* (New York: Oxford University Press, 1998), pp. 1–15.

23. See Daron Acemoglu, Simon Johnson, and James A. Robinson, "The colonial origins of comparative development: An empirical investigation," *American Economic Review* 91 (2001): 1369–1401, and "Reversal of fortune: Geography and institutions in the making of the modern world income distribution," *Quarterly Journal of Economics* 117 (2002): 1231–1294.

24. For an interesting and provocative analysis of the critical role of "ideas" and "ingenuity" in long-term economic growth, see Paul M. Romer, "Idea gaps and object gaps in economic development," *Journal of Monetary Economics* 32 (1993): 543–573, and Thomas Homer-Dixon, "The ingenuity gap: Can poor countries adapt to resource scarcity?" *Population and Development Review* 21 (1995): 587–612.

25. Romer, "Idea gaps," 543. An extensive review of the important role of knowledge and information in promoting economic development with a focus on "knowledge gaps" and "information problems" as these affect poor nations can be found in World Bank, *World Development Report, 1998/99*. A theoretical contribution to the literature on historical growth and its relevance to contemporary developing countries can be found in Marvin Goodfriend and John McDermott, "Early development," *American Economic Review* 85 (March 1995): 116-133. Goodfriend and McDermott argue that long-term economic development involves four fundamental processes: the exploitation of

Information on current economic, social, and demographic trends within individual developing countries and regions can best be obtained from the annual *World Development Report* and *World Development Indicators* published by the World Bank, available online at http://www.worldbank.org, as well as the annual *World Economic Outlook*, published by the International Monetary Fund, and various United Nations publications, including the annual *Statistical Yearbook*, the UNDP's annual *Human Development Report*, and the regular publications of the UN's Economic Commission for Latin America (ECLA), Economic Commission for Africa (ECA), and Economic and Social Commission for Asia and the Pacific (ESCAP). Concise statistical summaries can also be obtained from the annual *World Bank Atlas*. The World Bank and International Monetary Fund also do studies of individual countries; see their current publications list for the most recent titles.

On the historical record of economic growth, the classic study is that of the Nobel Prize–winning Harvard economist Simon Kuznets, whose lifetime work is best revealed in two volumes: *Modern Economic Growth: Rate, Structure, and Spread* (New Haven, Conn.: Yale University Press, 1966) and *Economic Growth of Nations: Total Output and Production Structure* (Cambridge, Mass.: Harvard University Press, 1971). A concise summary of his findings is given in Simon Kuznets, "Modern economic growth: Findings and reflections," *American Economic Review* 63 (1973): 247–258.

A provocative historical perspective on the possible backlash generated by rapid globalization accompanied by rising inequality can be found in Jeffrey G. Williamson, "Globalization and inequality: Past and present," *World Bank Research Observer* 12 (1997): 117–135. For the long-term overview of historical growth and development, see Angus Maddison, *The World Economy: A Millennial Perspective* (Paris: Development Center of the Organization for Economic Cooperation and Development, 2001). See also David Landes, *The Wealth and Poverty of Nations: Why Some Are So Rich and Some So Poor* (New York: Norton, 1998). For the best comparative incomes data across countries and the methodological issues in its construction, see Alan Heston, Robert Summers, and Bettina Aten, *Penn World Table*, version 6.1 (Philadelphia: Center for International Comparisons at the University of Pennsylvania, 2002).

An attempt to model long-term economic growth focusing on the new growth theory ideas of increasing returns and human capital accumulations can be obtained from Marvin Goodfriend and John McDermott, "Early development," *American Economic Review* 85 (1995): 116–133. For an interesting review of the history of ideas concerning policies for encouraging growth in developing countries, see William Easterly, *The Elusive Quest for Growth* (Cambridge, Mass.: MIT Press, 2001).

Appendix 2.1

Components of Economic Growth

Three components of economic growth are of prime importance in any society; these are capital and labor "factor accumulation," and technological progress:

1. Capital accumulation, including all new investments in land, physical equipment, and human resources through improvements in health, education, and job skills

2. Growth in population and hence eventual growth in the labor force

3. Technological progress—broadly, new ways of accomplishing tasks. In this appendix, we look briefly at each.

Capital Accumulation

Capital accumulation results when some proportion of present income is saved and invested in order to augment future output and income. New factories, machinery, equipment, and materials increase the physical **capital stock** of a nation (the total net real value of all physically productive capital goods) and make it possible for expanded output levels to be achieved. These directly productive investments are supplemented by investments in what is known as social and economic **infrastructure**—roads, electricity, water and sanitation, communications, and the like—which facilitates and integrates economic activities. For example, investment by a farmer in a new tractor may increase the total output of the vegetables he can produce, but without adequate transport facilities to get this extra product to local commercial markets, his investment may not add anything to national food production.

There are less direct ways to invest in a nation's resources. The installation of irrigation facilities may improve the quality of a nation's agricultural land by raising productivity per hectare. If 100 hectares of irrigated land can produce the same output as 200 hectares of nonirrigated land using the same other inputs, the installation of such irrigation is the equivalent of doubling the quantity of nonirrigated land. Use of chemical fertilizers and the control of insects with pesticides may have equally beneficial effects in raising the productivity of existing farmland. All these forms of investment are ways of improving the quality of existing land resources. Their effect in raising the total stock of productive land is, for all practical purposes, indistinguishable from the simple clearing of hitherto unused arable land.

Similarly, investment in human resources can improve its quality and thereby have the same or even a more powerful effect on production as an increase in human numbers. Formal schooling, vocational and on-the-job training programs, and adult and other types of informal education may all be made more effective in augmenting human skills as a result of direct investments in buildings, equipment, and materials (e.g., books, film projectors, personal computers, science equipment, vocational tools, and machinery such as lathes and grinders). The advanced and relevant training of teachers, as well as good textbooks in economics, may make an enormous difference in the quality, leadership, and productivity of a given labor force. Improved health can also significantly augment productivity. The concept of investment in human resources and the creation of **human capital** is therefore analogous to that of improving the quality and thus the productivity of existing land resources through strategic investments.

All of these phenomena and many others are forms of investment that lead to capital accumulation. Capital accumulation may add new resources (e.g., the clearing of unused land) or upgrade the quality of existing resources (e.g., irrigation), but its essential feature is that it involves a trade-off between present and future consumption—giving up a little now so that more can be had later, such as giving up current income to stay in school.

Population and Labor Force Growth

Population growth, and the associated eventual increase in the labor force, has traditionally been considered a positive factor in stimulating economic growth. A larger labor force means more productive workers, and a large overall population increases the potential size of domestic markets. However, it is questionable whether rapidly growing supplies of workers in developing countries with a surplus of labor exert a positive or a negative influence on economic progress (see Chapter 6 for an in-depth discussion of the pros and cons of population growth for economic development). Obviously, it will depend on the ability of the economic system to absorb and productively employ these added workers—an ability largely associated with the rate and kind of capital accumulation and the availability of related factors, such as managerial and administrative skills.

Given an initial understanding of these first two fundamental components of economic growth and disregarding for a moment the third (technology), let us see how they interact via the **production possibility curve** to expand society's potential total output of all goods. For a given technology and a given amount of physical and human resources, the production possibility curve portrays the *maximum* attainable output combinations of any two commodities, say, rice and radios, when all resources are fully and efficiently employed. Figure A2.1 shows two production possibility curves for rice and radios.

Suppose now that with unchanged technology, the quantity of physical and human resources were to double as a result of either investments that improved the quality of the existing resources or investment in new resources—land, capital, and, in the case of larger families, labor. Figure A2.1 shows that this doubling of total resources will cause the entire production possibility curve to shift uniformly outward from PP to $P'P'$. More radios and more rice can now be produced.

Because these are assumed to be the only two goods produced by this economy, it follows that the gross domestic product (the total value of all goods and services produced) will be higher than before. In other words, the process of economic growth is under way.

Note that even if the country in question is operating with underutilized physical and human resources as at point X in Figure A2.1, a growth of productive resources can result in a higher total output combination as at point X', even though there may still be widespread unemployment and underutilized or idle capital and land. But note also that there is nothing deterministic about resource growth leading to higher output growth. This is not an economic law, as attested by the poor growth record of many contemporary developing countries. Nor is resource growth even a necessary condition for *short-run* economic growth because the better utilization of idle existing resources can raise output levels substantially, as portrayed in the movement from X to X' in Figure A2.1. Nevertheless, in the *long run*, the improvement and upgrading of the quality of existing resources and new investments designed to expand the quantity of these resources are principal means of accelerating the growth of national output.

Now, instead of assuming the proportionate growth of *all* factors of production, let us assume that, say, only capital or only land is increased in quality and quantity. Figure A2.2 shows that if radio manufacturing is a relatively large user of capital equipment and rice production is a relatively land-intensive process, the shifts in society's production possibility curve will be more pronounced for radios when capital grows rapidly (Figure A2.2a) and for rice when the growth is in land quantity or quality Figure A2.2b). However, because un-

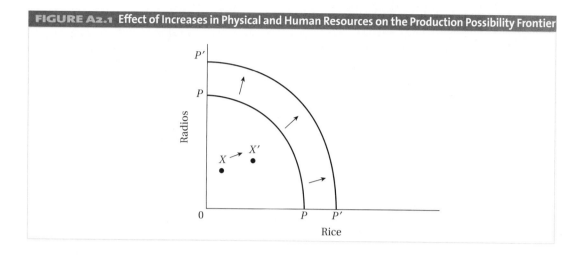

FIGURE A2.1 Effect of Increases in Physical and Human Resources on the Production Possibility Frontier

der normal conditions both products will require the use of both factors as productive inputs, albeit in different combinations, the production possibility curve still shifts slightly outward along the rice axis in Figure A2.2a when only capital is increased and along the radio axis in Figure A2.2b when only the quantity or quality of land resources is expanded.

Technological Progress

It is now time to consider the third, and to many economists the most important, source of economic growth, **technological progress**. In its simplest form, technological progress results from new and improved ways of accomplishing traditional tasks such as growing crops, making clothing, or building a house. There are three basic classifications of technological progress: neutral, laborsaving, and capital-saving.

Neutral technological progress occurs when higher output levels are achieved with the same quantity and combinations of factor inputs. Simple innovations like those that arise from the division of labor can result in higher total output levels and greater consumption for all individuals. In terms of production possibility analysis, a neutral technological change that, say, doubles total output is conceptually equivalent to a doubling of all productive inputs. The outward-shifting production possibility curve of Figure A2.2 could therefore also be a diagrammatic representation of neutral technological progress.

By contrast, technological progress may result in savings of either labor or capital (i.e., higher levels of output can be achieved with the same quantity of labor or capital inputs). Computers, the Internet, automated looms, high-speed electric drills, tractors, and mechanical ploughs—these and many other kinds of modern machinery and equipment can be classified as products of **laborsaving technological progress**. Technological progress since the late nineteenth century has consisted largely of rapid advances in laborsaving technologies for producing everything from beans to bicycles to bridges.

Capital-saving technological progress is a much rarer phenomenon. But this is primarily because almost all of the world's scientific and technological research is conducted in developed countries, where the mandate is to save labor, not capital. In the labor-abundant (capital-scarce) developing countries, however, capital-saving technological progress is what is needed most. Such progress results in more efficient (lower-cost) labor-intensive methods of production—for example, hand- or rotary-powered weeders and threshers, foot-operated bellows pumps, and back-mounted mechanical sprayers for small-scale agriculture. The indigenous LDC development of low-cost, efficient, labor-intensive (capital-

FIGURE A2.2   Effect of Growth of Capital Stock and Land on the Production Possibility Frontier

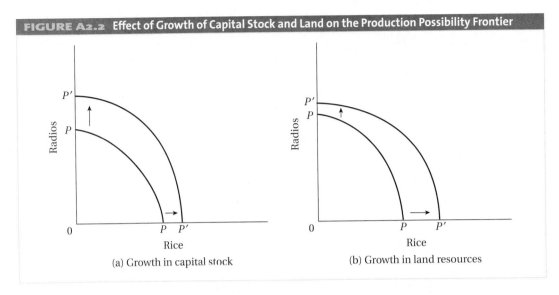

(a) Growth in capital stock   (b) Growth in land resources

saving) techniques of production is one of the essential ingredients in any long-run employment-oriented development strategy (see Appendix 5.1).

Technological progress may also be labor- or capital-augmenting. **Labor-augmenting technological progress** occurs when the quality or skills of the labor force are upgraded—for example, by the use of videotapes, televisions, and other electronic communications media for classroom instruction. Similarly, **capital-augmenting technological progress** results in the more productive use of existing capital goods—for example, the substitution of steel for wooden plows in agricultural production.

We can use our production possibility curve for rice and radios to examine two very specific examples of technological progress as it relates to output growth in developing countries. In the 1960s, agricultural scientists at the International Rice Research Institute in the Philippines developed a new and highly productive hybrid rice seed, known as IR-8, or "miracle rice." These new seeds, along with later further scientific improvements, enabled some

FIGURE A2.3   Effect of Technological Change in the Agricultural Sector on the Production Possibility Frontier

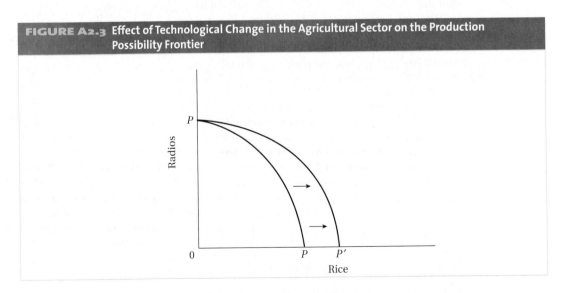

FIGURE A2.4 **Effect of Technological Change in the Industrial Sector on the Production Possibility Frontier**

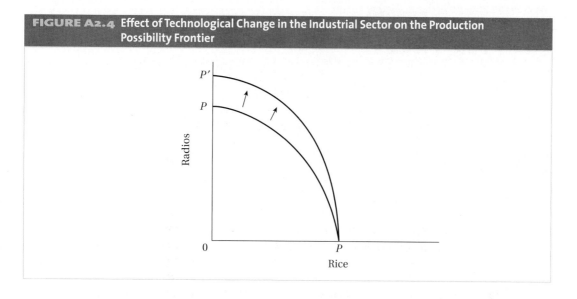

rice farmers in parts of South and Southeast Asia to double and triple their yields in a matter of a few years. In effect, this technological progress was "embodied" in the new rice seeds (one could also say it was "land-augmenting"), which permitted higher output levels to be achieved with essentially the same complementary inputs (although more fertilizer and pesticides were recommended). In terms of our production possibility analysis, the higher-yielding varieties of hybrid rice could be depicted, as in Figure A2.3, by an outward shift of the curve along the rice axis with the intercept on the radio axis remaining essentially unchanged (i.e., the new rice seeds could not be directly used to increase radio production).

In terms of the technology of radio production, the invention of transistors has probably had as significant an impact on communications as the development of the steam engine had on transportation. Even in the remotest parts of Africa, Asia, and Latin America, the transistor radio has become a prized possession. The introduction of the transistor, by obviating the need for complicated, unwieldy, and fragile tubes, led to an enormous growth of radio production. The production process became less complicated, and workers were able to increase their total productivity significantly. Figure A2.4 shows that, as in the case of higher-yielding rice seeds, the technology of the transistor can be said to have caused the production possibility curve to rotate outward along the vertical axis. For the most part, the rice axis intercept remains unchanged (although perhaps the ability of rice paddy workers to listen to music on their transistor radio while working may have made them more productive!).

Conclusion

We can summarize the discussion so far by saying that the sources of economic progress can be traced to a variety of factors, but by and large, investments that improve the quality of existing physical and human resources, increase the quantity of these same productive resources, and raise the productivity of all or specific resources through invention, innovation, and technological progress have been and will continue to be primary factors in stimulating economic growth in any society.[44] The production possibility framework conveniently allows us to analyze the production choices open to an economy, to understand the output and opportunity cost implications of idle or underutilized resources, and to portray the effects on economic growth of increased resource supplies and improved technologies of production.

CHAPTER THREE

Classic Theories of Economic Development

It matters little how much information we possess about development if we have not grasped its inner meaning.

—Denis Goulet, *The Cruel Choice*

Development must be redefined as an attack on the chief evils of the world today: malnutrition, disease, illiteracy, slums, unemployment and inequality. Measured in terms of aggregate growth rates, development has been a great success. But measured in terms of jobs, justice and the elimination of poverty, it has been a failure or only a partial success.

—Paul P. Streeten, Former Director, World Development Institute

Our new framework is a holistic and integrated approach to development strategies and programs that highlights the interdependence of all aspects of development strategy— social, structural, human, institutional, environmental, economic, and financial.

—James D. Wolfensohn, President, World Bank

Every nation strives after development. Economic progress is an essential component, but it is not the only component. As we discovered in Chapter 1, development is not purely an economic phenomenon. In an ultimate sense, it must encompass more than the material and financial side of people's lives. Development should therefore be perceived as a multidimensional process involving the reorganization and reorientation of entire economic and social systems. In addition to improvements in incomes and output, it typically involves radical changes in institutional, social, and administrative structures as well as in popular attitudes and, in many cases, even customs and beliefs. Finally, although development is usually defined in a national context, its widespread realization may necessitate fundamental modification of the international economic and social system as well.

In this chapter, we explore the historical and intellectual evolution in scholarly thinking about how and why development does or does not take place. We do this by examining four major and often competing development theories. In addition to presenting these differing approaches, we will discover how each offers valuable insights and a useful perspective on the nature of the development process. Newer models of development and underdevelopment often draw eclectically on the classic theories, and we consider them in the following chapter.

Classic Theories of Economic Development: Four Approaches

The post–World War II literature on economic development has been dominated by four major and sometimes competing strands of thought: (1) the linear-stages-of-growth model, (2) theories and patterns of structural change, (3) the international-dependence revolution, and (4) the neoclassical, free-market counterrevolution. In recent years, an eclectic approach has emerged that draws on all of these classic theories.

Theorists of the 1950s and early 1960s viewed the process of development as a series of successive stages of economic growth through which all countries must pass. It was primarily an economic theory of development in which the right quantity and mixture of saving, investment, and foreign aid were all that was necessary to enable developing nations to proceed along an economic growth path that had historically been followed by the more developed countries. Development thus became synonymous with rapid, aggregate economic growth.

This linear-stages approach was largely replaced in the 1970s by two competing economic (and ideological) schools of thought. The first, which focused on theories and patterns of structural change, used modern economic theory and statistical analysis in an attempt to portray the internal process of structural change that a "typical" developing country must undergo if it is to succeed in generating and sustaining a process of rapid economic growth. The second, the international-dependence revolution, was more radical and political in orientation. It viewed underdevelopment in terms of international and domestic power relationships, institutional and structural economic rigidities, and the resulting proliferation of dual economies and dual societies both within and among the nations of the world. Dependence theories tended to emphasize external and internal institutional and political constraints on economic development. Emphasis was placed on the need for major new policies to eradicate poverty, to provide more diversified employment opportunities, and to reduce income inequalities. These and other egalitarian objectives were to be achieved within the context of a growing economy, but economic growth per se was not given the exalted status accorded to it by the linear-stages and structural-change models.

Throughout much of the 1980s and early 1990s, a fourth approach prevailed. This neoclassical (sometimes called neoliberal) counterrevolution in economic thought emphasized the beneficial role of free markets, open economies, and the privatization of inefficient public enterprises. Failure to develop, according to this theory, is not due to exploitive external and internal forces as expounded by dependence theorists. Rather, it is primarily the result of too much government intervention and regulation of the economy. Today's eclectic approach draws on all of these perspectives, and we will highlight the strengths and weaknesses of each.

Development as Growth and the Linear-Stages Theories

When interest in the poor nations of the world really began to materialize following the Second World War, economists in the industrialized nations were caught off guard. They had no readily available conceptual apparatus with which to analyze the process of economic growth in largely agrarian societies characterized by the virtual absence of modern economic structures. But they did have the recent experience of the Marshall Plan, under which massive amounts of U.S. financial and technical assistance enabled the war-torn countries of Europe to rebuild and modernize their economies in a matter of a few years. Moreover, was it not true that all modern industrial nations were once undeveloped agrarian societies? Surely their historical experience in transforming their economies from poor agricultural subsistence societies to modern industrial giants had important lessons for the "back ward" countries of Asia, Africa, and Latin America. The logic and simplicity of these two strands of thought—the utility of massive injections of capital and the historical pattern of the now developed countries—was too irresistible to be refuted by scholars, politicians, and administrators in rich countries to whom people and ways of life in the developing world were often no more real than UN statistics or scattered chapters in anthropology books. Because of its emphasis on the central role of accelerated capital accumulation, this approach is often dubbed "capital fundamentalism."

Rostow's Stages of Growth

Out of this somewhat sterile intellectual environment, fueled by the cold war politics of the 1950s and 1960s and the resulting competition for the allegiance of newly independent nations, came the stages-of-growth model of development. Its most influential and outspoken advocate was the American economic historian Walt W. Rostow. According to the Rostow doctrine, the transition from underdevelopment to development can be described in terms of a series of steps or stages through which all countries must proceed. As Rostow wrote in the opening chapter of *The Stages of Economic Growth:*

> This book presents an economic historian's way of generalizing the sweep of modern history. . . . It is possible to identify all societies, in their economic dimensions, as lying within one of five categories: the traditional society, the pre-conditions for take-off into self-sustaining growth, the take-off, the drive to maturity, and the age of high mass consumption. . . . These stages are not merely descriptive. They are not merely a way of generalizing certain factual observations about the sequence of development of modern societies. They have an inner logic and continuity. . . . They constitute, in the end, both a theory about economic growth and a more general, if still highly partial, theory about modern history as a whole.[1]

The advanced countries, it was argued, had all passed the stage of "takeoff into self-sustaining growth," and the underdeveloped countries that were still in either the traditional society or the "preconditions" stage had only to follow a certain set of rules of development to take off in their turn into self-sustaining economic growth.

One of the principal strategies of development necessary for any takeoff was the mobilization of domestic and foreign saving in order to generate sufficient investment to accelerate economic growth. The economic mechanism by which more investment leads to more growth can be described in terms of the **Harrod-Domar growth model**,[2] today often referred to as the *AK* model because it is based on a linear production function with output given by the capital stock *K* times a constant, often labeled *A*. In one form or another, it has frequently been applied to policy issues facing developing countries, such as in the two-gap model examined in Chapter 15.

The Harrod-Domar Growth Model

Every economy must save a certain proportion of its national income, if only to replace worn-out or impaired capital goods (buildings, equipment, and materials). However, in order to grow, new investments representing net additions to the capital stock are necessary. If we assume that there is some direct economic relationship between the size of the total capital stock, *K*, and total GDP, *Y*—for example, if $3 of capital is always necessary to produce a $1 stream of GDP—it follows that any net additions to the capital stock in the form of new investment will bring about corresponding increases in the flow of national output, GDP.

Suppose that this relationship, known in economics as the **capital-output ratio**, is roughly 3 to 1. If we define the capital-output ratio as *k* and assume further that the national **savings ratio**, *s*, is a fixed proportion of national output (e.g., 6%) and that total new investment is determined by the level of total savings, we can construct the following simple model of economic growth:

1. Saving (*S*) is some proportion, *s*, of national income (*Y*) such that we have the simple equation

$$S = sY \tag{3.1}$$

2. Net investment (*I*) is defined as the change in the capital stock, *K*, and can be represented by ΔK such that

$$I = \Delta K \tag{3.2}$$

But because the total capital stock, *K*, bears a direct relationship to total national income or output, *Y*, as expressed by the capital-output ratio, *k*, it follows that

$$\frac{K}{Y} = k$$

or

$$\frac{\Delta K}{\Delta Y} = k$$

or, finally,

$$\Delta K = k\Delta Y \tag{3.3}$$

3. Finally, because net national savings, S, must equal net investment, I, we can write this equality as

$$S = I \tag{3.4}$$

But from Equation 3.1 we know that $S = sY$ and from Equations 3.2 and 3.3 we know that

$$I = \Delta K = k\Delta Y$$

It therefore follows that we can write the "identity" of saving equaling investment shown by Equation 3.4 as

$$S = sY = k\Delta Y = \Delta K = I \tag{3.5}$$

or simply as

$$sY = k\Delta Y \tag{3.6}$$

Dividing both sides of Equation 3.6 first by Y and then by k, we obtain the following expression:

$$\frac{\Delta Y}{Y} = \frac{s}{k} \tag{3.7}$$

Note that the left-hand side of Equation 3.7, $\Delta Y/Y$, represents the rate of change or rate of growth of GDP.

Equation 3.7, which is a simplified version of the famous equation in the Harrod-Domar theory of economic growth, states simply that the rate of growth of GDP ($\Delta Y/Y$) is determined jointly by the national savings ratio, s, and the national capital-output ratio, k. More specifically, it says that in the absence of government, the growth rate of national income will be directly or positively related to the savings ratio (i.e., the more an economy is able to save—and invest—out of a given GDP, the greater the growth of that GDP will be) and inversely or negatively related to the economy's capital-output ratio (i.e., the higher k is, the lower the rate of GDP growth will be).

The economic logic of Equation 3.7 is very simple. In order to grow, economies must save and invest a certain proportion of their GDP. The more they can save and invest, the faster they can grow. But the actual rate at which they can grow for any level of saving and investment—how much additional output can be had from an additional unit of investment—can be measured by the inverse of the capital-output ratio, k, because this inverse, $1/k$, is simply the output-capital or output-investment ratio. It follows that multiplying the rate of new investment, $s = I/Y$, by its productivity, $1/k$, will give the rate by which national income or GDP will increase.

Obstacles and Constraints

Returning to the stages-of-growth theories and using Equation 3.7 of our simple Harrod-Domar growth model, we learn that one of the most fundamental strategies of economic growth is simply to increase the proportion of national income saved (i.e., not consumed). If we can raise s in Equation 3.7, we can increase $\Delta Y/Y$, the rate of GDP growth. For example, if we assume that the national capital-output ratio in some less developed country is, say, 3 and the aggregate saving ratio is 6% of GDP, it follows from Equation 3.7 that this country can grow at a rate of 2% per year because

$$\frac{\Delta Y}{Y} = \frac{s}{k} = \frac{6\%}{3} = 2\% \tag{3.8}$$

Now if the national net savings rate can somehow be increased from 6% to, say, 15%—through increased taxes, foreign aid, and/or general consumption sacrifices—GDP growth can be increased from 2% to 5% because now

$$\frac{\Delta Y}{Y} = \frac{s}{k} = \frac{15\%}{3} = 5\% \tag{3.9}$$

In fact, Rostow and others defined the takeoff stage in precisely this way. Countries that were able to save 15% to 20% of GDP could grow ("develop") at a much faster rate than those that saved less. Moreover, this growth would then be self-sustaining. The mechanisms of economic growth and development, therefore, are simply a matter of increasing national savings and investment.

The main obstacle to or constraint on development, according to this theory, was the relatively low level of new capital formation in most poor countries. But if a country wanted to grow at, say, a rate of 7% per year and if it could not generate savings and investment at a rate of 21% of national income (assuming that k, the final aggregate capital-output ratio, is 3) but could only manage to save 15%, it could seek to fill this "savings gap" of 6% through either foreign aid or private foreign investment.

Thus the "capital constraint" stages approach to growth and development became a rationale and (in terms of cold war politics) an opportunistic tool for justifying massive transfers of capital and technical assistance from the developed to the less developed nations. It was to be the Marshall Plan all over again, but this time for the underdeveloped nations of the developing world.

Necessary versus Sufficient Conditions: Some Criticisms of the Stages Model

Unfortunately, the mechanisms of development embodied in the theory of stages of growth did not always work. And the basic reason they didn't work was not because more saving and investment isn't a **necessary condition** for accelerated rates of economic growth—it is—but rather because it is not a **sufficient condition**. The Marshall Plan worked for Europe because the European countries receiving aid possessed the necessary structural, institutional, and attitudinal conditions (e.g., well-integrated commodity and money markets, highly developed transport facilities, a well-trained and educated workforce, the motivation to succeed, an efficient government bureaucracy) to convert new capital effectively into higher levels of output. The Rostow and Harrod-Domar models implicitly assume the existence of these same attitudes and arrangements in underdeveloped nations. Yet in many cases they are lacking, as are complementary factors such as managerial competence, skilled labor, and the ability to plan and administer a wide assortment of development projects. But at an even more fundamental level, the stages theory failed to take into account the crucial fact that contemporary developing nations are part of a highly integrated and complex international system in which even the best and most intelligent development strategies can be nullified by external forces beyond the countries' control.

Structural-Change Models

Structural-change theory focuses on the mechanism by which underdeveloped economies transform their domestic economic structures from a heavy emphasis on traditional subsistence agriculture to a more modern, more urbanized, and more industrially diverse manufacturing and service economy. It employs the tools of neoclassical price and resource allocation theory and modern econometrics to describe how this transformation process takes place. Two well-known representative examples of the structural-change approach are the "two-sector surplus labor" theoretical model of W. Arthur Lewis and the "patterns of development" empirical analysis of Hollis B. Chenery and his coauthors.

The Lewis Theory of Development

Basic Model One of the best-known early theoretical models of development that focused on the **structural transformation** of a primarily subsistence economy was that formulated by Nobel laureate W. Arthur Lewis in the mid-1950s and later modified, formalized, and extended by John Fei and Gustav Ranis.[3] The **Lewis two-sector model** became the general theory of the development process in surplus-labor Third World nations during most of the 1960s and early 1970s. It still has many adherents today.

In the Lewis model, the underdeveloped economy consists of two sectors: a traditional, overpopulated rural subsistence sector characterized by zero marginal labor productivity—a situation that permits Lewis to classify this as **surplus labor** in the sense that it can be withdrawn from the traditional agricultural sector without any loss of output—and a high-productivity modern urban industrial sector into which labor from the subsistence sector is gradually transferred. The primary focus of the model is on both the process of labor transfer and the growth of output and employment in the modern sector. (The modern sector could include modern agriculture, but we will call the sector "industrial" as a shorthand). Both labor transfer and modern-sector employment growth are brought about by output expansion in that sector. The speed with which this expansion occurs is determined by the rate of industrial investment and capital accumulation in the modern sector. Such investment is made possible by the excess of modern-sector profits over wages on the assumption that capitalists reinvest all their profits. Finally, the level of wages in the urban industrial sector is assumed to be constant and determined as a given premium over a fixed average subsistence level of wages in the traditional agricultural sector. (Lewis assumed that urban wages would have to be at least 30% higher than average rural income to induce workers to migrate from their home areas.) At the constant urban wage, the supply curve of rural labor to the modern sector is considered to be perfectly elastic.

We can illustrate the Lewis model of modern-sector growth in a two-sector economy by using Figure 3.1. Consider first the traditional agricultural sector portrayed in the two right-side diagrams of Figure 3.1b. The upper diagram shows how subsistence food production varies with increases in labor inputs. It is a typical agricultural **production function** where the total output or product (TP_A) of food is determined by changes in the amount of the only variable input, labor (L_A), given a fixed quantity of capital, $\overline{K}_A$, and unchanging traditional technology, $\overline{t}_A$. In the lower right diagram, we have the **average** and **marginal product** of labor curves, AP_{LA} and MP_{LA}, which are derived from the total product curve shown immediately above. The quantity of agricultural labor (Q_{LA}) available is the same on both horizontal axes and is expressed in millions of workers, as Lewis is describing an underdeveloped economy where 80% to 90% of the population lives and works in rural areas.

Lewis makes two assumptions about the traditional sector. First, there is surplus labor in the sense that MP_{LA} is zero, and second, all rural workers share *equally* in the output so that the rural real wage is determined by the average and not the marginal product of labor (as will be the case in the modern sector). Metaphorically, this may be thought of as passing around the family rice bowl at dinnertime, from which each takes an equal share (this need not be literally equal shares for the basic idea to hold). Assume that there are L_A agricultural workers producing TP_A food, which is shared equally as W_A food per person (this is the average product, which is equal to TP_A/L_A). The marginal product of these L_A workers is zero, as shown in the bottom diagram of Figure 3.1b; hence the surplus-labor assumption applies to all workers in excess of L_A (note the horizontal TP_A curve beyond L_A workers in the upper right diagram).

The upper-left diagram of Figure 3.1a portrays the total product (production function) curves for the modern industrial sector. Once again, output of, say, manufactured goods (TP_M) is a function of a variable labor input, L_M, for a given capital stock $\overline{K}_M$ and technology, $\overline{t}_M$. On the horizontal axes, the quantity of labor employed to produce an output of, say, TP_{M1}, with capital stock K_{M1}, is expressed in thousands of urban workers, L_1. In the Lewis model, the modern-sector capital stock is allowed to increase from K_{M1} to K_{M2} to K_{M3} as a result of the reinvestment of profits by industrial capitalists. This will cause the total product curves in Figure 3.1a to shift upward from $TP_M(K_{M1})$ to $TP_M(K_{M2})$ to $TP_M(K_{M3})$. The process that will generate these capitalist profits for reinvestment and growth is illustrated in the lower-left diagram of Figure 3.1a. Here we have modern-sector marginal labor

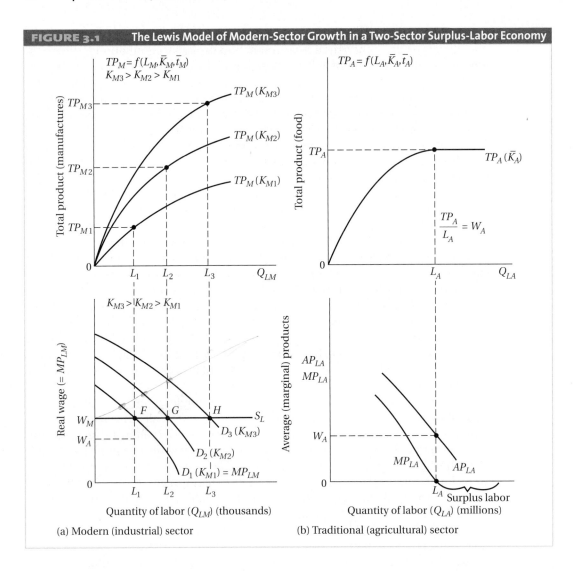

FIGURE 3.1   The Lewis Model of Modern-Sector Growth in a Two-Sector Surplus-Labor Economy

(a) Modern (industrial) sector

(b) Traditional (agricultural) sector

product curves derived from the TP_M curves of the upper diagram. Under the assumption of perfectly competitive labor markets in the modern sector, these marginal product of labor curves are in fact the actual demand curves for labor. Here is how the system works.

W_A in the lower diagrams of Figures 3.1a and 3.1b represents the average level of real subsistence income in the traditional rural sector. W_M in Figure 3.1a is therefore the real wage in the modern capitalist sector. At this wage, the supply of rural labor is assumed to be unlimited or perfectly elastic, as shown by the horizontal labor supply curve $W_M S_L$. In other words, Lewis assumes that at urban wage W_M above rural average income W_A, modern-sector employers can hire as many surplus rural workers as they want without fear of rising wages. (Note again that the quantity of labor in the rural sector, Figure 3.1b, is expressed in millions whereas in the modern urban sector, Figure 3.1a, units of labor are expressed in thousands.) Given a fixed supply of capital K_{M1} in the initial stage of modern-sector growth, the demand curve for labor is determined by labor's declining marginal product and is shown by the negatively sloped curve $D_1(K_{M1})$ in the lower-left diagram. Because profit-maximizing modern-sector employers are assumed to hire laborers to the point where their marginal physical product is equal to the real wage (i.e., the point F of intersection between the labor demand and supply curves), total modern-sector employment will be equal to L_1. Total modern-sector output, TP_{M1}, would be given by the area bounded by points OD_1FL_1. The share of this total output paid to workers in the form of wages would be equal, therefore, to the area of the rectangle OW_MFL_1. The balance of the output shown by the area W_MD_1F would be the total profits that accrue to the capitalists. Because Lewis assumes that all of these profits are reinvested, the total capital stock in the modern sector will rise from K_{M1} to K_{M2}. This larger capital stock causes the total product curve of the modern sector to shift to $TP_M(K_{M2})$, which in turn induces a rise in the marginal product demand curve for labor. This outward shift in the labor demand curve is shown by line $D_2(K_{M2})$ in the bottom half of Figure 3.1a. A new equilibrium modern-sector employment level will be established at point G with L_2 workers now employed. Total output rises to TP_{M2} or OD_2GL_2 while total wages and profits increase to OW_MGL_2 and W_MD_2G, respectively. Once again, these larger (W_MD_2G) profits are reinvested, increasing the total capital stock to K_{M3}, shifting the total product and labor demand curves to $TP_M(K_{M3})$ and to $D_3(K_{M3})$, respectively, and raising the level of modern-sector employment to L_3.

This process of modern-sector **self-sustaining growth** and employment expansion is assumed to continue until all surplus rural labor is absorbed in the new industrial sector. Thereafter, additional workers can be withdrawn from the agricultural sector only at a higher cost of lost food production because the declining labor-to-land ratio means that the marginal product of rural labor is no longer zero. Thus the labor supply curve becomes positively sloped as modern-sector wages and employment continue to grow. The structural transformation of the economy will have taken place, with the balance of economic activity shifting from traditional rural agriculture to modern urban industry.

Criticisms of the Lewis Model Although the Lewis two-sector development model is simple and roughly reflects the historical experience of economic growth in the West, four of its key assumptions do not fit the institutional and economic realities of most contemporary developing countries.

First, the model implicitly assumes that the rate of labor transfer and employment creation in the modern sector is proportional to the rate of modern-sector capital accumulation. The faster the rate of capital accumulation, the higher the growth rate of the modern sector and the faster the rate of new job creation. But what if capitalist profits are reinvested in more sophisticated laborsaving capital equipment rather than just duplicating the existing capital as is implicitly assumed in the Lewis model? (We are, of course, here accepting the debatable assumption that capitalist profits are in fact reinvested in the local economy and not sent abroad as a form of "capital flight" to be added to the deposits of Western

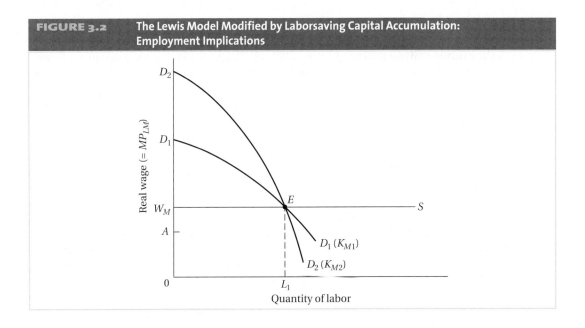

FIGURE 3.2 The Lewis Model Modified by Laborsaving Capital Accumulation: Employment Implications

banks.) Figure 3.2 reproduces the lower, modern-sector diagram of Figure 3.1a, only this time the labor demand curves do not shift uniformly outward but in fact cross. Demand curve $D_2(K_{M2})$ has a greater negative slope than $D_2(K_{M1})$ to reflect the fact that additions to the capital stock embody laborsaving technical progress—that is, KM_2 technology requires much less labor per unit of output than KM_1 technology does.

We see that even though total output has grown substantially (i.e., OD_2EL_1, is significantly greater than OD_1EL_1), total wages (OW_MEL_1) and employment (L_1) remain unchanged. All of the extra output accrues to capitalists in the form of profits. Figure 3.2 therefore provides an illustration of what some might call "anti-developmental" economic growth—*all* the extra income and output growth are distributed to the few owners of capital, while income and employment levels for the masses of workers remain largely unchanged. Although total GDP would rise, there would be little or no improvement in aggregate social welfare measured, say, in terms of more widely distributed gains in income and employment.

The second questionable assumption of the Lewis model is the notion that surplus labor exists in rural areas while there is full employment in the urban areas. Most contemporary research indicates that there is little general surplus labor in rural locations. True, there are both seasonal and geographic exceptions to this rule (e.g., parts of China and the Asian subcontinent, some Carribean islands, and isolated regions of Latin America where land ownership is very unequal), but by and large, development economists today agree that Lewis's assumption of rural surplus labor is generally not valid.

The third unreal assumption is the notion of a competitive modern-sector labor market that guarantees the continued existence of constant real urban wages up to the point where the supply of rural surplus labor is exhausted. Prior to the

1980s, a striking feature of urban labor markets and wage determination in almost all developing countries was the tendency for these wages to rise substantially over time, both in absolute terms and relative to average rural incomes, even in the presence of rising levels of open modern-sector unemployment and low or zero marginal productivity in agriculture. Institutional factors such as union bargaining power, civil service wage scales, and multinational corporations' hiring practices tend to negate competitive forces in LDC modern-sector labor markets.

A final concern with the Lewis model is its assumption of diminishing returns in the modern industrial sector. Yet there is much evidence that increasing returns prevail in that sector, posing special problems for development policymaking, as we examine in Chapter 4.

We conclude, therefore, that when one takes into account the laborsaving bias of most modern technological transfer, the existence of substantial capital flight, the widespread nonexistence of rural surplus labor, the growing prevalence of urban surplus labor, and the tendency for modern-sector wages to rise rapidly even where substantial open unemployment exists, the Lewis two-sector model—though extremely valuable as an early conceptual portrayal of the development process of sectoral interaction and structural change—requires considerable modification in assumptions and analysis to fit the reality of contemporary developing nations.

Structural Change and Patterns of Development

Like the earlier Lewis model, the **patterns-of-development analysis** of structural change focuses on the sequential process through which the economic, industrial, and institutional structure of an underdeveloped economy is transformed over time to permit new industries to replace traditional agriculture as the engine of economic growth. However, in contrast to the Lewis model and the original stages view of development, increased savings and investment are perceived by patterns-of-development analysts as necessary but not sufficient conditions for economic growth. In addition to the accumulation of capital, both physical and human, a set of interrelated changes in the economic structure of a country are required for the transition from a traditional economic system to a modern one. These structural changes involve virtually all economic functions, including the transformation of production and changes in the composition of consumer demand, international trade, and resource use as well as changes in socioeconomic factors such as urbanization and the growth and distribution of a country's population.

Empirical structural-change analysts emphasize both domestic and international constraints on development. The domestic ones include economic constraints such as a country's resource endowment and its physical and population size as well as institutional constraints such as government policies and objectives. International constraints on development include access to external capital, technology, and international trade. Differences in development level among developing countries are largely ascribed to these domestic and international constraints. However, it is the international constraints that make the transition of currently developing countries differ from that of now industrialized countries. To the extent that developing countries have access to the opportunities presented by the industrial countries as sources of capital, technology, and manufactured imports as well as markets for exports, they can make the transition at an even faster rate than that achieved by the industrial countries during the early periods of their economic development. Thus, unlike the earlier stages model, the structural-change model recognizes the fact that developing countries are part of an integrated international system that can promote (as well as hinder) their development.

The best-known model of structural change is the one based largely on the empirical work of the late Harvard economist Hollis B. Chenery and his colleagues, who examined patterns of development for numerous developing countries during the postwar period.[4] Their empirical studies, both cross-sectional (among countries at a given point in time) and time-series (over long periods of time), of countries at different levels of per capita income led to the identification of several characteristic features of the development process. These included the shift from agricultural to industrial production, the steady accumulation of physical and human capital, the change in consumer demands from emphasis on food and basic necessities to desires for diverse manufactured goods and services, the growth of cities and urban industries as people migrate from farms and small towns, and the decline in family size and overall population growth as children lose their economic value and parents substitute child quality (education) for quantity (see Chapter 6), with population growth first increasing and then decreasing in the process of development. Proponents of this school often call for development specialists to "let the facts speak for themselves," rather than get bogged down in the arcana of theories such as the stages of growth. This is a valuable counterbalance to empty theorizing, but it also has its own limits.

Conclusions and Implications

The structural changes that we have described are the "average" patterns of development Chenery and colleagues observed among countries in time-series and cross-sectional analyses. The major hypothesis of the structural-change model is that development is an identifiable process of growth and change whose main features are similar in all countries. However, as mentioned earlier, the model does recognize that differences can arise among countries in the pace and pattern of development, depending on their particular set of circumstances. Factors influencing the development process include a country's resource endowment and size, its government's policies and objectives, the availability of external capital and technology, and the international trade environment.

One limitation to keep in mind is that by emphasizing patterns rather than theory, this approach runs the risk of leading practitioners to draw the wrong conclusions about causality, in effect, to "put the cart before the horse." Observing developed-country patterns such as the decline of the share of the labor force in agriculture over time, many developing-country policymakers have been inclined to neglect that vital sector. But as we will see in Chapter 9, that is precisely the opposite conclusion than should be drawn. Observing the important role of higher education in developed countries, policymakers may be inclined to emphasize the development of an advanced university system even before a majority of the population has gained basic literacy, a policy that has led to gross inequities even in countries at least nominally committed to egalitarian outcomes, such as Tanzania.

Empirical studies on the process of structural change lead to the conclusion that the pace and pattern of development can vary according to both domestic and international factors, many of which lie beyond the control of an individual developing nation. Yet despite this variation, structural-change economists argue that one can identify certain patterns occurring in almost all countries during the development process. And these patterns, they argue, may be affected by the choice of development policies pursued by LDC governments as well as the international trade and foreign-assistance policies of developed nations. Hence structural-change analysts are basically optimistic that the "correct" mix of economic policies will generate beneficial patterns of self-sustaining growth. The international-dependence school to which we now turn is, in contrast, much less sanguine and is in many cases downright pessimistic.

The International-Dependence Revolution

During the 1970s, international-dependence models gained increasing support, especially among developing-country intellectuals, as a result of growing disenchantment with both the stages and structural-change models. While this theory to a large degree went out of favor during the 1980s and 1990s, versions of it have enjoyed a resurgence in the early years of the twenty-first century, as some of its views have been adopted, albeit in modified form, by theorists and leaders of the antiglobalization movement.[5] Essentially, international-dependence models view developing countries as beset by institutional, political, and economic rigidities, both domestic and international, and caught up in a **dependence** and **dominance** relationship with rich countries. Within this general approach are three major streams of thought: the neocolonial dependence model, the false-paradigm model, and the dualistic-development thesis.

The Neocolonial Dependence Model

The first major stream, which we call the **neocolonial dependence model**, is an indirect outgrowth of Marxist thinking. It attributes the existence and continuance of **underdevelopment** primarily to the historical evolution of a highly unequal international capitalist system of rich country–poor country relationships. Whether because rich nations are intentionally exploitative or unintentionally neglectful, the coexistence of rich and poor nations in an international system dominated by such unequal power relationships between the **center** (the developed countries) and the **periphery** (the LDCs) renders attempts by poor nations to be self-reliant and independent difficult and sometimes even impossible.[6] Certain groups in the developing countries (including landlords, entrepreneurs, military rulers, merchants, salaried public officials, and trade union leaders) who enjoy high incomes, social status, and political power constitute a small elite ruling class whose principal interest, knowingly or not, is in the perpetuation of the international capitalist system of inequality and conformity in which they are rewarded. Directly and indirectly, they serve (are dominated by) and are rewarded by (are dependent on) international special-interest power groups, including multinational corporations, national bilateral-aid agencies, and multilateral assistance organizations like the World Bank or the International Monetary Fund (IMF), which are tied by allegiance or funding to the wealthy capitalist countries. The elites' activities and viewpoints often serve to inhibit any genuine reform efforts that might benefit the wider population and in some cases actually lead to even lower levels of living and to the perpetuation of underdevelopment. In short, the neo-Marxist, neocolonial view of underdevelopment attributes a large part of the developing world's continuing poverty to the existence and policies of the industrial capitalist countries of the northern hemisphere and their extensions in the form of small but powerful elite or **comprador** **groups** in the less developed countries.[7] Underdevelopment is thus seen as an *externally* induced phenomenon, in contrast to the linear-stages and structural-change theories' stress on *internal* constraints such as insufficient savings and investment or lack of education and skills. Revolutionary struggles or at least major restructuring of the world capitalist system are therefore required to free dependent developing nations from the direct and indirect economic control of their developed-world and domestic oppressors.

One of the most forceful statements of the international-dependence school of thought was made by Theotonio Dos Santos:

> Underdevelopment, far from constituting a state of backwardness prior to capitalism, is rather a consequence and a particular form of capitalist development known as dependent capitalism. . . . Dependence is a conditioning situation in which the economies of one group of countries are conditioned by the development and expansion of others. A relationship of interdependence between two or more economies or between such economies and the world trading system becomes a dependent relationship when some countries can expand through self-impulsion while others, being in a dependent position, can only expand as a reflection of the expansion of the dominant countries, which may have positive or negative effects on their immediate development. In either case, the basic situation of dependence causes these countries to be both backward and exploited. Dominant countries are endowed with technological, commercial, capital and sociopolitical predominance over dependent countries—the form of this predominance varying according to the particular historical moment—and can therefore exploit them, and extract part of the locally produced surplus. Dependence, then, is based upon an international division of labor which allows industrial development to take place in some countries while restricting it in others, whose growth is conditioned by and subjected to the power centers of the world.[8]

Curiously, a similar but obviously non-Marxist perspective was expounded by Pope John Paul II in his widely quoted 1988 encyclical letter (a formal, elaborate expression of papal teaching) *Sollicitude rei socialis* (The Social Concerns of the Church), in which he declared:

One must denounce the existence of economic, financial, and social mechanisms which, although they are manipulated by people, often function almost automatically, thus accentuating the situation of wealth for some and poverty for the rest. These mechanisms, which are maneuvered directly or indirectly by the more developed countries, by their very functioning, favor the interests of the people manipulating them. But in the end they suffocate or condition the economies of the less developed countries.

The False-Paradigm Model

A second and a less radical international-dependence approach to development, which we might call the **false-paradigm model**, attributes underdevelopment to faulty and inappropriate advice provided by well-meaning but often uninformed, biased, and ethnocentric international "expert" advisers from developed-country assistance agencies and multinational donor organizations. These experts offer sophisticated concepts, elegant theoretical structures, and complex econometric models of development that often lead to inappropriate or incorrect policies. Because of institutional factors such as the central and remarkably resilient role of traditional social structures (tribe, caste, class, etc.), the highly unequal ownership of land and other property rights, the disproportionate control by local elites over domestic and international financial assets, and the very unequal access to credit, these policies, based as they often are on mainstream, neoclassical (or perhaps Lewis-type surplus labor or Chenery-type structural-change) models, in many cases merely serve the vested interests of existing power groups, both domestic and international.

In addition, according to this argument, leading university intellectuals, trade unionists, high-level government economists, and other civil servants all get their training in developed-country institutions where they are unwittingly served an unhealthy dose of alien concepts and elegant but inapplicable theoretical models. Having little or no really useful knowledge to enable them to come to grips in an effective way with real development problems, they often tend to become unknowing or reluctant apologists for the existing system of elitist policies and institutional structures. In university economics courses, for example, this typically entails the perpetuation of the teaching of many "irrelevant" Western concepts and models, while in government policy discussions, too much emphasis is placed on attempts to measure capital-output ratios, to increase savings and investment ratios, to privatize and deregulate the economy, or to maximize GDP growth rates. As a result, proponents argue that desirable institutional and structural reforms, many of which we have discussed, are neglected or given only cursory attention.

The N

Cl
ar

The Dualistic-Development Thesis

Implicit in structural-change theories and explicit in international-dependence theories is the notion of a world of dual societies, of rich nations and poor nations and, in the developing countries, pockets of wealth within broad areas of poverty. **Dualism** is a concept widely discussed in development economics. It represents

the privatization of public corporations. In developing countries, it called for freer markets and the dismantling of public ownership, statist planning, and government regulation of economic activities. Neoclassicists obtained controlling votes on the boards of the world's two most powerful international financial agencies—the World Bank and the International Monetary Fund. In conjunction and with the simultaneous erosion of influence of organizations such as the International Labor Organization (ILO), the United Nations Development Program (UNDP), and the United Nations Conference on Trade and Development (UNCTAD), which more fully represent the views of LDC delegates, it was inevitable that the neoconservative, free-market challenge to the interventionist arguments of dependence theorists would gather momentum.

The central argument of the neoclassical counterrevolution is that underdevelopment results from poor resource allocation due to incorrect pricing policies and too much state intervention by overly active developing-nation governments. Rather, the leading writers of the counterrevolution school, including Lord Peter Bauer, Deepak Lal, Ian Little, Harry Johnson, Bela Balassa, Jagdish Bhagwati, and Anne Krueger, argue that it is this very state intervention in economic activity that slows the pace of economic growth. The neoliberals argue that by permitting competitive **free markets** to flourish, privatizing state-owned enterprises, promoting free trade and export expansion, welcoming investors from developed countries, and eliminating the plethora of government regulations and price distortions in factor, product, and financial markets, both economic efficiency and economic growth will be stimulated. Contrary to the claims of the dependence theorists, the neoclassical counterrevolutionaries argue that the Third World is underdeveloped not because of the predatory activities of the First World and the international agencies that it controls but rather because of the heavy hand of the state and the corruption, inefficiency, and lack of economic incentives that permeate the economies of developing nations. What is needed, therefore, is not a reform of the international economic system, a restructuring of dualistic developing economies, an increase in foreign aid, attempts to control population growth, or a more effective development planning system. Rather, it is simply a matter of promoting free markets and laissez-faire economics within the context of permissive governments that allow the "magic of the marketplace" and the "invisible hand" of market prices to guide resource allocation and stimulate economic development. They point both to the success of countries like South Korea, Taiwan, and Singapore as "free market" examples (although, as we shall see later, these Asian Tigers are far from the laissez-faire neoconservative prototype) and to the failures of the public-interventionist economies of Africa and Latin America.[10]

The neoclassical challenge to the prevailing development orthodoxy can be divided into three component approaches: the free-market approach, the public-choice (or "new political economy") approach, and the "market-friendly" approach. **Free-market analysis** argues that markets alone are efficient—product markets provide the best signals for investments in new activities; labor markets respond to these new industries in appropriate ways; producers know best what to produce and how to produce it efficiently, and product and factor prices reflect accurate scarcity values of goods and resources now and in the future. Competition is effective, if not perfect; technology is freely available and nearly costless to absorb; information is also perfect and nearly costless to obtain. Under these circumstances, any government intervention in the economy is by definition distortionary and counterproductive. Free-market development economists have tended to assume that developing-world markets are efficient and that whatever imperfections exist are of little consequence.

Public-choice theory, also known as the **new political economy approach**, goes even further to argue that governments can do nothing right. This is because public-choice theory assumes that politicians, bureaucrats, citizens, and states act solely from a self-interested perspective, using their power and the authority of government for their own selfish ends. Citizens use political influence to obtain special benefits (called "rents") from government policies (e.g., import licenses or rationed foreign exchange) that restrict access to important resources. Politicians use government resources to consolidate and maintain positions of power and authority. Bureaucrats and public officials use their positions to extract bribes from rent-seeking citizens and to operate protected businesses on the side. Finally, states use their power to confiscate private property from individuals. The net result is not only a misallocation of resources but also a general reduction in individual freedoms. The conclusion, therefore, is that minimal government is the best government.[11]

The **market-friendly approach** is the most recent variant on the neoclassical counterrevolution. It is associated principally with the writings of the World Bank and its economists, many of whom were more in the free-market and public-choice camps during the 1980s.[12] This approach recognizes that there are many imperfections in LDC product and factor markets and that governments do have a key role to play in facilitating the operation of markets through "nonselective" (market-friendly) interventions—for example, by investing in physical and social infrastructure, health care facilities, and educational institutions and by providing a suitable climate for private enterprise. The market-friendly approach also differs from the free-market and public-choice schools of thought by accepting the notion that market failures are more widespread in developing countries in areas such as investment coordination and environmental outcomes. Moreover, phenomena such as missing and incomplete information, externalities in skill creation and learning, and economies of scale in production are also endemic to LDC markets. In fact, it is the recognition of these last three phenomena that gives rise to the newest schools of development theory, the *new* or *endogenous growth* school of thought, and the coordination failure approach, to which we turn in Chapter 4.

Traditional Neoclassical Growth Theory

Another cornerstone of the neoclassical free-market argument is the assertion that liberalization (opening up) of national markets draws additional domestic and foreign investment and thus increases the rate of capital accumulation. In terms of GDP growth, this is equivalent to raising domestic savings rates, which enhances **capital-labor ratios** and per capita incomes in capital-poor developing countries.

Traditional neoclassical models of growth are a direct outgrowth of the Harrod-Domar and Solow models, which both stress the importance of savings.[13]

The **Solow neoclassical growth model** in particular represented the seminal contribution to the neoclassical theory of growth and later earned Robert Solow the Nobel Prize in economics. It expanded on the Harrod-Domar formulation by adding a second factor, labor, and introducing a third independent variable, technology, to the growth equation. Unlike the fixed-coefficient, constant-returns-to-scale assumption of the Harrod-Domar model, Solow's neoclassical growth model exhibited diminishing returns to labor and capital separately and constant returns to both factors jointly. Technological progress became the residual factor explaining long-term growth, and its level was assumed by Solow and other growth theorists to be determined exogenously, that is, independently of all other factors.

More formally, the Solow neoclassical growth model uses a standard aggregate production function in which

$$Y = K^\alpha (AL)^{1-\alpha} \tag{3.10}$$

where Y is gross domestic product, K is the stock of capital (which may include human capital as well as physical capital), L is labor, and A represents the productivity of labor, which grows at an exogenous rate. For developed countries, this rate has been estimated at about 2% per year. It may be smaller or larger for developing countries, depending on whether they are stagnating or catching up with the developed countries. Because the rate of technological progress is given exogenously (at 2% per year, say), the Solow neoclassical model is sometimes called an "exogenous" growth model, to be contrasted with the endogenous growth approach (discussed at the beginning of Chapter 4). In Equation 3.10, α represents the elasticity of output with respect to capital (the percentage increase in GDP resulting from a 1% increase in human and physical capital). The physical capital component is usually measured statistically as the share of capital in a country's national income accounts. Since α is assumed to be less than 1 and private capital is assumed to be paid its marginal product so that there are no external economies, this formulation of neoclassical growth theory yields diminishing returns both to capital and to labor. The Solow neoclassical growth model is examined in detail in Appendix 3.1.

According to **traditional neoclassical growth theory**, output growth results from one or more of three factors: increases in labor quantity and quality (through population growth and education), increases in capital (through saving and investment), and improvements in technology (see Chapter 2). **Closed economies** (those with no external activities) with lower savings rates (other things being equal) grow more slowly in the short run than those with high savings rates and tend to converge to lower per capita income levels. **Open economies** (those with trade, foreign investment, etc.), however, experience income convergence at higher levels as capital flows from rich countries to poor countries where capital-labor ratios are lower and thus returns on investments are higher. Consequently, by impeding the inflow of foreign investment, the heavy-handedness of LDC governments, according to neoclassical growth theory, will retard growth in the economies of the developing world.

Conclusions and Implications

Like the dependence revolution of the 1970s, the neoclassical counterrevolution of the 1980s had its origin in an economics-cum-ideological view of the developing world and its problems. Whereas dependence theorists (many, but not all, of whom were LDC economists) saw underdevelopment as an externally induced phenomenon, neoclassical revisionists (most, but not all, of whom were Western economists) saw the problem as an internally induced LDC phenomenon, caused by too much government intervention and bad economic policies. Such finger-pointing on both sides is not uncommon in issues so contentious as those that divide rich and poor nations.

But what of the neoclassical counterrevolution's contention that free markets and less government provide the basic ingredients for development? On strictly efficiency (as opposed to equity) criteria, there can be little doubt that market price allocation usually does a better job than state intervention. The problem is that many LDC economies are so different in structure and organization from their Western counterparts that the behavioral assumptions and policy precepts of traditional neoclassical theory are sometimes questionable and often incorrect. Competitive markets simply do not exist, nor, given the institutional, cultural, and historical context of many LDCs, would they necessarily be desirable from a long-term economic and social perspective (see Chapter 11). Consumers as a whole are rarely sovereign about anything, let alone about what goods and services are to be produced, in what quantities, and for whom. Information is limited, markets are fragmented, and much of the economy is still nonmonetized.[14] There are widespread externalities of both production and consumption as well as discontinuities in production and indivisibilities (i.e., economies of scale) in technology. Producers, private or public, have great power in determining market prices and quantities sold. The ideal of competition is typically just that—an ideal with little substance in reality. Although monopolies of resource purchase and product sale are pervasive in the developing world, the traditional neoclassical theory of monopoly also offers little insight into the day-to-day activities of public and private corporations. Decision rules can vary widely with the social setting, so that profit maximization may be a low-priority objective especially in state-owned enterprises, in comparison with, say, the creation of jobs or the replacement of foreign managers with local personnel (see Chapter 16). Finally, the invisible hand often acts not to promote the general welfare but rather to lift up those who are already well-off while pushing down the vast majority.

Much can be learned from neoclassical theory with regard to the importance of elementary supply-and-demand analysis in arriving at "correct" product, factor, and foreign-exchange prices for efficient production and resource allocation. However, do not confuse free markets with price allocation. Enlightened governments can also make effective use of prices as signals and incentives for influencing socially optimal resource allocations. Indeed, we will often demonstrate the usefulness of various tools of neoclassical theory in our later analysis of problems such as population growth, agricultural stagnation, unemployment and underemployment, the environment, educational demands, export promotion versus import substitution, devaluation, project planning, monetary policy, and economic privatization. Nevertheless, the reality of the institutional and political structure of many developing-world economies—not to mention their differing value systems and ideologies—often makes the attainment of appropriate economic policies based either on markets or on enlightened public intervention an exceedingly difficult endeavor. In an environment of widespread institutional rigidity and severe socioeconomic inequality, *both* markets and governments will typically fail. It is not simply an either-or question based on ideological leaning; rather it is a matter of assessing each individual country's situation on a case-by-case basis. Developing nations will need to adopt local solutions in response to local constraints.[15] Development economists must therefore be able to distinguish between textbook neoclassical theory and the institutional and political reality of contemporary LDCs.[16] They can then choose the neoclassical concepts and models that can best illuminate issues and dilemmas of development and discard those that cannot. This will be our task in Parts Two and Three.

Classic Theories of Development: Reconciling the Differences

In this chapter, we have reviewed a range of competing theories and approaches to the study of economic development. Each approach has its strengths and weaknesses. The fact that there exists such controversy—be it ideological, theoretical, or empirical—is what makes the study of economic development both challenging and exciting. Even more than other fields of economics, development economics has no universally accepted doctrine or paradigm. Instead, we have a continually evolving pattern of insights and understandings that together provide the basis for examining the possibilities of contemporary development of the diverse nations of Africa, Asia, and Latin America.

You may wonder how consensus could emerge from so much disagreement. Although it is not implied here that such a consensus exists today or can indeed ever exist when such sharply conflicting values and ideologies prevail, we do suggest that something of significance can be gleaned from each of the four approaches that we have described. For example, the linear-stages model emphasizes the crucial role that saving and investment play in promoting sustainable long-run growth. The Lewis two-sector model of structural change underlines the importance of attempting to analyze the many linkages between traditional agriculture and modern industry, and the empirical research of Chenery and his associates attempts to document precisely how economies undergo structural change while identifying the numerical values of key economic parameters involved in that process. The thoughts of international-dependence theorists alert us to the importance of the structure and workings of the world economy and the many ways in which decisions made in the developed world can affect the lives of millions of people in the developing world. Whether or not these activities are deliberately designed to maintain developing nations in a state of dependence is often beside the point. The fact of their very dependence and their vulnerability to key economic decisions made in the capitals of North America, Western Europe, or Japan (not to mention those made by the IMF and the World Bank) forces us to recognize the validity of many of the propositions of the international-dependence school. The same applies to arguments regarding the dualistic structures and the role of ruling elites in the domestic economies of the developing world.

Although a good deal of conventional neoclassical economic theory needs to be modified to fit the unique social, institutional, and structural circumstances of developing nations, there is no doubt that promoting efficient production and distribution through a proper, functioning price system is an integral part of any successful development process. Many of the arguments of the neoclassical counterrevolutionaries, especially those related to the inefficiency of state-owned enterprises and the failures of development planning (see Chapter 11) and the harmful effects of government-induced domestic and international price distortions (see Chapters 7, 13, and 15) are as well taken as those of the dependence and structuralist schools. By contrast, the unquestioning exaltation of free markets and open economies along with the universal disparagement of public-sector leadership in promoting growth with equity in the developing world is open to serious challenge. As we shall discover all too often in Parts Two and Three, successful development requires a skillful and judicious balancing of market pricing and promotion where markets can indeed exist and operate efficiently, along with intelligent and equity-oriented government intervention in areas where unfettered market forces would lead to undesirable economic and social outcomes.

In summary, each of these approaches to understanding development has something to offer. Their respective contributions will become clear later in the book when we explore in detail both the origins of and possible solutions to a wide range of problems such as poverty, population growth, unemployment, rural development, international trade, and the environment. They also inform contemporary models of development and underdevelopment, to which we turn in the next chapter.

Schools of Thought in Context: South Korea and Argentina

A closer examination of two countries confirms the conclusion that each of the first four broad approaches to development— stages of growth, structural patterns of development, dependence, and neoclassical—provides important insights about development processes and policy.* South Korea and Argentina are reasonably well matched for such a comparison; for example, both are midsize in population (38 million in Argentina and 48 million in South Korea in 2002), and until 1997, both were classified as middle-income countries. But South Korea, now designated by the World Bank as a high-income country, has almost double the per capita income of Argentina, whereas 30 years earlier the reverse was true. Can the four classic approaches to development explain this reversal?

South Korea

Stages of Growth South Korea confirms some linear-stages views, albeit in a limited way. In recent years, its share of investment in

national income has been among the highest in the world, and this is a crucial part of the explanation of the nation's rapid ascent. To remind us of just how rapid this ascent has been, we should consider that the country did not even rate a mention in Rostow's *Stages of Economic Growth*, and in 1960, when the book was published, few of the "preconditions for takeoff" were in place. Investment has been very high over the past three decades. But as a share of GNI, the investment ratio, at 15%, was still below takeoff levels in 1965. Yet it rose dramatically to 37% of GNI by 1990 and remained at a high 28% in the early 2000s. Still, South Korea today does seem well characterized by Rostow's notion of an economy in the midst of a "drive to maturity," well on its way toward mastering the range of currently available technologies, and by the early 2000s appeared to be entering an "age of high mass consumption."

Rostow claimed that maturity is attained some 60 years after takeoff begins, but he never denied unique experiences for each country, and it may well be that the gap between traditional and advanced technology can actually be crossed more quickly at later stages of development. The larger the productivity gap between countries, the quicker that income can grow once takeoff has been achieved. Korea certainly meets the "maturity" criterion of becoming integrated with

*The new models of endogenous growth theory and multiple equilibria are not treated systematically here, although the importance of human capital development, externalities, economies of scale, and the Big Push have obvious relevance to South Korea's growth experience, and, to date, little relevance for Argentina, except to illustrate how government can become part of a bad equilibrium. See Chapter 4.

the world economy through new types of exports and imports. Although the fact that India, rather than South Korea, was picked by Rostow for takeoff shows the limits of the predictive powers of the stages theory, the case of Korea nonetheless offers some confirmation of their value.

Structural Patterns South Korea also confirms some patterns-of-development structural-change models. In particular, South Korea's rise over the past generation has been characterized by rapidly increasing agricultural productivity, shifts of labor from agriculture to industry, the steady growth of the capital stock and of education and skills, and the demographic transition from high to low fertility. These changes occurred while South Korea's per capita income grew by more than 7% annually for the whole 1965–1990 period. Even in the 1990–2002 period, as a more mature economy, and in the face of the Asian financial crisis of 1997-1998, the economy grew at a 5.8% rate. In the late 1940s and 1950s, South Korea carried out a thoroughgoing land reform, so agriculture was not neglected; but otherwise its growth through rapid expansion of the percentage of the labor force in industry has broadly conformed with the Lewis model of development. After about 1970, productivity growth in agriculture also increased rapidly, owing in part to a successful integrated rural development program.

Dependence Revolution But South Korea poses a serious challenge to the dependence revolution models. Here is a poor country that became tied in with the international economy: It was strongly dependent in international relations—it was a Japanese colony until 1945 and thereafter wholly dependent on maintaining the goodwill of the United States for defense against invasion by North Korea. It received a large part of its national budget in the form of U.S. aid in the 1950s and both exported and imported a great deal from developed countries, especially the United States and Japan. The shape of the nation's development was thus "conditioned" in large part by export opportunities to developed countries, and dependence theory would predict that retarded development opportunities should result. Yet South Korea today is widely considered a candidate for developed-country status (its income is comparable to that of Greece and Portugal. Of course, dependence theorists could and do claim that South Korea is an exception because of the magnitude of aid it received and the self-interests of the advanced countries in seeing its full successful development because of its role as a bulwark against communism. And the Korean government pursued some particular policies that the dependence school would by and large applaud, including carrying out an extremely active industrial upgrading policy, sharply limiting the role of multinational corporations and deliberately establishing indigenous industries as an alternative, and using debt rather than direct foreign equity investment to finance extraordinary levels of investment. South Korea also implemented one of the most ambitious land reform programs in the developing world and placed strong emphasis on primary rather than university education, two policies of exceptional importance. But this does not explain how South Korea was able to adopt such policies to break out of dependence in the first place. And when too many exceptions start to be made in any theory, it usually indicates that the theory doesn't reflect the whole truth.

Neoclassical Counterrevolution South Korea likewise poses a strong challenge to the neoclassical counterrevolution models. Although some members of this school have tried to claim South Korea as their own, by now an overwhelmingly large body of scholarship makes it clear that the nation was highly interventionist at home and in international trade, with the government making extensive use of development planning, using a wide range of tax breaks and incentives to induce firms to follow government directives and interventions, setting individual company export targets, orchestrating efforts in various industries to upgrade the average technological level, coordinating foreign technology licensing agreements, using monopoly power to get the best deal from competing multinationals, and generally inducing firms to move rapidly up the ladder of (dynamic) comparative advantage (see Chapter 13). These policies addressed real technology and skill-raising market failure problems of development, and at least prior to the 1997 Asian currency crisis, from which Korea quickly recovered, very few cases of glaring government failure can be pointed to in this experience. Of course, it does confirm that firms respond to economic incentives. But it may also be claimed with at least equal force that South Korea provides an object lesson in government's role in overcoming coordination failures, as examined in Chapter 4.

Argentina

In contrast, for Argentina, stages and patterns theories illuminate relatively little economic history, whereas the dependence revolution and neoclassical counterrevolution theories together offer important insights.

Stages of Growth The history of Argentina poses a strong challenge to the linear-stages approach. Rostow defined takeoff as "the interval when the old blocks and resistances to steady growth are finally overcome. . . . Growth becomes its normal condition." In 1870, Argentina ranked eleventh in the world in per capita income (ahead of Germany); to-

day, it is not even in the top 50. Although Rostow said that in determining a country's stage, technology absorption, not income per inhabitant, is what matters, he dated Argentina's preconditions for takeoff as an extended period before 1914 and concluded that takeoff "in some sense" began in the First World War, but "in the mid 1930s . . . a sustained takeoff was inaugurated, which by and large can now [1960] be judged to have been successful," concluding that "in Latin America the take-off has been completed in two major cases (Mexico and Argentina)." Rostow attributes the fact that preconditions were there for some time before takeoff to excessive import of foreign capital over too long a period without increasing domestic savings. (But South Korea was also a heavy foreign borrower until very recently.) Argentina certainly satisfied Rostow's criterion of developing manufacturing sectors at a rapid rate.

But now let's look at what happened in Argentina since Rostow put the country forward as an example. According to World Bank data, Argentina had a *negative* growth rate throughout the 1965–1990 period, and in the 1980s, domestic investment shrank at a −8.3% rate, falling back well below Rostow's threshold takeoff investment levels. Although Argentina grew at 3.6% in 1990–2001, it defaulted on its debt in 2002, and the economy shrank 11%, followed by a modest recovery. Like many other Latin American and African countries in the 1970s and 1980s, Argentina demonstrated that development progress is not irreversible and that sustained growth can come to an end.

Structural Patterns Argentina did exhibit many of the usual structural patterns of development as agricultural productivity rose, industrial employment grew (albeit slowly), urbanization took place, fertility fell, and so on. But the fact that many structural regularities of development were observed even as living standards in the country stagnated illustrates some of the shortcomings of relying too much on selected pieces of data without the assistance of guiding theory on how the parts fit together.

Dependence Revolution In contrast to South Korea, the case of Argentina offers some vindication for dependence theories in that the country relied to a large extent on exporting primary goods, and the real prices of these goods fell compared to imports. Multinational corporations played a large role, and Argentina was unable to create its own viable manufacturing *export* industries, ultimately having to submit to stringent structural-adjustment programs, sell state industries to foreign companies, and other constraints. Dependence theorists can claim with some justification that Argentina's conditioned development fell victim to developed-country economic interests, especially those of British and American corporations.

Neoclassical Counterrevolution But Argentina also offers some vindication for neoclassical counterrevolution theory in that faulty interventionist restrictions, inefficient state enterprise, bias against production for exports, and unnecessary red tape ended up hurting industry and entrepreneurship. Government policy consistently seemed to support privileged interests rather than broad goals of development, and government failure was usually worse than market failure in the country. In the mid-1990s, a large-scale liberalization and privatization program seemed to be beginning to reinvigorate growth in Argentina. Unfortunately, by 2002 four years of recession culminated in economic implosion as the economy collapsed under the weight of rising internal fiscal and external trade deficits, caused in part by the linking of the peso to a strong U.S. dollar. Dependency theorists claimed vindication. The subsequent recovery despite the default showed that single explanations for development success and failure are rarely adequate.

Summary

It is interesting that as South Korea provides a challenge to both dependence and neoclassical theory, the starkest opposites in many ways, Argentina can be viewed more as a vindication for these two theories; and South Korea serves more to confirm linear stages of growth and conclusions about structural patterns of development, whereas Argentina poses challenges to their universal importance. Yet each of these four approaches has added something vital to our understanding of development experiences and prospects in just these two countries. South Korea also illustrates the role of government in overcoming coordination failures, while Argentina illustrates how government can become part of a bad equilibrium, topics explored in the next chapter. ∎

Sources

Financial Times, Various issues.

Fishlow, Albert, et al. *Miracle or Design? Lessons from the East Asian Experience*. Washington, D.C.: Overseas Development Council, 1994.

Porter, Michael. *Competitive Advantage of Nations*. New York: Free Press, 1990.

Rodrik, Dani. "Coordination failures and government policy: A model with applications to East Asia and Eastern Europe." *Journal of International Economics* 40 (1996): 1–22.

Rostow, Walt W. *The Stages of Economic Growth: A Non-Communist Manifesto*. London: Cambridge University Press, 1960.

Smith, Stephen C. *Industrial Policy in Developing Countries: Reconsidering the Real Sources of Expert-Led Growth.* Washington, D.C.: Economic Policy Institute, 1991.

Thurow, Lester. *Head to Head.* New York: Morrow, 1992.

Washington Post, various issues.

World Bank. *Korea: Managing the Industrial Transition.* Washington, D.C.: World Bank, 1987.

Concepts for Review

Autarky	Lewis two-sector model	Production function
Average product	Marginal product	Public-choice theory
Capital-labor ratio	Market-friendly approach	Savings ratio
Capital-output ratio	Necessary condition	Self-sustaining growth
Center	Neoclassical counterrevolu-	Solow neoclassical growth
Closed economy	tion	model
Comprador groups	Neocolonial dependence	Stages-of-growth model of
Dependence	model	development
Dominance	New institutionalism	Structural-change theory
Dualism	New political economy ap-	Structural transformation
False-paradigm model	proach	Sufficient condition
Free market	Open economy	Surplus labor
Free-market analysis	Patterns-of-development	Traditional neoclassical
Harrod-Domar growth	analysis	growth theory
model	Periphery	Underdevelopment

Questions for Discussion

1. Explain the essential distinctions among the stages-of-growth theory of development, the structural-change models of Lewis and Chenery, and the theory of international dependence in both its neo-Marxist and false-paradigm conceptualizations. Which model do you think provides the best explanation of the situation in most developing nations? Explain your answer.

2. Explain the meaning of *dualism* and *dual societies*. Do you think that the concept of dualism adequately portrays the development picture in most developing countries? Explain your answer.

3. Some people claim that international dualism and domestic dualism are merely different manifestations of the same phenomenon. What do you think they mean by this, and is it a valid conceptualization? Explain your answer.

4. What is meant by the term *neoclassical counterrevolution*? What are its principal arguments, and how valid do you think they are? Explain your answer.

5. Given the diversity of developing countries, do you think that there could ever be a single, unified theory of development? Explain your answer.

6. Is the neoclassical, free-market theory necessarily incompatible with dependence theory? How might these two approaches work together?

Notes

1. Walt W. Rostow, *The Stages of Economic Growth: A Non-Communist Manifesto* (London: Cambridge University Press, 1960), pp. 1, 3, 4, and 12. For an extensive and critical review of the Rostow stages doctrine from a Marxist perspective, see Paul Baran and Edward Hobsbawm, "The stages of economic growth," *Kyklos* 14 (1961): 234–242.

2. This model is named after two economists, Sir Roy Harrod of England and Professor Evesey Domar of the United States, who separately but concurrently developed a variant of it in the early 1950s.

3. W. Arthur Lewis, "Economic development with unlimited supplies of labour," *Manchester School* 22 (1954): 139–191; John C. H. Fei and Gustav Ranis, *Development of the Labor Surplus Economy: Theory and Policy* (Homewood, Ill.: Irwin, 1964). In fact, many of the basic ideas of the Lewis and Fei-Ranis model were originally expounded by Ragnar Nurkse in his famous little book *Problems of Capital Formation in Underdeveloped Countries* (New York: Oxford University Press, 1953). We are indebted to Professor Harold Votey for reminding us of this often forgotten fact.

4. See Hollis B. Chenery, *Structural Change and Development Policy* (Baltimore: Johns Hopkins University Press, 1979); Hollis B. Chenery and Moshe Syrquin, *Patterns of Development, 1950–70* (London: Oxford University Press, 1975); Moshe Syrquin, "Patterns of structural change," in *Handbook of Development Economics*, ed. Hollis B. Chenery and T. N. Srinivasan (Amsterdam: Elsevier, 1989), vol. 1, pp. 205–273, and the landmark magnum opus of this school, *Industrialization and Growth: A Comparative Study*, by Hollis B. Chenery, Sherman Robinson, and Moshe Syrquin (New York: Oxford University Press, 1986).

5. See, for example, Sarah Anderson, John Cavanagh, Thea Lee, and the Institute for Policy Studies, *Field Guide to the Global Economy* (New York: New Press, 2000); Robin Broad (ed.) *Global Backlash: Citizen Initiatives for a Just World Economy* (Lanham, Md.: Rowman & Littlefield, 2002); and John Gray, *False Dawn: The Delusions of Global Capitalism* (New York: New Press, 2000).

6. For a comprehensive introduction to the neo-Marxist view of international development and underdevelopment, see Paul Baran, *The Political Economy of Neo-Colonialism* (London: Heinemann, 1975). An outstanding literature review is contained in Keith Griffin and John Gurley, "Radical analysis of imperialism, the Third World, and the transition to socialism: A survey article," *Journal of Economic Literature* 23 (1985): 1089–1143. See also Ted C. Lewellen, *Dependency and Development: An Introduction to the Third World* (Westport, Conn.: Bergin & Garvey, 1995).

7. A provocative and well-documented application of this argument to the case of Kenya can be found in Colin Leys, *Underdevelopment in Kenya: The Political Economy of Neo-Colonialism* (London: Heinemann, 1975).

8. Theotonio Dos Santos, "The crisis of development theory and the problem of dependence in Latin America," in *Underdevelopment and Development*, ed. Henry Bernstein (Harmondsworth, U.K.: Penguin, 1973), pp. 57–80. See also Benjamin J.

Cohen, *The Question of Imperialism: The Political Economy of Dominance and Dependence* (New York: Basic Books, 1973).

9. Hans W. Singer, "Dualism revisited: A new approach to the problems of dual societies in developing countries," *Journal of Development Studies* 7 (1970): 60–61.

10. For examples of the literature of neoclassical counterrevolutionaries, see Peter T. Bauer, *Reality and Rhetoric: Studies in the Economics of Development* (London: Weidenfield & Nicolson, 1984); Deepak Lal, *The Poverty of Development Economics* (Cambridge, Mass.: Harvard University Press, 1985); Ian Little, *Economic Development: Theories, Policies, and International Relations* (New York: Basic Books 1982); and any mid-1980s issue of the World Bank's *World Development Report* (New York: Oxford University Press) and the International Monetary Fund's *Annual World Economic Outlook*. An outstanding critique of this literature can be found in John Toye, *Dilemmas of Development: Reflections on the Counter-Revolution in Development Theory and Policy* (Oxford: Blackwell, 1987). See also Ziya Onis, "The limits of neoliberalism: Toward a reformulation of development theory," *Journal of Economic Issues* 29 (1995): 97–119; Lance Taylor, "The revival of the liberal creed: The IMF and the World Bank in a globalized economy," *World Development* 25 (1997): 45–152; and Alexandro Portes, "Neoliberalism and the sociology of development: Emerging trends and unanticipated facts," *Population and Development Review* 23 (1997): 229–259.

11. For a good explication of the tenets of the public-choice theory, see Merilee S. Grindle and John W. Thomas, *Public Choices and Public Policy Change: The Political Economy of Reform in Developing Countries* (Baltimore: Johns Hopkins University Press, 1991). The classic article in the field is by Nobel laureate James M. Buchanan, "Social choice, democracy and free markets," *Journal of Political Economy* 62 (1954): 114–123. For a critique, see Paul P. Streeten, "Markets and states: Against minimalism," *World Development* 21 (1993): 1281–1298, and Amartya Sen, "Rationality and social choice," *American Economic Review* 85 (1995): 1–24.

12. See any of the 1990s *World Development Reports* and also World Bank, *The East Asian Miracle* (New York: Oxford University Press, 1993). For a critique of this approach, see Ajit Singh, "State intervention and 'market-friendly' approach to development: A critical analysis of the World Bank theses," in *The States, Markets and Development*, ed. Amitava K. Dutt, Kwan S. Kim, and Ajit Singh (London: Elgar, 1994).

13. The Solow model is set forth in Robert Solow, "A contribution to the theory of economic growth," *Quarterly Journal of Economics* 70 (1956): 65–94.

14. For a discussion of these and related issues, see Heinz W. Arndt, "'Market failure' and underdevelopment," *World Development* 16 (1988): 210–229.

15. On identifying and addressing local constraints, see Dani Rodrik, Ricardo Hausmann, and Andres Velasco, "Growth Diagnostics," http://ksghome.harvard.edu/~drodrik/barcelonaoct19.pdf.

16. A possible fourth component of the neoclassical counterrevolution—one that goes to the essence of development issues—has been called the **new institutionalism**. The institutions include property rights, prices and market structures, money and financial institutions, firms and industrial organization, and relationships between government and markets. The basic message of the new institutionalism is that even in a

neoclassical world, the success or failure of development efforts will depend on the nature, existence, and proper functioning of a country's fundamental institutions. The origins of the new institutionalism can be found in the theory of institutions pioneered by the work of Nobel laureate Ronald Coase. See Ronald H. Coase, "The institutional structure of production," *American Economic Review* 82 (1992): 713–719; Howard Stein, "Theories of institutions and economic reform in Africa," *World Development* 22 (1994): 889–904; Oliver E. Williamson, "The institutions and governance of economic development and reform," in *Proceedings of the World Bank Annual Conference on Development Economics, 1994* (Washington, D.C.: World Bank, 1995); and Jean-Jacques Laffont, "Competition, conformation and development," *Annual World Bank Conference on Development Economics, 1998* (Washington, D.C.: World Bank, 1999).

Further Reading

Thoughtful analyses of the evolution of development thinking can be found in Gerald M. Meier and Joseph E. Stiglitz (eds.), *Frontiers of Development Economics: The Future in Perspective* (New York: Oxford University Press, 2000); Amartya Sen, *Development as Freedom* (New York: Knopf, 1999); Amartya Sen, "Development: Which way now?" *Economic Journal* 93 (1983): 745–762; Heinz W. Arndt, *Economic Development: The History of an Idea* (Chicago: University of Chicago Press, 1987); Diana Hunt, *Economic Theories of Development* (Totawa, N.J.: Rowman & Littlefield, 1987); Nicholas Stern, "The economics of development: A survey," *Economic Journal* 99 (1989): 597–685; Robert Dorfman, "Economic development from the beginning to Rostow," *Journal of Economic Literature* 29 (1991): 573–591; Hollis B. Chenery and T. N. Srinivasan (eds.), *Handbook of Development Economics* (Amsterdam: Elsevier, 1989), vol. 1, pt. 1 (articles by Sen, Lewis, Bardhan, and Ranis); and Jean Waelbroeck, "Half a century of development economics: A review based on the *Handbook of Development Economics*," *World Bank Economic Review* 12 (1998): 323–335.

For an excellent summary statement of the concept of dualism and dual societies, see Hans Singer, "Dualism revisited: A new approach to the problems of dual society in developing countries," *Journal of Development Studies* 7 (1970): 60–61.

Among surveys of the dependence literature as applied to problems of underdevelopment, the following are among the best: Keith Griffin and John Gurley, "Radical analysis of imperialism, the Third World, and the transition to socialism: A survey article," *Journal of Economic Literature* 23 (1985): 1089–1143; Samir Amin, *Imperialism and Unequal Development* (New York: Monthly Review Press, 1977); Patrick O'Brien, "A critique of Latin American theories of dependency," in *Beyond the Sociology of Development*, ed. Iver Oxaal et al. (London: Routledge, 1975); Sanjaya Lall, "Is 'dependence' a useful concept in analyzing underdevelopment?" *World Development* 3 (1975): 799–810; G. Kay, *Development and Underdevelopment: A Marxist Analysis* (London: Macmillan, 1975); Gabriel Palma, "Dependency: A formal theory of underdevelopment or a methodology for the analysis of concrete situations of underdevelopment?" *World Development* 6 (1978): 881–924; Celso Furtado, "Underdevelopment: To conform or reform?" in *Pioneers in Development: Second Series*, ed. Gerald M. Meier (New York: Oxford University Press, 1987), pp. 203–207; and Ted C. Lewellen, *Dependency and Development: An Introduction to the Third World* (Westport, Conn.: Bergin & Garvey, 1995).

Readings on the neoclassical counterrevolution, in addition to those cited in note 10, include Peter T. Bauer, *Dissent on Development* (London: Weidenfeld & Nicolson, 1972); Julian Simon, *The Ultimate Resource* (Princeton, N.J.: Princeton University Press, 1981); Ian Little, "An economic renaissance," in *Economic Growth and Structural Change in Taiwan,* ed. W. Galenson (Ithaca, N.Y.: Cornell University Press, 1979); and World Bank, *World Development Report, 1982, 1983,* and *1987.* (New York: Oxford University Press, 1982,1983, 1987). For a wide-ranging and fascinating discussion of both the power and the inherent limitations of markets, see John McMillan, *Reinventing the Bazaar: A Natural History of Markets* (New York: Norton, 2002).

Appendix 3.1

The Solow Neoclassical Growth Model

The Solow neoclassical growth model, for which Robert Solow of the Massachusetts Institute of Technology received the Nobel Prize, is probably the best-known model of economic growth.[1] Although in some respects Solow's model describes a developed economy better than a developing one, it remains a basic reference point for the literature on growth and development. It implies that economies will conditionally converge to the same level of income, given that they have the same rates of savings, depreciation, labor force growth, and productivity growth. Thus the Solow model is the basic framework for the study of convergence across countries (see Chapter 2). In this appendix, we consider this model in further detail.

The key modification from the Harrod-Domar (or AK) growth model, considered earlier in Chapter 2, is that the Solow model allows for substitution between capital and labor. In the process, it assumes that there are diminishing returns to the use of these inputs.

The aggregate production function, $Y = F(K, L)$ is assumed characterized by constant returns to scale. For example, in the special case known as the Cobb-Douglas production function, at any time t we have

$$Y(t) = K(t)^\alpha (A(t)L(t))^{1-\alpha} \qquad (A3.1)$$

where Y is gross domestic product, K is the stock of capital (which may include human capital as well as physical capital), L is labor, and $A(t)$ represents the productivity of labor, which grows over time at an exogenous rate.

Because of constant returns to scale, if all inputs are increased by the same amount, say 10%, then output will increase by the same amount (10% in this case). More generally,

$$\gamma Y = F(\gamma K, \gamma L)$$

where γ is some positive amount (1.1 in the case of a 10% increase).

Because γ can be any positive real number, a mathematical trick useful in analyzing the implications of the model is to set $\gamma = 1/L$ so that

$$Y/L = f(K/L, 1) \quad \text{or} \quad y = f(k) \qquad (A3.2)$$

Note that the symbol k is used for K/L, not for K/Y as it was in the Ak or Harrod-Domar model. This simplification allows us to deal with just one argument in the production function. For example, in the Cobb-Douglas case introduced in Equation 3.1,

$$y = Ak^\alpha \qquad (A3.3)$$

This represents an alternative way to think about a production function, in which everything is measured in quantities per worker. Equation A3.3 states that output per worker is a function that depends on the amount of capital per worker. The more capital with which each worker has to work, the more output that worker can produce. The labor force grows at rate n per year, say, and labor productivity growth, the rate at which the value of A in the production function increases, occurs at rate λ. The total capital stock grows when savings are greater than depreciation, but capital per worker grows when savings are also greater than what is needed to equip new workers with the same amount of capital as existing workers have.

The Solow equation (Equation A3.4) gives the growth of the capital-labor ratio, k (known as capital deepening), and shows that the growth of k depends on savings $sf(k)$, after allowing for the amount of capital required to service depreciation, δk, and after capital widening, that is, providing the existing amount of capital per worker to net new workers joining the labor force, nk. That is,

$$\Delta k = sf(k) - (\delta + n)k \qquad\qquad (A3.4)$$

Versions of the Solow equation are also valid for other growth models, such as the Harrod-Domar model.

For simplicity, we are assuming for now that A remains constant. In this case, there will be a state in which output and capital per worker are no longer changing, known as the steady state. (If A is increasing, the corresponding state will be one in which capital per effective worker is no longer changing. In that case, the number of effective workers rises as A rises; this is because when workers have higher productivity, it is as if there were extra workers on the job.) To find this steady state, set $\Delta k = 0$:

$$sf(k^*) = (\delta + n)k^* \qquad\qquad (A3.5)$$

The notation k^* means the level of capital per worker when the economy is in its steady state. That this equilibrium is stable can be seen from Figure A3.1.[2]

The capital per worker k^* represents the steady state. If k is higher or lower than k^*, the economy will return to it; thus k^* is a stable equilibrium. This stability is seen in the diagram by noting that to the left of k^*, $k < k^*$. Looking at the diagram, we see that in this case, $(n + \delta)k < sf(k)$. But now looking at the Solow equation (Equation A3.4), we see that when $(n + \delta)k < sf(k)$, $\Delta k > 0$. As a result, k in the economy is growing toward the equilibrium point k^*. By similar reasoning, to the right of k^*, $(n + \delta)k > sf(k)$, and as a result, $\Delta k < 0$ (again refer to Equation A3.4), and capital per worker is actually shrinking toward the equilibrium k^*.[3]

It is instructive to consider what happens in this model if we increase the rate of savings, s. A temporary increase in the rate of output growth is realized as we increase k by raising the rate of savings. We return to the original steady-state growth rate later, though at a higher level of output per worker in each later year. The key implication is that unlike in the

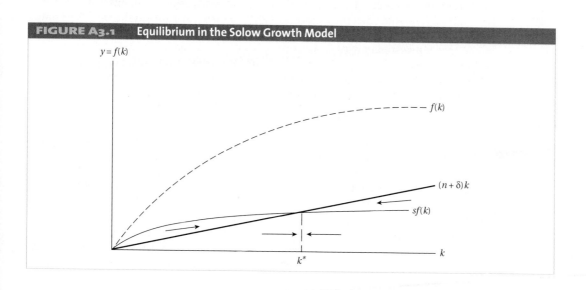

FIGURE A3.1   Equilibrium in the Solow Growth Model

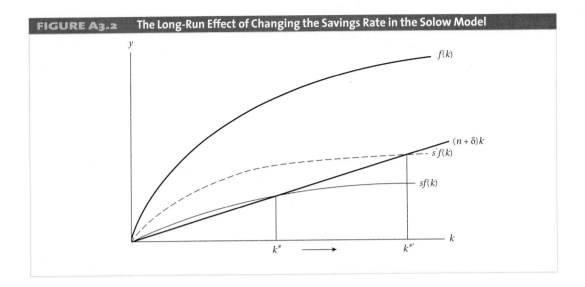

FIGURE A3.2   The Long-Run Effect of Changing the Savings Rate in the Solow Model

Harrod-Domar (or *AK*) analysis, in the Solow model an increase in *s* will not increase growth in the long run; it will only increase the equilibrium k^*. That is, after the economy has time to adjust, the capital-labor ratio increases, and so does the output-labor ratio, but not the rate of growth. The effect is shown in Figure A3.2, in which savings is raised to S'.

Note carefully that an increase in *s* does raise equilibrium output per person—which is certainly a valuable contribution to development—just not the equilibrium rate of growth. And the growth rate does increase temporarily as the economy kicks up toward the higher equilibrium capital per worker. Moreover, simulations based on cross-national data suggest that if *s* is increased, the economy may not return even halfway to its steady state for decades.[4] That is, for practical purposes of policymaking in developing countries, even if the Solow model is an accurate depiction of the economy, an increase in savings may substantially increase the growth rate for many decades to come. (Both theoretically and empirically, the link between the rate of savings and the rate of growth remains controversial).

Finally, it is possible that the rate of savings (and hence investment) is positively related to the rate of technological progress itself, so that the growth of *A* depends on *s*. This could be the case if investment uses newer-vintage capital and hence is more productive, if investment represents innovation in that it solves problems faced by the firm, and if other firms see what the investing firm has done and imitate it ("learning by watching"), generating externalities. This leads to a model somewhere between the standard Solow model and the endogenous growth models examined in Chapter 4.

Notes to Appendix 3.1

1. Robert M. Solow, "A contribution to the theory of economic growth," *Quarterly Journal of Economics* 70 (1956): 65–94.

2. Readers with more advanced mathematical training may note that Figure A3.1 is a phase diagram, which applies given that the Inada conditions hold: that the marginal product of *k* goes to infinity as *k* goes to zero and goes to zero as *k* goes to infinity (this follows from Inada conditions assumed separately for capital and labor inputs). This diminishing returns feature drives results of the Solow model.

3. Note that in the Solow model with technological progress, that is, growth of A, the capital-labor ratio grows to keep pace with the effective labor force, which is labor power that is augmented by its increasing productivity over time.

4. See N. Gregory Mankiw, David Romer, and David N. Weil, "A contribution to the empirics of economic growth," *Quarterly Journal of Economics* 107 (1992): 407–437. This article shows that when human capital is accounted for, as well as physical capital, the Solow model does a rather good job of explaining incomes and growth across countries. For a critical view see William Easterly and Ross Levine, "It's not factor accumulation: Stylized facts and growth models," *World Bank Economic Review* 15 (2001): 177–219, with the reply by Robert M. Solow, "Applying growth theory across countries," *World Bank Economic Review* 15 (2001): 283–288. For time-series evidence that the Solow model does a good job of explaining even the case of South Korean growth, see Edward Feasel, Yongbeom Kim, and Stephen C. Smith, "Investment, exports, and output in South Korea: A VAR approach to growth empirics," *Review of Development Economics* 5 (2001): 421–432.

CHAPTER FOUR

Contemporary Models of Development and Underdevelopment

Individuals need not make the right tradeoffs. And whereas in the past we thought the implication was that the economy would be slightly distorted, we now understand that the interaction of these slightly distorted behaviors may produce very large distortions. The consequence is that there may be multiple equilibria and that each may be inefficient.
—Karla Hoff and Joseph E. Stiglitz, writing in *Frontiers in Development Economics*, 2000

The unconventional themes put forth by the high development theorists—their emphasis on strategic complementarity in investment decisions and on the problem of coordination failure—did in fact identify important possibilities that are neglected in competitive equilibrium models.
—Paul Krugman, *Development, Geography, and Economic Theory*, 1995

After more than a half century of experience with attempting to encourage modern development, we have learned that development is both possible and extremely difficult to achieve. Thus an improved understanding of impediments and catalysts of development is of the utmost importance. Since the late 1980s, significant strides have been made in the analysis of economic development and underdevelopment. In some cases, ideas of the classic theories reviewed in Chapter 3 have been formalized, and in the process, their logical structure and their significance for policy have been clarified and refined. At the same time, the analysis has also led to entirely new insights into what makes development so hard to achieve (as witnessed in sub-Saharan Africa) but also possible to achieve (as witnessed in East Asia). Indeed, this is what makes the study of economic development so very important: It does not happen automatically; it requires systematic effort. But development is far from a hopeless cause; we know it can be done. Theory helps us think systematically about how to organize our efforts to help achieve development—a goal second to none in its importance to humanity.

In this chapter, we review a sample of some of the most influential of the new models of economic development. In some ways, these models show that development is harder to achieve, in that it faces more barriers than had previously been recognized. But greater understanding itself facilitates improvements in development strategy, and the new models have already influenced development policy and modes of international assistance.

The new research has broadened considerably the scope for modeling a market economy in a developing-country context. One of its major themes is incorporating problems of coordination among **agents**, such as among groups of firms, workers, or firms and workers together. Other key themes, often but not always in conjunction with the coordination problem, include the formal exploration of situations in which increasing returns to scale, a finer division of labor, the availability of new economic ideas or knowledge, learning by doing, and monopolistic competition or other forms of industrial organization other than perfect competition predominate and in which special, explicit requirements of long-run growth (rather than only static efficiency) are separately or jointly important. The new perspective also incorporates work in the "new institutional economics," such as that of Nobel laureate Douglass C. North, and work in the economics of imperfect information, building on earlier insights of theorists such as Nobel laureate George Akerlof. All of these approaches depart to some degree from conventional neoclassical economics, at least in its assumptions of perfect information, the relative insignificance of externalities, and the uniqueness and optimality of equilibria.[1]

We begin with a look at endogenous growth models, which offer alternative perspectives to those of the neoclassical growth theories reviewed at the end of Chapter 3. We then turn attention to modern models of development traps.

The New Growth Theory: Endogenous Growth

Motivation for the New Growth Theory

The poor performance of neoclassical theories in illuminating the sources of long-term economic growth has led to dissatisfaction with traditional growth theory (see Chapter 3). In fact, according to traditional theory, there is no intrinsic characteristic of economies that causes them to grow over extended periods of time. The literature is instead concerned with the dynamic process through which capital-labor ratios approach long-run equilibrium levels. In the absence of external "shocks" or technological change, which is not explained in the neoclassical model, all economies will converge to zero growth. Hence rising per capita GNI is considered a temporary phenomenon resulting from a change in technology or a short-term equilibrating process in which an economy approaches its long-run equilibrium.

Any increases in GNI that cannot be attributed to short-term adjustments in stocks of either labor or capital are ascribed to a third category, commonly referred to as the **Solow residual**. This residual is responsible for roughly 50% of historical growth in the industrialized nations.[2] In a rather ad hoc manner, neoclassical theory credits the bulk of economic growth to an exogenous or completely independent process of technological progress. Though intuitively plausible, this approach has at least two insurmountable drawbacks. First, using the neoclassical framework, it is impossible to analyze the determinants of technological advance because it is completely independent of the decisions of economic agents. And second, the theory fails to explain large differences in residuals across countries with similar technologies.

According to neoclassical theory, the low capital-labor ratios of developing countries promise exceptionally high rates of return on investment. The free-market reforms impressed on highly indebted countries by the World Bank and the International Monetary Fund should therefore have prompted higher investment, rising productivity, and improved standards of living. Yet even after the prescribed liberalization of trade and domestic markets, many LDCs experienced little or no growth and failed to attract new foreign investment or to halt the flight of domestic capital. The anomalous behavior of developing-world capital flows (from poor to rich nations) helped provide the impetus for the development of the concept of **endogenous growth theory** or, more simply, the **new growth theory**. The new growth theory represents a key component of the emerging development theory.

The new growth theory provides a theoretical framework for analyzing endogenous growth, persistent GNI growth that is determined by the system governing the production process rather than by forces outside that system. In contrast to traditional neoclassical theory, these models hold GNI growth to be a natural consequence of long-run equilibrium. The principal motivations of the new growth theory are to explain both growth rate differentials across countries and a greater proportion of the growth observed. More succinctly, endogenous growth theorists seek to explain the factors that determine the size of λ, the rate of growth of GDP that is left unexplained and exogenously determined in the Solow neoclassical growth equation (i.e., the Solow residual).

Models of endogenous growth bear some structural resemblance to their neoclassical counterparts, but they differ considerably in their underlying assumptions and the conclusions drawn. The most significant theoretical differences stem from discarding the neoclassical assumption of diminishing marginal returns to capital investments, permitting increasing returns to scale in aggregate production, and frequently focusing on the role of externalities in determining the rate of return on capital investments.[3] By assuming that public and private investments in human capital generate external economies and productivity improvements that offset the natural tendency for diminishing returns, endogenous growth theory seeks to explain the existence of increasing returns to scale and the divergent long-term growth patterns among countries. And whereas technology still plays an important role in these models, exogenous changes in technology are no longer necessary to explain long-run growth.

A useful way to contrast the new (endogenous) growth theory with traditional neoclassical theory is to recognize that many endogenous growth theories can be expressed by the simple equation $Y = AK$, as in the Harrod-Domar model. In this formulation, A is intended to represent any factor that affects technology, and K again includes both physical and human capital. But notice that there are no diminishing returns to capital in this formula; so the possibility exists that investments in physical and human capital can generate external economies and productivity improvements that exceed private gains by an amount sufficient to offset diminishing returns. The net result is sustained long-term growth—an outcome prohibited by traditional neoclassical growth theory. Thus even though the new growth theory reemphasizes the importance of savings and human capital investments for achieving rapid growth, it also leads to several implications for growth that are in direct conflict with traditional theory. First, there is no force leading to the equilibration of growth rates across closed economies; national growth rates remain constant and differ across countries depending on national savings rates and technology levels. Furthermore, there is no tendency for per capita income levels in capital-poor countries to catch up with those in rich countries with similar savings and population growth rates. A serious consequence of these facts is that a temporary or prolonged recession in one country can lead to a permanent increase in the income gap between itself and wealthier countries.

But perhaps the most interesting aspect of endogenous growth models is that they help explain anomalous international flows of capital that exacerbate wealth disparities between developed and developing countries. The potentially high rates of return on investment offered by developing economies with low capital-labor ratios are greatly eroded by lower levels of **complementary investments** in human capital (education), infrastructure, or research and development (R&D).[4] In turn, poor countries benefit less from the broader social gains associated with each of these alternative forms of capital expenditure.[5] Because individuals receive no personal gain from the positive externalities created by their own investments, the free market leads to the accumulation of less than the optimal level of complementary capital. (We examine these issues further in subsequent sections of this chapter.)

Where complementary investments produce social as well as private benefits, governments may improve the efficiency of resource allocation. They can do this by providing public goods (infrastructure) or encouraging private investment in knowledge-intensive industries where human capital can be accumulated and subsequent increasing returns to scale generated. Unlike the Solow model, new growth theory models explain technological change as an endogenous outcome of public and private investments in human capital and knowledge-intensive industries. Thus in contrast to the neoclassical counterrevolution theories examined in Chapter 3, models of endogenous growth suggest an active role for public policy in promoting economic development through direct and indirect investments in human capital formation and the encouragement of foreign private investment in knowledge-intensive industries such as computer software and telecommunications.

The Romer Model

To illustrate the endogenous growth approach, we examine the **Romer endogenous growth model** in detail because it addresses technological spillovers that may be present in the process of industrialization. Thus it is not only the seminal model of endogenous growth but also one of particular relevance for developing countries. We use a simplified version of Romer's model that keeps his main innovation—in modeling technology spillovers—without presenting unnecessary details of savings determination and other general equilibrium issues.

The model begins by assuming that growth processes derive from the firm or industry level. Each industry individually produces with constant returns to scale, so the model is consistent with perfect competition; and up to this point it matches assumptions of the Solow model. But Romer departs from Solow by assuming that the economywide capital stock, $\overline{K}$, positively affects output at the industry level, so that there may be increasing returns to scale at the economywide level.

It is valuable to think of each firm's capital stock as including its knowledge. The knowledge part of the firm's capital stock is essentially a **public good**, like A in the Solow model, that is spilling over instantly to the other firms in the economy. As a result, this model treats learning by doing as "learning by investing." You can think of Romer's model as spelling out—endogenizing—the reason why growth might depend on the rate of investment (as in the Harrod-Domar model). In this simplification, we abstract from the household sector, an important feature of the original model, in order to concentrate on issues concerning industrialization.[6] Formally,

$$Y_i = AK_i^\alpha L_i^{1-\alpha} \overline{K}^\beta \tag{4.1}$$

We assume symmetry across industries for simplicity, so each industry will use the same level of capital and labor. Then, we have the aggregate production function:

$$Y = AK^{\alpha+\beta}L^{1-\alpha} \tag{4.2}$$

To make endogenous growth stand out clearly, we assume that A is constant rather than rising over time; that is, we assume for now that there is no technological progress. With a little calculus,[7] it may be shown that the resulting growth rate for per capita income in the economy would be

$$g - n = \beta n / [1 - \alpha - \beta], \tag{4.3}$$

where g is the output growth rate and n is the population growth rate. Without spillovers, as in the Solow model with constant returns to scale, $\beta = 0$, and so per capita growth would be zero (without technological progress).[8]

Romer assumes, however, that taking the three factors together, including the capital externality, $\beta > 0$; thus $g - n > 0$, and Y/L is growing. Now we have endogenous growth, not driven exogenously by increases in productivity. If we also allowed for technological progress, so that λ in the Solow model is greater than zero, growth would be increased to that extent.[9]

Criticisms of the New Growth Theory

An important shortcoming of the new growth theory is that it remains dependent on a number of traditional neoclassical assumptions that are often inappropriate for LDC economies. For example, it assumes that there is but a single sector of production or that all sectors are symmetrical. This does not permit the crucial growth-generating reallocation of labor and capital among the sectors that are transformed during the process of structural change.[10] Moreover, economic growth in developing countries is frequently impeded by inefficiencies arising from poor infrastructure, inadequate institutional structures, and imperfect capital and goods markets. Because endogenous growth theory overlooks these very influential factors, its applicability for the study of economic development is limited, especially when country-to-country comparisons are involved. For example, existing theory fails to explain low rates of factory capacity utilization in low-income countries where capital is scarce. In fact, poor incentive structures may be as responsible for sluggish GNI growth as low rates of saving and human capital accumulation. Allocational inefficiencies are common in economies undergoing the transition from traditional to commercialized markets. However, their impact on short- and medium-term growth has been neglected due to the new theory's overemphasis on the determinants of long-term growth rates. Finally, empirical studies of the predictive value of endogenous growth theories have to date offered only limited support.[11]

Underdevelopment as a Coordination Failure

Many newer theories of economic development that became influential in the 1990s and the early years of the twenty-first century have emphasized **complementarities** between several conditions necessary for successful development. These theories often highlight the problem that several things must work well enough, at the same time, to get sustainable development under way. They also stress that in many important situations, investments must be undertaken by many agents in order for the results to be profitable for any individual agent. Generally, when complementarities are present, an action taken by one firm, worker, or organization increases the incentives for other agents to take similar actions.

Models of development that stress complementarities are related to some of the models used in the endogenous growth approach, in ways we will point out later in the chapter, but the **coordination failure** approach has evolved relatively independently and offers some significant and distinct insights.[12] Put simply, a coordination failure is a state of affairs in which agents' inability to coordinate their behavior (choices) leads to an outcome (equilibrium) that leaves all agents worse off than in an alternative situation that is also an equilibrium. This may occur even when all agents are fully informed about the preferred alternative equilibrium: They simply cannot get there because of difficulties of coordination, sometimes because people hold different expectations and sometimes because everyone is better off waiting for someone else to make the first move. This section spells out the meaning and implications of these perspectives in detail, through both simple models and examples.

When complementarities are present, an action taken by one firm, worker, organization, or government increases the incentives for other agents to take similar actions. In particular, these complementarities often involve investments whose return depends on other investments being made by other agents. In development economics, such network effects are common, and we consider some important examples later in this chapter, including the model of the **big push**, in which production decisions by modern-sector firms are mutually reinforcing, and the **O-ring model**, in which the value of upgrading skills or quality depends on similar upgrading by other agents. Curiously, such effects are also common in analyses of frontier technologies in developed countries, particularly information technologies, in which the value of using an operating system, word-processing, spreadsheet program, instant messaging, and other software or product standard depends on how many other users also adopt it. In both cases, the circular causation of positive feedback is common. Thus these models often seem most applicable to problems of the least developed and the most developed economies, though in different ways.[13]

An important example of a complementarity is the presence of firms using specialized skills and the availability of workers who have acquired those skills. Firms will not enter a market or locate in an area if workers do not possess the skills the firms need, but workers will not acquire the skills if there are no firms to employ them. This coordination problem can leave an economy stuck in a bad equilibrium—that is, at a low average income or growth rate or with a class of citizens trapped in extreme poverty. Even though all agents would be better off if workers acquired skills and firms invested, it may not be possible to get to this better equilibrium without the aid of government. As we will see, such coordination problems are also common in initial industrialization, as well as in upgrading skills and technologies, and may extend to issues as broad as changing behavior to modern "ways of doing things." Such problems are further compounded by other market failures, particularly those affecting capital markets.[14]

Another example typical of rural developing areas concerns the commercialization of agriculture. As Adam Smith already understood, specialization is one of the sources of high productivity. Indeed, specialization and a detailed division of labor are hallmarks of an advanced economy. But we can specialize only if we can trade for the other goods and services we need. Producers must somehow get their products to markets while convincing distant buyers of their quality. As Shahe Emran and Forhad Shilpi stress, in the development of agricultural markets, middlemen play a key role by effectively vouching for the quality of the products they sell; they can do this because they get to know the farmers from whom they buy as well as the product. It is difficult to be an expert in the quality of many products, so in order for a specialized agricultural market to emerge, there needs to be a sufficient number of concentrated producers with whom a middleman can work effectively. But without available middlemen to whom the farmers can sell, they will have little incentive to specialize in the first place and will prefer to continue producing their staple crop or a range of goods primarily for personal consumption or sale within the village. The result can be an **underdevelopment trap** in which a region remains stuck in subsistence agriculture.[15]

In many cases, the presence of complementarities creates a classic "chicken and egg" problem: Which comes first, the skills or the demand for skills? Often the answer is that the complementary investments must come at the same time, through coordination. This is especially true when, as is generally the case, there is a lag between making an investment and realizing the return on that investment.[16] In this case, even if, for some reason, all parties expect a change to a better equilibrium, they will still be inclined to wait until other parties have made their investments. Thus there can be an important role for government policy in coordinating joint investments, such as between the workers who want skills that employers can use and the employers who want equipment that workers can use.

Neither may be in a position (or find it in their self-interest) to take the first step; each may be better off waiting for the other parties to invest first.

As another example, a new or modernizing firm using new technologies may provide benefits to other firms that the adopting firm cannot capture; so each firm has an incentive to underinvest in the new technology, unless a sufficient number of others invest. Some of these benefits may include raising demand for key industrial products such as steel, helping pay for the fixed costs of an essential infrastructure such as railroads or container ports, or learning from others' experiences. We will take a closer look at this problem later in the chapter.

The new work expands the scope for potentially valuable government policy interventions, but it does not take their success for granted. Rather, government itself is increasingly analyzed in contemporary development models as one of the components of the development process that may contribute to the problem as well as to the solution; government policy is understood as partly determined by (endogenous to) the underdeveloped economy (see Chapter 11). For example, a dictator such as Mobutu Sese Seko, the former ruler of the Democratic Republic of Congo when it was known as Zaire, may prefer to keep his country in an underdevelopment trap, knowing full well that as the economy developed, he would lose power. But rather than concluding that government generally exacerbates underdevelopment rather than facilitates development (as in extreme versions of the neoclassical counterrevolution school), many development specialists look actively for cases in which government policy can still help, even when government is imperfect, by pushing the economy toward a self-sustaining, better equilibrium. Such **deep interventions** move an economy to a preferred equilibrium, or even to a higher permanent rate of growth, in which there is no incentive to go back to the behavior associated with the bad equilibrium. In these cases, government has no need to continue the interventions, because the better equilibrium will be maintained automatically. Government could then concentrate its efforts on other crucial problems in which it has an essential role (e.g., in addressing problems of public health). This onetime-fix character of some multiple-equilibrium problems makes them worthy of special focus because they can make government policy that much more powerful in addressing problems of economic development. But it also makes the policy choices more momentous, because a bad policy today could mire an economy in a bad equilibrium for years to come.

In much of economics, such complementarities are not present. For example, in competitive markets, when there is excess demand, there is counterpressure for prices to rise, restoring equilibrium. Whenever **congestion** may be present, these counterpressures are very strong: The more people fishing in one lake, the more fishers try to move to another lake that is less crowded; the more people using one road, the more commuters try to find an alternative route. But in the process of economic development, joint externalities are common: Underdevelopment begets underdevelopment, while processes of sustainable development, once under way, tend to stimulate further development.

Coordination problems are illustrated by the **where-to-meet dilemma**: Several friends know that they will all be in Buenos Aires on a certain day but have neglected to settle on a specific location within the city. Now they are out of communication and can arrive at a common meeting point only by chance or by very clever guessing. They want to meet and consider themselves better off if they can do so; there is no incentive to "cheat."[17] But the fact that all gain from coordination does not make the where-to-meet dilemma easy to solve. There are many famous places in Buenos Aires: the Plaza de Mayo, the Cathedral, the colorful Caminito neighborhood, the Cafe Tortoni, the Cemeterio de la Recoleta, even the casino. Only with luck would the friends end up making the same guesses and meeting in the same place. Arriving at, say, the center of Caminito and not finding the others there, one of our travelers may decide to try the Plaza de Mayo instead. But en route she may miss another of the other travelers, who at that moment may be on her way to check out the Cemeterio. So the friends never meet. Something analogous happens when farmers in a region do not know what to specialize in. There may be several perfectly good products from which to choose, but the critical problem is for all the farmers to choose *one* so that middlemen may profitably bring the village's produce to market.

The story may lose a bit of its power in the age of cell phones and e-mail. For example, as long as the friends know each other's e-mail addresses, they can go to cybercafes, access their accounts, contact each other, and come to an agreement about where to meet. Sometimes, what seems at first a complex problem of coordination is really a simpler one of communication. But anyone who has tried to establish a meeting time by e-mail among a large number of participants with no formal leader knows that this can be a slow and cumbersome process. Without a clear leader and with a large enough number of participants, no meeting place may be agreed to on such short notice before it is too late. And in real economic problems, the people who need to "meet"—perhaps to coordinate investments—do not even know the identity of the other key agents.[18] However, the e-mail example does point up possibilities for improved prospects for development with the advent of modern computing and telecommunications technology. Of course, peasant farmers usually have no access to cell phones or e-mail (but see the case study for Chapter 5).

Multiple Equilibria: A Diagrammatic Approach

The standard diagram to illustrate **multiple equilibria** with possible coordination failure is shown in Figure 4.1. This diagram, in one version or another, has become almost as ubiquitous in discussions of multiple equilibria as the famous Marshallian supply-and-demand scissors in discussions of single equilibrium analysis.[19]

The basic idea reflected in the S-shaped function of Figure 4.1 is that the benefits an agent receives from taking an action depend positively on how many other agents are expected to take the action or on the extent of those actions. For example, the price a farmer can hope to receive for his produce depends on the number of middlemen who are active in the region, which in turn depends on the number of other farmers who specialize in the same product.

To take as a simple metaphor a situation often faced by students, your decision about whether to sign up for an instant messaging (IM) system depends on how many of your friends are signing up (or that you expect will sign up). In this example, the x-axis would show the number of friends expected to sign up, and the

FIGURE 4.1   Multiple Equilibria

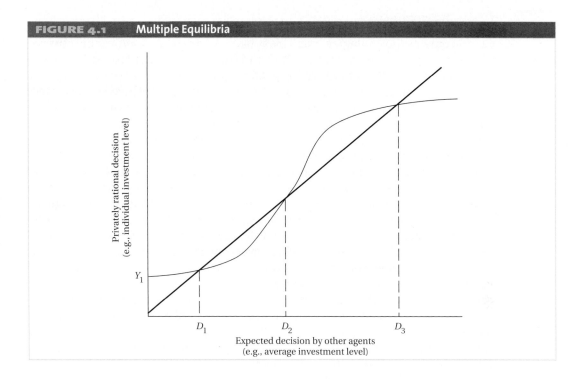

y-axis would show how many will sign up as a function of the number expected to sign up. If all of your friends would like to be on an IM format with you, but none of you thinks the others will be interested or sign up, then no one may get it started. Actually, in the case drawn in the diagram, some people might sign up even if they think none of their friends will, perhaps because they hope to meet some new friends online. This gives a positive intercept at Y_1. After that, the function has a positive slope because the more friends expected to sign up, the more there will be who want to do so.[20] In addition to deciding whether to sign up at all, choosing the format also requires coordination. In the case of your group of friends, coordination is really not that difficult. For example, one person can sign up for one of the systems (maybe ICQ, AOL, Yahoo, or MSN) and then suggest that everyone else do the same. As suggested by this simple example of leadership, coordination is really not much of a problem when the group to be coordinated is small, the parties know each other and share common interests, and they can communicate with each other at low cost. Unfortunately, as we will see, when the problem is as complex as achieving successful economic development, the solutions to coordination problems are far more difficult: By analogy, "signing up for a service" comes with a high and nonrefundable price, with a gamble your friends will choose the same service.[21]

So how do we find the equilibria in this type of problem? In the Marshallian supply-and-demand scissors diagram, equilibrium is found where the supply-and-demand curves cross. In the multiple equilibrium diagram, equilibrium is found where the "privately rational decision function" (the S-shaped curve in Figure 4.1) crosses the 45-degree line. This is because, in these cases, agents observe what they expected to observe. As drawn in this case, it is not an equilibrium to have no one sign up. Suppose you expected none of your friends to sign up, but some people did anyway (this is what it means to have a positive vertical intercept—in our analogy, that some people [Y_1] will find it in their self-interest to sign up even if none of their friends does so). But then, seeing that some people in fact have signed up, it would not be reasonable to continue to expect that no one would sign up! We would have to revise our expectations upward, matching our expectations to the number of participants we actually see. But if people now expect that larger number to sign up, even more would want to join. This process of adjustment of expectations would continue until the number observed to sign up would just equal the number expected to sign up: In that case, there is no reason for people to adjust their expectations any further. So the idea of an equilibrium in such cases is one of a situation in which everyone is doing what is best for them, given what they expect others to do, which in turn matches what others are actually doing. This happens when the function crosses the 45-degree line. At these points the values on the x-axis and y-axis are equal, implying in our case that the number expected to take an action is equal to the number that actually take that action.

In the diagram, the function cuts the 45-degree line three times. Any of these points could be an equilibrium: That is what we mean by the possibility of multiple equilibria. Of the three, D_1 and D_3 are "stable" equilibria. They are stable because if expectations were slightly changed to a little above or below these levels, people would adjust their behavior—sign up or get off the system, in the case of instant messaging—in a way to bring us back to the original equilibrium levels. Note that in each of these two stable equilibria, the S-shaped function cuts the 45-degree line from above—a hallmark of a stable equilibrium.

At the middle equilibrium at D_2, the function cuts the 45-degree line from below, and so it is unstable. This is because, in our example, if a few less were expected to join, the equilibrium would be D_1, and if a few more, the equilibrium would move to D_3. D_2 could therefore be an equilibrium only by chance. Thus in practice we think of an unstable equilibrium such as D_2 as a way of dividing ranges of expectations over which a higher or lower stable equilibrium will hold sway.

Typically, the S-shaped "privately rational decision function" first increases at an increasing rate and then at a decreasing rate, as in the diagram. This shape reflects what is thought to be the typical nature of complementarities. In general, some agents may take the complementary action (such as joining or investing) even if others in the economy do not, particularly when interactions are expected to be with foreigners, such as through exporting or messaging with people in other countries. If only a few agents take the action, each agent may be isolated from the others, so spillovers may be minimal. Thus the curve does not rise quickly at first as more agents take the action. But after enough join or invest, there may be a snowball effect, in which most agents begin to provide spillover benefits to neighboring agents, and the curve increases at a much faster rate. Finally, after most potential investors have been positively affected and the most important gains have been realized, the rate of increase starts to slow down.

In many cases, the shape of the function in Figure 4.1 could be different, however. For example, a very "wobbly" curve could cut the 45-degree line several times. In the case of telephone service, getting on e-mail or instant messaging, or buying a fax machine, where the value of taking the action steadily increases with the number of others on the system, the function may only increase at an increasing rate (like a quadratic or exponential function). Depending on the slope of the function and whether it cuts the 45-degree line, there could be a single equilibrium or multiple equilibria, including cases in which either no one ever adopts a new technology or (virtually) everyone does. In general, the value (utility) of the various equilibria (two in this case) is not the same. For example, it is very possible that everyone is better off in the equilibrium in which more people use the network; in this case, we say the equilibria are Pareto-ranked, with the higher rank to the equilibrium giving higher utility to everyone.

The classic example of this problem in economic development concerns coordinating investment decisions when the value (rate of return) of one investment depends on the presence or extent of other investments. All are better off with more investors or higher rates of investment, but the market may not get us there without the influence of certain types of government policy (but note that we may also not arrive at the preferred solutions if we have the wrong kinds of government policy). The difficulties of investment coordination give rise to various government-led strategies for industrialization that we consider both in this chapter and later in the text (see especially Chapters 7 and 13).

The investment coordination perspective helps clarify the nature and extent of problems posed when technology spillovers are present, such as seen in the Romer model described in the section on endogenous growth. Think now of the x-axis in Figure 4.1 as representing the average rate of investment expected of other key firms or in the economy as a whole and the y-axis as the profitable rate of investment for a particular firm, given what the other firms are expected to invest on average. In this case, the points where the S-shaped function crosses the 45-degree line depict equilibrium investment rates.[22] Then, given what we have learned in examining endogenous growth theory about the possible relation between investment and growth, we can see that an economy can get stuck in a low growth rate largely because the economy is expected to have a low investment rate. Strategies for coordinating a change from a less productive to a more productive set of mutually reinforcing expectations can vary widely, as the example in Box 4.1 illustrates. However, changing expectations may not be sufficient if it is more profitable for a firm to wait for others to invest rather than to be a "pioneer" investor. In that case, government policy is generally needed in addition to a change of expectations. This explains why attention to the potential presence of multiple equilibria is so important. Market forces can generally bring us to one of the equilibria, but they are not sufficient to ensure that the best equilibrium will be achieved, and they offer no mechanism to become unstuck from a bad equilibrium and move toward a better one.

BOX 4.1 Synchronize Your Expectations: Resetting "Latin American Time"

Kaushik Basu and Jorgen Weibull argue that while the importance of culture is undeniable, the innateness of culture is not. They present a model that shows that punctuality may be "simply an equilibrium response of individuals to what they expect others to do" and that the same society could benefit from a "punctual equilibrium" or get caught in a lateness equilibrium.

Estimates suggested that Ecuador lost between 4% and 10% of its GDP due to chronic lateness. As one commentator put it, "Tardiness feeds on itself, creating a vicious cycle of *mañana, mañana.*" Lately, Ecuador has tried to make up for lost time. Inspired by some in the younger generation who were fed up with "Latin American time," government and business have joined in a private-sector-funded drive to get people to show up at their scheduled appointment times. The country has launched a national "Campaña Contra la Impuntualidad," or campaign against lateness, coordinated by Participacíon Ciudadana (Citizen Participatíon). The result is a test of the idea that a society can consciously switch from a bad to a good equilibrium through a change in expectations.

The campaign was a timely one. A newspaper is publishing a list each day of officials who are late for public events. A popular poster for the campaign against lateness describes the disease and says, "Treatment: Inject yourself each morning with a dose of responsibility, respect and discipline. Recommendation: Plan, organize activities and repair your watches." Hundreds of public and private institutions have signed up to a promise to be punctual. A popular notice for meeting rooms in the style of hotel "Do Not Disturb" signs has been making the rounds. On one side it says "Come in: You're on time." When the meeting begins at its scheduled time, it is turned around to the other side, which reads, "Do not enter: The meeting began on time."

If the campaign against lateness proves successful, it will be more than about time. If a social movement to change expectations about punctuality can be made to work, something similar might be tried around the world for fixing even more pernicious problems, such as public corruption.

Sources: Kaushik Basu and Jorgen Weibull, "Punctuality: A cultural trait as equilibrium," in *Economics for an Imperfect World: Essays in Honor of Joseph Stiglitz,* ed. Richard Arnott et al. (Cambridge, Mass.: MIT Press, 2003); Scott Wilson, "In Ecuador, a timeout for tardiness drive promotes punctuality," *Washington Post Foreign Service,* November 4, 2003, p. A22; "The price of lateness," *Economist,* November 22, 2003, p.67; *"Punctuality Pays,"* New Yorker, April 5, 2004, p. 31.

We will also encounter a similar multiple equilibrium situation in the analysis of the Malthus population trap in Chapter 6. In this population trap, fertility decisions need in effect to be coordinated across families—all are better off if the average fertility rate declines, but any one family may be worse off by being the only one to have fewer children. We also see coordination failures in processes of urbanization and other key elements of economic development.

In general, when jointly profitable investments may not be made without coordination, multiple equilibria may exist, in which the same individuals with access to the same resources and technologies could find themselves in either a good or a bad situation. In the view of many development economists, it is very plausible that many of the least developed countries, including many in sub-Saharan Africa, are essentially caught in such circumstances. Of course, other problems are also present. For example, political pressures from potential losers in the modernization process can also prevent shifts to better equilibria. In addition, modern technology may not yet be available in the country. The technology transfer problem is another important concern in economic development. In fact, another problem illustrated by the graph in Figure 4.1 could be that the amount of effort each firm in a developing region expends to increase the rate of technology transfer depends on the effort undertaken by other firms; bringing in modern technology from abroad often has spillover effects for other firms (the Romer growth model could apply here). But the presence of multiple equilibria shows that making better technology available is a necessary but not a sufficient condition to achieve development goals.

Starting Economic Development: The Big Push

Whether an economy has already been growing sustainably for some time or has been stagnant seems to make a very big difference for subsequent development. If growth can be sustained for a substantial time, say, a generation or more, it is much rarer for economic development to later get off track for long (though, of course, there will be setbacks over the business cycle as the economy is affected by temporary shocks). Certainly, we have had too many disappointing experiences to assume, with Rostow, that once economic development is under way, it can in effect never be stopped. As noted in the case study in Chapter 3, a century ago, Argentina was regarded as a future powerhouse of the world economy, yet it later experienced relative stagnation for more than half a century. A look at the record, however, allows us to agree with Rostow at least in that it is very difficult to get modern economic growth under way in the first place and much easier to maintain it once a track record has been established.

Why should it be so difficult to start modern growth? Many models of development that were influential in earlier years, such as the Lewis model examined in Chapter 3, effectively assume perfectly competitive conditions in the industrial sector. Under perfect competition, it is not clear why starting development would be so difficult, provided at least that the needed human capital is developed, the technology transfer problem is adequately addressed, and government provides other essential services. But development seems hard to initiate even when better technologies are available—they often go unused. Apparently, people do not have the incentives to put the new technology to work. Beyond this, perfect competition does not hold under conditions of increasing returns-to-scale. And yet looking at the industrial revolution, it is clear that taking advantage of returns to scale has been key. Many development economists have concluded that several market failures work to make economic development difficult to initiate, notably **pecuniary externalities**, which are spillover effects on costs or revenues.

Perhaps the most famous coordination failures model in the development literature is that of the "big push," pioneered by Paul Rosenstein-Rodan, who first raised some of the basic coordination issues. He pointed out several problems associated with initiating industrialization in a subsistence economy, of the type introduced in Chapter 1. The problem is easiest to perceive if we start with the simplifying assumption that the economy is not able to export. In this case, the question becomes, who will buy the goods produced by the first firm to industrialize? Starting from a subsistence economy, no workers have the money to buy the new goods. The first factory can sell some of its goods to its own workers, but no one spends all of their income on a single good. Each time an entrepreneur opens a factory, the workers spend some of their wages on products of the other sectors of the economy. So the profitability of one factory depends on whether another one opens, which in turn depends on its own potential profitability, and that in turn depends on the profitability of still other factories. Such circular causation should now be a familiar pattern of a coordination failure problem. Moreover, the first factory has to train its workers, who are accustomed to a subsistence way of life. The cost of training puts a limit on how high a wage the factory can pay and still remain profitable. But once the first firm trains its workers, other entrepreneurs, not having to recoup training costs, can offer a slightly higher wage to attract them to their own new factories. However, the first entrepreneur, anticipating this likelihood, does not pay for training in the first place. No one is trained, and industrialization never gets under way.

The big push is a model of how the presence of market failures can lead to a need for a concerted economywide and probably public-policy-led effort to get the long process of economic development under way or to accelerate it. Put differently, coordination failure problems work against successful industrialization, a counterweight to the push for development. A big push may not always be needed, but it is helpful to find ways to characterize cases in which it will be.

Rosenstein-Rodan's arguments became a major part of the way development economists thought about development problems in the 1950s and 1960s, and they have continued to be taught in development courses. But while some of the basic intuition has thus been around for decades, the approach received a huge boost following the 1989 publication of a technical paper by Kevin Murphy, Andrei Shleifer, and Robert Vishny, which for the first time demonstrated the formal logic of this approach more clearly.[23] Its recent appeal is also due in part to its perceived value in explaining the success of the East Asian miracle economies, notably that of South Korea. One value of using a formal model is to get a clearer sense of when the need for coordination is more likely to present a serious problem. The approach of these authors was in turn simplified and popularized by Paul Krugman in his 1995 monograph, *Development, Geography, and Economic Theory* and became the classic model of the new development theories of coordination failure of the 1990s.[24]

The Big Push: A Graphical Model

Assumptions In any model (indeed, in any careful thinking), we need to make some assumptions, sometimes seemingly large assumptions, to make any progress in our understanding. The analysis of the big push is no exception to this rule. The assumptions we use for the big push analysis here can be relaxed somewhat, though at the expense of requiring more mathematical technique, but it should be noted that we cannot relax our assumptions as much as we are accustomed to doing in simpler microeconomic problems, such as those that assume perfect competition. Here we cannot meaningfully assume perfect competition in the modern sector, where increasing returns to scale and hence natural monopoly, or at least monopolistic competition, prevail. To paraphrase Paul Krugman, if we think development has something significant to do with increasing returns to scale, then we will have to sacrifice some generality to address it. We will make six types of assumptions.

1. *Factors.* We assume that there is only one factor of production—labor. It has fixed total supply, L.

2. *Factor payments.* The labor market has two sectors. We assume that workers in the traditional sector receive a wage of "1" (or normalized to 1, treating the wage as the numeraire; that is, if the wage is 19 pesos per day, we simply call this amount of money "1" to facilitate analysis using the geometry in Figure 4.2). Workers in the modern sector receive a wage $w > 1$. As a stylized fact, this wage differential is found in every developing country, even if it needs some explanation (see Chapter 7). The underlying reason for this differential *may be* a compensation for disutility of modern factory types of work. If so, in equilibrium workers would receive no net utility benefits from switching sectors during industrialization; but if economic profits are generated, this will represent a **Pareto improvement** (in this case because investors are better off and no one is worse off), and average income would rise (there can also be income redistribution so that everyone may be made better off, not just no one worse off). Moreover, if there is surplus labor in the economy or if modern wages are higher than opportunity costs of labor for some other reason,[25] the social benefits of industrialization are all the greater.[26] Finally, note that we are examining one example of a model in which a driving force for an underdevelopment trap is the relatively high wages that have to be paid in the modern sector. We do this because it is an approach that is easy to characterize graphically and that has received a lot of attention. As will be described later, however, high modern wages is only one circumstance in which a coordination problem may

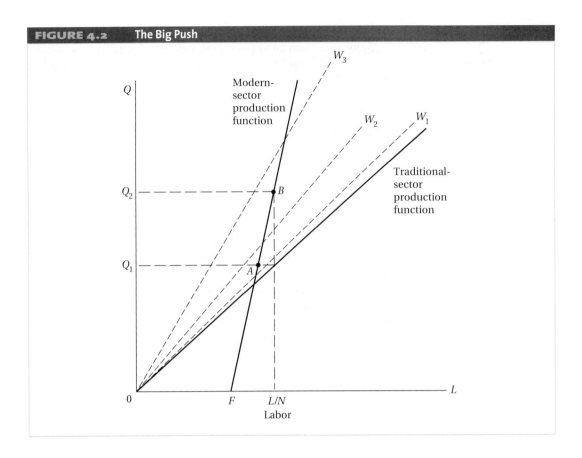

FIGURE 4.2   The Big Push

exist. In fact, we will see that there may be coordination failure problems even if modern-sector wages are no higher than those in the traditional sector.

3. *Technology.* We assume that there are N types of products, where N is a large number.[27] In each market in the traditional sector, one worker produces one unit of output (this is a less stringent assumption than it appears because again we have a certain freedom in choosing our unit of measurement; if a worker produces three pairs of shoes per day, we call this quantity one unit). This is a very simple example of constant-returns-to-scale production. In the modern sectors, there are increasing returns to scale. We want to introduce increasing returns in a very simple way. Assume that no product can be produced unless a minimum of, say, F workers are employed. This is a fixed cost. Because we are keeping things simple to facilitate analysis of the core issues, we have not put capital explicitly in the model; thus the only way to introduce a fixed cost is to require a minimum number of workers. After that, there is a linear production function, in which workers are more productive than those in the traditional sector. Thus labor requirements in any sector take the form $L = F + cQ$, where

$c < 1$ is the marginal labor required for an extra unit of output. The trade-off is that modern workers are more productive, but only if a significant cost is paid up front. As this fixed cost is amortized over more units of output, average cost declines, which is the effect of increasing returns to scale. We assume symmetry: The same production function holds for each sector (note that each sector produces one type of good).

4. *Domestic demand.* We assume that each good receives a constant and equal share of consumption out of national income. There is only one period in the model and no assets; thus there is no saving in the conventional sense. As a result, if national income is Y, then consumers spend an equal amount, Y/N, on each good.[28]

5. *International supply and demand.* We assume that the economy is closed. This makes the model easy to develop. The most important conclusions will remain when trade is allowed, provided that there are advantages to having a domestic market. These advantages likely include initial economies of scale and learning to achieve sufficient quality, favorable product characteristics, and better customer support before having to produce for distant and unknown consumers. These are very realistic considerations: Evidence suggests that export-led economies such as South Korea have benefited enormously from the presence of a substantial domestic market to which early sales are directed.[29] Moreover, export-led economies have benefited from active industrial policy aimed at overcoming coordination failures (see Chapter 13). The points will also hold if there are necessary inputs that are not tradable, such as certain types of services. Alternative models focusing on infrastructure investments can also imply the need for a big push even with a fully open world economy.[30]

6. *Market structure.* We assume perfect competition in the traditional (cottage industry) sector. This means that there is free entry and no economic profits. Therefore, the price of each good will be 1—that is, the marginal cost of labor (which is the only input). We assume that, at most, one modern-sector firm can enter each market. This limitation is a consequence of increasing returns to scale. Given the assumptions about preferences, the monopolist faces unit-elastic demand, so if this monopolist *could* raise its price above 1, it would be profitable to do so.[31] However, if price is raised above 1, competition from the traditional-sector producers will cause the modern-sector firm to lose all of its business. Therefore, the monopolist will also charge a price of 1 if it decides to enter the market.[32] Because the monopolist charges the same price, it will monopolize this particular market if it enters but will also produce the same quantity that was produced by the traditional producers. Because this firm is the only one using modern techniques and in all other sectors workers receive a wage of 1, national income will be essentially the same, so more units of output cannot be sold.[33] We also assume that at the point the monopolist would choose to produce, it is able to produce at least as much output as the traditional producers for that same level of labor; otherwise, it would make no sense to switch out of the traditional techniques.

Conditions for Multiple Equilibria With these six assumptions, we can characterize cases that will require a big push. To begin, suppose that we have a traditional economy with no modern production in any market. A potential producer with modern technology (i.e., a technology like the one described previously, with fixed costs and increasing returns) considers whether it is profitable to enter the market. Given the size of the fixed cost, the answer depends on two considerations: (1) how much more efficient the modern sector is than the traditional sector and (2) how much higher wages are in the modern sector than in the traditional sector.

In Figure 4.2, production functions are represented for the two types of firms for any industry.[34] The traditional producers use a linear technique with slope 1, with each worker producing one unit of output. The modern firm requires F workers before it can produce anything, but after that it has a linear technique with slope $1/c > 1$. Price is 1, so revenues PQ can be read off the Q axis. For the traditional firm, the wage bill line lies coincident with the production line (both start at the origin and have a slope of 1). For the modern firm, the wage bill line has slope $w > 1$. At point A, we see the output that the modern firm will produce if it enters, provided there are traditional firms operating in the rest of the economy. Whether the modern firm enters depends, of course, on whether it is profitable to do so.

Using Figure 4.2, first consider a wage bill line like w_1 passing below point A. With this relatively low modern wage, revenues exceed costs, and the modern firm will pay the fixed cost F and enter the market. In general, this outcome is more likely if the firm has lower fixed costs or lower marginal labor requirements as well as if it pays a lower wage. By assumption, all the sectors are symmetrical, so if a modern firm finds it profitable to enter in one sector, the same incentives will be present in all sectors, and the whole economy will industrialize through market forces alone; demand is now high enough that we end up at point B in each sector. This shows that a coordination failure need not always happen: It depends on the technology and prices (including wages) prevailing in the economy.

If a wage bill line like w_2 holds, passing between points A and B, the firm would not enter if it were the only modern firm to do so in the economy because it would incur losses. But if modern firms enter in each of the markets, then wages are increased to the modern wage in all markets, and income expands. We may assume that price remains 1 after industrialization. To motivate this, note that the traditional technique still exists and would be profitable with a price higher than 1. So to prevent traditional firms from entering, modern firms cannot raise prices above 1.[35] Firms in each sector can now sell all of their expanded output (at point B), produced by using all of their available labor allocation (L/N), because they have sufficient demand from workers and entrepreneurs in the other industrializing sectors. As can be seen in Figure 4.2, with prevailing wage w_2, point B is profitable after industrialization because it lies above the w_2 line. Workers are also at least as well off as when they worked in the traditional sector because they can afford to purchase an additional quantity of goods in proportion to their increased wage,[36] and they have changed sectors voluntarily. All of the output is purchased because all of national income is spent on output; national income is equal to wages plus profits, the value of which is output per sector times the number of sectors N.[37]

Thus with a prevailing wage like w_2, there are two equilibria: one in which producers with modern techniques enter in all markets, and profits, wages, and output are higher than before; and one in which no modern producer enters, and wages and output remain lower. The equilibrium with higher output is unambiguously better, but in general the market will not get there by itself.

A final possibility is found in a wage bill line like w_3, passing above point B. In this case, even if a modern producer entered in all sectors, all of these firms would still lose money, so again the traditional technique would continue to be used. In general, whenever the wage bill line passes below point A, the market will lead the economy to modernize, and whenever it passes above A, it will not. The steeper (i.e., the more efficient) the modern-sector production technique or the lower the fixed costs, the more likely it is that the wage bill will pass below the corresponding point A. If the line passes above B, it makes no sense to industrialize. But if the wage line passes between points A and B, it is efficient to industrialize, but the market will not achieve this on its own. Be sure to note that these are three different wages that might exist depending on conditions in a particular economy at one point in time, not three wages that occur successively.

Again, the problematic cases occur when the wage bill line passes between A and B, thus creating two equilibria: one in which there is industrialization and the society is better off (point B) and one without industrialization (point A). However, the market will not get us from A to B because of a coordination failure.[38] In this case, there is a role for policy in starting economic development. There is no easy test to determine where a traditional economy, such as Mozambique, is located on this continuum. But at least we can begin to understand why development often has not gotten under way, even when technology was available.

Note that in general, it is not necessary for all sectors to industrialize to get a sufficient push for some to do so. It is only necessary that a sufficient number industrialize in order to generate enough national income (through the higher industrial wage and positive profits from the industrialized sectors) to make industrialization minimally profitable. Also note that each firm's failure to take into account the impact of its investments on demand for other firms' goods represents a very small distortion by itself. But when added up across all of the sectors, the resulting distortion, namely the failure to industrialize at all, is very large indeed.

We could also have cases of semi-industrialization, in which benefits or costs accrue in different amounts to different sectors, or in which there are different types of spillovers, from firm to firm. For example, this is plausible when the level of required fixed costs declines the more sectors industrialize, because there are more local examples from which to learn.[39] With this alternative type of externality, no wage premium is necessary for multiple equilibria to be present. In this case, if there are clusters of two or more firms that have large effects on each other's fixed costs F but not on firms outside of the cluster, the result could be an equilibrium in which only the industries in this cluster change to modern techniques. Thus in this circumstance, we could have three or more equilibria; we could also have enclave economies, in which a modern sector exists side by side with traditional cottage industries in other sectors.[40]

Notice that this model has not assumed the existence of any type of **technological externalities,** in which the presence of one advanced firm can, through "learning by watching" other firms' production methods or some similar effect, generate spillovers to other firms that can raise their productivity as well as lower their costs. This is another type of market failure that can also lead to inefficiently low investment; we considered one such possibility when we examined the Romer endogenous growth model earlier in the chapter.

Other Cases in Which a Big Push May Be Necessary The need for a big push can result from four conditions beyond those described previously.

1. *Intertemporal effects.* Even if the industrial wage rate is 1 (i.e., the same as the traditional-sector wage), multiple equilibria can occur if investment must be undertaken in the current period to get a more efficient production process in the next period.[41] Investment in the first period depresses aggregate demand in the first period but increases it in the second (or later) period. But investment will be undertaken only if it is profitable, that is, if demand is expected to be high enough in the second period, and this may require that many sectors invest simultaneously. Once again, however, the market does not ensure that industrialization will occur, even when it is (Pareto-) preferred, because of pecuniary externalities. Again the source of the multiple equilibria is that one firm's profits do not capture its external contribution to overall demand for modern-sector products because it also raises wage income in the future periods when other entering modern firms will be seeking to sell their own products. When there is a case for a big push, industrialization makes the society better off (is Pareto-preferred) because first-period income is decreased only by the fixed cost, but second-period income is sufficiently increased by both the wage and profits in other sectors to more than offset this.[42] Note that a part of profits can, in principle, also be subject to income redistribution so that everyone may be made better off rather than just some people made better off and no one made worse off.

2. *Urbanization effects.* If some of the traditional cottage industry is rural and the increasing-returns-to-scale manufacturing is urban, urban dwellers' demand may be more concentrated in manufactured goods (e.g., foods must be processed to prevent spoilage due to the time needed for transportation and distribution). If this is the case, one needs a big push to urbanization to achieve industrialization.[43]

3. *Infrastructure effects.* By using infrastructure such as a railroad or a port, an investing modern firm helps defray the large fixed costs of that infrastructure. The existence of the infrastructure helps investing firms lower their own costs. But investing firms thereby contribute indirectly to lowering the costs of other firms (by lowering the average cost of infrastructure use). Infrastructure, such as roads, railroads, and ports, is not tradable; by definition it is located in a particular region. And openness to foreign investment cannot always solve the problem because investors do not know whether firms will develop to make use of the infrastructure.[44] The critical point is that when one sector industrializes, it increases the size of the market for the use of infrastructure services that

would be used by other sectors and so makes the provision of these services more profitable. But it is also possible that efficient industrialization may not take place, even if the infrastructure is built, if other coordination problems are present.

4. *Training effects.* There is underinvestment in training facilities because entrepreneurs know that the workers they train may be enticed away with higher wages offered by rival firms that do not have to pay these training costs. There is also too little demand by workers for training because they do not know in what skills to acquire. (In addition to not knowing whether firms will make investments requiring these skills, people are not born with perfect information about their comparative advantage; basic education helps workers discover it.) This is part of the economic case for mandatory public education. Note that in this case, openness to trade cannot resolve the coordination failure unless there is free mobility of labor across borders, which has yet to develop even within the European Union, where there are no formal barriers to such mobility, and is far from emerging for any developing country. In any case, relying on expatriate skilled workers is hardly an adequate solution to a country's own underdevelopment. Actually, infrastructure and trained workers are subsets of a general case of jointly used intermediate goods. Another example is joint research facilities for small firms in an "industrial district" (see Chapter 7).

Why the Problem Cannot Be Solved by a Super-Entrepreneur

Some readers may wonder, why can't one agent solve the coordination failure problems by capturing all the rent? In other words, why not have a super-entrepreneur who enters into all of the markets that need to be coordinated and receives the profits from all of them? For some types of coordination failures, this solution is ruled out in advance. For example, regarding education and skill development, there is a legal constraint on bonded labor. But in terms of our industrialization problem, why can't one agent become a super-entrepreneur in each of the N markets simultaneously? There are at least four significant theoretical answers and one decisive empirical answer.

First, there may be capital market failures. How could one agent assemble all the capital needed to play the super-entrepreneur role? Even if this were logistically imaginable, how would lenders have confidence in their investments? In particular, how could a penalty for default be imposed?

Second, there may be costs of monitoring managers and other agents and designing and implementing schemes to ensure compliance or provide incentives to follow the wishes of the employer; these are often referred to as **agency costs**. Monitoring is too expensive once the scale of a firm gets too large. Even if the plan is to sell off the industries, these industries must be developed simultaneously. The super-entrepreneur is likely to know more about the firms than will the potential buyers. In other words, if the firm is so profitable, why would its owners be selling? Thus potential purchasers of the industries face a problem of **asymmetric information**, often known as a "lemons problem."[45]

Third, there may be communication failures. Suppose someone says to you, "I am coordinating investments, so work with me." Should you do so? How do you know this person will eventually be the coordinator? There is a potentially huge profit to be made by assuming the super-entrepreneur role, so many agents might wish to play it. If many try to claim the role, with which one should you coordinate? Even if each agent personally encounters only one pretender to the super-entrepreneur role, that pretender may still not be the right one (i.e., the coordinator with whom you can make money).

Fourth, there are limits to knowledge. Even if we stipulate that the economy as a whole has access to modern technology ideas, this does not mean that one individual can gain sufficient knowledge to industrialize (or even gain enough knowledge about whom to hire to industrialize).

Finally, there is the empirical reason that no private agent has been observed playing the role of super-entrepreneur. Whether because of problems of monitoring, knowledge, capital markets, or other diseconomies of scope, "solving" problems with ever-larger firms clearly provides no answer. For example, it is rare enough to find a firm producing steel and even a significant fraction of the products using steel, let alone one firm owning all the industries backwardly linked from steel or forwardly linked from steel-using industries into industries further down the production chain. Nor can the problem be solved by direct government production, as the extreme case of the former Soviet Union demonstrates. Rather, public coordination of actions of private investors is generally needed to solve the problem, a common interpretation of the role of industrial policy in East Asia.

Thus we have seen that under some conditions, pecuniary externalities associated with the development process can lead to multiple equilibria, which may create a case for a big push policy. Our main example (the moderate wage premium case) and each of the other examples have as a common feature a process by which an investing (industrializing) firm captures only part of the contribution of its investment to the profits of other investing firms. In these examples, firms adopting increasing-returns-to-scale technologies are having one or more of the following effects: raising total demand, shifting demand toward manufactured goods, redistributing demand toward the (later) periods in which other industrializing firms sell, or helping defray the fixed costs of an essential infrastructure. Each of these has external beneficial effects on other industrializing firms.

Further Problems of Multiple Equilibria

Inefficient Advantages of Incumbency The presence of increasing returns in modern industries can also create another kind of bad equilibrium. Once a modern firm has entered, it has an advantage over any rivals because its large output gives it low average costs. So if an even better modern technology becomes available to a potential rival, it may not be easy for the new technology to supplant the old. Even though the new technique has a lower per-unit cost for any given level of output, the firm with the old technique has an advantage because its large output lets it produce at a lower per-unit cost than that of the new technique, which starts out with a small customer base and a large fixed cost. As a result, firms may need access to significant amounts of capital to cover losses while they build their customer base. If capital markets do not work well, as they often do not in developing countries (see Chapter 16), the economy may be stuck with backward, less cost-effective industries.[46]

Behavior and Norms Movement to a better equilibrium is especially difficult when it involves many individuals changing their behavior from one of rent seeking or corruption to honesty and the value of building a reputation to reap the gains from cooperation (e.g., with business partners). Your choice of partner may determine much. If you naively cooperate with an opportunistic, predator type, you may be worse off than by going it alone. Only by cooperating with other good willed cooperators may you reach the best outcome. Moreover, past experience may lead people to expect opportunistic behavior at least among certain groups of potential business partners, which in turn raises the incentives for the potential partners to actually act that way. If there is nothing to be gained and something to be lost by being honest, clearly the incentives lie in being dishonest. On the other hand, in some settings, individuals take it on themselves to enforce norms rather than leaving this task to government. If many people work to enforce a norm such as honesty, each individual's enforcement burden is relatively low. You can have equilibria where most people resist corruption, and so corruption is rare; and you can have equilibria where few resist corruption, and corruption is common.

We cannot rely on good organizations to prevail in competition if the rules of the game tend to reward the bad organizations. Rather, the critical importance of policies for developing or reforming institutions is highlighted, such as reform of the framework of property rights, antitrust, clean government rules, and other laws, regulations, and industry association norms that create the rules of the game for economic life. Once the new behavior assumes the status of a norm, it is much easier to maintain. Some neoclassical theorists have at times implied that good institutions would be developed through the market mechanism. Bad institutions would be outcompeted by good institutions. But reform of institutions aiding and abetting coordination failure—for example, by permitting or encouraging corruption—is itself subject to coordination failure.

Once cooperative relationships (e.g., in business) become a norm, more people may adopt cooperative behavior. But norms of all kinds are subject to inertia. Although norms might have been adaptive when they originated, they are hard to change, even when they become dysfunctional. An example is a value such as that to be a good citizen (or a good Hindu, Muslim, Christian, animist, etc.), one must have a large number of children. This value may have been adaptive at a premodern stage, but today it inhibits development. Another example may be to distrust anyone who is not a member of your family. This may be helpful in a tribal period, and caution is always advisable, but this extreme injunction hardly encourages the formation of successful business partnerships in a modern economy.

Linkages There are several ways to undertake a big push, encouraging the simultaneous expansion of the modern sector in many industries. One strategy for solving coordination problems is to focus government policy on encouraging the development of sectors with key backward or forward **linkages.** This could mean subsidies or quid pro quos for domestic industries to enter these key sectors, as was done in South Korea; it could mean incentives for multinational firms to enter in key sectors and provide advanced training, a policy followed in Singapore; or it could mean establishing a few key public enterprises to act as pioneers in an industry (that could later be sold), as was done in South Korea and Taiwan.[47] The theory of linkages stresses that when certain industries are developed first, their interconnections or linkages with other sectors will induce or at least facilitate the development of new industries. Backward linkages raise demand for an activity, while forward linkages lower the costs of using an industry's output; both may involve interactions between the size of the market and increasing returns to scale and hence pecuniary externalities. In other words, linkages are especially significant for industrialization strategy when one or more of the sectors involved have increasing returns to scale, of which a larger market may take advantage. For example, when the manufacture of power looms expands, enabling a reduction in the price of power looms, there are forward linkage effects due to increased output of woven cloth made by the power looms. When increased demand for chemicals used in textile manufacture causes expansion of the chemical industry that enables it to produce at a larger scale and hence lower cost, a backward linkage can occur. Both examples illustrate a pecuniary externality effect (a lowering of cost) when there are increasing returns in the linked industry.

The linkage approach targets investment in a key linkage as a start to overcoming a coordination failure and generating positive feedback. Such a policy would select industries with a larger number of links to other industries and greater strength of those links. In choosing among industries with several strong links (and passing a cost-benefit test), one policy would generally select sectors that have a smaller likelihood of private-sector investment, because that is where the most intransigent bottlenecks are most likely to be found: If an investment is profitable, it is more likely that an entrepreneur will come along to fill that niche.[48] This observation provides a reason to interpret with some caution studies that show government enterprises to be less efficient than private ones. If government systematically enters vital but less profitable industries because of their beneficial effects on development, it is unreasonable to hold these enterprises to the same profit standards as those of the private sector. This is certainly not to say that state-owned enterprises are generally as efficient as privately owned ones; in fact, there is much evidence to the contrary.[49] We can say, however, that a blanket statement, such as has often been made in publications from agencies such as the World Bank, that government should never be in the business of production, even temporarily or in any sector, is sometimes unreasonable in the light of linkages and other strategic complementarities that a developing economy needs to address.

Inequality, Multiple Equilibria, and Growth Other important work being done on growth and multiple equilibria addresses the impact of inequality on growth. The traditional view has been that some inequality may enhance growth because the savings of the rich are higher than those of the poor. If at least some savings to be mobilized for investment purposes must come from within a country, then according to this view, too high a degree of equality could compromise growth. However, the poor save at much higher rates than previously believed, when savings are properly measured to include expenditures on health, children's education, and improvements on a home.

Moreover, where inequality is great, the poor may not be able to obtain loans because they lack collateral; indeed, one definition of what it means to be poor is to be entirely or mostly lacking in a source of collateral. Poor persons unable to get a loan to start a business due to such capital market imperfections may get stuck in subsistence or wage employment, although they (and perhaps potential employees) could do much better if they had access to financing or if there were a more even distribution of income. For example, Abhijit Banerjee and Andrew Newman show that multiple equilibria, including equilibria involving outcomes with virtually all citizens enjoying high incomes and outcomes with predominantly low-income people, can exist when imperfect credit markets provide too few people with the opportunity to become entrepreneurs.[50]

Similarly, if the poor lack access to credit, they may not be able to obtain loans to finance otherwise very productive schooling. If the poor are unable to bequeath much to their next generation, families can be trapped in poverty from generation to generation; however, if schooling could somehow be achieved, they could escape from this **poverty trap**. It is best to keep in mind a rather expansive definition of what is meant by a *transfer* from parents to be used for human capital accumulation by their children. It is more than tuition and more than forgone wages or work on the farm to help the family because it goes well beyond the cost of formal schooling and may be thought of as the building of a whole array of "capabilities" (see Chapter 1) that one acquires almost as a simple by-product of growing up in an affluent, educated family.

In a formal model of this problem, Oded Galor and Joseph Zeira examined the implications of missing credit markets for growth and the distribution of both income and human capital. They developed an endogenous growth model that points up the importance of both human capital and distribution, and of the interaction between the two, for economic growth and development as well as for more short-term macroeconomic adjustments. Their analysis contains two critical assumptions: (1) imperfect capital markets, which, as will be described in detail in Chapter 16, is a typical condition of these markets, and (2) indivisibilities in human capital investment, which means that markets treat investment in human capital as coming in discrete packages, such as a year of school, if not larger blocks, such as primary, secondary, and tertiary education. The second assumption does not seem unreasonable, both because of the nature of learning and because of the screening nature of markets for human capital. A threshold level of knowledge is necessary before an employer will be willing to pay for it. Further, because education acts as a screen for inherent ability, as will be discussed in Chapter 8, we have the well-known "sheepskin effect"; that is, there is a very large jump in the return to human capital when an individual passes primary school and again when the person obtains a secondary school diploma and so on. This is not because the last course taken conveys so much more knowledge than the ones preceding it but because the degree itself is what enables the individual to prove that an entire regimen of requirements has been met. Note that indivisibilities in amounts of investment imply a region of increasing returns to scale, as in the fixed costs of the big push model. Once again, increasing returns plays a key role in generating multiple equilibria.[51] Empirically, many studies have found a negative impact of inequality on growth, especially for the period after 1980.[52]

Kremer's O-Ring Theory of Economic Development

Another innovative and influential model that provides important insights into low-level equilibrium traps was provided by Michael Kremer.[53] The notion is that modern production (especially in contrast to traditional crafts production) requires that many activities be done well together in order for any of them to amount to high value. This is a form of strong complementarity and is a natural way of thinking about specialization and the division of labor, which along with economies of scale is another hallmark of developed economies in general and industrial production in particular. The name for Kremer's model is taken from the 1986 *Challenger* disaster, in which the failure of one small, inexpensive part caused the space shuttle to explode. The O-ring theory is interesting in part because it explains not only the existence of poverty traps but also the reasons that countries caught in such traps might have such exceptionally low incomes compared with high-income countries.

The O-Ring Model

The key feature of the O-ring model is the way it models production with strong complementarities among inputs. We start by thinking of the model as describing what is going on inside a firm, but as we will see, this model also provides valuable insights into the impact of complementarities across firms or sectors of the economy.

Suppose a production process is broken down to n tasks. There are many ways of carrying out these tasks, which for simplicity we order strictly by level of skill q required, where $0 \le q \le 1$. The higher the skill, the higher the probability that the task will be "successfully completed" (which may mean, for example that the part created in this task will not fail). Kremer's concept of q is quite flexible. Other interpretations may include a quality index for characteristics of the good: Consumers would be willing to pay more for higher-quality characteristics. For example, suppose that $q = 0.95$. Among other interpretations, this could mean (1) that there is a 95% chance that the task is completed perfectly, so the product keeps maximum value, and a 5% chance that it is completed so poorly that it has no value; (2) that the task is always completed well enough that it keeps 95% of its maximum value; or (3) that the product has a 50% chance of having full value and a 50% chance of an error reducing the value of the product to 90%. For simplicity, assume that the probability of mistakes by different workers is strictly independent. The production function assumed is a simple one: Output is given by multiplying the q values of each of the n tasks together, in turn multiplied by a term, say B, that depends on the characteristics of the firm and is generally larger with a larger number of tasks.

Suppose also that each firm hires only two workers. Then the **O-ring production function** looks like this:[54]

$$BF(q_i q_j) = q_i q_j \qquad (4.4)$$

To make things simple, for the moment we let the multiplier, B, equal 1. In addition to the form of the production function, we make three other significant types of simplifying assumptions: (1) Firms are risk-neutral, (2) labor markets are competitive, and (3) workers supply labor inelastically (i.e., they work regardless of the wage). If we consider capital markets, we assume that they are competitive as well. For now, we also assume that the economy is closed.

One of the most prominent features of this type of production function is what is termed *positive assortative matching*. This means that workers with high skills will work together and workers with low skills will work together. When we use the model to compare economies, this type of matching means that high-value products will be concentrated in countries with high-value skills. In this model, everyone would like to work with the more productive workers, because if your efforts are multiplied by those of someone else, as they are in Equation 4.4, you will be more productive when working with a more productive person. In competitive markets, your pay is based on how productive you are. A firm with a higher-productivity worker can more afford to pay a higher wage and has the incentive to bid higher to do so, because the value of output will be higher with two productive workers, say, than with one low- and one high-productivity worker. As a result, there will be a strong tendency for the most productive workers to work together.

This can be seen easily if we imagine a four-person economy. Suppose this economy has two high-skill q_H–workers and two low-skill q_L–workers. The four workers can be arranged either as matched skill pairs or unmatched-skill pairs. Total output will always be higher under a matching scheme because

$$q_H^2 + q_L^2 > 2q_H q_L \qquad (4.5)$$

(Try it! Just plug in any values $q_H > q_L$.) This generalizes to larger numbers of workers in the firms and the economy; the result is that workers sort out by skill level.[55]

Because total value is higher when skill matching takes place, the firm that starts with high-productivity workers can afford to bid more to get additional high-productivity workers, and it is profitable to do so. Of course, every firm would like to hire the most productive worker, but it would be in that worker's interest to team up with other high-productivity workers. Think of firms being formed while workers try to determine for which firm they want to work. After the high-productivity workers pair off, they are out of the picture. The less productive workers are then stuck with each other. If there are many classes of skill or productivity, first the highest-skill workers get together, then the next highest, and so on, such that skill matching results as a cascading process. For example, a symphony orchestra would be adversely affected as a whole by hiring one single poor performer. So an otherwise excellent orchestra has every incentive to bid the most for an outstanding performer to replace the poor performer. Similarly, the best jazz performers play and record together rather than each lead a group of poorer players. The restaurant with the very best chef also hires mature, highly trained, full-time waiters, while a fast-food restaurant does not hire a famous chef.

This sorting process is perhaps most vividly easy to remember by analogy to Nobel laureate Gary Becker's famous "marriage market" model, which is a somewhat different case but offers some additional intuition. If prospective spouses care only about attractiveness, every man wants to marry the most attractive woman, and every woman wants to marry the most attractive man, so the most attractive man and woman will marry. They are now out of the picture, so next, the second most attractive man and woman marry. This process continues until the least attractive man and woman marry.[56] Of course, beauty is in the eye of the beholder, and most people care about a lot of other things besides attractiveness in a mate (kindness, intelligence, wealth, beliefs, interests, commitment, sense of humor), so the model is more plausible for workers in firms than for marriage partners, but it creates a memorable analogy. The result is that some firms and workers, even an entire low-income economy, can fall into a trap of low skill and low productivity, while others escape into higher productivity.

Although this model may seem abstract, a numerical example can show how the firms with high-skill workers could and would pay more to get other high-skill workers or would have more incentive to upgrade skills among existing workers. Suppose that there are six workers; three have $q = 0.4$ and are grouped together in equilibrium, while the other three have $q = 0.8$. Now suppose that the q of one of the workers in the first firm rises from 0.4 to 0.5 (perhaps due to training). Similarly, suppose the q of one worker in the second firm rises from 0.8 to 1.0. In each case, we have a 25% increase in the quality of one worker. As you might expect, a 25% increase in the quality of one worker leads to a 25% increase in output quality. But starting from a higher level of quality, that 25% clearly translates into a much larger point increase: In the example, the first firm goes from $(0.4)(0.4)(0.4) = 0.064$ to $(0.4)(0.4)(0.5) = 0.080$; this is a difference of $0.080 - 0.064$, which is a point change of 0.016; and $0.016/0.064 = 0.25$, which is a 25% increase. For the second firm, we move from $(0.8)(0.8)(0.8) = 0.512$ to $(0.8)(0.8)(1.0) = 0.640$; the change in this case is 0.128, which is again 25%. However, the point value of the increase is much greater—eight times greater—for a doubled point-value investment (0.2 in the second firm versus 0.1 in the first firm). If a firm can increase quality in percentage terms at constant marginal cost, or even not too quickly rising cost, there is a virtuous circle in that the more you upgrade overall, the more value you obtain by doing so. As Kremer shows, this model is consistent with competitive equilibrium.

The O-ring result of positive assortative matching relies on some rather strong assumptions. How important are each of these, and how much can they be relaxed? Two points are crucial: (1) Workers must be sufficiently imperfect substitutes for each other, and (2) we must have sufficient complementarity of tasks. As long as these conditions hold, the basic results will follow.

To see why workers must be imperfect substitutes, suppose they were perfect substitutes. Specifically, suppose there are two skill levels, q_L and $q_H = 2q_L$, so every q_H worker can be replaced by two q_L workers with no other change. Thus q_H workers will be paid twice the amount that q_L workers are paid. We can draw no predic-

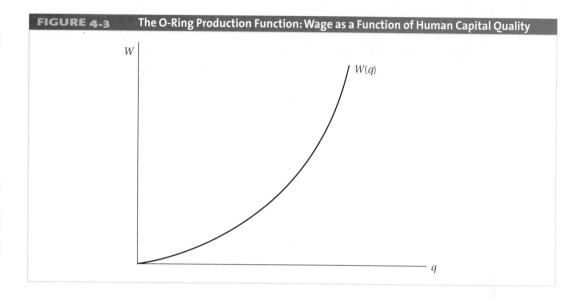

FIGURE 4.3   **The O-Ring Production Function: Wage as a Function of Human Capital Quality**

tions about what combination of worker skill levels a firm—or an economy—will use, so we can learn nothing about low-skill-level equilibrium traps. In fact, there is empirical evidence for imperfect substitutability across worker types in firms.

To see why we must have complementarity of tasks, suppose there are two tasks indexed by g and h but with no complementarity between them. To be specific, suppose our q_H worker is hired for the g task, and a q_L worker is hired for the h task; then

$$F(q_H q_L) = g(q_H) + h(q_L)$$

Here skills are imperfect substitutes for each other, because only one type of worker can be hired for each task (i.e., no two-for-one type of substitution is possible here). However, because tasks are not complementary, the optimal choice of skill for the g task is independent of that of the h task, and again no strategic complementarities are present.[57]

Implications of the O-Ring Theory

The analysis has several important implications:

- Firms tend to employ workers with similar skills for their several tasks.

- Workers performing the same task earn higher wages in a high-skill firm than in a low-skill firm.

- Because wages increase in q at an increasing rate, wages will be more than proportionally higher in developed countries than would be predicted from some objective measure of skill. Figure 4.3 shows the relationship between skill and wages found in the O-ring model.

- If workers can improve their skill level and make such investments, and if it is in their interests to do so, they will consider the level of human capital investments made by other workers as a component of their own decision about how much skill to acquire. Put differently, when those around you have higher average skills, you have a greater *incentive* to acquire more skills. This type of complementarity should by now be a familiar condition in which multiple equilibria can emerge; it parallels issues raised in our analysis of the big push model.

- One can get caught in economywide low-production-quality traps. This will occur when there are (quite plausibly) O-ring effects across firms as well as within firms. Because there is an externality at work, there could thus be a case for an industrial policy to encourage quality upgrading, as some East Asian countries have undertaken in the past (see Chapter 13).

- O-ring effects magnify the impact of local production bottlenecks because such bottlenecks have a multiplicative effect on other production.

- Bottlenecks also reduce the incentive for workers to invest in skills by lowering the expected return to these skills.

Following Kremer, consider a simple illustration of these bottleneck effects. Suppose that n tasks are required to produce a good. Let q be the standard skill level of these n tasks. But now let the actual skill level of two workers be cut in half in all firms. With an O-ring production function, output would fall by 75% (the result of cutting output in half once and then again). But then the marginal product of quality also falls by 75% for all the remaining $n - 2$ tasks, and thus so does the incentive to invest in increasing skill. The strong assumption of our simple O-ring production function may overstate the case, but the point that strategic complementarities can cause low-skill equilibria remains.

As workers reduce their skill investments, they further reduce the level of skill in the economy and thereby lower further the incentive to invest in skill. To some extent, such bottlenecks could be ameliorated by international trade and investment, because foreign inputs and investors provide an alternative source of inputs from outside the bottlenecked economy. One explanation of why economies that have cut themselves off from the international economy, such as India until recent years, have not fared as well as those that are more integrated, such as South Korea, could well be their failure to take advantage of foreign inputs or investments; the O-ring analysis helps explain why the impact could be so great. Trade cannot solve all problems of industrialization, but the O-ring model helps explain why trade can play a key role as a part of an industrialization strategy.

The model also has implications for the choice of technology. When skill is scarce, a firm is less likely to choose a technique with higher value but complicated production technology with many tasks, because the costs of doing any one of those tasks poorly are magnified. In this way, the value of production is increasing in the complexity of the product, assuming that the product is completed successfully. Given positive assortative matching, firms producing products or using technologies requiring a large size or many steps will be induced to employ high-quality employees. Mistakes are costly to firms with large numbers of workers and production steps; therefore, such firms place exceptional value on high-quality, skilled workers who are unlikely to make mistakes.[58] This indicates one reason why rich countries with high-skill workers tend to have larger firms and specialize in more complex products; it also explains why firm size and wages are positively correlated within and across countries.

Finally, under some additional assumptions, the model can also help explain the international brain drain. It is often observed that when a worker of any given skill moves from an LDC to a developed country, he or she immediately receives a higher wage for using those same skills. A version of the O-ring model is one way of explaining this.

Thus Kremer's O-ring model points out many of the implications of strong complementarities for economic development and the distribution of income across countries. As Kremer concludes, "If strategic complementarity is sufficiently strong, microeconomically identical nations or groups within nations could settle into equilibria with different levels of human capital."[59]

Conclusions: Multiple Equilibria and Coordination Failures

The important point is not that people keep doing inefficient things. This is not in itself very surprising. The deeper point is that people keep doing inefficient things because it is rational to keep doing them, and it will remain rational as long as others keep doing inefficient things. This leads to a fundamental problem of coordination failure. Sometimes firms and other economic agents will be able to coordinate to achieve a better equilibrium on their own. But in many cases, government policy and aid will be necessary to overcome the resulting vicious circles of underdevelopment.

The purpose of economic development theory is not only to understand underdevelopment but also to devise effective policies to redress it. The analysis of coordination failure problems in this chapter offers some important overall lessons for policy, but they are not simple lessons with easy applicability, and indeed they present something of a two-edged sword. On one side, the analysis shows that the potential for market failure, especially as it affects the prospects for economic development, is broader and deeper than had been fully appreciated in the past. Rather than the small "deadweight triangle losses" of conventional economic analysis of monopoly, pollution externalities, and other market failures, coordination failure problems can have more far-reaching effects and consequently much greater costs.[60] For example, the interactions of slightly distorted behaviors by potential investors failing to consider the income effects of the wages they pay may produce very large distortions, such as the outright failure to industrialize. This makes the potential benefit of an active role for government larger in the context of multiple equilibria.

The coordination failures that may arise in the presence of complementarities highlight potential policies for deep interventions that move the economy to a preferred equilibrium or even to a higher permanent rate of growth that can then be self-sustaining. For example, once a big push has been undertaken, government coordination may no longer be necessary. The unaided market can often maintain industrialization once it is achieved, even when it cannot initiate or complete the process of industrialization. For another example, in Chapter 8 we will see that in some cases, the presence of child labor represents a kind of bad equilibrium among the families with children who work, one that might be fixed with appropriate policy. After successfully abolishing child labor, in some cases child labor regulations will not have to be enforced to keep child labor from making a resurgence. If there is no incentive to go back to the behavior associated with the bad equilibrium, then in these cases government has no need to continue the interventions designed to escape it. Instead, government can then concentrate its efforts on other crucial problems in which it has an essential role (e.g., in addressing problems of public health). This onetime-fix character of some multiple-equilibrium problems makes them worthy of special focus because they can make government policy that much more powerful in addressing problems of economic development. Among other implications, the prospect of deep interventions can mean that the costs of implementing policy can be reduced and that carefully targeted development assistance could have more effective results.

The other edge of the sword, however, is that with deep interventions, the potential costs of a public role are also much larger. Policy choices are more momentous because a bad policy today could push an economy into a bad equilibrium for years to come. This is partly because government can be a major part of the problem, playing a key role in perpetuating a bad equilibrium such as a high-corruption regime, in part because some government officials and politicians may benefit personally from it. Bad policy can even initiate a move to a worse equilibrium than a country began with. To expect government to be the source of reform that moves the economy to a better equilibrium in countries where government has been part of the complex nexus of a bad equilibrium can be naive. For example, as 2001 Nobel laureate Joseph Stiglitz pointed out, development officials should have been more suspicious of corrupt government officials' embracing of the World Bank's doctrine of thoroughgoing privatization in the late 1980s and early 1990s. Why would corrupt officials have done so if they benefited from a stream of rents captured from public enterprises? The answer, Stiglitz suggests, is that these officials found that by corrupting the process of privatization, they could get not only a stream of corrupt rents from the annual operations of the enterprise but also a share of the present discounted value of the whole future operations of the enterprise.[61] The results of corrupt privatization in Russia in particular have been devastating for its economy, preventing it from enjoying the benefits of the market and potentially keeping it in a suboptimal equilibrium for many years to come. Even when a government is not corrupt, the potential impact of a well-intentioned but flawed government policy is much greater when it could push the economy to a fundamentally different equilibrium, which may be difficult to reverse. This is all the more problematic in the many cases in which "history matters" in a developing economy—that is, when past conditions determine what is possible today.

Both government failure and market failure are real, but public- and private-sector contributions to development are also vital. Therefore, we need to work toward the development of institutions in which actors in the public and private sectors have incentives to work productively together (directly and indirectly) in such a way as to create the conditions necessary to break out of poverty traps. In achieving this goal, the international community also has a vital role to play, providing ideas and models and serving as a catalyst for change, as well as providing some of the necessary funding.

In sum, the contributions of the new models of development reviewed in this chapter include a better understanding of the causes and effects of poverty traps, achieved by more precisely pinning down roles of different types of strategic complementarities, explaining the role of expectations, illuminating the potential scope for deep interventions, and of equal importance, improving our understanding of both the potential role of government and the constraints on the effectiveness of that role—when government itself becomes a player in an underdevelopment trap. Finally, the new approaches point out more clearly the real potential contributions of outside development assistance that extend beyond provision of capital to modeling new ways of doing things. The chief limitation of the new models to date is that they are long on analysis but still short on practical policy implications not previously recognized. But perhaps it is still too early to expect detailed policy recommendations from these approaches.

Nevertheless, as democratic government spreads in the developing world, the new understandings of underdevelopment traps can make for a more effective guide to policy design than was available even a few years ago. As Karla Hoff has aptly summarized, "Governments fail, even in democracies, just as markets do. But a positive development of recent years is to try more limited interventions to harness the spillovers among agents, and to try to sequence policy reforms in a way that makes it more likely for good equilibria to emerge."[62]

In Parts Two and Three, as we consider pressing issues affecting developing countries today, we will be using the insights provided by both the classic theories and the new models of development and underdevelopment to inform our understanding of both the nature of the problems faced and the potential benefits and pitfalls of policies designed to help overcome them.

Understanding a Development Miracle: China

From 1978 to 2004, the economy of China grew at an average rate of 9% a year, an unprecedented achievement for any economy in history, let alone the world's most populous nation. China's income *per capita* by 2004 was about *five times* higher than it was in 1978. Growth threatened to become explosive by 2004, igniting inflation, and the government was trying to slow growth back to 9%—three times the rate that would be considered respectable by the recent standards of most low-income countries.

Skeptics such as Thomas Rawski of the University of Pittsburgh cast doubt on some of the official statistics. Given other available information about the Chinese economy, such as price deflation, unemployment, and demand for certain goods, Rawski argued that growth has been just under half the official totals at least during the period from 1998 to 2002, that is, about 4% per year. But even in the most pessimistic reading, the unprecedented scale of China's growth and transformation is clear, and by 2004, the main concerns were inflation and unsustainably rapid growth.

China has also experienced the world's most dramatic reductions in poverty. China's official estimates show a sensational decrease in residents living in poverty from 260 million in 1978 to just 42 million in 1998. An independent World Bank estimate has the number of poor in China falling from some 303 million in 1987 to 213 million in 1998. Whichever estimates and thresholds for the poverty line are used, the reductions in poverty in China are far faster and greater than anywhere else in the world.

For such a stunning record, the roots of China's success remain a source of deep disagreement. The Chinese experience seems to change everything—but does it? And if so, how? Success has a thousand fathers, and all the major traditional and new schools of thought on development want to claim China as their most important case in point. China is hailed as an example of the benefits of markets, trade, and globalization. There is no doubt that manufactured exports are key to China's growth, and market incentives have played the key motivational role in business decisions. But China has also adopted active industrial policies, pushing exports of increasingly higher skill and technology content, and it started its period of rapid growth around 1980, more than a decade before trade liberalization. Moreover, much of China's growth in the 1980s and 1990s was due to rural township and village enterprises, which have had a quasi-cooperative character. There has been less privatization of state-owned enterprises than in most developing countries (in some countries, privatization has been made to work, but in other countries, privatization has been little more than the theft of public assets). In the meantime, countries in Africa, Latin America, and elsewhere that have most closely followed the free-market model have generally not done particularly well. While all schools may find something in China to let them claim it as vindication of their favored development policies, it is also clear that if China were performing dismally, everyone could (and no doubt would) equally find reasons why their own theories, including free-market theory, predicted such a failure.

There have been many special explanations for China's remarkable success. Many of them contain part of the truth, but such dramatic success is more than the sum of these parts. Let us review some of the explanations.

The presence of regional "demonstration" models has been crucial. Japan was emulated by other countries in the East Asian region. Hong Kong provided an additional example for China, as did China's archrival Taiwan. Taiwan, Hong Kong, and South Korea focused on export-oriented industrialization at a time when world trade was growing rapidly. Then, by the late 1980s, the locus of regional growth shifted to China as investors began to pour investments into China in large part because of the allure of its eventual market of 1 billion or more consumers. Although the market was limited at first both by low incomes and by government policies, early investors found high incentives to export from several special economic zones on the southeast coast. These investors discovered that China offered very cheap labor with unusually high skills and work habits for its income level. Once early investments built up a sufficient critical mass, agglomeration benefits of concentrated economic activity kicked in (see Chapter 7). The more producers located in China, the greater the benefits for an increasing number of suppliers to operate there. At this point, investments started to feed on themselves in a cumulative causation. In the meantime, when wages began to rise, companies could set up production farther west, or migrants from the west could move to the new industrial centers. Given China's population of hundreds of millions of low-income farmers, expectations were formed that this process of wage restraint could continue for an extended time.

The central planning of China's first decades after the 1949 revolution were by most measures a failure. Industry was highly inefficient. As many as 30 million people died in a late-1950s famine caused by poor planning decisions, and political pressures that led party and government officials to regularly overstate the harvest prospects. As Amartya Sen stresses, famines rarely occur in democratic countries with a free press. Such disasters were only partly offset by the early and ongoing emphasis on basic health and education in China and then on reductions of fertility through China's one-child policy (see the case study for Chapter 6). But these basic first steps on education, health, and fertility helped set the stage for growth and poverty reduction when later combined with market incentives. One of the results is the apparently higher educational and skill level of factory workers for given wages in China in comparison to its competitor countries. In addition, government negotiation of licenses and other business agreements helped ensure that China got more favorable deals than many other developing countries; in this, the role model lessons from South Korea and other East Asian countries was a benefit.

There has been considerable debate about whether rapid growth in other East Asian countries is the result of capital accumulation or productivity gains. Alwyn Young, Paul Krugman, and others have concluded that South Korea and other Asian Tigers grew more from investing heavily in capital assets such as machinery and factories than by improved worker efficiency. But for the case of China, Zuliu Hu and Mohsin Khan concluded that productivity gains explained more than 42% of China's growth in the 1979–1994 period and that productivity had overtaken investment by the early 1990s as the largest source of growth. This was considered surprising in part because of the breathtaking pace of capital investments in China. But on the other hand, when China's rapid growth began in the late 1970s in the areas close to Hong Kong, while it was clear that a large volume of investment funds were flowing from capital-abundant Hong Kong (still a British crown colony) to capital-scarce China, the bigger story was the flow of productive ideas over the Hong Kong border, a barrier that had long prevented the flow of both capital and know-how. Of these two factors, it often seemed that the ideas were more important than the finance. There is widespread concern that by now, China had entered into an investment bubble stage, in which many investments are of dubious quality. Even so, the rapid pace of development in China has been unprecedented.

In a separate study, Ashoka Mody and Fang-Yi Wang of the World Bank examined the causes of industrial growth in China and concluded that

> Although industry-specific features—the degree of specialization and competition—had some influence on growth, much of the action came from region-specific influences and regional spillovers. Regional influences included the open-door policies and special economic zones that successfully attracted investments from overseas Chinese to particular locations. Existing regional strengths, especially high-quality human capital and infrastructure, also contributed to growth. Our results illuminate the interplay between conditions conducive for growth—for example, the contribution of foreign expertise is greatly enhanced by available human capital. China made judicious use of the advantages of backwardness by targeting areas that were less developed and less encumbered by the legacy of existing institutions,

although it was fortunate in this regard that the backward regions were in close proximity to Hong Kong and Taiwan.

Government played off potential investors who wanted access to China's billion-plus consumers, demanding and getting extensive technology transfer, public and private Chinese business partnerships, local content, and other concessions in exchange for the right to sell to Chinese citizens.

However, Wing Thye Woo concluded that most of China's growth came from the reallocation of labor, particularly from surplus in agriculture to other activities; and that sustainable total factor productivity progress was much lower, on the order of 2% per year.

In China, the *way* that market incentives were introduced and used seems to have been almost as important as the fact *that* they were introduced. One of the most important features of the past quarter century of economic history in China has been the painstaking, gradual, systematic implementation of reforms. China's approach has been the opposite of that of many Eastern European countries such as Russia and Poland, which opted for a "big bang," a sudden comprehensive changeover to a free-market economy. (Hungary and Slovenia are two countries in that region that pursued a more gradualist strategy.) China has introduced new and transitional institutions that exist side by side with previous institutions of central planning for extended periods. In the former Soviet Union and Eastern Europe, central planning was abolished almost immediately, and economic depression, with drops in output of up to 50%, ensued before gradual recovery. In contrast, China kept the central planning system partially intact for an extended period. Previous quotas for buyers and sellers at fixed planned prices were maintained. Reform was instead introduced on the margin. After filling their quotas, producers were free to buy and sell at market-determined prices; resales were generally not prohibited. This "dual track" system simulated the allocational efficiency of a more competitive market economy and created strong incentives for firms to improve efficiency and increase output.

Moreover, while in other transition and developing countries state-owned enterprises (SOEs) were sold off to private investors fairly quickly, in China these remained in government hands for an extended period. The government tried to reform them internally, though with limited success. But at the same time, China has allowed and encouraged a new, more efficient sector to grow up around them. In recent years, China has privatized or closed many of the smaller SOEs. Many larger SOEs continue to operate in a relatively inefficient manner, and some economists suspect that their accumulating indebtedness will eventually pose significant financial risks to the economy. But if the economy can continue to grow rapidly, it is also possible that China may stay ahead of this problem without experiencing a financial crash. Eventually, as employment opportunities continue to expand, more of the larger SOEs can be privatized or closed.

Further, for the first nearly two decades of reform, from the late 1970s to the mid 1990s, at the local level, township and village enterprises (TVEs) were encouraged. Vaguely owned by local government, private entrepreneurs and employees of TVEs also held "vaguely defined" property rights. These TVEs accounted for a very large share of industrial output growth in China. Finally, after the Chinese economy had grown nearly fourfold, the majority of these TVEs were privatized in the 1990s. But the TVEs played a unique role in spurring growth and spreading the benefits of development to rural areas. It should be noted that early reforms favored agriculture in the rural areas where most of the poor live, and poverty fell as income rose. From the late 1980s on, the terms of trade shifted toward industry, and the rate of poverty reduction fell. In 2004, over half the population was still involved in agriculture.

As outlined by Yingyi Qian of the University of California-Berkeley, China's transitional institutions have served a dual purpose: to improve efficiency while compensating the losers (and thereby preserving legitimacy or at least reducing the chance of political backlash). Provided that the quotas were enforced—and for the most part they seem to have been in the transition in China—the dual-track allocation system protected the interests of those who had benefited from and planned on receiving inputs at fixed, low prices. As a result, these agents did not oppose or undermine reforms and indeed could benefit further from them to the degree they could learn to produce more efficiently and operate on markets effectively. The system was largely phased out only many years later, after the economic landscape had changed dramatically.

The vaguely local-government-owned TVEs provided protection for investors who feared the hostility of many in the government to private property and worried about expropriation. The image that these companies were owned by the township or village protected the de facto full or partial private owners. Once reform proceeded to a certain point, these de facto owners were able to "take off the red hat," as the saying went in China, and assume ownership in exchange for considerations to local government; and taxes replaced direct revenue transfer out of the TVEs. Qian shows how similar arguments apply to fiscal and financial reforms. Under the reforms, local government continued to have a responsibility to provide revenue to the central government, but local government was allowed to keep a large share of collections on the margin before fully separating local and central revenue collection. Government also allowed anonymous banking accounts for a long transition period, to credibly constrain the ability of the government to arbitrarily impose high individual taxes on successful entrepreneurs; Qian judged the program a success despite the fact that this diverges from what is considered normal best practice in advanced Western countries.

Yingyi Qian's insightful explanation is that

although building best-practice institutions is a desirable goal, getting institutions right is a process involving incessant changes interacting with initial conditions. The difference between China and Russia is not at all that China has established best-practice institutions and Russia has not. The difference lies in the institutions in transition. . . . The real challenge in reform facing transition and developing countries is not so much knowing where to end up, but searching for a feasible path toward the goal. Therefore, it focuses on transitional institutions, not best-practice institutions. . . . The general principle of efficiency-improving and interest-compatible institutional change is simple, but the specific forms and mechanisms of transitional institutions often are not. Successful institutional forms usually are not a straightforward copy of best-practice institutions. They need not be and sometimes should not be. They need not be because room exists for efficiency improvement that does not require fine tuning at the beginning. They should not be because the initial conditions are country- and context-specific, requiring special arrangements. . . . Understanding these mechanisms sometimes needs an appeal to the counterintuitive second best argument, which states that removing one distortion may be counterproductive in the presence of another distortion.

Finally, for peasants in parts of China where the rural sector has done well, earlier land reforms have been among the causes—with the revolution setting the stage and the late-1970s reforms giving greater incentives to individual farmers. Land reform has been notoriously difficult to implement in other parts of the world. Remittances from migrant workers have fueled a service sector boom in some rural areas, and prices received by farmers have generally risen, particularly near urban areas.

There are some other limits and caveats to China's success, and to the lessons that other countries can learn from it. Life can indeed be harder than ever for millions of those still remaining in extreme poverty, such as rural peasants in some parts of the country facing the loss of security, official corruption including reports of official land grabs from peasants, and rising local taxes, and receiving few improvements in technology or skills.

The huge indebtedness of the SOE sector and other public debt may eventually lead to a significant financial crisis. Moreover, China is quite homogeneous, overwhelmingly populated by members of the Han ethnic group. In Africa and other parts of the world, ethnic diversity is associated with slower growth, though only in countries that also have incomplete or nonexistent political freedoms. Clearly, China is lacking in many freedoms. There may be limits to the ability of other countries to carry out China's brand of centrally designed and implemented policies for transition and directed growth when either broader democratic freedoms are in place or greater ethnic diversity is present. Finally, China, like much of the rest of East Asia, has a relatively poor endowment of natural resources. Many development specialists have concluded that this lack is actually more of a benefit than a drawback. Natural resource abundance encourages political infighting for control over the revenues, while manufacturing success is more important when you don't have natural resources to fall back on. It requires more initiative and more efforts to upgrade technology and skill. In terms of geographical advantages, East Asia is also much less plagued than Africa and other developing regions by problems such as malaria and other tropical diseases for which medicines are not readily available, the difficulties and disadvantages of tropical agriculture, and the problems of landlocked countries.

In sum, China does change the way we think about development. It assures us that the East Asian miracle is not a fluke due to special local factors in economies such as South Korea and Taiwan. It gives us much greater confidence when we say that "real development is possible." On the other hand, there are clear limits to the ability of other developing regions to emulate the success of China. Not only do other developing countries differ in geography, demography, institutions, and allure to foreign investors, but other regions may find themselves starved for investments that are redirected to China while remaining unable to compete with China's impressive combination of low wages and high skills and know-how. The shakeout from the end to textile quotas in 2005 as the international multifibre arrangement is abolished is a dramatic example of negative effects of China's success on other developing countries. Some East Asian countries have greatly benefited from the surge in import demand from China. And China itself has a good chance of continued high growth. But for most developing countries, the success of China today appears to be as much of a threat as an opportunity. ■

Sources

Brandt, Loren, and Xiaodong R. Zhu. "Distribution in a decentralized economy: Growth and inflation in China under reform." *Journal of Political Economy* 108 (2000): 422–439.

Byrd, William, and Lin Qingsong (eds.). *China's Rural Industry: Structure, Development, and Reform.* New York: Oxford University Press, 1990.

Chen, B., and Y. Feng. "Determinants of economic growth in China: Private enterprise, education, and openness." *China Economic Review* 11 (2000): 1–15.

Goodman, Peter S. "Financial enterprise in China at odds with party politics." *Washington Post*, January 2, 2004, p. 1.

Harney, Alexandra, "Going home: Chinese migrant workers shun long factory hours and low pay," *Financial Times*, November 3, 2004, p. 15.

Hu, Zuliu, and Mohsin S. Khan. "Why is China growing so fast?" IMF Working Paper No. 96/75, 1996.

Krugman, Paul. "The myth of Asia's miracle," MIT Working Paper, 1998.

Lau, Lawrence J., Yingyi Qian, and Gerald Roland. "Pareto-improving economic reforms through dual track liberalization." *Economics Letters* (1997): 285–292.

Lau, Lawrence J., Yingyi Qian, and Gerald Roland. "Reform without losers: An interpretation of China's dual-track approach to transition." *Journal of Political Economy* 108 (2000): 120–143.

Lu, D. "Industrial policy and resource allocation: Implications of China's participation in globalization." *China Economic Review* 11 (2000): 342–360.

Mody, Ashoka, and Fang-Yi Wang. "Explaining industrial growth in coastal China: Economic reforms . . . and what else?" *World Bank Economic Review* 11 (1997): 293–325.

Qian, Yingyi. "How reform worked in China." In *In Search of Prosperity: Analytic Narratives on Economic Growth*, ed. Dani Rodrik. Princeton, N.J.: Princeton University Press, 2003.

Rawski, Thomas. "Measuring China's recent GDP growth: Where do we stand?" October 2002. http://www.pitt.edu/~tgrawski/papers2002/measuring.pdf.

Roland, Gerald. *Transition and Economics: Politics, Markets, and Firms*. Cambridge, Mass.: MIT Press 2000.

Romer, Paul M. "Two strategies for economic development: Using ideas versus producing ideas." Supplement to *World Bank Economic Review:* Proceedings of the 1992 World Bank Development Economics Conference, Washington D.C., 1993, pp. 63–91.

Romer, Paul M. "Idea gaps and object gaps in economic development," *Journal of Monetary Economics* 32 (1993): 543–573.

Smith, Stephen C. "Employee participation in China's township and village enterprises." *China Economic Review* 6 (1995): 157–167.

Smith, Stephen C. "Industrial policy and export success: Third World development strategies reconsidered." In *U.S. Trade Policy and Global Growth*, ed. Robert Blecker. New York: Sharpe, 1996.

United Nations Development Program. *Human Poverty Report, 2000*. New York: United Nations, 2000.

Vogel, Ezra. *One Step Ahead in China*. Cambridge, Mass.: Harvard University Press, 1989.

Weitzman, Martin L., and Chenggang Xu. "Chinese township and village enterprises as vaguely defined cooperatives." *Journal of Comparative Economics* 20 (1994): 121–145.

Woo, Wing Thye. "Chinese economic growth: Sources and prospects." In *The Chinese Economy*, ed. Michel Fouquin and Francoise Lemoine. London: Economica, 1998.

Young, Alwyn. "The tyranny of numbers: Confronting the statistical realities of the East Asian growth experience." *Quarterly Journal of Economics* 110 (1995): 641–680.

Zhou, Ning, Yunshi Wang, and Lester Thurow. "The PRC's real economic growth rate." Cambridge, Mass.: MIT, 2002 (unpublished).

Concepts for Review

Agency costs
Agent
Asymmetric information
Big push
Complementarity
Complementary investments
Congestion
Coordination failure

Deep intervention
Endogenous growth theory
Linkage
Multiple equilibria
New growth theory
O-ring model
O-ring production function
Pareto improvement
Pecuniary externality

Poverty trap
Prisoners' dilemma
Public good
Romer endogenous growth model
Solow residual
Technological externality
Underdevelopment trap
Where-to-meet dilemma

Questions for Discussion

1. How does the endogenous (new) growth approach differ from the traditional (neo-classical or Solow) approach reviewed in Chapter 3? What are the implications for public policy in each case?

2. Can you think of additional examples of complementarities from everyday life? Does the S-shaped curve of Figure 4.1 shed any light on them? Do you think your examples help as a metaphor for economic development problems?

3. What role do you think international trade and foreign investment can play in solving some of the problems identified in the big push model? In the O-ring model? What limitations to your arguments can you think of?

4. The word *trap* suggests that there is a way to escape. Do you think developing countries can escape all of the traps described in this chapter? Which ones would be most difficult to escape? How could the developed world be of assistance in these cases? Could developed countries do more?

5. Why might high levels of inequality lead to lower rates of growth and development? Why might it be difficult to get out of this kind of trap?

6. Why is the government sometimes a part of the problem of coordination failure rather than the solution? Does this make the problem hopeless? What could be done in this case?

7. One of the characteristics of some developing economies is the relatively low level of trust of people outside one's extended family. How might the models explored in this chapter shed light on this problem?

8. Can you think of an example of O-ring production from everyday life? Do you think your example is a good metaphor for development problems?

9. Modern economic models sometimes require strong assumptions. What do you think are some of the trade-offs between a more rigorous, logically cohesive model with strong assumptions but clear inferences and a description of problems followed by a verbal discussion of possible implications? Do you think the two approaches can be used together to inform each other?

10. As you read later chapters, think about whether the models described in this chapter are useful in shedding additional light on the nature of problems considered. Some of the later problems you might consider are child labor, poor health and nutrition among the poor, high fertility, environmental degradation, availability of credit for the poor, urbanization, protectionism in international trade by developed and developing countries, reform of government, and land reform.

Notes

1. See Karla Hoff and Joseph E. Stiglitz, "Modern economic theory and development," in *Frontiers in Development Economics,* ed. Gerald M. Meier and Joseph E. Stiglitz (New York: Oxford University Press, 2000). The Hoff and Stiglitz header quote is drawn from this source, p. 390.

2. Oliver J. Blanchard and Stanley Fischer, *Lectures on Macroeconomics* (Cambridge, Mass.: MIT Press, 1989).

3. For a short history of the evolution of theoretical models of growth, see Nicholas Stern, "'The determinants of growth," *Economic Journal* 101 (1991): 122–134. For a more detailed but technical discussion of endogenous growth models, see Robert Barro and Xavier Sala-i-Martin, *Economic Growth,* 2nd ed. (Cambridge, Mass.: MIT Press, 2003), and Elhanan Helpman, "Endogenous macroeconomic growth theory," *European Economic Review* 36 (1992): 237–268.

4. See also Paul M. Romer, "Increasing returns and long-run growth," *Journal of Political Economy* 94 (1986): 1002–1037; Robert B. Lucas, "On the mechanics of economic development," *Journal of Monetary Economics* 22 (1988): 3–42; and Robert Barro, "Government spending in a simple model of endogenous growth," *Journal of Political Economy* 98 (1990): 5103–5125. See also the Further Reading selections at the end of this chapter.

5. For a concise technical discussion of the importance of human capital as a complementary input, see Robert B. Lucas, "Why doesn't capital flow from rich to poor countries?" *AEA Papers and Proceedings* 80 (1990): 92–96.

6. Cobb-Douglas production functions will be assumed for simplicity.

7. By the chain rule,

$$\dot{Y} = \frac{dY}{dt} = \frac{\partial Y}{\partial K}\frac{\partial K}{\partial t} + \frac{\partial Y}{\partial L}\frac{\partial L}{\partial t}$$

By the exponent rule, we know that

$$\frac{\partial Y}{\partial K} = A(\alpha + \beta)K^{\alpha+\beta-1}L^{1-\alpha}$$

$$\frac{\partial Y}{\partial L} = AK^{\alpha+\beta}(1 - \alpha)L^{1-\alpha-1}$$

Combining these three equations, we have

$$\dot{Y} = dY/dt = [AK^{\alpha+\beta}L^{1-\alpha}]\left[(\alpha + \beta)\frac{\dot{K}}{K} + (1 - \alpha)\frac{\dot{L}}{L}\right]$$

The first term in brackets in the preceding expression is of course output, Y. For a steady state, $\dot{K}/K$, $\dot{L}/L$, and $\dot{Y}/Y$ are all constant. From earlier discussion of the Harrod-Domar and Solow models, we know that

$$\dot{K} = I - \delta K = sY - \delta K$$

Dividing this expression through by K, we have

$$\frac{\dot{K}}{K} = \frac{sY}{K} - \delta a$$

For $\dot{K}/K$ constant in the preceding expression, we must have Y/K constant. If this ratio is constant, we have

$$\frac{\dot{K}}{K} = \frac{\dot{Y}}{Y} = g, \text{ a constant growth rate}$$

So from the expression for dY/dt above, for the aggregate production function, with $\dot{L}/L = n$, which is also a constant, we have

$$\frac{\dot{Y}}{Y} = (\alpha + \beta)\left(\frac{\dot{K}}{K}\right) + (1 - \alpha)\frac{\dot{L}}{L} \rightarrow g = (\alpha + \beta)g + (1 - \alpha)n$$

$$\rightarrow g - n = \left[\frac{(1 - \alpha) + (\alpha + \beta) - 1}{[1 - (\alpha + \beta)]}\right]n$$

which is Equation 4.3 in the text. This may also be expressed as

$$g = n(1 - \alpha)/(1 - \alpha - \beta)$$

8. Recall that there is no technological progress, so λ in the Solow model is zero.

9. In a more complex model, decisions about and effects of factors such as R&D investment can be modeled explicitly. Firms would decide on general investment and R&D investment. The effect of the latter on overall output would enter in a manner similar to $\bar{K}$ in Equation 4.1. For a discussion and references, see Gene M. Grossman and Elhanan Helpman, "Endogenous innovation in the theory of growth" in the symposium on new growth theory, in the *Journal of Economic Perspectives* 8 (1994): 3–72.

10. Syed Nawab Haider Naqvi, "The significance of development economics," *World Development* 24 (1996): 977.

11. For an excellent review and empirical critique of the new growth theory, see Howard Pack, "Endogenous growth theory: Intellectual appeal and empirical shortcomings," *Journal of Economic Perspectives* 8 (1994): 55–72. See also articles by Paul M. Romer

and Robert M. Solow in the same issue. For an argument that endogenous theory performs well in explaining differences in growth rates among countries, see Barro and Sala-i-Martin, *Economic Growth*. An excellent survey of quantitative growth research disputing this claim and indicating widening gaps between rich and poor countries can be found in Jonathan Temple, "The new growth evidence," *Journal of Economic Literature* 37 (1999): 112–156.

12. For example, the two approaches have converged when low-growth paths resulting from a coordination failure have been explicitly examined within an endogenous growth framework. For example, see Oded Galor and Joseph Zeira, "Income distribution and macroeconomics," *Review of Economic Studies* 60 (1993): 35–52.

13. For an insightful discussion of how many of the perspectives of this approach are applied to "new economy" issues, see Carl Shapiro and Hal Varian, *Information Rules: A Strategic Guide to the Network Economy* (Boston: Harvard Business School Press, 1999).

14. The problems cannot be solved even by perfect labor contracting (which is generally impossible in any case) if there is a risk of involuntary separations between firms and their employees (e.g., firm bankruptcies or death or serious illness of an employee). For a particularly insightful formal model, see Daron Acemoglu, "Training and innovation in an imperfect labour market," *Review of Economic Studies* 64 (1997): 445–464.

15. For an interesting formal model of this problem with supporting empirical evidence from rural Bangladesh, see Shahe Emran and Forhad Shilpi, "Marketing externalities, multiple equilibria, and market development," a paper presented at the Northeast Universities Development Conference, Boston University, September 2001.

16. Alicia Adsera and Debraj Ray, "History and coordination failure," *Journal of Economic Growth* 3 (1998): 267–276; Debraj Ray, *Development Economics* (Princeton, N.J.: Princeton University Press, 1998), ch. 5.

17. Thus the where-to-meet problem is much different from that of **prisoners' dilemma**, which is a situation in which all parties would be better off cooperating than competing, but each would gain the most by cheating, provided that others stick to cooperative agreements, causing any agreement to unravel.

18. Even under perfect information conditions, however, coordination can remain a problem.

19. Technically, this diagram assumes that agents are homogeneous and depicts a symmetrical Nash equilibrium, but this can be generalized to cases in which agents differ.

20. There is no reason why the curve has to take an S-shape in this case, but that shape is common in many coordination problems; the S-shape reflects the idea that increasing returns are present at first, as one takes advantage of the best opportunities afforded by, say, the presence of the first middleman. In this range, one sees a more than proportional individual response to an expected increase in average behavior among the other agents; but after the best opportunities are exhausted, the response is positive but less than proportional, giving rise to the latter, concave part of the S-shaped curve. The curve might actually wobble several times, for example, at each point that a new middleman enters the market.

21. If the IM providers make good on their pledge to ensure interoperability of their systems, this illustration may lose some of its power.

22. Technically, what is depicted is a set of symmetrical Nash equilibria. The S-shaped curve is the reaction curve of a representative agent to the average behavior of the other agents.

23. Kevin M. Murphy, Andrei Shleifer, and Robert W. Vishny, "Industrialization and the big push," *Journal of Political Economy* 97 (1989): 1003–1026. The seminal article is Paul Rosenstein-Rodan, "Problems of industrialization of Eastern and Southeastern Europe," *Economic Journal* 53 (1943): 202–211.

24. Paul Krugman, *Development, Geography, and Economic Theory* (Cambridge, Mass.: MIT Press, 1995), ch. 1. For an alternative exposition and an algebraic development of the model, see Kaushik Basu, *Analytical Development Economics* (Cambridge, Mass.: MIT Press, 1997), pp. 17–33.

25. One reason could be an efficiency wage effect, in which workers work harder to avoid being fired when paid a high wage, thereby raising productivity enough to pay for the higher wage.

26. In this we are assuming that modern-sector workers would be changing the sectors in which they work voluntarily; that is, they are not slave labor.

27. In the formal model of Murphy, Shleifer, and Vishny, there is a continuum of sectors, and hence of products, but that need not concern us here.

28. This consumption pattern means that there is unit-elastic demand; this is the type of demand function that follows from a Cobb-Douglas utility function with equal preference weights for all goods, such as a utility function given by the products of the amounts of each type of good consumed. Technically, Murphy, Shleifer, and Vishny assume that there is one representative consumer who supplies all labor and receives all profits, and with their other assumptions, set up the model so that Figure 4.2 and other parts of the analysis can be thought of either as the economy as a whole or as any particular market; but these considerations need not concern us here.

29. See, for example, Hollis B. Chenery, Sherman Robinson, and Moshe Syrquin, *Industrialization and Growth: A Comparative Study* (New York: Oxford University Press, 1986).

30. For work in this field, see, for example, Andres Rodriguez-Clare, "The division of labor and economic development," *Journal of Development Economics* 49 (1996): 3–32. Rodriguez-Clare starts with three plausible conditions that have had wide theoretical and empirical support since Adam Smith in the first two cases and Alfred Marshall in the third: There are productivity gains from the division of labor, the division of labor is limited by the extent of the market, and efficiency gains are derived from the proximity of suppliers and users of certain inputs. Given these assumptions, Rodriguez-Clare then shows that a small, open economy may be caught in an underdevelopment trap in which a "shallow division of labor" (i.e., a low variety of specialized inputs) is self-reinforcing. This in turn leads to a low rate of return to capital, so foreign investment or domestic capital accumulation may not materialize to help solve the problem. For another illustration, see Dani Rodrik, "Coordination failures and government policy: A model with applications to East Asia and Eastern Europe,"

Journal of International Economics 40 (1996): 1–22. See also Murphy, Schleifer, and Vishny, "Industrialization," sec. 6.

31. Recall from microeconomics that we can write marginal revenue as $P(Q)[1 - 1/\eta]$, where P is price and η is the (absolute value of) price elasticity of demand, with $\eta = 1$; then note that this producer has positive constant marginal costs. Therefore, profits may be indefinitely increased by decreasing output and raising price accordingly.

32. In other words, the producer acts as a limit-pricing monopolist.

33. Wages have risen to w in this sector, but this sector is by definition a very small part of the economy, so we can ignore income effects, which are very small.

34. The graph was first suggested by Krugman in *Development, Geography, and Economic Theory*.

35. Thus conditions for monopoly limit pricing are still present.

36. With a price of 1, the amount of goods purchased by workers is equal to the wage bill.

37. To see this, note that after the big push, total wages in the economy are $w_2(L/N)N$, and total profits are $[1Q_2 - w_2(L/N)]N$. Summing these, we get $1Q_2N$, the value of total output.

38. Expressed differently, the problem is that market failure is present. In particular, as Krugman points out, the interaction between a firm's internal economies of scale and the existence of perfectly elastic labor supplies at low wages together generate pecuniary externalities that inhibit the entry of modern firms. In other words, by generating an increase in aggregate demand, each firm makes a contribution to a mutually profitable big push to industrialization, even though individually each firm would lose money by industrializing alone. Thus although the economies of scale are internal to the firm, when combined with the presence of a traditional sector paying low wages, de facto external *pecuniary* positive externalities are generated. Again, this is because each firm's production has the effect of raising other firms' revenues, making them more profitable.

39. Formally, $F = F(N)$, where F is falling as N rises.

40. For details of one insightful formal model that casts the big push model into relatively accessible algebraic terms, see Stefano Paternostro, "The poverty trap: The dual externality model and its policy implications," *World Development* 25 (1997): 2071–2081.

41. Note that formally, in this case, *efficient* means "laborsaving," but the point is more general.

42. As Murphy, Schleifer, and Vishny show, there is also a plausible equilibrium condition that an increased interest-rate effect is not too large.

43. Openness to trade will not resolve this problem because the development of cities in *other* countries does not generally assist with national development. Urbanization is discussed further in Chapter 7.

44. In principle, if it is known that a sufficient number of modern firms will enter, the infrastructure problem could be solved by using perfect price discrimination, but if firms have different fixed costs that are not observable by the infrastructure provider

or if perfect price discrimination is not possible for some other reason, the infrastructure may not be built, even when it is efficient to do so. See Murphy, Schleifer, and Vishny, "Industrialization," sec. 6. For an accessible algebraic derivation using a diagram similar to Figure 4.2, see Pranab Bardhan and Chris Udry, *Development Microeconomics* (New York: Oxford University Press, 1999), pp. 208–211.

45. The term *lemons* derives from poor-quality used cars. As is well known, new cars lose a significant part of their value as soon as they leave the showroom. This is because the mere fact that a car is offered for sale is taken as valuable information about the car in itself. People wanting to buy a car are generally not expert mechanics, so they need to search for some shorthand information to help them decide what a car is worth; obviously, owners of a poor-quality car are more likely to offer it for sale. Analogies to this "lemons problem" have many other applications in economics, such as in financial markets (see Chapter 16). Also see George Akerlof, "The market for lemons," *Quarterly Journal of Economics* 84 (1970): 488–500.

46. For an excellent survey of some of the new developments covered in this section, see Hoff and Stiglitz, "Modern economic theory and development." Another good discussion of this and related topics is found in Ray, *Development Economics,* ch. 5.

47. Alice Amsden, *Asia's Next Giant: South Korea and Late Industrialization* (Oxford: Oxford University Press, 1989) and *The Rise of the Rest,* (New York: Oxford University Press, 2001); Carl J. Dahlman, Bruce Ross-Larson, and Larry E. Westphal, "Managing technical development: Lessons from the newly industrializing countries," *World Development* 15 (1987): 759–775; Richard Luedde-Neurath, *Import Controls and Export-Oriented Development: A Reassessment of the South Korean Case* (Boulder, Colo.: Westview Press, 1986); Howard Pack and Larry E. Westphal, "Industrial strategy and technological change: Theory versus reality," *Journal of Development Economics* 22 (1986): 87–128; Michael Porter, *The Competitive Advantage of Nations* (New York: Free Press, 1990); Joseph Stern et al., *Industrialization and the State: The Korean Heavy and Chemical Industry Drive* (Cambridge, Mass.: Harvard University Press, 1995); Gordon White (ed.), *Developmental States in East Asia* (New York: St. Martin's Press, 1988); Paul M. Romer, "Two strategies for economic development: Using ideas vs. producing ideas," in *Proceedings of the Annual World Bank Conference on Development Economics, 1992* (Washington, D.C.: World Bank, 1993); World Bank, *The East Asian Miracle: Economic Growth and Public Policy* (New York: Oxford University Press, 1993); Stephen C. Smith, "Industrial policy and export success: Third World development strategies reconsidered," in *U.S. Trade Policy and Global Growth,* ed. Robert Blecker (New York: Sharpe, 1996), pp. 267–298.

48. This perspective helps account for the popularity of input-output analysis in development planning and policy formulation, especially in earlier years, although it is an imperfect tool for this purpose (see Chapter 11).

49. For some evidence, see William L. Megginson and Jeffry M. Netter, "From state to market: A survey of empirical studies on privatization," *Journal of Economic Literature* 39 (2001): 321–390.

50. See Abhijit V. Banerjee and Andrew F. Newman, "Occupational choice and the process of development," *Journal of Political Economy* 101 (1993): 274–298.

51. Galor and Zeira's model rests on an alternative way to characterize imperfect capital markets—that the rate of interest for borrowers is greater than that for lenders. One can verify the reasonableness of this assumption with a brief visit to any bank. The model is a simple two-period, overlapping-generations model. See Oded Galor and Joseph Zeira, "Income distribution and macroeconomics," *Review of Economic Studies* 60 (1993): 35–52.

52. Torsten Persson and Guido Tabellini, "Is inequality harmful for growth?" *American Economic Review* 84 (1994): 600–621; see also Chapter 5.

53. Michael Kremer, "The O-ring theory of economic development," *Quarterly Journal of Economics* 108 (1993): 551–575. A good exposition of the model, which provides alternative proofs to the ones found in Kremer, is found in Basu, *Analytical Development Economics.*

54. More generally, there are *n* tasks; for simplicity, we continue to assume that one and only one worker must perform each of the *n* tasks; but conceptually, *n* should be thought of as tasks rather than number of workers. If, and only if, all tasks are performed successfully, then output per worker is given by *B*, which is given in value terms (or if thought of in quantity terms, price is normalized to 1). Conventional capital *k* may also be used (if not, simply set $k = 1$), which is introduced in the formula, with diminishing returns (of course, capital might also be of varying quality). Expected output *y* is given by

$$E(y) = K^{\alpha} \left(\prod_{i=1}^{n} q_i \right) nB$$

In general, we must multiply by *n* because otherwise the firm can only lose value by adding more differentiated tasks. In the "O-ring theory," Kremer analyzes what happens when $B = B(n)$, where $B'(n) > 0$, as a way of endogenizing technology choice.

55. For a more formal and more general demonstration that firms would choose to employ workers of the same skill level (or as close to identical as possible), let us continue the example from note 54. A necessary condition for a maximum with respect to each of the labor qualities *q* is

$$dw(q_i)/dq_i \equiv dy/dq_i = \left(\prod_{j \neq i} q_j \right) nBK^{\alpha}$$

This equation tells us that in equilibrium, the value of the marginal product of skill is equal to the marginal cost of skill in wage payments. In other words, the firm finds that the added value of replacing one worker with another with higher skill while leaving the skill levels of all other workers constant is equal to the resulting increase in the wage bill. Next, note that the second derivative, or the derivative of the marginal product of skill for the *i*th worker with respect to the skill level of any other worker, is positive; that is,

$$d^2y/dq_i d\left(\prod_{j \neq i} q_j \right) = nBK^{\alpha} > 0$$

This positive cross-derivative indicates that firms with high-skilled workers in all but one task receive the greatest benefits from having a high-skilled worker in the remaining task, and so they can and would bid the most for high-skilled workers.

56. Technically, this type of marriage market matching process does not depend on the presence of positive cross-derivatives as in note 55 but results only from individual preferences, along with the assumption of nontransferable utility (meaning that there can be no side payments). Thus there are two types of situations in which positive assortative matching may occur.

57. See Michael Kremer and Eric Maskin, "Wage inequality and segregation by skill," NBER Working Paper No. 5718, 1996.

58. See Kremer, "O-ring theory," for a formal statement of this result and for extensions to cases of endogenous skill investments under imperfect information.

59. Kremer, "O-ring theory," p. 574.

60. Hoff and Stiglitz, "Modern economic theory and development."

61. Seminar presentation by Joseph E. Stiglitz at the World Bank, May 27, 1999; and Hoff and Stiglitz, ibid., p. 421.

62. Hoff, Karla, "Beyond Rosenstein-Rodan: The modern theory of coordination problems in development," in *Annual World Bank Conference on Development Economics* (Washington, D.C.: World Bank, 2000), p. 146.

Further Reading

See the readable symposium on new growth theory, in the *Journal of Economic Perspectives* 8 (1994): 3–72, which includes the following four articles: Paul M. Romer, "The origins of endogenous growth"; Gene M. Grossman and Elhanan Helpman, "Endogenous innovation in the theory of growth"; Robert M. Solow, "Perspectives on growth theory"; and Howard Pack, "Endogenous growth theory: Intellectual appeal and empirical shortcomings." Important contributions to endogenous growth theory include Robert B. Lucas, "On the mechanics of economic development," *Journal of Monetary Economics* 22 (1983): 3–42; Paul M. Romer, "Increasing returns and long run growth," *Journal of Political Economy* 94 (1986): 1002–1037; Paul M. Romer, "Idea gaps and object gaps in economic development," *Journal of Monetary Economics* 32 (1993): 543–573; Robert B. Lucas, "Why doesn't capital flow from rich to poor countries?" *American Economic Review* 80 (1990): 92–96; Paul M. Romer, "Are nonconvexities important for understanding economic growth?" *American Economic Review* 80 (1990): 97–103; Robert B. Lucas, "Making a miracle," *Econometrica* 61 (1993): 251–272.

A concise history of the evolution of growth theory is offered in Nicholas Stern, "The determinants of growth," *Economic Journal* 101 (1991): 122–134. See also Pranab Bardhan, "The contributions of endogenous growth theory to the analysis of development problems: An assessment," in *Handbook of Development Economics*, ed. J. Behrman and T. N. Srinivasan (Amsterdam: Elsevier, 1995). A more advanced text is Robert Barro and Xavier Sala-i-Martin, *Economic Growth*, 2nd ed. (Cambridge, Mass.: MIT Press, 2003).

For an excellent review of recent developments in strategic complementarities and multiple equilibria, see Karla Hoff and Joseph E. Stiglitz, "Modern economic theory and development," in *Frontiers in Development Economics*, ed. Gerald M. Meier and Joseph E. Stiglitz (New York: Oxford University Press, 2000). The approach to graphing the big push can be seen in Paul Krugman, *Development, Geography and Economic Theory* (Cambridge, Mass.: MIT Press, 1995). Additional algebraic derivations may be found in Kaushik Basu, *Analytical Development Economics* (Cambridge, Mass.: MIT Press, 1997). Basu also presents an accessible derivation of the O-ring theory proofs. Related material may be found in Pranab Bardhan and Chris Udry, *Development Microeconomics* (New York: Oxford University Press, 1999), ch. 16.

PART TWO

Problems and Policies: Domestic

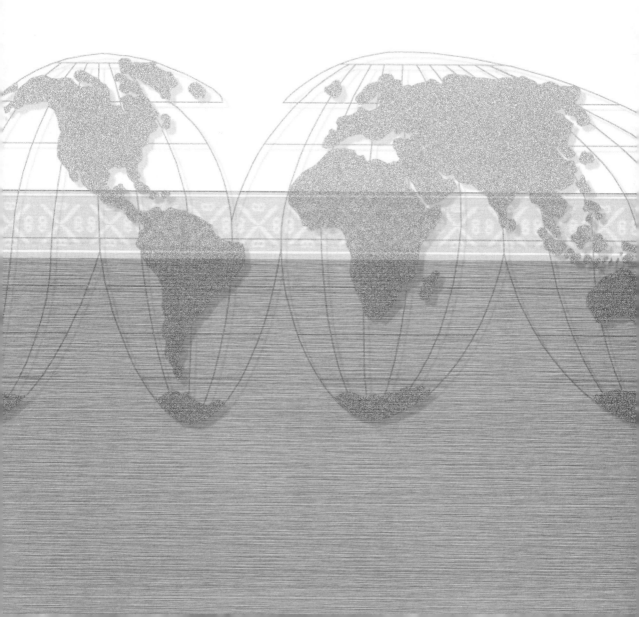

CHAPTER FIVE

Poverty, Inequality, and Development

No society can surely be flourishing and happy, of which by far the greater part of the numbers are poor and miserable.

—Adam Smith, 1776

A society that is not socially just and does not intend to be puts its own future in danger.

—Pope John Paul II, Brazil, 1980

The unfinished business of the twenty-first century is the eradication of poverty.

—Juan Somavia, United Nations World Summit for Social Development, 1995

In Chapters 1 and 2, we saw that despite significant improvements over the past half century, extreme poverty remains widespread in the developing world. More than 1.2 billion people live on less than $1 per day at purchasing power parity, and more than 2.8 billion—almost half the world's population—live on less than $2 a day. As we will see in the next few chapters, these impoverished people often suffer from undernutrition and poor health, have little or no literacy, live in environmentally degraded areas, have little political voice, and attempt to earn a meager living on small and marginal farms or in dilapidated urban slums. In this chapter, we set the stage with an in-depth examination of the problems of poverty and of highly unequal distributions of income.

That development requires a higher GNI and a faster growth rate is obvious. The basic issue, however, is not only how to make GNI grow but also who would make it grow, the few or the many. If it were the rich, it would most likely be appropriated by them, and poverty and inequality would continue to worsen. But if it were generated by the many, they would be its principal beneficiaries, and the fruits of economic growth would be shared more evenly. Thus many developing countries that had experienced relatively high rates of economic growth by historical standards discovered that such growth brought little in the way of significant benefits to their poor.

In September 1994, the Program of Action at the Cairo International Conference on Population and Development asserted that "despite decades of development efforts, both the gap between rich and poor nations and inequalities within nations have widened. . . . Widespread poverty remains the major challenge to development efforts."[1] This view was echoed at the United Nations World Summit for Social Development held in Copenhagen in March 1995 and attended by more than 134 heads of state. The Millennium Declaration in 2000 symbolized the growing commitment to end extreme poverty and gross inequality, as we saw at the end of Chapter 1.

Because the elimination of widespread poverty and high and even growing income inequality are at the core of all development problems and in fact define for many people the principal objective of development policy, we begin Part Two by focusing on the nature of the poverty and inequality problem in developing countries. Although our main focus is on economic poverty and inequalities in the distribution of incomes and assets, it is important to keep in mind that this is only a small part of the broader inequality problem in the developing world. Of equal or even greater importance are inequalities of power, prestige, status, gender, job satisfaction, conditions of work, degree of participation, freedom of choice, and many other dimensions of the problem that relate more to our second and third components of the meaning of development, self-esteem and freedom to choose. But as in most social relationships, we cannot really separate the economic from the noneconomic manifestations of inequality. Each reinforces the other in a complex and often interrelated process of cause and effect.

After introducing appropriate measures of inequality and poverty, we define the nature of the poverty and income distribution problem and consider its quantitative significance in various developing nations. We then set forth possible goals and objectives, examine in what ways economic analyses can shed light on the problem, and finally explore alternative possible policy approaches directed at the elimination of poverty and the reduction of excessively wide disparities in LDC distributions of income. A thorough understanding of these two fundamental economic manifestations of underdevelopment provides the basis for analysis in subsequent chapters of more specific development issues including population growth, rural development, education, international trade, and foreign assistance.

In this chapter, therefore, we will examine the following critical questions about the relationship between economic growth, income distribution, and poverty:

1. What is the extent of relative inequality in developing countries, and how is this related to the extent of absolute poverty?

2. Who are the poor, and what are their economic characteristics?

3. What determines the nature of economic growth—that is, who benefits from economic growth, and why?

4. Are rapid economic growth and more equitable distributions of income compatible or conflicting objectives for low-income countries? To put it another way, is rapid growth achievable only at the cost of greater inequalities in the distribution of income, or can a lessening of income disparities contribute to higher growth rates?

5. Do the poor benefit from growth, and does this depend on the type of growth a developing country experiences? What could be done to help the poor benefit (even more)?

6. What is so bad about high levels of inequality?

7. What kinds of policies are required to reduce the magnitude and extent of absolute poverty?

We begin the chapter by defining *inequality* and *poverty*, terms that are commonly used in informal conversation but need to be measured more precisely to have a meaningful understanding of how much progress has already been made, how much more remains to be achieved, and how to set incentives for government officials to focus on the most pressing needs. We will see that the most important measures of poverty and inequality used by development economists satisfy properties that most would agree are of fundamental importance. After a discussion of why attention to inequality as well as poverty is important, we then use the measures of poverty and inequality that we developed to evaluate the welfare significance of alternative patterns (or "typologies") of growth. After reviewing the evidence on the degrees of poverty and inequality in the developing world, we conclude with an overview of the key issues in poverty policy. Some important principles of effective poverty policies are considered, together with some initial examples of programs that have worked well in practice. We conclude the chapter with a case study of the Grameen Bank of Bangladesh, one of the most acclaimed efforts to bring microfinance and related services to the poor.

Measuring Inequality and Poverty

In this section, we define the dimensions of the income distribution and poverty problems and identify some similar elements that characterize the problem in many developing nations. But first we should be clear about what we are measuring when we speak about the distri-bution of income and absolute poverty.

Measuring Inequality

Economists usually distinguish between two principal measures of income distribution for both analytical and quantitative purposes: the personal or size distribution of income and the functional or distributive factor share distribution of income.

Size Distributions The **personal** or **size distribution of income** is the measure most commonly used by economists. It simply deals with individual persons or households and the total incomes they receive. The way in which that income was received is not considered. What matters is how much each earns irrespective of whether the income was derived solely from employment or came also from other sources such as interest, profits, rents, gifts, or inheritance. Moreover, the locational (urban or rural) and occupational sources of the income (e.g., agriculture, manufacturing, commerce, services) are neglected. If Ms. X and Mr. Y both receive the same personal income, they are classified together irrespective of the fact that Ms. X may work 15 hours a day as a doctor while Mr. Y doesn't work at all but simply collects interest on his inheritance.

Economists and statisticians therefore like to arrange all individuals by ascending personal incomes and then divide the total population into distinct groups, or sizes. A common method is to divide the population into successive **quintiles** (fifths) or **deciles** (tenths) according to ascending income levels and then determine what proportion of the total national income is received by each income group. For example, Table 5.1 shows a hypothetical but fairly typical distribution of income for a developing country. In this table, 20 individuals (or more commonly, households), representing the entire population of the country, are arranged in order of ascending annual personal income, ranging from the individual with the lowest income (0.8 units) to the one with the highest (15.0 units). The total or national income of all individuals amounts to 100 units and is the sum of all entries in column 2. In column 3, the population is grouped into quintiles of four individuals each. The first quintile represents the bottom 20% of the population on the income scale. This group receives only 5% (i.e., a total of 5 money units) of the total national income. The second quintile (individuals 5–8) receives 9% of the total income. Alternatively, the bottom 40% of the population (quintiles 1 plus 2) is receiving only 14% of the income, while the top 20% (the fifth quintile) of the population receives 51% of the total income.

A common measure of income inequality that can be derived from column 3 is the ratio of the incomes received by the top 20% and bottom 40% of the population. This ratio, sometimes called a Kuznets ratio after Nobel laureate Simon Kuznets, is often used as a measure of the degree of inequality between high- and low-income groups in a country. In our example, this inequality ratio is equal to 51 divided by 14, or approximately 3.64.

To provide a more detailed breakdown of the size distribution of income, decile (10%) shares are listed in column 4. We see, for example, that the bottom 10% of the population (the two poorest individuals) receives only 1.8% of the total income, while the top 10% (the two richest individuals) receives 28.5%. Finally, if we wanted to know what the top 5% receives, we would divide the total population into 20 equal groups of individuals (in our example, this would simply be each of the 20 individuals) and calculate the percentage of total income received by the top group. In Table 5.1, we see that the top 5% of the population (the twentieth individual) receives 15% of the income, a higher share than the combined shares of the lowest 40%.

Lorenz Curves Another common way to analyze personal income statistics is to construct what is known as a **Lorenz curve**.[2] Figure 5.1 shows how it is done. The numbers of income recipients are plotted on the horizontal axis, not in absolute terms but in *cumulative percentages*. For example, at point 20 we have the lowest (poorest) 20% of the population, at point 60 we have the bottom 60%, and at the end of the axis all 100% of the population has been accounted for. The vertical axis shows the share of total income received by each percentage of population. It is

| TABLE 5.1 | Typical Size Distribution of Personal Income in a Developing Country by Income Shares—Quintiles and Deciles |

| Individuals | Personal Income (money units) | Percentage Share in Total Income | |
		Quintiles	Deciles
1	0.8		
2	1.0		1.8
3	1.4		
4	1.8	5	3.2
5	1.9		
6	2.0		3.9
7	2.4		
8	2.7	9	5.1
9	2.8		
10	3.0		5.8
11	3.4		
12	3.8	13	7.2
13	4.2		
14	4.8		9.0
15	5.9		
16	7.1	22	13.0
17	10.5		
18	12.0		22.5
19	13.5		
20	15.0	51	28.5
Total (national income)	100.0	100	100.0

Note: Measure of inequality = ratio of top 20% to bottom 40% = 51/14 = 3.64.

also cumulative up to 100%, meaning that both axes are the same length. The entire figure is enclosed in a square, and a diagonal line is drawn from the lower left corner (the origin) of the square to the upper right corner. At every point on that diagonal, the percentage of income received is *exactly equal* to the percentage of income recipients—for example, the point halfway along the length of the diagonal represents 50% of the income being distributed to exactly 50% of the population. At the three-quarter point on the diagonal, 75% of the income would be distributed to 75% of the population. In other words, the diagonal line in Figure 5.1 is representative of "perfect equality" in size distribution of income. Each percentage group of income recipients is receiving that same percentage of the total income; for example, the bottom 40% receives 40% of the income, while the top 5% receives only 5% of the total income.[3]

The Lorenz curve shows the *actual* quantitative relationship between the percentage of income recipients and the percentage of the total income they did in fact receive during, say, a given year. In Figure 5.1, we have plotted this Lorenz curve using the decile data contained in Table 5.1. In other words, we have divided both the horizontal and vertical axes into ten equal segments corresponding to each of the ten decile groups. Point *A* shows that the bottom 10% of the population

FIGURE 5.1   The Lorenz Curve

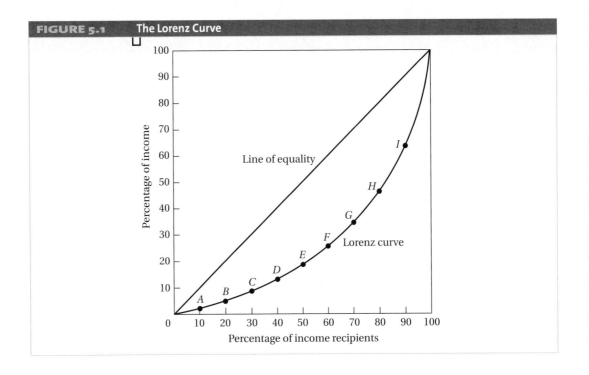

receives only 1.8% of the total income, point *B* shows that the bottom 20% is receiving 5% of the total income, and so on for each of the other eight cumulative decile groups. Note that at the halfway point, 50% of the population is in fact receiving only 19.8% of the total income.

The more the Lorenz line curves away from the diagonal (perfect equality), the greater the degree of inequality represented. The extreme case of perfect inequality (i.e., a situation in which one person receives all of the national income while everybody else receives nothing) would be represented by the congruence of the Lorenz curve with the bottom horizontal and right-hand vertical axes. Because no country exhibits either perfect equality or perfect inequality in its distribution of income, the Lorenz curves for different countries will lie somewhere to the right of the diagonal in Figure 5.1. The greater the degree of inequality, the greater the bend and the closer to the bottom horizontal axis the Lorenz curve will be. Two representative distributions are shown in Figure 5.2, one for a relatively equal distribution (Figure 5.2a) and the other for a more unequal distribution (Figure 5.2b). (Can you explain why the Lorenz curve could not lie above or to the left of the diagonal at any point?)

Gini Coefficients and Aggregate Measures of Inequality A final and very convenient shorthand summary measure of the relative degree of income inequality in a country can be obtained by calculating the ratio of the area between the diagonal and the Lorenz curve divided by the total area of the half-square in which the

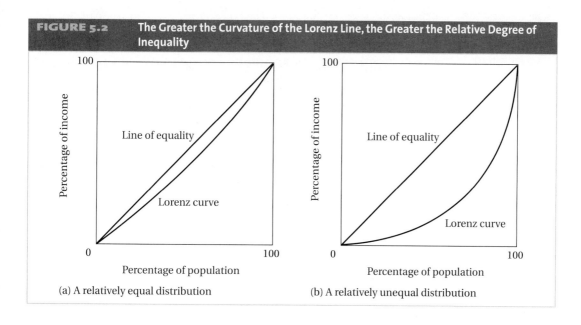

FIGURE 5.2   **The Greater the Curvature of the Lorenz Line, the Greater the Relative Degree of Inequality**

(a) A relatively equal distribution

(b) A relatively unequal distribution

curve lies. In Figure 5.3, this is the ratio of the shaded area *A* to the total area of the triangle *BCD*. This ratio is known as the *Gini concentration ratio* or **Gini coefficient**, named after the Italian statistician who first formulated it in 1912.

Gini coefficients are aggregate inequality measures and can vary anywhere from 0 (perfect equality) to 1 (perfect inequality). In fact, as we shall soon discover, the Gini coefficient for countries with highly unequal income distributions typically lies between 0.50 and 0.70, while for countries with relatively equitable distributions, it is on the order of 0.20 to 0.35. The coefficient for our hypothetical distribution of Table 5.1 and Figure 5.1 is approximately 0.44—a relatively unequal distribution.

Four possible Lorenz curves such as might be found in international data are drawn in Figure 5.4. In the "Lorenz criterion" of income distribution, whenever one Lorenz curve lies above another Lorenz curve, the economy corresponding to the upper Lorenz curve is more equal than that of the lower curve. Thus economy *A* may unambiguously be said to be more equal than economy *D*. Whenever two Lorenz curves cross, such as curves *B* and *C*, the Lorenz criterion states that we "need more information" or additional assumptions before we can determine which of the underlying economies is more equal. For example, we might argue on the grounds of the priority of addressing problems of poverty that curve *B* represents a more equal economy, since the poorest are richer, even though the richest are also richer (and hence the middle class is "squeezed"). But others might start with the assumption that an economy with a stronger middle class is inherently more equal, and that observer might select economy *C*.

One could also use an aggregate measure such as the Gini coefficient to decide the matter. As it turns out, the Gini coefficient is among a class of measures that

FIGURE 5.3 Estimating the Gini Coefficient

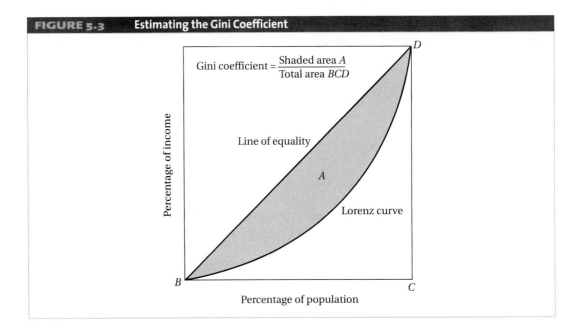

satisfy four highly desirable properties: the anonymity, scale independence, population independence, and transfer principles.[4] The *anonymity principle* simply means that our measure of inequality should not depend on who has the higher income; for example, it should not depend on whether we believe the rich or the poor to be good or bad people. The *scale independence principle* means that our measure of inequality should not depend on the size of the economy or the way we measure its income; for example, our inequality measure should not depend on whether we measure income in dollars or in cents or in rupees or rupiahs or for that matter on whether the economy is rich on average or poor on average—because if we are interested in inequality, we want a measure of the dispersion of income, not its magnitude (note that magnitudes are very important in poverty measures). The *population independence principle* is somewhat similar; it states that the measure of inequality should not be based on the number of income recipients. For example, the economy of China should be considered no more or less equal than the economy of Vietnam simply because China has a larger population than Vietnam. Finally, we have the *transfer principle* (sometimes called the *Pigou-Dalton principle* after its creators); it states that, holding all other incomes constant, if we transfer some income from a richer person to a poorer person (but not so much that the poorer person is now richer than the originally rich person), the resulting new income distribution is more equal. If we like these four criteria, we can measure the Gini coefficient in each case and rank the one with the larger Gini as more unequal. However, this is not always a perfect solution, because the Gini coefficient can, in theory, be identical for two Lorenz curves that cross; can you see why by looking at curves *B* and *C* in Figure 5.4?

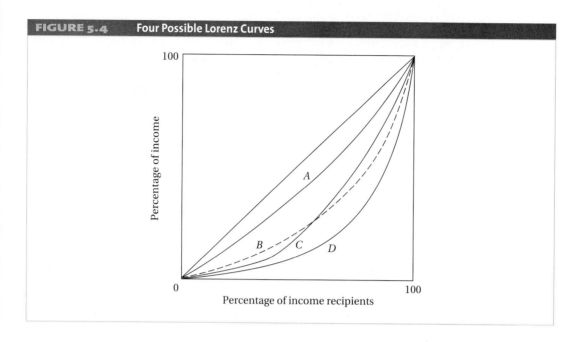

FIGURE 5.4   **Four Possible Lorenz Curves**

Note that a measure of dispersion common in statistics, the coefficient of variation (CV), which is simply the sample standard deviation divided by the sample mean, is another measure of inequality that also satisfies the four criteria. The CV is sometimes used in studies of international convergence of income (see Chapter 2) or convergence of other development indicators such as life expectancy and literacy. Although the CV is more commonly used in statistics, the Gini coefficient is often used in studies of income and wealth distribution due to its convenient Lorenz curve interpretation. Note that we can also use Lorenz curves to study inequality in the distribution of land (as in Chapter 9), in education and health (as in Chapter 8), and in other assets.

Functional Distributions   The second common measure of income distribution used by economists, the **functional** or **factor share distribution of income**, attempts to explain the share of total national income that each of the **factors of production** (land, labor, and capital) receives. Instead of looking at individuals as separate entities, the theory of functional income distribution inquires into the percentage that labor receives as a whole and compares this with the percentages of total income distributed in the form of rent, interest, and profit (i.e., the returns to land and financial and physical capital). Although specific individuals may receive income from all these sources, that is not a matter of concern for the functional approach.

A sizable body of theoretical literature has been built up around the concept of functional income distribution. It attempts to explain the income of a factor of production by the contribution that this factor makes to production. Supply and demand curves are assumed to determine the unit prices of each productive factor. When these unit prices are multiplied by quantities employed on the assumption of efficient (minimum-cost) factor utilization, we get a measure of the total payment to each factor. For example, the supply of and demand for labor are assumed to determine its market wage. When this wage is then multiplied by the total level of employment, we get a measure of total wage payments, also sometimes called the *total wage bill*.

Figure 5.5 provides a simple diagrammatic illustration of the traditional theory of functional income distribution. We assume that there are only two factors of production: capital, which is a fixed (given) factor, and labor, which is the only variable factor. Under competitive market assumptions, the demand for labor will be determined by labor's marginal product (i.e., additional workers will be hired up to the point where the value of their marginal product equals their real wage). But in accordance with the principle of diminishing marginal products, this demand for labor will be a declining function of the numbers employed. Such a negatively sloped labor demand curve is shown by line D_L in Figure 5.5. With a traditional neoclassical upward-sloping labor supply curve S_L, the equilibrium wage will be equal to W_E and the equilibrium level of employment will be L_E. Total national output (which equals total national income) will be represented by the area $0REL_E$.[5] This national income will be distributed in two shares: $0W_EEL_E$ going to workers in the form of wages and W_ERE remaining as capitalist profits (the return to owners of capital). Hence in a competitive market economy with constant-returns-to-scale production functions (a doubling of all inputs doubles output), factor prices are determined by factor supply and demand curves, and factor shares always combine to exhaust the total national product. Income is distributed by function—laborers receive wages, owners of land receive rents, and capitalists obtain profits. It is a neat and logical theory in that each and every factor gets paid only in accordance with what it contributes to national output, no more and no less. In fact, as you may recall from Chapter 3, this model of income distribution is at the core of the Lewis theory of modern-sector growth based on the reinvestment of rising capitalist profits.

Unfortunately, the relevance of the functional theory is greatly diminished by its failure to take into account the important role and influence of nonmarket forces such as power in determining these factor prices—for example, the role of collective bargaining between employers and trade unions in the setting of modern-sector wage rates and the power of monopolists and wealthy landowners to manipulate prices on capital, land, and output to their own personal advantage. Later in this chapter we will have more to say about the relative strengths and weaknesses of the size and functional approaches to analyzing income distribution.

Measuring Absolute Poverty

Now let's switch our attention from relative income shares of various percentile groups within a given population to the arguably more significant question of the extent and magnitude of **absolute poverty** in developing countries. In Chapter 2, we defined the extent of absolute poverty as the number of people who are unable to command sufficient resources to satisfy basic needs. They are counted as the to-

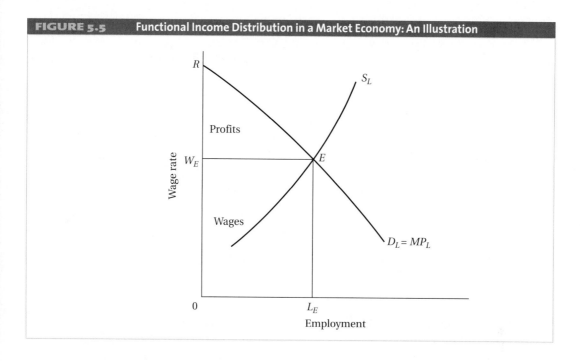

FIGURE 5.5   Functional Income Distribution in a Market Economy: An Illustration

tal number living below a specified minimum level of real income—an international poverty line. That line knows no national boundaries, is independent of the level of national per capita income, and takes into account differing price levels by measuring poverty as anyone living on less than $1 a day or $2 per day in PPP dollars. Absolute poverty can and does exist, therefore, as readily in New York City as it does in Calcutta, Cairo, Lagos, or Bogotá, although its magnitude is likely to be much lower in terms of percentages of the total population.

Absolute poverty may be measured by the number, or "headcount," H, of those whose incomes fall below the absolute poverty line, Y_p. When the headcount is taken as a fraction of the total population, N, we define the **headcount index**, H/N. The poverty line is set at a level that remains constant in real terms so that we can chart our progress on an absolute level over time. The idea is to set this level at a standard below which we would consider a person to live in "absolute human misery," such that one's health is in jeopardy.

Of course, to define a "minimum health standard" that is invariant across historical epochs is an impossibility, in part because technology changes over time. For example, today we have 15-cent oral rehydration therapy packets that can save the life of a child in Malawi. Not many years ago, the death of a child after a diarrheal disease would be taken as a sad but inevitable part of life, whereas today we regard such a death as a catastrophic moral failure of the international community. We simply come as close as we can to establishing a reasonable minimum standard that might hold over a few decades so that we can estimate more carefully how much progress we have made on a (more) absolute rather than a (highly) relative scale.

FIGURE 5.6   Measuring the Total Poverty Gap

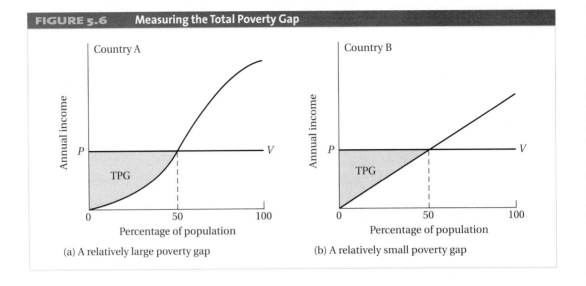

(a) A relatively large poverty gap

(b) A relatively small poverty gap

Certainly one would not accept the international poverty level of $1 per day in an unquestioning way when planning local poverty work. One practical strategy for determining a local absolute poverty line is to start by defining an adequate basket of food, based on nutritional requirements from medical studies of required calories, protein, and micronutrients. Then, using local household survey data, one can identify a typical basket of food purchased by households that just barely meet these nutritional requirements. One then adds other expenditures of this household for basic needs, such as clothing, shelter, and medical care, to determine the local absolute poverty line. Depending on how these calculations are done, the resulting poverty line may come to more than $1 per day at PPP.

In many respects, however, simply counting the number of people below an agreed-on poverty line can have its limitations. For example, if the poverty line is set at U.S. $360 per person, it makes a big difference whether most of the absolute poor earn $350 or $300 per year. Both are accorded the same weight when calculating the proportion of the population that lies below the poverty line; clearly, however, the poverty problem is much more serious in the latter instance. Economists therefore attempt to calculate a **total poverty gap (TPG)** that measures the total amount of income necessary to raise everyone who is below the poverty line up to that line. Figure 5.6 illustrates how we could measure the total poverty gap as the shaded area between poverty line, PV, and the annual income profile of the population.

Even though in both country A and country B, 50% of the population falls below the same poverty line, the TPG in country A is greater than in country B. Therefore, it will take more of an effort to eliminate absolute poverty in country A.

The TPG—the extent to which the incomes of the poor lie below the poverty line—is found by adding up the amounts by which each poor person's income, Y_i, falls below the absolute poverty line, Y_p, as follows:

$$TPG = \sum_{i=1}^{H} (Y_p - Y_i) \tag{5.1}$$

We can think of the TPG in a simplified way (i.e., no administrative costs or general equilibrium effects are accounted for) as the amount of money per day it would take to bring every poor person in an economy up to our defined minimum income standards. On a per capita basis, the *average poverty gap* (APG) is found by dividing the TPG by the total population:

$$APG = TPG / N \tag{5.2}$$

Often we are interested in the size of the poverty gap in relation to the poverty line, so that we would use as our income shortfall measure the *normalized poverty gap*: (NPG) = APG/Y_p; this measure lies between 0 and 1 and so can be useful when we want a unitless measure of the gap for better comparisons across countries or across time.

Another important poverty gap measure is the *average income shortfall* (AIS), which is the total poverty gap divided by the headcount of the poor: AIS = TPG/H. The AIS tells us the average amount by which the income of a poor person falls below the poverty line. This measure can also be divided by the poverty line to yield a fractional measure, the *normalized income shortfall* (NIS): NIS = AIS/Y_p.

The Foster-Greer-Thorbecke Measure   We are also often interested in the degree of income inequality among the poor, such as the Gini coefficient among those who are poor, G_p, or alternatively, the coefficient of variation (CV) of incomes among the poor, CV_p. The Gini or CV among the poor can be important because the impact on poverty of economic shocks can differ greatly, depending on the level and distribution of resources among those who are poor. For example, if the price of rice rises, as it did in 1998 in Indonesia, low-income rice producers, who sell a little of their rice on local markets and whose incomes are below, but not too far below, the absolute poverty line, may find that this price rise increases their incomes to bring them out of absolute poverty. On the other hand, for those with too little land to be able to sell any of the rice they grow and who are net buyers of rice on markets, this price increase can greatly worsen their poverty. Thus the most desirable measures of poverty would also be sensitive to the distribution of income among the poor.

As was the case with inequality measures, there are criteria for a desirable poverty measure that are widely accepted by development economists: the anonymity, population independence, monotonicity, and distributional sensitivity principles. The first two principles are very similar to the properties we examined for inequality indexes: Our measure of the extent of poverty should not depend on who is poor or on whether the country has a large or small population. The monotonicity principle means that if you add income to someone below the poverty line, all other incomes held constant, poverty can be *no higher* than it was.[6] The distributional sensitivity principle states that, other things being equal, if you transfer income from a poor person to a richer person, the resulting economy should be deemed strictly poorer. The headcount ratio measure satisfies anonymity, population independence, and monotonicity, but it fails on distributional sensitivity. The simple headcount fails even to satisfy the population independence principle.

Two well-known poverty indexes that satisfy all four criteria are the Sen index and certain forms of the **Foster-Greer-Thorbecke (FGT) index**, often called the P_α class of poverty measures.[7] The P_α index is given by

$$P_\alpha = \frac{1}{N} \sum_{i=1}^{H} \left(\frac{Y_p - Y_i}{Y_p} \right)^\alpha \tag{5.3}$$

where Y_i is the income of the ith poor person, Y_p is the poverty line, and N is the population. Depending on the value of α, the P_α index takes on different forms. If $\alpha = 0$, the numerator is equal to H, and we get the headcount ratio, H/N. If $\alpha = 1$, we get the normalized poverty gap.

If $\alpha = 2$, the impact on measured poverty of a gain in income by a poor person increases in proportion to the distance of the person from the poverty line. For example, raising the income of a person from a household living at half the per capita poverty line by, say, one penny per day would have five times the impact on poverty reduction as would raising by the same amount the income of a person living at 90% of the poverty line.

If $\alpha = 2$, the resulting measure, P_2, can be rewritten as

$$P_2 = (H/N)[\text{NIS}^2 + (1 - \text{NIS})^2 \, (\text{CV}_p)^2] \tag{5.4}$$

As equation 5.4 shows, P_2 contains the CV_P measure, and it satisfies all four of the poverty axioms.[8] Clearly, P_2 increases whenever H/N, NIS, or CV_P increases. Note from the formula that there is a greater emphasis on the distribution of income among the poor (CV_p) when the normalized income shortfall is small and a smaller emphasis when the NIS is large.

The P_2 measure is increasingly used as a standard poverty measure by the World Bank, the regional development banks, and most UN agencies, and it is used in most empirical work on poverty because of its sensitivity to the depth and severity of poverty. For the same reason, the P_2 measure has now become part of the Mexican constitution (Chapter V, Article 34). Mexico uses the P_2 poverty measure to allocate funds for education, health, and welfare programs for the poor (in particular in the Progresa program, described at the end of Chapter 8), in accordance with the regional intensity of poverty.[9]

Values of P_0 and P_2 for selected developing countries are found in Table 5.4 later in this chapter.

The Human Poverty Index One final measure of poverty that was introduced by the United Nations Development Program (UNDP) in its 1997 *Human Development Report* demands our attention.[10] Not satisfied with the dollar-a-day World Bank income measures, the UNDP sought to substitute a measure of "human" poverty for the Bank's "income" poverty. It therefore constructed the **Human Poverty Index (HPI)**, analogous in many ways to its Human Development Index (HDI), discussed in Chapter 2. The UNDP argued that human poverty should be measured in terms of three key deprivations—of *life* (over 30% of people in the least developed countries are unlikely to live beyond 40 years of age), of *basic education* (as measured by the percentage of adults who are illiterate), and of overall *economic provisioning* (measured by the percentage of people without access to health services and safe water plus the percentage of children under 5 who are underweight). Using a formula to calculate the HPI for 95 developing countries, the 2004 report ranked these countries from lowest to highest HPI and found that these rankings could differ substantially from both the World Bank's income poverty rankings and the UNDP's own HDI rankings. Since the HPI value indicates the proportion of the population adversely affected by the three key deprivations (survival, knowledge, and economic provisions), a low HPI is good (i.e., a smaller percentage of the population is deprived), and a higher HPI is reflective of greater deprivation.

Consider some striking examples from the 2004 *Human Development Report's* rankings for these 95 developing countries: Côte d'Ivoire ranked 24 places higher (worse) in the country rankings based on income poverty than on human poverty; Morocco ranked 36 places higher; Algeria, 30 higher; and Yemen, 15 higher. The implication is that poverty is worse in these countries than standard headcount ratio measures pick up. In contrast, some of the countries that perform better with the human poverty ranking include Nigeria (27 places lower), Ghana (23 lower), Venezuela (20 lower), and Honduras (17 lower). According to the UNDP approach, these countries are performing better in the eradication of poverty than the headcount ratio measures would suggest. Of course, measures that account for the intensity as well as average level of poverty (such as P_2) also help make adjustments to the income measures that may have analogous effects.

A final approach to accounting for the distribution of income in assessing the quality of growth is to value increases in income for all individuals, but to assign a higher weight to income gains by lower-income individuals than to gains by higher-income individuals. Perhaps the best known example is the Ahluwalia-Chenery Welfare Index, which is explained in Appendix 5.2.

Poverty, Inequality, and Social Welfare

What's So Bad about High Inequality?

Throughout this chapter, we are assuming that social welfare depends positively on the level of income per capita but negatively on poverty and negatively on the level of inequality, as these terms have just been defined. The problem of absolute poverty is obvious. No civilized people can feel satisfied with a state of affairs in which their fellow humans exist in conditions of such absolute human misery, which is probably why every major religion has emphasized the importance of working to alleviate poverty and is at least one of the reasons why international development assistance has the universal support of every democratic nation. But it may reasonably be asked, if our top priority is the alleviation of absolute poverty, why should *relative inequality* be a concern? We have seen that inequality among the poor is a critical factor in understanding the depth of poverty and the impact of market and policy changes on the poor, but why should we be concerned with inequality among those *above* the poverty line?

There are three major answers to this question. First, extreme income inequality leads to economic inefficiency. This is partly because at any given average income, the higher the inequality, the smaller the fraction of the population that qualifies for a loan or other credit. Indeed, one definition of *relative poverty* is the lack of collateral. When low-income individuals (whether they are absolutely poor or not) cannot borrow money, they generally cannot adequately educate their children or start and expand a business. Moreover, with high inequality, the overall rate of saving in the economy tends to be lower, because the highest rate of marginal savings is usually found among the middle classes. Although the rich may save a larger dollar amount, they typically save a smaller fraction of their incomes, and they certainly save a smaller fraction of their marginal incomes. Landlords, business leaders, politicians, and other rich elites are known to spend much of their incomes on imported luxury goods, gold, jewelry, expensive houses, and foreign travel or to seek safe havens abroad for their savings in what is known as capital flight.[11] Such savings and investments do not add to the nation's productive resources; in fact, they represent substantial drains on these resources. In short, the rich do not generally save and invest significantly larger proportions of their incomes (in the real economic sense of productive domestic saving and investment) than the middle class or even the poor.[12] Furthermore, inequality may lead to an inefficient allocation of assets. As we will see in Chapter 8, high inequality leads to an overemphasis on higher education at the expense of quality universal primary education, and this in turn begets still more inequality in incomes. Moreover, as we will see in Chapter 9, high inequality of land ownership—characterized by the presence of huge *latifundios* (plantations) alongside tiny *minifundios* that are incapable of supporting even a single family—also leads to inefficiency, because the most efficient scales for farming are family and medium-size farms. The result of these factors can be a lower average income and a lower rate of economic growth when inequality is high.[13]

The second reason to be concerned with inequality among those above the poverty line is that extreme income disparities undermine social stability and solidarity. Worse, high inequality strengthens the political power of the rich, as well as their economic bargaining power. Usually this power will be used to encourage outcomes favorable to themselves. High inequality facilitates "rent seeking," including actions such as excessive lobbying, large political donations, bribery, and cronyism. When resources are allocated to such rent-seeking behaviors, they are diverted from productive purposes that could lead to faster growth, Of course, high inequality may also lead the poor to support populist policies that can be self-defeating. Countries with extreme inequality, such as El Salvador and Iran, have undergone upheavals or extended civil strife that have cost countless lives and set back development progress by decades. In sum, with high inequality, the focus of politics often tends to be on the redistribution of the existing economic pie rather than on policies to increase its size (Chapter 11 examines these concerns in more detail).

Finally, extreme inequality is generally viewed as unfair. The philosopher John Rawls proposed a thought experiment to help clarify why this is so.[14] Suppose that before you were born into this world, you had a chance to select the overall level of inequality among the earth's people—but not your own identity. That is, you might be born as Bill Gates, but you might be born as the most wretchedly poor person in rural Ethiopia with equal probability. Rawls calls this uncertainty the "veil of ignorance." The question is, facing this kind of risk, would you vote for an income distribution that was more equal or less equal than the one you see around you? If the degree of equality had no effect on the level of income or rate of growth, most people would vote for nearly perfect equality. Of course, if everyone had the same income no matter what, there would be little incentive to work hard, gain skills, or innovate. As a result, most people vote for *some* inequality of income outcomes, to the extent that these correspond to incentives for hard work or innovation. But even so, most vote for *less* inequality than seen in the world (or in virtually any country) today. This is because much of the inequality we observe in the world is based on luck or extraneous factors, such as inborn ability to kick a football, or simply the identity of one's great-grandparents.

For all of these reasons, for this part of the analysis we will write welfare, W, as

$$W = W(Y, I, P) \qquad (5.5)$$

where Y is income per capita and enters our welfare function positively, I is inequality and enters negatively, and P is absolute poverty and also enters negatively. These three components have distinct significance, and we need to consider all three elements to achieve an overall assessment of welfare in developing countries.

Dualistic Development and Shifting Lorenz Curves: Some Stylized Typologies

In his classic book *Poverty, Inequality and Development,* Gary Fields demonstrates how Lorenz curves can be used to analyze three limiting cases of dualistic development.[15] He distinguishes among three stylized development typologies:

1. The *modern-sector enlargement* growth typology, in which the two-sector economy develops by enlarging the size of its modern sector while maintaining constant wages in both sectors. This is the case depicted by the Lewis model in Chapter 3. It corresponds roughly to the historical growth pattern of Western developed nations and, to a lesser extent, the pattern in countries like South Korea and Taiwan.

2. The *modern-sector enrichment* growth typology, in which the economy grows but such growth is limited to a fixed number of people in the modern sector, with both the numbers of workers and their wages held constant in the traditional sector. This roughly describes the experience of many Latin American and African economies.

3. The *traditional-sector enrichment* growth typology, in which all of the benefits of growth are divided among traditional-sector workers, with little or no growth occurring in the modern sector. This process roughly describes the experiences of countries whose policies focused on achieving substantial reductions in absolute poverty even at very low incomes and with relatively low

FIGURE 5.7   **Improved Income Distribution under the Traditional-Sector Enrichment Growth Typology**

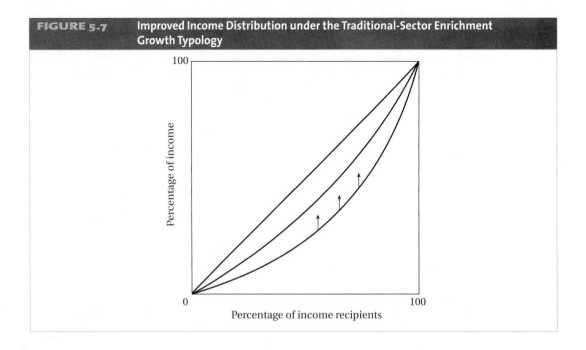

growth rates, such as Sri Lanka in the 1960s and 1970s and other regions such as the state of Kerala in southwest India.

Using these three special cases and Lorenz curves, Fields is able to demonstrate the validity of the following propositions (reversing the order just presented):

1. In the *traditional-sector enrichment* typology, growth results in higher income, a *more equal* relative distribution of income, and less poverty. Traditional-sector enrichment growth causes the Lorenz curve to shift uniformly upward and closer toward the line of equality, as portrayed in Figure 5.7.

2. In the *modern-sector enrichment* growth typology, growth results in higher incomes, a *less equal* relative distribution of income, and no change in poverty. Modern-sector enrichment growth causes the Lorenz curve to shift downward and farther from the line of equality, as shown in Figure 5.8.

3. Finally, in the case of Lewis-type *modern-sector enlargement* growth, absolute incomes rise and absolute poverty is reduced, but the Lorenz curves will always cross so that we cannot make any unambiguous statement about changes in relative inequality. It may improve or worsen. Fields shows that in fact, if this style of growth experience is predominant, inequality is likely first to worsen in the early stages of development and then to improve. The crossing of the Lorenz curves is demonstrated in Figure 5.9.

The explanation for the crossing in Figure 5.9 is as follows: The poor who remain in the traditional sector have their incomes unchanged, but these incomes

FIGURE 5.8   Worsened Income Distribution under the Modern-Sector Enrichment Growth Typology

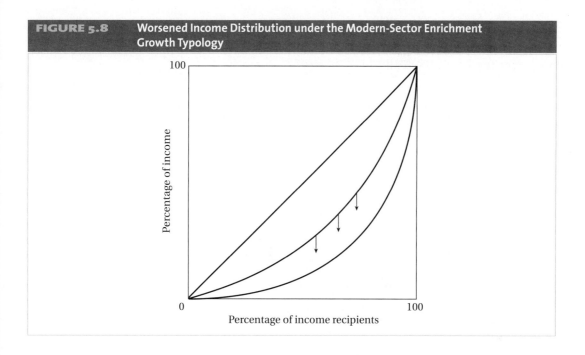

are now a smaller fraction of the larger total, so that the new Lorenz curve, L_2, lies below the old Lorenz curve, L_1, at the lower end of the income distribution scale. Each modern-sector worker receives the same absolute income as before, but now the share received by the richest income group is smaller, so the new Lorenz curve lies *above* the old one at the higher end of the income distribution scale. Therefore, somewhere in the middle of the distribution, the old and new Lorenz curves must cross.[16]

These three typologies offer different predictions about what will happen to inequality in the course of economic growth. With modern-sector enrichment, inequality would rise steadily, while under traditional-sector enrichment, inequality would fall steadily. Under modern-sector enlargement, inequality would first rise and then fall.[17] If this admittedly highly stylized process of development were occurring, we would not be concerned about the temporary rise in inequality because in addition to being temporary, it would be reflecting a process in which citizens are, one by one, achieving incomes above the absolute poverty line.[18]

These observations tell us that we have to qualify our conclusion that inequality is bad. In particular, in some cases inequality may increase on a temporary basis due to causes that will eventually make everyone better off and ultimately lower inequality. On the other hand, with modern-sector enrichment growth, the increase in inequality is not later reversed, and the poor do not escape their poverty.[19] As a result, we need to be careful about drawing conclusions from short-run changes in economic statistics before we know more about the underlying changes in the real economy that gave rise to these statistics. The process of mod-

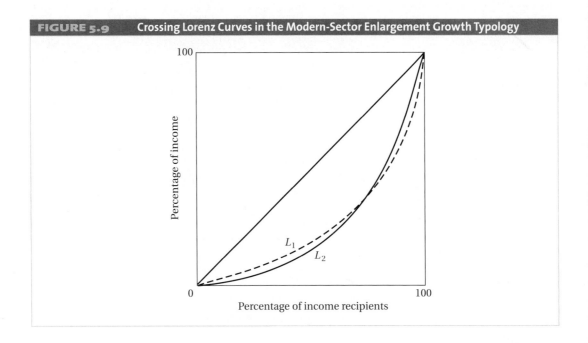

FIGURE 5.9 Crossing Lorenz Curves in the Modern-Sector Enlargement Growth Typology

ern-sector enlargement growth suggests a possible mechanism that could give rise to Kuznets's "inverted-U" hypothesis, so we turn to this question next.

Kuznets's Inverted-U Hypothesis

Simon Kuznets suggested that in the early stages of economic growth, the distribution of income will tend to worsen; only at later stages it will improve.[20] This observation came to be characterized by the "inverted-U" **Kuznets curve** because a longitudinal (time-series) plot of changes in the distribution of income—as measured, for example, by the Gini coefficient—seemed, when per capita GNI expanded, to trace out an inverted U-shaped curve in some of the cases Kuznets studied, as illustrated in Figure 5.10.

Explanations as to why inequality might worsen during the early stages of economic growth before eventually improving are numerous. They almost always relate to the nature of structural change. Early growth may, in accordance with the Lewis model, be concentrated in the modern industrial sector, where employment is limited but wages and productivity are high.

As we have just seen, the Kuznets curve could be generated by a steady process of modern-sector enlargement growth, as a country develops from a traditional to a modern economy. Alternatively, returns to education may first rise as the emerging modern sector demands skills and then fall as the supply of educated workers increases and the supply of unskilled workers falls. So while Kuznets did not specify the mechanism by which his inverted-U hypothesis was supposed to occur, it

FIGURE 5.10   The "Inverted-U" Kuznets Curve

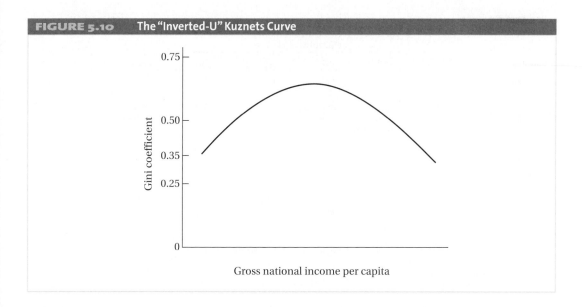

could in principle be consistent with a sequential process of economic development. But as we have seen, traditional- and modern-sector enrichment would tend to pull inequality in opposing directions, so the net change in inequality is ambiguous, and the validity of the Kuznets curve remains an empirical question.

Disregarding the merits of the methodological debate, few development economists would argue that the Kuznets sequence of increasing and then declining inequality is inevitable. There are now enough case studies and specific examples of countries such as Taiwan, South Korea, Costa Rica, and Sri Lanka to demonstrate that higher income levels can be accompanied by falling and not rising inequality. It all depends, as we shall see, on the nature of the development process.

Evidence on the Inverted-U Hypothesis Let us look at data collected from 15 countries on the percentage shares in total national income going to different percentile groups (see Table 5.2). Though methods of collection, degree of coverage, and specific definitions of personal income may vary from country to country, the figures recorded in Table 5.2 give a first approximation of the magnitude of **income inequality** in these developing countries. For example, we see from the last row that in Zambia, the poorest 20% (first quintile) of the population receives only 3.3% of the income, while the highest 10% and 20% (fifth quintile) receive 41.0% and 56.6%, respectively. By contrast, in a developed country like Japan, the poorest 20% receives a much higher 8.7% of the income while the richest 10% and 20% get only 22.4% and 37.5%, respectively.

Consider now the relationship, if any, between levels of per capita income and degree of inequality. Are higher incomes associated with greater or lesser inequality, or can no definitive statement be made? Table 5.3 provides data on income

TABLE 5.2	Some Income Distribution Estimates, Late 1990s and Early 2000s						
	Quintile						
Country	1st	2nd	3rd	4th	5th	Highest 10%	Year
Bangladesh	9.0	12.5	15.9	21.2	41.3	25.4	2000
Botswana	2.2	4.9	8.2	14.4	70.3	56.6	1993
Brazil	2.0	5.7	10.0	18.0	64.4	46.7	1998
Colombia	2.7	6.6	10.8	18.0	61.9	46.5	1999
Costa Rica	4.2	8.9	13.7	21.7	51.5	34.8	2000
Ghana	5.6	10.1	14.9	22.8	46.6	30.0	1999
Guatemala	2.6	5.9	9.8	17.6	64.1	48.3	2000
Honduras	2.7	6.7	11.8	19.9	58.9	42.2	1999
India	8.9	12.3	16.0	21.2	41.6	27.4	2000
Jamaica	6.7	10.7	15.0	21.7	46.0	30.3	2000
Pakistan	8.8	12.5	15.9	20.6	42.3	28.3	1999
Peru	2.9	8.3	14.1	21.5	53.2	37.2	2000
Philippines	5.4	8.8	13.1	20.5	52.3	36.3	2000
South Africa	2.0	4.3	8.3	18.9	66.5	46.9	1995
Zambia	3.3	7.6	12.5	20.0	56.6	41.0	1998

Source: World Bank, *World Development Indicators, 2004* (Washington, D.C., World Bank, 2004), tab. 2.7, pp. 60–62. Copyright © 2004 by the World Bank. Reprinted with the permission of the World Bank via the Copyright Clearance Center.

distribution in relation to per capita GNI for a sample of ten developing countries. Income distribution is measured in three ways: as the total share of income received by the poorest 40% of the population, as the ratio of the share going to the richest 20% divided by that of the poorest 20%, and as measured by the Gini coefficient. The countries are arranged from lowest to highest in terms of 2002 per capita income.

What clearly emerges from Table 5.3 is that per capita incomes are not highly correlated with any of our three measures of inequality. For example, Bangladesh

TABLE 5.3	Per Capita Income and Inequality in Developing Countries, 1990–2000s		
Country	GNI Per Capita 2002 (U.S. $)	Income Share of Lowest 40% of Households	Ratio of Highest 20% to Lowest 20%	Gini Coefficient
Kenya	360	14.9	9.1	0.45
Bangladesh	380	21.5	4.6	0.32
Indonesia	710	20.3	5.2	0.34
Sri Lanka	850	19.8	5.4	0.34
Philippines	1,030	14.2	9.7	0.46
Paraguay	1,170	8.7	27.4	0.38
Jamaica	2,690	17.4	6.7	0.38
Brazil	2,830	7.7	32.2	0.59
Malaysia	3,540	12.5	12.3	0.49
Costa Rica	4,070	13.1	12.3	0.47

Source: World Bank, *World Development Indicators, 2004* (Washington, D.C.: World Bank, 2004), tabs. 1.1 and 2.7, pp. 14, 60. Copyright © 2004 by the World Bank. Reprinted with the permission of the World Bank via the Copyright Clearance Center.

and Kenya have about the same (low) level of income, but Kenya is much more un-equal. Among middle-income countries, a similar observation holds for Jamaica and Brazil. We can therefore conclude that there is no strong relationship between levels of per capita income and the degree of income concentration over a rele-vant range of LDC incomes. But although inequality is not highly correlated with per capita income, there may still be a slight nonlinear correlation, as the in-verted-U hypothesis suggests, when high-income countries are also considered.

For years, the validity of the Kuznets curve has been controversial. In the cross-section work, it is commonly noted that many of the middle-income countries are found in Latin America, the region that traditionally has the highest average level of inequality in the world. Could the Kuznets curve that is seen in the data be a mere statistical fluke resulting from the fact that for extraneous historical reasons, most Latin American countries just happened to have both a middle level of in-come and a high level of inequality? And could a combination of both cross-sectional and longitudinal (time-series) data help resolve the question? Gary Fields and George Jakubson undertook to examine just this question. Figure 5.11 plots a combination of data from the 35 countries in Fields and Jakubson's data set, where reliable estimates of the Gini coefficient have been available for various developing countries at different points in time. The inverted-U relationship, tracing the trian-gles, is a computer-generated parabola that best fits the data under standard statis-tical criteria. Observations on Latin American countries are circled: All of the high-est-inequality countries in their data come from that region. Statistically, when the Latin American identity of the country is controlled for, the inverted-U drawn in Figure 5.11 tends to disappear in this data set and others as well.[21]

So, the question is, what happens over time? In Figure 5.12, selected countries from the data in Figure 5.11 have been isolated. As can be seen, only the data from Brazil, which have the label *1* in the diagram, plainly show an inverted-U pattern. Data from Hong Kong and Singapore, in contrast, labeled *4* and *5* in the diagram, appear to reflect a U-pattern. But when these separate experiences are merged into one picture, the eyes (and the computer) misleadingly trace an inverted-U in the data taken as a whole. This reinforces the great importance of understanding what gives rise to the statistical patterns in the data rather than taking them at face value. Detailed longitudinal studies of developing countries similarly show a very mixed pattern. Juan Luis Lonondro found an inverted-U for Colombia, but Harry Oshima found no particular pattern among several Asian countries.[22]

As a result of this work, the dominating influence of the "Latin America effect" has been confirmed. In fact, for many countries there is no particular tendency for inequality to change much at all in the process of economic development. In-equality seems to be a rather stable part of a country's socioeconomic makeup, al-tered significantly only as a result of a substantial upheaval. East Asia achieved its relatively low inequality largely from exogenous forces: the U.S. occupation of Japan, the Nationalist takeover of Taiwan, and the expulsion of the Japanese in South Korea. China's low inequality resulted from a social revolution and resis-tance to the Japanese invasion, which resulted in the Communist takeover of 1949. In all four cases, thoroughgoing land reform was implemented that had far-reaching effects on inequality (we return to these events when we examine land reform in Chapter 9).

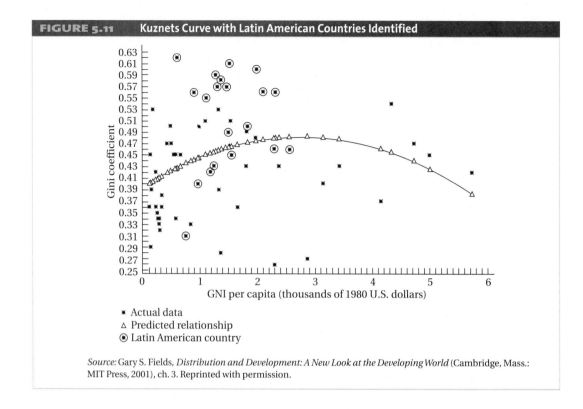

FIGURE 5.11 Kuznets Curve with Latin American Countries Identified

* Actual data
△ Predicted relationship
⊛ Latin American country

Source: Gary S. Fields, *Distribution and Development: A New Look at the Developing World* (Cambridge, Mass.: MIT Press, 2001), ch. 3. Reprinted with permission.

Growth and Inequality

Having examined the relationship between inequality and levels of per capita income, let us look now at the relationship, if any, between economic growth and inequality. In Figure 5.13, we have plotted rates of growth of GNI for 13 developing countries on the horizontal axis and the growth rate of income of the lowest 40% of their population along the vertical axis. The data are for the time span shown in parentheses after each country, and the scatter is intended to reveal any obvious relationships between GNI growth rates and improvements in relative income levels for the poor. Each country's data, therefore, are plotted in the figure at a point reflecting its combination of GNI growth and the income growth of the lowest 40% of its population. Countries above the 45-degree line are those where the distribution of income improved—that is, the incomes of the bottom 40% grew faster than the overall GNI growth rate—whereas countries below the 45-degree line experienced a worsening of their income distributions over the indicated period.

The scatter of points in Figure 5.13 does not reveal any strong or obvious relationship between GNI growth and the distribution of income.[23] High growth rates do not necessarily worsen the distribution of income, as some observers have suggested. Indeed, countries like Taiwan and South Korea experienced relatively high rates of GNI growth and exhibited improved or at least unchanged distributions of income. Nevertheless, countries like Mexico and Panama grew just as fast but ex-

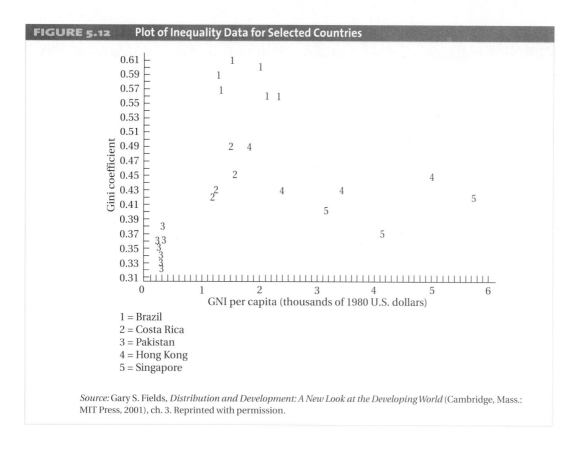

FIGURE 5.12   Plot of Inequality Data for Selected Countries

1 = Brazil
2 = Costa Rica
3 = Pakistan
4 = Hong Kong
5 = Singapore

Source: Gary S. Fields, *Distribution and Development: A New Look at the Developing World* (Cambridge, Mass.: MIT Press, 2001), ch. 3. Reprinted with permission.

perienced a deterioration of their income distribution. However, there does not seem to be a necessary relationship between low GNI growth and improved income distribution. In developing countries like India, Peru, and the Philippines, low rates of GNI growth appear to have been accompanied by a deterioration of the relative income shares of the bottom 40%. And yet Sri Lanka, Colombia, Costa Rica, and El Salvador, with similarly low GNI growth rates, managed to improve the relative economic well-being of their low-income populations. Note that in all cases, the poor did share in some of the benefits of economic growth even though there is no direct, positive relationship between rate of growth and degree of improvement.

Figure 5.14 provides long-run data covering the mid-1960s and the mid-1990s. It also shows that inequality, as measured by Gini coefficients, seems unrelated to aggregate GNI per capita growth rates. During these periods, per capita growth in East Asia averaged 5.5% while that of Africa declined by 0.2%, yet both Gini coefficients remained essentially unchanged. The data from Figures 5.13 and 5.14 suggest once again that it is the **character of economic growth** (how it is achieved, who participates, which sectors are given priority, what institutional arrangements are designed and emphasized, etc.) that determines the degree to which

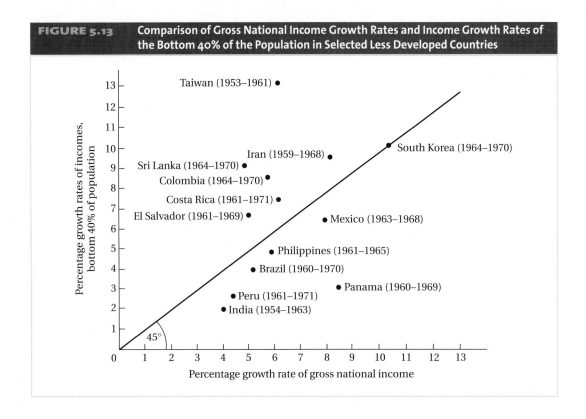

FIGURE 5.13   Comparison of Gross National Income Growth Rates and Income Growth Rates of the Bottom 40% of the Population in Selected Less Developed Countries

that growth is or is not reflected in improved living standards for the very poor. It is not the mere fact of rapid growth per se that determines the nature of its distributional benefits.

Absolute Poverty: Extent and Magnitude

Like so much in economic development, the critical problem of eradicating absolute poverty is one of bad news and good news—of a glass that may be seen as either half empty or half full. Look back at Table 2.7 in Chapter 2, which shows that the number of the absolutely poor barely changed at all between 1987 and 1998 but actually rose slightly from 1.183 billion to 1.199 billion people, using the headcount measure. But as we have seen, the headcount is an imperfect measure; the headcount ratio is better, at least in that it satisfies the population independence principle. Using this measure, it becomes clear that some progress has been made: While 28.3% of the world's population was absolutely poor in 1987, this ratio had fallen to 24.0% by 1998. This was an impressive achievement, because the world's population increased by nearly a billion people during this period—from a population of just over 5 billion to just under 6 billion—and virtually all of that increase occurred

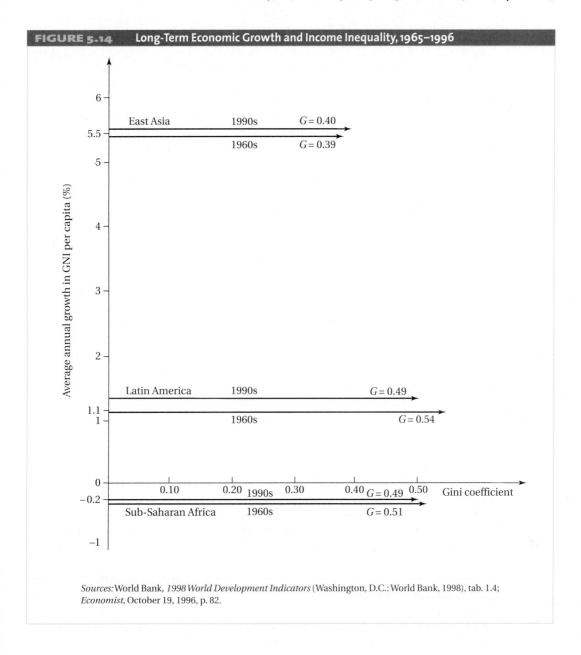

FIGURE 5.14   Long-Term Economic Growth and Income Inequality, 1965–1996

Sources: World Bank, *1998 World Development Indicators* (Washington, D.C.: World Bank, 1998), tab. 1.4; *Economist,* October 19, 1996, p. 82.

in the developing world, much of that in the low-income countries where poverty is concentrated.

Table 2.7 also shows that significant gains were made in East Asia, where the headcount fell from 417.5 million to 278.3 million during this 11-year period, which corresponded to an impressive drop in the headcount ratio from 26.6% to 15.3%. Gains were substantial whether or not China, with its large population and low income but very rapid growth, was included in the totals. Notable gains were also made in the Middle East and North Africa. But elsewhere the picture was not as encouraging. Although the headcount ratio in South Asia declined from 44.9% to 40.0%, population growth continued at a rapid enough pace that the number of people in absolute poverty rose—from 474.4 million to 522.0 million—meaning that more poor people live in South Asia than anywhere else in the world. In sub-Saharan Africa, absolute poverty increased substantially, from 217.2 million people to 290.9 million; although there was essentially no change in the headcount ratio, at over 46% this incidence is the highest in the world, and current projections actually anticipate an increase in the incidence of poverty in the region to over 50% in coming years. Finally, absolute poverty increased from a minuscule 0.2% of the population in Europe and Central Asia to a worrying 5.1% in the aftermath of the breakup of the Soviet Union and the difficult transition period that followed. Figure 5.15 provides a visual picture of where poverty has fallen and where it has not. The result of these different experiences with changes in absolute poverty has been a shift in the location of the poor, away from East Asia and toward sub-Saharan Africa and South Asia as well as Europe and Central Asia, as clearly seen in Figure 5.16.

It should also be noted that the normalized poverty gap tends to be worse in sub-Saharan Africa, where the share in poverty is stable or rising, than in South Asia, where it is falling. For example, in the three large South Asian countries, we find that for India, the NPG at the $1-per-day poverty line is 8.2%; in Bangladesh, 8.1%; and in Pakistan, 2.4%. But the poverty gap in some significant African countries is much larger, such as in Nigeria at 34.9%; in Madagascar, 18.3%; in Mali, 37.4%; and in Zambia, 32.7%. Table 5.4 shows the population, the percentages in poverty at the $1 and $2 poverty lines, and the NPG for the most recently available data for selected countries. Note the far greater extent and depth of poverty when the $2-per-day poverty line is used.

Most current projections call for the number of persons living in poverty to rise over the current decade before declining throughout the rest of the century, hopefully to be banished forever by century's end. This outcome depends critically on two factors: first, the rate of economic growth—provided it is undertaken in a sustainable way—and second, the level of resources devoted to poverty programs and the quality of those programs. The world's leaders have committed to the very achievable Millennium Development Goal of halving poverty by 2015 (see Chapter 1). Indeed, rapid high-quality and sustainable growth and timely, well-designed poverty programs could reduce absolute poverty even more quickly; without these two factors, however, the goal could be missed by a wide mark. Let us consider each of these dimensions in turn.

Growth and Poverty

Are the reduction of poverty and the acceleration of growth in conflict? Or are they complementary? Traditionally, a body of opinion held that rapid growth is bad for the poor, because they would be bypassed and marginalized by the structural changes of modern growth. Beyond this, there had been considerable concern in

FIGURE 5.15   Where Poverty Has Fallen and Where It Has Not

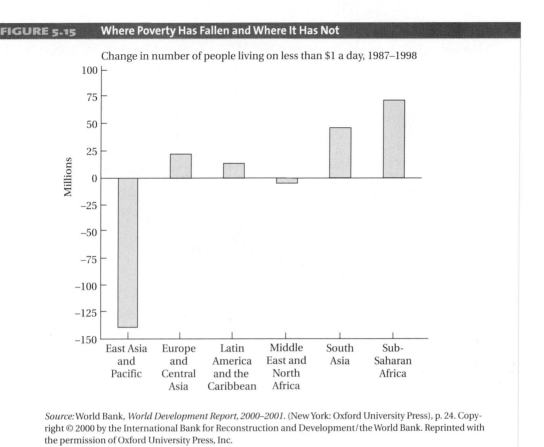

Change in number of people living on less than $1 a day, 1987–1998

Source: World Bank, *World Development Report, 2000–2001.* (New York: Oxford University Press), p. 24. Copyright © 2000 by the International Bank for Reconstruction and Development/the World Bank. Reprinted with the permission of Oxford University Press, Inc.

policy circles that the public expenditures required for the reduction of poverty would entail a reduction in the rate of growth. The concerns that concentrated efforts to lower poverty would slow the rate of growth paralleled the arguments that countries with lower inequality would experience slower growth. In particular, if there were redistribution of income or assets from rich to poor, even through progressive taxation, the concern was expressed that savings would fall. However, while the middle class generally has the highest savings rates, the marginal savings rates of the poor, when viewed from a holistic perspective, are not small. In addition to financial savings, the poor tend to spend additional income on improved nutrition, education for their children, improvements in housing conditions, and other expenditures that, especially at poverty levels, represent investments rather than consumption. There are at least five reasons why policies focused toward reducing poverty levels need not lead to a slower rate of growth.

First, widespread poverty creates conditions in which the poor have no access to credit, are unable to finance their children's education, and, in the absence of physical or monetary investment opportunities, have many children as a source

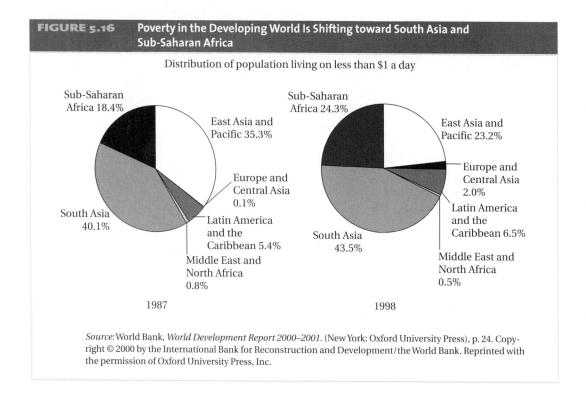

FIGURE 5.16   **Poverty in the Developing World Is Shifting toward South Asia and Sub-Saharan Africa**

Distribution of population living on less than $1 a day

Sub-Saharan Africa 18.4%
East Asia and Pacific 35.3%
Europe and Central Asia 0.1%
Latin America and the Caribbean 5.4%
Middle East and North Africa 0.8%
South Asia 40.1%

1987

Sub-Saharan Africa 24.3%
East Asia and Pacific 23.2%
Europe and Central Asia 2.0%
Latin America and the Caribbean 6.5%
Middle East and North Africa 0.5%
South Asia 43.5%

1998

Source: World Bank, *World Development Report 2000–2001.* (New York: Oxford University Press), p. 24. Copyright © 2000 by the International Bank for Reconstruction and Development/the World Bank. Reprinted with the permission of Oxford University Press, Inc.

of old-age financial security. Together these factors cause per capita growth to be less than what it would be if there were greater equality.

Second, common sense, supported by a wealth of recent empirical data, bears witness to the fact that unlike the historical experience of the now developed countries, the rich in contemporary poor countries are generally *not* noted for their frugality or for their desire to save and invest substantial proportions of their incomes in the local economy.

Third, the low incomes and low levels of living for the poor, which are manifested in poor health, nutrition, and education, can lower their economic productivity and thereby lead directly and indirectly to a slower-growing economy. Strategies to raise the incomes and levels of living of the poor would therefore contribute not only to their material well-being but also to the productivity and income of the economy as a whole.[24] (These issues are considered further in Chapter 8.)

Fourth, raising the income levels of the poor will stimulate an overall increase in the demand for locally produced necessity products like food and clothing, whereas the rich tend to spend more of their additional incomes on imported luxury goods. Rising demand for local goods provides a greater stimulus to local production, local employment, and local investment. Such demand thus creates the conditions for rapid economic growth and a broader popular participation in that growth.[25]

TABLE 5.4	Population, Headcount Ratio, and Poverty Gap at the $1 and $2 Poverty Lines, Selected Countries, Late 1990s and Early 2000s						
	Population			International Poverty Line			
Economy	Millions, 2002	Average Annual Growth, 1980–2002 (%)	Survey Year	Population below $1 a Day (%)	NPG at $1 a Day (%)	Population below $2 a Day (%)	NPG at $2 a Day (%)
Armenia	3	0.0	1998	12.8	3.3	49.0	17.3
Bangladesh	136	2.1	2000	36.0	8.1	82.8	36.3
Bolivia	9	2.3	1999	14.4	5.4	34.3	14.9
Botswana	2	2.9	1993	23.5	7.7	50.1	22.8
Brazil	176	1.6	2001	8.2	2.1	22.4	8.8
Burkina Faso	12	2.4	1998	44.9	14.4	81.0	40.6
Central African Republic	4	2.3	1993	66.6	38.1	84.0	58.4
China	1,280	3.2	2001	16.6	3.9	46.7	18.4
Colombia	44	2.0	1999	8.2	2.2	22.6	8.8
Costa Rica	4	2.5	2000	2.0	0.7	9.5	3.0
Côte d'Ivoire	17	3.2	1998	15.5	3.8	50.4	18.9
Dominican Republic	9	1.9	1998	<2	<0.5	<2	<0.5
Ecuador	13	2.2	1998	17.7	7.1	40.8	17.7
Egypt	66	2.2	2000	3.1	<0.5	43.9	11.3
El Salvador	6	1.5	2000	31.1	14.1	58.0	29.7
Estonia	1	−0.4	1998	<2	<0.5	5.2	0.8
Ethiopia	67	2.6	2000	26.3	5.7	80.7	31.8
Ghana	20	2.8	1999	44.8	17.3	78.5	40.8
Guatemala	12	2.6	2000	16.0	4.6	37.4	16.0
Honduras	7	2.9	1998	23.8	11.6	44.4	23.1
Hungary	10	−0.2	1998	<2	<0.5	7.3	1.7
India	1,049	1.9	2000	34.7	8.2	79.9	35.3
Indonesia	212	1.6	2002	7.5	0.9	52.4	15.7
Jamaica	3	0.9	2000	<2	<0.5	13.3	2.7
Kazakhstan	15	0.0	2001	<2	<0.5	8.5	1.4
Kenya	31	2.9	1997	23.0	6.0	58.6	24.1
Laos	6	2.5	1997	26.3	6.3	73.2	29.6
Lesotho	2	1.5	1995	36.4	19.0	56.1	33.1
Madagascar	16	2.8	1999	49.1	18.3	83.3	44.0
Mali	11	2.5	1994	72.8	37.4	90.6	60.5
Mauritania	3	2.5	2000	25.9	7.6	63.1	26.8
Mexico	101	1.8	2000	9.9	3.7	26.3	10.9
Moldova	4	0.3	2001	22.0	5.8	63.7	25.1
Mongolia	2	1.8	1995	13.9	3.1	50.0	17.5
Mozambique	18	1.9	1996	37.9	12.0	78.4	36.8
Namibia	2	3.0	1993	34.9	14.0	55.8	30.4
Nepal	24	2.3	1995	37.7	9.7	82.5	37.5
Niger	11	3.3	1995	61.4	33.9	85.3	54.8
Nigeria	133	2.8	1997	70.2	34.9	90.8	59.0
Pakistan	145	2.5	1998	13.4	2.4	65.6	22.0
Panama	3	1.9	2000	7.2	2.3	17.6	7.4
Paraguay	6	2.6	1999	14.9	6.8	30.3	14.7

continued

TABLE 5.4	(continued)	Population			International Poverty Line			
Economy	Millions, 2002	Average Annual Growth, 1980–2002 (%)	Survey Year	Population below $1 a Day (%)	NPG at $1 a Day (%)	Population below $2 a Day (%)	NPG at $2 a Day (%)
Peru	27	2.0	2000	18.1	9.1	37.7	18.5
Russian Federation	144	0.2	2000	6.1	1.2	23.8	8.0
Rwanda	8	2.1	1983–85	35.7	7.7	84.6	36.7
Senegal	10	2.7	1995	26.3	7.0	67.8	28.2
Sierra Leone	5	2.2	1989	57.0	39.5	74.5	51.8
South Africa	45	2.3	1995	7.1	1.1	23.8	8.6
Sri Lanka	19	1.2	1995	6.6	1.0	45.4	13.5
Tanzania	35	2.9	1993	19.9	4.8	59.7	23.0
Turkey	70	2.0	2000	<2	<0.5	10.3	2.5
Turkmenistan	5	2.3	1998	12.1	2.6	44.0	15.4
Ukraine	49	−0.1	1999	2.9	0.6	31.0	8.0
Venezuela	25	2.3	1998	15.0	6.9	32.0	15.2
Yemen	19	3.5	1998	15.7	4.5	45.2	15.0
Zambia	10	2.6	1998	63.7	32.7	87.4	55.4
Zimbabwe	13	2.7	1990–91	36.0	9.6	64.2	29.4

Source: Adapted from World Bank, *World Development Indicators, 2004* (New York: Oxford University Press, 2004), tabs. 2.5 and 2.1. Copyright © 2004 by the World Bank. Reprinted with the permission of the World Bank via the Copyright Clearance Center.

Fifth and finally, a reduction of mass poverty can stimulate healthy economic expansion by acting as a powerful material and psychological incentive to widespread public participation in the development process. By contrast, wide income disparities and substantial absolute poverty can act as powerful material and psychological disincentives to economic progress. They may even create the conditions for an ultimate rejection of progress by the masses, impatient at the pace of progress or its failure to alter their material circumstances.[26]

We can conclude, therefore, that promoting rapid economic growth and reducing poverty are not mutually conflicting objectives. The World Bank reached a similar conclusion in its 1990 report on poverty when it declared:

> Discussions of policy toward the poor usually focus on the trade-off between growth and poverty. But the review of country experience suggests that this is not a critical trade-off. With appropriate policies, the poor can participate in growth and contribute to it, and when they do, rapid declines in poverty are consistent with sustained growth.[27]

That dramatic reductions in poverty need not be incompatible with high growth is seen both in case studies and in the cross-national comparisons of data. Over the past 20 years, China has experienced the highest growth rate in the world, and also the most dramatic reductions in poverty. As can be seen in Table 2.7 (by subtracting the second line from the first), the headcount of the poor in China fell from 303.4 million to 213.2 over the 1987–1998 period alone. This did not occur merely as a result of high growth. China has worked with the World Bank to improve its poverty reduction programs throughout this period and has built on its long-standing efforts to provide at least minimal education and health care for its people as a firm foundation for long-term progress. While the plight of many peasants has worsened in recent years, especially in interior regions, the positive overall results of China's efforts to fight extreme poverty are apparent. The recent dramatic reductions of poverty in Vietnam follow a similar pattern. Figure 5.17 shows the cross-country evidence.[28] Figure 5.17a shows that the higher the per capita income in the country, the higher the average incomes of the poor; that is, the poverty gap falls as the overall income per capita in the economy rises. Figure 5.17b shows the relationship between per capita income growth and the growth rates of incomes of the poor.

Certainly, the close relationship between economic growth and progress among the poor does not by itself indicate causality. Some of the effect may run from improved incomes, education, and health among the poor to faster overall growth (as suggested by some of the arguments listed previously). Moreover, as we have seen, poverty reduction is possible without rapid growth. But whatever the causality, it is clear that growth and poverty reduction are entirely compatible objectives.

Economic Characteristics of Poverty Groups

So far we have painted a broad picture of the income distribution and poverty problem in developing countries. We argued that the magnitude of absolute poverty results from a combination of low per capita incomes and highly unequal distributions of that income. Clearly, for any given distribution of income, the higher the level of per capita income, the lower the numbers of the absolutely poor. But as we have seen, higher levels of per capita income are no guarantee of lower levels of poverty. An understanding of the nature of the size distribution of income, therefore, is central to any analysis of the poverty problem in low-income countries.

But painting a broad picture of absolute poverty is not enough. Before we can formulate effective policies and programs to attack poverty at its source, we need some specific knowledge of these poverty groups and their economic characteristics.[29]

Rural Poverty

Perhaps the most valid generalizations about the poor are that they are disproportionately located in rural areas, that they are primarily engaged in agricultural and associated activities, that they are more likely to be women and children than adult males, and that they are often concentrated among minority ethnic groups and indigenous peoples. Data from a broad cross section of developing nations support these generalizations. We find, for example, that about two-thirds of the very poor scratch out their livelihood from subsistence agriculture either as small farmers or as low-paid farm workers. Some of the remaining one-third are also located in rural areas but engaged in petty services, and others are located on the fringes and in

FIGURE 5.17 Growth and the Poor

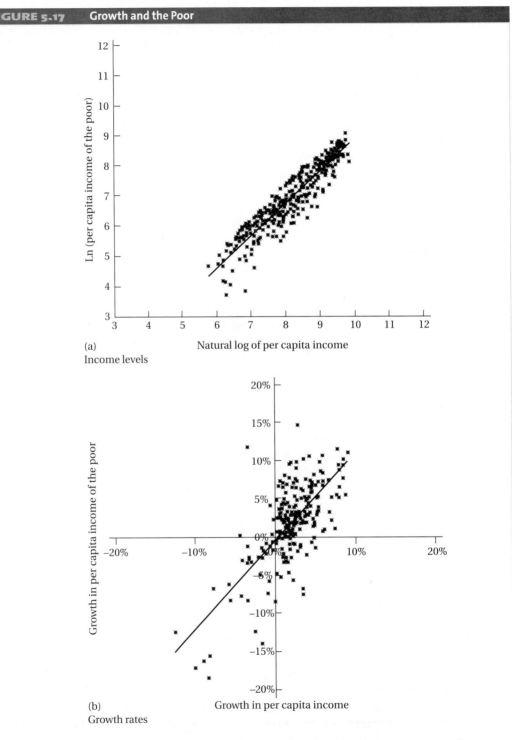

(a)
Income levels

(b)
Growth rates

Source: David Dollar and Aart Kraay, "Growth Is Good for the Poor," World Bank Working Paper, presented at George Washington University, Economics Department, October 9, 2001. Reprinted with the permission of the authors.

TABLE 5.5	Rural Poverty as a Percentage of Total Poverty	
Region and Country	Rural Population as a Percentage of the Total Population, 2003	Rural Poor as a Percentage of the Total Poor, 1991–2000.
Sub-Saharan Africa		
Burkina Faso	85	96
Ghana	63	80
Kenya	80	82
Asia		
Bangladesh	77	82
India	72	76
Philippines	53	73
Thailand	69	82
Latin America		
Guatemala	61	81
Panama	38	66
Paraguay	46	60
Peru	31	41

Source: World Bank, *World Development Indicators, 2004* (New York: Oxford University Press, 2004), tab. 25 and Population Data Sheet. Copyright © 2004 by the World Bank. Reprinted with the permission of the World Bank via the Copyright Clearance Center. Calculations for the rural poor were done by the authors using these data.

marginal areas of urban centers where they engage in various forms of self-employment such as street-hawking, trading, petty services, and small-scale commerce. On the average, we may conclude that in Africa and Asia, about 80% of all target poverty groups are located in the rural areas, as are about 50% in Latin America. Some data for specific countries are provided in Table 5.5.

It is interesting to note, in light of the rural concentration of absolute poverty, that the largest share of most LDC government expenditures over the past quarter century has been directed toward the urban area and especially toward the relatively affluent modern manufacturing and commercial sectors. Whether in the realm of directly productive economic investments or in the fields of education, health, housing, and other social services, this urban modern-sector bias in government expenditures is at the core of many of the development problems that will be discussed in succeeding chapters. We need only point out here that in view of the disproportionate number of the very poor who reside in rural areas, any policy designed to alleviate poverty must necessarily be directed to a large extent toward rural development in general and the agricultural sector in particular (we will discuss this matter in detail in Chapter 9).

Women and Poverty

Women make up a substantial majority of the world's poor. If we compared the lives of the inhabitants of the poorest communities throughout the developing world, we would discover that virtually everywhere, women and children experience the harshest deprivation. They are more likely to be poor and malnourished and less likely to receive medical services, clean water, sanitation, and other benefits.[30] The prevalence of female-headed households, the lower earning capacity of women, and their limited control over their spouses' income all contribute to this disturbing phenomenon. In addition, women have less access to education, formal-sector employment, social security, and government employment programs. These facts combine to ensure that poor women's financial resources are meager and unstable relative to men's.

The poorest segments of LDC populations live in households headed by women, in which there are generally no male wage earners. Women head roughly 20% of households in India, 17% in Costa Rica, and 40% in rural Kenya, and the proportion is rising throughout most of the developing world. Because the earning potential of women is considerably below that of their male counterparts, women are more likely to be among the very poor. In general, women in female-headed households have less education and lower incomes. Furthermore, the larger the household, the greater the strain on the single parent and the lower the per capita food expenditure.

A portion of the income disparity between male- and female-headed households can be explained by the large earnings differentials between men and women. In addition to the fact that women are often paid less for performing similar tasks, they are essentially barred from higher-paying occupations. In urban areas, women are much less likely to obtain formal employment in private companies or public agencies and are frequently restricted to illegal, low-productivity jobs. The illegality of piecework, as in the garment industry, prevents it from being regulated and renders it exempt from minimum-wage laws or social security benefits. Similarly, rural women have less access to the resources necessary to generate stable incomes and are frequently subject to laws that further compromise earning potential. Legislation and social custom often prohibit women from owning property or signing financial contracts without a husband's signature, and women are typically ineligible for institutionally provided resources such as credit and training. With a few notable exceptions, government employment or income-enhancing programs are accessible primarily if not exclusively by men, exacerbating existing income disparities between men and women.

But household income alone fails to describe the severity of women's relative deprivation. Because a higher proportion of female-headed households are situated in the poorest areas, which have little or no access to government-sponsored services such as piped water, sanitation, and health care, household members are more likely to fall ill and are less likely to receive medical attention. In addition, children in female-headed households are less likely to be enrolled in school and more likely to be working in order to provide additional income.

The degree of economic hardship may also vary widely within a household. We have already discussed the fact that GNI per capita is an inadequate measure of development because it fails to reflect the extent of absolute poverty. Likewise, household income is a poor measure of individual welfare because the distribution of income within the household may be quite unequal. In fact, among the poor, the economic status of women provides a better indication of their own welfare, as well as that of their children. Existing studies of intrahousehold resource allocation clearly indicate that in many regions of the world, there exists a strong bias against females in areas such as nutrition, medical care, education, and inheritance. For example, it is estimated that in India, girls are four times as likely to suffer from acute malnutrition and boys are 40 times more likely to be taken to a hospital when ill. Moreover, empirical research has shown that these gender biases in household resource allocation significantly reduce the rate of survival among female infants. As a result, recorded female-male sex ratios in countries like China are so much below their expected values that 100 million girls and women are said to be "missing."[31] The favor shown toward boys in part reflects the fact that men are perceived to have a greater potential for contributing financially to family survival. This is not only because well-paying employment for women is unavailable but also because daughters are often married to families outside the village, after which they become exclusively responsible to their in-laws and thus cease contributing to their family of origin.

The extent of these internal biases is strongly influenced by the economic status of women. Studies have found that where women's share of income within the home is relatively high, there is less discrimination against girls, and women are better able to meet their own needs as well as those of their children. When household income is marginal, virtually 100% of women's income is contributed toward household nutritional intake. Since this fraction is considerably smaller for men, a rise in male earnings leads to a less than proportionate increase in the funds available for the provision of daily needs. It is thus unsurprising that programs designed to increase nutrition and family health are more effective when targeting women than when targeting men. In fact, significant increases in total household income do not necessarily translate into improved nutritional status (see Chapter 8). The persistence of low levels of living among women and children is common where the economic status of women remains low. Box 5.1 provides some views of the poor on gender relations.

Women's control over household income and resources is limited for a number of reasons. Of primary importance is the fact that a relatively large proportion of the work performed by women is unremunerated—for example, collecting firewood and cooking—and may even be intangible, as with parenting. Women's control over household resources may also be constrained by the fact that many women from poor households are not paid for the work they perform in family agriculture or business. For example, in Mexico, it has been estimated that 22.5% of women in the agricultural sector and 7.63% of women in the nonagricultural sectors work full time without pay. These figures are greatly understated in that they do not include women who work part time in family production. It is common for the male head of household to control all funds from cash crops or the family business, even though a significant portion of the labor input is provided by his spouse. In addition, in many cultures, it is considered socially unacceptable for women to contribute significantly to household income, and hence women's work may remain concealed or unrecognized. These combined factors perpetuate the low economic status of women and can lead to strict limitations on their control over household resources.

Development policies that increase the productivity differentials between men and women are likely to worsen earnings disparities as well as further erode women's economic status within the household. Since government programs to

BOX 5.1 Gender Relations in Developing Countries: Voices of the Poor

Sister, if you don't beat them they'll stop being good. And if they're good and you beat them, they'll stay that way.

—A man in Bangladesh

When my husband died, my in-laws told me to get out. So I came to town and slept on the pavement.

—A middle-aged widow in Kenya

When I was working, I used to decide. When she is working, she owns her money and does anything she wishes.

—A man from Vila Junqueira, Brazil

Problems have affected our relationship. The day my husband brings in money we are all right together. The day he stays at home [out of work] we are fighting constantly.

—A woman from El Gawaber, Egypt

The unemployed men are frustrated because they can no longer play the part of family providers and protectors. They live on the money made by their wives and feel humiliated because of this.

—An elderly woman from Uchkun, Kyrgyzstan

When a woman gives her opinion, they [men] make fun of her and don't pay attention. If women go to a meeting, they don't give their opinion.

—A woman in Las Pascuas, Bolivia

alleviate poverty frequently work almost exclusively with men, they tend to exacerbate these inequalities. In urban areas, training programs to increase earning potential and formal-sector employment are generally limited to men, while agricultural extension programs promote male-dominated crops, frequently at the expense of women's vegetable plots. Studies have shown that development efforts can actually increase women's workload while at the same time reduce the share of household resources over which they exercise control. Consequently, women and their dependents remain the most economically vulnerable group in developing countries.

The fact that the welfare of women and children is strongly influenced by the design of development policy underscores the importance of integrating women into development programs. To improve living conditions for the poorest individuals, women must be drawn into the economic mainstream. This would entail increasing female participation rates in educational and training programs, formal-sector employment, and agricultural extension programs. It is also of primary importance that precautions be taken to ensure that women have equal access to government resources provided through schooling, services, employment, and social security programs. Legalizing informal-sector employment where the majority of the female labor force is employed would also improve the economic status of women.

The consequences of declines in women's relative or absolute economic status has both ethical and long-term economic implications. Any process of growth that fails to improve the welfare of the people experiencing the greatest hardship, broadly recognized to be women and children, has failed to accomplish one of the principal goals of development. In the long run, the low status of women is likely to translate into slower rates of economic growth. This is true because the educational attainment and future financial status of children are much more likely to reflect those of the mother than those of the father. Thus the benefits of current investments in human capital are more likely to be passed on to future generations if women are successfully integrated into the growth process. And considering that human capital is perhaps the most important prerequisite for growth, education and enhanced economic status for women are critical to meeting long-term development objectives. (We examine these issues in greater detail in Chapter 8.)

Ethnic Minorities, Indigenous Populations, and Poverty

A final generalization about the incidence of poverty in the developing world is that it falls especially heavily on minority ethnic groups and indigenous populations. We pointed out in Chapter 2 that some 40% of the world's nation-states have more than five sizable ethnic populations, one or more of which faces serious economic, political, and social discrimination. In recent years, domestic conflicts and even civil wars have arisen out of ethnic groups perceptions that they are losing out in the competition for limited resources and job opportunities. The poverty problem is even more serious for indigenous peoples, whose numbers exceed 300 million in over 5,000 different groups in more than 70 countries.[32]

Although detailed data on the relative poverty of minority ethnic and indigenous peoples is difficult to obtain (for political reasons, few countries wish to highlight these problems), researchers have compiled data on the poverty of indigenous people in Latin America.[33] The results clearly demonstrate that most indigenous groups live in extreme poverty and that being indigenous greatly increases the chances that an individual will be malnourished, illiterate, in poor health, and unemployed. For example, the research showed that in Mexico, over 80% of the indigenous population is poor, compared to 18% of the nonindigenous population. Table 5.6 shows that similar situations exist in countries such as Bolivia, Guatemala, and Peru (not to mention Native American populations in the United States and Canada). Whether we speak of Kurds in Iraq, Tamils in Sri Lanka, Karens in Myanmar, Untouchables in India, or Tibetans in China, the poverty

TABLE 5.6 Indigenous Poverty in Latin America		
	Percentage of Population below the Poverty Line	
Country	Indigenous	Nonindigenous
Bolivia	64.3	48.1
Guatemala	86.6	53.9
Mexico	80.6	17.9
Peru	79.0	49.7

Source: George Psacharopoulos and Harry A. Patrinos, "Indigenous people and poverty in Latin America," *Finance and Development* 31 (1994): 41. Reprinted with permission.

plight of ethnic minorities is as serious as that of indigenous peoples. Being an indigenous, rural woman is the worst-case poverty scenario of all.

Finally, it should be noted that the poor come from poor countries. Although this may seem like a trivial observation, it is actually a useful note of optimism. Figure 5.18 shows the relationship between per capita income in 1993 PPP dollars and the headcount index at the $1-per-day poverty line for 65 developing countries. The negative relationship in the graph suggests that if higher incomes can be achieved, poverty will be reduced, if only because of the greater resources that countries will have available to tackle poverty problems. Unfortunately, as we have seen, a high level of absolute poverty can also retard a country's growth prospects. Moreover, many of the poorest countries in sub-Saharan Africa are not growing but are experiencing outright declines in per capita income. Among those that are growing, at current growth rates it would take decades to reach the levels of income at which poverty tends to be eradicated. After all, Brazil, which has had a solidly upper-middle income for many years, still has 9% of its population living on less than $1 per day. As a result, poverty still needs to be addressed directly.

The Range of Policy Options: Some Basic Considerations

Developing countries that aim to reduce poverty and excessive inequalities in their distribution of income need to know how best to achieve their aim. What kinds of economic and other policies might LDC governments adopt to reduce poverty and inequality while maintaining or even accelerating economic growth rates? As we are concerned here with moderating the size distribution of incomes in general and raising the income levels of, say, the bottom 40% of the population in particular, it is important to understand the various determinants of the distribution of income in an economy and see in what ways government intervention can alter or modify their effect.

Areas of Intervention

We can identify four broad areas of possible government policy intervention, which correspond to the following four major elements in the determination of a developing economy's distribution of income:

FIGURE 5.18   Poverty Declines as National Income Rises

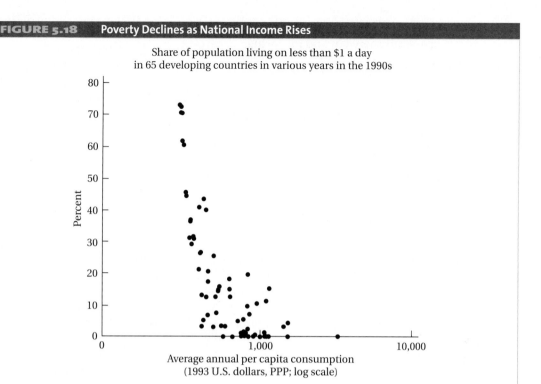

Share of population living on less than $1 a day
in 65 developing countries in various years in the 1990s

Source: From World Bank, *World Development Report, 2000–2001.* (New York: Oxford University Press), p. 46. Copyright © 2000 by the International Bank for Reconstruction and Development/the World Bank. Reprinted with the permission of Oxford University Press, Inc.

1. *Altering the functional distribution*—the returns to labor, land, and capital as determined by factor prices, utilization levels, and the consequent shares of national income that accrue to the owners of each factor.

2. *Mitigating the size distribution*—the functional income distribution of an economy translated into a size distribution by knowledge of how ownership and control over productive assets and labor skills are concentrated and distributed throughout the population. The distribution of these asset holdings and skill endowments ultimately determines the distribution of personal income.

3. *Moderating (reducing) the size distribution at the upper levels* through progressive taxation of personal income and wealth. Such taxation increases government revenues and converts a market- and asset-determined level of personal income into a fiscally corrected "disposable" personal income. An individual or

family's **disposable income** is the actual amount available for expenditure on goods and services and for saving.

4. *Moderating (increasing) the size distribution at the lower levels* through public expenditures of tax revenues to raise the incomes of the poor either directly (e.g., by outright money transfers) or indirectly (e.g., through public employment creation or the provision of free or subsidized primary education and health care for both men and women). Such public policies raise the real income levels of the poor above their market-determined personal income levels.

Policy Options

Developing-country governments have many options and alternative possible policies to operate in the four broad areas of intervention just outlined. Let us briefly identify the nature of some of them.

Altering the Functional Distribution of Income through Policies Designed to Change Relative Factor Prices Altering the functional distribution represents the traditional economic approach. It is argued that as a result of institutional constraints and faulty government policies, the relative price of labor is higher than what would be determined by the free interplay of the forces of supply and demand. For example, the power of trade unions to raise minimum wages to artificially high levels (higher than those that would result from supply and demand) even in the face of widespread unemployment is often cited as an example of the "distorted" price of labor. From this it is argued that measures designed to reduce the price of labor relative to capital (e.g., through market-determined wages in the public sector or public wage subsidies to employers) will cause employers to substitute labor for capital in their production activities. Such factor substitution increases the overall level of employment and ultimately raises the incomes of the poor, who have been excluded from modern sector employment and typically possess only their labor services. Put differently, artificially increased modern-sector wages reduce the rate of modern-sector enlargement growth, thus harming the poor. Note that minimum wages are never enforced in practice in the traditional sector.

However, often the price of capital equipment is "institutionally" set at artificially low levels (below what supply and demand would dictate) through various public policies such as investment incentives, tax allowances, subsidized interest rates, overvalued exchange rates, and low tariffs on capital goods imports such as tractors and automated equipment relative to tariffs set on consumer goods. If these special privileges and capital subsidies were removed so that the price of capital would rise to its true "scarcity" level, producers would have a further incentive to increase their utilization of the abundant supply of labor and lower their uses of scarce capital. Moreover, owners of capital (both physical and financial) would not receive the artificially high economic returns they now enjoy.

Because factor prices are assumed to function as the ultimate signals and incentives in any economy, correcting these prices (i.e., lowering the relative price of labor and raising the relative price of capital) would not only increase productivity and efficiency but would also reduce inequality by providing more wage-paying jobs for currently unemployed or underemployed unskilled and semiskilled workers. It would also lower the artificially high incomes of owners of capital. Removal of such *factor-price distortions* would therefore go a long way toward combining more growth, efficiently generated, with higher employment, less poverty, and greater equality (see Appendix 5.1).

We may conclude that there is much merit to the traditional factor-price distortion argument and that correcting prices should contribute to a reduction in poverty and an improved distribution of income. How much it actually contributes will depend on the degree to which firms and farms switch to more labor-intensive production methods as the relative price of labor falls and the relative price of capital rises. This is an important empirical question, the answer to which will vary from country to country. But some improvement can be expected.

Modifying the Size Distribution through Progressive Redistribution of Asset Ownership Given correct resource prices and utilization levels for each type of productive factor (labor, land, and capital), we can arrive at estimates for the total earnings of each asset. But to translate this functional income into personal income, we need to know the distribution and ownership concentration of these assets among and within various segments of the population. Here we come to what is probably the most important fact about the determination of income distribution within an economy: The ultimate cause of the unequal distribution of personal incomes in most developing countries is the unequal and highly concentrated patterns of **asset ownership** (wealth) in these countries. The principal reasons why less than 20% of their population receives over 50% of the national income is that this 20% probably owns and controls well over 90% of the productive and financial resources, especially physical capital and land but also financial capital (stocks and bonds) and human capital in the form of better education and health. Correcting factor prices is certainly not sufficient to reduce income inequalities substantially or to eliminate widespread poverty where physical and financial asset ownership and education are highly concentrated.[34]

It follows that the second and perhaps more important line of policy to reduce poverty and inequality is to focus directly on reducing the concentrated control of assets, the unequal distribution of power, and the unequal access to educational and income-earning opportunities that characterize many developing countries. A classic case of such **redistribution policies** as they relate to the rural poor, who comprise 70% to 80% of the target poverty group, is **land reform**. The basic purpose of land reform is to transform tenant cultivators into smallholders who will then have an incentive to raise production and improve their incomes. But as we shall see in Chapter 9, land reform may be a weak instrument of income redistribution if other institutional and price distortions in the economic system prevent small farm holders from securing access to much needed critical inputs such as credit, fertilizers, seeds, marketing facilities, and agricultural education. Similar reforms in urban areas could include the provision of commercial credit at affordable rates (rather than through traditional, high-interest moneylenders) to small entrepreneurs (so-called microcredit—see the case study at the end of this chapter and Chapter 16) so that they can expand their business and provide more jobs to local workers.

In addition to the redistribution of existing productive assets, dynamic redistribution policies could be gradually pursued. For example, LDC governments could transfer a certain proportion of annual savings and investments to low-income groups so as to bring about a more gradual and perhaps politically more acceptable redistribution of additional assets as they accumulate over time. This is what is often meant by the expression "redistribution from growth." Whether such a gradual redistribution from growth is any more possible than a redistribution of existing assets is a moot point, especially in the context of very unequal power structures. But some form of asset redistribution, whether static or dynamic, seems to be a necessary condition for any significant reduction of poverty and inequality in most developing countries.

Human capital in the form of education and skills is another example of the unequal distribution of productive asset ownership. Public policy should therefore promote wider access to educational opportunities (for girls as well as boys) as a means of increasing income-earning potential for more people. This investment in human capital as a principal strategy for alleviating poverty has been widely promoted (along with accelerating economic growth) by the World Bank in its various poverty reports, especially *World Development Report 1998/99: Knowledge for Development*. But as in the case of land reform, the mere provision of greater access to education is no guarantee that the poor will be any better off, unless complementary policies—for example, the provision of more productive employment opportunities for the educated—are adopted to capitalize on this increased human capital. The relationship among education, employment, and development is discussed further in Chapter 8.

Reducing the Size Distribution at the Upper Levels through Progressive Income and Wealth Taxes Any national policy attempting to improve the living standards of the bottom 40% must secure sufficient financial resources to transform paper plans into program realities. The major source of such development finance is the direct and progressive taxation of both income and wealth. Direct **progressive income taxes** focus on personal and corporate incomes, with the rich required to pay a progressively larger percentage of their total income in taxes than the poor. Taxation on wealth (the stock of accumulated assets and income) typically involves personal and corporate property taxes but may also include progressive inheritance taxes. In either case, the burden of the tax is designed to fall most heavily on the upper-income groups.

Unfortunately, in many developing countries (and developed countries as well), the gap between what is supposed to be a progressive tax structure and what different income groups actually pay can be substantial. Progressive tax structures on paper often turn out to be **regressive taxes** in practice, in that the lower- and middle-income groups pay a proportionately larger share of their incomes in taxes than the upper-income groups. The reasons for this are simple. The poor are often taxed at the source of their incomes or expenditures (by withholding taxes from wages, general poll taxes, or **indirect taxes** levied on the retail purchase of goods such as cigarettes and beer). By contrast, the rich derive by far the largest part of their incomes from the return on physical and financial assets, which often go unreported. They often also have the power and ability to avoid paying taxes without fear of government reprisal. Policies to enforce progressive rates of direct taxation on income and wealth, especially at the highest levels, are what are most needed in this area of redistribution activity (see Chapter 16 for a further discussion of taxation for development).

Direct Transfer Payments and the Public Provision of Goods and Services The direct provision of tax-financed **public consumption** goods and services to the very poor is another potentially important instrument of a comprehensive policy designed to eradicate poverty. Examples include public health projects in rural villages and urban fringe areas, school lunches and preschool nutritional supplementation programs, and the provision of clean water and electrification to remote rural areas. Direct money transfers and subsidized food programs for the urban and rural poor, as well as direct government policies to keep the price of essential foodstuffs low, represent additional forms of public consumption **subsidies**.

Direct transfers and subsidies can be highly effective, but they need to be designed carefully. Four significant problems require attention. First, when resources for attacking poverty are limited—as they always are—resources need to be directed to those who are genuinely poor. Second, it is important that beneficiaries not become unduly dependent on the poverty program; in particular, we do not want to give the poor less incentive to build the assets, such as education, that can enable them to stay out of poverty. But a "safety net" can also be valuable to encourage the poor to accept a more entrepreneurial attitude toward their microenterprises. This is much more possible when the poor do not fear that their children will suffer terrible consequences if their small businesses fail. Third, we do not want to divert people who are productively engaged in alternative economic activities to participate in the poverty program instead. Finally, poverty policies are often limited by resentment from the nonpoor, including those who are working hard but are not very far above the poverty line themselves.

When a subsidy of goods consumed by the poor is planned, it should be targeted to the geographic areas where the poor are found and should emphasize goods that nonpoor people do not consume. This helps conserve resources for the program and minimizes efforts by nonpoor people to benefit from the program. For example, nutritional supplements can be provided for any woman who brings her baby to the neighborhood poverty program center located in villages and neighborhoods with high incidence of absolute poverty. Although more affluent mothers could use the program, few would risk the stigma of venturing into the poorer villages and neighborhoods, let alone the center itself. The nutritional supplements help poor mothers and their small children stay healthy, helping break the cycle of poverty.

In addition, it may be useful to impose a work requirement before food aid is provided. This is done in the well-known Bangladesh Food for Work Program and in the Maharashtra Employment Guarantee Scheme in India. In these programs, the poor are put to work building infrastructure, such as roads from outlying areas (where the poor live) to market towns, that will ultimately benefit the poor and others in the region. Although the administrative costs are sometimes higher and the skills of the workers significantly lower than would be the case with a commercially procured construction contract, in many cases these valuable infrastructure projects would never be tackled at all in the absence of the program. The high work requirement and minimum in-kind payment in basic foodstuffs discourage the nonpoor from participating, thus conserving resources. This characteristic is known as the "screening" function of **workfare programs**. These requirements also help preserve the program's political sustainability: When people see that the poor are getting "a hand up rather than a handout," the programs tend to maintain wider public support.

In sum, we can say that workfare, such as the Food for Work Program, represents a better policy than welfare or direct handouts when the following criteria are met:

1. The program does not reduce or seriously undermine incentives for the poor to acquire human capital and other assets.

2. There are greater *net* benefits of the work output of the program.

3. It is harder to screen the poor without the workfare requirement.

4. There is lower opportunity cost of time for poor workers (so the economy loses little output when they join the workfare program).

5. There is higher opportunity cost of time for nonpoor workers (so they won't avail themselves of the benefits).

6. The fraction of the population living in poverty is smaller (so the extra costs of universal welfare scheme would be high).

7. There is less social stigma attached to participating in a workfare program, so that the poor do not suffer undue humiliation or even be deterred from seeking the help that their families need (otherwise, a discrete welfare transfer may be preferable to a highly visible workfare scheme).[35]

We will be continuing our examination of policies for poverty reduction throughout the remainder of this text. Appropriate agricultural development policies represent a crucial strategy for attacking poverty because such a high fraction of the poor are located in rural areas and engaged in agricultural pursuits. Strategies for agricultural development are examined in Chapter 9. In addition, the poor in urban as well as rural areas suffer from degraded environmental conditions, which lowers opportunities for economic growth and also worsens the health of the poor; these problems are examined in Chapter 10.

Another set of viable policies involve targeted poverty programs to increase the capabilities and human and social capital of the poor. An important example centers on helping the poor develop their microenterprises, on which a large fraction of the nonagricultural poor depend for their survival. It has been found that credit is the binding constraint for many of these tiny firms. By building up the working capital and other assets of microenterprises, the poor can substantially improve their productivity and incomes. The village banking strategy for accomplishing this goal, as exemplified by the Grameen Bank of Bangladesh, is examined in this chapter's case study. In addition, relatively new approaches to attacking poverty focus on an integrated approach to achieving higher incomes together with improved education, health, and nutrition among the poor; these approaches are considered in Chapter 8. Finally, strategies to assist the development of the urban informal sector are examined in Chapter 7.

Summary and Conclusions: The Need for a Package of Policies

To summarize our discussion of alternative policy approaches to the problems of poverty and inequality in development, the need is not for one or two isolated policies but for a "package" of complementary and supportive policies, including the following four basic elements.[36]

1. A policy or set of policies designed to correct factor-price distortions so as to ensure that market or institutionally established prices provide accurate (i.e., socially correct) signals and incentives to both producers and resource suppliers. Correcting distorted prices should contribute to greater productive efficiency, more employment, and less poverty. The promotion of indigenous technological research and development of efficient, labor-intensive methods of production may also be valuable.

2. A policy or set of policies designed to bring about far-reaching structural changes in the distribution of assets, power, and access to education and associated income-earning (employment) opportunities. Such policies go beyond the realm of economics and touch on the whole social, institutional, cultural, and political fabric of the developing world. But without such fundamental structural changes and substantive asset redistributions, whether immediately achieved (e.g., through public-sector interventions) or gradually introduced over time (through redistribution from growth), the chances of improving significantly the living conditions of the masses of rural and urban poor in any reasonable time frame will be highly improbable, perhaps even impossible.

3. A policy or set of policies designed to modify the size distribution of income at the upper levels through the enforcement of legislated progressive taxation on incomes and wealth and at the lower levels through direct transfer payments and the expanded provision of publicly provided consumption goods and services, including workfare programs. The net effect is to create a social "safety net" for people who may be bypassed by the development process.

4. A set of targeted policies to directly improve the well-being of the poor and their communities, particularly those caught in poverty traps, that goes beyond safety net schemes, to offer programs that build capabilities and human and social capital of the poor, such as microfinance, health, education, agricultural development, environmental sustainability, and community development and empowerment programs, as described throughout this text. These can be carried out either by government or by nongovernmental organizations through local and international support.

Although the task of ending extreme poverty will be difficult, it is quite possible, if we can only muster the will. As noted by James Speth, the executive director of the United Nations Development Program, in his foreword to the 1997 *Human Development Report:*

> Poverty is no longer inevitable. The world has the material and natural resources, the know-how and the people to make a poverty-free world a reality in less than a generation. This is not woolly idealism but a practical and achievable goal.[37]

Making Microfinance Work for the Poor: The Grameen Bank of Bangladesh

One of the major obstacles facing the poor is access to credit. For the poor urban peddler, access to credit can mean a chance to build a bigger inventory, so she has items on hand when customers request them, and can eventually move from the insecurity of being a petty street hawker to the stability of being an established vendor. For the poor rural peasant, access to credit can mean a chance to purchase tools, a draft animal, and small capital goods that can enable him to greatly improve his productivity, diversify crops and move toward commercial farming by producing some cash crops for the market, and eventually move from marginal peasant to established commercial farmer. For the poor rural landless laborer, access to credit can mean a chance to learn skills, purchase raw materials (such as cloth) and tools (such as a sewing machine), and eventually become an established businessperson.

In a working-capital poverty trap, a microentrepreneur has too little inventory to be very productive at sales. For example, she does not have styles or sizes that match what the customers she encounters that day want. But this means that she will also have too little net income to acquire the resources to hold a larger inventory in the future.

The Grameen Bank of Bangladesh is an excellent illustration of how credit can be provided to the poor while minimizing the risk that resources will be wasted. Microfinance institu-

tions (MFIs) targeting the poor such as Grameen have expanded rapidly throughout the developing world since the 1980s. But nowhere has this expansion been more striking than in Bangladesh, which has been transforming itself from a symbol of famine to a symbol of hope, due in part to the success of its MFIs. In this case study, we examine the strategies of one of them, the Grameen Bank. (In Chapter 11, we examine the education, empowerment, and other activities of BRAC, an important Bangladeshi NGO that integrates microfinance with many other poverty programs.)

Muhammad Yunus conceived of the Grameen Bank in the mid-1970s when he was a Chittagong University economics professor. Yunus had become convinced from his research that the lack of access to credit on the part of the poor was one of the key constraints on their economic progress, a conclusion that has been supported by later studies from around the developing world. Yunus wanted to demonstrate that it was possible to lend to the poor without collateral. To determine the best system for doing so, he created Grameen as an "action and research project." Today Grameen is a chartered financial institution with over 3 million borrowers among the poor and formerly poor.

Yunus said in an interview that "all human beings are born entrepreneurs. Some get the opportunity to find this out, but some never get this opportunity. A small loan can be a ticket to exploration of personal ability. All human beings have a skill—the survival skill. The fact that they are alive proves this. Just support this skill and see how they will choose to use it."

Yunus began the operation in 1976 after convincing the Bangladesh agricultural development bank to provide initial loan money, the first loans guaranteed personally by Yunus. A series of expansions convinced the government of Grameen's value, and the Grameen Bank was formally chartered as a financial institution in 1983.

The public-cooperative bank continued to grow rapidly and now has over 2,000 branch offices throughout the country. The branch office, covering 15 to 20 villages, is the basic organizational unit and is responsible for its profits and losses. Each branch has a number of village or neighborhood centers, comprised of about eight solidarity groups. Each solidarity group has five members, so there are about 40 borrowers in each center. The five-person group size was not decided arbitrarily but on the basis of experimentation. Initially, loans were awarded directly to individuals, but this required too much staff time to control the use and repayment of the loan. After the idea of mutual responsibility was developed, groups of ten or more were tried at first, but this proved too large for intimate and informal peer-to-peer monitoring to be effective. Groups of five proved in practice to work best. Since 1998, Grameen has again been placing greater emphasis on individual liability.

Since its founding, the Grameen Bank has enabled several million poor Bangladeshis to start or upgrade their own small businesses. Today some 95% of the borrowers are women. Borrowers are generally limited to those who own less than half an acre, and this seems to hold for 96% of borrowers. Representatives of Grameen branches often go door to door in the villages they cover to inform people, who are often illiterate and very reticent about dealing with banks, about Grameen's services.

Before opening a branch, the new branch manager is assigned to prepare a socioeconomic report covering the economy, geography, demographics, transportation and communications infrastructure, and politics of the area. Among other things, this ensures that the branch manager becomes familiar with the region and its potential borrowers before the branch begins operations.

Grameen, which means "rural" or "village" in Bengali, is incorporated as a publicly supported credit union, with borrowers owning 75% of the bank's stock and the government owning the remainder. Once borrowers reach a certain borrowing level, they are entitled to purchase one share of Grameen stock. The bank sets its own policy with strong borrower input, independent of government control. Grameen's total annualized interest rate on its basic working-capital loans has been kept at 16%. The current rate of interest on home loans is 8%. The average annual inflation rate in Bangladesh has been falling over time; it was nearly 10% in the 1980s, falling to about 4% for the 1990s and closer to 3% today; thus the real interest rate appears to have been rising over time.

To qualify for uncollateralized loans, potential borrowers form five-member groups. Each member must undergo a two-week training session before any member can secure a loan, and the training sessions are followed up with weekly group meetings with a bank officer. Grameen relies on what could be called the "collateral of peer pressure." Contrary to widely cited reports, currently borrowers in the solidarity groups do *not* have to cosign or jointly guarantee each other's loans. However, it is clear that strong social pressure is placed on members to repay. Members know the character of other group members and generally only join groups with members they believe are likely to repay their loans.

Peer oversight has contributed to Grameen's high repayment rate of over 90%. Although the exact repayment rate has been a matter of some controversy in the literature, there is no doubt that repayment has been far higher than the national average for bank loans to much wealthier borrowers.

There are also additional financial incentives to repay loans in a timely manner. Each individual borrower can increase by 10% the amount she can borrow each year if she has repaid loans in a timely manner. For the group, if there is 100% attendance at meetings and all loans are repaid, each borrower can increase her borrowing by an additional 5%, thus raising her borrowing ceiling at a rate of 15% per year. An additional increment is provided when there is a perfect record from each of the eight or so borrowing groups in a center. The desire of many borrowers to take advantage of these higher borrowing ceilings presumably does lead to some peer pressure for all to repay in a timely manner.

A member who is unable to repay is allowed to restructure her loan, repaying at a slower rate, with some limited refinancing as needed. This has reduced defaults to essentially zero, according to the Grameen Bank. In addition to peer pressure, most borrowers wish to reestablish their credit and resume their rights to borrow increasing sums, so they work hard to get and keep their loans up to date.

The group structure facilitates the formation of cooperative ventures among the participants, permitting the undertaking of ventures too large or too risky for poor individuals to shoulder alone. Grameen also works to facilitate the accumulation of savings among its members through savings requirements or incentives for its borrowers to save.

Group members are trained in such practical matters as bank procedures, the group savings program, the role of the center chief and the chairperson of the five-member group, and even how to write their signa-tures. In addition, training has a moral component, stressing the bank's 16 principles, known as "decisions," to be adhered to by each member. These decisions were formulated in a national conference of 100 female center chiefs in 1984. They emphasize mutual assistance and other modern values, including self-discipline and hard work, hygiene, and refusal to participate in backward practices like demanding dowries. Adherence to these principles and attendance at rallies featuring the chanting of the decisions are not formal requirements for receiving loans, but they are said to have become effective, implicit requirements.

The 16 decisions cover a wide range of activities. Here are a few:

3. We shall not live in dilapidated houses. We shall repair our houses and work toward constructing new houses as soon as possible.

4. We shall grow vegetables all the year round. We shall eat plenty of them and sell the surplus.

6. We shall plan to keep our families small.

8. We shall always keep our children and the environment clean.

11. We shall not take any dowry in our sons' weddings, neither shall we give any dowry in our daughters' weddings. We shall not practice child marriage.

13. For higher income, we shall collectively undertake higher investments.

The full list, with their pictorial presentation for villagers, may be found on the Grameen Web site at http://www.grameen-info.org.

There has been a major debate in the microfinance community about whether microcredit institutions should just make loans or also engage in other social development activities. Grameen, which is technically a bank rather than an NGO, is usually grouped among the minimalist institutions, but the 16 decisions show that there is a much broader social component at Grameen as well. Other institutions have sought to actively combine other very different activities. Examples include Freedom from Hunger, which has combined credit with its basic education campaigns, Project Hope, which has combined credit with its maternal and child health campaigns, and BRAC, one of the world's most comprehensive NGOs working with the poor in Bangladesh (see the case study in Chapter 11).

Starting loans are typically for about $50 to $100. The average loan size in 1994 was $140, over half the annual income of many borrowers. In 1995, loans over $100 were common but generally did not exceed $300.

Mahabub Hossain found that 46% of loans went for livestock and poultry raising, 25% for processing and light manufacturing, and 23% for trading and shopkeeping; thus almost no loans went to finance farm crop activities. Grameen borrowers have had notable success in capital accumulation. Cattle raising is a major activity of borrowers. Hossain found that the number of cattle owned increased by 26% per year. Though the numbers involved are small—going from 61 per 100 borrowers before becoming a Grameen member to 102 per 100 borrowers at the time of the survey—these are impressive improvements for Bangladesh's poor. The working capital of borrowers tripled on average within 27 months.

But completely landless agricultural laborers appear to remain significantly underrepresented in the pool of borrowers: Hossain found that they represent 60% of Grameen's target group but only 20% of its actual borrowers—and this includes those who reported hired agricultural labor as a secondary economic activity as well as those who reported it a primary economic activity. Note that in Bangladesh, most laborers own a small plot of land for their house but too little to form the basis for a viable farm. Some 60% of Bangladeshis are "functionally landless" in this sense. Landless farm laborers are extremely hard to reach for any development program in any country. They also tend to be the least educated and are probably the least well prepared to move into viable entrepreneurial activities.

Grameen's emphasis on serving poor women is especially impressive. According to Hossain's survey, half the women borrowers said they were unemployed at the time they became Grameen members (compared with less than 7% of the men). The share of women among borrowers has climbed steadily over the years and reached 94% by the end of 1995. An impact evaluation carried out by Mark Pitt and Shahidur Khandker concluded that microcredit for women from Grameen and two other lenders had a larger effect on the behavior of poor households in Bangladesh than for men. In a representative finding, they concluded that annual household consumption expenditure increases 18 taka for every additional 100 taka borrowed by women from credit programs, compared with just 11 taka for men. In addition, availability of microcredit also helps households smooth consumption over time so that family members can reduce suffering during lean periods. In other research, Pitt and collaborators found that credit for women had a positive effect on children's health in Bangladesh, but credit for men had no comparable effect. (Related issues are examined in Chapter 8.)

Is Grameen subsidized, and how much subsidy makes sense? Some analysts argue that microfinance institutions should not provide loans at subsidized rates, so that as many total loans can be made as possible, ploughing back all the profits into new loans. Others argue that the poorest of the poor cannot afford to borrow at unsubsidized rates because they do not yet have access to sufficiently profitable activities. Although Grameen seems uneasy with the idea that they provide, or pass through, subsidies, Jonathan Morduch has examined the evidence and concluded that there are indeed subsidies, at least in the 1990s. In 1996, for example, he calculated that total subsidies, evaluated at the economic opportunity cost of capital, amounted to $26 million to $30 million. Morduch also offers an excellent discussion of the issues in his essay, "The Microfinance Schism."

Costs at the Grameen Bank are quite high by commercial bank standards. They have been estimated at 26.5% of the value of loans and advances. This is some 10% higher than the nominal interest rate charged, meaning that 39% of the costs of lending are subsidized from all sources. Adding in estimated opportunity costs, Hossain has calculated an effective subsidy of 51%. About half of the excess of costs over interest receipts is attributable to the expense of opening new branches, which should be treated as a capital cost. Whether a significant fraction of poor borrowers could pay higher interest rates and remain profitable remains uncertain.

Since funds for subsidies are limited, the more the subsidy per loan, the fewer subsidized loans can be made. There may be some combination of reduced operating costs, modest increases in interest rates, and continued subsidy that is optimal for creating the most welfare gains with the available resources. However, a public subsidy of Grameen loans may be justified on the basis of the loans' effect on absolute poverty alleviation and other positive externalities.

The Grameen Phone Ladies

Until recently in Bangladesh, telephones were an unimaginable luxury for most people. Even if you were in an urban area that had been wired, landlines cost hundreds of dollars—plus the need to pay huge bribes to get the phone at all, which put a phone beyond the means of even members of the middle class. Lack of phones meant that most business had to be conducted in person. Valuable time was used up just going to the town or city to talk with someone. Most villages are still without a landline phone system. The poor, meanwhile, were simply cut off from the world. In a strikingly original idea, Grameen's Telecom subsidiary had a simple business plan: "to provide the poorest woman in each village with a cellular phone." "Now you may wonder," Muhammad Yunus said in 1995, "what would the poorest woman in such a Bangladesh village want with a cellular phone? Well, everyone in the village who wants to make a call will have to come to her!"

By 2003, more than 25,000 phone ladies, all of them Grameen Bank members, were active in nearly as many villages around the country. Grameen estimates that each phone lady makes phone usage possible for more than 1,000 fellow villagers, more than a quarter of the rural population overall. Revenue per phone lady is about $140 per month, which nets out at about $60 per month after expenses. This is double the country's monthly per capita income.

Yunus commented in 2003 that "when we put this in place on the ground, we found that to make it work the woman had to be able to do accounts. It is very difficult to teach this to the poorest woman in the village, who is illiterate, must work all the time, and has not learned to think in an entrepreneurial way. You at least have to have an educated person in the family. We decided to leave it up to our Centers to decide who should become the phone lady." Yunus also noted that "we are now serving 34,000 villages with over one million subscribers; 32,000 of these are our phone ladies. That might not sound like a lot, but if you look at it by airtime, 17% is on the phones managed by the phone ladies. This is phone use by the poor."

Despite a published list of rates, reports are that there is some price discrimination going on—some of it socially beneficial. A lower price may be charged to the very poor if it is all they can afford. The practice of some phone ladies is apparently that bad news may be phoned for free, but a premium is charged for good news.

The phone lady system makes use of the knowledge of the poor and of their organizations, in this case the local Grameen Bank organization. The phone ladies were usually

Grameen members of some standing, who had previously demonstrated that they were able and willing to build up microenterprises, were capable of basic bookkeeping, and were generally known and had a good location. Women seem to trust using a phone operated by another woman—especially putting trust in them to answer the phone and contact them right away when a return call comes through—though men seem perfectly happy to use the phone ladies' mobiles as well. As the market grows, new competitors can be expected to enter the market, driving down prices, which should be good for the villagers as a whole.

In fact, as the number of villages with phone ladies has steadily grown, demand for phone use in each village has grown with it. This is partly because the more villages that have a phone, the more villages there are that could potentially be called. This is an example of a complementarity such as reflected in the models of Chapter 4. Grameen is responding to other opportunities of new technology by creating a renewable energy company and an Internet service provider.

Future Challenges

Grameen does face some challenges. In 2004, major flooding hit the country again, and recovery will again test the resiliency of Grameen's borrowers—and Grameen itself—in the face of shocks. As MFIs expand and new private and quasi-private credit providers enter the market, competition among microcredit providers is growing. Adapting to this new environment will be a challenge. In Bolivia, another country where microfinance is highly developed, increases in competition, especially from private consumer credit companies eager to piggyback on MFI membership lists, was widely viewed as at least partly responsible for a financial crisis there.

Cultural challenges are also important. Rising women's incomes, self-esteem, and business clout have begun to cause some backlash in the conservative Islamic culture of rural Bangladesh, in which under the purdah system women are expected to be secluded from social activities. Grameen and other programs, such as the nontraditional schools run by BRAC (see Chapter 11), are seen as a challenge to this traditional status quo over which men have traditionally presided. Schools have been burned, and women have been driven out of their villages or even harmed for challenging traditional cultural norms, including participating in market activities. Yunus has stated that some husbands have viewed Grameen as a threat to their authority. In some cases "the husband thought we had insulted him and were destroying his family. We had cases of divorce just because the woman took loans." A fundamentalist cleric in Dhaka claimed that "we have no objection to improving the lot of women, but the motives of the Grameen Bank and other organizations are completely different. They want to eradicate Islam, and they want to do this through women and children." The future of the Grameen Bank will depend on a creative response to this difficult environment of economic and cultural change.

Grameen has proved flexible and responsive to the borrowing needs of its members. For example, the Grameen Bank is also pioneering a low-cost cooperative health insurance scheme, in which an annual fee of $1.25 provides half of the health costs for an entire family for a variety of services. The Grameen housing program can lend up to 30,000 takas (about $500) as home loans. To date there have been more than a half million Grameen-financed houses built or rebuilt, adding iron roofs, cement pillars, and sanitary latrines. The houses generally have mud walls, but these are thick and, properly maintained, and can last many years. The houses are substantial in size, with an electric fan overhead and usually other basic appliances in electrified villages. Grameen has also started offering higher education loans for its members. An increasing number of parents are witnessing the first members of their families to ever go to college graduate in fields such as computer science and accounting. It is a remarkable transformation. ■

Sources

Banerjee, Abhijit V., Timothy Besley, and Timothy W. Guinnane. "Thy neighbor's keeper: The design of a credit cooperative with theory and a test." *Quarterly Journal of Economics* 109 (1994): 491–515.

Ghatak, Maitreesh, and Timothy W. Guinnane. "The economics of lending with joint liability: A review of theory and practice." *Journal of Development Economics* 60(1999): 195–228.

Grameen Bank Web page, http://www.grameen.org

"Grameen dream washed away." *Financial Times*, October 1, 1998.

Hossain, Mahmoub. Credit for Alleviation of Rural Poverty: The Grameen Bank in Bangladesh. Washington, D.C.: International Food Policy Research Institute, 1988.

Khandker, Shahidur R. *Fighting Poverty with Microcredit: Experience in Bangladesh.* New York: Oxford University Press, 1998.

Khandker, Shahidur R., Hussain A. Samad, and Zahed H. Khan. "Income and employment effects of microcredit programs: Village-level evidence from Bangladesh." *Journal of Development Studies* 35 (1998): 96–124.

Morduch, Jonathan. "The Microfinance Promise." *Journal of Economic Literature* 37 (1999): 1569–1614.

Morduch, Jonathan. "The role of subsidies in microfinance: Evidence from the Grameen Bank." *Journal of Development Economics* 60 (1999): 229–248.

Morduch, Jonathan. "The Microfinance Schism." *World Development* 28 (2000): 617–629.

Osmani, S. R. "Limits to the alleviation of poverty through non-farm credit." *Bangladesh Development Studies* 17 (1989): 1–17.

Pearl, Daniel. "Bank that pioneered loans for the poor hits repayment snag." *Wall Street Journal*, November 27, 2001, p. AI.

Pitt, Mark M., and Shahidur R. Khandker. "Credit programs for the poor and seasonality in rural Bangladesh." *Journal of Development Studies* 39, No. 2 (2002): 1–24

Pitt, Mark M., and Shahidur R. Khandker. "The impact of group-based credit programs on poor households in Bangladesh: Does the gender of participants matter?" *Journal of Political Economy* 106 (1998): 958–996.

Pitt, Mark M., Shahidur R. Khandker, Omar Haider Choudhury, and Daniel Millimet. "Credit programs for the poor and the health status of children in rural Bangladesh." *International Economic Review* 44 (2003): 87–118.

Singh, Inderjit. *The Great Ascent: The Rural Poor in South Asia.* Baltimore: Johns Hopkins University Press, 1990.

Smith, Stephen C. *Ending Global Poverty: A Guide to What Works.* New York: Palgrave Macmillan, 2005.

Smith, Stephen C. "Village banking and maternal and child health: Evidence from Ecuador and Honduras." *World Development* 30 (2002): 707–723.

Wahid, Abu N. M. *The Grameen Bank: Poverty Alleviation in Bangladesh.* Boulder, Colo: Westview, 1993.

Wahid, Abu N. M. "The Grameen Bank and poverty alleviation in Bangladesh: Theory, evidence, and limitations." *American Journal of Economics and Sociology* 53 (1994): 1–15.

Yunus, Muhammad. Speech and interview at the World Bank, October 4, 1995.

Yunus, Muhammad. *Grameen II.* Dhaka, Bangladesh: Grameen Bank, 2001.

Yunus, Muhammad, and Alan Jolis. *Banker to the Poor: Micro-Lending and the Battle against World Poverty.* New York: Public Affairs, 1999.

Concepts for Review

Absolute poverty	Functional distribution of income	Progressive income tax
Asset ownership	Gini coefficient	Public consumption
Character of economic growth	Headcount index	Quintiles
Deciles	Human Poverty Index (HPI)	Redistribution policies
Disposable income	Income inequality	Regressive tax
Elasticity of factor substitution	Indirect taxes	Size distribution of income
Factor-price distortions	Kuznets curve	Subsidy
Factor share distribution of income	Land reform	Total poverty gap (TPG)
Factors of production	Lorenz curve	Workfare programs
Foster-Greer-Thorbecke (FGT) index	Neoclassical price-incentive model	
	Personal distribution of income	

Questions for Discussion

1. Most development economists now seem to agree that the level and rate of growth of GNI and per capita income do not provide sufficient or even accurate measures of a country's development. What is the essence of their argument? Give some examples.

2. Distinguish between size and functional distributions of income in a nation. Which do you feel is the more appropriate concept? Explain your answer.

3. What is meant by absolute poverty? What is the poverty gap? How do these measures differ from the UNDP's Human Poverty Index (HPI)? Why should we be concerned with the measurement of poverty in developing nations?

4. What are the principal economic characteristics of poverty groups? What do these characteristics tell us about the possible nature of a poverty-focused development strategy?

5. Describe Kuznets's inverted-U hypothesis. Discuss the conceptual merits and limitations of this hypothesis for contemporary developing countries.

6. In the text, when we examined statistics from a wide range of developing countries, we found no direct relationship (positive or negative) between a country's level of GNI, GNI per capita, and rate of economic growth, on the one hand, and its extent of absolute poverty or the degree of equality in its distribution of income, on the other. Assuming that these data are indeed correct, what do they tell us about the importance of the character of a nation's growth process and about its institutional structure?

7. What is the relationship between a Lorenz curve and a Gini coefficient? Give some examples of how Lorenz curves and Gini coefficients can be used as summary measures of equality and inequality in a nation's distribution of income.

8. It is asserted in the text that the major determinant of a country's income distribution is its distribution of productive and income-earning assets. Explain the meaning of this statement, giving examples of different kinds of productive and income-earning assets.

9. Are rapid economic growth (as measured by either GNI or per capita GNI) and a more equitable distribution of personal income necessarily conflicting objectives? Summarize the arguments both for and against the presumed conflict of objectives, and state and explain your own view.

10. Is progress being made in the fight against poverty? Why or why not?

11. What types of poverty policies have proved most effective?

12. Economic growth is said to be a necessary but not sufficient condition to eradicate absolute poverty and reduce inequality. What is the reasoning behind this argument?

13. Outline the range of major policy options available to LDC governments to alter and modify the size distribution of their national income. Which policy or policies do you believe are absolutely essential, and which are important but not crucial? Explain your answer.

14. How would you design a program aimed at eradicating absolute poverty in the next two decades?

Notes

1. United Nations, *International Conference on Population and Development: Program of Action* (New York: United Nations, 1994), pp. 3.11, 3.13.

2. The Lorenz curve is named for Conrad Lorenz, an American statistician who in 1905 devised this convenient and widely used diagram to show the relationship between population groups and their respective income shares.

3. A more precise definition of perfect equality would take into account the age structure of a population and expected income variations over the "life cycle" of all households within that population. See Morton Paglin, "The measurement and trend of inequality: A basic revision," *American Economic Review* 65 (1975):598–609.

4. For the details, see Gary S. Fields, *Distribution and Development: A New Look at the Developing World* (Cambridge, Mass.: MIT Press, 2001), ch. 2.

5. The sum of all workers' marginal product must equal total gross national income (GNI). For the mathematically inclined, GNI is simply the integral of the marginal product curve between 0 and L_E. This is because the marginal product function is the derivative of the GNI curve: $GNI = f(L, \bar{K})$; $MP_L = f'(L)$.

6. If measured poverty is always *strictly lower* after such transfers, this property is called *strong* monotonicity. The headcount ratio satisfies monotonicity but not strong monotonicity.

7. For the technical details, see James Foster, Joel Greer, and Erik Thorbecke, "A class of decomposable poverty measures," *Econometrica* 52 (1984): 761–766.

8. It is similar in spirit to the Sen index, $S = (H/N)[\text{NIS} + (1 - \text{NIS})G_p]$, which also satisfies all four axioms. For the technical details and derivations of the P_2 and S poverty measures, see Amartya Sen and James E. Foster, *On Economic Inequality*, expanded ed. (Oxford: Clarendon Press, 1997), pp. 165–194.

9. *Cornell Chronicle,* May 11, 2000; author interview with Erik Thorbecke.

10. United Nations Development Program, *Human Development Report, 1997* (New York: Oxford University Press, 1997), ch. 1 and 2.

11. For a study and documentation of the substantial magnitude of capital flight in the 1980s, see Donald R. Lessard and John Williamson, *Capital Flight: The Problem and Policy Responses* (Washington, D.C.: Institute for International Economics, 1987). We discuss capital flight in greater detail in Chapter 14.

12. Various UN studies on sources of savings in developing nations show that small farmers and individuals seem to be among the highest savers. See Andrew Mason, "Savings, economic growth and demographic change," *Population and Development Review* 14 (1988): 113–144.

13. Two technical articles that address the mechanisms by which higher inequality may lead to lower growth or incomes are Abhijit V. Banerjee and Andrew F. Newman, "Occupational choice and the process of development," *Journal of Political Economy* 101 (1993): 274–298, and Oded Galor and Joseph Zeira, "Income distribution and macroeconomics," *Review of Economic Studies* 60 (1993): 35–52. See also Fields, *Distribution and Development,* ch. 10.

14. John Rawls, *A Theory of Justice* (Cambridge, Mass.: Belknap Press, 1971).

15. Gary S. Fields, *Poverty, Inequality and Development* (Cambridge: Cambridge University Press, 1980), pp. 46–56.

16. Ibid., p. 52.

17. This can perhaps be visualized most easily by considering a traditional economy in which everyone is "equally poor," each claiming their share of, say, 50 cents per day. If the absolute poverty line is $1 per day, all are in absolute poverty. Then, modernization begins, and the modern sector absorbs workers one by one, where the wage is, say $2 per day. Starting from the line of perfect equality, the Lorenz curve bows out more and more until nearly half the people are in the modern sector. At that point, as more go to the modern sector, the Lorenz curve is less bowed in until finally everyone has been absorbed into the modern sector, and all once again have equal incomes but now at a higher level of $2 per day. In the process, all of the people have been pulled out of poverty. (Students should try this as an exercise, plotting the Lorenz curves as this process takes place, say, for an eight-person economy.)

18. In fact, some would go further and say that an increase in relative inequality is not objectionable as long as everyone has a higher income, even though the rich get a larger share—even in proportion to their larger starting income—of the gains. This situation is called "first-order stochastic dominance" in the literature. However, even in this case, incomes might be increased even more with less inequality.

19. Of course, in real economies, all three of these growth typologies may take place at the same time, and the net result may be little or no change in inequality. (Or in more

unfortunate cases, with economies with negative growth, like many of those in sub-Saharan Africa, there may be modern and traditional sector impoverishment, accompanied by a shrinking modern sector.)

20. Simon Kuznets, "Economic growth and income inequality," *American Economic Review* 45 (March 1955): 1–28, and "Quantitative aspects of the economic growth of nations," *Economic Development and Cultural Change* 11 (1963): 1–80. Cross-sectional studies supporting the Kuznets hypothesis include Harry Oshima, "The international comparison of size distribution of family incomes with special reference to Asia," *Review of Economics and Statistics* (1962): 439–445; Felix Paukert, "Income distribution at different levels of development: A survey of evidence," *International Labor Review* 108 (1973): 97–125; and Montek S. Ahluwalia, Nicholas G. Carter, and Hollis B. Chenery, "Growth and poverty in developing countries," *Journal of Development Economics* 16 (1979): 298–323. Studies arguing against the hypothesis include Ashwani Saith, "Development and distribution: A critique of the cross-country U-hypothesis," *Journal of Development Economics* 13 (1983): 367–382, and Sudhir Anand and S. M. R. Kanbur, "The Kuznets process and the inequality-development relationship," *Journal of Development Economics* 40 (1993): 25–42.

21. The parabola plotted results from an ordinary least-squares regression. For details on the derivation of Figures 5.11 and 5.12, see Fields, *Distribution and Development*, ch. 3. Fields (pp. 42–43) reports results showing that, in using a country fixed-effect specification, the estimated inverted-U flips to an estimated U-pattern.

22. These studies are cited by Fields, ibid., p. 35.

23. This finding is strongly supported by a much more rigorous empirical study of both cross-sectional and time-series data for 83 countries. See Gustav Papanek and Oldrich Kyn, "The effect on income distribution of development, the growth rate, and economic strategy," *Journal of Development Economics* 23 (1986): 55–65. For evidence that higher growth is more often associated with *lower* inequality, see World Bank, *World Development Report, 1991* (New York: Oxford University Press, 1991), fig. 7.2. See also Roberto Perotti, "Growth, income distribution, and democracy: What the data say," *Journal of Economic Growth* 1 (1996):149–187.

24. For a theoretical argument that lower poverty and greater equality in income distribution can lead to improved nutrition, more employment, and greater output growth, see Partha Dasgupta and Debraj Ray, "Inequality as a determinant of malnutrition and unemployment policy," *Economic Journal* 97 (1987): 177–188.

25. An empirical study of variables explaining LDC growth during the 1960–1973 period provides strong econometric confirmation of the argument that policies designed to promote better distribution and reduce poverty are, on balance, growth-stimulating rather than growth-retarding. See Norman L. Hicks, "Growth vs. basic needs: Is there a trade-off?" *World Development* 7 (1979): 985–994, and Adriana Marshall, "Income distribution, the domestic market and growth in Argentina," *Labour and Society* 13 (1988): 79–103.

26. For robust empirical evidence on how improved distribution can increase domestic demand, promote political stability, and generate higher growth rates, see Alberto Alesina and Roberto Perotti, "The political economy of growth: A critical survey of the

recent literature," *World Bank Economic Review* 8 (1994): 351–371, and Alberto Alesina and Dani Rodrik, "Distributive policies and economic growth," *Quarterly Journal of Economics* 109 (1994): 465–490.

27. World Bank, *World Development Report, 1990* (New York: Oxford University Press, 1990), pp. 51–52. See also Albert Fishlow, "Inequality, poverty, and growth: Where do we stand?" in *Proceedings of the World Bank Annual Conference on Development Economics, 1995*, ed. Michael Bruno and Boris Pleskovic (Washington, D.C.: World Bank, 1996); Nancy Birdsall, David Ross, and Richard Sabot, "Inequality and growth reconsidered: Lessons from East Asia," *World Bank Economic Review* 9 (1995): 477–508; and George R. G. Clarke, "More evidence on income distribution and growth," *Journal of Development Economics* 47 (1995): 403–427.

28. The data reflect 370 observations on 125 countries, each observation on the same country separated by at least five years.

29. For an excellent overview of the nature, magnitude, and incidence of poverty in the developing world, see World Bank, *World Development Report, 2000–2001* (New York: Oxford University Press, 2000).

30. For a comprehensive analysis of how poverty directly affects women's lives in developing countries, see Irene Tinker, *Persistent Inequalities: Women and World Development* (New York: (Oxford University Press, 1990); Mayra Buvinic, Margaret A. Lycette, and William P. McGreevey (eds.), *Women and Poverty in the Third World* (Baltimore; Johns Hopkins University Press, 1983); Judith Bruce and Daisy Dwyer (eds.), *A Home Divided: Women and Income in the Third World* (Stanford, Calif.: Stanford University Press, 1988); Janet Momsen, *Women and Development in the Third World* (New York: Routledge, 1991); and Diane Elson, "Gender-aware analysis and development economics," *Journal of International Development* 5 (1993): 237–247. An excellent statistical survey can be found in United Nations, *The World's Women, 1995: Trends and Statistics* (New York: United Nations, 1995).

31. Amartya Sen, "Missing women," *British Medical Journal* 304 (1992): 587–588.

32. The International Fund for Agricultural Development provides basic statistics and links to key resources on indigenous peoples and development at http://www.iFad.org/pub/factsheet/ip/e.pdf.

33. See, for example, Haeduck Lee, *The Ethnic Dimension of Poverty and Income Distribution in Latin America* (Washington, D.C.: World Bank, 1993), and George Psacharopoulos and Harry A. Patrinos, "Indigenous people and poverty in latin America," *Finance and Development* 31 (1994): 41–43.

34. It is interesting to note that in the United States, which has the greatest inequality of wealth ownership in the developed world, one individual, Bill Gates, the CEO of Microsoft, had a net worth in 1997 about equal to that of the 40 million American households at the bottom of the wealth distribution! If data were available, one could imagine what it would be like in many LDCs. For U.S. data see Edward N. Wolff, "Recent trends in the size distribution of household wealth," *Journal of Economic Perspectives* 12 (1998): 131–150.

35. For the classic analytical treatment of the workfare-versus-welfare problem, see Timothy J. Besley and Stephen Coate, "Workfare versus welfare: Incentive arguments for

work requirements in poverty alleviation programs," *American Economic Review* 82 (1992): 249–261.

36. For other discussions of poverty policies, see Arne Bigsten, "Poverty, inequality and development," in *Surveys in Development Economics,* ed. Norman Gemmell (Oxford: Blackwell, 1987), pp. 157–163; Irma Adelman and Cynthia T. Morris, *Economic Growth and Social Equality in Developing Countries* (Stanford, Calif.: Stanford University Press, 1973), pp. 54–65; Jagdish N. Bhagwati, "Poverty and public policy," *World Development* 16 (1988): 539–555; World Bank, *World Development Report, 1990,* ch. 7 and 8; Irma Adelman and Sherman Robinson, "Income distribution and development," in *Handbook of Development Economics,* vol. 2, ed. Hollis B. Chenery and T. N. Srinivasan (Amsterdam: Elsevier, 1989), pp. 982–996; and especially Paul P. Stre-eten, *Strategies for Human Development: Global Poverty and Unemployment* (Copenhagen: Handelshojskølens Forlag, 1994), and United Nations, *Report on the World Social Situation* (New York: United Nations, 1997) ch. 6.

37. United Nations Development Program, *Human Development Report, 1997,* p. iii.

Further Reading

A comprehensive description of the various meanings and measurements of poverty and income distribution can be found in Gary S. Fields, *Distribution and Development: A New Look at the Developing World* (Cambridge, Mass.: MIT Press, 2001). Another outstanding although rather technical source is Amartya Sen and James E. Foster, *On Economic Inequality,* expanded ed. (Oxford: Clarendon Press, 1997). See also Anthony B. Atkinson, *The Economics of Inequality* (New York: Oxford University Press, 1975); Irma Adelman and Sherman Robinson "Income distribution and development," in *Handbook of Development Economics,* vol. 2, ed. Hollis B. Chenery and T. N. Srinivasan (Amsterdam: Elsevier, 1989), pp. 950–1008; Gary S. Fields, "Data for measuring poverty and inequality changes in developing countries," *Journal of Development Economics* 44 (1994): 87–102; and Martin Ravallion and Shaohua Chen, "What can new survey data tell us about recent changes in distribution and poverty?" *World Bank Economic Review* 11 (1997): 357–382.

For some readable and insightful inquiries into the problem of absolute poverty and policies to eradicate it, see Amartya Sen, *Development as Freedom* (New York: Random House, 1999); Partha Dasgupta, *An Inquiry into Well-Being and Destitution* (New York: Oxford University Press, 1993); and World Bank, *World Development Report, 2000–2001* (New York: Oxford University Press, 2001). See also Martin Ravallion, "Famines and economics," *Journal of Economic Literature* 35 (1997): 1205–1242; Jonathan Morduch, "The microfinance promise," *Journal of Economic Literature* 37 (1999): 1569–1614; and Fields, *Distribution and Development,* ch. 10.

For summaries of the poverty and income distribution problem in LDCs using cross-country data with appropriate analysis and alternative policy strategies, see World Bank, *Poverty Reduction and the World Bank* (Washington, D.C.: World Bank, 1996); United Nations, *Report on the World Social Situation, 1997* (New York: United Nations, 1997), chap. 6; Eliana Cardoso and Ann Helwege, "Below the line: Poverty in Latin America," *World Development* 20 (1992): 19–37; and R. M. Sundrum, *Income Distribution in Less Developed*

Countries (London: Routledge, 1992). See also Hollis B. Chenery, John Duloy, and Richard Jolly (eds.), *Redistribution with Growth: An Approach to Policy* (Washington, D.C.: World Bank, 1974); Mahbub ul-Haq, *The Assault on World Poverty* (Baltimore: Johns Hopkins University Press, 1975); Montek S. Ahluwalia, Nicholas G. Carter, and Hollis B. Chenery, "Growth and poverty in developing countries," *Journal of Development Economics* 16 (1979): 298–323; Gary S. Fields, *Poverty, Inequality and Development* (Cambridge: Cambridge University Press, 1980); Arne Bigsten, "Poverty, inequality and development," in *Surveys in Development Economics,* ed. Norman Gemmell (Oxford: Blackwell, 1987), ch. 4; "Poverty and Well-Being in Developing Countries" (symposium), *American Economic Review* 84 (1994): 211–231; Albert Fishlow, "Inequality, poverty, and growth: Where do we stand?" in *Proceedings of the World Bank Annual Conference on Development Economics, 1995,* ed. Michael Bruno and Boris Pleskovic (Washington, D.C.: World Bank, 1996).

Other useful works include Arne Bigsten, *Income Distribution and Development Theory, Evidence and Policy* (London: Heinemann, 1983); Gary S. Fields, "Employment, income distribution, and economic growth in seven small economies," *Economic Journal* 94 (1984): 74–83; Emanuel De Kadt, "Of markets, might, and mullahs: A case for equity, pluralism, and tolerance in development," *World Development* 13 (1985): 549–556; Gustav Papanek and Oldrich Kyn, "The effect on income distribution of development, the growth rate, and economic strategy," *Journal of Development Economics* 23 (1986): 55–65; Irma Adelman, "A poverty-focused approach to development policy," in *Development Strategics Reconsidered,* ed. John P. Lewis and Valeriana Kaleb (Washington, D.C.: Overseas Development Council, 1986), pp. 49–65; Jagdish N. Bhagwati, "Poverty and public policy," *World Development* 16 (1988): 539–555; Pranab Bardhan, "Efficiency, equity, and poverty alleviation: Policy issues in less developed countries," *Economic Journal* 106 (1996): 1344–1356; and Werner Baer and William Maloney, "Neoliberalism and income distribution in Latin America," *World Development* 25 (1997): 311–327.

Two valuable surveys of women and poverty in the developing world are World Resources Institute, *World Resources, 1994–1995* (New York: Oxford University Press, 1994), ch. 3; and especially United Nations Development Program, *Human Development Report, 1995* (New York: Oxford University Press, 1995). Compelling discussions of the special circumstances faced by poor women and children are presented in Judith Bruce and Daisy Dwyer (eds.), *A Home Divided: Women and Income in the Third World* (Stanford, Calif.: Stanford University Press, 1988); and Mayra Buvinic, Margaret A. Lycette, and William P. McGreevey (eds.), *Women and Poverty in the Third World* (Baltimore: Johns Hopkins University Press, 1983). For more detailed analysis of discrimination in intrahousehold resource allocation, see Meera Chatterjee, *Indian Women, Health, and Productivity* (Washington, D.C.: World Bank, 1990); Angus Deaton, *The Allocation of Goods within the Household: Adults, Children, and Gender* (Washington, D.C.: World Bank, 1987); Duncan Thomas, *Gender Differences in Household Resource Allocations* (Washington, D.C.: World Bank, 1991); and Lawrence Haddad, *Gender and Poverty in Ghana: A Descriptive Analysis* (Washington, D.C.: World Bank, 1991).

For a survey of poverty traps and programs designed to help the poor escape from them, see Stephen C. Smith, *Ending Global Poverty: A Guide to What Works* (New York: Palgrave Macmillan, 2005).

Appendix 5.1

Appropriate Technology and Employment Generation: The Price-Incentive Model

Choice of Techniques: An Illustration

The basic proposition of the **neoclassical price-incentive model** is quite simple and in the best tradition of the neoclassical theory of the firm. Following the principle of economy, producers (firms and farms) are assumed to face a given set of relative factor prices (e.g., of capital and labor) and to use the combination of capital and labor that minimizes the cost of producing a desired level of output. They are further assumed to be capable of producing that output with a variety of technological production processes, ranging from highly labor-intensive to highly capital-intensive methods. Thus if the price of capital is very expensive relative to the price of labor, a relatively labor-intensive process will be chosen. Conversely, if labor is relatively expensive, our economizing firm or farm will use a more capital-intensive method of production—it will economize on the use of the expensive factor, which in this case is labor.

The conventional economics of technical choice is portrayed in Figure A5.1. Assume that the firm, farm, industry, or economy in question has only two techniques of production from which to choose: technique or process $0A$, which requires larger inputs of (homogeneous) capital relative to (homogeneous) labor; and technique or process $0B$, which is relatively labor-intensive. Points F and G represent *unit* output levels for each process, and the line Q_1FGQ_1' connecting F and G is therefore a unit-output isoquant. (Note that in the traditional neoclassical model, an infinite number of such techniques or processes are assumed to exist so that the isoquant or equal-product line takes on its typical convex curvature.)

According to this theory, optimum (least-cost) capital-labor combinations (efficient or appropriate technologies) are determined by relative factor prices. Assume for the moment that market prices of capital and labor reflect their scarcity or shadow values and that the desired output level is Q_1 in Figure A5.1. If capital is cheap relative to labor (price line KL), production will occur at point F using capital-intensive process $0A$. Alternatively, if the market prices of labor and capital are such that labor is the relatively cheap (abundant) factor (line $K'L'$), optimal production will occur at point G, with the labor-intensive technique, $0B$, chosen. It follows that for any technique of production currently in use, a fall in the relative price of labor, all other things being equal, will lead to a substitution of labor for capital in an optimal production strategy. (Note that if capital-intensive process $0A$ "dominates" labor-intensive process $0B$—that is, if technology $0A$ requires less labor and less capital than $0B$ for all levels of output—then for any factor price ratio, the capital-intensive technique will be chosen.)

Factor-Price Distortions and Appropriate Technology

Given that most developing countries are endowed with abundant supplies of labor but possess very little financial or physical capital, we would naturally expect production methods to be relatively labor-intensive. But in fact we often find production techniques in both agriculture and industry to be heavily mechanized and capital-intensive. Large tractors and combines dot the rural landscape of Asia, Africa, and Latin America while people stand idly by. Gleaming new factories with the most modern and sophisticated automated machinery and equipment are a common feature of urban industries while idle workers congregate outside the factory gates. Surely, this phenomenon could not be the result of a lesser degree of economic rationality on the part of LDC farmers and manufacturers.

The explanation, according to the price-incentive school, is simple. Because of a variety of structural, institutional, and political factors, the actual market price of labor is higher and that of capital is lower than their respective true scarcity, or shadow, values would dictate. In Figure A5.1, the shadow price ratio would be given by line $K'L'$, whereas the actual (distorted) market price ratio is shown by line KL. Market wage structures are relatively high because of trade union pressure, politically motivated minimum-wage laws, an increasing range of employee fringe benefits, and the high-wage policies of multinational corporations. In former colonial nations, high-wage structures are often relics of expatriate remuneration scales based on European levels of living and "hardship" premiums. By contrast, the price of (scarce) capital is kept artificially low by a combination of liberal capital depreciation allowances, low or even negative real interest rates, low or negative effective rates of protection on capital goods imports, tax rebates, and overvalued foreign-exchange rates (see Chapter 13).

The net result of these **factor-price distortions** is the encouragement of inappropriate capital-intensive methods of production in both agriculture and manufacturing. Note that from the private-cost-minimizing viewpoint of individual firms and farms, the choice of a capital-intensive technique is correct. It is their rational response to the existing structure of price signals in the market for factors of production. However, from the viewpoint of society as a whole, the social cost of underutilized capital and, especially, labor can be very substantial. Government policies designed to "get the prices right"—that is, to remove factor-price distortions—would contribute not only to more employment but also to a better

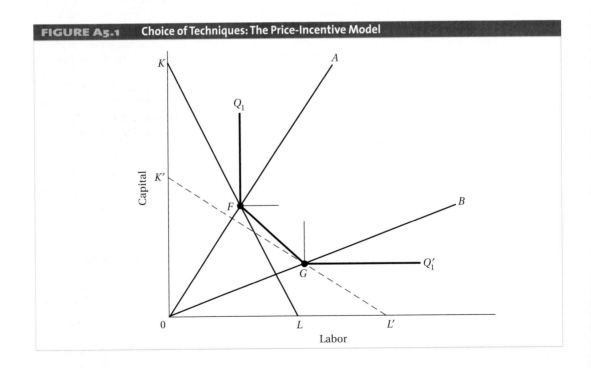

FIGURE A5.1   Choice of Techniques: The Price-Incentive Model

overall utilization of scarce capital resources through the adoption of more appropriate technologies of production.

The Possibilities of Labor-Capital Substitution

The actual employment impact of removing factor-price distortions will depend on the degree to which labor can be substituted for capital in the production processes of various developing-world industries. Economists refer to this as the **elasticity of factor substitution** and define it roughly as the ratio of the percentage change in the proportion of labor used relative to capital (labor-capital or L/K ratio) compared to a given percentage change in the price of capital relative to labor (P_K/P_L). Algebraically, the elasticity of substitution, η_{LK} can be defined as follows:

$$\eta_{LK} = \frac{d(L/K)/(L/K)}{d(P_K/P_L)/(P_K/P_L)} \tag{A5.1.1}$$

For example, if the relative price of capital rises by 1% in the manufacturing sector and the labor-capital ratio rises as a result by, say, 1.5%, the elasticity of substitution in the manufacturing industry will be equal to 1.5. If P_K/P_L falls by, say, 10% while L/K falls by only 6%, the elasticity of substitution for that industry would be 0.6. Relatively high elasticities of substitution (ratios greater than about 0.7) are indicative that factor-price adjustments can have a substantial impact on levels and combinations of factor utilization. In such cases, factor-price modifications may be an important means of generating more employment opportunities.

In general, most empirical studies of the elasticity of substitution for manufacturing industries in less developed countries reveal coefficients in the range 0.5–1.0. These results indicate that a relative reduction in wages (either directly or by holding wages constant while letting the price of capital rise) of, say, 10% will lead to a 5% to 10% increase in employment.

Appendix 5.2

The Ahluwalia-Chenery Welfare Index

The necessity of reorienting development priorities away from an exclusive preoccupation with maximizing rates of GNI growth and toward broader social objectives such as the eradication of poverty and the reduction of excessive income disparities is now widely recognized throughout the developing world. Figures for GNI per capita give no indication of how national income is actually distributed and who is benefiting most from the growth of production. We have seen, for example, that a rising level of absolute and per capita GNI can camouflage the fact that the poor are no better off than before.

The calculation of the rate of GNI growth is largely a calculation of the rate of growth of the incomes of the upper 40% of the population, who receive a disproportionately large share of the national product. Therefore, the GNI growth rates can be a very misleading index of improved welfare. To give an extreme example, suppose that an economy consisted of only ten people and that nine of them had no income at all and the tenth received 100 units of income. The GNI for this economy would be 100 and per capita GNI would be 10. Now suppose that everyone's income increases by 20% so that GNI rises to 120 while per capita income grows to 12. For the nine individuals with no income before and still no income now ($1.20 \times 0 = 0$), such a rise in per capita income provides no cause for rejoicing. The one rich individual still has all the income. And GNI instead of being a welfare index of society as a whole, is merely measuring the welfare of a single individual!

The same line of reasoning applies to the more realistic situation where incomes are very unequally distributed, although not perfectly unequal as in our example. Taking the figures from Table 5.1, where we divided the population into quintiles that received 5%, 9%, 13%, 22%, and 5% income shares, respectively, we found that these income shares are a measure of the relative economic welfare of each income class and that the rate of income growth in each quintile is a measure of the economic welfare growth of that class. We can approximate the growth in the total welfare of society as the simple weighted sum of the growth of income in each class. This is in fact what the rate of GNI growth measures—the weights applied to each income class are their respective shares of national income. To be specific, in the case of a population divided into quintiles according to rising income levels, we would have

$$G = w_1 g_1 + w_2 g_2 + w_3 g_3 + w_4 g_4 + w_5 g_5 \qquad \text{(A5.2.1)}$$

where G = a weighted index of growth of social welfare, g_i = the growth rate of income of the ith quintile (where the i quintiles are ordered 1, 2, 3, 4, and 5 in our example), and w_i = the "welfare weight" of the ith quintile (in our example, $w_1 = 0.05$, $w_2 = 0.09$; $w_3 = 0.13$, $w_4 = 0.22$, and $w_5 = 0.51$). As long as the weights add up to unity and are nonnegative, our overall measure of the growth of social welfare, G, must fall somewhere between the maximum and minimum income growth rates in the various quintiles. In the extreme case of all income accruing to one individual or one group of individuals in the highest quintile and where the welfare weights are the income shares (as they are with GNI growth calculations), Equation A5.2.1 would be written as

$$G = 0g_1 + 0g_2 + 0g_3 + 0g_4 + 0g_5 = 1g_5 \qquad \text{(A5.2.2)}$$

The growth of social welfare would therefore be associated exclusively with the growth of incomes of the top quintile of the population!

In the example derived from Table 5.1, the GNI income share weighted index of social welfare would be written as

$$G = 0.05g_1 + 0.09g_2 + 0.13g_3 + 0.22g_4 + 0.51g_5 \qquad \text{(A5.2.3)}$$

New suppose that the income growth rate of the bottom 60% of the population is zero ($g_1 = g_2 = g_3 = 0$) while that of the top 40% is 10% ($g_4 = g_5 = 0.10$). Equation A5.2.3 could therefore be written as

$$G = 0.05(0) + 0.09(0) + 0.13(0) + 0.22(0.10) + 0.51(0.10) = 0.073 \qquad \text{(A5.2.4)}$$

and the social welfare index would rise by more than 7%, which is the rate of growth of GNI (i.e., GNI would rise from 100 in Table 5.1 to 107.3 if the incomes of the 4th and 5th quintiles grew by 10%). Thus we have an illustration of a case where GNI rises by 7.3%, implying that social well-being has increased by this same proportionate amount even though 60% of the population is no better off than before. This bottom 60% still has only 5, 13, and 22 units of income, respectively. Clearly, the distribution of income would be worsened (the relative shares of the bottom 60% would fall) by such a respectable growth rate of GNI.

The numerical example given by Equation A5.2.4 illustrates our basic point. The use of the growth rate of GNI as an index of social welfare and as a method of comparing the development performance of different countries can be misleading, especially where countries have markedly different distributions of income. The welfare weights attached to the growth rates of different income groups are unequal, with a heavy social premium being placed on the income growth of the highest-quintile groups. In the example of Equation A5.2.3, a 1% growth in the income of the top quintile carries more than ten times the weight of a 1% growth in the lowest quintile (0.51 compared with 0.05) because it implies an absolute increment that is ten times larger. In other words, using the measure of GNI growth as an index of improvements in social welfare and development accords to each income group a welfare valuation that corresponds to its respective income share (i.e., a 1% increase in the income of the richest 20% of the population is implicitly assumed to be more than ten times as important to society as a 1% increase in the income of the bottom 20%). It follows that the best way to maximize social welfare growth is to maximize the rate of growth of the incomes of the rich while neglecting the poor! If ever there was a case for *not* equating GNI growth with development, this example should provide a persuasive illustration.

Constructing a Poverty-Weighted Index of Social Welfare

An alternative to using a simple GNI growth rate or distributive share index of social welfare would be to construct an equal-weights or even a poverty-weighted index. The latter two indexes might be especially relevant for countries concerned with the elimination of poverty as a major development objective. As its name indicates, an equal-weights index weights the growth of income in each income class not by the proportion of total income in that class but rather by the proportion of the total population—that is, all people are treated ("weighted") equally. In an economy divided into quintiles, such as index would give a weight of 0.2 to the growth of income in each quintile. So a 10% increase in the income of the lowest 20% of the population would have the same bearing on the overall measure of social welfare improvements as a 10% increase in the top 20% group or in any other quintile group, even though the absolute increase in income for the bottom group will be much smaller than for the upper groups.

Using an equal-weights index in our example of a 10% income growth of the top two quintiles with the bottom three remaining static, we would have

$$G = 0.20g_1 + 0.20g_2 + 0.20g_3 + 0.20g_4 + 0.20g_5 \qquad \text{(A5.2.5)}$$

or, inserting growth rates for g_1, through g_5,

$$G = 0.20(0) + 0.20(0) + 0.20(0) + 0.20(0.10) + 0.20(0.10) = 0.04 \qquad \text{(A5.2.6)}$$

Social welfare will have increased by only 4%, compared to the 7.3% increase recorded by using the distributive shares or GNI growth rate index. Even though recorded GNI still grows by 7.3%, this alternative welfare index of development shows only a 4% rise.

Finally, consider a developing country that is genuinely and solely concerned with improving the material well-being of say, the poorest 40% of its population. Such a country might wish to construct a poverty-weighted index of development, which places "subjective" social values on the income growth rates of only the bottom 40%. In other words, it might arbitrarily place a welfare weight on w_1, of 0.60 and on w_2 of 0.40 while giving w_3, w_4, and w_5 zero weights. Using our same numerical example, the social welfare growth index for this country would be given by the expression

$$G = 0.60g_1 + 0.40g_2 + 0g_3 + 0g_4 + 0g_5 \qquad \text{(A5.2.7)}$$

which, when substituting $g_1 = g_2 = g_3 = 0$ and $g_4 = g_5 = 0.10$, becomes

$$G = 0.60(0) + 0.40(0) + 0(0) + 0(0.10) = 0(0 - 10) \qquad \text{(A5.2.8)}$$

The poverty-weighted index therefore records *no* improvement in social welfare (no development), even though recorded GNI has grown by 7.3%!

Although the choice of welfare weights in any index of development is purely arbitrary, it does represent and reflect important social value judgments about goals and objectives for a given society. It would certainly be interesting to know, if this were possible, the real implicit welfare weights of the various development strategies of different developing countries. Our main point, however, is that as long as the growth rate of GNI is explicitly or implicitly used to compare development performances, we know that a "wealthy weights" index is actually being employed.

To put some real-world flavor into the discussion of alternative indexes of improvements in economic welfare and to illustrate the usefulness of different weighted growth indexes in evaluating the economic performance of various countries, consider the data in Table A5.2 compiled by Montek Ahluwalia and Hollis Chenery. The table shows the growth of income in 12 countries as measured first by the rate of growth of GNI (GNI weights), second by an equal-weights index, and third by a poverty-weighted index where the actual weights assigned to income growth rates of the lowest 40%, the middle 40%, and the top 20% of the population are 0.6, 0.4, and 0.0, respectively. Some interesting conclusions emerge from a review of the last three columns of Table A5.2.

1. Economic performance as measured by equal-weights and poverty-weighted indexes was notably worse in some otherwise high-GNI-growth countries like Brazil, Mexico, and Panama. Because these countries all experienced a deterioration in income distribution and a growing concentration of income growth in the upper groups over this period, the equal-weights and poverty-weighted indexes naturally show a less impressive development performance than the simple GNI measure.

2. In five countries (Columbia, Costa Rica, El Salvador, Sri Lanka, and Taiwan), the weighted indexes show a better performance than GNI growth because the relative in-

TABLE A5.2	Income Distribution and Growth in Twelve Selected Countries					
	Income Growth			Annual Increase in Welfare		
Country	Upper 20%	Middle 40%	Lowest 40%	GNI Weights	Equal Weights	Poverty Weights
Brazil	6.7	3.1	3.7	5.2	4.1	3.5
Colombia	5.2	7.9	7.8	6.2	7.3	7.8
Costa Rica	4.5	9.3	7.0	6.3	7.4	7.8
El Salvador	3.5	9.5	6.4	5.7	7.1	7.4
India	5.3	3.5	2.0	4.2	3.3	2.5
Mexico	8.8	5.8	6.0	7.8	6.5	5.9
Panama	8.8	9.2	3.2	8.2	6.7	5.2
Peru	3.9	6.7	2.4	4.6	4.4	3.8
Philippines	5.0	6.7	4.4	5.5	5.4	5.2
South Korea	12.4	9.5	11.0	11.0	10.7	10.5
Sri Lanka	3.1	6.3	8.3	5.0	6.5	7.6
Taiwan	4.5	9.1	12.1	6.8	9.4	11.1

Source: Montek S. Ahluwalia and Hollis B. Chenery, "A conceptual framework for economic analysis," in *Redistribution with Growth: An Approach to Policy*, ed. Hollis B. Chenery, John Duloy, and Richard Jolly (Washington, D.C.: World Bank, 1974), p. 5. Copyright © 2004 by the World Bank. Reprinted with the permission of the World Bank via the Copyright Clearance Center.

come growth of lower-income groups proceeded more rapidly over the period in question in those five countries than that of the higher-income groups.

3. In three countries (Peru, the Philippines, and South Korea), little change in income distribution during the period in question resulted in little variation between the GNI measure and the two alternative weighted indexes of social welfare.

We may conclude, therefore, that a useful summary measure of the degree to which economic growth is biased toward the relative improvement of high-income or low-income groups is the positive or negative divergence between a weighted social welfare index and the actual growth rate of GNI.

CHAPTER SIX

Population Growth and Economic Development: Causes, Consequences, and Controversies

The central issue of our time may well turn out to be how the world addresses the problem of ever-expanding human numbers.

—James Grant, Former Director General, UNICEF

Population-related goals and policies are integral parts of cultural, economic and social development.

—Program of Action, 1994 United Nations International Conference on Population and Development

As the twenty-first century began, the world's population was estimated to be almost 6.1 billion people. Projections by the United Nations placed the figure at more than 9.2 billion by the year 2050 before reaching a maximum of 11 billion by 2200. Over 90% of that population will inhabit the developing world. What will be the economic and social implications for levels of living, national and personal esteem, and freedom of choice—in short, for development—if such projections are realized? Are such projections inevitable, or will they depend on the success or failure of development efforts? Finally, even more significant, is rapid population growth per se as serious a problem as many people believe, or is it a manifestation of more fundamental problems of underdevelopment and the unequal utilization of global resources between rich and poor nations, as others argue?

In this chapter, we examine many of the issues relating population growth to economic development. We begin, however, by looking at historical and recent population trends and the changing geographic distribution of the world's people. After explaining basic demographic concepts, we present some well-known economic models and hypotheses regarding the causes and consequences of rapid population growth in contemporary LDCs. Controversies surrounding the significance of the population factor in general and these models and hypotheses in particular are then explored. Finally, we evaluate a range of alternative policy options that developing countries may wish to adopt to influence the size and growth of their populations, as well as ways in which industrialized countries can contribute to a more manageable global population and resource environment. Population policies in China and India with the largest populations in the world, is this chapter's case study.

The Basic Issue: Population Growth and the Quality of Life

Every year approximately 80 million people are being added to the world's population. Almost all of this net population increase—97%—is in developing countries. Increases of such magnitude are unprecedented. But the problem of population growth is not simply a problem of numbers. It is a problem of human welfare and of development as defined in Chapter 1. Rapid population growth can have serious consequences for the well-being of all of humanity. If development entails the improvement in people's levels of living—their incomes, health, education, and general well-being—and if it also encompasses their self-esteem, respect, dignity, and freedom to choose, then the really important question about population growth is this: How does the contemporary population situation in many developing countries contribute to or detract from their chances of realizing the goals of development, not only for the current generation but also for future generations? Conversely, how does development affect population growth?

Among the major issues relating to this basic question are the following:

1. Will developing countries be capable of improving the levels of living for their people with the current and anticipated levels of population growth? To what extent does rapid population increase make it more difficult to provide essential social services, including housing, transport, sanitation, and security?

2. How will the developing countries be able to cope with the vast increases in their labor forces over the coming decades? Will employment opportunities be plentiful, or will it be a major achievement just to keep unemployment levels from rising?

3. What are the implications of higher population growth rates among the world's poor for their chances of overcoming the human misery of absolute poverty? Will world food supply and its distribution be sufficient not only to meet the anticipated population increase in the coming decades but also to improve nutritional levels to the point where all humans can have an adequate diet?

4. Given the anticipated population growth, will developing countries be able to extend the coverage and improve the quality of their health and educational systems so that everyone can at least have the chance to secure adequate health care and a basic education?

5. To what extent are low levels of living an important factor in limiting the freedom of parents to choose a desired family size? Is there a relationship between poverty and family size?

6. To what extent is the growing affluence among the economically more developed nations an important factor preventing poor nations from accommodating their growing populations? And is the inexorable pursuit of increasing affluence among the rich more detrimental to the global environment and to rising living standards among the poor than the absolute increase in their numbers?

A Review of Numbers: Population Growth—Past, Present, and Future

World Population Growth through History

Throughout most of the more than 2 million years of human existence on earth, humanity's numbers have been few. When people first started to cultivate food through agriculture some 12,000 years ago, the estimated world population was no more than 5 million (see Table 6.1). At the beginning of the common era 2,000 years ago, world population had grown to nearly 250 million, less than a fifth of the population of China today. From A.D. 1 to the beginning of the industrial revolution around 1750, it tripled to 728 million people, well under the total number living in India today. During the next 200 years (1750–1950), an additional 1.7 billion people were added to the earth's numbers. But in just four decades thereafter (1950–1990), world population more than doubled again, bringing the total figure to around 5.3 billion. The world entered the twenty-first century with almost 6.1 billion people. Figure 6.1 shows how rapidly total population grew in the four decades after 1950 in comparison with the two centuries before that. It vividly portrays the magnitude of population growth in the less developed regions of the world since 1950, both as a percentage of the total (Figure 6.1a) and in terms of absolute increases (Figure 6.1b). Finally, it provides projections to the year 2200, when world population is expected to stabilize at around 11 billion (some recent estimates are somewhat smaller).

Turning from absolute numbers to percentage growth rates, we can see from Table 6.2 that for almost the whole of human existence on earth until approximately 300 years ago, population grew at an annual rate not much greater than zero (0.002%, or 20 per million). Naturally, this overall rate was not steady; there were many ups and downs as a result of natural catastrophes and variations in growth rates among regions. By 1750, the population growth rate had accelerated by 150 times, from 0.002% to 0.3% per year. By the 1950s, the rate had again accelerated, tripling to about 1.0% per year. It continued to accelerate until around 1970, when it peaked at 2.35%.[1] Today the world's population growth rate remains at a historically high rate of 1.3% per year, but the rate of increase is slowing. However, the population growth rate in Africa is still an extremely high 2.4% per year.

The relationship between annual percentage increases and the time it takes for a population to double in size, or **doubling time**, is shown in the rightmost column of Table 6.2. We see that before 1650, it took nearly 36,000 years, or about 1,400 generations, for the world population to double. Today, in less than 53 years, or two generations, world population will double.[2] Moreover, whereas it took almost 1,750 years to add 480 million people to the world's population between

		Estimated Annual Percentage Increase in the Intervening Period
Year	**Estimated Population (millions)**	
10,000 B.C.	5	
A.D. 1	250	0.04
1650	545	0.04
1750	728	0.29
1800	906	0.45
1850	1,171	0.53
1900	1,608	0.65
1950	2,576	0.91
1970	3,698	2.09
1980	4,448	1.76
1990	5,292	1.73
2000	6,090	1.48
2050 (projected)	9,036	0.45

TABLE 6.1   Estimated World Population Growth through History

Sources: Warren S. Thompson and David T. Lewis, *Population Problems*, 5th ed. (New York: McGraw-Hill, 1965), p. 384: United Nations, *Demographic Yearbook for 1971* (New York: United Nations, 1971); United Nations, *Report on the World Social Situation, 1997* (New York: United Nations, 1997), p. 14; Population Reference Bureau, *World Population Data Sheet* (Washington, D.C.: Population Reference Bureau, 1998, 2001).

A.D. 1 and the onset of the industrial revolution, at current growth rates this same number of people is being added to the earth's population every six years!

The reason for the sudden change in overall population trends is that for almost all of recorded history, the rate of population change, whether up or down, had been strongly influenced by the combined effects of famine, disease, malnutrition, plague, and war—conditions that resulted in high and fluctuating death rates. In the twentieth century, such conditions came increasingly under technological and economic control. As a result, human mortality (the death rate) is now lower than at any other point in human existence. It is this decline in mortality resulting from rapid technological advances in modern medicine and the spread of modern sanitation measures throughout the world, particularly within the past half century, that has resulted in the unprecedented increases in world population growth, especially in developing countries. For example, death rates in Africa, Asia, and Latin America have fallen by as much as 50% during the past 30 to 40 years, whereas birthrates have only recently begun to decline.

In short, population growth today is primarily the result of a rapid transition from a long historical era characterized by high birth and death rates to one in which death rates have fallen sharply but birthrates, especially in developing countries, are only just beginning to fall from their historically high levels.

Structure of the World's Population

The world's population is very unevenly distributed by geographic region, by fertility and mortality levels, and by age structures.

Geographic Region   More than three-quarters of the world's people live in developing countries; fewer than one person in four lives in an economically developed

FIGURE 6.1 Population Growth, 1750–2200: World, Less Developed Regions, and More Developed Regions

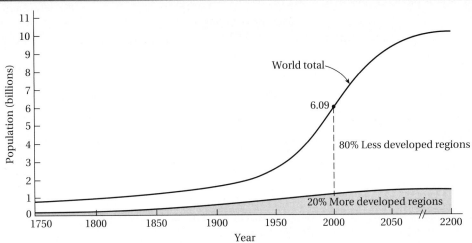

(a) Absolute size

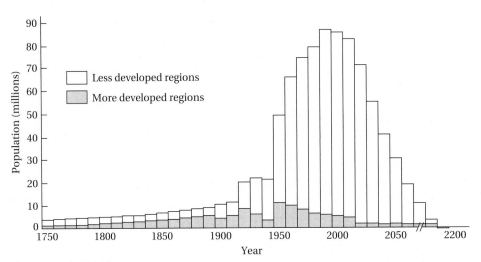

(b) Increase by decade

Sources: Thomas W. Merrick, "World population in transition," *Population Bulletin* 41 (1986): 4, and United Nations, *Report on the World Social Situation, 1997* (New York: United Nations, 1997), pp. 14–15.
Note: The less developed regions are Africa, Asia (minus Japan), and Latin America; the more developed regions are Europe, the former USSR, Japan, Oceania (including Australia and New Zealand), and North America (Canada and the United States).

Period	Approximate Growth Rate (%)	Doubling Time (years)
Appearance of humans to early historical times	0.002	36,000
1650–1750	0.3	240
1850–1900	0.6	115
1930–1950	1.0	72
1960–1980	2.3	31
Present	1.3	54

TABLE 6.2   World Population Growth Rates and Doubling Times

Sources: Warren S. Thompson and David T. Lewis, *Population Problems*, 5th ed. (New York: McGraw-Hill, 1965), p. 384; Population Reference Bureau, *2001 World Population Data Sheet* (Washington, D.C.: Population Reference Bureau, 2001).

nation. Figure 6.2 shows the regional distribution of the world's population as it existed in 2003 and as it is projected for 2050.

Given current population growth rates in different parts of the world (significantly higher in the LDCs), the regional distribution of the world's population will inevitably change by 2050. By that time, it is likely that there will be 6.6 billion more people on the earth than in 1950 and 3.1 billion more than in 2000. Africa will experience the largest percentage increase (184%), and its projected population of 2.1 billion will be almost three times its 1998 population and almost 10 times its 1950 population. Latin America and Asia are projected to grow by 70% and 50%, respectively. Together these three continents will probably hold over 88% of the world's population by 2050, as contrasted with 70% in 1950 and 82% in

FIGURE 6.2   World Population Distribution by Region, 2003 and 2050

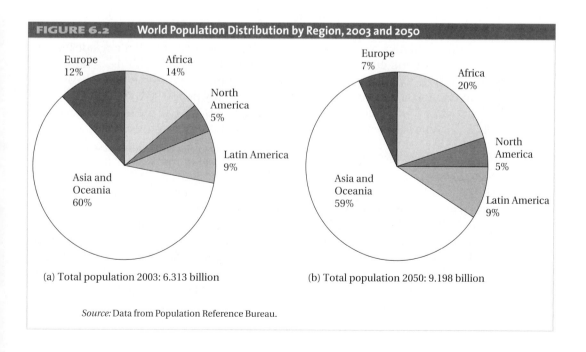

(a) Total population 2003: 6.313 billion

(b) Total population 2050: 9.198 billion

Source: Data from Population Reference Bureau.

Rank	Country	2003 Population (millions)	Rate of Increase (%)
1	China	1,289	0.6
2	India	1,069	1.7
3	United States	292	0.6
4	Indonesia	221	1.6
5	Brazil	177	1.3
6	Pakistan	149	2.7
7	Bangladesh	147	2.2
8	Russia	146	−0.7
9	Nigeria	134	2.8
10	Japan	128	0.1
11	Mexico	105	2.4
12	Germany	83	−0.1
13	Philippines	82	2.2
14	Vietnam	81	1.3
15	Egypt	72	2.1

TABLE 6.3 The Fifteen Largest Countries and Their Annual Population Increases

Source: Population Reference Bureau, *2003 World Population Data Sheet* (Washington, D.C.: Population Reference Bureau, 2003). Reprinted with permission.

1998. Correspondingly, the proportion of the world's population living in Europe, the former Soviet Union, and North America will have fallen from 17% to less than 12% of the total.

Consider, finally, the distribution of national populations. Table 6.3 lists the 15 largest countries in the world in 2003. Together they account for over 40% of the world's population.

Although these countries are on all the continents and in both developed and underdeveloped regions, it is instructive to note that in terms of annual increases in world population, countries such as India, Indonesia, Brazil, Bangladesh, Pakistan, and Nigeria all add more to the world's annual population increase than most of the economically more developed countries do. For example, Pakistan, ranked sixth in size, adds more than twice as many people to the absolute growth of the world's population than the United States, which ranks third. Similarly, Mexico, ranked eleventh, adds more people annually than the combined total of Russia, Germany, Japan, and the United States.

World population distribution is put into dramatic perspective by the map in Figure 6.3. Each box represents one million inhabitants. The ever-growing population share of the developing world is revealed by the large size of India in comparison with Europe. China is bordered on the north and west by a thin strip of land that represents Russia. Mexico looms very large in comparison with Canada—a dramatic reversal of conventional maps; taken together, even the Caribbean islands are larger than Canada. Bangladesh, smaller in size than the U.S. state of Wisconsin, appears larger than Germany and France combined. In Africa, the prominence of Nigeria stands out. Indonesia, which gets comparatively little international attention, dwarfs its neighbor Australia while appearing nearly as large as the United States.

TOTAL WORLD POPULATION = 6,446,131,400

1 grid square = 1 million people

Countries with more than 10 million people have their populations labeled on the map

Countries with less than 1 million people not shown on map:

Andorra	Cyprus	Kiribati	Sao Tome and Principe
Antigua and Barbuda	Djibouti	Liechtenstein	Seychelles
Bahamas	Dominica	Luxembourg	Solomon Islands
Bahrain	Equatorial Guinea	Maldives	Suriname
Barbados	Fiji	Malta	Tonga
Belize	Grenada	Marshall Islands	Tuvalu
Brunei	Guyana	Micronesia	Vanuatu
Cape Verde	Iceland	Monaco	Vatican City
Comoros		Nauru	
		Palau	
		Qatar	
		St Kitts & Nevis	
		St Lucia	
		St Vincent & the Grenadines	
		Samoa	
		San Marino	

Sources: U.S. Bureau of the Census, International Data Base 2005 population estimates; Tibet Information Network, Free Tibet Campaign

Source: **Copyright © ODT, Inc., 2005, http://www.odt.org.**

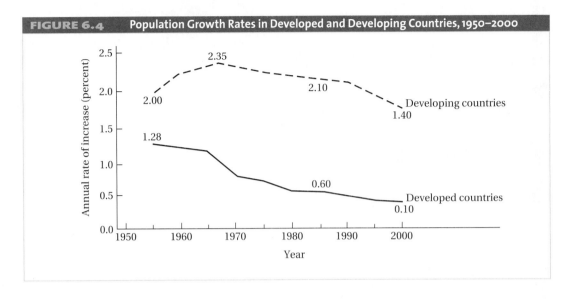

FIGURE 6.4   Population Growth Rates in Developed and Developing Countries, 1950–2000

Fertility and Mortality Trends The **rate of population increase** is quantitatively measured as the percentage yearly net relative increase (or decrease, in which case it is negative) in population size due to **natural increase** and **net international migration**. Natural increase simply measures the excess of births over deaths or, in more technical terms, the difference between fertility and mortality. Net international migration is of negligible, though growing, importance today (although in the nineteenth and early twentieth centuries it was an extremely important source of population increase in North America, Australia, and New Zealand and corresponding decrease in Western Europe). Population increases in developing countries therefore depend almost entirely on the difference between their birth and death rates.

The difference between developing and developed nations in terms of rates of population growth can be explained simply by the fact that **birthrates** (**fertility rates**) in developing countries are generally much higher than in the rich nations. LDC **death rates** (**mortality rates**) are also higher. However, these death rate differences are substantially smaller than the differences in birthrates. As a result, the average rate of population growth in the developing countries is now about 1.3% per year (1.6% excluding China), whereas the economically developed countries have an annual average natural growth rate of only 0.1%. Figure 6.4 shows recent and projected trends in population growth for both developed and less developed nations. Note that the overall population growth rate in developing countries appears to have peaked at an annual rate of 2.35% around 1970 and is now declining.

As just noted, the major source of difference in population growth rates between the less developed and the more developed countries is the sizable difference in their birthrates. Recall from Chapter 2 that most developing nations have birthrates ranging from 20 to 40 per 1,000. By contrast, in almost all developed countries, the rate is less than 15 per 1,000. Moreover, LDC birthrates today are often higher than they were in preindustrial Western Europe. This is largely because

TABLE 6.4	Fertility Rate for Selected Countries, 1970 and 2002	
	Total Fertility Rate[a]	
Country	1970	2002
Bangladesh	7.0	3.6
Colombia	5.3	2.7
Indonesia	5.5	2.6
Jamaica	5.3	2.4
Mexico	4.9	2.8
Thailand	5.5	1.7
Zimbabwe	7.7	4.0

Sources: World Bank, *World Development Report, 1994* (New York: Oxford University Press, 1994), tab. 26; Population Reference Bureau, *2003 World Population Data Sheet* (Washington, D.C.: Population Reference Bureau, 2004).
[a]Average number of children born to women who live beyond age 49.

of early and almost universal marriage in contemporary developing countries. But there has been a substantial decline in LDC fertility over the past two decades, not only in countries like Taiwan, South Korea, and Singapore, where rapid economic and social development have taken place, but also in nations where growth has been less rapid, including Mexico and Bangladesh, and in some where growth has stagnated, such as Zimbabwe. Table 6.4 lists seven countries that experienced significant fertility declines between 1970 and 2002. Nevertheless, the **total fertility rate** (the average number of children a woman would have assuming that current age-specific birthrates remain constant throughout her childbearing years, 15–49 years of age) remains very high in sub-Saharan Africa (5.6) and Western Asia (3.7).

While fertility has been declining in many LDCs, there has been a rapid narrowing of the gap in mortality rates between developed and less developed countries. The primary reason is undoubtedly the improvement in health conditions throughout the developing world. Modern vaccination campaigns against malaria, smallpox, yellow fever, and cholera as well as the proliferation of public-health facilities, clean water supplies, improved nutrition, and public education have all worked together over the past three decades to lower death rates by as much as 50% in parts of Asia and Latin America and by over 30% in much of Africa and the Middle East. Nevertheless, the average life span remains almost 13 years greater in the developed countries. But even this gap has been sharply reduced in recent decades. For example, in 1950, **life expectancy at birth** for people in developing countries averaged 35 to 40 years, compared with 62 to 65 years in the developed world. By 1980, the difference had fallen to 16 years as life expectancy in the LDCs increased to 56 years (a gain of 42%) while in the industrial nations it had risen to 72 years (an increase of 13%). Today, because of still relatively high **infant mortality rates** and the AIDS epidemic sub-Saharan Africa has the lowest life expectancy, 46 years, while in the high-income countries life expectancy at birth now averages about 78 years. Nevertheless, for many LDCs, infant mortality rates have declined dramatically over the past few decades (see Table 6.5), creating the basis for longer life expectancies. In East Asia and Latin America life expectancies have reached an impressive 69 and 71 years, respectively.

TABLE 6.5	Infant Mortality Rates, 1970 and 2003		
		Infant Mortality (per 1,000 live births)	
Country		1970	2003
Bangladesh		140	66
Bolivia		163	61
China		69	32
Ghana		111	56
India		137	66
Kenya		102	66
Nigeria		139	75
Sri Lanka		53	13
Zambia		106	95

Sources: World Bank, *World Development Indicators, 2003* (Washington, D.C.: World Bank, 2003), tab. 1d; Population Reference Bureau, *2004 World Population Data Sheet* (Washington, D.C.: Population Reference Bureau, 2004).

Age Structure and Dependency Burdens World population today is very youthful, particularly in the developing world. Children under the age of 15 constitute more than 31% of the total population of developing countries but just 18% of developed nations. For example, 46% of Ethiopia's population, 44% of Nigeria's, and 41% of Pakistan's was under 15 in 2002; for Mexico and India, the comparable figure is 33%, and for Iran it is 31%. In countries with such an age structure, the **youth dependency ratio**—the proportion of youths (under age 15) to economically active adults (ages 15 to 64)—is very high. Thus the workforce in developing countries must support almost twice as many children as it does in the wealthier countries. For example, in Sweden and the United Kingdom, the workforce age group (15 to 64) amounts to about 65% of the total population. This workforce has to support only about 18% of the population as youthful dependents. Their main problems relate more to their low population growth and old-age dependents (over age 65), who represent 18% to 16% of their populations. By contrast, in countries like Nigeria, Bangladesh, and Ghana, the economically active workforces and the child dependents each make up about 40% of the total population. In general, the more rapid the population growth rate, the greater the proportion of dependent children in the total population and the more difficult it is for people who are working to support those who are not. This phenomenon of youth dependency also leads to an important concept, the **hidden momentum of population growth**.

The Hidden Momentum of Population Growth

Perhaps the least understood aspect of population growth is its tendency to continue even after birthrates have declined substantially. Population growth has a built-in tendency to continue, a powerful momentum that, like a speeding automobile when the brakes are applied, tends to keep going for some time before coming to a stop. In the case of population growth, this momentum can persist for decades after birthrates drop.

There are two basic reasons for this. First, high birthrates cannot be altered substantially overnight. The social, economic, and institutional forces that have influenced fertility rates over the course of centuries do not simply evaporate at

FIGURE 6.5   Population by Age and Sex (Population Pyramids): Less Developed and More Developed Countries, 1998

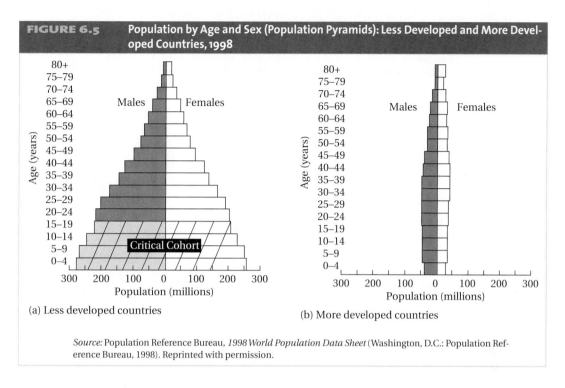

(a) Less developed countries

(b) More developed countries

Source: Population Reference Bureau, *1998 World Population Data Sheet* (Washington, D.C.: Population Reference Bureau, 1998). Reprinted with permission.

the urging of national leaders. We know from the experience of European nations that such reductions in birthrates can take many decades. Consequently, even if developing countries assign top priority to the limitation of population growth, it will still take many years to lower national fertility to desired levels.

The second and less obvious reason for the hidden momentum of population growth relates to the age structure of LDC populations. Figure 6.5 illustrates the great difference between age structures in less developed and more developed countries by means of two **population pyramids** for 1998. Each pyramid rises by five-year age intervals from 0 to 80+ years for both males and females, with the total number in each age cohort measured on the horizontal axis. We see from the LDC pyramid that in 1998 there were over 2 billion young people below the age of 20 and over 400 million youths aged 15 to 19. By contrast, in more developed countries there were fewer than 75 million youths aged 15 to 19. In terms of future population growth, this enormous numerical difference is compounded by the fact that the number of teens giving birth can run as high as 18% to 24% of all teenagers in many LDCs, while in some the ratio is less than 1%.

We saw earlier that nations with high birthrates have large proportions of children and adolescents in their population, sometimes as high as 50%. In such a high-fertility population, young people greatly outnumber their parents, and when their generation reaches adulthood, the number of potential parents will inevitably be much larger than at present. It follows that even if these new parents have only enough children to replace themselves (two per couple, as compared with their parents, who may have had four children), the fact that the total number of couples having two children is much greater than the number of couples

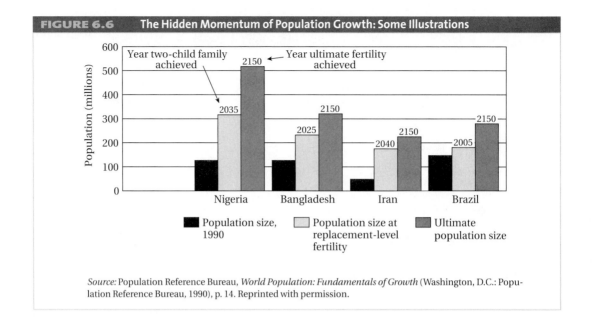

FIGURE 6.6   **The Hidden Momentum of Population Growth: Some Illustrations**

Source: Population Reference Bureau, *World Population: Fundamentals of Growth* (Washington, D.C.: Population Reference Bureau, 1990), p. 14. Reprinted with permission.

who previously had four children means that the total population will still increase substantially before leveling off.

Some examples of the hidden momentum process are illustrated in Figure 6.6 The first bar for each of the four countries gives the 1990 population. The second bar portrays the population size that will be reached when replacement-level fertility (two children per family) is finally achieved according to World Bank estimates. The final bar shows the ultimate projected level of population stability. We see, for example, that if Bangladesh reaches replacement fertility in 2025 at a population of slightly over 200 million, its population will not ultimately stabilize until 2150, when it will have grown by another 100 million people! Nigeria, with its very youthful population and rapid growth rate, can expect an almost fourfold increase in its population before stability is finally attained. Iran can expect a quadrupling of its population, and Brazil's will more than double from present levels. Globally, estimates by demographer John Bongaarts indicate that population momentum alone would increase the number of people in the developing world from 4.5 billion in 1995 to 7.3 billion in 2100 before stabilization would occur.[3]

These illustrations vividly demonstrate the extent to which most developing countries are *already* virtually assured of substantial population increases, whatever happens to fertility levels. As they set goals for desirable future population sizes, they must accept the fact that increases on the order of 60% to 125% are coming regardless of the policy strategies they adopt. But this should not be a cause for despair or a diminished commitment on the part of countries that believe that slowing population growth is in their best national interest. The important message of population momentum is that every year that passes without a reduction in fertility means a larger multiple of the present total population size before it can eventually level off.

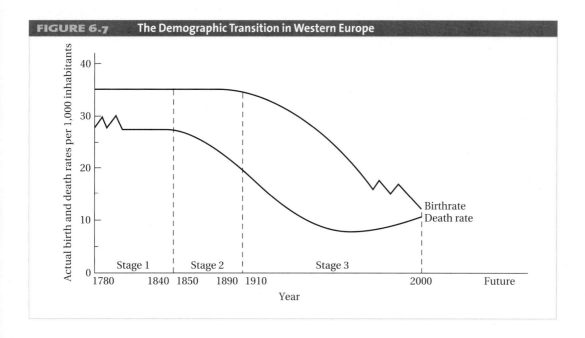

FIGURE 6.7 The Demographic Transition in Western Europe

The Demographic Transition

The process by which fertility rates eventually decline to replacement levels has been portrayed by a famous concept in economic demography called the **demographic transition**. The demographic transition attempts to explain why all contemporary developed nations have more or less passed through the same three stages of modern population history. Before their economic modernization, these countries for centuries had stable or very slow growing populations as a result of a combination of high birthrates and almost equally high death rates. This was stage 1. Stage 2 began when modernization, associated with better public-health methods, healthier diets, higher incomes, and other improvements, led to a marked reduction in mortality that gradually raised life expectancy from under 40 years to over 60 years. However, the decline in death rates was not immediately accompanied by a decline in fertility. As a result, the growing divergence between high birthrates and falling death rates led to sharp increases in population growth compared to past centuries. Stage 2 thus marks the beginning of the demographic transition (the transition from stable or slow-growing populations first to rapidly increasing numbers and then to declining rates). Finally, stage 3 was entered when the forces and influences of modernization and development caused the beginning of a decline in fertility; eventually, falling birthrates converged with lower death rates, leaving little or no population growth.

Figure 6.7 roughly depicts the three historical stages of the demographic transition in Western Europe. Before the early nineteenth century, birthrates hovered around 35 per 1,000 while death rates fluctuated around 30 per 1,000. This resulted in population growth rates of around 5 per 1,000, or less than 0.5% per year.

FIGURE 6.8   The Demographic Transition in Developing Countries

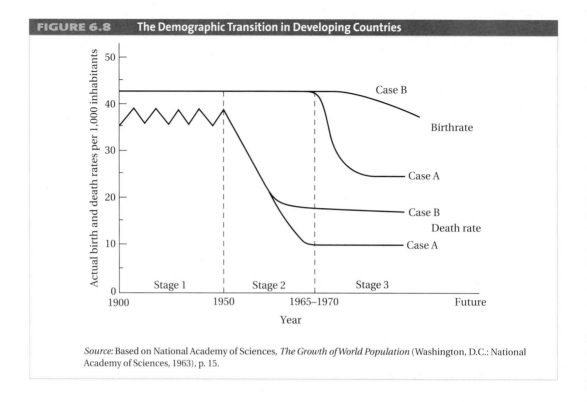

Source: Based on National Academy of Sciences, *The Growth of World Population* (Washington, D.C.: National Academy of Sciences, 1963), p. 15.

Stage 2, the beginning of Western Europe's demographic transition, was initiated around the first quarter of the nineteenth century by slowly falling death rates as a result of improving economic conditions and the gradual development of disease and death control through modern medical and public-health technologies. The decline in birthrates (stage 3) did not really begin until late in the nineteenth century, with most of the reduction many decades after modern economic growth had begun and long after death rates began their descent. But since the initial level of birthrates was generally low in Western Europe as a result of either late marriage or celibacy, overall rates of population growth seldom exceeded the 1% level, even at their peak. By the end of Western Europe's demographic transition in the second half of the twentieth century, the relationship between birth and death rates that marked the early 1800s had reversed, with birthrates fluctuating and death rates remaining fairly stable or rising slightly. This latter phenomenon is simply due to the older age distributions of contemporary European populations.

Figure 6.8 shows the population histories of contemporary developing countries, which contrast with those of Western Europe and fall into two patterns.

Birthrates in many underdeveloped countries today are considerably higher than they were in preindustrial Western Europe. This is because women tend to marry at an earlier age. As a result, there are both more families for a given population size and more years in which to have children. Beginning in the 1940s and especially in the 1950s and 1960s, stage 2 of the demographic transition occurred throughout most of the developing world. The application of highly effective imported modern medical and public-health technologies caused LDC death rates to fall much more rapidly than in nineteenth-century Europe. Given their historically high birthrates (over 40 per 1,000 in many countries), this has meant that stage 2 of the LDC demographic transition has been characterized by population growth rates well in excess of 2.0% per annum.

With regard to stage 3, we can distinguish between two broad classes of developing countries. In case A in Figure 6.8, modern methods of death control combined with rapid and widely distributed rises in levels of living have resulted in death rates falling as low as 10 per 1,000 and birthrates also falling rapidly, to levels between 20 and 30 per 1,000. These countries, most notably Taiwan, South Korea, Costa Rica, China, Cuba, Chile, and Sri Lanka, have thus entered stage 3 of their demographic transition and have experienced rapidly falling rates of overall population growth. In the 1980s and 1990s, several other countries, including Colombia, Indonesia, the Dominican Republic, Thailand, Malaysia, Mexico, Kenya, South Africa, and Brazil, appeared to be entering a period of sustained fertility decline consistent with case A.

But some developing countries fall into case B of Figure 6.8. After an initial period of rapid decline, death rates have failed to drop further, largely because of the persistence of widespread absolute poverty and low levels of living and more recently because of the AIDS epidemic. Moreover, the continuance of high birthrates as a result of these low levels of living causes overall population growth rates to remain relatively high. These countries, including many of those in sub-Saharan Africa and the Middle East, are still in stage 2 of their demographic transition. Though fertility is declining, it remains very high in these parts of the world.

The important question, therefore, is this: When and under what conditions are developing nations likely to experience falling birthrates and a slower expansion of population? To answer this question, we need to ask a prior one. What are the principal determinants or causes of high fertility rates in developing countries, and can these determinants of the "demand" for children be influenced by government policy? To try to answer this critical question, we turn to a very old and famous classical macroeconomic and demographic model, the Malthusian "population trap," and a contemporary and highly influential neoclassical microeconomic model, the household theory of fertility.

The Causes of High Fertility in Developing Countries: The Malthusian and Household Models

The Malthusian Population Trap

Two centuries ago, the Reverend Thomas Malthus put forward a theory of the relationship between population growth and economic development that still survives today. Writing in 1798 in his *Essay on the Principle of Population* and drawing on the concept of diminishing returns, Malthus postulated a universal tendency for the population of a country, unless checked by dwindling food supplies, to grow at a geometric rate, doubling every 30 to 40 years.[4] At the same time, because of diminishing returns to the fixed factor, land, food supplies could expand only at a

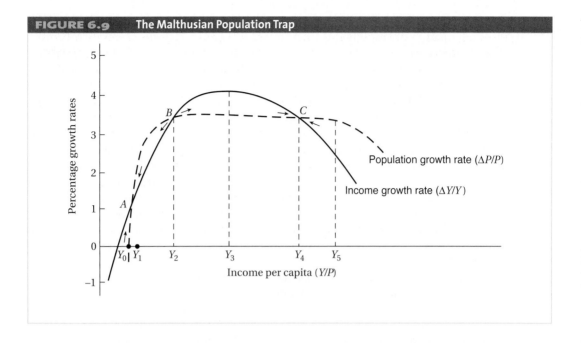

FIGURE 6.9   The Malthusian Population Trap

roughly arithmetic rate. In fact, as each member of the population would have less land to work, his or her marginal contribution to food production would actually start to decline. Because the growth in food supplies could not keep pace with the burgeoning population, per capita incomes (defined in an agrarian society simply as per capita food production) would have a tendency to fall so low as to lead to a stable population existing barely at or slightly above the subsistence level. Malthus therefore contended that the only way to avoid this condition of chronic low levels of living or absolute poverty was for people to engage in "moral restraint" and limit the number of their progeny. Hence we might regard Malthus, indirectly and inadvertently, as the father of the modern birth control movement.

Modern economists have given a name to the Malthusian idea of a population inexorably forced to live at subsistence levels of income. They have called it the *low-level equilibrium population trap* or, more simply, the **Malthusian population trap**. Diagrammatically, the basic Malthusian model can be illustrated by comparing the shape and position of curves representing population growth rates and aggregate income growth rates when these two curves are each plotted against levels of per capita income. This is done in Figure 6.9.

On the vertical axis, we plot numerical percentage changes, both positive and negative, in the two principal variables under consideration (total population and aggregate income). On the horizontal axis are levels of per capita income. Look first at the dashed curve portraying the assumed relationship between rates of population growth $\Delta P/P$ (measured vertically) and levels of per capita income, Y/P (measured horizontally). At a very low level of per capita income, Y_0, the rate of population change will be nil, and a stable population will exist.[5] Thus Y_0 might represent our concept of absolute poverty. Birth and death rates are equal, and the population is barely holding its own absolute level. The situation is analogous to stage 1 of the demographic transition theory. At per capita income levels beyond (to the right of) Y_0, it is assumed that population size will begin to increase under the pressure of falling death rates. Higher incomes means less starvation and disease. And with birthrates always assumed to be at the biological maximum, falling death rates provide the impetus for an expanding population (i.e., stage 2).

In Figure 6.9, population growth achieves its maximum rate, roughly 3.3%, at a per capita income level of Y_2. It is assumed to remain at that level until much higher per capita income levels are realized. Thereafter (beyond Y_5), in accordance with stage 3 of the demographic transition, birthrates will begin to decline, and the population growth rate curve becomes negatively sloped and once again approaches the horizontal axis.

The other part of the Malthusian theory requires us to plot a relationship between the growth rate of aggregate income (in the absence of population growth) and levels of per capita income. We can then compare the two rates (aggregate income and total population). If aggregate income (total product) is rising faster, per capita income by definition must be increasing; if total population is growing faster than total income, per capita income must be falling. In Figure 6.9, the rate of aggregate income growth (also measured vertically) is assumed at first to be positively related to levels of per capita income; that is, the higher the level of per capita income, the higher the rate of increase in aggregate income. The economic reason for this positive relationship is the assumption that savings vary positively with income per capita. Countries with higher per capita incomes are assumed to be capable of generating higher savings rates and thus more investment. Given a Harrod-Domar-type model of economic growth (see Chapter 3), higher savings rates mean higher rates of aggregate income growth. Beyond a certain per capita income point (Y_3), however, the income growth rate curve is assumed to level off and then begin to decline as new investments and more people are required to work with fixed quantities of land and natural resources. This is the point of diminishing returns in the Malthusian model (note that the possibility of technological progress is not considered). The aggregate income growth curve is therefore conceptually analogous to the total product curve in the basic theory of production.

Observe that in Figure 6.9, the curves are drawn so that they intersect at three points, A, B, and C. Point A represents the point at which the Malthusian population trap level of per capita income (Y_1) is attained. It is a stable equilibrium point—any small movement to the left or right of point A will cause the per capita income equilibrium point to return to Y_1. For example, as per capita income rises from Y_1 toward Y_2, the rate of population increase will exceed the rate of aggregate income growth (the $\Delta P/P$ curve is vertically higher than the $\Delta Y/Y$ curve). We know that whenever population is growing faster than income, per capita income must fall. The arrow pointing in the direction of A from the right therefore shows that per capita income must fall back to its very low level at Y_1 for all points between Y_1 and Y_2. Similarly, to the left of point A, incomes grow faster than population, causing the equilibrium per capita income level to rise to Y_1.

According to the neo-Malthusians, poor nations will never be able to rise much above their subsistence levels of per capita income unless they initiate **preventive**

checks (birth control) on their population growth. In the absence of such preventive checks, Malthusian **positive checks** (starvation, disease, wars) on population growth will inevitably provide the restraining force.

Completing our description of the population trap portrayed in Figure 6.9, we see that point B is an "unstable" equilibrium point. If per capita income can somehow jump rapidly from Y_1 to Y_2 (e.g., as a result of "big push" investment and industrialization programs) before Malthusian positive checks take their toll, it will continue to grow until the other stable equilibrium point C at per capita income level Y_4 is reached. Point B is an unstable equilibrium point in the sense that any movement to the left or right will continue until either A or C is reached.

Figure 4.1 in Chapter 4 is also relevant to understanding high-fertility traps. In the diagram, we can relabel the x-axis average (expected) fertility and the y-axis the family's own fertility decision. The upward-sloping response of own fertility to average fertility may be caused by at least two important factors. If others have high fertility, this may increase the number of formal-sector job seekers without (proportionately) increasing the number of formal-sector jobs. Each family may feel it needs a larger number of children to raise the probability that one child will get a modern job. In addition, families often follow local social norms about fertility and tend to model their own behavior on the behavior of others in their community. If the fertility response curve cuts the 45-degree line from above at least twice, then there are at least two stable equilibria (see Chapter 4), one with high and another with low levels of average fertility.

Criticisms of the Malthusian Model

The Malthusian population trap provides a theory of the relationship between population growth and economic development. Unfortunately, it is based on a number of simplistic assumptions and hypotheses that do not stand the test of empirical verification. We can criticize the population trap on two major grounds.

First, and most important, the model (and, indeed, Malthus) assumes away or ignores the enormous impact of technological progress in offsetting the growth-inhibiting forces of rapid population increases. As we discovered in Chapter 2, the history of modern economic growth has been closely associated with rapid technological progress in the form of a continuous series of scientific, technological, and social inventions and innovations. Increasing rather than decreasing returns to scale have been a distinguishing feature of the modern growth epoch. While Malthus was basically correct in assuming a limited supply of land, he did not—and in fairness could not at that time—anticipate the manner in which technological progress could augment the availability of land by raising its quality (its productivity) even though its quantity might remain roughly the same.

In terms of the population trap, rapid and continuing technological progress can be represented by an upward shift of the income growth (total product) curve so that at *all* levels of per capita income it is vertically higher than the population growth curve. This is shown in Figure 6.10. As a result, per capita income will grow steadily over time. All countries therefore have the potential of escaping the Malthusian population trap.

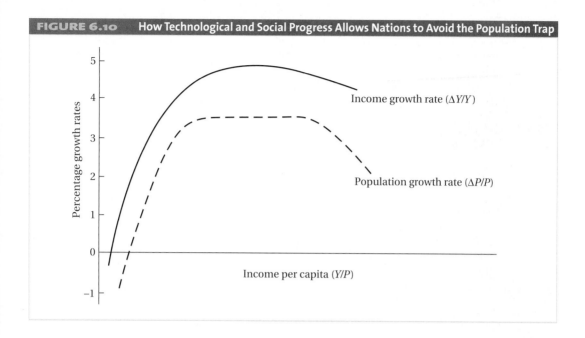

FIGURE 6.10   How Technological and Social Progress Allows Nations to Avoid the Population Trap

The second basic criticism of the trap focuses on its assumption that national rates of population increase are directly (positively) related to the level of national per capita income. According to this assumption, at relatively low levels of per capita income, we should expect to find population growth rates increasing with increasing per capita income. But research on LDCs indicates that there appears to be no clear correlation between population growth rates and levels of per capita income. As a result of modern medicine and public-health programs, death rates have fallen rapidly and have become less dependent on the level of per capita income. Moreover, as we can readily observe from Figure 6.11, birthrates seem to show no rigid relationship with per capita income levels. Note how widely fertility rates vary for countries with the same per capita income, especially in the relevant range of incomes below $1,000. Our conclusion, therefore, is that it is not so much the aggregate level of per capita income that matters for population growth but rather how that income is distributed. It is the level of household income, not the level of per capita income, that seems to matter most. The social and economic institutions of a nation and its philosophy of development are probably greater determinants of population growth rates than aggregate economic variables and simple models of macroeconomic growth.

We can thus largely reject the Malthusian and neo-Malthusian theories as applied to contemporary developing nations on the following grounds:

1. They do not take adequate account of the role and impact of technological progress.

2. They are based on a hypothesis about a macro relationship between population growth and levels of per capita income that does not stand up to empirical testing.

FIGURE 6.11 Fertility in Relation to Income in Developing Countries

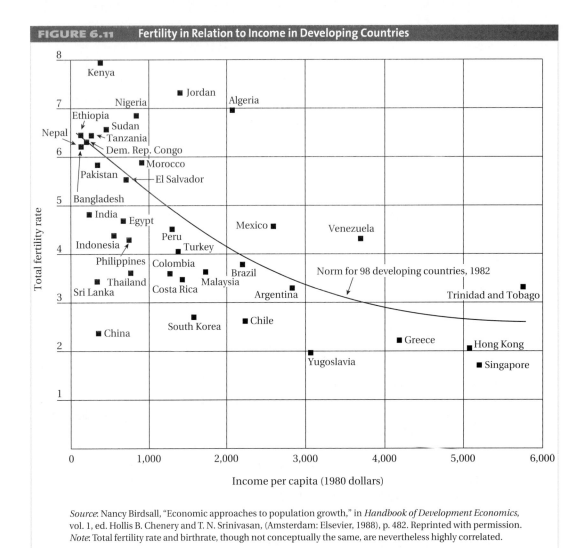

Source: Nancy Birdsall, "Economic approaches to population growth," in *Handbook of Development Economics*, vol. 1, ed. Hollis B. Chenery and T. N. Srinivasan, (Amsterdam: Elsevier, 1988), p. 482. Reprinted with permission.
Note: Total fertility rate and birthrate, though not conceptually the same, are nevertheless highly correlated.

3. They focus on the wrong variable, per capita income, as the principal determinant of population growth rates. A much better and more valid approach to the question of population and development centers on the microeconomics of family size decision making in which individual, and not aggregate, levels of living become the principal determinant of a family's decision to have more or fewer children.

The Microeconomic Household Theory of Fertility

In recent years, economists have begun to look more closely at the microeconomic determinants of family fertility in an attempt to provide a better theoretical and empirical explanation for the observed falling birthrates associated with stage 3 of the demographic transition. In doing this, they have drawn on the traditional neoclassical theory of household and consumer behavior for their basic analytical model and have used the principles of economy and optimization to explain family size decisions.

The conventional theory of consumer behavior assumes that an individual with a given set of tastes or preferences for a range of goods (a "utility function") tries to maximize the satisfaction derived from consuming these goods subject to his or her own income constraint and the relative prices of all goods. In the application of this theory to fertility analysis, children are considered as a special kind of consumption (and in LDCs, investment) good so that fertility becomes a rational economic response to the consumer's (family's) demand for children relative to other goods. The usual income and substitution effects are assumed to apply. That is, if other factors are held constant, the desired number of children can be expected to vary directly with household income (this direct relationship may not hold for poor societies; it depends on the strength of demand for children relative to other consumer goods and to the sources of increased income, such as female employment), inversely with the price (cost) of children, and inversely with the strength of tastes for other goods relative to children. Mathematically, these relationships can be expressed as follows:

$$C_d = f(Y, P_c, P_x, t_x), x = 1, \ldots, n \tag{6.1}$$

where C_d, the demand for surviving children (an important consideration in low-income societies where infant mortality rates are high), is a function of the given level of household income (Y), the "net" price of children (the difference between anticipated costs, mostly the opportunity cost of a mother's time, and benefits, potential child income and old-age support, P_c), the prices of all other goods (P_x), and the tastes for goods relative to children (t_x). Under normal (neoclassical) conditions, we would expect the following (expressed both mathematically and in words):

$\partial C_d / \partial Y > 0$	The higher the household income, the greater the demand for children.
$\partial C_d / \partial P_c < 0$	The higher the net price of children, the lower the quantity demanded.
$\partial C_d / \partial P_x > 0$	The higher the prices of all other goods relative to children, the greater the quantity of children demanded.
$\partial C_d / \partial t_x < 0$	The greater the strength of tastes for goods relative to children, the fewer children demanded.

Figure 6.12 provides a simplified diagrammatic presentation of the **microeconomic theory of fertility**. The number of desired (surviving) children, C_d, is measured along the horizontal axis, and the total quantity of goods consumed by the parents, G_p, is measured on the vertical axis.

Household desires for children are expressed in terms of an indifference map representing the subjective degree of satisfaction derived by the parents for all possible combinations of commodities and children. Each individual indifference curve portrays a locus of commodity-child combinations that yield the same

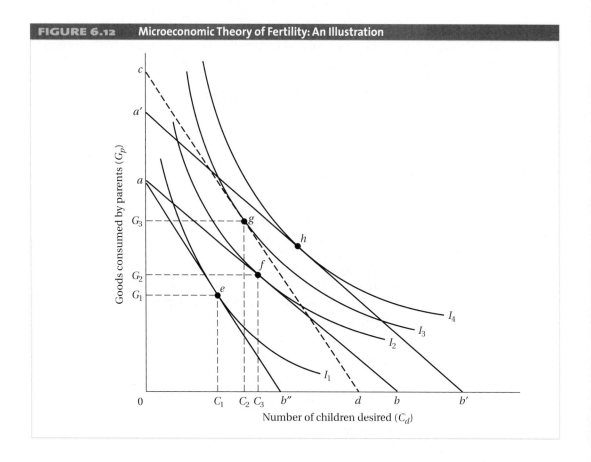

FIGURE 6.12   Microeconomic Theory of Fertility: An Illustration

amount of satisfaction. Any point (or combination of goods and children) on a "higher" indifference curve—that is, on a curve farther out from the origin—represents a higher level of satisfaction than any point on a lower indifference curve. But each indifference curve is a "constant satisfaction" locus.

In Figure 6.12, only four indifference curves, I_1, to I_4, are shown; in theory, there is an infinite set of such curves, filling the whole quadrant and covering all possible commodity-child combinations. The household's ability to "purchase" alternative combinations of goods and children is shown by the budget constraint line, *ab*. Thus all combinations on or below line *ab* (within the triangular area 0*ab*) are financially attainable by the household on the basis of its perceived income prospects and the relative prices of children and goods, as represented by the slope of the *ab* budget constraint. The steeper the slope of the budget line, the higher the price of children relative to goods.

According to the demand-based theory of fertility, the household chooses from among all attainable combinations the one combination of goods and children that maximizes family satisfaction on the basis of its subjectively determined preferences. Diagrammatically, this optimal combination is represented by point *f*, the tangency point between the budget constraint, *ab*, and indifference curve, I_2. Therefore, C_3 children and G_2 goods will be demanded.

A rise in family income, represented in Figure 6.12 by the parallel outward shift of the budget line from *ab* to *a′b′*, enables the household to attain a higher level of satisfaction (point *h* on curve I_4) by consuming more of *both* commodities and children—that is, if children, like most commodities, are assumed to be normal goods (demand for them rises with income), an important if in low-income countries where children are often in demand primarily as a source of future financial security. Note that as income rises, parents may spend more on each child, preferring a smaller number of children, each of higher "quality," for example, healthier and better-educated.

Similarly, an increase in the price (opportunity cost) of children relative to other goods will cause households to substitute commodities for children. Other factors (namely, income and tastes) being constant, a rise in the relative price of children causes the household utility-maximizing consumption combination to occur on a lower indifference curve, as shown by the movement of the equilibrium point from *f* to *e* when the budget line rotates around point *a* to *ab″*.

Note, finally, that if there is a simultaneous increase in household income and net child price as a result of, say, expanding female employment opportunities and a rise in wages coupled with a tax on children beyond a certain number per family, there will be *both* an outward shift and downward rotation of the budget constraint line of Figure 6.12 to, say, dashed line *cd*. The result is a new utility-maximizing combination that includes fewer children per family (point *g* compared with point *f*). In other words, higher levels of living for low-income families in combination with a relative increase in the price of children (whether brought about directly by fiscal measures or indirectly by expanded female employment opportunities) will motivate households to have fewer children while still improving their welfare. This is just one example of how the economic theory of fertility can shed light on the relationship between economic development and population growth as well as suggest possible lines of policy.

The Demand for Children in Developing Countries

As we have seen, the economic theory of fertility assumes that the household demand for children is determined by family preferences for a certain number of surviving (usually male) children (i.e., in regions of high mortality, parents may produce more children than they actually desire in the expectation that some will not survive), by the price or "opportunity cost" of rearing these children, and by levels of family income. Children in poor societies are seen partly as economic investment goods in that there is an expected return in the form of both child labor and the provision of financial support for parents in old age.[6] However, in many developing countries, there is a strong intrinsic psychological and cultural determinant of family size, so that the first two or three children should be viewed as "consumer" goods for which demand may not be very responsive to relative price changes.

The choice mechanism in the economic theory of fertility as applied to LDCs is assumed, therefore, to exist primarily with regard to the additional or marginal children who are considered as investments. In deciding whether or not to have *additional* children, parents are assumed to weigh private economic benefits against private costs, where the principal benefits are, as we have seen, the expected income from child labor, usually on the farm, and eventual financial support for elderly parents. Balanced against these benefits are the two principal elements of cost: the opportunity cost of the mother's time (the income she could earn if she were not at home caring for her children) and the opportunity and actual cost of educating children—the financial trade-off between having fewer "high-quality," high-cost, educated children with high-income-earning potentials versus more "low-quality," low-cost, uneducated children with much lower earning prospects.

Using the same thought processes as in the traditional theory of consumer behavior, the theory of family fertility as applied to LDCs concludes that when the price or cost of children rises as a result of, say, increased educational and employment opportunities for women or a rise in school fees or the establishment of minimum-age child labor laws or the provision of publicly financed old-age social security schemes, parents will demand fewer additional children, substituting, perhaps, quality for quantity or a mother's employment income for her child-rearing activities. It follows that one way to induce families to desire fewer children is to raise the price of child rearing by, say, providing greater educational opportunities and a wider range of higher-paying jobs for young women.

Some Empirical Evidence

Statistical studies in a broad spectrum of developing countries have provided strong support for the economic theory of fertility.[7] For example, it has been found that high female employment opportunities outside the home and greater female school attendance, especially at the primary and secondary levels, are associated with significantly lower levels of fertility. As women become better educated, they tend to earn a larger share of household income and to produce fewer children. Moreover, these studies have confirmed the strong association between declines in child mortality and the subsequent decline in fertility. Assuming that households desire a target number of surviving children, increased female education and higher levels of income can decrease child mortality and therefore increase the chances that the firstborn will survive. As a result, fewer births may be necessary to attain the same number of surviving children. This fact alone underlines the importance of educating women and improving public-health and child nutrition programs in reducing fertility levels.

Implications for Development and Fertility

All of the foregoing can be summarized by saying that the effect of social and economic progress in lowering fertility in developing countries will be the greatest when the majority of the population and especially the very poor share in its benefits. Specifically, birthrates among the very poor are likely to fall where there is

1. An increase in the education of women and a consequent change in their role and status

2. An increase in female nonagricultural wage employment opportunities, which raises the price or cost of their traditional child-rearing activities

3. A rise in family income levels through the increased direct employment and earnings of a husband and wife or through the redistribution of income and assets from rich to poor

4. A reduction in infant mortality through expanded public-health programs and better nutritional status for both mother and child and better medical care

5. The development of old-age and other social security systems outside the extended family network to lessen the economic dependence of parents, especially women, on their offspring

6. Expanded schooling opportunities so parents can better substitute child "quality" for large numbers of children

In short, expanded efforts to make jobs, education, and health more broadly available to poverty groups in general and women in particular will not only contribute to their economic and psychic well-being (i.e., to their development) but can also contribute substantially to their motivation for smaller families (i.e., their freedom to choose), which is vital to reducing population growth rates. Where such motivation exists, well-executed **family-planning programs** can then be an effective tool.[8] But before discussing policy issues and what government might or might not do, we should point out that while there seems to be considerable agreement regarding the determinants or causes of population growth, substantial disagreement and controversy remain regarding its consequences.

The Consequences of High Fertility: Some Conflicting Opinions

For many years, development economists and other social scientists have debated the seriousness of the consequences of rapid population growth. Nowhere was this debate more vocal than at the first World Population Conference held in Bucharest, Romania, in 1974.[9] On the one hand, we must recognize that population growth is not the only, or even the primary, source of low levels of living, eroding self-esteem, and limited freedom in developing nations. On the other hand, it would be equally naive to think that rapid population growth in many countries and regions is not a serious intensifier and multiplier of those integral components of underdevelopment, especially the first and third. The following discussion summarizes some of the main arguments for and against the idea that the consequences of rapid population growth lead to serious development problems. It then considers whether some consensus can be reached so that specific policy goals and objectives can be postulated.[10]

Population Growth Is Not a Real Problem

We can identify three general lines of argument on the part of people who assert that population growth is not a cause for concern:

1. The problem is not population growth but other issues.

2. Population growth is a false issue deliberately created by dominant rich-country agencies and institutions to keep LDCs in their underdeveloped, dependent condition.

3. For many developing countries and regions, population growth is in fact desirable.

Other Issues Many knowledgeable people from both rich and poor nations argue that the real problem is not population growth per se but one or all of the following four issues.

Underdevelopment If correct strategies are pursued and lead to higher levels of living, greater self-esteem, and expanded freedom, population will take care of itself. Eventually, it will disappear as a problem, as it has in all of the present economically advanced nations. According to this argument, underdevelopment is the real problem, and development should be the only goal. With it will come economic progress and social mechanisms that will more or less automatically regulate population growth and distribution. As long as the vast majority of people in developing countries remain impoverished, uneducated, and physically and psychologically weak, the large family will constitute the only real source of social security (i.e., parents will continue to be denied the freedom to choose a small family if they so desire). Proponents of the underdevelopment argument then conclude that birth control programs will surely fail, as they have in the past, when there is no motivation on the part of poor families to limit their size.

World Resource Depletion and Environmental Destruction Population can only be an economic problem in relation to the availability and utilization of scarce natural and material resources. The fact is that developed countries, with less than one-quarter of the world's population, consume almost 80% of the world's resources. For example, the average North American or European consumer uses up, directly and indirectly, almost 16 times as much of the world's food, energy, and material resources as his or her counterpart in developing countries. In terms of the depletion of the world's limited resources, therefore, the addition of another child in the developed countries is as significant as the birth of 16 additional children in the underdeveloped countries. According to this argument, developed nations should curtail their excessively high consumption standards instead of asking less developed nations to restrict their population growth. The latter's high fertility is really due to their low levels of living, which are in turn largely the result of the "overconsumption" of the world's scarce resources by rich nations. This combination of rising affluence and extravagant consumption habits in rich countries and among rich people in poor countries, and not population growth, should be the major world concern. We will analyze issues of the environment and development in Chapter 10.

Population Distribution According to this third argument, it is not the number of people per se that is causing population problems but their distribution in space. Many regions of the world (e.g., parts of sub-Saharan Africa) and many regions within countries (e.g., the northeastern and Amazon regions of Brazil) are in fact underpopulated in terms of available or potential resources. Others simply have too many people concentrated in too small an area (e.g., central Java or most urban concentrations in LDCs). Governments should therefore strive not to moderate the rate of population growth but rather to reduce rural-urban migration and to bring about a more natural spatial distribution of the population in terms of available land and other productive resources.

Subordination of Women As we have seen in Chapter 5 and will discover again later, women often bear the disproportionate burdens of poverty, poor education, lack of jobs, and limited social mobility. In many cases, their inferior roles, low status, and restricted access to birth control are manifested in their high fertility. According to this argument, population growth is a natural outcome of women's lack of economic opportunity. If women's health, education, and economic well-being are improved along with their role and status in both the family and the community, this **empowerment of women** will inevitably lead to smaller families and lower population growth. This was the principal message of the United Nations International Conference on Population and Development held in Cairo in 1994.[11]

A Deliberately Contrived False Issue

The second main line of argument denying the significance of population growth as a major development problem is closely allied to the neocolonial dependence theory of underdevelopment discussed in Chapter 3. Basically, it is argued that the frenetic overconcern in the rich nations with the population growth of poor nations is really an attempt by the former to hold down the development of the latter in order to maintain an international status quo that is favorable to their self-interests. Rich nations are pressuring poor nations to adopt aggressive population control programs even though they themselves went through a period of sizable population increase that accelerated their own development processes.

A radical neo-Marxist version of this argument views population control efforts by rich countries and their allied international agencies as racist or genocidal attempts to reduce the relative or absolute size of the poor, largely nonwhite populations of the world who may someday pose a serious threat to the welfare of the rich, predominantly white societies. Worldwide birth control campaigns are seen as manifestations of the fears of the developed world in the face of a possible radical challenge to the international order by the people who are its first victims.

A Desirable Phenomenon

A more conventional economic argument is that of population growth as an essential ingredient to stimulate economic development. Larger populations provide the needed consumer demand to generate favorable economies of scale in production, to lower production costs, and to provide a sufficient and low-cost labor supply to achieve higher output levels. Population "revisionist" economists of the neoclassical counterrevolution school argue, for example, that free markets will always adjust to any scarcities created by population pressures.[12] Such scarcities will drive up prices and signal the need for new cost-saving production technologies. In the end, free markets and human ingenuity (Julian Simon's "genius" as the "ultimate resource") will solve any and all problems arising from population growth. This revisionist viewpoint was clearly in contrast with the traditional "orthodox" argument that rapid population growth had serious economic consequences that, if left uncorrected, would slow economic development.

At the other end of the political spectrum, it has been argued by some developing-world neo-Marxist pronatalists that many rural regions in developing countries are in reality underpopulated in the sense that much unused but arable land could yield large increases in agricultural output if only more people were available to cultivate it. Many regions of tropical Africa and Latin America and even parts of Asia are said to be in this situation. With respect to Africa, for example, some observers have noted that many regions had larger populations in the remote past than exist today.[13] Their rural depopulation resulted not only from the slave trade but also from compulsory military service, confinement to reservations, and the forced-labor policies of former colonial governments. For example, the sixteenth-century Congo kingdom is said to have had a population of approximately 2 million. But by the time of the colonial conquest, which followed 300 years of slave trade, the population of the region had fallen to less than one-third of that figure. Today parts of the Democratic Republic of Congo (formerly Zaire) have barely caught up to the sixteenth-century numbers.[14] Other regions of western and eastern Africa provide similar examples—at least in the eyes of advocates of rapid population growth in Africa.

In terms of ratios of population to arable land (land under cultivation, fallow land, pastures, and forests), Africa south of the Sahara is said by these supporters of population expansion to have a total of 1.4 billion arable hectares. Land actually being cultivated amounts to only 170 million hectares, or about 1 hectare per rural inhabitant. Thus only 12% of all potential arable land is under cultivation, and this very low rural population density is viewed as a serious drawback to raising agricultural output.[15] Similar arguments have been expounded with regard to such Latin American countries as Brazil and Argentina.

Three other noneconomic arguments, each found to some degree in a wide range of developing countries, complete the "population growth is desirable" viewpoint. First, many countries claim a need for population growth to protect currently underpopulated border regions against the expansionist intentions of neighboring nations. Second, there are many ethnic, racial, and religious groups in less developed countries whose attitudes favoring large family size have to be protected for both moral and political reasons. Finally, military and political power are often seen as dependent on a large and youthful population.

Many of these arguments have a certain realism about them—if not in fact, then at least in the perceptions of vocal and influential individuals in both the developed and the developing worlds. The important point is that they represent a considerable range of opinions and viewpoints and therefore need to be seriously weighed against the counterarguments of theorists who believe that rapid population growth is indeed a real and important problem for underdeveloped countries. Let us now look at some of these counterarguments.

Population Growth Is a Real Problem

Positions supporting the need to curtail population growth because of the negative economic, social, and environmental consequences are typically based on one of the following three arguments.

The Extremist Argument: Population and the Global Crisis The extreme version of the population-as-problem position attempts to attribute almost all of the world's economic and social evils to excessive population growth. Unrestrained population increase is seen as the major crisis facing humankind today. It is regarded as the principal cause of poverty, low levels of living, malnutrition, ill health, environmental degradation, and a wide array of other social problems. Value-laden and incendiary terms such as "population bomb" and "population explosion" are tossed around. Indeed, dire predictions of world food catastrophes and ecological disaster are attributed almost entirely to the growth in world numbers.[16] Such an extreme position leads some of its advocates to assert that "world" (i.e., LDC) population stabilization or even decline is the most urgent contemporary task even if it requires severe and coercive measures such as compulsory sterilization to control family size in some of the most populated developing countries like India and Bangladesh.

The Theoretical Argument: Population-Poverty Cycles and the Need for Family-Planning Programs The **population-poverty cycle** theory is the main argument advanced by economists who hold that too rapid population growth yields negative economic consequences and thus should be a real concern for developing countries. Advocates start from the basic proposition that population growth intensifies and exacerbates the economic, social, and psychological problems associated with the condition of underdevelopment. Population growth is believed to retard the prospects for a better life for the already born by reducing savings rates at the household and national levels. It also severely draws down limited government revenues simply to provide the most rudimentary economic, health, and social services to the additional people. This in turn further reduces the prospects for any improvement in the levels of living of the existing generation and helps transmit poverty to future generations of low-income families.

The basic model that economists use to demonstrate these adverse consequences of rapid population growth is a simplification of the standard Solow-type neoclassical growth equation.[17] Using the standard production function, $Y = f(K, L, R, T)$, that is, output is a function of capital, labor, resources, and technology, and holding the resource base fixed, we can derive the result that

$$y - l = \alpha(k - l) + t \qquad (6.2)$$

where y = rate of GNI growth, l = rate of labor force (population) growth, k = rate of growth of the capital stock, α = capital elasticity of output (usually found to be constant), and t = the effect of technological change (the Solow residual in empirical studies of sources of economic growth in MDCs—see Chapter 3).

Assuming constant returns to scale, Equation 6.2 simply states that the rate of per capita income growth $(y - l)$ is directly proportional to the rate of growth of the capital-labor ratio $(k - l)$ plus the residual effects of technological progress (including improved human and physical capital). Therefore, in the absence of technological change, the higher the rate of population growth (l), the more rapid the rate of capital stock growth (k) must be and thus the greater the concomitant savings and investment rate just to maintain constant levels of per capita income (note the similarity to the Harrod-Domar model in Chapter 3). Moreover, because k may not be independent of l as is traditionally assumed in neoclassical growth models but may in fact be inversely related due to the reduced savings impact implied by the higher dependency burden effects of rapid population growth, it follows that the negative economic impact of population growth may even be greater than these models imply. Finally, if low incomes induce poor families to have more children as a source of cheap labor and old-age security, then we have another vicious cycle in progress—poor people have large families partly to compensate for their poverty, but large families mean greater population growth, higher dependency burdens, lower savings, less investment, slower economic growth, and ultimately greater poverty. Population growth is thus seen as both a cause and a consequence of underdevelopment!

Because widespread absolute poverty and low levels of living are thus seen as a major cause of large family size, and large families retard economic growth, it follows that more egalitarian economic and social development is a necessary condition for bringing about an eventual slowing or cessation of population growth at low levels of fertility and mortality. But according to this argument, it is not a sufficient condition—that is, development provides people with the incentives and motivations to limit their family size, but family-planning programs are needed to provide them with the technological means to avoid unwanted pregnancies. Even though countries like France, Japan, the United States, Great Britain, and, more recently, Taiwan and South Korea were able to reduce their population growth rates without widespread family-planning clinics, it is argued that the provision of these services will enable other countries desiring to control excessive population growth to do so more rapidly than if these family-planning services were not available.

The Empirical Argument: Seven Negative Consequences of Population Growth

According to the latest empirical research, the potential negative consequences of population growth for economic development can be divided into seven categories: its impact on economic growth, poverty and inequality, education, health, food, the environment, and international migration.[18]

Economic Growth Evidence shows that rapid population growth lowers per capita income growth in most LDCs, especially those that are already poor, dependent on agriculture, and experiencing pressures on land and natural resources.

Poverty and Inequality Even though aggregate statistical correlations between measures of poverty and population growth at the national level are often inconclusive, at the household level the evidence is strong and compelling. The negative consequences of rapid population growth fall most heavily on the poor because they are the ones who are made landless, suffer first from cuts in government health and education programs, bear the brunt of environmental damage, and are the main victims of job cuts due to the slower growth of the economy. Poor women once again bear the greatest burden of government austerity programs, and another vicious cycle is set in motion. To the extent that large families perpetuate poverty, they also exacerbate inequality.

Education Although the data are sometimes ambiguous on this point, it is generally agreed that large family size and low incomes restrict the opportunities of parents to educate all their children. At the national level, rapid population growth causes given educational expenditures to be spread more thinly, lowering quality for the sake of quantity. This in turn feeds back on economic growth because the stock of human capital is reduced by rapid population growth.

Health High fertility harms the health of mothers and children. It increases the health risks of pregnancy, and closely spaced births have been shown to reduce birth weight and increase child mortality rates.

Food Feeding the world's population is made more difficult by rapid population growth—over 90% of additional LDC food requirements are caused by population increases. New technologies of production must be introduced more rapidly, as the best lands have already been cultivated. International food relief programs become more widespread.

Environment Rapid population growth contributes to environmental degradation in the form of forest encroachment, deforestation, fuel-wood depletion, soil erosion, declining fish and animal stocks, inadequate and unsafe water, air pollution, and urban congestion (see Chapter 10).

International Migration Many observers consider the rapid increase in international migration, both legal and illegal, to be one of the major consequences of developing countries' population growth. Though many factors cause migration (see Chapter 7), an excess of job seekers (caused by rapid population growth) over job opportunities in the LDC economy is surely one of them. However, unlike the first six consequences listed here, some of the economic and social costs of international migration fall on recipient countries—increasingly in the developed world. It is not surprising, therefore, that this issue has recently taken on political importance in North America and Europe (see Chapters 2 and 18).

Goals and Objectives: Toward a Consensus

In spite of what may appear to be seriously conflicting arguments about the positive and negative consequences of population growth, during the past decade there emerged a common ground on which many people on both sides of the debate could agree. This position is best characterized by Robert Cassen in *Population Policy: A New Consensus*:

> After decades of controversy over the issue of population policy, there is a new international consensus among and between industrial and developing countries that individuals, countries, and the world at large would be better off if population were to grow more slowly. The consequences of rapid population growth should be neither exaggerated nor

minimized. Some past expressions of alarm have been counterproductive, alienating the very audiences they were intended to persuade; at the same time, claims that population growth was not all that important have had the effect of diminishing a proper concern for the subject.[19]

The following three propositions constitute the essential components of this intermediate or consensus opinion.

1. Population growth is not the primary cause of low levels of living, gross inequalities, or the limited freedom of choice that characterize much of the developing world. The fundamental causes of these problems must be sought, rather, in the plight of poor families, especially women, and failure of other aspects of domestic and international development policy.

2. The problem of population is not simply one of numbers but involves the quality of life and material well-being. Thus LDC population size must be viewed in conjunction with developed-country affluence in relation to the quantity, distribution, and utilization of world resources, not just in relation to indigenous resources of the LDCs.

3. But rapid population growth does serve to intensify problems of underdevelopment and make prospects for development that much more remote. As we have seen, the momentum of growth means that, barring catastrophe, the population of developing countries will increase dramatically over the coming decades, no matter what fertility control measures are adopted now. It follows that high population growth rates, though not the principal cause of underdevelopment, are nevertheless important contributing factors in specific countries and regions of the world.

In view of these three propositions, we may conclude that the following three policy goals and objectives might be included in any realistic approach to the issue of population growth in developing countries.

1. In countries or regions where population size, distribution, and growth are viewed as an existing or potential problem, the primary objective of any strategy to limit further growth must deal not only with the population variable per se but also with the underlying social and economic conditions of underdevelopment. Problems such as absolute poverty, gross inequality, widespread unemployment (especially among women), limited female access to education, malnutrition, and poor health facilities must be given high priority. Their amelioration is both a necessary concomitant of development and a fundamental motivational basis for the expanded freedom of the individual to choose an optimal—and, in many cases, smaller—family size.

2. To bring about smaller families through development-induced motivations, family-planning programs providing both the education and the technological means to regulate fertility for people who wish to regulate it should be established.

3. Developed countries should assist developing countries to achieve their lowered fertility and mortality objectives not only by providing contraceptives and

funding family-planning clinics but, more important, by curtailing their own excessive depletion of nonrenewable world resources through programs designed to cut back on the unnecessary consumption of products that intensively use such resources; by making genuine commitments to eradicating poverty, illiteracy, disease, and malnutrition in developing countries as well as their own; and by recognizing in both their rhetoric and their international economic and social dealings that development is the real issue, not simply population control.

Some Policy Approaches

In view of these broad goals and objectives, what kinds of economic and social policies might LDC and developed-country governments and international assistance agencies consider to bring about long-term reductions in the overall rate of world population growth? Three areas of policy can have important direct and indirect influences on the well-being of present and future world populations:

1. General and specific policies that LDC governments can initiate to influence and perhaps even control their population growth and distribution

2. General and specific policies that developed-country governments can initiate in their own countries to lessen their disproportionate consumption of limited world resources and promote a more equitable distribution of the benefits of global economic progress

3. General and specific policies that developed-country governments and international assistance agencies can initiate to help developing countries achieve their population objectives.

Let us deal with each of these areas in turn.

What Developing Countries Can Do

Earlier discussions have led to the conclusion that the principal variables influencing the demand for children at the family level are the ones most closely associated with the concept of development as we have defined it in Part One of this book. Thus certain development policies are particularly crucial in the transition from a high-growth to a low-growth population. These policies aim at eliminating absolute poverty; lessening income inequalities; expanding educational opportunities, especially for women; providing increased job opportunities for both men and women; bringing the benefits of modern preventive medicine and public-health programs, especially the provision of clean water and sanitation, to the rural and urban poor; improving maternal and child health through more food, better diets, and improved nutrition so as to lower infant mortality; and creating a more equitable provision of other social services to wide segments of the population. Again, it is not numbers per se or parental irrationality that is at the root of the LDC "population problem." Rather, it is the pervasiveness of absolute poverty and low levels of

TABLE 6.6	Countries Adopting Family-Planning Programs to Reduce Rates of Population Growth, 1960–1990					
	Date of Adoption of National Family-Planning Program					
Region	Before 1960	1960–1964	1965–1969	1970–1974	1975–1979	1980–1990
Asia and Pacific	India	China Fiji South Korea Pakistan	Indonesia Iran Malaysia Nepal Singapore Sri Lanka Taiwan Turkey	Bangladesh Hong Kong Philippines Thailand	Vietnam	Yemen

Caribbean and Latin America			Barbados
			Dominican
			  Republic
			Jamaica
			Trinidad
			  and Tobago
				Colombia
				El Salvador
				Mexico
				Puerto Rico
					Guatemala	Haiti
						Honduras
						Peru
						Brazil

Africa			Egypt Ghana Kenya Mauritius Morocco Tunisia	Botswana		Algeria Burundi Gambia Lesotho Rwanda Senegal Uganda Zimbabwe
Totals	1	4	18	9	2	13

Source: Population Council, *Data Bank, 1992* (Washington, D.C.: Population Council, 1992). Reprinted with permission.

living that provides the economic rationale for large families and burgeoning populations. And it is the spillover effects or negative social externalities of these private parental decisions (e.g., for education, health care, food supplies, resource degradation, job creation, and income distribution) that provide the strictly economic justification (in terms of "market failure" arguments) for government intervention in population matters. Clearly, there are noneconomic justifications as well.

Although long-run development policies of the kind just outlined are essential to ultimate population stabilization, there are some more specific policies that LDC governments might try to adopt to lower birthrates in the short run.[20] Governments can attempt to control fertility in five ways.

First, they can try to *persuade people* to have smaller families through the media and the educational process, both formal (school system) and informal (adult education).

Second, they can *establish family-planning programs* to provide health and contraceptive services to encourage the desired behavior. Such publicly sponsored or officially supported programs now exist in most developing countries (see Table 6.6). Today only a few large countries, such as Myanmar, Ethiopia, Nigeria, and the Democratic Republic of Congo, do not have such publicly sponsored or officially endorsed family-planning programs.

Third, they can deliberately *manipulate economic incentives and disincentives* for having children—for example, through the elimination or reduction of maternity leaves and benefits, the reduction or elimination of financial incentives, or the imposition of financial penalties for having children beyond a certain number; the establishment of old-age social security provisions and minimum-age child labor laws; the raising of school fees and the elimination of heavy public subsidies for secondary and higher education; and the subsidization of smaller families through direct money payments. Although some form of population-related incentive or disincentive schemes now exist in over 30 LDCs, Singapore, India, Bangladesh, South Korea, and China have been especially prominent in experimenting with policies to reduce family size. For example, Singapore allocated scarce public housing without giving consideration to family size. It also limited paid maternity leave to a maximum of two children, scaling the delivery fee according to number of children, and reducing income tax relief from five to three children. In 1984, it even went so far as to give special priority in school admission to all children born to women with university degrees while penalizing non-degree-holding women with more than two children. The presumed but dubious rationale was that educated women have brighter children whose births should be encouraged while discouraging the less educated (and presumably less intelligent) women from bearing more children. But fertility fell so dramatically that by 2004 the city-state had introduced incentives to *increase* fertility (as with Japan and Europe, relaxed controls on immigration would be more cost-effective).

In India, a tea estate in the mid-1970s experimented with making deposits into savings accounts for individual female workers during their periods of nonpregnancy. The deposits were scaled according to the number of children, and the whole account could be canceled if a woman bore too many children. These accumulated savings were then paid out when the woman reached the age of 45, as a form of social security in the place of children. Later, in northern India, women (or, more usually, their husbands) were provided with cash incentives for sterilization. In Taiwan, a rural township conducted an experiment in which the local government deposited funds into bank accounts for young couples to cover the costs of educating their first two children. However, if the couple had a third child, part of this money was forfeited, and *all* of it was forfeited at the birth of a fourth child. The program was expressly designed to encourage families to have fewer but better-educated children. South Korea also initiated a national system of rewards and penalties to encourage small family size. It offered educational allowances and free medical care to all two-child families provided that one of the parents was sterilized.

China has by far the most comprehensive set of state-enforced incentives and disincentives; they are described in the case study at the end of this chapter.

Fourth, governments can attempt to *coerce people* into having smaller families through the power of state legislation and penalties. For obvious reasons, few governments would attempt to engage in such coercion; not only is it often morally repugnant and politically unacceptable, but it is also almost always extremely difficult to administer. The defeat of Indian Prime Minister Indira Gandhi's government in 1977 was largely due to popular resentment of the government's forced-sterilization program. China's current policy borders on overt coercion and in some regions continues to be met with widespread resistance (again see the case study at the end of the chapter).

Finally, no policy measures will be successful in controlling fertility unless efforts are made to *raise the social and economic status of women* and hence create conditions favorable to delayed marriage and lower marital fertility.[21] A crucial ingredient in any program designed to lower fertility rates is the increased education of women, followed by the creation of jobs for them outside the home. The availability of income-earning opportunities can lead young women to delay marriage by enabling them to become economically self-sufficient and therefore in a better position to exercise control over the choice of partner and the timing of marriage. It can also reduce family pressures for early marriage by allowing women to make a contribution to parental household income. An independent source of income also secures a stronger position for married women in the household, reducing their dependence on other family members, particularly male offspring, for economic security. Furthermore, it enables women to consider the opportunity costs of additional children when childbearing competes with income-generating activities. In general, the availability of outside sources of income offers women genuine alternatives to early marriage and frequent childbearing, which are often motivated by their lack of resources. An additional benefit of employment outside the home is that it reduces women's isolation, which is often an impediment to the provision of family-planning services.

The importance of these policies to improve the role and status of women was underlined at the 1994 Cairo International Conference on Population and Development, where, unlike the first two conferences, held in Bucharest in 1974 and in Mexico City in 1984, less emphasis was placed on the provision of family-planning services and more on the general empowerment of women, especially in the area of **reproductive choice**. The Cairo Program of Action summarized this position in the following manner:

> The empowerment and autonomy of women and the improvement of their political, social, economic and health status . . . [are] essential for the achievement of sustainable development and . . . for the long-term success of population programs. Experience shows that population and development programs are most effective when steps have simultaneously been taken to improve the status of women.[22]

What the Developed Countries Can Do: Resources, Population, and the Global Environment

When we view the problems of population from the perspective of global resources and the environment, as we should, the question of the relationship between population size and distribution and the depletion of many nonrenewable resources in developed and underdeveloped countries assumes major importance. In a world where 4.6% of the population, located in one country, the United States, accounts for 40% of annual world resource use and where under 20% of the world's population accounts for 80% of annual resource use, we are clearly not dealing only or even primarily with a problem of numbers. We must also be concerned with the impact of rising affluence and the very unequal worldwide distribution of incomes on the depletion of many nonrenewable resources such as petroleum, certain basic metals, and other raw materials essential for economic growth.

In terms of food consumption, basic grains like wheat, corn, and rice are by far the most important source of humanity's direct food energy supply (52%). Consumed indirectly (e.g., grain is fed to livestock, which is then consumed as beef, poultry, pork, and lamb or indirectly as milk, cheese, and eggs), they make up a significant share of the remainder. In resource terms, more than 70% of the world's cropland goes into grain production. Yet the average North American directly and indirectly consumes five times as much grain and the corresponding agricultural resources—land, fertilizer, water—as his or her counterpart in India, Nigeria, or Colombia. With regard to energy, probably the second most essential resource to modern society, the average American's consumption of energy fuels (fossil oil and coal, nuclear, and hydroelectric) in 1990 was 25 times the average Brazilian's, 60 times the average Indian's, 191 times the average Nigerian's, and 351 times the average Ethiopian's consumption level! This use of fossil fuel energy to power private automobiles, operate home and office air conditioners, and activate electric toothbrushes in the developed nations is by far the major contributor of carbon dioxide (CO_2) gases into the atmosphere and to the phenomenon of ozone depletion and greenhouse global warming.[23] It also means that there is potentially that much less to fertilize small family farms in the less developed nations. Alternatively, it means that poor families will have to pay more to obtain these valuable resource inputs.

Many similar examples could be given of the gross inequalities in global resource use. Perhaps more important, one could cite innumerable instances of the unnecessary and costly waste of many scarce and nonrenewable resources by the affluent developed nations. The point, therefore, is that any worldwide program designed to engender a better balance between resources and people by limiting LDC population growth through social intervention and family planning must also include the responsibility of rich nations systematically to simplify their own consumption demands and lifestyles. Such changes would free resources that could then be used by poor nations to generate the social and economic development essential to slow population growth.

In addition to simplifying lifestyles and consumption habits, one other positive but unlikely internal policy that rich nations could adopt to mitigate current world population problems would be to liberalize the legal conditions for the international immigration of poor, unskilled workers and their families from Africa, Asia, and Latin America to North America, Europe, Japan, and Australia. The international migration of peasants from Europe to North America, Australia, and New Zealand in the nineteenth and early twentieth centuries was a major factor in moderating the problems of underdevelopment and population pressure in European countries. No such safety valve or outlet exists today for developing countries. In fact, what few outlets existed have over the past two decades been progressively closed. Yet clearly, many underpopulated regions of the world and many labor-scarce societies could benefit economically from international migration, and the benefits to developing countries would be enormous. For example, the United Nations has estimated that legal barriers to international migration from the developing to the developed world cost developing nations at least $250 billion a year.[24]

How Developed Countries Can Assist Developing Countries with Their Population Programs

There are also a number of ways in which the governments of rich countries and multilateral donor agencies can help the governments of developing countries achieve their population policy objectives in shorter periods of time. The most important of these concerns the willingness of rich countries to be of genuine assistance to poor countries in their development efforts. Such genuine support would consist not only of expanded public and private financial assistance but also of improved trade relations, such as tariff- and quota-free access to developed-country markets, more appropriate technology transfers, assistance in developing indigenous scientific research capacities, better international commodity-pricing policies, and a more equitable sharing of the world's scarce natural resources. (These and other areas of international economic relations between rich and poor countries will be examined in Part Three.)

There are two other activities more directly related to fertility moderation in which rich-country governments, international donor agencies, and private nongovernmental organizations (NGOs) can play an important assisting role. The first is the whole area of research into the technology of fertility control, the contraceptive pill, modern intrauterine devices (IUDs), voluntary sterilization procedures, and, particularly for Africa in the age of AIDS, effective barrier contraception. Research has been going on in this area for a number of years, almost all of it financed by international donor organizations, private foundations, and aid agencies of developed countries. Further efforts to improve the effectiveness of this contraceptive technology while minimizing the health risks should be encouraged.

The second area includes financial assistance from developed countries for family-planning programs, public education, and national population policy research activities in the developing countries. This has traditionally been the primary area of developed-country assistance in the field of population. Total resources devoted to these activities have risen dramatically from around $2 million in 1960 to around $3 billion by the 1990s. It remains an open question, however, whether such resources (especially those allocated to premature family-planning programs) might not have been more effectively used to achieve their fertility goals had they instead been devoted directly to helping LDCs raise the levels of living of their poorest people. As we have seen, it is of little value to have sophisticated family-planning programs when people are not motivated to reduce family size.

Conclusion

We conclude with a note of optimism. In the past decade, fertility rates in many of the poorest countries, such as Bangladesh and most of the countries in sub-Saharan Africa, have experienced an impressive decline. Population experts are now busy lowering, to at least a modest extent, their estimates of world population growth for coming decades. In no small part, this decline is the result of more widespread availability of family planning. This change helps set the stage for an opportunity for successful development efforts in the coming years, but developed countries need to do their part in providing expanded development assistance, especially efforts focused on the need and opportunity to greatly reduce the incidence of poverty, which remains the biggest cause of high rates of fertility.

Population, Poverty, and Development: China and India

In 2000, India's population reached 1 billion, triple the number at independence despite introducing the world's first family-planning policy in the 1950s. China's population remains larger, but its harsh one-child policy, despite being fairly successful at slowing fertility, has apparently been less successful than approaches based on women's empowerment and education in some parts of India, such as the state of Kerala. What can we learn about population and development from the world's most populous countries?

In India, it is common to hear the view that "everything is growing faster in China than India, except for population." India, which had well under two-thirds of China's population half a century ago, is projected to surpass China's population by 200 million people by 2050. Like most developing countries, both countries' populations grew rapidly when their mortality rates fell and their birthrates fell much more slowly. Both countries have viewed population pressures as threatening prospects for future development. What would lead their fertility rates to fall faster?

It is well known that as incomes rise, fertility falls, due largely to the increased opportunity cost of women's time. But despite national growth, incomes have been stagnant in some parts of India, and the same has been true in China until the past decade. The causality between fertility and growth runs in both direc-

tions. China's rapid economic growth has also been attributed in part to its lower fertility rate. India's increased growth rate since the mid-1980s may also be related to its more moderate decline in fertility. Thus population policy can potentially play an important role in setting the stage for growth. Moreover, to the degree that we accept Amartya Sen's view that development is freedom, the greater opportunities available to young women when fertility is reduced or delayed is itself a key indicator of development success; and population policy can help realize these goals. In this case study, then, we focus attention on population policies in the two largest countries in the world, China and India.

Population Policy in China

China has been the world's most populous nation for centuries. After the Communist takeover in 1949, Chinese leaders led by Mao Zedong took a broadly pronatalist stance, believing that a communist society could solve any population problems and that a larger population would mean a more powerful country. Mao went so far as to send advocates of population control to jail. However, in the face of famine in the late 1950s, these policies moderated.

In 1980, China initiated a tough new drive to deter births with a goal of lowering the annual birthrate to 1% during the decade. Stringent and often draconian measures to achieve that goal were introduced in 1982 and 1983 as the Chinese government adopted a policy of one child per family. Social and political pressures to limit family size to one child have included requiring women to appeal to the neighborhood committee or council for formal permission to become pregnant. Although first births are routinely approved, second births are usually approved only if the first child has a serious birth defect or if the woman has remarried. Economic incentives include giving priority to one-child families in housing, medical care, and education. Mothers of two or more children are often denied promotions, and steep fines, sometimes in excess of ten times China's per capita income, are levied for second and third children. Given such rigid national policies and a strong preference for male children, there have been reports of an alarming increase in female infanticide, with estimates, based on the normal ratio of women to men of 1.022, that there are 44 million "missing women" in China.

The full impact of China's population control programs is uncertain. Only time will tell whether the benefits of reduced population growth achieved through severe social and economic pressures for one-child families will be worth the cost of a harsh break with traditional family norms and perceptions regarding the value of children. Resistance in rural areas, where 80% of the population still resides, was apparently so widespread that in August 1988, when the Chinese government discovered to its surprise that the population had already passed the 1 billion mark, it decided to increase its enforcement of the one-child norm in rural as well as urban areas. However, popular opposition again caused it to relax its stringent controls and to focus more on elevating the status of women and providing greater old-age security.

By the mid-1990s, China's fertility rate seemed to have stabilized at 1.9, where it remained in 2002; this rate is slightly below replacement level and consistent with a slow long-term decline in population growth. Because of population momentum, China's population has continued to grow as larger, younger cohorts replace smaller, older ones. However, the country's largest cohorts are now passing out of their childbearing years. The population growth rate has slowed dramatically, and the population is not expected to exceed 1.5 billion at its peak.

In practice, many families have two children rather than one, and others in rural areas, including ethnic minorities exempted from the one-child policy, have more than two children. But fertility rates are extremely low in the urban areas to which an increasing share of the rural population is moving. The overall impact of the policy on significantly reducing fertility is clear.

The apparent success of China's tough if not coercive fertility policies have led some observers to see advantages of dictatorship rather than democracy in spurring development. But in fact there are several ways in which the lack of a free press in particular and democracy more generally has held back China's development. In Mao's "Great Leap Forward," at least 30 million people died due to poor government decisions and incentives for bureaucrats to send overly optimistic reports from the field. Democratic India, by contrast, has not had a famine since independence in 1947. Amartya Sen attributes China's lead in economic growth to its massive investments in health and education, which India has lacked. Dictatorship can be good or bad for fertility programs or any other aspects of development. But the risks of a very bad outcome are probably much lower with democracy.

Successful population control in China comes with its own risks as well as rewards.

By 2050, China will have almost twice as many people above age 50 as below age 20.* In addition, while fertility has fallen, preference for boys over girls has intensified. Many Chinese families seem to feel that if they are to have only one child, it should be a boy, to carry on the family name and help support the parents in their old age. The result is a ratio of 115 boys for every 100 girls and far fewer family resources going toward girl children than boys. This is partly the result of selective abortion but also discrimination in nutrition and health care (see Chapter 8).

Although rapid growth and coercion in family planning may account for part of China's drop in fertility, other factors include greater female literacy, improved child health, and greater economic opportunities for women. These have also been factors in the strong success in fertility reduction in the Indian state of Kerala.

Population Policy in India

India was the first country to implement a national family-planning program, shortly after its independence in 1949. Nevertheless, family planning has been relatively ineffective and has proceeded in fits and starts. By the early 1970s, observers were becoming increasingly alarmed by the very high rate of population growth in India.

When Prime Minister Indira Gandhi tried to implement drastic population control in 1975–1977, a period during which she seized dictatorial powers, it proved a failure. Reports of forced sterilizations, sometimes in mass "sterilization camps," and other coercive measures ended up giving family planning itself a bad reputation in many areas of the country. Indeed, public revulsion toward these coercive fertility policies helped bring the "emergency" period to an end more quickly, and when elections were held in 1977, Gandhi was voted out of office. Her return to power in the elections of 1980 was made possible in part by her commitment not to reintroduce coercive birth control policies. Years later, villagers in some parts of India avoided health workers out of fear of forced sterilization.

However, family planning did become more widely practiced. Some of the acceptance of limits on family size reflected rising incomes among the 200 million or more middle-class Indians and somewhat improved conditions among a significant fraction of the poor. Some of it reflected modest moves back to policy incentives to encourage smaller families. There have been variations from state to state. In Madhya Pradesh, individuals who had a third or subsequent child after January 2001 were banned from running for election to village council posts, spurring considerable controversy. In 2004, an uproar over reported higher fertility among Muslims than among Hindus—reports that turned out to be greatly exaggerated—revealed the continuing political sensitivity of the issue.

As fertility has fallen, a preference for boys over girls, not much different from that in China, has developed, particularly in the Hindi belt in northern India. The result is a "missing women" problem parallel to China's. Stronger male bias is actually found in the better-off states of India; and researchers Jean Drèze, Anne-Catherine Guio, and Mamta Murthi found that "female disadvantage in child survival is significantly lower in districts with higher poverty levels."

Mari Bhat and Francis Zavier analyzed data from the National Family Health Survey and estimated that "in northern India, girls currently constitute about 60% of the unwanted births and that the elimination of unwanted fertility has the potential to raise the

*To get a sense of the dramatic changes in China's demography, watch population change in China unfold over the 100-year period between 1950 and 2050 in an animated population pyramid at http://www.iiasa.ac.at/Research/LUC/ChinaFood/data/anim/pop_ani.htm.

sex ratio at birth to 130 boys per 100 girls." Such a dramatic imbalance seems likely to lead to future social stress.

Kerala, a state on India's southwest coast that has emphasized poverty reduction and human development, is an important case in point. By the mid-1990s, Kerala's fertility rate had fallen to just 1.7 births per woman and has remained low, implying a slowly falling population over time (in the absence of in-migration). Thus Kerala's fertility rate was significantly less than that of China, but unlike China, the dramatic reductions in fertility in Kerala were achieved without coercion, let alone China's huge direct economic incentives for lowered fertility.

Norms of behavior can be highly influential, and multiple equilibria resulting from different expected norms of behavior are possible, as explored in Chapter 4. Amartya Sen has observed that "there is much evidence that the sharp decline in fertility rates that has taken place in the more literate states in India has been much influenced by public discussion of the bad effects of high fertility rates, especially on the lives of young women and also on the community at large. If the view has emerged in, say, Kerala or Tamil Nadu that a happy family in the modern age is a small family, much discussion and debate have gone into the formation of these perspectives."

While television, billboard, and other advertising in India has promoted family planning, and there is some evidence that these campaigns can have some positive impact on their own, such efforts have been far more successful when the social climate has changed enough to be receptive to the message. This helps explain why nongovernmental organizations working for comprehensive rural development have often apparently had more success than many government programs. In Kerala, if the official campaigns supporting small families have seemed more effective than elsewhere, it is largely because both social and economic conditions on the ground changed previously or simultaneously. More than 85% of women in Kerala are literate, which means they have more power in the household and opportunities in the workforce as well as the ability to read print materials about fertility and family planning. Some of Kerala's success is due to the traditionally higher status of women in the local culture. But Kerala still had a total fertility rate exceeding 4 births per woman in 1970. There is no reason that Kerala's success cannot be duplicated elsewhere in India if there is the political and social will.

Sen concluded that Kerala's impressive results in fertility reduction were achieved "mainly through the emergence of new values—a process in which political and social dialogues have played a major part. The high level of literacy of the Kerala population, especially female literacy, which is higher than that of every province of China, has greatly contributed to making such social and political dialogues possible."

The success of Kerala suggests that successful fertility reductions may depend not on rapid economic growth or even, in its absence, on draconian governmental policies but rather on successful grassroots human development in which civil society plays a leading role. ■

Sources

Acharya, Keya. "Sterilisation in India." *Contemporary Review* 279 (2001): 26.

Barro, Robert J. *Determinants of Economic Growth: A Cross-Country Empirical Study.* Cambridge, Mass.: MIT Press, 1997.

"Can advertising create social change?" *Businessline,* January 20, 2000, p. 1.

Dasgupta, Partha. "The population problem: Theory and evidence." *Journal of Economic Literature* 33 (1995): 1879–1902.

Drèze, Jean, and Mamta Murthi. "Fertility, education, and development: Evidence from India." *Population and Development Review* 27 (2001): 33–63.

Drèze, Jean, Anne-Catherine Guio, and Mamta Murthi. "Mortality, fertility, and gender bias in India: A district-level analysis." *Population and Development Review* 21 (1995): 745–782.

Kremer, Michael. "Population growth and technological change: One million B.C. to 1990." *Quarterly Journal of Economics* 108 (1993): 681–716.

Pritchett, Lant H. "Desired fertility and the impact of population policies." *Population and Development Review* 20 (1994): 1–55.

Mari Bhat, P. N., and Francis Zavier, A. J. "Fertility decline and gender bias in northern India." *Demography* 40 (2003): 637–657.

Sen, Amartya. "Missing Women." *British Medical Journal* 304 (1992): 587–588.

Sen, Amartya. *Development as Freedom.* New York: Knopf, 1999.

Sunil, T. S., V. K. Pillai, and A. Pandey. "Do incentives matter? Evaluation of a family planning program in India." *Population Research and Policy Review* 18 (1999): 563–577.

Concepts for Review

Birthrate	Infant mortality rate	Population-poverty cycle
Death rate	Life expectancy at birth	Population pyramid
Demographic transition	Malthusian population trap	Positive checks
Doubling time	Microeconomic theory of	Preventive checks
Empowerment of women	fertility	Rate of population increase
Family-planning programs	Mortality rate	Reproductive choice
Fertility rate	Natural increase	Total fertility rate (TFR)
Hidden momentum of popu-	Net international migration	Youth dependency ratio
lation growth		

Questions for Discussion

1. Population growth in developing nations has proceeded at unprecedented rates over the past few decades. Compare and contrast the present rate of population growth in less developed countries with that of the modern developed nations during their early growth years. What has been the major factor contributing to rapid LDC population growth since the Second World War? Explain your answer.

2. What is the relationship between the age structure of a population and its dependency burden? Is the dependency burden higher or lower in developing countries? Why?

3. Explain the notion of the hidden momentum of population growth. Why is this an important concept for projecting future population trends in different developing nations?

4. Describe briefly the theory of the demographic transition. At what stage in this transition do most developing countries seem to be? Explain your answer.

5. How does the microeconomic theory of fertility relate to the theory of consumer choice? Do you think that economic incentives and disincentives influence family size decisions? Explain your answer, giving some specific examples of such incentives and disincentives.

6. "The world population problem is not just a matter of expanding numbers but also one of rising affluence and limited resources. It is as much a problem caused by developed nations as it is one deriving from developing countries." Comment on this statement.

7. List and briefly describe the principal causes of high population growth in LDCs and the major consequences.

8. Explain why fertility rates are failing in some developing countries and not in others.

9. Outline and comment briefly on some of the arguments *against* the idea that population growth is a serious problem in developing nations.

10. Outline and comment briefly on some of the arguments *in support of* the idea that population growth is a serious problem in developing nations.

11. Outline and comment briefly on the various policy options available to LDC governments in their attempt to modify or limit the rate of population growth.

Notes

1. The 1970s marked the apogee in the history of world population growth. By the end of the decade, rates had begun to decline in a large number of developing countries, and it became clear that the pace of world population growth had finally peaked. For some evidence of this turning point, see Bernard Berelson, W. Parker Mauldin, and Sheldon Segal, "Population: Current status and policy options," *Social Science and Medicine* (1980): 71–97, and World Bank, *World Development Report, 1984* (New York: Oxford University Press, 1984), ch. 4.

2. A convenient shorthand method of calculating doubling time is simply to divide any growth rate into the number 70. For example, something (an asset, population, GNI, etc.) growing at 2% per year will double its value in approximately 35 years. See Chapter 2, note 9.

3. John Bongaarts, "Population policy options in the developing world," *Science* 263 (1994): 771–776.

4. A geometric progression is simply a doubling (or some other multiple) of each previous number, as in 1, 2, 4, 8, 16, 32, 64, 128, 256, 512, 1,024, and so on. Like compound interest, geometric progressions have a way of reaching large numbers very rapidly.

5. Actually, between Y_0 and Y_1, population would be growing ever so slightly as a result of positive income growth. See the text discussion of equilibrium points *A*, *B*, and *C* in the figure.

6. See Simon Kuznets, *Fertility Differentials between Less Developed and Developed Regions: Components and Implications* (New Haven, Conn.: Economic Growth Center, Yale University, 1974).

7. See, for example, T. Paul Schultz, *Fertility Determinants: A Theory, Evidence, and Application to Policy Evaluation* (Santa Monica, Calif.: RAND Corp., 1974); Nancy Birdsall, "Economic approaches to population growth," in *Handbook of Development Economics*, vol. 1, ed. Hollis B. Chenery and T. N. Srinwasan (Amsterdam: Elsevier, 1988), pp. 478–542; Jean Drèze, Anne-Catherine Guio, and Mamta Murthi, "Mortality, fertility and gender bias in India: A district-level analysis," *Population and Development Review* 21 (1995): 745–782; and Partha Dasgupta, "The population problem: Theory and evidence," *Journal of Economic Literature* 33 (1995): 1879–1902.

8. For strong empirical evidence that low fertility results mostly from economic, social, cultural, and educational improvements in a population and only slightly from the availability of family planning programs, see Lant H. Pritchett, "Desired fertility and the impact of population policies," *Population and Development Review* 20 (1994): 1–55.

9. For an analysis of this conflict, see Jason L. Finkle and Barbara Crane, "The politics of Bucharest: Population, development and the new international economic order," *Population and Development Review* 1 (1975): 87–114. Although this conflict was less visible in the Second World Population Conference held in Mexico City in August 1984 and was a minor issue beneath that of reproductive choice and the empowerment of women at the Third Conference held in Cairo in 1994, it remained prominent in the thoughts and discussions of many developing-world delegates.

10. For a more detailed discussion of these divergent opinions, see Michael S. Teitelbaum, "Population and development: Is a consensus possible?" *Foreign Affairs 52* (1974): 749–757. See also Timothy King and Allen Kelley, *The New Population Debate: Two Views on Population Growth and Economic Development* (Washington, D.C.: Population Reference Bureau, 1985), and Robert H. Cassen, *Population Policy: A New Consensus* (Washington, D.C.: Overseas Development Council, 1994).

11. See United Nations, *International Conference on Population and Development: Program of Action* (New York: United Nations, 1994). The full text of this declaration is reprinted at http://www.unfpa.org/icpd/icpd_poa.htm. For an analysis of the politics of the Cairo Conference, see C. Alison McIntosh and Jason L. Finkle, "The Cairo Conference on population and development: A new paradigm?" *Population and Development Review* 21 (1995): 223–260.

12. See, for example, Colin Clark, "The 'population explosion' myth," *Bulletin of the Institute of Development Studies* Vol. 1 (1969); Julian Simon, *The Ultimate Resource* (Princeton, N.J.: Princeton University Press, 1981); Nick Eberstadt, "Population and economic growth," *Wilson Quarterly,* Winter 1986, pp. 95–129; and National Research Council, *Population Growth and Economic Development: Policy Questions* (Washington, D.C.: National Academy Press, 1986).

13. Samir Amin, "Underpopulated Africa," paper presented at the African Population Conference, Accra, December 1971.

14. Ibid., fn. 2.

15. Ibid., p. 3. For another perspective on long-run benefits of greater population density via faster technological progress, see Michael Kremer, "Population growth and technological change: One million B.C. to 1990," *Quaterly Journal of Economics* 108 (1993): 681–716.

16. For example, see Paul R. Ehrlich and Anne H. Ehrlich, *Population, Resources, and Environment: Issues in Human Ecology,* 2nd ed. (New York: Freeman, 1972); Lester R. Brown, *In the Human Interest: A Strategy to Stabilize World Population* (New York: Norton, 1974); and Paul R. Ehrlich and Anne H. Ehrlich, *The Population Explosion* (New York: Simon & Schuster, 1990).

17. We are grateful to Professor Harold Votey for suggesting this illustration.

18. For a detailed review of this evidence, see Cassen, *Population Policy,* pp. 14–22; Dennis A. Ahlburg et al., *Population and Economic Development: A Report to the Government of the Commonwealth of Australia* (Canberra: Australian International Development Assistance Bureau, 1994); and Geoffrey McNicoll, "Effects of population growth: Visions and revisions," *Population and Development Review* 21 (1995): 307–340. As

the Ahlburg report demonstrates, not all of these consequences are unambiguously negative. Much depends on the particular country and its demographic situation.

19. Cassen, *Population Policy*, p. 12.

20. See Birdsall, "Economic approaches to population growth," pp. 523–529.

21. Sousan Abadian, "Women's autonomy and its impact on fertility," *World Development* 24 (1996): 1793–1809. See also Shireen J. Jeejeebhoy, *Women's Education, Autonomy, and Reproductive Behavior: Experiences from Developing Countries* (Oxford: Clarendon Press, 1995).

22. United Nations, *International Conference*, para. 4.1. See also Nancy Folbre, "Engendering economics: New perspectives on women, work and demographic change," in *Proceedings of the World Bank Annual Conference on Development Economics, 1995*, ed. Michael Bruno and Boris Pleskovic (Washington, D.C.: World Bank, 1996).

23. For a highly informative analysis of the relative responsibilities of developed and less developed countries as well as the role of population growth in contributing to global environmental damage, see John Bongaarts, "Population growth and global warming," *Population and Development Review* 18 (1992): 299–319.

24. United Nations Development Program, *Human Development Report, 1992* (New York: Oxford University Press, 1992), p. 58.

Further Reading

For an introduction to the study of population, including basic concepts, analysis, and statistical trends, see Helen Daugherty and Kenneth Kammeyer, *An Introduction to Population* (New York: Guilford Press, 1995). See also Thomas W. Merrick, "World population in transition," *Population Bulletin* 41 (1986): 1–51; Paul Demeny, "The world demographic situation," in *World Population and U.S. Policy*, ed. Jane Menken (New York: Norton, 1986), pp. 27–66; and United Nations Population Fund, *The State of World Population, 1998* (New York: United Nations, 1998). A handy statistical summary is found in the annual *World Population Data Sheet* (Washington, D.C.: Population Reference Bureau).

An excellent early survey article on the various interrelationships between population and economic development is Robert H. Cassen, "Population and development: A survey," *World Development* 4 (1976): 785–830. Two additional volumes of readings on the subject are Ronald Ridker (ed.), *Population and Development: The Search for Selective Interventions* (Baltimore: Johns Hopkins University Press, 1976), and Richard Easterlin (ed.), *Population and Economic Change in Developing Countries* (Chicago: University of Chicago Press/National Bureau of Economic Research, 1980). The best overall more recent reviews are Nancy Birdsall, "Economic approaches to population growth," in *Handbook of Development Economics*, vol. 1, ed. Hollis B. Chenery and T. N. Srinivasan (Amsterdam: Elsevier, 1988), pp. 478–542; Dennis A. Ahlburg et al., *Population and Economic Development: A Report to the Government of the Commonwealth of Australia* (Canberra: Australian International Development Assistance Bureau, 1994); and Partha Dasgupta, "The population problem: Theory and evidence," *Journal of Economic Literature* 33 (1995): 1879–1902.

On the new microeconomics of fertility, see Harvey Leibenstein, "An interpretation of the economic theory of fertility: Promising path or blind alley?" *Journal of Economic Literature* 12 (1974): 457–479; T. Paul Schultz, *Fertility Determinants: A Theory, Evidence, and Application to Policy Evaluation* (Santa Monica, Calif.: RAND Corp., 1974); Richard A. Easterlin, "An economic framework for fertility analysis," *Studies in Family Planning* 6 (1975): 54–63; Marc Nerlove, "Household and economy: Toward a new theory of population and economic growth," *Journal of Political Economy* 82 (1974): S200–S218; and Susan H. Cochrane, "A review of some microeconomic models of fertility," *Population Studies* 29 (1975): 373–390.

For a survey of how population relates to resources and the environment, see United Nations Population Fund, *Population, Resources and the Environment: The Critical Challenges* (New York: United Nations, 1991); John Bongaarts, "Population growth and global warming," *Population and Development Review* 18 (1992): 299–319; and World Resources Institute, *World Resources, 1994–95* (New York: Oxford University Press, 1994), ch. 2.

For a concise and informative summary of the debate on population and development, see Michael S. Teitelbaum, "Population and development: Is a consensus possible?" *Foreign Affairs* (1974): 749–757, Timothy King and Allen Kelley, *The New Population Debate: Two Views on Population Growth and Economic Development* (Washington, D.C.: Population Reference Bureau, 1985); and Robert H. Cassen, *Population Policy: A New Consensus* (Washington, D.C.: Overseas Development Council, 1994). For an analysis of the positive effects of greater population density on technological progress, see Michael Kremer, "Population growth and technological change: One million B.C. to 1990," *Quarterly Journal of Economics* 108 (1993): 681–716.

Two informative analyses of the fertility impact of family-planning programs are John Bongaarts, W. Parker Mauldin, and James Phillips, *The Demographic Impact of Family Planning Programs* (Washington, D.C.: Population Council, 1990), and W. Parker Mauldin and John A. Ross, *Family Planning Programs: Efforts and Results, 1982–89* (Washington, D.C.: Population Council, 1991). For an economic critique of the effectiveness of family planning in developing countries, see Lant H. Pritchett, "Desired fertility and the impact of population policies," *Population and Development Review* 20 (1994): 1–55. For a feminist critique, see Betsy Hartmann, *Reproductive Rights and Wrongs: The Global Politics of Population Control and Contraceptive Choice* (New York: Harper & Row, 1987), and Gita Sen, Adrienne Germain, and Lincoln Chen (eds.), *Population Policies Reconsidered* (New York: International Women's Health Coalition, 1994).

CHAPTER SEVEN

Urbanization and Rural-Urban Migration: Theory and Policy

Cities will increasingly become the main players in the global economy.
—Kofi Annan, Secretary General of the United Nations and 2001 Nobel Laureate for Peace

In the early 1990s, approximately half the governments of the world, mostly those of developing countries, considered the patterns of population distribution to be unsatisfactory. A key issue was the rapid growth of urban areas.
—Program of Action, 1994 International Conference on Population and Development

Poverty is becoming increasingly urbanized: Within twenty-five years, the number of urban poor will increase from an estimated 400 million to over 1 billion.
—James D. Wolfensohn, President, World Bank, 1998

The Migration and Urbanization Dilemma

In this chapter, we focus on one of the most complex and nuanced dilemmas of the development process: the phenomenon of massive and historically unprecedented movements of people from the rural countryside to the burgeoning cities of Africa, Asia, and Latin America. In Chapter 6 we documented the extraordinary increase in world and especially developing-country population over the past few decades. By 2050, world population could reach over 9 billion people, and nowhere will population growth be more dramatic than in the major cities of the developing world.

After reviewing trends and prospects for overall urban population growth, we examine in this chapter the potential role of cities—both the modern sector and the urban informal sector—in fostering economic development. We then turn to a well-known theoretical model of rural-urban labor transfer in the context of rapid growth and high urban unemployment. In the final section, we evaluate various policy options that LDC governments may wish to pursue in their attempts to curtail the heavy flow of rural-to-urban migration and to ameliorate the serious un-

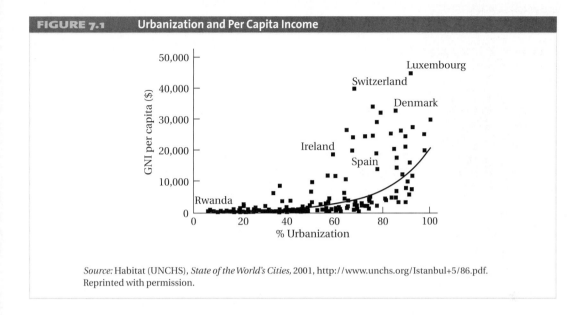

FIGURE 7.1   Urbanization and Per Capita Income

Source: Habitat (UNCHS), *State of the World's Cities,* 2001, http://www.unchs.org/Istanbul+5/86.pdf. Reprinted with permission.

employment problems that continue to plague their crowded cities. This chapter's case study looks at patterns of migration in India and Botswana.

Urbanization: Trends and Projections

The positive association between urbanization and per capita income is one of the most obvious and striking "stylized facts" of the development process. Generally, the more developed the country, measured by per capita income, the greater the share of population living in urban areas. Figure 7.1 shows urbanization versus GNI per capita; the highest-income countries, such as Denmark, are also among the most urbanized, while the very poorest countries, such as Rwanda, are among the least urbanized. At the same time, while individual countries become more urbanized as they develop, today's poorest countries are far more urbanized than today's developed countries were when they were at a comparable level of development, as measured by income per capita; and LDCs are urbanizing at a faster rate.

Figure 7.2 shows urbanization over time and across income levels over the quarter century from 1970 to 1995. The figure, from the World Bank 1999–2000 *World Development Report,* gives real income per capita (in constant 1987 U.S. dollars) but does not adjust for purchasing power parity. Each line segment represents the trajectory of one country, starting from the solid dots, which represent the 1970 income and urbanization level for a given country, and ending at the end of the line segments (marked by a diamond), which represent the corresponding 1995 income and urbanization level for the same country. Although the World Bank captioned the figure "Urbanization Is Closely Associated with Economic Growth," the figure may also be interpreted as showing that urbanization is occurring everywhere, at high and low levels of income and whether growth is positive

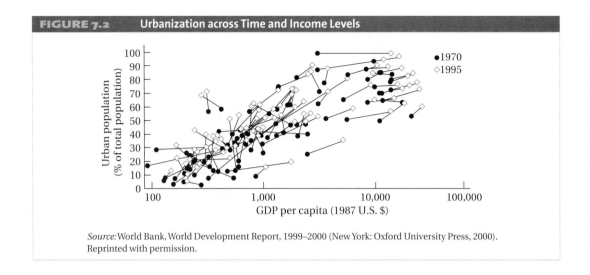

FIGURE 7.2   Urbanization across Time and Income Levels

Source: World Bank, World Development Report, 1999–2000 (New York: Oxford University Press, 2000). Reprinted with permission.

or negative. Even when the lines point to the left, indicating shrinking incomes per capita over the period, they still generally point upward, indicating that urbanization continued. In short, urbanization is happening everywhere in the world, although at differing rates. So we need to consider urbanization carefully—is it only correlated with economic development, or is causation also at work?

Indeed, one of the most significant of all postwar demographic phenomena and the one that promises to loom even larger in the future is the rapid growth of cities in developing countries. In 1950, some 275 million people were living in cities in the developing world, 38% of the 724 million total urban population. According to UN estimates, the world's urban population had reached nearly 3 billion by 2003, with well over two-thirds living in metropolitan areas of developing countries. The United Nations projects that in 2025, over 4.1 billion, or 80%, of the urban dwellers of the world will reside in less developed regions. This will represent an overall increase of 178%, or 1.8 billion new urbanites, in Africa, Asia, and Latin America. Depending on the nature of development strategies pursued, the final total could be substantially higher or lower than the 4.1 billion estimate. Table 7.1 presents data on this growth of urban populations by major world regions from 1950 to 1995 with projections to the year 2025.

With regard to particular cities, current rates of urban population growth range from under 1% per annum in two of the world's largest cities, New York and Tokyo, to over 6% per annum in many African cities including Nairobi, Lagos, and Accra. In Asia and Latin America, many cities are growing at rates in excess of 4% or 5%. Table 7.2 provides data on the world's 15 largest cities (defined as greater metropolitan areas) in 1995 with UN projections to 2015. Note that in 1995, only 4 of the 15 were in the developed countries. The remaining 11 cities are located in developing countries and had a combined population of 141 million. However, in contrast to the moderate growth of developed-nation cities, 9 of these plus 4 new LDC entries on the list of the 15 largest cities in the year 2015 are projected to grow to

TABLE 7.1	Urban Population in Major World Regions, 1950–2025 (millions)						
Region	1950	1960	1970	1980	1995	2000	2025
World	724	1,012	1,352	1,807	2,584	2,860	5,065
More developed regions	449	573	698	834	875	900	1,040
Less developed regions	275	439	654	972	1,709	1,960	4,025
Africa	32	50	83	133	250	295	804
Latin America	68	107	162	241	358	391	601
Asia	218	342	407	596	1,101	1,376	2,615

Sources: United Nations, *Patterns of Urban and Rural Population Growth* (New York: United Nations 1980); Pii Eina Berghäll, *Habitat II and the Urban Economy: A Review of Recent Developments and Literature* (Helsinki: United Nations University World Institute for Development Economics Research, 1995) tabs. 2 and 4; World Resources Institute, World Resources, 1996–97. *The Urban Environment* (New York: Oxford University Press, 1996), tab. A.1.: United Nations, *World Urbanization Prospects* (New York: United Nations, 2001).

244 million, for an additional 103 million inhabitants. Looking at specific cities, we find that three of the four largest cities in the year 2015 will be Bombay, Lagos, and Shanghai, with a projected population of 27.4, 24.4, and 23.4 million, respectively. Karachi, Dhaka, Delhi, and Manila, which didn't even appear on the 1995 list, are projected to rank seventh, ninth, thirteenth, and fifteenth, respectively. Of the 15 largest cities in 2015, only two, Tokyo and New York, will be from the more developed world.

TABLE 7.2	The World's Largest Cities, 1995 and 2015				
	1995 Population		Average Annual Growth Rate 1990–1995 (%)	2015 Population[a]	
City	Rank	Millions of Inhabitants		Rank	Millions of Inhabitants
Tokyo, Japan	1	26.8	1.41	1	28.7
São Paulo, Brazil	2	16.4	2.01	6	20.8
New York, United States	3	16.3	0.34	11	17.6
Mexico City, Mexico	4	15.6	0.73	10	18.8
Bombay, India	5	15.1	4.22	2	27.4
Shanghai, China	6	15.1	2.29	4	23.4
Los Angeles, United States	7	12.4	1.60	—	—
Beijing, China	8	12.4	2.57	8	19.4
Calcutta, India	9	11.7	1.67	12	17.6
Seoul, South Korea	10	11.6	1.95	—	—
Jakarta, Indonesia	11	11.5	4.35	5	21.2
Buenos Aires, Argentina	12	11.0	0.68	—	—
Tianjin, China	13	10.7	2.88	14	17.0
Osaka, Japan	14	10.6	0.23	—	—
Lagos, Nigeria	15	10.3	5.68	3	24.4
Karachi, Pakistan	—	—	—	7	20.6
Dhaka, Bangladesh	—	—	—	9	19.0
Delhi, India	—	—	—	13	17.1
Manila, Philippines	—	—	—	15	14.7

Sources: World Resources Institute, *World Resources, 1996–97*: The Urban Environment (New York: Oxford University Press, 1996), tab. 1.1; United Nations, *World Urbanization Prospects: The 1994 Revision* (New York: United Nations, 1995), tab. 1.
[a]Projections made in 1995.

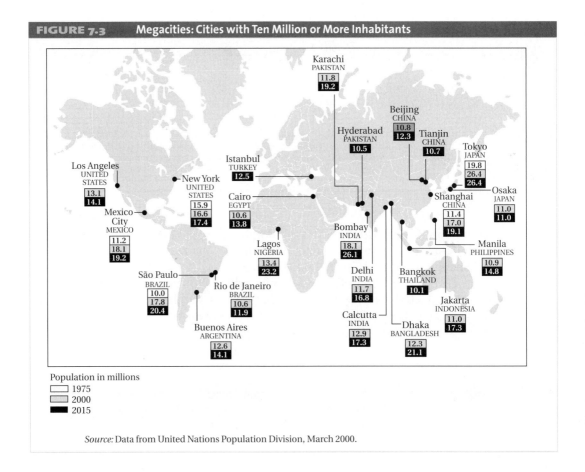

FIGURE 7.3   Megacities: Cities with Ten Million or More Inhabitants

Karachi
PAKISTAN
11.8
19.2

Beijing
CHINA
10.8

Hyderabad
PAKISTAN
10.5

Tianjin
CHINA
12.3

Tokyo
JAPAN
19.8
26.4
26.4

Istanbul
TURKEY
12.5

Los Angeles
UNITED
STATES
13.1
14.1

New York
UNITED
STATES
15.9
16.6
17.4

Cairo
EGYPT
10.6
13.8

Shanghai
CHINA
11.4
17.0
19.1

Osaka
JAPAN
11.0
11.0

Mexico
City
MEXICO
11.2
18.1
19.2

Lagos
NIGERIA
13.4
23.2

Bombay
INDIA
18.1
26.1

Manila
PHILIPPINES
10.9
14.8

São Paulo
BRAZIL
10.0
17.8
20.4

Rio de Janeiro
BRAZIL
10.6
11.9

Delhi
INDIA
11.7
16.8

Bangkok
THAILAND
10.1

Jakarta
INDONESIA
11.0
17.3

Buenos Aires
ARGENTINA
12.6
14.1

Calcutta
INDIA
12.9
17.3

Dhaka
BANGLADESH
12.3
21.1

Population in millions
☐ 1975
▨ 2000
■ 2015

Source: Data from United Nations Population Division, March 2000.

Figure 7.3 provides a map locating megacities, the largest cities in the world containing a population of at least 10 million people. As the figure shows, in 1975 there were only 5 megacities, but by 2000 there were 19 such metropolises. Of these 19, all but 2, New York and Tokyo, were located in the developing world. By 2015, at least 4 more giant cities are projected to join their ranks: Istanbul in Turkey, Hyderabad in Pakistan, Bangkok in Thailand, and Tianjin in China. (Note that lists of the largest cities, even across UN agencies, may differ, owing to alternative definitions of a metropolitan area, but any way they are counted, the trend toward an increasing number of urban giants in the developing world is unmistakably clear.) The world's urban population is now approximately as large as its rural population for the first time in history. Moreover, as Figure 7.4 shows, almost all of the increments to the world's population will be accounted for by the growth of urban areas as migrants continue to stream into the cities from rural areas and as urbanization rates in the developing world continue to approach those of the developed world.

A central question related to the unprecedented size of these urban agglomerations is how these LDC cities will cope—economically, environmentally, and polit-

FIGURE 7.4   **Estimated and Projected Urban and Rural Population of the More and Less Developed Regions, 1950–2030**

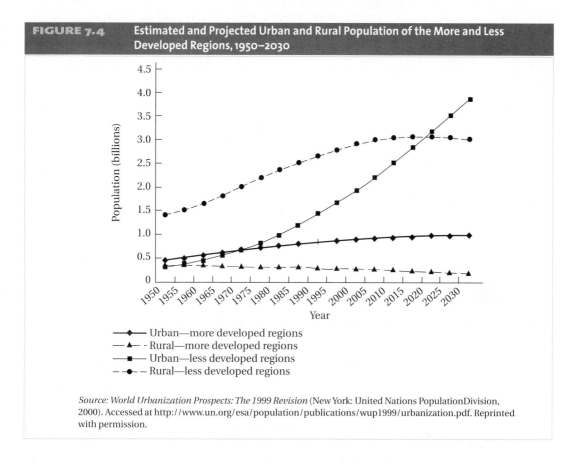

Source: *World Urbanization Prospects: The 1999 Revision* (New York: United Nations PopulationDivision, 2000). Accessed at http://www.un.org/esa/population/publications/wup1999/urbanization.pdf. Reprinted with permission.

ically—with such acute concentrations of people. While it is true that cities offer the cost-reducing advantages of agglomeration economies and economies of scale and proximity as well as numerous economic and social externalities (e.g., skilled workers, cheap transport, social and cultural amenities), the social costs of a progressive overloading of housing and social services, not to mention increased crime, pollution, and congestion, tend gradually to outweigh these historical urban advantages. Former World Bank president Robert McNamara expressed his skepticism that huge urban agglomerations could be made to work at all:

> These sizes are such that any economies of location are dwarfed by costs of congestion. The rapid population growth that has produced them will have far outpaced the growth of human and physical infrastructure needed for even moderately efficient economic life and orderly political and social relationships, let alone amenity for their residents.[1]

Along with the rapid spread of urbanization and the **urban bias** in development strategies has come the prolific growth of huge slums and shantytowns. From the *favelas* of Rio de Janeiro and the *pueblos jovenes* of Lima to the *bustees* of Calcutta and the *bidonvilles* of Dakar, such makeshift communities have been

City	Slum Dwellers as a Percentage of the Population
TABLE 7.3 Slum Dwellers and Squatters as a Percentage of the Urban Population	
Latin America	
Bogotá, Colombia	60
Mexico City, Mexico	46
Caracas, Venezuela	54
Rio de Janeiro, Brazil	20
Middle East and Africa	
Addis Ababa, Ethiopia	79
Casablanca, Morocco	70
Ankara, Turkey	60
Cairo, Egypt	60
Dar es Salaam, Tanzania	53
Asia	
Calcutta, India	67
Karachi, Pakistan	44
Manila, Philippines	35
Jakarta, Indonesia	26

Sources: Population Crisis Committee, *World Population Growth and Global Security*, Report No. 13 (Washington, D.C.: Population Crisis Committee, 1983), p. 2; Daniel Litvin, "Dirt poor: A survey of development and the environment," *Economist*, March 21, 1998, p. 8.

doubling in size every five to ten years. Today slum settlements represent over one-third of the urban population in all developing countries; in many cases they account for more than 60% of the urban total (see Table 7.3). During the late 1980s, fully 72 out of every 100 new households established in urban areas of developing countries were located in shanties and slums. In Africa, the number was 92 out of every 100. Most of the settlements are without clean water, sewage systems, or electricity. For example, metropolitan Cairo is attempting to cope with a population of more than 10 million people with a water and sanitation system built to serve 2 million.

Although population growth and accelerated **rural-urban migration** are chiefly responsible for the explosion in urban shantytowns, part of the blame rests with LDC governments. Their misguided urban-planning policies and outmoded building codes often means that 80% to 90% of new urban housing is "illegal." For example, colonial-era building codes in Nairobi, Kenya, make it impossible to build an "official" house for less than $3,500. The law also requires every dwelling to be accessible by car. As a result, two-thirds of Nairobi's land is occupied by 10% of the population, while 100,000 slum dwellings cannot legally be improved. Similarly in Manila, Philippines, 88% of the population is too poor to be able to buy or rent an officially "legal" house.[2]

Statistics show that rural migrants constitute anywhere from 35% to 60% of recorded urban population growth (see Table 7.4). Accordingly, 90 out of 116 developing countries responding to the UN survey indicated that they had initiated policies to slow down or reverse their accelerating trends in rural-urban migration.

Given the widespread dissatisfaction with rapid urban growth in developing countries, the critical issue that needs to be addressed is the extent to which national governments can formulate development policies that can have a definite

TABLE 7.4   Importance of Rural-Urban Migration as a Source of Urban Population Growth in Selected Developing Countries

Country	Annual Urban Growth (%)	Share of Growth Due to Migration (%)
Argentina	2.0	35
Brazil	4.5	36
Colombia	4.9	43
India	3.8	45
Indonesia	4.7	49
Nigeria	7.0	64
Philippines	4.8	42
Sri Lanka	4.3	61
Tanzania	7.5	64
Thailand	5.3	45

Source: K. Newland, *City Limits: Emerging Constraints on Urban Growth,* Worldwatch Institute, Worldwatch Paper No. 38. Copyright © 1980, http://www.worldwatch.org. Reprinted with permission.

impact on trends in urban growth. It is clear that the unquestioning pursuit of the orthodox development strategies of the past few decades, with their emphasis on industrial modernization, technological sophistication, and metropolitan growth, created a substantial geographic imbalance in economic opportunities and contributed significantly to the steadily accelerating influx of rural migrants into urban areas. Is it possible and or even desirable now to attempt to reverse these trends by pursuing a different set of population and development policies? With birthrates beginning to decline in many LDCs, the serious and worsening problem of rapid urban growth and accelerated rural-urban migration will undoubtedly be one of the most important development and demographic issues of the coming decades. And within urban areas, the growth and development of the informal sector as well as its role and limitations for labor absorption and economic progress will assume increasing importance.

Before examining conditions in developing-country cities more closely, we first consider the potential advantages offered by cities. Urban areas have played a highly constructive role in the economies of today's developed countries, and they offer huge and still largely untapped potential to do the same for developing countries. We take a detailed look at the informal sector in developing cities, considering its potential as an engine of growth. We also consider in more detail what has been different—and what has gone wrong—with urban development in LDCs. We examine the important phenomenon of excessively rapid rural-urban migration. Finally, we conclude with a look at constructive urban policies to realize the potential of cities to foster successful development, while at the same time giving more balanced treatment to development in rural areas.

The Role of Cities

What explains the strong association between urbanization and development? To a large degree, cities are formed because they provide cost advantages to producers and consumers through what are called **agglomeration economies**. As noted by the pioneering regional economist Walter Isard, these agglomeration economies come in two forms. **Urbanization economies** are effects associated with the general growth of a concentrated geographic region. **Localization economies** are effects captured by particular sectors of the economy, such as finance or automobiles, as they grow within an area. Localization economies often take the form of backward and forward linkages of the type introduced in Chapter 4. When transportation costs are significant, users of the outputs of an industry may benefit from a nearby location to save on these costs. This benefit is a type of forward linkage. In addition, firms of the same or related industries may benefit from being located in the same city, so they can all draw on a large pool of workers with the specific skills used in that sector or from specialized infrastructure. This is a type of backward linkage. Workers with specialized skills appropriate to the industry prefer to be located there as well so that they can easily find a new job or be in a position to take advantage of better opportunities.

Industrial Districts

Firms often also prefer to be located where they can learn from other firms doing similar work. Learning takes place in both formal relationships, such as joint ventures, and informal ones, such as from tips learned in evening social clubs or while "doing lunch." These spillovers are also agglomeration economies, part of the benefits of what Alfred Marshall called "industrial districts," and they play a big role in Michael Porter's "clusters" theory of competitive advantage.[3] Firms located in such industrial districts also benefit from the opportunity to contract out work easily when an unusually large order materializes. Thus a firm of modest size does not have to turn down a big job due to lack of capacity, an arrangement that provides "flexible specialization."[4] Further, firms may wish to operate in well-known districts for the marketing advantages of locating where consumers of their goods know to shop to get the best selection.

It may not matter so much where such industrial districts are located as that they somehow got an early start there, perhaps because of a historical accident. For example, in the United States, many innovative computer firms located in Silicon Valley, California, simply because other such firms were already located there. Analogously, suppliers to shoe firms locate in the Sinos Valley in southern Brazil and in Guadalajara in Mexico because so many shoe firms are located in those regions. Some of the benefits are gained simply by the fact of location—Khalid Nadvi has termed this "passive collective efficiency"—but other benefits must be achieved through collective action, such as developing training facilities or lobbying government for needed infrastructure as an industry rather than as individual firms ("active collective efficiency").

A growing body of evidence shows that industrial clusters are now common in developing countries, at stages of industrial development ranging from cottage industry to advanced manufacturing techniques, and appear to be significant factors in emerging industrial competitiveness.[5] Nevertheless, the dynamism of these clusters has varied widely. Some of the identified districts are traditional clusters of artisans that have shown little ability to innovate, export, or expand.

Traditional cottage industries are often grouped together by village, a phenomenon found throughout the developing world that is particularly prominent in Java. But such groupings often remain one-family microenterprises with little division of labor or use of modern techniques. Producers in a village are better off sharing a common specialization than producing a random assortment of goods, in part because intermediaries work with villages with a high concentration of producers in their sector. But such traditional producers benefit little from "internal" divisions of labor within the firm, generally producing a largely complete product within the household and remaining at very low productivity and incomes. For example, a small town in Kenya may have a dozen or more families fabricating wheelbarrows, each family starting with timber and a few simple purchased metal inputs and producing a final product for sale.

In other cases, such traditional township specializations have evolved into clusters, with still modest-size but somewhat larger firms using a more detailed division of labor, such as a group of wheelbarrow producers with some specialization, each employing a few workers. Eventually, the cluster might expand in scope and become a low-tech metal products industrial district selling products throughout the country as the town grows into a small city. These clusters are reminiscent of the industrial districts of developed countries but require that sufficient financing be gathered to invest in core firms using somewhat larger-scale capital goods.

As Hermine Weijland found in her study of Java, Indonesia, "it needs only a few fortunate years of market expansion to create gains from externalities and joint action."[6] She cites as examples local clusters that have upgraded and now competitively produce such goods as roof tiles, rattan furniture, cast metal, and textiles. Similarly, Dorothy McCormick concluded from a study of six representative clusters in Africa that "groundwork clusters prepare the way; industrializing clusters begin the process of specialization, differentiation, and technological development; and complex industrial clusters produce competitively for wider markets."[7] In some cases, the evidence suggests that coordination failures are not overcome, and so there may be a role for government policy in encouraging the upgrading of clusters. In other cases, it is the government itself that shares blame for cluster stagnation when it enforces irrational and stifling regulations, which are far more damaging than the usual policy of benign neglect toward nascent clusters in the informal sector. Examples of clusters in developing countries that are widely considered successful include surgical instruments in Sialkot, Pakistan; software in the Bangalore area in India; and footwear in the Sinos Valley, Brazil (although this last industry is also known for its use of child labor). Clusters of all kinds, however, face substantial challenges from globalization and trade liberalization.

Again, not all of the collective efficiency advantages of an industrial district are realized through passive location. Others are actively created by joint investments and promotional activities of the firms in the district. One factor determining the dynamism of a district is the ability of its firms to find a mechanism for such collective action. While the government can provide financial and other important services to facilitate cluster development, **social capital** is also critical, especially group trust and a shared history of successful collective action, which requires time to develop. Government can help by bringing parties together and helping them gain experience cooperating on more modest goals before tackling larger ones, but social capital normally grows organically in an economic community and cannot be created forcibly. Even with collective action to supplement passive benefits of agglomeration, traditional clusters may not survive in their current form into more advanced stages of industrialization. Nonetheless, as Hubert Schmitz and Khalid Nadvi note, even if transitional, districts in the informal sector may still play a crucial role in mobilizing underused human and financial resources.[8]

Statistical estimates show that such benefits of agglomeration can be quite substantial in practice. For example, studies have demonstrated that "if a plant moves from a location shared by 1,000 workers employed by firms in the same industry to one with 10,000 such workers, output will increase an average of 15%, largely because the pool of specialized workers and inputs deepens." Moreover, "productivity rises with city size, so much so that a typical firm will see its productivity climb 5% to 10% if city size and the scale of local industry double."[9]

Efficient Urban Scale

Localization economies do not imply that it would be efficient for all of a country's industries to be located together in a single city! These economies extend across closely related industries, such as those with strong backward and forward linkages, but there are fewer productivity benefits for unrelated industries to locate together. One notable exception is the potential spillover from technological progress in one industry to its adaptation for different uses in another industry. But there are also some important **congestion** costs. The higher the urban density, the higher the costs of real estate. It is much more expensive to build vertically than horizontally, increasingly so as skyscraper scale is reached, so that when market forces work properly, tall buildings are built primarily when urban land costs become high. (Note that skyscrapers and other buildings of monumental scale are sometimes built for political show rather than for economic efficiency, such as the world's tallest buildings in Taipei, Taiwan, and Kuala Lumpur, Malaysia.) In large urban areas, workers may find themselves with longer and longer commutes and greater transportation costs and may demand higher wages to cover these costs. In addition, the costs of infrastructure such as water and sewer systems are higher in concentrated urban areas. In theory, if costs of transportation of finished goods are high and consumers wish to be located in the largest city to avoid paying those transportation costs as much as possible, economic activity could become indefinitely concentrated within a city (called the "black hole" effect), but it is generally much less costly to improve the transportation system of a country than to pay the costs of maintaining a gargantuan urban complex. Under competitive forces and other things being equal, if workers are mobile, a worker in a large city with higher wages but higher costs of living (such as higher housing prices) is no better off in real material terms than a worker with comparable education, experience, ability, and health in a small city who has lower wages and lower costs of living.[10]

Thus the concentrating, or "centripetal," forces of urban agglomeration economies are opposed by the dispersing, or "centrifugal," forces of diseconomies featuring increasing costs with greater concentration, because some of the factors of production, most obviously land, are not mobile. We can "create" more central city land by building skyscrapers, but only to a certain scale and only at substantial cost. Thus it is normal for an economy to have a range of cities, with sizes dependent on the scale of the industries it sponsors and the extent of agglomeration economies found for that industry or cluster of industries.

Two well-known theories of city size are the urban hierarchy model (central place theory) and the differentiated plane model.[11] In the urban hierarchy model, originated by August Losch and Walter Christaller, plants in various industries have a characteristic market radius that results from the interplay of three factors: economies of scale in production, transportation costs, and the way the demand for land is spread over space. The larger the economies of scale in production and the lower the transportation costs, the larger the radius of territory that will be served by that industry to minimize costs. In contrast, if the price of real estate is bid up to high levels in the resulting cities, this will tend to create smaller radii. As a result, small cities contain activities with short market radii, while large cities emerge to contain activities of both small and large radii. Generally speaking, activities of a national scope, such as government and finance, will be located in a single city (though not necessarily the *same* large city because of the effect of congestion costs). Clearly, the urban hierarchy approach applies better to nonexport industries than to export industries. When countries have different specializations in the international market or are at different stages of economic development, the size distribution of cities may potentially differ. For example, a developing country that still overwhelmingly specializes in agriculture might reasonably have one or two large cities serving national industries such as finance and government and many smaller towns serving local agricultural areas. A country with a highly differentiated manufacturing and service base might have a large number of medium-size cities.

In the differentiated plane model, originated by Alfred Weber, Walter Isard, and Leon Moses, the limited number of transportation routes linking the industries within an economy plays a key role. The model predicts urban concentrations where the scarce transportation routes cross, called "internal nodes." The hierarchy of urban sizes depends on the pattern of nodes and the industrial mix. Primary processing industries have few inputs and are usually located near the source of the primary resource. However, there will also be incentives for industries with strong backward or forward linkages to locate in the same city.

The Urban Giantism Problem

In the case of developing countries, the main transportation routes are often a legacy of colonialism. Theorists of the dependency school (see Chapter 3) have compared colonial transportation networks to drainage systems, emphasizing ease of extraction of the country's natural resources. In many cases, the capital city will be located near the outlet of this system on the seacost. This type of transportation system is also called a "hub-and-spoke system," which is especially visible when the capital city is located in the interior of the country. Many nations have inherited a hub-and-spoke system from ancient colonial times, such as that of Paris and London, as well as more recent colonial experiences, such as cities in Africa and Latin America. In the case of London and Paris, these transportation systems were designed in the time of the Roman Empire to facilitate movement of troops from the capital to the outlying towns to suppress revolts. A similar motivation was likely present in the more recent designs of the African colonies of Britain and France and the Central and South American colonies of Spain.

The differentiated plane approach emphasizes the lasting impact of historical accidents. In this case, it helps explain where the most oversized cities are found in the developing world and suggests where policies of urban decentralization may be most helpful. Note that not all countries have such a hub-and-spoke system; Germany does not, for the historical reason that it was never conquered by Rome; the United States does not, in part because it is the result of the merger of 13 separate British colonies, which retained some measure of local autonomy, as do the federal states of Germany. The recent development of the United States makes the emergence of cities such as Atlanta from the crossing of transportation routes especially clear, but the same principle has applied elsewhere over longer historical epochs.

Sometimes one urban core grows to become too large to keep the costs of the industries located there to a minimum. In developed countries, other cores are often developed within the broad metropolitan region, enabling the region as a whole to continue to receive benefits of agglomeration while lowering some of the costs; or new cities may develop in entirely different parts of the country. But this creation of new urban cores does not happen automatically if there are advantages to locating where other firms and residents are already located today. This is another chicken-and-egg coordination problem of the type described in Chapter 4. Who will be the pioneer if it is less costly to stay where you are and wait for other pioneers to settle in the new city first? In economic terms, the agglomeration economies of cities are externalities, which must somehow be internalized or the market will fail. How can this possibly be done?

In the United States, developers frequently internalize the externality by creating a new "edge city" within a metropolitan area, financing and building a new center where land is still relatively inexpensive, perhaps 10 to 50 kilometers from the original urban core. This takes place within a context of public oversight in the form of zoning regulations and inducements such as tax breaks. In LDCs, however, capital markets generally do not (yet) work well enough for this process of development to take place. In Europe, the public sector plays a much larger role in coordinating new towns and large developments.

In developing countries, however, governments are less involved in the dispersal of economic activity to more manageable sizes or, if they are involved, are often less effective. For example, government may seek to disperse industry without regard to the nature of agglomeration economies, giving incentives for dispersal but no attention to clustering relevant industries together, a problem seen in industrial parks in Pakistan. And all too often, the incentives are for firms to concentrate in the capital city or other "urban giants." A key problem of countries such as Peru and Argentina is that their giant capitals suffer from enormous levels of congestion, but there are no adequate midsize cities to provide alternative locations for growth. A well-designed infrastructure development program, including more efficient links between medium-size cities and better roads, utilities, and telecommunications within these cities, can help alleviate this problem.

A more detailed comparison of North and South America is instructive. The largest urban area in the United States, the New York metropolitan area, has about 6% of the national population (3% in New York City itself and about the same percentage in its suburbs). Toronto, the largest metropolitan area in Canada, has 4.3 million residents, some 14% of the Canadian population. But Mexico City holds more than one-fifth of the population of Mexico, Montevideo two-fifths of the population of Uruguay, Lima about one-fifth of the population of Peru, and Buenos Aires and Santiago more than a third of the populations of Argentina and Chile, respectively.[12]

First-City Bias

A form of urban bias that has often caused considerable harm might be termed *first-city bias*. This means that the country's largest or "first" city receives a disproportionately large share of public investment and incentives for private investment, in relation to the country's second city and other smaller cities. As a result, the first city receives a disproportionately, and inefficiently, large share of population and economic activity.

Table 7.5 shows the largest and second-largest cities in the United States, Canada, and major Latin American countries. Notice that in all of the outsized capital cities—Buenos Aires, Santiago, Mexico City, and Lima—the first city also serves as the capital. Patterns are similar in many other developed and developing countries. Although two European countries, the former colonial powers of the United Kingdom and France, have exceptionally large first cities, some seven times the size of the second city in both cases, in virtually all other European countries, the second city is about half, or more, the size of the first city.[13] Some other developing countries have remarkably outsized first cities, notably Thailand, where Bangkok has a population nearly 20 times the size of the second city of Nakhon Ratchasima.

Causes of Urban Giantism

Why have first cities often swelled to such a large multiple of second cities in developing countries? Overall, urban giantism probably results from a combination of a hub-and-spoke transportation system and the location of the political capital in the largest city, thus combining the effects of the urban hierarchy model with the differentiated plane model. This is further reinforced by a political culture of rent seeking and the capital market failures that make the creation of new urban centers a task that markets cannot complete. Other more detailed explanations also gener-

TABLE 7.5	Population of the Largest and Second-Largest Cities in Selected Countries (millions)		
Country	Largest-City Population	Second-City Population	Ratio
Canada	Toronto, 4.3	Montreal, 3.3	1.3
United States	New York, 19.7	Los Angeles, 15.3	1.3
Argentina	Buenos Aires, 10.7	Rosario, 1.1	9.7
Brazil	São Paulo, 9.8	Rio de Janeiro, 5.5	1.8
Chile	Santiago, 4.3	Concepcion, 0.3	14.3
Mexico	Mexico City, 15.0	Guadalajara, 2.9	5.2
Peru	Lima, 6.4	Arequipa, 0.6	10.7

Source: Data from United Nations demography Web page, http://www.un.org/Depts/unsd/demog/city.htm.
Note: Definitions of city size differ across studies.

ally involve unfortunate consequences of political economy (see Chapter 11). One argument, featured in the work of Paul Krugman, stresses that under import substitution industrialization (see Chapter 13), with a high level of protection, there is much less international trade, and population and economic activity have an incentive to concentrate in a single city, largely to avoid transportation costs. Thus firms wish to set up operations in the city where the most consumers already live, which attracts more people to the region in search of jobs and perhaps lower prices (made possible because there are fewer transport costs to be passed on to consumers); this concentration in turn attracts still more firms and consumers in a circle of causation. However, when trade barriers are reduced, the incentive to focus production on the home market is also reduced, and exporters and their suppliers have much less incentive to be located in the country's biggest population center. This moves production toward ports and borders, or elsewhere in the country, to escape the overly large congestion costs of the largest city.[14]

Another recent explanation for urban giants focuses on the consequences of dictators' efforts to remain in power. As Figure 7.5 shows, on average, a much larger share of a country's urbanized population (37%) lives in the first city in unstable dictatorships than in stable democracies (23%). In interpreting this finding, Alberto Ades and Edward Glaeser argue that unstable dictatorships (fearing overthrow) must provide "bread and circuses" for the first city (usually the capital) to prevent unrest; this extreme urban bias in turn attracts more migrants to the favored city and a still larger need for bread and circuses. It should be noted that although the authors attempt to control for reverse causality, it may still be the case that unstable dictatorships also tend to emerge in countries with high first-city concentrations.[15]

In the developing world, until recently relatively few countries were effective democracies. In the 1970s, almost all developing countries had authoritarian governments of one form or another. To remain in power and prevent popular uprisings and coups, which were generally thought to be most threatening when launched from the capital city, governments had an incentive to "buy off" the population of the largest city. This focus of national government spending on the capital city is the bread-and-circuses effect, recalling the phrasing of "rent-sharing" policies in ancient Rome in its period of expansion. The availability of better opportunities, whether the equivalent of the grain handouts in ancient Rome or

FIGURE 7.5	Politics and Urban Concentration

STABLE DEMOCRACIES	STABLE DICTATORSHIPS
Urban concentration = 0.23	Urban concentration = 0.3
(0.032)	(0.03)
Number of observations = 24	Number of observations = 16
UNSTABLE DEMOCRACIES	UNSTABLE DICTATORSHIPS
Urban concentration = 0.35	Urban concentration = 0.37
(0.07)	(0.02)
Number of observations = 6	Number of observations = 39

Source: Alberto F. Ades and Edward L. Glaeser, "Trade and circuses: Explaining urban giants," *Quarterly Journal of Economics* 110 (1995): 196. Copyright © 1995 by the President and Fellows of Harvard College and the Massachusetts Institute of Technology. Reprinted with permission.
Note: Urban concentration is the share of the urban population in the largest city. Standard errors are in parentheses.

jobs, wages, infrastructure, and other government services concentrated in the capital city of many of today's developing countries, attracts an ever-growing migrant population, in turn leading to larger precautionary government spending as the fear of political instability grows.

A final political economy factor contributes to capital city giantism: It becomes advantageous for firms to be located where they have easy access to government officials, to curry political favor from a regime that can be induced to give companies special favors for a price or that simply demands bribes to function at all. The resulting first-city giantism may be viewed as a form of underdevelopment trap, which may be escaped fully only with a return to democratic rule together with a better balance of incentives to compete for exports as well as home consumption. Democracy does not eliminate political benefits of location in the national capital, but while lobbyists still congregate in the political capital, there may be less incentive for production to become overconcentrated there. Moreover, a free press tends to expose corruption and generate public pressure to root it out, as recent experience in many democratizing countries in Latin America and East Asia makes clear.

The four explanations for urban giantism—production for the home market in the face of high protection and transport costs, few adequate smaller cities as alternative locations for firms reflecting infrastructure patterns, location of the capital in the largest city, and the political logic of unstable dictatorships—are complementary and help explain some of the advantages of democracies with more balanced economic policies, including well-planned investments in infrastructure. Such countries are able to avoid some of the costs of urban giantism.

The Urban Informal Sector

As noted in Chapter 3, a major focus of development theory has been on the dualistic nature of developing countries' national economies—the existence of a modern urban capitalist sector geared toward capital-intensive, large-scale production and a traditional rural subsistence sector geared toward labor-intensive, small-scale production. In recent years, this dualistic analysis has also been applied specifically to the urban economy, which has been decomposed into a formal and an informal sector.

The existence of an unorganized, unregulated, and mostly legal but unregistered **informal sector** was recognized in the 1970s, following observations in several developing countries that massive additions to the urban labor force failed to show up in formal modern-sector unemployment statistics. The bulk of new entrants to the urban labor force seemed to create their own employment or to work for small-scale family-owned enterprises. The self-employed were engaged in a remarkable array of activities, ranging from hawking, street vending, letter writing, knife sharpening, and junk collecting to selling fireworks, prostitution, drug peddling, and snake charming. Others found jobs as mechanics, carpenters, small artisans, barbers, and personal servants. Still others were highly successful small-scale entrepreneurs with several employees (mostly relatives) and high incomes. Some could even eventually graduate to the formal sector, where they become legally registered, licensed, and subject to government labor regulations. With the unprecedented rate of growth of the urban population in developing countries expected to continue and with the increasing failure of the rural and urban formal sectors to absorb additions to the labor force, more attention is being devoted to the role of the informal sector in serving as a panacea for the growing unemployment problem.

The informal sector continues to play an important role in developing countries, despite decades of benign neglect at best and outright hostility at worst. In many developing countries, about half of the employed urban population works in the informal sector. Figure 7.6 shows the relative importance of informal unemployment in selected cities. Most of these cities reflect the typical range of informal-sector employment share, from about 30% to 70%. (The only exception is Ljubljana, a virtually developed city near Austria and Italy.) We find a similar pattern of high informal-sector employment in cities throughout the developing world. For example, in India, the urban informal sector comprises 28.5% of employment in Calcutta, 46.5% in Ahmedabad, 49.5% in Bombay, 53.8% in Madras, 61.4% in Delhi, and 65.5% in Bangalore.

The informal sector is characterized by a large number of small-scale production and service activities that are individually or family-owned and use simple, labor-intensive technology. They tend to operate like monopolistically competitive firms with ease of entry, excess capacity, and competition driving profits (incomes) down to the average supply price of labor of potential new entrants. The usually self-employed workers in this sector have little formal education, are generally unskilled, and lack access to financial capital. As a result, worker productivity and in-

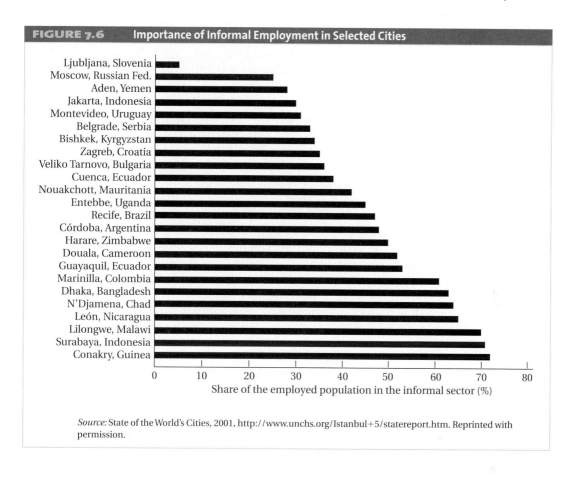

FIGURE 7.6   Importance of Informal Employment in Selected Cities

Source: State of the World's Cities, 2001, http://www.unchs.org/Istanbul+5/statereport.htm. Reprinted with permission.

come tend to be lower in the informal sector than in the formal sector. Moreover, workers in the informal sector do not enjoy the measure of protection afforded by the formal modern sector in terms of job security, decent working conditions, and old-age pensions. Many workers entering this sector are recent migrants from rural areas unable to find employment in the formal sector. Their motivation is often to obtain sufficient income for survival, relying on their own indigenous resources to create work. As many members of the household as possible are involved in income-generating activities, including women and children, and they often work very long hours. A large fraction inhabit shacks that they themselves have built in slums and squatter settlements, which generally lack minimal public services such as electricity, water, drainage, transportation, and educational and health services. Others are even less fortunate. Many millions are homeless, living on the pavements of Calcutta, Manila, Dakar, Nairobi, Rio de Janeiro, and Bogotá—to mention just a few major developing-country cities. They find sporadic temporary employment in the informal sector as day laborers and hawkers, but their incomes are insufficient to provide even the most rudimentary shelter.

Policies for the Urban Informal Sector

In terms of its relationship with other sectors, the informal sector is linked with the rural sector in that it allows excess labor to escape from extreme rural poverty and underemployment, although under living and working conditions and for incomes that are often not much better. It is closely connected with the formal urban sector: The formal sector depends on the informal sector for cheap inputs and wage goods for its workers, and the informal sector in turn depends on the growth of the formal sector for a good portion of its income and clientele.

Informal-sector incomes have remained persistently higher than those in the poorest rural regions despite continued flow of rural-urban migration. Concern about urban bias goes back at least to the seminal writings of Nobel laureate Sir Arthur Lewis in the 1950s. Lewis viewed traditional-sector workers, the petty traders like newspaper hawkers, as unproductive and essentially as engaged in distractions from the main urban work of industrialization. But if wages are persistently higher in very competitive activities such as informal work, this must reflect higher productivities as well.

Table 7.6 shows that urban poverty rates, as measured by the headcount ratio, are quite high in many low-income countries, ranging from 14.5% to 56.0% in the

TABLE 7.6 Income Poverty in Seven African Countries, Various Years			
		Share of Population below the National Poverty Line[a] (%)	
Country (Dates of years 1 and 2)	Area	Year 1	Year 2
Burkina Faso (1994, 1998)	Rural	51.1	50.7
	Urban	10.4	15.8
	Total	44.5	45.3
Ghana (1991–92, 1998–99)	Rural	45.8	36.2
	Urban	15.3	14.5
	Total	35.7	29.4
Mauritania (1996, 2000)	Rural	65.5	61.2
	Urban	30.1	25.4
	Total	50.0	46.3
Nigeria (1992, 1996)	Rural	45.1	67.8
	Urban	29.6	57.5
	Total	42.8	65.6
Uganda (1992, 1997)	Rural	59.4	48.2
	Urban	29.4	16.3
	Total	55.6	44.0
Zambia (1996, 1998)	Rural	82.8	83.1
	Urban	46.0	56.0
	Total	69.2	72.9
Zimbabwe (1991, 1996)	Rural	51.5	62.8
	Urban	6.2	14.9
	Total	37.5	47.2

Sources: World Bank, *World Development Report 2000–2001* (New York: Oxford University Press, 2001); World Bank, *World Development Indicators, 2004* (New York: Oxford University Press, 2004). Reprinted with permission.
[a]Nutrition-based poverty lines. Comparisons between countries are not valid.

most recent years in this sampling of African countries. However, in all cases, rural poverty rates remain markedly higher than urban poverty rates.

Possibly taking a cue from such observations, recently a revisionist view espousing the constructive role of cities in economic development has begun to take hold. This approach has been championed by the Dar es Salaam–based UN Habitat, in its new series, the *State of the World's Cities* reports.[16] The 2001 report systematically criticized what it termed the "anti-urban bias of the development agencies." Acting on the strong development tradition beginning with the Lewis skepticism of the urban informal sector, developed with the Todaro migration model (examined later in this chapter) emphasizing the negative consequences of urban bias for both efficiency and equity, continuing with the influential work of the integrated rural development school (see Chapter 8) of the 1970s and recast and reemphasized in recent years under the Wolfensohn presidency at the World Bank, development agencies have indeed stressed rural development rhetorically. Many scholars have concluded, however, that this rhetoric often goes untranslated into real resources for the rural areas. Thus any pro-rural bias of development agencies is in general little more than a partial correction to the overriding forces for urban bias.

However, the new pro-urban offensive by UN Habitat is likely to prove influential. Indeed, the World Bank, in its 1999–2000 *World Development Report*, signaled its own attention to urban issues by devoting chapters to urban development for the first time. The new attention focused on how to make cities in developing countries more dynamic engines of growth and more livable environments promises to be one of the more important streams of emerging research in economic development in coming years. In any case, while medium-size cities undoubtedly have a much larger role to play in the development process than has been appreciated in the past, the revisionist view does not obviate the problem of overconcentration of activities in first-city urban giantism.

The important role that the informal sector plays in providing income opportunities for the poor is clear. There is some question, however, as to whether the informal sector is merely a holding ground for people awaiting entry into the formal sector and as such is a transitional phase that must be made as comfortable as possible without perpetuating its existence until it is itself absorbed by the formal sector or whether it is here to stay and should in fact be promoted as a major source of employment and income for the urban labor force.[17]

There seems to be a good argument in support of the latter view. The formal sector in developing countries has a small base in terms of output and employment. To absorb future additions to the urban labor force, the formal sector must be able to generate employment at a very high rate of at least 10% per annum, according to estimates made by the International Labor Organization (ILO). This means that output must grow at an even faster rate, since employment in this sector increases less than proportionately in relation to output. This sort of growth seems highly unlikely in view of current trends. Thus the burden on the informal sector to absorb more labor will continue to grow unless other solutions to the urban unemployment problem are provided.

Moreover, the informal sector has demonstrated its ability to generate employment and income for the urban labor force. As pointed out earlier, it is already absorbing an average of 50% of the urban labor force. Some studies have shown the informal sector generating almost one-third of urban income.

Several other arguments can be made in favor of promoting the informal sector. First, scattered evidence indicates that the informal sector generates surpluses even under the currently hostile policy environment, which denies it access to the advantages offered to the formal sector, such as credit, foreign exchange, and tax concessions. Thus the informal sector's surplus could provide an impetus to growth in the urban economy. Second, as a result of its low capital intensity, only a fraction of the capital needed in the formal sector is required to employ a worker in the informal sector, offering considerable savings to developing countries so often plagued with capital shortages. Third, by providing access to training and apprenticeships at substantially lower costs than that provided by formal institutions and the formal sector, the informal sector can play an important role in the formation of human capital. Fourth, the informal sector generates demand for semiskilled and unskilled labor whose supply is increasing in both relative and absolute terms and is unlikely to be absorbed by the formal sector with its increasing demands for a skilled labor force. Fifth, the informal sector is more likely to adopt appropriate technologies and make use of local resources, allowing for a more efficient allocation of resources. Sixth, the informal sector plays an important role in recycling waste materials, engaging in the collection of goods ranging from scrap metals to cigarette butts, many of which find their way to the industrial sector or provide basic commodities for the poor. Finally, promotion of the informal sector would ensure an increased distribution of the benefits of development to the poor, many of whom are concentrated in the informal sector.

Promotion of the informal sector is not, however, without its disadvantages. One of the major disadvantages in promoting the informal sector lies in the strong relationship between rural-urban migration and labor absorption in the informal sector. Migrants from the rural sector have both a lower unemployment rate and a shorter waiting period before obtaining a job in the informal sector. Promoting income and employment opportunities in the informal sector could therefore aggravate the urban unemployment problem by attracting more labor than either the desirable parts of the informal or the formal sector could absorb. Furthermore, there is concern over the environmental consequences of a highly concentrated informal sector in the urban areas. Many informal-sector activities cause pollution and congestion (e.g., pedicabs) or inconvenience to pedestrians (e.g., hawkers and vendors). Moreover, increased densities in slums and low-income neighborhoods, coupled with poor urban services, could cause enormous problems for urban areas. Any policy measures designed to promote the informal sector must be able to cope with these various problems. Finally, it is an almost universal observation that when regular formal-sector employment becomes available, informal-sector microentrepreneurs switch sectors to take these jobs—clear evidence of "revealed preference."

There has been little discussion in the literature as to what sorts of measures might be adopted to promote the informal sector. The International Labor Organization has made some general suggestions. To begin with, governments will have to dispense with the currently hostile attitude toward the informal sector and maintain a more positive and sympathetic posture. For example, in Latin America, bureaucratic red tape and an inordinate number of administrative procedures needed to register a new business typically result in delays up to 240 days in Ecuador, 310 days in Venezuela, and 525 days in Guatemala. Brazil, Mexico, and Chile all require more than 20 applications before a company can be approved for business. These procedures not only cause excessive delays but can also inflate the costs of doing business by up to 70% annually. So informal-sector businesses simply skirt the law.

Because access to skills plays an important role in determining the structure of the informal sector, governments should facilitate training in the areas that are most beneficial to the urban economy. In this way, the government can play a role in shaping the informal sector so that it contains production and service activities that provide the most value to society. Specifically, such measures might promote legal activities and discourage illegal ones by providing proper skills and other incentives. It could also generate taxes that now go unpaid.

The lack of capital is a major constraint on activities in the informal sector. The provision of credit would therefore permit these enterprises to expand, produce more profit, and hence generate more income and employment. Access to improved technology would have similar effects. Providing infrastructure and suitable locations for work (e.g., designating specific areas for stalls) could help alleviate some of the environmental consequences of an expanded informal sector. Most important, better living conditions must be provided, if not directly, then by promoting growth of the sector on the fringes of urban areas or in smaller towns where the population will settle close to its new area of work, away from the urban density. Promotion of the informal sector outside the urban areas may also help redirect the flow of rural-urban migration, especially if carried out in conjunction with the policies discussed at the end of this chapter.

Women in the Informal Sector

In some regions of the world, women predominate among rural-urban migrants and may even comprise the majority of the urban population. Though historically many of these women were simply accompanying their spouses, a growing number of unattached women in Latin America, Asia, and Africa migrate to seek economic opportunity. With the exception of the export enclaves of East Asia and a few other cities, where everything from computers to running shoes are manufactured, few of these migrants are able to find employment in the formal sector, which is generally dominated by men. As a consequence, women often represent the bulk of the informal-sector labor supply, working for low wages at unstable jobs with no employee or social security benefits. The increase in the number of single female migrants has also contributed to the rising proportion of urban households headed by women, which tend to be poorer, experience tighter resource constraints, and retain relatively high fertility rates. The changing composition of migration flows has important economic and demographic implications for many urban areas of the developing world.

Because members of female-headed households are generally restricted to low-productivity informal-sector employment and experience higher dependency burdens, they are more likely to be poor and malnourished and less likely to obtain formal education, health care, or clean water and sanitation. Among the Brazilian poor, for example, male-headed households are four times as likely as female-headed households to have access to government-sponsored health services. Dropout rates among children from households headed by women are much higher because they are more likely to be working to contribute to household income.

Many women run small business ventures or *microenterprises* that require little or no start-up capital and often involve the marketing of homemade foodstuffs and handicrafts. Though women's restricted access to capital leads to high rates of return on their tiny investments, the extremely low capital-labor ratios confine women to low-productivity undertakings. Studies in Latin America and Asia have found that where credit is available to women with informal-sector microenterprises, repayment rates have equaled or exceeded those for men (see Chapter 16). And because women are able to make more productive use of capital and start from a much lower investment base, their rates of return on investments often surpass those for men.

Despite the impressive record of these credit programs, they remain far too rare. The vast majority of institutional credit is still channeled through formal-sector agencies, and as a result, women generally find themselves ineligible for even small loans. Government programs to enhance income in poor households will inevitably neglect the neediest households so long as governments continue to focus on formal-sector employment of men and allocation of resources through formal-sector institutions. To solve the plight of poor urban women and their children, it is imperative that efforts be made to integrate women into the economic mainstream. Ensuring that women benefit from development programs will require that women's special circumstances be considered in policy design.

The legalization and economic promotion of informal-sector activities, where the majority of the urban female labor force is employed, could greatly improve women's financial flexibility and the productivity of their ventures. However, to enable women to reap these benefits, governments must repeal laws that restrict women's rights to own property, conduct financial transactions, or limit their fertility. Likewise, barriers to women's direct involvement in technical training programs and extension services must be eradicated. Finally, the provision of affordable child-care and family-planning services would lighten the burden of women's reproductive roles and permit them a greater degree of economic participation.

Urban Unemployment

One of the major consequences of the rapid urbanization process has been the burgeoning supply of job seekers into both the modern (formal) and informal sectors of the urban economy. In many developing countries, the supply of workers far exceeds the demand, the result being extremely high rates of unemployment and underemployment in urban areas. Table 7.7 provides some detailed data on urban unemployment for 20 countries. Note that the table focuses solely on rates of open unemployment. It thus excludes the very many more people who are chronically underemployed in the informal sector. The problem is therefore much more serious than even these data suggest. Unfortunately, reliable information on unem-

TABLE 7.7	Urban Open-Unemployment Rates in Twenty Developing Countries, 1993–1998	
Country	Year	Unemployment Rate (%)
Algeria	1995	23.8
Argentina	1994	18.6
Barbados	1994	21.9
Chile	1994	6.3
Colombia	1994	9.2
Egypt	1993	8.3
Indonesia	1998	10.0
Jamaica	1994	15.4
Morocco	1998	15.5
Nicaragua	1995	20.2
Panama	1995	14.3
Peru	1994	8.8
Philippines	1995	9.5
Saudi Arabia	1993	15.5
South Africa	1995	33.0
South Korea	1998	6.4
Sri Lanka	1995	13.6
Thailand	1998	5.8
Uruguay	1994	10.7
Venezuela	1994	10.3

Sources: International Labor Office, *World Employment, 1996–97* (Geneva: International Labor Office, 1996), tabs. 5.1a and 5.1d; *Economist*, April 25, 1998, p. 72; United Nations, *Report on the World Social Situation, 1997* (New York: United Nations, 1997), pp. 108–109.

ployment in Africa and in some of the most populated Asian cities (e.g., Calcutta, Karachi, Shanghai), where rates are likely to be high, is unavailable.[18] Nevertheless, 15 of the 20 countries listed in Table 7.7 had rates above 9%, and 13 countries had rates in excess of 10%. If we had included scattered information on the very substantial numbers of the urban labor force who were underemployed in part-time informal-sector service activities, the overall figures for urban surplus labor (both openly unemployed and underemployed) would exceed 30% in many developing countries. For example, UN data indicate that the combined urban unemployment and underemployment rate in 1995 was 28.7% for Argentina, more than 30% in the Philippines, and 42% in Cameroon. Finally, had we focused on residents in the 15–24 age bracket (the majority of whom are recent migrants), the rate would typically exceed 50%—as it did in Colombia, Ethiopia, Indonesia, Mexico, Algeria, and Panama, for example, during the 1990s.

Because a major contributing factor to both high rates of urban growth and high rates of unemployment and underemployment is rural-urban migration, it is essential to investigate this issue in some detail.

Migration and Development

As we have seen earlier in the chapter, rural-urban migration has been dramatic, and urban development plays an important role in economic development. Rates of rural-urban migration in developing countries have exceeded rates of urban job creation and thus surpassed greatly the absorption capacity of both industry and urban social services. Migration today, particularly to the largest LDC cities, must be seen as the major factor contributing to the ubiquitous phenomenon of urban surplus labor, a force that continues to exacerbate already serious urban unemployment problems.

Migration worsens rural-urban structural imbalances in two direct ways. First, on the supply side, internal migration disproportionately increases the growth rate of urban job seekers relative to urban population growth, which itself is at historically unprecedented levels, because of the high proportion of well-educated young people in the migrant system. Their presence tends to swell the urban labor supply while depleting the rural countryside of valuable human capital. Second, on the demand side, urban job creation is generally more difficult and costly to accomplish than rural job creation because of the need for substantial complementary resource inputs for most jobs in the industrial sector. Moreover, the pressures of rising urban wages and compulsory employee fringe benefits in combination with the unavailability of appropriate, more labor-intensive production technologies means that a rising share of modern-sector output growth is accounted for by increases in labor productivity. Together this rapid supply increase and lagging demand growth tend to convert a short-run problem of resource imbalances into a long-run situation of chronic and rising urban surplus labor.

But the impact of migration on the development process is much more pervasive than its exacerbation of urban unemployment and underemployment. In fact, the significance of the migration phenomenon in most developing countries is not necessarily in the process itself or even in its impact on the sectoral allocation of human resources. Rather, its significance lies in its implications for economic growth in general and for the character of that growth, particularly its distributional manifestations.

We must therefore recognize that migration in excess of job opportunities is both a symptom of and a contributor to underdevelopment. Understanding the causes, determinants, and consequences of internal rural-urban labor migration is thus central to understanding the nature and character of the development process and to formulating policies to influence this process in socially desirable ways. A simple yet crucial step in underlining the centrality of the migration phenomenon is to recognize that any economic and social policy that affects rural and urban real incomes will directly or indirectly influence the migration process. This process will in turn itself tend to alter the pattern of sectoral and geographic economic activity, income distribution, and even population growth. Because all economic policies have direct and indirect effects on the level and growth of urban or rural incomes or both, they all will have a tendency to influence the nature and magnitude of the migration stream. Although some policies may have a more direct and immediate impact (e.g., wages and income policies and employment promotion programs), there are many others that, though less obvious, may in the long run be no less important. Included among these policies, for example, would be land tenure arrangements; commodity pricing; credit allocation; taxation; export promotion; import substitution; commercial and exchange-rate policies; the geographic distribution of social services; the nature of public investment programs; attitudes toward private foreign investors; the organization of population and family-planning programs; the structure, content, and orientation of the educational system; the functioning of labor markets; and the nature of public policies toward international technology transfer and the location of new industries. There is thus a clear need to recognize the central importance of internal and, for many countries, even international migration and to integrate the two-way relationship between migration and population distribution on the one hand and economic variables on the other into a more comprehensive framework designed to improve development policy formulation.

In addition, we need to understand better not only why people move and what factors are most important in their decision-making process but also what the consequences of migration are for rural and urban economic and social development. If all development policies affect migration and are affected by it, which are the most significant, and why? What are the policy options and trade-offs among different and sometimes competing objectives (e.g., curtailing internal migration and expanding educational opportunities in rural areas)? Part of our task in the following sections will be to seek answers to these and other questions relating to migration, unemployment, and development.

Migration patterns are complex. The most important type of migration from the standpoint of long-run development is rural-urban migration, but a great deal of rural-rural, urban-urban, and even urban-rural migration also takes place. Rural-urban migration is most important because the population share of cities is growing, despite the fact that fertility is much lower in urban areas, and the difference is accounted for by rural-urban migration. It is also important because of the potential development benefits of economic activity of cities, due to agglomeration economies and other factors. However, urban-rural migration is important to understand because it usually occurs when hard times in cities coincide with increases in output prices from the country's cash crops; the recent experience of Ghana is a notable example. Thus the overall picture is one of a remarkable amount of "churning," or continuous movements of many people within developing countries, especially over short distances. These movements contradict the popular image of stasis in traditional societies. The composition of internal migration for several countries is shown in Figure 7.7.

In addition to wage differentials, age, and education, migration is also explained partly by relocation upon remarrying; prior emigration of family members; distance and costs of relocation, occurrence of famine, disease, violence, and other disasters; and relative standing in the origin community, with those lower on the social order more likely to migrate. Migration can also be a form of portfolio diversification of families who seek to settle some members in areas where they may not be affected by economic shocks in the same way as if they had stayed at home.[19] And one researcher has found that in Thailand, at least, insurance motives play an important role in explaining migration patterns.[20]

Toward an Economic Theory of Rural-Urban Migration

The economic development of Western Europe and the United States was closely associated with the movement of labor from rural to urban areas. For the most part, with a rural sector dominated by agricultural activities and an urban sector focus-

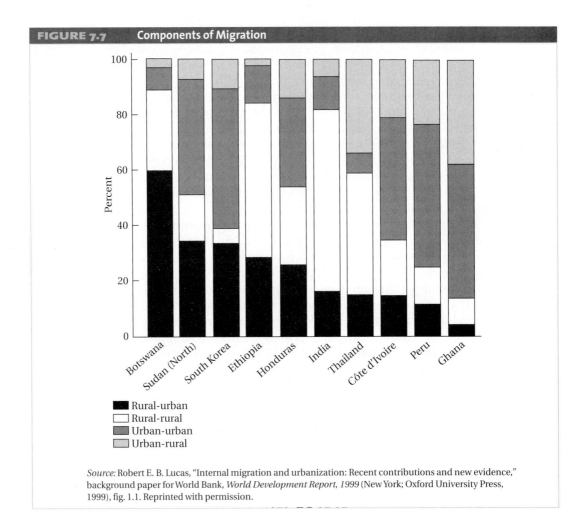

FIGURE 7.7　Components of Migration

Legend:
- ■ Rural-urban
- □ Rural-rural
- ▨ Urban-urban
- ▨ Urban-rural

Source: Robert E. B. Lucas, "Internal migration and urbanization: Recent contributions and new evidence," background paper for World Bank, *World Development Report, 1999* (New York; Oxford University Press, 1999), fig. 1.1. Reprinted with permission.

ing on industrialization, overall economic development in these countries was characterized by the gradual reallocation of labor out of agriculture and into industry through rural-urban migration, both internal and international. Urbanization and industrialization were in essence synonymous. This historical model served as a blueprint for the development of LDCs, as evidenced, for example, by the original Lewis theory of labor transfer (see Chapter 3).

But the overwhelming evidence of the past several decades, when developing nations witnessed a massive migration of their rural populations into urban areas despite rising levels of urban unemployment and underemployment, lessens the validity of the Lewis two-sector model of development.[21] An explanation of the phenomenon, as well as policies to address the resulting problems, must be sought elsewhere. In a series of articles, one of us developed a theory to explain the apparently paradoxical relationship of accelerated rural-urban migration in the context of rising urban unemployment.[22] This theory has come to be identified in the literature as the **Todaro migration model**, and in its equilibrium form as the **Harris-Todaro model.**

A Verbal Description of the Todaro Model

Starting from the assumption that migration is primarily an economic phenomenon, which for the individual migrant can be a quite rational decision despite the existence of urban unemployment, the Todaro model postulates that migration proceeds in response to urban-rural differences in **expected income** rather than actual earnings. The fundamental premise is that migrants consider the various labor market opportunities available to them in the rural and urban sectors and choose the one that maximizes their expected gains from migration. A schematic framework showing how the varying factors affecting the migration decision interact is given in Figure 7.8.

In essence, the theory assumes that members of the labor force, both actual and potential, compare their expected incomes for a given time horizon in the urban sector (the difference between returns and costs of migration) with prevailing average rural incomes and migrate if the former exceeds the latter. (See Appendix 7.1 for a mathematical formulation.)

Consider the following illustration. Suppose that the average unskilled or semi-skilled rural worker has a choice between being a farm laborer (or working his own land) for an annual average real income of, say, 50 units or migrating to the city, where a worker with his skill or educational background can obtain wage employment yielding an annual real income of 100 units. The more commonly used economic models of migration, which place exclusive emphasis on the income differential factor as the determinant of the decision to migrate, would indicate a clear choice in this situation. The worker should seek the higher-paying urban job. It is important to recognize, however, that these migration models were developed largely in the context of advanced industrial economies and hence implicitly assume the existence of full or near-full employment. In a full-employment environment, the decision to migrate can be based solely on the desire to secure the highest-paid job wherever it becomes available. Simple economic theory would then indicate that such migration should lead to a reduction in wage differentials through the interaction of the forces of supply and demand, in areas of both emigration and immigration.

Unfortunately, such an analysis is not realistic in the context of the institutional and economic framework of most developing nations. First, these countries are beset by a chronic unemployment problem that a typical migrant cannot expect to secure a high-paying urban job immediately. In fact, it is much more likely that on entering the urban labor market, many uneducated, unskilled migrants will either become totally unemployed or will seek casual and part-time employment as vendors, hawkers, repairmen, and itinerant day laborers in the urban traditional or informal sector, where ease of entry, small scale of operation, and relatively competitive price and wage determination prevail. In the case of migrants with considerable human capital in the form of a secondary or university certificate,

FIGURE 7.8 Schematic Framework for Analyzing the Migration Decision

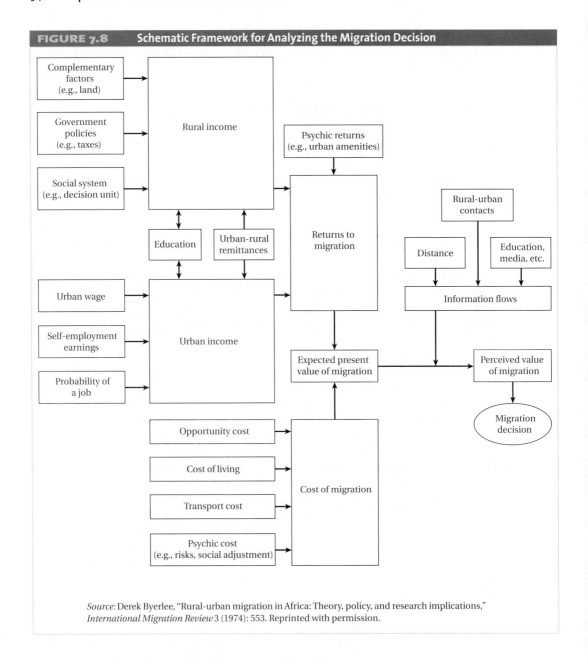

Source: Derek Byerlee, "Rural-urban migration in Africa: Theory, policy, and research implications," *International Migration Review* 3 (1974): 553. Reprinted with permission.

opportunities are much better, and many will find formal-sector jobs relatively quickly. But they constitute only a small proportion of the total migration stream. Consequently, in deciding to migrate, the individual must balance the probabilities and risks of being unemployed or underemployed for a considerable period of time against the positive urban-rural real income differential. The fact that a typical migrant who gains a modern-sector job can expect to earn twice the annual real income in an urban area than in a rural environment may be of little consequence if the actual probability of his securing the higher-paying job within, say, a one-year period is one chance in five. Thus the actual probability of his being successful in securing the higher-paying urban job is 20%, and therefore his expected urban income for the one-year period is in fact 20 units and not the 100 units that an urban worker in a full-employment environment would expect to receive. So with a one-period time horizon and a probability of success of 20%, it would be irrational for this migrant to seek an urban job, even though the differential between urban and rural earnings capacity is 100%. However, if the probability of success were 60% and the expected urban income therefore 60 units, it would be entirely rational for our migrant with his one-period time horizon to try his luck in the urban area, even though urban unemployment may be extremely high.

If we now approach the situation by assuming a considerably longer time horizon—a more realistic assumption, especially in view of the fact that the vast majority of migrants are between the ages of 15 and 24—the decision to migrate should be represented on the basis of a longer-term, more permanent income calculation. If the migrant anticipates a relatively low probability of finding regular wage employment in the initial period but expects this probability to increase over time as he is able to broaden his urban contacts, it would still be rational for him to migrate, even though expected urban income during the initial period or periods might be lower than expected rural income. As long as the **present value** of the net stream of expected urban income over the migrant's planning horizon exceeds that of the expected rural income, the decision to migrate is justifiable. This, in essence, is the process portrayed in Figure 7.8.

Rather than equalizing urban and rural wage rates, as would be the case in a competitive model, we see that rural-urban migration in our model acts as an equilibrating force that equates rural and urban expected incomes. For example, if average rural income is 60 and urban income is 120, a 50% urban unemployment rate would be necessary before further migration would no longer be profitable. Because expected incomes are defined in terms of both wages and employment probabilities, it is possible to have continued migration despite the existence of sizable rates of urban unemployment. In our example, migration would continue even if the urban unemployment rate were 30% to 40%.

A Diagrammatic Presentation

This process of achieving an unemployment equilibrium between urban expected wages and average rural income rather than an equalized rural-urban wage as in the traditional neoclassical free-market model can also be explained by a diagrammatic portrayal of the basic Harris-Todaro model. This is done in Figure 7.9.[23] Assume only two sectors, rural agriculture and urban manufacturing. The demand for labor (the marginal product of labor curve) in agriculture is given by the negatively sloped line AA'. Labor demand in manufacturing is given by MM' (reading from right to left). The total labor force is given by line $O_A O_M$. In a neoclassical, flexible-wage, full-employment market economy, the equilibrium wage would be established at $W_A^* = W_M^*$, with $O_A L_A^*$ workers in agriculture and $O_M L_M^*$ workers employed in urban manufacturing. All available workers are therefore employed.

FIGURE 7.9   The Harris-Todaro Migration Model

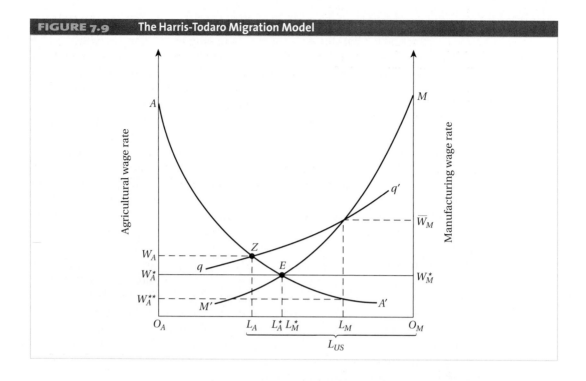

But what if urban wages are institutionally determined (inflexible downward) as assumed by Todaro at a level $\overline{W}_M$, which is at a considerable distance above W_M^*? If for the moment we continue to assume that there is no unemployment, $O_M L_M$ workers would get urban jobs, and the rest, $O_A L_M$, would have to settle for rural employment at $O_A W_A^{**}$ wages (below the free-market level of $O_A W_A^*$). So now we have an urban-rural real wage gap of $\overline{W}_M - W_A^{**}$, with $\overline{W}_M$ institutionally fixed. If rural workers were free to migrate (as they are almost everywhere except China), then despite the availability of only $O_M L_M$ jobs, they are willing to take their chances in the urban job lottery. If their chance (probability) of securing one of these favored jobs is expressed by the ratio of employment in manufacturing, L_M, to the total urban labor pool, L_{US}, then the expression

$$W_A = \frac{L_M}{L_{US}} (\overline{W}_M)$$ (7.1)

shows the probability of urban job success necessary to equate agricultural income W_A with urban expected income $(L_M / L_{US}) (\overline{W}_M)$, thus causing a potential migrant to be indifferent between job locations. The locus of such points of indifference is given by the qq' curve in Figure 7.9.[24] The new unemployment equilibrium now occurs at point Z, where the urban-rural actual wage gap is $\overline{W}_M - W_A, O_A L_A$ workers are still in the agricultural sector, and $O_M L_M$ of these workers have modern (formal)-sector jobs paying $\overline{W}_M$ wages. The rest, $O_M L_A - O_M L_M$, are either unemployed or engaged in low-income informal-sector activities. This explains the existence of urban unemployment and the private economic rationality of continued rural-to-urban migration despite this high unemployment. However, although it may be privately rational from a cost-benefit perspective for an individual to migrate to the city despite high unemployment, it can, as we shall soon discover, be socially very costly. Finally, note that if instead of assuming that all urban migrants are the same, we incorporate the reality of different levels of human capital (education), we can understand why a higher proportion of the rural educated migrate than the uneducated—because they have a better chance (a higher probability) of earning even higher urban wages than unskilled migrants.

We often observe that migrants from the same rural region tend to settle in common cities, even the same neighborhoods of cities, that are relatively distant from the migrants' place of origin. In a model proposed by William Carrington, Enrica Detragiache and Tara Vishwanath, earlier migrants create a positive externality for later potential migrants from their home region by lowering their costs of moving by helping with resettlement and lowering their probability of unemployment by providing them with jobs or information about available jobs. Thus the search for employment, selection into the migration decision, and forward-looking behavior may all be incorporated into an equilibrium migration model.[25]

The Todaro and Harris-Todaro models are relevant to developing countries even if the wage is not fixed by institutional forces, such as a minimum wage. Recent theoretical research on rural-urban migration has confirmed that the emergence of a high modern-sector wage alongside unemployment or an urban traditional sector as seen in these models can also result from market responses to imperfect information, labor turnover, and other common features of labor markets.[26]

To sum up, the Todaro migration model has four basic characteristics:

1. Migration is stimulated primarily by rational economic considerations of relative benefits and costs, mostly financial but also psychological.

2. The decision to migrate depends on expected rather than actual urban-rural real-wage differentials where the expected differential is determined by the interaction of two variables, the actual urban-rural wage differential and the probability of successfully obtaining employment in the urban sector.

3. The probability of obtaining an urban job is directly related to the urban employment rate and thus inversely related to the urban unemployment rate.

4. Migration rates in excess of urban job opportunity growth rates are not only possible but also rational and even likely in the face of wide urban-rural expected income differentials. High rates of urban unemployment are therefore inevitable outcomes of the serious imbalance of economic opportunities between urban and rural areas in most underdeveloped countries.

Five Policy Implications

Although the Todaro theory might at first seem to devalue the critical importance of rural-urban migration by portraying it as an adjustment mechanism by which workers allocate themselves between rural and urban labor markets, it does have important policy implications for development strategy with regard to wages and incomes, rural development, and industrialization.

First, imbalances in urban-rural employment opportunities caused by the urban bias, particularly first-city bias, of development strategies must be reduced. Because migrants are assumed to respond to differentials in expected incomes, it is vitally important that imbalances between economic opportunities in rural and urban sectors be minimized. Permitting urban wage rates to rise at a greater pace than average rural incomes will stimulate further rural-urban migration in spite of rising levels of urban unemployment. This heavy influx of people into urban areas not only gives rise to socioeconomic problems in the cities but may also eventually create problems of labor shortages in rural areas, especially during the busy seasons. These social costs may exceed the private benefits of migration.

Second, urban job creation is an insufficient solution for the urban unemployment problem. The traditional (Keynesian) economic solution to urban unemployment (the creation of more urban modern-sector jobs without simultaneous attempts to improve rural incomes and employment opportunities) can result in the paradoxical situation where more urban employment leads to higher levels of urban unemployment! Once again, the imbalance in expected income-earning opportunities is the crucial concept. Because migration rates are assumed to respond positively to *both* higher urban wages *and* higher urban employment opportunities (or probabilities), it follows that for any given positive urban-rural wage differential (in most LDCs, urban wages are typically three to four times as large as rural wages), higher urban employment rates will widen the expected differential and induce even higher rates of rural-urban migration. For every new job created, two or three migrants who were productively occupied in rural areas may come to the city. Thus if 100 new jobs are created, there may be as many as 300 new migrants and therefore 200 more urban unemployed. Hence a policy designed to reduce urban unemployment may lead not only to higher levels of urban unemployment but also to lower levels of agricultural output due to **induced migration**.

Third, indiscriminate educational expansion will lead to further migration and unemployment. The Todaro model also has important policy implications for curtailing investment in excessive educational expansion, especially at the higher levels. The heavy influx of rural migrants into urban areas at rates much in excess of new employment opportunities has necessitated a rationing device in the selection of new employees. Although within each educational group such selection may be largely random, many observers have noted that employers tend to use educational attainment or number of years of completed schooling as the typical rationing device. For the same wage, they will hire people with more education in preference to those with less, even though extra education may not contribute to better job performance. Jobs that could formerly be filled by those with a primary education (sweepers, messengers, filing clerks, etc.) now require secondary training; those formerly requiring a secondary certificate (clerks, typists, bookkeepers, etc.) must now have a university degree. It follows that for any given urban wage, if the probability of success in securing a modern-sector job is higher for people with more education, their expected income differential will also be higher, and they will be more likely to migrate to the cities. The basic Todaro model therefore provides an economic rationale for the observed fact in most LDCs that rural inhabitants with more education are more likely to migrate than those with less.

From the viewpoint of educational policy, it is safe to predict that as job opportunities become scarce in relation to the number of applicants, students will experience increasing pressure to proceed further up the educational ladder. The private demand for education, which in many ways is a derived demand for urban jobs, will continue to exert tremendous pressure on governments to invest in postprimary school facilities. But for many of these students, the specter of joining the ranks of the "educated unemployed" becomes more of a reality with each passing year. Government overinvestment in postprimary educational facilities thus often turns out to be an investment in idle human resources. Chapter 8 will focus on this and other issues related to the economics of education in greater detail.

Fourth, wage subsidies and traditional scarcity factor pricing can be counterproductive. As we have seen in Chapter 5 and Appendix 5.1, a standard economic policy prescription for generating urban employment opportunities is to eliminate factor-price distortions by using "correct" prices, perhaps implemented by wage subsidies (fixed government subsidies to employers for each worker employed) or direct government hiring. Because actual urban wages generally exceed the market or "correct" wage as a result of a variety of institutional factors, it is often argued that the elimination of wage distortions through price adjustments or a subsidy system will encourage more labor-intensive modes of production. Although such policies can generate more labor-intensive modes of production, they can also lead to higher levels of unemployment in accordance with our argument about induced migration. The overall welfare impact of a **wage subsidy** policy when both the rural and urban sectors are taken into account is not immediately clear. Much will depend on the level of urban unemployment, the size of the urban-rural expected-income differential, and the magnitude of induced migration as more urban jobs are created.

Finally, programs of integrated rural development should be encouraged. Policies that operate only on the demand side of the urban employment picture, such as wage subsidies, direct government hiring, elimination of factor-price distortions, and employer tax incentives, are probably far less effective in the long run in alleviating the unemployment problem than policies designed directly to regulate the supply of labor to urban areas. Clearly, however, some combination of both kinds of policies is most desirable.

Policies of rural development are crucial to this aim. Many informed observers agree on the central importance of rural and agricultural development if the urban unemployment problem is to be solved. Most proposals call for the restoration of a proper balance between rural and urban incomes and for changes in government policies that currently give development programs a strong bias toward the urban industrial sector (e.g., policies in the provision of health, education, and social services).

Conceptually, it may be useful to think of cities and their surrounding rural areas as integrated systems. There are significant complementarities between town and country (see Chapter 9). Agricultural and raw materials grown and extracted in rural areas are inputs for urban industry. Although there is some urban agriculture, most food consumed in urban areas is grown in agricultural regions. Towns are needed to allow sufficient agglomeration economies, as well as economies of scale, to produce and exchange many goods and services that are needed in rural areas. In turn, when rural incomes grow, markets for urban manufactures expand. People come from their rural residences to work in the city by the day or the week. City residents temporarily migrate to nearby agricultural regions during peak planting and harvesting seasons. Thus rural-urban linkages are extensive. And while investment in urban areas can accelerate migration to cities, investment in agriculture can raise productivity and incomes, making labor redundant, and also accelerate migration. As a result, for policy purposes, it may make a great deal of sense to take account of rural impacts when devising urban policies and vice versa.

At the same time, as globalization proceeds (see Chapter 12), cities tend to trade more with other cities, often in distant parts of the world, and less with nearby rural areas. Moreover, cities generally get the upper hand when urban and rural areas are treated as a bloc, reinforcing urban bias. And rural hinterlands, far from significant cities and from the attention of distant governments, whether national or regional, often suffer from benign neglect at best and systematic exploitation at worst, such as forced sale of food at low prices. Thus rural areas need to retain their own autonomy, and poverty programs need to be tailored to the needs of rural citizens.

Every effort must be made to broaden the economic base of the rural economy. The present unnecessary economic incentives for rural-urban migration must be minimized through creative and well-designed programs of integrated rural development. These should focus on both farm and nonfarm income generation, employment growth, health-care delivery, educational improvement, infrastructure development (electricity, water, roads, etc.), and the provision of other rural amenities. Successful rural development programs adapted to the socioeconomic and environmental needs of particular countries and regions seem to offer the only viable long-run solution to the problem of excessive rural-urban migration.

To assert, however, that there is an urgent need for policies designed to curb the excessive influx of rural migrants is not to imply an attempt to reverse what some observers have called inevitable historical trends. Rather, the implication of the Todaro migration model is that there is a growing need for a policy package that does not exacerbate these historical trends toward urbanization by artificially creating serious imbalances in economic opportunities between urban and rural areas.

Summary and Conclusions: The Shape of a Comprehensive Migration and Employment Strategy

Based on long-term trends, comparisons with developed countries, and still-strong individual incentives, continued urbanization and rural-urban migration are probably inevitable. Urban bias spurs migration, but focused investment in agriculture raises rural productivity sufficiently to require less labor; most alternative areas of employment expansion tend to be concentrated in urban areas because of agglomeration effects. Moreover, as education increases in rural areas, workers gain the skills they need, and perhaps the rising aspirations, to seek employment in the city. But rural-urban migration is still often excessive from the social viewpoint, particularly to urban giants.

At various points throughout this chapter, we have looked at possible policy approaches designed to improve the very serious migration and employment situation in developing countries. We conclude with a summary of what appears to be the consensus of most economists on the shape of a comprehensive migration and employment strategy.[27] This would appear to have seven key elements:

1. *Creating an appropriate rural-urban economic balance.* A more appropriate balance between rural and urban economic opportunities appears to be indispensable to ameliorating both urban and rural unemployment problems and to slowing the pace of rural-urban migration. The main thrust of this activity should be in the integrated development of the rural sector, the spread of small-scale industries throughout the countryside, the reorientation of economic activity and social investments toward the rural areas, and the development of more modest-size cities.

2. *Expansion of small-scale, labor-intensive industries.* The composition or "product mix" of output has obvious effects on the magnitude (and in many cases the location) of employment opportunities because some products (often basic consumer goods) require more labor per unit of output and per unit of capital than others. Expansion of these mostly small-scale and labor-intensive industries in both urban and rural areas can be accomplished in two ways: directly, through government investment and incentives, particularly for activities in the urban informal sector, and indirectly, through income redistribution (either directly or from future growth) to the rural poor, whose structure of consumer demand is both less import-intensive and more labor-intensive than that of the rich.

3. *Eliminating factor-price distortions.* There is ample evidence to demonstrate that correcting factor-price distortions primarily by eliminating various capital subsidies and curtailing the growth of urban wages through market-based pricing would increase employment opportunities and make better use of scarce capital resources. But by how much or how quickly these policies would work is not clear. Moreover, their migration implications would have to be ascertained. Correct pricing policies by themselves are insufficient to fundamentally alter the present employment situation.[28]

4. *Choosing appropriate labor-intensive technologies of production.* One of the principal factors inhibiting the success of any long-run program of employment creation in both urban industry and rural agriculture is the almost complete technological dependence of developing nations on imported (typically laborsaving) machinery and equipment from the developed countries. Both domestic and international efforts must be made to reduce this dependence by developing technological research and adaptation capacities in the developing countries themselves. Such efforts might first be linked to the development of small-scale, labor-intensive rural and urban enterprises. They could

also focus on the development of low-cost, labor-intensive methods of meeting rural infrastructure needs, including roads, irrigation and drainage systems, and essential health and educational services. This is an area where scientific and technological assistance from the developed countries could prove extremely helpful.

5. *Modifying the linkage between education and employment.* The emergence of the phenomenon of the educated unemployed is calling into question the appropriateness of the massive quantitative expansion of educational systems, especially at the higher levels. Formal education has become the rationing tunnel through which all prospective jobholders must pass. As modern-sector jobs multiply more slowly than the numbers of persons leaving the educational tunnel, it becomes necessary to extend the length of the tunnel and to narrow its exit. Although a full discussion of educational problems and policies must await the next chapter, one way to moderate the excessive demand for additional years of schooling (which in reality is a demand for modern-sector jobs) would be for governments, often the largest employers, to base their hiring practices and their wage structures on other criteria. Moreover, the creation of attractive economic opportunities in rural areas would make it easier to redirect educational systems toward the needs of rural development. At present, many developing-country educational systems, being transplants of Western systems, are oriented toward preparing students to function in a small modern sector employing at the most 20% to 30% of the labor force. Many of the skills needed for development remain largely neglected.

6. *Reducing population growth* through reductions in absolute poverty and inequality, particularly for women, along with the expanded provision of family-planning and rural health services. Clearly, any long-run solution to LDC employment and urbanization problems must involve a lowering of current high rates of population growth. Even though the labor force size for the next two decades is already determined by today's birthrates, the hidden momentum of population growth applies equally as well to labor force growth. Together with the demand policies identified in points 1 through 5, the population and labor supply reduction policies described in Chapter 6 provide an essential ingredient in any strategy to combat the severe employment problems that developing countries face now and in future years.

7. *Decentralizing authority to cities and neighborhoods.* Experience shows that decentralizaton of authority to municipalities is an essential step in the improvement of urban policies and the quality of public services. Local conditions vary greatly among small and large cities, as well as across different national regions, and policies need to be designed to reflect these differences. Local officials have greater information about evolving local conditions; and when officials are held accountable for local fiscal performance and know they must answer to recipients of the services they provide, they also have greater incentives to carry out their responsibilities effectively. Decentralization, with increased authority of cities and regions, has been a major international trend in the organization of government (see Chapter 11).

Rural-Urban Migration and Urbanization in Developing Countries: India and Botswana

About half of the world's population lives in cities; by 2025, nearly two-thirds will live in urban areas. Most of the urban growth is taking place in the developing world. The patterns of this growth and its implications are complex. Urban population growth in the developing world is far more rapid than population growth generally; about half the urban growth is accounted for by migrants from rural areas. Unchecked urbanization of the developing world is placing a strain on infrastructure and public health and threatens social stability. Shantytowns and similar makeshift settlements represent over one-third of developing country urban residences. About half of the urban labor force works in the informal sector of low-skilled, low-productivity, often self-employed jobs in petty sales and services. Still, this sector may generate up to a third of urban income and features a low capital intensity, low-cost training, waste recycling, and creation of surplus as well as employment creation. What drives migration? The cases of India and Botswana are instructive in showing the value of the probabilistic theory of migration, and suggesting ways of extending it.

Any economic or social policy that affects rural and urban incomes will influence migration; this, in turn, will affect sectoral and geographic economic activity, income distribution, and even population growth. Before the Todaro and Harris-Todaro migration models were introduced, migration was widely viewed as irrational or driven by noneconomic motivations, sometimes termed the "bright city lights." Noneconomic factors influence migration decisions, but economic factors are now understood to be primary. In the economic version of the bright-city-lights theory, people rationally migrated on the basis of costs and benefits. In this approach, it was assumed that if migrants appeared to be worse off, this was because other benefits were being overlooked, with the effect of making the migrants feel better off (or raising their overall utility).

The Todaro migration models postulate that observed migration is individually rational but that migrants respond to urban-rural differences in expected rather than actual earnings. Urban modern-sector earnings are much higher than rural earnings, which may in turn be even higher than urban traditional-sector earnings. Migration occurs until average or expected rather than actual incomes are equal across regions, generating equilibrium unemployment or underemployment in the urban traditional-sector. The extension of the model to consider equilibrium and effects of actions like increases in wages and probability of employment in the urban areas, undertaken by Harris and Todaro, shows that under some conditions, notably elastic supply of labor, creation of employment opportunities in cities can actually lead to an *increase* in unemployment by attracting more migrants than there are new jobs. Despite being individually rational, extensive rural-urban migration generates social costs for crowded cities, while excessive migration also imposes external costs on the rural areas emptied of better-educated, more venturesome young people as well as external costs on urban infrastructure and lost output.

One set of relevant migration and employment policies emphasizes rural development, rural basic-needs strategies, elimination of factor-price distortions, and appropriate technology choice as well as appropriate education. Each is intended to increase the incentives for rural residents to remain in rural areas rather than migrate to cities. But even if rural development is successful, fewer rural laborers will ultimately be needed, and demand for products of the cities will grow, which will fuel migration anyway. So other policies seek to influence the pattern of urban development to gain the most benefits for the fewest costs from migration that is probably inevitable.

India provides an interesting setting for a case study because future urban migration is potentially so vast and because a number of interesting studies have been undertaken there. Botswana offers a good counterpoint because it has better published data and more advanced statistical analysis of those data has been undertaken there than for most developing regions.

India

One of the most detailed studies of rural-urban migration, providing some tests of the Todaro migration models and depicting the characteristics of migrants and the migration process, is Biswajit Banerjee's *Rural to Urban Migration and the Urban Labour Market: A Case Study of Delhi.*

Everyone who has been to a major city in a developing country has noticed the sharp inequality between residents with modern-sector jobs and those working in the informal sector. But can the informal sector be seen as a temporary way station to the formal sector, or can the barriers between these sectors be explained by education and skill requirements that informal-sector workers cannot hope to meet? Banerjee found that the idea of segmented formal-informal rural labor markets could be substantiated statistically. After carefully controlling for human-capital variables, Banerjee was still left with earnings in the formal sector 9% higher than in the informal sector that were not explained by any standard economic factor. Even so, the earnings differences found in India were not nearly so dramatic as implied in some of the migration literature.

In much of the literature on urbanization, the typical laborer is characterized as self-employed or working on some type of piecework basis. But Banerjee found that only 14% of his informal-sector sample worked in nonwage employment. Interestingly, average monthly incomes of nonwage workers were 47% higher than those of formal-sector workers.

Banerjee argued that entry into nonwage employment was not easy in Delhi. Some activities required significant skills or capital. Those that did not were often controlled by cohesive "networks" of operators that controlled activities in various enterprises. Entry barriers to self-employment in petty services are probably lower in other developing-country cities.

Consistent with these findings, Banerjee found that mobility from the informal to the formal sector was low: There was little evidence that more than a very small minority of informal-sector workers were actively seeking jobs in the formal sectors, and only 5% to 15% of rural migrants into the informal sector had moved over to the formal sector in a year's time.

Moreover, the rate of entrants into the formal sector from the informal sector was just one-sixth to one-third that of the rate of direct entry to the urban formal sector from outside the area.

Informal-sector workers tended to work in the same job almost as long as those in the formal sector; the average informal-sector worker had worked 1.67 jobs over a period of 61 months in the city, while formal sector workers averaged 1.24 jobs over an urban career of 67 months.

Banerjee's survey data suggested that a large number of informal-sector workers who had migrated to the city were attracted by the informal rather than the formal sector, coming to work as domestic servants, informal construction laborers, and sales people. Of those who began nonwage employment upon their arrival, 71% had expected to do so. The fact that only a minority of informal-sector workers continued to search for formal-sector work was taken as further evidence that migrants had come to Delhi expressly to take up informal-sector work.

Workers who appear underemployed may not consider themselves as such, may perceive no possibility of moving into the modern sector, may be unable to effectively search for modern-sector work while employed in the informal sector, and hence do not create as much downward pressure on modern-sector wages as it would at first appear. This may be one factor keeping modern-sector wages well above informal-sector wages for indefinite periods of time despite high measured urban underemployment.

One reason for this focus on the informal sector was concluded to be the lack of contacts of informal-sector workers with the formal sector. About two-thirds of direct entrants into the formal sector and nearly as many of those switching from the informal to the formal sector found their jobs through personal contacts. This overwhelming importance of contacts was taken to explain why some 43% of Banerjee's sample migrated after receiving a suggestion from a contact,

which suggests that job market information can become available to potential migrants without their being physically present in the city. An additional 10% of the sample had a prearranged job in the city prior to migration.

Finally, the duration of unemployment following migration is usually very short. Within one week, 64% of new arrivals had found employment, and although a few were unemployed for a long period, the average waiting time to obtain a first job was just 17 days.

Banerjee also found that migrants kept close ties to their rural roots. Some three-quarters of the migrants visited their villages of origin and about two-thirds were remitting part of their urban incomes, a substantial 23% of income on average. This indicates that concern for the whole family appeared to be a guiding force in migration. It also suggests a source of the rapid flow of job market information from urban to rural areas.

In a separate study, A. S. Oberai, Pradhan Prasad, and M. G. Sardana examined the determinants of migration in three states in India—Bihar, Kerala, and Uttar Pradesh. Their findings were consistent with the ideas that migrants often have a history of chronic underemployment before they migrate, migrate only as a measure of desperation, and have the expectation of participating in the informal urban sector even in the long run. Remittances were found to be substantial, and considerable levels of return migration were also documented, among other evidence of continued close ties of migrants to their home villages.

But Banerjee's fascinating findings do not necessarily represent a challenge to the applicability of Harris-Todaro or other "probabilistic migration models." Instead, they suggest that they need to be extended to accommodate the apparently common pattern of migrating with the ultimate aim of urban informal-sector employment. As Ira Gang and Shubhashis Gangopadhyay have noted, one can modify the model to include in the urban area not only a formal sector but also a highly paid informal-sector, as well as a low-paid (or unemployed) sector. In this case, people will migrate looking for either a formal-sector job or a high-paid informal-sector job. This seems to be consistent with Banerjee's evidence. The assumption that keeps the essence of the probabilistic models intact is that the wage of the formal urban sector exceeds the high-paid informal wage, which in turn exceeds the agricultural wage, which in turn exceeds the low-paid informal (or unemployed) wage. In fact, if rural wages remain below all urban opportunities, this suggests that we are well out of equilibrium, and much additional migration must occur before expected incomes can be equalized across sectors. The particular formulations of the Todaro models are really no more than examples of a general principle: that migrants go where they expect in advance to do better, not where they do better after the fact. The basic ideas of the Todaro models do not depend on a particular notion of an informal or a formal sector.

Oded Stark's ideas on a family's use of migration can be a useful supplement to the Todaro models and may apply to some of Banerjee's findings. In his view, a family will send members to different areas as a "portfolio diversification" strategy, to reduce the risk that the family will have no income. This approach is useful to explain any observed migration from higher- to lower-wage areas and into higher-wage areas but not necessarily the area with the highest expected wage. The basic idea of the Todaro models still applies, but this approach looks at families rather than individuals and stresses risk aversion. Some evidence for this in Thailand has been identified by Anna Paulson.

In other studies, the Todaro migration models have held up well without modification in other parts of the world. A survey by Deepak Mazumdar showed that the evidence is overwhelming that migration decisions are made according to rational economic motivations.

Botswana

A study of migration behavior conducted by Robert E. B. Lucas in Botswana addressed such problems in the most economically and statistically sophisticated empirical study of migration in a developing country. His econometric model consisted of four groups of equations—for employment, earnings, internal migration, and migration to South Africa. Each group was estimated from microeconomic data on individual migrants and nonmigrants. Very detailed demographic information was available in the survey used.

Rural migrants in Botswana move to five urban centers (they would be called towns rather than cities in many parts of the world) as well as to neighboring South Africa. Lucas found that unadjusted urban earnings are much higher than rural earnings—68% higher for males—but these differences become much smaller when schooling and experience are controlled for.

Lucas's results confirm that the higher a person's expected earnings and the higher the estimated probability of employment given a move to an urban center, the greater the chances that the person will migrate. And the higher the estimated wage and probability of employment for a person in his or her home village, the lower the chances that the person will migrate. This result was very "robust"—not sensitive to which subgroups were examined or the way various factors were controlled for—and statistically significant. It represents clear evidence in support of Todaro's original hypothesis.

Moreover, Lucas estimated that at current pay differentials, the creation of one job in an urban center would draw more than one new migrant from the rural areas, thus confirming the Harris-Todaro effect. Earnings were also found to rise significantly the longer a migrant had been in an urban center, holding education and age constant. But the reason was because of increases in the rate of pay rather than in the probability of modern-sector employment.

Taken together, the best-conducted studies of urbanization confirm the value of probabilistic migration models as the appropriate place to start seeking explanations of rural-to-urban migration in developing countries. But these studies underscore the need to expand these explanations of migration, considering that many people today migrate to participate in the informal rather than the formal urban sector, and that workers may face a variety of different risks in different settings. ■

Sources

Banerjee, Biswajit. "The role of the informal sector in the migration process: A test of probabilistic migration models and labour market segmentation for India." *Oxford Economic Papers* 35 (1983): 399–422.

Banerjee, Biswajit. *Rural to Urban Migration and the Urban Labour Market: A Case Study of Delhi.* Bombay: Himalaya Publishing House, 1986.

Cole, William E., and Richard D. Sanders. "Internal migration and urban employment in the Third World." *American Economic Review* 75 (1985): 481–494.

Corden, W. Max, and Ronald Findlay. "Urban unemployment, intersectoral capital mobility, and development policy." *Economica* 42 (1975): 37–78.

Gang, Ira N., and Shubhashis Gangopadhyay. "A model of the informal sector in development." *Journal of Economic Studies* 17 (1990): 19–31.

Gang, Ira N., and Shubhashis Gangopadhyay, "Optimal policies in a dual economy with open unemployment and surplus labour." *Oxford Economic Papers* 39 (1987): 378–387.

Habitat (UNCHS), *State of the World's Cities,* 2001, http://www.unchs.org/Istanbul+5/86.pdf

Harris, John, and Michael P. Todaro. "Migration, unemployment, and development: a two-sector analysis." *American Economic Review* 60 (1970): 126–142 .

Lucas, Robert E. B. "Migration amongst the Batswana." *Economic Journal* 95 (1985): 358–382.

Lucas, Robert E. B. "Emigration to South Africa's mines." *American Economic Review* 77 (1987): 313–330.

Mazumdar, Deepak. "Rural-urban migration in developing countries." *Handbook of Regional and Urban Economics,* vol. 2. New York: Elsevier, 1987.

Oberai, A. S., Pradhan Prasad, and M. G. Sardana. *Determinants and Consequences of Internal Migration in India: Studies in Bihar, Kerala and Uttar Pradesh.* Delhi: Oxford University Press, 1989.

Paulson, Anna. "Insurance motives for migration: Evidence from Thailand." Unpublished manuscript, Northwestern University, 2000.

Stark, Oded. *The Migration of Labor.* Cambridge, Mass.: Blackwell, 1991.

Todaro, Michael P. "A model of labor migration and urban unemployment in LDCs." *American Economic Review* 59 (1969): 138–148.

United Nations. *An Urbanizing World: Global Report on Human Settlements.* Report presented to the Habitat II conference, Istanbul, 1996.

United Nations Population Division. *World Urbanization Prospects: The 1999 Revision.* New York: United Nations Population Division, 2000.

Concepts for Review

Agglomeration economies	Informal sector	Todaro migration model
Congestion	Labor turnover model	Urban bias
Efficiency wage	Localization economies	Urbanization economies
Expected income	Present value	Wage subsidy
Harris-Todaro model	Rural-urban migration	
Induced migration	Social capital	

Questions for Discussion

1. Why might the problem of rapid urbanization be a more significant population policy issue than curtailing LDC population growth rates over the next two decades? Explain your answer.

2. Describe briefly the essential assumptions and major features of the Todaro model of rural-urban migration. One of the most significant implications of this model is the paradoxical conclusion that government policies designed to create more urban employment may in fact lead to more urban unemployment. Explain the reasons for such a paradoxical result.

3. "The key to solving the serious problem of excessive rural-urban migration and rising urban unemployment and underemployment in developing countries is to restore a proper balance between urban and rural economic and social opportunities." Discuss the reasoning behind this statement, and give a few specific examples of government policies that would promote a better balance between urban and rural economic and social opportunities.

4. For many years, the conventional wisdom of development economics assumed an inherent conflict between the objectives of maximizing output growth and promoting rapid industrial employment growth. Why might these two objectives be mutually supportive rather than conflicting? Explain your answer.

5. What is meant by the expression "getting prices right"? Under what conditions will eliminating factor-price distortions generate substantial new employment opportunities? (Be sure to define factor-price distortions.)

6. The informal sector is becoming an ever-larger part of the urban economy. Distinguish between the urban formal and informal sectors, and discuss both the positive and negative aspects of the informal urban labor market.

7. Why are capital cities in many LDCs often disproportionately large? Which factors can be addressed with better policies?

8. What is an industrial district? How might government in LDCs help them succeed?

Notes

1. Robert S. McNamara, "The population problem: Time bomb or myth?" Foreign Affairs 62 (1984): 1107–1131. For additional information on the problems of rapid urban population growth, see Bertrand Renaud, *National Urbanization Policy in Developing Countries* (New York: Oxford University Press, 1981). A less concerned viewpoint is expressed in Jeffrey G. Williamson, "Migration and urbanization," in *Handbook of Development Economics,* vol. 1, ed. Hollis B. Chenery and T. N. Srinivasan (Amsterdam: Elsevier, 1988), pp. 426–465.

2. United Nations Population Fund, *Population, Resources, and the Environment* (New York: United Nations, 1991), p. 61.

3. See Michael Porter, *The Competitive Advantage of Nations* (New York: Free Press, 1990); his theory is reviewed further in Chapter 13.

4. See Michael Piore and Charles Sabel, *The Second Industrial Divide* (New York: Basic Books, 1984).

5. The significance of industrial districts in developing countries is difficult to pin down, in part because such clusters overlap traditional political jurisdictions for which data are collected. The best source on this topic is Hubert Schmitz and Khalid Nadvi (eds.), "Special issue on clustering and industrialization," *World Development* 27 (1999): 1503 ff.

6. See Hermine Weijland, "Microenterprise clusters in rural Indonesia: Industrial seedbed and policy target," in ibid., p. 1519.

7. Dorothy McCormick, "African enterprise and industrialization: Theory and reality," in ibid., pp. 1531–1551.

8. Schmitz and Navdi, "Introduction: Clustering and Industrialization" in ibid., pp. 1505–1506, summarize it this way:

   In the early stage, both the mobilizations and use of resources occur in small amounts at a time. This is where clustering becomes significant because it facilitates specialization and effective investment in small steps. Producers do not have to acquire equipment for the entire production process; they can concentrate on particular stages, leaving other stages to other entrepreneurs. Specialized workshops that can repair and upgrade existing machinery further help to reduce technological discontinuities. It follows that investment [and working] capital is needed in small, rather than big, lumps ["riskable steps"]. . . . One producer's investment in specialized skill renders returns because others have invested in complementary expertise. Specialization does not mean isolation, however, because without interaction no one can sell their products or services. . . . Clustering draws out the less exceptional and more common "ordinary" entrepreneurs.

9. World Bank, *World Development Report, 1999–2000* (New York: Oxford University Press, 2000), ch. 6.

10. Ibid.

11. For an introductory overview of urban economics, see, for example, Arthur M. O'Sullivan, *Urban Economics*, 5th ed. (New York: McGraw-Hill/Irwin, 2002). For recent formal models of some of these ideas, see Masahisa Fujita, Paul Krugman, and Anthony J. Venables, *The Spatial Economy: Cities, Regions, and International Trade* (Cambridge, Mass.: MIT Press, 1999). We would like to thank Anthony Yezer for his very helpful suggestions on these sections.

12. In this comparison, it is no accident that a relatively modest scale of the largest city tends to be found in countries in which the political capital is not found in the largest city, as we shall see shortly. This has been true in Canada and the United States nearly since their founding; it is more recently true in Brazil, where much recent urban growth has been diverted to the new capital, Brasilia, which was inaugurated in 1960 and has reached a population of over 2 million.

13. Examples—Italy: Rome 2.7 million, Milan 1.4 million; Germany: Berlin 3.5 million, Hamburg 1.7 million; the Netherlands: Rotterdam and Amsterdam 1.1 million each; Portugal: Lisbon 2.6 million, Porto 1.2 million; Spain: Madrid 3.0 million, Barcelona 1.6 million.

14. For example, while Mexico City continues to expand, it has a smaller share of industry than in decades past. A major reason is the growing concentration of export industries in northern Mexico along the U.S. border, especially following implementation of NAFTA (see Chapter 13) and, even more recently, the move of low-skill industries to southern Mexico.

15. Alberto F. Ades and Edward L. Glaeser, "Trade and circuses: Explaining urban giants," *Quarterly Journal of Economics* 110 (1995): 195–227. Urban concentration is defined as the average share of urbanized population living in the main city from 1970 to 1985. Stable countries are defined as those whose average number of revolutions and coups is below the worldwide median. Dictatorships are countries whose average Gastil index for the period is higher than 3. In Figure 7.5 standard errors are in parentheses. See also Rasha Gustavsson, "Explaining the phenomenon of Third World urban giants: The effects of trade costs," *Journal of Economic Integration* 14 (1999): 625–650.

16. Habitat (UNCHS), *State of the World's Cities*, 2001, http://www.unchs.org/Istanbul+5/statereport.htm.

17. For a concise review of this debate, see Cathy A. Rakowski, "Convergence and divergence in the informal sector debate: A focus on Latin America, 1984–92," *World Development* 22 (1994): 501–516. See also Donald C. Mead and Christian Morrisson, "The informal sector elephant," *World Development* 24 (1996): 1611–1619, and Edward Funkhauser, "The urban informal sector in Central America: Household survey evidence," *World Development* 24 (1996): 1737–1751.

18. For evidence of the deteriorating urban employment situation in Latin America and sub-Saharan Africa, see International Labor Organization, *World Employment Report 1996–97* (Geneva: International Labor Organization, 1996), ch. 5; and Charles M. Becker, Andrew M. Hammer, and Andrew R. Morrison, *Beyond Urban Bias in Africa: Urbanization in an Era of Structural Adjustment* (Portsmouth, N.H.: Heinemann, 1994).

19. See Robert E. B. Lucas, "Internal migration and urbanization: Recent contributions and new evidence," background paper for World Bank, *World Development Report, 1999* (New York: Oxford University Press, 1999), fig. 1.1.

20. Anna Paulson, "Insurance motives for migration: Evidence from Thailand," unpublished manuscript, Northwestern University, 2000.

21. Although the *rate* of rural-urban migration slowed during the 1980s, especially in Latin America and sub-Saharan Africa, as a result of declining urban real wages and fewer formal-sector employment opportunities, the actual number of migrants continued to expand.

22. See Michael P. Todaro, "A model of labor migration and urban unemployment in less developed countries," *American Economic Review* 59 (1969): 138–148, and John R. Harris and Michael P. Todaro, "Migration, unemployment, and development: A two-sector analysis," *American Economic Review* 60 (1970): 126–142.

23. This graph was first introduced in W. Max Corden and Ronald Findlay, "Urban unemployment, intersectoral capital mobility, and development policy," *Economica* 42 (1975): 59–78. It reflects Harris and Todaro, "Migration, unemployment, and development."

24. Note that qq' is a rectangular hyperbola, a unitary-elasticity curve showing a constant urban wage bill; that is, $L_M \times W_M$ is fixed.

25. William J. Carrington, Enrica Detragiache, and Tara Vishwanath, "Migration with endogenous moving costs," *American Economic Review* 86 (1996): 909–930.

26. Whereas the Todaro model focuses on the institutional determinants of urban wage rates above the equilibrium wage, several other authors have sought to explain this phenomenon by focusing on the high costs of labor turnover (the so-called **labor turnover model**) in urban areas and the notion of an **efficiency wage**; an above-equilibrium urban wage enables employers to secure a higher-quality workforce and greater productivity on the job. For a review of these various models, see Joseph E. Stiglitz, "Alternative theories of wage determination and unemployment in LDCs: The labor turnover model," *Quarterly Journal of Economics* 88 (1974): 194–227, and Janet L. Yellen, "Efficiency wage models of unemployment," *American Economic Review* 74 (1984): 200–205. For recent evidence of the existence and importance of an institutionally determined urban-rural wage gap, see Francis Teal, "The size and sources of economic rents in a developing country manufacturing labour market," *Economic Journal* 106 (1996): 963–976.

  In an influential study, Valerie R. Bencivenga and Bruce D. Smith make the alternative assumption that urban modern firms do not know the productivity of migrants but that some potential migrants from rural areas are highly productive and others are unproductive within formal-sector (say, industrial) firms. In this scenario, firms will be motivated through competitive forces to (in effect) offer migrants a package of a wage and a probability of employment. Modern-sector firms hire labor until their marginal products are equal to the resulting high wage rate, and unemployment ensues. Moreover, if modern-sector labor demand increases, both modern- and traditional-sector workforces expand proportionately, inducing additional migration. See Valerie R. Bencivenga and Bruce D. Smith, "Unemployment, migration and growth," *Journal of Political Economy* 105 (1997): 582–608. An alternative perspective within the economics of information framework, based on moral hazard problems, is offered by Hadi S. Esfahani and Djavad Salehi-Ifsahani, "Effort observability and worker productivity: Toward an explanation of economic dualism," *Economic Journal* 99 (1989): 818–836.

27. See, for example, Gary S. Fields, "Public policy and the labor market in less developed countries," in *The Theory of Taxation for Developing Countries*, ed. David P. Newbery and Nicholas Stern (New York: Oxford University Press, 1987); Becker, Hammer, and Morrison, *Beyond Urban Bias in Africa*, ch. 4–7; David Turnham, *Employment and Development: A New Review of Evidence* (Paris: Organization for Economic Coordination and Development, 1993), pp. 245–253; Paul P. *Streeten, Strategies for Human Development: Global Poverty and Unemployment* (Copenhagen: Handelshøjskolens Forlag, 1994), pp. 50–64; and Cedric Pugh, "Poverty and progress: Reflections on housing and urban policies in developing countries, 1976–96," *Urban Studies* 34 (1997): 1547–1595.

28. The literature has also examined strategies to eliminate excessive migration through wage subsidies; these would prove expensive and difficult to administer, but their analysis has yielded interesting insights into the nature of the Harris-Todaro migration model. See, for example, Ira Gang and Shubhashis Gangopadhyay, "Optimal policies in a dual economy with open unemployment and surplus labour," *Oxford Economic Papers* 39 (1987): 378–387, which also contains references to important earlier work.

Further Reading

An excellent source for current information is the UN-Habitat website and *State of the World's Cities* reports at http://www.unhabit.org.

Useful surveys of urbanization issues in developing nations are George S. Tolley and Vinod Thomas, *The Economics of Urbanization and Urban Policies in Developing Countries* (Washington, D.C.: World Bank, 1987); Alan Gilbert and Josef Gugler, *Cities, Poverty, and Development*, 2nd ed. (New York: Oxford University Press, 1992); Pradip K. Ghosh (ed.), *Urban Development in the Third World* (Westport, Conn.: Greenwood Press, 1984); Charles M. Becker, Andrew M. Hammer, and Andrew R. Morrison, *Beyond Urban Bias in Africa: Urbanization in an Era of Structural Adjustment* (Portsmouth, N.H.: Heinemann, 1994); and Pii Elina Berghäll, *Habitat II and the Urban Economy: A Review of Recent Development and Literature* (Helsinki: United Nations University, World Institute for Development Economics Research, 1995).

Among the many readings on the critical problem of rural-urban migration in developing countries, the following are perhaps the most comprehensive: Derek Byerlee, "Rural-urban migration in Africa: Theory, policy, and research implications," *International Migration Review* 3 (1974): 543–566; John R. Harris and Michael P. Todaro, "Migration, unemployment, and development: A two-sector analysis," *American Economic Review* 60 (1970): 126–142; Michael P. Todaro, *Internal Migration in Developing Countries: A Review of Theory, Evidence, Methodology and Research Priorities* (Geneva: International Labor Organization, 1976); Nanda R. Shrestha, "Institutional policies and migration behavior: A selective review," *World Development* 15 (1987): 329–345. Oded Stark, *The Migration of Labour* (Oxford: Blackwell, 1991); Valerie R. Bencivenga and Bruce D. Smith, "Unemployment, migration and growth," *Journal of Political Economy* 105 (1997): 582–608; and John L. Gallup, "Theories of migration," Discussion Paper No. 569, *Harvard Institute for International Development*, January 1997.

For a suggested national and international strategy to combat developing-world poverty and unemployment, see International Labor Organization, *Employment, Growth and Basic Needs: A One-World Problem* (Geneva: International Labor Organization, 1976); Lyn Squire, *Employment Policy in Developing Countries: A Survey of Issues and Evidence* (New York: Oxford University Press, 1981); Subbiah Kannappan, *Employment Problems and the Urban Labor Market in Developing Nations* (Ann Arbor: University of Michigan Press, 1983); Gary S. Fields, "Public policy and the labor market in less developed countries," in *The Theory of Taxation for Developing Countries,* ed. David P. Newbery and Nicholas Stern (New York: Oxford University Press, 1987); and United Nations, *Report on the World Social Situation,* 1997 (New York: United Nations, 1997), ch. 7.

Readings on the informal sector include Salem V. Sethuraman, *The Urban Informal Sector in Developing Countries: Employment, Poverty and Environment* (Geneva: International Labor Organization, 1981); Harry W. Richardson, "The role of the informal sector in developing countries: An overview," *Regional Development Dialogue* 5 (1984): 3–40; Alejandro Portes and Richard Schauffler, "Competing perspectives on the Latin American informal sector," *Population and Development Review* 19 (1993): 33–60; Cathy A. Rakowski, "Convergence and divergence in the informal sector debate: A focus on Latin America, 1984–92," *World Development* 22 (1994): 501–516; and Donald C. Mead and Christian Morrisson, "The informal sector elephant," *World Development* 24 (1996): 1611–1619. A classic book on the potential contribution of the informal sector, and the ways that misdirected government policies can thwart it is Hernando de Soto, *Other Path: The Economic Answer to Terrorism* (New York: Basic Books, 1989).

Appendix 7.1

A Mathematical Formulation of the Todaro Migration Model

Consider the following mathematical formulation of the basic Todaro model discussed in this chapter. Individuals are assumed to base their decision to migrate on considerations of income maximization and what they perceive to be their expected income streams in urban and rural areas. It is further assumed that the individual who chooses to migrate is attempting to achieve the prevailing average income for his or her level of education or skill attainment in the urban center of his or her choice. Nevertheless, the migrant is assumed to be aware of the limited chances of immediately securing wage employment and the likelihood that he or she will be unemployed or underemployed for a certain period of time. It follows that the migrant's expected income stream is determined by both the prevailing income in the modern sector and the probability of being employed there, rather than being underemployed in the urban "informal" sector or totally unemployed.

If we let $V(0)$ be the discounted present value of the expected "net" urban-rural income stream over the migrant's time horizon; $Y_u(t)$ and, $Y_r(t)$ the average real incomes of individuals employed in the urban and the rural economy, respectively; n the number of time periods in the migrant's planning horizon; and r the discount rate reflecting the migrant's degree of time preference, then the decision to migrate or not will depend on whether

$$V(0) = \int_{t=0}^{n} [p(t)Y_u(t) - Y_r(t)]e^{-rt}dt - C(0) \tag{A7.1.1}$$

is positive or negative, where $C(0)$ represents the cost of migration and $p(t)$ is the probability that a migrant will have secured an urban job at the average income level in period t.

In any one time period, the probability of being employed in the modern sector, $p(t)$, will be directly related to the probability π of having been selected in that or any previous period from a given stock of unemployed or underemployed job seekers. If we assume that for most migrants the selection procedure is random, then the probability of having a job in the modern sector within x periods after migration, $p(x)$, is $p(1) = \pi(1)$ and $p(2) = \pi(1) + [1 - \pi(1)]\pi(2)$ so that

$$p(x) = p(x-1) + [1 - p(x-1)]\pi(x) \tag{A7.1.2}$$

or

$$p(x) = \pi(1) + \sum_{t=2}^{x} \pi(t)\prod_{s=1}^{t-1}[1 - \pi(s)] \tag{A7.1.3}$$

where $\pi(t)$ equals the ratio of new job openings relative to the number of accumulated job aspirants in period t.

It follows from this probability formulation that for any given level of $Y_u(t)$ and $Y_i(t)$, the longer the migrant has been in the city, the higher his or her probability p of having a job and the higher, therefore, his or her expected income in that period.

Formulating the probability variable in this way has two advantages:

1. It avoids the "all or nothing" problem of having to assume that the migrant either earns the average income or earns nothing in the periods immediately following migration: consequently, it reflects the fact that many underemployed migrants will be able to generate some income in the urban "informal" or traditional sector while searching for a regular job.

2. It modifies somewhat the assumption of random selection since the probability of a migrant's having been selected varies directly with the time the migrant has been in the city. This permits adjustments for the fact that longer-term migrants usually have more contacts and better information systems so that their expected incomes should be higher than those of newly arrived migrants with similar skills.

Suppose that we now incorporate this behavioristic theory of migration into a simple aggregate dynamic equilibrium model of urban labor demand and supply in the following manner. We once again define the probability π of obtaining a job in the urban sector in any one time period as being directly related to the rate of new employment creation and inversely related to the ratio of unemployed job seekers to the number of existing job opportunities, that is:

$$\pi = \frac{\lambda N}{S - N} \qquad (A7.1.4)$$

where λ is the net rate of urban new job creation, N is the level of urban employment, and S is the total urban labor force. If w is the urban real wage rate and r represents average rural real income, then the "expected" urban-rural real-income differential d is

$$d = w\pi - r \qquad (A7.1.5)$$

or, substituting Equation A7.1.4 into Equation A7.1.5,

$$d = w\frac{\lambda N}{S - N} - r \qquad (A7.1.6)$$

The basic assumption of our model once again is that the supply of labor to the urban sector is a function of the urban-rural *expected* real-income differential, that is,

$$S = f_s(d) \qquad (A7.1.7)$$

If the rate of urban job creation is a function of the urban wage w and a policy parameter a, such as a concentrated governmental effort to increase employment through a program of import substitution, both of which operate on labor demand, we have

$$\lambda = f_d(w; a) \qquad (A7.1.8)$$

where it is assumed that $\partial \lambda / \partial a > 0$. If the growth in the urban labor demand is increased as a result of the governmental policy shift, the increase in the urban labor supply is

$$\frac{\partial S}{\partial a} = \frac{\partial S}{\partial d} \frac{\partial d}{\partial \lambda} \frac{\partial \lambda}{\partial a} \qquad \text{(A7.1.9)}$$

Differentiating Equation A7.1.6 and substituting into Equation A7.1.9, we obtain

$$\frac{\partial S}{\partial a} = \frac{\partial S}{\partial d} w \frac{N}{S-N} \cdot \frac{\partial \lambda}{\partial a} \qquad \text{(A7.1.10)}$$

The absolute number of urban employed will increase if the increase in labor supply exceeds the increase in the number of new jobs created, that is, if

$$\frac{\partial S}{\partial a} > \frac{\partial(\lambda N)}{\partial a} = \frac{N \partial \lambda}{\partial a} \qquad \text{(A7.1.11)}$$

Combining Equations A7.1.10 and A7.1.11, we get

$$\frac{\partial S}{\partial d} w \frac{N}{S-N} \cdot \frac{\partial \lambda}{\partial a} > \frac{N \partial \lambda}{\partial a} \qquad \text{(A7.1.12)}$$

or

$$\frac{\partial S/S}{\partial d/d} > \frac{d}{w} \cdot \frac{S-N}{S} \qquad \text{(A7.1.13)}$$

or, finally, substituting for d:

$$\frac{\partial S/S}{\partial d/d} > \frac{w\pi - r}{w} \cdot \frac{S-N}{S} \qquad \text{(A7.1.14)}$$

Expression A7.1.14 reveals that the absolute level of unemployment will rise if the elasticity of urban labor supply with respect to the expected urban-rural income differential $(\delta S/S)/(\delta d/d)$—what has been called elsewhere the "migration response function"—exceeds the urban-rural differential as a proportion of the urban wage times the unemployment rate, $(S - N)/S$. Alternatively, Equation A7.1.14 shows that the higher the unemployment rate, the higher must be the elasticity to increase the level of unemployment for any expected real-income differential. But note that in most developing nations, the inequality in Equation A7.1.14 will be satisfied by a very low elasticity of supply when realistic figures are used. For example, if the urban real wage is 60, average rural real income is 20, the probability of getting a job is 0.50, and the unemployment rate is 20%, then the level of unemployment will increase if the elasticity of urban labor supply is greater than 0.033; that is, substituting into Equation A7.1.14, we get

$$\frac{\partial S/S}{\partial d/d} = \frac{(0.5 \times 60) - 20}{60} (0.20) = \frac{2}{60} = 0.033 \qquad \text{(A7.1.5)}$$

Much more needs to be known about the empirical value of this elasticity coefficient in different developing nations before one can realistically predict what the impact of a policy to generate more urban *employment* will be on the overall level of urban *unemployment*.

CHAPTER EIGHT

Human Capital: Education and Health in Economic Development

What makes for a good health system? What makes a health system fair? And how do we know whether a health system is performing as well as it could? These questions are the subject of public debate in most countries around the world.

—Gro Harlem Brundtland, Director General, World Health Organization, 2000

Education is fundamental to enhancing the quality of human life and ensuring social and economic progress.

—United Nations, *Report on the World Social Situation*, 1997

Education is the key to creating, adapting and spreading knowledge.... But the gains in access to education have been unevenly distributed, with the poor seldom getting their fair share.

—World Bank, *World Development Report*, 1998–99

The Central Roles of Education and Health

Education and health are basic *objectives of development;* they are important ends in themselves. Health is central to well-being, and education is essential for a satisfying and rewarding life; both are fundamental to the broader notion of expanded human capabilities that lie at the heart of the meaning of development (see Chapter 1). At the same time, education plays a key role in the ability of a developing country to absorb modern technology and to develop the capacity for self-sustaining growth and development. Moreover, health is a prerequisite for increases in productivity, while successful education relies on adequate health as well. Thus both health and education can also be seen as vital *components of growth and development*—as inputs to the aggregate production function. Their dual role as both

363

inputs and outputs gives health and education their central importance in economic development.

It is hard to overstate how truly dramatic the improvements in world health and education have been over the past half century. In 1950, some 280 of every 1,000 children in the developing world as a whole died before their fifth birthday. By 2002, that number had fallen to 120 per 1,000 in low-income countries, and 37 per 1,000 in middle-income countries (compared with 7 per 1,000 in high-income countries).[1] Some important killers have been eradicated, or nearly eliminated. Smallpox used to kill more than 5 million people every year; the virus no longer exists outside a few laboratory samples. Major childhood illnesses such as rubella and polio have been largely controlled through the use of vaccines. In addition, recent decades have witnessed a historically unprecedented extension of **literacy** and other basic education to a majority of people in the developing world. The United Nations reports that although there were still a staggering 875 million illiterate people aged 15 or older in the world in 2000, the good news is that 80% of all people are literate today, compared to just 63% as recently as 1970.

Despite such outstanding achievements, the developing world continues to face great challenges as it seeks to continue to improve the health and education of its people. The distribution of health and education within countries is as important as income distribution; life expectancy may be quite high for better-off people in developing countries but far lower for the poor. Child mortality rates in developing countries remain more than ten times higher than those found in the rich countries. These deaths generally result from conditions that are easily treatable, including millions who continue to die needlessly each year from dehydration caused by diarrhea. If child death rates in developing countries fell to those prevailing in the developed countries, the lives of more than 10 million children would be saved each year. Many children who survive nonetheless suffer chronic problems of malnutrition, debilitating parasitic infections, and other recurrent illnesses. Problems caused by lack of key micronutrients such as iodine, as well as protein, affect some 2 billion people, but children are particularly vulnerable. Whereas a child in Europe, North America, or Japan can expect to receive more than 12 years of schooling, the average child in sub-Saharan Africa and South Asia can expect to spend less than four years in school—before taking account of teacher absenteeism and making no adjustment for the lack of schoolbooks and other resources even when a teacher is present. Box 8.1 conveys some of the impact of deprivation in health and education on people's lives.

In this chapter, we examine the roles of education and health in economic development. As we will see in the next section, these two **human capital** issues are treated together because of their close relationship. The connections between health and education include similar analytical treatment, because both are forms of human capital; the dual impacts of effects of health spending on the effectiveness of the educational system and vice versa; and the fundamental fact that when we speak of investing in a person's health and investing in a person's education, we are after all talking about the same person. We then consider the relationships between income on the one hand and health and education on the other. Despite

BOX 8.1   Health and Education: Voices of the Poor

If you don't have money today, your disease will take you to your grave.

—An old woman from Ghana

The children keep playing in the sewage.

—Sacadura Cabral, Brazil

In the hospitals, they don't provide good care to the indigenous people like they ought to; because of their illiteracy they treat them badly ... They give us other medicines that are not for the health problem you have.

—A young man from La Calera, Ecuador

The school was OK, but now it is in shambles; there are no teachers for weeks. ... There is no safety and no hygiene.

—Vila Junqueira, Brazil

If parents do not meet these payments, which are as high as 40 to 50 rupees per month, the teachers were reported to beat the student or submit a failing grade for her/him.

—Pakistan ("Voice of the Poor")

Teachers do not go to school except when it is time to receive salaries.

—Nigeria ("Voice of the Poor")

Before everyone could get health care, but now everyone just prays to God that they don't get sick because everywhere they just ask for money.

—Vares, Bosnia-Herzegovina

their close relationship, we will see that the record shows that higher household income is no guarantee of improved health and education: Human capital must be given direct attention in its own right, even in economies that are growing rapidly. Health and education may be distributed very unequally, just as income and wealth are. But improved health and education help families escape some of the vicious cycles of poverty in which they are trapped. At the same time, the most important root cause of poor health in developing countries is poverty itself. Finally, we take a systematic look at educational and health systems in developing countries, to understand the sources of the severe inequalities and inefficiencies that continue to plague them. We will find compelling evidence that investments in human capital have to be undertaken with both equity and efficiency for them to successfully realize their potential impact on incomes.

Education and Health as Joint Investments for Development

Health and education are closely related in economic development.[2] On the one hand, greater health capital may improve the return to investments in education, in part because health is an important factor in school attendance and in the formal learning process of a child. A longer life raises the return to investments in education; better health at any point during working life may in effect lower the rate of depreciation of education capital. On the other hand, greater education capital may improve the return to investments in health, because many health programs rely on basic skills often learned at school, including personal hygiene and sanitation, not to mention basic literacy and numeracy; education is also needed for the formation and training of health personnel. Finally, an improvement in productive efficiency from investments in education raises the return on a lifesaving investment in health. Box 8.2 summarizes the linkages between investments in health and education.

The past half century witnessed unprecedented advances in human capital. Health and education levels improved in both developed and developing countries, but by most measures they have improved more rapidly in developing countries. As a result, there has been some international convergence in these measures. Only in sub-Saharan Africa have falling life expectancies cast doubt on the trend toward catching up in health. As primary enrollments rise in developing countries, education is catching up, though some observers believe that the quality gap may be larger than ever.

The progress made in health and education is in strong contrast to per capita income, which shows little sign of convergence across countries (see Chapter 2).

BOX 8.2   Linkages between Investments in Health and Education

- Health and education are investments made in the same individual.
- Greater health capital may raise the return on investment in education because
    - Health is an important factor in school attendance
    - Healthier children are more successful in school and learn more efficiently
    - Deaths of school-age children also increase the cost of education per worker
    - Longer life spans raise the return to investments in education
    - Healthier individuals are more able to productively use education at any point in life
- Greater education capital may raise the return to investment in health because
    - Many health programs rely on skills learned in school (including literacy and numeracy)
    - Schools teach basic personal hygiene and sanitation
    - Education is needed for formation and training of health personnel
- Improvement in productive efficiency from investment in education raises the return on a lifesaving investment in health.

But even though the health and education gap between developed and developing countries remains large and further improvements may prove difficult, the progress to date has been unmistakable.[3]

Improving Health and Education: Why Increasing Income Is Not Sufficient

Health and education levels are much higher in high-income countries. There are good reasons to believe that the causality runs in both directions: With higher income, people and governments can afford to spend more on education and health; with greater health and education, higher productivity and incomes are possible. Because of these relationships, development policy needs to focus on income, health, and education simultaneously. This conclusion is parallel to our finding in Chapter 5 that we need a multipronged strategy to address the stubborn problems of absolute poverty.

People will spend more on human capital when income is higher. But the evidence shows clearly that even if we were able to raise incomes without a large improvement in health and education, we could not count on that income increase being used to adequately invest in children's education and health. The market will not solve this problem automatically, and in many cases, household consumption choices themselves may lead to a surprisingly small link between income and nutrition, especially for children.[4] There is a substantial economic literature on the income elasticity of the demand for calories, that is, in estimating the percentage change in calories consumed for a percentage change in family incomes, under a range of scenarios. Estimates of this income elasticity among low-income people range from near zero to about 0.5, depending on the region and the statistical strategy used by the researchers.[5] This less than proportional response is due to two factors: Income is spent on other goods besides food, and part of the increased food expenditures is used to increase food variety without necessarily increasing the consumption of calories. If the relationship between income and nutrition is indeed quite low, as some studies suggest, then development policies that emphasize increasing incomes of the poor, without attention to the way these additional resources are expended within the family, may not lead to improved health, and successful development more generally, at least not very quickly.[6] As discussed further in the Chapter 5 case study and Chapter 16, credit for microenterprises has been one of the most popular poverty-alleviation strategies in recent years. In this case, credit may help the poor improve their nutrition, for example, because seasonal price fluctuations are also shown to be an important determinant of calorie consumption along with average income among the very poor, but it will not be sufficient if nutrition remains inadequate and does not improve automatically with higher income.

Note that even if income elasticities for calories are higher than the traditional, close-to-zero estimates imply—say, on the order of 0.3 to 0.5, as Shankar Subramanian and Angus Deaton estimated using a newer statistical strategy[7]—calories are not the same as nutrition, and the nutrition of earners is not the same as the nutrition of their children. The income elasticity of "convenience" foods is greater than unity.[8] An increase in income frequently allows families in developing countries to switch consumption from nutritious foods such as beans and rice to nonnutritious "empty calories" such as candy and soda, which may be perceived as modern and a symbol of economic success. Parents may then fail to place restrictions on children's consumption of such items or to place positive restrictions on consumption of nutritious foods.

Howarth Bouis found that intake of vitamins A and C is not positively associated with income in the Philippines and argued that consumer education was important. Moreover, morbidity (incidence of sickness) did not necessarily decrease significantly with income in that country.[9] A major problem is that poor health (e.g., diarrheal diseases) can negate the health advantages of better nutrition. A study of the Gambia found that diarrhea is associated with reduced nutritional status even after calorie intake is controlled for.[10]

There is considerable evidence that the better the education of the mother, the better the health of her children. Usually, formal education is needed in complementary relationship with ongoing access to current information. Paul Glewwe found in an analysis of data from Morocco that a mother's basic health knowledge had a positive effect on her children's health. This finding paralleled that of many other previous studies. But Glewwe went beyond this finding to examine the sources of this connection. Several mechanisms were possible, such as that "formal education directly teaches health knowledge to future mothers; literacy and numeracy skills acquired in school assist future mothers in diagnosing and treating child health problems; and exposure to modern society from formal schooling makes women more receptive to modern medical treatments." But, Glewwe concludes, "mother's health knowledge alone appears to be the crucial skill for raising child health. In Morocco, such knowledge is primarily obtained outside the classroom, although it is obtained using literacy and numeracy skills learned in school; there is no evidence that health knowledge is directly taught in schools. This suggests that teaching of health knowledge skills in Moroccan schools could substantially raise child health and nutrition in Morocco." Thus there are still opportunities for improving health through simple activities in school that have not been utilized.[11]

Health status, once attained, also affects school performance, as has been shown in studies of many developing countries. Better health and nutrition leads to earlier and longer school enrollment, better school attendance, and more effective learning. For example, it has been found that the probability of attending school among nutritionally stunted children in Nepal is just 5%, but this rises to 27% for nonstunted students.[12] Undernourished children were found to lag 20% in test score gains in northeast Brazil, one of the worst pockets of poverty in Latin America.[13] Children with low height for their age, an indicator of undernutrition, have been found to lag in school grade attainment in many parts of the world, including rural China and Thailand. Thus to improve the effectiveness of schooling, we must improve the health of children in developing countries. Indeed, advances in statistical methods are showing that the links from health to educational attainment in developing countries are stronger than had been believed until very recently. These effects are large for both boys and girls but especially so for girls.[14] In a careful randomized evaluation carried out in rural Kenya, Michael Kremer and Edward Miguel found that low-cost deworming of parasite-infected schoolchildren caused significant improvements in their school attendance and other outcomes. In fact, the study demonstrated that deworming actually increases attendance in neighboring school districts that were not treated, due to reduced contagion through contaminated water.[15]

Finally, there are other important spillover benefits to investment in one's health or education. An educated person provides benefits to people around him or her, such as reading for them or coming up with innovations that benefit the community.[16] As a result, there are significant market failures in education. Moreover, a healthy person is not only less contagious but can also benefit the community in many ways that a sick person cannot. Because of such spillover effects, the market cannot be counted on to deliver the socially efficient levels of health and education. Thus, as the World Health Organization (WHO) concluded in its 2000 *World Health Report* on health systems, "Ultimate responsibility for the performance of a country's health system lies with government."[17] Developing-country officials are drawing lessons from the many studies showing the interrelationships among health, education, and incomes and are devising integrated strategies.

Investing in Education and Health: The Human Capital Approach

The analysis of investments in health and education is unified in the human capital approach. *Human capital* is the term economists often use for education, health, and other human capacities that can raise productivity when increased. An analogy is made to conventional investments in physical capital: After an initial investment is made, a stream of higher future income can be generated from both expansion of education and improvements in health. As a result, a rate of return can be deduced and compared with returns to other investments. This is done by estimating the present discounted value of the increased income stream made possible by these investments and then comparing it with their direct and indirect costs. Of course, health and education also contribute directly to well-being, but the human capital approach focuses on their indirect ability to increase utility by increasing incomes. In this section, we will generally illustrate points with educational investments, but the same principles apply to health investments.

The impact of human capital investments in developing countries can be quite substantial. Figure 8.1 shows the age-earnings profiles by levels of education in Venezuela. The chart shows how incomes vary over the life cycle for people with various levels of education. Note that those with higher levels of education start full-time work at a later age, but as the graph shows, their incomes quickly outpace those who started working earlier. But such income gains from education must be compared with the total costs incurred to understand the value of human

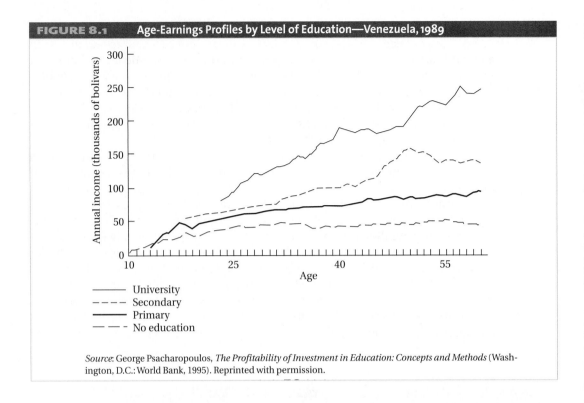

FIGURE 8.1   Age-Earnings Profiles by Level of Education—Venezuela, 1989

——— University
– – – – Secondary
——— Primary
— — - No education

Source: George Psacharopoulos, *The Profitability of Investment in Education: Concepts and Methods* (Washington, D.C.: World Bank, 1995). Reprinted with permission.

capital as an investment. Education costs include any direct tuition or other expenditures specifically related to education, such as books, and indirect costs, primarily income foregone because the student could not work while in school.

Formally, the income gains can be written as follows, where E is income with education, N is income without the extra education, t is year, and the summation is over expected years of working life:

$$\sum \frac{E_t - N_t}{(1 + i)^t} \tag{8.1}$$

An analogous formula applies to health, with the direct and indirect cost of resources devoted to health compared with the extra income gained in the future as a result of higher health (such as improved nutritional status).

Figure 8.2 provides a schematic representation of the trade-offs involved in the decision to continue in school. It is assumed that the individual works from the time he or she finishes school until he or she is unable to work or dies. This is taken to be the current world life expectancy of 66 years. Two earnings profiles are presented—for those with primary school but no secondary education and for those with a full secondary (but no higher) education. Primary graduates are assumed to begin work at age 13, secondary graduates at age 17. For an individual in a developing country deciding whether to go on from primary to secondary education,

FIGURE 8.2   Financial Trade-Offs in the Decision to Continue in School

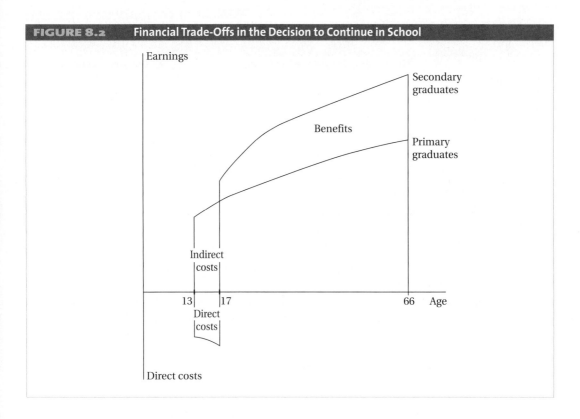

four years of income are foregone. This is the indirect cost, as labeled in the diagram. The child may work part time, a possibility ignored here for simplicity, but if so, only part of the indirect-cost area applies. There is also a direct cost, such as fees, school uniforms, books, and other expenditures that would not have been made if the individual had left school at the end of the primary grades. Over the rest of the person's life, he or she makes more money each year than would have been earned with only a primary education. This differential is labeled "Benefits" in the diagram. Before comparing costs with benefits, note that a dollar today is worth more to an individual than a dollar in the future, so those future income gains must be discounted accordingly, as is done in Equation 8.1. Although a simple analytical formula for the rate of return would rely on unrealistic assumptions, the rate of return will be higher whenever the discount rate is lower, the direct or indirect costs are lower, or the benefits are higher.

This analysis is performed from the individual's point of view in the three right-hand columns of Table 8.1. Notice that in sub-Saharan Africa and Asia the private rate of return to primary education is about 40%! Despite this extraordinary return, many families do not make this investment because they have no ability to borrow even the meager amount of money that a working child can bring into the family. Note that the higher rates of return for developing countries reflect that the

TABLE 8.1	Rates of Return to Investment in Education by Level of Education, Country, Type, and Region (percent)					
Country Type and Region	Social Rate of Return			Private Rate of Return		
	Primary	Secondary	Higher	Primary	Seondary	Higher
Developing						
Sub-Saharan Africa	24	18	11	41	27	28
Asia	20	13	12	39	19	20
Latin America	18	13	12	26	17	20
Developed	14	10	9	22	12	12

Source: George Psacharopoulous. "Returns to investment in education: A global update," *World Development* 22 (1994): 1325—1343, tab. 1. Copyright © 1994. Reprinted with the permission of Elsevier.
Note: How these rates of return are calculated is explained in note 19 at the end of this chapter.

income differential between those with more and less schooling is greater on average than for the developed countries.[18]

The first three columns of Table 8.1 indicate the social rate of return. This is found by reducing the benefits by the amount of public subsidy for the individual's education, because this is part of the investment from the social point of view (and also by considering pretax rather than after-tax incomes).[19] It should be noted that these social returns are probably understated because they do not take into account the externality that educated people confer on others (e.g., being able to read for other family members). This raises two important questions: How large are public subsidies for education, and are they allocated in a way that is most helpful for achieving development objectives? We will consider these matters later in the chapter.

Child Labor

Child labor is a widespread problem in developing countries. When children under age 14 work, their labor time disrupts their schooling and in a majority of cases prevents them from attending school altogether. Compounding this, the health of child workers is significantly worse, even accounting for their poverty status, than that of children who do not work; physical stunting among child laborers is very common. In addition, a large fraction of laboring children are subject to especially cruel and exploitative working conditions.

The International Labor Office (ILO), a UN body that has played a leading role on the child labor issue, recently estimated that some 120 million children in developing countries between the ages of 5 and 14 are working full time, with another 130 million working half time.[20] Some 61% of the 250 million working children, or nearly 153 million, live in Asia, while 32%, or 80 million, live in Africa, and 7%, or over 17 million, live in Latin America. Although Asia has the largest number of child laborers, in relative terms, Africa has the highest child labor rate, estimated at about 41% of all children between 5 and 14 years old. The rates for Asia and Latin America are 21% and 17%, respectively. These numbers do not even include the many children who work full time at home for their parents or guardians. Working conditions are often horrendous; the ILO reports that some of its surveys show that more than half of working children toil for nine or more hours per day. Moreover, at least 180 million child laborers are either under 14 years of age or work in conditions that endangers their health or well-being, involving hazards, sexual exploitation, trafficking, and debt bondage. This includes 110 million children under the age of 15 doing hazardous work. Some 73 million working children are under 10 years of age. The Human Rights Commission of Pakistan estimated that in 1994, there were 11 to 12 million children, half of whom were under the age of 10, effectively working as indentured servants. They earned less than half the adult wage and often worked in excess of 80 hours per week, many in carpet- and brick-making factories. Thus child labor is not an isolated problem, but a pervasive one, especially in Africa and South Asia.

Nevertheless, it is not obvious that an immediate ban on all forms of child labor is always in the best interests of the child. Without work, a child may become severely malnourished; with work, school fees as well as basic nutrition and health care may be available. But there is one set of circumstances under which both the child laborer and the family as a whole may be unambiguously better off with a ban on child labor: multiple equilibria. Kaushik Basu has provided such an analysis, and we first consider his simple model that shows how this problem may arise.[21]

To model child labor, we make two important assumptions: First, a household with a sufficiently high income would not send its children to work. As one might hope, there is strong evidence that this is true, at least most of the time. Second, child and adult labor are substitutes. In fact, children are not as productive as adults, and adults can do any work that children can do. This assertion is not an assumption; it is a finding of many studies of the productivity of child laborers in many countries. It is important to emphasize this, because one rationalization for child labor often heard is that children have special productive abilities, such as small fingers, that make them important for the production of rugs and other products. However, there is no support for this view. In essentially every task that has been studied, including carpet weaving, adult laborers are significantly more productive. As a result, we can consider the supply of adult and child labor together in an economic analysis of the problem.

The child labor model is graphed in Figure 8.3. On the x-axis, we have the supply of labor in adult equivalents. Because we are interested in understanding the impact of the demand for labor, in a graph it is best to consider homogeneous units of labor. So if a child laborer is γ times as productive as an adult worker, we consider one child the productive equivalent of γ adult workers. According to our assumptions, $\gamma < 1$. For example, if a child laborer is half as productive as an adult worker, then $\gamma = 0.5$.

We start with the assumption that in the region in question, all (unskilled) adults work, regardless of the wage. This gives us a perfectly inelastic, vertical adult labor supply curve, called AA' in the diagram. Highly inelastic supply is a very reasonable assumption among families so poor that their children work. While the parents may not have modern-sector jobs, every adult is involved in

FIGURE 8.3 **Child Labor as a Bad Equilibrium**

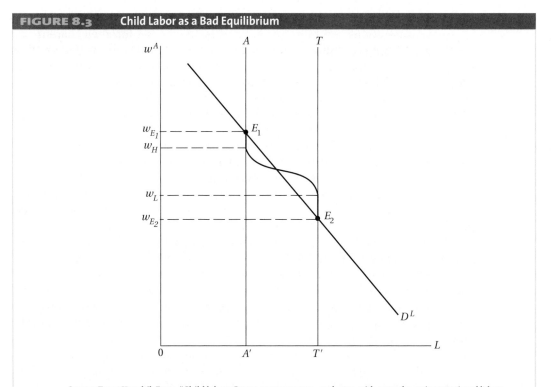

Source: From Kaushik Basu, "Child labor: Cause, consequence, and cure, with remarks on international labor standards," *Journal of Economic Literature* 37 (1999): 1101. Reprinted with the permission of the American Economic Association.

some type of activity to help the family survive. This adult supply AA' is simply the number of unskilled adults. If the adult wage falls to w_H, then some of the families find they are poor enough that they have to send their children to work. As the wage continues to fall, more families do the same, and labor supply expands along the S-shaped curve, until a wage of w_L is reached, at which point all of the children are working. At this point, we are on the vertical line labeled TT', which is the aggregate labor supply of all the adults and all the children together. This sum is the number of adults, plus the number of children multiplied by their lower productivity, $\gamma < 1$. The resulting supply curve for children and adults together is very different from the standard ones that we usually consider in basic microeconomics, such as the supply curve seen in Figure 5.5 (in Chapter 5), but it is highly relevant for the developing-country child labor context. To summarize, as long as the wage is above w_H, the supply curve is along AA'; if the wage is below w_L, the supply curve is along TT', and in between, it follows the S-shaped curve between the two vertical lines.

Now consider the labor demand curve, D^L; if demand is inelastic enough to cut the AA' line above w_H and also cut the TT' line below w_L, then there will be two stable equilibria, labeled E_1 and E_2 in the diagram.[22] When there are two equilibria, if we start out at the bad equilibrium E_2, an effective ban on child labor will move the region to the good equilibrium E_1. Moreover, once the economy had moved to the new equilibrium, the child labor ban would be self-enforcing, because by assumption the new wage is high enough for no family to have to send its children to work. If poor families could coordinate with each other and refuse to send their children to work, each would be better off; but in general, with a large number of families, they will be unable to achieve this.

Banning child labor when there is an alternative equilibrium in which all children go to school might seem like an irresistible policy, but note that while all the families of child laborers are better off, employers may now be worse off, because they have to pay a higher wage. Thus employers may use political pressure to prevent enactment of child labor laws. In this sense, child labor, even its worst forms, could actually be Pareto-optimal—a discovery that should remind us that Pareto optimality is sometimes a very weak condition on which to base development policy! In the same sense, many other problems of underdevelopment, including extreme poverty itself, may at times also be Pareto-optimal, in that solving these problems may make the rich worse off.[23]

While these child labor models are probably reasonable depictions of many developing areas, we do not know enough about conditions in unskilled labor markets to say how significant these types of multiple equilibria and severe credit constraints really are as explanations for child labor. Thus it would be potentially counterproductive, if even enforceable, to seek an immediate ban on all child labor in all parts of the world today. As a result, an intermediate approach is currently dominant in international policy circles.[24]

There are four main approaches to child labor policy current in development policy. The first recognizes child labor as an expression of poverty and recommends an emphasis on eliminating poverty rather than directly addressing child labor; this position is generally associated with the World Bank (poverty policy is discussed further in Chapters 5, 9, and 16). The second approach emphasizes strategies to get more children into school, including expanded school places, such as new village schools, and incentives to induce parents to send their children to school, such as the PROGRESA program in Mexico, discussed later in the chapter. This strategy has wide support from many international agencies and development bodies. It is probably a more effective approach than making basic education compulsory, because without complementary policies, the incentives to send children to work would still remain strong and enforcement is likely to be weak, for the same reasons that regulation of the informal sector has proved almost impossible in many other cases. Compulsory schooling is a good idea, but it is not an effective solution to child labor.

The third approach considers child labor inevitable, at least in the short run, and stresses palliative measures such as regulating it to prevent abuse and to provide support services for working children. This approach is most commonly associated with UNICEF, which has prepared a checklist of regulatory and social approaches that could meet the "best interest of the child." The regulations included on UNICEF's checklist include expanding educational opportunities through "time off" for standard or workplace schooling, encouraging stricter law enforcement against illegal child labor trafficking, providing support services for parents and for children working on the streets, and working to develop social norms against the economic exploitation of children.

The fourth approach, most often associated with the ILO, favors banning child labor. If this is not possible, however, and recognizing that child labor may not always result from multiple equilibria, this approach favors banning child labor *in its most abusive forms*. The latter approach has received much attention in recent years; the ILO's "Worst Forms of Child Labor Convention" was adopted in 1999. The worst forms covered under the convention include "all forms of slavery or practices similar to slavery, such as the sale and trafficking of children, debt bondage and serfdom and forced or compulsory labor"; child prostitution and pornography; other illicit activities, such as drug trafficking; and work that, "by its nature or the circumstances . . . is likely to harm the health, safety or morals of children."

Finally, many activists in developed countries have proposed the imposition of trade sanctions against countries that permit child labor or at least banning the goods on which children work. This approach is well intentioned, but if the objective is the welfare of children, it needs to be considered carefully, because if children cannot work in the export sector, they will almost certainly be forced to work in the informal sector, where wages and other working conditions are generally worse. Export restrictions may also make it more difficult for poor countries to grow their way out of poverty. Finally, if efforts at banning imports from developing countries were channeled instead into working to secure more public and private development assistance for nongovernmental organizations that work with child laborers, much more would be accomplished to help these children.

The Gender Gap: Women and Education

Young females receive considerably less education than young males in almost every developing country. In a recent year, in 66 out of 108 countries, women's enrollment in primary and secondary education was lower than that of men by at least 10 percentage points. This **educational gender gap** is the greatest in the poorest countries and regionally in the Middle East and North Africa. Table 8.2 provides data on female-male gaps in literacy, mean years of schooling, and enrollments for eight developing countries. For all developing countries taken together, the female literacy rate was 29% lower than male literacy, women's mean years of schooling were 45% lower than men's, and females' enrollment rates in primary, secondary, and postsecondary schools were 9%, 28%, and 49% lower, respectively, than the corresponding male rate. So even though progress has been made, a substantial gender gap persists.

Why is female education important? Is it simply a matter of equity? The answer is that there now exists ample empirical evidence that educational discrimination against women hinders economic development in addition to reinforcing social

TABLE 8.2 The Educational Gender Gap: Female Rates as a Percentage of Male Rates

Country	Adult Literacy	Mean Years of Schooling	Primary Enrollment	Secondary Enrollment	Tertiary Enrollment
Algeria	76	18	97	106	—
Bangladesh	62	29	102	110	50
Egypt	65	41	96	95	—
Mexico	96	96	101	103	95
Morocco	61	37	93	83	80
Nigeria	80	28	—	—	—
South Korea	—	61	100	100	60
Sudan	69	45	83	—	92

Source: United Nations Development Program, *Human Development Report, 2004* (New York: Oxford University Press, 2004), tab. 9. Reprinted with permission.
Notes: All figures are expressed in relation to the male average, which is indexed to equal 100. The smaller the figure, the bigger the gap. Mean years of schooling are for 1994.

inequality. Closing the educational gender gap by expanding educational opportunities for women, a key plank of the Millennium Development Goals, is economically desirable for four reasons:[25]

1. The rate of return on women's education is higher than that on men's in most developing countries.

2. Increasing women's education not only increases their productivity on the farm and in the factory but also results in greater labor force participation, later marriage, lower fertility, and greatly improved child health and nutrition.

3. Improved child health and nutrition and more educated mothers lead to multiplier effects on the quality of a nation's human resources for many generations to come.

4. Because women carry a disproportionate burden of the poverty and landlessness that permeates developing societies, any significant improvements in their role and status via education can have an important impact on breaking the vicious cycle of poverty and inadequate schooling.

Consequences of Gender Bias in Health and Education

Studies from around the developing world consistently show that expansion of basic education of girls earns among the very highest rates of return of any investment—much larger, for example, than most public infrastructure projects.[26] This is one reason why discrimination against girls in education, as well as health, is not just inequitable but very costly from the standpoint of achieving development goals.

Education of girls has also been shown to be one of the most cost-effective means of improving local health standards. Studies by the United Nations, the World Bank, and other agencies have concluded that the social benefits alone of increased education of girls is more than sufficient to cover its costs—even before considering the added earning power this education would bring. However, evidence from Pakistan, Bangladesh, and other LDCs shows that we cannot assume that education of girls will increase automatically with increases in family income.

Inferior education and health care access for girls shows the interlinked nature of economic incentives and the cultural setting. In rural Asia, a boy provides future economic benefits, such as support of parents in their old age and possible receipt of a dowry upon marriage, and often continues to work on the farm into adulthood. A girl, in contrast, may require a dowry upon marriage, often at a young age, and will then move to the village of her husband's family, becoming responsible for the welfare of her husband's parents rather than her own. A girl from a poor rural family in South Asia will in many cases perceive no suitable alternatives in life than serving a husband and his family; indeed, a more educated girl may be considered "less marriageable." For the parents, treatment of disease may be expensive and may require several days lost from work to go into the town for medical attention. Empirical studies demonstrate what we might guess from these perverse incentives: Often more strenuous efforts are made to save the life of a son than a daughter, and girls generally receive less schooling than boys.

The bias toward boys helps explain the "missing women mystery." In Asia, the United Nations has found that there are far fewer females as a share of the population than would be predicted by demographic norms. In developed countries, there are about 105 girls for every 100 boys. But in Asia there are about 110 boys for every 100 girls, and in China the ratio has reached about 116 to 100 and is rising. Estimating from developed-country gender ratios, Nobel laureate Amartya Sen concluded that worldwide "many more than" 100 million women are "missing."[27] Other methods of calculation, such as using historical developed-country data as a reference point rather than data from contemporary developed countries, generate smaller numbers, but these still approach 100 million missing women. Evidence shows that these conditions are continuing to worsen in China and India, implying that tens of millions of young males will be unable to marry, increasing the chances of future social instability. As Sen notes, that dearth of women is not just a matter of poverty per se because in Africa, where poverty is most severe, there are actually about 2% more women than men. Although this number is not as high as in Western Europe and North America, it is still much higher than in Asia, which has higher income on average. Reasons for the smaller number of women in Asia include female infanticide and selective abortion, but a larger part of the explanation is poorer treatment of girls. Figure 8.4 shows the female-male ratios in the total population in selected countries. These ratios show that even though women have a higher life expectancy than men, there are more men than women in many Asian countries. The evidence on gender bias in Africa is mixed, with some studies finding a small pro-female bias and others a small and possibly rising pro-male bias.[28]

Greater mothers' education, however, generally improves prospects for both her sons' and daughters' health and education. Studies show that mothers' education plays a decisive role in raising nutritional levels in rural areas. The level of child stunting, a valid indicator of child undernutrition, is much lower with higher education attainment of the mother at every income level. Harold Alderman and

FIGURE 8.4   **Female-Male Ratios in Total Population in Selected Communities**

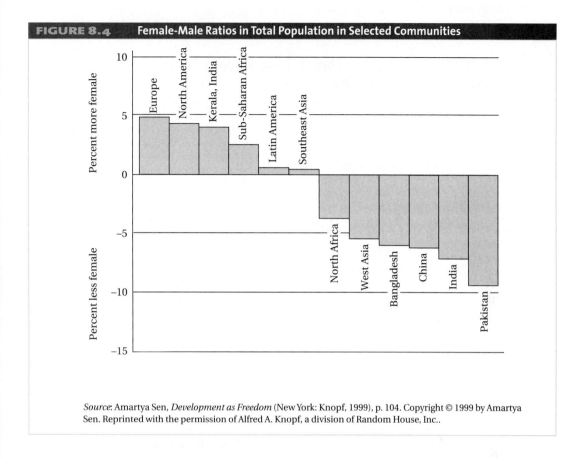

Source: Amartya Sen, *Development as Freedom* (New York: Knopf, 1999), p. 104. Copyright © 1999 by Amartya Sen. Reprinted with the permission of Alfred A. Knopf, a division of Random House, Inc..

Marito Garcia report that the incidence of child stunting would be reduced by a quarter of current levels (from 63.6% to 47.1% in their sample in Pakistan) if women were to attain a primary-level education. They note that this is almost ten times the projected impact of a 10% increase in per capita income. Coupled with the result that in many countries mothers' education tends to make a disproportionately larger health difference toward daughters than sons, as Duncan Thomas has reported, we can expect major benefits for girls.[29]

Taken together, the evidence shows that increases in family income do not automatically result in improved health status or educational attainment. If higher income cannot be expected to necessarily lead to higher health and education, as we will see in subsequent sections, there are no guarantees that higher health or education will lead to higher productivities and incomes. Much depends on the context, on whether gains from income growth and also the benefits of public investments in health and education and other infrastructure are shared equitably. Thus in the remainder of this chapter, we examine issues of education and health systems in turn. Even though health and education will be examined separately, it is important to keep their mutually reinforcing roles in mind.

Educational Systems and Development

Much of the literature and public discussion about education and economic development in general, and education and employment in particular, revolves around two fundamental economic processes: (1) the interaction between economically motivated demands and politically responsive supplies in determining how many school places are provided, who gets access to these places, and what kind of instruction they receive, and (2) the important distinction between social and private benefits and costs of different levels of education and the implications of these differentials for educational investment strategy.

Educational Supply and Demand: The Relationship Between Employment Opportunities and Educational Demands

The amount of schooling received by an individual, although affected by many nonmarket factors, can be regarded as largely determined by demand and supply, like any other commodity or service.[30] However, because most education is publicly provided in less developed countries, the determinants of the amount demanded turn out to be much more important than the determinants of supply. On the demand side, the two principal influences on the amount of schooling desired are (1) a more educated student's prospects of earning considerably more income through future modern-sector employment (the family's **private benefits of education**) and (2) the educational costs, both direct and indirect, that a student or family must bear. The amount of education demanded is thus in reality a **derived demand** for high-wage employment opportunities in the modern sector. This is because access to such jobs is largely determined by an individual's education. Most people (especially the poor) in less developed nations do not demand education for its intrinsic noneconomic benefits but simply because it is the only means of securing modern-sector employment. These derived benefits must in turn be weighed against the costs of education.

On the supply side, the quantity of school places at the primary, secondary, and university levels is determined largely by political processes, often unrelated to economic criteria. Given mounting political pressure throughout the developing world for greater numbers of school places, we can for convenience assume that the public supply of these places is fixed by the level of government educational expenditures. These are in turn influenced by the level of aggregate private demand for education.

Because it is the amount of education that is demanded that largely determines the supply (within the limits of government financial feasibility), let us look more closely at the economic (employment-oriented) determinants of this derived demand.

The amount of schooling demanded that is sufficient to qualify an individual for modern-sector jobs appears to be related to or determined by the combined influence of four variables: the wage or income differential, the probability of success in finding modern-sector employment, the direct private costs of education, and the indirect or opportunity costs of education.

Although several other important variables, many of them noneconomic (e.g., cultural traditions, gender, social status, education of parents, and size of family), certainly influence the amount of education demanded, concentrating on the four variables just identified can give important insights into the relationship between the quantity of education demanded and the supply of employment opportunities.

For example, suppose that we have a situation in an LDC where the following conditions prevail:

1. The modern-traditional or urban-rural wage gap is of the magnitude of, say, 100% for secondary versus primary school graduates.

2. The rate of increase in modern-sector employment opportunities for primary school dropouts is slower than the rate at which such individuals enter the labor force. The same may be true at the secondary level and even the university level in countries such as India, Mexico, Egypt, Pakistan, Ghana, Nigeria, and Kenya.

3. Employers, facing an excess of applicants, tend to select by level of education. They will choose candidates with secondary rather than primary education even though satisfactory job performance may require no more than a primary education.

4. Governments, supported by the political pressure of the educated, tend to bind the going wage to the level of educational attainment of jobholders rather than to the minimum educational qualification required for the job.

5. School fees at the early primary level are often nominal or even nonexistent. They tend to rise sharply at the late primary and secondary level and then decline again at the university level as the state bears a larger proportion of the college student's costs.

Under these conditions, which conform closely to the realities of the employment and education situation in many developing nations, we would expect the quantity of education demanded for the formal sector to be substantial. This is because the anticipated private benefits of more schooling would be large compared to the alternative of little or no schooling, while the direct and indirect private educational costs are relatively low. And the demand spirals upward over time. As job opportunities for the uneducated diminish, individuals must safeguard their position by acquiring a complete secondary education. This may suffice for a while, but the internal dynamics of the employment demand-supply process eventually lead to a situation in which job prospects for those with only primary education begin to decline. This in turn increases the demand for higher education. But the amount of secondary education must increase concurrently, as some people who were previously content with no education are now being squeezed out of the labor market.

The irony is that the more unprofitable a given level of education becomes as a terminal point, the greater the demand among the elite for it as an intermediate stage or precondition to the next level of education! This puts great pressure on governments to expand educational facilities at all levels to meet the growing demand. If they cannot respond fast enough, the people may do so on their own, as evidenced, for example, by the Harambee school self-help movement in Kenya, where community-sponsored secondary schools were built throughout the country with the knowledge that their maintenance would be taken over later by the government.

The upshot of all this is the chronic tendency for some developing nations to expand their educational facilities at a rate that is extremely difficult to justify either socially or financially in terms of optimal resource allocations. Supply and amount demanded are equated not by a price-adjusting market mechanism but rather institutionally, largely by the state. The **social benefits of education** (the payoff to society as a whole) for all levels of schooling fall far short of the private benefits (see Table 8.1). Each worsening of the employment situation calls forth an increased amount demanded for (and supply of) more formal education at all levels. Over time, there is an inexorable tendency for the average educational level of unemployed urban elites to rise as the supply of school graduates continues to exceed the demand for middle- and high-level workers. The better-educated must, after varying periods of unemployment during which aspirations are scaled downward, take jobs requiring lower levels of education. The diploma and degree thus become basic requirements for employment; they no longer provide entree into a high-paid job, nor do they provide the education they were intended to signify.

Governments and formal-sector private employers in many LDCs tend to reinforce this trend by continuously upgrading formal educational entry requirements for jobs previously filled by less educated workers. Excess educational qualification becomes formalized and may resist downward adjustment. Moreover, to the extent that trade unions succeed in binding going wages to the educational attainments of jobholders, the going wage for each job will tend to rise (even though worker productivity in that job does not significantly increase). Existing distortions in wage differentials will be magnified, thus stimulating the amount of education demanded even further. Egypt presents a classic case of this phenomenon with its government guaranteed and budget-busting employment in the public sector and its massive civil service overstaffing of overcredentialized school graduates.[31]

As a result of this **educational certification** and displacement phenomenon, students who for some reason (primarily poverty) are unable to continue their education will fall by the wayside as school dropouts. At the same time, the more affluent continue to overqualify themselves through more years of education. In the extreme case, a situation evolves like that of contemporary India, Pakistan, and Bangladesh, where the higher education system is in effect an "absorber of last resort" for the great numbers of the urban educated unemployed.[32] This is a terribly expensive form of unemployment compensation. Moreover, because people cannot remain students until they retire, these great masses will eventually have to emerge from behind the walls of academia into a world of tight labor markets. The result will be more visible unemployment among people who are both highly educated and highly vocal. For example, a study in Bangladesh revealed that the unemployment rate among university graduates was 47%.[33]

Finally, it should be pointed out that many individuals tend to resist what they see as a downgrading of their job qualifications. Consequently, even though on the demand-for-labor side employers will attempt to substitute the more educated for the less educated for a given job, on the supply side there will be many job seekers whose expectations exceed the emerging realities of the labor market. They might prefer to remain unemployed for some time rather than accept a job that they feel is beneath them. It follows that as a result of these frictional effects and lags in adjustment on the supply side, unemployment will exist at all levels of education even though it is concentrated at lower levels and, in general, is inversely related to educational attainment.

Social versus Private Benefits and Costs

The inexorable attraction of ever-higher levels of education is even more costly than this simple picture suggests. Typically in developing countries, the **social costs of education** (the opportunity cost to society as a whole resulting from the need to finance costly educational expansion at higher levels when these limited funds might be more productively used in other sectors of the economy) increase rapidly as students climb the educational ladder. The **private costs of education** (those borne by students themselves) increase more slowly or may even decline.

This widening gap between social and private costs provides an even greater stimulus to the demand for higher education than it does for education at lower levels. But educational opportunities can be accommodated to these distorted demands only at full social cost. As demands are generated progressively through the system, the social cost of accommodation grows much more rapidly than the places provided. More and more resources may be misallocated to educational expansion in terms of social costs, and the potential for creating new jobs will consequently diminish for lack of public financial resources.

Figure 8.5 provides an illustration of this divergence between private and social benefits and costs. It also demonstrates how this divergence can lead to a misallocation of resources when private interests supersede social investment criteria. In Figure 8.5a, expected private returns and actual private costs are plotted against years of completed schooling. As a student completes more and more years of schooling, expected private returns grow at a much faster rate than private costs, for reasons explained earlier. To maximize the difference between expected benefits and costs (and thereby the private rate of return to investment in education), the optimal strategy for a student would be to secure as much schooling as possible.

Now consider Figure 8.5b, where social returns and social costs are plotted against years of schooling. The social benefits curve rises sharply at first, reflecting the improved levels of productivity of, say, small farmers and the self-employed that result from receipt of a **basic education** and the attainment of literacy, arithmetic skills, and elementary vocational skills. Thereafter, the marginal social benefit of additional years of schooling rises more slowly, and the social returns curve begins to level off. By contrast, the social cost curve shows a slow rate of growth for early years of schooling (basic education) and then a much more rapid growth for

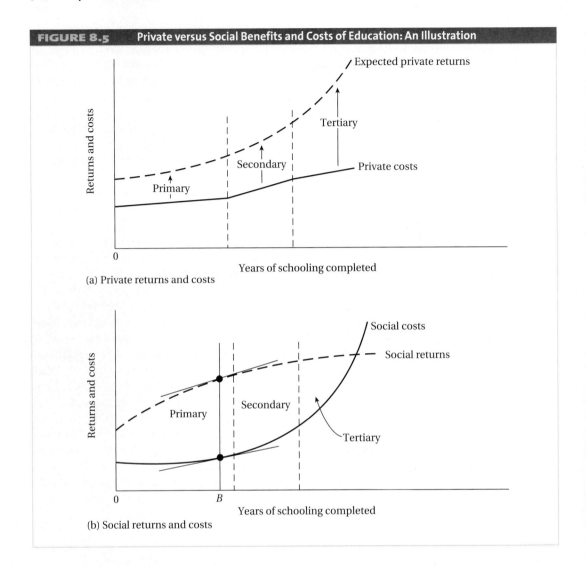

FIGURE 8.5   Private versus Social Benefits and Costs of Education: An Illustration

(a) Private returns and costs

(b) Social returns and costs

higher levels of education. This rapid increase in the marginal social costs of post-primary education is the result both of the much more expensive capital and re-current costs of higher education (buildings and equipment) and, more impor-tant, of the fact that much postprimary education in developing countries is heavily subsidized.[34]

It follows from Figure 8.5b that the optimal strategy from a social viewpoint, the one that maximizes the net social rate of return to educational investment, would be one that focuses on providing all students with at least B years of schooling. Be-yond B years, *marginal* social costs exceed *marginal* social benefits, so additional public educational investment in new, higher-level school places will yield a *negative* net social rate of return.

Figure 8.5 therefore illustrates the inherent conflict between optimal private and social investment strategies—a conflict that will continue to exist as long as private and social valuations of investment in education continue to diverge as students climb the educational ladder (see Table 8.1 for evidence of the magnitude of these divergences).

To a large degree, the problem of divergent social versus private benefits and costs has been artificially created by inappropriate public and private policies with regard to wage differentials, educational selectivity, and the pricing of educational services. As a result, private calculations of the value of education exceed its social value, which must take account of unemployment. As long as artificial and nonmarket incentives in the form of disproportionate expected benefits and subsidized costs continue to exist and place a premium on the number of years one spends getting an education, the individual will decide that it is in his or her best private interests to pursue a lengthy formal education process even though he or she may be aware that modern-sector jobs are becoming more scarce and unemployment rates are rising. Unless these various price signals are made to conform more closely to social realities, the misallocation of national resources (in this case, too much public expenditure on formal education) will persist and possibly increase.

What is needed is a properly functioning reward and cost structure that develops and allocates human resources in accordance with requirements and opportunities in various segments of the economy. Where this is absent (where high wage premiums are paid to workers in the modern urban sector and scarce jobs are allocated on the basis of ever-increasing educational credentials), two obvious misallocations of human resources are likely to occur. First, with the output of the educational system at higher levels, greatly in excess of what the economy can absorb, many students will emerge seeking jobs for which they may be educationally qualified but which have been preempted by others with even more education. They become temporarily unemployed for as long as it takes for their aspirations and status requirements, partly perhaps instilled in them by the educational system itself, to adjust to the stinging realities of unemployment in the modern sector. Second, those who adjust their sights downward and secure modern-sector employment normally have to take jobs for which they are overeducated in terms of the number of years spent in school. Those who fail to get modern-sector jobs at all swell the ranks of the permanently unemployed or become self-employed in the informal sector. They are thus denied the opportunity to contribute productively to the society that invested so heavily in their education. This combination of the overpaid and, in many cases, overeducated employed and the impoverished and unproductive educated unemployed reflects a serious misallocation of scarce national resources. The resources allocated to the expansion of the educational system might alternatively have been spent on needed rural public works projects or on increasing the quality of basic *primary* education in rural areas. Such investment would provide emergency employment opportunities for recent graduates as well as for people with less education.

It seems clear that the expansion of educational opportunities at all levels has contributed to aggregate economic growth by (1) creating a more productive labor force and endowing it with increased knowledge and skills; (2) providing widespread employment and income-earning opportunities for teachers, school and construction workers, textbook and paper printers, school uniform manufacturers, and related workers; (3) creating a class of educated leaders to fill vacancies left by departing expatriates or otherwise vacant positions in governmental services, public corporations, private businesses, and professions; and (4) providing the kind of training and education that would promote literacy and basic skills while encouraging "modern" attitudes on the part of diverse segments of the population.[35] Even if alternative investments in the economy could have generated greater growth, this would not detract from the important contributions, noneconomic as well as economic, that education can make and has made to promoting aggregate economic growth. That an educated and skilled labor force is a necessary condition of sustained economic growth cannot be denied.

However, any evaluation of the role of education in the process of economic development should go beyond the analysis of the single statistic of aggregate growth. We must also consider the structure and pattern of that economic growth and its distribution implications—who benefits.

Distribution of Education

The preceding analysis of forces operating for overeducation in developing countries should not lead us to despair over the possibility of fostering development through greater education. Countries that have developed successfully have generally ensured that educational benefits are more broadly available in the economy—to the poor as well as the rich, in the rural areas as well as the urban. Thus we turn attention to examining the distribution of educational benefits in developing countries.

Just as we can derive Lorenz curves for distribution of income (see Chapter 5), we can also develop Lorenz curves for the distribution of education. Figure 8.6, shows Lorenz curves for education in India and South Korea, using comparable data from 1990. By analogy with income Lorenz curves, we write the cumulative proportion of the population on the x-axis and the cumulative proportion of years of schooling on the y-axis. Along the 45-degree line of perfect equality, everyone in the economy would have the same number of years of schooling; for example, everyone would have finished a basic eight years of school, but no one would have started secondary education. In a highly unequal economy, many people might have no years of schooling at all, while a few might have received a Ph.D. from foreign universities. The closer the Lorenz curve is to the 45-degree line, the more equal the distribution of education.

As can be seen from Figure 8.6, South Korea had a much more equal distribution of education than India. For example, as of 1990, well over half of the population of India had received no schooling at all. In South Korea, less than 10% had received no schooling. Yet both countries were producing significant numbers of Ph.D. diplomates. One may also derive an education Gini coefficient, again by analogy with the derivation of the Gini coefficient for income inequality examined in Chapter 5; it is given by the area A above the education Lorenz curve, divided by

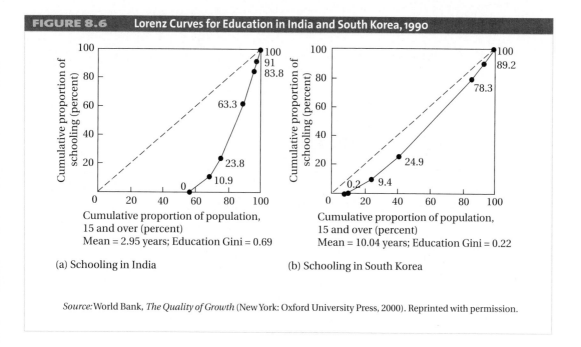

FIGURE 8.6   Lorenz Curves for Education in India and South Korea, 1990

(a) Schooling in India

Mean = 2.95 years; Education Gini = 0.69

(b) Schooling in South Korea

Mean = 10.04 years; Education Gini = 0.22

Source: World Bank, *The Quality of Growth* (New York: Oxford University Press, 2000). Reprinted with permission.

the whole area $A + B$ below the 45-degree line of perfect equality. Clearly, India had a much higher educational inequality as measured by the education Gini (in fact, the Gini was about 0.75) than South Korea did (about 0.25). Plotting the Gini coefficient for education against the average years of education, as in Figure 8.7, we see that there is no inverted-U curve for education. Instead, educational inequality tends to fall steadily as average years of education in the population rises.[36]

The precision of the relationship in Figure 8.7 is due in part to the "quantitative" way that education is measured—by the number of years of schooling. No allowance is made for the fact that some secondary school systems, for example, do a much more effective job of teaching than others. Certainly, educational quality is higher in high- than in low-income countries—in Europe than Africa, for example. However, it is also likely that the variability of educational quality is higher in a country such as Mali, where elite schools offer excellent college preparation while many rural public schools may have only one textbook for each five or six students. Although quality differs from school to school in developed countries as well, the differences are not as extreme, on average, as they are in developing countries.

Indeed, research by Jere Behrman and Nancy Birdsall indicates that it is the quality of education (the quality of teaching, facilities, and curricula) and not its quantity alone (years of schooling) that best explains differential earnings and productivity.[37] The implication is that governments should spend more to upgrade existing schools and less to expand the number of school places—that is, they should deepen the investment in human capital rather than extend it to more

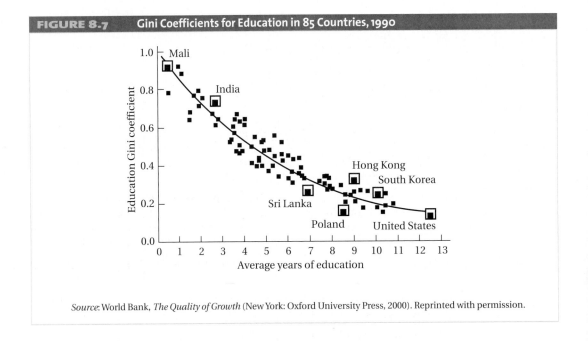

FIGURE 8.7   Gini Coefficients for Education in 85 Countries, 1990

Source: World Bank, *The Quality of Growth* (New York: Oxford University Press, 2000). Reprinted with permission.

people. Unfortunately, this raises serious equity questions, and their findings remain controversial. A balanced policy would be to emphasize the extension of quality primary education to all before embarking on rapid expansion of the quantity of secondary schools.

Education, Inequality, and Poverty

Recent studies have also demonstrated that contrary to what might have been assumed, the educational systems of many developing nations sometimes act to increase rather than to decrease income inequalities.[38]

The basic reason for this perverse effect of formal education on income distribution is the positive correlation between level of education and level of lifetime earnings. This correlation holds especially for workers who are able to complete secondary and university education where income differentials over workers who have completed only part or all of their primary education can be on the order of 300% to 800%. And as levels of earned income are clearly dependent on years of completed schooling, it follows that large income inequalities will be reinforced if students from the middle- and upper-income brackets are represented disproportionately in secondary and university enrollments. In short, if for financial or other reasons the poor are effectively denied access to secondary and higher educational opportunities, the educational system can actually perpetuate and even increase inequality in developing countries.

There are two fundamental economic reasons why one might suspect that many LDC educational systems are inherently inegalitarian, in the sense that poor students have less chance of completing any given educational cycle than more affluent students. First, the private costs of primary education (especially in view of the opportunity cost of a child's labor to poor families) are higher for poor students than for more affluent students. Second, the expected benefits of primary education are lower for poor students. Together, the higher costs and lower expected benefits of education mean that a poor family's rate of return from investment in a child's education is lower than it is for other families. The poor are therefore more likely to drop out during the early years of schooling. Let's examine in slightly more detail the reason why costs might be relatively higher and benefits relatively lower for a poor child.

First, the higher opportunity cost of labor to poor families means that even if the first few years of education are free, they are not without cost to the family. Children of primary school age are typically needed to work on family farms, often at the same times as they are required to be at school. If a child cannot work because he or she is at school, the family will either suffer a loss of valuable subsistence output or be required to hire paid labor to replace the absent child. In either case, there is the real cost to a poor family of having an able-bodied child attend school when there is productive work to be done on the farm—a cost not related to tuition and of much less significance to higher-income families, many of whom may live in urban areas where child work is not needed.

As a result of these higher opportunity costs, school attendance, and therefore school performance, tends to be much lower for children of poor families than for those from higher-income backgrounds. Thus in spite of the existence of free and universal primary education in many LDCs, children of the poor, especially in rural areas, are seldom able to proceed beyond the first few years of schooling. Their relatively poor school performance may have nothing to do with a lack of cognitive abilities; it may merely reflect their disadvantaged economic circumstances.

This financial process of eliminating the relatively poor during their first few years of schooling is often compounded by the substantial tuition charged at the secondary level. In many developing countries, annual tuition (especially at the better private schools) is roughly equivalent to the per capita national income. The cost of education therefore becomes prohibitive to lower-income families, who are often unable to borrow funds to finance their children's education. This in effect amounts to a system of educational advancement and selection based not on any criteria of merit but strictly on family income levels. It thus perpetuates concentration of income within certain population groups and means that earned income will accrue primarily to people who already possess the bulk of unearned income and wealth—those whose assets already place them in the upper deciles of the personal income distribution scale.[39]

The inegalitarian nature of many developing-country educational systems is compounded even further at the university level, where the government may pay the full cost of tuition and fees and even provide university students with income grants in the form of stipends. Because most university students already come from the upper-income brackets (and were so selected at the secondary level), highly subsidized university education using public funds often amounts to a transfer payment from the poor to the wealthy in the name of "free" higher education![40]

Table 8.3 shows how government educational spending benefits different occupational (and thus income) groups in various developing regions. The last three columns are the most significant. Each shows the ratio of the percentage of public educational resources received by (1) low-income farmers, (2) middle-income manual workers and traders, and (3) higher-income white-collar workers to their percentage representation in the population. A subsidy-benefit ratio of 1.00 would mean, for example, that a group comprising 25% of the working population receives 25% of all government spending on education. The data clearly show that the children of white-collar families receive disproportionate public educational benefits, whereas farm children are undersubsidized. For example, in Francophone Africa, children from (mostly urban) white-collar families receive more than ten times as much in state subsidies than children from rural farm families. When we combine this information with data measuring the incidence of direct and indirect taxation, which, as we shall see in Chapter 16, is often regressive in developing countries, it becomes clear that the educational system is not a vehicle for promoting greater equality. It often works in the opposite direction to reinforce or widen inequality.

Education, Internal Migration, and the Brain Drain

Education seems to be an important factor influencing rural-urban migration. Numerous studies of migration in diverse countries have documented the positive relationship between the educational attainment of an individual and his or her propensity to migrate from rural to urban areas. Basically, individuals with higher levels of education face wider urban-rural real-income differentials and higher probabilities of obtaining modern-sector jobs than those with lower levels of education (recall from Chapter 7 how income differentials and job probabilities interact to determine migration patterns). The probability variable in particular accounts for the growing proportion of the more educated rural migrants in the face of rising levels of urban unemployment among the less educated.

Education also plays a powerful role in the growing problem of the international migration of high-level educated workers—the so-called **brain drain**—from poor to rich countries. This is particularly true in the case of scientists, engineers, academics, and physicians, many thousands of whom have been trained in home-country institutions at considerable social cost only to reap the benefits from and contribute to the further economic growth of the already affluent nations.

The international brain drain deserves mention not only because of its effects on the rate and structure of LDC economic growth but also because of its impact on the style and approach of educational systems in the developing world. The brain drain, broadly construed, has not merely reduced the supply of vital professional people available within developing countries (see Chapter 2); perhaps even more serious, it has diverted the attention of the scientists, physicians, architects, engineers, and academics who remain in their homeland from important local problems and goals. These include the development of appropriate technology; the promotion of low-cost preventive health care; the construction of low-cost housing, hospitals, schools, and other service facilities; the design and building of

TABLE 8.3 Share of Public Resources for Education Appropriated by Different Socioeconomic Groups, by Region

Region	Percentage in the Population			Percentage of Public School Resources			Ratio between Percentage of Resources and of Population		
	Farmers	Manual Workers and Traders	White-Collar Workers	Farmers	Manual Workers and Traders	White-Collar Workers	Farmers	Manual Workers and Traders	White-Collar Workers
Africa									
Anglophone	76	18	6	56	21	23	0.73	1.19	3.78
Francophone	76	18	6	44	21	36	0.58	1.15	5.93
Asia	58	32	10	34	38	28	0.59	1.19	2.79
Latin America	36	49	15	18	51	31	0.49	1.04	2.03
Middle East and North Africa	42	48	10	25	46	29	0.60	0.35	2.87
Members of the Organization for Economic Cooperation and Development (OECD)	12	53	35	11	46	42	0.95	0.87	1.2

Source: Emmanuel Jimenez, "The public subsidization of education and health in developing countries: A review of equity and efficiency," *World Bank Research Observer* 1 (1986): 111–129, tab. 3. Reprinted with permission.

functional yet inexpensive labor-intensive roads, bridges, and machinery; the development of relevant university teaching materials such as appropriate introductory economics texts; and the promotion of problem-oriented research on vital domestic development issues. Such needs are often neglected as, dominated by rich-country ideas as to what represents true professional excellence, those highly educated and highly skilled LDC professionals who do not physically migrate to the developed nations nevertheless migrate intellectually in terms of the orientation of their activities. This "internal" brain drain is much more serious than the external one.

For example, developing nations often have numerous physicians specializing in heart diseases while preventive tropical medicine is considered a second-rate specialty. Architects are concerned with the design of national monuments and modern public buildings while low-cost housing, schools, and clinics remain an area of remote interest. Engineers and scientists concentrate on the newest and most modern electronic equipment while simple machine tools, hand- or animal-operated farm equipment, basic sanitation and water-purifying systems, and labor-intensive mechanical processes are relegated to the attention of "foreign experts." Finally, some academic economists teach and research totally irrelevant, sophisticated mathematical models of nonexistent competitive economies while problems of poverty, unemployment, rural development, and education are considered less intellectually interesting. In all these diverse professional activities, performance criteria are often based not on contributions to national development but rather on praise from the international community (professional mentors in the developed nations). The verdict, then, is clear: In many dimensions, the educational systems of most developing countries is in need of thoroughgoing reform.

Health Systems and Development

Measurement and Distribution

Earlier in the chapter, we followed standard practice by measuring health with infant survival rates and, especially, with life expectancy. The latter measure has the advantage that it is available for most countries, at least as an estimate; however, this measure can be very misleading. The extension of life expectancy can provide extended years of vitality in one country while providing only additional years of extremely poor health or suffering in another. The infant survival rate is a better measure but clearly omits consideration of the general health status of the population beyond early childhood, although it is sometimes argued that both of these measures also proxy for this status reasonably well. For example, some children who survive early deprivations suffer lifetime health consequences.

The **World Health Organization** (WHO), the key United Nations agency concerned with global health matters, prominently displays its definition of health on its Web page: "A state of complete physical, mental, and social well-being and not merely the absence of disease and infirmity."[41] This approach may put us on a better conceptual foundation but does not in itself provide a better measure. An al-

FIGURE 8.8 **Mortality of Children Two Years Old and Younger by Wealth, Brazil, 1996**

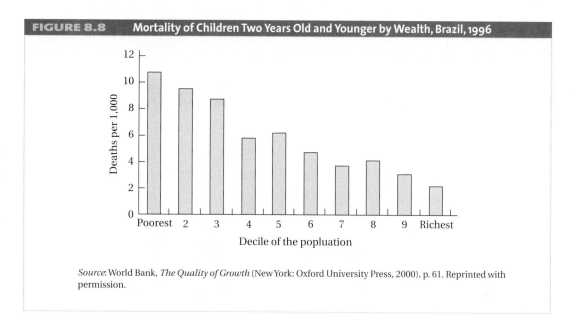

Source: World Bank, *The Quality of Growth* (New York: Oxford University Press, 2000), p. 61. Reprinted with permission.

ternative measure of health promoted by the WHO is the DALY, which stands for *disability-adjusted life year*. There are doubts about the quality of data used in these measures, especially for some of the poorest countries, and the use of DALYs to compare health across countries is controversial. But a well-known World Bank study for the 1993 *World Development Report* estimated that a staggering total of 1.36 billion DALYs were lost in the baseline study year, 1990. Premature deaths represented about two-thirds of lost DALYs, and disabilities accounted for the remaining third. Using a DALY measure, the study calculated that about one-quarter of the global burden of disease was represented by diarrhea, childhood diseases including measles, respiratory infections, parasitic worm infections, and malaria, all major health problems in developing countries. Even though impressive progress has continued to be made on most of these disease categories, such numbers show that an ongoing effort is needed.

However, average health levels can mask great inequality. For example, in some countries minorities and indigenous populations can have life expectancies a decade or more shorter than the dominant groups, while their infant mortality rates can be more than triple the national average.[42] Thus as is the case with income and education, the distribution of health among the population, not just averages, is what matters. As one might expect, the poor are significantly less healthy than the more affluent. Figure 8.8 shows that health gaps between the rich and poor are large in a highly unequal economy such as Brazil, with infant mortality more than triple for the poorest 40% than for the richest 30%. This difference does not merely reflect conditions in the poorer and richer regions of the country; Figure 8.9 shows dramatically higher infant and adult mortality in poor than in nonpoor neighborhoods in the Brazilian city of Porto Alegre.

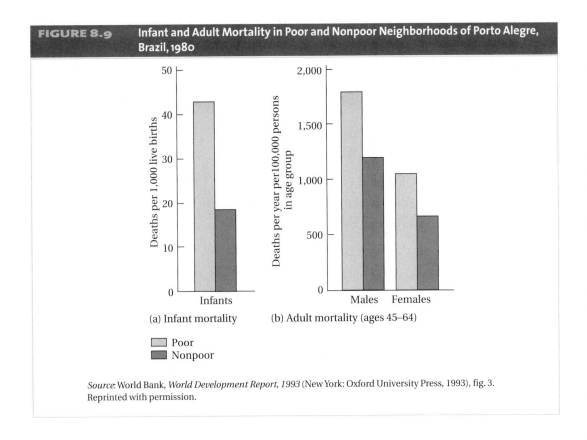

FIGURE 8.9 **Infant and Adult Mortality in Poor and Nonpoor Neighborhoods of Porto Alegre, Brazil, 1980**

(a) Infant mortality   (b) Adult mortality (ages 45–64)

Poor
Nonpoor

Source: World Bank, World Development Report, 1993 (New York: Oxford University Press, 1993), fig. 3. Reprinted with permission.

Disease Burden

As Figures 8.8 and 8.9 suggest, developing countries face a much more crippling disease burden than developed countries, especially regarding infectious diseases. AIDS, malaria, and parasites are three major problems that we consider in this section. Some of the other health challenges faced by developing countries are also surveyed in Box 8.3.

Every year, about 12 million children under the age of 5 die in developing countries. Because most of these children die of causes that could be prevented for just a few cents per child, it has been rightly claimed that their real underlying disease was poverty.

Health problems are particularly severe in sub-Saharan Africa, where about 20 countries are poorer than they were a generation ago. Water is generally as contaminated as it is scarce. Infant mortality is still over 100 deaths per 1,000 live births in these countries, and in some cases, such as Niger and Sierra Leone, it is nearly 200 per 1,000. In at least 16 sub-Saharan African countries a child is more likely to die before the age of 5 than to attend secondary school. About 40% of children in sub-Saharan Africa are malnourished. Life expectancy at birth in the region is only 46 years and is currently plunging toward levels of a generation ago, in

BOX 8.3   Health Challenges Faced by Developing Countries

Absolute poverty. Poverty plays such a central role in most health problems faced by developing countries that it has its own designation in the International Classification of Diseases: code Z59.5—extreme poverty.

AIDS. Now the leading cause of death of working-age adults in the developing world, if unchecked it may condemn sub-Saharan Africa, the hardest-hit region, to grinding poverty for at least another generation.

Malaria. Once in retreat, its most deadly strand is now making a big comeback, particularly in Africa; it still kills about 2 million people each year.

Tuberculosis. TB currently claims about 3 million lives each year. The WHO estimates that one-third of the world's population is infected with the TB bacillus and that each year about 8 million new cases result from this "reservoir of infection." New, multidrug-resistant strains of TB, difficult and expensive to treat, are spreading in about 40 "TB hot zones" in the developing world.

Hepatitis B. Hepatitis B may now kill over 1 million people each year.

Ascariasis. *Ascaris* roundworm parasites cause clinical symptoms in as many as 21.4 million people at any one time, most commonly infecting children aged 3 to 8 years, who often become infected by putting their hands to their mouths after playing in contaminated soil or by eating uncooked food grown in contaminated soil or irrigated with unsanitary water. The worst infections cause about 60,000 deaths per year, the overwhelming majority of them children.

Cholera. Once largely in retreat, cholera has been on the upsurge in recent years in many countries in Africa, Asia, and Latin America, as it has spread rapidly in this, its seventh pandemic. Untreated, dehydration from severe diarrhea causes death.

Dengue. While many serious diseases have been in retreat, dengue and dengue hemorrhagic fever are now spreading rapidly, with millions of cases each year, and thousands of deaths; about a half million cases require hospital treatment.

Leprosy (Hansen disease). There are still about 600,000 new cases of leprosy each year. Between 2 and 3 million people have been disabled by leprosy, including those who have been cured but crippled prior to treatment, in India and many other developing countries.

Dracunculiasis (guinea worm disease). A debilitating illness infecting about 3 million people, largely among the poorest of the poor, who lack access to even minimally safe water.

Chagas. A disease afflicting an estimated 17 million people in Latin America, causing about 45,000 deaths annually.

Leishmaniasis. A group of parasitic diseases infecting about 13 million people. Visceral leishmaniasis, also known as kala-azar, is the most severe form. Almost always fatal if untreated, it causes an estimated 80,000 deaths per year.

Lymphatic filariasis (elephantiasis). A disfiguring parasitic disease that still affects around 100 million people in the developing world.

Many other parasites are active, including *Trichuris,* now found in about 133 million people, and hookworm, which infects an estimated 96 million people.

Source: WHO data.

large part because of the impact of the AIDS epidemic. For example, by 2010 life expectancy in Namibia is projected to fall from 70.1 without AIDS to 38.9 with AIDS; in Zimbabwe, from 69.5 to 38.8; in Botswana, from 66.3 to 37.8; and in Malawi, from 56.8 to 34.8.[43]

Some diseases are especially deadly when combined with other diseases. Malnutrition is a form of disease, and its presence is a major factor among children in both contracting disease and dying of it. While the death certificate may cite dehydration from diarrhea or an infectious disease, in many cases death would not have occurred without the contributing factor of malnutrition. The interaction between malaria and acute respiratory infections or anemia is also deadly. Another important lethal interaction is between AIDS and tuberculosis. Failure to control either of these diseases will make each more likely to be fatal. Moreover, the spread of HIV has been demonstrated to be significantly promoted by the presence of other sexually transmitted diseases, whose sores facilitate viral invasion.

The WHO has found that five conditions—acute respiratory infections (ARIs), diarrhea, measles, malaria, and malnutrition—account for 70% of deaths among children less than 5 years of age. The WHO estimates that if current trends continue, by 2020 these conditions among African children alone will account for about 30% of childhood deaths worldwide. To address these problems, the WHO, in cooperation with other major international agencies and national health authorities, has been implementing its Integrated Management of Childhood Illness (IMCI) program, aimed at improving the training and performance of national health organizations and personnel in disease prevention and the treatment of sick children. The program emphasizes education on practices such as breastfeeding and use of oral rehydration therapy.

We turn now to consider three major scourges of the developing world—malaria, parasitic worms, and AIDS.

Malaria and Parasitic Worms

Malaria directly causes an estimated 1 million deaths each year, most of them among impoverished African children. The WHO reported that "malaria, directly or indirectly, causes up to 2 million deaths a year, the vast majority among young impoverished children in Africa, and some 400 million cases annually. Globally more than 2 billion people are threatened." The estimated direct cost of the disease in Africa alone reached more than $3 billion annually by 2000. Severe cases of malaria leave about 15% of the children who survive the disease with substantial neurological problems and learning disabilities.

Africa faces a resurgent presence of the most lethal strain of malaria. In a recent year, one-third of the population of Zambia was infected with malaria. Desmond McCarthy, Holger Wolf, and Yi Wu found that while the impact of malaria on economic growth differs sharply across countries, it exceeds a 0.25% per year in a quarter of their sample countries. Most of these were located in sub-Saharan Africa.[44]

The WHO's Roll Back Malaria program seeks to eradicate this disease at its source. In addition, major efforts are under way to increase international funding for a war on malaria, emphasizing the development of a malaria vaccine. With proper funding, specialists believe that an effective vaccine might be just a few years away, but because victims of malaria tend to come from low-income countries that cannot afford expensive drugs, there has been little incentive for pharmaceutical companies to emphasize research in this field. However, citizen and government pressure in developed countries, a desire to score public relations points, and perhaps some awakening of conscience has led some drug companies to begin to offer drugs at lower costs in low-income countries, and this may expand to a more balanced portfolio of research.

The incidence of debilitating parasitic worms has been nearly ubiquitous, though fortunately much progress is being made. Among the many parasitic diseases plaguing people in the developing world, schistosomiasis (also called bilharziasis or snail fever) may be the worst in terms of its human and development impact (following malaria, which is also classified as a parasitic disease). Schistosomiasis in humans is caused by water-borne flatworms (also known as blood flukes) called schistosomes. According to WHO estimates, the disease still affects more than 200 million people in 74 developing countries, of whom about 120 million are symptomatic and some 20 million suffer severe consequences, including about 200,000 deaths each year. Horrifying as these numbers are, it is important to recognize that they represent a substantial improvement over conditions of just a couple of decades ago, when the infection rates of many parasitic diseases, including schistosomiasis, were triple or more what they are today. Still, in many rural and periurban areas, especially in Africa, schistosomiasis continues to afflict a large percentage of all children. Growth in infected children is retarded, and if they are in school, their school performance is harmed. The WHO reports that the stunting effects of schistosomiasis are 90% reversible with effective treatment, which is still all too often entirely lacking. Effects on adults can also be serious. According to the WHO, the work capacity of rural laborers in Egypt, Sudan, and northeastern Brazil, for example, is severely reduced due to weakness and lethargy caused by the disease. If this were not enough, the WHO's International Agency for Research on Cancer has determined that urinary schistosomiasis causes bladder cancer: In some areas of sub-Saharan Africa, the incidence of schistosomiasis-linked bladder cancer is about 32 times higher than the incidence of bladder cancer in the United States.

Another long-standing scourge, African trypanosomiasis, or sleeping sickness, still affects up to a half million people in sub-Saharan Africa, mostly in remote areas. Tragically, because the disease is endemic where health systems are weakest, most people who contract sleeping sickness die before they are even diagnosed. The WHO recently estimated that sleeping sickness kills some 55,000 people a year. The impact of trypanosomiasis on economic development can be severe; in addition to the loss of human life and vitality, the disease kills cattle and leads to the abandonment of fertile but infected land. In this case, the parasites (*Trypanosoma*) are protozoa transmitted to humans by tsetse flies. The disease is being attacked with drugs donated to international organizations from a pharmaceutical company. In recent years, public pressure and attention have played an important role in getting drug companies to be more active and constructive in developing countries and in making donations to key agencies such as the WHO.

The sleeping sickness initiative is a good example, with Aventis Pharma providing three key drugs—pentamidine, melarsoprol, and eflornithine—that are each essential for treating sleeping sickness.

HIV and AIDS

Despite nearly two decades of intensive efforts, the AIDS epidemic continues to spread rapidly in the developing world, threatening to halt or even reverse years of hard-won human and economic development progress in numerous countries. Though usually thought of as an issue of health-care systems and delivery, AIDS is equally an issue of economic development. **Acquired immunodeficiency syndrome (AIDS)** is the final and fatal stage of infection with the **human immunodeficiency virus (HIV)**. In the developing countries as a whole, AIDS is transmitted primarily through heterosexual intercourse; contact with infected blood and drug needles, both by drug abusers and in hospitals, and perinatal transmission (from mother to fetus) also play significant roles. In low-income countries, average survival once AIDS symptoms set in has been under one year. Despite recent progress in making expensive antiretroviral medication available to low-income countries at much reduced prices (or even free of charge), because of slow implementation and an inadequate health-system infrastructure, these lifesaving drugs are still not available to a large majority of the infected in Africa and South Asia. Otherwise, treatments have generally been limited to aspirin, antibiotics for infections, and cortisone for skin rashes.

Even today, AIDS is still widely perceived in the developing world as a disease of developed countries and one primarily afflicting homosexuals. However, the WHO estimated that by the end of 2003, nearly 20 million people had died of AIDS since the disease was identified in the early 1980s, with the large majority of deaths occurring in sub-Saharan Africa. Throughout the region, AIDS is now the leading cause of death of adult males in the economically active years. Although infectious childhood diseases still kill far more people in developing countries, AIDS strikes those who have successfully run this gauntlet of child killers. Their societies are counting on the energies and skills of precisely the part of the population most afflicted. At the end of 2003, some 40 million people worldwide were infected with HIV, more than 25 million of them in sub-Saharan Africa. There, the adult prevalence rate is now estimated at 7.7% of the population, with women representing 55% of the infected. The impact of the disease in this region is now approaching that of the bubonic plague of the Middle Ages in Europe. Although many policymakers in LDCs continue to view HIV/AIDS as a "foreigner's disease," today more than 95% of all HIV cases and AIDS deaths occur in the developing world.

Fortunately, HIV has progressed more slowly in Asia than earlier projections had feared. However, if trends are not reversed, Asia may still become the next epicenter of the disease. Already, UNAIDS estimate that new infections in Asia now total close to a million cases per year, with some 6 million people already HIV-positive.[45]

Table 8.4 provides a breakdown of the incidence of AIDS in various parts of the world, showing the total number of cases and new cases in 2003, along with the main source of transmission of the disease. Table 8.5 indicates some recent estimates of the incidence of the disease in selected developing countries, including several of the hardest-hit African countries, and other major developing countries around the world.

AIDS is creating a virtual generation of orphans in some African countries. There were over 11 million AIDS orphans in sub-Saharan Africa as of 2001. Providing basic needs for these orphans, ensuring that they are not discriminated against out of irrational fears, and seeing that they are able to obtain the few years of schooling that will help rescue them from absolute poverty will be a major development challenge. It is not a challenge that Africa, with all its problems, is accustomed to. Extended family networks have provided privately for children who have lost their parents. In some parts of East Africa, this traditional family adaptation to death appears on the verge of collapse due to the scope of the AIDS crisis. Political analysts claim that conditions are ripe not only for child abuse and exploitation but also for recruiting of children for guerilla armies led by unscrupulous aspiring dictators or mercenary groups. The resulting destabilization and diversion of resources can have a devastating impact on social and economic development. An excellent recent strategy developed by church groups in Zimbabwe is to have volunteers visit and provide basic care for these orphans in the homes where they live, which can be homes of child-headed households, foster parents, grandparents, or other relatives. These visits provide a much needed combination of emotional and material support for these orphans.

Now that the world's attention is finally focusing on AIDS in the developing world, it is important to keep in mind that an effective response to the problems of AIDS and development requires a careful balancing act of policymaking. Despite the human tragedy and development catastrophe of the AIDS epidemic, it is important not to let resources for HIV programs overshadow other worthwhile development efforts, including attention to other parts of the disease burden.

Health and Productivity

The devastating effects of poor health on child mortality are clear enough. But do poor health conditions in developing countries also harm the productivity of adults? The answer appears to be yes. Studies show that healthier people earn higher wages. For example, daily wage rates in Côte d'Ivoire have been estimated to be about 19% lower among men whose health status makes them likely to lose a day of work per month because of illness than daily wage rates of healthier men. Careful statistical methods have shown that a large part of the effect of health on raising earnings is due to productivity differences: It is not just the reverse causality that higher wages are used in part to purchase better health. A study in Bangladesh found that the higher productivity of healthier workers allows them to get better-paying jobs. In another study, the elimination of deformity from leprosy was estimated to more than triple earnings of workers in India.[46]

Nobel laureate Robert Fogel has found that citizens of developed countries are substantially taller today than they were two centuries ago and has argued that stature is a useful index of the health and general well-being of a population. Increases in height also have been found in developing countries in recent decades

TABLE 8.4 Regional HIV/AIDS Statistics and Features, 2003

Region	Epidemic Started	Adults and Children Living with HIV/AIDS	Adults and Children Newly Infected with HIV	Adult Prevalence Rate[a]	Adult and Child Deaths due to AIDS	Main Modes of Transmission for Adults Living with HIV/AIDS[b]
Sub-Saharan Africa	Late '70s-early '80s	25.0–28.2 million	3.0–3.4 million	7.5–8.5%	2.2–2.4 million	Hetero
North Africa and Middle East	Late '80s	470,000–730,000	43,000–67,000	0.2–0.4%	35,000–50,000	Hetero, IDU
South and Southeast Asia	Late '80s	4.6–8.2 million	610,000–1.1 million	0.4–0.8%	330,000–590,000	Hetero, IDU
East Asia and Pacific	Late '80s	700,000–1.3 million	150,000–270,000	0.1%	32,000–58,000	IDU, hetero, MSM
Latin America	Late '70s-early '80s	1.3–1.9 million	120,000–180,000	0.5–0.7%	49,000–70,000	MSM, IDU, hetero
Caribbean	Late '70s-early '80s	350,000–590,000	45,000–80,000	1.9–3.1%	30,000–50,000	Hetero, MSM
Eastern Europe and Central Asia	Early '90s	1.2–1.8 million	180,000–280,000	0.5–0.9%	23,000–37,000	IDU
Western Europe	Late '70s-Early '80s	520,000—680,000	30,000–40,000	0.3%	2,600–3,400	MSM, IDU
North America	Late '70s-early '80s	790,000–1.2 million	36,000–54,000	0.5–0.7%	12,000–18,000	MSM, IDU, hetero
Australia and New Zealand	Late '70s-early '80s	12,000–18,000	700–1,000	0.1%	<100	MSM
Totals		40 million	5 million	1.1%	3 million	

Source: World Health Organization, http://www.WHO.int/hiv/pub/epidemiology/en/epi 2003_2_full.jpg. Reprinted with permission.

[a]Proportion of adults (15 to 49 years of age) living with HIV/AIDS in 2003, using 2003 population numbers.

[b]Hetero (heterosexual transmission), IDU (transmission through injecting drug use), MSM (sexual transmission among men who have sex with men).

TABLE 8.5		Percentage of Adult Population with HIV or AIDS, Selected Developing Countries, end 2001					
Botswana:	38.8	Kenya:	15.0	Democratic Republic		Argentina:	0.7
Zimbabwe:	33.7	Mozambique:	13.0	of Congo:	7.2	Brazil:	0.7
Namibia:	22.5	Central African		Haiti:	6.1	Mexico:	0.3
Zambia:	21.5	Republic:	12.9	Uganda:	5.0	Vietnam:	0.3
South Africa:	20.1	Côte d'Ivoire:	9.7	Thailand:	1.8	China:	0.1
Malawi:	15.0	Rwanda:	8.9	India:	0.8	Indonesia:	0.1

Source: WHO data; UNAIDS data, http//www.unaids.org/hivaidsinfo/statistics/june00/fact_sheets/index.html
Note: For comparative purposes, the infection rate in the United States is about 0.6, in Canada, 0.3, in the United Kingdom 0.1, and in Japan < 0.1.

as health conditions have improved. In most cases, rapid increases in average height earlier in the twentieth century gave way to smaller increases by midcentury. Figure 8.10 shows the trends in height over time for four countries, the United States, Côte d'Ivoire, Brazil, and Vietnam; scales in the charts differ across countries, but trends are comparable. The changes over time within countries reflect nutritional and other health improvements.

If height is an indicator of general health status, to the extent that increases in health lead to higher productivity, taller people should earn more (unless height also proxies other productivity characteristics). John Strauss and Duncan Thomas found that taller men earn more money in Brazil, even after controlling for other important determinants of income such as education and experience (Figure 8.11, panels A1 and A2). A 1% increase in height is associated with a 7% increase in wages in that middle-income country. In the United States, there is also an association, but a much smaller one, with a 1% increase in height associated with a 1% increase in wages. Moreover, shorter individuals are more likely to be unemployed altogether. Height reflects various benefits achieved early in life; thus one is not seeing just the impact of current income on current height. In particular, taller people receive significantly more education than shorter people (see Figure 8.11, panels B1 and B2). Note also that these relationships carry over to alternative health measures such as the body-mass index, which reflects short-term as well as long-term health and nutrition. Strauss and Thomas draw on these results and a survey of the literature to conclude that health and nutrition do increase productivity, with the greatest improvements for those who are initially least educated and poorest.[47]

Thus the preponderance of the evidence is that health and nutrition do affect employment, productivity, and wages and very substantially so among the poorest of the poor. This finding magnifies the policy priority of health in development; not only is health a major goal in itself, but it has a significant impact on income levels as well. After their exhaustive review of the literature and its complex statistical and data problems, Strauss and Thomas conclude that "the balance of evidence points to a positive effect of elevated nutrient intakes on wages, at least among those who are malnourished."[48] A healthy population is a prerequisite for successful development.

FIGURE 8.10   Adult Stature by Birth Cohort

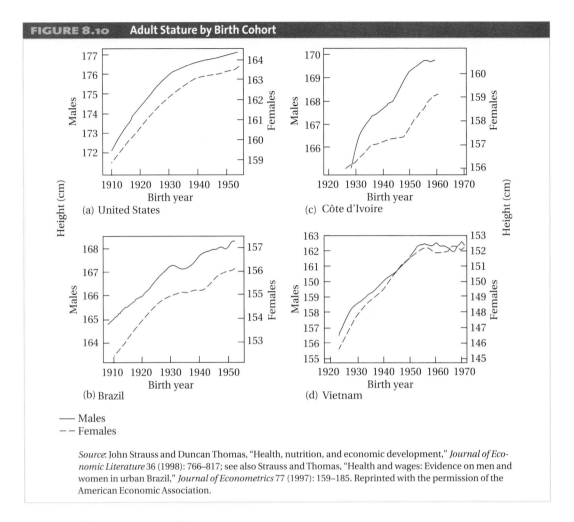

(a) United States

(b) Brazil

(c) Côte d'Ivoire

(d) Vietnam

—— Males
- - Females

Source: John Strauss and Duncan Thomas, "Health, nutrition, and economic development," *Journal of Economic Literature* 36 (1998): 766–817; see also Strauss and Thomas, "Health and wages: Evidence on men and women in urban Brazil," *Journal of Econometrics* 77 (1997): 159–185. Reprinted with the permission of the American Economic Association.

Health Systems Policy

In the WHO's definition, a health system is "all the activities whose primary purpose is to promote, restore, or maintain health." Health systems include the components of public health departments, hospitals and clinics, and offices of doctors and paramedics. Outside this formal system is an informal network used by many poorer citizens, which includes traditional healers, who may practice with the use of somewhat effective herbal remedies, or other methods that provide some medical benefits, such as acupuncture, but who also may practice techniques for which there is no evidence of effectiveness beyond the placebo effect.

It has long been understood that some developing countries' health systems were far more effective than others in achieving health goals. Figure 8.12 shows that some countries, such as China and Sri Lanka, and some regions, such as Kerala state in India, have achieved life expectancies of more than 70 years despite their low-income status. At the same time, some middle-income countries, such

FIGURE 8.11   Wages, Education, and Height of Males in Brazil and the United States

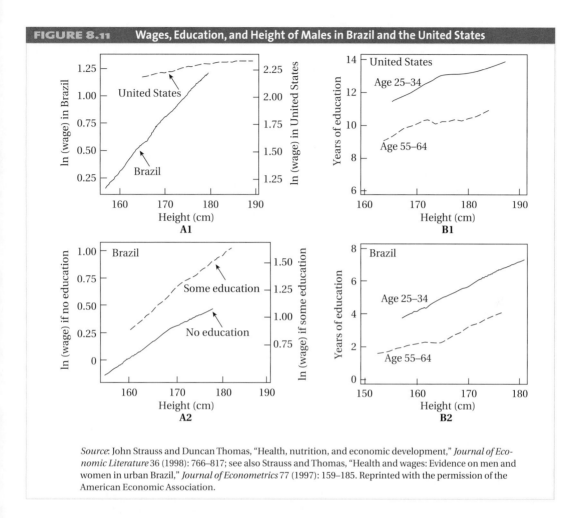

Source: John Strauss and Duncan Thomas, "Health, nutrition, and economic development," *Journal of Economic Literature* 36 (1998): 766–817; see also Strauss and Thomas, "Health and wages: Evidence on men and women in urban Brazil," *Journal of Econometrics* 77 (1997): 159–185. Reprinted with the permission of the American Economic Association.

as Brazil, South Africa, and Gabon, have only been able to achieve significantly lower life expectancies despite their much greater resources. The latter countries all have far more inequitable access to health care than China, Sri Lanka, and Kerala.

In 2000, the WHO released its first detailed report comparing health systems around the world. They found great variability in the performance of health systems at each income level. For example, Singapore was ranked 6th, Morocco, 29th, Colombia 22nd, Chile 33rd, and Costa Rica 36th—all of these developing countries ranked higher than the United States. Clearly much can be done with relatively modest incomes.[49]

The study used five performance indicators to measure health systems in the 191 WHO member states: (1) the overall level of health of the population; (2) health inequalities within the population; (3) health-system responsiveness (a

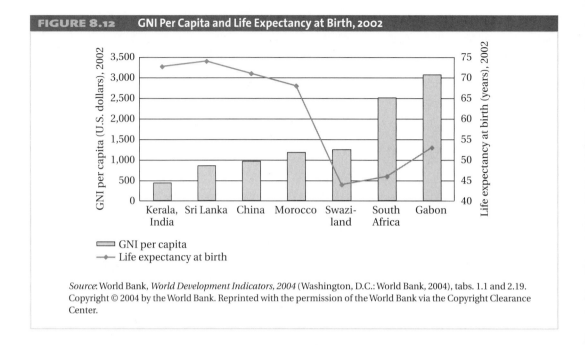

FIGURE 8.12   GNI Per Capita and Life Expectancy at Birth, 2002

Source: World Bank, *World Development Indicators, 2004* (Washington, D.C.: World Bank, 2004), tabs. 1.1 and 2.19. Copyright © 2004 by the World Bank. Reprinted with the permission of the World Bank via the Copyright Clearance Center.

combination of patient satisfaction and system performance); (4) the distribution of responsiveness within the population (how well people of varying economic status find that they are served by the health system); and (5) the distribution, or fairness, of the health system's financial burden within the population.

Many aspects of the resulting rankings, which are similar in spirit to the Human Development Index but with an exclusive focus on health, depend crucially on the level of income. However, the report concluded that, "dollar for dollar spent on health, many countries are falling short of their performance potential. The result is a large number of preventable deaths and lives stunted by disability. The impact of this failure is born disproportionately by the poor." At any given income level, there was wide variation in country performance, showing that a low-income country can achieve fairness in allocating the resources that it has. In fact, in equity of financial contribution, Colombia was the top-rated country overall. But several developing countries were judged to have the least fair financing of health systems, including Sierra Leone, Myanmar, Brazil, China, Vietnam, Nepal, the Russian Federation, Peru, and Cambodia. In Brazil and Peru, people make high out-of-pocket payments for health care, so poor households pay a large fraction of their income on health.

Formal public health measures have played a very important role in developing countries. Ministries of health, sometimes complemented by the services of nongovernmental organizations, have played vital roles in extending vaccines to remote rural areas, greatly reducing once lethal diseases such as smallpox. But like educational systems, public health operations have often favored the wealthy and well connected. Partly as a result, health systems often use public funds inefficiently. In effect, subsidies turn out to be focused on expensive curative measures for older (and generally richer) patients, such as those with heart disease or cancer, who are influential enough to get into the right hospitals. Too often ignored or at best underfunded are cost-effective preventive health campaigns and basic medical care for those not currently attended to by any health professionals. Doctors trained with public subsidies often choose to practice a speciality in affluent areas of the cities or emigrate to developed countries. And as the World Bank concluded, "In some countries a single teaching hospital can absorb 20 percent or more of the budget of the ministry of health, even though almost all cost-effective interventions are best delivered at lower-level facilities."[50]

In addition to its direct positive effect on national health standards, basic health is also an effective means to achieve goals of poverty reduction. Although both parents may be employed or self-employed long hours, if parents are too weak, unhealthy, and unskilled to be productive enough to support their family, the children have to work. But if the children work, they cannot get the education they need, so when they grow up, they will have to send their own children to work. Thus the bad equilibrium of child labor examined earlier in the chapter may extend across the generations, as a family is effectively locked into a vicious cycle of poverty. Calculations of benefits of health investments need to keep these long-term spillovers in mind.

An effective government role in health systems is critical for at least three important reasons. First, health is central to poverty alleviation, because people are often uninformed about health, a situation compounded by poverty. Second, households spend too little on health because they may neglect externalities (such as, literally, contagion problems). Third, the market would invest too little in health infrastructure and research and development and technology transfer to developing countries due to market failures. Government has different roles in different countries, but as the WHO concluded, "The careful and responsible management of the well-being of the population—stewardship—is the very essence of good government. . . . The health of people is always a national priority: government responsibility for it is continuous and permanent."

Policies for Health, Education, and Income Generation

In the coming years, the clear evidence that health and education are joint investments may offer scope for a more integrated policy approach. It may be that one of the most effective investments we can make in education quality is to improve child health. Similarly, one of the most effective investments we could make in health may be to improve the quality of education. In fact, a number of prominent poverty programs in developing countries now explicitly integrate incentives for the development of health and education human capital among low-income families.

A well-known example is that of the Mexican Program on Education, Health and Nutrition (known by its Spanish acronym, PROGRESA). The PROGRESA program has as one of its central features the promotion of an integrated package to promote the education, health, and nutrition status of poor families. It provides cash transfers to poor families, family clinic visits, and other in-kind nutritional supplements and other health benefits for pregnant and lactating women and their children under age 5. Some of these benefits are conditional on children's regular school attendance; in effect, parents are paid to send their children to school. From its launching in August 1997, the program has covered over 3 million households. PROGRESA affects child nutrition through four "pathways": cash transfers, which may be used in part for improved nutrition; nutritional supplements given to all participating children under age 2 and to those between ages 2 and 5 who show signs of malnutrition; growth monitoring, which provides feedback to parents; and participation in regular meetings where health knowledge is disseminated. Evaluations of this program indicate that its integrated approach has been highly successful, with large improvements in the well-being of participants. Nutrition has improved, school attendance is up significantly, and the dropout rate has declined substantially, especially in the critical "transition" grades 6 through 9.[51]

Another integrated strategy seeks to link highly successful microcredit systems (see Chapter 16) with health and education programs. Project HOPE, an international nongovernmental organization, started a village banking and income-generation project in Ecuador and Honduras in 1993. HOPE developed the project in part on the premise that earlier maternal and child health programs were often limited in providing *sustained* improvements in health and nutrition because of constraints due to poverty. HOPE's "village health banks" combine loans and basic business training with maternal and child health promotion activities. The banks sponsor health-promotion activities focusing on maternal and child health in addition to providing credit and basic business skills to low-income women for use in productive activities. The health banks provide access to basic health services and knowledge, which may include basic hygiene, maternal health, family planning, and women's preventive health care, as well as child survival interventions, including acute respiratory infections, immunization, control of diarrheal diseases, breast-feeding, and nutrition. The health interventions take the form of 15-minute health lectures and other activities at each biweekly meeting of the bank. Health messages for each 16-week loan cycle are printed in simple language on the reverse of each borrower's account booklet. In addition, each bank designates a member to monitor immunizations of children and women, record births and deaths, weigh children under age 2 on a quarterly basis, and refer members to local health services. The business and health education components of the project are intended to reinforce behaviors conducive to sustained improvements in the health status and income of the family. Improved health status is at least implicitly also intended to improve efficiency on the job and to decrease time lost from work due to child illness. The evidence suggests that this integrated strategy is effective in raising health and business skills, as well as family income, among participants.[52]

There is much hope for achieving a healthy, educated, and productive developing world as we look ahead.

AIDS—Economic Development Impact and the Needed Response: Uganda and South Africa

The global AIDS pandemic is much far-ther-reaching than many epidemiologists believed possible in the early 1990s. By 2004, life expectancies in sub-Saharan Africa were just 46 years, compared with the 62 years that might have occurred without the disease, and are still falling. In this case study, we examine the impact of AIDS on two African countries near the center of the epidemic, Uganda and South Africa. While the latter is in the grips of one of the largest health crises in the world over AIDS, Uganda has managed to reverse the unfortunate status it once held as the country most badly affected by the disease to become a bright spot for hope.

AIDS is both an issue of health-care systems and delivery and of economic development. The case of Uganda shows that even a massive AIDS epidemic need not devastate an African economy. Implementing the right policies can help restore growth and development. Creative solutions and a resolute determination can succeed in bringing compassionate care to children and others most affected by the disease. But a policy of AIDS prevention is the best strategy for successful economic development, and Uganda illustrates each of these objectives. At the same time, the case of South Africa shows that even for a country with more

resources, a failure to respond to the threat of an AIDS breakout at an early stage, particularly when accompanied by a misguided view of the nature of the disease, can make it difficult to prevent catastrophic health and economic development repercussions. The case of South Africa also illustrates the consequences of inequality in access to health care.

AIDS is now the leading cause of death of working-age adults in the developing world. If unchecked, it may condemn sub-Saharan Africa, the hardest-hit region, to grinding poverty for at least another generation.

Although the statistics from various sources do reflect general trends, the degree of measurement error can mean a difference, for, say, Uganda, of as many as half a million individuals. Even the officially reported cumulative Uganda AIDS death toll of nearly one million may be an underestimate due to deaths having been attributed to proximate causes rather than their root cause of AIDS. But even that is about 5% of the nation's population. Tragically, this is one reason why the infection rate is no longer as high as it was: So many victims have already died. But a more important reason is that the rate at which the infection is spreading has slowed due to public awareness and public policy.

The problem of AIDS for development is an inherently multidisciplinary one involving not just medicine and medical research but also economics and most of the social and behavioral sciences. Sociologists or anthropologists must determine who the prime infection-spreading groups are in various regions, what is most risky about their behavior, and how to effectively change that behavior. Simulation models may also be useful in designing strategy. These models suggest that more significant reductions in the spread of HIV can be realized through changes in sexual behavior than through needle sterilization efforts.

Uganda

In the 1980s and early 1990s, Uganda had the highest infection rate in Africa. Today, the rate in Uganda is below average for the region: 8.3%, less than in the mid-1990s.

When economically active adults die of AIDS they leave behind dependents, including children and seniors, who become more vulnerable to absolute poverty. There were over 11 million AIDS orphans in Africa as of 2001. Uganda still has one of the highest number of orphans. Well over a million children under 15 years of age have lost their mothers to AIDS; many have lost their fathers as well. The World Bank has estimated that in Uganda and the rest of East Africa, each woman dying of AIDS leaves three children orphaned. In Uganda, the response to the orphan problem has been to try to keep rural children on their farms so they can later support themselves and otherwise to place children with relatives even if they are not immediate family. The policy to keep orphans living on their farmland is productive in some ways, but serious problems remain. These children are often in need of counseling, and social workers carry staggering caseloads. Horrifyingly, orphaned teenage girls living alone on their farmland are sometimes preyed on by thieves and by rapists who may

carry HIV. Teenagers are the group most vulnerable to HIV infection, and teenage girls have several times the infection rate of teenage boys.

AIDS is likely to lead to national dissavings as earnings fall and the sick have to be cared for. This may be balanced in part by foreign savings. Aid may increase; on the other hand, direct foreign investment may very well decrease. Uganda has received considerable new support, in part because of its very severe AIDS epidemic. The concern in the mid-1990s was that as many other countries reached and surpassed the magnitude of Uganda's AIDS epidemic, resources would be diverted to those regions. Indeed, aid did fall from $750 million in 1994 to $690 million in 1999. This still sounds like a significant amount, but the latter figure represented a mere $27 per person in aid. However, this problem has been considerably offset by Uganda's impressive growth, especially for a country in the stagnant sub-Saharan Africa region. Per capita growth of output has averaged nearly 4% for the past decade, a result that is due in part to its unusually effective AIDS response.

The spread of HIV is strongly facilitated by active movements of migrant labor. Migrants, especially young males, are more likely to adopt high-risk behaviors, including frequent visits to prostitutes and intravenous drug use. They may bring HIV infection with them when they visit their home village. Truck drivers were responsible for a significant part of the early spread of HIV in Uganda.

Uganda illustrates that the course of the disease cannot be separated from the socioeconomic context in which it propagates. Uganda had a history of disastrous development decisions, and reversing some of these would mitigate the development impact of the AIDS crisis. In 1972, the unbalanced dictator Idi Amin expelled a majority of South Asian entrepreneurs from the country and confiscated their property. Asians had formed the nucleus of commercial agriculture and commerce in Uganda, and the moves drove about 70,000 of them into exile. The economy suffered severe hardships following these expulsions and other perverse economic policy decisions, some of which led indirectly to the AIDS epidemic. Commercial controls led to an extremely active smuggling industry. Illegal, highly paid smugglers, often stranded for days in towns along smuggling truck routes, made frequent visits to prostitutes, encouraging the rapid spread of the disease. At the same time, the harshly dependent status of women, widespread polygyny, and generally weak foundations of marriage as an institution led to high rates of divorce, prostitution, and other types of rapid sexual partner changes.

Women's de facto inability to own land despite the fact that they do most of the farmwork created incentives for both sexes that anthropologists claim leads to the pattern of rapid sexual partner changes. This behavior is conducive to the spread of HIV while reinforcing low and declining agricultural productivity. There is little doubt that the poor conditions of rural women in Uganda, and Africa in general, is a crucial root cause of the rapid spread of HIV there.

The government of Uganda, a largely Catholic country, long resisted the promotion of condom use and was slow even to acknowledge the widespread presence of the disease. But by the early 1990s, the Ugandan government had devised one of the most active and comprehensive AIDS prevention programs in Africa, a priority that continues. Programs are coordinated by the Ugandan AIDS Commission secretariat. The commission is charged with "policy formulation and setting of priorities as well as overseeing, coordinating and facilitating all AIDS prevention, control and management activities throughout the country." Funding has been provided by UNICEF, WHO, USAID, the World Bank, and the UNDP. Donor countries including the United States were probably more active on AIDS in Uganda than other countries as a result of the extensive attention to the problem there. But in contrast to the government's early failures to stem the epidemic, in the late 1990s and early 2000s, the more progressive government deserves a significant part of the credit in reversing the trends and has been working effectively with NGOs and development donors to combat the disease.

NGOs are playing the leading role in developing creative, effective responses at the grassroots level. A Ugandan private voluntary organization, The AIDS Support Organization (TASO), has played a crucial role in treatment, family assistance, and counseling, as well as education and awareness. Recently, TASO gathered much attention thanks to a visit by U.S. Secretary of State Colin Powell in 2001 and by President George W. Bush in 2003.

Mass media were used in Uganda in the HIV awareness efforts, sometimes to good effect, but unpretested commercials have sometimes been misinterpreted or have even backfired. A famous example promoted "zero grazing," a locally sophisticated way of saying "stay with one partner" that many ordinary people did not understand.

But there will be no opportunity for either government or private organizations to rest in the near future, as the challenges remain great. The rate of mother-to-child transmission of HIV in Uganda has been estimated at 15% to 25% and access to antiretroviral drugs to reduce this rate remains very limited. The under-5 mortality rate was a staggering 162 per 1,000 in 1999.

Condom use has increased in Uganda and some other African countries but is still very limited. In particular, acceptance of condom use is very low among married or regular partners, regardless of the amount of extramarital sexual activity. Teen condom use reportedly remains less than 2%. But the AIDS film *It's Not Easy* was a great success, viewed by some 90% of Uganda's formal-sector workforce. Together, these public and private efforts do have a real effect. T-shirts with slogans such as "Love Carefully" became popular. In Uganda, the prostitution industry in towns known to be highly infected has dropped dramatically. These campaigns have paid off. Several studies showed that the rate of AIDS infection among teenagers in Uganda dropped steeply from 1990 to 1995, most likely due to the adoption of at least comparatively safer sex practices. Other statistics show that the proportion of pregnant women testing positive for HIV in prenatal clinics has also dropped significantly.

Tony Barnett and Piers Blaikie's report on studies of AIDS in Uganda shows the extent of the challenges. It is widely believed among Ugandans that people who discover they have AIDS deliberately infect others sexually. There is at least some evidence that this actually happens, as men with the disease have admitted trying to infect women, including through rape. This is reportedly motivated by anger at having to "die alone." Women infected with HIV are reported to take a gamble at bearing children so they do not "feel cheated by death." If ghastly attitudes like these are indeed commonplace, it will be a formidable task to get the epidemic under control, whatever economic incentives and social programs are put in place.

In sum, as the case of Uganda reveals, each sector of the developing economy, and indeed every aspect of human development, will be severely, if sometimes indirectly, affected by the AIDS epidemic. AIDS is much more than a health issue, and all agencies concerned with development must work with health officials to halt its spread. The later the development of an effective AIDS policy, the greater the ultimate costs, including for med-

ical care, output loss, and the longer-term impact of the undereducation of orphans.

South Africa

The AIDS epidemic is continuing almost unchecked in South Africa. In fact, at this point Botswana and South Africa are among a small but growing number of countries that are now considered likely to see actual population declines as a result of AIDS deaths, according to a 2004 U.S. Census Bureau study. Until recently passed by India, which has almost 24 times as many people, South Africa has had the largest number of HIV-infected people in the world. Despite the country's much better position to afford and deliver antiretroviral drugs, millions of South Africa's citizens have already died of AIDS. Between 5 and 6 million South Africans are infected with HIV, more than 11% of the entire population. Infection in prime-age adults is much higher. Surveys undertaken at prenatal clinics found that an alarming 27.9% of pregnant women tested HIV-positive in 2003, up from 26.5% in 2002. The adult death rate has increased by more than 50% since the late 1990s, primarily as a result of AIDS. At least 1.5 million people have already died of AIDS in South Africa. Twice as many women as men are infected with the virus.

Since 1990, the contrast with Uganda could not have been starker. In 2000, South African President Thabo Mbeki triggered domestic and international outrage by suggesting that the HIV virus does not cause AIDS. He elaborated that AIDS in Africa is essentially a label for diseases aggravated by lack of sanitation and malnutrition. He even claimed that anti-HIV drugs are toxic and may even cause AIDS. In this he was echoing long-discredited crank theories. This was just symbolic of a foot-dragging approach to responding to the problem that may also have had the unfortunate effect of encouraging people not to take precautions for safe sex and clean needle use. Although Mbeki later backed down from these statements, he has since made other comments, such as that he knows no one who has died of AIDS, that have led critics to label him an "AIDS denialist." In 2004, despite his poor record on AIDS, Mbeki was reelected to a second term as president. He failed to even mention the country's overwhelming problem with AIDS in his inaugural address. The government recently claimed that 3.8 million people are infected, rather than the 5.3 million estimated by UNAIDS. Another government study by the Department of Health put the 2003 figure at 5.6 million. All these figures are estimates based on assumptions about the rates at which the disease has been spreading. The lack of more accurate information has been another impediment to progress.

Jolene Skordis and Nicoli Nattrass recently concluded that contrary to widely held opinion, medicines to reduce mother-to-child transmission of HIV are affordable even if the government has no additional resources. They estimated that in South Africa, each HIV-positive child "costs the government more in terms of health and welfare expenses than it does to reduce mother-to-child transmission of HIV through the use of antiretroviral regimens" when the mother continues to breast-feed.

Despite its initial slow response, the South African government by 2004 seemed to have made combating AIDS a genuine top priority. Its AIDS program contained many of the elements of Uganda's earlier success, along with an ambitious program to expand the number of recipients of antivirals. The more serious effort came not a moment too soon. But it continued to be met with ambiguous policies and statements by government officials. In September 2004 the Vice-President Jacob Zuma praised virginity testing of women as a response to the crisis, even though men are mostly responsible for the spread of the disease and women most commonly contract the virus from their husbands. AIDS activists said that Zuma's implied support for the practice of virginity testing was an affront to women's dignity. Sharon Ekambaram of the AIDS Consortium, a leading activist group, was quoted in the *Financial Times* as saying that growing support for this practice was counterproductive and had led young women to become more willing to submit to unprotected anal sex. Clearly, it will take much more effort to ensure the constructive and realistic social and political response to this epidemic that is desperately needed.

Despite the human devastation, a recent macroeconometric model of the South African economy analyzed by Ellis, Smit, and Laubscher suggested that the impact of HIV/AIDS in South Africa on economic performance over the next 10 to 15 years may not be catastrophic. While such models project on the basis of current trends, the problem is that the underlying conditions have been deteriorating. The encouraging thing about such findings is that they suggest that if the deterioration can be halted, much of the economic damage done so far can be largely reversed. Reports of an irreclaimably lost generation seem to have been greatly exaggerated. South Africa can still benefit from following the example of Uganda.

An effective response to the problems of AIDS and development will require a careful balancing act of policymaking. Despite the human tragedy and development catastrophe of the AIDS epidemic, it is important not to let resources for HIV programs overshadow other worthwhile development projects. At the same time, the potential problem is severe enough that development project planners need to keep the problem at the forefront of attention. Each new health, population, and basic needs project is now required by several development agencies to either contain an HIV component or to justify why this is not relevant or cost-effective for the project. This requirement is likely to be adopted by virtually all development agencies in the near future. ∎

Sources

Ainsworth, Martha, and Mead Over. "AIDS and African development." *World Bank Research Observer* 9 (1994): 203–240.

Armstrong, Jill. "Socioeconomic implications of AIDS in developing countries." *Finance and Development* 28, 4 (1991): 14–17.

Arndt, Channing, and Jeffrey D. Lewis. "The HIV/AIDS pandemic in South Africa: Sectoral impacts and unemployment." *Journal of International Development* 13, (2001) 427-449

Barnett, Tony, and Piers Blaikie. *AIDS in Africa: Its Present and Future Impact.* New York: Guilford Press, 1992.

Ellis, L. L., B. W. Smit, and P. Laubscher. "The macro-economic impact of HIV/AIDS in South Africa." *Journal for Studies in Economics and Econometrics* 27, 2 (2003): 1–28.

Kambou, Gerard, Shanta Devarajan, and Mead Over. "The economic impact of AIDS in an African country: Simulations with a CGE model of Cameroon." *Journal of African Economies* 1 (1993): 109–130.

Lamboray, Jean-Louis, and A. Edward Elmendorf. *Combating AIDS and other Sexually Transmitted Diseases in Africa.* Washington, D.C.: World Bank, 1992.

Lewis, Maureen A., et al. *AIDS in Developing Countries: Cost Issues and Policy Trade-Offs.* Washington, D.C: Urban Institute, 1989.

Over, Mead. *The Macroeconomic Impact of AIDS in Sub-Saharan Africa.* Washington, D.C.: World Bank, 1993.

Population and Development. Special issue on "A Cultural Perspective on HIV Transmission," January 1993.

"Report on AIDS offers dire prognosis." *Washington Post*, July 3, 2002, p. A3.

Skordis, Jolene, and Nicoli Nattrass. "Paying to waste lives: The affordability of reducing mother-to-child transmission of HIV in South Africa." *Journal of Health Economics* 21 (2002): 405-421.

Timberg, Craig. "Mbeki marks decade of democracy, AIDS is not mentioned in South African's 2nd inaugural address." *Washington Post*, April 28, 2004, p. A14.

Uganda AIDS Commission, http://www.aidsuganda.org

UNAIDS, *2004 Report on the Global AIDS Epidemic*, http://www.unaids.org/bangkok2004/report.html

United Nations Development Program. *HIV and Development.* New York: Oxford University Press, 1993.

United Nations Development Program. *Human Development Report, 2001.* New York: Oxford University Press, 2001.

World Bank. *Report on a Workshop on the Economic Impact of Fatal Adult Illness in Sub-Saharan Africa.* Washington, D.C.: World Bank, 1993.

World Bank. *World Development Indicators, 2001, 2004.* Washington, D.C.: World Bank, 2001, 2004.

Concepts for Review

Acquired immunodeficiency
   syndrome (AIDS)
Basic education
Brain drain
Derived demand
Educational certification

Educational gender gap
Human capital
Human immunodeficiency
   virus (HIV)
Literacy
Private benefits of education

Private costs of education
Social benefits of education
Social costs of education
World Health Organization
   (WHO)

Questions for Discussion

1. What reasons would you give for the rather sizable school dropout rates in developing countries? What might be done to lower these rates?

2. What are the differences between formal and nonformal education? Give some examples of each.

3. It is often asserted that LDC educational systems, especially in rural areas, are unsuited to the real social and economic needs of development. Do you agree or disagree with this statement? Explain your reasoning.

4. How would you explain the fact that relative costs of and returns to higher education are so much higher in LDCs than in developed countries?

5. What is the supposed rationale for subsidizing higher education in many developing countries? Do you think that it is a legitimate rationale from an economic viewpoint? Explain your answer.

6. Early-childhood environmental factors are said to be important determinants of school performance. What are some of these factors, how important do you think they are, and what might be done to ensure that these factors are not negative?

7. What do we mean by the economics of education? To what extent do you think educational planning and policy decisions ought to be guided by economic considerations? Explain, giving hypothetical or actual examples.

8. What is meant by the statement "The demand for education is a 'derived demand' for high-paying modern-sector job opportunities"? Many educational specialists claim that families and children in LDCs demand education not so much as an investment good but as a consumption good. What do you think this statement means, and what do you think is the relative importance of the consumption demand for education among your student friends?

9. What are the links among educational systems, labor markets, and employment determination in many developing countries? Describe the process of educational job displacement.

10. Distinguish carefully between private and social benefits and costs of education. What economic factors give rise to the wide divergence between private and social benefit-to-cost valuations in most developing countries? Should governments attempt through their educational and economic policies to narrow the gap between private and social valuations? Explain.

11. Describe and comment on each of the following education-development relationships:

    a. Education and economic growth: Does education promote growth? How?

    b. Education, inequality, and poverty: Do educational systems typical of most LDCs tend to reduce, exacerbate, or have no effect on inequality and poverty? Explain with specific reference to a country with which you are familiar.

    c. Education and migration: Does education stimulate rural-urban migration? Why?

    d. Education and fertility: Does the education of women tend to reduce their fertility? Why?

    e. Education and rural development: Do most LDC formal educational systems contribute substantially to the promotion of rural development? Explain.

    f. Education and the brain drain: What factors cause the international migration of high-level educated workers from LDCs to developed countries? What do we mean by the internal brain drain? Explain, giving examples.

12. Governments can influence the character, quality, and content of their educational systems by manipulating important economic and noneconomic factors or variables both outside of and within educational systems. What are some of these external and internal factors, and how can government policies make education more relevant to the real meaning of development?

13. What explains the large gains in health and education in recent decades? To what extent do you think these measured gains represent authentic improvement, and to what extent are they more of a mirage?

14. Why are health and education so closely linked in the development challenge?

15. What are the most pressing health and education challenges today? What makes them so difficult to solve?

16. What makes for a good and fair health system? Education system?

17. What are the consequences of gender bias in health and education?

18. What is the human capital approach to health and education? What do you think are its most important strengths and weaknesses?

19. What are the strategies being discussed to address the problem of child labor? What are the strengths and weaknesses of these approaches?

20. What are the relationships between health and education, on the one hand, to productivity and incomes, on the other?

21. What can government do to make health systems more equitable?

Notes

1. United Nations Development Program, *Human Development Report, 2004* (New York: Oxford University Press, 2004), p. 171.

2. Selma Mushkin, "Health as an investment," *Journal of Political Economy* 70 (1962): 129–157.

3. See Randa Sab and Stephen C. Smith, "Human capital convergence: International evidence," http://www.imf.org/external/pubs/ft/wp/2001/wp0132.pdf; the paper presents evidence that the relative improvement in health and education in the developing world is pronounced enough to conclude that slow but steady convergence is taking place across countries. See also Randa Sab and Stephen C. Smith,"Human capital convergence: A joint estimation approach," *IMF Staff Papers* 49 (2002): 200-211, and Robert J. Barro and Jong-Wha Lee, "International comparisons of educational attainment," *Journal of Monetary Economics* 32 (1993): 363–394.

4. This discussion draws on Stephen C. Smith, "Microcredit and health programs: To integrate or not to integrate?" in *Microenterprise Development for Better Health Outcomes*, ed. Rosalia Rodriguez-Garcia, James A. Macinko, and Willium F. Waters (Westport, Conn.: Greenwood Press, 2001), pp. 41–50.

5. See Howarth E. Bouis and Lawrence J. Haddad, "Are estimates of calorie-income elasticities too high? A recalibration of the plausible range," *Journal of Development Economics* 39 (1992): 333–364; Jere Behrman and Anil Deolalikar, "Will developing country nutrition improve with income? A case study for rural south India," *Journal of Political Economy* 95 (1987): 108–138; and Shankar Subramanian and Angus Deaton, "The demand for food and calories," *Journal of Political Economy* 104 (1996): 133–162.

6. For a review of some of this literature, see Tonia Marek, *Ending Malnutrition: Why Increasing Income Is Not Enough* (Washington, D.C.: World Bank, 1992).

7. Subramanian and Deaton, "The demand for food and calories."

8. See Maurice Schiff and Alberto Valdes, "Nutrition: Alternative definitions and policy implications," *Economic Development and Cultural Change* 38 (1990): 281–292; and Marek, *Ending Malnutrition*.

9. Howarth E. Bouis, *The Determinants of Household-Level Demand for Micronutrients: An Analysis for Philippine Farm Households* (Washington, D.C.: International Food Policy Research Institute, 1991).

10. Joachim von Braum, Detlev Peutz, and Patrick Webb, *Irrigation Technology and Commercialization of Rice in the Gambia: Effects on Income and Nutrition* (Washington, D.C.: International Food Policy Research Institute, 1989).

11. Paul Glewwe, "Why does mother's schooling raise child health in developing countries? Evidence from Morocco," *Journal of Human Resources* 34 (1999): 124–159. See also Ravi Kanbur and Lyn Squire, "The evolution of thinking about poverty," in *Frontiers of Development Economics: The Future in Perspective*, ed. Gerald M. Meier and Joseph E. Stiglitz (New York: Oxford University Press, 2001).

12. World Bank, *World Development Report, 1993* (New York: Oxford University Press, 1993), p. 18.

13. Ibid., p. 19.

14. See Ernesto Pollitt, *Malnutrition and Infection in the Classroom* (Paris: UNESCO, 1990); Harold Alderman, Jere Behrman, Victor Lavy, and Rekha Menon, "Child health and school enrollment: A longitudinal analysis," *Journal of Human Resources* 36 (2001): 185–201; Jere Behrman, "The impact of health and nutrition on education," *World Bank Researcher* 11 (1996): 23–37; and Paul Glewwe and Hanan G. Jacoby, "An economic

analysis of delayed primary school enrollment in a low-income country: The role of early childhood nutrition," *Review of Economics and Statistics* 77 (1995): 156–169.

15. Michael Kremer and Edward Miguel, "Worms: Identifying impact on education and health in the presence of treatment externalities," *Econometrica* 72 (2004): 159–217.

16. See Kaushik Basu and James Foster, "On measuring literacy," *Economic Journal* 108 (1998): 1733–1749.

17. World Health Organization, *World Health Report, 2000* (Geneva: World Health Organization, 2000), p. 4.

18. This also reflects the finding that developing countries have a more unequal income distribution on average than developed countries (see Chapter 5).

19. For a detailed review of the empirical studies of rates of returns to investment in education, see George Psacharopoulos, "Returns to education: An updated international comparison," *Comparative Education* 17 (1981): 321—341, and "Returns to investment in education: A global update," *World Development* 22 (1994): 1325–1343; Christopher Colclough, "The impact of primary schooling on economic development: A review of the evidence," *World Development* 10 (1982): 167–185; and Rati Ram, "Level of development and rates of return to schooling: Some estimates from multicountry data," *Economic Development and Cultural Change* 44 (1996): 839–857. As Psacharopoulos explains in "Education as investment," *Finance and Development* (1982): 40:

> Estimates of the private rate of return to a given level of education are calculated by comparing the discounted benefits over the lifetime of an educational investment "project" to the costs of such a project. Thus, for a calculation of the private rate of return to four years of university education, benefits are estimated by taking the difference between existing statistics on the mean post-tax earnings of university graduates by age and those of a sample group of secondary school graduates. The earnings of the latter also represent the opportunity costs of staying in school. Direct costs are obtained from statistics on a student's out-of-pocket expenditures that are strictly due to the costs of college attendance. Given these data, the rate of return to investment in a college degree compared with a secondary school qualification is the rate of interest that reduces to zero the net present value of the discounted difference between the costs and benefits. A simple equation for the private rate of return is
>
> $$\text{Private rate of return} = \frac{\left(\begin{array}{c}\text{Mean annual post-tax}\\\text{earnings of university}\\\text{graduates}\end{array}\right) - \left(\begin{array}{c}\text{Mean annual post-tax}\\\text{earnings of secondary}\\\text{school graduates}\end{array}\right)}{\left(\begin{array}{c}\text{Four}\\\text{years}\\\text{of study}\end{array}\right) \times \left(\begin{array}{c}\text{Mean annual post-tax}\\\text{earnings of second}\\\text{school graduates}\end{array}\right) + \left(\begin{array}{c}\text{Mean annual}\\\text{provate direct}\\\text{cost of study}\end{array}\right)}.$$
>
> A social rate of return to college education could be calculated in the same way, although earnings should be pretax (as taxes are a transfer from the point of view of society at large) and the direct cost should include the full amount of resources committed per student for higher education, rather than the usually smaller part of expenditure borne by the student.

20. Unless otherwise noted, child labor statistics come from the International Labor Office; see its child labor Web site at http://www.ilo.org/public/english/standards/ipec/index.htm. Also see http://www.ilo.org/public/english/bureau/inf/childlabour/factssheet.htm and http://www.ilo.org/dyn/declaris/DECLARATIONWEB.DOWNLOAD_BLOB?Var_DocumentID=1566. More recent updates may be found on the ILO web page.

21. For further details on the model, and an excellent survey, see Kaushik Basu, "Child labor: Cause, consequence, and cure, with remarks on international labor standards," *Journal of Economic Literature* 37 (1999): 1083–1120.

22. Notice that the demand curve also cuts the labor supply curve a third time, through the S-shaped part of the supply curve, but this is an unstable equilibrium; see Chapter 4 for a discussion of unstable equilibria.

23. Another influential theoretical model was provided by Jean-Marie Baland and James Robinson, who point out that with highly imperfect capital markets such as those faced by many impoverished rural families, child labor is one of the few ways families have to borrow from the future. The result is that child labor, which reduces future earning opportunities because the working child receives less schooling, may exist only because of market failures. The authors formally derive conditions under which a ban on child labor may be Pareto-improving in general equilibrium. See Jean-Marie Baland and James A. Robinson, "Is child labor inefficient?" *Journal of Political Economy* 108 (2000): 663–679.

24. The following paragraphs draw on ILO, UNICEF, and World Bank Web pages.

25. Wadi D. Haddad et al., *Education and Development: Evidence for New Priorities* (Washington, D.C.: World Bank, 1990), pp. 12–15. The Millennium Development Goals (MDGs) are described in Chapter 1.

26. Although human capital investment rate of return estimates are often fraught with errors and regularly present serious problems of interpretation, results such as those on the benefits of educating girls, when consistent across time and space and methods of evaluation, still offer useful guidance for policy. See, for example, George Psacharopoulos, "Education and development: A review," *World Bank Research Observer* 3 (January 1988): 99–116; and Stephen C. Smith, *Case Studies in Economic Development*, 2nd ed. (Boston: Addison-Wesley, 1997), ch. 16.

27. Amartya Sen, "Missing women", *British Medical Journal* 304 (1992): 587–588. See also Sen's *Development as Freedom* (New York: Knopf, 1999), p. 104.

28. For more on this debate, see Stephan Klasen, "Nutrition, health, and mortality in sub-Saharan Africa: Is there a gender bias?" and "Rejoinder," *Journal of Development Studies* 32 (1996): 913–933, 944–948; and Peter Svedberg, "Gender biases in sub-Saharan Africa: Reply and further evidence," *Journal of Development Studies* 32 (1996): 934–943. On the social instability and security implications of the 12% to 15% of the adult male population in China and India projected by 2020 to find itself unable to marry, see Valerie M. Hudson and Andrea M. Den Boer, *Bare Branches: The Security Implications of Asia's Surplus Male Population* (Cambridge, Mass.: MIT Press, 2004).

29. Harold Alderman and Marito Garcia, *Food Security and Health Security: Explaining the Levels of Nutrition in Pakistan* (Washington, D.C.: World Bank, 1992); Duncan

Thomas, *Gender Differences in Household Resource Allocations* (Washington, D.C.: World Bank, 1991).

30. Much of the material in this section is drawn from Michael P. Todaro and Edgar O. Edwards, "Educational demand and supply in the context of growing unemployment in less developed countries," *World Development* 1 (1973): 107–117.

31. See, for example, Ragui Assaad, "The effects of public sector hiring and compensation policies on the Egyptian labor market," *World Bank Economic Review* 11 (1997): 85–118.

32. For a penetrating analysis of the Indian education and employment problems, see Marc Blaug et al., *Causes of Graduate Unemployment in India* (Harmondsworth, England: Penguin, 1967).

33. Rizwanul Islam, "Graduate unemployment in Bangladesh: A preliminary analysis," *Bangladesh Development Studies* 8, 4 (1980): 47–74.

34. For evidence of this, see Emmanuel Jimenez, "The public subsidization of education and health in developing countries: A review of equity and efficiency," *World Bank Research Observer* 1 (1986): 123.

35. Psacharopoulos, "Education and development," pp. 100–102.

36. See World Bank, *The Quality of Growth* (New York: Oxford University Press, 2000), pp. 56–66; and Vinod Thomas, Yan Wang, and Xibo Fan, *Measuring Education Inequality: Gini Coefficients of Education* (Washington, D.C.: World Bank Institute, 2000). It is also worth noting that human capital tends to be more equally distributed than other assets, such as land.

37. Jere Behrman and Nancy Birdsall, "The quality of schooling: Quantity alone is misleading," *American Economic Review* 73 (1983): 928–946. See also Eric A. Hanushek, "Interpreting recent research on schooling in developing countries," *World Bank Research Observer* 10 (1995): 227–246, and Paul Glewwe, "The relevance of standard estimates of rates of return to schooling for educational policy," *Journal of Development Economics* 51 (1996): 267–290.

38. See, for example, Jagdish N. Bhagwati, "Education, class structure and income equality," *World Development* 1 (1973): 21–36; Jimenez, "Public subsidization"; and Alberto Alesina and Roberto Perotti, "The political economy of growth: A critical survey of the recent literature," *World Bank Economic Review* 8 (1994): 360.

39. Another explanation is that where perfect capital markets exist, all individuals can borrow for their education in anticipation of high future earnings. But in LDCs with very imperfect capital markets, limited information about individual abilities, and poor loan enforcement, it is extremely difficult for the poor to borrow to finance their education. This is not, however, a problem for the rich, who can rely on their own resources to invest in education. So the system of inequality has a built-in tendency to reproduce itself with each generation.

40. For some evidence of the regressive nature of educational subsidies in Latin America, see Jean-Pierre Jallade, *Public Expenditures on Education and Income Distribution in Colombia* (Baltimore: Johns Hopkins University Press, 1974), and *Basic Education and Income Inequality in Brazil: The Long-Term View* (Washington, D.C.: World Bank, 1977).

41. See http://www.who.int/aboutwho/en/definition.html. In earlier years, the WHO has offered other, at least equally expansive definitions of health, such as "the healthy organism seeks and solves problems."

42. The same types of measures used for studying the distribution of income (reviewed in Chapter 5) could also be used to examine the distribution of health and education, but for some reason this is rarely done. But see R. Andrew Allison and James Foster, *Measuring Health Inequality Using Qualitative Data* (Cambridge, Mass.: Harvard Center for Population and Development Studies, 1999).

43. Other countries facing dramatic declines in life expectancy include Zambia, from 60.1 to 37.8; South Africa, from 68.2 to 48.0; and Tanzania, from 60.7 to 46.1. "AIDS is declared threat to security: White House fears epidemic could destabilize world," *Washington Post*, April 30, 2000, p. A1.

44. See F. Desmond McCarthy, Holger Wolf, and Yi Wu, *Malaria and Growth* (Washington, D.C.: World Bank, 2000). Much of the information in the following sections derives from WHO sources, including its *World Health Reports,* and its Web pages.

45. In 1996, the AIDS programs of several international agencies were merged into the Joint United Nations Program on HIV/AIDS, commonly referred to as UNAIDS, which is a kind of joint venture between the WHO, UNDP, UNICEF, UNESCO, UNFPA, UNDCP, and the World Bank.

46. World Bank, *World Development Report, 1993*; T. Paul Schultz and Aysit Tansel, "Wage and labor supply effects of illness in Côte d'Ivoire and Ghana: Instrumental variable estimates for days disabled," *Journal of Development Economics* 53 (1997): 251–286; Emmanuel Max and Donald S. Shepard, "Productivity loss to deformity from leprosy in India," *International Journal of Leprosy* 57 (1989): 476–482.

47. John Strauss and Duncan Thomas, "Health, nutrition, and economic development," *Journal of Economic Literature* 36 (1998): 766–817; see also Strauss and Thomas, "Health wages: Evidence on men and women in urban Brazil," *Journal of Econometrics* 77 (1997): 159–185. Note however that height could be independently associated with physical strength (e.g., through muscle length) which would tend to overstate the effect of health per se.

48. Strauss and Thomas, "Health, nutrition, and economic development," p. 806. Note that some statements to the contrary were found in earlier literature reviews and continue to persist in some economics textbooks, but those reports fail to take into account the most recent, rigorous studies that do a better job of accounting for the joint determination of health and income.

49. The study ranked France in first place and found that the "U.S. health system spends a higher portion of its gross domestic product than any other country but ranks 37 out of 191 countries according to its performance." While the United States spends almost 14% of its GDP on health, the United Kingdom, which spends just 6% of GDP on health services, ranked 18th in the report. Note that this study has been highly controversial; it seems that almost all countries are unhappy about some aspect of their ratings. The report may be found at http://www.who.int/whr/2001/archives/2000/en/index.htm.

50. World Bank, *World Development Report, 1993*, p. viii.

51. See, for example, Secretaria de Desarrollo Social (SEDESOL), Government of Mexico, Programa de Educación, Salud y Alimentación (PROGRESA), 2001, at http://www.progresa.gob.mx; John Hoddinott and Emmanuel Skoufias, "Preliminary evidence on the impact of PROGRESA on consumption," paper presented at the American Economic Association annual meeting, New Orleans, January 2001; T. Paul Schultz, "The impact of PROGRESA on school enrollment," paper presented at the American Economic Association annual meeting, New Orleans, January 2001; and John Hoddinott and Jere Behrman, "Program evaluation with unobserved heterogeneity, selective implementation, and imperfectly targeted beneficiaries: The Mexican PROGRESA impact on child nutrition," paper presented at the NEUDC conference, Boston University, September 2001.

52. See Stephen C. Smith, "Village banking and maternal and child health: Evidence from Ecuador and Honduras," *World Development* 30 (2002): 707–723.

Further Reading

For an analysis of the revolution in information and communications technology and the skill requirements to compete globally in the 1990s, see Ajit Singh, "Global economic changes, skills and international competitiveness," *International Labour Review* 133 (1994): 167–183; and Graciela Chichilnisky, "The knowledge revolution," *Journal of International Trade and Development* 7 (1998): 39–54.

Excellent surveys of economic issues relating education to development can be found in John Simmons, "Education for development reconsidered," *World Development* 7 (1979): 1005–1016; Marc Blaug, *An Introduction to the Economics of Education* (Harmondsworth, England: Penguin, 1970); George Psacharopoulos and Maureen Woodhall, *Education for Development: An Analysis of Investment Choices* (New York: Oxford University Press, 1987); World Bank, *The Financing of Education in Developing Countries: An Exploration of Policy Options* (Washington, D.C.: World Bank, 1986); Wadi D. Haddad et al., *Education and Development: Evidence for New Priorities* (Washington, D.C.: World Bank, 1990); and Martin Carnoy, "Structural adjustment and the changing face of education," *International Labour Review* 134 (1995): 653–673.

A good review of the empirical research on the economic returns to investment (both private and social) in education can be found in George Psacharopoulos, "Returns to investment in education: A global update," *World Development* 22 (1994): 1325–1343, and "Education and development: A review," *World Bank Research Observer* 3 (1988): 99–116; an alternative view focusing on the quality rather than quantity of education is contained in Jere Behrman and Nancy Birdsall, "The quality of schooling: Quantity alone is misleading," *American Economic Review* 73 (1983): 928–946.

For a broad analysis of how education can promote rural development, see Philip H. Coombs and Manzoor Ahmed, *Attacking Rural Poverty: How Nonformal Education Can Help* (Baltimore: Johns Hopkins University Press, 1974).

A challenging and critical view of the role of education in society can be found in Ivan Illich, *Deschooling Society* (New York: Harper & Row, 1970), in Ronald Dore, *The Diploma Disease* (Berkeley: University of California Press, 1976), and in Paolo Friere, *Pedagogy of the Oppressed* (New York: Seabury Press, 1970).

A good summary of the issues involved in the question of education and inequality can be obtained from Jagdish N. Bhagwati, "Education, class structure and income equality," *World Development* 1 (1973): 21–36, and from Alain Mingat and Jee-Peng Tan, "On equity in education again: An international comparison," *Journal of Human Resources* 20 (1985): 298–308.

In addition to the references in the chapter notes, the World Health Organization's annual *World Health Reports* are excellent sources for further reading on health and development. Similarly, the ILO's *World Employment Reports* are highly informative on education issues, as are UNESCO reports.

CHAPTER NINE

Agricultural Transformation and Rural Development

It is in the agricultural sector that the battle for long-term economic development will be won or lost.

—Gunnar Myrdal, Nobel Laureate in Economics

The main burden of development and employment creation will have to be borne by the part of the economy in which agriculture is the predominant activity, that is, the rural sector.

—Francis Blanchard, Director General, International Labor Organization

The Imperative of Agricultural Progress and Rural Development

If the migration of people with and without school certificates to the cities of Africa, Asia, and Latin America is proceeding at historically unprecedented rates, a large part of the explanation can be found in the economic stagnation of the outlying rural areas. Over 2 billion people in the developing world grind out a meager and often inadequate existence in agricultural pursuits. Well over 3.3 billion people lived in rural areas in 2003. People living in the countryside comprise considerably more than half the population of such diverse Latin American and Asian nations as Bolivia, Guatemala, India, Indonesia, Myanmar, Ecuador, Sri Lanka, Pakistan, the Philippines, and China. In Africa, the ratios are much higher, with most countries having rural dwellers in excess of three-quarters of the total population.

Of greater importance than sheer numbers is the fact that over two-thirds of the world's poorest people are also located in rural areas and engaged primarily in subsistence agriculture. Their basic concern is survival. Many hundreds of millions of people have been bypassed by whatever economic progress has been attained. It is estimated that more than 800 million of these people do not have enough food to meet their basic nutritional needs.[1] In their daily struggle to subsist, their behavior may have often seemed irrational to many observers who, until recently, had little comprehension of the precarious nature of subsistence living and the importance of avoiding risks. If development is to take place and become self-sustaining, it will have to include the rural areas in general and the agricultural sector in particular. The core problems of widespread poverty, growing inequality, rapid population growth, and rising unemployment all find their origins in the stagnation and too often retrogression of economic life in rural areas.

Traditionally, the role of agriculture in economic development has been viewed as passive and supportive. Based on the historical experience of Western countries, economic development was seen as requiring a rapid structural transformation of the economy from one predominantly focused on agricultural activities to a more complex modern industrial and service society. As a result, agriculture's primary role was to provide sufficient low-priced food and manpower to the expanding industrial economy, which was thought to be the dynamic "leading sector" in any overall strategy of economic development. Lewis's famous two-sector model discussed in Chapter 3 is an example of a theory of development that places heavy emphasis on rapid industrial growth with an agricultural sector fueling this industrial expansion by means of its cheap food and surplus labor.

Today, development economists have come to realize that far from playing a passive, supporting role in the process of economic development, the agricultural sector in particular and the rural economy in general must play an indispensable part in any overall strategy of economic progress, especially for the low-income developing countries.

An agriculture- and employment-based strategy of economic development requires at a minimum three basic complementary elements: (1) accelerated output growth through technological, institutional, and price incentive changes designed to raise the productivity of small farmers; (2) rising domestic demand for agricultural output derived from an employment-oriented urban development strategy; and (3) diversified, nonagricultural, labor-intensive rural development activities that directly and indirectly support and are supported by the farming community.[2] To a large extent, therefore, agricultural and rural development has come to be seen by many as the sine qua non of national development. Without such **integrated rural development**, industrial growth either would be stultified or, if it succeeded, would create such severe internal imbalances in the economy that the problems of widespread poverty, inequality, and unemployment would become even more pronounced.

Six main questions, therefore, need to be asked about agriculture and rural development as it relates to overall national development:

1. How can total agricultural output and productivity per capita be substantially increased in a manner that will directly benefit the average small farmer and the landless rural dweller while providing a sufficient food surplus to support a growing urban, industrial sector?

2. What is the process by which traditional low-productivity peasant farms are transformed into high-productivity commercial enterprises?

3. When traditional family farmers and peasant cultivators resist change, is their behavior stubborn and irrational, or are they acting rationally within the context of their particular economic environment?

4. What are the effects of the high risks faced by farmers in low-income countries, how do farm families cope with these risks, and what policies are appropriate to lessen risk?

5. Are economic and price incentives sufficient to elicit output increases among peasant agriculturalists, or are institutional and structural changes in rural farming systems also required?

6. Is raising agricultural productivity sufficient to improve rural life, or must there be concomitant off-farm employment creation along with improvements in educational, medical, and other social services? In other words, what do we mean by *rural development*, and how can it be achieved?

Our approach in this chapter is to start with an examination of the basic characteristics of agrarian systems in Latin America, Asia, and Africa to identify some important similarities and differences. We then look at the economics of peasant subsistence agriculture and discuss the stages of transition from subsistence to commercial farming in developing nations. Our focus here is not only the economic factors but also the social, institutional, and structural requirements of small-farm modernization. We then explore the meaning of rural development and review alternative policies designed to raise levels of living in rural areas. The chapter concludes with a case study on agricultural extension for women farmers in Africa.

Agricultural Growth: Past Progress and Current Challenges

We have seen that many developing countries experienced respectable rates of GNI growth during the past few decades. The greatest proportionate share of this overall growth occurred in the manufacturing and commerce sectors, where recorded rates of annual output growth often exceeded 10%. In contrast, agricultural output growth for most developing regions was much less robust during these decades, and the share of agricultural output in total GNI declined. Table 9.1 reveals that in spite of the fact that the agricultural sector accounts for most of the employment in developing countries, it accounts for a much lower share of the output. In fact, in no developing region does agricultural production constitute more than 30% of the total national product. This is in marked contrast to the historical experience of advanced countries, where agricultural output in their early stages of growth always contributed at least as much to total output as the share of the labor force engaged in these activities. The fact that contemporary agricultural employment in developing countries is typically two to three times as large in proportion to the total as is agricultural output simply reflects the relatively low levels of labor productivity compared with those in manufacturing and commerce.

Agricultural production continues to rise around the world, broadly keeping pace with the rising population. But progress has been very uneven, as seen in Figure 9.1. In East Asia and the Pacific, by 2000 food output was two and a half times

	Percentage of the Labor Force in Agriculture	Output of Agriculture as a Percentage of Gross National Income
TABLE 9.1 Output and Employment in Developing-World Agriculture, 2002		
Region		
South Asia	64	23
East Asia (including China)	70	15
Latin America	25	7
Sub-Saharan Africa	68	18

Sources: World Bank, *World Development Report, 1997: The State in a Changing World* (New York: Oxford University Press, 1997). Reprinted with the permission of Oxford University Press, Inc. World Bank, *World Development Indicators, 2004* (Washington, D.C.: World Bank, 2004). Copyright © 2004 by the World Bank. Reprinted with the permission of the World Bank via the Copyright Clearance Center.

what it was in 1980, and hunger in China and elsewhere fell. In South Asia, progress made possible by the **green revolution** continued, albeit at an uneven and slower pace; gains were sufficient to provide a continued increase in food output per capita. But in sub-Saharan Africa, output was only about 50% higher in the early 2000s than it was in 1980, while population increased by more than 75%. Thus in the poorest region of the world, per capita food production continued its steady decline. One of the causes is that in many areas of Africa, the population has reached a size where traditional slash- and-burn agricultural practices are no

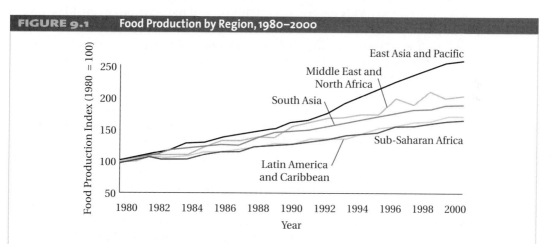

FIGURE 9.1 Food Production by Region, 1980–2000

Food production has outpaced population growth in recent decades, but the progress has been uneven. And despite the more than 80% increase in food production in low-income countries, hunger persists in parts of the world. Among developing regions, East Asia and the Pacific have had the highest growth in food production, sub-Saharan Africa the lowest.

Source: World Bank, *World Development Indicators, 2003* (Washington, DC: World Bank, 2004), p. 131. Copyright © 2004 by the World Bank. Reprinted with the permission of the World Bank via the Copyright Clearance Center.

longer feasible without reusing land with too little rest, resulting in significant deterioration of soil nutrients. But subsistence farmers cannot purchase modern seeds, fertilizers, and other essentials of modern agriculture; the result is a poverty trap in which farmers must work harder and harder just to stay in place.

The United Nations Food and Agriculture Organization (FAO) has repeatedly warned of catastrophic food shortages. In a majority of African countries, the average per capita calorie intake has now fallen below minimal nutritional standards. The FAO recently estimated that of Africa's 750 million people, more than 270 million suffer from some form of malnutrition associated with inadequate food supplies. Whereas the severe famine of 1973–1974 took the lives of hundreds of thousands and left many more with permanent damage from malnutrition, its geographic impact was limited to the Sahelian belt that stretches below the Sahara from Cape Verde, off the coast of Senegal in the west, across the continent to Ethiopia. By contrast, in 1982–1984 and again in 1987–1988, 1991–1992, and 1993–1994, the food crisis became much more widespread, with more than 22 nations threatened by severe famine, including, in addition to the Sahelian nations, Zambia, Tanzania, Malawi, Uganda, Botswana, Mozambique, Zimbabwe, and Angola. In the early 2000s, famine seriously affected African countries as widely separated as Mauritania in the northwest, Ethiopia and Eritrea in the east, and Angola, Zambia, Zimbabwe, Malawi, and Mozambique across the south.[3]

A major reason for the relatively poor performance of agriculture in low-income regions has been the neglect of this sector in the development priorities of their governments. This neglect of agriculture and the accompanying bias toward investment in the urban industrial economy can in turn be traced largely to the misplaced emphasis on rapid industrialization via import substitution and exchange rate overvaluation (see Chapter 13) that permeated development thinking and strategy during the postwar decades. For example, during the 1950s and 1960s, the share of total national investment allocated toward the agricultural sector in a sample of 18 LDCs was approximately 12%, even though agriculture in these countries accounted for almost 30% of GNI and more than 60% of total employment.[4] As we saw in Chapter 7, one significant manifestation of this rural neglect and the corresponding emphasis on urban growth has been the massive migration of rural peasants into the teeming cities of developing nations.

As a result of this disappointing experience and the realization that the future of most underdeveloped countries will depend to a large extent on what happens to their agriculture, there has been a marked shift in development thinking and policymaking. This shift, which began in the late 1970s, has been away from the almost exclusive emphasis on rapid industrialization toward a more realistic appreciation of the overwhelming importance of agricultural and rural development for national development. In many areas, significant progress has been achieved. Even so, progress has been very slow in the least developed countries that most need increased attention to the agricultural sector. A first step toward understanding what is needed for agricultural and rural development must be a comprehension of the nature of agricultural systems in diverse developing regions and, in particular, of the economic aspects of the transition from subsistence to commercial agriculture.

The Structure of Agrarian Systems in the Developing World

Two Kinds of World Agriculture

When we look at the state of contemporary agriculture in most poor countries, we realize the enormity of the task that lies ahead. A brief comparison between agricultural productivity in the developed nations and the least developed nations makes this clear. World agriculture, in fact, comprises two distinct types of farming: (1) the highly efficient agriculture of the developed countries, where substantial productive capacity and high output per worker permit a very small number of farmers to feed entire nations, and (2) the inefficient and low-productivity agriculture of developing countries, where in many instances the agricultural sector can barely sustain the farm population, let alone the burgeoning urban population, even at a minimum level of subsistence.[5] Between these extremes, a steadily growing number of developing regions, such as the Punjab in India, newly cultivated areas of the Brazilian southwest, and many export-oriented sectors in Latin America and Asia, have been achieving much higher productivity levels and growth. Recently, advances in biotechnology are beginning to have an impact. Although controversial, biotechnology has the potential to launch a new phase of the green revolution.

Nevertheless, the gap between the two types of agriculture is immense. This is best illustrated by the disparities in labor productivity. In 1960, the agricultural population of the developed nations was about 115 million people, who produced a total output of $78 billion, or about $680 per capita. In contrast, the per capita product of the agricultural population in the underdeveloped countries in 1960 was only $52. In other words, agricultural labor productivity in developed countries was more than 13 times that in the less developed countries. By 2000, this **productivity gap** had widened to more than 50 to 1. For example, in low-income countries, the value added per agricultural worker in 1999 was $346, while in countries like the United Kingdom, Sweden, and Japan, it was $34,730, $34,285, and $30,620, respectively. Another manifestation of the productivity gap relates to land productivity. Table 9.2 shows variations in land productivity (measured as kilograms of grain harvested per hectare of agricultural land) between three developed countries (United Kingdom, Japan, and the United States) and nine developing countries. Despite the far smaller number of farm workers per hectare in the United Kingdom, its grain yield per hectare was 3 times that of India, 6 times that of Nigeria, and almost 12 times that of Sudan.

In the developed countries, there has been a steady growth of agricultural output since the mid-eighteenth century. This growth has been spurred by technological and biological improvements, which have resulted in ever-higher levels of labor and land productivity. The growth rate accelerated after the First World War and particularly after the Second World War. The end result is that fewer farmers are able to produce more food. This is especially the case in the United States, where in 2002 only 2% of the total workforce was engaged in agriculture, compared to more than 70% in the early nineteenth century. For example, in 1820, the American farmer could produce only four times his own consumption. A century

TABLE 9.2 Land Productivity in Developed and Developing Countries, 2002

Country	Average Grain Yield (kilograms per hectare)	Population (million)
United Kingdom	6,841	59
Japan	5,879	127
United States	5,830	288
Indonesia	4,141	212
Bangladesh	3,312	136
Brazil	3,081	174
Mexico	2,870	101
India	2,390	1,065
Russia	1,846	144
Nigeria	1,105	133
Congo (Dem. Rep.)	774	52
Sudan	600	33

Source: World Bank, *World Development Indicators, 2004* (Washington D.C.: World Bank, 2004), tabs. 1.1, 3.3. Copyright © 2004 by the World Bank. Reprinted with the permission of the World Bank via the Copyright Clearance Center.

later, in 1920, his productivity had doubled, and he could provide enough for eight persons. It took only another 32 years for this productivity to double again and then only 12 more years for it to double once more. By 2000, a single American farmer could provide enough food to feed nearly 100 people. Moreover, during the entire period, average farm incomes in North America rose steadily.[6]

The picture is different when we turn to the agricultural production experience of low-income nations. In many poor countries, agricultural production methods have changed relatively slowly over time. Later in this chapter, we will discover that much of this technological stagnation can be traced to the special circumstances of peasant agriculture, with its high risks and uncertain rewards. Rapid rural population growth has compounded the problem by causing great pressure to be exerted on existing resources. Where fertile land is scarce, especially throughout South and Southeast Asia but also in many parts of Latin America and Africa, rapid population growth has led to an increase in the number of people living on each unit of land. Given the same farming technology and the use of traditional nonlabor inputs (e.g., simple tools, animal power, traditional seeds), we know from the principle of diminishing returns that as more and more people are forced to work on a given piece of land, their marginal (and average) productivity will decline. The net result is a continuous deterioration in real living standards for rural peasants in some areas.

Peasant Agriculture in Latin America, Asia, and Africa

In many developing countries, various historical circumstances have led to a concentration of large areas of land in the hands of a small class of powerful landowners. This is especially true in Latin America and parts of the Asian subcontinent. In Africa, both historical circumstances and the availability of relatively more unused land have resulted in a different pattern and structure of agricultural activity.

A common characteristic of agriculture in all three regions, and for that matter in many developed countries, is the position of the family farm as the basic unit of production. As Raanan Weitz points out:

> For the vast number of farm families, whose members constitute the main agricultural work force, agriculture is not merely an occupation or a source of income; it is a way of life. This is particularly evident in traditional societies, where farmers are closely attached to their land and devote long, arduous days to its cultivation. Any change in farming methods perforce brings with it changes in the farmer's way of life. The introduction of biological and technical innovations must therefore be adapted not only to the natural and economic conditions, but perhaps even more to the attitudes, values, and abilities of the mass of producers, who must understand the suggested changes, must be willing to accept them, and must be capable of carrying them out.[7]

Thus in spite of the obvious differences between agricultural systems in Asia, Latin America, and Africa and among individual nations within each region, certain broad similarities enable us to make some generalizations and comparisons. In particular, **agrarian systems** in many parts of Asia and Latin America show more structural and institutional similarities than differences, and subsistence farmers in all three regions exhibit many of the same economic behavior patterns. We examine first the major features of agricultural systems in Latin America and Asia.

Latin America and Asia: Similarities and Differences Although Latin America and Asia have very different heritages and cultures, peasant life in impoverished areas of these two regions is in many ways similar. Francis Foland has succinctly described these similar features:

> Both the Latin American and Asian peasant is a rural cultivator whose prime concern is survival. Subsistence defines his concept of life. He may strive to obtain his and his family's minimal needs by tilling an inadequate piece of land which is his own or, more often, which is rented from or pawned to a landlord or moneylender, or by selling his labour for substandard wages to a commercial agricultural enterprise. Profits which might come to him through the fortunes of weather or market are windfalls, not preconceived goals. Debt rather than profit is his normal fate, and therefore, his farming techniques are rationally scaled to his level of disposable capital: human and animal power rather than mechanized equipment; excrement rather than chemical fertilizers; traditional crops and seeds rather than experimental cultivation.
>
> No effective social security, unemployment insurance, or minimum wage law ease his plight. His every decision and act impinge directly upon his struggle for physical survival. In countries with a high proportion of peasantry, traditional food crops which a rural family can itself convert readily into the daily fare for its grain- or tuber-based diet dominate the agriculture; corn in Mexico, rice in Indonesia, mandioca in Brazil, soybeans in China.[8]

Although the day-to-day struggle for survival permeates the lives and attitudes of peasants in both Latin America and Asia (and also Africa, although the rural structure and institutions are considerably different), the nature of their agrarian existence differs markedly. In Latin America, the peasants' plight is rooted in the *latifundio-minifundio* system (to be explained shortly). In Asia, it lies primarily in fragmented and heavily congested dwarf parcels of land. As Table 9.3 shows, the average farm size in Latin America is far larger than in Asia; in all the Asian countries surveyed, average operation farm size was under 4 hectares, with farm size in Indonesia just 1.1 hectares. In contrast, average-operation farm size ranged from 16.9 to 214.1 hectares in the Latin American countries surveyed. Nevertheless, a substantial number of farms in Latin America consisted of less than 5 hectares, including 36.8% of farms in Brazil and 78.0% of farms in Peru. This is possible because of the huge farmlands controlled by the largest farms in Latin America.

Just as we can draw income Lorenz curves from data on the distribution of income, we can draw land Lorenz curves from data on the distribution of farmholdings among farmers. Figure 9.2 shows representative land Lorenz curves for two highly equal agrarian systems (Japan and Taiwan), two highly unequal systems (Brazil and Colombia), and three agrarian systems of intermediate inequality (Mexico, India, and Pakistan). The *x*-axis reports the proportion of total holdings, and the *y*-axis reports the proportion of total area. A land Gini may be calculated in a manner analogous to that of the income Gini: It is the ratio of the area between the land Lorenz curve and the 45-degree line, and the whole triangle. Table 9.3 presents land Ginis for representative countries in Asia and Latin America.

The *Latifundio-Minifundio* Pattern and Resource Underutilization in Latin America   In Latin America, as in Asia and Africa, agrarian structures are not only part of the production system but also a basic feature of the entire economic, social, and political organization of rural life. The agrarian structure that has prevailed in Latin America since colonial times and has provided much of the region with its social organization is the pattern of agricultural dualism known as *latifundio-minifundio*.[9] Basically, **latifundios** are very large landholdings. They are defined in Latin America as farms large enough to provide employment for more than 12 people, though some employ thousands. In contrast, **minifundios** are the smallest farms. They are defined as farms too small to provide employment for a single family (two workers) with the typical incomes, markets, and levels of technology and capital prevailing in each country or region.

According to the FAO, 1.3% of landowners in Latin America hold 71.6% of the land under cultivation. If we exclude countries that have carried out drastic land reforms during the last century (Mexico, Bolivia, and Cuba), Latin America's agrarian structure seems to follow a uniform pattern. This pattern is basically one in which a small number of *latifundios* control a large proportion of the agricultural land while a vast number of *minifundios* must scratch out a survival existence on a meager fraction of the occupied land.

Table 9.4 provides a dramatic picture of this unequal distribution of landholdings in seven Latin American countries during the late 1960s. In no case did *minifundios*, which accounted for up to 90% of the farms, occupy more than 17% of the total agricultural land. In countries with dense indigenous populations like Ecuador, Guatemala, and Peru, *minifundios* were particularly widespread. In all countries, the *latifundios* made up less than 7% of all farms, yet they occupied as much as 82% of the agricultural land. The average size of the *latifundios* in Argentina was 270 times that of the *minifundios* in Guatemala, and the *latifundio* was often as much as 1,732 times the size of the *minifundio*. More recent data on

TABLE 9-3   Distribution of Farms and Farmland by Operational Farm Size and Land Tenure Status in Selected Developing Countries in Asia and Latin America

Country	Average Operational Farm Size (hectare)	Percentage of Farms and Farmland				Gini Coefficient of Land Concentration	Percentage of Tenanted Area in Total Farmland		Percentage of Share Tenancy in Tenanted Land[b]
		Below 5 Hectares		Above 50 Hectares			Pure Tenancy	Total[a]	
		Farms	Area	Farms	Area				
Asia									
Bangladesh	1.6	90.6	67.6	n.a.	n.a.	0.42	n.a	20.9	91.0
India	2.3	88.7	46.7	0.1	3.7	0.62	2.4	8.5	48.0
Indonesia	1.1	97.9	68.7	0[c]	13.6	0.56	2.1	23.6	60.0
Nepal	1.0	97.2	72.1	0[c]	0.8	0.56	1.5	13.2	48.3
Philippines	3.6	84.8	47.8	0.2	13.9	0.51	21.4	32.8	79.3
Thailand	3.7	72.3	39.4	0	0.9	0.45	6.0	15.5	29.0
Latin America									
Brazil	59.7	36.8	1.3	16.3	84.6	0.84	6.1	10.2	n.a.
Costa Rica	38.1	48.9	1.9	14.5	79.7	0.82	1.2	9.0	9.4
Colombia	26.3	59.6	3.7	8.4	77.7	0.86	5.3	11.5	49.4
Peru	16.9	78.0	8.9	1.9	79.1	0.91	4.5	13.6	0[c]
Uruguay	214.1	14.3	0.2	37.6	95.8	0.82	19.1	46.3	4.7
Venezuela	91.9	43.8	0.9	13.6	92.5	0.91	4.5	2.4	n.a.

Source: Kejiiro Otsuka, Hiroyuki Chuma, and Yujiro Hayami, "Land and labor contracts in agrarian economies: Theories and facts," *Journal of Economic Literature* 30 (1992): 1972. Reprinted with the permission of the American Economic Association.

[a] Area in pure tenant farms plus area in owner-as-tenant farms.

[b] Percent in area of pure tenant farms, except percent in total tenanted area for Bangladesh.

[c] Less than 0.05%.

n.a. = not available.

FIGURE 9.2 Lorenz Curves of Agricultural Land Distribution by Operational Holdings

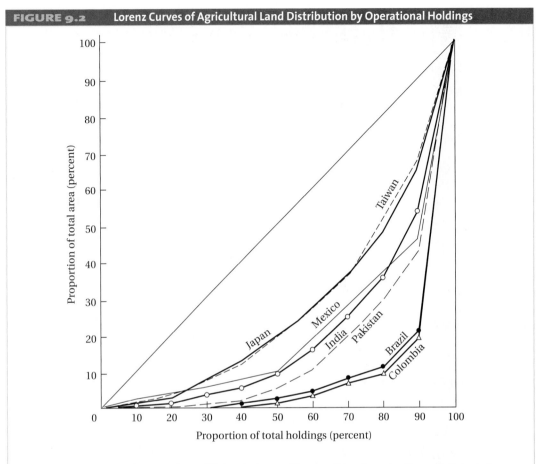

Source: Bruce F. Johnston and Peter Kilby, *Agriculture and Structural Transformation: Economic Strategies in Late-Developing Countries* (London: Oxford University Press, 1975), tab.1.2. Reprinted with permission.

land distribution in Latin America underline the continuing gross inequality in holdings. Using Gini coefficients to measure the degree of land concentration, as seen in Table 9.3, researchers report that the coefficient for Colombia is 0.86, for Brazil 0.84, for Costa Rica 0.82, for Uruguay 0.82, for Peru 0.91, and for Venezuela 0.91. Other countries are even more unequal; the Gini for Paraguay is an almost perfectly unequal 0.94.[10] These are by far the highest regional Gini coefficients in the world, and they dramatically reflect the degree of land ownership inequality (and thus, in part, income inequality) throughout Latin America.

But *latifundios* and *minifundios* do not constitute the entire gamut of Latin American agricultural holdings. A considerable amount of production is also earned on **family farms** and **medium-size farms**. The former provide work for

TABLE 9.4   *Minifundios* and *Latifundios* in the Agrarian Structure of Selected Latin American Countries (percent)

Country	Minifundios		Latifundios	
	Farms	Occupied Land	Farms	Occupied Land
Argentina	43.2	3.4	0.8	36.9
Brazil	22.5	0.5	4.7	59.5
Chile	36.9	0.2	6.9	81.3
Colombia	64.0	4.9	1.3	49.5
Ecuador	89.9	16.6	0.4	45.1
Guatemala	88.4	14.3	0.1	40.8
Peru	88.0	7.4	1.1	82.4

Source: Celso Furtado, *Economic Development in Latin America* (New York: Cambridge University Press, 1970), p. 54. Reprinted with permission.

two to four people (recall that the *minifundio* could provide work for fewer than two people), and the latter, also sometimes known as *multifamily farms,* employ 4 to 12 workers (just below the *latifundio*). In Venezuela, Brazil, and Uruguay, these intermediate farm organizations account for almost 50% of total agricultural output and employ similar proportions of agricultural labor. These farms use a more efficient balance between labor and land, and studies show they have a much higher total factor productivity than either *latifundios* or *minifundios,* as the law of diminishing returns would suggest.

The economic and social ramifications of heavy land concentration in the hands of a few large landowners are compounded by the relative inefficiency of *latifundios* in comparison with other Latin American farm organizations. Some economists have assumed that large farms (or firms) use productive resources more efficiently than small ones on the grounds that large enterprises can take advantage of economies of large-scale production and thereby lower costs. In terms of agriculture, the efficient utilization of large tractors and combine harvesters requires large tracts of land—otherwise this capital equipment will be grossly underutilized. Evidence from a wide range of developing countries, however, clearly demonstrates that small farms are more efficient (lower-cost) producers of most agricultural commodities.[11] For example, *minifundios* in Argentina, Brazil, and Chile yield more than twice the value of output per hectare under cultivation than the *latifundios* and more than 10 times the value per hectare of total farmland.[12] Moreover, a 1990s land survey in Brazil showed that small farms of under 10 hectares had production of $85 per hectare, while the largest farms, in excess of 500 hectares, had a gross output of only $2 per hectare. These findings do not contradict the theory that most large farms in developed countries are lower-cost producers than small family farms. Rather, the explanation lies in the poor utilization of productive farm resources in developing nations—especially land resources on *latifundios* in Latin America. In terms of farm yields per unit of land actually under cultivation, the *latifundios* of Argentina, Brazil, Chile, Colombia, and Guatemala were all below not only the *minifundios* but also the medium-size farms.[13] Moreover, in Brazil it has been estimated that the *latifundios*, with an average area 31.6 times larger than that of the family farm, invest only 11 times as much. A considerable portion of the arable *latifundio* land is thus underutilized. The net result is that total factor productivity on family farms was twice as high (and, therefore, unit costs half as high) as on the large *latifundio* tracts of land. It follows from this inverse relation between productivity and farm size that a redistribution of these large unused arable lands to family and medium-size farms would probably raise national agricultural output and productivity, provided that basic support such as training and access to credit and markets is made available.

A major explanation for the relative economic inefficiency of farming the fertile land on the *latifundios* in comparison with *minifundios* is simply that the wealthy landowners often value these holdings not for their potential contributions to national agricultural output but rather for the considerable power and prestige that they bring. (And as will be seen, this problem is not unique to Latin America.) Much of the land is left idle or farmed less intensively than *minifundios*. Also, *latifundio* **transaction costs**, especially the cost of supervising hired labor, are much higher than the low effective cost of using family labor on peasant farms. It follows that raising agricultural production and improving the efficiency of Latin American agrarian systems in particular will require much more than direct economic policies that lead to the provision of better seeds, more fertilizer, less distorted factor prices, higher output prices, and improved marketing facilities. It will also require a reorganization of rural social and institutional structures to provide Latin American peasants, who now constitute almost 70% of the rural population, a real opportunity to lift themselves out of their present state of economic subsistence and social subservience.

Although many *minifundio* owners remain in poverty and many *latifundios* continue to operate well below their productivity potential, a more dynamic sector is emerging. For example, Brazil is now the fourth-largest soybean exporter, as a growing number of efficient farms develops in the southwest. Chile has dynamic nontraditional agriculture export industries, and some parts of Mexico have made substantial progress since NAFTA was initiated.[14]

Fragmentation and Subdivision of Peasant Land in Asia If the major agrarian problem of Latin America can be identified as too much land under the control of too few people, the basic problem in Asia is one of too many people crowded onto too little land. For example, the per capita availability of arable land in 1994 in India, China, and Bangladesh was 0.19, 0.08, and 0.07 hectares, respectively. Central Java in Indonesia is an extreme example of the pressure of population on limited land that characterizes the Asian agrarian scene. It has the dubious distinction of possessing the world's highest population density—over 1,500 persons per square kilometer.[15] The land is distributed more equally in Asia than in Latin America but still with substantial levels of inequality. As seen in Table 9.3, the Gini coefficients for land distribution in Asia range from 0.42 in Bangladesh and 0.45 in Thailand to 0.62 in India and 0.56 in Indonesia and Nepal.

Throughout much of the twentieth century, at least until its last two decades, rural conditions in Asia deteriorated. Gunnar Myrdal identified three major interrelated forces that molded the traditional pattern of land ownership into its present fragmented condition: (1) the intervention of European rule, (2) the progressive introduction of monetized transactions and the rise in power of the moneylender, and (3) the rapid growth of Asian populations.[16]

The traditional Asian agrarian structure before European colonization was organized around the village. Local chiefs and peasant families each provided goods and services—produce and labor from the peasants to the chief in return for protection, rights to use community land, and the provision of public services. Decisions on the allocation, disposition, and use of the village's most valuable resource, land, belonged to the tribe or community, either as a body or through its chief. Land could be redistributed among village members as a result of either population increase or natural calamities such as drought, flood, famine, war, or disease. Within the community, families had a basic right to cultivate land for their own use, and they could be evicted from their land only after a decision by the whole village.

The arrival of the Europeans (mainly the British, French, and Dutch) led to major changes in the traditional agrarian structure, some of which had already begun. As Myrdal points out, "Colonial rule acted as an important catalyst to change, both directly through its effects on property rights and indirectly through its effects on the pace of monetization of the indigenous economy and on the growth of population."[17] In the area of property rights, European land tenure systems of private property ownership were both encouraged and reinforced by law. One of the major social consequences of the imposition of these systems was, as Myrdal explains, the

> breakdown of much of the earlier cohesion of village life with its often elaborate, though informal, structure of rights and obligations. The landlord was given unrestricted rights to dispose of the land and to raise the tribute from its customary level to whatever amount he was able to extract. He was usually relieved of the obligation to supply security and public amenities because these functions were taken over by the government. Thus his status was transformed from that of a tribute receiver with responsibilities to the community to that of an absolute owner unencumbered by obligations toward the peasants and the public, other than the payment of land taxes.[18]

Contemporary **landlords** in India and Pakistan are able to avoid much of the taxation on income derived from their ownership of land. Today the typical landlord in South Asia is an absentee owner who lives in the town and turns over the working of the land to **sharecroppers** and **tenant farmers**. In many respects, therefore, his position of power in the economic, political, and social structure of the rural community is analogous to that of the Latin American *patrón*. There is a difference in that the former is an absentee owner, whereas the latter often lives on his *latifundio*. But the efficiency and productivity implications are similar.

Sharecropping is widespread in both Asia and Latin America but more pervasive in Asia. It has been estimated that of all tenanted land, some 84.5% is sharecropped in Asia while only 16.1% is sharecropped in Latin America. Moreover, this institution is almost unknown in Africa, where farms operated under tribal or communal tenure forms continue to be dominant.[19] For example, as shown in

Table 9.3, about 48% of all tenanted land is sharecropped in India, 60% in Indonesia, and 79% in the Philippines. Though common in Colombia, sharecropping is unusual elsewhere in Latin America; for example, it is almost unheard of in Peru.

The creation of individual titles to land made possible the rise to power of another dubious agent of change in Asian rural socioeconomic structures, the **moneylender**. Once private property came into effect, land became a negotiable asset that could be offered by peasants as security for loans and, in the case of default, could be forfeited and transferred to the often unscrupulous moneylender. At the same time, Asian agriculture was being transformed from a subsistence to a commercial orientation, both as a result of rising local demand in new towns and, more important, in response to external food demands of colonial European powers. With this transition from subsistence to commercial production, the role of the moneylender changed drastically. In the subsistence economy, his activities had been restricted to supplying the peasant with money to tide him over a crop failure or to cover extraordinary ceremonial expenditures such as family weddings or funerals. Most of these loans were paid in kind (in the form of food) at very high rates of interest. With the development of commercial farming, however, the peasants' cash needs grew significantly. Money was needed for seeds, fertilizer, and other inputs. It was also needed to cover his food requirements if he shifted to the production of cash crops such as tea, rubber, or jute. Often moneylenders were more interested in acquiring peasant lands as a result of loan defaults than they were in extracting high rates of interest. By charging exorbitant interest rates or inducing peasants to secure larger credits than they could manage, moneylenders were often able to drive the peasants off their land. They could then reap the profits of land speculation by selling this farmland to rich and acquisitive landlords. Largely as a consequence of the moneylenders' influence, Asian peasant cultivators have seen their economic status deteriorate steadily over time.[20]

The final major force altering the traditional agrarian structure in Asia has been the rapid rate of population growth. Myrdal notes in reference to the population phenomenon that

> when and where expansion in the cultivated area was a feasible alternative—whether for physical, technical, social, economic, or institutional reasons—population growth was reflected, in the first instance, in the cumulative subdivision and fragmentation of the acreages already under cultivation. Later this process, in combination with the emergence of private property and the rise of commercial agriculture and moneylending, often contributed to the rise of large landowners, the demise of small peasant proprietors, and the increase of the landless.[21]

The ultimate impoverishment of the peasantry was the inevitable consequence of this process of fragmentation, economic vulnerability, and loss of land to rich and powerful landlords.

To understand the deterioration of rural conditions in some Asian countries during the twentieth century, consider the cases of India, Indonesia, and the Philippines. In 1901, there were 286 million Indians; a century later, there were $3\frac{1}{2}$ times that number. The Indonesian population grew from 28.4 million in 1900 to 210 million in 2000. The population of central Luzon in the Philippines has increased more than tenfold from its level of 1 million in 1903. In each case, severe fragmentation of landholdings inevitably followed, so that today average peasant holdings in many areas of these countries are less than 1 hectare.

As these holdings shrink even further, production falls below the subsistence level, and chronic poverty becomes a way of life. Peasants are forced to borrow even more from the moneylender at interest rates ranging from 50% to 200%. Most cannot repay these loans. They are then compelled to sell their land and become tenants with large debts. Because land is scarce, they are forced to pay high rents. If they are sharecroppers, they typically have to give the landlord 50% to 80% of their crop. And because labor is abundant, wages are extremely low. Peasants thus get trapped in a vise of chronic poverty from which, in the absence of major rural reconstruction and reform, there is no escape. Like their Latin American counterparts, many rural Asians are gradually being transformed from small proprietors to tenant farmers and sharecroppers, then landless rural laborers, then jobless vagrants, and finally migrant slum dwellers on the fringes of modern urban areas.[22] Not only have their levels of living deteriorated, but their sense of self-esteem and freedom from exploitation, which may previously have been relatively high despite low incomes, has also vanished. These many hundreds of millions of people in Asia and Latin America have therefore been largely bypassed by whatever economic development and social progress the region has experienced. Sociologist Mead Cain, who returned after a two-year absence to a small rural village, Char Gopalpur, in Bangladesh, where he had done earlier research, vividly depicts the precarious existence of a typical peasant farmer's life in South Asia.

> This past year has indeed been a poor one economically for Bangladesh, with a succession of poor harvests. . . . The tranquillity of the village setting hides an enduring, harsh existence, and a number of persistent degenerative social processes. The recent drought, bringing with it a series of poor harvests, accelerated the process of economic differentiation; the process by which marginal farmers lose their land and eventually become landless, while at the same time, larger farmers accumulate land. A typical example from the village will illustrate the process of economic differentiation and the kinds of effects generated among marginal farmers by this past year's drought. The case is that of Amir Hossain, a man who is about 50 years old, who owns slightly less than two acres of arable land, and who lives with his wife, one married son, the son's wife, and several unmarried children. In a good year, the produce from the two acres will just about provide for the consumption needs of Amir's family. This past year, because of poor harvests, Amir's son had to work as an agricultural wage laborer for a period. In addition, Amir took a loan from a local bank in order to purchase paddy for consumption; he also used part of the loan to purchase paddy, have his wife husk paddy, and then resell the processed rice for a profit. The distress of Amir and his family was compounded when a bull that he had purchased for 900 taka in January contracted a disease and died in April of this year. The combination of the poor harvest, the untimely death of the bull, and the inadequacy of the various supplementary sources of income that the family collectively exploited forced Amir to sell one tenth of an acre of land.
>
> The experience of Amir Hossain and his family is significant because it is not at all unusual among farmers with similar or smaller land holdings. With as little land as they own, small differences in yield can force such families into debt or the distress sale of land. The case also illustrates the importance of luck and the ominous uncertainty of the environ-

ment in which the villagers live. The death of the bull was unrelated to the drought. The value of the bull was 900 taka and the value of the land sold was 1,300 taka. It is unlikely that the family would have been forced to sell the land if the bull had not died. Even in a normal or relatively good agricultural year, the individual experience of particular farmers will vary widely. The distribution among farmers of good and bad experiences in a given year is largely random. However, the ability of families to absorb dips in fortune depends very much on the size of a family's land holdings and on the size and composition of the family. Other things [being] equal, those with smaller holdings and with certain demographic characteristics (e.g., few able-bodied males) are less resilient and are more at risk of enduring loss in times of hardship.[23]

Subsistence Agriculture and Extensive Cultivation in Africa As in Asia and Latin America, **subsistence farming** on small plots of land is the way of life for the vast majority of African people. However, the organization and structure of African agricultural systems differ markedly from those found in contemporary Asia or Latin America. Except in former colonial settlement areas like White Highlands of Kenya and some of the large sugar, cocoa, and coffee plantations of East and West Africa, the great majority of farm families in tropical Africa still plan their output primarily for their own subsistence. Since the basic variable input in African agriculture is farm family and village labor, African agriculture systems are dominated by three major characteristics: (1) the importance of subsistence farming in the village community; (2) the existence of some (though rapidly diminishing) land in excess of immediate requirements, which permits a general practice of shifting cultivation and reduces the value of land ownership as an instrument of economic and political power; and (3) the rights of each family (both nuclear and extended) in a village to have access to land and water in the immediate territorial vicinity, excluding from such access use by families that do not belong to the community even though they may be of the same tribe.

The low-productivity subsistence farming characteristic of most traditional African agriculture results from a combination of three historical forces restricting the growth of output:

1. In spite of the existence of some unused and potentially cultivable land, only small areas can be planted and weeded by the farm family at a time when it uses only traditional tools such as the short-handled hoe, the ax, and the long-handled knife or *panga*. In some countries, use of animals is impossible because of the notorious tsetse fly or a lack of fodder in the long dry seasons, and traditional farming practices must rely primarily on the application of human labor to small parcels of land.

2. Given the limited amount of land that a farm family can cultivate in the context of a traditional technology and the use of primitive tools, these small areas tend to be intensively cultivated. As a result, they are subject to rapidly diminishing returns to increased labor inputs. In such conditions, **shifting cultivation** is the most economic method of using limited supplies of labor on extensive tracts of land. Under shifting cultivation, once the minerals are drawn out of the soil as a result of numerous croppings, new land is cleared, and the

process of planting and weeding is repeated. In the meantime, formerly cropped land is allowed to recover fertility until it can be used again. Under such a process, manure and chemical fertilizers are unnecessary, although in most African villages some form of manure (mostly animal waste) is applied to nearby plots that are intensively cultivated in order to extend their period of fertility.

3. Labor is scarce during the busiest part of the growing season, planting and weeding times. At other times, much of the labor is underemployed. Because the time of planting is determined by the onset of the rains and because much of Africa experiences only one extended rainy season, the demand for workers during the early weeks of this rainy season usually exceeds all available rural labor supplies.

The net result of these three forces had been a relatively constant level of agricultural total output and labor productivity throughout much of Africa. As long as population size remained relatively stable, this historical pattern of low productivity and shifting cultivation enabled most African tribes to meet their subsistence food requirements. But the feasibility of shifting cultivation has now broken down as population densities increase. It has largely been replaced by sedentary cultivation on small owner-occupied plots. As a result, the need for other nonhuman productive inputs and new technologies grows, especially in the more densely populated agricultural regions of Kenya, Nigeria, Ghana, and Uganda. Moreover, with the growth of towns, the penetration of the monetary economy, soil erosion and deforestation of marginal lands, and the introduction of land taxes, pure subsistence-agricultural practices are no longer viable. Mixed and modern commercial farming must appear, as indeed they have in parts of sub-Saharan Africa.

Of all the major regions of the world, Africa has suffered the most from its inability to expand food production at a sufficient pace to keep up with its rapid population growth.[24] As a result of declining production, African per capita food consumption fell dramatically during the 1980s and 1990s while dependence on imports—particularly wheat and rice—increased.[25]

Conclusions

Although traditional African communal social systems differ markedly from agrarian structures prevalent throughout much of Asia and Latin America, the contemporary economic status of most poor farmers is not very different among the three regions. Achieving subsistence is still the major objective of peasant agriculture. Even though the small African farmer once had more room in which to maneuver than his typical Asian or Latin American counterpart, the rapid growth of rural populations throughout sub-Saharan Africa has led to a similar fragmentation of smallholder agriculture. Unless low-productivity peasant agriculture can be transformed rapidly into higher-productivity farming in Asia and Latin America (primarily through judicious land reform accompanied by concomitant structural changes in socioeconomic institutions) and Africa (basically through improved farming practices and greater price incentives), the hundreds of millions of impoverished and increasingly landless rural dwellers face an even more precarious existence in the years ahead.

The Important Role of Women

A major and often overlooked feature of LDC agrarian systems, particularly in Africa and Asia, is the crucial role played by women in agricultural production.[26] In Africa, where subsistence farming is predominant and shifting cultivation remains important, nearly all tasks associated with subsistence food production are performed by women. Although men who remain home generally perform the initial task of cutting trees and bushes on a potentially cultivable plot of land, women are responsible for all subsequent operations, including removing and burning felled trees, sowing or planting the plot, weeding, harvesting, and preparing the crop for storage or immediate consumption. In her pioneering work on women and development, Ester Boserup examined many studies on African women's participation in agriculture and found that in nearly all cases recorded, women did most of the agricultural work. In some cases, they were found to do around 70% and in one case nearly 80% of the total. Typically, these tasks are performed only with the most primitive tools and require many days of long, hard labor simply to produce enough output to meet the family's subsistence requirements, while the men often attempt to generate cash income through work on nearby plantations or in the cities.[27]

Women provide an important source of labor for cash crop production, cultivate food for household consumption, raise and market livestock, generate additional income through cottage industries, collect firewood and water, and perform household chores, including the processing and cooking of foods. Due to the time-consuming nature of their diverse responsibilities, women tend to work longer hours than their male counterparts. Studies concerning the allocation of women's time among different activities have greatly increased recognition of the importance of rural women's economic contribution. It has become clear that since women produce a large share of agricultural output, successful agricultural reform will require raising women's productivity.

The diversity of women's duties makes it difficult to determine their share of agricultural production, much less place an economic value on their work. However, current estimates underscore the importance of women's agricultural labor. It is estimated that in addition to work within the household, women provide 60% to 80% of agricultural labor in Africa and Asia and about 40% in Latin America. Much of this work, however, is statistically "invisible" in that women often receive no payment for the work they perform.

Women make an important contribution to the agricultural economy through the labor they supply in the cultivation of **cash crops**. Though the production and profits from commercial crops are generally controlled by men, women are usually responsible for the strenuous jobs of weeding and transplanting. As population density increases and land becomes more fragmented, the length of time that women must spend walking to and from the fields increases, often in very hot climates that make strenuous work exceedingly difficult. In addition to commercial crops, women frequently cultivate small vegetable gardens that provide food for domestic consumption. Though the cash value of produce from these gardens may be small, it often represents an important component of the total resources available to women.

Women's work in the low-income household involves a range of demanding tasks including processing and pounding raw grains, tending livestock, cooking, and caring for children. Collecting increasingly scarce firewood and water from distant sources may add several hours to the workday. To raise additional income, it is common for women to engage in household production of goods for sale in village markets. These items are specific to each region, but a few examples are homemade beer, processed foods, handicrafts, and textiles.

Perhaps the most important role of women is providing food security for the household. This is accomplished through the supplementation of household earnings, diversification of household income sources, and raising of livestock to augment household assets. The production of vegetables for household consumption helps insulate households from dramatic swings in food prices and reduces cash outlays for the purchase of household necessities during periods of slack income. Women's investments in revenue-generating projects and livestock are crucial to stabilizing household income, especially in female-headed households, where resource constraints are the most severe.

However, financial investments are inherently risky, and the poorer the household, the more averse its members are to taking any kind of risk. When credit and resources are unavailable, reducing the variability of household earnings generally entails choosing less efficient methods of production and thus lower income. This trade-off occurs most frequently in female-headed households, where resource constraints are greatest. Thus as a consequence of their restricted range of choices, women tend to retain traditional modes of economic activity. The upshot is that their productivity has stagnated while that of men has continued to improve.

Where the structure of agriculture is becoming more commercialized, women's roles and thus their economic status are changing. In many developing regions, women are still unremunerated for the long hours they contribute to the tending of commercial crops. As revenue-generating cash cropping rises in importance, the proportion of resources controlled by women tends to diminish. This is largely due to the fact that household resources, such as land and inputs, are transferred away from women's crops in order to promote the production of cash crops.

Government extension programs that provide resources exclusively to men tend to exacerbate existing disparities between men's and women's access to resources. If credit is provided solely or preferentially to men for the purpose of cash cropping, commercial production will increase at the expense of women's vegetable gardens. Since homegrown vegetables must be replaced by purchased substitutes, significant increases in a male spouse's cash contribution are necessary to offset a woman's losses. If the market price of vegetables increases markedly (there are now fewer producers) and the increase in the husband's contribution is not sufficient to compensate for the increased need for cash, the welfare of the woman and her children will decline.

This fall in the well-being of household members is due to the fact that a considerably higher proportion of women's income than men's is used for nutrition and basic necessities. Thus if men's incomes rise at the expense of women's resources, as many studies have indicated, an increase in household income will not necessarily lead to improvements in health and nutrition. Changes in land use that increase household income but reduce women's economic status can be detrimental to the welfare of both women and children. Consequently, it is important that the design of government extension programs reflect the interests of all household members.

Yet government-sponsored programs continue to exclude women, often because women lack collateral for loans or are barred by law from owning property or conducting financial transactions without their husband's permission. Agricultural inputs and training are rarely provided to female applicants. Even efforts to reduce poverty through land reforms have been found to reduce female income and economic status because they distribute land titles only to male heads of household. Cultural and social barriers to women's integration into agricultural programs remain strong because in many countries, women's income is perceived as a threat to men's authority. While men are taught new agricultural techniques to increase their productivity, women, if involved at all, are trained to perform low-productivity tasks that are considered compatible with their traditional roles, such as sewing, cooking, or basic hygiene. Women's components of development projects are frequently little more than welfare programs that fail to improve economic well-being. Furthermore, these projects tend to depend on the unpaid work of women, while men are remunerated for their efforts.

Though efforts to increase the income of women by providing direct access to credit and inputs have experienced considerable success, programs that work indirectly with women have frequently fallen short of their stated goals. Studies have found that projects are most likely to elicit the cooperation of women when resources are placed directly under their control. Clearly, projects that depend on the unremunerated labor of women are likely to obtain only minimal support. Adoption of new crops and technologies will be more effective where patterns of production are consistent with the interests of female household members. Because the active participation of women is critical to agricultural prosperity, policy design should ensure that women benefit equally from development efforts.

The Economics of Agricultural Development: Transition from Peasant Subsistence to Specialized Commercial Farming

For expository convenience, we can identify three broad stages in the evolution of agricultural production.[28] The first and most primitive is the pure, low-productivity, mostly subsistence-level peasant farm. The second stage is what might be called diversified or mixed family agriculture, where part of the produce is grown for consumption and part for sale to the commercial sector. The third stage represents the modern farm, exclusively engaged in high-productivity specialized agriculture geared to the commercial market.

Agricultural modernization in mixed-market developing economies may be described in terms of the gradual but sustained transition from subsistence to diversified and specialized production. But such a transition involves much more than reorganizing the structure of the farm economy or applying new agricultural technologies. We have seen that in most traditional societies, agriculture is not just an economic activity; it is a way of life. Any government attempting to transform its traditional agriculture must recognize that in addition to adapting the farm structure to meet the demand for increased production, profound changes affecting the entire social, political, and institutional structure of rural societies will often be necessary. Without such changes, agricultural development will either never get started or, more likely, simply widen the already sizable gap between the few wealthy large landholders and the masses of impoverished tenant farmers, smallholders, and landless laborers.

Before analyzing the economics of agricultural and rural development, therefore, we need to understand how the agricultural system of a developing nation tends to evolve over time from a predominately subsistence-level and small-scale peasant orientation to more diversified and larger extended-family operations and eventually to the dominance in total production of large-scale commercial enterprises.

Subsistence Farming: Risk Aversion, Uncertainty, and Survival

On the classic peasant subsistence farm, most output is produced for family consumption (although some may be sold or traded in local markets), and a few **staple foods** (usually including wheat, barley, sorghum, rice, or corn) are the chief sources of nutrition. Output and productivity are low, and only the simplest traditional methods and tools are used. Capital investment is minimal; land and labor are the principal factors of production. The law of diminishing returns is in operation as more labor is applied to shrinking (or shifting) parcels of land. The failure of the rains, the appropriation of his land, and the appearance of the moneylender to collect outstanding debts are the banes of the peasant's existence and cause him to fear for his survival. Labor is underemployed for most of the year, although workers may be fully occupied at seasonal peak periods such as planting and harvest. The peasant usually cultivates only as much land as his family can manage without the need for hired labor, although many peasant farmers intermittently employ one or two landless laborers. The environment is harsh and static. Technological limitations, rigid social institutions, and fragmented markets and communication networks between rural areas and urban centers tend to discourage higher levels of production. Any cash income that is generated comes mostly from nonfarm wage labor.[29]

Throughout much of the developing world, agriculture is still in this subsistence stage. But in spite of the relative backwardness of production technologies and the misguided convictions of some foreigners who attribute the peasants' resistance to change as a sign of incompetence or irrationality, the fact remains that given the static nature of the peasants' environment, the uncertainties that surround them, the need to meet minimum survival levels of output, and the rigid social institutions into which they are locked, most peasants behave in an economically rational manner when confronted with alternative opportunities. As one informed observer of peasant agricultural systems has noted:

> Despite the almost infinite variety of village-level institutions and processes to be found around the world, they have three common characteristics which are pertinent to change: 1, they have historically proven to be successful, i.e., the members have survived; 2, they are relatively static, at least the general pace of change is below that which is considered desirable today; and 3, attempts at change are frequently resisted, both because these institutions and processes have proven dependable and because the various elements constitute something akin to an ecological unity in the human realm.[30]

Some insight into the economics of subsistence agriculture is provided by the traditional two-factor neoclassical theory of production in which land (and perhaps capital) is fixed, labor is the only variable input, and profit is maximized. Specifically, the theory provides an economic rationale for the observed low productivity of traditional agriculture in the form of the law of diminishing marginal productivity.

Unfortunately, this theory does not satisfactorily explain why small-scale farmers are often resistant to technological innovation in farming techniques or to the introduction of new seeds or different cash crops. According to the standard theory, a rational income or profit-maximizing farm or firm will always choose a method of production that will increase output for a given cost (in this case, the available labor time) or lower costs for a given output level. But the theory is based on the crucial assumption that farmers possess "perfect knowledge" of all technological input-output relationships as well as current information about prevailing factor and product prices. This is the point at which the theory loses a good deal of its validity when applied to the environment of subsistence agriculture in much of Asia, Africa, and Latin America. Furthermore, when access to information is highly imperfect, the transaction costs of obtaining this information are usually high. Given price uncertainty, peasant farmers often face **price bands** (wide ranges) rather than a single input price. Along with limited access to credit and insurance, such an environment is not conducive to the type of behavior posited by neoclassical theory and goes a long way toward explaining the actual risk-averse behavior of peasant farmers, including their caution in the use of purchased inputs such as fertilizer.[31]

Subsistence agriculture is thus a highly risky and uncertain venture. It is made even more so by the fact that human lives are at stake. In regions where farms are extremely small and cultivation is dependent on the uncertainties of variable rainfall, average output will be low, and in poor years the peasant and his family will be exposed to the very real danger of starvation. In such circumstances, the main motivating force in the peasant's life may be the maximization not of income but rather of his family's chances of survival. Accordingly, when risk and uncertainty are high, a small farmer may be very reluctant to shift from a traditional technology and crop pattern that over the years he has come to know and understand to a new one that promises higher yields but may entail greater risks of crop failure.

FIGURE 9.3 **Small-Farmer Attitudes toward Risk: Why It Is Sometimes Rational to Resist Innovation and Change**

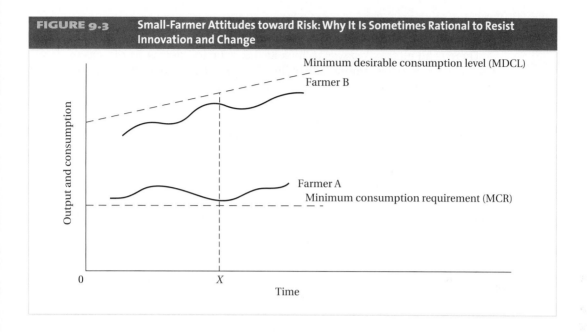

When sheer survival is at stake, it is more important to avoid a bad year (total crop failure) than to maximize the output in better years. Risk-avoiding peasant farmers are likely to prefer a technology of food production that combines a low *mean* per-hectare yield with low *variance* (fluctuations around the average) to alternative technologies and crops that may promise a higher mean yield but also present the risk of a greater variance.

Figure 9.3 provides a simple illustration of how attitudes toward risk among small farmers may militate against apparently economically justified innovations.[32] In the figure, levels of output and consumption are measured on the vertical axis and different points in time on the horizontal axis, and two straight lines are drawn. The lower horizontal line measures the minimum consumption requirements (MCR) necessary for the farm family's physical survival. This may be taken as the starvation minimum fixed by nature. Any output below this level would be catastrophic for the peasant and his family. The upper, positively sloped straight line represents the minimum level of food consumption that would be desirable given the prevailing cultural factors affecting village consumption standards. It is assumed that the minimum desirable consumption level (MDCL) rises over time to reflect rising expectations as traditional societies are opened up to external influences. The producer's attitude toward risk will be largely conditioned by his historical output performance relative to these two standards of reference.

Looking at Figure 9.3 we see that at time *X*, farmer A's output levels have been very close to the MCR. He is barely getting by and cannot take a chance of any crop failure. He will have a greater incentive to minimize risk than farmer B, whose output performance has been well above the minimum subsistence level and is close to the culturally determined MDCL. Farmer B will therefore be more likely to innovate and change than farmer A. The result may be that farmer A remains in a self-perpetuating poverty trap.[33]

There is an alternative way to look at risk-aversion decisions of peasant farmers. In Figure 9.4, two graphs portraying hypothetical probabilities for crop yields are depicted. The higher graph (technique A) shows a production technology with a lower mean crop yield (10) than that of technique B (12), shown by the lower graph. But it also has a lower variance around that mean yield than technique B. Clearly, the chances of starving are much greater with technique B, so risk-averse peasant farmers would naturally choose technique A, the one with the lower mean yield.[34]

Many programs to raise agricultural productivity among small farmers have suffered because of failure to provide adequate insurance (both financial credit and physical "buffer" stocks) against the risks of crop shortfalls, whether these risks are real or imagined. An understanding of the major role that risk and uncertainty play in the economics of subsistence agriculture would have prevented early and unfortunate characterizations of subsistence or traditional farmers as technologically backward, irrational producers with limited aspirations or just plain "lazy natives" as in the colonial stereotype. Moreover, in many parts of Asia and Latin America, a closer examination of why peasant farmers have apparently not responded to an "obvious" economic opportunity will often reveal that (1) the landlord secured all the gain, (2) the moneylender captured all the profits, (3) the government's "guaranteed" price was never paid, or (4) complementary inputs (fertilizers, pesticides, assured supplies of water, adequate nonusurious credit, etc.) were never made available.

We may conclude that peasant farmers do act rationally and are responsive to economic incentives and opportunities. Where innovation and change fail to occur, we should not assume that peasants are stupid, irrational, or conservative; instead, we should examine carefully the environment in which the small farmer operates to search for the particular institutional or commercial obstacles that may be blocking or frustrating constructive change.[35] Efforts to minimize risk and remove commercial and institutional obstacles to small-farmer innovation are therefore essential requirements of agricultural and rural development.

Sharecropping and Interlocking Factor Markets   The phenomenon of risk aversion among peasant farmers also helps explain the prevalence of sharecropping throughout much of Asia and Latin America.[36] Although different forms of relationships may arise between the owners of land and the people who work on them (e.g., the farmers could rent or act as wage laborers), sharecropping is widespread. Sharecropping occurs when a peasant farmer uses the landowner's farmland in exchange for a share of food output, such as half of the rice or wheat he grows. The landlord's share may vary from less than a third to more than two-thirds of output, depending on local labor availability and the other inputs (such as credit, seeds, and hoes) that the landlord provides.

The poor incentive structure of sharecropping lends itself to inefficiency. Alfred Marshall observed that the farmer was in effect paid only part, rather than all, of his marginal product and would rationally reduce work effort accordingly.[37] This effect can be seen graphically in Figure 9.5. Labor input is found along the x-axis,

FIGURE 9.4 **Crop Yield Probability Densities of Two Different Farming Techniques**

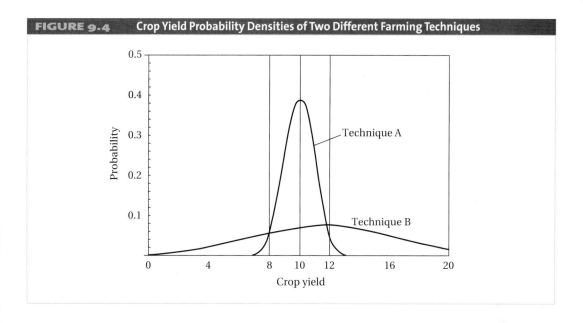

which may be interpreted as number of hours of work, or of total effort; output per unit of labor is found along the y-axis. A farmer who owned his own farm would work until his value marginal product of labor (VMP_L) was equal to his alternative wage, or opportunity cost of labor, w^A, and so would put in an efficient amount of labor effort L^F. However, a sharecropper receives only a fraction, γ, of his effort; for example, under 50–50 sharecropping, the sharecropper's share would be $\gamma = 0.5$. Thus the sharecropper would receive only γ of his value marginal product, or $\gamma \, VMP_L$. As a result, the sharecropper would have an incentive to put in an inefficiently low level of effort L^S, as seen in Figure 9.5.

This view was challenged in the 1960s by Steven Cheung, who argued that profit-maximizing landlords would establish contracts requiring adequate work effort from the tenant as well as stipulating each party's share of the output.[38] If, as Cheung argued, effort is not too difficult to monitor, then if one tenant failed to live up to his part of the bargain, he would be replaced by another tenant who was willing to work harder; as a result, sharecropping would be as efficient as any other contractual form. Cheung's theory is known as the *monitoring approach*, in contrast to the *Marshallian approach* to the analysis of sharecropping illustrated in Figure 9.5; Cheung argued that labor effort L^F would also obtain under sharecropping.

The monitoring approach was popular for two decades, and it was difficult to test because of endogeneity. For example, only low-productivity people may choose to enter into sharecropping contracts. In fact, some scholars believe that landlords may offer tenants an option of either sharecropping or pure rental contracts precisely because higher-ability people more often choose pure rental arrangements: High-ability farmers are able to get the full value of their high mar-

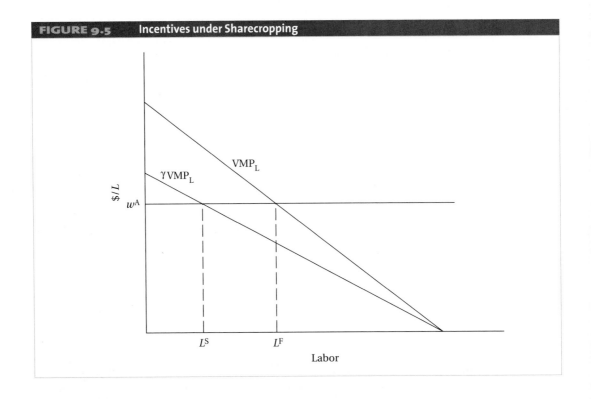

FIGURE 9.5   Incentives under Sharecropping

ginal product, while this is not as attractive to lower-ability farmers. If landlords are not sure which farmers have high ability, they may find out by observing which ones choose the pure rental contract. The motivation may be to enable landlords to squeeze more profits out of the renters, charging higher effective rents for pure rental contracts than for sharecropping contracts—but not *too* high or even high-ability farmers would choose sharecropping. This approach is known as the *screening hypothesis* of sharecropping.[39]

However, in a well-known study, Radwan Ali Shaban identified farmers who farmed plots that they owned and who also leased out additional farmland under a sharecropping contract. By comparing the *same* farmers' behavior under different contractual arrangements, Ali Shaban controlled for factors specific to individual farmers that cannot be easily observed. He found that farmers used fewer inputs and produced less output on the sharecropped land than on their own land, all else being equal. These results provide strong evidence that sharecropping is less efficient than farming one's own land, just as Marshall predicted.[40]

A final approach suggests that sharecropping is relatively efficient after all, in that it makes the best out of an inherently uncertain and risky situation for both parties.[41] If the landlord pays the tenant a straight wage, which would be efficient if the tenant always gave his full effort and it didn't cost the landlord anything to make sure of this, the tenant has every incentive to accept the money and not work hard. If the tenant pays a straight rent for the land, he faces the appalling risk that there will be a particularly lean year, such as a drought, and there will not be enough food left after the rent is paid to prevent starvation. Thus sharecropping represents a compromise between two types of risk: the risk to the landlord that the tenant will not do much work and the risk to the tenant that a fixed rent will in some years leave him no income. So even though sharecropping would be inefficient in a world of perfect certainty, in the real world, with high inequality, it is "as efficient as we can get." However, this arrangement is necessary only because of extreme inequality of land ownership. Farmers who own their own farms do not choose sharecropping contracts for themselves. As a result, the enormous efficiency loss, as seen in Figure 9.5, is not negated by this important explanation of why sharecropping arises.

More broadly, the economic and social framework in which sharecropping takes place is one of extraordinary social inequality and far-reaching market failure. When the peasant faces his landlord, he faces not only the individual whom he must persuade to rent him productive land but at the same time his prospective employer, his loan officer, and often his ultimate customer for any crops he wishes to sell. These are the conditions known as **interlocking factor markets**, and they provide the rural landlord with abundant sources of monopoly and monopsony power, making traditional rural economic and social organization hardly resistant to efforts at reform. The consequences of this have been explored with economic theory and with case studies of agrarian regions. Suppose that a well-meaning government puts a cap on the interest rates that the landlord can charge. The landlord may simply respond by lowering the wage, the tenant's share of the crop, or the price the landlord pays for any crops the tenant seeks to sell or by raising the implicit price of seeds and tools advanced to the tenant. Under plausible conditions—in particular, the availability of a perfectly elastic supply of tenants and the ability of the landlord to subdivide his land into as many plots as he chooses—the peasant is forced to the same *reservation utility level*, or next-best income opportunity, as before. One key feature of this analysis is that the peasant's effort per hectare increases with decreases in plot size. Interlocked-factor-market sharecropping does have the resource allocation advantage that it is in the landlord's interest to see to it that his sharecropper receives credit from the lowest-cost source. Attempting to regulate several of these interlocked markets at once in an uncertain economy will often aggravate inefficiency, if not leave most tenants unemployed as landlords switch to entirely different uses for their land. The analysis often concludes that nothing short of land reform will affect the tenant's welfare. We discuss the pros and cons of land reform later in the chapter.[42]

The Transition to Mixed and Diversified Farming

It is neither realistic nor necessarily desirable to think of instantly transforming a traditional agrarian system that has prevailed for many generations into a highly specialized commercial farming system. Attempts to introduce cash crops indiscriminately in subsistence farms have often resulted in the peasants' loss of land to moneylenders or landlords. Subsistence living is merely substituted for subsistence production. For small farmers, exclusive reliance on cash crops can be even more precarious than pure subsistence agriculture because the risks of price fluctuations are added to the uncertainty of nature.

Diversified or **mixed farming** therefore represents a logical intermediate step in the transition from subsistence to specialized production. In this stage, the staple crop no longer dominates farm output, and new cash crops such as fruits, vegetables, coffee, tea, and pyrethrum are established, together with simple animal husbandry. These new activities can take up the normal slack in farm workloads during times of the year when disguised unemployment is prevalent. This is especially desirable in many developing nations where rural labor is abundantly available for better and more efficient use.

For example, if the staple crop occupies the land during only parts of the year, new crops can be introduced in the slack season to take advantage of both idle land and family labor. And where labor is in short supply during peak planting seasons, as in many parts of Africa, simple laborsaving devices (such as small tractors, mechanical seeders, or animal-operated steel plows) can be introduced to free labor for other farm activities. Finally, the use of better seeds, fertilizers, and simple irrigation to increase the yields of staple crops like wheat, maize, and rice can free part of the land for cash crop cultivation while ensuring an adequate supply of the staple food. The farm operator can thus have a marketable surplus, which he can sell to raise his family's consumption standards or invest in farm improvements. Diversified farming can also minimize the impact of staple crop failure and provide a security of income previously unavailable.

The success or failure of such efforts to transform traditional agriculture will depend not only on the farmer's ability and skill in raising his productivity but, even more important, on the social, commercial, and institutional conditions under which he must function. Specifically, if he can have reasonable and reliable access to credit, fertilizer, water, crop information, and marketing facilities; if he receives a fair market price for his output; and if he can feel secure that he and his family will be the primary beneficiaries of any improvements, there is no reason to assume that the traditional farmer will not respond to economic incentives and new opportunities to improve his standard of living. Evidence from such diverse countries as Colombia, Mexico, Nigeria, Ghana, Kenya, India, Pakistan, Thailand, and the Philippines shows that under proper conditions, small farmers are responsive to price incentives and economic opportunities and will make radical changes in what they produce and how they produce it.[43] Lack of innovation in agriculture, as we have seen, is usually due not to poor motivation or fear of change but to inadequate or unprofitable opportunities.

From Divergence to Specialization: Modern Commercial Farming

The specialized farm represents the final and most advanced stage of individual holding in a mixed market economy. It is the most prevalent type of farming in advanced industrial nations. It has evolved in response to and parallel with development in other areas of the national economy. General rises in living standards, biological and technical progress, and the expansion of national and international markets have provided the main impetus for its emergence and growth.

In **specialized farming**, the provision of food for the family with some marketable surplus is no longer the basic goal. Instead, pure commercial profit becomes the criterion of success, and maximum per-hectare yields derived from synthetic (irrigation, fertilizer, pesticides, hybrid seeds, etc.) and natural resources become the object of farm activity. Production, in short, is entirely for the market. Economic concepts such as fixed and variable costs, saving, investment and rates of return, optimal factor combinations, maximum production possibilities, market prices, and price supports take on quantitative and qualitative significance. The emphasis in resource utilization is no longer on land, water, and labor as in subsistence and often mixed farming. Instead, capital formation, technological progress, and scientific research and development play major roles in stimulating higher levels of output and productivity.

Specialized farms vary in both size and function. They range from intensively cultivated fruit and vegetable farms to the vast wheat and corn fields of North America. In most cases, sophisticated laborsaving mechanical equipment, ranging from huge tractors and combine harvesters to airborne spraying techniques, permits a single family to cultivate many thousands of hectares of land.

The common features of all specialized farms, therefore, are their emphasis on the cultivation of one particular crop, their use of capital-intensive and in many cases laborsaving techniques of production, and their reliance on economies of scale to reduce unit costs and maximize profits. In some ways, specialized farming is no different in concept or operation from large industrial enterprises. In fact, some of the largest specialized farming operations in both the developed and especially the less developed nations are owned and managed by large agribusiness multinational corporate enterprises. But for smallholder farmers, strategies for dealing with risk, and in some cases overcoming coordination failures in specialization as described in Chapter 4, remain prerequisites for successful specialization.

Conclusions

Although we can find all three types of farms—subsistence, mixed, and specialized commercial—coexisting in almost all LDCs at any given time, for the majority of low-income countries, contemporary agricultural systems are still dominated by peasant subsistence and small-scale mixed family farms. The further transition to a preponderance of commercial enterprises may be difficult to achieve, depending as it does on the solution to many other short- and intermediate-term problems. We may conclude, therefore, that the improvement of small- and medium-scale mixed farming practices that will not only raise farm incomes and average yields but, if labor-intensive, also effectively absorb underutilized rural labor offers the major immediate avenue toward the achievement of real people-oriented rural development.

Large-scale commercial farms will continue to increase in number, but given the population, poverty, and urban employment problems of developing nations, they should not form the basis of most agricultural development strategies.

Toward a Strategy of Agricultural and Rural Development: Some Main Requirements

If the major objective of agricultural and rural development in developing nations is the progressive improvement in rural levels of living achieved primarily through increases in small-farm incomes, output, and productivity, it is important to identify the principal sources of agricultural progress and the basic conditions essential to its achievement. These are necessarily interrelated, but for purposes of description we may separate them and further divide each into three components:

Sources of Small-Scale Agricultural Progress

1. Technological change and innovation

2. Appropriate government economic policies

3. Supportive social institutions

Conditions for General Rural Advancement

1. Modernizing farm structures to meet rising food demands

2. Creating an effective supporting system

3. Changing the rural environment to improve levels of living

Let us look at each of these six interrelated components.

Improving Small-Scale Agriculture

Technology and Innovation In most developing countries, new agricultural technologies and innovations in farm practices are preconditions for sustained improvements in levels of output and productivity. In many parts of Africa and Latin America, however, increased output in earlier years was achieved without the need for new technology simply by extending cultivation into unused but potentially productive lands. Almost all of these opportunities have by now been exploited, however, and there is not much scope for further significant improvement.

Two major sources of technological innovation can increase farm yields. Unfortunately, both have somewhat problematic implications for LDC agricultural development. The first is the introduction of mechanized agriculture to replace human labor. The introduction of laborsaving machinery can have a dramatic effect on the volume of output per worker, especially where land is extensively cultivated and labor is scarce. For example, one man operating a huge combine harvester can accomplish in a single hour what would require hundreds of workers using traditional methods.

But in the rural areas of most developing nations, where land parcels are small, capital is scarce, and labor is abundant, the introduction of heavily mechanized techniques is not only often ill suited to the physical environment but, more important, often also has the effect of creating more rural unemployment without necessarily lowering per-unit costs of food production.[44] Importation of such machinery can therefore be antidevelopmental in that its efficient deployment requires large tracts of land (and thus the consolidation of small holdings) and tends to exacerbate the already serious problems of rural poverty and unemployment. And if mechanized techniques exclude women, the male-female productivity gap could widen further, with serious repercussions.[45]

By contrast, biological (hybrid seeds), water control (irrigation), and chemical (fertilizer, pesticides, insecticides, etc.) innovations—the second major source— are not without their own problems. They are land-augmenting; that is, they improve the quality of existing land by raising yields per hectare. Only indirectly do they increase output per worker. Improved seeds; advanced techniques of irrigation and crop rotation; the increasing use of fertilizers, pesticides, and herbicides; and new developments in veterinary medicine and animal nutrition represent major scientific advances in modern agriculture. These measures are technologically **scale-neutral**; theoretically, they can be applied equally effectively on large and small farms. They do not necessarily require large capital inputs or mechanized equipment. They are therefore particularly well suited for tropical and subtropical regions and offer enormous potential for raising agricultural output in developing nations, and indeed have been highly effective in doing so, particularly in Asia.

Institutional and Pricing Policies: Providing the Necessary Economic Incentives
Unfortunately, although the new hybrid "miracle seed" varieties of wheat, corn, and rice, together with needed irrigation and chemicals (often collectively referred to as the green revolution) are scale-neutral and thus offer the potential for small-farm progress, the social institutions and government economic policies that accompany their introduction into the rural economy are often *not* scale-neutral.[46] On the contrary, they often merely serve the needs and vested interests of the wealthy landowners. Because the new hybrid seeds require access to complementary inputs such as irrigation, fertilizer, insecticides, credit, and agricultural extension services, if these are provided only to a small minority of large landowners, the effective impact of the green revolution can be (as in parts of South Asia and Mexico) the further impoverishment of many peasants. Large landowners, with their disproportionate access to these complementary inputs and support services, are able to gain a competitive advantage over smallholders and eventually drive them out of the market. Large-scale farmers obtain access to low-interest government credit, while smallholders are forced to turn to moneylenders. The inevitable result is the further widening of the gap between rich and poor and the increased consolidation of agricultural land in the hands of a very few so-called progressive farmers. A developmental innovation with great potential for alleviating rural poverty and raising agricultural output can thus turn out to be antidevelopmental if public policies and social institutions militate against the active participation of the small farmer in the evolving agrarian structure.[47]

Another critical area calling for major improvements in government policies relates to the pricing of agricultural commodities, especially food grains and other staples produced for local markets. Many LDC governments, in their headlong pursuit of rapid industrial and urban development, maintained low agricultural prices in an attempt to provide cheap food for the urban modern sector. Farmers were paid prices below either world competitive or free-market internal prices. The relative internal price ratio between food and manufactured goods (the domestic terms of trade) thus turned against farmers and in favor of urban manufacturers. With farm prices so low—in some cases below the costs of production—there was no incentive for farmers to expand output or invest in new productivity-raising technology. As a result, local food supplies continually fell short of demand, and many developing nations, especially in sub-Saharan Africa, that were once self-sufficient in food production had to import food. This caused further strains on their international balance of payments situation and contributed to the foreign-exchange and international debt crises of the 1980s and 1990s (see Chapters 13 and 14 for further analysis of the international trade and debt problems).

Economists therefore argue that if LDC governments are to promote increases in agricultural production through new green revolution technologies, they must not only make the appropriate institutional and credit market adjustments but also provide incentives for small- and medium-size farmers by implementing pricing policies that truly reflect internal market conditions.[48] This often means less government intervention (especially in Africa) in the form of public agricultural marketing boards, which monopolize the purchase and distribution of farm output and set producer prices that are typically well below world market prices.[49]

Conditions for Rural Development

Let us now collect what has already been said to formulate three conclusions that in essence constitute the necessary conditions for the realization of a people-oriented agricultural and rural development strategy.[50]

Land Reform

Conclusion 1: Farm structures and land tenure patterns must be adapted to the dual objectives of increasing food production and promoting a wider distribution of the benefits of agrarian progress.

Agricultural and rural development that benefits the masses of people can succeed only through a joint effort by the government and *all* farmers, not just the large farmers. A first step in any such effort, especially in Latin America and Asia, is the provision of secured tenure rights to the individual farmer. A small farmer's attachment to his land is profound. It is closely bound up with his innermost sense of self-esteem and freedom from coercion. When he is driven off his land or is gradually impoverished through accumulated debts, not only is his material well-being damaged, but more important, his sense of self-worth and his desire for self- and family improvement can be permanently destroyed.

It is for these humane reasons as well as for reasons of higher agricultural output and the simultaneous achievement of both greater efficiency and more equity that **land reform** is often proposed as a necessary first condition for agricultural development in many LDCs. In most countries, the highly unequal structure of land ownership is probably the single most important determinant of the existing highly inequitable distribution of rural income and wealth. It is also the basis for the character of agricultural development. When land is very unevenly distributed, rural peasants can have little hope for economic advancement.

Land reform usually entails a redistribution of the rights of ownership or use of land away from large landowners in favor of cultivators with very limited or no landholdings. It can take many forms: the transfer of ownership to tenants who already work the land to create family farms (Japan, South Korea, Taiwan); transfer of land from large estates to small farms (Mexico), rural cooperatives (Cuba), or state farms (Peru); or the appropriation of large estates for new settlement (Kenya). All go under the heading of land reform and are designed to fulfill one central function: the transfer of land ownership or control directly or indirectly to the people who actually work the land.

There is widespread agreement among economists and other development specialists on the need for land reform. To Gunnar Myrdal, land reform was the key to agricultural development in Asia. The Economic Commission for Latin America (ECLA) has repeatedly identified land reform as a necessary precondition for agricultural and rural progress. An FAO report concluded that in many developing regions, land reform remains a prerequisite for development. The report argued that such reform was more urgent today than ever before, primarily because (1) income inequalities and unemployment in rural areas have worsened, (2) rapid population growth threatens further to worsen existing inequalities, and (3) recent and potential technological breakthroughs in agriculture (the green revolution) can be exploited primarily by large and powerful rural landholders and hence can result in an increase in their power, wealth, and capacity to resist future reform.[51] Finally, as noted earlier, from a strict view of economic efficiency and growth, there is ample empirical evidence that land redistribution not only increases rural employment and raises rural incomes but also leads to greater agricultural production and more efficient resource utilization.

Unfortunately, *minifundio* or landless farmers cannot directly purchase land from the big landowners because of market failures. Credit markets do not function well enough to provide a potentially efficient family farmer with a loan; even if they did, the price of *latifundio* land is too high because *latifundio* ownership confers many benefits beyond the income from farming activities, such as disproportionate political influence.

If programs of land reform can be legislated and effectively implemented by the government, the basis for improved output levels and higher standards of living for rural peasants will be established. Unfortunately, many land reform efforts have failed because LDC governments (especially those in Latin America) bowed to political pressures from powerful landowning groups and failed to implement the intended reforms.[52] But even an egalitarian land reform program alone is no guarantee of successful agricultural and rural development.[53] This leads to our second proposition.

Supportive Policies

Conclusion 2: The full benefits of small-scale agricultural development cannot be realized unless government support systems are created that provide the necessary incentives, economic opportunities, and access to needed credit and inputs to enable small cultivators to expand their output and raise their productivity.

Though land reform is essential in many parts of Asia and Latin America, it is likely to be ineffective and perhaps even counterproductive unless there are corresponding changes in rural institutions that control production (e.g., banks, moneylenders, seed and fertilizer distributors), in supporting government aid services (e.g., technical and educational extension services, public credit agencies, storage and marketing facilities, rural transport and feeder roads), and in government pricing policies with regard to both inputs (e.g., removing factor-price distortions) and outputs (paying market-value prices to farmers). Even where land reform is not necessary but where productivity and incomes are low (as in most of Africa and parts of Southeast Asia), this broad network of external support services, along with appropriate governmental pricing policies related to both farm inputs and outputs, is an essential condition for sustained agricultural progress.

Integrated Development Objectives

Conclusion 3: Rural development, though dependent primarily on small-farmer agricultural progress, implies much more. It encompasses (a) efforts to raise both farm and nonfarm rural real incomes through job creation, rural industrialization, and the increased provision of education, health and nutrition, housing, and a variety of related social and welfare services; (b) a decreasing inequality in the distribution of rural incomes and a lessening of urban-rural imbalances in incomes and economic opportunities; and (c) the capacity of the rural sector to sustain and accelerate the pace of these improvements over time.

This conclusion is self-explanatory. We need only add that the achievement of its three objectives is vital to national development. This is not only because the majority of populations in the developing world are located in rural areas but also because the burgeoning problems of urban unemployment and population congestion must find their ultimate solution in the improvement of the rural environment. By restoring a proper balance between urban and rural economic opportunities and by creating the conditions for broad popular participation in national development efforts and rewards, developing nations will have taken a giant step toward the realization of the true meaning of development.

Improving Agricultural Extension for Women Farmers: Kenya

As seen in Chapter 5, absolute poverty is disproportionately concentrated among women, in rural areas, and in the agricultural sector. Improvements in the productivity and incomes of women farmers are therefore key to a strategy for poverty reduction. The role of women in agriculture is particularly important in sub-Saharan Africa. But this is also the region that has benefited least from the green revolution of high-yielding crop varieties and other modern farming practices that has had such a large impact in many parts of Asia over the past three decades.

The crucial importance of a solid agricultural extension program for successful rural development and increased yields has been appreciated by development specialists for decades. Support for agricultural extension has played a central role in the activities of most multilateral and bilateral development agencies. Historically, agricultural extension programs played a vital development role in the United States, one of the world's great agricultural productivity success stories.

For decades, extension in developing countries was aimed almost exclusively at training men, even though women do most of the agricultural work. In sub-Saharan Africa, women are responsible for well over two-thirds of staple food production. They are also active in growing and marketing cash crops, in food processing, and in animal husbandry. In part, the prominent role of women in agriculture reflects tradition, but women's roles have expanded in recent years as men have increasingly migrated to urban areas and taken on other nonagricultural tasks. Where men and women both do agricultural work, there still tends to be a gender-based division of labor. As a result, techniques relevant to the work of men are often not relevant to the work of women. Where they are relevant, for various reasons men in the region have tended to pass on to their wives ("trickle across") surprisingly little of what they have learned.

The focus on training men has generally been more by default than by design. For example, training has been copied from developed countries like the United States, where men do the majority of agricultural work. There may be religious or cultural constraints on men training women, and male extension agents may simply be more comfortable talking to men. A World Bank study showed that most male African extension agents have perceived women as "wives of farmers" rather than as farmers in their own right. And almost all extension agents have been male. Female agents must be trained. A major problem is the segregation and exclusion of women in large parts of Africa as well as Asia.

The success of women in agriculture in sub-Saharan Africa is at the very core of

457

prospects for genuine development and poverty reduction. But the agricultural extension program response to the problem has been slow. And in some countries, program design reflects explicit bias against providing women with too much independence.

One important strategy of the past 20 years has been to make use of radio, audiotapes, and then television and videotapes. Women may listen to or watch the materials in groups in homes or village centers. Katrin Saito and her colleagues reported that female farmers question extension agents in Ghana about subjects they have heard discussed on the radio.

Agricultural extension for women is interconnected with a number of other important rural development and women in development issues. Five key issues are the following:

1. *Human capital.* Women have less education than men on average in most rural developing areas. The bias in agricultural extension may in some part be a bias to train the more educated spouse, but the practice has also exacerbated this relative deficiency.

2. *Appropriate technology.* Because women tend to be involved in different farm activities than men, they will often have different technology requirements. Most technology development has been focused on activities of men.

3. *Land reform and agrarian design.* On average, women farm on much smaller, more fragmented plots than men; are less likely to have secure ownership; and often cultivate less fertile soil. This distribution is likely to be inefficient as well as distributionally inequitable.

4. *Credit.* Women have little access, if any, to financial credit, a key input in efficient agriculture.

5. *Work requirements.* Many women who work as many hours per day as men in agricultural pursuits also have to perform several hours of domestic work that men do not do. Working days for poor women farmers in Africa have been estimated at 16 to 19 hours. The attention mothers can give to children is limited by long agricultural hours. The implication may be that women should receive an even higher priority for technical education and technology development and access.

As Rekha Mehra has noted, one intent of structural adjustment programs in many African countries has been to encourage the shift to exportable cash crops. But these are the crops over which men tend to exercise control. A woman's profit share after working with these crops may be as little as 5%. But she is still responsible for growing consumption crops and feeding her children. Mehra concludes that structural adjustment programs tend to place even more time requirements on women already burdened with 16-hour days.

Removal of agricultural price controls in Africa, allowing prices farmers receive for their crops to move toward world market levels, has provided more accurate price signals to farmers and encouraged a switch to more economically productive crops. But an International Food Policy Research Institute (IFPRI) study showed that after diversification to commercial crops, Kenyan women still try to grow the same amount of consumption crops. Thus more is needed than price adjustments featured under structural adjustment programs; reform must address structural problems faced by women that will prevent them from responding to price signals efficiently. A good example is the larger profit share taken by the husband and often not shared with his wife or wives.

None of these problems is limited to Africa. For example, Carmen Deere, in a review of 13 Latin American agrarian reform experiences, found that most have benefited only men. This was mostly because farmers were thought of as men and the reforms were designed to target only men as beneficiaries. Her review found that women benefit only in the rare instances when their well-being is a specific objective of the reform and rural women are made an explicit part of the design of programs from the outset.

Taken as a whole, these points show why women farmers need the help of extension programs. It is also efficient to do this because of an application of the law of diminishing returns to training for men. The evidence suggests that the trickle-across theory—that trained husbands will in turn train their wives–rarely occurs in practice, at least in sub-Saharan Africa.

In Kenya, the ministry of agriculture operates a national extension system (NES) in concert with its agricultural research efforts. Before 1983, the NES worked almost exclusively with male farmers, while a separate "home economics branch" advised women on household and cottage industry management and domestic hygiene but only peripherally on farming matters. Research by the Institute of Development Studies in Nairobi and other agencies confirmed that extension was much more likely to have reached men than women farmers. In 1983, Kenya's training and visit (T&V) system was established with the express purpose of training women as well as men in efficient agricultural practices. After two decades, the case provides an example both of the necessary ingredients of progress but also of how much remains to be accomplished.

The design of the T&V system is based on providing "technical messages" to selected "contact farmers," who are regularly visited on their farms. Unfortunately, resources are insufficient to reach all farmers, and even if the T&V system did try to reach all farmers, the quality of training would be poor. As a result, only 10% of all farmers are chosen to adopt advice brought to them in these messages and then to help spread this new technical knowledge by persuading other farmers in the villages to adopt them as well. A number of "follower farmers" are expected to attend meetings with T&V officials on the contact farmer's land. In this way, it is hoped that technical "diffusion" is maximized in a cost-effective manner. The selection process is vital. Farmers must be selected who are capable, likely to diligently follow through on new information, and locally respected so as to encourage emulation. In choosing contact farmers, T&V officials meet with farmers and consult with local communities and their leaders. In recent years, T&V outreach has focused more on working with traditional community farmer self-help groups, which can provide greater flexibility, better diffusion, and group reinforcement.

At first, messages focused on procedures offering the prospect of significant productivity gains but not requiring cash expenditure, such as ground preparation, spacing, seed varieties, and pruning. The messages being diffused in any one month are linked to farm activities under way in the annual crop cycle, such as planting or harvesting the crops being cultivated at any given point in the course of the year. The training process builds step by step: Simpler messages are imparted in early stages, more complex messages later in the program. Moreover, only after farmers see results from this initial advice and so come to trust the T&V messages are measures requiring modest cash outlays introduced, such as fertilizer use and crop spraying. In a later stage, measures requiring purchase of capital goods may be introduced. Increasing numbers of women function officially as contact farmers. Even more serve unofficially in this role, as their husbands farm only part time or not at all.

The messages of the T&V program, at least ideally, are supposed to be transmitted in both directions. T&V agents are supposed to gather information about how well previous advice has worked in practice and about continued problems in order to guide research efforts. This is in the spirit of the often touted but seldom fulfilled development participation ideal.

In 1997, Vishva Bindlish and Robert Evenson reported that T&V-type extension programs operated in more than 30 countries in sub-Saharan Africa. They concluded from their statistical evidence that the experience of "Kenya and Burkina Faso shows that T&V management enhances the effectiveness of extension and that such programs support agricultural growth and produce high returns on investments." They found that "areas served by extension have higher yields and that within these areas the highest yields are achieved by farmers who participate directly in extension activities. As a result, extension helps to close the gap between the yields attainable with existing technologies and those actually realized by farmers." But they find that while this makes improvements in the short run, there are limits to what the program can achieve without "the development of improved technologies that are relevant to local conditions."

Another study by Evenson and Germano Mwabu found that the impact of T&V in Kenya on productivity was positive but, interestingly, strongest among farmers of highest and lowest ability (measured by the portion of productivity unexplained by the use of farm inputs). They hypothesize that high ability overcomes diminishing returns to extension inputs; perhaps extension is complementary with high (unobserved) management ability. But the relatively high impact on the lower-ability farmers is noteworthy, even if data drawing conclusions about possible impacts such as on poverty are not available.

Economic advancement of women farmers is also important for promoting environmentally sustainable development. In addition to their responsibility for agriculture, especially on more marginal and often ecologically fragile lands, women have a customary role in traditional societies as the guardians of natural resources such as the water supply. This is also an important domain for agricultural extension work with women. In Kenya, the T&V system is not yet strongly involved in environmental problems.

Christina Gladwin and Della McMillan argue that much more must be done; for example, women should be consulted at the design stage of technology development, extension specialists should receive training on how to approach a male farmer about training his wife or wives, and governments should target funds to women's organizations and clubs.

Another shortcoming of the T&V system is that it has made too little progress in the field of women's credit, and private voluntary organizations have not been able to take up the slack. A study by Kathleen Staudt found that of 84 female farm managers interviewed in the Kakamega District in Kenya's Western Province, only one knew about the credit program, and no female manager had received any credit. Informal indications are that this is the area that has improved least over the subsequent years. But rural credit, often run by local NGOs, has recently been expanding in Kenya at a rapid rate that has surprised many long-term observers.

The strategy of involving women in public agriculture initiatives has shown some results in environment and credit as well as agricultural productivity. For example, the United Nations Population Fund reports that "women are now the principal participants in Kenya's National Soil Conservation Program. Since the mid-1980s, women have terraced more than 360,000 small farms, or 40 per cent of the country's total. Rural collectives, run by women, are now getting bank loans and agricultural extension services tailored to their specific needs and interests."

The Women in Development Service of the United Nations' Food and Agriculture Organization (FAO) reports that "in Kenya, following a national information campaign targeted at women under a National Extension Project, yields of corn increased by 28 percent, beans by 80 percent and potatoes by 84 percent." The way forward also includes a greater emphasis on more general knowledge. The FAO also reports on a study in Kenya showed that farm "yields among rural women could be increased by 24 percent if all women farmers completed primary school."

Nevertheless, the agricultural extension program in Kenya has remained weak by international standards. The World Bank audited its programs in this field in 1999 and found it severely wanting in many respects, including low cost-effectiveness. The audit called for more efficient targeting of extension services where the impact is likely to be greatest, using improved information systems, and empowering farmer clients by giving them a greater voice in the design of the services. The World Bank also called for more cost recovery, but this is likely to prove controversial. Kenya eliminated user fees on primary education in 2002, making it at least nominally free for all—despite 1980s-era encouragement by the World Bank and other agencies to seek "cost recovery" from impoverished parents of primary pupils. As a vital part of poverty alleviation, cost recovery from impoverished women farmers is a dubious strategy. It may also be noted that structural adjustment in Kenya is cited by other critics as a cause of declining T&V budgets in the late 1980s and 1990s, severely crippling the capacities of this program.

In Kenya and elsewhere in sub-Saharan Africa, public extension programs have been supplemented in recent years by a growing presence of nongovernmental organizations (see Chapter 11). For example, in western Kenya, the NGO Africa Now is actively recruiting and training farmers to participate in beekeeping as an alternative means of income generation. Broad participation of many civil society actors with diverse knowledge bases and connections with various ethnic and other social groupings is essential to success in an ecologically and socially diverse region such as sub-Saharan Africa.

Regarding government extension, a World Bank evaluation concluded that "progress on gender issues has been mixed. The earlier bias against women farmers has been rectified, but some bias persists in the selection of contact farmers. The proportion of female field-extension agents has remained largely unchanged since 1982." Though a better performance than many African and Asian countries and than Kenya exhibited in the past, it leaves much to be desired. Real progress has been made, but there is a pressing need for systematic follow-up and expansion.

But the role of women is strengthening throughout Kenya. Thousands of women are taking part in the Green Belt Movement (GBM), established in 1977 by the National Council of Women in Kenya at the behest of the visionary leader Wangari Maathai. Its simple objective, in Maathai's words, is to "halt desertification by encouraging tree planting and soil and water conservation in rural communities." The GBM also works to promote sustainable development and poverty alleviation in parallel projects. Although the program is run through the NGO or citizen sector, seedlings are provided by the government at low prices, and GBM volunteers receive advice and support from government forestry officials. For her work in supporting sustainable agriculture and forestry that benefits women and children, Maathai was awarded the 2004 Nobel Prize for Peace.

The GBM emphasizes grassroots participation and self-help and strives to educate people on the link between deforestation, erosion, poor soil quality, and subsequent low crop yields. With the help of outside funding, women are paid to work at about 1,000 nurseries. Seedlings grown at these nurseries are given to small farmers, schools, and churches, which have planted tens of millions of trees. The estimated survival rate is 70% to 80%. The GBM has had striking success in scalability, that is, bringing the model to service throughout Kenya and then disseminating it widely in Africa. This success was noted by the Nobel committee when awarding the laureate to Maathai. ∎

Sources

Bindlish, Vishva, and Robert E. Evenson, "The impact of T&V extension in Africa: The experience of Kenya and Burkina Faso," *World Bank Research Observer* 12 (1997): 183–201.

Bindlish, Vishva, and Robert E. Evenson, *Evaluation of the Performance of T&V Extension in Kenya* (Washington, D.C.: World Bank, 1994).

Davison, Jean (ed.), *Agriculture, Women, and Land: The African Experience* (Boulder, Colo.: Westview Press, 1989).

Deere, Carmen Diana, "The division of labor by sex in agriculture: A Peruvian case study," *Economic Development and Cultural Change* 30 (1982): 795–781.

Deere, Carmen Diana, "Rural women and state policy: The Latin American agrarian reform experience," *World Development* 13 (1985): 1037–1053.

Due, Jean M., and Christina H. Gladwin, "Impacts of structural adjustment programs on African women farmers and female-headed households," *American Journal of Agricultural Economics* 73 (1991): 1431–1439.

Evenson, Robert E., and Germano Mwabu, "The effect of agricultural extension on farm yields in Kenya," *African Development Review* 13 (2001): 1–23.

Food and Agriculture Organization, *Improving Extension Work with Rural Women* (Rome: Food and Agricultural Organization, 1996), http://www.fao.org/DOCREP/x0249e/x0249e01.htm.

Gladwin, Christina H., and Della McMillan, "Is a turnaround in Africa possible without helping African women to farm?" *Economic Development and Cultural Change* 37 (1989): 345–369.

Kennedy, Eileen T., and Bruce Cogill, *Income and nutritional effects of the commercialization of agriculture in southwestern Kenya*, Research Report No. 63, International Food Policy Research Institute, Washington, D.C., 1987.

Maathai, Wangari, "Kenya's Green Belt Movement, ecological movement headed by Women," *UNESCO Courier*, March 1992.

Mehra, Rekha, "Can structural adjustment work for women farmers?" *American Journal of Agricultural Economics* 73 (1991): 1440–1447.

Sahn, David E., and Lawrence Haddad, "The gendered impacts of structural adjustment programs in Africa: Discussion," *American Journal of Agricultural Economics* 73 (1991): 1448–1451.

Saito, Katrin, and C. Jean Weidemann, *Agricultural Extension for Women Farmers in Sub-Saharan Africa* (Washington, D.C.: World Bank, 1990).

Saito, Katrin, Hailu Mekonnen, and Daphne Spurling, *Raising the productivity of women farmers in Sub-Saharan Africa*, World Bank Discussion Paper, No. 230, Africa Technical Department Series, Washington, D.C., 1994.

Staudt, Kathleen K., *The Effects of Government Agricultural Policy on Women Farmers: Preliminary Findings from Idakho Location in Kakamega District.* (Nairobi: Institute of Development Studies, 1975).

Staudt, Kathleen K., "Women farmers and inequities in agricultural services," in *Women and Work in Africa*, ed. Edna Bay (Boulder, Colo.: Westview Press, 1982).

United Nations Population Fund, "Women as Land Stewards" (New York: UNPF, n.d.).

von Braun, Joachim, *Commercialization of Smallholder Agriculture: Policy Requirements for Capturing Gains for the Malnourished Poor* (Washington, D.C.: International Food Policy Research Institute, 1989).

World Bank, *World Bank Agricultural Extension Projects in Kenya* (Washington, D.C.: World Bank, 1999).

Concepts for Review

Agrarian systems	Land reform	Scale-neutral
Cash crops	*Latifundio*	Sharecropper
Diversified farming	Medium-size farms	Shifting cultivation
Family farms	*Minifundio*	Specialized farming
Green revolution	Mixed farming	Staple foods
Integrated rural develop-	Moneylender	Subsistence farming
ment	*Patrón*	Tenant farmer
Interlocking factor markets	Price bands	Transaction costs
Landlord	Productivity gap	

Questions for Discussion

1. Why should any analysis of development problems place heavy emphasis on the study of agricultural systems, especially peasant agriculture, and the rural sector?

2. What were the principal reasons for the relative stagnation of developing-country agriculture during the so-called development decades of the 1960s and 1970s? How can this disappointing performance be improved on in the future? Explain your answer.

3. It is sometimes said that the world consists of two kinds of agriculture. Explain what is meant by this statement, and indicate how it might be illustrated. Be specific.

4. Compare and contrast the nature of peasant or small-scale agriculture in Asia, Africa, and Latin America. How do overall agricultural systems differ among these regions? What are the common characteristics?

5. Explain the meaning of Gunnar Myrdal's quote at the beginning of this chapter: "It is in the agricultural sector that the battle for long-term economic development will be won or lost."

6. It is sometimes asserted that small peasant farmers are backward and ignorant because they seem to resist agricultural innovations that could raise farm yields substantially. Does this resistance stem from an inherent irrationality on their part, or might it be attributable to some other factors often overlooked by Western economists? Explain your answer.

7. We described three stages in the transition from subsistence to specialized agriculture. What are the principal characteristics of each of these stages?

8. There appears to be widespread agreement that in regions where the distribution of land ownership is highly unequal (mainly Latin America but also parts of Asia), land reform is a necessary but not sufficient condition for promoting and improving small-scale agriculture. What is meant by this statement and by the concept of land reform? Give some examples of supportive policy measures that might accompany land reform.

9. What is meant by comprehensive or integrated rural development? What criteria would you use to decide whether or not such integrated rural development was or was not taking place?

10. What explains sharecropping? To what extent do you think your explanation justifies the practice?

11. If land reform is efficient, why do you think it is so rare?

12. Why is a proper understanding of risks faced by smallholder farmers of such fundamental importance to agricultural development policy?

Notes

1. United Nations Food and Agricultural Organization, "Rome Declaration on World Food Security," *Population and Development Review* 22 (1996): 807–809. See also Lester R. Brown, "Facing the prospect of food scarcity," in Worldwatch Institute, *State of the World, 1997* (New York: Norton, 1997), pp. 23–41; Nikos Alexandratos, "The world food outlook: A review Essay," *Population and Development Review* 23 (1997): 877–888; and United Nations Food and Agriculture Organization "The state of food insecurity in the world, 2003," http://www.fao.org/documents/show_cdr.asp?url_file=/docrep/006/j0083e/j0083e00.htm.

2. John W. Mellor, "Agriculture on the road to industrialization," in *Development Strategies Reconsidered,* ed. John P. Lewis and Valeriana Kallab (Washington, D.C.: Overseas Development Council, 1986), pp. 67–89; see also Subrata Ghatak, "Agriculture and economic development," in *Surveys in Economic Development,* ed. Norman Gemmell (Oxford: Blackwell, 1987), ch. 10, and Charles P. Timmer, "The agricultural transformation," in *Handbook of Development Economics*, vol. 1, ed. Hollis B. Chenery and T. N. Srinivasan (Amsterdam: Elsevier, 1988), pp. 276–331.

3. For a quantitative review of recent trends in food and agricultural production, see World Resources Institute, *World Resources, 1996–97* (New York: Oxford University Press, 1997), ch. 10. For projections of future trends, see Alexandratos, "World food outlook." For reports on recent famine problems in Africa, see United Nations Food and Agriculture Organization, "State of food insecurity," and BBC, "Africa's famine: Country by country," November 11, 2002, http://news.bbc.co.uk/1/hi/world/africa/2027079.stm.

4. E. F. Scepanik, "Agricultural capital formation in selected developing countries," *Agricultural Planning Studies* 11 (1970).

5. See Raanan Weitz, *From Peasant to Farmer: A Revolutionary Strategy for Development* (New York: Columbia University Press, 1971), pp. 6–9. This statement is not meant to imply that no high-productivity farming is done in LDCs or that no low-productivity family farms operate in developed countries. Rather, it is meant to emphasize the enormous productivity differences that exist when we look at the overall distribution of farm structures and aggregate productivity across the entire agricultural sector for both less developed and developed countries.

6. Ibid., pp. 7–8 (U.S. Census Bureau data). Although much of the success of developed-country agriculture is the result of the application of advanced farm technology, such

factors as agricultural protectionism, massive price supports, and huge "pork barrel" public investment programs have also contributed to developed-country output expansion.

7. Ibid., p. 9.

8. Francis M. Foland, "Agrarian unrest in Asia and Latin America," *World Development* 2 (1974): 56. Copyright © 1974. Reprinted with permission from Elsevier Science Ltd.

9. Beginning in the early 1960s, many countries in Latin America initiated land reform programs that did not alter the highly unequal distribution of land ownership but did do away with some of the more feudal patron-client social relationships associated with *latifundios* and *minifundios*. For pedagogical purposes, we will continue to use these terms more as a designation of the dualistic agrarian structure that still permeates Latin America than as a description of contemporary rural social relationships.

10. United Nations Development Program, *Human Development Report, 1996* (New York: Oxford University Press, 1996), p. 98. See also Keijiro Otsuka, Hiroyuki Chuma, and Yujiro Hayami, "Land and labor contracts in agrarian economies: Theories and facts," *Journal of Economic Literature* 30 (1992): 1965–2018.

11. For a summary of the empirical evidence on this point, see R. Albert Berry and William Cline, *Agrarian Structure and Productivity in Developing Countries* (Baltimore: Johns Hopkins University Press, 1979), ch. 3 and app. B; G. A. Cornia, "Farm size, land yields and the agricultural production function: An analysis of fifteen developing countries," *World Development* 13 (1985): 513–534; Nancy L. Johnson and Vernon Ruttan, "Why are farms so small?" *World Development* 22 (1994): 691–705; and, United Nations Development Program, *Human Development Report, 1996*, p. 95.

12. Celso Furtado, *Economic Development in Latin America* (New York: Cambridge University Press, 1970), p. 56.

13. Ibid., pp. 57–58.

14. For evidence that land redistribution is likely to lead to greater output and higher productivity levels, see Cornia, "Farm size, land yields."

15. Foland, "Agrarian unrest," 57. Only the city-state of Singapore has a denser population than Bangladesh.

16. Gunnar Myrdal, *Asian Drama* (New York: Pantheon, 1968), pp. 1033–1052.

17. Ibid., p. 1035.

18. Ibid.

19. Otsuka, Chuma, and Hayami, "Land and labor contracts," tab. 1.

20. A somewhat more positive view of the efficiency of land leases and access to credit through moneylenders and other informal sources of credit in Asia (and Latin America) was the focus of the "new agrarian economics" of the late 1970s and 1980s. In general, the position of this school of thought was that land contracting and usurious moneylending are efficient given the existence of other market failures, imperfect information, high transaction costs, moral hazards, and the like. Whether or not they were as efficient as these theorists claimed was far from clear, but their ultimate exploitive nature is difficult to deny. For an example of this literature, see Pranab Bardhan, *Land, Labor, and Rural Poverty: Essays in Development Economics* (New York: Columbia University Press, 1984); Keijiro Otsuka and Yujiro Hayami, "Theories of shared

tenancy: A critical survey," *Economic Development and Cultural Change* (1988); Karla Hoff and Joseph E. Stiglitz, "Imperfect information and rural credit markets: Puzzles and policy perspectives," *World Bank Economic Review* 4 (1990): 235–250; and Timothy Besley, "How do market failures justify interventions in rural credit markets?" *World Bank Research Observer* 9 (1994): 27–47.

21. Myrdal, *Asian Drama*, p. 1048.

22. For a discussion of the phenomenon of landlessness in developing countries with a particular emphasis on Asia, see Mahmood H. Khan, "Landlessness and rural poverty in underdeveloped countries," *Pakistan Development Review* 25 (1986): 371–394.

23. Mead Cain, "Char Gopalpur revisited," diary notes, Center for Policy Studies, Population Council, October 1979. Reprinted with permission.

24. See World Bank, *World Development Indicators (WDI) 2003*, p. 1311, and *WDI 2004*, Tables 2.1, 3.3, and 4.1 (Washington, D.C.).

25. World Resources Institute, *World Resources 1996–97* (New York: Oxford University Press, 1997), Table 10.1; and *World Resources 1987* (New York: Basic Books, 1987).

26. An especially informative book on women's role in developing-country agriculture is Carolyn Sachs, *The Invisible Farmers: Women in Agriculture* (Totowa, N.J.: Rowman & Littlefield, 1983). The classic and still influential treatment of the subject can be found in Ester Boserup, *Women's Role in Economic Development* (New York: St. Martin's Press, 1970).

27. Boserup, *Women's Role*.

28. See Weitz, *From Peasant to Farmer*, pp. 15–28, from which much of the following material is drawn. The three stages of farm evolution outlined in this section should not be interpreted as inevitable periods or sequences of time in which all farms are simultaneously in one of these stages before moving on to the next. In reality, of course, all three types of farms exist in every country at all points in time. Clearly, however, peasant farming predominates in most LDCs, whereas commercial agriculture tends to dominate in most developed countries.

29. See Carmen Diana Deere and Alain de Janvry, "A conceptual framework for the empirical analysis of peasants," *American Journal of Agricultural Economics* 61 (1979): 602–612, where it is reported in tab. 5 that in Latin America almost 50% of the income generated by smallholders came from their wage labor. See also Alain de Janvry, Elisabeth Sadoulet, and Linda Wilcox Young, *Rural Labor in Latin America* (Geneva: International Labor Organization, 1986), tab. 24.

30. Clifton R. Wharton Jr., "Risk, uncertainty, and the subsistence farmer," *Development Digest* 7 (1969): 3.

31. For an outstanding analysis, see Marcel Fafchamps, *Rural Poverty, Risk and Development* (Northampton, Mass.: Elgar, 2004). Important earlier contributions include Alain de Janvry, Marcel Fafchamps, and Elisabeth Sadoulet, "Peasant household behavior with missing markets: Some paradoxes explained," *Economic Journal* 101 (1991): 1400–1417, and Alain de Janvry and Elisabeth Sadoulet, "Structural adjustment under transaction costs," paper presented at the 29th Conference of the European Association of Agricultural Economists, September 1992.

32. See Marvin P. Miracle, "Subsistence agriculture: Analytical problems and alternative concepts," *American Journal of Agricultural Economics* 50 (1968): 292–310.

33. For a rigorous analysis of how such farmer productivity traps operate, see Frederick J. Zimmerman and Michael R. Carter, "Asset smoothing, consumption smoothing, and the reproduction of inequality under risk and subsistence constraints," *Journal of Development Economics* 71 (2003): 233–260.

34. We are grateful to Professor Frank Thompson for this suggestion.

35. Keith Griffin, "Agrarian policy: The political and economic context," *World Development* 1 (1973): 6.

36. Joseph E. Stiglitz first formulated the argument that sharecropping represents a compromise between landlord and tenant in which the landlord assumes some of the production risk but the tenant accepts some degree of work incentive given that monitoring is costly; see Stiglitz, "Incentives and risk sharing in sharecropping," *Review of Economic Studies* 41 (1974): 219–255.

37. Alfred Marshall, *Principles of Economics,* 8th ed. (London: Macmillan 1920).

38. Steven N. S. Cheung, "Private property rights and sharecropping," *Journal of Political Economy* 76 (1968): 1107–1122.

39. The classic article in this literature is William S. Hallagan, "Self-selection by contractual choice and the theory of sharecropping," *Bell Journal of Economics* 9 (1978): 344–354.

40. Radwan Ali Shaban, "Testing between competing models of sharecropping," *Journal of Political Economy* 95 (1987): 893–920.

41. See, for example, Nirviker Singh, "Theories of sharecropping," in *Theories of Agricultural Institutions*, ed. Pranab Bardhan (Oxford: Oxford University Press, 1992); David M. Newberry, "Risk-sharing, sharecropping, and uncertain labor markets," *Review of Economic Studies* (1977): 585–594; and Joseph E. Stiglitz, "Sharecropping," in *Economic Development,* ed. John Eatwell, Murray Milgate, and Peter Newman (London: Macmillan, 1989), pp. 308–315.

42. A succinct but rather technical overview of the competing theories is found in Singh, "Theories of sharecropping."

43. For a detailed analysis of the responsiveness of farmers in developing countries to price incentives, see World Bank, *World Development Report, 1986* (New York: Oxford University Press, 1986), ch. 4 and 5. For an analysis of the role of risk, see also Fafchamps, *Rural Poverty, Risk and Development,* p. 28.

44. For an extensive analysis of these adverse effects of premature mechanization, see Montague Yudelman et al., *Technological Change in Agriculture and Employment in Developing Countries* (Paris: Organization for Economic Cooperation and Development, 1971), and Yujiro Hayami and Vernon Ruttan, *Agricultural Development: An International Perspective* (Baltimore: Johns Hopkins University Press, 1985).

45. Two informative articles on appropriate mechanization for development are Hans P. Binswanger, "Agricultural mechanization: A comparative historical perspective," *World Bank Research Observer* 1 (1986): 81–98, and Hans P. Binswanger and Prabhu

Pingali, "Technological priorities for farming in sub-Saharan Africa," *World Bank Research Observer* 3 (1988).

46. An excellent analysis of the role of institutions in rural development can be found in Brian van Arkadie, "The role of institutions in development," *Proceedings of the World Bank Annual Conference on Development Economics, 1989* (Washington, D.C.: World Bank, 1989), pp. 153–192.

47. For an analysis of the impact of the green revolution in the developing world, see Keith Griffin, *The Political Economy of Agrarian Change* (London: Macmillan, 1974); Chris Manning, "Rural employment creation in Java: Lessons from the green revolution and oil boom," *Population and Development Review* 14 (1988): 17–18; and Donald K. Freebairn, "Did the green revolution concentrate incomes? A quantitative study of research reports," *World Development* 23 (1995): 265–279.

48. An informative discussion of the important role of appropriate pricing policies in stimulating agricultural production can be found in A. Drazen and Z. Eckstein, "On the organization of rural markets and the process of economic development," *American Economic Review* 78 (1988): 431–443. A massive five-volume research report, *The Political Economy of Agrarian Pricing Policy*, published by the World Bank in 1991, found similar results in the 18 developing countries investigated.

49. For an extensive critique of inappropriate government policies hindering agricultural development in sub-Saharan Africa as well as elsewhere in the developing world, see World Bank, *World Development Report, 1986*, ch. 4 and 5, and especially Hans P. Binswanger and Klaus Deininger, "Explaining agricultural and agrarian policies in developing countries," *Journal of Economic Literature* 35 (1997): 1958–2005.

50. For a more comprehensive review of integrated programs for rural development, see Alain de Janvry, *The Economics of Investment in Rural Development: Private and Social Accounting Experiences from Latin America* (Berkeley: Department of Agricultural and Resource Economics, University of California, 1988).

51. Myrdal, Gunnar, *Asian Drama* and "The Equality Issue in World Development," Nobel Prize Lecture, in *Nobel Lectures, Economics 1969–1980*. Assar Lindbeck (ed.) (Singapore: World Scientific Publishing Co., 1992; United Nations Food and Agriculture Organization), http://www.Fao.org/sd/Ltdirect/landrE.htm.

52. See Alain de Janvry, *The Agrarian Question and Reformism in Latin America* (Baltimore: Johns Hopkins University Press, 1981).

53. For an analysis of the successes and failures of various reform efforts, see World Bank, *World Development Report, 1990: Poverty* (New York: Oxford University Press, 1990), pp. 64–73; and Peter Dorner, *Latin American Land Reforms in Theory and Practice: A Retrospective Analysis* (Madison: University of Wisconsin Press, 1992).

Further Reading

An excellent survey of agrarian systems in developing countries can be found in Dharam Ghai et al. (eds.), *Agrarian Systems and Rural Development* (New York: Holmes & Meier, 1979). There are also a number of studies on agriculture and agrarian systems in specific developing regions. For Africa, see Peter Robson and Dennis A. Lury (eds.), *The Economies of Africa* (London: Allen & Unwin, 1969). For Asia, see Gunnar Myrdal, *Asian Drama* (New York: Pantheon, 1968), ch. 22, 23, and 26. For Latin America, see Rodolfo Stavenhagen (ed.), *Agrarian Problems and Peasant Movements in Latin America* (New York: Doubleday, 1970); Celso Furtado, *Economic Development in Latin America* (New York: Cambridge University Press, 1970), ch. 7 and 14; Solon Barraclough, *Agrarian Structure in Latin America* (Lexington, Mass.: Lexington Books, 1973), and Alain de Janvry, *The Agrarian Question and Reform in Latin America* (Baltimore: Johns Hopkins University Press, 1981). Comparative analyses of landlessness and rural poverty can be found in Milton J. Esman, *Landlessness and Near-Landlessness in Developing Countries* (Ithaca, N.Y.: Cornell University Press, 1978); Erick Eckholm, *The Dispossessed of the Earth: Land Reform and Sustainable Development* (Washington, D.C., Worldwatch Institute, 1979); and Mahmood H. Khan, "Landlessness and rural poverty in underdeveloped countries," *Pakistan Development Review* 25 (1986): 371–394.

For an outstanding comparative study of developing agrarian systems, see Thomas P. Tomich, Peter Kilby, and Bruce F. Johnston, *Transforming Agrarian Economies: Opportunities Seized, Opportunities Missed* (Ithaca, N.Y.: Cornell University Press, 1995).

For a general introduction to the economics of agricultural and rural development in developing countries, see Carl Eicher and John Stoatz (eds.), *Agricultural Development in the Third World* (Baltimore: Johns Hopkins University Press, 1984); Erik Thorbecke (ed.), *The Role of Agriculture in Economic Development* (New York: Columbia University Press, 1969): Raanan Weitz, *From Peasant to Farmer: A Revolutionary Strategy for Development* (New York: Columbia University Press, 1971); Bruce F. Johnston, "Agriculture and structural transformation in developing countries: A survey of research," *Journal of Economic Literature* 8 (1970): 369–404; John W. Mellor, *The Economics of Agricultural Development* (Ithaca, N.Y.: Cornell University Press, 1966); Theodore W. Schultz, *Transforming Traditional Agriculture* (New Haven, Conn.: Yale University Press, 1964); World Bank, *World Development Report, 1986* (New York: Oxford University Press, 1986), which contains an examination of trends in agriculture in developing countries; C. Peter Timmer, Walter Falcon, and Scott Pearson, *Food Policy Analysis* (Baltimore: Johns Hopkins University Press, 1983); Subrata Ghatak, "Agriculture and economic development," in *Surveys in Development Economics*, ed. Norman Gemmell (Oxford: Blackwell, 1987), ch. 10; Yair Mudlak, Donald Larson, and Al Crego, "Agricultural development: Issues, evidence and consequences," memorandum, World Bank International Economics Department, Washington, D.C., 1996; and Hans P. Binswanger and Klaus Deininger, "Explaining agricultural and agrarian policies in developing countries," *Journal of Economic Literature* 35 (1997): 1958–2005.

Descriptions of the policies and problems associated with integrating women into agricultural reforms are provided in Mahabub Hossain, *Credit for Alleviation of Rural Poverty: The Grameen Bank in Bangladesh* (Washington, D.C.: International Food Policy Research Institute, 1988); Monica Fong and Heli Perrett, *Women and Credit* (Milan: Finafrica, 1991); and Sharon Holt and Helena Ribe, *Developing Financial Institutions for the Poor and Reducing Barriers to Access for Women* (Washington, D.C.: World Bank, 1991).

For an excellent if relatively technical analysis of risk in rural developing regions, see Marcel Fafchamps, *Rural Poverty, Risk and Development* (Northampton, Mass.: Elgar, 2004).

CHAPTER TEN

The Environment and Development

Environmental damage almost always hits those living in poverty the hardest.
—United Nations, *Human Development Report, 1998*

Sustainability must be strengthened as a guiding principle of development.
—Boutros Boutros-Ghali, Secretary General, United Nations, 1994

The old notion of "development versus environment" has given way to a new view in which ... better environmental stewardship is essential to sustain development.
—World Bank, *World Bank Atlas, 1997*

Economics and the Environment

In recent years, economists have become increasingly aware of the important implications of environmental issues for the success of development efforts. We now understand that the interaction between poverty and environmental degradation can lead to a self-perpetuating process in which, as a result of ignorance or economic necessity, communities may inadvertently destroy or exhaust the resources on which they depend for survival. Rising pressures on environmental resources in developing countries can have severe consequences for self-sufficiency, income distribution, and future growth potential in the developing world.

Environmental degradation can also detract from the pace of economic development by imposing high costs on developing countries through health-related expenses and the reduced productivity of resources. The poorest 20% of the world's population will experience the consequences of environmental ills most acutely. Severe environmental degradation, due to population pressures on marginal land, has led to falling farm productivity and per capita food production. Since the cultivation of marginal land is largely the domain of lower-income groups, the losses are suffered by those who can least afford them. Similarly, the inaccessibility of sanitation and clean water mainly affects the poor and is believed to be responsible for 80% of disease worldwide. Because the solutions to these and many other environmental problems involve enhancing the productivity of resources and improving living conditions among the poor, achieving environmentally sustainable growth is synonymous with our definition of economic development.

Though there is considerable dispute concerning the environmental costs associated with various economic activities, consensus is growing among development economists that environmental considerations should form an integral part of policy initiatives.[1] The exclusion of environmental costs from calculations of GNI is largely responsible for the historical absence of environmental considerations from development economics. Damage to soil, water supplies, and forests resulting from unsustainable methods of production can greatly reduce long-term national productivity but will have a positive impact on current GNI figures. It is thus very important that the long-term implications of environmental quality be considered in economic analysis. Rapid population growth and expanding economic activity in the developing world are likely to do extensive environmental damage unless steps are taken to mitigate their negative consequences.

The growing consumption needs of LDC populations may have global implications as well. There is increasing concern in the MDCs that the destruction of the world's remaining forests, which are concentrated in a number of highly indebted developing countries in Africa as well as such countries as Indonesia, Brazil, Peru, and the Philippines, will greatly contribute to global warming and the greenhouse effect. In this chapter, we examine the economic causes and consequences of environmental devastation and explore potential solutions to the cycle of poverty and resource degradation. We begin, as in previous chapters, with a survey of basic issues, including discussions of sustainable development and the linkages among population, poverty, economic growth, rural development, urbanization, and the LDC environment. We next look at the applicability of traditional economic models of the environment, depict some typical environmental situations, and provide some relevant data. We then broaden our scope to examine the global environment and explore policies for seeking worldwide sustainable development. The environmental problems of the Philippines and the emerging policy response are the focus of this chapter's case study.

Environment and Development: The Basic Issues

Seven basic issues define the environment of development. Many grow out of the discussions in the preceding chapters. The seven issues are (1) the concept of sustainable development and linkages between the environment and (2) population and resources, (3) poverty, (4) economic growth, (5) rural development, (6) urbanization, and (7) the global economy. We briefly discuss each in turn.

Sustainable Development and Environmental Accounting

Environmentalists use the term *sustainability* to characterize the desired balance between economic growth and environmental preservation. Although many definitions exist,[2] *sustainability* generally refers to "meeting the needs of the present generation without compromising the needs of future generations."[3] For economists, a development path is sustainable "if and only if the stock of overall capital assets remains constant or rises over time."[4] Implicit in these statements is the fact that future growth and overall quality of life are critically dependent on the quality of the environment. The natural resource base of a country and the quality of its air, water, and land represents a common heritage for all generations. To destroy that endowment indiscriminately in the pursuit of short-term economic goals penalizes both present and, especially, future generations. It is therefore important that development policymakers incorporate some form of **environmental accounting** into their decisions. For example, the preservation or loss of valuable environmental resources should be factored into estimates of economic growth and human well-being. Alternatively, policymakers may set a goal of no net loss of environmental assets. In other words, if an environmental resource is damaged or depleted in one area, a resource of equal or greater value should be regenerated elsewhere.

An example of environmental accounting is offered by David Pearce and Jeremy Warford.[5] Overall capital assets are meant to include not only manufactured capital (machines, factories, roads) but also human capital (knowledge, experience, skills) and **environmental capital** (forests, soil quality, rangeland). By this definition, **sustainable development** requires that these overall capital assets not be decreasing and that the correct measure of **sustainable net national income (NNI*)** is the amount that can be consumed without diminishing the capital stock. Symbolically,

$$NNI^* = GNI - D_m - D_n \tag{10.1}$$

where NNI* is sustainable national income, D_m is depreciation of manufactured capital assets, and D_n is depreciation of environmental capital—the monetary value of environmental decay over the course of a year.

An even better measure, though more difficult to calculate with present data collection methods, would be

$$NNI^* = GNI - D_m - D_n - R - A \tag{10.2}$$

where D_m and D_n are as before, R is expenditure required to restore environmental capital (forests, fisheries, etc.), and A is expenditure required to avert destruction of environmental capital (air pollution, water and soil quality, etc.)

In light of rising consumption levels worldwide combined with high rates of population growth, the realization of sustainable development will be a major challenge. We must ask ourselves, what are realistic expectations about sustainable standards of living? From present information concerning rapid destruction of many of the world's resources, it is clear that meeting the needs of a world population that is projected to grow by an additional 3 billion in the next 50 years will require radical and early changes in consumption and production patterns. We discuss these needed changes later in the chapter.

Population, Resources, and the Environment

Much of the concern over environmental issues stems from the perception that we may reach a limit to the number of people whose needs can be met by the earth's finite resources. This may or may not be true, given the potential for new technological discoveries, but it is clear that continuing on our present path of accelerating environmental degradation would severely compromise the ability of present and future generations to meet their needs. A slowing of population growth rates would help ease the intensification of many environmental problems. However, the rate and timing of fertility declines, and thus the eventual size of world population, will largely depend on the commitment of governments to creating economic and institutional conditions that are conducive to limiting fertility (see Chapter 6).

Rapidly growing populations have led to land, water, and fuelwood shortages in rural areas and to urban health crises stemming from lack of sanitation and clean water.[6] In many of the poorest regions of the globe, it is clear that increasing population density has contributed to severe and accelerating degradation of the very resources that these growing populations depend on for survival. To meet expanding LDC needs, environmental devastation must be halted and the productivity of existing resources stretched further so as to benefit more people. If increases in GNI and food production are slower than population growth, per capita levels of production and food self-sufficiency will fall. Ironically, the resulting persistence of poverty would be likely to perpetuate high fertility rates, given, as we discovered in Chapter 6, that the poor are often dependent on large families for survival.

Poverty and the Environment

Too often, however, high fertility is blamed for problems that are attributable to poverty itself. For example, China's population density per acre of arable land is twice that of India, yet yields are also twice as high. Though it is clear that environmental destruction and high fertility go hand in hand, they are both direct outgrowths of a third factor, absolute poverty. For environmental policies to succeed in developing countries, they must first address the issues of landlessness, poverty, and lack of access to institutional resources. Insecure land tenure rights, lack of credit and inputs, and absence of information often prevent the poor from making resource-augmenting investments that would help preserve the environmental assets from which they derive their livelihood. Hence preventing environmental degradation is more often a matter of providing institutional support to the poor than fighting an inevitable process of decay.[7] For this reason, many goals on the international environmental agenda are very much in harmony with the three objectives of development articulated in Chapter 1.

Growth versus the Environment

If, in fact, it is possible to reduce environmental destruction by increasing the incomes of the poor, is it then possible to achieve growth without further damage to the environment? Evidence indicates that the worst perpetrators of environmental destruction are the billion richest and billion poorest people on earth. It has even been suggested that the bottom billion are more destructive than all four billion people in between. It follows that increasing the economic status of the poorest group would provide an environmental windfall. However, as the income and consumption levels of everyone else in the economy also rise, there is likely to be a net increase in environmental destruction. Meeting increasing consumption demand while keeping environmental degradation at a minimum will be no small task.

Rural Development and the Environment

To meet the expanded food needs of rapidly growing LDC populations, it is estimated that food production in developing countries will have to increase by at least 50% between 2005 and 2025. Because land in many areas of the developing world is being unsustainably over-exploited by existing populations, meeting these output targets will require radical changes in the distribution, use, and quantity of resources available to the agricultural sector. And because women are frequently the caretakers of rural resources such as forests and water supplies and provide much of the agricultural supply of labor, it is of primary importance that they be integrated into environmental programs. In addition, poverty alleviation efforts must target women's economic status in particular to reduce their dependence on unsustainable methods of production.

The increased accessibility of agricultural inputs to small farmers and the introduction (or reintroduction) of sustainable methods of farming will help create attractive alternatives to current environmentally destructive patterns of resource use. Land-augmenting investments can greatly increase the yields from cultivated land and help ensure future food self-sufficiency.

Urban Development and the Environment

Chapter 7 demonstrated that rapid population increases accompanied by heavy rural-urban migration is leading to unprecedented rates of urban population growth, sometimes at twice the rate of national growth. Consequently, few governments are prepared to cope with the vastly increased strain on existing urban water supplies and sanitation facilities. The resulting environmental ills pose extreme health hazards for the growing numbers of people exposed to them. Such conditions threaten to precipitate the collapse of the existing urban infrastructure and create circumstances ripe for epidemics and national health crises. These conditions are exacerbated by the fact that under existing legislation, much urban housing is illegal. This makes private household investments risky and renders large portions of urban populations ineligible for government services.

Congestion, vehicular and industrial emissions, and poorly ventilated household stoves also inflate the tremendously high environmental costs of urban crowding. Lost productivity of ill or diseased workers, contamination of existing water sources, and destruction of infrastructure, in addition to increased fuel expenses incurred by people's having to boil unsafe water, are just a few of the costs associated with poor urban conditions. Research reveals that the urban environment appears to worsen at a faster rate than urban population size increases, with the result that the marginal environmental cost of additional residents rises over time.[8] The importance of urban as well as rural environmental protection is recognized in the seventh MDG (p. 24).

The Global Environment

As total world population grows and incomes rise, net global environmental degradation is likely to worsen. Some trade-offs will be necessary to achieve sustainable world development. By using resources more efficiently, a number of environmental changes will actually provide economic savings, and others will be achieved at relatively minor expense. However, because many essential changes will require substantial investments in pollution abatement technology and resource management, significant trade-offs between output and environmental improvements will occasionally become necessary. The poorer the country, the more difficult it will be to absorb these costs. Yet a number of issues, including biodiversity, rain forest destruction, and population growth, will focus international attention on some of the most economically strapped countries in the world. In the absence of substantial assistance to low-income countries, environmental efforts will necessarily have to be funded at the expense of other social programs, such as education, health services, and employment schemes, that themselves have important implications for the preservation of the global environment.

Exactly what sacrifices need to be made and who should make them will continue to be matters of great controversy. Nowhere was this more evident than at the second United Nations Conference on Environment and Development (UNCED)—the so-called Earth Summit—held in Rio de Janeiro in June 1992 and follow-up conferences in Kyoto, Japan, in 1997 and Johannesburg in 2002. Most cumulative environmental destruction to date has been caused by the developed world. However, with high fertility rates, rising average incomes, and increasing greenhouse gas emissions in the developing world, this pattern is likely to reverse sometime in this century.[9] It is thus unclear how the costs of global reform should be divided. Apportionment of responsibility for reducing environmental damage essentially hinges on the manner in which the question is framed. For example, if a limit is placed globally on levels of per capita pollution emissions, the approach would clearly favor lower-income countries that have much lower per capita consumption levels. Conversely, if international pressures try to limit the growth rate of per capita emissions or even to impose limits on the growth of national emissions, any movement in that direction would tend to freeze incomes in the developing world at a small fraction of those of their developed-world counterparts.

The Scope of Environmental Degradation: An Overview

The most pressing environmental challenges in developing countries in the next few decades will be caused by poverty. These will include health hazards created by lack of access to clean water and sanitation, indoor air pollution from biomass stoves, and deforestation and severe soil degradation—all most common where households lack economic alternatives to unsustainable patterns of living. Table 10.1 summarizes the principal health and productivity consequences of environmental damage in the developing world. It divides this damage into seven categories: water pollution and scarcity, air pollution, solid and hazardous wastes, soil degradation, deforestation, loss of biodiversity, and atmospheric changes.

In the 1980s, per capita levels of arable land fell by 1.9% annually, leading to worsening land shortages, which have forced many of the poorest onto marginal land with extremely limited cultivability. It is estimated that over 60% of the poorest peoples residing in developing countries struggle for survival on agriculturally marginal soils. This trend is greatly worsened in some areas of the developing world by strong inequalities in the distribution of land, which force an ever-growing class of landless workers onto increasingly taxed, ecologically sensitive soils. The growing intensification of cultivation on fragile lands leads to rapid soil degradation and loss of productivity. Roughly 270,000 square kilometers of soil lose virtually all of their productivity each year. An area greater than the size of India and China combined, over 1.2 billion acres, has been significantly degraded. The resulting annual loss in agricultural productivity is estimated to be between 0.5% and 1.5% of annual worldwide GNI. As a result of rapid population increases and the failure of agricultural production to keep pace, per capita food production declined in sub-Saharan Africa during the 1980s and 1990s (see Chapter 9).[10]

An environmental problem shared by both the urban and rural poor is the prevalence of unsanitary conditions created by the lack of clean water and sanitation. This in turn contributes greatly to the spread of infectious diseases. It has been estimated that waterborne pathogens that contribute to typhoid, cholera, amoebic infections, bacillary dysentery, and diarrhea account for 80% of all disease in developing countries and at least in part for up to 90% of the 13 million child deaths each year. Deteriorating environmental conditions were cited as a contributing factor to the spread of cholera epidemics in a number of countries in Latin America and Africa in the 1990s (see Chapter 8).

Rapid population growth and heavy rural-urban migration make it difficult to extend urban services to many people who need them. For example, to provide clean water to all urban dwellers in Latin American cities by 2030, the numbers served by public facilities will have to be increased by 250%. Though this figure itself is staggering, it excludes the 1.2 billion rural individuals whose needs must also be met. A comparable aim for the provision of sanitation would require 400% and 900% increases for urban and rural communities, respectively. On average throughout the developing world, 72% of all new urban households are located in shanties or slums. In Africa, the proportion is even greater, and most of these households have no access to public services.

Airborne pollutants also take a high toll on the health of citizens in developing countries. Dependence on **biomass fuels** such as wood, straw, and manure is closely related to poverty. The burning of biomass fuels for cooking and the boiling of water create dangerously high levels of indoor pollution to which 400 million to 700 million people, mostly women and children, are exposed each year. Smoke and fumes from indoor stoves are believed to contribute significantly to up to 4.3 million childhood deaths each year from respiratory diseases and to an ever-larger number of chronic respiratory illnesses (see Table 10.1).[11]

In urban areas, other sources of pollution pose serious threats to physical well-being. According to the World Health Organization, 1.3 billion people live in urban areas with unsafe levels of airborne pollutants. Yet it is projected that by 2030, manufacturing in developing countries will expand to 600% of 2000 levels, vastly increasing potential concentrations of pollutants. Just to maintain current urban air standards until 2030 (which means conceding to conditions much worse than those existing in the urban centers of developed countries), average emissions

TABLE 10.1	Principal Health and Productivity Consequences of Environmental Damage	
Environmental Problem	**Effect on Health**	**Effect on Productivity**
Water pollution and water scarcity	More than 2 million deaths and billions of illnesses a year attributable to pollution; poor household hygiene and added health risks caused by water scarcity	Declining fisheries; rural household time and municipal costs of providing safe water; aquifer depletion leading to irreversible compaction; constraint on economic activity because of water shortages
Air pollution	Many acute and chronic health impacts: Excessive urban particulate matter levels are responsible for 300,000 to 700,000 premature deaths annually and for half of childhood chronic coughing; 400 million to 700 million people, mainly women and children in poor rural areas, affected by smoky indoor air	Restrictions on vehicle and industrial activity during critical episodes; effect of acid rain on forests and water bodies
Solid and hazardous wastes	Diseases spread by rotting garbage and blocked drains; risks from hazardous wastes typically local but often acute	Pollution of groundwater resources
Soil degradation	Reduced nutrition for poor farmers on depleted soils; greater susceptibility to drought	Field productivity losses of 0.5% to 1.5% of GNI common on tropical soils; off-site siltation of reservoirs, river-transport channels, and other hydrologic investments
Deforestation	Localized flooding, leading to death and disease	Loss of sustainable logging potential and of erosion prevention, watershed stability, and carbon sequestration provided by forests
Loss of biodiversity	Potential loss of new drugs	Reduction of ecosystem adaptability and loss of genetic resources
Atmospheric changes	Possible shifts in vector-borne diseases; risks from climatic natural disasters; diseases attributable to ozone depletion (perhaps 300,000 additional cases of skin cancer a year worldwide; 1.7 million cases of cataracts)	Sea-rise damage to coastal investments; regional changes in agricultural productivity; disruption of marine food chain

Source: World Bank, *World Development Report, 1992: Development and the Environment* (New York: Oxford University Press, 1992), tab. 1. Copyright 1992 by the International Bank for Reconstruction and Development/the World Bank. Reprinted with the permission of Oxford University Press, Inc.

from LDC industries and electric generators would have to be reduced by 90% to 95% per unit of output.

Rural Development and the Environment: A Tale of Two Villages

To clarify how rural poverty and environmental degradation interact, let us take a brief look at two hypothetical developing-world villages, one in Africa and the other in South America.

The residents of the African village, located in a semiarid landscape, have been warned by international experts that cutting the remaining trees and cultivating marginal land will only worsen the hardships that they already endure. The advice runs counter to each family's first priority, which remains obtaining the basic necessities for survival. Here trees serve many functions, the most important of which is to provide firewood for cooking. Without wood, it would be impossible to prepare many foods, make cornmeal (*posho*), or boil water. As a result of the intensification of land use by a rapidly growing population, the cutting of trees for firewood, and the clearing of marginal land for cultivation, the soil is increasingly exposed to destructive environmental forces. The loss of vegetation, which helps mitigate the destructive impact of heavy winds, rain, and desiccation by the sun, leads to more rapid erosion of precious topsoil needed for cultivation. Good yields are more difficult to obtain, and the consequences of drought years are more intense. **Desertification**—encroachment of the desert into areas where erosion has been most severe—threatens to consume even the more productive land.

As a result of the loss of precious topsoil and declining output, there are fewer crops to bring to market to barter for necessities. In many households, there is less food for the children. Yet the family must spend longer hours trying to obtain enough income to survive. Paid work is scarce, although some households earn a small amount of additional income by sending family members to work on larger, more prosperous farms.

It is generally the job of women to collect enough firewood for the day's cooking. It may take several hours to walk to and from an area where it is available, adding considerably to the day's work. Though this is a relatively inefficient use of a woman's time, no alternative forms of fuel are available in the local market, and even if they were, household funds would be insufficient to purchase them. In fact, many women spend additional time collecting precious firewood to make charcoal, which can then be sold in the cities for the equivalent of a few pennies, which helps buy household necessities. The low opportunity cost of a woman's time perpetuates the wasteful use of forests and worsens local environmental conditions.[12]

Consider now the other hypothetical village, on the edge of a vast rain forest in South America. The great majority of farmers here are newcomers, drawn by government promises of land and prosperity. The public resettlement program, which distributes property titles to settlers willing to clear the land, is designed to reduce the overcrowding of cities and stem the flow of rural-to-urban migrants. In contrast to the African village, this settlement has no shortage of rainfall, wildlife, or trees. In fact, the forest is an obstacle for migrant farmers and is regularly burned to make room for cultivation.

Though burning the forest may temporarily provide the landless with a modest source of income, the land, like 90% of rain forest soil worldwide, is very infertile and can sustain intensive cultivation for only a few years. Complementary inputs and farming know-how that might help improve levels of output are in short supply, and yields begin to drop rapidly after the first few years. Settlers are then forced to burn their way deeper into the forest. Because the settlers are located on marginal soils and must constantly seek new fertile ground, with little prospect of rising above a subsistence existence, the government program may be antidevelopmental in the long run. Household incomes remain low and unstable, there is little or no gain in average productivity, and the migrating population leaves environmental devastation in its wake, further reducing the productivity of all.

Although heavy urbanization is leading to rapid demographic changes, the majority of the very poor live in rural areas similar to the two villages we described. Frequently, 70% to 80% of the poor in LDCs reside in the agricultural sector, where economic necessity often forces small farmers to use resources in ways that guarantee short-term survival but reduce the future productivity of environmental assets. Unsustainable patterns of living may be imposed by economic necessity. In periods of prolonged and severe food shortages, desperately hungry farmers have been known to eat the seeds with which they would have planted the next year's crop, knowingly paving the way for future disaster. Because it happens more slowly, the tendency of impoverished peoples to degrade agricultural resources on which they depend for survival is less dramatic, but it is motivated by similar circumstances.

The causes and consequences of rural environmental destruction vary greatly by region. However, persistent poverty is frequently the root cause. The majority of the poor in developing countries survive on the meager yield obtained from cultivation of small plots of land whose soil may be too shallow, too dry, or too sandy to sustain permanent cultivation. If the land is not in some way replenished through either shifting cultivation or the use of manufactured fertilizers, it becomes exhausted, and yields decrease with successive harvests. But the poor generally do not have the wherewithal to increase the productivity of the land by allowing it to lay fallow or by making investments in irrigation and fertilizer. In addition, where fertility rates are high and children provide a vital economic contribution through wages or on-farm labor, population and the intensity of cultivation are likely to increase over time, speeding the rate at which the soil becomes exhausted.

One immediate result of this type of environmental pressure is **soil erosion**. With little plant cover to protect it from wind and water, precious topsoil may be blown or washed away, further reducing the productivity of the land. This process of environmental degradation leads to persistent declines in local per capita food production and may eventually lead to desertification. This phenomenon is likely to spur increases in rural-to-urban migration and may force the remaining local population onto even less fertile land, where the process is repeated.

Another factor in the cycle of rural poverty and environmental destruction is **deforestation**. The vast majority of wood cut in the developing world is used as fuel for cooking. Loss of tree cover has two potentially devastating environmental implications for predominantly poor rural populations. Deforestation can lead to a number of environmental maladies that over time can greatly lower agricultural yields and increase rural hardships. On a day-to-day basis, however, the increasing scarcity of firewood means that women must spend large portions of the day in search of fuel, diverting time from other important activities such as income generation and child care. In the worst cases, fuel shortages are sufficient to require the burning of biomass or natural fertilizers, such as manure, which are important farm inputs for maintaining crop yields.

Environmental degradation that begins on a local scale can quickly escalate into a regional problem. For example, clearing of vegetation at high elevations may increase the exposure of cultivated lands at lower altitudes. Soil that has been carried away by heavy rains may silt rivers and pollute drinking water. Plants help retain rainfall, which percolates down through the soil into underground reserves of groundwater. The water is in turn tapped by a variety of plants during dry seasons in arid regions. A loss of vegetation leads to a decrease in the rate at which groundwater is replenished. The subsequent drop in the water level leads to the death of plants with shallow root systems, including young trees. This self-perpetuating process can spread the malady to previously unaffected regions. Not surprisingly, the increase in natural disasters associated with environmental degradation, including floods, droughts, and mudslides, can have a devastating impact on both the local and the regional agricultural economy.

Traditional Economic Models of the Environment

Privately Owned Resources

We will review some common economic models of the environment. In each model, the market's failure to account for environmental externalities is the exception rather than the rule, and neoclassical theory is then applied in order to cure or circumvent an inefficiency.[13] Neoclassical theory has been applied to environmental issues to determine what conditions are necessary for the efficient allocation of resources and how market failures lead to inefficiencies and to suggest ways in which these distortions can be corrected.

Figure 10.1 demonstrates how the market determines the optimal consumption of a natural resource. Finding the optimal market outcome involves maximizing the total net benefits to society from a resource, which is the difference between the total benefits derived from a resource and the total costs to producers of providing it. This is equal to the shaded area in Figure 10.1. **Total net benefit** is maximized when the **marginal cost** of producing or extracting one more unit of the resource is equal to its marginal benefit to the consumer. This occurs at Q^*, where the demand and supply curves intersect. In a perfectly competitive market, the "invisible hand" will ensure that Q^* is the quantity produced. The marginal cost curve in Figure 10.1 is upward-sloping because extraction costs increase as a resource becomes more scarce. The resulting **producer surplus** is called a **scarcity rent**. In the diagram, the producer surplus is area aPb, and the **consumer surplus** is area DPb. Together they yield a maximum net benefit equal to Dab. In principle, some of these scarcity rents could be taxed and used for environmental protection or other socially useful purposes.

If resources are scarce and are rationed over time, scarcity rents may arise even when the marginal cost of production is constant, as in Figure 10.2. The owner of a scarce resource has a finite volume of a resource X to sell (75 units) and knows that by saving a portion of it for future sales, he or she can charge a higher price today. The price of a good that is being rationed intertemporally (over time) must equate

FIGURE 10.1   Static Efficiency in Resource Allocation

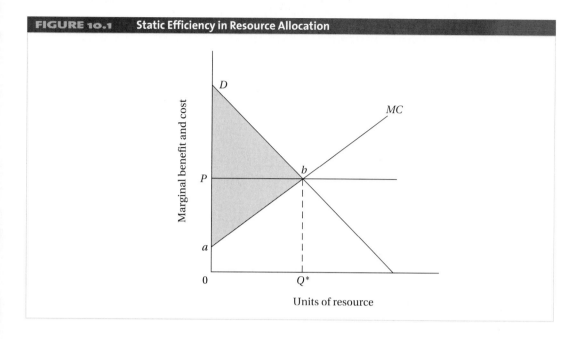

the **present value** of the **marginal net benefit** of the last unit consumed in each period. That is, the consumer must be indifferent between obtaining the next unit today and obtaining it tomorrow. In Figure 10.2, assume that a resource owner has 75 units available. If he or she is willing to offer only 50 units for sale today, the market price for the scarce resource is P_s. The scarcity rent collected by the owner of the resource is equal to $P_s abP$, the shaded region in the diagram between price and marginal cost. It is the owner's ability to collect this rent that creates the rationing effect and is thus necessary to ensure the efficient allocation of resources over time. In the absence of scarcity, all of the resource will be sold at the extraction cost $P = MC$, 75 units will be consumed at one time, and no rent will be collected.

The proponents of neoclassical free-market theory stress that inefficiencies in the allocation of resources result from impediments to the operation of the free market or imperfections in the property rights system. So long as all resources are privately owned and there are no market distortions, resources will be allocated efficiently. Perfect **property rights** markets are characterized by four conditions:

1. *Universality*—all resources are privately owned.

2. *Exclusivity*—it must be possible to prevent others from benefiting from a privately owned resource.

3. *Transferability*—the owner of a resource may sell the resource when desired.

FIGURE 10.2   Optimal Resource Allocation over Time

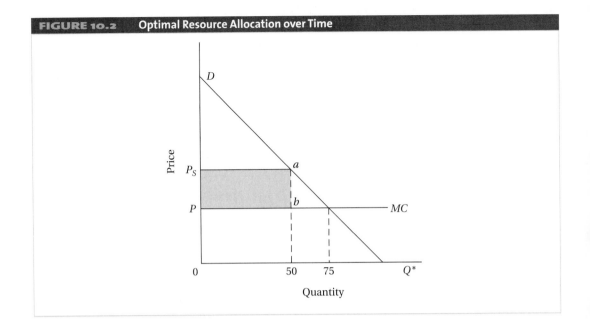

4. *Enforceability*—the intended market distribution of the benefits from resources must be enforceable.

Under these conditions, the owner of a scarce resource has an economic incentive to maximize the net benefit from its sale or use. For example, a farmer who owns his land will choose the levels of investment, technology, and output that maximize the net yield from the land. Because the value of the land may be used as collateral, any viable farm investment can be financed by obtaining a loan at the prevailing market rate of interest.

If the foregoing conditions are not met simultaneously, inefficiencies are likely to arise. Thus the way to correct the misallocation of resources is generally to remove any market distortions. A number of models have been designed to explain apparent inefficiencies in resource allocation. We next look at two simple models of inefficiency arising from imperfections in property markets.

Common Property Resources

If a scarce resource (such as arable land) is publicly owned and thus freely available to all (for, say, farming or grazing animals), as is the case with a **common property resource**, any potential profits or scarcity rents will be competed away. As we have noted, neoclassical theory suggests that in the absence of scarcity rents, inefficiencies will arise. Using a somewhat different framework, we will investigate the misallocation of resources under a common property system. Figure 10.3 describes the

FIGURE 10.3   Common Property Resources and Misallocation

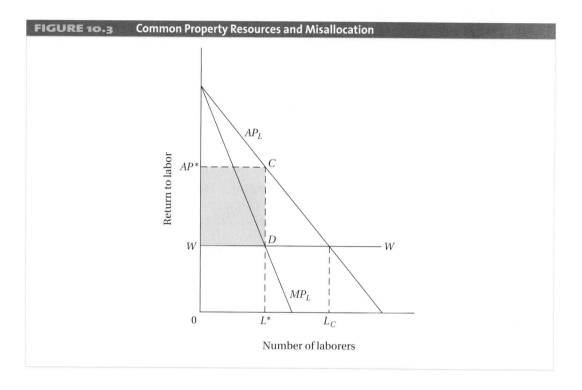

relationship between the returns to labor on a given piece of land and the number of laborers cultivating it.

Suppose for the moment that this piece of land is privately held. Conventional wisdom tells us that the landowner will hire additional labor to work the land until the marginal product of the last worker is equal to the market wage, W, at point L^*. The workload is shared equally among the employees, each of whom produces the *average* product. However, assuming decreasing returns to labor, each new worker hired reduces the average product of all workers. The *marginal* product of each additional worker is thus equal to his average product minus the decrease in the average product across all other workers. If an additional employee is hired beyond L^*, his cost to the producer, W, will be greater than his marginal product, and the difference will represent a net loss to the landowner. A profit maximizer will thus hire L^* workers, with a total output equal to average product AP^* multiplied by the number of workers, L^*. Scarcity rents collected by the landowner will equal AP^*CDW.

Society's total net benefit from land will be lower under a system of common property, unless workers can coordinate their resource use decisions in a cooperative manner. Generally, if land is commonly owned, each worker is able to appropriate the entire product of his work, which is equal to the average product of all workers. Worker income will continue to exceed the wage until enough workers are attracted so that the average product falls to the level of the wage, at which point the labor force equals L_C. Though total farm output may either rise or fall (depending on whether MP_L is positive or negative—it is negative as drawn in Figure 10.3), the marginal product of the additional workers is below the wage. Because we are assuming that all workers could be employed elsewhere with productivity equal to or greater than W, it follows that social welfare must fall when marginal product falls below W. No scarcity rent is collected at L_C. The implication of the common property resource model is that where possible, privatization of resources will lead to an increase in aggregate welfare and an efficient allocation of resources.

Note that these neoclassical models are strictly concerned with efficiency and do not address issues related to equity. Income distribution is not considered, and the theory is unconcerned with the distributional issues arising when all scarcity rents from national resources accrue to a few private owners. Although neoclassical theorists have sometimes suggested that an optimal outcome may be achieved through the taxation and then "lump sum" redistribution of the gains accruing to the owners of scarce natural resources, the historical record for such efforts is not encouraging. This is especially true where the authorities responsible for legislating and coordinating such redistributions are also the owners. Thus the large-scale commercial privatization of resources does not necessarily ensure an improvement in standards of living for the impoverished majority.

Beyond the standard neoclassical arguments, there are a number of alternative reasons why individuals making use of publicly owned resources may make inefficient use of them within the context of farming systems in developing countries. Family farmers, who, as we saw in Chapter 9, are generally the most efficient cultivators of land, may be reluctant to make land-augmenting investments if they are afraid of losing tenure on the common property plot. They may also have insufficient funds to hire additional labor or purchase complementary resources due to a lack of collateral, a factor that frequently excludes the poor from competitive credit markets (see Chapter 16). It is therefore possible that conferring extended tenancy rights or ownership of land to family farmers would raise productivity. The relevant question for the property rights structure is then, who should obtain title to the land if privatization is to occur? A simple auction of publicly owned land to the highest bidder is unlikely to be consistent with development objectives.

Public Goods and Bads: Regional Environmental Degradation and the Free-Rider Problem

In the preceding discussion, each additional worker who joined those cultivating commonly held land created a negative **externality** by lowering the returns to all other workers without providing any compensation. An externality occurs when one person's consumption or production behavior affects that of another without any compensation. The benefits and costs of one's actions are said to be internalized when one is made to bear them in full. In the previous common property problem, the externalities associated with decreasing average product were easily internalized by reestablishing perfect property markets through the privatization of public property. In many cases, the **internalization** of externalities is not so easily accomplished. This is especially the case where the consequences of an individual's actions constitute a public good or a public bad. A **public good** is anything that provides a benefit to everyone and the availability of which is in no way diminished by its simultaneous enjoyment by others. Common examples include clean air and national defense. A **public bad** is any product or condition that decreases the well-being of others in a nonexhaustive manner. Air pollution and water pollution are examples. Intuitively, it is clear that given the fact that individuals do not pay the full costs associated with their actions, too much of a public bad will be produced. The result is a socially nonoptimal outcome. We will demonstrate this shortly using a diagrammatic representation.

Let us consider the case of a particular public bad, regional environmental degradation caused by deforestation. Increased exposure to the forces of erosion, excessive drying of the soil, regional loss of groundwater, silting or pollution of public water supplies, and potential climatic changes are all public bads associated with the clear-cutting or burning of trees. Whether these trees are on private or commonly held property, the clearing of protective ground cover, either for cultivation or for the extraction of timber, may lead to more widespread regional environmental degradation. To simplify our analysis, we will translate this public-bad problem into a public-good framework. Environmental conservation through the protection of trees provides a benefit to all and is thus a public good.

The most obvious difference between a public good and a purely private good is that aggregate demand for the public resource is determined by summing individual demand curves vertically as in Figure 10.4a rather than horizontally, as is the case for private goods as illustrated in Figure 10.4b. The difference results from the fact that many individuals may enjoy the same unit of a public good but only one may benefit from a unit of a normal, private consumption good. Through vertical summation, we are sure to capture all benefits accruing to all individuals from each unit of a public good. The marginal cost associated with the preservation of an additional tree is equal to the forestry maintenance cost plus the opportunity cost of the tree, that is, the most valuable alternative use of the tree, such as for firewood, charcoal, animal fodder, or lumber. Figure 10.4 illustrates the problem of pricing public goods.

In Figure 10.4a, the socially optimal number of trees is Q^*. It is determined by the intersection of the (vertically summed) aggregate demand curve with the supply (MC) curve. At Q^*, total net benefits to society from the public good, $P_M Dc$, are maximized. However, due to what we call the **free-rider problem**, the free market will not lead to this optimal quantity. Because individuals are able to enjoy the benefits of trees provided by others, each will contribute less than what he or she would if acting independently. At a price of P_M, the free market will satisfy person B's demand Q_B while not denying person A's requirements of Q_A; that is, A can free ride on B's contribution. The market will therefore provide a suboptimal level of forest preservation, Q_B. To restore optimality (Q^* of the public good), some form of government intervention is required. The most effective solution is to charge each consumer just enough per unit, P_A and P_B for individuals A and B, respectively, to entice each of them to demand the preservation of the optimal quantity of trees,

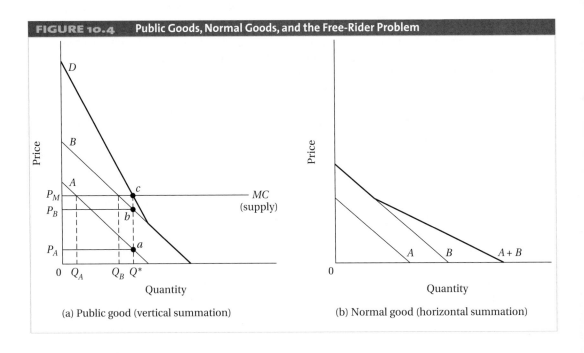

FIGURE 10.4   Public Goods, Normal Goods, and the Free-Rider Problem

(a) Public good (vertical summation)

(b) Normal good (horizontal summation)

Q^*. Their joint payments, $P_A \times Q^*$ for A plus $P_B \times Q^*$ for B, represent a total contribution equal to $P_M \times Q^*$, exactly the sum required to purchase the socially optimal level of preservation.

Limitations of the Public-Good Framework

The problem with the public-good pricing mechanism is, of course, how to know which prices to charge. People have no incentive to divulge how much they really benefit from a public good because by shirking they may free ride on the contributions of others and avoid paying their full share. A government may be capable of reducing market inefficiencies, but it is unlikely to be able to produce a perfect allocation of resources due to deficiencies in the information available to it. Hypothetically, collected fees can be used to provide a public good by preserving existing forests or managing a sustainable timber production program that will supply the community's needed timber. Although charging fees to the people benefiting from the preservation of a resource may sound practical, it is exceedingly difficult. In a development context, the problems become even more complicated. When the collection of fees entails taxing deeply impoverished populations with little or no cash income, such a program becomes an impossibility. It would be equally difficult to collect payment from people who are cutting trees to meet subsistence needs. However, neoclassical theory can be useful for explaining why market failures lead to the inefficient allocation of resources in highly commercialized economies and how these inefficiencies may be mitigated.

Urban Development and the Environment

The Ecology of Urban Slums

In some ways, life among the poor in urban slums is similar to that of the poor in rural villages: Families work long hours, income is uncertain, and difficult trade-offs must be made between expenditures on nutrition, medical care, and education. Though on average, urban dwellers are likely to have higher incomes, the poorest are frequently at greater risk of being exposed to dangerous environmental conditions. Let us contrast our earlier look at environmental conditions in an African and a South American rural community with those of an Asian urban shanty.

> In a typical urban slum in an Asian metropolis, health-threatening pollutants are commonplace both inside and outside the home. Women are scarcely aware that the smoke from the fuels they burn in the home to cook and boil water may have severe long-term consequences for the health of their children. However, even if they did, knowledge alone would do little to alter the economic necessity of cooking with relatively dirty but cheap and accessible fuels. Conditions resulting from poor ventilation in the home are equivalent to smoking several packs of cigarettes per day, and women and their children are exposed to these fumes for long portions of each day. Though some children actually avoid much of this exposure by attending school, many are kept out of school to assist their mothers in market work or the production of goods at home. Thus from an early age, chronic and acute bronchitis are a cruel fact of life. Debilitating and ultimately fatal respiratory infections among the poor are commonplace.
>
> But it is not only in the home that individuals are exposed to harmful pollutants. Street vendors and market workers are constantly exposed to high levels of other pollutants. Untreated sewage runs in open drains along the roads, providing a conduit for infectious diseases. Because food and drinking water are frequently contaminated, diarrhea is common, especially in young children. Frequent spells of the illness cause malnourishment, even when food is more plentiful, making the young more susceptible to other diseases. Many of the weakest children die from severe dehydration. Because the fuels used to cook foods and boil water must be purchased in the market and consume a large portion of the daily earnings, there is sometimes insufficient fuel to boil the household's drinking water, increasing the chance of infection. The costs associated with obtaining medical treatment for sick children may be very high, involving the opportunity cost of time spent traveling to and from clinics and long hours in crowded waiting rooms, in addition to medical fees. For many households, the forgone earnings can be ill afforded. In many of the poorest households, only boys receive medical attention because they are expected to contribute more to household income. It is thus not surprising that they are more likely than their sisters to survive to adulthood.
>
> Children playing in the streets and others working outdoors are also exposed to the combined emissions from automobiles and factories. Dangerously high levels of atmospheric lead are common because few cars are equipped with the expensive catalytic converters now mandated in the West. Due both to physical and mental impairments suffered as a result of exposure to environmental factors and to repeated absence from school, children in the poorest neighborhoods will find it difficult to meet basic academic standards. And with many thousands of new migrants locating their families in this urban shanty each year, the conditions are likely to worsen in the future.

The urban centers of the developing world will absorb over 80% of future increases in world population. Much of the intensification of urban congestion, however, will result from heavy rural-urban migration. It is expected that by 2010, the rural population of developing countries will stabilize at 2.8 billion, at which point rural-urban migration will be sufficient to counteract any additional population growth. The rapid expansion of urban centers has placed increasing strain on the resources of developing-country governments attempting to provide adequate infrastructure and services to their inhabitants.

Though the health implications of environmental degradation are currently highest in rural areas, due to rapid urbanization the vast bulk of future increases in human exposure to unsafe conditions will occur in the cities. Unsanitary environmental conditions exacerbated by rapidly increasing urban congestion and industrial emissions pose severe health hazards (see Table 10.1). Exposure to high concentrations of toxic pollutants as well as pathogens in contaminated air and water can cause a variety of health problems at tremendous cost to a struggling economy. Left unchecked, environmental hazards tend to grow exponentially as the size of cities in developing countries increases.

Because the urban poor are much less able than the wealthy to insulate themselves from the negative effects of a tainted environment, they are more likely to suffer serious consequences resulting from environmental degradation. In addition, malnutrition and poor health among people living in urban shantytowns tend to reduce individual resistance to environmental hazards. Though at least 43% of people residing in the cities of developing countries already live in squatter settlements, this number may rise in the future because a much higher proportion of new housing each year is located in shantytowns.[14]

The bulk of any increases in mortality and morbidity in urban areas will result from health complications due to chronic exposure to factors that weaken the body's defenses. Thus bronchitis and diarrhea, which afflict large portions of LDC populations, are likely to impose greater burdens on the poor than fatalities resulting from sudden exposure to toxins. It is therefore important to concentrate our analysis on the conditions experienced by urban populations on a day-to-day basis.

Much of the environmental degradation of urban areas and the consequences for economic growth and human health are avoidable. However, to explore viable solutions, it is necessary to have a clear understanding of the sources of problems and the ways in which they interact. The causes of severe urban environmental problems are numerous, but for simplicity of analysis we will divide these factors into two categories—those associated with urbanization and industrial growth and those that must be dealt with in any community but tend to be exacerbated by the congestion of urban settings.

Industrialization and Urban Air Pollution

The early stages of urbanization and industrialization in developing countries are generally accompanied by rising incomes and worsening environmental conditions. Cross-sectional analysis of numerous countries at different levels of income suggest that urban pollution tends first to rise with national income levels and then to fall.[15] This effect has been dubbed the "environmental Kuznets curve." According to the World Bank, pollution levels for even the worst quartile of high-income cities are better than for the best quartile of low-income cities.[16] Indeed, at higher incomes it is easier to afford expensive **clean technologies**. However, there is nothing inevitable about the trend. Air (and water) quality is closely related to the extent of government regulation, in both high- and low-income countries. Moreover, some environmental resources, such as rain forests, may be irretrievably lost unless action is taken immediately.

The principal sources of air pollution, which pose the greatest health threat associated with modernization, are energy use, vehicular emissions, and industrial production. Industrialization can lead to increases in waste either directly through emissions or indirectly by altering patterns of consumption and boosting demand for manufactured goods. The production of manufactured goods generally entails the creation of by-products that may be detrimental to the environment. The extent to which they degrade the environment will depend on a number of factors, including the type of by-products produced, their quantities, and their means of disposal. Unfortunately, in the absence of regulation, the cheapest way to dispose of unwanted by-products is usually to release them untreated into the air and waterways or to dump them on the ground where runoff is free to sink into groundwater or wash into rivers. Due to the broader transmission of ideas, greater availability of goods, and increased incomes, changes in patterns of consumption and their environmental consequences are likely to appear first in cities. Until technologies and infrastructures capable of coping with environmental consequences are introduced, modernization is likely to lead to high urban environmental costs. (Some representative examples of the extreme disparities in per capita consumption of various goods in selected high-, middle-, and low-income countries are found in Table 10.2 later in this chapter.)

We have already looked briefly at the issue of externalities and the fact that many of the costs of pollutants are borne by someone other than the polluter. This suggests that the price paid for the consumption of a good is below the social cost associated with the good. Figure 10.5 depicts the typical supply and demand curves. In this case, however, we have labeled the supply curve $S = MC_P$ because it represents the marginal **private costs** associated with producing good X. The free-market equilibrium output and price are Q_M and P_M, respectively. If there are externalities associated with the consumption or production of each unit of good X, the MC_P curve does not represent the true costs of the good to society. If each unit of good X imposes a cost of $2 on a third party, we can obtain the true marginal social cost curve MC_S by legislating a $2-per-unit sales tax on the output. This **pollution tax** shifts the private cost curve upward by $2 at every point to MC_S in Figure 10.5. At the new intersection between the demand curve and the marginal **social cost** curve, Q^* is the efficient outcome and P^* the price. Therefore, by incorporating the social costs of pollution into the analysis, the actual output of the polluting product is reduced to the socially optimal level while the price charged to the consumer rises from P_M to P^* and the price received by the producer falls from P_M to P_C. Depending on the relative elasticities of the demand and supply

FIGURE 10.5 Pollution Externalities: Private versus Social Costs and the Role of Taxation

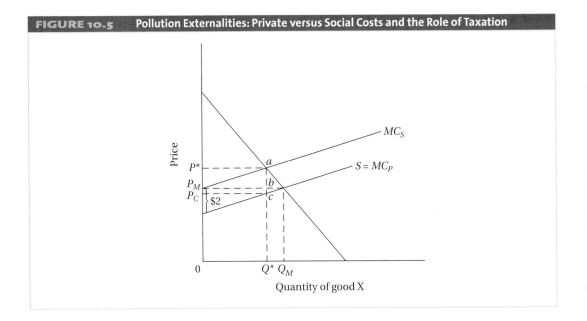

curves, the burden of the pollution tax is shared by both consumers and producers. In Figure 10.5, the consumer pays ab and the producer bc of the ac tax.

At sufficiently high levels, most emissions will be toxic to humans or otherwise damaging to the environment, whereas at low levels, per-unit costs may be insignificant. This is due to the fact that humans have some tolerance for most toxins, although the ability to tolerate exposure may rapidly decline as concentrations in drinking water and air increase. The environment also has an **absorptive capacity** that enables it to assimilate a quantity of most pollutants. Once this critical quantity has been exceeded, however, concentrations and hence toxicity are likely to rise rapidly. A more realistic marginal social cost curve is drawn in Figure 10.6. As concentrations of pollutants increase (as total output increases), the gap between the social and private cost curves increases. While aggregate demand remains low, this differential will be small. However, as the demand curve shifts outward from D to D' with rapid urbanization and rising incomes, the importance of externalities rises at an increasing rate. This would suggest that the costs associated with curing urban ills caused by congestion will increase faster than the rate of increase of the population.

Health hazards are created by toxic air emissions as well as increasing volumes of waste that contaminate water supplies and land. Though research on the issue has been scanty, there is increasing evidence that in the absence of regulation, current and future increases in LDC manufacturing and transport will have serious consequences for public health. It is estimated that in the latter half of the 1980s, by World Health Organization (WHO) standards, 1.3 billion people lived in cities with unsafe levels of airborne particulate matter and 1 billion were exposed to unacceptably high levels of sulfur dioxide.[17] Other compounds, such as nitrous

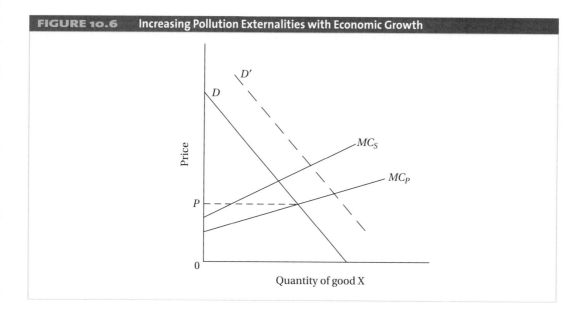

FIGURE 10.6   Increasing Pollution Externalities with Economic Growth

oxides and organic compounds, rise in importance as industrialization proceeds. By contaminating water supplies, contributing to dangerous levels of air pollution, and damaging public and private property, industrial pollution can exact a high toll in terms of human health and economic prosperity.

A number of case studies indicate the potential severity of industrial pollution. In Bangkok, high levels of airborne lead have caused such severe consequences for the development of small children that the average child's IQ has been lowered by four or more points by the age of 7. Seventy percent of children in Mexico City have abnormally high blood levels of lead by WHO standards. Due to serious air pollution in 1980, the industrial town of Cubatao, Brazil, reported 10,000 medical emergencies involving respiratory ailments in a total population of 80,000. Health complications caused by smog tend to be worse in developing countries, where poor nutrition and general ill health greatly lower individual tolerance to pollutants. The implications for health are the worst for young children, who inhale roughly twice as many pollutants per unit of body weight as adults do.

Problems of Congestion and the Availability of Clean Water and Sanitation

Though rising levels of industrial emissions of pollution pose a serious threat to the health of urban inhabitants in developing countries, at present the two most important environmental factors affecting the health of the urban poor are the inaccessibility of clean water and the lack of sanitation. In 2000, 42% of people in sub-Saharan Africa had no access to an improved water source, even though millions of urban residents were counted as having access if they shared a single faucet with over 1,000 residents at a considerable distance from their homes. In South Asia, 66% of the population had no access to improved sanitation facilities.[18] Because there are no alternative sources, many of the poor collect drinking water from rivers, streams, and canals that are polluted with human excreta and chemicals.

Although the poorest urban dwellers experience many of the same adverse environmental conditions as the rural poor, including heavy indoor pollution and unsanitary conditions, crowding can intensify exposure. Raw sewage runs in the streets, mixing with garbage and contributing to the spread of disease. This is reflected in the fact that death rates in urban shanties are occasionally higher than in rural areas, even though the latter generally have fewer services. Though survival rates in developing countries have been improving, these achievements are now being threatened by rapidly increasing numbers of poor with no access to clean water or sanitation.

The health and economic costs associated with these conditions are enormous and represent formidable obstacles to the improvement of living standards. The prevalence of disease and the potential for epidemics is closely linked to the accessibility of clean water and the success of a community in eliminating exposure to sources of infectious diseases. Some 900 million cases of diarrheal diseases, 200 million cases of schistosomiasis, and 900 million cases of hookworm occur each year. Cholera, typhoid, and paratyphoid also contribute greatly to human suffering. Provision of clean water and sanitation can greatly reduce mortality rates. For example, children in households with adequate facilities are 60% less likely to die from diarrhea than those in households without such facilities.

The enormous economic costs resulting from lost productivity and expensive medical care represent a drag on economic development. Chronic ill health is both a consequence and a cause of poverty. It can contribute to poor nutrition, poor school performance, reduced productivity, and permanent disability and thus give little hope for economic advancement (see Chapter 8). In addition to averting fatalities, improvements in the supply of water and sanitation reduce the incidence and severity of illnesses, thereby reducing other costs associated with waterborne disease.

Although higher-income households generally have access to either publicly or privately provided services, the poorest are usually without services. This is frequently due to the illegal status of much low-income housing, which renders it ineligible for government services and makes it risky for private individuals to invest in upgrading equipment. It is estimated that as much as 70% of new urban housing in the LDCs is in some way illegal. As a result, the majority of the poor must purchase water, which is frequently contaminated, from vendors at an average of 10 times the cost of piped water.

To take a typical example, in Lima, Peru, poor households consume one-sixth as much water as higher-income households, but their water bills are on average three times higher. In addition, this low-quality water must be boiled, leading to expensive fuel bills and adding to indoor pollution. If these households were to boil water for periods of time recommended by the government, the additional fuel costs would consume 29% of household income. In Jakarta, Indonesia, $50 million is spent per year on boiling water. Much of these costs could be avoided, and total expenditures on water could be decreased, if clean water were made widely available.

Postponement of investments in the infrastructure required for provision of urban water and sanitation can lead to much greater costs in the future. Poor access to water has led to widespread systems of private wells, which can overtax existing groundwater supplies. In a number of large cities including Bangkok, Mexico City, and Jakarta, this phenomenon has led to the collapse of existing infrastructure and the destruction of property through subsidence of the land and flooding. In coastal areas, overuse can draw salt water into supplies, leading to their permanent salinization. Where raw sewage is untreated and is improperly disposed of, underground and surface water is frequently contaminated, creating long-term shortages of clean water and threatening public health.

Foreign-exchange earnings may also be severely threatened by contaminated water supplies. Strict health standards in developed countries may prohibit the importation of agricultural goods produced with potentially contaminated water. For example, an outbreak of cholera in Peru in 1991 led to an estimated $1 billion combined loss in export and tourism markets within a few months.

In light of these problems, it is not surprising that the costs of preventive measures are much lower than those associated with lost revenues, resources, and infrastructure. Investment in clean water and sanitation can essentially provide economic returns because relatively small initial outlays may be used to avert the much larger costs associated with urban crises. It is imperative, however, that efforts to provide improved urban sanitation and clean water be carried out simultaneously in rural areas. This leads us to consider needed policy reforms and the crucial question of financial feasibility.

The Need for Policy Reform

Recognition is growing that insufficient action has been taken to reduce environmental hazards through primary health care, education, and the provision of services such as clean water and sanitation. According to one estimate, expenditure on these programs will have to double over the next few years just to maintain the current situation. But the structure of some existing programs may actually hinder progress. Currently, few low-budget grassroots services are provided, even though they tend to be more cost-effective, especially when community organizations become involved. Annually, only about 0.5% of developing-country GDP is spent on sanitation and water services; 80% is spent on programs costing at least $550 per person, and less than 20% is spent on programs costing less than $30 per person. Despite the emphasis on improved water and sanitation access in the Millennium Development Goals (see Chapter 1), few increases in budgets for these goals were apparent by 2005. Similar patterns occur in the health professions. As a consequence, government schemes tend to reach a relatively select group of constituents while falling far short of providing universal access for the poor, who, as we have described, are subject to the worst environmental conditions. Unless governments vastly increase the breadth of the population served by programs, these disparities will tend to worsen with increased urbanization in the future. Unfortunately, the poor generally lack the clout to demand their share of environmental protection efforts.

To meet their targets in the face of increasing financial shortages, governments will have to radically change the manner in which scarce resources are managed. In the past, many policies designed to cure environmental ills have actually worsened the problems that they were designed to alleviate. Where scarce resources have been provided to recipients at prices far below the cost of provision, artificial scarcities have arisen. For example, on average in developing countries, the price paid for piped water is only 35% of the total cost of supplying it. Due to rationing, such subsidies frequently benefit only people with higher incomes. The poor are thus forced to buy water from vendors at a price ten times that of piped water. Many governments provide free water service at little or no charge, even in areas with water shortages. The result is the waste of precious resources. In Cairo, Jakarta, Lima, Manila, and Mexico City, among other cities, more than half of urban water supplies remain unaccounted for. Ironically, while chronic water shortages affect 2 billion people annually, overirrigation and waterlogging have contributed to the salinization of roughly 25% of all irrigated land, greatly reducing its productivity.

Similar patterns are repeated for energy and agricultural inputs. The average price paid for electricity in developing countries, which, again, is usually available only to the relatively well-to-do, represents less than half the cost of supplying it, and losses in transmission are three to four times higher than in industrialized countries.

Better pricing policies and efficiency requirements would lead to improvements in the allocation of resources, as well as substantial savings on fuel imports. Fertilizer and pesticide subsidies, which most frequently benefit larger farmers, tend to promote monocultures that deplete soils and to discourage the use of sustainable methods such as integrated pest management. Used excessively, they can lead to the contamination of underground and surface water supplies.[19]

Another factor that needs more careful consideration in the design of environmental policy is the important role of women in the management of resources. Through their roles as managers of fuel and water supplies, agricultural producers, and guardians of household health, women control the fate of many of the world's resources. Yet they are rarely consulted in the design of government services or have access to extension programs. Women in the developing world, who commonly work 60 to 90 hours a week, will have little or no use for resources unless they are made easily accessible. Further investments in the educational attainment of women, which is closely related to the health of their children, can thus greatly enhance environmental efforts.

The Global Environment: Rain Forest Destruction and Greenhouse Gases

Though early Malthusian predictions of environmental calamity proved to be overly pessimistic, recent scientific studies indicate that there is cause for concern with respect to the limited ability of the earth's ecosystem to regenerate itself. Increasing evidence regarding the extent of **ozone depletion** and encroaching **global warming** present alarming implications for the global climate. Concerns range from an increase in the incidence of skin cancer to desertification and rising oceans. The potential costs of climate changes are likely to vary from region to region, with losses being greatest for people already living in semiarid regions. Because most developing countries have predominantly agricultural economies and so many are located in warm semiarid regions of the globe, any increase in temperatures is likely to have harsh implications for LDC incomes and food self-sufficiency.

Goods (or bads) such as ozone depletion and global warming whose benefits (or costs) reach across national borders, generations, and population groups are known as **global public goods**. In addition to world environmental quality, health, knowledge, and peace may also qualify as global public goods.[20]

It is through changes in patterns of land use that the developing countries currently make their largest contribution to global concentrations of **greenhouse gases**. It is estimated that deforestation alone accounts for roughly 25% of CO_2 emissions worldwide.[21] Also of great significance is the fact that deforestation leads to the destruction of a vital source of atmospheric oxygen. Because trees consume carbon dioxide and release oxygen during the process of photosynthesis, the tropical rain forests represent an important mechanism through which the ecosystem regenerates itself. Clearing the rain forests will reduce the environment's absorptive capacity for CO_2.

The majority of tropical rain forest destroyed, about 60%, is cleared for cultivation by small farmers. Each year, 4.5 million hectares are cleared for this purpose, much of it, like 90% of rain forest land worldwide, so infertile that it will be cultivable for no more than a few years. The land is then frequently sold to large farmers who use it for grazing cattle, often under heavy government subsidy, leading to further desertification. The previous tenants are then forced to clear additional forest areas in a desperate attempt to derive a livelihood for the next few years. In the past, rain forest settlement programs have regularly been encouraged and financed by LDC governments, often with the assistance of international development banks. A review by the World Bank of its own support for settlement programs found that they were exceptionally expensive—on average, $10,000 per household—and could be environmentally destructive. Policymakers in countries with large rain forests, including Brazil, Bolivia, Costa Rica, the Philippines, and Ecuador, are therefore experiencing increasing pressure from foreign public and private agencies to implement policies that will reduce the rate of tropical forest destruction. It is argued that the resulting decrease in the growth of concentration of greenhouse gases will be in everyone's interests. Thus rain forest preservation provides a public good.

Because the political and economic costs of preserving the rain forests are often masked or ambiguous, maintaining a forest may appear to be an almost costless venture. In fact, because of the important roles that rain forests play in LDCs' domestic economies, the true costs of preserving all remaining forests may be extraordinarily high. The opportunity costs arising from the preservation of rain forests will involve the loss of an important source of domestic fuel, forgone foreign-exchange earnings from timber and beef, and the loss of a temporary solution to the problem of land shortages and population pressures. It is therefore unreasonable to assume that the few highly indebted countries that contain the majority of remaining rain forests should be responsible for single-handedly providing this global public good.

Several steps must be taken to preserve the rain forests. Developing countries could vastly increase the efficiency of their economic use of rain forests by managing them (less than 1% of rain forests have been replanted or cut in a sustainable manner) and by developing alternative markets for other rain forest products such as meats, nuts, fruits, oils, sweeteners, resins, tannin, fibers, construction materials, and natural medicinal compounds. The international community should also assist in the preservation effort. By reducing trade barriers to the alternative goods just mentioned, developed countries reduce the dependence of LDCs on unsustainable modes of production. Forgiving debt and debt-for-nature swaps (to be explained shortly) also reduce the need for the rapid exploitation of forests to raise foreign exchange. Finally, funds for the preservation and maintenance of tropical rain forests are necessary to guarantee the success of conservation programs that provide a public good. It is important that such funds not be viewed as aid because the ultimate benefits are to be shared by all.

The heavy indebtedness of many LDCs may make it exceptionally difficult for governments with large debt burdens to finance the expenses of environmental programs designed to protect natural resources. In total, developing countries owe in excess of $2.1 trillion (see Chapter 14). In 1996, total long-term debt of countries in sub-Saharan Africa was 56% of their combined GDPs, the highest in the developing world. Slowdowns in the downward movement of fertility rates in the Philippines, India, Tunisia, Morocco, Colombia, and Costa Rica have been attributed to cuts in health care and family-planning programs arising from efforts to reduce foreign debt. The result is the persistence of environmentally destructive poverty and population pressures. Ironically, heavy debt servicing can undermine the long-term creditworthiness of borrower nations by diverting domestic funds away from programs designed to maintain the productivity of national resources.

Because they require dramatic cuts in services and programs, the structural adjustment and stabilization policies required of highly indebted countries by conditionality agreements with the World Bank and the International Monetary Fund (policies detailed in Chapter 14) have often intensified poverty and its environmental consequences. In recent years, however, a number of international assistance agencies, including the World Bank, have established environmental divisions to promote more environmentally conscientious patterns of lending. They have also initiated their own programs to address environmental issues directly. Their success in the future may largely depend on the compatibility of such efforts with the economic realities confronting LDC governments.

Policy Options in Developing and Developed Countries

What Less Developed Countries Can Do

A range of policy options is available for LDC governments. Six stand out: (1) proper resource pricing, (2) community involvement, (3) clearer property rights and resource ownership, (4) improving economic alternatives for the poor, (5) raising the economic status of women, and (6) policies to abate industrial emissions. Let's briefly examine each in turn.[22]

Proper Resource Pricing   The most obvious area for reform is probably government pricing policy, which can exacerbate resource shortages or encourage unsustainable methods of production. Often programs that were ostensibly designed to reduce hardships for the very poor have had little impact on poverty and have worsened existing inequalities. High-income households have frequently been the predominant beneficiaries of energy, water, and agricultural subsidies. The results have often included the wasteful and unsustainable use of resources. Even though elimination of misdirected subsidies is a relatively costless (or profitable) way of protecting the environment, the political stakes are high where powerful elites stand to lose lucrative government transfers.

Community Involvement   Programs to improve environmental conditions are likely to be most effective when they work in tandem with community networks, ensuring that program design is consistent with both local and national objectives. The experience of development agencies has demonstrated that grassroots efforts can be more cost-effective because they generally involve the use of low-cost alternatives and provide jobs to local populations. When poor communities truly benefit from public-works programs, residents are often willing and able to contribute much or all of the program costs.

Clearer Property Rights and Resource Ownership   Investments in household sanitation and water and on-farm improvements often represent a large portion of lifetime savings for the poor, the loss of which can impose harsh economic consequences on households. Hence the lack of secure tenure on rural or urban property can greatly hinder investment in environmental upgrading. Legalization of tenure can lead to improved living conditions for the poor and increases in agricultural investments.

In many cases, however, land reform may be necessary (see Chapter 9). It is not uncommon for renters or sharecroppers to lose the economic gains from their farm investments because it is relatively easy for landlords to extract higher rents once the productivity of the land has been improved. Transferring title to tenants may be the only means of ensuring that financial rewards from land-augmenting investments accrue to the investor. Land reform may also be required where unequal distribution of land has led to large tracts of uncultivated high-quality land in close proximity to overexploited marginal lands cultivated by large numbers of landless workers.

Programs to Improve the Economic Alternatives of the Poor   Further environmental devastation in rural areas may be avoidable in many cases through on-farm investments in irrigation and sustainable farming techniques, the use of alternative fuels, and the creation of barriers to erosion. However, the economic costs of each of these alternatives is prohibitive for the vast majority of impoverished family producers. Ironically, the greater the environmental devastation, the less likely that a rural population will be able to afford alternative methods of production. It is therefore important that government programs make credit and land-augmenting inputs accessible to small farmers. By providing rural economic opportunities outside the home, governments can also create alternative employment opportunities so that the very poor are not forced to cultivate marginal lands. For example, programs to build rural infrastructure (roads, storage facilities, etc.) create local jobs, alleviate population pressures on ecologically sensitive land, stimulate rural development, and reduce the flow of rural-to-urban migration.

Raising the Economic Status of Women Improving the educational attainment of women and increasing their range of economic alternatives raise the opportunity cost of their time and may lead to decreases in desired family size (see Chapter 6). Education also tends to increase women's access to information concerning child nutrition and hygiene, a factor that has been linked to rapid declines in child mortality. It is important that community-based environmental programs work closely with women because their own day-to-day activities may largely determine patterns of resource use and their ability to meet the needs of their families is dependent on the sustainable management of water and fuel supplies.

Industrial Emissions Abatement Policies A range of policy options is available to developing-country governments for the purpose of limiting industrial pollution, including the taxation of emissions, tradable emissions permits, quotas, and standards. There is some evidence to suggest that the first two policies, which are market-based, are more effective because they tend to reward the more efficient producers, allow greater flexibility for firms, and are generally easier to enforce. Regulations should be as simple as possible and must be enforceable. Additional incentives to adopt clean technologies may be provided through tax credits and subsidies specifically tied to the purchase or development of pollution abatement technologies. Ironically, the hardest industries to regulate are those run by governments themselves because the profit motive is often not a consideration and, as a general rule, it is difficult for any group to regulate itself.[23]

How Developed Countries Can Help LDCs

Industrial countries can help developing nations in their efforts to improve the environment of development in three areas: (1) trade liberalization, (2) debt relief, and (3) financial and technological assistance.

Trade Policies The focus of much current discussion concerning the environment is the desperate need to break the cycle of poverty and environmental destruction in developing countries. However, the increasing protectionism of MDCs caused international markets for LDC products, and thus earning capacity, to shrink dramatically (see Chapters 12 and 13). According to a 2001 United Nations estimate, annual losses of the developing world due to the lack of access to the goods markets of the developed world were more than double the total amount of aid received in 2000 from all sources. If lack of access to capital and labor markets is also included, annual losses total about $500 billion. Eliminating trade barriers against developing-country exports, by stimulating economic growth in the developing world, creating new jobs, and encouraging rural development, could significantly reduce the level of absolute poverty.

In addition to trade barriers, the industrialized countries penalize developing-country exports by heavily subsidizing their own agricultural sectors. The resulting large surpluses are often dumped on international markets, unfairly undercutting the agricultural exports of developing countries in markets for which they are presumed to have a comparative advantage. Reducing the estimated $500 billion in annual agricultural subsidies in developed countries could help guarantee the success of rural development efforts in LDCs by reducing poverty and the environmental decay that it causes. Wider access to international markets would not only raise incomes but also improve the ability of heavily indebted countries to service their debt. They would thereby reduce their dependence on the unsustainable exploitation of rain forests and other resources to raise foreign exchange.

Debt Relief Heavy debt servicing drastically reduces funds available to LDC governments for domestic social programs, including those designed to alleviate poverty and reduce environmental degradation (see Chapter 14). Debt forgiveness may be required if LDC governments are to be given the flexibility to make the sweeping changes necessary to achieve sustainable development.

Debt-for-nature swaps offer an attractive and mutually beneficial way for the developing world to retire its foreign-denominated debt while guaranteeing the protection of tropical rain forests.[24] In a debt-for-nature swap, a foreign private environmental organization such as the U.S.-based Rainforest Alliance or the Nature Conservancy, working in conjunction with a local environmental organization, purchases developing-country debt on financial markets at a fraction, say, 30%, of the face value. The debt is then exchanged for government bonds denominated in the debtor-country currency but worth the full value of the original foreign debt. The environmental organization purchasing the debt is thus able to leverage its funds by 230%. Income from the securities is used to maintain forest or wildlife reserves. In this way, the developing country no longer owes debt in scarce hard currencies and is able to set up endowments for the preservation of national resources. The foreign donor is able to make an effective contribution several times larger than the actual outlay of cash and obtains a verbal guarantee that the endowment will be used to protect natural resources. By 1997, debt-for-nature swaps had amounted to $152.7 million and had been negotiated in 15 countries, including Costa Rica, Ecuador, the Philippines, Mexico, and Ghana. However, after reaching a peak of $43.9 million in 1989, these swaps declined precipitously so that by 1997 they amounted to only $576,000 and only one country, Mexico, was participating.[25] Though debt-for-nature swaps provided an exciting, albeit partial, solution to tropical deforestation, a number of persistent economic and political obstacles limited the potential scope of such schemes, not the least of which was fear of foreign control over domestic resource decisions.

Development Assistance Substantial new development assistance is necessary in developing countries to achieve sustainable development. These investments would be used for a variety of programs to alleviate poverty, provide services, and promote sustainable patterns of production. Additional aid from developing countries earmarked for these purposes could have a positive impact on developing-country environments (see Chapter 15). Even greater sums would be necessary to maintain tropical rain forests, which provide benefits to the entire international community through reduced CO_2 emissions. As mentioned earlier, external funds provided for this purpose should not be considered aid because they are in the interests of all living beings.

What Developed Countries Can Do for the Global Environment

Perhaps most important, developed countries, which currently consume over 70% of the earth's resources, can directly contribute to global environmental improvement through their own efforts to (1) reduce harmful emissions, (2) develop clean technologies for themselves and for LDCs, and (3) alter their own environmentally harmful patterns of demand.

Table 10.2 shows per capita consumption of various goods in selected high-, middle-, and low-income countries. These consumption disparities, reported in the 2001 *World Resources Report,* are staggering.[26] The United States consumed a portly 6,902 kilograms (kg) per person of fossil fuels in oil equivalents in 1997, while China consumed only one-tenth as much, despite its enormous industrial inefficiencies. India consumed only 268 kg, and Bangladesh consumed a mere 67 kg per capita, less than 1% of U.S. levels. Indonesia and Nigeria, important oil-exporting countries, consumed only 450 kg and 186 kg per person, respectively. Similarly, while the United States consumed a staggering 293 kg of paper per person, China again consumed just one-tenth as much, while India consumed only about 1% as much per person. The United States and other developed countries consume a similarly disproportionate share of other environmentally sensitive products, such as ocean fish; consumption of raw materials is strikingly disproportionate. A substantial part of developed-country consumption is wasteful. It seems clear that the world as a whole cannot consume at current U.S. or other developed-country levels; responsible consumption on the part of the developed countries is not just setting a good example but an ecological necessity. This does not mean that economies cannot continue to grow indefinitely—clearly they can, as more consumption becomes knowledge-based and more modest in its use of raw materials. It is rather that the patterns of consumption must change. As we have seen, price signals alone will not guide resource use when substantial externalities and public goods are involved.

Emission Controls Beyond responsible consumption, perhaps the greatest contribution that MDCs can make to the global environment will be through a clear demonstration of their own commitment to a cleaner environment. Because they remain the main polluters of air and sea, developed countries must lead the way to global changes in current and future patterns of production. If wealthy nations do not achieve significant and sustained reductions in the production of greenhouse gases and ozone-depleting chemicals, there will be little reason for the developing world to do so, considering that per capita emissions levels are far below those in the industrialized countries.

TABLE 10.2   Disparities in Consumption: Annual Per Capita Consumption (in PPP dollars) in Selected High-, Medium-, and Low-Income Nations

Country	Total Value of Private Consumption (1997)	Fish (kg) (1997)	Meat (kg) (1998)	Cereals (kg) (1997)	Paper (kg) (1998)	Fossil Fuels (kg of oil equivalent) (1997)	Passenger Cars (per 1,000 people) (1996)
United States	$21,680	21.0	122.0	975.0	293.0	6,902	489.0
Singapore	$16,340	34.0	77.0	159.0	168.0	7,825	120.0
Japan	$15,554	66.0	42.0	334.0	239.0	3,277	373.0
Germany	$15,229	13.0	87.0	496.0	205.0	3,625	500.0
Poland	$5,087	12.0	73.0	696.0	54.0	2,585	209.0
Trinidad and Tobago	$4,864	12.0	28.0	237.0	41.0	6,394	94.0
Turkey	$4,377	7.2	19.0	502.0	32.0	952	55.0
Indonesia	$1,808	18.0	9.0	311.0	17.0	450	12.2
China	$1,410	26.0	47.0	360.0	30.0	700	3.2
India	$1,166	4.7	4.3	234.0	3.7	268	4.4
Bangladesh	$780	11.0	3.4	250.0	1.3	67	0.5
Nigeria	$692	5.8	12.0	228.0	1.9	186	6.7
Zambia	$625	8.2	12.0	144.0	1.6	77	17.0

Sources: World Resources Institute *2001 World Resources Report* (Washington, D.C.: World Resources Institute, 2001), p. 27. Reprinted with permission. Additional updates from World Resources Institute, "Earth Trends," http://earthtrends.wri.org.

Research and Development The MDCs must also take a leadership role in research and development efforts. Growing public support for stricter environmental regulation in the industrialized world is likely to lead to the development of both cheaper emissions abatement technologies and cleaner production processes. Innovations resulting from research and development will enhance LDC efforts to reduce emissions if they are adopted in developing countries. Currently, many clean technologies are prohibitively expensive for the developing world's industries. It is thus unrealistic to expect low-income countries to attain standards set in high-income countries. However, it is not necessary for developing countries to reproduce environmental debacles endured during the onset of industrialization in the developed world, as depicted, for example, in Charles Dickens's *Hard Times*. Making cheaper, cleaner abatement technologies accessible to LDCs can help limit a principal source of global emissions—the rapid industrialization of the developing world.

Import Restrictions Through its importation of products that are associated with environmentally unsustainable production, the developed world has an indirect but important impact on the global environment. International treaties to limit the destruction of endangered resources will have little effect if wealthy nations continue to provide lucrative markets for the sale of such goods. Import restrictions are an effective way of reducing undesired international trade. Consumer sovereignty expressed through boycotts and other forms of pressure on corporations can be effective. However, they require strong leadership and tend to focus on large firms, which represent only a relatively small portion of the overall problem.

Economic Growth and Environmental Sustainability: The Philippines*

Elizabeth M. Remedio, Ph.D.

Department of Economics, University of San Carlos, Cebu City, Philippines

This case study examines the state of Philippine natural resources and environment during the early years of the twenty-first century. After the 1992 Earth Summit, the Philippines launched its own version of Agenda 21, known as the Sustainable Development Framework and referred to as PA 21. This laudable effort took off during the presidency of Fidel V. Ramos and continued during the Gloria Macapagal-Arroyo presidency. The status of PA 21 in addressing civil society, environmental management, and sustainable development concerns is considered here.

The case of the Philippines provides evidence that there is a strong link between poverty, fertility, malnourishment, environmental damage, and civil struggle. Partha Dasgupta has emphasized that traditional and resource economics is not sufficient to explain the needs of the developing world. Dasgupta stresses that the gap between the

rich and poor nations is so wide that attempts at analyzing LDC circumstances using MDC premises becomes irrelevant and often inappropriate.

Strapped by a multitude of development constraints, the Philippines has recorded an average GDP growth rate of just 3.1% for 30 years to 2004, along with low savings, high population growth, high unemployment, pale performance of the agriculture sector, and weak governance. Paul Hutchcroft referred to the Philippines as a "longstanding developmental bog" inasmuch as it was experiencing very low and even negative rates of economic growth compared to its many Asian neighbors in the 1980s and 1990s. Moreover, the persistence of natural resource depletion and environmental degradation is both serious and alarming.

Beyond the Ten-Point Agenda: Long-Term Economic Development Goals

President Macapagal-Arroyo set a Ten-Point Agenda for her six-year term that began in 2001, encompassing provisions for job creation, providing scholarship opportunities

---

*Elizabeth M. Remedio, "How Much More Can the Philippines Take? Revisiting Philippine Natural Resources, Environment, and PA 21." Reprinted with the permission of the author.

and educational facilities, balancing the budget, decentralization, universal provision of electricity and water, decongestion of metropolitan Manila, development of international service and logistic centers, automation of the electoral process, peace in conflict-torn Mindanao, and political reconciliation.

Alongside the president's agenda is the implementation of PA 21. The strong correlation between development and environmental consequences has long been recognized. Industrialization, urbanization, economic growth, and development lead to such problems as air and water pollution; depletion and losses in flora and fauna species; greenhouse gas emissions; and biodiversity imbalances. Hence environmental management and conservation, particularly through public policy, are supposed to set up an equation so that a sustainable economic development can be achieved. As a framework, therefore, PA 21 is encompassing, yet the Philippine environment is in grave distress, and hence the call for environment restoration and regeneration must be addressed with serious urgency. PA 21 is the Philippines agenda for the twenty-first century.

More than Seven Thousand Islands

The Philippines archipelago covers approximately 300,000 square kilometers of land area in Southeast Asia between the Philippine Sea and the South China Sea. The three main island groups are Luzon, Visayas, and Mindanao. Terrain consists mostly of mountains with narrow to extensive coastal lowlands. The country sits astride a typhoon belt and is hit by 20 to 30 typhoons annually. Other natural hazards include landslides, active volcanoes, and earthquakes.

As of July 2004, total population stood at 86,241,697, with a growth rate of 2.36%, and is expected to double within the next 29 years; it is the world's fourteenth most populous country. The population is young: 36% of the

population is 0 to 14 years old, 60% is between 15 and 64 years old, and only 4% is aged 65 years and over.

The Philippines was ceded from Spain to the United States in 1898 after the Spanish-American War. The country gained its independence in 1946 soon after the Japanese Occupation in World War II. A popular revolution in 1986 ousted Ferdinand Marcos, the dictator, who ruled for 21 years. Corazon Aquino replaced him as president. Three presidential elections followed in the period 1992–2004.

The Philippine archipelago was proclaimed by Conservation International as one of the 17 "mega diverse" countries of the world. It ranked twelfth among the 80 top fish-producing countries in the world according to a 1995 FAO study. In 2003, Francisco and de los Angeles reported that the marine community and coastal resources around the islands host 74% of the world's mangrove species and 98% of the world's coral species, making it a fertile breeding ground for marine life. The country's coral reefs are second only to Australia's Great Barrier Reef in terms of diversity of coral and fish species. Coxhead and Jayasuriya disclosed that the country is also home to 67% of species in the major group of animals and plants not found elsewhere in the world, 6% of the world's birds, 5% of the world's flora species, and 4% of its mammals. Moreover, the Philippines has the second highest number of seagrass species in the world. To a certain extent, the country is thus abundantly blessed with a diverse and ecologically rich environment; however, the situation of Philippine environment is dismal. Environmental degradation and overexploitation of natural resources have resulted in an alarming state of deterioration and decline.

Natural Resources and the Environment in the Philippines

Forest and Upland Ecosystem
The Philippine forest and upland ecosystem is known to be one of the richest and most di-

verse in the world inasmuch as it contains some of the most unique flora and fauna in the world. Coxhead and Jayasuriya mentioned that about 30% of the total population of the country, particularly the poor, depends on upland and forest resources for their survival. However, only 3% of the original forest covers remains. The figures in the literature vary, depending on definitions, classifications, and the availability and accuracy of data, but by any measure, the rate at which resources are diminishing remains astounding. Citing NSCB 1998 figures, Danilo Israel noted a total forest cover of 5.7 million hectares, representing 19% of the total national land area of 30 million hectares (and 39% of the land classified as forestland, estimated at 15 million hectares). Hence Israel calculates that forest cover is only half of what it was 20 years ago. Despite the lack of accurate data, David Kummer stressed that it is "plausible" that the country had a 24.7% forest cover in 2004, based on Japan Forest Technical Association reports.

The World Bank reported a 1.4% annual deforestation rate, roughly equivalent to 89,000 hectares, for the period 1900–2000. Deforestation could result in reduced biodiversity, land degradation, soil erosion, and negative impacts on watershed cycles. Philippine government sources claim that the average annual deforestation rate is 2%. Kummer reported that between 1900 and 1950, national forest cover was reduced from 70% to 50% and that by the 1980s, only 25% remained.

Deforestation is caused by many factors. Population pressure to move upland, implying massive land clearance for agricultural purposes, is one primary reason. It is expected that the 1990 upland population figure of 18 million will double to 37.8 million by 2015 if left unchecked. Aside from population and migration patterns, commercial exploitation of forest resources, including legal and illegal logging, is also responsible for the loss of valuable forest timber such as old-growth dipterocarp. Poor forest management control schemes and weak enforcement of regulations are also to be blamed. Lastly, pricing schemes that reflect the true scarcity values of forest resources are likewise inadequate.

Agriculture and Lowland Ecosystem

Overall productivity growth rates of Philippine agriculture have been low. According to Coxhead and Jayasuriya, cereal and root crop yields and the rate of fertilizer use are among the lowest in Asia. Out of the 30 million hectares of national land area, the National Economic Development Authority (NEDA) declared a total of 10.3 million hectares as agricultural land in 1998: 33% lowland and 45% upland. Agriculture remains the largest sector in the Philippines, employing more than half of its population, especially the poor, who depend on it for food and income. The degradation and deterioration of agricultural land resources cast doubts on the food security of the country.

The growing population, the move toward more industrialization, and the pursuit of other economic activities all exert pressure on the land resources by converting forestlands to agricultural and other types of land use. These moves have inadvertent watershed consequences and over time give rise to serious environmental problems such as soil erosion. Eroded matter ends up as sediment and causes water pollution problems. Pesticides, fertilizers, and other chemicals are major pollutants. Current estimates by the Forest Management Bureau indicate that 74 to 81 million tons of soils are lost annually and that 63% to 77% of the country's land area is affected by soil erosion. All in all, 45% of the national land area is classified as eroded. Sedimentation has negatively affected irrigation, household water consumption levels, and power generation; notwithstanding the fact that agricultural productivity has experienced a serious decline.

Coxhead and Jayasuriya likewise indicated a growing trend toward the use of inorganic fertilizers and pesticides, particularly in rice cultivation areas. In many instances, the use of such fertilizers and pesticides has been inappropriate and unrestrained, causing health-related problems such as skin, respiratory, eye, and other illnesses among farmers and their families. Water pollution brought about by inorganic fertilizer and chemical use is thus a huge risk to the entire ecosystem. Also, from a long-term perspective, the Filipino practice of intensive monoculture (of rice and grain) is another factor in the decline in farm yields.

Coastal and Marine Ecosystem

The archipelago has a total coastline of about 33,900 kilometers, with a continental shelf of about 244,500 square kilometers. Marine territorial waters cover 2.2 million square kilometers. This vast coastline is home to bountiful marine and coastal resources that are a major source of economic growth. More than a million Filipinos depend on it as a source of livelihood, food, and income. Fish is the second staple food in the Philippines, after rice. The fishery sector is also one of the major export earners of the country. Aside from the economic value, the marine community also performs "critical ecological functions" according to Coxhead and Jayasuriya, such as breakwater and erosion control, nutrient recycling, and beach sand deposition. It also provides resources such as mangroves, seagrass beds, coral reefs, and tourism and recreation. Its biodiversity is part of the global ecology. Coastal and marine resource productivity, however, has gradually diminished over time. Fish stock depletion is a particular case in point. The deterioration is due to overfishing, pollution, abuse, coral and mangrove destruction, and seagrass degradation, among other causes.

Mangrove forests covered 500,000 hectares in 1918, but 57% was destroyed in the 1970s so that by 1998, only 112,400 hectares remained. As more and more mangrove areas are converted into fishponds and given over to aquaculture and tourism-related development, mangrove forests will continue to diminish. Seagrass beds have also suffered the impacts of destructive fishing technologies, coastal land conversion, coastal mining activities, and runoff due to deforestation.

Coral reef destruction is often brought about by overfishing, destructive fishing methods, pollution, sediment deposits caused by deforestation, and coastal development. A survey conducted in 1991 by the Department of Environment and Natural Resources (DENR) showed that out of 742 coral reef sites, only 39 sites, or 5.3% were in good condition, while 226 sites, or 30.5%, were in bad shape. In Manila Bay, total coliform counts exceed the standards set by the DENR. Red tides cause economic losses as well.

Freshwater Ecosystem

The Philippines' inland water resource consists of rivers and lakes. There are 384 principal river systems and 59 lakes throughout the country, claiming a total area of 569,600 hectares. Laguna de Bay, the largest lake in Southeast Asia, covers 90,000 hectares. Four major river basins (the Cotabato, Cagayan, Central Luzon, and Agusan) serve as reservoirs and are currently used for irrigation, power generation, water supply, and fisheries. Many of the freshwater resources, river systems, and inland water bodies in the country, however, are experiencing problems due to pollution and watershed degradation, and water supplies are therefore seriously at risk. It has been reported that of the country's 421 existing rivers, 50 are biologically dead.

Rapid industrialization, increasing population, cropland intensification, and other manufacturing and production-related endeavors all involve human activities that lead to harmful/household waste disposal practices, poor sewerage systems, industrial waste and industrial effluent generation due to noncompliance with pollution standards, and pollution with mine tailings, heavy metals and agricultural runoff.

Laguna de Bay is a case in point. It is the only lake in the country placed under a government agency, the Laguna Lake Development Authority (LLDA). The lake covers 90,000 hectares and extends to metropolitan Manila and other small cities where rivers and streams flow into it. There are about 1,400 to 1,600 factories located in the catchment area. Beverage and food processing plants, hog farms and slaughterhouses, and textile manufacturers have all contributed to the pollution of the lake. Pollution policies and regulations were once widely ignored, but in 1997, the LLDA launched an environmental user fee system whereby polluters now must pay and put up waste treatment facilities.

Urban Ecosystem

Cities and population centers make up the urban ecosystem. Rapid industrialization, increases in population, rising living standards, and lack of serious attention to the environment have all contributed to the mounting urban environmental problems. Improper solid waste disposal and air and water pollution are among the problems associated with such environmental deterioration. In the Philippines, the primary sources of solid waste are household and commercial activities. Indiscriminate dumping of commercial and residential wastes contaminates surface and groundwater supplies. Furthermore, in most urban areas, solid waste clogs drainage systems, causing flooding, particularly during the rainy season. Stagnant water is also a breeding ground for insects, thereby posing health and safety issues. Human fecal matter is commonly found in municipal waste. Risks

of dengue fever and cholera are high whenever one is exposed to contaminated food or water carried by insects or rodents attracted by municipal waste. Contact with contaminated water through bathing, drinking, eating, and other means can expose individuals to health risks. The problem of air pollution is also pronounced in metropolitan Manila. In 1992, the city recorded annual average total suspended particulate (TSP) concentrations more than five times higher than World Health Organization air quality guidelines recommend. Rising population growth that leads to increases in vehicular requirements and greater traffic congestion are the major factors that bring about air pollution.

Mineral Resources

The Philippines is endowed with vast mineral deposits, and the mining industry is a significant economic sector, employing over 100,000 workers. Exploitation of mineral resources, however, have caused a number of environmental problems, including soil erosion, habitat destruction, mine waste, damage to cropland ecosystems, and changes in terrain. All lead to the pollution, sedimentation, and siltation of bodies of water.

PA 21 and the Environmental Health of the Country

The Asian Development Bank wants governments in Asia to reevaluate their environmental policies so as to be able to avoid serious economic penalties. According to one of the bank's senior environmental specialists, pervasive, accelerating, and unabated environmental degradation in much of Asia is being caused primarily by a lack of political will and overpopulation.

For the Philippines, the ADB sketched a scenario whereby environment and development policies are to be integrated at the national and regional levels and that development should, by design, guide sustainable development (guiding urban and industrial development according to integrated environmental and economic development plans that are publicly accepted). In other words, regulation and governance are the keys to resolving the Philippines' environmental predicament. The ADB's 2001 Asian Environmental Outlook pinpointed overexploitation of natural resources, poor management, unchecked industrial expansion, and urbanization as the culprits in the nation's environmental deterioration. These factors compound poverty issues, widen the gap between rich and poor, threaten food security, and increase pollution, among other negative results.

A number of sectors, institutions, and personalities are heavily engaged in projects and activities promoting the goals of sustainable development in the country. The Philippine Council for Sustainable Development is mandated to formally adopt PA 21 and to develop national sustainability plans and programs. Rio's Agenda 21 indicates that the conservation and management of natural resources and environment is but one major component. Three others are examining social and demographic dimensions, strengthening the role of major groups, and determining appropriate means of implementation. Thus the problem of natural resource and environmental protection, management, and conservation is not a stand-alone problem. It is closely related to the problems of poverty, people empowerment, financial and economic resources, and information and education.

A PA 21 review was undertaken in preparation for the Johannesburg Earth Summit of 2002 or what was referred to as Rio plus 10. The Philippine case showed that the extent and quality of implementation of PA 21 *commitments* appeared to be generally high, while the impact of *implementation* has been low. These circumstances had a threefold ex-

planation: (1) The full effects of PA 21 need time to take root, develop, and bear fruit; (2) PA 21 strategies and instrumentalities appear to be inappropriate; and (3) the external environment may not be fully conducive to sustainable development.

Some progress has been made in arresting natural resource depletion and degradation as shown by the higher environment-adjusted net domestic product as opposed to unadjusted net domestic product. However, pressures on the environment and natural resources continue to mount, manifested by increasing water pollution, air pollution, and soil erosion.

Progress that has been made includes (1) the integration of Agenda 21 principles into the country's national, regional, and local development plans, programs, and budgets; (2) the creation of the Philippine Inter-Agency Committee on Climate Change, devoted to efforts to protect the atmosphere; (3) expansion of the membership of the Technical Committee on Land Use matters to include other agencies of the Department of Agriculture to review applications for land conversions and land use; (4) adoption of the Master Plan for Forestry Department, which provides the framework for combating deforestation and guiding long-term development of the forestry sector in the Philippines; (5) implementation of the Key Production Area for sustainable agriculture and Integrated Pest Management for an ecological approach to crop cultivation; (6) establishment of the National Biodiversity Strategy and Action Plan and the National Integrated Protected Areas System to recognize the need to confront problems and issues relating to the conservation of biodiversity; (7) implementation of the Coastal Environment Program by the Department of Environment and Natural Resources to integrate programs, projects, and initiatives related to or concerning coastal environments; and (8) adoption of the Clean Air Act, the Solid Waste Management Act, the

Water Quality Management Policy, and many other laws reflecting efforts toward cleaner production in the Philippines.

Walden Bello and his colleagues have argued, however, that "the clash between protecting the environment and protecting business interests is best illustrated by the content of PA 21 and the Medium-Term Philippine Development Plan (MTPDP), 2001–2004." In a way, the MTPDP assumes that GDP increases will eventually trickle down to the poor; PA 21, by contrast, is committed to direct poverty reduction and redistribution of income. Further, the MTPDP focuses on export orientation as the engine for growth and thus the modernization of the countryside; PA 21, however, implies that it is by tapping the local market that growth can best be achieved and therefore emphasizes "nurturing the inherent strengths of local and indigenous knowledge."

Addressing the multiple faces of poverty vis-à-vis economic growth and development targets is a herculean task where time is crucial due to the irreversibility of the processes of nature. Solving the poverty, malnourishment, health, income distribution, and education problems are steps toward arresting environmental degradation and deterioration, particularly in the case of the Philippines. But commitment, political will, and well articulated and conscious education and information, coupled with vigilant legislation, implementation, and monitoring, are essential in achieving these ends. These should come not only from government, although much should come from the government; even more important, however, is that they should emanate from an empowered citizenry. After all, the environment is not made up of natural resources alone; it includes people, its caretakers and managers. Such is the framework of Agenda 21; the sustainability of development goes beyond the gifts of nature to include the managers of nature and their respective cultures and societies. ■

Sources

Bello, Walden, et al., "Unsustainable development," in *The Anti-Development State: The Political Economy of Permanent Crisis in the Philippines* (Quezon City: University of the Philippines, 2004).

Broad, Robin and John Cavanagh, *Plundering Paradise: The Struggle for the Environment in the Philippines*, (Berkeley: University of California Press, 1994).

Coxhead, Ian, and Sisira Jayasuriya, "Environment and natural resources," in *The Philippine Economy: Development, Policies, and Challenges*, eds. Arsenio M. Balisacan and Hal Hill (Diliman: University of the Philippines, 2003).

Dasgupta, Partha, "Environmental and resource economics in the world of the poor," lecture delivered for Resources for the Future, Washington, D.C., October 9, 1997, http://www.econ.cam.ac.uk.

Francisco, Herminia, and Marian S. de los Angeles, "The Natural Resource Situation in the Philippines," in *Economy and Environment: Selected Readings in the Philippines*, eds. Herminia Francisco and Marian de los Angeles (Quezon City: Resources, Environment and Economics Center for Studies, 2003).

Hutchcroft, Paul, *Booty Capitalism: The Politics of Banking in the Philippines* (Quezon City: Ateneo de Manila University Press, 1998).

IBON Foundation, *The State of the Philippine Environment* (Manila: IBON Foundation, 1991).

Israel, Danilo C., "The quest for a better environment: Past experiences and future challenges," PIDS Discussion Paper Series No. 2002-14, Philippine Institute for Development Studies, http://www.pids.gov.ph.

Kummer, David M., "Deforestation in the Philippines, 1950–2000," in *Muddied Waters: Historical and Contemporary Perspectives on Man-*

agement of Forests and Fisheries in Island Southeast Asia, eds. Peter Boomgaard, David Henley, and Manon Osseweijer (Leiden: KITLV Press, in press).

"Philippines: ADB Calls for Re-Evaluation of Government Environmental Policies," *Asia Environmental Review*, July 7, 2001, http://www.environmental-center.com/magazine/aet/aer/sample.

World Bank, "The Philippines environment monitor" vol. 1, Working Paper No. 22192, World Bank Group, 2000, http://www.worldbank.org.

Concepts for Review

Absorptive capacity	Free-rider problem	Producer surplus
Biomass fuels	Global public goods	Property rights
Clean technologies	Global warming	Public bad
Common property resource	Greenhouse gases	Public good
Consumer surplus	Internalization	Scarcity rent
Debt-for-nature swap	Marginal cost	Social costs
Deforestation	Marginal net benefit	Soil erosion
Desertification	Ozone depletion	Sustainable development
Environmental accounting	Pollution tax	Sustainable net national
Environmental capital	Present value	income (NNI*)
Externality	Private costs	Total net benefit

Questions for Discussion

1. Is sustainable development a practical and feasible goal for nations? What might be some of the difficulties and possible trade-offs? Explain your answer.

2. In what ways does poverty lead to environmental degradation? What types of environmental problems do the rural and urban poor share? What are some differences in the conditions they face?

3. How are population growth, poverty, and land pressures interrelated? Explain how these problems can create a vicious cycle of events.

4. What steps might governments in less developed countries take to reduce overexploitation of natural resources? What impact do pricing policies have?

5. Why are national environmental concerns in LDCs likely to focus increasingly on urban problems in the future? How are urban conditions related to rural-to-urban migration?

6. Why are the objectives of economic development and sustainable growth mutually reinforcing?

7. In what ways does neoclassical theory provide a useful framework for analyzing environmental issues? What are some of its limitations?

8. What are some of the costs associated with environmental degradation? How might they detract from economic growth? What are the developmental implications?

9. Why are children more susceptible than adults to health risks posed by their environment?

10. In what ways can developed nations best contribute to the alleviation of global and domestic LDC environmental problems? Be specific.

Notes

1. For a comprehensive view of the range of issues linking the environment to economic development, see World Bank, *World Development Report, 1992 and 2003* (New York: Oxford University Press, 1992, 2003); David W. Pearce, Edward Barbier, and Alvin Markandya, *Sustainable Development: Economics and Environment in the Third World* (Cheltenham, England: Elgar, 1990); John M. Antle and Gregg Heidebrink, "Environment and development: Theory and international evidence," *Economic Development and Cultural Change* 43 (1995): 603–625; Herman E. Daly, *Beyond Doubt: The Economics of Sustainable Development* (Boston: Beacon Press, 1996); and Daniel Litvin, "Dirt poor: A survey of development and the environment," *Economist,* March 21, 1998, pp. 3–16.

2. For a comparative analysis of various definitions of sustainable development, see Sharachchandra A. Lele, "Sustainable development: A critical review," *World Development* 19 (1991): 607–621, and Lance Taylor, "Sustainable development: An introduction," *World Development* 24 (1996): 215–225.

3. World Commission on Environment and Development, *Our Common Future* (New York: Oxford University Press, 1987), p. 4.

4. David W. Pearce and Jeremy J. Warford, *World without End: Economics, Environment, and Sustainable Development—A Summary* (Washington, D.C.: World Bank, 1993), p. 2.

5. Ibid., pp. 2–3.

6. See United Nations Population Fund, *Population, Resources, and the Environment: The Critical Challenge* (New York: United Nations, 1991), for a review and an analysis of these critical population-environment linkages. See also Maureen L. Cropper and Charles Griffiths, "The interaction of population growth and environmental quality," *American Economic Review* 84 (1994): 250–254.

7. For analysis of these issues, see Karl-Göran Mäler, "Environment, poverty and growth," in *Annual World Bank Conference on Development Economics, 1997* (Washington, D.C.: World Bank, 1998), pp. 251–284, and, in the same volume, Ramon E. Lopez, "Where development can or cannot go: The role of poverty-environment linkages," pp. 285–306.

8. See World Resources Institute, *World Resources, 1996–97: The Urban Environment* (New York: Oxford University Press, 1996).

9. A description of the factors leading to the production of greenhouse gases in developing countries is offered in John Bongaarts, "Population growth and global warming," *Population and Development Review* 18 (1992): 299–319.

10. For a detailed statistical and descriptive portrait of environmental damage in the developing world, see World Resources Institute, *World Resources 1998–99: A Guide to the Global Environment* (New York: Oxford University Press, 1998). Most of the data quoted in this and succeeding sections of the chapter come from the 1994–1995 edition, as well as from World Bank, *World Development Report, 1992*; United Nations, *Population, Resources, and the Environment*; and World Resources Institute, *World Resources, 2000–2001* (New York: Oxford University Press, 2000).

11. An interesting analysis of the market for biomass fuels is Elizabeth M. Remedio and Terrence G. Bensel, "The woodfuel supply system for Cebu City, Philippines: A preliminary analysis," *Philippine Quarterly of Culture and Society* 20 (1992): 157–169.

12. For a provocative look at the issue of gender and the environment, see Cecile Jackson, "Doing what comes naturally: Women and environment in development," *World Development* 21 (1993): 1947–1963.

13. For a basic and detailed presentation of models of environmental economics, see Tom Tietenberg, *Environmental and Natural Resources Economics* (Glenview, Ill.: Scott, Foresman, 1990); John M. Hartwick and N. Olewiler, *The Economics of Natural Resource Use* (New York: Harper & Row, 1986); G. Tyler Miller, *Living in the Environment* (Belmont, Calif.: Wadsworth, 1990); and Maureen L. Cropper and Wallace E. Oates, "Environmental economics: A survey," *Journal of Economic Literature* 30 (1992): 675–740.

14. See UN-HABITAT, *The Challenge of Slums: Global Report on Human Settlements, 2003* (New York: United Nations, 2003).

15. World Bank, *World Development Report, 1992*, fig. 4. Note that for the most part, the Coase theorem does not apply to these discussions due to the high transaction costs involved.

16. Ibid.

17. Ibid., fig. 2.4.

18. World Bank, *World Development Indicators, 2004* (New York: Oxford University Press, 2004), tab. 1.3.

19. A discussion of the dangers of pesticide misuse in developing countries is presented in Ruth Norris (ed.), *Pills, Pesticides, and Profits* (Croton-on-Hudson, N.Y.: North River Press, 1982), and Ruth Norris, *Sustainability: The Case for Reducing the Use of Chemical Pesticides* (Rome: Pesticide Action Network, 1987).

20. For an excellent overview, see Inge Kaul, Isabelle Grunberg, and Marc A. Stern (eds.), *Global Public Goods: International Cooperation in the 21st Century* (New York: Oxford University Press, 1999).

21. Two excellent sources of information concerning tropical deforestation are World Resources Institute, *World Resources, 1994–95*, ch. 7, and World Bank, *World Development Report, 1992*, ch. 7.

22. For an extensive discussion of public environment policies that LDC governments might pursue, see World Bank, *World Development Report, 1992*, ch. 3 and 7; and World Resources Institute, *World Resources, 1992–93*, ch. 3 and 14.

23. An interesting and lucid discussion of government policy options in this area can be found in Stephen W. Salant, "The economics of natural resource extraction: A primer for development economists," *World Bank Research Observer* 10 (1995): 93–111.

24. For more information concerning debt-for-nature swaps, see World Resources Institute, *World Resources, 1992–93*, pp. 122–123 and tab. 20.6, and World Bank, *World Debt Tables, 1991–1992* (Washington, D.C.: World Bank, 1992), box 4.5. See also Chapter 14.

25. World Bank, *Global Development Finance, 1998* (Washington, D.C.: World Bank, 1998), p. 89.

26. The annual reports of the World Resources Institute and its Web site (http://earthtrends.wri.org) are excellent sources of data and information on global environmental and resource trends.

Further Reading

For a lively and easy-to-follow economics-based review of environment and development issues, see David W. Pearce and Jeremy J. Warford, *World without End: Economics, Environment, and Sustainable Development—A Summary* (Washington, D.C.: World Bank, 1993), and Herman E. Daly, *Beyond Growth: The Economics of Sustainable Development* (Boston: Beacon Press, 1996). An advanced and thorough overview of the literature relating to current models of the environment and their policy implications is provided in Maureen L. Cropper and Wallace E. Oates, "Environmental economics: A survey," *Journal of Economic Literature* 30 (1992): 675–740.

For an excellent overview of the concept of global public goods, see Inge Kaul, Isabelle Grunberg, and Marc A. Stern (eds.), *Global Public Goods: International Cooperation in the 21st Century* (New York: Oxford University Press, 1999).

Comprehensive discussions of developing-world environmental problems, including desertification, deforestation, access to clean water and sanitation, and soil degradation, are offered in World Bank, *World Development Report, 2003, Sustainable Development in a Dynamic World. Transforming Institutions, Growth, and Quality of Life* (New York: Oxford University Press, 2003), and World Resources Institute, *World Resources, 1998–99* and *World Resources, 2000–2001* (New York: Oxford University Press, 1998, 2000).

For more detailed information concerning the causes and consequences of environmental degradation in developing countries, see Scott Barrett, "Optimal soil conservation and the reform of agricultural pricing policies," *Journal of Development Economics* 36 (1991): 167–187; Gordon McGranahan, "Fuelwood, subsistence foraging, and the decline of common property," *World Development* 19 (1991): 1275–1285; and Steven L. Rhodes, "Rethinking desertification: What do we know and what have we learned?" *World Development* 19 (1991): 1137–1143.

Careful descriptions of the socioeconomic causes of deforestation may be found in Nicholas Guppy, "Tropical deforestation: A global view," *Foreign Affairs* (1984): 928–965, and Robert Repetto, "Deforestation in the tropics," *Scientific American*, April 1990, pp. 36–42.

For a general description of the application of economics to global warming, see Thomas C. Schelling, "Some economics of global warming," *American Economic Review* 82 (1992): 1–14. A variety of suggestions concerning the policy implications of global warming for developed-world governments are available in Dieter Helm (ed.), *Economic Policy towards the Environment* (Cambridge: Blackwell, 1991). For analysis of the growing contribution of developing countries to the production of greenhouse gases, see John Bongaarts, "Population growth and global warming," *Population and Development Review* 18

(1992): 299–319, and Stephen W. Salant, "The economics of natural resource extraction: A primer for development economists," *World Bank Research Observer* 10 (1995): 93–111.

For additional information concerning the impact of population on the environment, see United Nations Population Fund, *Population, Resources, and Environment: The Critical Challenges* (New York: United Nations, 1991). See also Kingsley Davis and Mikail S. Bernstam (eds.), *Resources, Environment, and Population,* supplement to *Population and Development Review* 16 (1990), Richard Bilsborrow and M. Geores, *Population, Land Use, and the Environment in Developing Countries: What Can We Learn from Cross-National Data?* (Washington, D.C.: National Academies Press, 1991). For an in-depth look at practical problems of managing environmentally sustainable economic development, see Phillip J. Cooper and Claudia Maria Vargas, *Implementing Sustainable Development: From Global Policy to Local Action* (Lantham, Md.: Rowman & Littlefield, 2004).

CHAPTER ELEVEN

Development Policymaking and the Roles of Market, State, and Civil Society

If we could first know where we are, and whither we are tending, we could better judge what to do, and how to do it.

—Abraham Lincoln

It is not a question of state or market: Each has a large and irreplaceable role.
—World Bank, *World Development Report, 1991*

National governments have played an important role in the successful development experiences of the countries in East Asia. In other parts of the world, including some countries in Africa, Latin America and the Carribean, and the transition countries, government appears to have been more of a hindrance to development than a help, stifling the market rather than facilitating its role in growth and development. This chapter examines the relationships between states and markets in the process of economic development.

Nobel laureate Amartya Sen has pointed out that to be generically against markets is almost as strange as to be generically against conversations. As he says, some conversations do harm, even to those doing the conversing, but this is not a reason to be against conversations in general. Analogously, government can also do harm as well as good, but this is no reason to be generically against a government role. A government role can facilitate the satisfaction of human wants and in many cases is essential to achieving them.

The problem is achieving the proper balance between private markets and public policy. In early years, a perception of the state as a benevolent supporter of development held sway, at least implicitly; but the record of corruption, poor governance, and state capture by vested interests in so many developing countries over the past few decades has made this view untenable as a "positive," or empirically accurate, description of government. More recently, a negative view of government has predominated, but it too has been based more on theory than fact and has failed to explain the important and constructive role that the state has played in many successful development experiences, particularly in East Asia. Finally, a middle ground is emerging, recognizing both strengths and weaknesses of public and private roles and providing a more empirically grounded analysis of what goes wrong with governance in development and the conditions under which these flaws can be rectified.

In this chapter, we examine the roles and limitations of planning and development policymaking as practiced in developing nations, consider the problems of economic transition to competitive free-market economies, and ask fundamental questions as to the proper role of the state and how public and private economic activity can best be made mutually supporting. We start with a brief review of the nature of development planning and a summary of general planning issues. After examining the main arguments for and against the role of planning in developing societies and briefly reviewing different models of planning and project appraisal, we examine the requirements of economic transition to market economies and evaluate the arguments for and against the role of the state in contemporary developing nations.

In particular, we examine the "Washington consensus" on development policy and its limitations and discuss progress toward a new consensus that began to crystalize at the Santiago Summit in 1998. Then we examine some recent theories of development policy formulation, including studies of the impact of political processes on the quality of policy decisions. We next examine three important trends in governance and reform: tackling the problem of corruption, implementing decentralization, and encouraging broad-based development participation. Finally, we examine the nature of the third sector—the civil society or citizen sector encompassing NGOs—and its growing role in economic development. The chapter concludes with a case study of the largest LDC-based development NGO, BRAC of Bangladesh.

The Planning Mystique

In the initial decades after the Second World War, the pursuit of economic development was reflected in the almost universal acceptance of development planning as the surest and most direct route to economic progress. Until the 1980s, few people in the developing world would have questioned the advisability or desirability of formulating and implementing a national development plan. Planning had become a way of life in government ministries, and every five years or so the latest development plan was paraded out with great fanfare.

But why has there been such an aura of mystique about development planning and such faith in its utility? Basically, because national planning was widely believed to offer the essential and perhaps the only institutional and organizational mechanism for overcoming the major obstacles to development and for ensuring a sustained high rate of economic growth. To catch up with their former rulers, poor nations were persuaded that they required a comprehensive national plan. The planning record, unfortunately, did not live up to its advance billing, and disillusionment with the planning mystique is now widespread. But a comprehensive development policy framework can play an important role in accelerating growth and reducing poverty.

The Nature of Development Planning

Basic Concepts

Economic planning may be described as a deliberate governmental attempt to co-ordinate economic decision making over the long run and to influence, direct, and in some cases even control the level and growth of a nation's principal economic variables (income, consumption, employment, investment, saving, exports, imports, etc.) to achieve a predetermined set of development objectives.[1] An **economic plan** is simply a specific set of quantitative economic targets to be reached in a given period of time, with a stated strategy for achieving those targets. Economic plans may be comprehensive or partial. A **comprehensive plan** sets its targets to cover all major aspects of the national economy. A **partial plan** covers only a part of the national economy—industry, agriculture, the public sector, the foreign sector, and so forth. Finally, the **planning process** itself can be described as an exercise in which a government first chooses social objectives, then sets various targets, and finally organizes a framework for implementing, coordinating, and monitoring a development plan.[2]

Proponents of economic planning for developing countries argued that the un-controlled market economy can, and often does, subject these nations to economic dualism, fluctuating prices, unstable markets, and low levels of employment. In particular, they claimed that the market economy is not geared to the principal operational task of poor countries: mobilizing limited resources in a way that will bring about the structural change necessary to stimulate a sustained and balanced growth of the entire economy. Planning came to be accepted, therefore, as an essential and pivotal means of guiding and accelerating economic growth in almost all developing countries.

Planning in Mixed Developing Economies

Most development plans have been formulated and carried out within the framework of the mixed economies of the developing world. These economies are characterized by the existence of an institutional setting in which some of the productive resources are privately owned and operated and some are controlled by the public sector. The actual proportionate division of public and private ownership varies from country to country, and neither the private nor the public sector can really be considered in isolation from the other. However, unlike market economies where only a small degree of public ownership usually exists, LDC mixed economies are often distinguished by a substantial amount of government ownership and control. The private sector typically comprises four distinct forms of individual ownership:

1. The traditional subsistence sector, consisting of small-scale private farms and handicraft shops selling a part of their production to local markets

2. Small-scale individual or family-owned commercial business and service activities in the formal and informal urban sectors

3. Medium-size commercial enterprises in agriculture, industry, trade, and transport owned and operated by local entrepreneurs

4. Large jointly owned or completely foreign-owned manufacturing enterprises, mining companies, and plantations, catering primarily to foreign markets but sometimes with substantial local sales (the capital for such enterprises usually comes from abroad, and a good proportion of the profits tends to be transferred overseas)

In the context of such an institutional setting, we can identify two principal components of development planning in mixed economies:

1. The government's deliberate use of domestic saving and foreign finance to carry out public investment projects and to mobilize and channel scarce resources into areas that can be expected to make the greatest contribution toward the realization of long-term economic objectives (e.g., the construction of railways, schools, hydroelectric projects, and other components of **economic infrastructure**, as well as the creation of import-substituting industries)

2. Governmental economic policy (e.g., taxation, industrial licensing, the setting of tariffs, and the manipulation of quotas, wages, interest rates, and prices) to stimulate, direct, and in some cases even control private economic activity so as to ensure a harmonious relationship between the desires of private business operators and the social objectives of the central government

The compromise nature of this situation between the extremes of market inducement and central control is readily evident from our simplified characterization of planning in mixed market economies.

The Rationale for Development Planning

The early widespread acceptance of planning as a development tool rested on a number of fundamental economic and institutional arguments. Of these we can single out four as the most often put forward.

Market Failure Markets in LDCs are permeated by imperfections of structure and operation. Commodity and factor markets are often badly organized, and the existence of distorted prices often means that producers and consumers are responding to economic signals and incentives that are a poor reflection of the real cost to society of these goods, services, and resources. It is therefore argued that governments have an important role to play in integrating markets and modifying prices. Moreover, the failure of the market to price factors of production correctly is further assumed to lead to gross disparities between social and private valuations of alternative investment projects. In the absence of governmental interference, therefore, the market is said to lead to a misallocation of present and future resources or, at least, to an allocation that may not be in the best long-run social interests. This **market failure** argument is perhaps the most often quoted reason for the expanded role of government in less developed countries.[3]

Various kinds of market and government failure are examined in several of the earlier chapters, but a brief review is in order here. There are three general forms in which market failure can be observed: The market cannot function properly or no market exists; the market exists but implies an inefficient allocation of resources; the market produces undesirable results as measured by social objectives other than the allocation of resources. Market failures can occur in situations in which social costs or benefits differ from the private costs or benefits of firms or consumers; public goods, externalities, and market power are the best known examples. With public goods, "free riders" who do not pay for the goods cannot be excluded except at high cost; it is economically inefficient to exclude nonpaying individuals from consuming these goods. With externalities, consumers or firms do not have to pay all the costs of their activities or are unable to receive all the benefits. Coordination failures occur when several agents would be better off if they could cooperate on actions if all or most agents participate but worse off taking the action if too few participate (see Chapter 4).[4] Market power occurs when firms can influence price by restricting quantity, a power most common under increasing returns to scale. Capital markets are particularly prone to failure due to their intrinsic connection to information generation and transmittal; information has public good properties (see Chapter 16). A more equal distribution of income itself can be considered a public good when it is an agreed social objective. This can also reflect a concern for the well-being of future generations, who cannot participate in today's economic or political markets. Merit goods, such as health, education, and basic welfare, can also be considered public goods or as social entitlements guaranteed by government. But concerns about distribution and merit goods are often treated as separate rationales for policy, because in themselves their levels are generally viewed as outside the realm of economic efficiency.

Unfortunately, we cannot jump to the conclusion that if economic theory says policy can fix market failures, it will do so in practice! Government failure may also occur in the many cases in which politicians and bureaucrats put their priority on their own private interests rather than the public interest. Analysis of incentives for government failure helps guide reforms such as constitution design and civil service rules. LDCs tend to have both high market failure and government failure.[5]

Resource Mobilization and Allocation Developing economies cannot afford to waste their very limited financial and skilled human resources on unproductive ventures. Investment projects must be chosen not solely on the basis of partial productivity analysis dictated by individual industrial capital-output ratios but also in the context of an overall development program that takes account of external economies, indirect repercussions, and long-term objectives. Skilled workers must be employed where their contribution will be most widely felt. Economic planning is assumed to help by recognizing the existence of particular constraints and by choosing and coordinating investment projects so as to channel these scarce factors into their most productive outlets. In contrast, it is argued, competitive markets will tend to generate less investment and to direct that investment into areas of low social priority (e.g., consumption goods for the rich).

Attitudinal or Psychological Impact It is often assumed that a detailed statement of national economic and social objectives in the form of a specific development plan can have an important attitudinal or psychological impact on a diverse and often fragmented population. It may succeed in rallying the people behind the government in a national campaign to eliminate poverty, ignorance, and disease. By mobilizing popular support and cutting across class, caste, racial, religious, or tribal factions with the plea to all citizens to work together toward building the nation, it is argued that an enlightened central government, through its economic plan, can best provide the needed incentives to overcome the inhibiting and often divisive forces of sectionalism and traditionalism in a common quest for widespread material and social progress.

Foreign Aid The formulation of detailed development plans has often been a necessary condition for the receipt of bilateral and multilateral foreign aid. With a shopping list of projects, governments are better equipped to solicit foreign assistance and persuade donors that their money will be used as an essential ingredient in a well-conceived and internally consistent plan of action.

The Planning Process: Some Basic Models

Most development plans have traditionally been based initially on some more or less formalized macroeconomic model. Such economywide planning models can conveniently be divided into two basic categories: (1) aggregate growth models, involving macroeconomic estimates of planned or required changes in principal economic variables, and (2) multisector input-output and computable general equilibrium (CGE) models, which ascertain (among other things) the production, resource, employment, and foreign-exchange implications of a given set of final demand targets within an internally consistent framework of interindustry product flows. Finally, probably the most important component of plan formulation is the detailed selection of specific investment projects within each sector through the technique of project appraisal and social cost-benefit analysis. These three "stages" of planning—aggregate, sectoral, and project—provided the main intellectual tools of the planning authority. All of these tools have been, and still are, extensively used by the World Bank and other development agencies.

Aggregate Growth Models: Projecting Macro Variables

The first and most elementary planning model used in almost every developing country is the **aggregate growth model**. It deals with the entire economy in terms of a limited set of macroeconomic variables deemed most critical to the determination of levels and growth rates of national output: savings, investment, capital stocks, exports, imports, foreign assistance, and so on. Aggregate growth models provide a convenient method for forecasting output (and perhaps also employment) growth over a three- to five-year period. Almost all such models represent some variant of the basic Harrod-Domar (or AK) model described in Chapter 3.

Given targeted GDP growth rates and a national capital-output ratio, the Harrod-Domar model can be used to specify the amount of domestic saving necessary to generate such growth. In most cases, this necessary amount of domestic saving is not likely to be realized on the basis of existing savings functions, and so the basic policy problem of how to generate additional domestic savings or foreign assistance comes into play. For planning purposes, the Harrod-Domar model is usually formulated as follows.[6]

We start with the assumption that the ratio of total output to reproducible capital is constant so that

$$K(t) = kY(t) \tag{11.1}$$

where $K(t)$ is capital stock at time t, $Y(t)$ is total output (GDP) at time t, and k is the average (equal to the marginal) capital-output ratio. We assume next that a constant share (s) of output (Y) is always saved (S), so that

$$I(t) = K(t + 1) - K(t) + \delta K(t) = sY = S(t) \tag{11.2}$$

where $I(t)$ is gross investment at the time t and δ is the fraction of the capital stock depreciated in each period. Now if g is the targeted rate of growth of output such that

$$g = \frac{Y(t + 1) - Y(t)}{Y(t)} = \frac{\Delta Y(t)}{Y(t)} \tag{11.3}$$

then capital must be growing at the same rate because from Equation 11.1 we know that

$$\frac{\Delta K}{K} = \frac{k\Delta Y}{K} = \frac{(K/Y)\Delta Y}{K} = \frac{\Delta Y}{Y} \tag{11.4}$$

Using Equation 11.2, we therefore arrive once again at the basic Harrod-Domar growth formula (though this time with a capital depreciation parameter):

$$g = \frac{sY - \delta K}{K} = \frac{s}{k} - \delta \tag{11.5}$$

Finally, because output growth can also be expressed as the sum of labor force growth (n) and the rate of growth of labor productivity (p), Equation 11.5 can be rewritten for planning purposes as

$$n + p = \frac{s}{k} - \delta \qquad (11.6)$$

Of course, much development policymaking does not take productivity as exogenous but is actively focused on raising it. But given an expected rate of labor force and productivity growth (labor force growth can be calculated from readily available demographic information, and productivity growth estimates are usually based either on extrapolations of past trends or on an assumed constant rate of increase), Equation 11.6 can then be used to estimate whether domestic savings will be sufficient to provide an adequate number of new employment opportunities to a growing labor force. One way of doing this is to disaggregate the overall savings function ($S = sY$) into at least two component sources of saving, normally, the propensity to save out of wage income, W, and profit income, π. Thus we define

$$W + \pi = Y \qquad (11.7)$$

and

$$s_\pi \pi + s_W W = I \qquad (11.8)$$

where s_π and s_W are the savings propensities from π and W, respectively. By manipulating Equation 11.5 and substituting Equations 11.7 and 11.8 into it, we arrive at a modified Harrod-Domar growth equation:

$$k(g + \delta) = (s_\pi - s_W)\left(\frac{\pi}{Y}\right) + s_W \qquad (11.9)$$

which can then serve as a formula for ascertaining the adequacy of current saving out of profit and wage income. For example, if a 4% growth rate is desired and if $\delta = 0.03$, $k = 3.0$, and $\pi/Y = 0.5$, Equation 11.9 reduces to $0.42 = s_\pi + s_W$.[7] If savings out of capital income amount to 25%, wage earners must save at a 17% rate to achieve the targeted rate of growth. In the absence of such a savings rate out of labor income, the government could pursue a variety of policies to raise domestic saving or seek foreign assistance.

In countries where inadequate foreign-exchange reserves are believed to be the principal constraint on economic growth, the aggregate growth model typically employed is some variant of the two-gap model, which will be described in Chapter 15. (Two-gap models are simply Harrod-Domar models generalized to take foreign-trade problems into account.) In either case, aggregate growth models can provide only a rough first approximation of the general directions an economy might take. Thus they rarely constitute the operational development plan. Perhaps more important, the simplicity and relatively low data collection cost of using aggregate growth models can often blind us to their very real limitations, especially when carried out in too mechanical a fashion. Average capital-output ratios are notoriously difficult to estimate and may bear little relation to marginal capital-output ratios, which are the relevant ratios for forecasting purposes, and savings rates can be highly unstable. The operational plan requires a more disaggregated multisector model of economic activity like the well-known input-output approach.

Multisector Models and Sectoral Projections

A much more sophisticated approach to development planning is to use some variant of the **interindustry** or **input-output model**, in which the activities of the major industrial sectors of the economy are interrelated by means of a set of simultaneous algebraic equations expressing the specific production processes or technologies of each industry. All industries are viewed both as producers of outputs and users of inputs from other industries. For example, the agricultural sector is both a producer of output (e.g., wheat) and a user of inputs from, say, the manufacturing sector (e.g., machinery, fertilizer). Thus direct and indirect repercussions of planned changes in the demand for the products of any one industry on output, employment, and imports of all other industries can be traced throughout the entire economy in an intricate web of economic interdependence. Given the planned output targets for each sector of the economy, the interindustry model can be used to determine intermediate material, import, labor, and capital requirements with the result that a comprehensive economic plan with mutually consistent production levels and resource requirements can, in theory, be constructed.

Interindustry models range from simple input-output models, usually consisting of 10 to 30 sectors in the developing economies and 30 to 400 sectors in advanced economies, to more complicated linear programming or activity analysis models where checks of feasibility (what is possible given certain resource constraints) and optimality (what is best among different alternatives) are also built into the model. But the distinguishing characteristic of the interindustry or input-output approach is the attempt to formulate an internally consistent, comprehensive development plan for the entire economy.[8]

Input-output analysis is often extended in two ways. First, by including data on factor payments, sources of household income, and the pattern of household goods consumption across various social groups (such as urban and rural households), a social accounting matrix (SAM) is created. This is accomplished by adding data from the system of national accounts, balance of payments, and flow-of-funds databases, often supplemented with household survey data, to the basic input-output table. A SAM therefore provides a comprehensive and detailed quantitative description of the interrelationships in an economy as they exist at a point in time, making it well suited as a tool for evaluating the impact of alternative development policies. SAMs for many countries can be found online. SAMs are often further elaborated with computable general equilibrium (CGE) models, which assume that households maximize utility and firms maximize profits. Utility (or demand) and production functions are assumed or estimated from national data. The resulting impact of the policy is then simulated using standard computer programs. The CGE approach is more complicated than a SAM, but its value lies in enabling policymakers to take into account the possible reactions of consumers and firms to the alternative policies being considered rather than assume that they will behave the way they did before the new policies were implemented.[9]

Project Appraisal and Social Cost-Benefit Analysis

The vast majority of day-to-day operational decisions with regard to the allocation of limited public investment funds are based on a microeconomic technique of analysis known as **project appraisal**. The intellectual as well as the operational linkage among these three major planning techniques, however, should not be overlooked. Macro growth models set the broad strategy, input-output analysis ensures an internally consistent set of sectoral targets, and project appraisal is designed to ensure the efficient planning of individual projects within each sector.

Basic Concepts and Methodology The methodology of project appraisal rests on the theory and practice of social **cost-benefit analysis**,[10] which is also used in the United States and other developed countries. The basic idea of cost-benefit analysis is simple: To decide on the worth of projects involving public expenditure (or, indeed, in which public policy can play a crucial role), it is necessary to weigh the advantages (benefits) and the disadvantages (costs) to society as a whole. The need for social cost-benefit analysis arises because the normal yardstick of commercial profitability that guides the investment decisions of private investors may not be an appropriate guide for public investment decisions. Private investors are interested in maximizing private profits and therefore normally take into account only the variables that affect net profit: receipts and expenditures. Both receipts and expenditures are valued at prevailing market prices for inputs and outputs.

The point of departure for social cost-benefit analysis is that it does not accept that actual receipts are a true measure of social benefits or that actual expenditures a true measure of social costs. Not only will actual market prices often diverge from their true value, but private investors do not take into account the external effects of their decisions. These externalities can be sizable and pervasive.[11] In other words, where social costs and benefits diverge from private costs and benefits, investment decisions based entirely on the criterion of commercial profitability may lead to wrong decisions from the point of view of social welfare, which should be the government's primary concern. Although social valuations may differ significantly from private valuations, the practice of cost-benefit analysis is based on the assumption that these divergences can be adjusted for by public policy so that the difference between social benefit and cost will properly reflect social profitability just as the difference between actual receipts and expenditures measures the private profitability of an investment.

Thus we can define **social profit** in any period as the difference between social benefits and social costs where these are measured both directly (the real costs of inputs and the real value of outputs) and indirectly (e.g., employment effects, distributional effects). The calculation of the social profitability of an investment is then a three-step process.[12]

1. We must first specify the objective function to be maximized—ordinarily, net social benefit—with some measure of how different benefits (e.g., per capita consumption, income distribution) are to be calculated and what the trade-off between them might be.

2. To arrive at calculations of net social benefit, we need social measures of the unit values of all project inputs and outputs. Such social measures are often called **accounting prices** or **shadow prices** of inputs and outputs to distinguish them from actual **market prices**.[13] In general, the greater the divergence between shadow and market prices, the greater the need for social cost-benefit analysis in arriving at public investment decision rules.

3. Finally, we need some decision criterion to reduce the stream of projected social benefit and cost flows to an index, the value of which can then be used to select or reject a project or to rank it relative to alternative projects.

Let us briefly examine each of these steps of project appraisal.

Setting Objectives Given the difficulty of attaching numerical values to such objectives as national cohesion, self-reliance, political stability, modernization, and quality of life, economic planners typically measure the social worth of a project in terms of the degree to which it contributes to the net flow of future goods and services in the economy—that is, by its impact on future levels of consumption.

Recently, a second major criterion, the project's impact on income distribution, has received increased attention. If preference is to be given to raising the consumption standards of low-income groups, the social worth of a project must be calculated as a weighted sum of the distribution of its benefits, where additional consumption by low-income groups may receive a disproportionately high weight in the social welfare objective function. (This procedure is analogous to that of constructing a poverty-weighted index of economic growth, discussed in Appendix 5.2.) Beginning in 1991, project analysis at the World Bank also included an environmental impact evaluation as a third criterion, along with future consumption and income distribution.

Computing Shadow Prices and Social Discount Rates The core of social cost-benefit analysis is the calculation or estimation of the prices to be used in determining the true value of benefits and the real magnitude of costs. There are many reasons for believing that in developing countries, market prices of outputs and inputs do not give a true reflection of social benefits and costs. Five such reasons, in particular, are often cited.

1. *Inflation and currency overvaluation.* Many developing countries are still beset by inflation and varying degrees of price controls. Controlled prices do not typically reflect the real opportunity cost to society of producing these goods and

services. Moreover, in many countries, the government manages the price of foreign exchange. With inflation and unaltered foreign-exchange rates, the domestic currency becomes overvalued (see Chapter 13), with the result that import prices underestimate the real cost to the country of purchasing foreign products and export prices (in local currency) understate the real benefit accruing to the country from a given volume of exports. Bubbles and crises can also lead to larger distortions. Public investment decisions based on this price will therefore tend to be biased against export industries and to favor import substitutions.

2. *Wage rates, capital costs, and unemployment.* Almost all developing countries exhibit factor-price distortions resulting in modern-sector wage rates exceeding the social opportunity cost (or shadow price) of labor and interest rates understating the social opportunity cost of capital. This leads to the widespread phenomenon of unemployment and underemployment and the excessive capital intensity of industrial production technologies. If governments were to use unadjusted market prices for labor and capital in calculating the costs of alternative public investment projects, they would underestimate the real costs of capital-intensive projects and tend to promote these at the expense of the socially less costly labor-intensive projects more favorable to the poor.

3. *Tariffs, quotas, and import substitution.* The existence of high tariffs, in combination with import quotas and overvalued exchange rates, discriminates against the agricultural export sector and favors the import-substituting manufacturing sector (see Chapter 13). It also encourages socially wasteful **rent seeking** on the part of competing exporters and importers. They vie with each other (often through bribes and threats as well as direct lobbying efforts) to capture the extra profits that can accrue to traders with import licenses, export subsidies, tariff protection, and industrial preferences.

4. *Savings deficiency.* Given the substantial pressures for providing higher immediate consumption levels to the masses of poor people, the level and rate of domestic savings in most developing countries is often thought to be suboptimal. According to this argument, governments should use a discount rate that is lower than the market rate of interest in order to promote projects that have a longer payoff period and generate a higher stream of investible surpluses in the future.[14]

5. *The social rate of discount.* In our discussion of the shadow price of savings, we mentioned the need for governments to choose appropriate discount rates in calculating the worth of project benefits and costs that occur over time. The **social rate of discount** (also sometimes referred to as *social time preference*) is essentially a price of time—the rate used to calculate the **net present value** of a time stream of project benefits and costs where the net present value (NPV) is calculated as

$$\text{NPV} = \sum_t \frac{B_t - C_t}{(1 + r)^t} \tag{11.10}$$

where B_t is the expected benefit of the project at time t, C_t is the expected cost (both evaluated using shadow prices), and r is the government's social rate of discount. Social discount rates may differ from market rates of interest (normally used by private investors to calculate the profitability of investments), depending on the subjective evaluation placed on future net benefits: The higher the future benefits and costs are valued in the government's planning scheme—for example, if government also represents future, unborn citizens—the lower will be the social rate of discount.

In view of these five forces leading to considerable product, factor, and money price distortions, as well as considerations of external economies and diseconomies of production and consumption (by definition, factors not taken into account in private investment decisions), it has been widely argued and generally agreed that a strong case can be made for concluding that a project's actual anticipated receipts and expenditures often do *not* provide an accurate measure of its social worth. It is primarily for this reason that the tools of social cost-benefit analysis for project appraisal are essential to an efficient process of project selection in developing countries.

Choosing Projects: Some Decision Criteria Having computed relevant shadow prices, projected a time stream of expected benefits and costs (including indirect or external effects), and selected an appropriate social discount rate, planners are in a position to choose from a set of alternative investment projects those thought to be most desirable. They therefore need to adopt a decision criterion to be followed. Normally, economists advocate using the net present value rule in choosing investment projects; that is, projects should be accepted or rejected according to whether their net present value is positive or negative. As we have seen, however, NPV calculations are very sensitive to the choice of a social discount rate. An alternative approach is to calculate the discount rate that gives the project an NPV of zero, compare this **internal rate of return** with either a predetermined social discount rate or the market rate of interest, and choose projects whose internal rates exceed the predetermined or market rate. This approach is widely used in evaluating educational investments.

Because most developing countries face substantial capital constraints, the choice of investment projects will normally also involve a ranking of all projects that meet the NPV rule. Projects are ranked by descending net present value (more precisely, by their benefit-cost ratios, which are arrived at by dividing NPV by the constraint on total capital cost, K—that is, an NPV/K ratio is calculated for each project). The project or set of projects (some investments should be considered as a package of projects) with the highest NPV/K ratio is chosen first, then the next highest, and so on down the line until all available capital investment funds have been exhausted.[15]

Conclusions: Planning Models and Plan Consistency

The process of formulating a comprehensive, detailed development plan is obviously a more complicated process than that described by our three-stage approach. It involves a constant dialogue and feedback mechanism between national leaders who set priorities and planners, statisticians, research workers, and departmental or ministry officials. Internal rivalries and conflicting objectives (not to mention political pressure from powerful vested-interest groups) are always to be reckoned with. Nevertheless, our presentation should at least serve to provide a feel for the mechanics of planning and to demonstrate the ways in which aggregate, input-output, and project planning models have been used to attempt to formulate an internally consistent and comprehensive development plan.

Problems of Plan Implementation and Plan Failure

The results of development planning have been generally disappointing.[16] The widespread rejection of development planning based on poor performance has had a number of practical outcomes, the most important of which is the adoption in a growing number of LDCs of a more free-market-oriented economic system and a precipitous decline in development planning.

What went wrong? Why has the early euphoria about planning gradually been transformed into disillusionment and dejection? We can identify two interrelated sets of answers, one dealing with the gap between the theoretical economic benefits and the practical results of development planning and the other associated with more fundamental defects in the planning process, especially as it relates to administrative capacities, political will, and plan implementation.

Theory versus Practice

The principal economic arguments for planning briefly outlined earlier in this chapter—market failure, divergences between private and social valuations, resource mobilization, investment coordination, and the like—have often turned out to be weakly supported by the actual planning experience. Commenting on this planning failure, Tony Killick has noted that

> it is doubtful whether plans have generated more useful signals for the future than would otherwise have been forthcoming; governments have rarely, in practice, reconciled private and social valuations except in a piecemeal manner; because they have seldom become operational documents, plans have probably had only limited impact in mobilizing resources and in coordinating economic policies.[17]

To take the specific case of the market failure argument and the presumed role of governments in reconciling the divergence between private and social valuations of benefits and costs, the experience of government policy in many LDCs has been one of often *exacerbating* rather than reconciling these divergences—**government failure** rather than market failure. Government policy has often tended to increase rather than reduce the divergences between private and social valuations. For example, public policies have raised the level of wages above labor's shadow price or scarcity value by various devices such as minimum-wage legislation, tying wages to educational attainment, and structuring rates of remuneration at higher levels on the basis of international salary scales. Similarly, investment depreciation and tax allowances, overvalued exchange rates, low effective rates of protection, quotas, and credit rationing at low interest rates all serve to lower the private cost of capital far below its scarcity or social cost (see Chapter 13). The net effect of these factor-price distortions has been to encourage private and public enterprises to adopt more capital-intensive production methods than would exist if public policy attempted to correct the prices.

As another example, we discovered in Chapter 8 that economic signals and incentives in many LDCs have served to exaggerate the private valuations of the returns to education at the secondary and tertiary levels to a point where the private demand for ever more years of schooling is greatly in excess of the social payoff. The tendency to ration scarce high-paying employment opportunities by level of completed education and the policy of most LDC governments to subsidize the private costs of education at the higher levels have together led to a situation in which the social returns to investment in further quantitative educational expansion seem hardly justified in comparison with alternative investment opportunities.

Reasons for Plan Failure

In view of the foregoing examples, we may conclude that the gap between the theoretical economic benefits of planning and its practical results in most developing countries has been quite large. The gap between public rhetoric and economic reality has been even greater. While supposedly concerned with eliminating poverty, reducing inequality, and lowering unemployment, many LDC planning policies have in fact unwittingly contributed to their perpetuation. Some of the major explanations for this have to do with failures of the planning process itself; these failures in turn arise out of certain specific problems.[18]

Deficiencies in Plans and Their Implementation Plans are often overambitious. They try to accomplish too many objectives at once without consideration that some of the objectives are competing or even conflicting. They are often grandiose in design but vague on specific policies for achieving stated objectives. In this they have much in common with the excessive lists of 60 to 100 or more issue areas in conditionality agreements set out by the World Bank and the International Monetary Fund (IMF). Finally, the gap between plan formulation and implementation is often enormous (many plans, for reasons to be discussed, are never implemented).

Insufficient and Unreliable Data The economic value of a development plan depends to a great extent on the quality and reliability of the statistical data on which it is based. When these data are weak, unreliable, or simply nonexistent, as in many poor countries, the accuracy and internal consistency of economywide quantitative plans are greatly diminished. And when these unreliable data are compounded by an inadequate supply of qualified economists, statisticians, and other planning personnel (as is also the situation in most poor nations), the attempt to formulate and carry out a comprehensive and detailed development plan is likely to be frustrated at all levels.

Unanticipated Economic Disturbances, External and Internal Because most LDCs are open economies dependent on the vicissitudes of international trade, aid, and private foreign investment, it becomes exceedingly difficult for them to engage in even short-term forecasting, let alone long-range planning. The oil price increases of 1974, 1979, and 1990 caused havoc in most LDC development plans. But the energy crisis was only an extreme case of a general tendency for economic factors over which most LDC governments have little control to determine the success or failure of their developmental policies.

Institutional Weaknesses The institutional weaknesses of the planning processes of most developing countries include the separation of the planning agency from the day-to-day decision-making machinery of government; the failure of planners, administrators, and political leaders to engage in a continuous dialogue and internal communication about goals and strategies; and the international transfer of institutional planning practices and organizational arrangements that may be inappropriate to local conditions. In addition, there has been much concern about incompetent and unqualified civil servants; cumbersome bureaucratic procedures; excessive caution and resistance to innovation and change; interministerial personal and departmental rivalries (e.g., finance ministries and planning agencies are often conflicting rather than cooperative forces in LDC governments); lack of commitment to national goals as opposed to regional, departmental, or simply private objectives on the part of political leaders and government bureaucrats; and in accordance with this lack of national as opposed to personal interest, the political and bureaucratic corruption that is pervasive in many governments.[19]

Lack of Political Will Poor plan performance and the wide gap between plan formulation and plan implementation are also attributable to a lack of commitment and **political will** on the part of many developing-country leaders and high-level decision makers.[20] Political will to develop entails much more than high-minded purposes and noble rhetoric. It requires an unusual ability and a great deal of political courage to challenge powerful elites and vested-interest groups and to persuade them that such development is in the long-run interests of *all* citizens even though some of them may suffer short-term losses. In the absence of their support, be it freely offered or coerced, a will to develop on the part of politicians is likely to meet with staunch resistance, frustration, and internal conflict.

Government Failure and the Resurgent Preference for Markets over Planning

As a result of the disenchantment with planning and the perceived failure of government intervention, many economists, some finance ministers in developing countries, and the heads of the major international development organizations advocated the increased use of the market mechanism as a key instrument for promoting greater efficiency and more rapid economic growth. U.S. President Ronald Reagan made a famous reference to the "magic of the marketplace" in a 1981 speech at Cancun, Mexico. If the decade of the 1970s could be described as a period of increased public-sector activity in the pursuit of more equitable development, the 1980s and 1990s witnessed the reemergence of free-market economics as part of the ever-changing development orthodoxy.

Among the early converts were Latin American countries, including Chile (1973), Uruguay (1974), and Argentina (1976), although the state retains an active economic role. Others have since jumped on the free-market bandwagon, ranging from traditionally more market-oriented countries such as Kenya, Peru, the Philippines, and Côte d' Ivoire to formerly socialist-inclined countries such as India, Sri Lanka, Tanzania, Jamaica, and Turkey, not to mention China and most of the former Soviet Union. As part of their domestic market liberalization programs, these countries have sought to reduce the role of the public sector, encourage greater private-sector activity, and eliminate distortions in interest rates, wages, and the prices of consumer goods. The intent of such changes is to lubricate the wheels of the market mechanism. In addition, these countries have sought to improve their comparative advantage in the international economy by lowering exchange rates, promoting exports, and eliminating protection.

Among the international organizations preaching the virtues of the free market are the IMF and the World Bank. The IMF is requiring substantial market liberalization programs and policies to improve comparative advantage and promote macroeconomic stabilization as conditions for access to its higher credit windows. The World Bank is carefully scrutinizing its project lending to ensure that the projects proposed could not otherwise be undertaken by the private sector. Furthermore, it is emphasizing joint ventures between governments and private enterprise as part of its structural adjustment lending.

In most developing countries, the public sector has grown dramatically since the 1970s, now accounting for 15% to 25% of GDP and some 40% to 50% of total investment. However, this growth has been accompanied by considerable inefficiency and waste. The returns to public investment, in terms of GDP growth, declined nearly 25% between 1960 and 1980. Much of this diminishing return has resulted from poor investment decisions, delays in construction, low-capacity utilization, and insufficient maintenance of public projects. Given these problems, many of the "free marketeers" assert that a greater role for private enterprise in undertaking projects could lead to more efficient utilization of resources.

With regard to price distortions, the World Bank has argued that these distortions slowed GDP growth in many developing countries. It has estimated that countries with highly distorted prices experienced growth rates 2% lower than the average for developing countries. Moreover, it found that credit allocations and subsidized interest rates resulted in a bias toward capital-intensive industries; minimum-wage requirements reduced the demand for labor; and subsidized prices for consumer goods, especially for food, frequently discouraged producers and thereby created widespread shortages. As a result, many people are calling for the elimination of government-induced distortions in interest rates, wages, and the prices of consumer goods, in the hope that the market mechanism would operate more smoothly and produce a more efficient allocation of resources.

Box 11.1 lists some of the problems attributed to state intervention in developing countries. But just as market failure does not always justify public intervention (because governments, as we have seen, can often make things worse), so too government failure is not necessarily an argument for private markets. For example, in South Korea, the Pohang Steel Company was publicly operated and highly efficient until its privatization in 2000, whereas the Steel Authority in India, also publicly owned and operated, is a model of inefficiency. Subsidized interest rates exist in both East Asia, where growth has accelerated, and in Latin America, where it has stagnated. Unproductive rent-seeking activities can just as easily be found in

BOX 11.1   Some Problems of Government Intervention in Developing Countries

- Individuals may know more about their own preferences and circumstances than the government.
- Government planning may increase risk by pointing everyone in the same direction—governments may make bigger mistakes than markets.
- Government planning may be more rigid and inflexible than private decision making because complex decision-making machinery may be involved in government.
- Governments may be incapable of administering detailed plans.
- Government controls may block private-sector individual initiative if there are many bureaucratic obstacles.
- Organizations and individuals require incentives to work, innovate, control costs, and allocate efficiently, and the discipline and rewards of the market cannot easily be replicated within public enterprises and organizations. Public enterprises are often inefficient and wasteful.
- Different levels and parts of government may be poorly coordinated in the absence of the equilibrating signals provided by the market, particularly where groups or regions with different interests are involved.
- Markets place constraints on what can be achieved by government; for example, resale of commodities on black markets and activities in the informal sector can disrupt rationing or other nonlinear pricing or taxation schemes. This is the general problem of "incentive compatibility."
- Controls create resource-using activities to influence those controls through lobbying and corruption—often called rent seeking or directly unproductive activities.
- Planning may be manipulated by privileged and powerful groups that act in their own interests, and planning creates groups with a vested interest in planning, for example, bureaucrats or industrialists who obtain protected positions.
- Governments may be dominated by narrow interest groups interested in their own welfare and sometimes actively hostile to large sections of the population. Planning may intensify their power.

Source: Adapted from Nicholas Stern, "The economics of development: A survey," *Economic Journal* 99 (1989): 597–685, tab. 4. Adapted with permission.

poorly functioning private markets as in inefficient state operations. Simple judgments about the relative merits of public versus private economic activities cannot therefore be made outside the context of specific countries and concrete situations. But for LDCs intent on pursuing market reforms, either because of their dissatisfaction with the performance of their public sectors or because of IMF or World Bank pressure, a number of sociocultural preconditions and economic practices must be met.

The Market Economy

Sociocultural Preconditions and Economic Requirements

A well-functioning market system requires special social, institutional, legal, and cultural preconditions often absent in developing nations. Fraud, corruption, and monopoly do not disappear with the wave of a magic neoclassical wand. Nathan Keyfitz and Robert Dorfman have identified 14 institutional and cultural requirements for the operation of effective private markets:[21]

1. Trust (in banks, insurance companies, suppliers, etc.)

2. Law and order (enforcement of contracts)

3. Security of persons and of property

4. Balancing competition with cooperation (for a safe workplace and a cleaner environment)

5. Division of responsibility and diffusion of power (an independent judiciary)

6. Community altruism (a social "safety net" for the impaired, chronically unemployed, elderly, etc.)

7. Social mobility, legitimation of ambition, and toleration of competitiveness

8. Materialistic values as a stimulus to greater production

9. Deferring gratification to generate private saving

10. Rationality unconstrained by tradition

11. Honesty in government

12. Efficient forms of competition, as opposed to monopolistic control

13. Freedom of information (along with protection of privacy)

14. Flows of information without restrictions or favoritism

Given the existence of these institutional and cultural preconditions, a well-functioning market system requires at least the following 11 market-facilitating legal and economic practices:[22]

1. Property rights clearly established and demarcated; procedures for establishing property rights and transferring them

2. Commercial laws and courts to enforce them, especially contract and bankruptcy laws

3. Freedom to establish businesses in all sectors except those with significant externalities, without excessive licensing requirements: analogous freedom to enter trades and professions and to attain government offices (equal economic opportunity)

4. A stable currency and a reliable and efficient system for making transfers (a banking system)

5. Public supervision or operation of natural monopolies (industries with increasing returns to scale) as occurs in industries where technological efficiency requires that a firm be large enough to supply 10% to 15% of the national market

6. Provision of adequate information in every market about the characteristics of the products offered and the state of supply and demand, to both buyers and sellers

7. Autonomous tastes—protection of consumers' preferences from influence by producers and purveyors

8. Public management of externalities (both harmful and beneficial) and provision of public goods

9. Instruments for executing stabilizing monetary and fiscal policies (see Chapter 16)

10. Safety nets—provisions for maintaining adequate consumption for individuals affected by certain economic misfortunes, especially involuntary unemployment, industrial injuries, and work disabilities

11. Encouragements to innovations, in particular, issuance and enforcement of patents and copyrights

So we see that market reforms involve much more than eliminating price distortions, privatizing public enterprises, and declaring markets free. The setbacks to market reforms in Eastern Europe and Russia as well as in many African and Asian economies is in no small measure attributable to the absence of some (or many) of the institutional preconditions and market practices.

Role and Limitations of the Market in LDCs

In general, developing countries will not be able to rely on the market mechanism to the extent that the industrial countries did during their early stages of development. Perhaps the most important reason is that in most developing countries, markets are in reality characterized by widespread imperfections.[23] One such imperfection not mentioned earlier is the lack of information and the presence of uncertainty that most individual producers and consumers face.[24] Thus in many developing countries, producers are often unsure about the size of local markets, the presence of other producers, and the availability of inputs, both domestic and imported. Consumers may be unsure about the quality and availability of products and their substitutes. Moreover, in contrast to their counterparts in developed countries, producers and consumers usually lack the tools to ferret out this information because little marketing is done. Under such circumstances, profit- and utility-maximizing behavior may be based on the wrong information and hence not lead to an efficient allocation of resources. The government may attempt to provide this information, or it may decide to intervene in the market by guiding producers and consumers. The 2001 Nobel Prize in economics was awarded to George Akerlof, Michael Spence, and Joseph Stiglitz for their compelling work in this field, which has had an especially large influence on development studies.

Another major imperfection in LDC markets is the presence of substantial externalities. Many goods may have a high social value that is not reflected in their market price. Because such goods, such as education and health services, must be provided at a price below their cost or even free, the private sector has no incentive to produce them. Thus the government must often be responsible for providing these goods in order to ensure a minimum of welfare. In view of the population growth and poverty that characterize many developing countries, it is likely that public-sector activity—what the World Bank calls "market-friendly" policies—in this area will continue to expand.

Even if the market operated relatively efficiently in allocating current resources, however, governments still have to contend with allocating resources over time. Capital formation is a fundamental requirement for economic development. Private savings are very low in the early stages of development, and hence governments, through their fiscal and monetary policies, must usually play a major role in accumulating capital (see Chapter 16). Investment in infrastructure, particularly during the early stages of development, is of crucial importance as it sets the framework for subsequent investment by both the private and public sectors.[25] Furthermore, even in the later stages of development, the private sector may not be able to generate the massive funding required to establish certain industries, despite their long-run profitability. The government may also need to create certain linkages that will permit the private sector to flourish in the future. Finally, the government must often assist in the creation of human capital through educating and training the labor force so that labor productivity will increase.

Another major concern in the debate over markets versus planning relates to income distribution. Although the market mechanism may result in a more efficient allocation of resources, it can also produce a distribution of income that is highly unequal. Most developing countries, as we have seen, have a very skewed pattern of income distribution. Excessive reliance on the market mechanism will not improve that distribution. In fact, it may tend to exacerbate the problem, for wealthy individuals with their monopoly of "dollar votes" determine the allocation of resources and hence income.

Finally, it is important to remember that economic development is a process of structural change. The market may be efficient in allocating resources at the margin, allowing certain industries to emerge and others to fail, but may be ineffective in producing large discontinuous changes in the economic structure, changes that may be crucial to the country's long-term development (see Chapter 4). The government may therefore have to intervene in sectors crucial to the country's development to ensure that they change over time and flourish.

The foregoing arguments have shown that the market mechanism can fail in the presence of the widespread imperfections and special concerns that characterize many developing countries. This does not mean that countries should not rely more on the market to allocate their products and resources. No central-planning agency is capable of regulating the vast array of goods and services, nor would this be desirable. Rather, it means greater and more effective *cooperation* between the public and private sectors. It also means that governments must seek to determine in which areas the market can most efficiently operate and in which areas the government itself can achieve the best results given its own limited human resources. This public-sector–private-sector cooperation through a proactive government industrial policy is a key lesson of the success stories of South Korea, Taiwan, and Singapore.[26]

In summary, there are degrees to which different developing countries will be able to rely on the market mechanism to foster economic development. It would appear that low-income countries in the early stages of development will have to continue to rely more on planning because the institutional and cultural preconditions for a market economy are in short supply and they face major structural changes in the future. Middle-income countries are likely gradually to become more market-oriented, although they will still remain mixed economies with a broad range of government participation. Countries in later stages of development, such as the industrializing countries of East Asia and Latin America, already have conditions that allow a greater reliance on private markets and competitive prices. But they too must remain wary of the pitfalls of relying solely on the private sector to allocate resources and distribute income in pursuit of both the economic and social objectives of long-term development. Commenting specifically on the Latin American experience of the 1980s, noted Chilean economist Alejandro Foxley made the following astute observation:

> Critical evaluations of past free market experiments are currently underway in Latin America. It is generally accepted now that a naive and radical hands-off attitude on the part of the governments leads to serious distortion in resource allocation: low investment, high capital flight, etc. This was often due to poor performance in specific markets, such as domestic capital markets that in some countries produced real interest rates in the range of 20%–50% for several years; to persistent goods and labor market disequilibrium, to unchecked speculative behavior by economic agents that led to capital flight, to imperfect world markets for key export products, etc. Thus it seems that an active regulatory role for the government is needed, as well as government intervention for the protection of the poorer sectors through vigorous development of social programs.
>
> The difference between this sort of active government presence and old-fashioned statism lies in the fact that what is stressed now is a decentralized, smaller government that opens channels for the private sector and organized labor to participate in the decision-making process. Discussions in Latin America today focus more on decentralized development, social pacts, and concerted action and less on an omnipresent state role or the advocacy of unrestricted free markets.[27]

We return to the themes of decentralization and participation at the close of this chapter.

The "Washington Consensus" on the State in Development and Its Limitations

For much of the 1980s and early 1990s, the "Washington Consensus" on development policy held sway. This consensus, encapsulated by John Williamson, reflected the free-market approach to development followed in those years by the IMF,

TABLE 11.1 The Washington Consensus and East Asia

Elements of the Washington Consensus	South Korea	Taiwan
1. Fiscal discipline	Yes, generally	Yes
2. Redirection of public expenditure priorities toward health, education, and infrastructure	Yes	Yes
3. Tax reform, including the broadening of the tax base and cutting marginal tax rates	Yes, generally	Yes
4. Unified and competitive exchange rates	Yes (except for limited time periods)	Yes
5. Secure property rights	President Park starts his rule in 1961 by imprisoning leading businessmen and threatening confiscation of their assets	Yes
6. Deregulation	Limited	Limited
7. Trade liberalization	Limited until the 1980s	Limited until the 1980s
8. Privatization	No. Government established many public enterprises during 1950s and 1960s.	No. Government established many public enterprises during 1950s and 1960s.
9. Elimination of barriers to direct foreign investment (DFI)	DFI heavily restricted	DFI subject to government control
10. Financial liberalization	Limited until the 1980s	Limited until the 1980s

Source: Dani Rodrik, "Understanding economic policy reform," *Journal of Economic Literature* 34 (1996): 9–41. Reprinted with the permission of the American Economic Association.

World Bank, and key U.S. government agencies. It contained ten points, summarized in column 1 of Table 11.1.

The ten points of the Washington Consensus are striking at least as much for what they do not contain as for what they do. There is no mention of shared growth, of the central need to focus on eliminating absolute poverty to achieve development in any meaningful sense, or of reducing inequality, as central ends in themselves as well as instruments of economic growth.[28] Driving the several components of the consensus was the conviction that government was more likely to make things worse than better. There also was the view that poverty would be taken care of by growth and was not a major obstacle in itself to growth and development; but this view, as we have seen in Chapters 4 and 5, is no longer considered adequate by most development specialists.

The Washington Consensus list is also striking in its free-market approach, even in fields in which market failure is prevalent, such as the financial sector (examined in Chapter 16). Moreover, the list is striking in its limited applicability to the most successful cases of economic development, South Korea and Taiwan. These cases not only represent the highest rates of economic growth over the past half century but also have often been cited as examples of shared growth, in which absolute poverty was eliminated early on, and the lower income groups have continued to benefit from the development process, despite an upturn in inequality since the late 1990s. (Hong Kong and Singapore have comparable growth records but are comparatively small city states; Singapore has been fairly interventionist. The historical record for high growth in China is shorter but in any case does not represent a triumph of the free market.) Indeed, as Dani Rodrik summarizes in Table 11.1, for about half of its elements, the Washington Consensus is at best of limited applicability to South Korea and Taiwan. It can be concluded that the state has had a broader role in the most successful development experiences than encapsulated by the Washington Consensus.

Toward a New Consensus

In recent years, there has been a major change in the Washington Consensus worldview in Washington as well as elsewhere. In the Americas, the new views were sometimes referred to, by World Bank President James Wolfensohn and others, as the New ("Santiago") Consensus, which was in some respects crystalized at the April 1998 Summit of the Americas in Santiago, Chile.[29] Note that the scholarly tradition in Continental Europe and Japan, as well as in many parts of the developing world, such as India, has remained more positive toward the role of the state throughout the period but has to a large degree also converged toward the New Consensus. The broad elements of the Santiago Consensus are summarized in Box 11.2.

Given that developing-country governments are highly constrained in their available resources, some of these Santiago Consensus objectives will have to receive less emphasis than others. An important dimension of the New Consensus is the emphasis on government's responsibility to focus on poverty alleviation. This is in part a return to the focus of the 1970s; one reason for this renewed focus is that free-market policies of the 1980s and early 1990s were viewed as inadequately helping the poor. The New Consensus also appears to reflect a growing sentiment that the goal of poverty eradication is finally achievable, especially given recent progress in health and education. But the New Consensus on the role of government in development borrows some important lessons from the Washington Consensus period. In particular, the stress on market-based development and limiting government's role in direct production continues to be the consensus view. And the new elements are not just a reprise of the old view of government as benevolent provider of social welfare. A sober view continues, emphasizing the importance of building state capacity and responsiveness by responding to government failure with judiciously designed reforms and encouraging the development of NGOs and civil society more generally.

For example, government has an important role in human capital. Health and education are critical to successful development (see Chapter 8). The ability of a society to make effective use of the market depends on the capabilities of its citizens. People who are ill or illiterate have limited capacity to take advantage of market opportunities when these emerge. India and China provide a valuable illustration. Both countries have had restraints on the market in the past. But China

---

BOX 11.2   The Santiago Consensus

1. Development must be market-based, but there are large market failures that cannot be ignored.
2. Government should not be in the business of direct production, as a general rule.
3. But there is a broad, eclectic role for government in the following areas:
   - Providing a stable macro environment
   - Infrastructure, though in fewer sectors than thought necessary in the past
   - Public health
   - Education and training
   - Technology transfer (and for advanced LDCs, the beginnings of original R&D)
   - Ensuring environmentally sustainable development and ecological protection
   - Providing export incentives
   - Helping the private sector overcome coordination failures
   - Ensuring "shared growth" by acting to reduce poverty and inequality and to ensure that as the economy grows, the poor share substantially in the benefits
   - Continued if more moderate regulation and support in financial sectors
   - Provision of fundamental public goods, such as legal structure, including the protection of property rights

---

invested heavily in basic education and health. When China liberalized, beginning in 1978, it started with a literate, numerate, and at least relatively healthy adult population, and the result has been high growth. When India finally began to liberalize around 1991 or somewhat thereafter, nearly half the adults were still illiterate and many were still lacking in nutrition and basic health care. As Amartya Sen has pointed out, this may be one explanation for China's better growth outcome after market liberalization than India's.[30]

The New Consensus also does not include some features that many commentators have considered significant to East Asian success, such as an active industrial policy—picking winners—to overcome coordination failures, because these remain controversial. There are widespread doubts about the replicability of industrial policy experiences of these countries, and the consensus is that industrial policy is ineffective when government is less capable or more constrained.

The new view represents in part a renewed recognition that markets do fail, that at times these failures cannot be addressed without a significant and ongoing role for government—that market failure can be significantly worse than government failure after all, and that when governance is poor, it can often be improved. Indeed, a key part of government's role is to help secure the foundations for economic development by ensuring that the requirements for an effective market-based economy are met. But there is no sense that government reform is easy and no swing toward widespread support for a dirigiste state such as prevailed prior to the 1980s. We further explore the roles of market and state in economic development in the next section.

Development Political Economy: Theories of Policy Formulation and Reform

Until recently, two extreme views seem often to have dominated the discussions of the role of government in economic development. The first view has been that effective government was not only necessary due to market failure but possibly even sufficient to achieve economic development. At least implicit in this view is the argument that if a particular regime could not be counted on to perform competently and honestly in this process, either the regime would eventually be forced to do so as a result of building political pressures or else it would lose power, through elections if available or through other means if not.

The second view, associated with the neoclassical counterrevolution or new orthodoxy school, which has its roots in Nobel laureate Friedrich von Hayek, was developed in the ideas of Nobel laureate James Buchanan and was applied to development policy by Anne Krueger, Deepak Lal, and others. In this view, participants in government, such as politicians and bureaucrats, were as selfish and self-interested as owners of companies but lacked the market to restrain them. Even when the economy was locked in a poverty trap, government itself played a key role in that bad equilibrium. While these points might enjoy broad agreement under some circumstances, this approach drew the strong conclusion that, as a rule, at least beyond a minimum role, governments could only make things worse.[31]

It is easy to see how such extreme views became popular: At least they offered a guiding framework. Development specialists with a more nuanced view of government's role lacked a clear theory. At the same time, most countries seemed to follow a particular "model" of development year after year, decade after decade, many reacting to colonial experiences: Governments in newly independent countries often either continued colonial policies or seemed to choose policies in angry reaction to those of the colonial period by emulating either Soviet policies or more moderate versions of them, as in India. In short, there was all too little on which to base a meaningful theory of development policy formulation.

The questions are insistent ones. Why did some developing countries reform quickly and effectively and others remain stuck year after year in an obviously counterproductive set of policies? Why did some adopt a course of aggrandizement for the rulers and others focus successfully on shared growth? Why did some reform programs become bogged down in squabbling among interest groups and others reach compromises that allowed for relatively efficient and equitable outcomes? Why were apparently good policy reforms abandoned in some countries after their adoption and stuck to diligently and unswervingly in others? Moreover, why did some governments that seemed to be following good advice on reform end up with an unequal and slow-growth outcome when they led to better outcomes elsewhere? Why were some countries such as Chile able to make a transition to a centrist, shared-growth regime after being stuck first in a stagnant import substitution mode and then in a dictatorship for which reducing poverty and inequality was not a priority? What makes for the dynamism of a Mauritius rather than the stagnation of a Guinea-Bissau? The recent progress of a Mozambique rather than the continued impasse of an Angola? A South Korea rather than a Philippines? A Thailand rather than a Myanmar? Most work in development economics has examined policies that make a constructive difference but not the process by which policies are adopted. There are better questions than answers, but a start has been made.

We have learned something from the mixed ways in which different countries have responded to the obvious need for policy reform—for example, under conditions of hyperinflation or debt crisis. The uneven experiences of the transition countries of Eastern Europe and the former Soviet Union have sharpened the debate. Progress has been made through careful case studies and theoretical analyses of political decision making. The new work sometimes claims too much, but important steps have been taken simply by asking some good questions, however tentative the answers.

The general framework of political economy analysis is that people may be assumed to oppose policy changes if they think they are likely to personally lose by them. Obviously, people do at times support policies that they believe are morally right, even if they will prove materially costly to them. As a rule of thumb, however, most work in this field begins with the assumption of material self-interest: the so-called self-interest standard of rationality. For example, an economic reform that benefits most people may not be adopted if the losers are relatively few in number but have a lot to lose and so have a great incentive to take actions—ranging from lobbying to bribery—to block the reform, while the many gainers each stand individually to benefit relatively little, so they do not have much of an incentive to take comparable political action in support of the reform. This pattern of diffuse gainers and concentrated losers has been identified repeatedly in postmortems of reform failure.[32]

Understanding Voting Patterns on Policy Reform

Sometimes reform is designed so as to maximize the benefits of the few. It is natural that the majority would oppose this, if they have the power to do so. Or they may think it likely that they will lose in the process of reform and, perhaps reflecting their previous experience, not believe that they will be adequately compensated through redistribution. But sometimes a majority of the public opposes policies that the majority would likely gain from. This may in part be due to lack of understanding of the nature of economic policy choices among the general public. It may be due to uncertainty over who will likely gain or lose from the policy. It is easy to understand that if voters are risk-averse, they may oppose a policy if they see a risk that they may turn out to be among those who will lose from it.

Raquel Fernandez and Dani Rodrik, however, offer a celebrated example of a situation in which even risk-neutral voters may vote against a policy from which a majority will benefit. The basic idea is that if a significant number, but still a minority, of voters know with certainty that they will gain from a policy, they will vote for the policy. But what of the majority who do not know? For example, most may be unsure what skills they will need in order to be successful in the still obscure postreform environment and therefore how competitive they can be. Suppose that these remaining voters can only estimate their chances of gaining. Even if the percentage of gainers is fully known—say, 55% will gain—in many cases if the uncertain voters estimate their chances of gaining as equal to that of the other uncertain voters, it will be rational to vote no.[33] A simple numerical example will illustrate.

> Let the economy have 100 voters and suppose that the reform in question will increase the incomes of 51 individuals by five zlotys each and decrease the incomes of the rest by one zloty each, leaving a net gain of $(5 \times 51 - 1 \times 49) = 206$ zlotys. In the absence of uncertainty, the majority of the population would vote in favor and the reform would be adopted. Assume that all of these consequences of reform are common knowledge. Now suppose that while 49 individuals know for sure that they will gain, the remaining 51 are in the dark as to which among them will gain and which will lose. However, because aggregate consequences are common knowledge, individuals in the latter group know that 2 of them will eventually benefit while 49 will lose out. This renders individuals in the second group identical *ex ante,* with an expected benefit from reform of $[(5 \times 2) - (1 \times 49)]/51 = -0.76$ zlotys each. Hence the individuals in the uncertain group will reject reform, blocking its adoption.[34]

Although this is a specific case, the result is quite general. In fact, this example is striking because the gains outweight the losses by so much—by a nearly 5-to-1 margin. Students can verify that in many cases, a large majority of 60% or more can gain from a policy, but when a sufficient number are already known with certainty to gain, this leaves a majority of voters with an expected loss, and they then block the policy.

In contrast to our relatively clearer understanding of the obstacles to constructive reform, we still understand too little about why constructive change takes place at all. If progress were rare, this would not be much of an empirical problem, because there would be little to explain. It would of course remain an important development problem because it would leave an important sphere of policy unaddressed. Fortunately, progress appears to be much more common than political economy theory would suggest. Democratization has been sweeping the developing world. In more countries, attention to the importance of shared growth has been visible, and development participation has been strengthening. Reforms that benefit the majority are sometimes implemented even over the strenuous resistance of powerful social and economic forces that stand to lose. This is what we need to understand better if successful development policy reform is to spread further in the developing world.[35]

A widely favored approach to understanding policy formation has been to examine the trade-off between short-term costs of reform and its long-term benefits, to both politicians and the economy. Politicians in particular are viewed as having a very short time horizon because of their limited time in office. Only when crises become sufficiently serious do discounted net benefits of reform become sufficiently large to induce change. The limitation of this literature is that the short-term costs of reform are rarely quantified, and the precise causes of increased growth remain difficult to identify.

It has been noted that reforms are often instituted after a crisis, and so the literature has considered whether "crisis can cause reform." Only when conditions are very serious, one view has it, will risk-averse politicians and voters be willing to try a different strategy. The debt crisis in Latin America is viewed as the catalyst to the adoption of more market-friendly policies, moving away from what had been, in most Latin American countries, failed experiments in import substitution. However, left unexplained is why even more severe debt crises in Africa did not promote analogous reforms. One part of the answer may be that greater outside pressure and resources were brought to bear on Latin America because of the greater threat its insolvency represented to major banks. But as Rodrik notes, "What we surely need to understand is why South Korea's politicians are ready to change course at the slightest hint of a crisis, while Brazil's will bring their economy to the brink of hyperinflation several times before they tackle the problem."[36] The political-economy literature recognizes this issue but is largely silent on it.

Institutions and Path Dependency

The framework suggested by Nobel laureate Douglass North is useful for understanding qualitative differences in policy formulation across countries. North distinguishes between institutions and organizations: Institutions are "formal and informal rules of the economic game." These are humanly devised constraints, notably property rights, that define incentives for savings, investment, production, and trade. These in turn affect benefits and costs and economic behavior that may lead to development or decline. Following from this, organizations spring up around the property rights, designed to help those who control the organization prosper under these existing property rights. Organizations emerge that are in large part defined and shaped by the incentives that emerge from these rules. In a widely cited quote North says, "If the institutional matrix rewards piracy, then [only] piratical organizations will come into existence."[37]

Once these inefficient rights are in place, there are generally no incentives for the people in power to change them, especially when these rights can provide leaders with greater private gains than an alternative regime that might be better for society as a whole. Thus inefficient institutions continue at the expense of overall welfare or of growth; the market cannot guarantee the evolution of efficient institutions. This trap is an example of **path dependency**, a condition in which the past condition of an individual or economy affects future conditions. Several examples of path dependency were examined in Chapters 4 (poverty and low productivity traps), 6 (Mathusian traps), and 8 (child labor traps). Specifically, North argues that the "inability of societies to develop effective low-cost enforcement of contracts is the most important source of both historical stagnation and contemporary underdevelopment."[38]

The individuals who control the state have the incentive to use it for private gain rather than for the public interest. But North argues that historically, on occasion, the interests of those with high bargaining power have coincided with the public interest; when this occurs, effective institutions emerge. While there is no way to ensure that this will happen, it appears that the more examples of successful institutions in neighboring countries, the greater the pressure on governments to adopt similar institutions. Clearly, the adoption of certain institutions, including human rights, property rights protection, and democracy, have spread over the objections of dictators because of their popular appeal.

An improved understanding of the political economy of successful policy reform and implementation will probably require continued and extensive interactions between political scientists, sociologists, and economists, each of whom have valuable insights to contribute from their research. In the process, more will have to be done to base theory on the experiences of the new governments of developing countries, which in many cases will be struggling with the early stages of democratization and expanding avenues for development participation, with higher levels of conflict and an ongoing threat of return to military government or other autocratic rule. As Merilee Grindle has noted, further progress in this field will require moving beyond political economy models that were developed primarily to study political processes in advanced economies with stable democratic traditions.[39]

Democracy versus Autocracy: Which Facilitates Faster Growth?

There has been much debate on the comparative merits of democratic or autocratic regimes for development performance. These debates have presented some of the trade-offs starkly. Under democracy, politicians seeking reelection have an incentive to reflect the will and interests of a majority of the people. On the other hand, a looming election gives an incentive to pursue short-term accomplishments that can be pointed to during a campaign, rather than what is necessarily good for long-term development. Worse, the corrupt politician who knows he or she will soon be voted out of office has an interest to steal as much as possible in the meantime. Under autocracy, there are fewer constraints on what can be stolen and for how long. But the politician who is reasonably confident of remaining in power for a long time can pursue long-term development strategies.

Some high-growth but autocratic countries such as Singapore, and South Korea and Taiwan prior to their transitions to democracy, appear to have enjoyed some of the potential benefits of autocracy for development. In these cases, corruption was present but to no greater extent than in most other developing countries and probably somewhat less than average. The positive effect of autocracy on growth-enhancing policies seems to have worked best when a regime sees that its greatest chance of remaining in power lies in achieving a maximum rate of growth; this is the case with South Korea, which has historically viewed economic development as a bulwark against the aggressive designs of North Korea, or of Taiwan, with its concern over possible invasion from the People's Republic of China. For that matter, China's current rulers have staked their political legitimacy and dreams of political recognition as a world power on a drive to modernization. But autocrats also have the power to use the state for strictly private gains, as Mobutu did in the Democratic Republic of Congo (formerly known as Zaire), following the example of the greedy and depraved Belgian colonial rule of that unfortunate country. And those who fear overthrow will have an incentive both to "steal fast" and to focus resources on fortifying their own power and crushing opponents rather than using state resources to develop institutions and make investments that foster development.

In such a nuanced problem, it is no wonder that the empirical results are closely divided. It seems that about a third of studies find a positive effect for democracy, a third a neutral effect, and the remaining third a negative effect. Ahmed Mobarak proposed not long ago that democratic regimes will be less volatile than autocratic ones. As a result, because more volatile economies are known to grow more slowly than more stable economies, the positive effect of democracy on growth may operate through this channel. But these benefits may be canceled by negative direct effects of democracy on growth.[40]

Jakob de Haan and Clemens Siermann point out that despite the arguments and also some evidence in the literature of a negative relationship between growth and democracy, such studies report that a *lack* of civil and political liberties is also negatively correlated with growth. They propose using better measures of democracy, including how deeply rooted it has become in the society, suggesting a measure based on the number of years that a country can be regarded as a democracy. They then offer various statistical tests of direct and indirect effects of "democratic liberties." Their main conclusion may speak for the literature in general: "The relationship between democracy and economic growth is not robust."[41]

Development Roles of NGOs and the Broader Citizen Sector

It is increasingly recognized that development success depends not only on a vibrant private sector and an efficient public sector but on a vigorous citizen sector as well. Relying on the former sectors alone has been compared to trying to sit on a two-legged stool. Organizations of the citizen sector are usually termed **nongovernmental organizations (NGOs)** in the development context but are also referred to as *nonprofit, voluntary, independent, civil society,* or *citizen organizations.*

A wide range of organizations fall under the NGO banner. The United Nations Development Program defines an NGO as

> any non-profit, voluntary citizens' group which is organized on a local, national or international level. Task-oriented and driven by people with a common interest, NGOs perform a variety of services and humanitarian functions, bring citizens' concerns to governments, monitor policies and encourage political participation at the community level. They provide analysis and expertise, serve as early warning mechanisms and help monitor and implement international agreements. Some are organized around specific issues, such as human rights, the environment or health.[42]

Whereas governments rely on authority to achieve outcomes and private sector firms rely on market mechanisms to provide incentives for mutually beneficial exchange, civil society actors, working through NGOs, rely on independent *voluntary* efforts and influence to promote their values and to further social and economic development.

The emergence of civil society actors such as NGOs as key players in global affairs is recognized by their prominent inclusion in the 2003 World Economic Forum and World Social Forum and in NGOs receiving the Nobel Peace Prize (Campaign to Ban Landmines in 1997, Doctors without Borders in 1999), as well as individual laureates who have played key roles in establishing NGOs and other citizen organizations.[43] A good example is the 2004 laureate, Wangari Maathai, who launched the Kenyan and now Africa-wide Green Belt Movement (see the case study in Chapter 9).

At least 2,250 NGOs had consultative status with the United Nations by 2003; international NGOs grew 20% in the 1990s and grew 20-fold from 1964 to 1998.[44] The potential impact of NGOs is also seen in their wide scope in activities and issues and their size as measured by number of employees as well as their large and growing budgets.

In contrast to private goods, public goods are nonexcludable (it is impossible to prevent individuals from consuming them except at excessive cost) and nonrival (consumption by individuals does not reduce the amount of the good available for consumption by others). Activities in which NGOs have comparative advantage typically lie between conventional private and public goods in these dimensions. In particular, they tend to be partially rival, partially excludable, rival but not excludable, or excludable but not rival. Figure 11.1 reflects this range of activities, again in these two dimensions. The result is a typology that includes "private goods" (high excludability, high rivalry) in the upper right-hand corner, referred to here as Type I goods, and "public goods" (low excludability, low rivalry) in the lower left-hand corner, referred to here as Type III goods. The production and distribution of these Type I and Type III goods are generally assigned to the market and the public sector, respectively. The other two corners represent goods that are hybrids of the other two.

In the lower right-hand corner are found common-pool (or common property) resources, characterized by low excludability but high rivalry. Examples of such Type II goods are natural resources such as fisheries, pastures, and forests, with open access. As explained in Chapter 10, because of open access, these resources tend to be overused (and underinvested).[45] Common property resources can be allocated through institutions in both public and private sectors, but NGOs play an important and growing role. Historically, common property resources were allocated by traditional (e.g., tribal) mechanisms, but these often broke down under colonialism and postcolonial government control in many developing countries.[46] Increasingly, NGOs are helping community-based organizations (CBOs) reclaim this role in common-pool resource allocation. Because they are organizations based on trust rather than coercion (government) or individual self-interest (market), NGOs may be able to arrive at efficient and socially acceptable allocations of common-pool resources at relatively low transaction costs.

Finally, in the upper left-hand corner are found another hybrid, Type IV goods. For example, productive ideas can be used by all without their becoming used up or degraded and so are nonrival, but they can often be effectively kept secret, so they are excludable.[47] A related example is technology transfer to developing countries. Technical knowledge is not a rival good once it is transferred and absorbed into the local economy, as ideas may often spread rather freely across

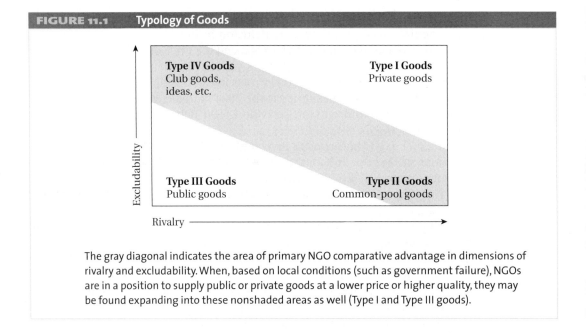

The gray diagonal indicates the area of primary NGO comparative advantage in dimensions of rivalry and excludability. When, based on local conditions (such as government failure), NGOs are in a position to supply public or private goods at a lower price or higher quality, they may be found expanding into these nonshaded areas as well (Type I and Type III goods).

firms within a locality, but it is excludable in that without active intervention, productive ideas often do not cross national boundaries (especially between developed and developing countries). One reason is the free-rider problem: One firm might pay to learn a new technology, but its local rivals could likely find a way to absorb their knowledge (such as hiring away employees) without sharing the cost. Type IV goods exhibit high excludability but low rivalry and are typically assigned to government-regulated private-sector or civil society actors.[48] For example, productive ideas are often developed by nonprofit universities, and technology transfer is often undertaken by specialized NGOs or nonprofit industry associations or consortia.

A special form of public good that operates at the local level or in a specialized subgroup of a wider society is known as a *local public good* or *club good*. Under some conditions, a decentralized solution to allocation problems for such goods may be found.[49] Club goods are excludable but exhibit only partial rivalry. One can find all three sectors active in producing and allocating local public and club goods. For example, local amenities may be provided by for-profit developers, local government, or local NGOs.

There are at least seven partially overlapping and mutually reinforcing types of organizational comparative advantage for international or national NGOs or local organizations such as federations of community-based organizations:

1. *Innovation.* NGOs can play a key role in the design and implementation of programs focused on poverty reduction and other development goals. For example, NGOs that work directly with the poor may design new and more effective programs that reach the poor, facilitated by this close working relationship. Indi-

vidual profit-making firms may lack incentives for poverty innovation, especially when the form of innovations that would be effective is so difficult to anticipate that no request for proposal could be written to draw them out. In many cases, government has an advantage in scaling up established programs. But government has been relatively less successful at significant program innovation, compared to (or at least without a prod from) the NGO sector. Often government programs have not reached the poorest families. More broadly, government tends to offer uniform services, whereas the poor may have special needs different from mainstream populations. Some of the most important innovations in poverty programs (such as microfinance) have been conceptualized and initially developed by domestic and international NGOs. In the sphere of education, for example, NGOs have played the pioneering role in such areas as nonformal education, community literacy campaigns, educational village theater, use of computer technology in urban slums, and subtitling of community center music videos for educational purposes.[50] A key question is whether the government or private sector is then capable of scaling up NGO innovations, once they have become established as working models, as effectively as or better than the innovating NGO. In any case, if governments or private-sector firms are unable or unwilling, the experience of BRAC (see the case study at the end of this chapter) shows that NGOs may do this scaling up to a substantial degree, at least until the government is finally ready to step in. Such innovations are nonrival but are potentially excludable, particularly if detailed information is not transmitted easily.

2. Program *flexibility*. An NGO can address development issues viewed as important for the communities in which it works. In principle, an NGO is not constrained by the limits of public policy or other agendas such as those of donor-country foreign-assistance priorities or by domestic national or local governmental programs. Indeed, national NGOs (such as BRAC, in this chapter's case study) are in principle also unconstrained by the preferences of the international NGOs (and vice versa). Moreover, once a potential solution to a development problem has been identified, NGOs may have greater flexibility in altering their program structure accordingly than would be the case for a government program. Flexibility can be interpreted as localized innovations or minor adaptations of program innovations to suit particular needs. NGOs may be better able to make use of participation mechanisms, unconstrained by limits placed on individual rights or prerogatives for elites that prevail in the public sphere. However, there are limits to this flexibility, as NGOs may have a tendency to tailor their programs to fit the available funding, a phenomenon known as *donor capture*.

3. Specialized technical *knowledge*. National and international NGOs may be greater repositories of technical expertise and specialized knowledge than local governments (or businesses). In particular, international NGOs can draw on the experiences of many countries that may offer possible models for problems of poverty faced by any one country, as well as possible solutions. Of course, this forms part of the basis for credibility. These technical skills may be used for developing effective responses to locally binding poverty traps and coordination problems. Specialized knowledge is acquired in the process of doing specialized work with local citizen groups, including those of the poor. Consider the Grameen

phone lady model, in which microcredit and training is provided to village women to purchase and operate a cell phone available to community members on a fee basis (see the case study in Chapter 5). This program reflects innovations coupled with local NGO advantages in technical knowledge. Knowledge, understood as an economic good, is also excludable but nonrival.

4. Targeted *local public goods*. Goods and services that are rival but excludable, including those targeted to socially excluded populations, may be best designed and provided by NGOs who know and work with these groups. Possible examples include local public health facilities, nonformal education, provision of specialized village telecommunications and computing facilities, codification and integration of traditional legal and governance practices, creating local markets, community mapping and property registration, and community negotiations with governments. Some examples of these goods may lie along the gray diagonal of Figure 11.1, but local public (or club) goods are generally nonrival but excludable.

5. *Common property* resource management design and implementation. NGOs, including federations of local CBOs, can play an important role in common property management and targeted local public goods provision. Throughout the developing world, both governments and the private sector have a poor track record in ensuring sustainability of forests, lakes, coastal fishing areas, pasturelands, and other commons. But a large fraction of the world's people still rely on local natural resources for most of their income and consumption. Targeted NGO and CBO programs, including training, assistance with organizational development, efforts to change noncooperative cultural characteristics, and initiating measures such as community and common property policing, can help address common property mismanagement and related problems. Common property resources are rival but nonexcludable.

6. *Trust* and credibility. In practice, NGOs may have other advantages over government in gaining the trust of and providing effective services to groups with special needs, notably those in extreme poverty. NGOs' local presence and relationships, frequent interaction and communication, and greater avenues for participation may generate greater trust among the poor and other citizens. Although in a decentralized and socially inclusive democratic setting, an elected government might be at least as trusted as "unelected" NGOs, government in many developing countries may be democratic in name only. But even majority rule can be of little benefit to the socially excluded, particularly when the majority population or its representatives actively marginalize the poor. When government resources are limited, trade-offs between benefits for established or excluded groups can take on added significance. Democracy may also provide little benefit to the socially excluded when they experience benign neglect and a lack of established communication channels with the government. Once such a history is established, it may be difficult for even a new and well-meaning government to overcome this legacy. NGOs, in contrast, may enjoy greater trust in assumed competence, benevolence, reliability, responsiveness, established personal contacts, and perception of consistent behavior in various settings that may not be possible to monitor. To

the degree that NGOs follow explicit bylaws requiring democratic practice, accountability, and responsiveness, credibility is enhanced over time. Partly as a result, NGOs may also be more trusted by local government than less responsive or less accessible official donors. At the same time, if governments are perceived as corrupt or incompetent, foundations and certain other donors may trust only NGOs to address poverty, environment, local health and education delivery, and other services. Thus NGOs help mobilize resources that would otherwise not be available for local residents, including those in structural poverty. Finally, the private sector may prefer to partner with NGOs than with governments or other official actors to gain credibility in socially responsible investment activities.[51] In sum, NGOs may enjoy higher trust than other organizations among all the major parties concerned, including the poor, developing-country local and national governments, and donors. Trust is related to the capability for effective advocacy.

7. Representation and *advocacy*. NGOs may hold advantages in understanding the needs of the poor, who otherwise are often excluded from political processes and even local community deliberations. NGOs may play a role in the aggregation of preferences and hence of representation of community needs. To the degree that NGOs have a better understanding of locally binding poverty traps, they should be in a position to more effectively represent the needs of the poor. This responsibility reflects the advocacy role of NGOs, including federations of CBOs, in advocating for the needs of poor and socially excluded peoples. Minorities may need special protections in majority-rule representative democracies, and existing constitutional protections are not always sufficient. It is not a comparative advantage of either the private or the public sector to advocate for the poor or excluded. The private sector is less likely to hold the trust of those whose interests are to be advocated. Individual donors, foundations, agencies, or other funders of advocacy will want to ensure that the advocates they sponsor are working diligently and with a broad understanding of the mission, as well as honestly. Finally, if it is government that needs to be lobbied or influenced, it is unlikely to be in the comparative advantage of government to fulfill this function—particularly to the degree that trust is at issue—although an office of ombudsman or citizen protection can play a valuable role. Advocacy for a given group is partly nonrival and nonexcludable.

Sometimes exceptional failures of either government or the private sector create situations under which NGOs can, and perhaps should, temporarily step in to fill the void. For example, BRAC is involved with producing private goods such as chalk, shoes, and seeds, under conditions of a dysfunctional private sector at least in rural areas (see the case study at the end of this chapter). In Africa, in the face of government neglect, the international NGO Africare is involved in what are normally government responsibilities such as road building. But in such cases, NGOs may eventually turn these functions over to local CBOs, to the private sector, or to government (through a transfer agreement) when conditions warrant. For example, Africare helps government and CBOs take over responsibility for road maintenance after construction of a road has been completed.

As we have seen, in the developing countries, both government and markets can be weak, and strengthening their capacity is essential. But the citizen sector is often even weaker in these countries, in part because people have less money and time to donate, because skills are lacking, and because sometimes the citizen sector is actively undermined by the government and business sectors. Short of embezzlement or other outright lawbreaking, NGOs are also vulnerable to weaknesses, termed **voluntary failure**. Instead of realizing their potential, NGOs may be insignificant, owing to small scale and reach, selective and exclusionary, elitist, and or ineffective.[52] One potential pitfall is the lack of adequate incentives to ensure effectiveness, which requires careful organizational design. Another is the ever-present danger of capture by the goals of funders rather than intended beneficiaries. This can reach the point where NGOs change their priorities from one year to the next.[53] NGOs can fail to live up to their organizational potential when means—such as fundraising—become ends in themselves or when means are given too little attention, as when poor fundraising keeps NGOs from realizing the scale they need to have a real impact. There are sometimes inadequate checks and balances to prevent these flaws. NGOs may not receive the immediate feedback from the market that private firms receive or that elected governments receive at the polls. This lack of rapid feedback can encourage these weaknesses or at least let them go on for some time before being corrected. Such problems must be addressed if NGOs are to achieve their potential for facilitating development and poverty alleviation.

In addition to the rapid rise to prominence of NGOs as key players in the development drama, three other major trends in governance have emerged: tackling corruption, fostering decentralization, and facilitating development participation in both the government and NGO sectors.

Trends in Governance and Reform

Tackling the Problem of Corruption

No examination of political economy issues would be complete without a consideration of problems of corruption. **Corruption** is the abuse of public trust for private gain; it is a form of stealing. Indexes of corruption regularly rate developing countries as having an average rate of corruption far higher than that of developed countries. This relationship is understood to reflect both cause and effect. An absence of corruption encourages investment and efforts to expand the pie rather than merely fight over its distribution and thus encourages growth; to this extent, improvements in governance in general and reduction of corruption in particular could be means to accelerate the process of development. In addition, as societies grow wealthier, good governance becomes more widely demanded by the population. This latter effect makes simple correlations between income and good governance difficult to interpret: Which causes which? Poor governance practices, such as bribery, controls over the press, and limits on civil liberties, are often found together and are clearly mutually reinforcing. But reform can also beget reform. For example, when Taiwan's press obtained substantial freedoms, many public scandals became publicized, which in turn helped generate public pressures for reform; the introduction of elections provided a mechanism to enforce this popular will.

The elimination of corruption is important for development for several reasons. Honest government may promote growth and sustainably high incomes. In addition, the association of eliminating corruption with public empowerment suggests that it is a direct objective of development: Good governance enhances what Sen calls the "capability to function" (see Chapter 1), providing a genuine lift out of poverty. Finally, the effects of corruption fall disproportionately on the poor and are a major restraint on their ability to escape from poverty. This is perhaps the most compelling reason for emphasizing the elimination of corruption and improvement of governance in general as part of an antipoverty strategy from the earliest stages of development. While the rich may pay large bribes under corrupt regimes, the poor generally pay much larger fractions of their incomes in bribes and other forms of extortion. In other words, corruption may be viewed as a regressive tax on the absolutely poor. In addition, government for sale means government for the highest bidder. The poor find fewer services in their communities, including poor education and health facilities, when corruption is rife. This makes it more difficult to accumulate the means to escape from poverty traps. In addition, microenterprises of the poor pay a much higher fraction of sales in bribes than larger firms do, and low-income households pay a much larger percentage of their incomes in bribes than higher income households, as Figure 11.2 illustrates for the case of Ecuador.

Good governance certainly includes an absence of corruption but is broader and is also comprised of the ability of the public sector to design and implement efficient and effective policies to realize development goals, government responsiveness and respect for citizens and the institutions of society, and mechanisms for the peaceful transfer of power in accordance with popular will, including widespread participation. These characteristics often, but not always, go together. Some dictatorial regimes such as Singapore have low levels of corruption and earn very high marks on other aspects of governance. Moreover, it is very possible for low-income countries to have noncorrupt and generally good governance, although the best examples are generally found among middle-income countries. Honest and high-quality governance has been observed in such widely dispersed middle-income countries as Chile, Costa Rica and Slovenia in recent years.[54]

Countries that have avoided or successfully tackled corruption in recent years have tended to promote competition and entry in the economy, avoiding too much power in the hands of large monopolies such as those in the energy sector in many countries, and have ensured that privatized firms faced competition; promoted civil service professionalism, with improved pay and incentives for public servants; made public expenditures transparent, with clear rules of procurement and budgeting; reduced immunity from prosecution of executive, legislative, and judicial figures; provided judicial independence; established and enforced meritocratic, transparent promotion policies; and eliminated inefficient regulations

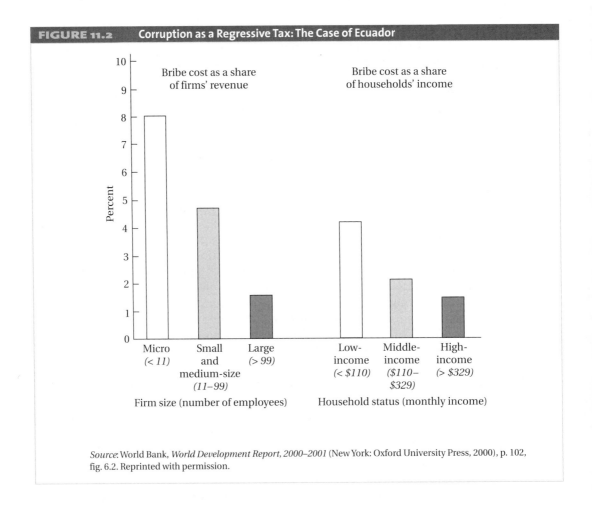

FIGURE 11.2   Corruption as a Regressive Tax: The Case of Ecuador

Source: World Bank, *World Development Report, 2000–2001* (New York: Oxford University Press, 2000), p. 102, fig. 6.2. Reprinted with permission.

and made needed ones more transparent. The relationship between the rule of law and per capita GDP is shown in Figure 11.3.

Decentralization

Decentralization has been a long-term trend in developed countries. The United States, Canada, and Germany have had significant powers at the state and local level enshrined in their constitutions. The European Union has been proceeding—officially, at least—on the principle of "subsidiarity," meaning that decisions are made at the most local level feasible. Decentralization has been steadily gaining momentum in most European countries. The United Kingdom has decentralized authority to Scotland and Wales and also to local authorities in England. In Italy, power has been transferred to the 20 regions and their provinces. Local governments are closer to the urban and rural problems they must address.

Recently, trends toward decentralization and greater urban self-government have been growing in the developing world as democracy has spread in Latin

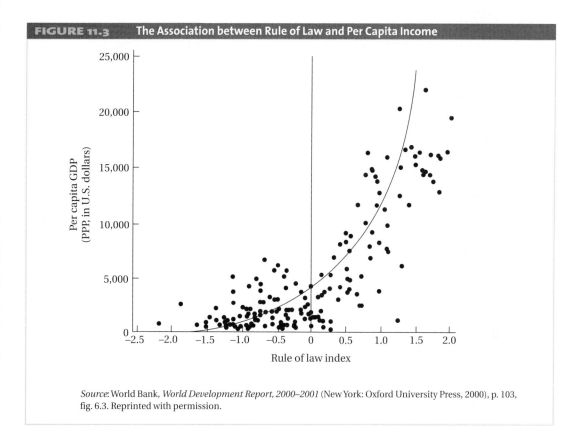

FIGURE 11.3   The Association between Rule of Law and Per Capita Income

Source: World Bank, *World Development Report, 2000–2001* (New York: Oxford University Press, 2000), p. 103, fig. 6.3. Reprinted with permission.

America, Eastern Europe, and elsewhere, and the political process has allowed for providing greater autonomy, notably more fiscal autonomy, for regional and local levels of government. The constitutional reform that has frequently accompanied democratization has in many cases provided an opportunity to codify greater local autonomy. In many cases, decentralization has been spurred by debt and structural adjustment crises of the past two decades (see Chapter 14) and the constitutional reforms that have often accompanied these measures. A major motivation of the central government has often been to share fiscal burdens with regions and cities, but decentralization has sometimes taken on a life of its own that has been difficult to contain.

In the developing world, decentralization has been especially significant in Latin America. Decentralization in Brazil to its 26 states and some 5,000 municipalities dates at least to the 1891 constitution, but the recent period of devolution of authority started with the constitutional reform of 1989, which gave new authority and responsibilities to the states and developed fiscal federalism, increasing the local share of government resources. The fiscal decentralization occurred in the wake of the debt crisis of the 1980s and the perceived need to carry out structural adjustment by lowering the federal budget deficit. As elsewhere, the federal government was motivated to spread some of the adjustment burden to the regions. However, many observers consider the resources available to states and cities too small in relation to responsibilities, with more burden than opportunity. Further definition of the rights and responsibilities of each level, and commensurate resources, are widely perceived as still needed in Brazil.

A wave of decentralization in Mexico also began in the late 1980s in the wake of the debt crisis, as a component of the broader programs of privatization, liberalization, and deregulation. Constitutional reforms transferred additional power—and responsibilities—to the states and municipalities. But as in Brazil, local governments complain that they have insufficient resources to carry out their added mandates.

A third Latin American example is the Bolivia decentralization of 1994, which recognized local forms of organization and citizen participation; encouragingly, indigenous and peasant organizations have begun to seek an active role under the new system. The decentralization resulted from a combination of pressures from local government and popular organizations and from international agencies.

The experience of Senegal is a well-known example of decentralization in Africa. In 1996, presidents of rural councils were made more accountable to their constituencies, and regional governments were established to develop and carry out regional development policy. However, the fiscal limitations of local government in Latin America are small compared to those faced in Senegal, and thoroughgoing fiscal reform remains a top priority.

In Asia, decentralization has proceeded apace with democratization, while long-standing democracies such as India have also provided greater local control, notably under India's 74th Constitutional Amendment. In China, decentralization has occurred to some extent but has been plagued by problems of corruption.

Development Participation

If the goal of economic growth is human development, then without participation, we could have economic growth without development. Indeed, many observers would agree that participation—a say in development policies by the people most affected by them—is in itself a chief end of development. Participation is also a means to further human capabilities and other goals of development as defined in Chapter 1. Moreover, economic growth is greatly facilitated by human development and impossible to sustain without it. Development participation has been shown to make projects work better. Participation plays a central role in the most successful development strategies, notably microcredit cooperatives such as the Grameen Bank of Bangladesh (see the case study in Chapter 5). With genuine and full participation by beneficiaries on what projects are chosen and in the way that development assistance gets used more generally, we should expect less corruption and greater development results per aid dollar spent. Indeed, participation would seem to offer a better way to achieve many of the purported goals of recent World Bank conditionality agreements, without their many drawbacks.

But development participation is anything but an *easy* alternative. It has been discussed by academics for decades; the United Nations has been promoting it since the 1970s; it was an academic fad in the early 1980s; and in the 1990s, the World Bank came out vocally for development participation. When everyone is in favor of something that involves substantial change, it is a good bet that the words mean different things to different actors and that if proposed solutions sound a little too easy, they are. Critics have complained that when the World Bank uses the term *participation,* it often seems meant as a strategy to reduce project costs or to deflect criticism. But the World Bank has clearly discovered the merits of getting governments and civil society to take ownership of development projects and reforms. Only then are reforms undertaken in a serious and sustainable way.

What are the potential objections to the principle of genuine participation? First, the poorest countries need to make some policy decisions immediately. The highly indebted poor countries need immediate debt relief. They are required by the World Bank and the IMF to implement special development plans to gain debt relief, and participation takes time. Even if the mechanisms of participation are already in place, it takes time to operate them, to make sure there is sufficient voice, to aggregate the preferences voiced, and to work out a means of implementation. But in most cases, mechanisms of genuine participation are not in place; doing so may take years, even with the full cooperation of national government and local powerbrokers.

Second, unhealthy and unskilled people are probably not able to effectively participate in development projects, let alone have a full voice in the decisions that affect them. A third objection is the costs of time: The poor are busy trying to survive. They may receive a low market wage, but that does not mean they have a low opportunity cost of time for volunteer work. This is especially true of women. They work long hours in both economic activity and at home because they cannot afford alternatives to household production. They may reasonably view expectations that they participate as unremunerated labor. Donors and LDC governments need to develop ways to reward participation, but a big part of the problem is the superficiality of what passes for participation in the field. These three objections suggest that participation may have limits, but the principle of its implementation whenever feasible stands.

Distinctions between different types of participation are a valuable starting point and have been suggested by a number of authors. For example, Cohen and Uphoff examine degrees of participation along three dimensions: kinds of participation (in decision making, implementation, benefits, and evaluation), the identity of participants (including residents, leaders, government personnel, and foreign personnel), and how participation occurs (the basis, form, extent, and effect of participation).[55] Deshler and Sock distinguish "genuine participation," which can include either citizen control or cooperation, with delegated power or partnership agreements between citizens and agencies, from "pseudo-participation," which can include placation, consultation, or information without power sharing, as well as "therapy" and manipulation. One objection could be that participation has been tried and found wanting, but these distinctions are valuable and point up that genuine participation has still been given very little chance.[56]

Genuine participation is often not in the interests of national or local government officials and other elites. One could start with the premise that aid should typically be channeled through local NGOs with substantial local beneficiary control. As a form of debt relief, interest and principal for debt service could be paid into an NGO drawdown account. These funds could be made available to NGOs for new programs or increments to existing ones, provided that they can show that the beneficiaries are participating in the design and administration of the programs. But this too is not as easy as it sounds.

Many NGOs are committed to the more complete forms of participation, at least on paper. But there are significant dilemmas even when these NGOs are involved. NGO staff often perceive, rightly or wrongly, that beneficiaries do not have the skills and experience needed to make fundamental decisions or administer projects efficiently. Administrative competence of beneficiaries is a less tangible outcome than, for example, the percentage of farmers who get linked up to irrigation canals; so staff, even with the best of motives, may not view genuine participation as a priority but more as a distraction. It is also obvious that staff owe their livelihoods to development work and do not have a material interest in working themselves out of a job. Thus staff have a motivation for encouraging participation to the extent that it increases the efficiency of the project but not necessarily beyond this point. Such a level of participation may bring benefits but not normally the socially transformative benefits of genuine participation.

Sarah White reports on an NGO in the Philippines that was committed to genuine participation in theory and enabled local people to develop and control their own organization. But when this organization wanted to bypass the NGO and interact directly with donors, the NGO would not allow it to do so.[57] Victoria Michener offers an insightful look at development participation in a case study of a nonformal education project run by an NGO (Save the Children/FDC in Burkina Faso). Participation itself is one of the six objectives of the project, to "increase community participation in educational decision making, and in the management of educational activities." Participants are expected to play an active role in recruiting teachers and students, determining curriculum, building and maintaining the schoolhouse, and paying costs such as teacher salaries. Overall, the projects would rank very high in participation typologies such as that of Cohen and Uphoff, providing for substantial participation in decision making, implementation, benefits, and evaluation. But at the same time, Michener notes that an undertone of "planner-centered participation" can be found, especially in the emphasis on the responsibilities of beneficiaries. As translated to field workers, participation means an obligation that recipients give something in return, payment in a sense, for the benefits of a project: financial, in-kind, or at least the donation of time. But participants naturally resent this requirement, at least coming in a context of paternalism. Typically, villagers cannot afford to repudiate the NGO; they do benefit from the assistance, and lack the resources to continue the project on their own.[58]

But even more obviously, they cannot throw out local government. NGOs generally offer an improvement on national or local government and an additional leverage that the poor desperately need. Though achievement of genuine participation will not come easily, as more NGOs become committed to it, and grants are targeted to these NGOs, we may reasonably expect to steadily approach it.

Genuine public participation at all levels provides a foundation for democratic and responsive government. Participation will not cure all of the ills of government, including the limits of democracy itself, but it will go some distance to alleviating the ills of the politics of development policy reform.

Development Policy and the State: Concluding Observations

In view of the record of recent decades, most development economists would now probably agree that their early and almost mystical belief in the efficacy and benefits of development planning and extensive public intervention has not been validated by experience. Moreover, as mentioned earlier, economic policies have more often than not tended to be ad hoc responses to recurring and often unexpected crises rather than the playing out of a grand economic design for development. We should never forget that political leaders and decision makers are human beings like the rest of us, with all the usual human idiosyncrasies, foibles, and weaknesses. Except in very unusual cases, they will tend to take a parochial (class, caste, tribal, religious, ethnic, regional, etc.) rather than national point of view. In democracies, politicians will respond first to their political constituencies and the vested-interest groups within their home areas. In more autocratic forms of government, be it military dictatorship or strict one-party rule, political leaders will still have a natural tendency to respond to the groups to whom they owe their power or on whom their continued power depends. We must always bear in mind that economic policies are ultimately made not by economists or planners but by politicians, who may well be more interested in "muddling through" each emerging crisis and staying in power than in instituting major social and economic reforms.

We must therefore be pragmatic about the role and limitations of economic policies in developing nations. On the one hand, we should avoid the tendency to assume that political leaders and decision makers place the national interest above their own private interests or base their policies on some notion of social welfare as opposed to the private welfare of the groups to whom they are primarily indebted. On the other hand, we should equally avoid the cynical view that the social interest, especially the interest of the poor, the weak, and the inarticulate, will never be considered short of revolution. Social and political revolutions are notorious vehicles by which one elite replaces another while the welfare of the poor typically remains largely unaffected. It appears more reasonable, therefore, to base our discussion of the role and limitations of the state on the proposition that most LDC governments are beset by conflicting forces, some elitist, others egalitarian, and that their economic policies will be largely a reflection of the relative strength of these competing forces. Although narrow elitist interests have tended to prevail in the past, the groundswell for a more egalitarian development process has now reached the point where politicians and planners can no longer ignore it or camouflage it behind noble but empty rhetoric.

Thus there seems to be general agreement today among economists that LDC governments should do what they are capable of doing better than in the past. Most observers would agree that the machinery of many LDC governments has become too cumbersome. There are too many ministries, often with competing interests, too many inefficient public corporations, and too many boards of one kind or another. Governments are criticized for being too centralized and too urban-oriented in both staff and outlook. Civil servants and other trained personnel are often poorly utilized, badly motivated, and less productive than they should be. There is too much corruption and too little innovation. Bureaucratic red tape and ossified procedures and processes sap originality and flexibility.

But whether we like it or not, LDC governments must inevitably assume an active responsibility for the future well-being of their countries. As their primary tasks of nation building and generating rapid economic growth are gradually supplemented by preoccupations with problems of debts and deficits as well as poverty, population, unemployment, the environment, and inequality, these governments are forging a new role, one that will require innovation and change on a scale that has rarely occurred in the past. Central to this new role will be institutional and structural reform in the fields of land tenure; taxation; asset ownership and distribution; educational and health delivery systems; credit allocation; labor relations; pricing policies; the organization and orientation of technology transfer, research, and experimentation; and the machinery of government itself.[59]

Successful economic development requires improved functioning of public, private, and citizen sectors. Each play essential and complementary roles in attaining balanced, shared, and sustainable development.

A National Development NGO: The BRAC Model

BRAC, originally known as the Bangladesh Rural Advancement Committee, is an extraordinary NGO whose mission is poverty reduction. The BRAC model illuminates how comparative advantages of NGOs can function to support poverty reduction and illustrates conditions under which NGOs extend that in the face of deficiencies of government and private-sector actors.

BRAC was founded in the early 1970s to aid displaced persons in the aftermath of civil war and famine. The organization's leaders soon understood that the problems of the rural poor were chronic and structural, and they turned their attention to long-term development and poverty alleviation efforts. BRAC operates primarily in the rural areas of Bangladesh, where government is charaterized by low capacity and high corruption. In contrast, BRAC has grown steadily, attracting funds for its reputation for competence, dedication, innovativeness, accountability, and effectiveness.

With tens of millions of people and whole regions of the country caught in complex poverty traps, BRAC has had to innovate continuously to bring needed services to the poor. Through helping the poor identify their own needs and priorities, BRAC has developed high-impact and widely emulated program innovations in education, nutrition, health, credit, legal rights, advocacy, and other fields.

By some measures, BRAC is now the largest NGO in the world. BRAC's activities contribute more than 1% of Bangladesh's GDP. Today BRAC has over 60,000 employees, making it the country's second-largest employer. More than half of BRAC employees are primary teachers in its widely emulated Nonformal Primary Education Program (NFPE). While BRAC programs such as "Microcredit-plus" have been widely replicated in other countries, none operate at BRAC's scale. BRAC is a complex organization, with some 4 million grassroots members (one woman per household). These members participate in BRAC's basic units, the Village Organization. There are some 115,000 of these VOs, each including about 35 to 50 women from a village or neighborhood. BRAC currently works in 64,000 of the country's 80,000 villages through a system of 14 training centers and over 1,500 field offices, with a budget of about $175 million.

Once highly dependent on donors, BRAC has responded to donor demands for greater self-reliance. BRAC is now more than 80% self-supporting, with donor contributions to its budget projected at just 18% in 2003, and this figure has been held to under 22% for several years. The major source of its internal revenue is a growing network of productive enterprises that it has established, with the twin aims of poverty reduction and net income generation for its poverty programs.

BRAC owns or co-owns and operates several small and medium-size enterprises with the explicit aim of direct or indirect poverty reduction as well as its income-generating mission. BRAC rural enterprises produce goods such as chalk, seeds, shoes, and sanitary napkins. Although these are all classic private goods, an extended role for NGOs has emerged due to Bangladesh's dysfunctional private sector. BRAC's activities supply needed inputs for nonformal schools and farms and more affordable basic consumer goods for local people while providing employment for poor women.

Fazle Hasan Abed originally founded BRAC to provide assistance to victims of famine and displacement. Soon, however, Abed and his organization concluded that poverty was a chronic and entrenched problem, and they turned their attention to development and poverty alleviation. Abed has won international recognition for his work, including the Ramon Magsaysay Award, the Noma Prize for Literacy, the Feinstein World Hunger Award, UNICEF's Maurice Pate Award, and the 2004 Gates Prize. Aware of the need for sustained leadership, BRAC is developing a new generation of professionals who continue to innovate in poverty alleviation programs while increasing the efficiency and effectiveness of existing programs.

Transparency International rated the Bangladesh government the most corrupt in the world in 2003. Though possibly an exaggeration, the rating does reflect genuine problems. In this context, BRAC has helped fill the vacuum left by government, taking on many of the functions of good governance—targeting public goods, providing common-pool goods, and advocating for the poor. The influence of BRAC has been so great that a popular saying in Bangladesh is that "we have two governments," the formal government and BRAC. Despite its size, BRAC remains very flexible. When catastrophic flooding hit the country in August 2004, BRAC temporar-ily reoriented virtually its entire organization to relief activities.

The linchpin program is microfinance for the poor, actually started two years before Grameen (see the case study in Chapter 5). The program is targeted to individuals owning very little land and typically involved in rural nonfarm activities such as door-to-door sales and small-scale vending from their homes or markets. These women borrowers often had very little inventory because they could afford to hold little; thus their sales would be so low that they could afford no more inventory the next day.

But people stuck in working-capital poverty traps may face several other types of poverty traps at the same time. Thus BRAC has designed a strategy that it calls microcredit-plus-plus to convey the scope of its interrelated village programs seeking to meet a variety of poverty reduction goals.

In Bangladesh just 25 years ago, attending school was an unimaginable luxury for most of the poor. Even in 1990, fewer than half of all children in the country completed primary school. By 2003, about two-thirds were completing school. BRAC has been one of the major driving forces in this transformation through its NFPE. BRAC began its highly innovative village nonformal primary schools in 1984, in response to the needs and requests of the village women with whom it works. A major reason that parents do not send their children to school is that their work is needed at home and on the small family farm plot to help the family survive. A second reason is the intimidation and alienation that uneducated parents and their children feel in traditional school settings. A third is harassment of girls.

The program structure was developed to respond to schooling problems identified by mothers taking part in other BRAC programs. BRAC schools teach the children of poor, often landless families. Well over two-thirds of the students are girls. Typically, the school operates for only a few hours a day so that the children can help at home and in farm or nonfarm activities. Parents decide whether classes will be held in the morning or the evening, depending on the nature of the village's needs. Little homework is assigned, as homework requirements were identified as a major stumbling block to keeping children in school. BRAC hopes to make up for shorter school hours with a higher-quality education featuring a significantly smaller class size of about 30 to 35, engaging teaching styles, and the care shown for the pupils.

The NFPE has grown steadily, and today there are over 1.1 million pupils currently enrolled in some 34,000 schools. There are about the same number of teachers—a few hundred less, as some teachers run two schools that meet at different hours. Over 2.6 million students have graduated since the NFPE programs began.

Many BRAC schools have bamboo walls and a thatched roof; others are bamboo-framed, with tin sheets for walls and roof. Inside, decorations are hung from the roof. Lessons and papers are posted on the walls. The children typically sit around the periphery of the room. In addition to lessons, all were expected to actively participate in recitations, traditional dances, and other engaging activities.

Nearly all the teachers (about 97%) are village women who are trained and supervised by professional staff. They are required to have had nine years of education, less than required by public schools but sufficient for the materials being taught. Outside evaluators of the program have concluded that the quality of teacher supervision is one of the keys to the program's consistent success. This program design keeps costs low and quality high while providing useful employment for village women who have obtained somewhat more education.

The NFPE program has evolved over the years to reflect the changing needs of the rural poor. At first, the program lasted three years, usually between the ages of 8 and 10. This was a year or two later than students start public school; the reason for this, BRAC officials explain, is to identify students who would for some reason likely never start public school or would drop out almost immediately. The greatest emphasis was on literacy and numeracy, health and hygiene, basic science, and social studies. The program was designed in part to establish a foundation from which students could enter the fourth grade of the public school system. There is also a system of basic education for somewhat older children, aged 11 to 14.

In 1998, the schools expanded to a four-year program covering the five-year primary curriculum in less time. This redesign was in response to the large number of BRAC graduates interested in continuing their education at the secondary level. BRAC says that today more than 90% of its graduates continue in the formal system.

To bring needed services to the poor, BRAC has had to innovate. Many of BRAC's programs, including its "microcredit-plus," nonformal primary education, and legal education programs, have been widely emulated in other countries, even if none has done so on the same scale. BRAC continues to innovate with new ventures such as the promising Targeting the Ultrapoor Program.

While one can question how it is possible for BRAC to do so many things without losing its management discipline, BRAC can hardly be blamed for taking so seriously the insistence of donors that it become more self-sufficient. And rather than charge the poor for "full cost recovery" of basic medical and other services for the poor, as the development agencies was advised in earlier years, BRAC views it as a better option to subsidize services for the desperately poor with profits from productive enterprises that themselves provide employment and guarantee inputs that poor farmers need and help find markets for the products of the poor. There are very strong penalties for unethical behavior, and BRAC is considered to hold to an unusually high standard of probity. However, it is difficult for an outsider to be sure where all the cross-subsidies are going under the current system of accounts.

An obvious question is how BRAC could do all of these activities without losing its focus on poverty programs, let alone operate such a variety of businesses without losing management focus. To the degree BRAC has been successful at this, perhaps the most important factor has been the high quality of BRAC management. Abed is one of the most impressive management talents in the country, and BRAC has been able to recruit many other extremely competent managers from all sectors of Bangladesh. BRAC has done this while paying comparatively modest salaries at all levels of the organization. It seems that BRAC is so much better than management in the private sector that it has repeatedly been able to find untapped opportunities and to profit from them. (This is true not just of BRAC but of other leading NGOs such as Grameen.) The most effective scope for a company depends not just on the type of activities it specializes in but on the management skills available in the rest of the country. If one organization's talent is high while that of its competitors is low, one company or NGO can participate in many activities that in another country would constitute a fatal distraction away from its "core competencies." But one can find no hint of a negative attitude toward the private sector at BRAC; instead, BRAC is actively working to foster its growth.

BRAC is working to improve the efficacy of government as well. Most notably, although the public schools are in some sense competitors of its NFPE program, BRAC is working actively with interested government officials to infuse the public schools with some of the secrets of its own success.

In one of its most recent new ventures, BRAC has established a university with a focus on the needs of national development. It also runs a bank and a growing program for assisting private small and medium-size enterprises. Finally, it has recently begun its first international venture, in Afghanistan.

BRAC faces several challenges. As BRAC's first generation of founders retires, replacements must be found who have the same special combination of talents and commitment. As BRAC continues to grow and diversify, it will continue to confront management problems that would prove challenging in any environment, but particularly for a poverty-focused organization operating in rural Bangladesh. But BRAC has consistently served as a pioneer, both in innovation of specific programs and in widening the vision of development practitioners around the world about the possible range and scope for the work of NGOs in developing countries. ■

Sources

Additional key references are:

BRAC, "Education programmes," http://www.brac.net/edf.htm.

Khandker, Shahidur R., and Baqui Khalily, *The Bangladesh Rural Advancement Committee's Credit Programs: Performance and Sustainability* (Washington, D.C.: World Bank, 1996).

Lovell, Catherine H., and Kaniz Fatema, *BRAC: Non-Formal Primary Education in Bangladesh* (New York: United Nations Children's Fund, 1989).

Matin, Imran, *Stories of Targeting: The BRAC Targeting the Ultrapoor Program* (Dhaka, Bangladesh: BRAC Research and Evaluation Division, 2003).

Matin, Imran, and David Hulme, "Programs for the poorest: Learning from the IGVGD program in Bangladesh," *World Development* 31 (2003): 647–665.

Quelch, John, and Nathalie Laidler, *The BRAC and Aarong Commercial Brands* (Cambridge, Mass.: Harvard Business School, 2003).

This case study is adapted from Stephen C. Smith, *Ending Global Poverty* (New York: Palgrave/Macmillan, 2005).

Concepts for Review

Accounting prices	Input-output model	Path dependency
Aggregate growth model	Interindustry model	Planning process
Comprehensive plan	Internal rate of return	Political will
Corruption	Market failure	Project appraisal
Cost-benefit analysis	Market prices	Rent seeking
Economic infrastructure	Net present value	Shadow prices
Economic plan	Nongovernmental organiza-	Social profit
Economic planning	tion (NGO)	Social rate of discount
Government failure	Partial plan	Voluntary failure

Questions for Discussion

1. Why do you think so many developing countries were convinced of the necessity of development planning? Were the reasons strictly economic? Comment.

2. Explain and comment on some of the major arguments or rationales, both economic and noneconomic, for planning in developing economies.

3. Planning is said to be more than just the formulation of quantitative economic targets. It is often described as a process. What is meant by the planning process, and what are some of its basic characteristics?

4. Compare and contrast the three basic types of planning models: aggregate growth models, input-output analysis, and project appraisal. What do you think are some of the strengths and weaknesses of these models from the standpoint of planning in developing nations?

5. There is much talk today about the demise of development planning. Many observers assert that development planning has been a failure. List and explain some of the major reasons for plan failures. Which reasons do you think are the most important? Explain your thinking.

6. Distinguish between market failure and government failure. Does rent-seeking behavior occur only as a result of government failure? Explain your answer.

7. What are some of the difficulties associated with the establishment of market economies in LDCs? In what type of country is the market more likely to succeed? Why?

8. What do you think should be the role of the state in contemporary LDCs? Is the choice between markets and government an either-or choice? Explain your answer.

9. What features of the political process make effective development policymaking so difficult?

10. Why is development participation not used more often despite its potentially decisive role in ensuring the success of development policies?

Notes

1. For a more detailed discussion of planning and planning models, see Michael P. Todaro, *Development Planning: Models and Methods* (Nairobi, Kenya: Oxford University Press, 1971), and J. Price Gittinger, *Economic Analysis of Agricultural Projects*, 2nd ed. (Baltimore: Johns Hopkins University Press, 1984).

2. United Nations Department of Economic Affairs, *Measures for the Economic Development of Underdeveloped Countries* (New York: United Nations Department of Economic Affairs, 1951), p. 63.

3. United Nations, *Planning the External Sector: Techniques, Problems, and Policies* (New York: United Nations, 1965), p. 12; R. Helfgoth and S. Schiavo-Campo, "An introduction to development planning," *UNIDO Industrialization and Productivity Bulletin* 16 (1970): 11. A more sophisticated version of the market failure argument as applied to contemporary LDCs can be found in Heinz W. Arndt, "Market failure and underdevelopment," *World Development* 16 (1988): 219–229. For a concise explication of the economic rationale for state intervention, stressing not only market failure and externalities but also public goods, natural monopolies, incomplete markets, and imperfect information, see World Bank, *World Development Report, 1997* (New York: Oxford University Press, 1997), box 1.4.

4. These failures differ from the familiar prisoner's dilemma model, in which there is an incentive to defect after coordination is achieved.

5. See Anthony Atkinson and Joseph E. Stiglitz, *Lectures on Public Economics*, (New York: McGraw-Hill, 1980); Karla Hoff and Joseph E. Stiglitz, "Modern economic theory and development," in *Frontiers in Development Economics*, ed. Gerald M. Meier and Joseph E. Stiglitz (New York: Oxford University Press, 2001); Oliver Williamson, *The Economic Institutions of Capitalism* (New York: Free Press, 1985); Stephen C. Smith, *The Firm, Human Development, and Market Failure* (Geneva: International Labor Office, 1995); and Carl Shapiro and Hal Varian, *Information Rules: A Strategic Guide to the Network Economy* (Boston: Harvard Business School Press, 1999).

6. Lance Taylor, "Theoretical foundations and technical implications," in *Economy-Wide Models and Development Planning*, ed. Charles R. Blitzer, Paul B. Clark, and Lance Taylor (London: Oxford University Press, 1975), pp. 37–42.

7. Ibid., p. 39.

8. For an introductory discussion of the nature and use of input-output models, see Todaro, *Development Planning*, ch. 5.

9. For good surveys, see F. Graham Pyatt and Erik Thorbecke, *Planning Techniques for a Better Future* (Geneva: International Labor Office, 1976), and Shantayanan Devarajan, Jeffrey D. Lewis, and Sherman Robinson, *Getting the Model Right: The General Equilibrium Approach to Adjustment Policy* (Washington, D.C.: World Bank, 1994). The International Food Policy Research Institute is a major contributor to recent work in this field; go to http://www.ifpri.cgiar.org/divs/tmd/method/sam.htm.

10. For a good introduction to cost-benefit analysis stressing links with economic theory, see Ajit K. Dasgupta and David W. Pearce, *Cost-Benefit Analysis: Theory and Practice* (London: Macmillan, 1972).

11. For an excellent assessment of the magnitude and policy significance of externalities in developing countries, see Frances Stewart and Ejaz Ghani, "How significant are externalities for development?" *World Development* 19 (1991): 569–591. Large-scale externalities are discussed in Chapter 4.

12. The classic analysis of project appraisal issues is Partha Dasgupta, Stephen Marglin, and Amartya Sen, *UNIDO Guidelines for Project Evaluation* (New York: United Nations Industrial Development Organization, 1972). An excellent survey of various techniques of project appraisal can be found in Ivy Papps, "Techniques of project appraisal," in *Surveys in Development Economics*, ed. Norman Gemmell (Oxford: Blackwell, 1987), pp. 307–338. For a look at contemporary issues in project appraisal, see Ian Little and James Mirrlees, "Project appraisal and planning twenty years on," *Proceedings of the World Bank Annual Conference on Development Economics, 1990* (Washington, D.C.: World Bank, 1991), pp. 351–382.

13. If you are familiar with the techniques of linear programming, you will recognize that shadow prices are merely the solution values of the dual to a linear-programming output or profit maximization problem; see Todaro, *Development Planning*, ch. 5.

14. This approach is advocated by Ian Little and James Mirrlees in their highly regarded book, *Project Appraisal and Planning in Developing Countries* (New York: Basic Books, 1974).

15. For a complete discussion, see Gittinger, *Economic Analysis of Agricultural Projects*. On social discount rates, see Dasgupta, Marglin, and Sen, *UNIDO Guidelines*.

16. Derek T. Healey, "Development policy: New thinking about an interpretation," *Journal of Economic Literature* 10 (1973): 761; I.M.D. Little, *Economic Development* (New York: Basic Books, 1982).

17. Tony Killick, "Possibilities of development planning," *Oxford Economic Papers* 41 (1976): 163–164.

18. Ibid., 164.

19. For an overview, see World Bank, *World Development Report, 2002* (New York: Oxford University Press, 2002). For an analysis of the effects of corruption, see M. Shahid Alam, "Some economic costs of corruption in LDCs," *Journal of Development Studies* 27 (1990): 89–97; Susan Rose-Ackerman, "Corruption and development," *Annual World Bank Conference on Development Economics, 1997* (Washington, D.C.: World Bank, 1998): pp. 35–68; and Pranab Bardhan, "Corruption and development: A review of issues," *Journal of Economic Literature* 35 (1997): 1320–1346.

20. Albert Waterston, *Development Planning: Lessons of Experience* (Baltimore: Johns Hopkins University Press, 1965), p. 367.

21. Nathan Keyfitz and Robert A. Dorfman, *The Market Economy Is the Best but Not the Easiest* (mimeograph, 1991), pp. 7–13. See also Robert Klitgaard, *Adjusting to Reality: Beyond "State versus Market" in Economic Development* (San Francisco: ICS Press, 1991), pp. 5–6.

22. Keyfitz and Dorfman, *Market Economy*, p. 14.

23. Arndt, "Market failure and underdevelopment."

24. See, for example, Bruce C. Greenwald and Joseph E. Stiglitz, "Externalities in economies with imperfect information and incomplete markets," *Quarterly Journal of Economics* 101 (1986): 229–264.

25. For an in-depth analysis of the role of infrastructure in development, see World Bank, *World Development Report, 1994: Infrastructure for Development* (New York: Oxford University Press, 1994).

26. An interesting commentary on this issue was provided by Alice Amsden, who noted that when the operations evaluation division of the World Bank reported that South Korea and Taiwan used extensive government intervention to industrialize, the bank refused to publish this analysis. See the essay by Alice H. Amsden, "From P.C. to E.C.," *New York Times*, January 12, 1993, p. A15, as well as Richard Grabowski, "The successful development state: Where does it come from?" *World Development* 22 (1994): 413–422; Ajit Singh, "Openness and market-friendly approach to development: Learning the right lessons from development experience," *World Development* 22 (1994): 1811–1823; and Jene Kwon, "The East Asia challenge to neoclassical orthodoxy," *World Development* 22 (1994): 635–644. See also the case studies for Chapters 12 and 13.

27. Alejandro Foxley, "Latin American development after the debt crisis," *Journal of Development Economics* 27 (1987): 211–212.

28. John Williamson, the original compiler of the list, has indicated that he would have wanted to add distributional considerations as a component of development policy but did not observe it as part of the consensus he sought to summarize.

29. Nicholas Stern, chief economist of the World Bank in 2000–2002, was an early proponent of what later became the New Consensus; see, for example, his "Public policy and the economics of development," *European Economic Review* 35 (1991): 250–257. Key elements of the New Censensus remained intact during the Bush administration, which offered expanded support for debt relief and health assistance.

30. Amartya Sen, *Development as Freedom* (New York: Knopf, 1999), p. 43.

31. Anne Krueger, "Government failures in development," *Journal of Economic Perspectives* 4 (1990): 9–24; Deepak Lal, *The Poverty of Development Economics* (Cambridge, Mass.: Harvard University Press, 1995); and Friedrich A. Hayek, *The Road to Serfdom* (Chicago: University of Chicago Press, 1994).

32. See Dani Rodrik, "Understanding economic policy reform," *Journal of Economic Literature* 34 (1996): 9–41, and Merilee S. Grindle, "In quest of the political: The political economy of development policymaking," in *Frontiers in Development Economics*, ed. Gerald M. Meier and Joseph E. Stiglitz (New York: Oxford University Press, 2001). See also the classic work by Mancur Olsen, *The Logic of Collective Action* (Cambridge, Mass.: Harvard University Press, 1965).

33. See Raquel Fernandez and Dani Rodrik, "Resistance to reform: Status quo bias in the presence of individual specific uncertainty," *American Economic Review* 81 (1991): 1146–1155.

34. Rodrik, "Understanding economic policy reform," 37.

35. There has been much emphasis in the development political economy literature on

the process by which Washington Consensus policies become adopted. Again see the surveys of Rodrik and Grindle cited in note 32. This has posed some difficulties for formulating a general theory of the establishment of good governance, because not all development specialists have agreed that all of these policies are best for development broadly construed. However, future studies might focus on a few variables that virtually all specialists agree to be good policies for development. One example, an element of the Washington Consensus that was also implemented in Taiwan and South Korea (see Table 11.1), is the "redirection of public expenditure priorities toward health, education, and infrastructure." Other candidates include the securing and regularizing of property rights (which may include legal protections for the urban informal sector and rural land reform) and a reasonable degree of fiscal discipline (so as not to generate hyperinflation or crowd out a large fraction of potential investment funds). To the extent that such a list can be agreed on, we can arrive at a widely appreciated analysis of the political economy of constructive policy reform rather than merely the process by which assorted policy changes are adopted for good or ill.

36. Rodrik, "Understanding economic policy reform," 26.

37. Douglass C. North, "Economic performance through time," *American Economic Review* 84 (1994): 361.

38. Douglass C. North, *Institutions, Institutional Change, and Economic Performance* (New York: Cambridge University Press, 1990), p. 54.

39. Grindle, "In quest of the political."

40. Ahmed Mobarak reports some results that confirm these ideas along with a good literature review; see his papers "Volatility and its implications for economic development," presented at the WIDER Conference on Growth and Poverty, Helsinki, May 2001, and "Why democracies are more stable: Models of policy choice and political conflict," working paper, University of Maryland, October 2001.

41. Jakob de Haan and Clemens L. J. Siermann, "New evidence on the relationship between democracy and economic growth," *Public Choice* 86 (1996): 175. See also Sen, *Development as Freedom.*

42. United Nations, *Human Development Report, 2003* (New York: United Nations, 2003), http://www.undp.org/hdr2003. The difficulty in sharply defining NGOs is reflected in the broad and diverse sector these actors have come to constitute. With a plethora of terms and acronyms to describe them—from *people's organizations* to *briefcase* or *nongovernmental individuals*—NGOs run the gamut from profit-seeking entrepreneurs to well-intentioned catalyst organizations to professional, streamlined, efficient service deliverers. Overall, while many NGOs retain their philanthropic origin and orientation, they have evolved into strategically managed development specialists, treading the fine line between the technical language and processes of the development industry on the one hand and responsiveness to developing-country clientele and individual contributors on the other. See Jennifer Brinkerhoff, *Partnership for Development: Rhetoric or Results?* (Boulder, Colo.: Rienner, 2002). Parts of this discussion draw on Jennifer Brinkerhoff, Stephen C. Smith, and Hildy Teegen, "Beyond the 'non': The strategic space for NGOs in development," unpublished manuscript, 2003. The authors would like to thank Professors Brinkerhoff and Teegen for many

helpful discussions. This section also draws on Stephen C. Smith, "Escape routes from poverty traps: Organizational comparative advantages of NGOs in eradicating extreme poverty and hunger," unpublished manuscript, 2004. Another interesting paper that develops some related themes is Inge Kaul, "Achieving the Millennium Development Goals: A Global Public Goods Perspective, Reflections on the Debate," GpgNet Discussion Forum Paper No. 5, (New York: UNDP, December 2003).

43. These include the 2003 laureate, Shirin Ebadi, who founded and served as first director of the Association for Protection of Children Rights in Iran, and 2002 laureate Jimmy Carter, who has been active in Habitat for Humanity as well as in resolving developing-country conflicts through the Carter Center.

44. See United Nations, *Human Development Report, 2001* and *2003*, and Susan Raymond, "The nonprofit piece of the global puzzle," *on Philanthropy*, October 15, 2001, http://www.onphilanthropy.com/op2001-10-15.html.

45. Other examples include modern-sector jobs in the Harris-Todaro migration model and effort expended in other types of winner-take-all markets.

46. Elinor Ostrom, *Governing the Commons: The Evolution of Institutions for Collective Action* (New York: Cambridge University Press, 1990).

47. See Paul Romer, "Idea gaps and object gaps in economic development," *Journal of Monetary Economics* 32 (1993): 543–573, and "Two strategies for economic development: Using ideas vs. producing ideas," *World Bank Economic Review Annual Supplement*, 1992.

48. Vincent Ostrom and Elinor Ostrom, "Public goods and public choice," in *Alternatives for Delivering Public Services*, ed. E. S. Savas (Boulder, Colo.: Westview Press, 1977, pp. 7–49; David L. Weimar and Aidan R. Vining, *Policy Analysis: Concepts and Practice*, 2nd ed. (Englewood Cliffs, N.J.: Prentice Hall, 1992).

49. Charles M. Tiebout, "A pure theory of local expenditures," *Journal of Political Economy* 64 (1956): 416–424; James M. Buchanan, "An economic theory of clubs," *Economica* 32 (1965): 1–14.

50. In addition to Grameen and BRAC in Bangladesh, international NGOs such as ACCION and FINCA pioneered village banking in Latin America. See Stephen C. Smith, *Ending Global Poverty* (New York: Palgrave Macmillan, 2005), where examples of several NGO educational innovations are also detailed.

51. Note, for example, the 2004 partnership between Starbucks and Oxfam UK. For a broad analysis, see Jonathan P. Doh and Hildy Teegen, *Globalization and NGOs: Transforming Business, Government, and Society* (Westport, Conn.: Praeger, 2003).

52. Ralph Kramer identifies four characteristic vulnerabilities: (1) institutionalization, or "a process of creeping formalization; (2) goal deflection, or the displacement of ends by means, such as fundraising; (3) minority rule, in which NGOs reflect their philanthropic origins (i.e., funders) rather than their clientele; and (4) ineffectuality. Lester Salamon outlines four similar voluntary failures: (1) philanthropic insufficiency, rooted in NGOs' limited scale and resources; (2) philanthropic particularism, reflecting NGOs' choice of clientele and projects; (3) philanthropic paternalism, where

those who control the most resources are able to control community priorities; and (4) philanthropic amateurism. See Ralph M. Kramer, *Voluntary Agencies in the Welfare State* (Berkeley: University of California Press, 1981), and Lester M. Salamon, "Of market failure, voluntary failure, and third-party government: Toward a theory of government-nonprofit relations in the modern welfare state," *Journal of Voluntary Action Research* 16 (1987): 29–49.

53. Ian Smillie and Henny Helmich call this phenomenon the "alms bazaar" (i.e., the development industry). See Smillie and Helmich (eds.), *Non-Governmental Organisations and Governments: Stakeholders for Development* (Paris: Development Center of the Organization for Economic Cooperation and Development, 1993).

54. World Bank, *The Quality of Growth* (New York: Oxford University Press, 2000), ch. 6.

55. John M. Cohen and Norman T. Uphoff, "Participation's place in rural development: Seeking clarity through specificity," *World Development* 8 (1980): 213–235.

56. David Deshler and Donald Sock, "Community development participation: A concept review of the international literature," paper presented at the conference of the International League for Social Commitment in Adult Education, Ljungskile, Sweden, July 22–26, 1985.

57. Sarah C. White, "Depoliticising development: The uses and abuses of participation," *Development in Practice* 6 (1996): 6–15.

58. Victoria J. Michener, "The participatory approach: Contradiction and cooption in Burkina Faso," *World Development* 26 (1998): 2105–2118.

59. It is ironic that the principal actor in the transition to more market-oriented economies will have to be the LDC government itself and that successful liberalization may require more intervention, at least during a transitional period. See Paul P. Streeten, "Markets and states: Against minimalism," *World Development* 21 (1993): 1281–1298; Ha-Joon Chang and Robert Rowthorn (eds.), *The Role of the State in Economic Change* (New York: Oxford University Press, 1995); and Joseph E. Stiglitz, "The role of government in economic development," in *Annual World Bank Conference on Development Economics, 1996* (Washington, D.C.: World Bank, 1997), pp. 11–26.

Further Reading

For good discussions of the political economy of development policymaking and reform, see Dani Rodrik, "Trade and industrial policy reform," in *Handbook of Development Economics*, vol. 3B, ed. Jere Behrman and T. N. Srinivasan (New York: Elsevier, 1995), pp. 2925–2982; Dani Rodrik, "Understanding economic policy reform," *Journal of Economic Literature* 34 (1996): 9–41; Merilee S. Grindle, "In quest of the political: The political economy of development policymaking," in *Frontiers in Development Economics*, ed. Gerald M. Meier and Joseph E. Stiglitz (New York: Oxford University Press, 2001); and Douglass C. North, *Institutions, Institutional Change, and Economic Performance* (New York: Cambridge University Press, 1990).

For a good overview of the role of instutions in development, see World Bank, *World Development Report, 2002: Building Institutions for Markets* (New York: Oxford University Press, 2002).

On the nature and role of development planning, see Jan Tinbergen, *Development Planning* (London: Weidenfeld & Nicolson, 1967); Michael P. Todaro, *Development Planning: Models and Methods* (Nairobi, Kenya: Oxford University Press, 1971); Hollis B. Chenery (ed.), *Studies in Development Planning* (Cambridge, Mass.: Harvard University Press, 1971); Pradip K. Ghosh (ed.), *Development Policy and Planning: A Third World Perspective* (Westport, Conn.: Greenwood Press, 1984); and Francisco R. Sagesti, "National development planning in turbulent times: New approaches and criteria for institutional design," *World Development* 16 (1988): 431–448.

For a more advanced treatment of the use of mathematical models in development planning, see Charles R. Blitzer, Paul B. Clark, and Lance Taylor (eds.), *Economy-Wide Models and Development Planning* (London: Oxford University Press, 1975).

An informative and thoughtful study of the methodology and use of cost-benefit analysis for project appraisal in developing countries can be found in Ian Little and James Mirrlees, *Project Appraisal and Planning for Developing Countries* (New York: Basic Books, 1974), and Ivy Papps, "Techniques of project appraisal," in *Surveys in Development Economics,* ed. Norman Gemmell (Oxford: Blackwell, 1987), ch. 9. See also Arnold C. Harberger, "Reflections on social project evaluation," in *Pioneers in Development: Second Series,* ed. Gerald M. Meier (New York: Oxford University Press, 1987), pp. 159–189, and Shantayanan Devarajan, Lyn Squire, and Sethaput Suthiwart-Narueput, "Beyond rate of return: Reorienting project appraisal," *World Bank Research Observer* 12 (1997): 35–46.

For a review of the planning experience of developing countries over the past decades as well as a critique of the "planning mystique," see Albert Waterston, *Development Planning: Lessons of Experience* (Baltimore: Johns Hopkins University Press, 1965); Mike Faber and Dudley Seers (eds.), *The Crisis in Planning* (London: Chatto & Windus, 1972), especially the article by Seers, "The prevalence of pseudo-planning"; and Tony Killick, "The possibilities of development planning," *Oxford Economic Papers* 41 (1976): 161–184.

Among the best references on the critical issue of markets versus planning, see Tony Killick, *A Reaction Too Far: Economic Theory and the Role of the State in Developing Countries* (London: Overseas Development Institute, 1989); "Development strategies: The role of the state and the private sector—a roundtable discussion," *Proceedings of the World Bank Annual Conference on Development Economics, 1990* (New York: Oxford University Press, 1991), pp. 421–435; World Bank, *World Development Report, 1991* (New York: Oxford University Press, 1991), ch. 7; Robert Klitgaard, *Adjusting to Reality: Beyond "State versus Market" in Economic Development* (San Francisco: ICS Press, 1991); Paul P. Streeten, *Strategies for Human Development* (Copenhagen: Handelshøjskolens Forlag, 1994), pt. 2; Ha-Joon Chang and Robert Towthorn (eds.), *The Role of the State in Economic Change* (New York: Oxford University Press, 1995); Joseph E. Stiglitz, "The role of government in economic development," *Annual World Bank Conference on Development Economics, 1996* (Washington, D.C.: World Bank, 1997), pp. 11–26; World Bank, *World Development Report, 1997: The State in a Changing World* (Washington, D.C.: World Bank, 1997); and Cedric Pugh, "The World Bank's millennial theory of the state: Further attempts to reconcile the political and the economic," *Third World Planning Review* 19 (1997): iii–xiv.

On NGOs in development, see David Hulme and Michael Edwards (eds.), *States and Donors: Too Close for Comfort?* (New York: St. Martin's Press/Save the Children Fund, 1997), pp. 107—127. Tim Brodhead, "NGOs: In One Year, Out the Other?" *World Development*, ed. Anne Gordon Drabek, 15 (Supplement 1987): 1–6. Jonathan A. Fox and L. David Brown, *The Struggle for Accountability: The World Bank, NGOs and Grassroots Movements* (Cambridge, Mass.: MIT Press, 1998). Inge Kaul, "Global Public Goods: What Role for Civil Society?" *Non-Profit and Voluntary Sector Quarterly* 30 (2001): 588–602. Marc Lindenberg and Coralie Bryant, *Going Global: Transforming Relief and Development NGOs.* (Bloomfield, Conn.: Kumarian Press, 2002). Lester M. Salamon, "The Rise of the Nonprofit Sector: A Global 'Associational Revolution,'" *Foreign Affairs* 73 (1999): 109–122.

PART THREE

Problems and Policies: International and Macro

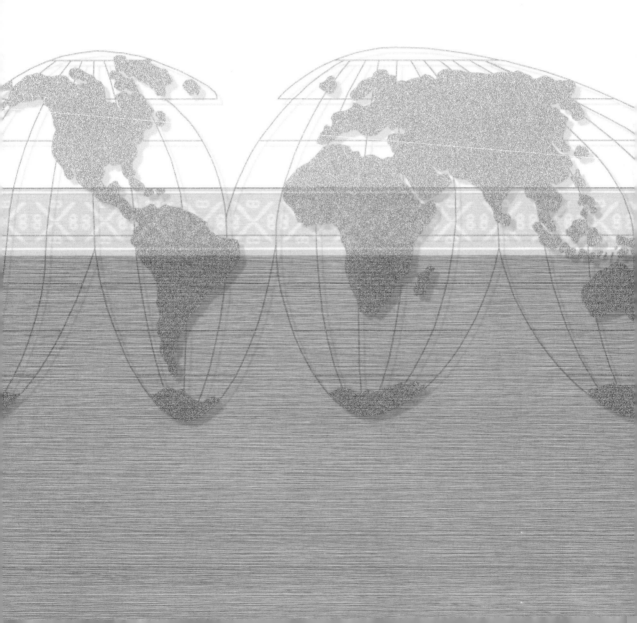

CHAPTER TWELVE

Trade Theory and Development Experience

Integration into the world economy has proven a powerful instrument for countries to promote economic growth.... These trends point to the need to liberalize trade further.

—Staffs of World Bank and IMF, *Market Access for Developing Countries' Exports, 2001*

Increasing polarization between the haves and have-nots has become a feature of our world. Reversing this shameful trend is the preeminent moral and humanitarian challenge of our age.

—Report of the U.N. High-Level Panel on Financing for Development, 2001

Made in one or more of the following countries: Korea, Hong Kong, Malaysia, Singapore, Taiwan, Mauritius, Thailand, Indonesia, Mexico, Philippines. The exact country of origin is unknown.

—Integrated Circuit Label[1]

Globalization: An Introduction

Over the past several decades, the economies of the world have become increasingly linked, through expanded international trade in services as well as primary and manufactured goods, through portfolio investments such as international loans and purchases of stock, and through direct foreign investment, especially on the part of large multinational corporations. At the same time, foreign aid has increased very little and indeed has become dwarfed by the now much larger flows of private capital. These linkages have had a marked effect on the developing world. Developing countries are importing and exporting more from each other, as well as from the developed countries, and in some parts of the developing world, especially East Asia but notably Latin America as well, investments have poured in from developed countries such as the United States, the United Kingdom, and Japan. We shall review how developing countries have been affected by these trends and examine theories of the effects of expanded international linkages for the prospects for development.

Globalization is one of the most frequently used words in discussions of development, trade, and international political economy.[2] As the form of the word implies, globalization is a *process* by which the economies of the world become increasingly integrated, leading to a global economy and, increasingly, global economic policymaking, for example, through international agencies such as the World Trade Organization (WTO). *Globalization* also refers to an emerging "global culture," in which people more often consume similar goods and services across countries and use a common language of business, English; these changes facilitate economic integration and are in turn further promoted by it. But in its core economic meaning, *globalization* refers to the increased openness of economies to international trade, financial flows, and direct foreign investment, the topics of Chapters 12–15. The growing interconnection of all kinds across national governments and firms and directly between peoples is a process that affects everyone in the world, one that so far seems more visible in the developed countries. But globalization can in many ways have a greater impact on people in developing countries.

For some people, the term *globalization* suggests exciting business opportunities, more rapid growth of knowledge and innovation, or the prospect of a world too interdependent to engage in war. In part, globalization may well turn out to be all of these things. For other people, however, globalization raises troubling concerns: that inequalities may be accentuated both across and within countries, that environmental degradation may be accelerated, that the international dominance of the richest countries may be expanded and locked in, and that some peoples and regions may be left behind. Some of these concerns have been exaggerated, but they represent legitimate issues that need to be addressed to prevent globalization from leading to some or all of these problems.

Thus globalization carries benefits and opportunities as well as costs and risks. This is true for all peoples in all countries but especially for people living in absolutely poor families and in low-income countries, for whom the stakes are much higher. The potential upside is perhaps also greatest for developing countries; globalization does present new possibilities for broad-based economic development. By providing many types of interactions with people in other countries, globalization can potentially benefit poor countries directly and indirectly through cultural, social, scientific, and technological exchanges, as well as through conventional trade and finance. A faster diffusion of productive ideas, such as a shorter time between innovation and adoption of new technologies around the world, might help developing countries catch up more quickly. In short, globalization makes it possible, at least in principle, for the less developed countries to more effectively absorb the knowledge that is one of the foundations of the wealth of developed countries. In addition, as Adam Smith wrote in1776, "the division of labor is limited by the extent of the market." The larger the market that can be sold to, the greater the gains from trade and the division of labor. Moreover, the greater is the incentive for innovation, because the potential return is much greater.

The downside of globalization is also greater for poorer countries, as there is a real possibility that poor countries may become locked into a pattern of dependence, that dualism in LDCs may sharpen, or that some of the poor may be entirely bypassed by globalization; in any case, the poor may be left in poverty traps that may be all the harder to break out of without concerted public action. The share of international investment received by the poorest countries has been steadily falling rather than rising. All countries may be affected by increased vulnerability to capital flows, but especially developing countries. All countries may experience certain threats to their cultural identities, but developing countries most so.

Certainly, some very important low-income countries, accounting for a large fraction of world population, notably China and India, have recently been using globalization as an opportunity to accelerate their rate of catch-up by growing faster than the developed world, thereby reducing some international inequalities. But by other measures, inequality may be accentuated both across and within countries. The decline in Africa and the extreme and growing disparities between coastal and inland China are important cases in point.

Legitimate and understandable concerns about globalization are based on the fact that previous great waves of globalization were extraordinarily uneven in their impact. The worst affected areas, such as Africa, are still reeling. The argument that there will be widespread general benefits from at least some form of globalization today must rest on what is different about this current wave. It is not enough simply to say that previous waves were associated with conquest and subordination by colonialism. Critics can and do contend that today's globalization is only superficially different. A claim that "things are different this time" must stand or fall on evidence that there are now effective rules of the game for international trade, investment, finance, and assistance to the poor—or if not, that these rules are steadily, convincingly, and irreversibly being put into place.

Formal processes of trade liberalization have been key to the encouragement of globalization thus far. As we will see, there have been a significant series of "rounds" of trade negotiations through the General Agreement on Tariffs and Trade (GATT), initiated in 1948, which led eventually to the creation of the WTO in 1995. The trade rules negotiated under the auspices of the WTO are key examples of creation of rules of the game. In practice, however, these rules have not been truly balanced. They have greatly benefited some countries but much less the very poor countries still trying to gain a foothold in growth and development through agriculture and textiles and facing barriers put up by the very countries most promoting the benefits of trade openness. Trade protectionism as practiced by developed countries tends to fall most heavily on the poorest developing countries. Developed-country protection focuses on agriculture and basic manufactured products such as textiles. The damage this tactic does to developing countries is immense.

To create genuinely fair as well as efficient rules of the game, much more needs to be done. International agreements are needed to level the globalization playing field for the poor. Some of this leveling process involves international change, and some involves national changes that can be facilitated by the international community—for example, to effectively prevent propping up corrupt governments and violent and exploitative rebels that stay in power through international trade in legal goods such as diamonds (mined with slave labor) as well as in illegal goods such as narcotics. Codes of conduct for multinational corporations, regarding political and other behavior, need to be developed further. And reasonable limits on the applicability of international property rights must be agreed to, such as those concerning provision of medicines in life-threatening emergencies in poor countries that cannot afford to pay monopoly rents, prices that far exceed production costs. In Chapter 15, we will learn that direct foreign investment by MNCs may contribute to development, but a country also eventually needs its own firms or at least a way of inducing international firms to treat the country as a home base.

It has also been asked whether more cannot be done for the poorest countries than to merely level the playing field. Many development advocates are calling for the immediate and full opening of developed-country markets to exports from the poorest countries. It may also be said that among the worst possible outcomes for a poor country is to be unaffected by the current round of globalization, having it bypass the country entirely. This situation is reflected in much of sub-Saharan Africa. Adversely affected by previous waves of globalization, this region has been little affected by the present wave, other than through a high debt burden.

International Trade and Finance: Some Key Issues

International trade has often played a central role in the historical experience of the developing world. In recent years, much of the attention to trade and development issues has been focused on understanding the spectacular export success of East Asia. Taiwan, South Korea, and other East Asian economies pioneered this strategy, which has been successfully followed by their much larger neighbor, China. The experiences of these countries are an important plot in the unfolding trade and development drama and will be examined in the next chapter.

At the same time, throughout Africa, the Middle East, and Latin America, primary product exports have traditionally accounted for a sizable proportion of individual gross national products. In some of the smaller countries, up to 25% or more of the monetary income is derived from the overseas sale of agricultural and other **primary products** or commodities such as coffee, cotton, cacao, sugar, palm oil, bauxite, and copper. In the special circumstances of the oil-producing nations in the Persian Gulf and elsewhere, the sale of unrefined and refined petroleum products to countries throughout the world accounts for over 70% of their national incomes. But unlike the oil-producing states and newly industrializing countries like South Korea, Taiwan, and now China, many developing countries must depend on nonmineral primary-product exports for much of their foreign-exchange earnings. This is a particularly serious problem in sub-Saharan Africa. Because the markets and prices for these exports are often unstable, primary-product **export dependence** carries with it a degree of risk and uncertainty that few nations desire. This is an important issue because the long-term trend for prices of primary goods is downward.

Some African countries continue to receive 3% or less of their merchandise export earnings from manufactures, including Mali, Niger, and Rwanda (none of which received more than 1% of their export earnings from fossil fuels in 2002).

TABLE 12.1	LDCs Receiving at Least 40 Percent of Export Earnings from One or Two Agricultural or Nonfuel Mineral Products	
Africa	**Asia and the Pacific**	**Latin America and the Carribean**
Burkina Faso (cotton)	Fiji (sugar)	Belize (sugar)
Burundi (coffee)	Maldives (fish)	Chile (copper, metal ores)
Côte d'Ivoire (cocoa, coffee)	Myanmar and the Pacific (wood, vegetables)	Costa Rica (coffee, fruit)
Ethiopia (coffee)	Papua New Guinea (gold, metal ores)	Cuba (sugar)
Ghana (cocoa, precious stones)	Solomon Islands (wood)	Dominica (iron, fruit)
Kenya (tea, coffee)	Tonga (vegetables)	Guadeloupe (sugar, fruit)
Madagascar (coffee, spices)		Guyana (gold, sugar)
Malawi (tobacco)		Honduras (fruit, coffee)
Mauritania (iron ore)		Jamaica (minerals)
Mozambique (fish, fruit)		Panama (fruit)
Reunion (sugar)		Paraguay (vegetable oil, cotton)
Rwanda (coffee)		Saint Lucia (fruit)
Senegal (fish, vegetable oil)		
Seychelles (fish)		
Sierra Leone (precious stones)		
Sudan (cotton, vegetables)		
Uganda (coffee)		

Source: Sarah Anderson, John Cavanagh, Thea Lee, and Barbara Ehrenreich, *Field Guide to the Global Economy* (New York: New Press, 2000). Reprinted with permission.

Nigeria received 100% of its export earnings from fossil fuels in 2002. Indeed, at least 35 LDCs received at least two-fifths of their export earnings from one or two agricultural or nonfuel mineral products, as indicated in Table 12.1.

In addition to their export dependence, many developing countries rely, generally to an even greater extent, on the importation of raw materials, machinery, capital goods, intermediate producer goods, and consumer products to fuel their industrial expansion and satisfy the rising consumption aspirations of their people. For most developing nations, import demands have exceeded their capacity to generate sufficient revenues from the sale of exports. This has led to chronic deficits on their balance of payments position vis-à-vis the rest of the world. Whereas such deficits on the **current account** (an excess of import *payments* over export *receipts* for goods and services) were often more than compensated for on their balance of payments table by a surplus on the **capital account** (a receipt of foreign private and public lending and investment in excess of repayment of principal and interest on former loans and investments), in recent years the debt burden of repaying earlier international loans and investments has become increasingly acute. In a number of LDCs, severe deficits on current and capital accounts have therefore led to a rapid depletion of their international monetary reserves, currency instability, and a slowdown in economic growth.

In the 1980s and 1990s, this combination of rising trade deficits, growing foreign debts, accelerated capital flight, and diminished international reserves led to the widespread adoption of fiscal and monetary austerity measures (often with the involvement of the International Monetary Fund), which may have further exacerbated the slowdown in economic growth and the worsening of poverty and unemployment in much of the developing world. The precise meaning of these various concepts of international economics will be explained later in this chapter and in the next two. Here the point is merely that a chronic excess of foreign expenditures over receipts (which may have nothing to do with an LDC's inability to handle its financial affairs but rather may be related to its vulnerability to global economic disturbances) can significantly retard development efforts. It can also greatly limit a poor nation's ability to determine and pursue its most desirable economic strategies.

But international trade and finance must be understood in a much broader perspective than simply the intercountry flow of commodities and financial resources. By opening their economies and societies to global trade and commerce and by looking outward to the rest of the world, developing countries invite not only the international transfer of goods, services, and financial resources but also the developmental or antidevelopmental influences of the transfer of production technologies; consumption patterns; institutional and organizational arrangements; educational, health, and social systems; and the more general values, ideals, and lifestyles of the developed nations of the world. The impact of such technological, economic, social, and cultural transfers on the character of the development process can be either benign or malignant. Much will depend on the nature of the political, social, and institutional structure of the recipient country and its development priorities. Whether it is best for LDCs to look outward and promote more exports, either passively or actively; to look inward and substitute domestic production for imports, as the protectionists and cultural nationalists propose; or to be simultaneously and strategically outward- and inward-looking in their international economic policies cannot be stated a priori. Individual nations must appraise their present and prospective situations in the world community realistically in the light of their specific development objectives. Only thus can they determine how to design the most beneficial trade strategy.

Small, low-income countries (which constitute well over half of all developing nations) have little choice about whether to opt in or opt out. Participation in the world economy is inevitable, but there is ample room for policy choice about what *kind* of participation to promote, and what policy strategies to pursue.

Five Basic Questions about Trade and Development

Our objective in this chapter is to focus on traditional and more contemporary theories of international trade in the context of five basic themes or questions of particular importance to developing nations.

1. How does international trade affect the rate, structure, and character of LDC economic growth? This is the traditional "trade as an engine of growth" controversy, set in terms of contemporary development aspirations.

2. How does trade alter the distribution of income and wealth within a country and among different countries? Is trade a force for international and domestic equality or inequality? In other words, how are the gains and losses distributed, and who benefits?

3. Under what conditions can trade help LDCs achieve their development objectives?

4. Can LDCs by their own actions determine how much they trade?

5. In the light of past experience and prospective judgment, should LDCs adopt an outward-looking policy (freer trade, expanded flows of capital and human resources, ideas and technology, etc.) or an inward-looking one (protectionism in the interest of self-reliance), or should they pursue some combination of both, for example, in the form of regional economic cooperation? What are the arguments for and against these alternative trade strategies for development?

Clearly, the answers or suggested answers to these five questions will not be uniform throughout the diverse economies of the developing world. The whole economic basis for international trade rests on the fact that countries do differ in their resource endowments, their preferences and technologies, their scale economies, their economic and social institutions, and their capacities for growth and development. Developing countries are no exception to this rule. Some are very populous yet deficient in natural resources and human skills. Others are sparsely populated yet endowed with abundant mineral and raw material resources. Still others—the majority—are small and economically weak, having at present neither the human nor the material resources on which to base a sustained and largely self-sufficient strategy of economic and social development. Yet with the notable exception of the now very wealthy oil nations of the Middle East and a few other countries rich in internationally demanded mineral resources, most developing nations face similar issues and choices in their international relations with the developed countries and with each other. Consequently, though an effort will be made here to place generalizations about LDC trade prospects and policy alternatives in the context of a broad typology of developing nations, the goal of being comprehensive in coverage will necessitate a number of sweeping generalizations, many of which may not hold for a particular country at a particular time. On balance, however, the benefits of this broad perspective outweigh the costs of having to make some analytical and policy generalizations.

Accordingly, we begin with a statistical summary of recent LDC trade performance and patterns. There follows a simplified presentation of the basic neoclassical theory of international trade and its effect on efficiency, equity, stability, and growth (four basic economic concepts related to the central questions outlined here). We then provide a critique of pure free-trade theories in the light of both historical experience and the contemporary realities of the world economy. Like free markets, **free trade** has many desirable theoretical features, not the least of which is the promotion of static economic efficiency and optimal resource allocation. But also like free markets and perfect competition, free trade exists more in theory than in practice—and today's developing nations have to function in the imperfect and often highly unequal real world of international commerce. Consequently, we will briefly discuss more recent alternative trade models, including North-South models of exchange that focus on the real world of imperfect competition, unequal trade, and the dynamic effects of differential human resource and technological growth. In Chapters 13 and 14, we will learn something about a country's balance of payments, review some issues in international finance, engage in an in-depth analysis of the debt crisis, and explore the range of commercial policies (tariffs, subsidies, quotas, exchange-rate adjustments, etc.) that LDCs might wish to adopt within the broader context of the ongoing debate about the relative merits of export promotion versus import substitution. An outstanding example of the benefits of world trade is illustrated at the conclusion of this chapter, where the sources of the pioneering success of Taiwan are examined.

Importance of Exports to Different Developing Nations

Although the overall LDC figures for export volumes and values are important indicators of patterns of trade for the group as a whole, the varying importance of exports to the economic well-being of individual nations is masked by these aggregate statistics. Table 12.2 has been compiled to provide a capsule picture of the relative importance of commodity export earnings to various developing nations of different sizes and in different regions. For purposes of comparison, three key developed countries are included at the bottom of the table.

Developing countries are generally more dependent on trade than developed countries are. As Table 12.2 indicates, while large countries are understandably less dependent on trade than small countries, at any given size, developing countries tend to devote a larger share of their output as merchandise exports than developed countries do. We see that large countries like Brazil and India, which have had unusually closed economies, tend to be less dependent on foreign trade in terms of national income than relatively small countries like those in tropical Africa and East Asia. As a group, however, less developed nations are more dependent on foreign trade in terms of its share in national income than the very highly developed countries are. This is shown clearly in the case of traditionally export-oriented Japan, whose exports amount to roughly 10% of GDP, whereas LDCs with somewhat larger populations such as Indonesia, Bangladesh, and Nigeria export a far higher share of output.

The greater share of developing-country exports in GDP is probably due in part to the much higher relative prices of nontraded services in developed than in developing countries. Nevertheless, the point remains that LDCs are generally more dependent on trade in international economic relations because most trade is in merchandise, for which price disparities are smaller across countries. Moreover, the exports of LDCs are much less diversified than those of the developed countries.

While total exports and the share of manufactures in merchandise exports have been rising for many developing countries, and important new exporters such as China have emerged, it is important to keep this rise in perspective. A few NICs still command a dominant position in developing-country exports. For example,

TABLE 12.2	Merchandise Export Earnings as a Percentage of GDP and Share of Primary and Manufactured Commodities in Total Merchandise Exports for Selected Countries, 2002		
Country	Exports as Percentage of GDP	Percentage Share of Primary Commodities	Percentage Share of Manufactures
Developing countries			
Malaysia	98.3	21	79
Philippines	46.5	50	50
Nigeria	34.7	100	0
South Korea	34.1	8	92
Indonesia	33.0	46	54
Togo	31.0	57	43
Venezuela	28.5	87	13
Sri Lanka	28.4	26	74
China (excluding Hong Kong)	25.7	10	90
Mexico	25.2	16	84
Kenya	17.0	76	24
Jamaica	14.0	36	64
Brazil	13.3	46	54
Bangladesh	12.8	8	92
India	9.7	25	75
Developed countries			
United Kingdom	17.9	21	79
Japan	10.4	7	93
United States	6.7	19	81

Sources: World Bank, *World Development Indicators,* 2004 (New York: Oxford University Press, 2004), tab. 6.1; World Bank, *World Development Report 2002* (New York: Oxford University Press, 2002), tabs. 4.2 and 4.5. Reprinted with permission.

in 2000, South Korea alone exported more than all of South Asia and sub-Saharan Africa combined. And South Korea and Taiwan together exported more manufactured goods in 2000 than the entire regions of Latin America, the Carribean, the Middle East, North Africa, South Asia, and sub-Saharan Africa combined.[3]

Demand Elasticities and Export Earnings Instability

We have an important clue here as to why the export performance of the majority of LDCs has been relatively weak compared with the export performance of rich countries. It relates to the concept of elasticity of demand. Most statistical studies of world demand patterns for different commodity groups reveal that in the case of primary products, the **income elasticity of demand** is relatively low: The percentage increase in quantity of primary products demanded by importers (mostly rich nations) will rise by less than the percentage increase in their GNIs. By contrast, for fuels, certain raw materials, and manufactured goods, income elasticity is relatively high.[4] For example, it has been estimated that a 1% increase in developed-country incomes will normally raise their import of foodstuffs by a mere 0.6%, agricultural raw materials such as rubber and vegetable oils by 0.5%, but of petroleum products and other fuels by 2.4%, and manufactures by about 1.9%. Consequently, when incomes rise in rich countries, their demand for food, food products, and raw materials from the developing nations goes up relatively slowly, whereas their own as well as LDC demand for manufactures, the production of which is dominated by the developed countries, goes up very rapidly.

The net result of these low income elasticities of demand is the tendency for the relative price of primary products to decline over time. Moreover, since the **price elasticity of demand** for (and supply of) primary commodities also tends to be quite low (i.e., inelastic), any shifts in demand or supply curves can cause large and volatile price fluctuations. Together these two elasticity phenomena contribute to what has come to be known as **export earnings instability**, which has been shown to lead to lower and less predictable rates of economic growth.

While almost all attention goes to merchandise exports, there has been a slow rise in the share of commercial services in the exports of both developed and developing countries. For the former, these are more likely to represent highly skilled activities such as investment banking and management consulting, while for the latter, construction and other less skill-intensive activities are more common.

The Terms of Trade and the Prebisch-Singer Thesis

The question of changing relative price levels for different commodities brings us to another important quantitative dimension of the trade problems historically faced by developing nations. The total value of export earnings depends not only on the volume of these exports sold abroad but also on the price paid for them. If export prices decline, a greater volume of exports will have to be sold merely to keep total earnings constant. Similarly, on the import side, the total foreign exchange expended depends on both the quantity and the price of imports.

Clearly, if the price of a country's exports is falling relative to the prices of the products it imports, it will have to sell that much more of its export product and enlist more of its scarce productive resources merely to secure the same level of imported goods that it purchased in previous years. In other words, the real or social opportunity costs of a unit of imports will rise for a country when its export prices decline relative to its import prices.

Economists have a special name for the relationship or ratio between the price of a typical unit of exports and the price of a typical unit of imports. This relationship is called the **commodity terms of trade**, and it is expressed as P_x/P_m, where P_x and P_m represent the export and import price indexes, respectively, calculated on the same base period (e.g., 2001 = 100). The commodity terms of trade are said to deteriorate for a country if P_x/P_m falls, that is, if export prices decline *relative to* import prices, even though both may rise. Historically, the prices of primary commodities have declined relative to manufactured goods.[5] As a result, the terms of trade have on the average tended to worsen over time for the non-oil-exporting developing countries while showing a relative improvement for the developed countries. Moreover, recent empirical studies suggest that real primary-product prices have declined at an average annual rate of 0.6% since 1900.[6]

The main theory for the declining commodity terms of trade is known as the **Prebisch-Singer thesis**, after two famous development economists who explored its implications in the 1950s.[7] They argued that there was and would continue to be a secular decline in the terms of trade of primary-commodity exporters due to a combination of low income and price elasticities of demand. This decline would result in a long-term transfer of income from poor to rich countries that could be combated only by efforts to protect domestic manufacturing industries through a process that has come to be known as import substitution (see Chapter 13).

Both because of this theory and because of the unfavorable terms of trade trends, developing countries have been doing their utmost over the past several decades to diversify into manufactures exports. After a slow and costly start, these efforts have resulted in a dramatic shift in the composition of developing-country exports, especially among middle-income LDCs. Led at first by the East Asian "tiger" economies of South Korea, Taiwan, Hong Kong, and Singapore and now followed by many other countries in Asia, including China and India, the share of merchandise exports accounted for by manufactured goods has risen strongly in many developing countries.

Unfortunately, this structural change has not brought as many benefits to most developing countries as they had hoped, because relative prices within manufactures have also diverged: Over the last quarter century, the prices of the basic manufactured goods exported by poor countries fell relative to the advanced products exported by rich countries. The price of textiles fell especially precipitously, and low-skilled electronic goods are not far behind.

Using alternative methods, the United Nations found that the real decline in developing-country export prices of manufactures in the 1980s was about 3.5% per year, or about 30% for the decade. In a detailed study, Alf Maizels discovered that the terms of trade in manufacturing goods for developing countries vis-à-vis the United States deteriorated over the 1981–1997 period. The declines in textile prices accelerated dramatically in the late 1990s.[8]

Having reviewed some of the international trade issues that developing countries face, we turn next to consider alternative theories of the role that trade plays in economic development.

The Traditional Theory of International Trade

The phenomenon of transactions and exchange is a basic component of human activity throughout the world. Even in the most remote villages of Africa, people regularly meet in the village market to exchange goods, either for money or for other goods through simple **barter transactions**. A transaction is an exchange of two things—something is given up in return for something else. In an African village, women may barter food such as cassava for cloth or simple jewelry for clay pots. Implicit in all transactions is a price. For example, if 20 kilos of cassava are traded for a meter of bark cloth, the implicit price (or terms of trade) of the bark cloth is 20 kilos of cassava. If 20 kilos of cassava can also be exchanged for one small clay pot, it follows that clay pots and 1-meter pieces of bark cloth can be exchanged on a one-to-one basis. A price system is already in the making.

Comparative Advantage

Why do people trade? Basically, because it is profitable to do so. Different people possess different abilities and resources and may want to consume goods in different proportions. Diverse preferences as well as varied physical and financial endowments open up the possibility of profitable trade. People usually find it profitable to trade the things they possess in large quantities relative to their tastes or needs in return for things they want more urgently. Because it is virtually impossible for individuals or families to provide themselves with all the consumption requirements of even the simplest life, they usually find it profitable to engage in the activities for which they are best suited or have a **comparative advantage** in terms of their natural abilities or resource endowments. They can then exchange any surplus of these home-produced commodities for products that others may be relatively more suited to produce. The phenomenon of **specialization** based on comparative advantage arises, therefore, to some extent in even the most primitive of subsistence economies.

These same principles of specialization and comparative advantage have long been applied by economists to the exchange of goods between individual nations. In answer to the question of what determines which goods are traded and why some countries produce some things while others produce different things, economists since the time of Adam Smith have sought the answer in terms of international differences in costs of production and prices of different products. Countries, like people, specialize in a limited range of production activities because it is to their advantage to do so. They specialize in activities where the gains from specialization are likely to be the largest.

But why, in the case of international trade, should costs differ from country to country? For example, how can Germany produce cameras, electrical appliances, and automobiles cheaper than Kenya and exchange these manufactured goods for Kenya's relatively cheaper agricultural produce (fruits, vegetables, coffee, and tea)? Again, the answer is to be found in international differences in the structure of costs and prices. Some things (manufactured goods) are relatively cheaper to produce in Germany and can profitably be exported to other countries like Kenya; other things (agricultural goods) can be produced in Kenya at a lower relative cost and are therefore imported into Germany in exchange for its manufactures.

The concept of *relative* cost and price differences is basic to the theory of international trade. The *principle of comparative advantage*, as it is called, asserts that a country should, and under competitive conditions will, specialize in the export of the products that it can produce at the lowest *relative cost*. Germany may be able to produce cameras and cars as well as fruits and vegetables at lower *absolute* unit costs than Kenya, but because the commodity cost differences between countries are greater for the manufactured goods than for agricultural products, it will be to Germany's advantage to specialize in the production of manufactured goods and exchange them for Kenya's agricultural produce. So even though Germany may have an **absolute advantage** in the cost of both commodities, its comparative cost advantage lies in manufactured goods. Conversely, Kenya may be at an absolute disadvantage vis-à-vis Germany in both manufacturing and agriculture in that its absolute unit costs of production are higher for both types of products. It can nevertheless still engage in profitable trade because it has a comparative advantage in agricultural specialization (or alternatively, because its absolute disadvantage is less in agriculture). It is this phenomenon of differences in comparative advantage that gives rise to beneficial trade even among the most unequal trading partners.

Relative Factor Endowments and International Specialization: The Neoclassical Model

The classical comparative advantage theory of free trade is a static model based strictly on a one-variable-factor (labor cost), complete-specialization approach to demonstrating the gains from trade. This nineteenth-century free-trade model, primarily associated with David Ricardo and John Stuart Mill, was modified and refined in the twentieth century by two Swedish economists, Eli Hecksher and Bertil Ohlin, to take into account differences in factor supplies (mainly land, labor, and capital) on international specialization. The Hecksher-Ohlin neoclassical (or variable-proportions) **factor endowment trade theory** also enables us to describe analytically the impact of economic growth on trade patterns and the impact of trade on the structure of national economies and on the differential returns or payments to various factors of production.

Unlike the classical labor cost model, however, where trade arises because of fixed but differing labor productivities for different commodities in different countries, the neoclassical factor endowment model assumes away inherent differences in relative labor productivity by postulating that all countries have access to the same technological possibilities for all commodities. If domestic factor prices were the same, all countries would use identical methods of production and would therefore have the same relative domestic product price ratios and factor productivities. The basis for trade arises not because of inherent technological differences in labor productivity for different commodities between different countries but because countries are endowed with different factor supplies. Given relative factor endowments, relative factor prices will differ (e.g., labor will be relatively cheap in labor-abundant countries), and so will domestic commodity price ratios and factor combinations. Countries with cheap labor will have a relative cost and price advantage over countries with relatively expensive labor in commodities that make intensive use of labor (e.g., primary products). They should therefore focus on the production of these labor-intensive products and export the surplus in return for imports of capital-intensive goods.

Conversely, countries well endowed with capital will have a relative cost and price advantage in the production of manufactured goods, which tend to require relatively large inputs of capital compared with labor. They can thus benefit from specialization in and export of capital-intensive manufactures in return for imports of labor-intensive products from labor-abundant countries. Trade therefore serves as a vehicle for a nation to capitalize on its abundant resources through more intensive production and export of commodities that require large inputs of those resources while relieving its factor shortage through the importation of commodities that use large amounts of its relatively scarce resources.

To summarize, the factor endowment theory is based on two crucial propositions:

1. Different products require productive factors in different relative proportions. For example, agricultural products generally require relatively greater proportions of labor per unit of capital than manufactured goods, which require more machine time (capital) per worker than most primary products. The proportions in which factors are actually used to produce different goods will depend on their relative prices. But no matter what factor prices may be, the factor endowment model assumes that certain products will always be relatively more capital-intensive while others will be relatively more labor-intensive. These relative factor intensities will be no different in India than in the United States; primary products will be the relatively labor-intensive commodities compared with secondary manufactured goods in both India and the United States.

2. Countries have different endowments of factors of production. Some countries, like the United States, have large amounts of capital per worker and are thus designated capital-abundant countries. Others, like India, Egypt, or Colombia, have little capital and much labor and are thus designated labor-abundant countries. In general, developed countries are relatively capital-abundant (one could also add that they are well endowed with skilled labor), while most developing countries are labor-abundant.

The factor endowment theory goes on to argue that capital-abundant countries will tend to specialize in such products as automobiles, aircraft, sophisticated electronic communication goods, and computers, which use capital intensively in their technology of production. They will export some of these capital-intensive products in exchange for the labor- or land-intensive products like food, raw materials, and minerals that can best be produced by countries that are relatively well endowed with labor or land.

This theory, which played a predominant role in the early literature on trade and development, encouraged developing countries to focus on their labor- and land-intensive primary-product exports. It was argued that by trading these primary commodities for the manufactured goods that developed countries were theoretically best suited to produce, developing nations could realize the enormous potential benefits to be had from free trade with the richer nations of the world.

The mechanism whereby the benefits of trade are transmitted across national boundaries under the factor endowment approach is analogous to that of the classical labor cost approach. However, in the factor endowment case, with the possibility of differing factor combinations for producing different commodities, nations are assumed to be operating initially at some point on their concave (or increasing opportunity cost) production possibility frontier determined by domestic demand conditions. For example, consider the standard two-country, two-commodity model. Let the two countries be "Developing World" and "Developed World" and the two commodities be agricultural goods and manufactured goods. Figure 12.1 portrays the theoretical benefits of free trade with the Developing World's domestic (no-trade) production possibility frontier shown in Figure 12.1a and Developed World's frontier in Figure 12.1b. Point A on Developing World production possibility frontier PP in Figure 12.1a provides the illustration. With full employment of all resources and under perfectly competitive assumptions, Developing World will be producing and consuming at point A, where the relative price ratio, P_a/P_m, will be given by the slope of the dotted line, $(P_a/P_m)T$, at point A.[9] Similarly, Developed World may be producing and consuming at point A' in Figure 12.1b, with a domestic price ratio, $(P_a/P_m)R$, that differs (agricultural goods are relatively more costly, or conversely, manufactured goods are relatively cheaper) from that of Developing World. Note that with a closed economy, both countries will be producing both commodities. However, Developing World, being poorer, will produce a greater proportion of food products in its (smaller) total output.

The relative difference in costs of production and prices at points A and A' (i.e., their different slopes) gives rise once again to the possibilities of profitable trade. As in the classical labor cost model, the international free-trade price ratio, $\overline{P}_a/\overline{P}_m$ will settle somewhere between $(P_a/P_m)T$ and $(P_a/P_m)R$, the domestic price ratios of Developing World and Developed World, respectively. The lines $\overline{P}_a/\overline{P}_m$ in both graphs in Figure 12.1 denote the common world price ratio. For Developing World, this steeper slope of $\overline{P}_a/\overline{P}_m$ means that it can get more manufactured goods for a unit of agriculture than in the absence of trade; that is, the world price of agricultural goods in terms of manufactures is higher than Developing World's domestic price ratio. It will therefore reallocate resources away from its costly capital-intensive manufacturing sector and specialize more on labor-intensive agricultural production. Under perfectly competitive assumptions, it will produce at point B on its production frontier, where its relative production (opportunity) costs are just equal to relative world prices. It can then trade along $\overline{P}_a/\overline{P}_m$, the prevailing international price line, exporting BD agricultural products in return for DC manufactured imports and arrive at a final consumption point C with more of *both* goods than before trade. To give a numerical example, suppose that the free-trade international price ratio, $\overline{P}_a/\overline{P}_m$, were 2 to 1. In other words, a unit of agricultural goods sells at a price twice that of a unit of manufactured goods. This means that for every unit of agriculture that Developing World exports to Developed World, it can import two units of manufactured goods. The slope of the international price line graphically portrays this trading ratio, these terms of trade. If Developing World exports BD agriculture (say, 30 units), it will receive DC manufactures (60 units) in return.

Similarly, for Developed World, the new international price ratio means more agricultural products in exchange for manufactured goods than at domestic prices. Graphically, the international price ratio has a lesser slope than Developed World's domestic price ratio (see Figure 12.1b). Developed World will therefore reallocate its abundant capital resources so as to produce more manufactured

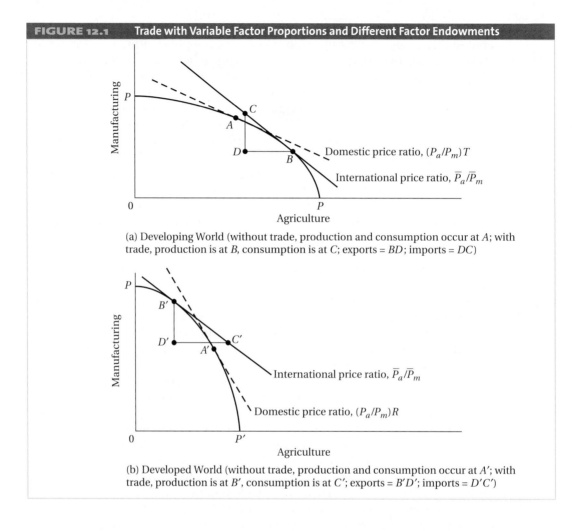

FIGURE 12.1 Trade with Variable Factor Proportions and Different Factor Endowments

(a) Developing World (without trade, production and consumption occur at A; with trade, production is at B, consumption is at C; exports $= BD$; imports $= DC$)

(b) Developed World (without trade, production and consumption occur at A'; with trade, production is at B', consumption is at C'; exports $= B'D'$; imports $= D'C'$)

goods and less agriculture, as at point B', where its relative domestic production costs are just equal to relative world prices. It can then trade $B'D'$ $(= DC)$ of these manufactures for $D'C'$ $(= BD)$ of Developing World's agricultural products. Developed World can therefore also move outside the confines of its production frontier and end up consuming at a point like C' in Figure 12.1b. Trade is balanced—the value of exports equals the value of imports for both regions. Moreover, it has resulted in increased consumption of both goods for both regions, as shown by a comparison between free-trade points C and C' and no-trade points A and A' in Figure 12.1.

The main conclusions of the neoclassical model of free trade are that all countries gain from trade and world output is increased. However, there are several others in addition to these two basic conclusions. First, due to increasing opportunity costs associated with resource shifting among commodities with different factor intensities of production, complete specialization will not occur as in the classical comparative-advantage model. Countries will tend to specialize in products that use their abundant resources intensively. They will compensate for their scarce resources by importing products that use these scarce resources most intensively. But rising domestic costs and therefore prices in excess of world prices will prevent complete specialization from occurring.

Second, given identical technologies of production throughout the world, the equalization of domestic product price ratios with the international free-trade price ratio will tend to equalize factor prices across trading countries. Wage rates, for example, will rise in labor-abundant Developing World as a result of the more intensive use of human resources in the production of additional agricultural output. But the price of scarce capital will decline due to the diminished production of manufactured goods, which are heavy users of capital. In Developed World, the price of its abundant capital will rise relative to its scarce labor as more emphasis is placed on the production of capital-intensive manufactured goods and less on labor-intensive agriculture.

The neoclassical factor endowment theory therefore makes the important prediction that international real wage rates and capital costs will gradually tend toward equalization.[10] In recent years, many highly paid manufacturing workers in the more developed countries were worried that freer trade and greater international competition would drive their wages down to LDC levels. However, the reality is that with the exception of a few Asian NICs, the wage gap between developed and less developed country workers remains as wide as ever.

Third, within countries, the factor endowment theory predicts that the economic return to owners of the abundant resources will rise in relation to owners of scarce resources as the abundant factor is more intensively used; in developing countries, this would generally mean a rise in the share of national income going to labor. In the absence of trade, labor's share might be smaller. Thus trade tends to promote more equality in domestic income distributions.

Finally, by enabling countries to move outside their production possibility frontiers and secure capital as well as consumption goods from other parts of the world, trade is assumed to stimulate economic growth. If developed countries have the comparative advantage in producing higher-skill capital goods, trade would lower the price of equipment and machinery and stimulate investment and growth for developing countries. Developing-country exporters learn from their customers in developed countries, who may also alert them to other products they might produce given their mix of skills, as the experience of Taiwan shows. Trade also enables a nation to obtain the domestically expensive raw materials and other products (as well as knowledge, ideas, new technologies, etc.) with which it is relatively less well endowed at lower world market prices. It can thus create the conditions for a more broadly based and self-sustaining growth of its industrial output.

Trade Theory and Development: The Traditional Arguments

We are now in a position to summarize the theoretical answers to our five basic questions about trade and development derived from the neoclassical free-trade model.

1. Trade is an important stimulator of economic growth. It enlarges a country's consumption capacities, increases world output, and provides access to scarce resources and worldwide markets for products without which poor countries would be unable to grow.

2. Trade tends to promote greater international and domestic equality by equalizing factor prices, raising real incomes of trading countries, and making efficient use of each nation's and the world's resource endowments (e.g., raising relative wages in labor-abundant countries and lowering them in labor-scarce countries).

3. Trade helps countries achieve development by promoting and rewarding the sectors of the economy where individual countries possess a comparative advantage, whether in terms of labor efficiency or factor endowments. It also lets them take advantage of economies of scale.

4. In a world of free trade, international prices and costs of production determine how much a country should trade in order to maximize its national welfare. Countries should follow the principle of comparative advantage and not try to interfere with the free workings of the market.

5. Finally, to promote growth and development, an outward-looking international policy is required. In all cases, self-reliance based on partial or complete isolation is asserted to be economically inferior to participation in a world of unlimited free trade.

Some Criticisms of Traditional Free-Trade Theory in the Context of Developing-Country Experience

The conclusions of traditional international trade theory are derived from a number of explicit and implicit assumptions that in many ways are often contrary to the reality of contemporary international economic relations. This theory therefore often leads to conclusions incompatible with both the historical and the contemporary trade experience of many developing nations. This is not to deny the potential benefits of a world of free trade but rather to recognize that the real world is beset by all sorts of national protection and international noncompetitive pricing policies.

What are the major and crucial assumptions of the traditional factor endowment theory of trade, and how are these assumptions violated in the real world? What are the implications for the trade and financial prospects of developing nations when a more realistic assessment of the actual mechanism of international economic and political relations is made?

Six basic assumptions of the traditional neoclassical trade model must be scrutinized:

1. All productive resources are fixed in quantity and constant in quality across nations and are fully employed.

2. The technology of production is fixed (classical model) or similar and freely available to all nations (factor endowment model). Moreover, the spread of such technology works to the benefit of all. Consumer tastes are also fixed and independent of the influence of producers (international consumer sovereignty prevails).

3. Within nations, factors of production are perfectly mobile between different production activities, and the economy as a whole is characterized by the existence of perfect competition. There are no risks or uncertainties.

4. The national government plays no role in international economic relations; trade is carried out among many atomistic and anonymous producers seeking to minimize costs and maximize profits. International prices are therefore set by the forces of supply and demand.

5. Trade is balanced for each country at any point in time, and all economies are readily able to adjust to changes in the international prices with a minimum of dislocation.

6. The gains from trade that accrue to any country benefit the nationals of that country.

We can now take a critical look at each of these assumptions in the context of the contemporary position of developing countries in the international economic system. Some of these criticisms form the rationale for other, nonneoclassical theories of trade and development, including vent-for-surplus, structuralist, and North-South models.

Fixed Resources, Full Employment, and the International Immobility of Capital and Skilled Labor

Trade and Resource Growth: North-South Models of Unequal Trade This initial assumption about the static nature of international exchange—that resources are fixed, fully utilized, and internationally immobile with same product production functions everywhere identical—is central to the traditional theory of trade and finance. In reality, the world economy is characterized by rapid change, and factors of production are fixed neither in quantity nor in quality. Critics point out that this is especially true with respect to resources most crucial to growth and development, such as physical capital, entrepreneurial abilities, scientific capacities, the ability to carry out technological research and development, and the upgrading of technical skills in the labor force.

It follows, therefore, that relative factor endowments and comparative costs are not given but are in a state of constant change. Moreover, they are often determine by, rather than themselves determine, the nature and character of international specialization. Any initial state of unequal resource endowments may be reinforced and exacerbated by the very trade that these differing resource endowments were supposed to justify. Specifically, if rich nations (the *North*) as a result of historical forces, are relatively well endowed with the vital resources of capital, entrepreneurial ability, and skilled labor, their continued specialization in products and processes that use these resources intensively can create the necessary conditions and economic incentives for their further growth. By contrast, developing-world countries (the *South*), endowed with abundant supplies of unskilled labor, by specializing in products that intensively use unskilled labor and for which world demand prospects and terms of trade may be very unfavorable, often find themselves locked into a stagnant situation that perpetuates their comparative advantage in unskilled, unproductive activities. This in turn inhibits the domestic growth of needed capital, entrepreneurship, and technical skills. Static efficiency can become dynamic inefficiency, and a cumulative process is set in motion in which trade exacerbates already unequal trading relationships, distributes the benefits largely to the people who already "have," and perpetuates the physical and human resource underdevelopment that characterizes most poor nations. As one well-known LDC scholar put it, "With few exceptions, the technological distance between the developing and the developed countries is widening. Neoclassical international trade theory, by postulating identical production functions for different products in various countries, assumes this problem away."[11]

In recent years, some economists have therefore challenged the static neoclassical model with alternative dynamic models of trade and growth that emphasize the process of factor accumulation and uneven development along the lines suggested in the preceding paragraphs. These so-called **North-South trade models** focus specifically on trade relations between rich and poor countries, whereas the traditional model was assumed to apply to all nations. The typical North-South model argues, for example, that initial higher endowments of capital in the industrialized North generate external economies in manufacturing output and higher profit rates. This, in combination with the rise in monopoly power, stimulates higher Northern growth rates (in accordance with Harrod-Domar and factor-share growth models discussed earlier) through further capital accumulation. As a result, the rapidly growing North develops a cumulative competitive advantage over the slower-growing South. If we then add differential income elasticities of demand (higher for Northern "capital goods" than for Southern "consumption goods") and capital mobility to the model (in the form of South-to-North capital flight, as occurred in the 1980s), the basis for the developing-world trade pessimism would be further enhanced.[12]

Some economies, like the Four Asian Tigers (Taiwan, South Korea, Singapore, and Hong Kong), have succeeded in transforming their economies through purposeful effort from unskilled-labor to skilled-labor to capital-intensive production. Other Asian countries, notably China, are following in their footsteps. However, for the vast majority of poor nations, the possibilities of trade itself stimulating similar structural economic changes are more remote without the application of judicious development policies.

Another interesting example of the new, postneoclassical genre of international trade models is contained in Michael Porter's *Competitive Advantage of Nations*.[13] Porter's fundamental departure from the standard, neoclassical factor endowment theory is to posit a *qualitative* difference between basic factors and advanced factors of production. He argues that standard trade theory applies only to basic factors like undeveloped physical resources and unskilled labor. For the advanced factors, which are more specialized and include highly trained workers with specific skills, and knowledge resources such as government and private research institutes, major universities, and leading industry associations, standard theory does not apply. Porter concludes that

> the central task facing developing countries is to escape from the straitjacket of factor-driven national advantage . . . where natural resources, cheap labor, locational factors and other basic factor advantages provide a fragile and often fleeting ability to export . . . [and are] vulnerable to exchange rate and factor cost swings. Many of these industries are also not growing, as the resource intensity of advanced economies falls and demand becomes more sophisticated. . . . Creation of advanced factors is perhaps the first priority.[14]

Unemployment, Resource Underutilization, and the Vent-for-Surplus Theory of International Trade The assumption of full employment in traditional trade models, like that of the standard perfectly competitive equilibrium model of microeconomic theory, violates the reality of unemployment and underemployment in developing nations. Two conclusions could be drawn from the recognition of widespread unemployment in the developing world. The first is that underutilized human resources create the opportunity to expand productive capacity and GNP at little or no real cost by producing for export markets products that are not demanded locally. This is known as the **vent-for-surplus theory of international trade**. First formulated by Adam Smith, it has been expounded more recently in the context of developing nations by the Burmese economist Hla Myint.

According to this theory, the opening of world markets to remote agrarian societies creates opportunities not to reallocate fully employed resources as in the traditional models but rather to make use of formerly *underemployed* land and labor resources to produce greater output for export to foreign markets. The colonial system of plantation agriculture as well as the commercialization of small-scale subsistence agriculture were made possible, according to this view, by the availability of unemployed and underemployed human resources. In terms of our production possibility analyses, the vent-for-surplus argument can be represented by a shift in production from point V to point B in Figure 12.2, with trade enlarging final domestic consumption from V to C.

We see that before trade, the resources of this closed developing-world economy were grossly underutilized. Production was occurring at point V, well within the confines of the production possibility frontier, and $0X$ primary products and $0Y$ manufactures were being produced and consumed. The opening up of the nation to foreign markets (probably as a result of colonization) provides the economic impetus to utilize these idle resources (mostly excess land and labor) and expand primary-product exportable production from $0X$ to $0X'$ at point B on the production frontier. Given the international price ratio P_a/P_m, $X' - X$ (equal to VB) primary products can now be exported in exchange for $Y' - Y$ (equal to VC) manufactures, with the result that the final consumption point, C, is attained with the same primary products (X) being consumed as before but with $Y' - Y$ more imported manufactures now available.

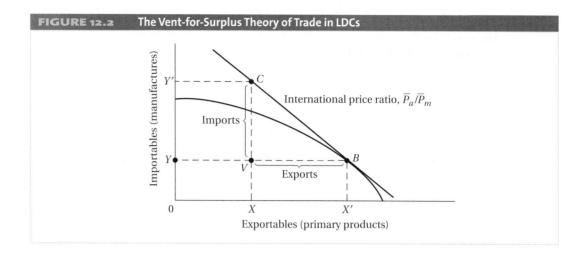

FIGURE 12.2 The Vent-for-Surplus Theory of Trade in LDCs

The vent-for-surplus argument does provide a more realistic analytical scenario of the historical trading experience of many LDCs than either the classical or the neoclassical model. However, in the short run, the beneficiaries of this process were often colonial and expatriate entrepreneurs rather than LDC nationals. And in the long run, the structural orientation of the LDC economy toward primary-product exports in many cases created an export "enclave" and inhibited needed structural transformation in the direction of a more diversified economy.

Fixed, Freely Available Technology and Consumer Sovereignty

Just as capital resources are rapidly growing and being dispersed to maximize the returns of their owners throughout the world, rapid technological change is profoundly affecting world trading relationships. One of the most obvious examples of the impact of developed-country technological change on developing-country export earnings is the development of synthetic substitutes for many traditional primary products. Over the past four or five decades, **synthetic substitutes** for such diverse commodities as rubber, wool, cotton, sisal, jute, hides, and skins have been manufactured in increasing quantities. The developing world's market shares of these natural products in all cases has fallen steadily. For example, between 1950 and 1980, the share of the natural rubber in total world rubber consumption fell from 62% to 28%, and cotton's share of total fiber consumption dropped from 41% to 29%. Technological substitution, together with the low income and price elasticities of demand for primary products and the rise of agricultural protection in the markets of developed nations, must be accounted for in a trade and industrialization strategy.

On the other side of the ledger, however, is the argument that the worldwide availability of new technologies developed in the West has given many newly industrializing countries the opportunity to capitalize on Western research and development expenditures. By first imitating products developed abroad but not on the frontiers of technological research, certain LDCs with sufficient human capital (e.g., the Asian NICs) can follow the **product cycle** of international trade. Using their relatively lower wages, they move from low-tech to high-tech production, filling manufacturing gaps left vacant by the more industrialized nations. Eventually, the hope is to catch up with the developed countries, as in the case of Japan.

The assumption of fixed worldwide consumer tastes and preferences dictating production patterns to market-responsive atomistic producers is unrealistic. Not only are the capital and production technologies disseminated throughout the world by means of the multinational corporations often aided by their home governments, but consumer preferences and tastes are often created and reinforced by the advertising campaigns of the powerful financial giants that dominate local markets. By creating demands for imported goods, market-dominating international enterprises can create the conditions for increased profitability. This is particularly significant in LDCs, where limited and imperfect information in both production and consumption creates a situation of highly incomplete markets. For example, it has been estimated that in many developing nations, more than 90% of all advertising is financed by foreign firms selling in the local market.

Internal Factor Mobility and Perfect Competition: Increasing Returns, Imperfect Competition, and Controlled Markets

The traditional theory of trade assumes that nations are readily able to adjust their economic structures to the changing dictates of world prices and markets. Movements along production possibility frontiers involving the reallocation of resources from one industry to another may be easy to make on paper, but according to structuralist arguments, such reallocations are extremely difficult to achieve in practice. This is especially true in developing nations, where production structures are often rigid and factor movements are largely restricted. The most obvious example of this is plantation and small-farm commercial agriculture. In economies that have gradually become heavily dependent on a few primary-product exports, the whole economic and social infrastructure (roads, railways, communications, power locations, credit and marketing arrangements, etc.) may be geared to facilitate the movement of goods from production locations to shipping and storage depots for transfer to foreign markets. Over time, cumulative investments of capital may have been sunk into these economic and infrastructure facilities, and they cannot easily be transferred to manufacturing activities located elsewhere. Thus the more dependent nations become on a few primary-product exports, the more inflexible their economic structures become, and the more vulnerable they are to the unpredictabilities of international markets. It may take many years to transform an underdeveloped economy from an almost exclusively primary-product, export-oriented reliance to a more diversified, multisector structure. In other words, history matters.

More generally, structuralists argue that all kinds of politically and institutionally generated structural rigidities, including product supply inelasticities, lack of intermediate products, fragmented money markets, limited foreign exchange, government licensing, import controls, poor transport and distribution facilities, and scarcities of managerial and skilled labor, often inhibit an LDC's ability to respond in the smooth and frictionless way of the neoclassical trade model to changing international price signals.[15]

Thus the internal processes of adjustment and resource reallocation necessary to capitalize on changing world economic conditions are much more difficult for the less diversified developing economies to realize than for their rich counterparts in the northern hemisphere. And yet, curiously enough, the LDCs that can expand their capacities to produce low-cost, labor-intensive manufactured goods for export in industries such as textiles, shoes, sporting goods, handbags, processed foodstuffs, wigs, and rugs often find these exports blocked by tariff and nontariff barriers erected by developed countries to restrict the entry of such low-cost goods into their home markets. The United Nations estimated in 2001 that such trade restrictions cost the LDCs at least $100 billion annually—2% of their GDP. The reasons usually given by the North are that this low-cost foreign competition will create unemployment among the higher-cost domestic industries of the developed country and that the problems of internal economic adjustment are too serious to permit such unfettered foreign competition!

Moreover, by assuming either fixed or diminishing **returns to scale** (fixed or increasing production costs as output is expanded), the labor cost and factor endowment theories of trade neglect one of the most important phenomena in international economic relations. This is the pervasive and income-widening effect of increasing returns to scale and hence decreasing costs of production. Decreasing production costs mean simply that large existing firms are able to underprice smaller or new firms and thus exert monopolistic control over world markets. Far from being a rare exception, economies of scale are a common factor in determining trade patterns. Economies of large-scale production lead to monopolistic and oligopolistic control of world supply conditions (just as they do in domestic markets) for a wide range of products.

In addition, **monopolistic** and **oligopolistic market control** of internationally traded commodities, along with widespread product differentiation, intraindustry trade, and external economies of production, means that large individual corporations are able to manipulate world prices and supplies (and often demands as well) in their own private interest. Instead of competition, we find joint producer activities and oliogopolistic bargaining among giant buyers and sellers as the most pervasive price-and quantity-determining force in the international economy.[16] But from the perspective of developing nations trying to diversify their economies and promote industrial exports in particular, the phenomenon of **increasing returns** and **product differentiation** (monopolistic competition), combined with the noneconomic power of large multinational corporations (their political influence with many governments—see Chapter 15), means that the first nations to industrialize (the rich nations) are able to take advantage of these economies of scale and differentiated products to perpetuate their dominant position in world markets.[17]

The second major limitation of the perfectly competitive assumption of trade models is its exclusion of **risk** and **uncertainty** in international trading arrangements. It may not be in the LCDs' long-run interest to invest heavily in primary-product export promotion, given the historical instability of world markets for primary commodities in comparison to those for manufactured goods. As was already pointed out, concentration on one or two vital primary exports can play havoc with LDC development plans when foreign-exchange earnings are largely unpredictable from one year to the next.

The Absence of National Governments in Trading Relations

In domestic economies, the coexistence of rich and poor regions, of rapidly growing and stagnating industries, and of the persistent disproportionate regional distribution of the benefits of economic growth can all, at least in theory, be counteracted and ameliorated by the intervention of the state. Cumulative processes for inequality within nation-states by which **growth poles** may grow rapidly while other regions stagnate can be modified by government through legislation, taxes, transfer payments, subsidies, social services, regional development programs, and so forth. But since there is no effective international government to play a comparable role across countries, the highly uneven gains from trade can easily become self-sustaining. This result is then reinforced by the uneven power of national governments to promote and protect the interests of their own countries. The spectacular export successes of South Korea and Taiwan, and, more recently, China, were in no small way aided and abetted by government promotion of export industries.[18]

Governments are often partisan players whose activist interventions in this area of **industrial policy** (guiding the market through strategic coordination of business investments to increase export market shares) are specifically designed to create a comparative advantage where none existed before but where world demand is likely to rise in the future. The history of industrial growth in Japan in the 1950s and 1960s with its famous Ministry of International Trade and Industry (MITI) and more recently in Taiwan and South Korea are widely cited examples of industrial policies.[19] This approach to industrialization strategy is examined in the next chapter.

Governments may also employ various instruments of commercial policy, such as **tariffs**, import **quotas**, and export **subsidies**, and can manipulate commodity prices and thus their trade position vis-à-vis the rest of the world. Moreover, when developed-nation governments pursue restrictive economic policies designed to deal with purely domestic issues like inflation or unemployment, these policies can have profound negative effects on the economies of poor nations.

The reverse, however, is not true. LDC domestic economic policies generally have little impact on the economies of rich nations. Moreover, governments of developed countries often join to promote their shared interests through coordinated trade and other economic ventures. Though these governments may not intend for such activities to promote their own welfare at the expense of that of poor countries, this is often the result.

Governments often serve to reinforce the unequal distribution of resources and **gains from trade** resulting from differences in size and economic power. Rich-country governments can influence world economic affairs by their domestic and international policies. They can resist countervailing economic pressures from weaker nations and can act in **collusion** and often in conjunction with their powerful multinational corporations to manipulate the terms and conditions of international trade to their own national interests. Despite the growing role of the World Trade Organization, there is no superagency or world government to protect and promote the interests of the weaker parties (the LDCs) in such international affairs. A trade and industrialization strategy must therefore take into account the powerful governmental forces of the developed world.

Balanced Trade and International Price Adjustments

The theory of international trade, like other perfectly competitive general-equilibrium models in economics, is not only a full-employment model but also one in which flexible domestic and international product and resource prices always adjust instantaneously to conditions of supply and demand. In particular, the terms of trade (international commodity price ratios) adjust to equate supply and demand for a country's exportable and importable products so that trade is always balanced; that is, the value of exports (quantity times price) is always equal to the value of imports. With **balanced trade** and no international capital movements, balance of payments problems never arise in the pure theory of trade. But the realities of the world economy, especially in the period following the rapid increase in international oil prices in the 1970s, were such that balance of payments deficits and the consequent depletion of foreign reserves (or the need to borrow foreign funds to cover commodity deficits) were a major cause of concern for all nations, rich and poor.

For the non-oil-producing poor nations in particular, a combination of declining terms of trade and sluggish international demands for their export products has meant chronic merchandise **trade deficits**. The gradual drying up of bilateral and multilateral foreign assistance and the growing concern of LDCs with the social costs of private foreign investment (see Chapter 15) have meant that severe balance of payments problems necessitate further departures from relatively free trade.

Trade Gains Accruing to Nationals

The sixth and final major assumption of traditional trade theory, that trade gains accrue to nationals in the trading countries, is more implicit than the other five. It is rarely spelled out, nor need it be if we accept the assumption that factors are internationally immobile. But we need to examine the implicit notion that if developing countries benefit from trade, it is the people of these countries who reap the benefits. The issue thus revolves around the question of who owns the land, capital, and skills that are rewarded as a result of trade. Are they nationals or foreigners? If both, in what proportions are the gains distributed?

We know, for example, that in the **enclave economies** in developing countries, such as those with substantial foreign-owned mining and plantation operations, foreigners often pay very low rents for the rights to use land, bring in their own foreign capital and skilled labor, hire local unskilled workers at subsistence wages, and have a minimal effect on the rest of the economy even though they may generate significant export revenues. Although mining and plantation enclaves are gradually disappearing, they are often being replaced by "manufacturing export enclaves" (personal computer assembly, shoe and toy manufacture, etc.) as a result of the economic penetrations of multinational corporations. The distinction, therefore, between gross domestic product (GDP), which is a measure of the value of output generated within defined geographic boundaries, and gross national income (GNI), which measures the income actually earned by nationals of that country, becomes extremely important. To the extent that the export sector, or for that matter any sector of the economy, is foreign-owned and -operated, GDP will be that much higher than GNI, and few of the benefits of trade will actually accrue to LDC nationals.

With the proliferation of multinational corporations and increasing foreign ownership of companies in a wide range of countries, aggregate statistics for LDC export earnings (and, indeed, GDP) may mask the fact that LDC nationals, especially those in lower income brackets, may not benefit at all from these exports. The major gains from trade may instead accrue to nonnationals, who often repatriate large proportions of these earnings. The inter- and intraindustry trade that is being carried out may look like trade between rich and poor nations. But in reality such trade is being conducted between rich nations and *other nationals of rich nations* operating in developing countries! Until recently, the activities of most mining and plantation operations had this characteristic. Manufactures exports are generally more effective at generating modern sector enlargement but some of the recent export enclave manufacturing activities in poor countries may merely be masking the fact that a large proportion of the benefits are still being reaped by foreign enterprises. In short, LDC export performances can be deceptive unless we analyze the character and structure of export earnings by ascertaining who owns or controls the factors of production that are rewarded as a result of export expansion.

Some Conclusions on Trade Theory and Economic Development Strategy

We can now attempt to provide some preliminary general answers to the five questions posed early in the chapter. Again, we must stress that our conclusions are general and set in the context of the diversity of developing countries. Many will not be valid for specific nations at any given point in time. But on the whole, these conclusions do appear to represent the consensus of current economic thinking, especially from developing-country economists, on the relationship between trade and development, as the latter term has been defined throughout this book.

First, with regard to the rate, structure, and character of economic growth, our conclusion is that trade can be an important stimulus to rapid economic growth. This has been amply demonstrated by the successful experiences of countries like China, Malaysia, Thailand, Brazil, Chile, Taiwan, Singapore, and South Korea. Access to the markets of developed nations (an important factor for developing nations bent on export promotion) can provide an important stimulus for the greater utilization of idle human and capital resources. Expanded **foreign-exchange earnings** through improved export performance also provide the wherewithal by which LDCs can augment their scarce physical and financial resources. In short, where opportunities for profitable exchange arise, foreign trade can provide an important stimulus to aggregate economic growth.[20]

But as we have seen in earlier chapters, rapid growth of national output may have little impact on development. An export-oriented strategy of growth, particularly when a large proportion of export earnings accrue to foreigners, may not only bias the structure of the economy in the wrong directions (by not catering to the real needs of local people) but also reinforce the internal and external dualistic and inegalitarian character of that growth. Therefore, the fact that free trade may promote expanded export earnings and even increase output levels does not mean that it is an unambiguously desirable strategy for economic and social development. It all depends on the nature of the export sector, the distribution of its benefits, and its linkages with the rest of the economy.

As for the distributional effects of trade, it is fair to claim that the principal benefits of world trade have accrued disproportionately to rich nations and, within poor nations, disproportionately to foreign residents and wealthy nationals. Factors such as the widespread existence of increasing returns, the highly unequal international distribution of economic assets and power, the growing influence of large multinational corporations, and the combined ability of both governments and businesses to manipulate international prices, levels of production, and patterns of demand are crucial. Together, they lead us to the general conclusion that many developing countries have in the past benefited disproportionately less from their economic dealings with developed nations.

It should be apparent by now that the answer to the third question—the question of the conditions under which trade can help LDCs achieve their development aspirations—is to be found largely in the ability of developing nations (probably as a group) to extract favorable trade concessions from the developed nations, especially in the form of the latter's elimination of barriers to LDC exports of labor-intensive manufactured goods. Here the Uruguay Round of the General Agreement on Tariffs and Trade (GATT) negotiations lowering worldwide tariff barriers and the later creation of the World Trade Organization provided a helpful but incomplete start (see Chapter 13). Also, the extent to which LDC exports can efficiently utilize scarce capital resources while making maximum use of abundant but presently underutilized labor supplies will determine the degree to which export earnings benefit the ordinary citizen. Links between export earnings and other sectors of the economy are crucial. For example, small-farm agricultural export earnings will expand the demand for domestically produced simple household goods, whereas export earnings from capital-intensive manufacturing industries are more likely to find their way back to rich nations in payment for luxury imports. Finally, much will depend on how well LDCs can influence and control the activities of private foreign enterprises. These nations' ability to deal effectively with multinational corporations in guaranteeing a fair share of the benefits to local citizens is extremely important.

The answer to the fourth question—whether LDCs can determine how much they trade—can only be speculative. For small and poor countries, the option of not trading at all, by closing their borders to the rest of the world, is obviously not realistic. Not only do they lack the resources and market size to be self-sufficient, but their very survival, especially in the area of food production, often depends on their ability to secure foreign goods and resources. Some 32 of the least developed countries face annual threats of severe famine for which international assistance is not a choice but a necessity. Whether to trade or to remain in isolation is not the major issue that developing countries face. All countries trade. As Graciella Chichilnisky and Geoffrey Heal note, the real issue is

> whether or not to expand exports, and if so which exports to promote. The question is often the right balance between the domestic sectors and the international sectors of the economy. . . . The neoclassical theory of gains from trade provides little guidance on such policy questions.[21]

These and other issues of trade policy are discussed in Chapter 13.

And even for the bulk of developing nations, the international economic system still offers the only real source of scarce capital and needed technological knowledge. The conditions under which such resources are obtained will greatly influence the character of the development process. As we show in Chapter 13, the long-run benefits from trade among developing countries themselves through the creation of **regional trading blocs** similar to the original Common Market or the European Union may offer prospects for a balanced and diversified development strategy. Finally, for the few countries rich in mineral resources and raw materials, especially those that have been able to establish an effective international bargaining stance against the large corporations that purchase their exports (e.g., the members of OPEC), trade has been and continues to be a vital source of development finance.

The fifth question—whether on balance it is better for developing countries to look outward toward the rest of the world or more inward toward their own capacities for development—turns out not to be an either-or question at all. It is possible to favor both genuinely free world trade among individual countries and mutual cooperation among groups of LDCs, in the form of greater **collective self-reliance**.[22] While exploring profitable opportunities for trade with the rest of the world, developing countries should seek ways to expand their share of world trade *and* extend their economic ties with one another. For example, by pooling their resources, small countries can overcome the limits of their small individual markets and their serious resource constraints while retaining an important degree of autonomy in pursuing their individual development aspirations. In this way, groups of small countries may have a better chance of achieving what China has been able to do in recent years: leveraging the bargaining power of its large market to insist on the best deal from potential foreign exporters and investors. Indeed, this strategy has likely been one of the factors helping China realize very high growth rates over the past quarter century.

Although the preceding argument is often overstated, it seems clear that if interregional political rivalries can be transcended, increased regional cooperation among developing nations at roughly equal stages of development offers an important component of a trade and industrialization strategy. In fact, the share of

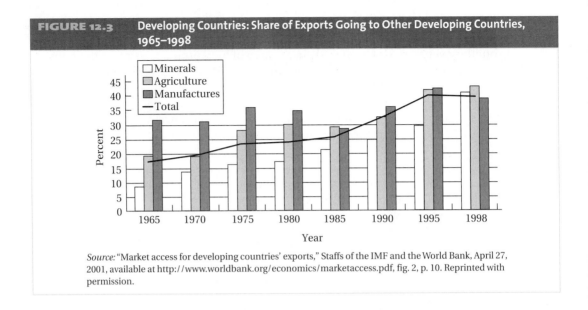

FIGURE 12.3 **Developing Countries: Share of Exports Going to Other Developing Countries, 1965–1998**

Source: "Market access for developing countries' exports," Staffs of the IMF and the World Bank, April 27, 2001, available at http://www.worldbank.org/economics/marketaccess.pdf, fig. 2, p. 10. Reprinted with permission.

developing-country exports going to other developing countries has increased dramatically since the 1960s, from about 17% to nearly 40%, as seen in Figure 12.3. Explicit developing-country policies including free-trade areas such as ASEAN in Southeast Asia and Mercosur in South America are at least partly responsible for this trend. Of course, the trend also reflects the development successes of LDCs in Asia, whose economies have been growing faster than those in North America and Europe throughout this period. Unfortunately, once again Africa has been left out of the game. Concerted development assistance is needed to help this important region reach the stage at which it can begin to benefit more actively from international trade.

We turn now to consider the advantages and disadvantages of alternative trade policies for developing countries in more detail.

Taiwan: A Development Success Story

Taiwan is one of the four East Asian "tiger economies" whose dramatic economic successes of recent decades have influenced the way economists think about development (the other three are South Korea, Singapore, and Hong Kong). The experience of Taiwan was a major impetus behind the changes in economic policy instituted in the People's Republic of China (PRC) beginning in 1978. With a population of about 22 million, Taiwan is a mountainous, 14,000-square-mile island off the coast of the Chinese mainland, about the size of Massachusetts, Connecticut, and Rhode Island combined.

Taiwan's claim to its status as a "development miracle" is as strong as that of any other economy in the world. The island racked up a measured annual economic growth rate averaging about 7% over the four decades from 1960 to 2000. Taiwan's economy grew nearly 10% annually in the 1965–1980 period, faster than any other economy's. Despite its now high-income status, with a per capita income of $13,925 in 2000 at market exchange rates ($22,646 in 2000 at PPP), Taiwan continued to grow, at a rapid rate of 5.7% on average over the 1996–2000 period. Sustaining such high rates over such a long stretch of time is unprecedented. At least as important, Taiwan has achieved universal elementary and middle school education (nine years are mandatory), a healthy population with a life expectancy of 75 years, and an infant mortality rate of only 5 per 1,000 live births. Absolute poverty has essentially been eliminated, unemployment is extremely low, and relative inequality is modest even by developed-country standards.

Taiwan has had to adjust to some of the changes that economies that reach the threshold of high-income status must confront. There has been "hollowing out" of basic manufacturing as plants have moved to mainland China in search of lower-wage labor. Production that has remained has been forced to shift rapidly to high-tech products and processes in the face of rising competition in basic industries from other developing countries. Continued uncertainty clouds the island's political future, given saber-rattling from the PRC, which continues to regard Taiwan as a renegade province, but so far the society has adapted. It has also transformed itself into a credibly and competitively democratic polity with far less corruption and more government transparency than its neighbors.

Taiwan's achievement stands in dramatic contrast to many other economies that started in similar—or even better—circumstances in the postwar world. How did the Taiwanese people do it?

Competing Explanations for Success

Taiwan's success has been ascribed to many factors, including an emphasis on education, extensive infrastructure development, early and thorough land reform, very high rates of saving and investment, a mixture of constructive foreign influences and diffusion of commercial ideas from Japan and the United States, an effective government industrialization strategy, the free market's release of human energies and creativity, the 1960s boom resulting from the Vietnam War, the initiation of an export-led growth strategy in the midst of the rapidly expanding world economy of the early 1960s, direct American aid—and Taiwan's use of that aid for investment rather than consumption, the work ethic and productive attitudes of the Taiwanese labor force, a long history as an entrepreneurial culture, the movement into entrepreneurship of capable local islanders who sought opportunities for advancement but were blocked from the political arena, and the survival instinct—the necessity of economic development as a defense against attack from the mainland People's Republic of China.

Instead of having to choose from just one or two of these factors, an alternative interpretation is that development success requires many things to work well together, and hence there may not be so many explanations after all. Many of the cited factors may reflect necessary but not sufficient conditions. In this view, the key is to understand the magnified impact of having many development factors operating successfully at the same time (see Chapter 4).

Let's examine the factors cited more closely.

Emphasis on education. Consistent with the historical Chinese cultural veneration for education, six years of education became compulsory on Taiwan in 1950. Especially impressive were enrollment rates for girls, which surpassed 90% for those aged 6 to 11 by 1956. (The comparable figure for boys in that year was over 96%.) Emphasis on girls' education is widely viewed as one of the most important factors in successful development.

When compulsory education was expanded to nine years in 1968, there were doubts that the economy could afford it. Today, while nine years remains a remarkable minimum educational standard for any developing economy, plans are being considered to expand compulsory schooling to 12 years.

Other features have also been in play. Students go to school seven hours a day, five and one-half days a week. In 2002, the overall student-teacher ratio was less than 20. Teacher salaries are relatively high, comparable to lower-middle management in Taiwan. The United States was Taiwan's model for general education and Japan for vocational education. Greater emphasis is placed on general than on job-specific skills. But incentives for close relationships between education and business are also stressed. Tax breaks are given for company donations of personnel and equipment to schools.

Assuming that the world development community is serious in its millennium development goal of enrolling all children in six years of elementary school by 2015, the early experience of Taiwan is instructive. Enrollment was real and not just on paper, students generally remained in school after they enrolled, teachers taught seriously, and corruption was kept to a minimum. The contrast in most of these respects to today's low-income countries is striking.

Extensive infrastructure development. Developement of infrastructure has been widely cited as a crucial factor in successful development. A major highway, for example, is argued to represent a "growth pole" around which industrial and commerical development can consolidate and grow. From the period of Japanese colonial rule (1905–1945), Taiwan inherited an infrastructure system that was far superior to that of most poor countries. The Japanese built roads, ports, and railroads to facilitate their own acquisition of rice and other farm products from the island. But this same infrastructure became a vehicle for national industrial growth from the 1950s. This endowment was supplemented by the government's own extensive program in the 1950s and 1960s. Taiwan's army was too large for the island, a legacy of the pre-1949 control of the mainland by the governing Kuomintang, or Chinese Nationalists. Thousands of soldiers participated in a voluntary program to retire from active military service to build infrastructure, including the technically challenging east-west highway projects, a program reckoned in Taiwan to be a major factor in its subsequent success. In more recent years, the emphasis has moved to telecoms and other high-tech infrastructure.

There was some waste, fraud, and abuse in infrastructure spending, though apparently less than average. When the press was freed, a number of infrastructure scandals were uncovered, many affecting Taiwan's capital, Taipei. The political openings have played a role in keeping infrastructure development and other development necessities on track, another reflection of the interactive roles played by several contributory factors in economic growth.

Early and thorough land reform. Not burdened by close political ties to landlords, the Taiwan government implemented a thoroughgoing land-to-the-tiller reform program in the 1950s. Landowners received stock in state-owned enterprises in return for transferring land to peasants. This was a major factor in the extremely rapid growth of agricultural productivity in this period—a crucial foundation for later industrialization. Other countries with similar land reform efforts, such as South Korea and Japan, have seen impressive results. The United States had similary benefited from nineteenth-century programs such as the Homestead Act. In contrast, development in Latin America, as well as in some neighboring countries, such as the Philippines, has been severely hampered by the lack of land reform.

Very high rates of saving and investment. Most analysts agree that capital formation is crucial to successful development. Developed countries have much higher levels of capital per head than less developed countries, one of the factors enabling developed countries to enjoy higher productivity and incomes. Taiwan's saving rates were among the hightest ever recorded, reaching 30% to 40% in the 1950s and 1960s.

The saving ethic is deeply rooted in Taiwanese culture. Parents teach children the overriding need to save for a rainy day. Public policies keep real interest rates for savers relatively high and tax-free. Interestingly, like fellow tiger South Korea, Taiwan has a relatively low foreign-capital share in total investment, about 10%. High rates of saving and investment are important factors in development, but not sufficient ones. India has substantially increased its rate of investment since independence in 1947 but not until recently its growth rate, partly because capital equipment has been expensive there and partly because investments have not been made in the most productive sectors at any point in time.

Diffusion of commercial ideas. High saving alone will not create a development miracle without productive ideas among entrepreneurs about what use to make of it. Taiwan has had considerable success at absorbing commercial ideas from Japan and the United States, largely due to the diligence of thousands of individual small companies. But government has also played a role, through agencies like the China External Trade Development Council (CETDC) that combed the world, especially the United States, for ideas on how Taiwanese firms could upgrade their technology and adapt to enter industrial markets. The World Bank's Donald Keesing has offered some fascinating insights into the CETDC's operation:

> Market research in CETDC's New York office as of 1980 was based on an active search for items that could be sold in the United States. The search began with an analysis of the size and origin of U.S. imports, followed by a preliminary study of the price and quality of the more competitive imported and U.S. products. From this the officers in New York reached an estimate of the likelihood of Taiwan, China, firms competing successfully against offerings already on the market. (They claimed to understand the manufacturing capabilities of Taiwan, China, firms well enough to do this.) Once a likely product was identified, the office asked firms in Taiwan, China, to send it samples of the product and price lists. Representatives of the office would then visit importers, wholesalers, and other traders with samples and price lists, prospecting for sales. They would try to get reactions to the product. If the buyers were interested, they would telex the manufacturers. If not, they would find out why and then suggest appropriate steps to the manufacturer.

These observations lead us to perhaps the most complex set of development issues, the roles of state and market in successful development.

Effective government industrial policies. A traditional explanation for Taiwan's success is the operation of the free market. In contrast, Robert Wade and others have shown that Taiwan employed extensive government industrial policies and have presented somewhat controversial evidence that Taiwan's success is due in large measure to the effectiveness of industrial policy.

Taiwan has had active industrial policy systems in place to license exports, control direct foreign investment both in and from Taiwan, establish export cartels, and provide fiscal incentives for investment in priority sectors and concessional credit for favored industries. The government plays a much less active role today, now that developed-country status has been nearly attained, but it is interesting to view the roles played in Taiwan's more formative development stages.

Taiwan's economic history began with a very highly *dirigiste*, or state-directed, import substitution–oriented industrialization in the 1949–1958 period. Reforms in 1958 switched intervention to export promotion and introduced market forces. But what emerged was not a free market but merely a less thoroughly planned economy. Into the 1980s, all imports and exports in Taiwan had to be covered by a license. Imports were categorized as "prohibited," "controlled," and "permissible." Controlled goods included luxuries and some goods produced locally with reasonable quality, in sufficient quantities, and whose prices are not more than a narrow margin (about 5%) above comparable import prices. Because the controlled list was larger than the published one, not all "permissibles" were automatically approved. As Wade shows, a potential importer of an item on the hidden list had to provide evidence that domestic suppliers could not meet foreign price, quality, and timing-of-delivery terms. Wade presents evidence that their function was to jump-start growth industries by providing domestic demand for products targeted by the government. Then aggressive incentives were provided to induce companies to begin to export these products.

Wade's interpretation of the relative success of this import substitution program is consistent with an emphasis on market incentives. He argues that because it controls quantities of foreign goods entering the local economy, the government can use international prices to discipline the price-setting behavior of protected domestic producers. The government demanded to know good reasons why domestic prices of protected items were significantly higher than international prices, especially in the case of inputs to be used for export production. In this way, domestic prices for controlled goods could be kept near world price levels through the threat of permitting imports, even without free trade of goods across national borders. Wade concluded that an effective government threat of allowing more goods in can itself be sufficient to hold prices down, despite trade protection. Thus the argument is that government is able to play an active role in industrial policy without compromising the vitality of market incentives.

Clearly, Taiwan's economy has been far from a free market, but explanations for Taiwan's success other than its actively interventionist policies can be given. In particular, general policies such as support of basic education and encouragement of high rates of saving cannot be ruled out as more important factors in Taiwan's success. Many small entrepreneurs in Taiwan seemed to feel that government has done more to harass them than to help them. And the stable, consistent macroeconomic policies in Taiwan and elsewhere in East Asia also stand in dramatic contrast to much of the rest of the developing world, especially the poorest-performing regions.

Market incentives.   Even if entrepreneurial dynamism is hard to measure precisely, it is in evidence throughout the island. Incentives to produce wealth rather than merely to seek a share of existing wealth (rent-seeking behavior) are established with solid property rights and not significantly undermined by other policies.

Taiwan's government has not always been a highly efficient engine of progress. The mere fact that the Republic of China (ROC) administers both a central and a provincial government covering exactly the same territory has presented many opportunities for inefficiency. This is a legacy of the Chinese civil war, which the ROC lost. Morever, until 1991, the government ruled Taiwan under martial law, creating opportunities for corruption. Indeed, in the 1990s, new corruption scandals were reported almost daily in Taiwan's many independent newspapers. The free election of Lee Teng-hui as president in 1996 was the culmination of a smooth five-year transition to democratic governance. Elections have been highly competitive since then and are generally viewed as having been free and fair.

Other factors.   The other explanations listed earlier were also somewhat important but unlikely to have been critical given the decisive role of the seven factors just discussed. They are also special features that other economies cannot easily encourage through policy measures. The 1960s Vietnam War boom affected countries such as the Philippines as much, if not more, than Taiwan, without lasting effect. American aid to Egypt has been far larger and substantially used for investment purposes but with less impressive results. Undoubtedly, the work ethic and attitudes of the labor force were important. At the same time, they could not be called into play without the right incentives being in place and without the availability of economically productive ideas. And a work ethic can be stimulated by the right incentives. A long history as an entrepreneurial culture may also be important, but in the long run these will similarly be influenced by incentives for entrepreneurship.

The fact that Taiwan benefited from beginning export-led growth in the early 1960s, a time of unequaled world growth and a wide-open American market, was an undoubted advantage. On the other hand, other countries such as Thailand successfully grew through manufactures exports in the 1980s, despite far slower U.S. and world income and trade growth rates. The People's Republic has grown faster over the past quarter century than Taiwan ever did, despite sometimes sluggish world trade growth. Many of the PRC's reform policies since 1978 have been copied from the experience of Taiwan.

The idea that local islanders had few opportunities outside of entrepreneurship has not been proved; in any case, Taiwan seems hardly to differ in this regard from the situation under many other authoritarian regimes around the developing world that have suffered negative per capita income growth.

As to the necessity of economic development as a defense strategy, one can hardly single out Taiwan. The United States guaranteed Taiwan's defense after President Truman sealed off the island in 1950 in response to the Korean crisis. Other developing countries lacking the natural defenses of an island and as gravely threatened by hostile neighbors have made little development progress in the same period. Military necessity more often represents a diversion of resources needed for development than a productive stimulus.

Conclusion

A combination of factors underlies Taiwan's success. Among them are an emphasis on education, absorption of productive ideas from abroad, extensive infrastructure development, a thoroughgoing land reform, very high rates of saving and investment, an effective industrial policy, and last but not least, ensuring that marketplace incentives to produce wealth rather than to seek a share of existing wealth are established with solid property rights and not undermined by other policies.

Recently, the government of Taiwan had focused on collaborating with the private sector on more advanced research and development as Taiwan moves into high-technology fields. Taiwan's dynamic firms have invested vast sums in the PRC. Taiwan has been striving to adapt to a future in which rela-

tively unskilled industrial jobs will no longer be available. The focus has been on education; high-technology production in several sectors including computers, software, and biotechnology; and financial development. The focus continues to be on development through increasingly sophisticated exports. As Erik Thorbecke and Henry Wan point out, Taiwan launched its competitive semiconductor industry by using government laboratories to develop basic know-how and then formed private spin-off companies from these laboratories. And as noted by Thorbecke, Tung, and Wan, the government has also provided indirect but effective incentives to local firms that are providing key inputs to high-tech exporters and achieved success notably in the synthetic fiber and semiconductor industries. Thus continued development of government competence and effectiveness in industrialization strategy may be critical as a developing economy approaches developed-country status.

The fact that Taiwan weathered the enormous storms of the East Asian financial crisis in 1997–1998 strongly signaled the economy's development and resilience. The biggest problems looming for Taiwan are the resolution of the conflict with the PRC and the wholesale moves of Taiwan's industrial base to that country. The two issues are interrelated, most notably because greater interdependence between these economies is likely to raise the costs of war.

Are there any drawbacks to Taiwan's growth? Certainly environmental considerations have taken a backseat to economic growth until very recently. Taipei suffers from exceedingly noxious air pollution, for example. Despite a nominal beginning at land use planning, a drive down the island's west coast reveals a dizzying jumble of agricultural, industrial, commercial, and residential uses, defying any economic rationale, let alone aesthetics. Industrial sites sit perched on landfill over rice paddies and prawn pools, into which some waste products inevitably seep. Only after much Western pressure was attention given to endangered species. Even with increased government attention, as one Taiwanese official frankly put it, "the private sector is flexible and vibrant in Taiwan—where there is profit, there is activity."

Housing remains small and basic in Taiwan. Homeless derelicts can be seen sleeping on the streets of Taipei and Kaohsiung. Again, with the opening of the PRC, many Taiwanese companies are moving lock, stock, and barrel to the mainland; fears of the hollowing out of the economy, such as has been seen in the United States and the United Kingdom, are being voiced. But investment in the PRC by Taiwanese firms is likely to bring as much opportunity as problems. And even with such caveats, Taiwan has come exceptionally far. Indeed, the caveats only qualify Taiwan's success and point to some necessary future directions; they do not in any way negate its impressive accomplishments.

In sum, Taiwan illustrates well the complex mix of factors behind the kind of rapid economic and social progress often termed a development miracle. The factors that stood out were education, infrastructure, land reform, high rates of saving and investment, absorption of commercial ideas, effective industrial policy in formative stages, market incentives, and recently policies and incentives for continued improvement and upgrading in skills, specialization in design skills, flexible production operations, productive knowledge, and efficiency. ∎

Sources

Amsden, Alice H. "Taiwan's economic history: A case of *étatisme* and a challenge to dependency theory." *Modern China* 5 (1979): 341–380.

Amsden, Alice H. "Taiwan," *World Development*, 12 (1984): 627–633.

Balassa, Bela. "The lessons of East Asian development: An overview." *Economic Development and Cultural Change* 36 (1988): S273–S290.

Bradford, Colin I. "Trade and structural change, NICs and next-tier NICs as transitional economies." *World Development* 15 (1987): 299–316.

Chenery, Hollis, Sherman Robinson, and Moses Syrquin. *Industrialization and Growth: A Comparative Study*. New York: Oxford University Press, 1986.

Chu, Wan-Wen. "Export-led growth and import dependence: The case of Taiwan, 1969–1981." *Journal of Development Economics* 28 (1988): 265–276.

Dahlman, Carl J., and Ousa Sananikone. "Taiwan, China: Policies and institutions for rapid growth," in *Lessons from East Asia*, ed. Danny M. Leipziger. Ann Arbor: University of Michigan Press, 1997.

Dahlman, Carl J., Bruce Ross-Larson, and Larry E. Westphal. "Managing technical development: Lessons from the newly industrializing countries." *World Development* 15 (1987): 759–775.

Jacobsson, Steffan. "Technical change and industrial policy: The case of computer numerically controlled lathes in Argentina, Korea and Taiwan." *World Development* 10 (1982): 991–1014.

Keesing, Donald B. "The four successful exceptions: Official export promotion and support for export marketing in Korea, Hong Kong, Singapore and Taiwan, China." United Nations Development Program–World Bank Trade Expansion Program Occasional Paper no. 2, 1988.

Mathews, John A. "The origins and dynamics of Taiwan's R&D consortia." *Research Policy* 31 (2002): 633–651.

Pack, Howard, and Larry E. Westphal. "Industrial strategy and technological change: Theory versus reality." *Journal of Development Economics* 22 (1986): 87–128.

Smith, Stephen C. *Industrial Policy in Developing Countries: Reconsidering the Real Sources of Export-Led Growth.* Washington, D.C.: Economic Policy Institute, 1991.

Taiwan Yearbook, 2004 and 1993, Taipei Government Information Office.

Thorbecke, Erik, An-Chi Tung, and Henry Wan. "Industrial targeting: Lessons from past errors and successes of Hong Kong and Taiwan." *World Economy* 25 (2002): 1047–1061.

Thorbecke, Erik, and Henry Wan. "Revisiting East (and Southeast) Asia's development model." Paper presented at the Cornell University Conference on Seventy-Five Years of Development, Ithaca, N.Y., May 7–9, 2004.

Wade, Robert. "The role of government in overcoming market failure: Taiwan, Republic of Korea and Japan," in *Achieving Industrialization in East Asia*, ed. Helen Hughes. New York: Cambridge University Press, 1988.

Wade, Robert. "State intervention in outward-looking development: Neoclassical theory and Taiwanese practice," in *Developmental States in East Asia*, ed. Gordon White. New York: St. Martin's Press, 1988.

Wade, Robert. *Governing the Market.* Princeton, N.J.: Princeton University Press, 1991.

Concepts for Review

Absolute advantage	Foreign-exchange earnings	Primary products
Balanced trade	Free trade	Product cycle
Barter transactions	Gains from trade	Product differentiation
Capital account	Globalization	Quotas
Collective self-reliance	Growth poles	Regional trading blocs
Collusion	Income elasticity of	Returns to scale
Commodity terms of trade	demand	Risk
Comparative advantage	Income terms of trade	Specialization
Current account	Increasing returns	Subsidies
Enclave economies	Industrial policy	Synthetic substitutes
Export dependence	Monopolistic market control	Tariffs
Export earnings instability	North-South trade models	Trade deficits
Factor endowment trade	Oligopolistic market control	Uncertainty
theory	Prebisch-Singer thesis	Vent-for-surplus theory of
Factor-price equalization	Price elasticity of demand	international trade

Questions for Discussion

1. The effects of international trade on a country's development are often related to four basic economic concepts: efficiency, growth, equity, and stability. Briefly explain what is meant by each of these concepts as it relates to the theory of international trade.

2. Compare and contrast the classical labor cost theory of comparative advantage with the neoclassical factor endowment theory of international trade. Be sure to include an analysis of both assumptions and conclusions.

3. Briefly summarize the major conclusions of the traditional theory of free trade with regard to its theoretical effects on world and domestic efficiency, world and domestic economic growth, world and domestic income distribution, and the pattern of world production and consumption.

4. Proponents of free trade, primarily developed-country economists, argue that the liberalization of trading relationships between rich and poor countries (the removal of tariff and nontariff barriers) would work toward the long-run benefit of *all* countries. Under what conditions might the removal of all tariffs and other impediments to trade work to the best advantage of developing countries? Explain.

5. What factors—economic, political, or historical—do you think will determine whether or not a particular developing nation is more or less dependent on international exchange? Explain your answer, giving a few specific examples of different LDCs.

6. Explain some of the reasons why most non-oil-producing countries of the developing world seem to have benefited relatively less than the developed nations over the past 30 years from their participation in international trade.

7. Traditional free-trade theories are based on six crucial assumptions, which may or may not be valid for developing nations (or for developed nations for that matter). What are these crucial assumptions, and how might they be violated in the real world of international trade?

8. Traditional free-trade theory is basically a *static* theory of international exchange leading to certain conclusions about the benefits likely to accrue to all participants. What *dynamic* elements in real-world economies will tend to negate the widespread distribution of the benefits of free trade? Explain this dynamic process.

9. Critics of international trade from developing countries sometimes claim that present trading relationships between developed and underdeveloped countries can be a source of "antidevelopment" for the latter and merely serve to perpetuate their weak and dependent status. Explain their argument. Do you tend to agree or disagree? Explain why.

10. Manufactures now account for a majority of exports from the developing world. Why do you think LDCs have not benefited more?

11. In what ways is the emergence of China as the "workshop of the world" an opportunity for other developing countries, and in what ways is it a threat?

Notes

1. This widely cited label, a symbol of the global factory, is attributed to former McDonnell Douglas chairman John F. McDonnell; Shari Caudron, "The Power of Global Markets," businessfinancemag.com, http://www.businessfinancemag.com/archives/appfilles/Article.cfm?IssueID=143&ArticleID=5352.

2. This discussion draws on and attempts to synthesize the diverse sources in World Bank, *Poverty in an Age of Globalization* (Washington, D.C.: World Bank, 2000); Sarah Anderson and John Cavanaugh, with Thea Lee, *Field Guide to the Global Economy* (New York: New Press, 2000); the *British Government White Papers on Globalisation* (http://www.globalisation.gov.uk); Jeffrey Sachs, "Making globalization work" (Washington, D.C.: George Washington University Press, 2000); the articles in *Symposium on Globalization in Perspective*, esp. Dani Rodrik, "An Introduction," *Journal of Economic Perspectives* 12 (1998): 3–8; Dani Rodrik, "Globalisation, social conflict and economic growth," *World Economy* 21 (1998): 143–158; and David Dollar and Aart Kraay, "Growth is good for the poor," World Bank Working Paper (Washington, D.C.: World Bank, 2000).

3. These comparisons are derived from World Bank, *World Development Report, 2002* (New York: Oxford University Press, 2002), pp. 236–239.

4. For data on relative income elasticities of demand for selected commodities in relation to manufactures, see World Bank, *1994 Global Economic Prospects and the Developing Countries* (Washington, D.C.: World Bank, 1994), tab. 2.5. A good discussion of primary-product export earnings instability can be found in ch. 2.

5. See Carmen M. Reinhart and Peter Wickham, "Commodity prices: Cyclical weakness or secular decline?" *International Monetary Fund Staff Papers* 41 (1994): 175–213; Rati Ram, "Trends in developing countries' commodity terms-of-trade since 1970," *Review of Radical Political Economics* 36 (2004): 241–253.

6. An alternative measure of the terms of trade is the **income terms of trade**, which measures the relative purchasing power of a country's exports. Some economists argue that this gives a better picture of the relationship between exports (and export earnings instability) and growth because it abstracts from relative price movements. For example, Matthias Lutz has found that there is a strong negative relationship between income terms of trade volatility and economic growth rates, confirming earlier studies that found a negative relationship between volatility in commodity terms of trade and economic growth. See Matthias Lutz, "The effects of volatility in the terms of trade on output growth," *World Development* 22 (1994): 1959–1975.

7. See Raul Prebisch, *The Economic Development of Latin America and Its Principal Problems* (New York: United Nations, 1950), and Hans W. Singer, "The distribution of gains between borrowing and investing countries," *American Economic Review* 40 (1950): 473–485.

8. See Alf Maizels, *The Manufactures Terms of Trade of Developing Countries with the United States, 1981–97* (Oxford: Oxford University Press, 2000), and Sarkar Prabirjit and Hans W. Singer, "Manufactured exports of developing countries and their terms of trade since 1965," *World Development* 19 (1991): 333–340.

9. Recall that the slope of a line tangent to any point on the concave production possibility frontier will show the opportunity or real costs of reducing the output of one commodity in order to produce more of the other. In a world of perfect competition, these relative costs would also equal relative market prices. Therefore, the slope of the dotted line tangent to point A also shows relative commodity prices. The steeper the slope, the higher would be the price of a relative to m. As we move from left to right (e.g., from point A to point B in Figure 12.1a), the slope of the tangent line becomes progressively steeper, indicating increasing opportunity costs of producing more food. Similarly, a right-to-left movement along the production frontier (from B to A) would represent increasing opportunity costs of producing more manufactured goods in terms of forgone food output.

10. The classic article on **factor-price equalization** is Paul A. Samuelson, "International trade and equalization of factor prices," *Economic Journal* 48 (1948): 163–184.

11. Manmohan Singh, "Development policy research: The task ahead," *Proceedings of the World Bank Annual Conference on Development Economics, 1989* (Washington, D.C.: World Bank, 1990), p. 12. Singh was secretary general of the South Commission, Geneva, at the time of this address.

12. For some representative literature on North-South trade models, as well as other nontraditional theories, see Paul Krugman, "Trade, accumulation and uneven development," *Journal of Development Economics* 8 (1981): 149–161; Graciella Chichilnisky, "A general equilibrium theory of North-South trade," in *Essays in Honor of Kenneth J. Arrow,* ed. Walter Heller et al. (New York: Cambridge University Press, 1986); Jose Antonio Ocampo, "New developments in trade theory and LDCs," *Journal of Development Economics* 22 (1986): 129–170; and Amitova K. Dutt, "Mo-

nopoly power and uneven development: Baran revisited," *Journal of Development Studies* 24 (1988): 161–176.

13. Michael E. Porter, *The Competitive Advantage of Nations* (New York: Free Press, 1990). The new trade theory that allows for increasing returns to scale and imperfect competition, pioneered by Paul Krugman, offers an analysis that is parallel in some ways and leads to some similar conclusions. For an overview, see Paul Krugman, "Increasing returns, imperfect competition and the positive theory of international trade, in *Handbook of International Economics, Handbooks in Economics,* vol. 3 (New York: Elsevier, 1995), pp. 1243–1277.

14. Porter, *Competitive Advantage of Nations,* pp. 675–676.

15. See Heinz W. Arndt, "The origins of structuralism," *World Development* 13 (1985): 151–159.

16. For a review of how imperfect competition pervades international trading relations, see Elhanan Helpman, "The noncompetitive theory of international trade and trade policy," *Proceedings of the World Bank Annual Conference on Development Economics, 1989,* pp. 193–216, and David Greenaway, "New trade theories and developing countries," in *Current Issues in Development Economics,* ed. V. N. Balasubramanyam and Sanjaya Lall (New York: St. Martin's Press, 1991), pp. 159–169. On the costs of protection, see Intergovernmental Group of 24 Communique on International Monetary Affairs and Development, April 28, 2001, available from http://www.un.org/esa/.

17. Helpman, "Noncompetitive theory," p. 196.

18. In this, they were building on the earlier success of Japan. For an analysis of the important role that governments played in the free-market export successes of the Four Asian Tigers, see Stephen C. Smith, *Industrial Policy in Developing Countries: Reconsidering the Real Sources of Export-Led Growth* (Washington, D.C.: Economic Policy Institute, 1991), and Robert Wade, *Governing the Market: Economic Theory and the Role of Government in East Asian Industrialization* (Princeton, N.J.: Princeton University Press, 1990). See also Chapter 13.

19. See Ajit Singh, "Openness and the market-friendly approach to development: Learning the right lessons from the development experience," *World Development* 22 (1994): 1814. Copyright © 1994. Reprinted with the permission of Elsevier Science Ltd.

20. For evidence that trade-oriented developing countries seem to have higher rates of aggregate economic growth (although in many cases it is difficult to isolate the true sources of that growth), see World Bank, *World Development Report, 1992* (New York: Oxford University Press, 1992), and Jagdish N. Bhagwati, "Export-promoting trade strategy: Issues and evidence," *World Bank Research Observer* 3 (1988): 27–57.

21. Graciella Chichilnisky and Geoffrey Heal, *The Evolving International Economy* (New York: Cambridge University Press, 1986), p. 44.

22. See, for example, the Santiago Declaration of Third World economists, April 1973, and the Communique of the Third World Forum, Karachi, 1975. A more recent presentation of a similar though less radical view can be found in United Nations, *Development and International Economic Cooperation: An Agenda for Development* (New York: United Nations, 1994).

Further Reading

For an explication of the traditional classical and neoclassical theories of free trade, as well as newer theories taking account of increasing returns to scale and other deviations from perfect competition, see Paul Krugman and Maurice Obstfeld, *International Economics: Theory and Policy*, 6th ed. (Reading, Mass.: Addison-Wesley, 2003).

An excellent overall review and critique of alternative models of trade and development is provided by Sheila Smith and John Toye, "Three stories about trade and poor economies," *Journal of Development Studies* 15 (1979): 1–18, and David Greenaway and Chris Milner, "Trade theory and the less developed countries," in *Surveys in Development Economics*, ed. Norman Gemmell (Oxford: Blackwell, 1987), ch. 1.

For a critique of the traditional theory of trade as applied to underdeveloped nations, see Hla Myint, "The classical theory of international trade and the underdeveloped countries," *Economic Journal* 68 (1958): 317–337; Gunnar Myrdal, *The Challenge of World Poverty* (New York: Pantheon, 1970), ch. 9; Hla Myint, "International trade and the developing countries," in *International Economic Relations*, ed. Paul A. Samuelson (London: Macmillan, 1969); Thomas Balogh, "Fact and fancy in international economic relations, part 1," *World Development* 1 (1973): 76–92; special issue on trade and poor economies, *Journal of Development Studies* 15 (April 1979); James Riedel, *Trade as an Engine of Growth in Developing Countries: A Reappraisal* (Washington, D.C.: World Bank, 1983); John Toye, *Dilemmas of Development: Reflections on the Counter-Revolution in Development Theory and Policy* (Oxford: Blackwell, 1987), pp. 82–89; Graciella Chichilnisky and Geoffrey Heal, *The Evolving International Economy* (New York: Cambridge University Press, 1986); United Nations Development Program, *Human Development Report, 1997* (New York: Oxford University Press, 1997), ch. 5; and United Nations Conference on Trade and Development, *Trade and Development Report, 1997: Globalization, Distribution and Growth* (New York: United Nations, 1997), pt. 2. A more popularized critique of free-trade theory can be found in William Greider, *One World, Ready or Not: The Manic Logic of Global Capitalism* (New York: Simon & Schuster, 1997).

Examples of the recent trend in trade theory to focus on noncompetitive markets and increasing returns include Elhanan Helpman, "The noncompetitive theory of international trade and trade policy," *Proceedings of the World Bank Annual Conference on Development Economics, 1989* (Washington, D.C.: World Bank, 1990), pp. 193–216; Paul Krugman and Elhanan Helpman, *Trade Policy and Market Structure* (Cambridge, Mass.: MIT Press, 1989); David Greenaway, "New trade theories and developing countries," in *Current Issues in Development Economics*, ed. V. N. Balasubramanyam and Sanjaya Lall (New York: St. Martin's Press, 1991); and Gene M. Grossman and Elhanan Helpman, "Endogenous innovation in the theory of growth," *Journal of Economic Perspectives* 8 (1994): 23–44.

A more in-depth but rather technical exposition is found in Paul Krugman, "Increasing returns, imperfect competition and the positive theory of international trade," in *Handbook of International Economics*, vol. 3, (New York: Elsevier, 1995), pp. 1243–1277.

CHAPTER THIRTEEN

The Trade Policy Debate: Export Promotion, Import Substitution, and Economic Integration

However misguided the old model of blanket protection intended to nurture import substitute industries, it would be a mistake to go to the other extreme and deny developing countries the opportunity of actively nurturing the development of an industrial sector.
—Report of the High-Level Panel on Financing for Development (Zedillo Commission), 2001

It is ironic that while national [LDC] markets are opening, global markets remain restricted. Where can developing nations sell their products unless global markets are also freed of protectionist restraints?
—William H. Draper III, United Nations Development Program Administrator, 1992

A large part of the developing world has not yet reaped the benefits of globalization: many countries have continued to lose ground.
—International Monetary Fund, *World Economic Outlook*, 1997

In this chapter we move from general trade theory considerations and overall trade strategies to specific trade policy issues by examining a wide range of LDC commercial policies, including import tariffs, physical quotas, export promotion versus import substitution, exchange-rate adjustments, bargaining over technology licensing and market access, international commodity agreements, and economic integration. Our objective is to ascertain the conditions under which these policies might help or harm developing countries in their dealings with the industrialized world and with one another. We then summarize the various positions in the ongoing debate between the "trade optimists" (free traders) and "trade pessimists" (protectionists), between outward- and inward-looking strategies of development. Finally, we look at the trade policies of developed countries to see in what ways they directly and indirectly affect the economies of the developing world. South Korea provides an outstanding example of successful trade policy over the past four decades. This chapter's case study seeks to understand the sources of South Korea's success with a trade-based industrialization strategy.

Trade Strategies for Development: Export Promotion versus Import Substitution

A traditional way to approach the complex issues of appropriate trade policies for development is to set these specific policies in the context of a broader LDC strategy of looking outward or looking inward.[1] In the words of Paul Streeten, **outward-looking development policies** "encourage not only free trade but also the free movement of capital, workers, enterprises and student . . ., the multinational enterprise, and an open system of communications."[2] By contrast, **inward-looking development policies** stress the need for LDCs to evolve their own styles of development and to control their own destiny. This means policies to encourage indigenous "learning by doing" in manufacturing and the development of technologies appropriate to a country's resource endowments. According to proponents of inward-looking trade policies, greater self-reliance can be accomplished only if "you restrict trade, the movement of people, and communications and if you keep out the multinational enterprise, with its wrong products and wrong want-stimulation and hence its wrong technology."[3]

Within these two broad philosophical approaches to development, a lively debate has been carried on in the development literature since the 1950s. This is the debate between the free traders, who advocate outward-looking export promotion strategies of industrialization, and the protectionists, who are proponents of inward-looking import substitution strategies. The balance of the debate has swung back and forth, with the import substitutors predominating in the 1950s and 1960s and the export promoters gaining the upper hand in the late 1970s and, especially among Western and World Bank economists, in the 1980s and 1990s. Among many developing-country economists and certain developed-country advocates of the "new" or "strategic" trade theories discussed in Chapter 12, however, the philosophical foundations of import substitution and collective self-reliance remain almost as strong as they were in prior decades.

Basically, the distinction between these two trade-related development strategies is that advocates of **import substitution** (IS) believe that LDCs should initially substitute domestic production of previously imported simple consumer goods (first-stage IS) and then substitute through domestic production for a wider range of more sophisticated manufactured items (second-stage IS)—all behind the protection of high tariffs and quotas on these imports. In the long run, IS advocates cite the benefits of greater domestic industrial diversification ("balanced growth") and the ultimate ability to export some previously protected manufactured goods as economies of scale, low labor costs, and the positive externalities of learning by doing cause domestic prices to become more competitive with world prices.

By contrast, advocates of **export promotion** (EP) of both primary and manufactured goods cite the efficiency and growth benefits of free trade and competition, the importance of substituting large world markets for narrow domestic markets, the distorting price and cost effects of protection, and the tremendous successes of the East Asian export-oriented economies of South Korea, Taiwan, Singapore, and Hong Kong. They stress that firms in these economies—and more recently in China—have learned a great deal from the firms in the United States, Japan, and other economies that have been their long-term customers.

In practice, the distinction between IS and EP strategies is much less pronounced than many advocates would imply. Most LDCs have employed both strategies with different degrees of emphasis at one time or another. For example, in the 1950s and 1960s, the inward-looking industrialization strategies of the larger Latin American and Asian countries such as Chile, Peru, Argentina, India, Pakistan, and the Philippines were heavily IS-oriented. By the end of the 1960s, some of the key sub-Saharan African countries like Nigeria, Ethiopia, Ghana, and Zambia had begun to pursue IS strategies, and some smaller Latin American and Asian countries also joined in.[4] However, since the mid-1970s, the EP strategy has been increasingly adopted by a growing number of countries. The early EP adherents—South Korea, Taiwan, Singapore, and Hong Kong—were thus joined by the likes of Brazil, Chile, Thailand, and Turkey, which switched from an earlier IS strategy. It must be stressed, however, that even the most successful East Asian export promoters have pursued protectionist IS strategies sequentially and simultaneously in certain industries, so it is inaccurate to call them free traders, even though they are outward-oriented.[5]

Against this background, we can now examine the issue of outward-looking export promotion versus inward-looking import substitution in more detail by applying the following fourfold categorization:

1. Primary outward-looking policies (encouragement of agricultural and raw material exports)

2. Secondary outward-looking policies (promotion of manufactured exports)

3. Primary inward-looking policies (mainly agricultural self-sufficiency)

4. Secondary inward-looking policies (manufactured commodity self-sufficiency through import substitution)

Then we turn our attention to eclectic strategies.

Export Promotion: Looking Outward and Seeing Trade Barriers

The promotion of LDC primary or secondary exports has long been considered a major ingredient in any viable long-run development strategy. The colonial territories of Africa and Asia, with their foreign-owned mines and plantations, were classic examples of primary outward-looking regions. It was partly in reaction to this enclave economic structure and partly as a consequence of the industrialization bias of the 1950s and 1960s that newly independent states, as well as older LDCs, put great emphasis on the production of manufactured goods initially for the home market (secondary inward) and then for export (secondary outward). Let us therefore look briefly at the scope and limitations of LDC export expansion, first with respect to primary products and then with respect to manufactured exports.

Primary-Commodity Export Expansion: Limited Demand, Shrinking Markets
As we discovered in Chapter 12, many low-income LDCs still rely on primary

products for most of their export earnings. With the notable exception of petro-leum exports and a few needed minerals, primary-product exports have grown more slowly than total world trade. Moreover, the LDC share of these exports has been falling over the past few decades. Because food, nonfood agricultural prod-ucts, and raw materials make up almost 40% of all LDC exports and for many poor countries constitute their principal source of foreign-exchange earnings, we need to examine the factors affecting the demand for and supply of primary-product exports.[6]

On the demand side, there appear to be at least five factors working against the rapid expansion of LDC primary-product and especially agricultural exports to the developed nations (their major markets). First, the income elasticities of de-mand for agricultural foodstuffs and raw materials are relatively low compared with those for fuels, certain minerals, and manufactures. For example, the income elasticities of demand for sugar, cacao, tea, coffee, and bananas have all been esti-mated at less than 1, with most in the range of 0.3–0.6. Inelastic demand means that only a sustained high rate of per capita income growth in the developed countries can lead to even modest export expansion of these particular commodi-ties from the LDCs. Such high growth rates prevailed in the 1960s but have not been matched since, although many primary exporters have benefited from the boom in China in the early years of the twenty-first century.

Second, developed-country population growth rates are now at or near the re-placement level, so little expansion can be expected from this source. Third, the price elasticity of demand for most primary commodities is relatively low. When relative agricultural prices are falling, as they have been during most of the past three decades, such low elasticities mean less total revenue for exporting nations. For example, between June 1980 and June 1982, the price of sugar fell by 78%, rub-ber by 37%, and copper by 35%. Between 1989 and 1991, commodity prices fell by about 20%. Tin prices were so low that smelting was no longer profitable, and the real prices of coffee and tea were lower than at any time since 1950. With the ex-ception of the mid-1970s, non-oil real commodity prices fell by almost 40% be-tween 1957 and 1998. Such a decline, especially in the 1980s and 1990s when prices fell by over 35%, has hurt the least developed countries the most. Oil prices have not fared much better. They reached a 13-year low in 1999 before rebounding to a 20-year peak in 2004 (while remaining far below their all time highs in real terms).

Fourth, with the exception of oil and a few minor commodities, **international commodity agreements** have not fared well. Such agreements are intended to set overall output levels, stabilize world prices, and assign quota shares to various producing nations for such items as coffee, tea, copper, lead, and sugar. To work effectively, they require cooperation and compromise among participants. Com-modity agreements can also provide greater protection to individual exporting nations against excessive competition and the overexpansion of world produc-tion. Such overexpansion of supply tends to drive down prices and curtail the growth of earnings for all countries. In short, commodity agreements attempt to guarantee participating nations a relatively fixed share of world export earnings and a more stable world price for their commodity. But proposals by the United

Nations Conference on Trade and Development (UNCTAD) for the establishment of a common fund to finance "buffer stocks" to support the prices of some 19 primary commodities (including sugar, coffee, tea, bauxite, jute, cotton, tin, and vegetable oil) produced by various developing nations have made little progress. Most existing non-oil commodity agreements have either failed (tin) or been largely ignored by producers (coffee, sugar). Even in the best scenarios, such agreements cannot be effective for perishable commodities. Imagine trying to operate a buffer stock of bananas!

The fifth and sixth factors working against the long-run expansion of LDC primary-product export earnings—the development of synthetic substitutes and the growth of agricultural protection in the developed countries—are perhaps the most important. **Synthetic substitutes** for commodities like cotton, rubber, sisal, jute, hide, skins, and recently copper (with glass fiberoptics for communication networks) act both as a brake against higher commodity prices and as a direct source of competition in world export markets. The synthetic share of world market export earnings has generally risen over time, while the share of natural products has fallen. In the case of agricultural protection, which usually takes the form of tariffs, quotas, and nontariff barriers such as sanitary laws regulating food and fiber imports, the effects can be devastating to LDC export earnings. The common agricultural policy of the European Union (EU), for example, is much more discriminatory against LDC food exports than the policies that had formerly prevailed in the individual member nations.

On the supply side, a number of factors also work against the rapid expansion of primary-product export earnings. The most important is the structural rigidity of many rural production systems in developing countries. We discussed rigidities—such as limited resources; poor climate; bad soils; antiquated rural institutional, social, and economic structures; and nonproductive patterns of land tenure—in Chapter 9. Whatever the international demand situation for particular commodities (which will differ from commodity to commodity), little export expansion can be expected when rural economic and social structures militate against positive supply responses from peasant farmers who are averse to risk. Furthermore, in developing nations with markedly dualistic farming structures (i.e., large corporate capital-intensive farms existing side by side with thousands of fragmented, low-productivity peasant holdings), any growth in export earnings is likely to be distributed very unevenly among the rural population. Small farmers are further disadvantaged in countries (mostly in Africa) in which agricultural marketing boards act as middlemen between the farmers and export markets. Marketing boards often constrain export expansion by forcing cultivators to sell their goods at a fixed price—usually well below world market prices. They thereby remove the incentive to increase output. Fortunately, these boards have been largely dismantled in recent years.

But primary export growth has remained modest, partly due to the pernicious effects of developed-country trade policies (such as the United States' sugar quota and cotton subsidies) and foreign aid policies that depress agricultural prices in LDCs and discourage production. For example, the EU's policy of selling subsidized beef to the nations of West Africa in the guise of foreign assistance has devastated cattle prices in those countries.[7]

We may conclude, therefore, that the successful promotion of primary-product exports cannot occur unless there is a reorganization of rural social and economic structures along the lines suggested in Chapter 9 to raise total agricultural productivity and distribute the benefits more widely. The primary objective of any LDC rural development strategy is widely accepted to be *first* to provide sufficient food to feed local people and only then to be concerned about export expansion. But having accomplished this difficult internal development task, LDCs may be able to realize the potential benefits of their comparative advantage in world primary commodity markets only if they can (1) cooperate with one another, (2) be assisted by developed nations in formulating and carrying out workable international commodity agreements, and (3) secure greater access to developed-country markets. Unfortunately, given the structure of world demands for primary products, the threat of local food shortages and thus the desire for agricultural self-sufficiency, the inevitability of the development of further synthetic substitutes, and the unlikelihood of significantly lower levels of agricultural protection among developed nations, the real scope for primary-product export expansion in individual LDCs seems limited.[8]

Expanding Exports of Manufactured Goods: Some Successes, Many Barriers The expansion of LDC manufactured exports has been given great stimulus by the spectacular export performances of countries like South Korea, Singapore, Hong Kong, Taiwan, and China over the past four decades.[9] For example, Taiwan's total exports grew at an annual rate of over 20%, and exports from South Korea grew even faster. In both cases, this export growth was led by manufactured goods, which contributed over 80% of both nations' foreign-exchange earnings. For the developing world as a whole, manufactured exports grew from 6% of total merchandise exports in 1950 to almost 64% by 2000. Taken together, by 2002, the low- and middle-income countries accounted for 25.7% of the world's manufactured exports; China commanded a fast-growing share. However, the low-income countries still accounted for just 3.3% of the world total.[10]

The export successes of recent decades, especially among the Asian Tigers, have provided the primary impetus for arguments by market fundamentalists (see Chapter 3)—particularly those at the World Bank and the IMF—that LDC economic growth is best served by allowing market forces, free enterprise, and open economies to prevail while minimizing government intervention. Unfortunately, evidence from East Asia does not support this view of how export success was achieved. In South Korea, Taiwan, and Singapore (as in Japan earlier), the production and composition of exports was not left to the market but resulted from carefully planned intervention by the government.[11] We return to this consideration later in the chapter.

The demand problems for LDC export expansion of manufactured goods, though different in basic economic content from those for primary products, are nonetheless similar. Although income and price elasticities of international demand for manufactured goods in the aggregate are higher than for primary commodities, they afforded little relief to many developing nations bent on expanding their exports. For many years, there was widespread protection in developed nations against the manufactured exports of LDCs—which was in part the direct result of the successful penetration of low-cost labor-intensive manufactures from countries like Taiwan, Hong Kong, and South Korea during the 1960s and 1970s.

Industrial-nation trade barriers have been pervasive. During the 1980s, for example, 20 of the 24 industrialized countries *increased* their protection against LDC manufactured or processed products. Moreover, their rates of protection were considerably higher against LDC exports than against those of other industrial nations. Making matters worse, MDC protection often increased with the level of processing (e.g., the tariff on processed cacao, or cocoa, is twice that of raw cacao, so chocolate imports are discouraged; raw sugar faces tariffs below 2% while processed sugar products are blocked by 20% tariffs). Then there are the nontariff barriers, which now form the main protection against LDC manufactured exports, affecting at least one-third of them. The most significant has been the **Multi-Fiber Arrangement (MFA)**, in effect until 2005, which was a complex system of mostly bilateral quotas against LDC exports of cotton, wool, and synthetic fiber products. The United Nations Development Program estimates that the MFA cost the developing world $24 billion a year in lost textile and clothing export earnings.[12] Paradoxically, many observers forecast that the end of the MFA would actually hurt most LDC textile exporters, as China grabbed market share that had been limited only by quotas.

Whether displaced high-wage workers in developed-country manufactures will continue to permit the unimpeded entry of low-wage LDC products remains to be seen.[13] WTO rules eliminated many formal barriers, but many implicit barriers remain. Antidumping "investigations" increased significantly, reaching a peak in 1999, and the United States was the largest user of these protectionist measures. Although the number of new investigations declined in the early years of the new century, they remained an important weapon in the protectionist arsenal. Countervailing duty investigations are also on the rise. Regional trading agreements, including the North American Free Trade Agreement (NAFTA) and the EU, may also have the effect of discriminating against exports from nonmember developing countries.[14]

As in the case of agricultural and other primary production, the uncertain export outlook should be no cause for curtailing the needed expansion of manufacturing production to serve local LDC markets. There is great scope for mutually beneficial trade in manufactures among developing countries themselves within the context of the gradual economic integration of their national economies. South-South trade in minerals and agriculture has been rising much more quickly than South-South manufactures trade (see Figure 12.3); there remains much scope for expansion.

Import Substitution: Looking Inward but Still Paying Outward

During the 1950s and 1960s, developing countries experienced a decline in world markets for their primary products and growing balance of payments deficits on their current accounts. Given a general belief in the magic of industrialization as well as the terms of trade arguments of the Prebisch-Singer hypothesis, they turned to an import substitution strategy of urban industrial development.

Some countries still follow this strategy for both economic and political reasons, although pressure from the WTO, IMF, and World Bank impose high opportunity costs on such endeavors. As we noted earlier, import substitution entails an attempt to replace commodities that are being imported, usually manufactured consumer goods, with domestic sources of production and supply. The typical strategy is first to erect tariff barriers or quotas on certain imported commodities and then to try to set up a local industry to produce these goods—items such as radios, bicycles, or household appliances. Typically, this involves joint ventures with foreign companies, which are encouraged to set up their plants behind the wall of tariff protection and given all kinds of tax and investment incentives. Although initial costs of production may be higher than former import prices, the economic rationale put forward for the establishment of import-substituting manufacturing operations is either that the industry will eventually be able to reap the benefits of large-scale production and lower costs (the so-called **infant industry** argument for tariff protection) or that the balance of payments will be improved as fewer consumer goods are imported. Often a combination of both arguments is advanced. Eventually, it is hoped, the infant industry will grow up and be able to compete in world markets. It will then be able to generate net foreign-exchange earnings once it has lowered its average costs of production. Let us see how the theory of protection can be used to demonstrate this process.

Tariffs, Infant Industries, and the Theory of Protection A principal mechanism of the import substitution strategy is the erection of protective **tariffs** (taxes on imports) or **quotas** (limits on the quantity of imports) behind which IS industries are permitted to operate. The basic economic rationale for such protection is the infant industry argument mentioned earlier. Tariff protection against the imported commodity is needed, so the argument goes, in order to allow the now higher-priced domestic producers enough time to learn the business and to achieve the economies of scale in production and the external economies of learning by doing that are necessary to lower unit costs and prices. With enough time and sufficient protection, the infant will eventually grow up, be directly competitive with developed-country producers, and no longer need this protection. Ultimately, as in the case of many formerly protected IS industries in South Korea and Taiwan, domestic LDC producers may be able not only to produce for the domestic market without a tariff wall or government subsidies but also to export their now lower-cost manufactured goods to the rest of the world. Thus for many LDC industries, in theory, an IS strategy becomes the prerequisite for an EP strategy. It is for this reason, among others (including the desire to reduce dependence and attain greater self-reliance, the need to build a domestic industrial base, and the ease of raising substantial tax revenue from tariff collections),[15] that import substitution has been appealing to so many LDC governments.

The basic theory of protection is an old and controversial issue in the field of international trade. It is relatively simple to demonstrate. Consider Figure 13.1. The top portion of the figure shows standard domestic supply and demand curves for the industry in question (say, shoes) if there were no international trade—that is, in a closed economy. The equilibrium home price and quantity would be P_1 and

FIGURE 13.1   **Import Substitution and the Theory of Protection**

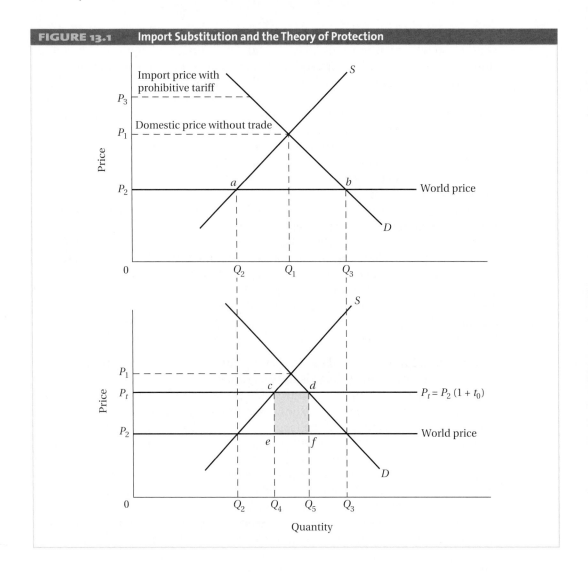

Q_1. If this LDC were then to open its economy to world trade, its small size in relation to the world market would mean that it would face a horizontal, perfectly elastic demand curve. In other words, it could sell (or buy) all it wanted at a lower world price, P_2. Domestic consumers would benefit from the lower price of imports and the resultant greater quantity purchased, while domestic producers and their employees would clearly suffer as they lose business to lower-cost foreign suppliers. Thus at the lower world price, P_2, quantity demanded rises from Q_1 to Q_3, whereas the quantity supplied by domestic producers falls from Q_1 to Q_2. The difference between what domestic producers are willing to supply at the lower P_2

world price (Q_2) and what consumers want to buy (Q_3) is the amount that will be imported—shown as line *ab* in Figure 13.1.

Facing the potential loss of domestic production and jobs as a result of free trade and desiring to obtain infant industry protection, local LDC producers will seek tariff relief from the government. The effects of a tariff (equal to t_0) are shown in the lower half of Figure 13.1. The tariff causes the domestic price of shoes to rise from P_2 to P_t—that is, $P_t = P_2 (1 + t_0)$. Local consumers now have to pay the higher price and will reduce their quantity demanded from Q_3 to Q_5. Domestic producers can now expand production (and employment) up to quantity Q_4 from Q_2. The rectangular area *cdfe* measures the amount of the tariff revenue collected by the government on imported shoes.

Clearly, the higher the tariff, the closer to the domestic price the sum of the world price plus the import tax will be. In the classic infant-industry IS scenario, the tariff may be so high that it raises the price of the imported produce above P_1 to, say, P_3 in the upper diagram of Figure 13.1, so that imports are effectively prohibited and the local industry is allowed to operate behind a fully protective tariff wall, once again selling Q_1 output at P_1 price. In the short run, it is clear that the impact of such a prohibitive tariff is to penalize consumers, who are in effect subsidizing domestic producers and their employees through higher prices and lower consumption. Alternatively, we can say that a tariff redistributes income from consumers to producers. However, in the longer run, advocates of IS protection for LDC infant industries argue that everyone will benefit as domestic and other shoe manufacturers reap the benefits of economies of scale and learning by doing so that ultimately the domestic price falls below P_2 (the world price). Production will then occur for *both* the domestic and the world market, domestic consumers as well as domestic producers and their employees will benefit, protective tariffs can be removed, and the government will be able to replace any lost tariff revenue with taxes on the now very much higher incomes of domestic manufactures. It all sounds logical and persuasive in theory. But how has it performed in practice?

The IS Industrialization Strategy and Results

Most observers agree that the import-substituting strategy of industrialization has been largely unsuccessful.[16] Specifically, there have been five undesirable outcomes. First, secure behind protective tariff walls and immune from competitive pressures, many IS industries (both publicly and privately owned) remain inefficient and costly to operate. Second, the main beneficiaries of the import substitution process have been the foreign firms that were able to locate behind tariff walls and take advantage of liberal tax and investment incentives. After deducting interest, profits, and royalty and management fees, most of which are remitted abroad, the little that may be left over usually accrues to the wealthy local industrialists with whom foreign manufacturers cooperate and who provide their political and economic cover.

Third, most import substitution has been made possible by the heavy and often government-subsidized importation of capital goods and intermediate products by foreign and domestic companies. In the case of foreign companies, much of this is purchased from parent and sister companies abroad. There are two immediate results. On the one hand, capital-intensive industries are set up, usually catering to the consumption habits of the rich while having a minimal employment effect. On the other hand, far from improving the LDCs' balance of payments situation and alleviating the debt problem, indiscriminate import substitution often worsens the situation by increasing a need for imported capital-good inputs and intermediate products while, as we have just seen, a good part of the profits is remitted abroad in the form of private transfer payments.

A fourth detrimental effect of many import substitution strategies has been their impact on traditional primary-product exports. To encourage local manufacturing through the importation of cheap capital and intermediate goods, **exchange rates** (the rate at which the central bank of a nation is prepared to purchase foreign currencies) have often been artificially overvalued. This has had the effect of raising the price of exports and lowering the price of imports in terms of the local currency. For example, if the free-market exchange rate between Pakistani rupees and U.S. dollars was 20 to 1 but the official exchange rate was 10 to 1, an item that cost $10 in the United States could be imported into Pakistan for 100 rupees (excluding transport costs and other service charges). If the **free-market exchange rate** (the exchange rate determined by the supply and demand for Pakistani rupees in terms of dollars) prevailed, that item would cost 200 rupees. Thus by means of an **overvalued exchange rate**, LDC governments have effectively lowered the domestic currency price of their imports. At the same time, their export prices have increased—for example, at an exchange rate of 10 to 1, U.S. importers would have to pay 10 cents for every 1-rupee item rather than the 5 cents they would pay if the hypothetical free-market ratio of 20 to 1 were in effect.

The net effect of overvaluing exchange rates in the context of import substitution policies is to encourage capital-intensive production methods still further (because the price of imported capital goods is artificially lowered) and to penalize the traditional primary-product export sector by artificially raising the price of exports in terms of foreign currencies. This overvaluation, then, causes local farmers to be less competitive in world markets. In terms of its income distribution effects, the outcome of such government policies may be to penalize the small farmer and the self-employed while improving the profits of the owners of capital, both foreign and domestic. Industrial protection thus has the effect of taxing agricultural goods in the home market as well as discouraging agricultural exports. Import substitution policies have in practice often worsened the local distribution of income by favoring the urban sector and higher-income groups while discriminating against the rural sector and lower-income groups.

Fifth and finally, import substitution, which may have been conceived with the idea of stimulating infant industry growth and self-sustained industrialization by creating "forward" and "backward" linkages with the rest of the economy, has often inhibited that industrialization. Many infants never grow up, content to hide behind protective tariffs and governments loath to force them to be more competitive by lowering tariffs. In fact, LDC governments themselves often operate protected industries as state-owned enterprises. Moreover, by increasing the costs of inputs to potentially forward-linked industries (those that purchase the output of the protected firm as inputs or intermediate products in their own productive process, such as a printer's purchase of paper from a locally protected paper mill) and by purchasing their own inputs from overseas sources of supply rather than through backward linkages to domestic suppliers, inefficient import-substituting firms may in fact block the hoped-for process of self-reliant integrated industrialization.[17]

Tariff Structures and Effective Protection Because import substitution programs are based on the protection of local industries against competing imports primarily through the use of tariffs and physical quotas, we need to analyze the role and limitations of these commercial policy instruments in developing nations. As we have already discussed, governments impose tariffs and physical quotas on imports for a variety of reasons. For example, tariff barriers may be erected to raise public revenue. In fact, given the administrative and political difficulties of collecting local income taxes, fixed-percentage taxes on imports collected at a relatively few ports or border posts often constitute one of the cheapest and most efficient ways to raise government revenue. In many LDCs, these foreign-trade taxes are thus a central feature of the overall fiscal system (see note 15). Physical quotas on imports like automobiles and other luxury consumer goods, though more difficult to administer and more subject to delay, inefficiency, and rent-seeking corruption (e.g., with regard to the granting of import licenses), provide an effective means of restricting the entry of particularly troublesome commodities. Tariffs, too, may serve to restrict the importation of nonnecessity products (usually expensive consumer goods). By restricting imports, both quotas and tariffs can improve the balance of payments. And like overvaluing the official rate of foreign exchange, tariffs may be used to improve a nation's terms of trade. However, in a small country unable to influence world prices of its exports or imports (in other words, most LDCs), this argument for tariffs (or devaluation) has little validity. Finally, as we have just seen, tariffs may form an integral component of an import substitution policy of industrialization.

Whatever the means used to restrict imports, such restriction always protects domestic firms from competition with producers from other countries. To measure the degree of protection, we need to ask by how much these restrictions cause the domestic prices of imports to exceed what their prices would be if there were no protection. There are two basic measures of protection: the nominal rate and the effective rate.

The **nominal rate of protection** shows the extent, in percentages, to which the domestic price of imported goods exceeds what their price would be in the absence of protection. Thus the nominal (ad valorem) tariff rate (t) refers to the final prices of commodities and can be defined simply as

$$t = \frac{p' - p}{p} \tag{13.1}$$

TABLE 13.1	Effective Protection Rate in Selected Developing Countries
Country	Average Effective Protection Rate (%)
Uruguay	384
Pakistan	356
India	69
Brazil	63
Côte d'Ivoire	41
Thailand	27
Singapore	22
Colombia	19
South Korea	-1

Source: David Greenaway and Chris Milner, "Trade theory and the less developed countries," in *Surveys in Development Economics*, ed. Norman Gemmell (Oxford: Blackwell, 1987), tab. 1.5. Reprinted with permission.

where p' and p are the unit prices of industry's output with and without tariffs, respectively.

For example, if the domestic price (p') of an imported automobile is $5,000 whereas the CIF (cost plus insurance and freight) price (p) when the automobile arrives at the port of entry is $4,000, the nominal rate of tariff protection (t) would be 25%. This is the kind of tariff depicted as t_0 in Figure 13.1.

By contrast, the **effective rate of protection** shows the percentage by which the **value added** at a particular stage of processing in a domestic industry can exceed what it would be without protection. In other words, it shows by what percentage the sum of wages, interest, profits, and depreciation allowances payable by local firms can, as a result of protection, exceed what this sum would be if these same firms had to face unrestricted competition (no tariff protection) from foreign producers.[18] The effective rate (g) can therefore be defined as the difference between value added (percent of output) in domestic prices and value added in world prices, expressed as a percentage of the latter, so that

$$g = \frac{v' - v}{v} \tag{13.2}$$

where v' and v are the value added per unit of output with and without protection, respectively. The result can be either positive or negative, depending on whether v' is greater or less than v. For most LDCs, it is highly positive.

Table 13.1 provides some estimates of effective protection in selected LDCs. In general, IS countries like Pakistan and Uruguay by definition have much higher rates of protection than EP countries like South Korea and Singapore.

The important difference between nominal and effective rates of protection can be illustrated by means of an example.[19] Consider a nation without tariffs in which automobiles are produced and sold at the international or world price of $10,000. The value added by labor in the final assembly process is assumed to be $2,000, and the total value of the remaining inputs is $8,000. Assume for simplicity that the prices of these nonlabor inputs are equal to their world prices. Suppose that a nominal tariff of 10% is now imposed on imported automobiles, which raises the domestic price of cars to $11,000 but leaves the prices of all the other importable intermediate units unchanged. The domestic process of automobile production can now spend $3,000 per unit of output on labor inputs, as contrasted with $2,000 per unit before the tariff. The theory of effective protection therefore implies that under these conditions, the nominal tariff of 10% on the final product (automobiles) has resulted in an effective rate of protection of 50% for the local assembly process in terms of its value added per unit of output. It follows that for any given nominal tariff rate, the effective rate is greater the smaller the value added of the process; that is, $g = t/(1 - a)$, where t is the nominal rate on final product and a is the proportionate value of the importable inputs in a free market where these inputs are assumed to enter the country duty-free.

Most economists argue that the effective rate is the more useful concept (even though the nominal or ad valorem rate is simpler to measure) for ascertaining the degree of protection and encouragement afforded to local manufacturers by a given country's tariff structure. This is because effective rates of protection show the net effect on a firm or industry of restrictions on the imports of both its outputs and its inputs. For most countries, developing and developed, the effective rate normally exceeds the nominal rate, sometimes by as much as 200%. For example, average levels of effective protection during the early 1960s exceeded 200% for India and Pakistan, 100% for Argentina and Brazil, 50% for the Philippines, 33% for Taiwan, and 25% for Mexico.[20]

Among the many implications of analyzing effective versus nominal tariff structures with regard to developing countries, two stand out as particularly noteworthy. First, most developing countries, as we have seen, have pursued import-substituting programs of industrialization with emphasis on the local production of final consumer goods for which a ready market was presumed to exist. Moreover, final goods production is generally less technically sophisticated than intermediate capital-goods production. The expectation was that in time, rising demand and economies of scale in finished-goods production would create strong backward linkages leading to the creation of domestic intermediate-goods industries. The record of performance, as we have also seen, has been disappointing for most developing countries. Part of the reason for this lack of success has been that developing-country tariff structures have afforded exceedingly high rates of effective protection to final-goods industries while granting considerably less effective protection to intermediate and capital goods. The net result is an attraction of scarce resources away from intermediate-goods production and toward the often inefficient production of highly protected final consumer goods. Backward linkages do not develop, intermediate-good import costs rise, and—perhaps most important in the long run—the development of an indigenous capital-goods industry focusing on efficient, low-cost, labor-intensive techniques is severely impeded.

Second, even though nominal rates of protection in developed countries on imports from the developing countries may seem relatively low, effective protection rates can be quite substantial. As we saw earlier in the cases of cacao and sugar, raw materials are usually imported duty-free, whereas processed products such as roasted and powdered coffee, coconut oil, and cocoa butter appear to have low nominal tariffs. The theory of effective protection suggests that in combination with zero tariffs on imported raw materials, low nominal tariffs on processed products can represent substantially higher effective rates of protection. For example, if a tariff of 10% is levied on processed coconut oil whereas copra (dried coconut) can be imported duty-free, and if the value added in making oil from copra is 5% of the total value of coconut oil, the *process* is actually being protected at 200%! This greatly inhibits the development of food and other raw-material-processing industries in developing nations and ultimately cuts back on their potential earnings of foreign exchange.

Effective rates of protection are also considerably higher than nominal rates in the developed countries. For example, the effective rate on thread and yarn, textile fabrics, clothing, wood products, leather, and rubber goods has averaged more than twice the nominal rate on these same items in the United States and the members of the European Union. In the EU, effective rates on coconut oil have been 10 times the nominal rate (150% compared with 15%), and those on processed soybeans have been 16 times the nominal rate (160% as opposed to 10%).

To sum up, the standard argument for tariff protection in developing countries has four major components:

1. Duties on trade are the major source of government revenue in most LDCs because they are a relatively easy form of taxation to impose and even easier to collect.

2. Import restrictions represent an obvious response to chronic balance of payments and debt problems.

3. Protection against imports is one of the most appropriate means for fostering economies of scale, positive externalities, and industrial self-reliance as well as overcoming the pervasive state of economic dependence in which most developing countries find themselves.

4. By pursuing policies of import restriction, developing countries can gain greater control over their economic destinies while encouraging foreign business interests to invest in local import-substituting industries, generating high profits and thus the potential for greater saving and future growth. They can also obtain imported equipment at relatively favorable prices and reserve an already established domestic market for local or locally controlled producers. Eventually, they may even become competitive enough to export to the world market.

Although these arguments can sound convincing and some protective policies have proved highly beneficial to the developing world, as we discovered, many have failed to bring about their desired results. Protection can have an important role to play in economic development, for both economic and noneconomic reasons, but it is a tool of economic policy that must be employed selectively and wisely, not as a panacea to be applied indiscriminately and without reference to both short- and long-term ramifications.

Foreign-Exchange Rates, Exchange Controls, and the Devaluation Decision

We have already briefly discussed the question of foreign-exchange rates. Remember that a country's **official exchange rate** is the rate at which its central bank is prepared to transact exchanges of its local currency for other currencies in approved foreign-exchange markets. Official exchange rates are usually quoted in terms of U.S. dollars—so many pesos, reals, pounds, shillings, rupees, bhat, or yen per dollar. For example, the official exchange rate of the South African rand for U.S. dollars in 1998 was approximately 5 rand per dollar, and the Indian rupee was officially valued at approximately 40 rupees per dollar. If a South African manufacturer wished to import fabrics from an Indian textile exporter at a cost of 40,000 rupees, he would need 5,000 rand to make the purchase. However, since almost all foreign-exchange transactions are conducted in U.S. dollars, the South African importer would need to purchase $1,000 worth of foreign exchange from the central bank of South Africa for his 5,000 rand and then transmit these dollars through official channels to the Indian exporter.

Official foreign-exchange rates are not necessarily set at or near the economic equilibrium price for foreign exchange—that is, the rate at which the domestic demand for a foreign currency such as dollars would just equal its supply in the absence of governmental regulation or intervention. In fact, as noted earlier, the currencies of most developing countries have usually been overvalued by the exchange rate. Whenever the official price of foreign exchange is established at a level that in the absence of any governmental restrictions or controls would result in an excess of local demand over the available supply of foreign exchange, the domestic currency in question is said to be overvalued.

In situations of excess demand, LDC central banks have three basic policy options to maintain the official rate of exchange. First, they can attempt to accommodate the excess demand by running down their reserves of foreign exchange (as Mexico did from 1991 to 1994 and Thailand, Malaysia, Indonesia, and the Philippines did from 1995 to 1997) or by borrowing additional foreign exchange abroad and thereby incurring further debts (as many African countries did in the 1980s and Indonesia and South Korea did in the 1990s). Second, they can attempt to curtail the excess demand for foreign exchange by pursuing commercial policies and tax measures designed to lessen the demand for imports (e.g., tariffs, physical quotas, licensing). Third, they can regulate and intervene in the foreign-exchange market by rationing the limited supply of available foreign exchange to "preferred" customers.[21] Such rationing is more commonly known as **exchange control**. The policy has been prevalent throughout the developing world, although it is much less common than it once was.

The mechanism and operation of exchange control can be illustrated diagrammatically with the aid of Figure 13.2. Under free-market conditions, the equilibrium price of foreign exchange would be P_e, with a total of M units of foreign exchange demanded and supplied. If, however, the government maintains an artificially low price of foreign exchange (i.e., an overvaluation of its domestic currency) at P_a, the supply of foreign exchange will amount to only M' units because exports are overpriced. But at price P_a the demand for foreign exchange will be M'' units, with the result that there is an "excess demand" equal to $M''- M'$ units. Un-

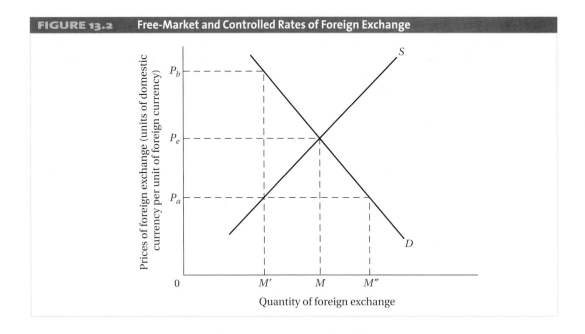

FIGURE 13.2   **Free-Market and Controlled Rates of Foreign Exchange**

less foreigners are willing to lend to or invest in the country to make up the difference, some mechanism will therefore have to be devised to ration the available supply of M'. If the government were to auction this supply, importers would be willing to pay a price of P_b for the foreign exchange. In such a case, the government would make a profit of $P_b - P_a$ per unit. However, such open auctions are rarely carried out, and limited supplies of foreign exchange are allocated through some administrative quota or licensing device. Opportunities for corruption, evasion, and the emergence of black markets are thus made possible because importers are willing to pay as much as P_b per unit of foreign exchange.

Why have most LDC governments at one time or another opted for an overvalued official exchange rate? Basically, as we have seen, they have done so as part of widespread programs of rapid industrialization and import substitution. Overvalued exchange rates reduce the domestic currency price of imports below the level that would exist in a free market for foreign exchange (i.e., by the forces of supply and demand). Cheaper imports, especially capital and intermediate producer goods, are needed to fuel the industrialization process. But overvalued exchange rates also lower the domestic currency price of imported consumer goods, especially expensive luxury products. LDCs wishing to limit such unnecessary and costly imports often need to establish import controls (mostly physical quotas) or to set up a system of **dual** or **parallel exchange rates** with one rate, usually highly overvalued and legally fixed, applied to capital and intermediate-good imports and the other, much lower and illegal (or freely floating), for luxury consumption good imports. Such dual exchange-rate systems make the domestic price of imported luxury goods very high while maintaining the artificially low and thus subsidized price of producer good imports. Needless to say, dual exchange-rate systems, like exchange controls and import licenses, present serious problems of administration and can promote black markets, corruption, evasion, and **rent seeking** (see note 21).[22]

However, overvalued currencies reduce the return to local exporters and to import-competing industries that are not protected by heavy tariffs or physical quotas. Exporters receive less domestic currency for their products than would be forthcoming if the free-market exchange rate prevailed. Moreover, in the absence of export subsidies to reduce the foreign-currency price of an LDC's exports, exporters, mostly farmers, become less competitive in world markets because the price of their produce has been artificially elevated by the overvalued exchange rate. In the case of import-competing but unprotected local industries, the overvalued rate artificially lowers the domestic currency price of foreign imports of the same product (e.g., radios, tires, bicycles, or household utensils).

Hence in the absence of effective government intervention and regulation of the foreign-exchange dealings of its nationals, overvalued exchange rates have a tendency to exacerbate balance of payments and foreign-debt problems simply because they cheapen imports while making exports more costly. Chronic payments deficits resulting primarily from current account transactions (exports and imports) can possibly be ameliorated by a currency **devaluation**. Simply defined, a country's currency is devalued when the official rate at which its central bank is prepared to exchange the local currency for dollars is abruptly increased. A currency **depreciation**, by contrast, refers to a gradual decrease in the purchasing power of a domestic currency in foreign markets relative to domestic markets; *appreciation* refers to a gradual increase.[23] For example, a devaluation of the South African rand and the Indian rupee would occur if their official exchange rates of approximately 5 rand and 40 rupees to the dollar were changed to, say, 8 rand and 50 rupees per dollar. Following these devaluations, U.S. importers of South African and Indian goods would pay fewer dollars to obtain the same products. But U.S. exports to South Africa and India would become more expensive, requiring more rand or rupees to purchase than before. In short, by lowering the *foreign*-currency price of its exports (and thereby generating more foreign demand) while raising the *domestic*-currency price of its imports (and thereby lowering domestic demand), LDCs that devalue their currency hope to improve their trade balance vis-à-vis the rest of the world. This is a principal reason why devaluation is always a key component of IMF stabilization policies when currencies are "pegged."

An alternative to a currency devaluation would be to allow foreign-exchange rates to fluctuate freely in accordance with changing conditions of international demand and supply. Freely fluctuating or **flexible exchange rates** in the past were not thought to be desirable, especially in developing nations heavily dependent on exports and imports, because they are extremely unpredictable, subject to wide and uncontrollable fluctuations, and susceptible to foreign and domestic currency speculation. Such unpredictable fluctuations can wreak havoc with both short- and long-range development plans. Nevertheless, during the global balance of payments and debt crises of the 1980s, a number of developing countries, including Mexico, Argentina, Chile, and the Philippines, were effectively forced by the IMF to let their exchange rates float freely in order to correct sizable payments imbalances and to prevent continued capital flight. The same phenomenon occurred again for Mexico in 1994 and for Thailand, the Philippines, South Korea, Malaysia, and Indonesia in 1997 and 1998 during the Asian currency crisis. In a matter of several months during 1997, the Thai baht lost one-third of its value against the dollar and the Philippine peso, South Korean won, Malaysian ringgit, and Indonesian rupiah fell by almost 30%.

The present international system of floating exchange rates, formally legalized at the 1976 Jamaica IMF meeting, represents a compromise between a fixed (artificially pegged) and a fully flexible exchange-rate system. Under this "managed" floating system, major international currencies are permitted to fluctuate freely, but erratic swings are limited through central bank intervention. Some developing countries, however, have continued to peg their currencies to those of developed countries. Some, like Kenya, have gone further and decided to tie their currencies to the movements of a weighted index of the world's major currencies rather than to tie them to a particular currency, like the U.S. dollar or the pound sterling. However, the trend for most LDCs is toward a **managed float** of their currencies.

One final point that should be made about currency devaluations concerns their probable effect on domestic prices. Devaluation has the immediate effect of raising prices of imported goods in terms of the local currency. Imported shirts, shoes, radios, records, foodstuffs, and bicycles that formerly cost x rupees now cost $(1 + d)x$ rupees, depending on the percentage magnitude of the devaluation, d. If, as a result of these higher prices, domestic workers seek to preserve the real value of their purchasing power, they are likely to initiate increased wage and salary demands. Such increases, if granted, will raise production costs and tend to push local prices up even higher. A **wage-price spiral** of domestic inflation is thereby set in motion. In fact, a vicious cycle of devaluation—domestic wage and price increases, higher export prices, and worsened balance of trade—could result. Thus the devaluation decision could simply exacerbate the external balance of payments problem while generating increased inflation domestically. For example, following the widespread IMF-induced currency devaluations during the 1997 Asian crisis, rates of inflation shot up in 1998 from 11% to 35% in Indonesia, from 6% to 12% in Thailand, and from 5% to 10% in the Philippines. Unemployment rates doubled, and workers took to the streets, demanding an end to the layoffs and a rise in wages to offset their lost purchasing power.

As for the distributional effects of a devaluation, it is clear that by altering the domestic price and returns of "tradable" goods (exports and imports) and creating incentives for the production of exports as opposed to domestic goods, devaluation will benefit certain groups at the expense of others. In general, urban wage earners, people with fixed incomes, the unemployed, and the small farmers and rural and urban small-scale producers and suppliers of services who do not participate in the export sector stand to be financially hurt by the domestic inflation that typically follows a devaluation. Conversely, large exporters (usually large landowners and foreign-owned corporations) and medium-size local businesses engaged in foreign trade stand to benefit the most. Although we cannot categorically assert that devaluation tends to worsen income distribution, we may conclude that the more that ownership of and control over the export sector is concentrated in private rather than public hands, the greater is the likelihood that devaluation will have an adverse effect on income distribution.[24] For this reason, among others, international commercial and financial problems (e.g., chronic balance of payments deficits) cannot be divorced from domestic problems (e.g., poverty and inequality) in LDCs. Policy responses to alleviate one problem can either improve or worsen others.

Summary and Conclusions: Trade Optimists and Trade Pessimists

We are now in a position to summarize the major issues and arguments in the great ongoing debate between advocates of free-trade, outward-looking development and export promotion policies—the **trade optimists**—and advocates of greater protection, more inward-looking strategies, and greater import substitution—the **trade pessimists**.[25] Let us begin with the latter school of thought.

Trade Pessimist Arguments

Trade pessimists tend to focus on three basic themes: (1) the limited growth of world demand for primary exports, (2) the secular deterioration in the terms of trade for primary producing nations, and (3) the rise of "new protectionism," against the exports of LDC manufactured and processed agricultural goods.

LDC exports grow slowly because of (1) a shift in developed countries from low-technology, material-intensive goods to high-technology, skill-intensive products, which decreases the demand for raw materials; (2) increased efficiency in industrial uses of raw materials; (3) the substitution of synthetics for natural raw materials like rubber, copper, and cotton; (4) the low income elasticity of demand for primary products and light manufactured goods; (5) the rising productivity of agriculture in developed countries; and (6) the rising tide of protectionism for both agriculture and labor-intensive developed-country industries.

The terms of trade deteriorate because of (1) oligopolistic control of factor and commodity markets in developed countries combined with increasing competitive sources of supply of LDC exportables and (2) a generally lower level of the income elasticity of demand for LDC exports.

The rise of **new protectionism** in the developed world results from the success of a growing number of LDCs in producing a wide range of both primary and secondary products at competitive world market prices, combined with the quite natural fears of workers in higher-cost developed-country industries that their jobs will be lost. They pressure their governments in North America, Europe, and Japan to curtail or prohibit competitive imports from the developing world. The trade pessimists therefore conclude that trade hurts developing countries because (1) the slow growth in demand for their traditional exports means that export expansion results in lower export prices and a transfer of income from poor to rich nations; (2) without import restrictions, the high elasticity of LDC demand for imports combined with the low elasticity for their exports means that developing countries must grow slowly to avoid chronic balance of payments and foreign-exchange crises; and (3) developing nations have their "static" comparative advantage in primary products, which means that export-promoting free-trade policies tend to inhibit industrialization, which is in turn the major vehicle for the accumulation of technical skills and entrepreneurial talents. Trade pessimists view trade liberalization under the WTO as limited in practice, with LDCs lacking the high-powered lawyers and other resources needed to pry developed markets open.

Trade Optimist Arguments

Trade optimists tend to underplay the role of international demand in determining the gains from trade. Instead, they focus on the relationship between LDC trade policy, export performance, and economic growth.[26] They argue that **trade liberalization** (including export promotion, currency devaluation, removal of trade restrictions, and generally "getting prices right") generates rapid export and economic growth because free trade provides a number of benefits:

1. It promotes competition, improved resource allocation, and economies of scale in areas where LDCs have a comparative advantage. Costs of production are consequently lowered.

2. It generates pressures for increased efficiencies, product improvement, and technical change, thus raising factor productivity and further lowering costs of production.

3. It accelerates overall economic growth, which raises profits and promotes greater saving and investment and thus furthers growth.

4. It attracts foreign capital and expertise, which are in scarce supply in LDCs.

5. It generates needed foreign exchange that can be used to import food if the agricultural sector lags behind or suffers droughts or other natural catastrophes.

6. It eliminates costly economic distortions caused by government interventions in both the export and foreign-exchange markets and substitutes market allocation for the corruption and rent-seeking activities that usually result from an overactive government sector.

7. It promotes more equal access to scarce resources, which improves overall resource allocation.

8. It enables LDCs to take full advantage of reforms under the WTO.

Trade optimists argue, finally, that even though export promotion may at first be difficult with limited gains—especially in comparison with the easy gains of first-stage import substitution—over the longer run, the economic benefits tend to gain momentum, whereas import substitution faces rapidly diminishing returns.

The Industrialization Strategy Approach to Export Policy

Since the mid-1980s, another important strand of thought has emerged concerning the relationship between trade and development. The **industrialization strategy approach** is outward-oriented and optimistic about export-led development but still envisions an active role for government in influencing the type and sequencing of exports as a country strives to produce more advanced products, adding higher value.

The industrialization strategy approach began primarily as an empirical literature but has developed a theory to help explain why an interventionist strategy toward exports can accelerate growth and improve development outcomes more than a strict free-trade approach. The theory is focused on identifying and redressing market failures encountered in the process of industrialization.

This strain of research has revealed that rather than operating on a free-market basis, the export-oriented East Asian economies, with the partial exception of Hong Kong, in fact had very active government interventions to encourage industrial exports and to attempt to move up the ladder of comparative advantage toward higher-skill and higher-technology content. Such programs are termed *industrialization strategies* or more narrowly as *industrial policies.*[27]

Why might an economy be better off using such policies, and why might these policies be better than available alternatives for achieving development goals? It has long been recognized that there are market failures in original research and development; some of the benefits of these expenditures are captured by other firms. This is the rationale for government research programs in the developed countries (such as the National Institutes of Health in the United States). But analogous market failures apply to the transfer of technology from developed to developing countries. In particular, if one firm absorbs technology from outside the region but then other firms benefit from learning by watching and similar spillover effects, then without outside support, we can expect too little technology transfer and other firm upgrading from the social viewpoint. This market failure forms part of the explanation for why a government industrialization strategy centered on absorbing technology from abroad might improve efficiency. In part, government can help solve a coordination problem.

The question, then, is why an *export-oriented* industrial strategy might be important. Of course, for small countries, one reason is to ensure a market of adequate size. But the full explanation goes well beyond this. The use of manufacturing exports of growing technological content as a yardstick of performance automatically emphasizes targets with very strong development benefits. In addition, the world export market is an arena in which performance is clearly, quickly, and rigorously tested while keeping government, whose resources and information capacities are inherently limited, tightly focused on relevant and manageable problems.

In this regard, export targets as a development policy mechanism hold the advantage of being easily observable. This fact has long been understood by LDC fiscal authorities, who have taxed exports precisely because they are observable and therefore not subject to the tax evasion that is so rampant in the developing world.

This distortion has a well-publicized (if not self-evident) antiexport bias effect. But East Asian countries put this "fiscal observability" to use as the centerpiece of their industrial policy system in a way that reversed the negative incentive effects of export taxes.

However, the literature has also stressed the continued importance of infant-industry support. Why might this sometimes be effective? First, empirically, import substitution often precedes export promotion. The influential study by Hollis Chenery, Sherwin Robinson, and Moshe Syrquin concluded that "periods of significant export expansion are almost always preceded by periods of strong import substitution."[28] This does not mean that across-the-board protection is viable today, even for large countries, but countries known primarily for their export prowess, such as South Korea, have often protected—for a limited time—the very industries in which they later became successful exporters.

Note that without proper attention to incentives (for both market and rent-seeking activities), these same industrial policies can prove counterproductive. Countries that cannot find the political will to use protection as a highly selective and strictly temporary instrument of industrial policy even in cases where large, identified market failures can be shown to exist may be better off abandoning this instrument altogether.

Evidence shows that Singapore, Taiwan, and South Korea have had especially active government industrialization strategies and specific industrial policies over a period of several decades. The experience in South Korea is examined in the case study at the conclusion of this chapter. The specific policies differ across countries but have common features in encouraging indigenous skills, technologies, and firms and not just promoting labor-intensive manufactures but actively and systematically seeking to upgrade over time.

In a globalizing economy, opportunities to grow through exporting by relying on free-market incentives are in some ways greater but in other ways less strong than before. For example, the end of the Multi-Fiber Arrangement most likely means that low-income countries will find it difficult to get manufactured exports under way through the traditional means of starting with textile exports. The growth of China as the "workshop of the world" suggests that it will likely be more difficult to break into exporting in other sectors as well.

Conditions for industrialization strategy also differ today from those that prevailed three decades ago, in that foreign investors are far more mobile and can quickly go wherever wages or other production costs are lowest. But as Sanjaya Lall has argued, "Increasing mobility does not mean factors spread themselves evenly over poor countries. Efficient production requires local capabilities to complement the mobile factors. Thus globalization needs efficient 'localization': Countries must provide the technical, skill, quality, and reliability needs of competitive production." Lall further argues that

"technologies cannot be effectively used by developing economies just by opening up to global trade, technology, or capital flows. Technology cannot be fully embodied in machines, licences, or people: It has strong tacit elements. These tacit elements need time, investment and effort: to understand, adapt, use and improve technologies—to build new capabilities. Such effort generally faces pervasive market and institutional failures: within the firm, between firms, and between enterprises and factor markets and institutions. Proactive strategies, often selective in nature, are essential for industrial success.[29]

As evidence has accumulated, the debate has shifted. Instead of opposing all government industrialization strategy, it has become a mainstream view to acknowledge the value of policies that effectively improve the position of all industrial exporters but to avoid what is termed "picking winners." In practice, Lall argues, this distinction is difficult to make because often the needed new organizations, skills, and infrastructure are specific to a given sector. But as a general starting point, nonpreferential but active government support for manufactures exporting as a development policy has gained wide acceptance.

Another issue is whether and to what degree the new WTO rules permit government actions like those of South Korea in the 1970s and 1980s (see the case study at the end of the chapter). Although general support for all industries that does not discriminate is permitted, and such support continues to be practiced by economies sufficiently advanced and governments sufficiently skilled to do so, such as Taiwan and South Korea, today's low-income countries that might benefit from exporting strategically in the way that Korea once did are not permitted to do so. There are, however, some important exceptions to these rules.

A third issue is whether other governments have the competence and political authority that South Korea did during its period of active industrial policy management. Where it is lacking, advocates have argued that the World Bank and other agencies should help governments build this competence. But some observers argue that if governments lack the needed skills (and are unable to get international assistance to develop the needed capabilities), they may ultimately be better off using less interventionist strategies.

Although the context of this debate has changed, with the far more competitive world environment and changes in trade rules, industrial policy considerations will continue to be important in the design of developing countries' export strategies.

Reconciling the Arguments: The Data and the Consensus

We can evaluate the debate on two levels, the empirical and the philosophical. Rostam Kavoussi argues that the empirical evidence demonstrates quite clearly that neither the trade optimists nor the trade pessimists are correct at all times. It all depends on fluctuations in the world economy.[30] Thus when the world economy was expanding rapidly during the period from 1960 to 1973, the more open-economy LDCs clearly outperformed (in terms of aggregate export and economic growth) the more closed-economy nations. The trade optimists' arguments appear validated during this period of rapid world growth. But when the world economy slowed down between 1973 and 1977, the more open economies (with the notable exception of the four Asian NICs) had a more difficult time and the trade pessimists fared better. A follow-up 1988 study by Hans Singer and Patricia Gray, which extended Kavoussi's empirical analysis for the period 1977–1983, when world economic conditions were even more unfavorable, supports the finding that high growth rates of export earnings occur only when external demand is strong.[31] Their conclusions seem validated to a considerable extent by subsequent history. LDC export growth was very strong during the high-growth late 1990s but fell off precipitously with the slowdown that began in 2000.

Changes in trade policy appear to have little or no effect. Furthermore, low-income countries were found to fare worse across all time periods. Singer and Gray argue that contrary to the position of the World Bank and other trade optimists, an outward-oriented policy is not necessarily valid for all LDCs. To conclude, therefore, that either export promotion or import substitution is always an unambiguously better strategy—even for promoting economic growth narrowly conceived, let alone our broader definition of development—is to miss a key conceptual and empirical insight that a growing number of development economists are beginning to recognize. The verdict on the impact of the WTO is still out.

In the final analysis, it is not a developing country's inward- or outward-looking stance vis-à-vis the rest of the world that will determine whether or not it develops. Inward-looking, protectionist policies such as tariffs, quotas and exchange-rate adjustments do not necessarily guarantee more jobs, higher incomes that are more equitably distributed, adequate nutrition and health, clean water, or relevant education any more than outward-looking, noninterventionist policies do. Policies of export promotion appear to have contributed more to GNP growth than import substitution did during the 1960s and 1970s. Similar results were not forthcoming in the slow-growth 1980s. Moreover, the success of export promotion in the 1990s globalization era varied widely from region to region and country to country. Some prospered, others stagnated, and some Asian economies that had prospered earlier through more open trade and financial liberalization policies (e.g., Thailand, Indonesia, Malaysia, and South Korea) found themselves in serious trouble when their currencies collapsed and foreign investors and speculators quickly withdrew their funds (see Chapter 16).

In short, the current consensus leans toward an eclectic view that attempts to fit the relevant arguments of both the free-trade and protectionist models to the specific economic, institutional, and political realities of diverse nations at different stages of development. What works for one may not work for another. For example, the East Asian success stories may have little relevance for other developing nations beyond the important conclusion reached by Colin Bradford:

> What seems to distinguish the East Asian development experiences is not the dominance of market forces, free enterprise, and internal liberalization, but effective, highly interactive relationships between the public and private sectors characterized by shared goals and commitments embodied in the development strategy and economic policy of the government. The dichotomy between market forces and government intervention is not only overdrawn: it misconceives the fundamental dynamic at work. It is the *degree of consistency* between the two sectors—rather than the extent of implicit or explicit conflict—that has been important in the successful development cases. A coherent development strategy was not only formulated but followed by both the government and the private

sector in providing an unusual degree of common direction to national energies in these cases.[32]

Finally, all of the foregoing discussion has left out perhaps one of the most viable long-run trade policies for small and medium-size developing economies. This is the expansion of trade among the developing countries—South-South rather than North-South trade alone—and the possibilities of economic integration in developing regions.

South-South Trade and Economic Integration: Looking Outward and Inward

The Growth of Trade among Developing Countries

Although trade among the LDCs still represents a meager 6.3% of total world trade, it grew rapidly during the 1980s. By 1990, South-South trade represented almost 33% of all developing-world exports. However, this share fell to about 23.5%, by 2002.[33] Nevertheless, much of the growth of these inter-LDC exports helped compensate for weak demand and protectionism in the developed world. Exports to China have provided an important opportunity in recent years for some developing countries.

Many development economists have argued that developing countries should orient their trade more toward one another.[34] Their arguments usually entail four basic points:

1. There are relative comparative-advantage changes to South-South as opposed to North-South trade.

2. There are greater dynamic gains to be realized from such trade.

3. Export instability resulting from fluctuations in developed-country economic activity can be reduced.

4. Greater collective self-reliance will be fostered.

Let us examine the nature of these arguments.

Economic Integration: Theory and Practice

One strong variant of the South-South trade hypothesis is that LDCs should go beyond greater trade with one another and move in the direction of **economic integration**. Economic integration occurs whenever a group of nations in the same region join together to form an **economic union** or **regional trading bloc** by raising a common tariff wall against the products of nonmember countries while freeing internal trade among members. In the terminology of integration literature, nations that levy common external tariffs while freeing internal trade are said to have formed a **customs union**. If external tariffs against outside countries differ among member nations while internal trade is free, the nations are said to have formed a **free-trade area**. Finally, a **common market** possesses all the attributes of a customs union (common external tariffs and free internal trade) plus the free movement of labor and capital among the partner states.

The theory of customs unions and economic integration is associated primarily with the work of Jacob Viner of Princeton University in the 1940s. The traditional core of this theory, which focuses on the static resource and production reallocation effects within highly integrated and flexible industrialized nations, is of limited value to contemporary developing nations intent on building up their industrial base. Yet many concepts of the theory of integration provide valid criteria on which to evaluate the probable short-run success or failure of economic cooperation among developing countries.

The basic economic rationale for the gradual integration of less developed economies is a long-term dynamic one: Integration provides the opportunity for industries that have not yet been established as well as for those that have to take advantage of economies of large-scale production made possible by expanded markets. Integration therefore needs to be viewed as a mechanism to encourage a rational division of labor among a group of countries, each of which is too small to benefit from such a division by itself. In the absence of integration, each separate country may not provide a sufficiently large domestic market to enable local industries to lower their production costs through economies of scale. In such cases, import-substituting industrialization will typically result, as we have seen, in the establishment of high-cost, inefficient local industries. Moreover, in the absence of integration, the same industry (e.g., textiles or shoes) may be set up in two or more adjoining small nations. Each will be operating at less than optimal capacity but will be protected against the imports of the other by high tariff or quota barriers. Not only does such duplication result in wasted scarce resources, but it also means that consumers are forced to pay a higher price for the product than if the market were large enough for high-volume, low-cost production to take place at a single location.

This leads to a second dynamic rationale for LDC economic integration. By removing barriers to trade among member states, the possibility of coordinated industrial strategy is created, especially in industries where economies of scale are likely to exist. Examples include fertilizer and petrochemical plants, heavy industry like iron and steel, capital goods and machine tool industries, and small-farm mechanical equipment. But the coordination of industrial expansion that enables all member states to accelerate their rates of industrial growth by assigning given industries to different members takes the partners that much closer to full economic and eventual political union. Problems of sovereignty and national self-interest impinge at this stage. To date, they have overwhelmed the economic logic of a close and coordinated union. However, as LDCs, especially small ones, continue to experience the limitations of either development in isolation (**autarky**) or full participation in the highly unequal world economy, it is likely that interest will increase in the coming decades in the long-run benefits of some form of economic (and perhaps political) cooperation. The recent expansion and deepening of cooperation in the Association of Southeast Asian Nations (ASEAN) is a case in point.

In addition to these two long-term dynamic arguments for integration, there are also the standard static evaluative criteria known as **trade creation** and **trade diversion**. Trade creation is said to occur when common external barriers and internal free trade lead to a shift in production from high- to low-cost member states. For example, before integration, both country A and country B may produce textiles for their respective local markets. Country A may be a lower-cost producer, but its exports to country B are blocked by the latter's high tariffs. If A and B form a customs union by eliminating all barriers to internal trade, country A's more efficient low-cost textile industry will service both markets. Trade will have been created in the sense that the removal of barriers has led to a shift in country B's consumption from its own relatively high-cost textiles to the lower-cost textiles of country A.

Similarly, trade diversion is said to occur when the erection of external tariff barriers causes production and consumption of one or more member states to shift from lower-cost nonmember sources of supply (e.g., a developed country) to higher-cost member producers. Trade diversion is normally considered undesirable because both the world and member states are perceived to be worse off as a result of diversion of production from more efficient foreign suppliers to the less efficient domestic industries of member states. However, because of potential economies of scale, the creation of local jobs, and the circular flow of income within the integrated region, static trade diversion may turn out to be dynamic trade creation. This is simply a variant of the standard infant-industry argument for protection, but with the more likely possibility that the infant will grow up as a result of the larger market in which it now operates. Moreover, if in the absence of integration, each member state were to protect its local import-substituting industry against all lower-cost foreign suppliers, the common external tariff of member states would cause no more trade diversion than would have happened anyway. But as we just saw, if there are scale economies, the possibility of dynamic trade creation can emerge.

Regional Trading Blocs and the Globalization of Trade

We may conclude, therefore, that developing countries at relatively equal stages of industrial development with similar market sizes and with a strong interest in coordinating and rationalizing their joint industrial growth patterns stand to benefit from the combined inward- and outward-looking trade policies represented by economic integration.[35] In particular, regional groupings of small nations like those of Central America and southern and western Africa can create the economic conditions (mainly in the form of larger internal markets) for accelerating their joint development efforts. Such groupings can also promote long-run development.

But even if such an integration strategy may seem economically logical and persuasive on paper, in practice it requires a degree of statesmanship and a regional rather than nationalistic orientation that is often lacking in many countries. The unfortunate demise of the East African Community in the 1970s demonstrates how political and ideological conflict—in this case among Kenya, Tanzania, and Uganda—can more than offset the economic logic of regional cooperation.

But prospects for the future are much more positive. As trade becomes increasingly globalized, even the largest industrialized nations now realize that they cannot go it alone. In Europe, a single economic market became a reality at the end of

1992 as all internal trade barriers were removed. Now the European Union has a single currency, requiring close monetary coordination and in effect creating the largest economic entity in the world. Similar efforts are under way in North America, where the North American Free Trade Agreement (NAFTA) represents a unique arrangement in that a large developing country, Mexico, has joined a developed-country trading bloc, Canada and the United States. (Chile, a NIC, is also seeking membership.)

Two major trading blocs now exist in Latin America. Argentina, Brazil, Paraguay, and Uruguay in 1994 finalized arrangements for a free-trade area called the Southern Cone Common Market, also known as Mercosur. In the six years after the original treaty was signed in 1990, regional trade in Mercosur more than quadrupled to $17.1 billion (see Table 13.2), and Brazil replaced the United States as Argentina's largest trading partner. Mercosur is taking advantage of sizable economies of scale and a new expanded market of 180 million people and $800 billion of economic activity. However, rivalries between Brazil and Argentina continue to put the future of Mercosur at risk. The other Latin American bloc, the Andean Group (consisting of Bolivia, Colombia, Ecuador, Peru, and Venezuela), established a full-fledged common market in 1995. Discussions also continue about creation of a hemisphere-wide Free Trade Area of the Americas. In Africa, moves are under way to promote regional economic integration, including the South African Development Community (SADC). Thanks to well-developed railroad and air links, the ten members of SADC—Angola, Botswana, Lesotho, Malawi, Mozambique, Namibia, South Africa, Swaziland, Zambia, and Zimbabwe—anticipate new and much greater trading opportunities.

The critical question about all these new regional trading blocs is not whether they will promote greater internal growth (which they likely will) but whether such regional groupings will fragment the world economy and run counter to the recent globalization of trade. Most economists believe that **globalization** is here to stay, particularly as multinational corporations set up subsidiaries throughout the world. For LDCs, effective regional blocs can provide a buffer against the negative effects of globalization while still permitting the dynamic benefits of intraunion specialization and greater equality among members to take place.

In any case, developing-country trading blocs have a tough road ahead. Trade among members of NAFTA and the European Union is much more significant, even in the relative amount of trade conducted among countries within the bloc. For example, in 2002, 56.7% of all trade of NAFTA members Canada, Mexico, and the United States were with each other, while the corresponding figure for the EU was 60.6% of its trade. In contrast, as seen in Table 13.2, the North American blocs each conduct only about one-tenth of their trade internally, and even ASEAN conducts only 23.7% of its trade among member nations. The rates are much lower for most other developing-country trading blocs. Moreover, the World Bank estimated that whereas in 1995, developed-country trade barriers cost developing countries $43.1 billion in lost welfare, *developing*-country trade barriers cost developing countries $65.1 billion in lost welfare. Thus LDCs cost each other about half again as much as developed countries cost LDCs—in spite of the much smaller size of the developing economies.[36]

TABLE 13.2   Trade within Selected Regional Trading Blocs, 1970–2002

Trading Bloc	1970		1980		1990		2002	
	Volume ($ millions)	Share of Total Exports (%)	Volume ($ millions)	Share of Total Exports (%)	Volume ($ millions)	Share of Total Exports (%)	Volume ($ millions)	Share of Total Exports (%)
Latin America								
Andean Group	97	1.8	1,161	3.8	1,312	4.1	5,026	9.5
Southern Cone Market (Mercosur)	451	9.4	3,424	11.6	4,127	8.9	10,341	11.6
Central American Common Market (CACM)	287	26.0	1,174	24.4	671	15.3	2,598	11.1
Latin American Integration Association (LAIA)	1,263	9.9	10,981	13.7	12,331	8.9	35,755	11.1
Africa								
Common Market for Eastern and Southern Africa (COMESA)	392	8.7	609	6.0	910	6.3	1,801	6.4
Economic Community of West African States (ECOWAS)	86	2.9	692	10.1	1,533	7.8	3,009	10.6
Southern African Development Community (SADC)	483	8.0	617	2.0	1,630	4.8	4,268	9.3[a]
Asia								
Association of Southeast Asian Nations (ASEAN)	1,456	22.9	13,350	18.7	28,648	19.8	95,473	23.7[a]

Sources: World Bank, *1998* and *2004 World Development Indicators* (Washington, D.C.: World Bank, 1998, 2004) tabs. 6.6 (1998) and 6.5 (2004). Reprinted with permission.
[a]2002 Figures are not fully comparable in that South Africa joined SADC in 1994 and Vietnam, Laos, Myanmar, and Cambodia joined ASEAN in the late 1990s.

It should also be noted that some development economists regard exporting to developed nations as inherently more valuable than exporting to other LDCs because of the learning that can occur when customers provide feedback on quality or suggest other products that firms might be able to export competitively. Part of the growth in Mexico in recent years has been attributed to greater learning from the U.S. and Canadian economies with which it now shares NAFTA membership. Ideally, a balance may be found allowing LDC trade blocs not only to continue to develop but also to gain improved access to developed-country markets.

Trade Policies of Developed Countries: The Need for Reform

We have seen that a major obstacle to LDC export expansion, whether in primary products or manufactures, has been the various trade barriers erected by developed nations against the principal commodity exports of developing countries. In the absence of economic integration or even in support of that effort, the prospects for future LDC trade and foreign-exchange expansion depend largely on the domestic and international economic policies of developed nations. Unfortunately, the rapid integration among NAFTA and EU members may itself pose one of the biggest impediments to LDC exports to North America and Europe. Although internal structural and economic reform may be essential to economic and social progress, an improvement in the competitive position of industries in which LDCs do have a dynamic comparative advantage will be of little benefit to them or the world as a whole so long as their access to major world markets is restricted by rich-country commercial policies.

Developed countries' economic and commercial policies are most important from the perspective of future LDC foreign-exchange earnings in three major areas:

1. Tariff and nontariff barriers to LDC exports

2. Adjustment assistance for displaced workers in developed-country industries hurt by freer access of labor-intensive, low-cost LDC exports

3. The general impact of rich-country domestic economic policies on developing economies

Rich-Nation Tariff and Nontariff Trade Barriers and the 1995 Uruguay Round GATT Agreement

Until 1995, the new-protectionist tariff and **nontariff trade barriers** (e.g., excise taxes, quotas, "voluntary" export restraints, sanitary regulations) imposed by rich nations on the commodity exports of poor ones were the most significant obstacles to the expansion of the latter's export-earning capacities. Moreover, as we have seen, many of these tariffs increased with the degree of product processing; that is, they were higher for processed foodstuffs than for basic foodstuffs (e.g., peanut oil compared with peanuts), higher for, say, shirts than for raw cotton. These high effective tariffs inhibited LDCs from developing and diversifying their own secondary-export industries and thus acted to restrain their industrial expansion.

The overall effect of developed-country tariffs, quotas, and nontariff barriers has been to lower the effective price received by LDCs for their exports, reduce the quantity exported, and diminish foreign-exchange earnings. Although the burdens that developed-country tariffs imposed on LDC primary- and secondary-product exports varied from commodity to commodity, it has been estimated that the net impact of trade barriers on all products reduced developing-world foreign-exchange earnings by more than $100 billion per year in 2000.

However, the final act of the **Uruguay Round** agreement that was signed in April 1994 and became effective in 1995 after passage by 124 national legislatures substantially reduced tariff and nontariff trade barriers in many sectors. It also established the **World Trade Organization (WTO)** to replace the 47-year-old **General Agreement on Tariffs and Trade (GATT)**. The Geneva-based WTO is intended to oversee the agreement and settle trade disputes. The three major provisions of the accord, from the perspective of developing nations, are the following:[37]

1. Developed countries cut tariffs on manufactures by an average of 40% in five equal annual reductions. Tariffs were eliminated in ten major sectors (beer, construction equipment, distilled spirits, farm machinery, furniture, medical equipment paper, pharmaceuticals, steel, and toys). Developing countries in turn agreed to not raise tariffs by "binding" in recent trade reforms. Despite these reductions, developing countries still face tariffs that are 10% higher than the global average while the least developed countries face tariffs that are 30% higher.[38]

2. Trade in agricultural products came under the authority of the WTO and were to be progressively liberalized. Developed-country nontariff barriers were to be converted into tariffs and reduced to 36% of the 1986–1988 level by the year 2000. The volume of subsidized agricultural exports was to be reduced, but only by 21%. Although much progress was made, agricultural subsidies have returned to record highs.

3. For textiles and apparel, the Multi-Fiber Arrangement quotas, which have long penalized exports of developing countries, were phased out by 2005, with most of the reductions taking effect toward the end of the period. But tariffs on textile imports were reduced only to an average of 12%—three times the average level of tariffs on other MDC imports. Moreover, textile exports looked set to increasingly originate from China rather than low-income countries.

One optimistic study that attempted to assess the quantitative impact of the agreement on developing-country economies concluded that the developing world's real income could grow by as much as $78 billion (in 1992 dollars).[39] But an evaluation by the UNDP in its 1997 *Human Development Report* led its authors to the following conclusion:

> Poor countries often lose out because the rules of the game are biased against them—particularly those relating to international trade. The Uruguay Round hardly changed the picture. Developing countries, with three-quarters of the world's people, will get only a quarter to a third of the income gains generated—and most of that will go to a few powerful exporters in Asia and Latin America.[40]

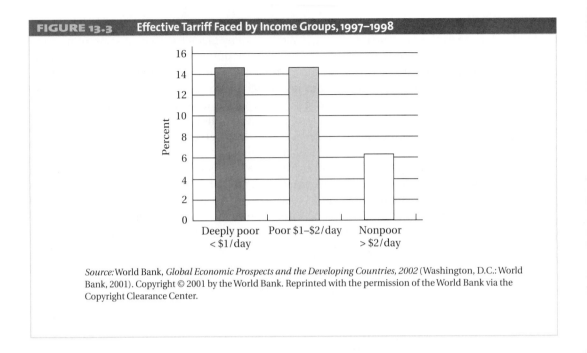

FIGURE 13.3   Effective Tariff Faced by Income Groups, 1997–1998

Source: World Bank, *Global Economic Prospects and the Developing Countries, 2002* (Washington, D.C.: World Bank, 2001). Copyright © 2001 by the World Bank. Reprinted with the permission of the World Bank via the Copyright Clearance Center.

Indeed, at the household level, the World Bank reported that the effective, trade-weighted tariffs faced by the poor are much higher than those faced by the nonpoor. Both those living on less than $1 a day, and those living on between $1 and $2 per day, faced effective tariffs of well over 14%, while those with higher incomes of over $2 per day face trade-weighted tariffs of only just over 6% on average, as shown in Figure 13.3.

Partly as a result, many governments, as well as companies and citizens, of developing countries believe that they got a bad deal in the Uruguay Round negotiations that culminated in the establishment of the WTO. There is the widespread conviction in the developing world that the rich countries did not live up to their part of the bargain, failing to open their markets fairly. Developing nations complain that governments and corporations of the developed world have the high-powered lawyers and other leverage to force developing countries to follow WTO requirements, while poor nations lack the resources to force the rich nations to do the same.

However, developing countries now represent more than three-quarters of the 142-member WTO. And whereas India and Brazil played high-profile, vocal roles in trade negotiations under the GATT, with perhaps three dozen other developing countries taking active, if relatively quiet roles, by 2001 the situation had changed palpably. The WTO director's own 2001 report noted that after eight trade liberalization rounds over the past half century, trade barriers remain in place in textiles and agriculture, the goods most affecting the developing world. As the world's trading nations began consideration of a new round of negotiations on reducing trade barriers, the developing world was insisting on a larger say. And they may well get it. Unlike the IMF and World Bank, the WTO operates on consensus, in effect giving even small, poor nations an equal vote—and an effective veto. It remains to be seen what this will mean in practice. But while there was much discord in WTO meetings in Seattle in 1999, *participation* was the watchword in the preparatory meetings for the November 2001 meeting that involved virtually all WTO members. Developing-country governments say they are reluctant to extend negotiations to what they term the "nontrade" issues of investment, competition, environment, and labor standards. Thus LDCs do not appear to be without bargaining power if they can learn to use it effectively.

The new negotiations have been named the Doha Development Round: *Doha* for the city in Qatar in which agreement on the agenda was reached in November 2001 and *Development* for the commitment to focus much more on the needs and aspirations of the developing world in this round of trade agreements. Whether this goal is achieved remains to be seen. But by 2005, leading developing countries were playing an active role in setting the agenda for trade talks as never before.

Industrial and Export Policy: South Korea

South Korea is one of the developing world's great long-term success stories. The country is now classified by the World Bank as a high-income economy, with PPP income at close to $18,000 in 2003. Korean consumer electronics and other brands have become synonymous with good quality at reasonable prices. Even more impressive are Korea's social development achievements. By 2004, Korea had attained the highest tertiary enrollment rate in the world, with graduates concentrated in technical fields. Life expectancy topped 75, and the country placed 26th on the human development index in 2002, nine places higher than would be predicted from income alone.

Exports, particularly manufactures in such key sectors as consumer electronics and motor vehicles and recently in high technology, have grown at an extraordinary rate in Korea. One apparent reason for South Korea's remarkable industrial achievements is the orientation of its national industrialization strategy toward the promotion of exports of increasingly sophisticated skill and technology content. Strong financial incentives for industrial firms to move up the ladder of skills and technology have been present in most of its policies.

In its years of rapid catch-up, South Korea used at least 19 major types of export promotion–oriented industrial policy interventions

(note that only some of these policies were in effect in any one industry and at any one time and that in recent years, effective subsidies have been considerably scaled back):

1. Currency undervaluation. The effective exchange rate (EER) for exporters was kept higher than that for importers. As early as 1964, South Korea's EER for exports was 281 and its EER for imports was 247—reflecting not trade neutrality but a pro-export bias.
2. Preferential access to imported intermediate inputs needed for producing exports, with strict controls to prevent abuse. Rebates were paid only after completion of the exports had been documented.
3. Targeted infant industry protection as a first stage before launching an export drive. South Korea has had a high dispersion of effective rates of protection even with a relatively low average.
4. Tariff exemptions on inputs of capital goods needed in exporting activities. This is a price incentive, whereas preferential access (intervention 2) is based on quantity restriction.
5. Tax breaks for domestic suppliers of inputs to exporting firms, which constitutes a domestic-content incentive.
6. Domestic indirect tax exemptions for successful exporters.

7. Lower direct tax on income earned from exports.
8. Accelerated depreciation for exporters.
9. Import entitlement certificates (exemptions from import restrictions) linked directly to export levels. South Korea long maintained an extensive list of items generally prohibited for import, including both luxury goods and import substitution targets. Profitable exemptions from this prohibition have often been available for firms exporting specified goods that have low profit margins.
10. Direct export subsidies for selected industries (no longer in use).
11. Monopoly rights granted to the firm first to achieve exports in targeted industries.
12. Subsidized interest rates and preferential credit access for exporters in selected industries, including automatic access to bank loans for the working capital needed for all export activities. Medium- and long-term loans for investment are rationed and often available only to firms that meet government export targets and pursue other requested activities.
13. A system of export credit insurance and guarantees, as well as tax incentives for overseas marketing and postshipment export loans by the Korean Export-Import Bank.
14. The creation of free-trade zones, industrial parks, and export-oriented infrastructure.
15. The creation of public enterprises to lead the way in establishing a new industry. Howard Pack and Larry Westphal found that "the share of public enterprises in [South] Korea's nonagricultural output is comparatively high, being similar to India's."
16. Activities of the Korean Traders Association and the Korea Trade Promotion Corporation to promote South Korean exports on behalf of South Korean firms worldwide.
17. General orchestration of sectorwide efforts to upgrade the average technological level through the use of a new generation of machinery.
18. Government coordination of foreign technology licensing agreements, using national bargaining power to secure better terms for the private sector in utilizing proprietary foreign technology.
19. The setting of export targets for firms (since the early 1960s). Firms set their own targets, which may be adjusted by the government.

Enforcement of export targets in South Korea was mostly based on moral suasion rather than administrative sanctions or economic incentives, but the evidence suggests that these have been among the most powerful incentives. South Korea as a whole has an extensive pattern of "rituals" reinforcing these economic incentives with cultural ones. In the period of rapid catch-up, a key ritual in the nation's economic life was the Monthly National Trade Promotion Meeting. According to Yung Whee Rhee, Bruce Ross-Larson, and Gary Pursell:

> Chaired by the president, the monthly trade promotion meetings are select gatherings of the ministers and top bureaucrats responsible for trade and the economy; the chief executives of export associations, research organizations, and educational institutions; and the heads of a few firms, mainly the general trading companies and other large firms. The prominence of those attending shows that the monthly meetings are far more than perfunctory meetings to improve coordination between the private and public sectors.

Firms were represented either by their particular export association or, in many cases for large firms, directly. After briefings, awards were typically presented for excellent export performance. Nationally, many types of annual export prizes were publicly awarded and proudly displayed by companies.

Richard Luedde-Neurath has described how South Korea maintained, in addition to domestic content regulations, an extensive system of import controls that lasted well into the 1980s. What he terms the "Korean kaleidoscope" included restrictive trader licensing, widespread quantitative controls, systematic foreign-exchange allocation under the Foreign Exchange Demand and Supply Plan, required advance deposits (which have been as high as 200% of import value), and capricious customs practices. For example, prospective importers had to achieve minimum export earnings before becoming eligible to import.

Pack and Westphal reported that "through import restrictions, selectively promoted infant industries were often initially granted whatever levels of effective protection were required to secure an adequate market for their output as well as a satisfactory rate of return on investment." They also found that after the export promotion reforms of the early 1960s, "imports . . . for the domestic market remained subject to tariffs and quantitative controls." As Wade notes, tariff rates appear much higher when they are averaged over non-export-related imports only. Peter Petri presented evidence that South Korea has had "an unusually protection-prone export bundle."

Sanjaya Lall concluded that in South Korea:

> Industrial targeting and promotion was pragmatic and flexible, and developed in concert with private industry. Moreover, only a relatively small number of activities were supported at a given time, and the effects of protection were offset by strong export orientation. . . . These features strongly differentiate its interventions from those in typical import substituting countries, where infant industry protection was sweeping and open-ended, non-selective, inflexible and designed without consultation with industry.

Thus in the South Korean case, import controls may be called a "handmaiden" of successful industrial export promotion. In the first instance, many export industries begin as infant industries requiring protection. Luedde-Neurath goes so far as to argue that the developing industrial sector functions as a whole and benefits from externalities and linkages between firms, making a market failure case for general protection of manufacturing at a critical stage of development. Amsden has pointed out that in South Korea, subsidization across divisions within firms as a company enters new export markets, such as shipbuilding, is intentionally facilitated by the government. Diversified companies were made to understand that they were expected to use the monopoly rents that they earn from these various import barriers as working capital for expansion into new sectors. The state also offered supplemental support for entering new markets as needed.

As Pack and Westphal summarize the evidence, "something approximating neutrality" applied to "established industries. . . . But there has been substantial industry bias in favor of the promoted infant industries."

Also important to South Korea's success was that it avoided the temptation to meddle in sectors, including new entrepreneurial ventures, that were not central to the current plan. If these private ventures proved successful, the government would include their sector in future strategy considerations.

A World Bank study by Westphal, Rhee, and Pursell concluded that South Korea's export industrialization "has overwhelmingly and in fundamental respects been directed and controlled by nationals" and that "technology has been acquired from abroad largely through means other than direct foreign investment." The role of multinational corporations in the economy has been much smaller than in most other middle-income countries.

As Lall concluded in 2003, the deliberate fostering of large conglomerates, known as *chaebol*, was also important to South Korea's industrial strategy:

> "The chaebol were hand picked from successful exporters and were given various subsidies and privileges, including the restriction of [foreign-firm] entry, in return for furthering a strategy of setting up capital- and technology-intensive activities geared to export markets. The rationale for fostering size was obvious: in view of deficient markets for capital, skills, technology and even infrastructure, large and diversified firms could internalize many of their functions. They could undertake the cost and risk of absorbing very complex technologies . . . further develop it by their own R&D, set up world-scale facilities and create their own brand names and distribution networks. . . . The risks were contained by the strict discipline imposed by the government: export performance, vigorous domestic competition and deliberate interventions to rationalize the industrial structure.

Moreover, Erik Thorbecke and Henry Wan concluded that the establishment of South Korean brand names rather than the contract (or original equipment) manufacturing were the result of government support of heavy industries.

Unquestionably, in the late 1980s and 1990s, South Korea substantially liberalized, particularly before but also after the 1997 financial crisis and subsequent severe recession. One open question is whether South Korea would have done as well had they liberalized sooner. Some economists have argued that South Korea would have industrialized even faster if it had maintained a free-trade policy from the beginning. Other analysts, such as Ha-Joon Chang, Hong-Jae Park, and Chul Gyue Yoo, argue that some aspects of mid-1990s liberalization were a major cause

of the 1997 crisis. In particular, capital account liberalization allowed first for speculative inflows and then for outflows once the crisis hit. But the effect was smaller than for many other countries that have experienced crises, partly because of the significant increase in saving and repatriation of South Korean capital abroad.

Active industrial policy continues emphasizing South Korean entry into leading-edge, high-technology fields. For example, the country's Highly Advanced National Projects Program supports the development of high-tech products that the government believes would successfully compete with those of advanced countries such as the United States and Japan within one to two decades and also supports development of core technologies believed essential for South Korea to achieve capabilities for independent national innovation. South Korea's Ministry of Trade and Industry has targeted new materials, computer-controlled machine tools, bioengineering, microelectronics, fine chemistry, optics, and aircraft as fields in which it predicted that the country could catch up with the United States and Japan economically and technologically. As Lall notes: "Korea alone accounts for some 53 percent of the developing world's total enterprise-financed R&D." He concludes that "the main stimulus to industrial R&D in [South] Korea came less from specific incentives than from the overall strategy that created large firms, gave them finance and protected markets, minimized their reliance on foreign direct investment, and forced them into export markets."

What stands out in the case of industrial policy in South Korea is the selective involvement of the government in projects in which technological progress (product, process, or organizational) has been a central concern. This policy theme may be traced from early attempts at achieving technology transfer in relatively basic industries to the current efforts of South Korea to develop original innovative capacity in high-technology sectors.

What are the alternative arguments? Beyond the claim that Korea could have grown even faster if government had stayed out of industrial strategy, one can also argue, like Joseph Stern and his colleagues, that the central role of the state was necessary in industrial policy in large part because of the way that government set up the rules of the economic game, including government allocation of credit, which ensured that major initiatives such as the chemical and heavy industry drive were impossible without government direction. Because South Korea often looked to the example of Japan in setting industrial policy, one can argue that the country followed a "patterns of development" analysis rather than a classic industrial policy. The costs of industrial policy in Japan did not become apparent until many years later, and the same could prove true of South Korea. The 1997 financial crisis may well have been abetted by some of the less sagacious of the industrial policy legacy.

But the interpretation that seems most favored by the evidence is that the South Korean industrial policy mix has served to overcome market failures involved in the process of technological progress.

By the 1997–1998 crisis, the chaebol came to be seen by many observers as liabilities to further growth. They were also seen as political liabilities or as companies that unfairly received government advantages in the past from which other companies did not benefit. Antitrust regulations that are now being enacted and enforced will probably make the South Korean economy much more competitive in the future. And as the economy matures, the government's role in the productive sector will continue to become more indirect. ■

Sources

Amsden, Alice H. *Asia's Next Giant: South Korea and Late Industrialization.* Oxford: Oxford University Press, 1989.

Amsden, Alice H. *The Rise of "the Rest": Challenges to the West from Late Industrializing Economies.* New York: Oxford University Press, 2001.

Chang, Ha-Joon, Hong-Jae Park, and Chul Gyue Yoo. "Interpreting the Korean crisis." *Cambridge Journal of Economics* 22 (1998): 735–746.

Chenery, Hollis, Sherwin Robinson, and Moses Syrquin. *Industrialization and Growth: A Comparative Study.* New York: Oxford University Press, 1986.

Cheng, Tun-jen, Stephan Haggard, and David Kang, "Institutions and growth in Korea and Taiwan: The bureaucracy." *Journal of Development Studies* 34 (1998): 87–111.

Cyhn, Jin. *Technology Transfer and International Production: The Development of the Electronics Industry in Korea.* Cheltenham, England: Elgar, 2001.

Dahlman, Carl J., Bruce Ross-Larson, and Larry E. Westphal. "Managing technical development: Lessons from the newly industrializing countries." *World Development* 15 (1987): 759–775.

Kim, L. "The dynamics of technology development: Lessons from the Korean experience," in *Competitiveness, FDI, and Technological Activity in East Asia*, ed. Sanjaya Lall and Shujiro Urata. Cheltenham, England: Elgar, 2003.

Lall, Sanjaya. "Technological capabilities and industrialization." *World Development* 20 (1992): 165–186.

Lall, Sanjaya. *Learning from the Asian Tigers.* London: Macmillan, 1996.

Lall, Sanjaya. *Competitiveness, Technology and Skills.* Cheltenham, England: Elgar, 2001.

Lall, Sanjaya. *The Role of Government Policy in Building Industrial Competitiveness in a Glob-*

alizing World. Oxford: International Development Centre, 2003.

Lall, Sanjaya, and M. Albaladejo. "China's export surge: The competitive implications for Southeast Asia." Report for the World Bank East Asia Department, 2003.

Lall, Sanjaya, and M. Teubal. "'Market stimulating' technology policies in developing countries: A framework with examples from East Asia." *World Development* 26 (1998): 1369–1385.

Luedde-Neurath, Richard. *Import Controls and Export-Oriented Development: A Reassessment of the South Korean Case.* Boulder, Colo.: Westview Press, 1986.

Mathews, John A., and Dong-Sung Cho. *Tiger Technology: The Creation of a Semiconductor Industry in East Asia,* New York: Cambridge University Press, 2000.

Noland, Marcus, and Howard Pack. *Industrial Policy in an Era of Globalization: Lessons from Asia.* Washington, D.C.: Institute for International Economics, 2003.

Pack, Howard, and Larry E. Westphal. "Industrial strategy and technological change: Theory versus reality." *Journal of Development Economics* 22 (1986): 87–128.

Petri, Peter. "Korea's export niche: Origins and prospects." *World Development* 16 (1988): 47–63.

Porter, Michael. *The Competitive Advantage of Nations.* New York: Free Press, 1990.

Presidential Commission on the Twenty-First Century. *Korea in the Twenty-First Century.* Seoul: Seoul Press, 1995.

Rhee, Yung Whee, Bruce Ross-Larson, and Gary Pursell. *Korea's Competitive Edge: Managing the Entry into World Markets.* Baltimore: Johns Hopkins University Press, 1984.

Rodrik, Dani. "Getting interventions right: How South Korea and Taiwan grew rich." *Economic Policy* 20 (1995): 53–101.

Smith, Stephen C. *Industrial Policy in Developing Countries: Reconsidering the Real Sources of Export-Led Growth.* Washington, D.C.: Economic Policy Institute, 1991.

Stern, Joseph, et al. *Industrialization and the State: The Korean Heavy and Chemical Industry Drive.* Cambridge, Mass.: Harvard University Press, 1995.

Stiglitz, Joseph E. "Some lessons from the East Asian miracle." *World Bank Research Observer* 11 (1996): 151–177.

Thorbecke, Erik, and Henry Wan. "Revisiting East (and Southeast) Asia's Development Model. "Paper presented at the Cornell University Conference on Seventy-Five Years of Development, Ithaca, N.Y., May 7–9, 2004.

Wade, Robert. "The role of government in overcoming market failure: Taiwan, Republic of Korea and Japan," in *Achieving Industrialization in East Asia,* ed. Helen Hughes. New York: Cambridge University Press, 1988.

Westphal, Larry E. "Industrial policy in an export propelled economy: Lessons from South Korea's experience." *Journal of Economic Perspectives* 4 (1990): 41–59.

Westphal, Larry E. "Technology strategies for economic development in a fast changing global economy." *Economics of Innovation and New Technology* 11 (2002): 275–320.

Westphal, Larry E., Yung Whee Rhee, and Gary Pursell. "Korean industrial competence: Where it came from." World Bank Staff Working Paper no. 469, 1981.

Westphal, Larry E., et al. "Exports of capital goods and related services from the Republic of Korea." World Bank Staff Working Paper no. 629, 1984.

White, Gordon (ed.). *Developmental States in East Asia.* New York: St. Martin's Press, 1988.

World Bank. *Korea: Managing the Industrial Transition.* Washington, D.C.: World Bank, 1987.

World Bank. *The East Asian Miracle: Economic Growth and Public Policy.* New York: Oxford University Press, 1993.

Concepts for Review

Autarky
Common market
Customs union
Depreciation
Devaluation
Dual exchange rate
Economic integration
Economic union
Effective rate of protection
Exchange control
Exchange rate
Export promotion
Flexible exchange rate
Free-market exchange rate
Free-trade area
General Agreement on Tariffs
and Trade (GATT)
Globalization

Import substitution
Industrialization strategy approach
Infant industry
International commodity agreements
Inward-looking development policies
Managed float
Multi-Fiber Arrangement (MFA)
New protectionism
Nominal rate of protection
Nontariff trade barriers
Official exchange rate
Outward-looking development policies
Overvalued exchange rate

Parallel exchange rate
Quotas
Regional trading bloc
Rent seeking
Synthetic substitutes
Tariffs
Trade creation
Trade diversion
Trade liberalization
Trade optimists
Trade pessimists
Uruguay Round
Value added
Wage-price spiral
World Trade Organization (WTO)

Questions for Discussion

1. Explain the distinction between primary and secondary inward- and outward-looking development policies.

2. Briefly summarize the range of commercial policies available to developing countries, and explain why some of these policies might be adopted.

3. What are the possibilities, advantages, and disadvantages of export promotion in developing nations with reference to specific types of commodities (e.g., primary food products, raw materials, fuels, minerals, manufactured goods)?

4. Most less developed countries in Latin America, Africa, and Asia have pursued policies of import substitution as major components of their development strategies. Explain the theoretical and practical arguments in support of import substitution policies. What have been some of the weaknesses of these policies in practice, and why have the results often not lived up to expectations?

5. Explain some of the arguments in support of the use of tariffs, quotas, and other trade barriers in developing countries.

6. What issues form the basis of the debate between trade optimists and trade pessimists? Is either side more correct? Explain your answer.

7. What are the basic static and dynamic arguments for economic integration in less developed countries? Briefly describe the various forms that economic integration can take (e.g., customs union, free-trade areas). What are the major obstacles to effective economic integration in developing regions?

8. How do the trade policies of developed countries affect the ability of less developed countries to benefit from greater participation in the world economy? How do non-trade domestic economic policies of rich nations affect the export earnings of developing countries? What is meant by adjustment assistance, and why is it so important to the future of LDC manufactured export prospects? Explain.

9. What factors do you think are most important in implementing a successful, outward-looking industrialization strategy?

Notes

1. For an excellent discussion of inward versus outward development policies, see Paul P. Streeten, "Trade strategies for development: Some themes for the seventies," *World Development* 1 (1973): 1–10, and Donald B. Keesing, *Trade Policy for Developing Countries*, (Washington, D.C.: World Bank, 1979). Among many informative reviews, two alternative perspectives are particularly noteworthy: Rudiger Dornbusch, "The case for trade liberalization in developing countries," *Journal of Economic Perspectives* 6 (1992): 69–85, and Dani Rodrik, "The limits of trade policy reform in developing countries," *Journal of Economic Perspectives* 6 (1992): 87–105.

2. Streeten, "Trade strategies," 1.

3. Ibid., 2.

4. Colin Kirkpatrick, "Trade policy and industrialization in LDCs," in *Surveys in Development Economics,* ed. Norman Gemmell (Oxford: Blackwell, 1987), pp. 71–72.

5. See, for example, Colin I. Bradford Jr., "East Asian 'models': Myths and lessons," in *Development Strategies Reconsidered,* ed. John P. Lewis and Valeriana Kallab (Washington, D.C.: Overseas Development Council, 1986), ch. 5; Stephen C. Smith, *Industrial Policy in Developing Countries* (Washington, D.C.: Economic Policy Institute, 1991); and Robert Wade, *Governing the Market: Economic Theory and the Role of Government in East Asian Industrialization* (Princeton, N.J.: Princeton University Press, 1990).

6. See Alfred Maizels, *Exports and Economic Growth of Developing Countries* (London: Cambridge University Press, 1968).

7. We are indebted to Professor Andreas Savvides for pointing this problem out to us.

8. For a good review of the difficulties that LDCs have had with primary-product exports, see United Nations Development Program, *Human Development Report, 1992* (New York: Oxford University Press, 1992), pp. 59–62; World Bank, *World Development Report, 1991* (Washington, D.C.: World Bank, 1991), pp. 105–110; and World Bank, *Global Economic Prospects and the Developing Countries* (Washington, D.C.: World Bank, 1994), ch. 2.

9. For a comprehensive empirical analysis extolling the growth-inducing benefits of manufactured export promotion based on the 1960s and 1970s experience, see Anne O. Krueger, *Trade and Employment in Developing Countries, Vol. 3: Synthesis and Conclusions* (Chicago: University of Chicago Press/National Bureau of Economics Research, 1983). See also Jagdish N. Bhagwati, "Export-promoting trade strategy: Issues

and evidence," *World Bank Research Observer* 3 (1988): 27–57; World Bank, *World Development Report, 1987* (Washington, D.C.: World Bank, 1987); and Anne O. Krueger, "Trade policy and economic development: How we learn," *American Economic Review* 87 (1997): 1–22. For an empirical critique of this research, however, see Sebastian Edwards, "Openness, trade liberalization, and growth in developing countries," *Journal of Economic Literature* 31 (1993): 1358–1393; Behzad Yaghmaian, "An empirical investigation of exports, development, and growth in developing countries: Challenging the neoclassical theory of export-led growth," *World Development* 22 (1994): 1977–1995; and Syed Nawab Haider Naqvi, "The significance of development economics," *World Development* 24 (1996): 978–980.

10. World Bank, *2004 World Development Indicators* (Washington, D.C.: World Bank 2004).

11. Bradford, "East Asian 'models'"; Smith, *Industrial Policy in Developing Countries;* Jene Kwon, "The East Asian challenge to neoclassical orthodoxy," *World Development* 22 (1994): 635–644; Paul Krugman, "The myth of Asia's miracle," *Foreign Affairs* 73 (1994): 62–78; Dani Rodrik, "Getting interventions right: How South Korea and Taiwan grew rich," *Economic Policy* 20 (1995): 53–97; and Henry J. Bruton, "A reconsideration of import substitution," *Journal of Economic Literature* 36 (1998): 903–936.

12. *Financial Times,* "The Textile Revolution," July 19, 2004.

13. For an interesting discussion of this issue, see "Working man's dread," *Economist,* October 1, 1994, pp. 14–19.

14. *World Trade Organization Annual Report, 2001* (Geneva: World Trade Organization, 2001). See subsequent editions for annual trends. For a comprehensive exposition, see Judith Czako, Johann Human, and Jorge Miranda, *A Handbook of Anti-Dumping Investigations* (Cambridge: Cambridge University Press, 2003).

15. For many LDCs, trade taxes represent a major source of government revenue. For details, see Chapter 16.

16. For a comprehensive analysis and critique of import substitution policies in developing countries, see Ian Little, Tibor Scitovsky, and Maurice Scott, *Industry and Trade in Some Developing Countries* (London: Oxford University Press, 1970). See also Kirkpatrick, "Trade policy and industrialization," pp. 71–75; Hubert Schmitz, "Industrialization strategies in less developed countries: Some lessons of historical experience," *Journal of Development Studies* 21 (1984): 1–21; and Dornbusch, "Case for trade liberalization."

17. It should be mentioned, however, that in light of some of the new trade theories, with their emphasis on economies of scale, externalities, and human capital investments, the arguments for selective tariff protection are coming back into vogue. See Bruton, "Reconsideration of import substitution," for a summary of these issues.

18. Little et al., *Industry and Trade,* p. 39.

19. Herbert G. Grubel, "Effective tariff protection: A non-specialist introduction to the theory, policy implications and controversies," in *Effective Tariff Protection,* ed. Herbert G. Grubel and Harry Johnson (Geneva: GATT, 1971), p. 2.

20. Little et al., *Industry and Trade,* p. 4. For later data, see tab. 13.1.

21. Such preferred customers are often identified in the literature as "rent seekers" because they spend a great amount of time and effort engaged in activities, such as bribery, designed to capture the "economic rent" generated by government-induced price distortions like overvalued exchange rates. See Anne O. Krueger, "The political economy of the rent-seeking society," *American Economic Review* 64 (1974): 291–303.

22. For an analysis of multiple exchange rates and their effects on the economy, see Miguel Kiguel and Stephen A. O'Connell, "Parallel exchange rates in developing countries," *World Bank Research Observer* 10 (1995): 21–52. Black market premiums in the 1980s ranged from 66% in Mexico and 173% in Brazil to 4,264% in Ghana.

23. For example, in December 1994, the Mexican government *devalued* its currency, the peso, by 35% against the dollar. By February 1995, the peso had *depreciated* by another 15% before recovering some of its losses in the foreign-exchange market.

24. For a concise discussion of some issues related to devaluation, see Karim Nashashibi, "Devaluation in developing countries: The difficult choices," *Finance and Development* 20 (1983): 14–17.

25. For an excellent review and analysis of these issues, from which much of the following discussion is drawn, see Rostam M. Kavoussi, "International trade and economic development: The recent experience of developing countries," *Journal of Developing Areas* 19 (1985): 379–392. See also Dornbusch, "Case for trade liberalization," and Rodrik, "Limits of trade policy reform."

26. A statement of these views can be found in Deepak Lal and Sarath Rajapatirana, "Foreign trade regimes and economic growth in developing countries," *World Bank Research Observer* 2 (1987): 189–217, and Bhagwati, "Export-promoting trade strategy."

27. See Alice Amsden, *The Rise of "the Rest": Challenges to the West from Late-Industrializing Economies* (New York: Oxford University Press, 2001); Howard Pack and Larry Westphal, "Industrial strategy and technological change: Theory versus reality," *Journal of Development Economics* 22 (1986): 87–128; Robert Wade, *Governing the Market* (Princeton, N.J.: Princeton University Press, 1991); Dani Rodrik, "Getting interventions right: How South Korea and Taiwan grew rich," *Economic Policy* 20 (1995): 53–101; and Sanjaya Lall, *Learning from the Asian Tigers* (London: Macmillan, 1996), and *The Role of Government Policy in Building Industrial Competitiveness in a Globalizing World*," (Oxford: International Development Centre, Oxford University, 2003).

28. Hollis Chenery, Sherwin Robinson, and Moshe Syrquin (eds.), *Industrialization and Growth: A Comparative Study* (New York: Oxford University Press, 1986), p. 178.

29. Sanjaya Lall, "Globalization and industrial performance," presentation at the Globelics Academy, Lisbon, May 2004.

30. Kavoussi, "International trade and economic development," 388–390.

31. Hans W. Singer and Patricia Gray, "Trade policy and growth of developing countries: Some new data," *World Development* 16 (1988): 395–403.

32. Bradford, "East Asian 'models,'" p. 123. Reprinted with the permission of the author.

33. World Bank *2004 World Development Indicators,* tab. 6.2.

34. See, for example, W. Arthur Lewis's Nobel Prize lecture, "The slowing down of the engine of growth," *American Economic Review* 70 (1980): 555–564, and Frances Stewart,

"The direction of international trade: Gains and losses for the Third World," in *A World Divided*, ed. Gerald K. Helleiner (Cambridge: Cambridge University Press, 1976).

35. For a useful analysis of developing-world regional integration, see "A symposium on regionalism and development," *World Bank Economic Review* 12 (1998): 177–320, which contains six articles on various aspects of regionalism. For an empirically based argument for expanded trade among developing countries as a stimulant to long-term growth and development, see Yves Sabolo, "Trade between developing countries, technology transfers and employment," *International Labour Review* 122 (1983): 593–609, and World Bank, *World Development Report, 1991*, pp. 105–108.

36. See World Bank, *2001 World Development Indicators* (Washington, D.C.: World Bank, 2001), p. 316. For information on progress toward achieving WTO goals in agriculture and other sectors, see *World Trade Organization Annual Report 2001*, (Geneva: WTO, 2001); agricultural subsidies of developing countries are discussed on p. 34.

37. International Monetary Fund, *World Economic Outlook, May 1994* (Washington, D.C.: International Monetary Fund, 1994), annex 1.

38. For an analysis of the many ways that poor countries will lose out, even under the Uruguay Round, because the rules of the game are biased against them, see United Nations Development Program, *Human Development Report, 1997* (New York: Oxford University Press, 1997), ch. 4.

39. Ian Goldin and Odin Knudson (eds.), *Agricultural Trade Liberalization: Implications for Developing Countries* (Paris: OECD Development Center, 1990). See also Will Martin and L. Alan Winters, *The Uruguay Round and the Developing Economies* (Washington, D.C.: World Bank, 1995).

40. United Nations Development Program, *Human Development Report, 1997*, p. 85. A similar conclusion was reached by even the most ardent advocate of open trade and globalization, the IMF, in its *World Economic Outlook* (Washington, D.C.: International Monetary Fund, 1997), p. 13.

Further Reading

Five of the best general sources of information on trade policies and strategies for development are Dani Rodrik, "Trade and industrial policy reform," in *Handbook of Development Economics*, vol. 3B, ed. Jere Behrman and T. N. Srinivasan (New York: Elsevier, 1995), pp. 2925–2982; Henry J. Bruton. "A reconsideration of import substitution," *Journal of Economic Literature* 36 (1998): 903–936; World Bank, *The East Asian Miracle* (New York: Oxford University Press, 1993); Colin Kirkpatrick, "Trade policy and industrialization in LDCs," in *Surveys in Development Economics*, ed. Norman Gemmell (Oxford: Blackwell, 1987), ch. 2; and Dominick Salvatore and Thomas Hatcher, "Inward-oriented and outward-oriented trade strategies," *Journal of Development Studies* 23 (1991): 7–25. See also Pradip K. Ghosh (ed.), *International Trade and Third World Development* (Westport, Conn: Greenwood Press, 1984); Ronald W. Jones and Peter B. Kenen, *Handbook of International Economics*

(Amsterdam: Elsevier, 1988), ch. 11, 12, 16, and 19, for a useful collection of readings and statistics; and Gerald K. Helleiner (ed.), *Trade Policy, Industrialization and Development: New Perspectives* (Oxford: Clarendon Press, 1992).

For a lively debate about the relative merits of trade policy, see Rudiger Dornbusch, "The case for trade liberalization in developing countries," *Journal of Economic Perspectives* 6 (1992): 69–85, and Dani Rodrik, "The limits of trade policy reform in developing countries," *Journal of Economic Perspectives* 6 (1992): 87–105.

For further reading on strategic policies and industrialization through trade, see the references in Note 27.

CHAPTER FOURTEEN

Balance of Payments, Developing-Country Debt, and the Macroeconomic Stabilization Controversy

The 1980s was a lost decade for Latin America.
                                        —Enrique Iglesias, President, Inter-American Development Bank, 2001

*The International Monetary Fund, the World Bank and the regional development banks
should write off in their entirety all claims against heavily indebted poor countries that
implement an effective economic and social development strategy in conjunction with the
World Bank and the regional development institutions.*
                                        —Report of the International Financial Institution Advisory Commission, 2000

In Chapters 12 and 13, we examined the scope, insights, and limitations of traditional trade theory and policy. In this chapter and the next, we extend this analysis in the following ways. First, in this chapter, after looking at a country's balance of payments accounts and recent trends in LDC trade balances, we dissect the dimensions and ramifications of the debt dilemma. Our focus will be on how the debt crisis emerged during the 1980s and remains a fundamental impediment to growth in Africa, what is being done about it, and who is bearing the burden of stabilization and adjustment programs induced by the International Monetary Fund (IMF). Specifically, we ask the question, "Is the debt crisis a nonissue, or has the problem simply receded from the headlines after developed-country commercial banks recovered and wrote down their bad loans?" We will discover that many LDCs continue to face serious debt problems requiring some form of relief. In Chapter 15, we will extend our analysis of the role of finance in trade to examine the international flow of financial resources, consisting of (1) the flow of private foreign direct investments, primarily via the carrier of the modern multinational corporation; (2) the recent resurgence of private financial "portfolio investments" in support of newly organized or refurbished "emerging" stock and bond markets;

(3) the flow of public financial and technical resources in the form of bilateral and multilateral foreign aid; and (4) the growing importance of private financial and technical assistance to the poorest LDCs in the form of nongovernmental organization foreign aid programs.

The Balance of Payments Account

General Considerations

The extension of our analysis beyond simple merchandise trade into areas related to the international flow of financial resources permits us to examine the **balance of payments (BOP)** of developing nations. A balance of payments table is designed to summarize a nation's financial transactions with the outside world. It is divided into three components, as shown by the summary in Table 14.1. Note that balance of payments tables are sometimes presented in a format that splits the current account into two parts (called the *current account* and the *capital account*) and renames what is here called the capital account as the *financial account*. We retain the traditional approach because most of the literature on developing-country debt is presented in that format. The **current account** focuses on the export and import of goods and services, investment income, debt-service payments, and private and public net remittances and transfers. Specifically, it subtracts the value of imports from exports (the *merchandise trade balance* of Chapter 12) and then adds flows of the net investment income received from abroad (e.g., the difference between interest and dividend payments on foreign stocks, bonds, and bank deposits owned by LDC nationals and brought into the country, as opposed to being left overseas, and those securities, if any, of the LDC owned by foreigners plus repatriated profits of multinational corporations). Taking this total ($A - B + C$ in Table 14.1), it subtracts item D, debt-service payments, which represents a major and growing component of developing-world current account deficits, and adds item E, net private and public remittances and transfers, such as money sent home by LDC nationals working abroad (e.g., Mexicans and Filipinos in the United States, Algerians in France, Pakistanis in Kuwait). The final result ($A - B + C - D + E$ in Table 14.1) yields the current account balance—a positive balance is called a **surplus**, a negative balance a **deficit**. The current account therefore allows us to analyze the impact of various commercial policies, primarily on merchandise trade but also indirectly on investment income, debt-service payments, and private transfers.

The **capital account** records the value of private foreign direct investment (mostly by multinational corporations), foreign loans by private international banks, and loans and grants from foreign governments (as in the form of foreign aid) and multilateral agencies such as the IMF and the World Bank. It then subtracts an extremely important item, especially for the major debtor countries of Africa and Latin America. This is what is called "resident capital outflow" in Table 14.1, otherwise known as **capital flight**. During the 1980s debt crisis, capital flight by wealthy LDC nationals, who sent vast amounts of money into developed-

TABLE 14.1 A Schematic Balance of Payments Account	
Exports of goods and services	A
Imports of goods and services	B
Investment income	C
Debt-service payments	D
Net remittances and transfers	E
Total *current account* balance ($A - B + C - D + E$)	F
Direct private investment	G
Foreign loans (private and public), minus amortization	H
Increase in foreign assets of domestic banking system	I
Resident capital outflow	J
Total *capital account* balance ($G + H - I - J$)	K
Increase (or decrease) in *cash reserve account*	L
Errors and omissions ($L - F - K$)	M

Source: Adapted from John Williamson and Donald R. Lessard, *Capital Flight: The Problem and Policy Responses* (Washington, D.C.: Institute for International Economics, 1987), tab. 1.

nation bank accounts, real estate ventures, and stock and bond purchases, is estimated to have had a value of up to half the total debt of some Latin debtor nations.[1] It dwarfed the receipt of private and public loans and investments and was a major contributor to the worsening balance of payments of many developing nations. The balance on capital account is therefore calculated as items $G + H - I - J$ in Table 14.1. Again, a positive balance is a surplus and a negative one a deficit.

Finally, the **cash account**, or **international reserve account** (item *L*), is the balancing item (along with the "errors and omissions" item *M*, which reconciles statistical inequalities) that is lowered (shows a net outflow of foreign reserves) whenever total disbursements on the current and capital accounts exceed total receipts. Table 14.2 presents a simple chart of what constitutes positive (credit) and negative (debit) items in a balance of payments table. Nations accumulate international cash reserves in any or all of the following three forms: (1) foreign **hard currency** (primarily U.S. dollars, but increasingly Japanese yen, pounds sterling, or the European **euro**)[2] whenever they sell more abroad than they purchase; (2) gold, mined domestically or purchased; and (3) deposits with the IMF, which acts as a reserve bank for individual nations' central banks.

TABLE 14.2 Positive and Negative Effects on Balance of Payments Accounts	
Positive Effects (Credits)	**Negative Effects (Debits)**
1. Any sale of goods or services abroad (export)	1. Any purchase of goods and services abroad (import)
2. Any earning on an investment in a foreign country	2. Any investment in a foreign country
3. Any receipt of foreign money	3. Any payment to a foreign country
4. Any gift or aid from a foreign country	4. Any gift or aid given abroad
5. Any foreign sale of stocks or bonds	5. Any purchase of stocks or bonds from abroad

Source: John Charles Pool and Stephen C. Stamos, *The ABCs of International Finance* (Lexington, Mass.: Lexington Books, 1987). Copyright © 1987 by D. C. Heath and Co., a division of Raytheon Company. Reprinted with the permission of Lexington Books/University Press of America.

TABLE 14.3   A Hypothetical Balance of Payments Table for a Developing Nation

Item			Amounts (millions of dollars)
Current Account			
Commodity exports			+35
Primary products	+25		
Manufactured goods	+10		
Commodity imports			−45
Primary products	−10		
Manufactured goods	−35		
Services (e.g., shipping costs)			-5
Investment income			+1
Debt-service payments			−15
Net remittances and transfers			+2
Balance on current account		−27	
Capital Account			
Private direct foreign investment			+3
Private loans and portfolio investments			+4
Government and multilateral flows (net)			+3
Loans	+9		
Debt amortization	−6		
Resident capital outflow			−8
Balance on capital account		+2	
Balance on current and capital accounts		−25	
Cash Account			
Net decrease in official monetary reserves			+25
Balance on cash account		+25	

A Hypothetical Illustration: Deficits and Debts

A numerical example might prove helpful at this point. In Table 14.3, a hypothetical balance of payments table for a developing country is portrayed. First, under the *current account,* there is a $10 million negative merchandise trade balance made up of $35 million of commodity export receipts (of which over 70%—$25 million— are derived from primary agricultural and raw material products), minus $45 million of mostly manufactured consumer, intermediate, and capital goods import payments. To this total we add $5 million in payments for the services of foreign shipping firms and $1 million of investment income receipts representing net interest transmitted on foreign bond holdings, subtract $15 million of debt-service payments representing this year's interest costs on the accumulated foreign debt of the LDC, and add $2 million of remittance and transfer receipts derived from payments of domestic workers living overseas who send home part of their earnings. Together, all of these items add up to a *deficit* on current account of $27 million.

Turning now to the *capital account,* we see that there is a net inflow of $7 million of foreign private investment, consisting of $3 million of direct investment from multinational corporations in the form of new local factories and $4 million in private loans (from international commercial banks) and private portfolio (stock and bond) investments by foreign individuals and mutual funds (see Chapter 15). There is also a net positive $3 million inflow of public loans in the form of

TABLE 14.4	The Lead-Up to the Debt Crisis and the Aftermath: Current Account Balances and Capital Account Net Financial Transfers of Developing Countries, 1978–1990 (billions of dollars)	
Year	Current Account	Capital Account Net Financial Transfers
1978	−32.1	33.2
1979	+10.0	31.2
1980	+30.6	29.5
1981	−48.6	35.9
1982	−86.9	20.1
1983	−64.0	3.7
1984	−31.7	−10.2
1985	−24.9	−20.5
1986	−46.4	−23.6
1987	−4.4	−34.0
1988	−22.4	−35.2
1989	−18.4	−29.6
1990	−3.0	−22.5

Sources: International Monetary Fund, *World Economic Outlook*, 1988 and 1992 (Washington, D.C.: International Monetary Fund, 1988, 1992), United Nations Development Program, *Human Development Report*, 1992 (New York: Oxford University Press, 1992), tab. 4.3.

foreign aid and multilateral agency assistance. Note that the gross *inflow* of $9 million in public loans and grants is partly offset by a $6 million capital *outflow* representing **amortization** (gradual reduction) of the principal on former loans. However, as shown in Table 14.4, which covers the 1980s debt crisis period, these figures were reversed in the 1980s—the outflow to repay accumulated debts exceeded the inflow of *both* public aid and new refinancing bank loans. As a result, a $35.9 billion net transfer from developed to developing countries in 1981 became a $22.5 billion transfer from poor to rich nations by 1990 (they turned positive again in the 1990s until substantial new problems emerged between 1997 and 2002).

Returning to Table 14.3, we see that a major reason for the perverse flow of financial capital from poor to rich nations was very high levels of resident capital outflow. This capital flight is estimated to have amounted to almost $100 billion during the first half of the 1980s from just five of the principal countries involved (Argentina, Brazil, Mexico, the Philippines, and Venezuela)[3] and almost $200 billion over the period 1976–1985. In Table 14.3, it is listed as an outflow of $8 million. The net result is a $2 million positive balance on capital account, bringing the total balance on current and capital accounts to a deficit of $25 million.

Financing and Reducing Payments Deficits

Some Initial Policy Issues

To finance this $25 million negative balance on combined current and capital accounts, our hypothetical country will have to draw down $25 million of its central bank holdings of official monetary reserves. Such reserves consist of gold, a few major foreign currencies, and special drawing rights at the IMF (these will be explained shortly). **International reserves** serve for countries the same purpose that bank accounts serve for individuals. They can be drawn on to pay bills and debts, they are increased with deposits representing net export sales and capital inflows, and they can be used as collateral to borrow additional reserves.

We see, therefore, that the balance on current account *plus* the balance on capital account must be offset by the balance on cash account. This is shown by the net *decrease* of $25 million in official monetary reserves. If the country is very poor, it is likely to have a very limited stock of these reserves. This overall balance of payments deficit of $25 million may therefore place severe strains on the economy and greatly inhibit the country's ability to continue importing needed capital and consumer goods. In the least developed nations of the world, which have to import food to feed a hungry population and possess limited monetary reserves, such payments deficits may spell disaster for millions of people.

Facing existing or projected balance of payments deficits on combined current and capital accounts, developing nations have a variety of policy options. First, they can seek to improve the balance on current account by promoting export expansion or limiting imports (or both). In the former case, there is the further choice of concentrating on primary or secondary product export expansion. In the latter case, policies of import substitution (the protection and stimulus of domestic industries to replace previously imported manufactured goods in the local market) and/or selective tariffs and physical quotas or bans on the importation of specific consumer goods may be tried. Alternatively, countries can seek to achieve both objectives simultaneously by altering their official foreign-exchange rates through a currency devaluation that lowers export prices and increases import prices. They can also follow very restrictive fiscal and monetary policies (called *structural adjustment* by the World Bank and *stabilization policies* by the IMF— see Appendix 14.1 for a history and description of these organizations). These policies are designed to reduce domestic demand so as to lower imports and reduce the inflationary pressures that may have contributed to the "overvalued" exchange rate that slowed exports and promoted imports.

A second alternative, often not exclusive of the first, is for developing countries to try to improve the balance on their capital account by encouraging more private foreign direct or portfolio investment, borrowing from international commercial banks, or seeking more public foreign assistance. But neither private foreign investment nor a major proportion of foreign aid comes in the form of gifts (outright grants). The receipt of loan assistance implies the necessity of future repayments of principal and interest. Directly productive foreign investments in, say, building local factories entail the potential repatriation of sizable proportions of the profits of the foreign-owned enterprise. Moreover, as shown in Chapter 15, the encouragement of private foreign investment has broader development implications than the mere transfer of financial or physical capital resources.

Finally, developing nations can seek to modify the detrimental impact of chronic balance of payments deficits by expanding their stocks of official monetary reserves. One way of doing this is through the acquisition of a greater share of international "paper gold" known as **special drawing rights (SDRs).** Traditionally, under the workings of the international monetary system, countries with deficits in their balance of payments were required to pay for these deficits by drawing down on their official reserves of the two principal international monetary assets, gold and U.S. dollars. But with the phenomenal growth in the volume and value of world trade, a new kind of international asset was needed to supplement the limited stock of gold and dollars. Consequently, in 1970 the IMF was given the authority to create $10 billion of these special drawing rights. These new international assets perform many of the functions of gold and dollars in settling balance of payments accounts. They are valued on the basis of a basket of currencies (a weighted average of the value of four different currencies—the U.S. dollar, the euro, the pound sterling, and the Japanese yen) and constitute claims on the IMF. They may thus be exchanged for convertible currencies to settle international official transactions. In 2004, one SDR was worth around $1.46. Eventually, the IMF would like to see all international financial settlements conducted in SDRs.

A major issue of great concern to developing countries, therefore, is the distribution of the benefits of SDRs. The present formula for distributing SDRs gives 75% of the total to the 25 industrialized nations. This leaves only 25% to be distributed among all the LDCs that participate in the international monetary system. Dissatisfied with this situation, these countries are now, as a group, exerting pressure on the developed nations to agree to the creation of supplementary SDRs that would be allocated in preferential amounts or on preferential terms to developing nations.

Having summarized some basic balance of payments concepts and issues as they relate to both commodity trade and international flows of financial resources, we can now briefly review some trends in the balance of payments of developing nations and then focus our attention on a detailed analysis of the debt problem.

Trends in LDC Balance of Payments

For most developing countries, the 1980s was an extraordinarily difficult period in their balance of payments accounts with the rest of the world. Prior to 1980, the conventional development strategy had LDCs operating with sizable current account deficits, for imports of capital and intermediate goods were required to provide the machinery and equipment for rapid industrialization. Export earnings paid for most, but not all, of these imports. The financing of these deficits was therefore made possible by large resource transfers in the capital account in the form of country-to-country (bilateral) foreign aid, direct private investment by multinational corporations, private loans by international banks to both LDC governments and local businesses, and multilateral loans from the World Bank and other international development agencies. Capital account surpluses, therefore, typically more than compensated for current account deficits so that international reserves were being accumulated.

However, during the 1980s, the developing world experienced a substantial deterioration in both current and capital account balances. As Table 14.4 shows, the net financial transfers component of the capital account (which includes everything in Table 14.3 except private direct foreign investment) turned sharply negative beginning in 1984. The overall transition amounted to more than $68 billion, comparing the positive $33.2 billion capital account balance in 1978 with the negative $35.2 billion balance in 1988. Meanwhile, the brief period of large current account surpluses, which reflects entirely OPEC's booming export revenues of

TABLE 14.5	Summary of LDC Payments Balances on Current Account, 1980–2003 (billions of dollars)					
	1980	1985	1990	1995	1996	1997
All developing countries	30.6	−24.9	−25.1	−96.2	−87.8	−82.9
By region						
Africa	−2.1	−1.2	−8.0	−16.6	−5.5	−6.5
Developing Asia	−14.4	−13.1	−16.4	−42.5	−38.6	9.2
Middle East	92.5	−7.6	0.6	—	11.4	10.3
Latin America	−29.8	−1.9	−1.3	−37.1	−39.1	−66.8
	1998	1999	2000	2001	2002	2003
All developing countries	−115.0	−18.1	88.1	37.9	83.6	121.0
By region						
Africa	−19.5	−15.9	5.4	−1.5	−7.4	−3.9
Developing Asia	48.9	48.1	45.4	38.1	68.1	61.8
Middle East	−25.3	11.5	69.6	38.1	29.0	51.7
Latin America	−91.2	−57.0	−47.0	−54.5	−15.8	3.8

Sources: International Monetary Fund, *World Economic Outlook, 1988, 2001,* and *2004* (Washington, D.C.: International Monetary Fund, 1988, 2001, 2004).

1979–1980, abruptly turned negative in 1981 and, as illustrated in Table 14.5, stayed negative until 2000. Recent positive balances (outside of Africa) have been possible largely because of the probably unsustainably large U.S. trade deficit.

The reasons for the decline in current account balances in the 1980s and 1990s included (1) a dramatic fall in commodity prices, including oil; (2) global recessions in 1981–1982 and 1991–1993, which caused a general contraction in world trade; (3) increasing protectionism in the developed world against LDC exports; and (4) some severely overvalued exchange rates, particularly among East Asian exporters and certain other key developing economies, such as Argentina.

The capital account showed its dramatic turn as a combined result of rising LDC debt-service obligations, sharp declines in lending by international banks, and massive capital flight. During the 1980s, these factors turned what had previously been a positive annual resource flow of $25 billion to $35 billion from developed to less developed countries into a negative annual flow of $25 billion to $35 billion from the developing to the developed world. Behind these trends, however, was the debilitating dilemma of developing-country debt.

The Debt Crisis of the 1980s

Background and Analysis

The accumulation of **external debt** is a common phenomenon of developing countries at the stage of economic development where the supply of domestic savings is low, current account payments deficits are high, and imports of capital are needed to augment domestic resources. Prior to the early 1970s, the external debt of developing countries was relatively small and primarily an official phenomenon, the majority of creditors being foreign governments and international financial institutions such as the IMF, the World Bank, and regional development banks. Most loans were on concessional (low-interest) terms and were extended for purposes of implementing development projects and expanding imports of capital goods. However, during the late 1970s and early 1980s, commercial banks began playing a large role in international lending by recycling surplus OPEC "petrodollars" and issuing general-purpose loans to LDCs to provide balance of payments support and expansion of export sectors.

Although foreign borrowing can be highly beneficial, providing the resources necessary to promote economic growth and development, it has its costs. In recent years, these costs have greatly outweighed the benefits for many developing nations. The main cost associated with the accumulation of a large external debt is **debt service.** Debt service is the payment of amortization (liquidation of the principal) and accumulated interest; it is a contractually fixed charge on domestic real income and savings. As the size of the debt grows or as interest rates rise, debt-service charges increase. Debt-service payments must be made with foreign exchange. In other words, debt-service obligations can be met only through export earnings, curtailed imports, or further external borrowing. Under normal circumstances, most of a country's debt-service obligations are met by its export earnings. However, should the composition of imports change or should interest rates rise significantly, causing a ballooning of debt-service payments, or should export earnings diminish, debt-servicing difficulties are likely to arise. This has been the experience of most of the heavily indebted LDCs.

However, before delving into the statistical details and tracing the origins of and consequences of the 1980s LDC debt crisis and other developing-country financial crises, it is necessary to understand a fundamental concept known as the **basic transfer.**[4] The basic transfer of a country is defined as the net foreign-exchange inflow or outflow related to its international borrowing. It is measured as the difference between the net capital inflow and interest payments on the existing accumulated debt. The net capital inflow is simply the difference between the gross inflow and the amortization on past debt. The basic transfer is an important concept because it represents the amount of foreign exchange that a particular LDC is gaining or losing each year from international capital flows. As we shall soon discover, the basic transfer turned very negative for developing nations during the 1980s, causing a loss of foreign exchange and a net outflow of capital.

The basic-transfer equation can be expressed as follows. Let the net capital inflow, F_N, be expressed as the rate of increase of total external debt, and let D represent the total accumulated foreign debt. If d is the percentage rate of increase in that total debt, then

$$F_N = dD \tag{14.1}$$

Because interest must be paid each year on the accumulated debt, let us let r equal the average rate of interest so that rD measures total annual interest payments. The basic transfer (BT) then is simply the net capital inflow minus interest payments, or

$$BT = dD - rD = (d - r)D \tag{14.2}$$

BT will be positive if $d > r$, and the country will be gaining foreign exchange. However if $r > d$, the basic transfer turns negative, and the nation loses foreign exchange. Any analysis of the evolution of and prospects for the LDC debt crisis requires an examination of the various factors that cause d and r to rise and fall.

In the early stages of debt accumulation, when an LDC has a relatively small total debt, D, the rate of increase, d, is likely to be high. Also, because most first-stage debt accumulation comes from official (as opposed to private) sources in the form of bilateral foreign aid and World Bank lending, most of the debt is incurred on concessional terms—that is, at below-market interest rates with lengthy repayment periods. Consequently, r is quite low and in any event less than d. As long as this accumulating debt is being used for productive development projects with rates of return in excess of r, the additional foreign exchange and rising foreign debt represented by the positive basic transfers pose no problems for recipient nations. In fact, as we have seen in earlier chapters, this process of debt accumulation for productive investments in both rural and urban areas represents an essential ingredient in any viable strategy of long-term development.

A serious problem can arise, however, when (1) the accumulated debt becomes very large so that its rate of increase, d, naturally begins to decline as amortization rises relative to rates of new gross inflows; (2) the sources of foreign capital switch from long-term "official flows" on fixed, concessional terms to short-term, variable-rate private bank loans at market rates that cause r to rise; (3) the country begins to experience severe balance of payments problems as commodity prices plummet and the terms of trade rapidly deteriorate; (4) a global recession or some other external shock, such as a jump in oil prices, a steep rise in U.S. interest rates on which variable-rate private loans are based, or a sudden change in the value of the dollar, in which most debts are denominated, takes place; (5) a loss in confidence in an LDC's ability to repay resulting from points 2, 3, and 4 occurs, causing private international banks to cut off their flow of new lending; and (6) a substantial flight of capital is precipitated by local residents who for political or economic reasons (e.g., expectations of currency devaluation) send great sums of money out of the country to be invested in developed-country financial securities, real estate, and bank accounts. All six factors can combine to lower d and raise r in the basic transfer equation, with the net result that the overall basic transfer becomes highly negative, and capital flows from the underdeveloped to the developed world (as shown in Table 14.5). The debt crisis then becomes a self-reinforcing phenomenon, and heavily indebted developing countries are forced into a downward spiral of negative basic transfers, dwindling foreign reserves, and stalled development prospects. The story of the debt crisis of the 1980s is largely told by the simple analysis of the factors affecting the basic transfer mechanism of Equation 14.2. Against this analytical background, we can now look at the specific details of the LDC debt crisis and the various efforts to deal with it.

Origins of the Debt Crisis

In the period 1970–2000, the external debt of developing nations grew from $68.4 billion to over $2.14 trillion, an increase of more than 3,000% (see Table 14.6). Debt-service payments increased by 2,527% to exceed $277 billion by 1997. Although a

TABLE 14.6	Dimensions of the LDC Debt Burden, 1970–2000						
	1970	**1975**	**1980**	**1985**	**1990**	**1995**	**2000**
Total external debt							
(billions of dollars)	68.4	180.0	635.8	949.0	1,182.3	1,808.9	2,140.6
Of which Africa	—	14.9	55.6	64.7	283.3	304.1	285.1
Debt-service payments[a]							
(billions of dollars)	11.0	25.8	102.4	128.0	140.5	237.5	315.2
Of which Africa	—	1.3	4.1	27.6	31.1	33.1	26.9
Debt-to export ratio[b]							
(percent)	99.4	76.4	81.9	154.5	178.6	136.9	162.0
Of which Africa	—	—	92.5	189.0	230.7	228.5	214.2
Debt-service ratio[c]							
(percent of exports)	13.5	9.5	13.2	20.9	9.4	27.5	25.6
Of which Africa	5.7	—	14.4	27.6	11.3	32.8	21.0
Debt-to-GDP ratio[d]							
(percent)	13.3	15.4	24.4	36.4	37.8	40.5	39.5
Of which Africa	20.9	—	28.3	46.6	61.4	74.2	64.8

Sources: International Monetary Fund, *World Economic Outlook, 1988* and *2001* (Washington, D.C.: International Monetary Fund, 1988, 2001).
[a]Actual payments of interest on total debt plus actual amortization payments on long-term debt.
[b]Ratio of external debt to exports of goods and services.
[c]Debt service as a percentage of exports of goods and services. Excludes service payments to the IMF.
[d]Ratio of external debt to gross domestic product (GDP).

great deal of the debt was concentrated in four Latin American nations (Brazil, Mexico, Argentina, and Venezuela), Table 14.7 highlights 14 severely indebted countries (SICs) among those identified as such by the World Bank in 2002. Their debts were deemed most vulnerable to default because of the very large share owed to commercial creditors at variable rates of interest. The debt problems of sub-Saharan Africa are made more troublesome by low and declining per capita incomes and stagnating economies. Their debt-to-export and debt-service ratios are both well above the overall LDC average and in some cases even above the ratios of other SICs (see the data for Africa in Table 14.6).

The seeds of the 1980s debt crisis were sown in the 1974–1979 period, when there was a virtual explosion in international lending, precipitated by the first major OPEC oil price increase. By 1974, developing countries had begun playing a larger role in the world economy, having averaged growth rates of 6.6% in 1967–1973. The newly industrializing countries, particularly those like Mexico, Brazil, Venezuela, and Argentina in Latin America, had growth rates well above the developing countries' average. To meet their growth needs, many countries had begun importing heavily, especially capital goods, oil, and food. Following outward-looking development strategies, they expanded their exports aggressively. In the face of high oil prices and a world recession, in which the growth rates of the industrialized countries fell from an average of 5.2% in 1967–1974 to an average of 2.7% for the rest of the 1970s, many developing countries sought to sustain their high growth rates through increased borrowing. Although lending from official sources, particularly nonconcessional lending, increased significantly, it was in-

	Debt Outstanding[a] (billions of U.S. dollars)	Public Debt Service[a]		Debt Indicators	
Country		Percentage of GNI	Percentage of Exports	Debt-to-GNI Ratio (%)	Debt-to-Exports Ratio (%)
Angola	10.1	8.7	9.8	118	125
Argentina	132.3	4.3	12.8	66	393
Brazil	227.9	5.0	29.4	48	342
Burundi	1.2	2.6	47.1	110	1,553
Côte d'Ivoire	11.8	4.5	8.6	91	188
Ecuador	16.5	5.7	20.9	95	300
Ethiopia	6.5	1.6	8.9	66	386
Indonesia	132.2	4.0	9.8	89	191
Malawi	2.9	1.5	5.7	51	183
Nicaragua	6.5	2.6	10.7	77	301
Nigeria	30.5	3.6	8.2	80	152
Peru	28.2	5.5	31.7	56	319
Sudan	16.4	0.0	0.0	136	851
Syria	21.5	0.8	1.9	114	270

TABLE 14.7   Public and Guaranteed Debt and Debt Service in Selected Severely Indebted Countries, 2002

Source: World Bank, *2004 World Development Indicators* (Washington, D.C.: World Bank, 2004), tab. 4.16 and 4.17. Copyright © 2004 by the World Bank. Reprinted with the permission of the World Bank via the Copyright Clearance Center.

[a]Debt, debt service, and interest include the use of IMF credit. Figures are based on actual payments on all external debt.

sufficient to meet the growth needs of the middle-income and newly industrializing developing countries. Furthermore, countries with an excess of imports over lagging exports were reluctant to approach official sources, such as the IMF, that might subject them to painful policy adjustments. So the middle-income and newly industrializing developing countries turned to commercial banks and other private lenders, which began issuing general-purpose loans to provide balance of payments support. Commercial banks, holding the bulk of the OPEC surplus (which had jumped from $7 billion in 1973 to $68 billion in 1974 and ultimately peaked at $115 billion in 1980) and facing a low demand for capital from the slower-growing industrialized countries, aggressively competed in lending to developing countries on comparatively permissive and favorable terms. Figure 14.1 portrays the mechanism by which OPEC petrodollars were recycled, starting with Middle Eastern oil export earnings being deposited in U.S. and European banks, which then lent these dollar balances to developing-world public- and private-sector borrowers. Over $350 billion was recycled from OPEC countries between 1976 and 1982.

As a result of all these factors, the total external debt of developing countries more than doubled from $180 billion in 1975 to $406 billion in 1979, increasing over 20% annually. More significant, an increasing portion of the debt was now on nonconcessional terms involving shorter maturities and market rates of interest, often variable rates. In 1971, about 40% of the total external debt was on nonconcessional terms. This increased to 68% by 1975, and by 1979, over 77% of the debt was on harder terms. Although the increase in nonconcessional lending by official

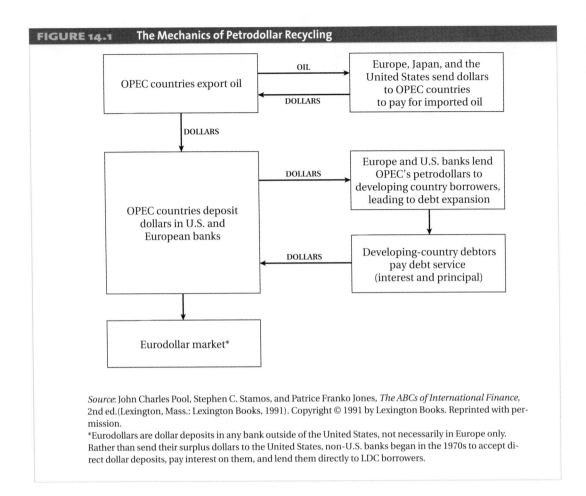

FIGURE 14.1   The Mechanics of Petrodollar Recycling

Source: John Charles Pool, Stephen C. Stamos, and Patrice Franko Jones, *The ABCs of International Finance*, 2nd ed.(Lexington, Mass.: Lexington Books, 1991). Copyright © 1991 by Lexington Books. Reprinted with permission.
*Eurodollars are dollar deposits in any bank outside of the United States, not necessarily in Europe only. Rather than send their surplus dollars to the United States, non-U.S. banks began in the 1970s to accept direct dollar deposits, pay interest on them, and lend them directly to LDC borrowers.

institutions was partly responsible for this rising proportion, the more than tripling of lending by private capital markets played the major role. Together, the large increase in the size of debt and the larger proportion scheduled on harder terms were responsible for the tripling of debt-service payments, which rose from $25 billion in 1975 to $75 billion in 1979.

Despite the sizable increases in debt-servicing obligations, the ability of most developing countries to meet their debt-service payments during the late 1970s remained largely unimpaired. This was primarily a function of the international economic climate during that period. A combination of declining real oil prices as a result of inflation, low or negative real interest rates, and increased export earnings narrowed current account deficits toward the end of the decade and enabled developing countries to sustain relatively high growth rates, averaging 5.2% during 1973–1979, through massive borrowing.

In sum, the surge in international lending following the first oil shock was largely during the period 1974–1979. In a congenial economic atmosphere, it permitted developing countries to maintain relatively high rates of growth with little debt-servicing difficulty. It also facilitated the recycling of a huge surplus from oil exporters to oil importers through the lending activities of private international banks, and it helped dampen the recession in industrialized countries by providing for increased export demand on the part of developing countries.

Unfortunately, this success was short-lived, and, in fact, the surge in international lending that occurred in 1974–1979 had laid the groundwork for all the problems that were to come. The second oil shock, which occurred in 1979, brought about a complete reversal of the economic conditions conducive to the success of international lending in the previous period. Now developing countries faced an abrupt increase in oil prices that added to oil import bills and affected industrial goods imports. There was also a huge increase in interest rates caused by the industrialized countries' economic stabilization policies and a decrease in LDC export earnings resulting from a combination of slowed growth in the more developed nations and a precipitous decline of over 20% in primary commodity export prices. Moreover, developing countries inherited from the previous period a huge debt and debt-service obligation, which was made even more onerous by burgeoning interest rates and more precarious as a result of the bunching of short-term maturities.

Finally, during the entire period of debt accumulation, one of the most significant and persistent trends was the tremendous increase in private capital flight. It is estimated that between 1976 and 1985, about $200 billion fled the heavily indebted countries.[5] This was the equivalent of 50% of the total borrowings by LDCs over the same period. Fully 62% of Argentina's and 71% of Mexico's debt growth are estimated to have resulted from capital flight. In fact, some researchers have argued that the 1985 level of Mexican debt would have been $12 billion (rather than the actual $96 billion) were it not for the huge private capital flight.[6]

Facing this critical situation, developing countries had two policy options. They could either curtail imports and impose restrictive fiscal and monetary measures, thus impeding growth and development objectives, or they could finance their widening current account deficits through more external borrowing. Unable, and sometimes unwilling, to adopt the first option as a means of solving the balance of payments crisis, many countries were forced in the 1980s to rely on the second option, borrowing even more heavily. As a result, massive debt-service obligations accumulated, so that countries like Nigeria, Argentina, Ecuador, and Peru were experiencing negative economic growth in the 1980s and consequently faced severe difficulties in paying even the interest on their debts out of export earnings (see Table 14.7). They could no longer borrow funds in the world's private capital markets. In fact, not only did private lending dry up, but by 1984, the developing countries were paying back $10.2 billion more to the commercial banks than they were receiving in new loans (see Table 14.4).

In the 1990s, experiences of developing countries were highly varied, with many experiencing positive net transfers, but other countries remained in crisis.

The statistical picture has become more complicated since the mid-1990s, with LDCs increasingly relying on foreign direct investment. Some countries in crisis have probably experienced negative net financial transfers in recent years.

Attempts at Alleviation: Macroeconomic Instability, IMF Stabilization Policies, and Their Critics

The IMF Stabilization Program

One course of action that was increasingly but often reluctantly used by countries facing serious **macroeconomic instability** (high inflation and severe government budget and foreign payments deficits) along with growing foreign-debt obligations was to renegotiate loans with private international banks. The basic idea was to stretch out the payment period for principal and interest or to obtain additional financing on more favorable terms. Typically, however, such debtor countries had to deal with the IMF before a consortium of international banks would agree to refinance or defer existing loan schedules. Relying on the IMF to impose its usual "conditionality" medicine of tough **stabilization policies** before it agreed to lend LDCs funds in excess of their legal IMF quotas, the private banks interpreted successful negotiations with the IMF as a sign that borrowing countries were making serious efforts to reduce payments deficits and earn the foreign exchange needed to repay earlier loans.[7] There are four basic components to the typical IMF stabilization program:

1. Abolition or liberalization of foreign exchange and import controls

2. Devaluation of the official exchange rate

3. A stringent domestic anti-inflation program consisting of (a) control of bank credit to raise interest rates and reserve requirements; (b) control of the government deficit through curbs on spending, including in the areas of social services for the poor and staple food subsidies, along with increases in taxes and in public enterprise prices; (c) control of wage increases, in particular abolishing wage indexing; and (d) dismantling of various forms of price controls and promoting freer markets

4. Greater hospitality to foreign investment and a general opening up of the economy to international commerce

In the early 1980s, numerous debtor countries with greatly depleted foreign reserves, including Mexico, Brazil, Argentina, Venezuela, Bangladesh, and Ghana, had to turn to the IMF to secure additional foreign exchange. By 1992, ten countries had arranged to borrow a total of $37.2 billion in special drawing rights (equal to approximately $27 billion) from the IMF. During the Asian crisis of 1997, the IMF had to intervene with substantially larger sums of money in an effort to stabilize the shaky economies of Thailand ($3.9 billion in IMF loans), Pakistan ($1.6 billion), the Philippines ($435 million), Indonesia ($10 billion), and South Korea ($21 billion). To receive their loans and, more important, to negotiate additional credits from private banks, all these nations were required to adopt some or all of the enumerated stabilization policies. Although such policies may be successful in reducing inflation and improving the LDCs' balance of payments situation, they can be politically very unpopular (as evidenced by anti-IMF riots in Venezuela, Nigeria, Indonesia, and South Korea in the 1990s) because they strike at the heart of development efforts by disproportionately hurting the lower- and middle-income groups.[8] Alternatively, they have often been viewed by LDC leaders as representing a double standard—harsh adjustment policies for LDC debtors and no adjustment of the huge budget or trade deficits for the world's greatest debtor, the United States. Finally, because IMF policies are being imposed by an international agency that is perceived by those of the dependence school to be merely an arm of the rich industrialized nations, stabilization policies are often viewed by this school as measures designed primarily to maintain the poverty and dependence of LDCs while preserving the global market structure for the international banks and private investors (and speculators) from the industrialized nations. For example, in an extensive dependence critique of the IMF and its stabilization programs, Cheryl Payer has argued that the IMF functions within a developed-world dominated global trading system "as the chosen instrument for imposing imperialist financial discipline upon poor countries" and thus creates a form of "international peonage" in which the balance of payments problems of LDCs are perpetuated rather than resolved. Payer further argues that the IMF encourages LDCs to incur additional debt from international financial institutions while it "blackmails" them (through threats of loan rejection) into antidevelopmental stabilization programs. This added debt burden thus becomes a source of future balance of payments problems, so that a vicious cycle sets in—one in which debtor nations have to run faster merely to stay in place.[9]

Less radical observers view the IMF as neither a developmental nor an antidevelopmental institution but simply an institution trying to carry out its original though somewhat outdated mandate to hold the global capitalist market together through the pursuit of orthodox short-term international financial policies. Its primary goal is the maintenance of an "orderly" international exchange system designed to promote monetary cooperation, expand international trade, control inflation, encourage exchange-rate stability, and help countries deal with short-run balance of payments problems through the provision of scarce foreign-exchange resources. Unfortunately, in a highly unequal trading world, the balance of payments problems of many developing nations may be structural and long-term in nature, with the result that short-term stabilization policies may easily lead to long-run development crises.[10] For example, between 1982 and 1988, the IMF strategy was tested in 28 of the 32 nations of Latin America and the Caribbean. It was clearly not working. During that period, Latin America financed $145 billion in debt payments but at a cost of economic stagnation, rising unemployment, and a decline in per capita income of 7%.[11] These countries "adjusted" but did not grow. By 1988, only two were barely able to make their payments. The same situation prevailed in much of Africa.[12]

In the absence of a major restructuring of both the domestic LDC economy (with perhaps the help of the World Bank's **structural adjustment loans**)[13] and the international economic order, the adoption of orthodox economic policies in pursuit of orthodox balance of payments objectives may in fact jeopardize the very system that the IMF seeks to preserve. Though its motives are probably not the sinister ones ascribed to it by Payer and other dependency theorists, the IMF's policies of severe financial austerity for debtor countries tended to inflict a harsh and often unnecessary economic burden on nations that in many cases could ill afford it.

Tactics for Debt Relief

LDC debt has become a worldwide problem with serious economic implications for both developed and less developed countries. In fact, the debt crisis of the 1980s, initiated by Mexico's declared moratorium on debt payments in 1982 (which came close to being repeated in 1995), called into question the stability and very viability of the international financial system. Fears were voiced that if one or two of the major debtor countries (Brazil, Mexico, or Argentina) were to default, if a group of debtor nations were jointly to repudiate their debts by forming a **debtors' cartel**, or if more countries followed Peru's early initiative to link debt servicing to export earnings, the economies of Western nations might be seriously affected. Following the onset of the debt crisis, most developing countries were cut off from the international capital market. Emergency meetings between international bankers and government officials of developed nations and LDC debtors were convened in the financial capitals of the world. This was because Latin American debts alone exceeded the net assets of the largest U.S. banks. Rumors of imminent default led currency speculators to purchase dollars, driving up the dollar's market value in 1983–1984 to a level well beyond its shadow value and adding even further to the dollar-denominated debt burdens of developing nations.

Numerous proposals for relieving or restructuring the debt burdens of highly indebted nations have been put forward.[14] These have ranged from a new allocation of special drawing rights to **restructuring** (on better terms for debtor countries) of principal payments falling due during an agreed-on consolidation period. Most notable have been the Paris Club arrangements, offering highly concessional conditions, the so-called Toronto terms. These bilateral arrangements for public loans permit creditor governments to choose from three alternative concessional options—partial cancellation of up to one-third of nonconcessional loans, reduced interest rates, or extended (25-year) maturity of payments—to generate cash flow savings for debtor countries. For commercial banks, the 1989 **Brady Plan** linked partial debt forgiveness for selected borrowers to IMF or World Bank financial support guaranteeing the payment of the remaining loans as well as LDC commitments to adopt stringent IMF-type adjustment programs, promote free markets, welcome foreign investors, and repatriate overseas capital. In addition, there has been much discussion of **debt-for-equity swaps**. These are the sale at a discount (sometimes in excess of 50%) of questionable LDC commercial bank debts to private investors (mostly foreign corporations) in secondary trading markets. These corporations then trade a debtor's IOU for a local state-owned asset, such as a steel mill or a telephone company. Commercial banks are now more willing to engage in such transactions because new interpretations and regulations for U.S. banks permit them to take a loss on the loan swap while not reducing the book value of other loans to that country. For the LDCs' part, they are able through debt-for-equity swaps to encourage private investments in local-currency assets from both foreign and resident investors as well as to reduce their overall debt obligations. Much of the privatization that has occurred in Latin American debtor countries has been financed through these swap arrangements. The flip side of these benefits, however, is the fact that foreign investors are buying up the state-owned real assets of developing nations, such as steel mills and telephone companies, at major discounts. Observers who worry about developed-country penetration into LDC economies or the exacerbation of domestic dualistic tendencies are naturally troubled by these debt-for-equity swaps. Between 1985 and 1992, they accounted for over 36% of all debt conversions.

An appealing but much less significant swap arrangement is the **debt-for-nature swap**, intended to win LDC government commitments to environmental preservation of such assets as the rain forests in Ecuador or a national park in Costa Rica (see Chapter 11). Most debt-for-nature swaps are carved out by nongovernmental organizations such as the World Wildlife Fund or the Nature Conservancy. They purchase the debtor nation's IOU at a discount from a local bank and then restructure it into local-currency payments, which are then used, say, to preserve an endangered natural resource. Unfortunately, the magnitude of debt-for-nature swaps has continuously declined since peaking at $43.9 million in 1989. By 1997, they had fallen to a mere $537,000. However, since 2000, new debt-for-nature exchanges have been worked out in several countries, including Jordan, Ghana, and Belize, and they are being actively negotiated in numerous new sites, including Madagascar, Indonesia, Russia, Argentina, Jamaica, Dominican Republic, the Philippines, and Thailand.

The problem with most proposals for debt alleviation, including debt-for-equity swaps, is that they require private international banks to initiate or endorse the policies. Most are unwilling to take any steps that would harm their short-run balance sheets. More significant, in the absence of unilateral **debt repudiation** by LDCs (a policy that surely would hurt both borrowers and lenders in both the short and the long term), most proposals (except debt-for-nature swaps) do not solve the debt problem but merely postpone the day when debts become once again due and another crisis erupts.

All in all, the debt crisis underlined the tremendous interdependence and political fragility of the international economic and financial system. It also demonstrated that not only were developing economies terribly vulnerable to small increases in U.S. interest rates but, perhaps more significant, that developed countries could indeed be harmed by the economic failures or public policies of key developing nations.

Although many developing countries can be held at least partly responsible for the massive accumulation of debt, the adverse economic conditions they face are often beyond their control. In fact, this adverse economic climate was in part precipitated by the industrialized countries' own economic stabilization policies, which led to soaring interest rates, worldwide economic recession, and the resulting decrease in demand for developing-country exports. William Cline has estimated, for example, that almost 85% ($401 billion) of the total increase ($480 billion) in the external debt of the non-oil-exporting LDCs between 1973 and 1982 can be attributed to four factors outside of their control: OPEC oil price increases, the rise in dollar interest rates in 1981–1982, the decline in LDC export volume as a result of the worldwide recession, and the dramatic fall in commodity prices and the consequent worsening of their terms of trade.[15]

Has the Debt Crisis Disappeared? Winners and Losers

Whereas the LDC debt problem was often referred to as the most significant international financial crisis of the 1980s, at least until 1997, LDC debt seemed to have all but disappeared from the pages of developed-country newspapers and magazines. This is because almost 80% of the outstanding debt owed to commercial banks by the most heavily indebted LDCs (Mexico, Argentina, Brazil, and Venezuela, among others), as well as a much smaller proportion owed to governments and multilateral institutions, had been restructured. Commercial bankers and financiers in the industrialized countries declared the debt crisis over and proclaimed that with the signing of a Brady-type restructuring accord with Argentina in April 1992 and with Brazil in July 1992, the banking industry could close its books on LDC debt. But the data contained in Tables 14.6 and 14.7 reveal that for many countries, especially those in Africa, the problem remained as serious as ever—perhaps even more so. Most poor countries have still seen little debt relief. The situation is particularly acute in sub-Saharan Africa, where the region's total debt is in many cases much larger than annual export earnings. Debt-service payments approach four times Africa's annual expenditure on health and education combined.[16] This represents a monstrous drain on the region's already depleted development finances.

Because of the large burden of repayment and the requirement that severely indebted LDCs swallow a heavy dose of IMF restrictive medicine, economic growth for many developing countries has turned negative, per capita consumption has steadily declined, and the investment necessary to generate the growth required to pay off debts and raise levels of living has all but disappeared. The crisis may be over for the developed-country commercial banks, whose outstanding LDC loans dropped from $67 billion in 1987 to $19 billion in 1992 when the crisis was declared over. For them, the IMF clearly did a good job. But for all the low- and middle-income citizens of the developing world whose economic welfare has been and continues to be sacrificed in order to prevent their indebted governments from sinking even further into insolvency, not only has the medicine been bitter, but many of the patients are clearly not recovering.[17] John Cavanagh put it this way:

> The IMF in many ways is like a medieval doctor where no matter what the ailment, you apply leeches and bleed the patient. My experience is that they [IMF quick fixes] are very successful in steering countries' resources toward paying debts to commercial banks, but they are disastrous in terms of the long-term economic health of these countries.[18]

Fortunately, by the late 1990s, the IMF had begun to show some flexibility and a willingness to modify its prescribed medicine to fit the varied illnesses of its patients.[19] This is a more logical, more humane, and ultimately more developmental course of action than the harsh prescriptions of the earlier stabilization packages.

But far from extinct, the debt crisis is, at best, only dormant. This was vividly revealed in late 1994 and early 1995 when one of the great "success stories" of debt rescheduling, Mexico, was forced to devalue its currency and seek special standby loans to pay off its short-term debt obligations. Almost half of the private portfolio investment capital that had flowed into Mexico (and other Latin American debtor nations, including Brazil, Argentina, and Venezuela) in the early 1990s was summarily withdrawn. Mexico was then forced to declare a new austerity program, further weakening the already deteriorating condition of its shrinking middle class and its working poor. As in 1982, the large commercial banks and Wall Street investors were once again surprised by Mexico's move. The "hot money" flows that had been universally hailed as a boon to the Mexican economic reform program now added to its burden of retrenchment as most investors withdrew their funds in the time that it took them to hit their computer keys. A similar process occurred during the Asian currency crisis of 1997.[20] The effective debt default in 2001 by Argentina, another "success story," showed that the LDC debt crisis continues to rear its head, even in Latin America.

At the same time, many severely indebted low-income LDCs, particularly those in Africa, have been caught in a vicious cycle in which the repayment of debt creates a drag on economic growth, yet accelerated growth is the only viable basis for escaping the confines of the debt trap. Perhaps more serious, their prolonged economic decline means that it will take at least a generation for them even to reestablish the low levels of living that they were experiencing in the late 1970s.

The first initiative to address the problems of **highly indebted poor countries (HIPCs)** was launched by the group of seven major industrialized countries (the Group of Seven or G7) in 1996. They set up an elaborate process for qualifying for expanded debt relief through the international financial institutions, but by 1999, despite extensive efforts, only 4 of the 36 poor countries initially deemed eligible had qualified. The G7 agreed at their meeting in Cologne, Germany, in 1999 to set aside approximately $100 billion for debt relief for those designated HIPC countries that demonstrated, to the satisfaction of the World Bank and the IMF, that they are both pursuing "sound policies" and are "committed" to reducing poverty. Commitment was to be demonstrated through what came to be called *poverty reduction strategy papers* (for the details, go to http://poverty.worldbank.org/prsp, or http://www.imf.org/external/nf/prsp/prsp.asp). But progress on committing these funds was slower than expected and is in any case unlikely to be sufficient to resolve the huge debt burden of sub-Saharan Africa.

Conclusions

The global debt burden must ultimately be shared by all. Many developing countries may have to continue a period of difficult adjustment. At the same time, industrialized countries will have to relax restrictive monetary policies and encourage imports from the developing world. Since research shows that along with political stability, the main determinant of LDC ability to repay debts and attract private investor capital is the level of global and domestic interest rates,[21] it is critical for creditor-country monetary authorities to keep this fact in mind as they pursue their macroeconomic strategies. Some additional debt relief (e.g., making interest payments in local currencies or putting a cap on real interest rates) will also be necessary. Commercial banks can no longer be permitted to pass on their losses to developed-country taxpayers. International organizations, primarily the IMF and the World Bank, will have to provide sufficient financial liquidity and policy flexibility so that the poorest developing countries can make the necessary adjustments without further sacrificing growth and equity. Indeed, if highly indebted African countries are to escape from their poverty trap, an essentially complete write-off of their external debt, in conjunction with viable poverty reduction strategies, is probably inevitable. Reduced agricultural protection and subsidies, along with better access to developed country export markets, will be necessary to reduce the risk of future crises. Whether Latin America can engineer a permanent escape from crisis remains to be seen.

Mexico: Crisis, Debt Reduction, and the Struggle for Renewed Growth

In August 1982, Mexico triggered a debt crisis when it announced that it could not service its debt and would begin a moratorium of at least three months on debt payments to private creditors. Creditor banks, led by Citibank, formed an advisory committee. Mexico sought and received emergency assistance from the International Monetary Fund and U.S. financial institutions. In September, Mexico nationalized its banks and introduced rigorous exchange controls.

In late September 1982, the annual World Bank–IMF meetings took place in Toronto in an atmosphere of panic. The greatest fear was that the stability of the international banking system was in peril if significant defaults on loans threatened the major banks. The crisis swept through Latin America, Africa, and developing countries such as the Philippines and Yugoslavia. A plan was devised that saved the banking system but led to what is often called the lost decade of development in Latin America and Africa.

Mexico was not only the first country to enter a debt crisis but also a pacesetter in resolving it. Despite some smaller crises, particularly the so-called Tequila Crisis of 1994, the country is considered one of the most successful cases of debt reduction with at least modest resumption of growth. The World Bank now classifies Mexico as a low-debt developing country. Capital inflows have very commonly assumed the form of long-term equity rather than debt. This case study will focus on the period of dramatic debt reduction in the late 1980s and early 1990s and will examine Mexico's strategies, following the framework of the excellent book on the subject by Sudarshan Gooptu.

Before 1973, Mexico's external debt, like that of most LDCs, was relatively small, primarily official, and often based on concessional lending. But major OPEC countries received a huge cash windfall from the 1973 oil price rise, and they deposited most of the funds in major American banks. Mexico and other Latin American countries had a ready demand for these funds. From 1970 to 1992, developing-country external debt grew from $68 billion to over $2000 billion.

Following Citibank chairman John Reed's dictum that "sovereign countries do not default," large banks lent to this region with abandon, often overlooking normal criteria of country lending risk. The value of outstanding loans increased tenfold in less than a decade.

Fate was sealed in the resulting crisis when Mexico and other borrowing countries failed to increase domestic investments apace with borrowing to levels capable of producing adequate levels of viable exports. Investment as a share of GDP hardly increased at all in this period of massive borrowing. Thus Mexico and other borrower countries did not have the added capacity to produce the exports that could have generated foreign exchange to repay the debt without necessitating a fall in living standards.

Problems in Mexico were aggravated by very large fiscal deficits and inflation. After Mexico discovered additional large oil reserves and began producing oil in larger amounts in 1977, the country was merely tempted to borrow more money with oil as an implicit collateral. But this money, too, was not wisely invested, and the oil industry was operated with considerable inefficiency. Exchange-rate appreciation hurt other exports (an example of the so-called *Dutch disease,* in which exports of a commodity raise exchange rates and crowd out manufacturing and agricultural exports), and non-oil industries were neglected.

If the first oil shock triggered international lending through the combination of loan demand and recycling petrodollars that expanded the supply of loanable funds, the second oil shock, in 1979, triggered a reversal of this process as interest rates rose, stagnation reduced the demand for LDC exports, and already high debt levels made further borrowing to accommodate high oil prices all the more difficult. When real interest rates rose dramatically after 1979, Mexico's debt burden became untenable. In early 1982, Mexico's financial position deteriorated rapidly. The country needed to borrow some $20 billion that year to finance its existing loans and meet its expected deficit. As the year progressed, bank loans were harder to arrange and required a substantially higher interest rate. Inflation rose and a series of devaluations began. When the crisis finally broke in August, it should not have come as a surprise. At its height in 1986, Mexican external debt approached 80% of GDP.

The early years of the crisis were harsh for Mexico. An economic adjustment program under IMF auspices restored economic order.

Elements of the typical IMF stabilization packages included liberalization of foreign-exchange and import controls, devaluation, interest rate increases, deficit reduction, wage restrictions, decreased price controls, and a general opening up of the economy. It was widely argued in Mexico that adjustment without growth would ensue, with negative development consequences. Indeed, Mexican leaders deeply resented this "austerity" program, but they saw no alternative.

This "IMF period" of the debt crisis had as its explicit objective the stability of the world financial system, and this meant ensuring the stability of the major money-center banks. Mexicans and the Mexican economy were clearly suffering. Real income fell dramatically from 1982 to 1985. The IMF was asked to provide funds under less stringent conditions. Its standard public relations reply was, "We are the fire department. You call us when your house is on fire. We are not the carpenter. You don't complain when we put an ax to your door or cause water damage with our hoses." But by 1985 it had become clear that although the fire was being contained, it was not going out. There had been some achievements; in particular, the public-sector deficit fell from about 17% to 8% as a share of GDP. But the level of GDP had fallen dramatically, and poverty and inequality had risen.

By 1985, the position of the banks was stabilizing. They were substantially reducing their exposure in developing-country debt in relation to their paid-up capital. The immediate crisis subsided somewhat in 1984 when a "multiyear rescheduling agreement" with foreign banks stretched out repayment terms for Mexico's debt. But growth showed no sign of resuming in Mexico or elsewhere among heavily indebted countries. No new capital flows were forthcoming to these countries, and it became clear that a new approach would be needed.

In 1985, U.S. secretary of state James Baker introduced a new initiative that became known as the Baker Plan. The idea was to get growth to resume in debtor countries so that they could "grow their way out of debt." Debt forgiveness was still a taboo subject. But new funds would be lent to indebted countries that would let growth resume, drawing on private banks, the World Bank, the IMF, and other sources. In return, Mexico and other indebted countries would introduce market reforms that were expected to facilitate the use of new funds in a more efficient and growth-enhancing manner.

Mexico became one of the first countries to participate in the Baker Plan. Mexico acceded to a major debt-restructuring and domestic economy reform program in June 1986. Commercial banks extended over $7 billion in loans and a new rescheduling agreement covering some $54 billion of outstanding debt. In return, the World Bank offered a loan of $500 million dollars. This represented the entry of the World Bank into structural adjustment loans as part of the Baker Plan. Previously, such general loans were seen as the exclusive province of the IMF, with the World Bank specializing in project lending.

The IMF also committed new funds. Mexico was being severely hurt by the big drop in the price of oil of the mid-1980s. The IMF agreed to a "special stand-by" agreement in which it would make some $600 million credit available to Mexico if the price of oil were to fall below $9 a barrel. The IMF also offered substantial new credit, to be matched by new credits from commercial banks. Mexico did introduce far-reaching market-oriented reforms in this period. The most important reason why this approach did not work in the end is that commercial banks proved unwilling to do their part in net new lending. These banks committed only a fraction of the loans anticipated in the Baker Plan. The banks' main intention at this time was still to reduce their exposure to developing-country debt, not to increase it.

Mexico had been one of the countries at the forefront of a major trend of the 1970s, passing laws limiting foreign firms' participation in most sectors to minority investments in preapproved joint ventures. One effect of the debt crisis was that these restrictions were largely lifted. Full subsidiaries were allowed. The level of direct foreign investment (DFI) increased steadily.

In the mid-1980s, Mexico became one of the pioneers of debt-for-equity swaps as an instrument of debt reduction. In these swaps, restrictions on DFI are lifted when foreign investors pay for the asset by presenting Mexican debt paper. These are acquired, usually at a substantial discount, from banks that wish to reduce their developing-country debt exposure. The secondary market for Latin American debt had an average discount of perhaps 50% of face value (sometimes with far steeper discounts). The investor presents the loan to the central bank, which in turn issues local currency (pesos in the case of Mexico) that can be used only to purchase a local firm's assets. Sometimes the firm may be a state-owned enterprise, so the transaction facilitates privatization. But debt-equity swaps carry the inherent risk of generating inflationary pressures because they usually involve swaps of public debt for private assets. Because the central bank issues funds for the investor to buy a local asset, this represents a direct addition to high-powered money.

Mexico suspended debt-equity swaps in November 1987, officially because of their inflationary effects. Part of the real reason may have been political pressures to limit the share of foreign ownership and control in the economy, though swaps of private debt for private equity continued to be permitted. In any case, concerns about large-scale foreign ownership would represent another limitation on the ability to use debt-equity swaps as a major element of a debt reduction program.

In 1988, as the swap strategy lost momentum, Mexico pioneered a new approach to debt reduction. Mexico would exchange some of its outstanding debt, perceived as high-risk, for new debt called "Aztec Bonds" that would be backed by U.S. Treasury bonds bought by Mexico as collateral. An auction would be held in which banks would bid on how much discount on the face amount of their existing loans they would accept in exchange for the new, more secure bonds. In March 1988, some $2.5 billion of bonds were exchanged for $3.6 billion in bank debt, an average discount of about 33%. A total of some $6.7 billion was offered by banks, but Mexico rejected some of these bids as offering too small a discount. If the results were disappointing in their magnitude, they represented an important innovation, later built on in the Brady Plan.

Eventually, all parties realized that substantial Mexican growth could not resume until the country's large debt burden was substantially reduced, not just rescheduled. With the major U.S. money-center banks out of immediate danger after several years of reducing developing-world exposure, debt reduction could be considered without risk of financial panic. A debt reduction plan was floated by U.S. Treasury secretary Nicholas Brady in March 1989. Although market-based, the plan had an important public role designed to help overcome free-rider problems. Each lender would like other lenders to reduce the amount of debt owed to them so as to increase the probability that its own debt would be repaid. But unilateral reduction of debt by any one bank only benefits other banks holding debt. Thus some coordinating role, generally of government, must be played to overcome this basic market failure.

Mexico was the first country to negotiate debt reduction under the new Brady Plan. Banks were given three options: (1) to exchange loans for floating-rate bonds with collateral at a 35% discount, (2) to exchange loans for bonds with the same par value but receiving a lower, fixed interest rate, or (3) to lend new money to finance Mexican interest payments, keeping nominal value of the debt they were owed intact. In 1990, some 49% of the banks exchanged $22 billion in debt for lower-interest, fixed-rate bonds, and 41% exchanged $20 billion in debt for the discounted floating-rate bonds. This constituted Mexico's creditor banks' "revealed preferences" from among the options.

Provided that Mexico continues to service this debt successfully, the bonds on deposit in Washington as collateral would earn interest that Mexico will receive, which can eventually be used for debt reduction or investment. These exchanges saved Mexico payments of about $1.3 billion per year. From the banks' point of view, the trade-off involved giving up higher-yielding but higher-risk debt for lower-yielding but lower-risk debt. Following Mexico's example, other countries reduced their required payments under the Brady Plan, and the debt crisis went into remission. Mexican debt was 63% of GDP in 1983 but fell to 32% by 1993 and was just 23% in 2003.

There was one major crisis along the way. In 1994 the government attempted to carry out a small, orderly devaluation of the peso. But the market saw this step as too little too late given the large current account deficit and concluded that the action was likely just a prelude to much larger devaluations in the near future. Speculators, acting on these expectations, forced the hand of the government, which let the peso float until it had lost over half its value. Instability spread across other countries in the so-called Tequila financial crisis. By mid-1996, the worst of the crisis had passed, and Mexico proved immune to the crises that rocked Argentina and Brazil in the first years of the twenty-first century. For Mexico, the special arrangements of NAFTA, with the particular benefits of bordering the world's largest economy, suggests that the country can now stay out of debt trouble with wise economic management. But it also suggests that the degree of its success will not be easy for other countries to emulate. And for all Mexico's advantages, output growth has remained sluggish, averaging less than 3% for 1990–2004. And real incomes remained well under one-quarter of those in the United States. ■

Sources

Central Intelligence Agency. *World Fact Book, Mexico, 2004.* Washington, D.C.: Government Printing Office, 2004.

Erzan, Refik. "Free trade agreements with the United States: What's in it for Latin America?" World Bank Policy Research Working Paper no. 827, 1992.

Gooptu, Sudarshan. *Debt Reduction and Development: The Case of Mexico.* Westport, Conn.: Praeger, 1993.

Hufbauer, Gary, and Jeffery Schott. *NAFTA: An Assessment.* Washington, D.C.: Institute for International Economics, 1993.

Kaminsky, Graciela L., Carmen M. Reinhart, and Carlos A. Vegh. "The unholy trinity of financial contagion." *Journal of Economic Perspectives,* 17 (2003): 51–74.

"The Mexican Worker." *Business Week,* April 19, 1993.

Pastor, Robert F., and Jorje G. Castenada. *Limits to Friendship: The United States and Mexico.* New York: Vintage Books, 1988.

World Bank. "World debt tables," various years, http://www.worldbank.org/data/countrydata/countrydata.html.

Concepts for Review

Amortization	Debt-for-nature swap	International reserve ac-
Balance of payments (BOP)	Debtors' cartel	count
Basic transfer	Debt repudiation	International reserves
Brady Plan	Debt service	Macroeconomic instability
Capital account	Deficit	Restructuring
Capital flight	Euro	Special drawing rights
Cash account	External debt	(SDRs)
Conditionality	Hard currency	Stabilization policies
Current account	Highly indebted poor coun-	Structural adjustment loans
Debt-for-equity swap	tries (HIPCs)	Surplus

Questions for Discussion

1. Draw up a balance of payments table similar in format to Table 14.3 using the most recent data from any developing country (consult the IMF's monthly publication *International Financial Statistic* for the most recent data). Explain the significance of the various entries in the current and capital accounts. What is the status of the country's international reserves, and how do they compare with those of one year ago?

2. Describe the basic-transfer mechanism. Using the list of credits and debits from Table 14.2, identify which ones would fit into the basic-transfer equation. How does the basic transfer help us analyze developing-world debt problems?

3. Trace the evolution of the LDC debt problem during the 1970s and 1980s. What were the key ingredients? Explain your answer.

4. Why was the problem of capital flight so serious in some highly indebted countries? What causes capital flight, and what do you think can be done about it?

5. Who should bear most of the burden of responsibility for (a) causing and (b) alleviating the debt crisis, LDCs or MDCs? And which agents within the LDCs and MDCs bear the blame for the crisis?

6. What is petrodollar recycling, and how did it contribute to the debt crisis? Why were LDCs so eager to borrow money from international banks? Explain your answer.

7. What is the significance of the debt-service ratio? Can indebted countries do anything to lower this ratio? Explain your answer.

8. Describe the typical IMF stabilization package for SICs. What are the objectives of these policies, and why are international banks so eager for IMF negotiations to precede their discussions with SICs? What are the economic and social costs of these programs? Explain your answer.

9. Is the debt crisis over? If so, what are the long-term implications for both lenders and borrowers? If not, what still needs to be done?

Notes

1. See, for example, John Williamson and Donald R. Lessard, *Capital Flight: The Problem and Policy Responses* (Washington, D.C.: Institute for International Economics, 1987), for an excellent review of data and issues.

2. In 1999, 11 European countries—Austria, Belgium, Finland, France, Germany, Ireland, Italy, Luxembourg, the Netherlands, Portugal, and Spain—adopted a common currency, the *euro*. In January 2002, the euro went into circulation and local currencies became obsolete.

3. Williamson and Lessard, *Capital Flight*, p. 56.

4. This discussion is based on Frances Stewart, "The international debt situation and North-South relations," *World Development* 13 (1985): 141–204.

5. John Charles Pool and Stephen C. Stamos, *The ABCs of International Finance: Understanding the Trade and Debt Crisis* (Lexington, Mass.: Lexington Books, 1987), pp. 55–57.

6. Ibid., p. 55.

7. For review and discussion of developing-nation stabilization programs from a developed-country perspective, see Rudiger Dornbusch, "Policies to move from stabilization to growth," and W. Max Corden, "Macroeconomic policy and growth: Some lessons of experience," in *Proceedings of the World Bank Annual Conference on Development Economics, 1990* (Washington D.C.: World Bank, 1991). For a lengthy economic critique of the IMF stabilization package and its effects on both the balance of payments and the overall economy, see Paul P. Streeten, "Stabilization and adjustment," *Labour and Society* 13 (1988): 1–18.

8. See, for example, James L. Dietz, "Debt and development: The future of Latin America," *Journal of Economic Issues* 20 (1986): 1029–1051, and Paul P. Streeten, *Strategies for Human Development* (Copenhagen: Handelshøjskolens Forlag, 1994), pt. 2.

9. Cheryl Payer, *The Debt Trap: The IMF and the Third World* (New York: Monthly Review Press, 1974), pp. 1–49.

10. For an analysis of how IMF stabilization programs are typically imposed on LDC debtors and how such policies can be counterproductive in a climate of macroeconomic instability, see Dani Rodrik, "The limits of trade policy reform in developing countries," *Journal of Economic Perspectives* 6 (1992): 87–105, and Lance Taylor, "The revival of the liberal creed and the IMF and the World Bank in a globalized economy," *World Development* 25 (1997): 145–152.

11. Part of the explanation for this decline in per capita income, according to researchers like Jeffrey Sachs, Paul Krugman, and Andreas Savvides, relates to the *debt overhang hypothesis*. The argument is that the external debt burden provided a disincentive to domestic investment in LDCs and thus slowed economic growth because any additional foreign-exchange earnings would have to be turned over to foreign creditors. For a brief discussion and empirical test of this hypothesis, see Andreas Savvides, "Investment slowdown in developing countries during the 1980s: Debt overhang or for-

eign capital inflows?" *Kyklos* 45 (1992): 363–378.

12. See Howard Stein, "Deindustrialization, adjustment, the World Bank and the IMF in Africa," *World Development* 20 (1992): 83–95, and Frances Stewart, "The many faces of adjustment," *World Development* 19 (1991): 1847–1864.

13. Unlike IMF stabilization policies, which are short-run in nature, the World Bank engages in what it calls long-run *structural adjustment* lending. The focus is on improving the macroeconomic policy environment with an emphasis on (a) mobilizing domestic savings through fiscal and financial policies, (b) improving public-sector efficiency by stressing price-determined allocation of public investments and improving the efficiency of public enterprises, (c) improving the productivity of public-sector investments by liberalizing trade and domestic economic policies, and (d) reforming institutional arrangements to support the adjustment process. For a description of the role of the bank in structural adjustment lending, see Appendix 14.1.

14. For a review and a description of debt-relief proposals, see World Bank, *Global Development Finance, 1998* (Washington, D.C.: World Bank, 1998), pp. 2–3.

15. William R. Cline, *International Debt and the Stability of the World Economy* (Washington, D.C.: Institute for International Economics, 1983).

16. Gary Gardner, "Third World debt is still growing," *World Watch*, January-February 1995, p. 37. See also Wayne Nafziger, *The Debt Crisis in Africa* (Baltimore: Johns Hopkins University Press, 1993); Gordon Brown, "Debt and development: Time to act, again," *Economist*, January 21, 1998, pp. 77–78; and World Bank, *2004 World Development Indicators.*

17. LDC nationals are not the only losers in the debt game. Taxpayers in the developed countries are increasingly absorbing the former debts of commercial banks through government loan guarantees generated by the Brady Plan. For an excellent discussion, see Benjamin J. Cohen, "What ever happened to the LDC debt crisis?" *Challenge*, May-June 1991, pp. 47–51.

18. Quoted in *New York Times*, April 26, 1992, sec. 3, p. 1.

19. Stewart, "Many faces of adjustment," 1857–1859. See also Jeffrey Sachs, "Beyond Bretton Woods: A new blueprint," *Economist*, October 1, 1994, pp. 23–27.

20. For an interesting analysis of what determines private capital flows (basically, the level of international interest rates) and why the debt crisis is far from dead, see Michael P. Dooley, Eduardo Fernandez-Arias, and Kenneth M. Kletzer, *Recent Private Capital Inflows to Developing Countries: Is the Debt Crisis History? World Bank Economic Review*, January 1996, pp. 27–50. For a review of the Mexican devaluation, see Independent Task Force, *Lessons of the Mexican Peso Crisis* (New York: Council on Foreign Relations, 1995).

21. Dooley, Fernandez-Arias, and Kletzer, ibid.

Further Reading

The best overall source of empirical information on the debt crisis can be found in the World Bank's annual edition of *Global Development Finance*. Two excellent books are Harold Lever and Christopher Huhne, *Debt and Danger: The World Financial Crisis* (New York: Atlantic Monthly Press, 1985), and John Charles Pool, Stephen C. Stamos, and Patrice Franko Jones, *The ABCs of International Finance*, 2nd ed. (Lexington, Mass.: Lexington Books, 1991). In addition to the numerous citations in the notes to this chapter, the following articles are recommended: Anne O. Kreuger, "Debt, capital flows, and LDC growth," *American Economic Review* 77 (1987): 159–164; Manuel Pastor Jr., "The effects of IMF programs in the Third World," *World Development* 15 (1987): 249–262; Alejandro Foxley, "Latin American development after the debt crisis," *Journal of Development Economics* 27 (1987): 201–225; the entire issue of the *Journal of Development Planning* 16 (1985), titled "The debt problem: Acute and chronic aspects," especially the articles by Carlos Massad, William R. Cline, and Albert Fishlow; Hans W. Singer, "Beyond the debt crisis," *Development* 18 (1992): 35–38; Wayne Nafziger, *The Debt Crisis in Africa* (Baltimore: Johns Hopkins University Press, 1993); Susan George, "Rethinking debt," *Development* 22 (1996): 54–58; Michael Dooley, Edwardo Fernandez-Aria, and Kenneth Kletzer, "Is the debt crisis history? Recent private capita inflows to developing countries," *World Bank Economic Review* 10 (1996): 27–50; and Graziela L. Kaminsky and Alfredo Pereira, "The debt crisis: Lessons of the 1980s for the 1990s," *Journal of Development Economics* 50 (1996): 1–24.

Appendix 14.1

A Brief History and Analysis of the International Monetary Fund and the World Bank

In July 1944, as World War II began to turn strongly in favor of the Allied forces, representatives from 45 countries convened in Bretton Woods, New Hampshire, to plan the terms of postwar international economic cooperation. The economic devastation of the Great Depression in the 1930s, followed by the ravages of the Second World War, had led to the collapse of international financial markets and precipitous declines in the volume of international trade. The International Monetary Fund (IMF) and World Bank were created to rebuild international goods and capital markets, as well as the war-torn economies of Western Europe.

The designated roles of the IMF and the World Bank were quite different, though to some extent they were intended to complement each other. It was the prevailing wisdom at the time of the Bretton Woods conference that the stabilization of international capital markets was essential to the resumption of lively international trade and investment. This concern led to the establishment of the IMF, which became responsible for monitoring and stabilizing the international financial system through the short-term financing of balance of payments deficits. The World Bank's complementary role involved financing the reconstruction and development of member nations, primarily through the rebuilding of national infrastructures. An attempt was also made to establish an international organization to encourage the liberalization of trade between countries, eventually leading to the creation of the General Agreement on Tariffs and Trade (GATT). It is widely recognized that the institutional structure provided by these organizations facilitated the international flow of goods and capital, though there remains considerable dispute over the extent of their effectiveness.

Though the policies of the IMF and the World Bank have changed considerably since their inception, the institutional framework laid out at Bretton Woods remains intact and continues to exert tremendous influence over the global economy. This applies especially to the countries of the developing world, whose ability to attract foreign capital is largely determined by the stance of the IMF and World Bank. Furthermore, the increasing interdependence between developed and developing countries has served to intensify the interaction between these international financial institutions and the developing world. Consequently, the IMF and the World Bank now play critical and evolving roles in the development process.

International Monetary Fund

The participants at the Bretton Woods conference established a system of fixed exchange rates in which each country was required to peg the value of its currency to the U.S. dollar, which remained directly convertible into gold at $35 per ounce. Initially, it was the responsibility of the IMF to finance temporary balance of payments deficits arising as a consequence of these pegged exchange rates. Any country experiencing a "fundamental disequilibrium" in trade as a result of an overvalued exchange rate was required to obtain approval from the IMF before devaluing its currency (see Chapter 13). In its capacity as overseer of exchange-rate policy and the financial conduct of member countries, the IMF was to stabilize international financial markets by ensuring convertibility between currencies. In addition, by financing trade imbalances, the IMF fulfilled the role of international lender of last resort, averting financial crises in countries experiencing acute foreign-exchange shortages. These activities were designed to maintain the viability of the international financial system created at Bretton Woods.

Progress toward international cooperation and compliance with the articles of agreement laid out at Bretton Woods continued until the mid-1960s, when a number of economic factors led many members to abandon their fixed exchange rates. Persistent declines in its gold reserves and chronic balance of payments deficits, in part resulting from overvaluation of the dollar, led the United States to abandon the convertibility of dollars into gold in August 1971. The ensuing collapse of the Bretton Woods system of exchange rates raised questions about the role of the IMF in international finance. The majority of the fund's resources had previously been used to maintain the value of several of the strongest currencies. The shift to a variety of floating-rate systems in the industrialized countries had obviated a principal IMF responsibility.

At the same time, however, the growing volume of international trade made it clear that a mechanism for expanding international liquidity was required. Therefore, in 1969, the IMF became responsible for the creation and allocation of a new international currency called *special drawing rights* (SDRs). The primary function of this new medium of exchange was to facilitate trade where shortages of international reserves of gold and dollars had imposed financial restrictions. In addition, the 1970s brought a new set of financial crises that helped reshape the role of the IMF in international markets. A combination of factors, including a world recession, rocketing OPEC fuel prices, and falling LDC exports, had led to large balance of payments deficits in many LDCs. This was a contributing factor in the decision by the IMF to more than double its total quota of SDRs. A substantial portion of the new funds were loaned through an agency, the Trust Fund, which provides concessional (low-interest) loans to finance trade deficits in the poorest developing countries.

Financing from the IMF is provisional in the sense that recipient countries must meet a set of requirements based on the purpose of the loan. During the IMF's first quarter century, the stipulations accompanying IMF funds were limited to exchange-rate behavior. However, following the demise of the system of fixed exchange rates and as the size and number of loans used for adjustment purposes increased, the restrictions placed on the economic policies of receiving countries also expanded and became known collectively as **conditionality**. These conditions are intended to increase the effectiveness of IMF resources by encouraging expedient behavior on the part of debtor governments facing chronic balance of payments troubles. Because the terms of conditionality are frequently draconian, imposing the greatest hardship on the poorest households in debtor countries, they have remained tremendously controversial.

The use of conditionality and the direct "surveillance" of LDC macroeconomic policy by the IMF marked its increasing involvement in the development process. Two other areas in which the fund began to expand its activities were in the provision of information services to the public and technical assistance to developing-country governments. These efforts were generally targeted toward achieving internal adjustments prescribed by the IMF to eliminate macroeconomic imbalances leading to payment deficits. Thus the direction of the IMF changed dramatically during the 1970s. According to a fund historian, "The use of resources was no longer undertaken in defense of a par value system but to promote effective and durable adjustment and restoration of the conditions for balanced and sustained economic growth."[1] Whether or not these policies were consistent with the development objectives of developing countries, they have at times helped avert financial crises arising in international capital markets.

By 1982, the external debt of non-oil-exporting developing countries stood at roughly $600 billion, and more than half that figure was owed on commercial terms. Imminent default in a number of heavily indebted developing countries experiencing high inflation, weak export markets, falling terms of trade, and large government deficits threatened to destabilize international financial markets. As the severity of crises in developing countries intensified, private sources of funding shrank rapidly, reducing the liquidity necessary to service debt. To avert widespread default and thus the threat of systemic failure in international capital markets, the IMF undertook exceptional measures to effect successful adjustment. Its role has been instrumental in the restructuring and financing of developing-country debt during the debt crisis of the 1980s and the Asian currency crisis of 1997–1998.

Perhaps the IMFs greatest influence has been exerted through its organization and negotiation of "financing packages." A financing package of stabilization policies is an agreement among the IMF, the debtor country, and private commercial banks designed to prevent default through the restructuring of macroeconomic policy and the garnering of new capital. In the negotiation and refinancing of loans, the IMF obtains prior commitment from private commercial banks to provide a portion of any new financing. Under this system, "debtor countries could obtain new loan commitments, especially from private creditors, only as part of 'financing packages.'"[2] Because each dollar provided by the IMF is matched with commercial money, the IMF essentially controls a much greater range of resources than those within its own budget. For this reason, the influence of the IMF among developing countries has increased dramatically over the past two decades.

World Bank

The structure of the World Bank is similar in a number of ways to that of the IMF. Each organization is jointly owned by its 184 member governments, and the voting power of each country depends on its annual contribution, which is proportional to the size of its economy. In addition, both institutions are primarily lending facilities. But they also serve as catalysts for outside investment and provide advice and expertise. Despite these similarities, the objectives of World Bank and IMF operations are quite different. Whereas the IMF was assigned a supervisory role over the external financial transactions of members of the international community created at Bretton Woods, internal reconstruction and development became the responsibility of the World Bank. The primary purpose of World Bank activity is to promote economic growth and prosperity by providing funds for investment in projects that help raise productivity and output. To push developing countries toward self-sustaining economic growth, the World Bank provides financial and technical assistance for the expansion of markets, construction of infrastructure, and creation of growth-oriented institutional frameworks.

Over the years, the institutional framework of the World Bank has changed considerably. Initially, all bank lending was channeled through the International Bank for Reconstruction and Development (IBRD), the branch of the World Bank established following Bretton Woods. At the time, its principal concern was rebuilding economies shattered during World War II. The structure of IBRD lending has been consistent since the 1940s, though the types of projects it supports have evolved. Loans are offered on commercial terms to borrowing governments or to private enterprises that have obtained government guarantees.

Largely due to the stunning success of the Marshal Plan, the reconstruction of Europe had become a fait accompli by the late 1950s, at which time the World Bank turned its primary focus toward investment in the poorer economies. The establishment in 1960 of the International Development Association (IDA), which provides additional support to the poorest countries, reflects this rising concern with the pace of economic development in the developing world. Though its responsibilities are much the same as those of the IBRD, the IDA differs in that the funds it lends, called *credits*, are offered on concessional terms to countries whose per capita incomes are below a critical level. These favorable terms involve repayment periods several times longer than those on IBRD loans and are interest-free. The preferred terms are an outgrowth of recognition that countries at the earliest stages of development are unable to borrow at commercial rates because they are more economically vulnerable and the financial returns to investment are slower to be realized.

Together the IBRD and IDA comprise what is known as the World Bank. A close affiliate of the World Bank is the International Finance Corporation (IFC), which shares the same staff but remains a separate entity both legally and financially. Established in 1956, the IFC was designed to complement the efforts of the World Bank by engaging in a range of economic activities from which the bank itself is restricted but which serve to further the interests of development. In contrast to the bank, the IFC lends directly to private enterprise in the absence of government guarantees. In addition, through a variety of activities such as underwriting or holding equity, it is capable of taking direct financial interests in the loan recipients. By spurring the development of new business activities among entrepreneurs who benefit directly from World Bank projects, the IFC helps magnify the economic rewards of World Bank investments.[3]

Changing Role

As previously mentioned, the original focus of the World Bank was on reviving economies destroyed during the Second World War. Though it was clearly expected that World Bank investments would lead to macroeconomic growth (and thus positive spillovers to international trade), the policies of the World Bank remained microeconomic in nature until the 1970s. For the first two decades following the war, the vast bulk of World Bank lending was used to finance the building of infrastructure related to energy and transportation. This should not be surprising, as much of Europe's infrastructure had been destroyed. Rising pressure to increase the flow of funds to poorer nations, following the economic recovery of Europe, led to a similar pattern of investment in developing countries.

It was discovered, however, that infrastructural investments in the developing world failed to produce the same returns as those in Europe (see Chapter 2), due largely to the lack of institutional framework and skilled labor. It became clear that a reordering of investment priorities specific to the needs of developing regions was necessary for successful development. This led to the diversification of investments and a general recognition that smaller-scale projects that target the livelihoods of the poorest populations are necessary to generate lasting economic prosperity.

Expansion of World Bank lending has been most rapid in the agricultural sector, especially in the production of cash crops for export. The bank's rationale for promoting cash crops is multifaceted: In addition to expanding the inflow of foreign currencies, the production of export crops is believed to enhance the incomes of the poor while improving food security. Recognition that the primary beneficiaries of past agricultural programs have been large farmers with the greatest access to credit and resources has led to increased interest in small-scale agriculture. A few of the other areas that have received additional resources are education, water supply and sewage, health care, and small-scale enterprise. Though recently these programs have received ample attention, funding by the World Bank lags behind its vocalized support.

The range of other services offered by the World Bank has also expanded. These include technical support, research, public provision of information and statistics, cofinancing of enterprise, and cooperative ventures with other nonprofit institutions. Since the late 1970s, there has been a dramatic increase in the transfer of funds and technical assistance for purposes of structural adjustment. These resources are designed to promote a fundamental restructuring of the economies of countries plagued by chronic trade and budget deficits. Critics of structural adjustment programs point to the fact that they frequently lead to increased hardships for the very poor and on occasion have substantially reversed the benefits of earlier economic progress. Though the World Bank has recently attempted to assist publics directly harmed by adjustment programs, the compensation measures remain ad hoc and are often severely limited in scope. Evidence suggests that adjustment tends to worsen income inequalities and can intensify poverty, even in countries experiencing economic recovery.

Cooperation between the IMF and the World Bank

Prior to the 1970s, the IMF policy prescription for a balance of payments deficit was a temporary infusion of foreign capital to meet currency shortfalls or currency devaluation where deficits had become chronic. Because the Bretton Woods conference had assigned the task of supervising foreign-exchange flows exclusively to the IMF, there was little overlap between fund and bank activities. Thus the IMF remained responsible for the balancing of external accounts through macroeconomic adjustments, while the World Bank influenced domestic production through microeconomic policy. Events during the past four decades however, have reduced the mutual exclusivity of these roles. Oil price shocks, falling exports, declining terms of trade, and capital flight experienced by developing countries made it clear that developing-world trade imbalances had become structural in nature.

To improve the status of developing countries vis-à-vis their developed-country trading partners, the IMF deemed it necessary that developing countries adopt stabilization policies to lower inflation, improve the efficiency of internal markets and institutions, lower domestic government spending, and review public investments, in addition to reforming their exchange-rate regimes. By becoming involved in these related negotiations, the IMF extended its activities into areas that had traditionally been within the sphere of influence of the World Bank. Similarly, the bank came to recognize that promoting domestic GNP growth would require consideration of external factors. Consequently, the structural adjustment programs of the World Bank began to include provisions for enhancing the international competitiveness of domestic products through the reform of trade policy and exchange-rates regimes. Thus in an analogous manner, the World Bank has intruded into the domain of the IMF.

Since maintaining equilibrium on external accounts is not conducive to long-term economic growth, fund and bank policies have not always been consistent with each other. The remarkable similarity between current IMF conditionality and World Bank structural adjustment policy is the result of a convergence in approaches that occurred during the 1970s and 1980s. There is a growing recognition that the successful resolution of both external and internal problems requires the simultaneous coordination of macroeconomic and microeconomic policies. This has led to greater cooperation between the World Bank and the IMF and a blurring of the distinctions in their roles.

In 1996, on the initiative of the G7, the World Bank and the IMF launched the highly indebted poor countries initiative (HIPC), enhanced in 1999, that is described in Chapter 14.

The Dissenting Views of Other Institutions

Although there is now greater congruence between World Bank and IMF policies, not all international development agencies have favored the reforms. Both structural adjustment and stabilization policies have been found to exacerbate hardships among the poorest groups in developing countries. This is generally due to cuts in government services, rising unemployment, falling real wages, and the elimination of food subsidies. As a result, numerous countries, including some experiencing economic recovery, have witnessed increasing infant mortality rates and malnutrition and declining school enrollment rates. Critics point out that the terms of conditionality associated with adjustment loans are antidevelopmental when they reverse or slow improvements in living conditions among the very poor.[4]

Many development agencies place greater emphasis on reducing or eradicating poverty and stress that it is misleading to include countries with rising rates of poverty and malnutrition among the adjustment success stories. In its 1990 *Human Development Report*, the United Nations Development Program introduced the Human Development Index, which it suggests should be used as an alternative measure of economic progress (see Chapter 2). Indicators of national income, life expectancy, and educational attainment are combined to provide a clearer picture of national economic well-being and may be used to determine the true benefits of adjustment. A study sponsored by UNICEF, *Adjustment with a Human Face*, found that children are frequently the group most vulnerable to the harsh consequences imposed by the restrictive macroeconomic policies of adjustment. Though structural changes are indeed necessary for economic recovery, it is argued that programs carefully designed to protect lower-income groups are needed to ensure that economic reforms are not achieved at the expense of the poor.[5]

Despite extensive criticism by the international community (especially by nongovernmental aid organizations) on humanitarian grounds,[6] the World Bank and the IMF were slow to restructure adjustment policies that hurt the poor. Though there is growing recognition of the importance of the problem within these institutions, compensatory programs such as HIPC have been modest.[7] For example, at a meeting of leaders of the seven major industrialized countries, or G7, held in Canada in June 1995, several proposals designed to enhance the role of the IMF and the World Bank in monitoring and responding to member-country (especially LDC) economic problems were put forward. These proposals initiated a longer-term review of both institutions to make them more responsive to the changing global economy of the twenty-first century. But the critical question, whether such institutional changes will actually reduce or promote poverty in LDCs rather than simply reinforce past policies that emphasized growth and fiscal austerity at the expense of lower-income groups, was not addressed. Until this issue is dealt with directly, the IMF and World Bank will continue to be perceived by some observers as agents of wealthy international bankers and investors with only limited interest in the plight of the poor.[8]

In 2000, the blue-ribbon International Financial Institution Advisory Commission (IFIAC), known as the Meltzer Commission, released its report to the U.S. Congress. The IFIAC findings reflected a broad consensus from many parts of the political spectrum. They concluded that the World Bank and the regional development banks needed thoroughgoing reform. The commission argued, "For the world's truly poor, the provision of improved levels of health care, primary education and physical infrastructure, once the original focus for development funding, should again become the starting points for raising living standards. Yet, poverty is often most entrenched and widespread in countries where corrupt and inefficient governments undermine the ability to benefit from aid or repay debt. Loans to these governments are, too often, wasted, squandered or stolen."

Accordingly, the commission made several recommendations, including the following:

- To underscore the shift in emphasis from lending to development, the name of the World Bank would be changed to World Development Agency. Similar changes should be made at the regional development banks.

- In poor countries without capital-market access, poverty alleviation grants to subsidize user fees should be paid directly to the supplier upon independently verified delivery of service. Grants should replace loans and guarantees for physical infrastructure and social service projects, and grant funding should be increased if grants are used effectively.

- Development services would be performed by outside private-sector providers (including nongovernmental and charitable organizations), as well as by public agencies, across the full range of activities, including vaccinations, road building, literacy, and water supply.

- Service contracts would be awarded on competitive bid. Failure to perform on earlier projects would weigh heavily against participation in future bids. Payments would be made directly to suppliers. Costs would be divided between recipient countries and the development agency, subsidized 10% to 90%, depending on capital market access and per capita income.

- Institutional reform loans should arise from decisions made by the LDC. If the development agency concurs in the merit of a proposal, the country would receive a loan with an interest rate 10% to 90% subsidized. Auditors, independent of both the borrowing government and the official lender, would be appointed to annually review implementation of the reform program.

- Development agencies should be precluded from financial-crisis lending.

- All country and regional programs in Latin America and Asia should be the primary responsibility of the area's regional bank.

- The World Bank should become the principal source of aid for the African continent until the African Development Bank is ready to take full responsibility.

- The World Development Agency should concentrate on producing global public goods and providing technical assistance to the regional development agencies. Global public goods include treatment of tropical diseases and AIDS, environmental protection, tropical climate agricultural programs, development of management and regulatory practices, and intercountry infrastructure.

- The income from paid-in capital and retained earnings should be reallocated to finance the increased provision of global public goods.

- Again, the World Bank and the regional development banks should write off in entirety their claims against all heavily indebted poor countries.

- The United States should be prepared to increase significantly its budgetary support for the poorest countries if they pursue effective programs of economic development.

Although the ultimate impact of the Meltzer Commission report remains to be seen, it has already become a basic starting point for discussions about reform of the World Bank and the IMF. The full report is available online at http://www.house.gov/jec/imf/meltzer.htm. Discussions concerning increasing the share of aid in the form of grants rather than loans have been active, but progress has been slow.

Notes to Appendix 14.1

1. M. Garritsen de Vries, *The IMF in a Changing World, 1945-85* (Washington, D.C.: International Monetary Fund, 1986), p. 120. This work provides a valuable presentation of the origins and evolution of the IMF.

2. Ibid., p. 188.

3. For a concise breakdown of the separate roles of the IBRD, IDA, and IFC, see World Bank, *The World Bank and the International Finance Corporation* (Washington, D.C.: World Bank, 1983). A comprehensive historical analysis is contained in Devesh Kapur, John P. Lewis, and Richard Webb, *The World Bank: Its First Half Century* (Washington, D.C.: Brookings Institution Press, 1997), vol. 1.

4. For poverty-oriented discussions of development efforts, see Frances Stewart, "The many faces of adjustment," *World Development* 19 (1991): 1847–1864; Giovanni A. Cornia, Richard Jolly, and Frances Stewart, *Adjustment with a Human Face* (Oxford: Clarendon Press, 1987); and United Nations Development Program, *Human Development Report, 1995* (New York: Oxford University Press, 1995).

5. Cornia et al., *Adjustment with a Human Face*.

6. See, for example, Hillary F. French, "The World Bank: Now fifty but how fit?" *World Watch*, July-August 1994, pp. 10–18; "Hunger and the World Bank," an NGO statement presented at the World Bank Hunger Conference, November 30, 1993; Jeffrey Sachs, "Beyond Bretton Woods: A new blueprint," *Economist*, October 1, 1994, pp. 23–27; Bruce Rich, *Mortgaging the Earth: The World Bank, Environmental Impoverishment, and the Crisis of Development* (Boston: Beacon Press, 1994); Catherine Caulfield, *The World Bank and the Poverty of Nations* (New York: Henry Holt, 1997); and Lance Taylor, "The revival of the liberal creed—the IMF and World Bank in a globalized economy," *World Development* 25 (1997): 145–152.

7. A more positive and supportive view of the activities of these two financial institutions, with recommendations for improved policies in the future, can be found in Anne O. Krueger, "Whither the World Bank and the IMF?" *Journal of Economic Literature* 36 (1998): 1983–2020.

8. It should be pointed out that beginning in 1997 under the leadership of its new president, James Wolfensohn, the World Bank began to move away from structural adjustment lending to more "project lending" that focused on issues like the environment, women's rights, labor standards, health and safety concerns, and cooperation with nongovernmental organizations. To that extent, the World Bank, more than the IMF, is currently giving greater recognition to poverty-related issues.

CHAPTER FIFTEEN

Foreign Finance, Investment, and Aid: Controversies and Opportunities

Foreign assistance must be linked to commonly agreed policy objectives—particularly to poverty reduction strategies.

—United Nations Development Program, *Human Development Report, 1994*

It is to perpetuate difficulties of the South for the North to relate to us as hapless victims to dictate to regarding loans and the employment of aid.

—Nelson Mandela, United Nations Social Summit, March 1995

The International Flow of Financial Resources

In Chapter 14, we learned that a country's international financial situation as reflected in its balance of payments and its level of monetary reserves depends not only on its current account balance (its commodity trade) but also on its balance on capital account (its net inflow or outflow of private and public financial resources). Because a majority of non-oil-exporting developing nations incur deficits on their current account balance, a continuous net inflow of foreign financial resources represents an important ingredient in their long-run development strategies.

In this chapter, we examine the international flow of financial resources, which takes two main forms: (1) *private foreign direct and portfolio investment*, consisting of (a) foreign "direct" investment by large multinational (or transnational) corporations, usually with headquarters in the developed nations, and (b) foreign **portfolio investment** (e.g., stocks, bonds and notes) in LDC "emerging" credit and equity markets by private institutions (banks, mutual funds, corporations) and individuals; and (2) *public and private development assistance (foreign aid)*, from (a) individual national governments and multinational donor agencies and, increasingly, (b) private *nongovernmental organizations (NGOs)*, most working directly with developing nations at the local level. We also examine the nature, significance, and controversy regarding private direct and portfolio investment and foreign aid in the context of the changing world economy. As in earlier chapters, our focus will be on ways in which private investment and foreign aid can contribute to development and on ways in which they may be harmful. We then ask how foreign investment and aid might best serve development aspirations. The chapter concludes with a case study examining the root causes of rapid development in Botswana, where foreign investment has played a key role.

Private Foreign Direct Investment and the Multinational Corporation

Few developments have played as critical a role in the extraordinary growth of international trade and capital flows during the past few decades as the rise of the **multinational corporation (MNC)**. An MNC is most simply defined as a corporation or enterprise that conducts and controls productive activities in more than one country. These huge firms, mostly from North America, Europe, and Japan but also increasingly from newly industrializing countries like South Korea, Taiwan, and Brazil, present a unique opportunity but may pose serious problems for the many developing countries in which they operate.

The growth of private **foreign direct investment (FDI)** in the developing world has been extremely rapid in recent decades. It rose from an annual rate of $2.4 billion in 1962 to $11 billion in 1980 and $35 billion in 1990 before surging to over $147 billion in 2002. Almost 60% of this total goes to Asia. Africa received less than 3% of the total, and the least developed countries got under 2%. This is not surprising given the fact that private capital gravitates toward countries and regions with the highest financial returns and the greatest perceived safety. Where debt problems are severe, governments are unstable, and economic reforms are only beginning, the risks of capital loss can be high. We must recognize that multinational corporations are not in the development business; their objective is to maximize their return on capital. This is why over 90% of global FDI goes to other industrial countries and the fastest-growing LDCs. MNCs seek out the best profit opportunities and are largely unconcerned with issues such as poverty, inequality, and unemployment alleviation.

FDI flows need to be understood in context. Figure 15.1 shows that FDI inflows to developing countries have remained a small fraction of these countries' total investment, most of which is accounted for by domestic sources. (Note, however, that foreign investment may be qualitatively different from domestic investment.) Moreover, in recent years, FDI has become far and away the largest source of foreign funds flowing to developing countries, as Figure 15.2 makes clear. In 2003, for example, FDI inflows were six times higher than official flows, and FDI accounted for some 72% of all resource flows to developing countries. This stands in sharp contrast to the late 1980s and early 1990s, when official flows and FDI flows were nearly equal. This is also a different picture in comparison with the mid-1990s, when portfolio flows and FDI flows were much more similar in magnitude, as can

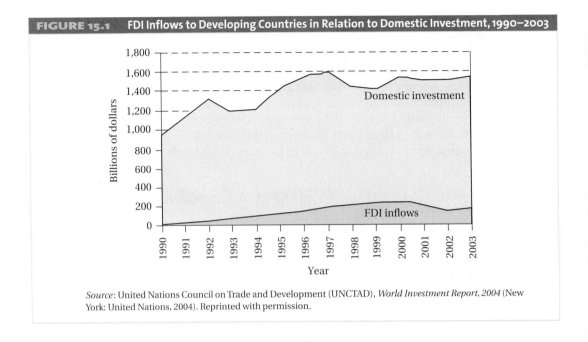

FIGURE 15.1 FDI Inflows to Developing Countries in Relation to Domestic Investment, 1990–2003

Source: United Nations Council on Trade and Development (UNCTAD), *World Investment Report, 2004* (New York: United Nations, 2004). Reprinted with permission.

be seen from Figure 15.2. Although FDI flows have fallen somewhat in the early years of the new century, they remained relatively strong.

MNCs employ a relatively small though rapidly growing number of people in LDCs. The jobs tend to be concentrated in the modern urban sector. These corporations often exert a disproportionate influence on urban salary scales and migrant worker perceptions.

But foreign direct investment involves much more than the simple transfer of capital or the establishment of a local factory in a developing nation. Multinationals carry with them technologies of production, tastes and styles of living, managerial philosophies, and diverse business practices, including cooperative arrangements, marketing restrictions, advertising, and "transfer pricing" (to be discussed shortly). They engage in a range of activities, many of which have little to do with the development aspirations of the countries in which they operate. But before analyzing some of the arguments for and against private foreign investment in general and multinational corporations in particular, let us examine the character of these enterprises.

Multinational Corporations: Size, Patterns, and Trends

Two central characteristics of multinational corporations are their large size and the fact that their worldwide operations and activities tend to be centrally controlled by parent companies. They are the major force in the rapid globalization of world trade. The 350 largest corporations now control more than 40% of that trade and dominate the production, distribution, and sale of many goods from develop-

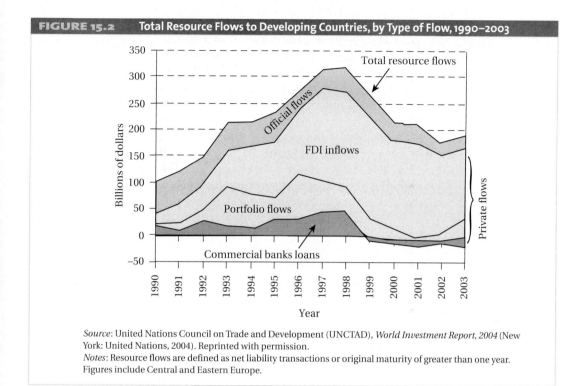

FIGURE 15.2   Total Resource Flows to Developing Countries, by Type of Flow, 1990–2003

Source: United Nations Council on Trade and Development (UNCTAD), *World Investment Report, 2004* (New York: United Nations, 2004). Reprinted with permission.

Notes: Resource flows are defined as net liability transactions or original maturity of greater than one year. Figures include Central and Eastern Europe.

ing countries (e.g., tobacco, electronics, footwear, and clothing). Almost one-fourth of international exchange involves intrafirm MNC sales of intermediate products or equipment from one nation's subsidiary to another. They have become, in effect, **global factories** searching for opportunities anywhere in the world. Many MNCs have annual sales volumes in excess of the GDP of the developing nations in which they operate.[1]

The scale of these corporations is immense. Seven of the top 10 MNCs, and 10 of the top 40, had worldwide sales in excess of $100 billion in 1999. Any 3 of them account for more sales than the gross national income of all of sub-Saharan Africa, and any 4 of them are larger than the economy of India. Four of the top 10 are individually larger than Indonesia. The top 7 together are larger than China. Most poorer countries are dwarfed in size by any of the major MNCs. This large scale of operations, combined with limited competition, conveys great bargaining power. Ownership of the largest MNCs is overwhelmingly concentrated in the developed countries. Five of the top 10 are based in the United States, with the remainder in the Netherlands, the United Kingdom, France, Germany, and Japan. All but 2 of the top 100 are in rich countries (number 91 on the list is Petroleos de Venezuela and number 100 is Cemex in Mexico), plus one other from an arguably developing region, Hong Kong. In fact, 97 of the top 100 are from North America, Western Europe, or Japan. The developing countries tend to believe, rightly or wrongly, that these corporations operate with the blessing of their home governments and with national resources at their disposal in the event of a significant dispute. LDCs, especially the smaller ones, understandably feel overwhelmed in attempting to bargain with such powerful entities. The success of China in negotiating better deals with MNCs regarding technology transfer and other conduct has been the exception that proves the rule, for no other LDC can match China's size and central government authority.

In sum, enormous size confers great economic (and sometimes political) power on MNCs vis-à-vis the countries in which they operate. This power is greatly strengthened by their predominantly oligopolistic market positions, that is, by the fact that they tend to operate in worldwide product markets dominated by a few sellers. This situation gives them the ability to manipulate prices and profits, to collude with other firms in determining areas of control, and generally to restrict the entry of potential competition by dominating new technologies, special skills, and, through product differentiation and advertising, consumer tastes. Although most MNC investments are directed to other developed countries, the LDCs, given their small economies, feel the presence of multinational corporations more acutely than the developed countries do.

Historically, multinational corporations, especially those operating in developing nations, focused on extractive and primary industries, mainly petroleum, nonfuel minerals, and plantation activities where a few "agribusiness" MNCs became involved in export-oriented agriculture and local food processing. Recently, however, manufacturing operations and services (banks, hotels, etc.) have occupied a dominant share of MNC production activities. Moreover, production for export to the MNC's home country and other developed markets today tends to predominate over production for LDC consumption.

Private Foreign Investment: Some Pros and Cons for Development

Few areas in the economics of development arouse so much controversy and are subject to such varying interpretations as the issue of the benefits and costs of private foreign investment. If we look closely at this controversy, however, we will see that the disagreement is not so much about the influence of MNCs on traditional economic aggregates such as GDP, investment, savings, and manufacturing growth rates (though these disagreements do indeed exist) as about the fundamental economic and social meaning of development as it relates to the diverse activities of MNCs. In other words, the controversy over the role and impact of foreign private investment often has as its basis a fundamental disagreement about the nature, style, and character of a desirable development process. The basic arguments for and against the developmental impact of private foreign investment in the context of the type of development it tends to foster can be summarized as follows.[2]

Traditional Economic Arguments in Support of Private Investment: Filling Savings, Foreign-Exchange, Revenue, and Management Gaps The pro-foreign-investment arguments grow largely out of the traditional neoclassical and new growth theory analysis of the determinants of economic growth. Foreign private investment (as well as foreign aid) is typically seen as a way of filling in gaps between the domestically available supplies of savings, foreign exchange, government revenue, and human capital skills and the desired level of these resources necessary to achieve growth and development targets. For a simple example of the "savings-investment gap" analysis, recall that the basic Harrod-Domar growth model postulates a direct relationship between a country's rate of net savings, s, and its rate of output growth, g, via the equation $g = s/k$, where k is the national capital-output ratio. If the desired rate of national output growth, g, is targeted at 7% annually and the capital-output ratio is 3, the needed rate of annual net saving is 21% (because $s = gk$). If the saving that can be domestically mobilized amounts to only, say, 16% of GDP, a "savings gap" equal to 5% can be said to exist. If the nation can fill this gap with foreign financial resources (either private or public), it will be better able to achieve its target rate of growth.

Therefore, the first and most often cited contribution of private foreign investment to national development (i.e., when this development is defined in terms of GDP growth rates—an important implicit conceptual assumption) is its role in filling the resource gap between targeted or desired investment and locally mobilized savings.

A second contribution, analogous to the first, is its contribution to filling the gap between targeted foreign-exchange requirements and those derived from net export earnings plus net public foreign aid. This is the so-called foreign-exchange or trade gap. ("Two-gap" models are discussed more fully later in the chapter.) An inflow of private foreign capital can not only alleviate part or all of the deficit on the balance of payments current account but also function to remove that deficit over time *if* the foreign-owned enterprise can generate a net positive flow of export earnings. Unfortunately, as we discovered in the case of import substitution, the overall effect of permitting MNCs to establish subsidiaries behind protective tariff and quota walls producing for domestic consumption is often a net *worsening* of both the current and capital account balances. Such deficits usually result both from the importation of capital equipment and intermediate products (normally from an overseas affiliate and often at inflated prices) and the outflow of foreign exchange in the form of repatriated profits, management fees, royalty payments, and interest on private loans. A large and growing share of MNC production in LDCs involves adding (labor-intensive) value to components for reexport, but this brings little foreign exchange into the economy.

The third gap said to be filled by foreign investment is the gap between targeted governmental tax revenues and locally raised taxes. By taxing MNC profits and participating financially in their local operations, LDC governments are thought to be better able to mobilize public financial resources for development projects.

Fourth, there is a gap in management, entrepreneurship, technology, and skill presumed to be partly or wholly filled by the local operations of private foreign firms. Not only do multinationals provide financial resources and new factories to poor countries, but they also supply a "package" of needed resources, including management experience, entrepreneurial abilities, and technological skills that can then be transferred to their local counterparts by means of training programs and the process of learning by doing. Moreover, according to this argument, MNCs can educate local managers about how to establish contact with overseas banks, locate alternative sources of supply, diversify market outlets, and become better acquainted with international marketing practices. Finally, MNCs bring with them the most sophisticated technological knowledge about production processes while transferring modern machinery and equipment to capital-poor developing countries. It has long been assumed that some of this knowledge leaks out to the broader economy when engineers and managers leave to start their own companies. Such transfers of knowledge, skills, and technology are assumed to be both desirable and productive for the recipient nations.[3]

Arguments against Private Foreign Investment: Widening Gaps There are two basic arguments against private foreign investment in general and the activities of MNCs in particular—the strictly economic and the more philosophical or ideological.

On the economic side, the four gap-filling pro-foreign-investment positions just outlined are countered by the following arguments:

1. Although MNCs provide capital, they may lower domestic savings and investment rates by stifling competition through exclusive production agreements with host governments, failing to reinvest much of their profits, generating domestic incomes for groups with lower savings propensities, and inhibiting the expansion of indigenous firms that might supply them with intermediate products by instead importing these goods from overseas affiliates. MNCs also raise a large fraction of their capital locally in the developing country itself, and this may lead to some crowding out of investment of local firms.

2. Although the initial impact of MNC investment is to improve the foreign-exchange position of the recipient nation, its long-run impact may be to reduce foreign-exchange earnings on both current and capital accounts. The current account may deteriorate as a result of substantial importation of intermediate products and capital goods, and the capital account may worsen because of the overseas repatriation of profits, interest, royalties, management fees, and other funds.

3. Although MNCs do contribute to public revenue in the form of corporate taxes, their contribution is considerably less than it should be as a result of liberal tax concessions, the practice of transfer pricing, excessive investment allowances, disguised public subsidies, and tariff protection provided by the host government.

4. The management, entrepreneurial skills, ideas, technology, and overseas contacts provided by MNCs may have little impact on developing local sources of these scarce skills and resources and may in fact inhibit their development by stifling the growth of indigenous entrepreneurship as a result of the MNCs' dominance of local markets.

LDC policies may be directed toward mitigating some of these concerns. Developing countries have commonly raised a number of more fundamental objections. First, the impact of MNCs on development is very uneven, and in many situations MNC activities reinforce dualistic economic structures and exacerbate income inequalities. They tend to promote the interests of a small number of local factory managers and relatively well-paid modern-sector workers against the interests of the rest by widening wage differentials. They divert resources away from needed food production to the manufacture of sophisticated products catering primarily to the demands of local elites and foreign consumers. And they tend to worsen the imbalance between rural and urban economic opportunities by locating primarily in urban export enclaves and contributing to excessive rural-urban migration.[4]

Second, it is argued that multinationals typically produce inappropriate products (those demanded by a small, rich minority of the local population), stimulate inappropriate consumption patterns through advertising and their monopolistic market power, and do this all with inappropriate (capital-intensive) technologies of production. This is perhaps the major criticism of MNCs in light of the growing employment problems of developing nations.

Third, as a result of the first two points, local resources tend to be allocated for socially undesirable projects. This in turn tends to aggravate the already sizable inequality between rich and poor and the serious imbalance between urban and rural economic opportunities.

Fourth, multinationals use their economic power to influence government policies in directions unfavorable to development. They are able to extract sizable economic and political concessions from competing LDC governments in the form of excessive protection, tax rebates, investment allowances, and the cheap provision of factory sites and essential social services. As a result, the private profits of MNCs may exceed social benefits. In some cases, these social returns to host countries may even be negative! Alternatively, an MNC can avoid much local taxation in high-tax countries and shift profits to affiliates in low-tax countries by artificially inflating the price it pays for intermediate products purchased from overseas affiliates so as to lower its stated local profits. This phenomenon, known as **transfer pricing**, is a common practice of MNCs and one over which host governments can exert little control as long as corporate tax rates differ from one country to the next. Some estimates place the lost revenue to LDC governments as a result of transfer pricing in the scores of billions of dollars.[5]

Fifth, MNCs may damage host economies by suppressing domestic entrepreneurship and using their superior knowledge, worldwide contacts, advertising skills, and range of essential support services to drive out local competitors and inhibit the emergence of small-scale local enterprises. In the context of recent LDC market reforms, the widespread privatization of public corporations, and the use of debt-for-equity swaps to reduce debt burdens, MNCs are today in a unique position to acquire some of the best and potentially most lucrative local businesses. They thereby can "crowd out" local investors and appropriate the profits themselves. For example, in a quantitative study of 11 developing countries outside the Pacific Basin, higher foreign direct investment was accompanied by lower domestic investment, lower national saving, larger current account deficits, and lower economic growth rates.[6]

Finally, at the political level, the fear is often expressed that powerful multinational corporations can gain control over local assets and jobs and can then exert

TABLE 15.1	Seven Key Disputed Issues about the Role and Impact of Multinational Corporations in Developing Countries

1. International capital movements (income flows and balance of payments)
   - Do they bring in much capital (savings)?
   - Do they improve the balance of payments?
   - Do they remit "excessive" profits?
   - Do they employ transfer pricing and disguise capital outflows?
   - Do they establish few linkages to the local economy?
   - Do they generate significant tax revenues?
2. Displacement of indigenous production
   - Do they buy out existing import-competing industries?
   - Do they use their competitive advantages to drive local competitors out of business?
3. Extent of technology transfer
   - Do they keep all R&D in home countries?
   - Do they retain monopoly power over their technology?
4. Appropriateness of technology transfer
   - Do they use only capital-intensive technologies?
   - Do they adapt technology to local factor endowments or leave it unchanged?
5. Patterns of consumption
   - Do they encourage inappropriate patterns of consumption through elite orientation, advertising, and superior marketing techniques?
   - Do they increase consumption of their products at the expense of other (perhaps more needed) goods?
6. Social structure and stratification
   - Do they develop allied local groups through higher wage payments, hiring (displacing) the best of the local entrepreneurs, and fostering elite loyalty and socialization through pressures for conformity?
   - Do they foster alien values, images, and lifestyles incompatible with local customs and beliefs?
7. Income distribution and dualistic development
   - Do they contribute to the widening gap between rich and poor?
   - Do they exacerbate urban bias and widen urban-rural differentials?

Source: Based on Thomas Biersteker, *Distortion or Development: Contending Perspectives on the Multinational Corporation* (Cambridge, Mass.: MIT Press, 1978), ch. 3.

considerable influence on political decisions at all levels. In extreme cases, they may even, either directly by payoffs to corrupt public officials at the highest levels or indirectly by contributions to "friendly" political parties, subvert the very political process of host nations (as occurred with International Telephone and Telegraph in the 1970s in Chile).

Table 15.1 attempts to summarize the debate about multinationals in terms of seven key issues and the questions that surround each of them: international capital movements (including income flows and balance of payments effects), displacement of indigenous production, extent of technology transfer, appropriateness of technology transfer, patterns of consumption, social structure and stratification, and income distribution and dualistic development.

Reconciling the Pros and Cons Although the foregoing discussion and Table 15.1 present a range of conflicting arguments, the real debate ultimately centers on different ideological and value judgments about the nature and meaning of economic development and the sources from which it springs. The advocates of private foreign investment tend to be free-market, private-enterprise, laissez-faire proponents who firmly believe in the efficacy and beneficence of the free-market mechanism, where this is usually defined as a hands-off policy on the part of host governments. As we have seen, however, the actual operations of MNCs tend to be monopolistic and oligopolistic. Price setting is achieved more as a result of international bargaining and collusion than as a natural outgrowth of free-market supply and demand.

Theorists who argue against the activities of MNCs are often motivated by a sense of the importance of national control over domestic economic activities and the minimization of dominance-dependence relationships between powerful MNCs and developing-country governments. They see these giant corporations not as needed agents of economic change but more as vehicles of antidevelopment. Multinationals, they argue, reinforce dualistic economic structures and exacerbate domestic inequalities with inappropriate products and technologies. Rightly or wrongly, they view MNCs as modern incarnations of colonial devices such as the British East India Company. Many analysts advocate a more stringent regulation of foreign investments, a tougher bargaining stance on the part of host governments, a willingness on the part of LDCs to "shop around" for better deals, the adoption of performance standards and requirements, increased domestic ownership and control, and a greater coordination of LDC strategies with respect to terms and conditions of foreign investment. One example of such coordinated strategies was a decision in the 1980s by the Andean Group in Latin America to require foreign investors to reduce their ownership in local enterprises to minority shares over a 15-year period. Tanzania adopted a similar policy of securing a controlling share of foreign enterprises, in line with its Arusha Declaration of 1967 on socialism and self-reliance. Not surprisingly, the annual flow of private foreign investment declined in both the Andean nations and Tanzania. Such "indigenization" requirements have since been rolled back throughout the developing world.

The arguments both for and against private foreign investment are still far from being settled empirically and may never be, as they ultimately reflect important differences in value judgments and political perceptions about desirable development strategies. Clearly, any real assessment of MNCs in development requires case studies of a given MNC in a specific country.[7] Perhaps the only valid general conclusion is that private foreign investment can be an important stimulus to economic and social development as long as the interests of MNCs and host-country governments coincide (assuming, of course, that they don't coincide along the lines of dualistic development and widening inequalities). As long as MNCs see their role in terms of global output or profit maximization with little interest in the long-run domestic impact of their activities, the accusations of the anti-private-investment school of thought will gain acceptance in the developing world. Maybe there can never be a real congruence of interest between the profit-maximizing objectives of MNCs and the development priorities of LDC governments. However, a strengthening of the relative bargaining powers of host-country governments through their coordinated activities, while probably reducing the overall magnitude and growth of private foreign investment, might make that investment better fit the long-run development needs and priorities of poor nations while still providing profitable opportunities for foreign investors.

Perhaps the strongest argument in favor of encouraging MNCs is that they facilitate the transfer of know-how from developed to developing countries. Dani

Rodrik surveyed the literature and concluded that so far, there has been little evidence of any horizontal spillovers, that is, transfers of knowledge from MNCs to local producers of the same type of product.[8] However, Garrick Blalock reported both statistical and managerial case study evidence for Indonesia that provides strong indications that MNCs strategically transfer technology to local vendors so that multinationals can procure high-quality inputs at low cost. Thus there is at least a suggestion that there may indeed be some significant technology spillovers, at least for Indonesia, but that the spillovers are vertical rather than horizontal in nature.[9]

The next decade should prove an interesting time to reassess the quantitative and qualitative impact of MNC investments in developing countries. As a result of the widespread adoption of market reforms, open economies, and privatization of state-owned enterprises, MNCs have been intensifying their global factory strategy, particularly in Asia and Latin America. They will add to national output, create some jobs, pay some taxes, and generally contribute to a more modern economy. But they will also gravitate toward the most profitable investment opportunities, purchase local factories of depressed LDC economies at "fire sale" prices, engage in transfer pricing, and repatriate profits. Whether the net outcome is more positive for development than in the past remains to be assessed. It is to be hoped that ways can be found in which MNC profits and broad-based national development can be simultaneously served.

Private Portfolio Investment: Boon or Bane for LDCs?

In addition to foreign direct investment, the most significant component of private capital flows has been in the area of portfolio investment.[10] With the increased liberalization of LDC domestic financial markets and the opening up of these markets to foreign investors, private portfolio investment now accounts for a significant and currently rising share of overall net resource flows to developing countries. Basically, portfolio investment consists of foreign purchases of the stocks (equity), bonds, certificates of deposit, and commercial paper of LDCs as seen in Figure 15.2. As usual, the middle-income countries have been the favored destination of these flows, with sub-Saharan African and South Asia all but neglected.

As in the case of the FDIs of multinational corporations, the benefits and costs of private portfolio investment flows to both the MDC investor and the LDC recipient have been subject to vigorous debate.[11] From the investor's point of view, investing in the stock markets of "emerging" countries (as some LDCs are called in the financial community) permits them to increase their returns while diversifying their risks. Early in the 1990s, annual returns on **emerging-country stock markets** were very high (e.g., 39% in Latin America between 1988 and 1993), but so was volatility. Many small investors in U.S.-based mutual funds were lured into the LDC stock markets to partake of these high rewards, only to be caught in a huge downdraft in December 1994 and January and February 1995 when the Mexican stock market collapsed after a 35% peso devaluation. Some investors lost as much as 60% of their money in dollar terms in a matter of weeks as both the Mexican Bolsa (stock market) plummeted and the peso continued to depreciate. Not surprisingly, in 1995, much of the money invested in emerging markets in the early 1990s was rapidly repatriated. The experience of these dramatic losses was reflected in the sharp downturn in total portfolio investment flows in 1995. The same phenomenon occurred in late 1997 and 1998 during the Asian economic crisis. Precipitous declines in the stock and bond markets in South Korea, Thailand, Indonesia, Malaysia, Hong Kong, and the Philippines scared foreign investors and panicked local citizens. In 1996, these countries received net capital inflows (both FDI and portfolio) of $93 billion. In 1997, they suffered a net outflow of $12 billion, mostly portfolio. The situation was even worse in 1998 as LDC stock markets collapsed around the world and foreign investors and speculators ran for cover. Similar volatility affected Argentina in 2001 and 2002.

From the perspective of the recipient LDC, private portfolio flows in local stock and bond markets are a potentially welcome vehicle for raising capital for domestic firms. Well-functioning local stock and bond markets also help domestic investors diversify their assets (an option usually open only to the wealthy) and can act to improve the efficiency of the whole financial sector by serving as a screening and monitoring device for allocating funds to industries and firms with the highest potential returns.

But from the policy perspective of developing-country governments, the key issue is whether large and volatile private portfolio flows into both local stock and short-term bond markets can be a destabilizing force for both the financial market and the overall economy. While some economists were arguing that these flows were not inherently unstable,[12] along came the Mexico crisis, and billions of dollars of these "hot money" flows disappeared from Mexico and much of the rest of Latin America in a matter of days—some say minutes! The lesson of the Mexican debacle was very clear: Developing countries that rely too heavily on private foreign portfolio investments to camouflage basic structural weakness in the economy (in Mexico and indeed later in Thailand, Malaysia, and Indonesia, a grossly overvalued foreign-exchange rate leading to high current account deficits and dwindling foreign reserves) are more than likely to suffer serious long-term consequences. Like multinational corporations, portfolio investors are not in the development business. If developed-country interest rates rise or perceived LDC profit rates decline, foreign speculators will withdraw their "investments" as quickly as they brought them in. What LDCs need is true long-run economic investment (plants, equipment, physical and social infrastructure, etc.), not speculative capital.

In summary, private portfolio financial flows have risen and fallen dramatically in recent decades. Their inherent volatility and the fact that they respond primarily to global interest-rate differentials, as well as to investor perceptions of political and economic stability, make them a very tenuous foundation on which to base medium- or long-term development strategies.[13] Asia's financial collapse in 1997, Russia's in 1998, Brazil's currency turmoil in 1999, and Argentina's crisis in 2001–2002 underlined the fragility of global capital markets.[14] Rather, LDCs need to focus first on putting fundamental conditions for development into place, because evidence shows that both MNCs and portfolio investors follow growth rather than lead it.[15]

Foreign Aid: The Development Assistance Debate

Conceptual and Measurement Problems

In addition to export earnings and private foreign direct and portfolio investment, the final two major sources of LDC foreign exchange are public (official) bilateral and multilateral development assistance and private (unofficial) assistance provided by nongovernmental organizations. Both of these activities are forms of **foreign aid**, although only public aid is usually measured in official statistics.

In principle, all governmental resource transfers from one country to another should be included in the definition of foreign aid. Even this simple definition, however, raises a number of problems.[16] For one thing, many resource transfers can take disguised forms, such as the granting of preferential tariffs by developed countries to LDC exports of manufactured goods. This permits LDCs to sell their industrial products in developed-country markets at higher prices than would otherwise be possible. There is consequently a net gain for LDCs and a net loss for developed countries, which amounts to a real resource transfer to the LDCs. Such implicit capital transfers, or disguised flows, should be counted in qualifying foreign aid flows. Normally, however, they are not.

However, we should not include *all* transfers of capital to LDCs, particularly the capital flows of private foreign investors. Private flows represent normal commercial transactions, prompted by commercial considerations of profits and rates of return, and therefore should not be viewed as aid to the LDCs. Commercial flows of private capital are *not* a form of foreign assistance, even though they may benefit the developing country in which they take place.

Economists have defined foreign aid, therefore, as any flow of capital to LDCs that meets two criteria: (1) Its objective should be noncommercial from the point of view of the donor, and (2) it should be characterized by **concessional terms**; that is, the interest rate and repayment period for borrowed capital should be softer (less stringent) than commercial terms.[17] Even this definition can be inappropriate, for it could include military aid, which is both noncommercial and concessional. Normally, however, military aid is excluded from international economic measurements of foreign aid flows. The concept of foreign aid that is now widely used and accepted, therefore, is one that encompasses all official grants and concessional loans, in currency or in kind, that are broadly aimed at transferring resources from developed to less developed nations on development or income distribution grounds. Unfortunately, there often is a thin line separating purely developmental grants and loans from sources ultimately motivated by security or commercial interests.

Just as there are conceptual problems associated with the definition of foreign aid, there are measurement and conceptual problems in the calculation of actual development assistance flows. In particular, three major problems arise in measuring aid. First, we cannot simply add up the dollar values of grants and loans; each has a different significance to both donor and recipient countries. Loans must be repaid and therefore cost the donor and benefit the recipient less than the nominal value of the loan itself. Conceptually, we should deflate or discount the dollar value of interest-bearing loans before adding them to the value of outright grants. Second, aid can be tied either by *source* (loans or grants have to be spent on the purchase of donor-country goods and services) or by *project* (funds can only be used for a specific project, such as a road or a steel mill). In either case, the real value of the aid is reduced because the specified source is likely to be an expensive supplier or the project is not of the highest priority (otherwise, there would be no need to tie the aid). Furthermore, aid may be tied to the importation of capital-intensive equipment, which may impose an additional real resource cost, in the form of higher unemployment, on the recipient nation. Or the project itself may require the purchase of new machinery and equipment from monopolistic suppliers while existing productive equipment in the same industry is being operated at very low levels of capacity. Finally, we always need to distinguish between the nominal and real value of foreign assistance, especially during periods of rapid inflation. Aid flows are usually calculated at nominal levels and tend to show a steady rise over time. However, when deflated for rising prices, the actual real volume of aid from most donor countries has declined substantially in recent decades.

Amounts and Allocations: Public Aid

The money volume of **official development assistance (ODA)**, which includes bilateral grants, loans, and technical assistance as well as multilateral flows, has grown from an annual rate of $4.6 billion in 1960 to $58 billion in 2002. However, in terms of the percentage of developed-country GNI allocated to official development assistance, there has been a steady decline from 0.51% in 1960 to 0.23% in 2002.[18] Table 15.2 shows the disbursement of ODA by principal donors both in total amount and as a percentage of GNI in 1985 and 2002. Although the United States (along with Japan) remains the largest donor in absolute terms, relative to others it provides the lowest percentage of GNI—0.13% in 2002, compared to an average of 0.23% for all industrial countries and well below the internationally agreed United Nations target of 0.70%. Only three countries are currently providing ODA in excess of this target: Sweden, the Netherlands, and Denmark contribute 0.83%, 0.81% and 0.96% of their 2002 GNI, respectively. Not only is the United States' ODA-to-GNI ratio the lowest among industrial countries, but it has also declined sharply from its level of 0.31% in 1970. But even an increase in U.S. aid to just 0.25% of GNI would provide more than $10 billion in additional funds, which if well-targeted could have a dramatic impact on development goals such as reduced infant mortality rates. Ten billion dollars is a huge sum by LDC standards, but it represents less than one-thousandth of U.S. income.

More interesting than the total amount of aid is the way in which it is distributed. ODA is allocated in some strange and arbitrary ways.[19] In terms of regional distribution, South Asia, where nearly 50% of the world's poorest people live, receives $5 per person in aid. The Middle East, with nearly five times South Asia's per

TABLE 15.2   Official Development Assistance Disbursements from Major Donor Countries, 1985 and 2002

Donor Country	1985		2002	
	Billions of U.S. Dollars	Percentage of GNI	Billions of U.S. Dollars	Percentage of GNI
Canada	1.6	0.49	2.0	0.28
Denmark	—	—	1.6	0.96
France	4.0	0.78	5.5	0.38
Germany	2.9	0.47	5.3	0.27
Italy	1.1	0.26	2.3	0.20
Japan	3.8	0.29	9.3	0.23
Netherlands	1.1	0.91	3.3	0.81
Sweden	—	—	2.0	0.83
United Kingdom	1.5	0.33	4.9	0.31
United States	9.4	0.24	13.3	0.13
Total (22 countries)	29.4	0.35	58.3	0.23

Sources: World Bank, *World Debt Tables, 1991–1992* (Washington, D.C.: World Bank, 1992), vol. 1, tab. 2. 1; World Bank, *2004 World Development Indicators* (Washington, D.C.: World Bank, 2004), tabs. 6.9 and 6.10.

capita income, receives four times the per capita aid. Europe and Central Asia, with more than four times the per capita income of sub-Saharan Africa, receives the same amount of aid. Table 15.3 shows the regional distribution of ODA in 2002.

In Table 15.4, we present data on over 40 selected developing countries that either receive large sums of aid or are heavily aid-dependent. The patterns of aid become even clearer when examined at the national level. Only 10 countries received more than U.S. $1 billion in aid in 2002. One of these, Israel, is actually classified as a developed country by the World Bank. India is included only because of its large population; it received only $1 per person in aid. China, although a richer country also received $1 per capita in aid. By contrast, middle-income countries such as Jordan and Poland received $103 and $30, respectively, in aid per person. These countries are of obvious strategic importance and receive aid out of convenience rather than need. Some desperately poor countries receive almost no aid. Others, however, have become heavily aid-dependent. Guinea-

TABLE 15.3   Official Development Assistance (ODA) by Region, 2002

Region	ODA per Capita (U.S. $)	GNI per Capita (U.S. $)	ODA as Share of GNI (%)
Middle East and North Africa	21	2,240	1.0
Sub-Saharan Africa	28	450	6.3
Latin America and Caribbean	10	3,280	0.3
East Asia and Pacific	4	960	0.5
South Asia	5	460	1.0
Europe and Central Asia	27	2,160	1.1

Source: World Bank, *2004 World Development Indicators* (Washington, D.C.: World Bank, 2004), tabs. 1.1 and 6.10. Copyright © 2004 by the World Bank. Reprinted with the permission of the World Bank via the Copyright Clearance Center..

Bissau and Mauritania received more than a quarter of their gross national income in the form of aid, and Nicaragua more than a third. Many LDCs are even more dependent on aid to finance investment and imports.

It is clear that the allocation of foreign aid is rarely determined by the relative needs of developing countries. Most bilateral aid seems unrelated to development priorities, being based largely on political and military considerations and the whims and ad hoc judgments of donor decision makers. Multilateral aid (e.g., from the World Bank and various UN agencies) is somewhat more economically rational, although here too the rich seem to attract more resources than the poor.

Because foreign aid is seen differently by donor and recipient countries, we must analyze the giving and receiving process from these two often contradictory viewpoints. One of the major criticisms of the literature on foreign aid is that it has concentrated almost exclusively on the motives and objectives of donor countries while devoting little attention to why LDCs accept aid and what they believe it will accomplish. After examining the aid question from both perspectives, we can summarize the conflicting views of the effects of traditional aid relationships over the past two decades.

Why Donors Give Aid

Donor-country governments give aid primarily because it is in their political, strategic, or economic self-interest to do so. Some development assistance may be motivated by moral and humanitarian desires to assist the less fortunate (e.g., emergency food relief programs), but there is no historical evidence to suggest that over longer periods of time, donor nations assist others without expecting some corresponding benefits (political, economic, military, etc.) in return. We can therefore characterize the foreign aid motivations of donor nations into two broad, but often interrelated, categories: political and economic.

Political Motivations Political motivations have been by far the more important for aid-granting nations, especially for the major donor country, the United States. The United States has viewed foreign aid from its beginnings in the late 1940s under the Marshall Plan, which aimed at reconstructing the war-torn economies of Western Europe, as a means of containing the international spread of communism. When the balance of cold-war interests shifted from Europe to the developing world in the mid-1950s, the policy of containment embodied in the U.S. aid program dictated a shift in emphasis toward political, economic, and military support for "friendly" less developed nations, especially those considered geographically strategic. Most aid programs to developing countries were therefore oriented more toward purchasing their security and propping up their sometimes shaky regimes than promoting long-term social and economic development. The successive shifts in emphasis from South Asia to Southeast Asia to Latin America to the Middle East and back to Southeast Asia during the 1950s and 1960s and then toward Africa and the Persian Gulf in the late 1970s, the Caribbean and Central America in the 1980s, and the Russian Federation, Bosnia, Ukraine, Asia (especially China), and the Middle East in the 1990s reflect changes in U.S. strategic, political, and economic interests more than changing evaluations of economic need.

TABLE 15.4 Large Recipients of Foreign Aid

| | Net Official Development Assistance or Official Aid ($ millions) | | Aid per Capita ($) | | Aid Dependency Ratios | | | | | |
| | | | | | Aid as a Percentage of GNI | | Aid as a Percentage of Gross Capital Formation | | Aid as a Percentage of Imports of Goods and Services | |
	1994	2002	1994	2002	1994	2002	1994	2002	1994	2002
Albania	165	317	52	101	8.4	6.4	46.4	28.8	21.3	15.1
Angola	450	421	42	32	23.1	4.3	66.7	11.6	11.9	4.5
Bangladesh	1,752	913	15	7	5.0	1.8	28.2	8.3	36.0	9.6
Benin	256	220	48	34	17.5	8.3	108.5	45.9	39.1	26.3
Bolivia	569	681	79	77	9.8	9.0	66.1	59.2	36.6	28.9
Bosnia and Herzegovina	391	587	107	143	—	10.0	—	53.4	—	12.1
Burkina Faso	433	473	44	40	23.5	15.2	113.4	82.8	83.1	65.1
Burundi	312	172	52	24	34.2	24.2	319.3	303.8	109.1	107.7
Cambodia	327	487	32	39	13.6	12.7	73.3	54.7	35.0	13.7
Central African Republic	165	60	51	16	19.9	5.8	165.6	38.6	61.9	—
Chad	213	233	33	28	18.5	11.8	108.5	19.8	50.3	—
China	3,225	1,476	3	1	0.6	0.1	1.4	0.3	2.7	0.4
Egypt	2,690	1,286	47	19	5.2	1.4	31.3	8.5	17.2	6.3
Eritrea	157	230	45	54	23.7	30.8	173.5	135.6	—	40.7
Ethiopia	1,071	1,307	20	19	22.2	21.7	144.4	105.2	90.2	21.0
Ghana	546	653	33	32	10.2	10.8	41.9	53.8	25.7	18.6
Guinea-Bissau	172	59	162	41	77.7	30.5	335.5	198.7	160.6	—
Haiti	601	156	86	19	30.7	4.5	899.8	22.1	243.8	—

Honduras	293	435	53	64	9.1	6.8	22.7	23.8	15.4	11.9
India	2,324	1,463	3	1	0.7	0.3	3.1	1.3	5.1	1.6
Indonesia	1,639	1,308	9	6	1.0	0.8	3.0	5.3	3.3	12.1
Israel	1,237	751	229	115	1.7	0.7	6.9	4.0	3.6	1.5
Jordan	369	534	91	103	6.2	5.8	17.8	25.0	7.7	8.1
Madagascar	289	373	22	23	10.2	8.6	89.1	59.4	28.0	33.8
Malawi	467	377	49	35	41.0	120.2	135.7	160.0	48.6	44.9
Mali	441	472	47	42	25.3	15.1	91.5	69.1	54.0	31.8
Mauritania	267	355	118	128	27.4	45.4	125.5	116.5	46.0	—
Mongolia	182	208	81	85	27.6	18.6	107.2	60.8	40.8	24.6
Nicaragua	597	517	139	97	46.5	13.6	143.9	40.3	42.1	23.7
Niger	377	298	43	26	24.6	13.8	231.9	107.7	80.9	—
Pakistan	1,605	2,144	13	15	3.0	3.6	15.8	24.7	12.6	14.3
Philippines	1,057	560	16	7	1.6	0.7	6.9	3.7	3.8	1.3
Poland	1,806	1,160	47	30	1.8	0.6	10.1	3.2	7.0	1.7
Russian Federation	1,847	1,361	12	9	0.6	0.4	2.2	1.8	2.6	1.3
Rwanda	714	356	115	44	95.3	20.8	809.8	109.2	149.7	77.1
Senegal	640	449	79	46	18.3	9.2	94.7	45.3	38.1	19.9
Sierra Leone	275	353	63	68	33.9	47.0	348.6	514.7	78.0	—
Tanzania	965	1,233	34	35	22.2	13.2	86.8	78.7	49.1	53.3
Thailand	578	296	10	5	0.4	0.2	1.0	1.0	0.9	0.4
Uganda	750	638	40	26	19.0	11.2	127.7	50.7	82.1	35.4
West Bank and Gaza	460	1,616	196	500	12.6	42.9	44.8	1,349.0	—	—
Zambia	718	641	82	63	23.1	18.1	260.4	99.4	41.6	36.6

Source: World Bank, *2004 World Development Indicators* (Washington, D.C.: World Bank, 2004), tab. 6.10. Copyright © 2004 by the World Bank. Reprinted with the permission of the World Bank via the Copyright Clearance Center.

After 2001, aid shifted toward countries with Islamist insurgencies or facing potential public support of terrorists. Recent increases in aid to African countries with public health crises may be due in part to concerns that disease may spread internationally or lead to destabilizing state collapse.

Even the Alliance for Progress, inaugurated in the early 1960s with great fanfare and noble rhetoric about promoting Latin American economic development, was in reality formulated primarily as a direct response to the rise of Fidel Castro in Cuba and the perceived threat of communist takeovers in other Latin American countries. As soon as the security issue lost its urgency and other more pressing problems came to the fore (the war in Vietnam, the growing dollar crisis, the rise in U.S. violence, etc.), the Alliance for Progress stagnated and began to fizzle out. Our point is simply that where aid is seen primarily as a means of furthering donor-country interests, the flow of funds tends to vary with the donor's political assessment of changing international situations and not the relative need of potential recipients.

The behavior of other major donor countries like Japan, Great Britain, and France has been similar to that of the United States. Although exceptions can be cited (Sweden, Denmark, the Netherlands, Norway, and perhaps Canada), by and large these Western donor countries have used foreign aid as a political lever to prop up or underpin friendly political regimes in developing countries, regimes whose continued existence they perceived as being in their national security interests.

Economic Motivations: Two-Gap Models and Other Criteria Within the broad context of political and strategic priorities, foreign aid programs of the developed nations have had a strong economic rationale. This is especially true for Japan, which directs most of its aid to neighboring Asian countries where it has substantial private investments and expanding trade. Even though political motivation may have been of paramount importance for other donors, the economic rationale was at least given lip service as the overriding motivation for assistance.

Let us examine the principal economic arguments advanced in support of foreign aid.

Foreign-Exchange Constraints External finance (both loans and grants) can play a critical role in supplementing domestic resources in order to relieve savings or foreign-exchange bottlenecks. This is the so-called two-gap analysis of foreign assistance.[20] The basic argument of the **two-gap model** is that most developing countries face either a shortage of domestic savings to match investment opportunities or a shortage of foreign exchange to finance needed imports of capital and intermediate goods. Most two-gap models assume that the **savings gap** (domestic real resources) and the **foreign-exchange gap** are unequal in magnitude and that they are independent, that is, that there is no substitutability between savings and foreign exchange. (This assumption is obviously unreal, but it greatly facilitates the mathematical analysis.)

The implication that follows is that one of the two gaps will be "binding" or "dominant" for any LDC at a given point in time. If, for example, the savings gap is dominant, this would indicate that the country is operating at full employment and is not using all of its foreign-exchange earnings. The Central Bank may have enough foreign exchange to purchase additional capital goods from abroad, but agents do not save enough income to purchase that foreign exchange and, with it, import capital goods. A country with a shortage of savings is incapable or unwilling to divert purchasing power from consumption goods to capital goods, either bought domestically or from abroad. As a result, "excess" foreign exchange, including foreign aid, might be spent on the importation of luxury consumption goods. An outstanding example of savings-gap nations would be the Arab oil states during the 1970s. Note, however, that the savings-gap analysis overlooks the possibility that excess foreign exchange can be used to purchase productive resources—for example, Saudi Arabia and Kuwait used their surplus petrodollars to pay for hired labor from non-oil-exporting countries in the region and overseas.

Most developing countries, however, are assumed to fall into the second category, where the foreign-exchange gap is binding. These countries have excess productive resources (mostly labor), and all available foreign exchange is being used for imports. The existence of complementary domestic resources would permit them to undertake new investment projects if they had the external finance to import new capital goods and associated technical assistance. Foreign aid can therefore play a critical role in overcoming the foreign-exchange constraint and raising the real rate of economic growth.

Algebraically, the simple two-gap model can be formulated as follows:

1. *The savings constraint or gap.* Starting with the identity that capital inflows (the difference between imports and exports) add to investible resources (domestic savings), the savings-investment restriction can be written as

$$I < F + sY \tag{15.1}$$

where F is the amount of capital inflows. If capital inflows (F) plus domestic saving (sY) exceeds domestic investment (I) and the economy is at full capacity, a savings gap is said to exist.

2. *The foreign-exchange constraint or gap.* If LDC investment has a marginal import share m_1 (typically ranging from 30% to 60% in most LDCs) and the marginal propensity to import out of a unit of noninvestment GNI (usually around 10% to 15%) is given by the parameter m_2, the foreign-exchange constraint or gap can be written as

$$(m_1 - m_2)I + m_2Y - E \leq F \tag{15.2}$$

where E is the exogenous level of exports.

The term F enters both inequality constraints and becomes the critical factor in the analysis. If F, E, and Y are initially assigned an exogenous current value, only one of the two inequalities will prove binding; that is, investment (and therefore the output growth rate) will be constrained to a lower level by one of the inequalities. Countries can therefore be classified according to whether the savings or foreign-exchange constraint is binding. More important from the viewpoint of foreign aid analysis is the observation that the impact of increased capital inflows will be greater where the foreign-exchange gap (Equation 15.2) rather than the savings gap (Equation 15.1) is binding. Two-gap models simply provide a crude methodology for determining the relative need and ability of different LDCs to use foreign aid effectively.

The problem is that such gap forecasts are very mechanistic and are themselves constrained by the necessity of fixing import parameters and assigning exogenous values to exports and net capital inflows. In the case of exports, this is particularly constricting because a liberalization of trade relations between the developed and the developing world would contribute more toward relieving foreign-exchange gaps than foreign aid. Although E and F are substitutable in Equation 15.2, they can have quite different indirect effects, especially in the case where F represents interest-bearing loans that need to be repaid. Thus the alteration of import and export parameters through both LDC and MDC government policy can in reality determine whether the savings or foreign-exchange constraint is restricting the further growth of national output (or, in fact, whether neither is binding).

Growth and Savings External assistance is also assumed to facilitate and accelerate the process of development by generating additional domestic savings as a result of the higher growth rates that it is presumed to induce. Eventually, it is hoped, the need for concessional aid will disappear as local resources become sufficient to make development self-sustaining. In reality, much aid is not invested, and if it is, the productivity of that investment is often very low.[21]

Technical Assistance Financial assistance needs to be supplemented by **technical assistance** in the form of high-level worker transfers to ensure that aid funds are used most efficiently to generate economic growth. This labor-gap-filling process is thus analogous to the financial-gap-filling process mentioned earlier.

Absorptive Capacity Finally, the amount of aid should be determined by the recipient country's **absorptive capacity**, a euphemism for its ability to use aid funds wisely and productively (often meaning as donors want them to be used). Typically, the donor countries decide which LDCs are to receive aid, how much, in what form (loans or grants, financial or technical assistance), for what purpose, and under what conditions on the basis of their donor countries' assessment of LDC absorptive capacities. But the total amount of aid rarely has anything to do with developing-country absorptive capacities; typically, foreign aid is a residual and low-priority element in donor-country expenditure. In most instances, the recipient countries have little say in the matter.

Economic Motivations and Self-Interest The arguments on behalf of foreign aid as a crucial ingredient for LDC development should not mask the fact that even at the strictly economic level, definite benefits accrue to donor countries as a result of their aid programs. The strong tendency toward providing loans instead of outright grants (interest-bearing loans now constitute some 80% of all aid, compared to less than 40% in earlier periods) and toward tying aid to the exports of donor countries has saddled many LDCs with substantial debt repayment burdens. It has also increased their import costs because aid tied to donor-country exports limits the receiving nation's freedom to shop around for low-cost and suitable capital and intermediate goods. **Tied aid** in this sense is clearly a second-best option to untied aid (and perhaps also to freer trade through a reduction of developed-country import barriers). A large fraction of U.S. aid has been spent on American consultants and other U.S. businesses.[22]

A former British minister of overseas development once noted that "about two-thirds of our aid is spent on goods and services from Britain. . . . Trade follows aid. We equip a factory overseas and later on we get orders for spare parts and replacements. . . . [Aid] is in our long-term interest."[23] Japan's aid programs in East Asia are even more closely tied to its economic interests.

In April 2001, the OECD Development Assistance Committee endorsed a proposal to untie aid to the least developed countries, but even this belated gesture covers only a fraction of spending, excluding food aid and technical cooperation.

Why LDC Recipients Accept Aid

The reasons why developing nations, at least until recently, have been eager to accept aid, even in its most stringent and restrictive forms, have been given much less attention than the reasons why donors provide aid. The major reason is probably economic. Developing countries have often tended to accept uncritically the proposition—typically advanced by developed-country economists, taught in all university development courses, and supported by reference to success stories like Taiwan, Israel, and South Korea to the exclusion of many more failures—that aid is a crucial and essential ingredient in the development process. It supplements scarce domestic resources, it helps transform the economy structurally, and it contributes to the achievement of LDC takeoffs into self-sustaining economic growth. Thus the economic rationale for aid in LDCs is based largely on their acceptance of the donor's perceptions of what the poor countries require to promote their economic development.

Conflicts generally arise, therefore, not out of any disagreement about the role of aid but over its amount and conditions. Naturally, LDCs would like to have more aid in the form of outright grants or long-term low-cost loans with a minimum of strings attached. This means not tying aid to donor exports and granting greater latitude to recipient countries to decide for themselves what is in their best long-run development interests. Unfortunately, a good deal of aid that comes in this form has either been wasted in showcase but unproductive projects (e.g., monuments to the ruling family, an elaborate parliamentary building, an oversized airport) or actually been plundered by corrupt government officials and their local cronies. Much of the criticism of foreign aid—that it wastes resources, that it bolsters corrupt regimes, that it is appropriated by the rich at the expense of the poor—is justified. Some LDC recipients in the past have accepted aid simply because it was there and they were not held accountable. A few leaders simply wish to leave no stone unturned in their quest for poverty alleviation, as perhaps describes Mozambique in the 1990s. They have been in the minority. The impact of the spread of democracy, press freedom and the rule of law, including anticorruption drives, on the effectiveness of aid remains an open question.

Second, in some countries, aid is seen by both donor and recipient as providing greater political leverage to the existing leadership to suppress opposition and maintain itself in power. In such instances, assistance takes the form not only of financial resource transfers but of military and internal security reinforcement as well. This phenomenon was clearly at work in Central America in the 1980s. The problem is that once aid is accepted, the ability of recipient governments to extricate themselves from implied political or economic obligations to donors and prevent donor governments from interfering in their internal affairs can be greatly diminished.

Finally, whether on grounds of basic humanitarian responsibilities of the rich toward the welfare of the poor or because of a belief that the rich nations owe the poor nations conscience money for past exploitation, many proponents of foreign aid in both developed and developing countries believe that rich nations have an obligation to support LDC economic and social development. They often link this moral obligation with the need for greater LDC autonomy with respect to the allocation and use of aid funds. An example was seen at the 1992 Earth Summit held in Rio de Janeiro, where developing nations pressed for substantial increases in foreign aid to permit them to pursue environmentally sustainable development programs. Implicit was the notion that industrialized countries were the major polluters and had no business telling LDCs to slow their growth to save the planet.

In sum, while there is no doubt that the least developed countries will need more assistance to escape from their vicious cycle of poverty, fresh approaches are needed to ensure effectiveness.

The Growing Role of Nongovernmental Organizations in International Aid

While there is much debate about the pros and cons of multinational corporate investment and public foreign aid in developing countries, few people doubt the value of one of the fastest-growing and most significant forces in the field of development assistance, private **nongovernmental organizations (NGOs)**. As we saw in Chapter 11, NGOs are voluntary organizations that work with and on behalf of mostly local grassroots people's organizations in developing countries. They also represent specific local and international interest groups with concerns as diverse as providing emergency relief, protecting child health, promoting women's rights, alleviating poverty, protecting the environment, increasing food production, and providing rural credit to small farmers and local businesses. NGOs build roads, houses, hospitals, and schools. They work in family-planning clinics and refugee camps. They teach in schools and universities and conduct research on increasing farm yields.

NGOs include religious groups, private foundations and charities, research organizations, and federations of dedicated doctors, nurses, engineers, agricultural scientists, and economists. Many work directly on grassroots rural development projects; others focus on relief efforts for starving or displaced peoples. Some familiar NGOs include Save the Children, CARE, Oxfam, Planned Parenthood, World Vision, the World Wildlife Fund, Habitat for Humanity, Africare, Heifer, Christian Aid, Project HOPE, and Amnesty International. Between 1970 and 1990, funding devoted to developed-country NGO projects and programs in LDCs grew from just under $1 billion to over $5 billion. Almost half of that total came from the United States, even though the highest per capita contributions to NGOs came from Sweden, Switzerland, Norway, and Germany.[24] Many give full local control to their LDC affiliates or other local groups they support. Increasingly, indigenous NGOs are taking the lead, such as BRAC in Bangledesh (see the case study for Chapter 11).

The great value of NGOs is twofold. First, being less constrained by political imperatives, most NGOs are able to work much more effectively at local levels with the people that they are trying to assist than massive bilateral and multilateral aid programs could. Second, by working directly with local people's organizations, many NGOs are able to avoid the suspicion and cynicism on the part of the mostly poor people that they serve that their help is less than sincere or likely to be short-lived. It is estimated that NGOs in developing countries are affecting the lives of some 250 million people; the fact that their voices are increasingly being listened to in the halls of developed-country governments and at international conferences on development, makes it clear that the nature and focus of foreign aid are changing rapidly.

The critical question is whether international NGOs can sustainably transfer their knowledge and capabilities to domestic NGOs, and other community-based organizations.[25]

The Effects of Aid

The issue of the economic effects of aid, especially public aid, like that of the effects of private foreign investment, is fraught with disagreement.[26] On one side are the economic traditionalists, who argue that aid has indeed promoted growth and structural transformation in many LDCs.[27] On the other side are critics who argue that aid does not promote faster growth but may in fact retard it by substituting for, rather than supplementing, domestic savings and investment and by exacerbating LDC balance of payments deficits as a result of rising debt repayment obligations and the linking of aid to donor-country exports.

Official aid is further criticized for focusing on and stimulating the growth of the modern sector, thereby increasing the gap in living standards between the rich and the poor in developing countries. Some critics on the left would even assert that foreign aid has been a positive force for antidevelopment in the sense that it both retards growth through reduced savings and worsens income inequalities.[28] Rather than relieving economic bottlenecks and filling gaps, aid—and for that matter private foreign investment—not only widens existing savings and foreign-exchange resource gaps but may even create new ones (e.g., urban-rural or modern-sector–traditional-sector gaps). Critics on the right charge that foreign aid has been a failure because it has been largely appropriated by corrupt bureaucrats, has stifled initiative, and has generally engendered a welfare mentality on the part of recipient nations.[29]

Quite apart from these criticisms, in the 1980s and 1990s, donor countries grew increasingly disenchanted with official foreign aid as domestic issues such as unemployment, government deficits, and balance of payments problems gained priority over international politics. The mood was one of **aid weariness**. Taxpayers wanted to focus on domestic economic problems, especially as they came to realize that their tax dollars allocated to foreign aid were often benefiting small elite groups in LDCs who in many cases were richer than themselves. However, in recent years, there has been an increasing willingness on the part of the public to donate development assistance via NGOs. And the development disaster in sub-Saharan Africa has mobilized public opinion in support of greater development assistance. As the United States announced a significant increase in aid in 2002, and many other countries donated growing contributions to global health funds, hope was renewed that more reasonable levels of aid might be forthcoming.

The attention to improved assistance to reduce extreme poverty at the G8 and UN meetings in 2005, coupled with some enhancement of resources, was widely viewed as a hopeful sign of progress.

Botswana: African Success Story at Risk

Botswana is a small, landlocked country in sub-Saharan Africa with high population growth and a high incidence of disease. Yet it has attained one of the highest average per capita growth rates in the world since obtaining its independence from Britain in 1966.

Botswana shows that mineral wealth can be a benefit in a country that has the appropriate political development in place. Botswana has experienced by far the highest rate of growth in sub-Saharan Africa: 8.4% per year over the entire 1965–1990 period and a still-high 5.1% in 1990–2002. Thus since its independence, Botswana has gone from being among the poorest countries in the world to one with a greater per capita income than Turkey, Thailand, or Brazil.

What explains this remarkable success? This is a case in which the theories of the modern neoclassical school have been borne out and the benefits of direct foreign investment for spurring growth are very clear. Moreover, success has been based on both favorable geography (huge diamond deposits) and favorable institutions (relatively effective protection of private property, rule of law, and good incentives for government to play a constructive role). When both are present, conditions for development are particularly auspicious.

Botswana's diamond wealth is vast, and hence the experience of Botswana shows that the "curse of natural resources" does not haunt all countries equally. Although diamonds have been a dictator's best friend in countries such as the Democratic Republic of Congo (formerly Zaire) and Sierra Leone, in Botswana diamond exports have been consistent with democracy and broad-based development. Jeffrey Herbst, a leading expert on African comparative political development, also notes that Botswana is one of the few African countries with a geography suitable for consolidating the power of the nation-state. The population is concentrated in the eastern part of the country, where Gaborone, the capital city, is located. In contrast, such countries as Nigeria and Congo have three widely dispersed centers of population.

Botswana is a multiparty democracy, although it has been dominated by one particular party, the Botswana Democratic Party. Elections have been held every five years since 1965. Amnesty International has consistently given Botswana the highest human rights rating in Africa. There is a free press, and there are no political prisoners. Botswana accomplished these impressive economic and political results while surrounded by white minority regimes (in South Africa, Zimbabwe, and Namibia) for the first half of its history—and even as nearby civil wars have spilled over into its territory and a steady stream of refugees has threatened to upset the social order.

Botswana has some geographic disadvantages that in other countries can act as a barrier to growth and development. It is a landlocked country with no access to seaports, a characteristic that is statistically associated with slow growth. It has generally poor conditions for agriculture. Only about 4% of the land can be easily cultivated. Most of the country is Kalahari Desert land, suitable only for summer grazing (almost all the rainfall takes place during the summer months). The five-year drought of the mid-1980s was very harsh by any standards, and other serious droughts have stricken the country with some regularity. The climate is tropical, and tropical countries have generally fared much more poorly in income levels and growth than temperate-zone countries. Botswana also shows that high population growth need not always forestall rapid growth in income per capita. Thus Botswana demonstrates that geography is not destiny and that good institutions can take advantage of opportunities of geography that are squandered or even make matters worse in countries with poor institutions. And it suggests that good institutions can overcome the constraints imposed by geography. Daron Acemoglu, Simon Johnson, and James Robinson attribute Botswana's success in large measure to favorable institutions, particularly protection of property rights.

Successful development requires both private and public goods. There is a need to prevent the government from doing harm, such as engaging in parasitic or predatory behavior, and at the same time to encourage the state to act in support of broad-based economic development, including provision of public goods needed for economic development. For this, minimal requirements are a cohesive society able to avoid substantial strife such as civil wars and a government that is both responsive and responsible to society. Achieving this state of affairs may not always require full-fledged democracy, but it clearly requires genuine accountability of the government to the governed.

As noted earlier, Botswana has been a well-functioning multiparty democracy. Although the Botswana Democratic Party has never lost national power, there is evidence that it responds to electoral threats by delivering improved government services. Government has played a constructive role in the economy by providing infrastructure, extension (information and training) services, and subsidized veterinary services and other support for the development of the cattle industry; these initiatives have been broad-based rather than earmarked for favored clientele. Government has also constructively managed relationships with mining interests, encouraging exploration by foreign companies and demanding and getting a share of profits without driving investors away. For example, favorable contracts were achieved with the De Beers diamond cartel that resulted in fully half of diamond profits going to the state in tax revenue. The government in turn managed these resources constructively, smoothing government services from good to bad periods and investing heavily in education. How a country spends its wealth matters, whether that wealth is large or small. Botswana has achieved essentially universal primary education, a rare achievement in Africa, and a respectable one-third of children enroll in secondary education, compared with the sub-Saharan Africa average of under 20%.

From 1982 to 1987, Botswana suffered a brutal drought that severely affected poor rural peoples. In many countries, their plight might have been ignored until significant starvation began and caught the attention of the world. But Botswana built on its social security system and provided relief to the rural poor through a three-pronged system of maintaining food availability, as detailed by Jean Dreze and Amartya Sen: (1) a guarantee of public employment for cash wages that could be spent on available food, (2) direct food distribution to selected groups, and (3) programs to increase agricultural productivity and restore food availability. Botswana's free press and democratic system seem to be major factors in this response.

On other human development indicators, such as infant mortality and health professionals per capita, Botswana also scores well. However, Botswana ranked only 128th out of 177 countries listed on the 2002 Human Development Index, a staggering 67 points lower than its GDP rank would predict; in other words, Botswana's human development is far lower than predicted by its level of real per capita income. Botswana has been falling rapidly in these rankings due to mortality from AIDS; the nation has the highest HIV infection rate in the world. But in other fields, its human development performance in the context of sub-Saharan Africa is extremely favorable; despite the AIDS epidemic, only seven countries in this region rate higher than Botswana in the UNDP Index.

The deeper question is why Botswana has been able to create and sustain better institutions. Acemoglu, Johnson, and Robinson surveyed Botswana's institutional history and suggest that the juxtaposition or interaction of five factors have been important.

1. Botswana possessed precolonial tribal institutions that encouraged broad-based participation and placed constraints on political elites. Commoners were allowed to make suggestions and criticize chiefs.

2. British colonialization had a limited effect on these precolonial institutions because of the peripheral nature of Botswana to the British Empire.

3. Upon independence, the most important rural interests, chiefs and cattle owners, were politically powerful, and it was in their economic interests to enforce property rights.

4. The revenues from diamonds generated enough rents for the main political actors, increasing the opportunity cost of and thereby discouraging further rent seeking.

5. Political leaders made sensible decisions. These included turning over diamond mining rights from tribal (Bangwato) to national control (this transition was initiated in a statesmanlike way by the postindependence leader Seretse Khama, who

was himself a member of the Bangwato tribe). Reduction of the powers of the tribal chiefs was another such decision. Each reduced the chances of internecine conflicts that have plagued so many other African countries. It might be said that in Botswana, although elites enjoyed a good share of the diamond eggs, they did not kill the goose that laid them, and they faced real constraints on their ability to take a larger share.

So unfavorable features of geography need not be destiny, natural resources need not be a curse, and good institutions can underpin dramatically superior economic performance.

With a clear, natural-resource-based comparative advantage and the requisite minimally supporting institutions, Botswana successfully struck a deal with foreign investors that was good for the national interest while avoiding serious corruption. As a result, the neoclassical paradigm—updated with emphasis on required human capital, support for exports, and shared growth—appears to do a good job of explaining this country's success.

But perhaps the most important question of all is left unsettled. What can countries without the favorable starting economic institutions and factors favoring development of good-quality state institutions do to get better institutions? Officials in other African countries who are seeking to reform their polities can work toward emulating some of the best features of governance in Botswana and publicize government and private-sector failures as well as relative success in neighboring countries. Societies as a whole can find themselves in poverty traps, in which government behavior itself is part of the vicious cycle of underdevelopment. The presence of a positive regional "role model" is of great importance in spreading successful development, as illustrated by the case of Japan in East Asia. (One blemish on Botswana's development record is that the minority Khoikhoi (Bushmen) fare much less well than the majority Batswana, though this problem is a very difficult one to remedy.)

Despite its successes, Botswana may now be facing its gravest crisis since independence. It now has a relatively high level of income inequality comparable to that of Latin America, as well as chronically high urban unemployment. But by far the worst problem is HIV/AIDS. According to UNDP reports, the HIV prevalence rate is 19% in the general population—and a stunning 36% in the 15–49 age group. Fortunately, the HIV prevalence rate among those aged 15 and below is less than 2%, a promising sign *if* new infections can be stopped with lifestyle changes and safe-sex practices. But the UN reports that "60% of the youth have no access to youth-friendly reproductive health services." Without AIDS, it is estimated that life expectancy in Botswana would be over 70 today. But as a result of the AIDS epidemic, life expectancy at birth in Botswana has plummeted to 47 years. In consequence, the UN projects that by 2010, one-fifth of all children in Botswana will have been orphaned.

It is reasonable to ask, if Botswana has such good institutions and government quality, how has the country allowed itself to reach the point at which more than a third of its prime-age population are HIV-positive? The failure of government to respond as decisively as in Uganda, despite the epidemic's later arrival in Botswana, may be viewed as a reflection of inconsistent government quality or of cultural characteristics. The test now is whether government quality and social development can halt the spread of HIV to the next generation. Botswana is at least responding to the challenge better than its neighbor, South Africa, and the case of Uganda shows that with determination, an African country with a high HIV infection rate can turn the tide (see the case study for Chapter 8). Botswana can learn from the lessons of Uganda. If it does, Botswana will recover its luster as a beacon of hope for broader development for Africa. ■

Sources

Acemoglu, Daron, Simon Johnson, and James Robinson, "An African success story: Botswana." In *In Search of Prosperity: Analytic Narratives on Economic Growth,* ed. Dani Rodrik (Princeton, N.J.: Princeton University Press, 2003), pp. 80–119.

Africa Research Bulletin, December 1993 and July 1995.

Dreze, Jean, and Amartya Sen. *Hunger and Public Action.* Oxford: Clarendon Press, 1989.

Edge, Wayne, and Mogopodi Lekorwe (eds.). *Botswana: Politics and Society.* Pretoria, South Africa: Schaik, 1998.

Goldsmith, Arthur. "Africa's overgrown state revisited: Bureaucracy and economic growth." *World Politics* 51 (1999): 520–546.

Greener, R., K. Jefferis, and H. Siphambe. "The impact of HIV/AIDS on poverty and inequality in Botswana." *South African Journal of Economics* 68 (2000): 888–915.

Harvey, Charles, and Stephen R. Lewis Jr. *Policy Choice and Development Performance in Botswana.* New York: St. Martin's Press, 1990.

Herbst, Jeffrey. *States and Power in Africa: Comparative Lessons in Authority and Control.* Princeton, N.J.: Princeton University Press, 2000.

Innocenti, Nicol D. "Compared to neighboring South Africa, Botswana is far ahead in implementing new retroviral and education programs," *Financial Times Online,* September 26, 2001.

Picard, Louis A. *The Politics of Development in Botswana: A Model for Success?* Boulder, Colo.: Rienner, 1987.

Porter, Michael. *Competitive Advantage of Nations.* New York: Free Press, 1990.

Stedman, Stephen J. (ed.). *Botswana: The Political Economy of Democratic Development.* Boulder, Colo.: Rienner, 1993.

United Nations Development Program, *Human Development Report, 2004,* http://hdr.undp.org/reports/global/2004.

Concepts for Review

Absorptive capacity	Foreign-exchange gap	Portfolio investment
Aid weariness	Global factories	Savings gap
Concessional terms	Multinational corporation	Technical assistance
Emerging-country stock	(MNC)	Tied aid
markets	Nongovernmental organiza-	Transfer pricing
Foreign aid	tions (NGOs)	Two-gap model
Foreign direct investment	Official development assis-	
(FDI)	tance (ODA)	

Questions for Discussion

1. The emergence of giant multinational corporations is said to have altered the very nature of international economic activity. In what ways do these MNCs affect the structure and pattern of trading relationships between the developed world and the underdeveloped world?

2. Summarize the arguments for and against the role and impact of private foreign investment in less developed countries. What strategies might LDCs adopt to make private foreign investment fit their development aspirations better without destroying all incentives for foreign investors?

3. What are private portfolio flows? What factors do you believe are most important in determining the amount and direction of such flows?

4. To what extent do private portfolio investments in LDCs benefit the recipient countries? What are the potential costs and risks to both investors and recipients? Explain your answer.

5. How important is foreign aid for developing economies in relation to their other sources of foreign-exchange receipts? Explain the various forms that official development assistance can take, and distinguish between bilateral and multilateral assistance. Which do you think is more desirable, and why?

6. What is meant by tied aid? Most nations have increasingly shifted from grants to loans and from untied to tied loans and grants. What are the major disadvantages of tied aid, especially when this aid comes in the form of interest-bearing loans?

7. Under what conditions and terms do you think LDCs should seek and accept foreign aid in the future? If aid cannot be obtained on such terms, do you think LDCs should accept whatever they can get? Explain your answer.

8. What are the differences between official development assistance (public foreign aid) and private development assistance from nongovernmental organizations (NGOs)? Which type of aid is more desirable from the perspective of recipient countries? Explain your answer.

9. How do you think the war on terrorism is likely to affect the pattern of development assistance?

10. What do you think would persuade the public to get over its "donor fatigue" and support more aid for the poorest countries?

Notes

1. The full list of the 100 largest firms and much additional data can be found at http://www.unctad.org. Note in making comparisons that sales figures include intermediate inputs, while GDP does not. The point is that the huge scale of MNCs conveys great bargaining power.

2. An excellent summary of the various issues, pro and con, surrounding MNCs can be found in Thomas Biersteker, *Distortion or Development: Contending Perspectives on the Multinational Corporation* (Cambridge, Mass.: MIT Press, 1978), ch. 1–3; Theodore H. Moran, "Multinational corporations and the developing countries: An analytical overview," in *Multinational Corporations,* ed. Theodore H. Moran (Lexington, Mass.: Heath, 1985), pp. 3–24; Mark Cassen and Robert D. Pearce, "Multinational enterprises in LDCs," in *Surveys in Development Economics,* ed. Norman Gemmell (Oxford: Blackwell, 1987), pp. 90–132; and David C. Korten, *When Corporations Rule the World,* 2nd ed. (San Francisco: Berrett-Kohler, 2001).

3. Recall from Chapter 4 the critical role that human capital plays in endogenous growth theories and the importance of concepts such as Romer's idea gap in explaining differential growth performance between developed and less developed countries.

4. Michael Lind, "To have and have not: Notes on the progress of the American class war," *Harper's,* June 1995, p. 39.

5. William Greider, *One World, Ready or Not: The Manic Logic of Global Capitalism* (New York: Simon & Schuster, 1997), p. 95.

6. Maxwell J. Fry, "Foreign direct investment, financing and growth," in *Investment and Financing in Developing Countries,* ed. Bernhard Fischer (Baden-Baden, Germany: Nomos, 1994), and *Foreign Direct Investment in Southeast Asia: Differential Impacts* (Singapore: Institute of Southeast Asian Studies, 1993).

7. For a discussion of the bargaining power of LDCs with MNCs, see Jan Svejnar and Stephen C. Smith, "The economics of joint ventures in less developed countries," *Quarterly Journal of Economics* 99 (1984): 149–167.

8. See Dani Rodrik, *The New Global Economy and Developing Countries: Making Openness Work* (Baltimore: Johns Hopkins University Press, 1999).

9. See Garrick Blalock, "Technology from foreign direct investment: Strategic transfer through supply chains," Hass School of Business, University of California, Berkeley, 2001; Garrick Blalock and Paul Gertler, "Learning from Exporting Revisited in a Less Developed Setting." *Journal of Development Economics* 75 (2004): 397–416; and Paolo Epifani, *Trade Liberalization, Firm Performance, and Labor Market Outcomes in the Developing World: What Can We Learn from Micro-Level Data?* (Washington, D. C.: World Bank, 2003). An example of finding few if any spillovers is Brian J. Aitken and Ann E. Harrison, "Do domestic firms benefit from direct foreign investment? Evidence from Venezuela," *American Economic Review* 89 (1999): 605–618.

10. For an excellent quantitative and analytical review of portfolio flows to LDCs, see Stijn Claessens, "The emergence of equity investment in developing countries: An overview," *World Bank Economic Review* 9 (1995): 1–17; Robert Feldman and Manmohan Kumar, "Emerging equity markets: Growth, benefits and policy concerns," *World Bank Research Observer* 10 (1995): 181–200; and World Bank, *Global Development Finance, 1998* (Washington, D.C.: World Bank, 1998), ch. 1. Current data on these flows may be found in World Bank, *2004 World Development Indicators* (Washington, D.C.: World Bank, 2004), tab. 6.7.

11. Claessens, "Emergence of equity investment," 11–14.

12. See, for example, Stijn Claessens, Michael Dooley, and Andrew Warner, "Portfolio flows: Hot or cold?" *World Bank Economic Review* 9 (1995): 153–174, and Mark P. Taylor and Lucio Sarno, "Capital flows to developing countries: Long- and short-term determinants," *World Bank Economic Review* 11 (1997): 451–470.

13. For a provocative account of how free-market policies and private investment flows in the early 1990s constituted a "speculative bubble," see Paul Krugman, "Dutch tulips and emerging markets," *Foreign Affairs* 74 (1995): 28–44.

14. For a perceptive analysis of why the Asian crisis occurred and how it was linked to failed LDC strategies to attract foreign capital inflows, see Walden Bellow, "The end of the Asian miracle," *Nation*, January 12, 1998, pp. 16–21. A more conventional analysis can be found in World Bank, *Global Development Finance, 1998* (Washington, D.C.: World Bank, 1998), ch. 2, and International Monetary Fund, *World Economic Outlook, May 1998* (Washington, D.C.: 1998), ch. 2.

15. World Bank, *Private Capital Flows to Developing Countries: The Road to Financial Integration* (Washington, D.C.: World Bank, 1997). For evidence that savings follows rather than leads growth more generally, see Ira S. Saltz, "An examination of the causal relationship between savings and growth in the Third World," *Journal of Economics and Finance* 23 (1999): 90–98.

16. Jagdish N. Bhagwati, "Amount and sharing of aid," in *Assisting Developing Countries: Problems of Debt, Burden-Sharing, Jobs, and Trade*, ed. Charles J. Frank Jr. et al.(New York: Praeger, 1972), pp. 72–73.

17. Ibid., p. 73.

18. Even these figures can be misleading and exaggerate the actual concessional aid component of developmental assistance. For a harsh critique of the accuracy of official development assistance statistics, see Gunnar Myrdal, *The Challenge of World Poverty* (New York: Pantheon, 1970), p. 10. See also J. Mohan Rao, "Ranking foreign donors: An index combining scale and equity of aid givers," *World Development* 25 (1997): 947–961.

19. United Nations Development Program, *Human Development Report, 1992* (New York: Oxford University Press, 1992), pp. 44–45.

20. See Hollis B. Chenery and Alan M. Strout, "Foreign assistance and economic development," *American Economic Review* 56 (1966): 680–733.

21. See William Easterly, "The ghost of financing gap: Testing the growth model used in the international financial institutions," *Journal of Development Economics* 60 (1999): 423–438.

22. William S. Gaud, "Foreign aid: What it is, how it works, why we provide it," *Department of State Bulletin* 59 (1968). It is important to note that the economic self-interests of foreign aid are often linked to the activities of MNCs in recipient countries. One interesting example of both the bargaining context of MNC-LDC negotiations and the link between foreign investment and foreign aid concerns the selection of an automobile MNC joint venture by the government of Egypt in the mid-1980s. Egypt was seeking a joint venture with one of the major automobile MNCs to develop a local plant for the production of cars. For many years, Fiat, the Italian multinational, had operated an assembly-only plant and was the sole auto firm in Egypt. General Motors, Nissan, Saab, Fiat, and several other auto MNCs submitted proposals to the Egyptian government. The central bargaining issues included tax breaks, profit remittances, the proportion of foreign versus Egyptian ownership, and most important, the proportion of component parts that would be manufactured by Egyptian firms. Egypt viewed this last issue as critical to its effort to promote domestic industrial growth. While the various proposals were being submitted, the United States Agency for International Development (USAID) announced that it had approved an aid package in support of the proposed GM project, in effect subsidizing the GM bid. With what it considered three equivalent bids, Egypt decided to award the contract to General Motors on the basis of the USAID subsidy. The decision in favor of GM was no doubt also influenced by the fact that U.S. military and economic aid to Egypt (the recipient of the largest annual package after Israel) was at that time still "pending" in the U.S. Congress. Thus foreign aid can be and often is used by developed-country governments as a leverage factor in support of their own domestic MNC investments. We are indebted to Professor Bruce Brunton for this illustration.

23. A staunch defender of the role of foreign aid in the development process, economist Hollis B. Chenery, noted that "in the most general sense, the main objective of foreign assistance, as of many other tools of foreign policy, is to produce the kind of political and economic environment in the world in which the United States can best pursue its own social goals." "Objectives and criteria of foreign assistance," in *The U.S. and the Developing Economies,* ed. Gustav Ranis (New York: Norton, 1964), p. 88.

24. For a thorough review of NGOs in developing nations, see United Nations Development Program, *Human Development Report, 1993* (New York: Oxford University Press, 1993), pp. 84–99. A more comprehensive analysis is provided in Mark Robinson and Roger C. Riddell, *Nongovernmental Organizations and Rural Poverty Alleviation* (New York: Oxford University Press, 1995). See also Michael Edwards and David Hulme, "Too close for comfort? The impact of official aid on nongovernmental organizations," *World Development* 24 (1996): 961–973.

25. For an examination of many of the most significant NGO programs, both international and domestic, see Stephen C. Smith, *Ending Global Poverty: A Guide to What Works* (New York: Palgrave Macmillan, 2005).

26. For reviews of the aid experience and the economic effects on recipient nations, see William Easterly, *The Elusive Quest for Growth: Economists' Adventures and Misadventures in the Tropics* (Cambridge, Mass.: MIT Press, 2001); Robert H. Cassen et al., *Does Aid Work?* (New York: Oxford University Press, 1986); Roger C. Riddell, "The contribution of foreign aid to development and the role of the private sector," *Development* 1

(1992): 7–15; and Tony Killick, *The Developmental Effectiveness of Aid to Africa* (Washington, D.C.: World Bank, 1991). For a specific review of the impact of aid on agricultural productivity, see George W. Norton, Jaime Ortiz, and Philip G. Pardey, "The impact of foreign assistance on agricultural growth," *Economic Development and Cultural Change* 40 (1992): 775–786.

27. See, for example, Hollis B. Chenery and Nicholas G. Carter, "Foreign assistance and development performance," *American Economic Review* 63 (1973): 459–468.

28. See, for example, Keith Griffin and John L. Enos, "Foreign assistance: Objectives and consequences," *Economic Development and Cultural Change* 18 (1970): 313–327.

29. See, for example, Peter T. Bauer, and Basil Yamey, "Foreign aid: What is at stake?" *Public Interest*, Summer 1982, pp. 57–70 and "Foreign aid: Rewarding impoverishment?" *Commentary*, September 1985, pp. 38–40. See also Easterly, "Ghost of financing gap."

Further Reading

A good collection of forty-one papers on multinational corporations is found in Stephen Young, ed., *Multinationals and Public Policy*, (Northampton, Mass.: Elgar, 2004). For an economic analysis of private foreign investment and the role and influence of multinational corporations, see Sanjaya Lall, "Less developed countries and private foreign direct investment: A review article," *World Development* 2 (1974): 43–48; Paul P. Streeten, *World Development* 1(1975): 393–397. "Policies toward Multinationals," Thomas Biersteker, *Distortion or Development: Contending Perspectives on the Multinational Corporation* (Cambridge, Mass.: MIT Press, 1978), and Mark Cassen and Robert D. Pearce, "Multinational enterprises in LDCs," in *Surveys in Development Economics*, ed. Norman Gemmell (Oxford: Blackwell, 1987), pp. 90–132. For a broad overview, see Richard Caves, *Multinational Enterprise and Economic Analysis*, 2nd ed. (New York: Cambridge University Press, 1996).

For an account of the power and inside workings of MNCs, whose decisions shape the lives of all peoples and often transcend national and international laws, see Richard J. Barnet and Ronald E. Muller, *Global Reach: The Power of Multinational Corporations* (New York: Simon & Schuster, 1975), and David C. Korten, *When Corporations Rule the World*, 2nd ed. (San Francisco: Berrett-Kohler, 2001). A strong defense of the economic benefits of MNCs for development can be found in Raymond Vernon, *Storm over the Multinationals* (London: Macmillan, 1977). Two useful surveys of the role and limitations of private portfolio investments and emerging stock markets in LDCs can be found in the entire issue of the *World Bank Economic Review* 9 (January 1995) and in the section "Latin America: The morning after," in *Foreign Affairs* 74 (1995): 28–75.

On the question of the benefits and costs of foreign aid, see Gunnar Myrdal, *The Challenge of World Poverty* (New York: Pantheon, 1970), ch. 10 and 11, Brandt Commission, *North-South: A Program for Survival* (Cambridge, Mass.: MIT Press, 1980); Anne O. Krueger, "Aid in the development process," *World Bank Research Observer* 1 (1986): 57–78; Roger C. Riddell, *Foreign Aid Reconsidered* (Baltimore: Johns Hopkins University Press, 1987); Robert H. Cassen et al., *Does Aid Work?* (New York: Oxford University Press, 1986); Roger C. Riddell, "The contribution of foreign aid to development and the role of the private sector," *Development* 1 (1992): 7–15; and William Easterly, *The Elusive Quest for Growth: Economists' Adventures and Misadventures in the Tropics* (Cambridge, Mass.: MIT Press, 2001).A penetrating analysis of the role of the World Bank and other major aid organizations in promoting market reforms as conditions of assistance in the 1980s can be found in Paul Mosley, Jane Harrington, and John Toye, *Aid and Power: The World Bank and Policy-Based Lending* (London: Routledge, 1991). On the activities of international and domestic NGOs, see Stephen C. Smith, *Ending Global Poverty: A Guide to What Works* (New York: Palgrave Macmillan, 2005).

CHAPTER SIXTEEN

Finance and Fiscal Policy for Development

The success of other market reforms depends on the health of the financial system.
—World Bank, *World Development Report, 1996*

I decided to set up my own bank. The government thought it was a funny idea; poor people cannot borrow money . . . Grameen is a mechanism for integrating people back into the marketplace. It opens up opportunities so that you can build your own life. Micro-credit brings people together.

—Muhammad Yunus, Founder of the Grameen Bank

It is increasingly recognized that the financial system plays a crucial role in the process of economic development. The government helps make this possible by adopting sound macroeconomic policies, including a sound fiscal as well as monetary policy, acting to establish financial markets where they do not yet exist, and providing prudential regulation of the financial system. In this chapter, we consider the role of finance and improvements in the workings of the financial system in the overall process of economic growth, modernization, and development. We examine the difficult road to macroeconomic stability on which many developing countries are now traveling. Then we examine developing-country financial systems in more detail. We take a look at stock markets in developing countries and consider the strengths and weaknesses of their expanding role. We examine special microfinancial institutions in developing countries, such as development banks, rotating savings and credit associations (ROSCAs), and village banking.

In this context, we look behind the scenes of LDC government attempts to stabilize their economies by focusing on the unique nature and structure of their financial and fiscal systems. We will discover why it is so difficult for most LDC governments to pursue traditional monetary and financial policies, how some financial policies have led to low domestic savings and widespread inefficiencies within the commercial banking system, and how current tax structures often work against attempts to restore fiscal balance through revenue increases. We also take a brief look at problems of public administration (a critical constraint in many developing countries), examine the debate over the privatization of state-owned enterprises, and consider the role of large military expenditures in promoting or retarding economic development. The chapter's case study compares the privatization experiences of Chile and Poland.

The Role of the Financial System

Generally, a distinction is made between the *real sector* and the *financial sector*. This terminology is unfortunate, because it suggests that the financial sector is something less than real. This impression has been abetted by the view that the financial sector is a mere appendage to the real economy. As the late Cambridge economist Joan Robinson famously put it, "Where industry treads, finance will follow." Certainly, there is some truth to this aphorism; to a large extent, demand for financial services is derived from the activities of nonfinancial firms. But increasingly, evidence suggests that finance can also be a limiting factor in economic development. From the impoverished mother in Zambia who attempts to feed her family with income from her credit-starved microenterprise and who could be much more productive with more working capital to the start-up firm in Bangalore, India, that cannot get established without private equity capital and may eventually wish to float a public offering to the farmer on the world's richest soil in Ukraine who cannot plant for want of credit to buy seeds to the budding family-owned shoe company in Brazil that needs better access to lower-cost loans to begin to export to the established publicly traded firm in Korea that wishes to sell more shares to provide funds for restructuring, the need for finance can be seen everywhere in the developing world.

Hugh Patrick offered a "stages of development" argument that financial development causes growth at the start of modern development, but once the financial system is established, it mainly follows the real sector. Most likely, the causality runs in both directions.

What is so important about finance? The financial sector provides six major functions that are important both at the firm level and at the level of the economy as a whole.[1]

1. *Providing payment services.* It is inconvenient, inefficient, and risky to carry around enough cash to pay for purchased goods and services. Financial institutions provide an efficient alternative. The most obvious examples are personal and commercial checking and check-clearing and credit and debit card services; each are growing in importance, in the modern sectors at least, of even low-income countries.

2. *Matching savers and investors.* Although many people save, such as for retirement, and many have investment projects, such as building a factory or ex-

panding the inventory carried by a family microenterprise, it would be only by the wildest of coincidences that each investor saved exactly as much as needed to finance a given project. Therefore, it is important that savers and investors somehow meet and agree on terms for loans or other forms of finance. This can occur without financial institutions; even in highly developed markets, many new entrepreneurs obtain a significant fraction of their initial funds from family and friends. However, the presence of banks, and later venture capitalists or stock markets, can greatly facilitate matching in an efficient manner. Small savers simply deposit their savings and let the bank decide where to invest them.

3. *Generating and distributing information.* One does not always think of it this way, but from a societywide viewpoint, one of the most important functions of the financial system is to generate and distribute information. Stock and bond prices in the daily newspapers of developing countries (and increasingly on the Internet as well in India and elsewhere) are a familiar example; these prices represent the average judgment of thousands, if not millions, of investors, based on the information they have available about these and all other investments. Banks also collect information about the firms that borrow from them; the resulting information is one of the most important components of the "capital" of a bank, although it is often unrecognized as such. In these regards it has been said that financial markets represent the "brain" of the economic system.[2]

4. *Allocating credit efficiently.* Channeling investment funds to uses yielding the highest rate of return allows increases in specialization and the division of labor, which have been recognized since the time of Adam Smith as key to the wealth of nations.

5. *Pricing, pooling, and trading risks.* Insurance markets provide protection against risk, but so does the diversification possible in stock markets or in banks' loan syndications.

6. *Increasing asset liquidity.* Some investments are very long-lived; in some cases—a hydroelectric plant, for example—such investments may last a century or more. Thus most investors in such plants would like to sell them at some point. In some cases, it can be quite difficult to find a buyer at the time one wishes to sell—at retirement, for instance. Financial development increases liquidity by making it easier to sell, for example, on the stock market or to a syndicate of banks or insurance companies.

Both technological and financial innovations have driven modern economic growth. Both were necessary conditions for the industrial revolution, as steam and water power required large investments facilitated by innovations in banking, finance, and insurance. Both are necessary for developing countries as they continue their struggle for economic development. But the effective functioning of the financial system requires, in turn, the precondition of macroeconomic stability.

The Painful Road to Macroeconomic Stability

In recent decades, a combination of large foreign debts, growing fiscal deficits, high inflation, and chronic balance of payments problems forced many governments in the developing world to undertake painful measures to stabilize their economies. **Macroeconomic stabilization** has three objectives: (1) getting inflation under control; (2) restoring fiscal balance through reduced government expenditures, raising personal and business taxes, and reforming the financial system; and (3) eliminating the current account deficit through control over the exchange rate (devaluation) and promotion of exports. As we learned in Chapter 13, the two principal catalysts for these stabilization and adjustment policies are the IMF, which holds the key to international private lending with its conditionality requirements, and the World Bank, which predicates the bulk of its multilateral development assistance on acceptance of its structural adjustment provisions. But all too often the requirements of fiscal austerity, competitive real exchange rates, sound financial markets, and the deregulation or privatization of industry in pursuit of macroeconomic stability and structural adjustment have meant a slowdown in economic growth, at least in the short-run, and a worsening of domestic poverty and inequality. Fiscal austerity typically involves severe cutbacks in government expenditures on social, educational, and health programs; massive layoffs of public-sector workers; disproportionate declines in real wages; and the elimination of critical economic safety nets for the poor and the disadvantaged. These actions may have helped highly indebted LDCs pay off part of their loans and thus resolve the debt crisis for developed-country private banks, but they invariably reduced levels of living for the rural and urban poor.[3]

Differences between MDC and LDC Financial Systems

In more developed nations, monetary and financial policy plays a major direct and indirect role in governmental efforts designed to expand economic activity in times of unemployment and surplus capacity and to contract that activity in times of excess demand and inflation.[4] Basically, **monetary policy** works on two principal economic variables: the aggregate supply of money in circulation and the level of interest rates. The **money supply** (currency plus commercial bank demand deposits) is thought to be directly related to the level of economic activity in the sense that a greater money supply induces expanded economic activity by enabling people to purchase more goods and services. This in essence is the *monetarist theory* of economic activity. Its advocates argue that by controlling the growth of the money supply, governments of developed countries can regulate their nations' economic activity and control inflation.

On the other side of the monetary issue are the *Keynesian economists*, who argue that an expanded supply of money in circulation increases the availability of loanable funds. A supply of loanable funds in excess of demand leads to lower interest rates. Because private investment is assumed to be inversely related to prevailing interest rates, businesspeople will expand their investments as interest rates fall and credit becomes more available. More investment in turn raises aggregate demand, leading to a higher level of economic activity (more employment and a higher GDP). Similarly, in times of excess aggregate demand and inflation, governments pursue restrictive monetary policies designed to curtail the expansion of aggregate demand by reducing the growth of the national money supply, lowering the supply of loanable funds, raising interest rates, and thereby inducing a lower level of investment and, it is hoped, less inflation.

Although this description of monetary policy in developed countries grossly simplifies a complex process, it does point out two important aspects that developing countries lack. First, the ability of developed-country governments to expand and contract their money supply and to raise and lower the costs of borrowing in the private sector (through direct and indirect manipulation of interest rates) is made possible by the existence of highly organized, economically interdependent, and efficiently functioning money and credit markets. Financial resources are continuously flowing in and out of savings banks, commercial banks, and other nationally regulated public and private financial intermediaries with a minimum of interference. Moreover, interest rates are regulated both by administrative credit controls and by market forces of supply and demand, so there tends to be consistency and a relative uniformity of rates in different sectors of the economy and in all regions of the country. Financial intermediaries are thus able to mobilize private savings and efficiently allocate them to their most productive uses. This is a critical ingredient in the promotion of long-term economic growth.

By contrast, markets and financial institutions in many developing countries are highly unorganized, often externally dependent, and spatially fragmented.[5] Many LDC commercial banks are merely overseas branches of major private banking institutions in developed countries. Their orientation, therefore, like that of multinational corporations, may be more toward external and less toward internal monetary situations. The ability of LDC governments to regulate the national supply of money is further constrained by the openness of their economies, in some cases the pegging of their currencies to the dollar or to a basket of MDC currencies, and the fact that the accumulation of foreign-currency earnings is a significant but highly variable source of their domestic financial resources. Even the money supply itself may be difficult to measure and more difficult to control when there are, as in many LDCs, problems of **currency substitution**, whereby foreign currencies serve as an alternative to the domestic currency (e.g., U.S. dollars in northern Mexico).[6] Most important, because of limited information and incomplete credit markets, the commercial banking system of many LDCs lacks **transparency** (full disclosure of the quality of loan portfolios) and often restricts its activities almost exclusively to rationing scarce loanable funds to medium- and large-scale enterprises in the modern manufacturing sector that are deemed more creditworthy. This lack of transparency, and the fact that many borrowers were *not* creditworthy, was a major factor in the 1997 Asian currency and banking crisis, especially in Thailand and Indonesia. As a result, small farmers and indigenous small-scale entrepreneurs and traders in both the formal and informal manufacturing and service sectors must normally seek financing elsewhere—sometimes from family members and relatives, but more typically from local moneylenders and loan sharks, who charge exorbitant rates of interest.

Thus most developing countries have operated under a dual monetary system: a small and often externally controlled or influenced **organized money market** with severely binding legal restrictions on nominal interest rate ceilings, catering to the financial requirements of a special group of middle- and upper-class local and foreign businesses in the modern industrial sector, and a large but amorphous **unorganized money market**, uncontrolled, illegal, and often usurious, to which most low-income individuals are obliged to turn in times of financial need. This is just another manifestation of the dual structure of many LDC economies and their tendency, intentional or not, to serve the needs of wealthy elites while neglecting the requirements of the relatively poor. One possible step toward the elimination of this major factor-price distortion would be the removal of artificially low nominal interest rate ceilings in the organized market as well as other related steps toward **financial liberalization** (e.g., liberalization of the foreign-exchange rate). Higher interest rates should generate more domestic savings, whereas greater transparency and more market-oriented real interest rates should better allocate loanable funds to the most productive projects. However, such coordinated liberalization of domestic financial and foreign-exchange markets is unlikely to solve the problem of channeling credit to small investors and entrepreneurs.[7] That will require more direct new initiatives. We will discuss both financial market reform and measures to improve finance for the informal economy later in the chapter.

The second major limitation of standard monetary theory and policy is the assumption of a direct link among lower interest rates, higher investment, and expanded output. In developing nations, investment decisions are often not very sensitive to interest rate movements. Moreover, as we will shortly discover, a number of larger countries in Latin America (e.g., Brazil and Argentina) have in the past followed a policy of inflation-financed industrial growth, in which expansionary monetary policy in conjunction with large budgetary deficits resulted in negative real interest rates (inflation rates exceeding nominal interest levels). The basic idea was that artificially low rates would encourage investment, finance the fiscal deficit, and promote industrial output growth. But there may be severe structural supply constraints (low elasticities of supply) inhibiting the expansion of output even when the demand for it increases. These constraints include poor management, the absence of essential (usually imported) intermediate products, bureaucratic rigidities, licensing restrictions, and an overall lack of industrial-sector interdependence. Whatever the reasons, structural supply rigidities mean that any increase in the demand for goods and services generated by rapid money creation will not be matched by increases in supply. Instead, the excess demand (in this case, for investment goods) will merely bid up prices and cause inflation. In some Latin American nations, such "structural" inflation has been a chronic problem made even worse on the cost side by the upward spiral of wages as workers attempt to protect their real income levels by indexing wage increases to price rises. Attempts to control inflation with fixed or slowly depreciating exchange rates led to major financial crises in Argentina in 2001–2002 and earlier in Brazil in 1999. Inflation now seems to be creeping upward again in both countries.

Despite some of these limitations, however, LDC financial systems remain an integral component of the general economic system. For example, in the context of severe macroeconomic instability of high inflation accompanied by large budget and trade deficits, they represent a key element in any overall stabilization effort. Moreover, as noted earlier, financial systems provide a variety of needed services, including savings mobilization, credit allocation, risk limitations, insurance protection, and foreign-exchange facilitation. Let's therefore begin our examination of the structure of LDC financial systems with a look at the central bank.

The Role of Central Banks

Role in Developed Nations In developed nations, **central banks**, such as the Federal Reserve Board in the United States, conduct a wide range of banking, regulatory, and supervisory functions. They have substantial public responsibilities and a broad array of executive powers. Their major activities can be grouped into five general functions:[8]

1. *Issuer of currency and manager of foreign reserves.* Central banks print money, distribute notes and coins, intervene in foreign-exchange markets to regulate the national currency's rate of exchange with other currencies, and manage foreign-asset reserves to maintain the external value of the national currency.

2. *Banker to the government.* Central banks provide bank deposit and borrowing facilities to the government while simultaneously acting as the government's fiscal agent and underwriter.

3. *Banker to domestic commercial banks.* Central banks also provide bank deposit and borrowing facilities to commercial banks and act as a lender of last resort to financially troubled commercial banks.

4. *Regulator of domestic financial institutions.* Central banks ensure that commercial banks and other financial institutions conduct their business prudently and in accordance with relevant laws and regulations. They also monitor reserve ratio requirements and supervise the conduct of local and regional banks.

5. *Operator of monetary and credit policy.* Central banks attempt to manipulate monetary and credit policy instruments (the domestic money supply, the discount rate, the foreign-exchange rate, commercial bank reserve ratio requirements, etc.) to achieve major macroeconomic objectives such as controlling inflation, promoting investment, or regulating international currency movements.

Sometimes these functions are handled by separate regulatory bodies.

Role in Developing Nations Central banks are capable of effectively carrying out their wide range of administrative and regulatory functions in developed nations primarily because these countries have a highly integrated, complex economy; a sophisticated and mature financial system; and a highly educated, well-trained, and well-informed population. In developing countries, the situation is quite different. As we have seen in earlier chapters, LDCs may be dominated by a narrow range of exports accompanied by a much larger diversity of imports, the relative prices (the terms of trade) of which are likely to be beyond local control. Their financial systems tend to be rudimentary and characterized by (1) foreign-owned commercial banks that mostly finance domestic and export industries, (2) an informal and often exploitive credit network serving the bulk of the rural and informal urban economy, (3) a central banking institution that may have been inherited from colonial rulers or operates either as a **currency board** issuing domestic currency for foreign exchange at fixed rates[9] or simply to finance budget deficits, (4) a money supply that is difficult to measure (because of currency substitution) and more difficult to regulate, (5) an unskilled and inexperienced workforce unfamiliar with the many complexities of domestic and international finance, and (6) a degree of political influence and control by the central government (over interest rates, foreign-exchange rates, import licenses, etc.) not usually found in more developed nations.

Under such circumstances, the principal task of a central bank is to instill a sense of confidence among local citizens and foreign trading partners in the credibility of the local currency as a viable and stable unit of account and in the prudence and responsibility of the domestic financial system. Unfortunately, many LDC central banks have limited control over the credibility of their currencies because fiscal policy—and large fiscal deficits—call the tune and must be financed either by printing money or through foreign or domestic borrowing. In either case, prolonged deficits inevitably lead to inflation and a loss of confidence in the currency.

Given the substantial differences in economic structure and financial sophistication between rich and poor nations, central banks in most of the least developed countries simply do not possess the flexibility or the independence to undertake the range of monetary macroeconomic and regulatory functions performed by their developed-country counterparts. What, then, can they do? And are there alternatives to a full-fledged central bank for the many small, export-oriented developing countries?

Alternatives to Central Banks   There are several alternatives to the standard central bank.[10] First, a *transitional central banking institution* can be formed as an intermediate step between a currency board and a central bank, with the government exerting a strong influence on its financial activities. The range of such activities, however, is checked by statutory limitations on the monetary authority's discretionary powers. British colonies and protectorates such as Fiji, Belize, Maldives, and Bhutan provide the most common examples of transitional central banks. Second, a *supranational central bank* may be created to undertake central banking activities for a group of smaller countries participating in a monetary union, perhaps also as part of a customs union (see Chapter 13). Examples of such monetary unions with regional central banks are the West African Monetary

TABLE 16.1 Central Banking Institutions

Institution	Function					
	Issuer of Currency	Banker to Government	Banker to Commercial Banks	Regulator of Financial Institutions	Operator of Monetary Policy	Promoter of Financial Development
Full-fledged central bank	3	3	3	3	3G	1
Supranational central bank	3E	2E	2	2	2E	2
Open-economy central banking institution	3C	2C	2	3	1	3
Transitional central banking institution	3CG	2C	2	1	2G	3
Currency enclave central banking institution	1,2CE	2CE	2	1	1	3
Currency board	3C	1	1	1	1	1

Source: Charles Collyns, *Alternatives to the Central Bank in the Developing World*, IMF Occasional Paper No. 20 (Washington, D.C.: International Monetary Fund, 1983), p. 22. Copyright © 1983 by the International Monetary Fund. Reprinted with the permission of the International Monetary Fund via the Copyright Clearance Center.
Key: 1 = limited involvement; 2 = substantial involvement; 3 = full involvement; C = considerable constitutional restrictions; E = considerable external influence; G = considerable government influence.

Union (franc zone), the Central African Monetary Area (also franc-related), and the East Caribbean Currency Authority. Third, a *currency enclave* might be established between an LDC central banking institution and a monetary authority of a larger trading partner, often the former colonial power. Such an arrangement provides a certain degree of stability to the LDC currency, but the dominating influence of the partner, with its own priorities, renders the enclave almost as dependent as a colony. Examples include Panama, and after 2000, Ecuador, which have "dollarized"—that is, they have adopted as legal tender currencies that are tied to the U.S. dollar, although there is no formal support agreement with the U.S. government. Finally, in an *open-economy central banking institution*, where both commodity and international capital flows represent significant components of national economic activity, the monetary environment is likely to be subject to fluctuations in world commodity and financial markets. As a result, the central banking institution will be engaged primarily in the regulation and promotion of a stable and respected financial system. Examples of such institutions are Singapore, Kuwait, Saudi Arabia, and the United Arab Emirates. Table 16.1 summarizes the major features of these four categories of central bank alternatives in comparison with the currency board and the central bank.

In the final analysis, however, it is not so much the organizational structure of the central banking institution or even its degree of political autonomy that matters. Rather, it is the extent to which such an institution is capable of financing and promoting domestic economic development, through its commercial and development banking system, in an international economic and financial environment characterized by various degrees of dominance and dependence. Commercial banks in developing countries must take a much more active role in promoting new industries and financing existing ones than is usual for banks in developed nations. They have to be sources of venture capital as well as repositories of the commercial knowledge and business skills that are typically in short supply domestically. It is because of their failure to do this that new financial institutions, known as development banks, have emerged over the past few decades in a wide variety of LDCs.

The Emergence of Development Banking

Development banks are specialized public and private financial institutions that supply medium- and long-term funds for the creation or expansion of industrial enterprises. They have arisen in many developing nations because the existing banks usually focus on either short-term lending for commercial purposes (commercial and savings banks) or, in the case of central banks, the control and regulation of the aggregate supply of money. Moreover, existing commercial banks set loan conditions that often are inappropriate for establishing new enterprises or for financing large-scale projects. Their funds are more often allocated to "safe" borrowers (established industries, many of which are foreign-owned or run by well-known local families). True venture capital for new industries rarely obtains approval.

To facilitate industrial growth in economies characterized by a scarcity of financial capital, development banks have sought to raise capital, initially focusing on two major sources: (1) bilateral and multilateral loans from national aid agencies like the U.S. Agency for International Development (USAID) and from international donor agencies like the World Bank and (2) loans from their own governments. However, in addition to raising capital, development banks have had to develop specialized skills in the field of industrial project appraisal. In many cases, their activities go far beyond the traditional banker's role of lending money to creditworthy customers. The activities of development banks often encompass direct entrepreneurial, managerial, and promotional involvement in the enterprises they finance, including government-owned and -operated industrial corporations. Development banks are thus playing an increasingly important role in the industrialization process of many LDCs.

The growth and spread of development banks in the developing world have been substantial. By 2000, their numbers had increased into the hundreds, and their financial resources had ballooned to billions of dollars. Moreover, although the initial sources of capital were agencies like the World Bank, bilateral aid agencies, and local governments (e.g., the Industrial Credit and Investment Corporation of India was established in 1954 with a 30-year interest-free advance of 75 million rupees from the Indian government), the growth of development bank finance has increasingly been facilitated by capital from private investors, institutional and individual, foreign and local. Almost 20% of the share capital of these banks was foreign-owned in 1990, with the remaining 80% derived from local investors.

In spite of their impressive growth and their increasing importance for LDC industrial expansion, development banks have come under mounting criticism for their excessive concentration on large-scale loans. Some privately owned finance companies (also categorized as development banks) refuse to consider loans of less than $20,000 to $50,000. They argue that smaller loans do not justify the time and effort involved in their appraisal. As a result, these finance companies almost totally remove themselves from the area of aid to small enterprises, even though such aid is of major importance to the achievement of broadly based economic development and often may constitute the bulk of assistance needed in the private sector. Small-scale entrepreneurs, often lacking technical, purchasing, marketing, organizational, and accounting skills, as well as access to bank credit, are thus forced to seek funds in the exploitive unorganized money markets. We may conclude, therefore, that in spite of the growth of development banks, there remains a need to channel more financial resources to small entrepreneurs, both on the farm and in the marginal or informal sector of urban areas, who often are excluded from access to credit at reasonable rates of interest.[11] In an attempt to respond to these needs of small-scale borrowers, a whole array of unique, informal credit arrangements has emerged in LDCs. Let us look briefly at some of them.

Informal Finance, Group Lending, and Microfinance Institutions for Small-Scale Enterprise

Much economic activity in developing nations comes from small-scale producers and enterprises. Recent studies indicate that they employ anywhere from 40% to 70% of the labor force and account for about one-third of domestic recorded output. Most are noncorporate, unlicensed, unregistered enterprises, including small farmers, producers, artisans, tradespeople, and independent traders operating in the informal urban and rural sectors of the economy. Their demands for financial services are unique and outside the purview of traditional commercial bank lending. For example, street vendors need short-term finance to buy inventories, small farmers require buffer loans to tide them over uncertain seasonal income fluctuations, and small-scale manufacturers need minor loans to purchase simple equipment or hire nonfamily workers. In such situations, traditional commercial banks are both ill equipped and reluctant to meet the needs of these small borrowers. Because the sums involved are small (usually less than $500) but administration and carrying costs are almost as high as for large loans, and because few informal borrowers have the necessary collateral to secure formal-sector loans, commercial banks simply are not interested. Most don't even have branch offices in rural villages, small towns, or on the periphery of cities where many of the informal activities take place. Thus most noncorporate borrowers have to turn to family or friends as a first line of finance and then warily to local professional moneylenders, pawnbrokers, and tradespeople as a backup. These latter sources of finance are extremely costly—moneylenders, for example, can charge up to 20% *a day* in interest for short-term loans to traders and vendors. In the case of small farmers requiring seasonal loans, the only collateral that they have to offer the moneylender or pawnbroker is their land or oxen. If these must be surrendered in the event of a default, peasant farmers become rapidly transformed into landless laborers, while moneylenders accumulate sizable tracts of land, either for themselves or to sell to large local landholders.

Fortunately, in recent years new, more reasonable, and more reliable forms of **informal finance** have emerged to replace the moneylender and pawnbroker in some instances.[12] These include local rotating savings and credit associations and group lending schemes. In the case of **rotating savings and credit associations** (ROSCAs), which can be found in such diverse countries as Mexico, Bolivia, Egypt, Nigeria, Ghana, the Philippines, Sri Lanka, India, China, and South Korea, a group of up to 50 individuals selects a leader who collects a fixed amount of savings from each member. This fund is then allocated on a rotating basis to each member as an interest-free loan. ROSCAs enable people to buy goods without having to save the full amount in advance. With a ROSCA, individuals can make their planned purchases in half the time, on average. Many low-income people prefer to save and borrow this way, repayment rates are extremely high, and participation is very active. Noting that ROSCAs are often formed by married women, Siwan Anderson and Jean-Marie Baland have proposed that they serve another important purpose when wives' bargaining power in the family is otherwise limited. Because the funds made available through membership in the ROSCA cannot be drawn on until the wife wins a turn to receive the kitty, this restriction prevents her husband from demanding access to her growing savings for immediate consumption before enough has been saved to purchase her targeted item, such as a sewing machine.[13]

Microfinance Institutions Microfinance is the supply of credit, saving vehicles, and other basic financial services made available to poor and vulnerable people who might otherwise have no access to them or could borrow only on highly unfavorable terms. Microfinance institutions (MFIs) specialize in delivering these services, in various ways and according to their own institutional rules.[14] In the case of village banking, or **group lending schemes**, a group of potential borrowers forms an association to borrow funds from a commercial bank, a government development bank, an NGO, or a private institution. The group then allocates the funds to individual members, whose responsibility is to repay the group. The group itself guarantees the loan to the outside lender; it is responsible for repayment. The idea is simple: By joining together, a group of small borrowers can reduce the costs of borrowing and, because the loan is large, can gain access to formal commercial credit. Group members have a vested interest in the success of the enterprise and therefore exert strong moral pressure on borrowing members to repay on time. The evidence shows that repayment rates compare favorably with formal-sector borrowers.

Economic research has consistently found that availability of credit is a binding constraint for microenterprise development. A majority of microenterprises are operated by women. But lack of credit particularly, though certainly not exclusively, affects women (microentrepreneur) borrowers, for reasons ranging from lack of property rights to local cultural practices, but lack of collateral is arguably the most important. Let's look a little more closely at how this works.

Three related factors have made it difficult to relax credit constraints to low-income women microenterpreurs: First, poor microentrepreneurs often have little or no collateral. Second, it is difficult for conventional lenders to determine borrower quality. Third, small loans are more costly to process per dollar lent.

Village banking seeks to solve these problems in part through the "collateral of peer pressure." Small microentrepreneurs are organized into credit cooperatives, to which seed capital is lent. Before qualifying for a loan, each member is required to identify several other members or potential members willing to cosign loans with them. Often, once a member of a cosigning group receives a loan, no other member may borrow until the first borrower has established a regular repayment record; and in any case no repeat loans are approved until all members' accounts are satisfactorily settled. Progressively larger loans are approved as borrowers gain experience and a credit history and identify productive uses for larger loans. Members know the characters of the cosigning group members they select and may be expected to join groups with members they believe likely to repay their loans. Thus the banks make use of the information "embedded" in the village or neighborhood about who is a reliable and capable borrower, getting villagers to reveal this information in an incentive-compatible way. At the same time, an implicit collateral is created by the pressure that members would be expected to place on each member in the group to repay funds. The goodwill of these relatives and friends of the borrower represents part of the borrowers' capital, which failure to pay the loan puts at risk. Finally, village banks extensively use volunteer member labor (as traditional consumer cooperatives do), thus lowering the bank's effective costs. Bank members reveal by participating that the value of the time thus spent is less than the value of the enhanced credit. An example of an MFI that uses this model is FINCA International.

Another outstanding example of an MFI is the Grameen Rural Bank in Bangladesh examined in the case study at the end of Chapter 5. Grameen uses solidarity groups and takes advantage of opportunities for peer pressure by granting loans to some group members first and extending loans to others only after the first borrowers have begun scheduled repayments. Increases in borrowing limits are allowed only if all members repay. But there is currently no cosigning requirement in Grameen.

Although these examples of successful informal finance programs are impressive, the fact remains that throughout the developing world, the majority of rural and urban poor have little or no access to credit. Until legal reforms are enacted making it easier for small enterprises to gain access to the formal credit system or more NGO- or government-supported credit programs are established to serve the needs of the noncorporate sector, the financial systems of most developing countries will remain unresponsive to the fundamental requirements of participatory national development.

MFIs: Two Current Policy Debates   A debate is under way in the microenterprise credit community about whether subsidies are appropriate. Known as the "microfinance schism," the debate pits the Consultative Group to Assist the Poor (CGAP), a donor consortium headquartered within the World Bank, and other mainstream donors against other NGOs and academic economists. CGAP effectively argues that one can reach more borrowers by requiring sustainability, so that available dollars go further. This argument is reasonable as far as it goes, but there is no reason to believe that the poorest borrowers can afford to pay the high interest rates that this would require with the business opportunities they realistically face. Put more precisely, the interest elasticity of the demand for credit on the part of the poor is not close to zero. And the poor generally lack opportunities to invest in high-return projects. Thus some subsidy is required to truly reach the poorest current and potential microentrepreneurs.[15]

But even subsidized credit is no guarantee of higher productivity and incomes. Some studies have suggested that the poorest of the poor may not be made better off by village banking and indeed may be made worse off if they take on additional debt that is for them unproductive but for which they must pay interest.[16]

Of course, it will be essential to ensure that these subsidized credit programs are run efficiently, that the credit is allocated to appropriate investments, and that credit actually ends up in the hands of poor households. In this regard, it may be useful to tie credit to social services that are demanded only by the poor and inherently require time for participation, for at least three reasons. First, such required participation can act as a kind of screening mechanism to ensure that nonpoor borrowers are not taking advantage of a subsidy not intended for them (analogous to workfare screening, described in Chapter 5). Second, the poor generally cannot make adequate use of credit without better health and education.[17] There is almost certainly going to be at least some subsidy in programs that offer health or educational services along with credit. Third, many of the poor appear not to recognize the importance of human capital, and the availability of credit may act as a "hook" to get them enrolled in health and education programs. But it may be less costly to keep these programs separate, in accordance with the comparative advantage of NGOs, and some low-income borrowers do not need these services. Accordingly, there is a growing debate in the microfinance community over whether to integrate credit with education, health, or other programs.[18] BRAC, the NGO examined in the case study in Chapter 11, provides a good example of an integrated approach with its Microcredit-Plus-Plus program.

Reforming Financial Systems

Financial Liberalization, Real Interest Rates, Savings, and Investment

The restriction of loans to a few large borrowers, together with the widespread existence of high inflation, growing budget deficits, and negative real interest rates, led to a serious LDC "credit crunch" during the 1980s. The global recessions of 1981–1982 and 1987 exposed the frailty of many development bank loans so that by the end of the decade almost half of these banks were reporting 50% or more of their loans in arrears and another quarter had delinquency rates in excess of 25%. With real interest rates on savings deposits in the negative and expectations of continued inflation and exchange-rate devaluation contributing to substantial capital flight, it is not surprising that few individuals were willing to save.

In addition, commercial banks and other financial intermediaries were subject to numerous lending restrictions and faced mandatory interest rate ceilings on loanable funds at levels well below market-clearing rates.[19] These artificial interest rate ceilings were often set by LDC governments seeking to finance their budget deficits through the sale of low-interest bonds to private commercial banks. These banks in turn had to resort to **rationing** the available credit beyond the normal credit rationing observed in developed economies as a response to ad-

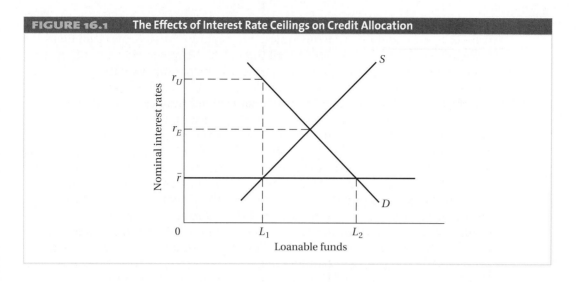

FIGURE 16.1   The Effects of Interest Rate Ceilings on Credit Allocation

verse selection. Figure 16.1 shows the impact of binding nominal interest rate ceilings at below-market-clearing levels. With the interest rate ceiling at $\bar{r}$, which is below the market-clearing equilibrium rate r_E, the demand for loanable funds, L_2, greatly exceeds the available supply, L_1. This excess demand leads to a need to ration the limited supply—a phenomenon known as **financial repression** because investment is limited or "repressed" by a shortage of savings, which in turn results from administered real interest rates below what would occur in a market setting. In the absence of outright corruption in the allocation of L_1 loanable funds, most commercial banks choose to allocate the available credit to a few large borrowers so as to minimize the administrative overhead costs as a proportion of the total costs of lending. Thus the net effect of government controls over lending rates is that even fewer loans will be allocated to small investors. Banks can cover the additional administrative costs and the added risks of smaller loans only by charging higher interest rates. Hence small farmers and urban entrepreneurs have no recourse but to seek finance from the unorganized money market, where, as we see from Figure 16.1, they are willing to pay above-market-clearing rates of r_U.

One suggested solution to the problem is to liberalize the financial sector by allowing nominal interest rates to rise to market-clearing levels. This would cause real interest rates to rise to positive levels and thus remove the explicit interest rate subsidy accorded to preferred borrowers (rent seekers) who are powerful enough to gain access to the rationed credit. Higher real rates should also generate more domestic saving and investment and permit some borrowers to shift from the unorganized to the organized credit market.[20] The World Bank cites evidence from countries such as Thailand, Turkey, and Kenya, where the liberalization of interest rates generated more saving and investment.[21] However, evidence of the effects of financial reform in Chile during the 1970s revealed many shortcomings of the process. These included the acquisition of numerous banks by large conglomerates, or *grupos*, who used their new financial resources to buy recently privatized firms or to expand their own companies. When many of their firms faced financial losses, these *grupos* had to resort to additional funding to avoid bankruptcy. This made the Chilean financial system particularly vulnerable when the debt crisis struck in the 1980s.

Reform and liberalization of the organized money sector is therefore no panacea for the financial systems of developing nations. The early success of South Korea and Taiwan (and, before them, Japan) with financial systems that exhibited many of the attributes of repression demonstrates that judicious and selective government intervention can be a stimulus to industrial development. Although there is evidence that the elimination of interest rate distortions can promote greater saving and more rapid economic growth, financial reform must always be accompanied by other more direct measures to make sure that small farmers and investors have access to needed credit. Furthermore, as shown in the next section, careful supervision of the banking and financial sectors is needed to prevent undue concentration by local elites. As we have already pointed out in this book, "getting prices right" is only one step, albeit an important one, in making development serve the needs of the forgotten majority.

Financial Policy and the Role of the State

Does financial liberalization mean that LDC governments have no role to play in the financial sector? In an effort to identify how these governments can work effectively within the context of liberalized financial markets, 2001 Nobel laureate Joseph Stiglitz isolated seven major market failures that imply a potential role for state intervention.[22] His basic argument is "that [LDC] financial markets are markedly different from other markets," "that market failures are likely to be more pervasive in these markets," and that "much of the rationale for liberalizing financial markets is based neither on a sound economic understanding of how these markets work nor on the potential scope for government intervention."[23] The seven market failures Stiglitz identified are the following:

1. *The "public good" nature of monitoring financial institutions.* Investors need information about the solvency and management of financial institutions. Like other forms of information, monitoring is a public good—everyone who places savings in a particular financial institution would benefit from knowing that the institution was prospering or close to insolvency. But like other public goods in free-market economies, there is an undersupply of monitoring information, and consequently, risk-averse savers withhold their funds. The net result is fewer resources allocated through these institutions.

2. *Externalities of monitoring, selection, and lending.* Benefits are often incurred by lenders who learn about the viability of potential projects from the monitoring, selection, and lending decisions of other lenders. Investors can also benefit from information generated by other investors on the quality of different financial institutions. Like other positive (or negative) externalities, the market provides too little information, and resources are underallocated or overallocated.

3. *Externalities of financial disruption.* In the absence of government insurance (whether or not an explicit policy has been issued), the failure of one major financial institution can cause a run on the entire banking system and lead to long-term disruptions of the overall financial system.

4. *Missing and incomplete markets.* In most developing countries, markets for insurance against a variety of financial (bank failure) or physical (e.g., crop failure) risks are missing. The basic problem is that information is imperfect and costly to obtain, so an LDC government has an important role in reducing these risks. It can, for example, force membership in insurance programs or require financial institutions as well as borrowers to disclose information about their assets, liabilities, and creditworthiness.

5. *Imperfect competition.* Competition in the banking sector of most developing countries is extremely limited, meaning that potential borrowers usually face only a small number of suppliers of loanable funds, many of which are unwilling or unable to accommodate new and unknown customers. This is particularly true of small borrowers in the informal urban and rural sectors.

6. *Inefficiency of competitive markets in the financial sector.* Theoretically, for perfectly competitive markets to function efficiently, financial markets must be complete (without uninsured risks) and information must be exogenous (freely available to all and not influenced by any one participant's action in the market). Clearly, there are special advantages to individuals or entities with privileged information in LDC financial markets, and risk insurance is difficult, if not impossible, to obtain. As a result, unfettered financial markets may not allocate capital to its most profitable uses, and there can be substantial deviations between social and private returns to alternative investment projects. In such cases, direct government intervention—for example, by restricting certain kinds of loans and encouraging others—may partly or completely offset these imbalances.

7. *Uninformed investors.* Contrary to the doctrine of consumer sovereignty, with its assumption of perfect knowledge, many investors in LDCs lack both the information and the appropriate means to acquire it in order to make rational investment decisions. Here again, governments can impose financial disclosure requirements on firms listed on local stock exchanges or require banks, for example, to inform customers of the differences between simple and compound interest rates or of the nature of penalties for early withdrawals of savings.

In each of these seven instances, Stiglitz argues, LDC governments have a proper role to play in regulating financial institutions, creating new institutions to fill gaps in the kinds of credit provided by private institutions (e.g., microloans to small farmers and tradespeople), providing consumer protection, ensuring bank solvency, encouraging fair competition, and ultimately improving the allocation of financial resources and promoting macroeconomic stability.

As in other areas of economic development, the critical issue for financial policy is not about free markets versus government intervention but rather about how both can work together to meet the urgent needs of poor people.

Debate on the Role of Stock Markets

Recent years have witnessed enormous growth in developing countries' stock markets. This has had both benefits and costs for development. It has increased volatility in the economy as funds have flowed in from abroad and even more dramatically flooded out. In this section, we take a look at stock markets in developing countries and consider some proposed policies to get the most benefits from these markets. We also consider some of the limitations of depending too heavily on stock markets as an engine of growth.

Some studies have suggested that stock market development can play a highly constructive role in encouraging growth. These studies show that greater past stock market development (measured by either past capitalization or turnover in relation to GDP) predicts faster subsequent economic growth, even after other variables known to influence growth, such as the rate of investment and education, are accounted for. Even more striking, both banking and stock market development were found to have independent positive effects on growth, suggesting that each plays a somewhat different role in the economy. A correlation between stock market development and growth would be expected by many theories, including the view that finance follows industry. Therefore, industrial growth and stock market growth would occur together, but in that case, stock market growth would merely reflect the growth of the real sector. The fact that there is faster growth after greater stock market development has already been realized is suggestive of causality but is not conclusive. This is because past financial depth is correlated with future depth: Countries that had well-developed stock markets in the past usually do in the future as well. So the correlation between growth and past depth could really be driven by a third factor, such as the protection of private property and the rule of law. However, the results suggest that stock markets do have a role to play. Moreover, we can expect that stock markets promote the more general availability of liquidity and risk diversification services, may serve to motivate entrepreneurs who may later go public, and provide incentives for managerial performance that make it easier for firms to raise capital in any form.[24]

The question, then, is, should government do anything to develop and promote such markets, given the remaining uncertainty about the importance of their role? It makes no sense to actively develop stock markets unless certain prerequisites are met. First, one needs macrostability; investors will not invest in equity without it. Second, policy credibility is needed. How will policymakers keep the economy stabilized, and how will they react in a financial crisis to prevent a meltdown? And third, one needs a solid domestic-firm base; there is no point to opening a stock market if there are few firms in which outside investors would wish to take an equity stake.

Given that these prerequisites are in place, it is reasonable to wonder why a country would need to promote stock markets; wouldn't these markets develop as a result of market forces? One rationale for a public policy promoting the development of stock markets could be to balance the effective tilt toward debt finance implicit in policy to date (for example, public deposit insurance, while clearly necessary, functions like an interest subsidy, which tilts the playing field away from equity markets). Although evidence of spillovers or other special benefits for the promotion of stock market development is probably not enough to make a case for public subsidies to expand stock markets, in many countries policymakers may conclude that the evidence is compelling enough to eliminate bias, explicit or implicit, that has operated against stock markets in the past.

In this regard, the first type of stock market development policy could be termed *barrier removal*. Rather than promoting stock markets directly, let alone subsidizing their development, this strategy would remove other impediments, generating stock market development on its own. In practice, this usually entails certain forms of deregulation. One must be careful here because, as we have seen earlier in the chapter, many regulations were put in place not necessarily because there was government failure but because of market failure in the financial sector. If some regulations responding to market failure are removed, others may have to be established in their place.

However, certain regulations probably do have the effect of retarding the development and expansion of the stock market. Prime examples are capital repatriation legislation limiting the amount of profit foreign investors can take out of a country, the existence of restrictions on investing directly, restrictions on foreign broker participation, entry restrictions on investment banking and brokering that are not rational or that encourage rent seeking, and the failure to ensure that regulations are transparent and evenly applied. Changing such regulations has potential costs as well as benefits and should be entered into carefully.

There are other significant problems with relying too strongly on stock markets as a development strategy. First, stock markets lead to substantial foreign-investor influence over domestic-company operations. A large percentage of shares of listed LDC companies are usually foreign-owned. Second, stock markets can lead to short-term speculation that can dominate trading and distort the decision making of managers, often inducing a short-time horizon. Third, relatedly, "hot money" that flows in and out of a country to speculate in markets can produce wide currency swings and destabilize the economy.

Many questions remain regarding the role of financial intermediation in general, and stock markets in particular, in economic development. This is sure to be an active area of policy discussion in the years ahead.

Fiscal Policy for Development

Macrostability and Resource Mobilization

Whereas financial policy deals with money, interest, and credit allocation, fiscal policy focuses on government taxation and expenditure. Together they represent the bulk of public-sector activities. Most stabilization attempts have concentrated on cutting government expenditures to achieve budgetary balance. But the burden of resource mobilization to finance essential public developmental efforts must come from the revenue side. Public domestic and foreign borrowing can fill some savings gaps. In the long run, it is the efficient and equitable collection of taxes on which governments must base their development aspirations.[25] In the absence of

TABLE 16.2 Comparative Average Levels of Tax Revenue, 1985–1997, as a Percentage of GDP		
Country Groups	**1985–1987**	**1995–1997**
OECD countries	**36.6**	**37.9**
America	30.6	32.6
Pacific	30.7	31.6
Europe	38.2	39.4
Developing Countries	**17.5**	**18.2**
Africa	19.6	19.8
Asia	16.1	17.4
Middle East	16.5	18.1
Western Hemisphere	17.6	18.0

Source: Vito Tanzi and Howell H. Zee, "Tax Policy for Emerging Markets: Developing Countries," International Monetary Fund Policy Working Paper WP/00/35, 2000, p. 8. Published in *National Tax Journal*, 53, no. 2 (2000): 299–322. Reprinted with the permission of the National Tax Association.

well-organized and locally controlled money markets, most developing countries have had to rely primarily on fiscal measures to stabilize the economy and to mobilize domestic resources.

Taxation: Direct and Indirect

Developed countries of the OECD collect a much higher percentage of GDP in the form of tax revenue than developing countries do, as can be seen in Table 16.2. In the period 1995–1997, developing countries collected some 18.2% of GDP in tax revenues, while OECD countries collected more than double this share, some 37.9%. Developed countries may have higher demand for public expenditures and also greater capacity to generate tax revenue, and thus the causality likely runs in large part from greater development to higher tax levels. But to the degree that government resources are spent wisely, such as on human capital and needed infrastructure investments, some of the causality may run the other way as well.

Typically, **direct taxes**—those levied on private individuals, corporations, and property—make up 20% to 40% of total tax revenue for most LDCs. **Indirect taxes**, such as import and export duties and excise taxes (purchase, sales, and turnover taxes), constitute the primary source of fiscal revenue for LDCs.

As can be seen in Table 16.3, developed OECD countries generally rely more strongly on direct taxes, but this pattern is much less pronounced in Europe, where reliance on indirect taxes is almost as great as on direct taxes. It is not clear whether direct or indirect taxation is better for economic development because their impacts on what is arguably the most important factor in economic development—human capital accumulation—is so complex. Avoiding extreme overreliance on any one form of taxation is a reasonable approach given the current state of knowledge.

The tax systems (both direct and indirect taxes combined) of many developing countries are far from progressive. In some, such as Mexico, they can be highly regressive (meaning that lower-income groups pay a higher proportion of their income in taxes than higher-income groups).

Taxation in developing countries has traditionally had two purposes. First, tax concessions and similar fiscal incentives have been thought of as a means of stim-

TABLE 16.3 Comparative Composition of Tax Revenue, 1985–1997, as a Percentage of GDP

Country Groups	1985–1987 Income Taxes			1985–1987 Consumption Taxes				Social Security	1995–1997 Income Taxes			1995–1997 Consumption Taxes				Social Security
	Total	Corporate	Personal	Total	General	Excises	Trade		Total	Corporate	Personal	Total	General	Excises	Trade	
OECD countries	**13.9**	**2.8**	**11.3**	**11.3**	**6.0**	**3.8**	**0.7**	**8.8**	**14.2**	**3.1**	**10.8**	**11.4**	**6.6**	**3.6**	**0.3**	**9.5**
America	14.0	2.5	11.4	7.6	3.4	2.2	0.6	5.8	15.4	3.0	12.3	7.0	3.7	2.0	0.3	6.1
Pacific	17.1	3.9	13.2	7.5	2.3	3.7	0.8	2.8	16.3	4.3	11.4	8.4	4.3	2.6	0.6	3.5
Europe	13.3	2.7	11.0	12.4	6.8	4.0	0.7	10.1	13.7	2.9	10.6	12.4	7.3	4.0	0.3	10.8
Developing countries	**4.9**	**2.8**	**1.7**	**10.3**	**2.3**	**2.6**	**4.2**	**1.2**	**5.2**	**2.6**	**2.2**	**10.5**	**3.6**	**2.4**	**3.5**	**1.3**
Africa	6.3	2.9	3.1	11.7	3.2	2.3	5.7	0.4	6.9	2.4	3.9	11.6	3.8	2.3	5.1	0.5
Asia	5.7	3.5	2.1	9.5	1.9	2.5	3.6	0.1	6.2	3.0	3.0	9.7	3.1	2.2	2.7	0.3
Middle East	4.7	4.3	1.0	9.1	1.5	2.4	4.4	1.2	5.0	3.2	1.3	10.3	1.5	3.0	4.3	1.1
Western Hemisphere	3.7	1.8	1.0	10.6	2.6	3.0	3.7	2.4	3.7	2.3	1.0	10.6	4.8	2.3	2.6	2.5

Source: Vito Tanzi and Howell H. Zee, "Tax Policy for Emerging Markets: Developing Countries," International Monetary Fund Policy Working Paper WP/00/35, 2000, p. 13. Published in *National Tax Journal*, 53, no. 2(2000): 299–322. Reprinted with the permission of the National Tax Association.

ulating private enterprise. Such concessions and incentives have typically been offered to foreign private investors to induce them to locate their enterprises in the less developed country. Such tax incentives may indeed increase the inflow of private foreign resources, but as we discovered in Chapter 15, the overall benefits of such special treatment of foreign firms are by no means self-evident.

The second purpose of taxation, the mobilization of resources to finance public expenditures, is by far the more important. Whatever the prevailing political or economic ideology of the less developed country, its economic and social progress depends largely on its government's ability to generate sufficient revenues to finance an expanding program of essential, non-revenue-yielding public services—health, education, transport, communications, and other components of the economic and social infrastructure. In addition, most LDC governments are directly involved in the economic activities of their nations through their ownership and control of public corporations and state trading agencies. Direct and indirect tax levies enable the government to finance the capital and recurrent expenditures of these public enterprises, many of which often operate at a loss.

In recent years, many LDCs faced problems of rising fiscal deficits—public expenditures greatly in excess of public revenues—resulting from a combination of ambitious development programs and unexpected negative external shocks. With rising debt burdens, falling commodity prices, growing trade imbalances, and declining foreign private and public investment inflows, developing-world governments had little choice but to undergo severe fiscal retrenchment. This meant cutting government expenditures (unfortunately mostly on social services) and raising revenues through increased or more efficient tax collections. In general, the taxation potential of a country depends on five factors:

1. The level of per capita real income

2. The degree of inequality in the distribution of that income

3. The industrial structure of the economy and the importance of different types of economic activity (e.g., the importance of foreign trade, the significance of the modern sector, the extent of foreign participation in private enterprises, the degree to which the agricultural sector is commercialized as opposed to subsistence-oriented)

4. The social, political, and institutional setting and the relative power of different groups (e.g., landlords as opposed to manufacturers, trade unions, village or district community organizations)

5. The administrative competence, honesty, and integrity of the tax-gathering branches of government

We now examine the principal sources of direct and indirect public tax revenues. We can then consider how the tax system might be used to promote a more equitable and sustainable pattern of economic growth.

Personal Income and Property Taxes Personal income taxes yield much less revenue as a proportion of GDP in the less developed countries than in the more developed nations. In the latter, the income tax structure is said to be progressive: People with higher incomes theoretically pay a larger percentage of that income in taxes.

It would be administratively too costly and economically regressive to attempt to collect substantial income taxes from the poor. But the fact remains that most LDC governments have not been persistent enough in collecting taxes owed by the very wealthy. Moreover, in countries where the ownership of property is heavily concentrated and therefore represents the major determinant of unequal incomes (e.g., most of Asia and Latin America), property taxes can be an efficient and administratively simple mechanism both for generating public revenues and for correcting gross inequalities in income distribution. But in a World Bank survey, in only one of the 22 countries surveyed did the property tax constitute more than 4.2% of total public revenues. Moreover, in spite of much public rhetoric about reducing income inequalities, the share of property taxes as well as overall direct taxation has remained roughly the same for the majority of developing countries over the past two decades. Clearly, this phenomenon cannot be attributed to government tax-collecting inefficiencies as much as to the political and economic power and influence of the large landowning and other dominant classes in many Asian and Latin American countries. The political will to carry out development plans must therefore include the will to extract public revenue from the most accessible sources to finance development projects. If the former is absent, the latter will be too.[27]

Corporate Income Taxes Taxes on corporate profits, of both domestically and foreign-owned companies, amount to less than 3% of GDP in most developing countries, compared with more than 6% in developed nations. LDC governments tend to offer all sorts of tax incentives and concessions to manufacturing and commercial enterprises. Typically, new enterprises are offered long periods (sometimes up to 15 years) of tax exemption and thereafter take advantage of generous investment depreciation allowances, special tax write-offs, and other measures to lessen their tax burden. In the case of multinational foreign enterprises, the ability of LDC governments to collect substantial taxes is often frustrated. These locally run enterprises are able to shift profits to partner companies in countries offering the lowest levels of taxation through transfer pricing (discussed in Chapter 15).

Indirect Taxes on Commodities The largest single source of public revenue in developing countries is the taxation of commodities in the form of import, export, and excise duties (see Table 16.3). These taxes, which individuals and corporations pay indirectly through their purchase of commodities, are relatively easy to assess and collect. This is especially true in the case of foreign-traded commodities, which must pass through a limited number of frontier ports and are usually handled by a few wholesalers. The ease of collecting such taxes is one reason why countries with extensive foreign trade typically collect a greater proportion of public revenues in the form of import and export duties than countries with limited external trade. For example, in open economies with up to 40% of GNI derived from foreign trade, an average import duty of 25% will yield a tax revenue equivalent of 10% of GNI. By contrast, in countries like India and Brazil with only about 7% of GNI derived from exports, the same tariff rate would yield only 2% of GNI in equivalent tax revenues. Although we discussed import and export duties in the context of LDC trade policies in Chapter 13, one further point about these taxes, often overlooked, must be mentioned. Import and export duties, in addition to representing a major source of public revenue in many LDCs, can also be a substitute for the corporate income tax. To the extent that importers are unable to pass on to local consumers the full costs of the tax, an import duty can serve as a proxy tax on the profits of the importer (often a foreign company) and only partly a tax on the local consumer. Similarly, an export duty can be an effective way of taxing the profits of producing companies, including locally based multinational firms that practice transfer pricing. But export duties designed to generate revenue should not be raised to the point of discouraging local producers from expanding their export production.

In selecting commodities to be taxed, whether in the form of duties on imports and exports or excise taxes on local commodities, certain general economic and administrative principles must be followed to minimize the cost of securing maximum revenue. First, the commodity should be imported or produced by a relatively small number of licensed firms so that evasion can be controlled. Second, the price elasticity of demand for the commodity should be low so that total demand is not choked by the rise in consumer prices that results from the tax. Third, the commodity should have a high income elasticity of demand so that as incomes rise, more tax revenue will be collected. Fourth, for equity purposes, it is best to tax commodities like cars, refrigerators, imported fancy foods, and household appliances, which are consumed largely by the upper-income groups, while forgoing taxation on items of mass consumption such as basic foods, simple clothing, and household utensils, even though these may satisfy the first three criteria.

The conventional wisdom in recent years has been that switching to a broad-based value added tax (VAT) would improve economic efficiency; such tax reforms have accordingly been undertaken in several LDCs. However, this approach has been challenged recently. In particular, welfare may be worsened when the ability of the informal economy to remain effectively untaxed introduces new distortions in the economy.[28] The impact on human capital accumulation raises further complexities.

Problems of Tax Administration In the final analysis, a developing nation's ability to collect taxes for public expenditure programs and to use the tax system as a basis for modifying the distribution of personal incomes will depend not only on the enactment of appropriate tax legislation but also on the efficiency and integrity of the tax authorities who must implement these laws. In other words, as Joel Slemrod has put it, we must consider "optimal tax systems" rather than "optimal taxes" in the abstract. Thus the "technology of tax collection" must be considered, which includes the cost of tax administration and enforcement of compliance.[29]

The ability of LDC governments to expand their tax nets to cover the higher-income groups and minimize tax evasion by local and foreign individuals and corporations will largely determine the efficiency of the tax system in achieving its dual function of generating sufficient public revenues to finance expanding development programs and transferring income from upper- to lower-income groups in order to reduce poverty and income inequality. Much will depend, once again, on the political will to enact and enforce such progressive tax programs.[30]

Public Administration: The Scarcest Resource

Many observers would argue that the shortage of public (and private) administrative capability is the single scarcest public resource in the developing world.[31] The problem is not only a lack of training or experience. It also arises out of the political instability of numerous developing nations. When power is constantly changing hands, considerations of efficiency and public welfare are likely to be subordinated to political loyalty. Moreover, the larger the group of officials affected by a change of power, the more difficult it will be to maintain continuity in the formulation and execution of policy.

Public administration is unlikely to function efficiently when the rule of law is in question, when there is public disorder, or when there is little consensus on fundamental issues. Acute conditions of class, tribal, or religious conflict within a society will usually be reflected in the management and operation of government departments and public agencies. In a highly traditional society, where kinship ties are strong and such concepts as statehood and public service have not yet taken firm root, there is little regard for a merit system. Similarly, where the dominant values are religious, traditional incentives to perform in the wider public interest may not have much appeal.

Many LDC governments may also have civil service goals other than performance: to break up traditional elites, to nationalize the civil service, to conform to ideological correctness, to reflect or favor an ethnic ratio, or to include or exclude minorities. Most governments also are organized in the traditional hierarchical form. But some have experimented with negative hierarchy (from bottom to top), ad hocracy (temporary arrangements), and polyarchy (cooperation with outside organizations), this last being attempted particularly when some special form of expertise is involved.

Many LDC bureaucracies are overstaffed at the bottom and understaffed at the top. There is a chronic and desperate shortage of skilled competent managers capable of independent decision making. The greater the number of parastatal organizations set up—the more state-owned enterprises and nationalized industries, quasigovernmental bodies, development corporations, and training institutions—the thinner this layer of managers is spread.

In the case of nationalized industries, most experiments have been economically disastrous and have resulted in all kinds of strains within the central civil service. Personnel systems in the public service are usually not adequate for the increased management complexities of an industrial enterprise. So parallel personnel systems have been set up, multiplying the public service systems, draining skills, leading to disparities in terms and conditions of service, and resulting in manpower shortages and morale problems. Political considerations often affect the ability to recruit competent managers with special technical skills. In short, nationalization in many instances has often added to the financial burden of the government budget.

But whatever the organizational and political problems of public administration, the sheer difficulty of efficiently managing complex modern economic systems is often cited when referring to critical public policy issues in the developing world. A striking example of the administration problem is provided by the case of the Tazara railroad through Tanzania and Zambia.

The Tazara railway, giving Zambia access to the sea at Dar es Salaam, the capital of Tanzania, was built in less than five years by the Chinese and was formally opened in July 1976. In October 1978, President Kaunda of Zambia announced that effective immediately and despite UN sanctions, OAU pressures, and the civil war in Zimbabwe, he was reopening Zambia's border with Zimbabwe and resuming the interrupted rail link with the south. The reason was that massive administrative breakdowns had so impaired the functioning of the railway that it was threatening to strangle the entire Zambian economy.

In early 1978, the European Community had granted Zambia $8 million for fertilizer desperately needed by its ailing agricultural sector. The first consignments from the United States were unloaded at Dar es Salaam, where the railway was unable to handle them, and they were left in the open to rot. As the pileup increased, Tanzania was reported to have increased storage and demurrage charges by 1,000%. Zambia then ordered the fertilizer rerouted through Beira, Mozambique, whence it went by rail to the town of Moatize and then by road through Malawi and Zambia. After 60,000 tons had been transported, it became clear that Mozambique's railways and Zambia's transporters, already short of fuel and spare parts, could not cope. Shippers refused to take the remaining 90,000 tons to Dar es Salaam because of the congestion there. Zambia then suggested it go to Maputo, Mozambique, from which it could be carried by South African Railways through South Africa via Pretoria and Mafeking to Francistown, where an armada of small Zambian truckers would carry it across the Kazungulu ferry. By the end of September, Zambia had spent an extra $25,000 in transport costs, Maputo and Francistown were drowning in fertilizer, only 2,000 tons had arrived in Zambia, and the plowing season had begun. In addition, some 100,000 tons of Zambian copper was either awaiting transportation or trapped somewhere on the line. Further stockpiles at the mines reached 70,000 tons by early October, causing cash shortages to the copper companies, which do not get paid until the copper is on the high seas. Production was hampered by shortages of spare parts and lubricating oil, which were held up elsewhere.

In four years' time, Tanzania and Zambia would have to start repaying their $400 million debt to China. About 100 Chinese specialists were brought back to try to restore the line to working order; they saw little chance of its paying its way unless its administration was completely overhauled. More than half the locomotives were under repair. A quarter of the 2,100 freight cars were off the line at any one time. The accounting department wasn't getting the bills out, and the railway was owed millions of dollars. Without huge spending on new equipment and training programs, there was little possibility of Tazara handling a fraction of its capacity; even massive spending would not necessarily guarantee results.

This is a dramatic example of an administrative shortfall in one sector, unanticipated in any feasibility study or economic blueprint, the effects of which were felt not only in other sectors of the Zambian economy but also in neighboring states. It serves to illustrate the crucial importance of the administrative component in economic development—not only in relation to the particular project under consideration but also in relation to the functioning of the entire public and private economic system.

State-Owned Enterprises

Associated with the problems of public administration in developing countries have been the widespread activities of **state-owned enterprises (SOEs)**, public corporations owned and operated by the government. In addition to their traditionally dominant presence in utilities (gas, water, and electricity), transportation (railroads, airlines, and buses), and communications (telephone, telegraph, and postal services), SOEs have become active in such key sectors as large-scale manufacturing, construction, finance, services, natural resources, and agriculture. Sometimes they may dominate these sectors, particularly in the areas of natural resources and manufacturing.[32] Even though China dramatically reduced the number of state-owned enterprises, in 1995 SOEs still employed most of the nation's 170 million urban workers and produced almost 30% of its industrial output, despite the fact that 43% of them were operating at a loss. Little progress has been made since.

Overall, it is clear that SOEs have played a major role in the economies of developing nations, contributing an average 7% to 15% of their GDP. In addition, SOEs account for a substantial amount of investment in developing countries, contributing one-fifth of the 1995 gross domestic investment. SOEs also absorb substantial amounts of resources and in many cases impose a heavy fiscal burden on governments. For example, a study of 27 developing countries revealed that the net budgetary payments to nonfinancial SOEs averaged more than 3% of GDP. Current spending alone represented 1.4% of GDP. And SOEs were found to be major borrowers of foreign exchange, accounting for 28% of all developing-world eurocurrency borrowing in the 1980s. They also absorbed a large part of domestic credit, particularly in small countries; in Benin, Guinea, Mali, and Senegal, for example, over 40% of domestic credit was absorbed by SOEs.

Given the strategic role state-owned enterprises play in the economies of developing countries and their demands on scarce resources, it is important to understand the reasons for their creation and the measures that might be undertaken to improve their efficiency and to help them meet their economic and social objectives.

Some of the rationale for the creation of SOEs were suggested in Chapter 11. One is the persistence of monopoly power in many developing countries. Direct government control has been intended to ensure that prices are not set above the marginal costs of producing the output. Moreover, as was also mentioned, certain goods that have a high social benefit are usually provided at a price below their costs or even free; hence the private sector has no incentive to produce such goods, and the government must be responsible for their provision.

The second rationale for the creation of SOEs is capital formation, which is particularly important at the early stages of development, when private savings are very low. Investment in infrastructure at this point is crucial, to lay the groundwork for further investment. And SOEs remain important at later stages in industries that require massive funds.

The lack of private incentives to engage in promising economic activities because of factors such as uncertainty about the size of local markets, unreliable sources of supply, and the absence of technology and skilled labor is a third major rationale for creating public enterprises. LDC governments may also seek to expand employment and facilitate training of their labor force by engaging in public production. They may desire to increase export earnings by creating export industries, particularly those that might otherwise be unable to compete. For reasons of income distribution, the government may seek to locate enterprises in certain regions, particularly in backward economic areas where there are no private incentives for creating such economic activities.

Other reasons for the creation of SOEs include the desire of some LDC governments to gain national control over strategic sectors of the economy such as defense, over foreign-owned enterprises (MNCs) whose interests may not coincide with those of the country, or over key sectors for development purposes. Government involvement may also come about as a result of bankruptcy in a major private industry. Ideological motivations may be an additional factor in the creation of state-owned enterprises.

Improving the Performance of SOEs

Despite these arguments, SOEs have come under sustained attack for wasting resources. As already mentioned, SOEs make significant demands on government finance, as well as on domestic and foreign credit. In many cases, the level of these demands is related to low profitability and inefficiency. Although it is difficult to generalize across countries, data from the World Bank for state-owned enterprises in 24 developing countries revealed only a small operating surplus.[33] And once factors such as interest payments, subsidized input prices, and taxes and accumulated arrears were taken into account, SOEs in many of these countries showed a large deficit. Turkish enterprises averaged net losses equivalent to 3% of GDP. Mexican SOEs showed a net loss of 1.2% of GDP. A study of SOEs in four African countries (Ghana, Senegal, Tanzania, and Zambia) also revealed generally poor performance. Most SOEs in these countries failed to show a profit. Operating at a deficit, they proved to be a massive drain on government resources. There was also evidence that labor and capital productivity were generally lower than in the private sector. These African SOEs were also found to be less successful in generating employment as a result of their bias toward capital intensiveness.[34]

Several factors contribute to the overall poor performance of SOEs in terms of profitability and efficiency. Perhaps the most important is that SOEs differ from private firms in that they are expected to pursue both commercial and social goals. Providing goods at prices below costs in an effort to subsidize the public or hiring extra workers to meet national employment objectives inevitably reduces profitability. Another factor adversely affecting the profitability and efficiency of SOEs is the overcentralization of their decision making, which allows little flexibility for managers in the everyday operation of the firm. An additional problem is the bureaucratization of management; many decision makers are not accountable for their performance, and little incentive is provided for improved decision making. Further, despite the abundant labor supply and the employment mandate, access to capital at subsidized interest rates has often encouraged unnecessary capital intensiveness, as in the cases of the four African nations cited. Finally, in very corrupt regimes, SOEs have provided a "tunnel" through which public assets may be stolen.

For the most part, however, the problems that have plagued many LDC public corporations are not beyond solution. Two alternative options typically mentioned are reorganization with a greater bottom-line focus for the SOE and the transfer of ownership and control from the public to the private sector, a process known as **privatization**. In the former option, decentralizing decision making to allow for more flexibility and providing better incentives for managers could increase production efficiency. Providing capital at its market rate may eliminate the bias toward capital intensiveness.

Privatization: Theory and Experience

The second option, the privatization of state-owned enterprises in the production and financial sectors, hinges on the neoclassical hypothesis that private ownership brings greater efficiency and more rapid growth. During the 1980s and 1990s, privatization was actively promoted by major international bilateral (USAID) and multilateral agencies (World Bank, IMF). Many LDCs followed this advice, although the extent of their philosophical agreement, as opposed to the financial pressures exerted by these funding agencies, remains unclear. In addition to the belief that privatization improves efficiency, increases output, and lowers costs, proponents argue that it curbs the growth of government expenditure, raises cash to reduce public internal and external debt, and promotes individual initiative while rewarding entrepreneurship. Finally, supporters of privatization see it as a way to broaden the base of ownership and participation in the economy, thereby encouraging individuals to feel that they have a direct stake in the system.[35] Between 1980 and 1992, more than 15,000 enterprises were privatized throughout the world, more than 11,000 of them in the former East Germany after reunification. In the developing nations, the number of privatized companies amounted to 450 in Africa, 900 in Latin America, and approximately 180 in Asia. Mexico, Chile, and Argentina have led the movement in Latin America. Among low-income countries, the speed of privatization has been much more cautious, with the majority of transfers coming in small, low-value firms. In Latin America in the late 1990s, the pace of privatization slowed, as most of the best candidates had been sold off.

Privatization has apparently been successful in promoting greater efficiency and higher output, especially in high- and middle-income countries.[36] In poorer LDCs, the results are less clear, though some positive results have been obtained. However, even though detailed data are yet to be compiled, privatization is likely to increase the gap between rich and poor, due to the fact that privatized assets are being concentrated in the hands of small groups of local and international elites. For example, many sales of former state-owned enterprises in Latin America were conducted without competitive bidding, often at predetermined concessionary ("fire sale") prices; corruption was often alleged. A similar situation occurred in the midst of the 1997 Asian crisis when large-scale currency depreciations allowed foreign investors to buy up valuable local enterprises. As a result, small groups of well-connected investors, both domestic and foreign, were enriched by the process. And some privatization merely replaced public monopolies with private monopolies, thereby allowing a few individuals to reap the monopoly profits that formerly accrued to the state while hundreds of thousands of workers lost their jobs.

Privatization has also been resorted to as a quick fix for fiscal deficits, but when the easy candidates for privatization have been exhausted, LDC governments have often found that the fiscal problems have returned. Privatization therefore raises many complex issues. There are questions of feasibility, appropriate financing, the structure of legal and property rights, the role of competing elites and interest groups (e.g., public officials and bureaucrats versus domestic and foreign private business interests), and whether or not widespread privatization promotes or ultimately weakens existing dualistic economic, social, and political structures. It is not sufficient to claim that privatization can lead to higher profits, greater output, or even lower costs. For one thing, while financial performance of firms generally improves after privatization, comparable SOEs in the same country that are not privatized may show similar improvements, and a study of matched firms in Egypt provided evidence for this. But the key issue is whether such privatization better serves the long-run development interests of a nation by promoting a more sustainable and equitable pattern of economic and social progress; the evidence so far is less than compelling.[37] Nevertheless, there has been great momentum toward privatization throughout the contemporary developing world, and few new state-owned enterprises are currently being created. (The experiences of privatization in Poland and Chile are described in the case study at the end of this chapter.)

Military Expenditures and Economic Development

Significance and Economic Impact

One important area of fiscal expenditures not often discussed in the development literature is that of mounting military outlays. Military expenditures by developing countries have been rising very rapidly. In 2000, total military expenditures by de-

				Developing Countries' Percentage of World
TABLE 16.4	**Trends in Global Military Spending, 1960–2000 (billions of dollars)**			
Year	Developing Countries	Industrial Countries	World	Expenditures
1960	35	385	420	8.3
1970	75	545	620	12.1
1980	137	618	755	18.1
1990	123	762	885	13.9
1995	154	644	798	19.3
2000	200	527	727	27.5

Sources: United Nations Development Program, *Human Development Report, 1992* and *1997* (New York: Oxford University Press, 1992, 1997). Copyright © 1992, 1997 by the United Nations Development Program. Reprinted with the permission of Oxford University Press. 2000 data derived from the Stockholm International Peace Research Institute military expenditure database at http://www.sipri.org.

veloping countries amounted to about \$200 billion, accounting for some 27.5% of world military expenditures (Table 16.4).[38]

Table 16.5 shows the trend in military expenditures in constant dollars over the period 1994–2003. In this period, the share of military expenditures accounted for by developing country spending has risen from under 20% to almost 25% of the world total.

Table 16.6 presents the results of a 1997 UNDP study that found that developing countries spend a higher share of GDP on military and have larger military budgets in relation to health and education budgets than developed countries. Moreover, as seen in Table 16.7, some developing countries spend particularly lavishly on their militaries. In 2002, these high-military-burden developing countries spent more on average on the military than on education and health combined. In contrast, low-military-burden developing countries spend more than 12 times as much on health and education as on the military. Not surprisingly, there is a tendency, though not uniform, to find higher Human Development Index standing

TABLE 16.5	**World Military Expenditures, 1994–2003 (in billions of constant 2000 U.S. dollars)**									
	1994	1995	1996	1997	1998	1999	2000	2001	2002	2003
World total	742	709	693	699	693	699	727	743	792	879
Income group (GNI per capita, 2000)										
Low (≤\$755)	29.3	30.1	31.1	30.2	27.8	29.4	32.7	33.4	34.3	36.1
Lower middle (\$756–\$2,995)	58.6	51.3	52.0	54.3	54.6	58.0	66.8	75.6	82.0	90.9
Upper middle (\$2,996–\$9,265)	65.7	66.9	66.0	73.0	74.4	73.1	76.1	79.6	78.9	79.5
High (≥\$9,266)	589	561	544	541	536	538	551	555	597	672
Development state in 2000 according to *World Development Report, 2002*										
Developing world	147	147	149	156	158	159	173	188	194	203
Industrial world	595	562	544	542	535	540	554	558	600	618

Source: Stockholm International Peace Research Institute military expenditure database at http://www.sipri.org.

TABLE 16.6 Military and Social Expenditures in Developing and Industrial Countries, 1995		
	Military Expenditures (% of GDP)	Military Expenditures as a Percentage of Combined Education and Health Expenditures
All developing countries	3.1	63
Least developed countries	2.7	71
Sub-Saharan Africa	2.6	44
Industrialized countries	2.7	33
World	2.8	38

Source: United Nations Development Program, *Human Development Report, 1997* (New York: Oxford University Press, 1997), tab. 19. Copyright © 1997 by the United Nations Development Program. Reprinted with the permission of Oxford University Press.

than predicted by per capita income among the low-burden countries and worse than expected human development performance among the low-military-burden countries.

Not only has military spending risen in recent decades, but there has also been a shift in its composition, away from paying armies and toward the procurement of sophisticated weaponry. Developing countries now account for more than 75% of the world's arms exports purchases; countries in the Middle East and North Africa are the leading arms importers. A few developing countries have emerged as arms exporters, including Brazil (now the world's sixth-largest arms exporter), India, China, Argentina, Pakistan, and South Korea, although 80% of all arms exports are still supplied by the industrialized world.

Apart from its political implications, the military expansion in the developing world has stirred debate over the economic impact of military expenditures on developing countries, where resources are scarce and the opportunity costs of military spending may therefore be high. Supporters of military spending argue that such expenditures have a positive impact on economic growth as a result of the relatively large benefits of increased aggregate demand generated by military spending, the creation of employment and training opportunities, and the construction of basic infrastructure. It is argued that the opportunity costs of military spending are relatively smaller because the resources devoted to military consumption might otherwise go to private consumption, which contributes little to current economic growth. Furthermore, it is argued that military spending has a relatively smaller opportunity cost because the resources used for military purposes might not otherwise be available for public use, considering that such resources are often available only through foreign military aid and loans.

The major empirical work in support of this view was a study conducted by Emile Benoit, which found a positive correlation between military expenditure and economic growth for 44 developing countries over the early period 1950–1965.[39] The study concluded that countries with a heavy defense burden had the most rapid rates of growth, whereas those with the lowest defense burdens tended to have the lowest growth rates.

TABLE 16.7	Countries with the Highest and Lowest Expenditures on the Military, 2002 (percentage of GDP)		
Country	Education	Health	Military
Highest			
Eritrea	4.8	2.8	23.5
Oman	3.9	2.3	12.3
Saudi Arabia	9.5	4.2	9.8
Jordan	5.0	4.2	8.4
Burundi	3.4	1.6	7.6
Liberia	n.a.	n.a.	7.5
Yemen	10.0	n.a.	7.1
Syria	4.1	1.6	6.1
Ethiopia	4.8	1.8	5.2
Turkey	3.5	3.6	4.9
Average	4.9	2.8	9.7
Lowest			
Costa Rica	4.4	4.4	0.0
Mauritius	3.7	1.9	0.2
Moldova	4.0	2.9	0.4
Mexico	4.4	2.5	0.5
Ghana	4.1d	2.2	0.6
Guatemala	1.7	2.3	0.6
Cape Verde	4.4	1.8	0.7
Honduras	4.0	4.3	0.8
El Salvador	2.3	3.8	0.8
Georgia	n.a.	0.7	0.9
Average	3.7	2.9	0.5

Source: Stockholm International Peace Research Institute military expenditure database at http://www.sipri.org.
n.a. = not available.

However, the purported benefits of military spending seem considerably smaller and may in fact become very costly in cases where military demand is diverted to foreign supplies or results in a shift away from the production of wage goods; where an increase in military expenditure is compensated by a decrease in public spending; where military demand diverts scarce skilled workers from other industries; or where it fails to create appropriate infrastructure. The costs of military spending are likely to be high in terms of reduced levels of human capital formation and private investment and hence lower long-term economic growth. One can certainly build infrastructure with greater development benefits without orienting it to military needs.

Most recent empirical work supports this view that military spending has had a negative effect on economic growth. For example, David Lim examined the relationship between defense spending and economic growth for 54 developing countries and concluded that there is a negative correlation between military spending and economic growth rates in developing countries.[40] Similar results were obtained by Riccardo Faine, Patricia Annez, and Lance Taylor in a study of 69 countries.[41] An empirical study of 83 developing countries by Alfred Maizels and Machiko Nissanke clearly demonstrated that the impact of military spending on economic growth in developing countries has been unambiguously negative.[42] It has been suggested that the earlier Benoit study's findings that military spending and economic growth have a positive correlation could be spurious because high military spending was correlated with high foreign aid during the period examined. With the decline in foreign aid since the 1970s, it is argued, the relationship between military expenditure and economic growth has been reversed. Finally, military buildups often seem to lead to war, which, as the many recent wars in Africa clearly show, has devastating consequences for economic and social development. Whatever the reasons, it is now clear that high military expenditures are draining developing economies of scarce resources needed to finance long-term development efforts.

Policies to promote progress include the imposition of defense conditionality on development assistance to ensure that economic aid is not diverted to military uses, stricter arms export policies in supplier countries, increased economic aid to LDCs to promote economic prosperity and thus internal political stability, and the reallocation of resources in developing countries away from the military and toward human investment.[43] The United Nations Development Program put a concise and appropriate perspective on the issue when it stated, "If a government chooses to spend more on its army than on its people, it cannot be regarded as committed to human development."[44]

Chile and Poland
Privatization: What, When, and to Whom?

By the late 1980s, there was widespread agreement that there had been an imbalance in favor of too much public ownership in developing countries. The need for privatization poses some difficult questions: Who should be able to purchase state-owned enterprises (SOEs)? Whatever party has the most ready cash? Or should market imperfections in who is able to raise immediate capital be taken into account? Does it matter if the purchaser is a domestic citizen or a multinational corporation? Managers and workers in the company or citizens at large? Are some modes of privatization politically easier to carry out than others? Can creative approaches to arranging and financing ownership transfer agreements widen the possibilities? Can privatization be carried out in isolation from other programs, or does it have to be conceived as part of an integrated development strategy? Does privatization simply mean a long-overdue diminution of the government ownership role, or is it optimally implemented as part of a reorganized and renewed nonownership, public role in development?

Domestic entrepreneurs and foreign investors will continue to be the purchasers of the largest part of shares sold. Some post-Communist countries such as the Czech Republic and a number of other developing countries have used a voucher scheme that entitled citizens to bid on shares of companies that they believed would be successful. These vouchers were distributed to citizens at no charge to them. But some countries are privatizing a significant part of companies' shares to employees. Part of this new trend reflects direct market forces in a changing world economy, part reflects public policy decisions in the face of identified market failures, and part reflects a quest for political consensus, especially for privatization. Legislation was pioneered in Asia and Latin America before the widespread adoption in transition economies. By 1994, there were laws or regulations in 50 developing and transition economies providing incentives, as well as some limitations, for employee ownership (EO), often, but not exclusively, in privatization initiatives. These EO provisions are varied in nature and extent. They range from seeking to restrain employee ownership to modest levels, such as 10%, to encouraging employee ownership participation to as much as 100% of certain companies.

We will explore the questions and issues of privatization by examining the experiences of Chile and Poland, countries that are remarkably different in many respects. But their per capita income and human development rankings are very similar: Chile's 2000 gross national income per capita was $4,600, while Poland's was $4,200; in PPP terms, the figures were \$9,110 and \$9,030, respectively. The 2001 *Human Development Report* ranks Poland 38th in the world and Chile 39th. More important, these countries have had two of the most sweeping privatization experiences to date and serve to represent the two types of privatization experiences we may expect to see implemented in transition and developing countries. The experiences of Chile and Poland also serve to illustrate the complexity of the privatization process and the development issues it raises.

Chile

For historically complex reasons, Chile, which pioneered the privatization movement, is well positioned economically and socially for successful long-term growth. It has a strongly market-based economy in which government competently plays an active but targeted role in the areas in which it is most needed.

The privatization program in Chile has been the most far-reaching in the developing world. It is an integral part of a major socioeconomic and political transformation that began with the 1973 military coup that brought the Pinochet dictatorship to power. Chile has changed from an economy with pervasive government intervention in the early 1970s to one of the most open and most market-oriented economies of Latin America. Every market (except the labor market) was largely freed from government control. Over an 18-year period, some 550 firms employing 5% of the country's workforce were privatized.

Even under Pinochet, Chile was never purely laissez-faire. Some hidden subsidies and inducements remained, including a massive government rescue of the financial sector, amounting to 4.6% of GDP from 1982 to 1986. Many banks that had been privatized in the preceding years had to be renationalized in the 1982 financial crash. In privatization itself, subsidies were offered to the private sector through the sale of assets at little

more than half their real value. Fishing companies were privatized in the 1970s, but an extensive government role remained, including export-market development, technical assistance, and ecosystem regulation. Agriculture is the sector in which the lion's share of new nontraditional exports have been realized, especially in fruits. There the government has played an active role in assisting potential export sectors, providing infrastructure, developing markets, supporting research, and providing extension services to help realize higher productivity.

This represented a modest but successful sector policy and played an important part in the favorable growth performance since the late 1980s. But it remains unclear if policies for exports of fruit and other specialty farm and forest products centering around larger farms (*latifundios* and agribusiness) provide a sufficient development strategy for the longer term. Most farms are very small, and most seem to have benefited little, though it is interesting that in the sugarbeet sector, agribusinesses have found it in their interest to provide small farmers with a secure market and a source of credit and technical assistance.

Chile's now democratic government is continuing a broad commitment to market-oriented reforms but is also responding to the apparent need to expand the supporting government role with a renewed commitment to shared growth. Thus privatization has an important role to play in most developing countries but must be understood in context and does not succeed by simply banishing government from the economic scene.

Privatization in Chile proceeded over several overlapping stages. In 1974 and 1975, some 360 firms that had been nationalized in the early 1970s were returned to their previous owners; most of the rest of these were reprivatized by 1978. This was far easier to carry out than the privatizations of long-term SOEs. Of the 110 enterprises divested in 1975–1983, a large share were SOEs founded in the early 1970s. Many others were existing private companies in which that government had bought shares. From 1978 to 1981, privatization of social services took place; the government officially continued to provide social services only for the poorest groups and focused on subsidizing demand rather than supply. By 1981, public enterprises represented 24% of GDP, down from 39% in 1973.

Chile experienced rapid growth in the 1976–1981 period, following three years of severe recession. But this expansion had the earmarks of a speculative bubble, including wild stock speculation. After the bubble burst in 1982, stocks crashed (falling 36% in 1982 and an additional 33% in 1983); there was a huge wave of bankruptcies, including one-fifth of all manufacturing companies employing 50 workers or more; and unemployment reached 24%.

In 1983–1986, many enterprises "rescued" (nationalized) by Pinochet in the 1982–1983 financial crash were reprivatized. Eight of the 15 largest corporations in Chile were privatized in the 1980s.

The renewed growth of the late 1980s had a qualitatively different character, owing to more judicious regulation of the financial system and macroeconomic management. Since 1986, at least 30 large industrial enterprises that had been in state hands for a longer time were privatized, two examples being an electricity-generating company and a railway company in 1996.

Privatization from the mid-1980s on was achieved through public auction, negotiation, sales to pension funds, "popular capitalism" (to small investors), and "labor capitalism" (to employees). Sales of the latter two types represented about 20% of privatization. Even SOEs not slated for privatization were subject to major internal reorganization, with the result that efficiency and profitability increased.

Popular capitalism was intended to spread ownership among many small individual investors, in part to increase popularity and acceptance of privatization. To become eligible for generous discounts, participants had to be taxpayers with no back taxes owed. Two major banks, Banco de Chile and Banco de Santiago, were privatized under this plan.

Under labor capitalism, workers could acquire a percentage of shares in their own company up to the value of 50% of a worker's pension fund that could be received in advance for this purpose. Retirement funds could be used as collateral for below-market government loans to buy additional shares. At retirement, workers could elect to trade these shares back for the value of their pension fund, so this gave the workers an essentially riskless investment. About 21,000 workers, 35% of those eligible, took part; other shares purchased by groups of workers were organized as investment societies. Between 1985 and 1990, a total of 15 SOEs were sold using some employee-ownership, including three that became 100% employee-owned. Three others became 44%, 33%, and 31% employee-owned, respectively, and the remaining nine had an average of about 12% employee ownership. These privatizations have been remarkably successful; not only have productivity and share values risen substantially, but employment has risen too. It remains to be seen whether significant employee ownership will continue in these firms into the future or if workers will resell their shares and ownership will become more concentrated among outsider investors. But for now the evidence is that employees are working more conscientiously (e.g., taking better care of company equipment), and in some cases firms are allowing workers to use greater judgment on the job.

To date, the conventional wisdom that EO may decrease attractiveness to foreign investors has not been borne out. An example is the National Sugar Industry in Chile, privatized in 1986, in which workers hold 45% of the shares. Despite this, several foreign investors purchased good-sized minority shares, and it is a highly regarded investment. Many firms are familiar with employee stock ownership plans (ESOPs) and similar programs in their own countries and may have introduced ESOPs themselves or seen firms with which they are familiar do so.

Indicators are conflicting, and Chile's wild swings of expansion and contraction make an accurate assessment of long-term trends difficult. But it would appear that Chile today is in an excellent position to move toward maturity. The country first placed a strong emphasis on education and human development in the 1920s; superior conditions of basic education and health survived the dictatorship period, and Chile is enjoying the fruits of this long-term program today. Despite some errors of excess, for which a price was paid in the form of the financial crash, many of the modern market institutions that are the foundation of a developed economy have been successfully created. It is hoped that other countries can follow the constructive features of its example within the democratic process, with protection of human rights. The democratic government is wisely giving greater attention to concerns for equity, reversing the cutbacks in social spending of the Pinochet regime by expanding programs in education, basic health care, nutrition, housing, water, and sewage. Tax reform raised $1 billion for social projects and increased pay for schoolteachers. The government is also expanding public investment in other vital infrastructure such as roads, ports, and irrigation systems. The country has traveled a rocky road, but today the outlook for Chile's extensively privatized economy, supported where needed by a constructive government role, is very bright indeed.

Poland

Despite serious socioeconomic problems, Chile began privatization with well-established legal and accounting frameworks; fully functioning labor, capital, and product markets; and many formal and informal socioeco-nomic institutions that are taken for granted in market economies. But in Eastern Europe, these background institutions had been systematically suppressed under communism. The severity of the impact of this problem varied; countries adjacent to the wealthy economies of Europe (including Poland) were able to overcome this handicap much more readily than more distant countries, including those in Central Asia and the Caucasus as well as Russia, Ukraine, Belarus, Moldova, and elsewhere in southeastern Europe.

To get a market economy under way, in early 1990 the Polish government launched a five-part radical stabilization plan consisting of price deregulation, introduction of a convertible currency, wage controls, increased interest rates, and budget-balancing measures. This was followed in the second half of 1990 by intensive legislative and administrative efforts to prepare for across-the-board privatization. GDP in Poland fell drastically in the early transition to a market economy—11.6% in 1990—and unemployment reached high levels. The World Bank found that a significant part of the declines was attributable to collapse of Soviet–Eastern European trade agreements; while reorganizing its internal economy, Poland has had to reorder its external trading economy as well. But by the end of 1995, there were signs that the economic freefall had come to an end and per capita growth averaged 4.5% over the 1990–2000 period. In 2004, Poland joined the European union, all but guaranteeing the success of its current drive to development. The Polish privatization plan was adopted in the summer of 1990. The first step in privatizing state enterprises, "commercialization," often requires the approval of the relevant ministry, management, and employees to set up a joint-stock company that can be sold. The stock is valued independently, and workers are then allowed to purchase up to 20% of the stock at half price. In capital-intensive companies, a subsidy limit based on the prior year's wages in the company may be set, making somewhat less than 20% of the stock eligible. This is done to avoid overly concentrating these subsidies among a few lucky employees.

An alternative strategy that circumvented administrative procedures, applying mainly to smaller firms, is "privatization through liquidation." This procedure permitted leveraged buyouts that could include substantial employee and management ownership. The process is initiated when the firm's managing director and the employees' council (an elected representative body) commissions a "preprivatization financial analysis." If financial conditions appear favorable, the firm petitions the government ministry that had control over the company under the central-planning system, which offers an opinion on the merits of the analysis and suggests a strategy for privatization. The old SOE is abolished, and the new firm buys some assets but normally leases others back from the state. The value of these leased assets is determined at the time of reorganization and does not change over the life of the contract (even to adjust for inflation). This constitutes a substantial subsidy to the new owners.

But of some 250 companies representing about 10% of employment commercialized by mid-1992, only 10% were fully privatized. And only about 175 firms had self-privatized by mid-1992, by which time the government was considering a large-scale privatization plan that would organize several hundred companies representing about 10% of industrial employment into a kind of closed-end mutual fund. That plan stalled until 1997, when the government resumed plans to sell 513 small manufacturing, construction, and trading companies to the public. For the equivalent of $7 per voucher, Polish citizens could purchase shares of these companies through listed national investment funds on the Warsaw stock exchange.

The task of privatization in Eastern Europe by any means has been daunting, and the countries have few resources to spare. In the early 1990s, the Polish privatization ministry had only 200 employees. This compared with 3,500 in the Treuhandanstalt, in charge of privatization in the former East Germany.

Summary

Despite the limitations on devising an optimal plan for privatization and market development, the experiences of Chile and Poland strongly suggest that privatization is best not implemented as an isolated part of a development strategy but rather as part of a general program for market development. The benefits of privatization will not occur automatically. The role of the state in the economy becomes significantly modified but is certainly not eliminated. The supporting institutions of the market will have to grow and develop. The proper balance will not be easy to find.

It makes a difference under what conditions state ownership came into being. Privatization is easiest when state ownership resulted from a historical accident rather than as a systematic policy or as a result of specific selections of a few industries intended to play a specific role in the development process. A good example is Bangladesh, in which the large state-owned sector resulted from the abandonment of factories by Pakistanis fleeing during the civil war or shortly thereafter; Bangladesh has had one of the largest-scale privatization programs. Another example is Mexico, which incidentally acquired many bank-owned companies when banks were nationalized in the financial crisis of 1982. This has provided part of the basis for that country's systematic privatization program. Privatization is also easier when SOEs started as nationalizations, especially recent ones, as in the case of Chile's reprivatizations of the 1970s; when markets are already well developed; when there is a strong political will for privatization; and when ordinary employees and citizens perceive themselves to have a positive stake in privatization. All of these, factors apply to a large extent to Chile. Privatization is most difficult in post-communist countries more distant from the European Union, where none of these facilitating characteristics seem to have been present. ■

Sources

Bogetic, Zejlko and Michael Conte, "Privatizing East European economies: A critical review and proposal," World Bank Report No. IDP-119 (Washington, D.C.: World Bank, 1992).

Foxley, Alejandro, *Latin American Experiments in Neoconservative Economics* (Berkeley: University of California, 1983).

Gindling, Timothy H. and Donald Robbins, "Patterns and Sources of Changing Wage Inequality in Chile and Costa Rica during Structural Adjustment," *World Development* 29, No. 4, (2001): 725–745.

Inter-American Development Bank, Chile, *Socioeconomic Report, August 1991*.

Kandilov, Ivan, "Do Exporters Pay More? Plant-level Evidence from an Export Refund Policy in Chile," unpublished manuscript, Economics Department, University of Michigan, 2005.

Lee, Barbara, *Should Employee Participation Be Part of Privatization?* Policy, Research, and External Affairs Working Paper WPS 664 (Washington D.C.: World Bank, 1991).

Lipton, David and Jeffrey D. Sachs, "Privatization in Eastern Europe: The case of Poland," *Brookings Papers Economic Activity* 2 (1990): 293–341.

Megginson, William L. and Jeffry M. Netter, "From state to market: A survey of empirical studies on privatization," *Journal of Economic Literature* 39 (2001): 321–389.

Smith, Stephen C., Beom-Cheol Cin, and Milan Vodopevic, "Privatization incidence, ownership forms, and firm performance: Evidence from Slovenia," *Journal of Comparative Economics* 25 (1997): 158–179.

Smith, Stephen C., "On the law and economics of employee ownership in privatization in developing and transition economies," *Annals Public and Cooperative Economics* 65 (1994): 437–468.

World Bank, *Techniques of Privatization of State-Owned Enterprises*, World Bank Technical Paper No. 90 (Washington D.C.: World Bank, 1988).

World Bank, *World Development Reports, 1996, 1997,* and *2002*.

Concepts for Review

Central bank	Indirect taxes	Privatization
Currency board	Informal finance	Rationing
Currency substitution	Macroeconomic stabiliza-	Rotating savings and credit
Development banks	tion	associations
Direct taxes	Microfinance	State-owned enterprises
Financial liberalization	Monetary policy	(SOEs)
Financial repression	Money supply	Transparency
Group lending schemes	Organized money market	Unorganized money market

Questions for Discussion

1. Explain the distinction between organized and unorganized money markets. In the context of development priorities, what are the relative roles of central banks, commercial banks, development banks, and informal sources of credit such as the Grameen Rural Bank of Bangladesh?

2. What is meant by financial repression, financial liberalization, currency substitution, and unorganized money markets, and how do they relate to financial policy in developing countries?

3. List and briefly discuss the seven market failures that, according to Stiglitz, justify a strong government role in LDC financial sectors. Do you agree or disagree with this assessment? Explain.

4. What is meant by the terms *inflation* and *recession*? Is it possible for an economy to experience inflation and recession simultaneously? If so, can you explain how this could come about and give some recent examples? If not, explain why.

5. What are the principal sources of government revenues in LDCs? Why are many taxes so difficult to collect? Discuss.

6. In what ways do you think LDC taxation and expenditure systems could be improved? Be specific.

7. If the scarcity of administrative capabilities is a serious constraint on development policy implementation, what can LDCs do to relieve this constraint? What are the options? Discuss.

8. Summarize the arguments for and against the establishment of state-owned enterprises (SOEs) in developing nations. Do you think that SOEs should be encouraged or discouraged? What are the arguments for and against privatization of the public sector in developing countries? Explain your answer.

9. Is military expenditure a positive or negative force in economic development? Do you think that international financial and technical assistance should be accorded to LDCs that spend more on their military than on social and educational services? Explain your answer.

10. What are the pros and cons of encouraging the development of stock markets in LDCs?

Notes

1. Some of this discussion is adapted from Ross Levine and Sara Zervos, "Stock markets, banks, and economic growth," *American Economic Review* 88 (1998): 537–558. Other useful references include World Bank, *World Development Report, 1989: Finance and development* (New York: Oxford University Press, 1989); Rudiger Dornbusch and Alejandro Reynoso, "Financial factors in economic development," *American Economic Review* 79 (1989): 204–209; Panicos Demetriades and Khaled Hussein, "Does financial development cause economic growth? Time series evidence from 16 countries," *Journal of Development Economics* 51 (1996): 387–411; Robert G. King and Ross Levine, "Finance and growth: Schumpeter might be right," *Quarterly Journal of Economics* 108 (1993): 717–737; Joseph E. Stiglitz, Jaime Jaramillo-Vallejo, and Yung Chal Park, "The role of the state in financial markets," *Annual Conference on Development Economics* (1993 suppl.): 19–61; Nouriel Roubini and Xavier Sala-i-Martin, "Financial repression and economic growth," *Journal of Development Economics* 39 (1992): 5–30; Carlos Diaz-Alejandro, "Goodbye financial repression, hello financial crash," *Journal of Development Economics* 19 (1985): 1–24; J. D. Von Pishke, *Finance at the Frontier* (Washington, D.C.: World Bank, 1991); Ross Levine, "Financial development and economic growth: Views and agenda," *Journal of Economic Literature* 35 (1997): 688–726; Raymond Atje and Boyan Jovanovic, "Stock markets and development," *European Economic Review* 37 (1993): 632–640; and Jack D. Glen and Brian Pinto, "Debt or equity? How firms in developing countries choose," IFC Discussion Paper 22 (Washington, D.C.: World Bank, 1994). For "stages of growth" approaches to financial market development, see Hugh T. Patrick, "Financial Development and Economic Growth in Underdeveloped Countries," *Economic Development and Cultural Change* 14, no. 2. (1966): 174–189, and Felix Rioja and Neven Valev, "Finance and the Sources of Growth at Various Stages of Economic Development," *Economic Inquiry* 42, no. 1 (2004): 27–40.

2. Stiglitz, Jaramillo-Vallejo, and Park, "Role of the state."

3. For an excellent account of how stabilization and adjustment measures adversely affected the poor and vulnerable during the 1980s, see Frances Stewart, "The many faces of adjustment," *World Development* 19 (1991): 1847–1864.

4. Space limitations prevent us from analyzing the possible relevance for LDCs of some of the more recent macroeconomic models of developed countries, including rational expectations and supply-side economics. However, given their widespread criticism as developed-country theories, their applicability to LDCs is very remote indeed. For an attempt, however, see W. Max Corden, "The relevance for developing countries of recent developments in macroeconomic theory," *World Bank Research Observer* 2 (1987): 171–188.

5. See Maxwell F. Fry, *Money, Interest, and Banking in Economic Development* (Baltimore: Johns Hopkins University Press, 1988), and World Bank, *World Development Report, 1991* (New York: Oxford University Press, 1991). One of the earliest and best descriptions of the unorganized and fragmented nature of money markets in developing countries can be found in U Tun Wai, "Interest rates outside the organized money markets," *IMF Staff Papers* 6 (1957): 80–125. For a modern description of the

persistence of fragmented financial markets in Africa, see Ernest Aryeetey et al., "Financial market fragmentation and reform in Ghana, Malawi, Nigeria, and Tanzania," *World Bank Economic Review* 11 (1997): 195–218.

6. For a discussion of the phenomenon of currency substitution and the impact of unorganized money markets on the developing world, see International Monetary Fund, *World Economic Outlook, October 1997* (Washington, D.C.: International Monetary Fund, 1997), pp. 92–93; Steven L. Green, "Monetary policies in developing countries and the new monetary economics," *Journal of Economic Development* 11 (1986): 7–23; and Guillermo Ortiz, "Currency substitution in Mexico: The dollarization problem," *Journal of Money, Credit, and Banking* 15 (1983): 174–185.

7. For a discussion of privatization and the liberalization of financial markets in LDCs, see Laurence H. White, "Privatization of financial sectors," in *Privatization and Development,* ed. Steven H. Hanke (San Francisco: Institute for Contemporary Studies, 1987), pp. 149–160.

8. Charles Collyns, *Alternatives to the Central Bank in the Developing World,* IMF Occasional Paper No. 20 (Washington, D.C.: International Monetary Fund, 1983), p. 2. Much of the discussion that follows is based on this informative report.

9. Currency boards were common in the British colonial nations of Africa and Asia prior to independence. They typically issued domestic currency for foreign exchange and offered limited banking facilities to commercial banks. They could not create new money, conduct monetary policy, give policy advice, or supervise the banking system. They simply acted as agents for the colonial banks and were charged with the responsibility of maintaining a fixed parity with the colonial power's currency. A contemporary example of a currency-based system was found in Argentina, where the peso was until 2000 pegged one-for-one with the U.S. dollar and was fully backed in the monetary base with international reserves. When the board was established in 1990, the purpose was to reduce inflation by controlling the money supply. A strong dollar and fiscal irresponsibility led to its demise.

10. Collyns, *Alternatives to the Central Bank,* p. 21.

11. For an extensive discussion of how to improve the monetary control system and mobilize and better allocate domestic savings in LDCs, see Delano Villanueva, "Issues in financial sector reform," *Finance and Development* 25 (1988): 14–17.

12. For a review of the growth of informal finance in developing countries in the context of "consumption-smoothing" strategies, see Timothy Besley, "Nonmarket institutions for credit and risk sharing in low-income countries," *Journal of Economic Perspectives* 9 (1995): 115–127.

13. Siwan Anderson and Jean-Marie Baland, "The economics of ROSCAs and intra-household resource allocation," *Quarterly Journal of Economics* 111 (2002): 963–995.

14. For details on MFIs and how they work, see Beatriz Armendriz de Aghion and Jonathan Morduch, *The Economics of Microfinance* (Cambridge, Mass.: MIT Press, 2005); Marguerite S. Robinson, *The Microfinance Revolution: Sustainable Finance for the Poor* (Washington, D.C.: World Bank, 2001); Robert Peck Christen and Deborah Drake, *Commercialization: The New Reality of Microfinance?* (Bloomfield, Conn.: Ku-

marian Press, 2002); and Elisabeth H. Rhyne, *Mainstreaming Microfinance: How Lending to the Poor Began, Grew, and Came of Age in Bolivia* (Bloomfield, Conn.: Kumarian Press, 2001).

15. See, for example, Microcredit Summit Fulfillment Campaign, "The Microcredit Summit: Declaration and Plan of Action 1997," http://www.microcreditsummit.org/declaration.htm; Jonathan Morduch, "The microfinance promise," *Journal of Economic Literature* 37(1999): 1569–1614; and Jonathan Morduch, "The microfinance schism," *World Development* 28 (2000): 617–629.

16. Shahidur Khandker, Baqui Khalily, and Zahed Khan, *Grameen Bank: Performance and Sustainability* (Washington, D.C.: World Bank, 1995).

17. Better access to credit can have a positive effect on health and education. Statistical evidence shows that growth patterns for children in landless households have been influenced by sudden gains or losses of wealth among credit-constrained households. A 1989 UN study concluded that the harvest from an irrigated rice project in the Gambia reduced seasonal fluctuations in food availability and that this resulted in improved nutritional status of children. There is some evidence that lack of access to credit can result in lower school attendance and poorer educational outcomes. See Andrew Foster, "Prices, credit markets and child growth in low-income rural areas," *Economic Journal* 105 (1993): 551–570, and Hanan G. Jacoby, "Borrowing constraints and progress through school: Evidence from Peru," *Review of Economics and Statistics* 76 (1994): 151–160.

18. For an evaluation of programs integrating microcredit with health, see Stephen C. Smith, "Village banking and maternal child health: Evidence from Ecuador and Honduras," *World Development* 30 (2002): 707–723.

19. In addition to setting interest rate ceilings, developing-country governments have often intervened in their financial markets in a variety of other ways. These have included directed credit programs, high bank reserve requirements that effectively tax the financial system, and forced lending to the government to finance high budget deficits—for example, by requiring banks to hold low-yielding government bonds. These and other policies are linked to interest rate ceilings. In the presence of high and variable inflation and negative real interest rates, they not only lead to lower savings and growth but also can cause the entire banking system to contract. We are grateful to Professor Valerie Bencivenga for these observations.

20. The classic writings on financial repression and the positive impact of financial liberalization on saving and investment are Ronald L. McKinnon, *Money and Capital in Economic Development* (Washington, D.C.: Brookings Institution, 1973), and Edward S. Shaw, *Financial Deepening in Economic Development* (New York: Oxford University Press, 1973). For a classic critique of this approach, see Carlos Diaz-Alexandro, "Good-bye financial repression, hello financial crash," *Journal of Development Economics* 19 (1985): 1–24. For a more recent debate on the merits and limitations of financial liberalization in general and the McKinnon-Shaw thesis in particular, see articles by Maxwell Fry and Ajit Singh in *Economic Journal* 107 (1997): 754–782. See also Bruce Greenwald, "Institutional adjustments in the face of imperfect financial markets," in *Annual World Bank Conference on Development Economics, 1998* (Washington, D.C.: World Bank, 1999).

21. World Bank, *World Development Report, 1987* (New York: Oxford University Press, 1987), pp. 117–122. However, for transnational evidence that interest rate levels have little or no effect on saving and investment, see Deena R. Khatkhata, "Assessing the impact of interest rates in less developed countries," *World Development* 16 (1988): 577–588; Gerado M. Gonzales Arrieta, "Interest rates, savings and growth in LDCs: An assessment of recent empirical research," *World Development* 16 (1988): 589–606; and Rudiger Dornbusch, "Policies to move from stabilization to growth," *Proceedings of the World Bank Annual Conference on Development Economics, 1990* (Washington, D.C.: World Bank, 1990), pp. 36–41.

22. Joseph E. Stiglitz, Jaime Jaramillo-Vallejo, and Yung Chal Park, "The role of the state in financial markets," *Proceedings of the World Bank Annual Conference on Development Economics, 1993* (Washington, D.C.: World Bank, 1994), pp. 7–52.

23. Ibid., p. 20.

24. Atje and Jovanovic, "Stock markets and development"; Levine and Zervos, "Stock markets, banks, and economic growth."

25. For an excellent collection of articles and essays related to taxation and development, see Donald Newberry and Nicholas Stern (eds.), *The Theory of Taxation for Developing Countries* (New York: Oxford University Press, 1987). See also World Bank, *World Development Report, 1988* (New York: Oxford University Press, 1988), pt. 2; "Symposium on tax policy in developing countries," *World Bank Economic Review* 5 (1991): 459–574; and Robin Burgess and Nicholas Stern, "Taxation and development," *Journal of Economic Literature* 31 (1993): 762–830.

26. Vito Tanzi, "Quantitative characteristics of the tax systems of developing countries," in *The Theory of Taxation for Developing Countries,* ed. David Newbery and Nicholas Stern (New York: Oxford University Press, 1987), and Vito Tanzi and Howell H. Zee, "Tax policy for emerging markets: Developing countries," *National Tax Journal* 53(2000): 299–322.

27. Tanzi, "Quantitative characteristics."

28. See two papers by M. Shahe Emran and Joseph E. Stiglitz; "VAT versus trade taxes: The (in)efficiency of indirect tax reform in developing countries," mimeo, Stanford University and Brookings Institution, 2000, and "On selective indirect tax reform in developing countries," Stanford University, 2001, and the references therein.

29. Joel Slemrod, "Optimal taxation and optimal tax systems," *Journal of Economic Perspectives* 4 (1990): 157–178.

30. For an interesting analysis and evaluation of ways to reform tax administration, see Dilip Mookherjee, "Incentive reforms in developing country bureaucracies: Lessons from tax administration," *Annual World Bank Conference on Development Economics, 1997* (Washington, D.C.: World Bank, 1998), pp. 108–125.

31. For an overview of some key issues in public administration and development, see World Bank, *World Development Report, 1997: The State in a Changing World* (New York: Oxford University Press, 1997), and Derick W. Brinkerhoff and Benjamin Crosby, *Managing Policy Reform: Concepts and Tools for Decision-Makers in Developing and Transitioning Countries* (Bloomfield, Conn.: Kumarian Press, 2002). The journal *Public Administration and Development* is a good source for current contributions to this evolving literature.

32. See World Bank, *World Development Report, 1983* (New York: Oxford University Press, 1983), figs. 5.4 and 5.5.

33. Ibid., ch. 8. See also the discussion of SOEs in *World Development Report, 1988*, ch. 8. See also Luke Haggarty and Mary M. Shirley, "A New Data Base on State-Owned Enterprises," *World Bank Economic Review* 11, no. 3 (1997): 491–513.

34. Tony Killick, "The role of the public sector in the industrialization of African developing countries," *Industry and Development* 7 (1983): 57–88.

35. For a review of privatization in LDCs in the late 1980s and early 1990s, see Sunita Kikeri, John Nellis, and Mary Shirley, "Privatization: Lessons from market economies," *World Bank Research Observer* 9 (1994): 241–272.

36. Ibid., 249–253. See also World Bank, *World Development Report, 1997* (New York: Oxford University Press, 1997), ch. 4, and William Megginson and Jeffrey N. Netter, "From state to market: A survey of empirical studies on privatization," *Journal of Economic Literature* 39 (2001): 321–389.

37. See, for example, Tony Killick, *A Reaction Too Far: Economic Theory and the Role of the State in Developing Countries* (London: Overseas Development Institute, 1989); Paul P. Streeten's review of the Killick book in *Economic Development and Cultural Change* 39 (1991): 421–439; Robert Klitgaard, *Adjusting to Reality: Beyond "State versus Market" in Economic Development* (San Francisco: ICS Press, 1991); and United Nations Development Program, *Human Development Report, 1993* (New York: Oxford University Press, 1993), pp. 49–51. See also Mohammed Omran, "The Performance of State-Owned Enterprises and Newly Privatized Firms: Does Privatization Really Matter?" *World Development* 32, no. 6 (2004): 1019–1041.

38. For national and regional data on military expenditures, an excellent source is the Website of Stockholm International Peace Research Institute (SIPRI), http://projects.sipri.se/milex/mex_data_index.html.

39. Emile Benoit, "Growth and defense in developing countries," *Economic Development and Cultural Change* 26 (1978): 271–280.

40. David Lim, "Another look at growth and defense in less developed countries," *Economic Development and Cultural Change* 31 (1983): 377–384.

41. Riccardo Faine, Patricia Annez, and Lance Taylor, "Defense spending, economic structure, and growth: Evidence among countries and over time," *Economic Development and Cultural Change* 32 (1984): 487–498.

42. Alfred Maizels and Machiko Nissanke, "The determinants of military expenditures in developing countries," *World Development* 14 (1986): 1125–1140.

43. Robert McNamara, "The post-Cold War world: Implications for military expenditure in the developing countries," *Proceedings of the World Bank Annual Conference on Development Economics, 1991* (Washington, D.C.: World Bank, 1992), pp. 95–125. See also Tamin Bayoumi, Daniel Hewitt, and Steven Symansky, *The Impact of Worldwide Military Spending Cuts on Developing Countries,* (Washington, D.C.: International Monetary Fund, 1994).

44. United Nations Development Program, *Human Development Report, 1991* (New York: Oxford University Press, 1991), p. 83.

Further Reading

On monetary and taxation issues as they relate to developing countries, consult the following books and articles: Maxwell J. Fry, *Money, Interest, and Banking in Economic Development* (Baltimore: Johns Hopkins University Press, 1988); W. Max Corden, "The relevance for developing countries of recent developments in macroeconomic theory," *World Bank Research Observer* 2 (1987): 171–188; Ross Levine, "Financial development and economic growth," *Journal of Economic Literature* 35 (1997): 688–726; Alison Harwood and Bruce L. R. Smith (eds.), *Sequencing? Financial Strategies for Developing Countries* (Washington, D.C.: Brookings Institution, 1997); Steven L. Green, "Monetary policy in developing countries and the new monetary economics," *Journal of Economic Development* 11 (1986): 7–23; Ronald I. McKinnon, *Money and Capital in Economic Development* (Washington, D.C.: Brookings Institution, 1973); Delano Villanueva, "Issues in financial sector reform," *Finance and Development* 25 (1988): 14–17; Rudiger Dornbusch and Alejandro Reynoso, "Financial factors in economic development," *American Economic Review* 79 (1989): 204–209; Nouriel Roubini and Xavier Sala-i-Martin, "Financial repression and economic growth," *Journal of Development Economics* 39 (1992): 5–30; Valerie R. Bencivenga and Bruce D. Smith, "Deficits, inflation, and the banking system in developing countries: The optimal degree of financial repression," *Oxford Economic Papers* 44 (1992): 767–790; Robert G. King and Ross Levine, "Finance, entrepreneurship, and growth," *Journal of Monetary Economics* 32 (1993): 717–737; Donald Newberry and Nicholas Stern (eds.), *The Theory of Taxation for Developing Countries* (New York: Oxford University Press, 1987); Norman Gemmell, "Taxation and development," in *Surveys in Development Economics*, ed. Norman Gemmell (London: Blackwell, 1987), ch. 8; Richard M. Bird, "A new look at indirect taxation in developing countries," *World Development* 15 (1987): 1151–1181; and World Bank, *World Development Report, 1989* (New York: Oxford University Press, 1989). For an excellent overview of tax policy issues and their implications for developing countries, see Vito Tanzi and Howell H. Zee, "Tax policy for emerging markets: Developing countries," *National Tax Journal* 53(2000): 299–322.

An excellent introduction to the economics and politics of public policy in developing nations can be found in Tony Killick, *Policy Economics: A Text for Developing Countries* (London: Heinemann, 1981). For a review and a critique of the role of the state in development activities, see World Bank, *World Development Report, 1997* (New York: Oxford University Press, 1997), pp. 41–127; T. N. Srinivasan, "Neoclassical political economy, the state and economic development," *Asian Development Review* 3 (1985): 38–58; Mahmood A. Ayub and Sven O. Hegstad, "Management of public industrial enterprises," *World Bank Research Observer* 2 (1987): 79–101; and Stanislaw Wellisz and Ronald Findlay, "The state and the invisible hand," *World Bank Research Observer* 3 (1988): 59–80. For an excellent in-depth analysis of the theory and operations of microfinance institutions in developing countries, see Beatriz Armendriz de Aghion and Jonathan Morduch, *The Economics of Microfinance* (Cambridge, Mass.: MIT Press, 2005).

In addition to the articles on privatization cited in notes 35 and 36, consult Richard Hemming and Ali M. Manson, *Privatization and Public Enterprises*, IMF Occasional Paper No. 56 (Washington, D.C.: International Monetary Fund, 1988); George Yarrow, "Privatization in theory and practice," *Economic Policy*, 2(1986): 323–377; and Jonas Prager, "Is privatization a panacea for LDCs? Market failure versus public sector failure," *Journal of Developing Areas* 26 (1992): 301–322.

Readings on defense and development include Emile Benoit, *Defense and Economic Growth in Developing Countries* (Boston: Heath, 1973); Shuja Nawaz, "Economic impact of defense," *Finance and Development* 20 (1983): 34–35; Pradip K. Ghosh (ed.), *Disarmament and Development: A Global Perspective* (Westport, Conn.: Greenwood Press, 1984); Riccardo Faine, Patricia Annez, and Lance Taylor, "Defense spending, economic structure, and growth: Evidence among countries and over time," *Economic Development and Cultural Change* 32 (1984): 487–498; Alfred Maizels and Machiko Nissanke, "The determinants of military expenditures in developing countries," *World Development* 14 (1986): 1125–1140; United Nations Development Program, *Human Development Report, 1994* (New York: Oxford University Press, 1994), pp. 47–60; and Tamin Bayoumi, Daniel Hewitt, and Steven Symansky, *The Impact of Worldwide Military Spending Cuts on Developing Countries* (Washington, D.C.: International Monetary Fund, 1994).

CHAPTER SEVENTEEN

Some Critical Issues for the Twenty-First Century

Global Interdependence and the Growth of Developing-World Markets

We live in an increasingly interdependent world. For developing countries, dependence on rich nations remains a stark fact of economic life. It is the principal reason for their heightened interest in promoting greater individual and collective self-reliance. At the same time, the developed world, which once prided itself on its apparent economic self-sufficiency, has come to realize that in an age of dramatically increased capital flows, diminishing natural and mineral resources, global environmental threats, accelerated international migration, and burgeoning world trade in manufactures and services, it is becoming ever more economically dependent on the developing world.

However, rich-nation dependence does not center solely on the need for energy and raw material supplies or on the ability of key nations like Brazil, India, and China to control their environmental damage. It is also manifested in the importance of LDCs as markets for developed-country exports. The United States exported more than $206 billion worth of merchandise exports to developing countries in 2002. Even more striking, the United States now receives nearly $500 billion in merchandise imports from developing countries.[1] These figures represent an already significant share of exports and imports and one that will grow steadily larger during this century.

The economic progress of developing countries now has both a direct and an indirect impact on the economic performance of industrialized nations. In this final chapter, we examine some of the major manifestations of global interdependence by focusing on three key issues that are likely to dominate international economic prospects in the near future: the global environmental threat, the worsening poverty and economic crisis in sub-Saharan Africa, and the globalization of international trade and finance.

The Global Environment and the Developing World

In recent years, rapidly rising global concentrations of atmospheric pollutants have threatened to cause severe damage to the ozone layer as well as dramatic climatic changes such as global warming. To reduce the severity of these environmental threats, global emissions must be sharply curtailed. Responsibility for reducing emissions must be divided across the members of a tremendously diverse international community that may be remarkably different in terms of stage of industrial development, income, social structure, and political orientation. As a consequence, there is great controversy over the extent to which each government is obliged to control the emissions produced by its domestic population. But given the potentially devastating effects of **global warming**, it is of paramount importance that steps be taken to limit emissions of **greenhouse gases**.

Pollutants and Their Consequences for the Global Environment

The rapid rise in the production of pollutants has led to dramatic increases in the levels of a number of greenhouse and ozone-depleting gases. For example, global concentrations of carbon dioxide (CO_2) have increased by nearly 30% since the start of the industrial revolution, and more than half of this increase has occurred since 1960. Total gaseous chlorides, usually ozone-depleting chlorofluorocarbons (CFCs), increased in concentration by 114% in the mere 16 years between 1975 and 1990. The level of another important greenhouse gas, methane, has increased by 143% since the start of the industrial revolution, and almost 30% of this increase has occurred since 1970. Due to rising incomes and rapid population growth, buildup of these chemicals will accelerate in the future unless sweeping international reforms are implemented.

A study jointly sponsored by the World Meteorological Organization and the United Nations Environment Program predicts that if current emission trends continue, mean global temperatures are likely to rise 0.3°C per decade, or 3°C (5.4°F) by the end of this century. Due to the delayed impact of current emissions, the study found that to stabilize CO_2 and CFC concentrations at current levels, immediate reductions in emissions from human activities of over 60% would be required.

Most of the warmest years on record have occurred in the past twenty-five years, particularly the last decade. Scientists are aware that some pollutants may actually slow warming by deflecting ultraviolet light back into space, so it is a matter of controversy whether we are experiencing a permanent change or a temporary phenomenon. Though statistically there is little proof that what appears to be recent warming is a significant trend, a scientific consensus has emerged that global warming of dramatic proportions will occur in this century without concerted action to prevent it.[2]

MDC and LDC Contributions to Greenhouse Gases

The burning of fossil fuels by automobiles and industry are obvious sources of greenhouse gases; less obvious sources include deforestation, animal husbandry, wet rice cultivation, decomposition of waste, and coal mining. A number of gases, including CFCs, carbon dioxide, methane, sulfur dioxide, and nitrous oxides, contribute significantly to the stock of greenhouse gases. However, CO_2 has the greatest impact, due to its relatively long lifetime in the atmosphere and the massive quantities produced globally. Sources of CO_2 emissions may be decomposed into two broad categories: industrial production (77% of emissions) and all others. Developing countries, with roughly three-quarters of the world's population, produce only about one-third of industrial CO_2—about one-fifth if we exclude China. Because incomes and consumption are higher in the wealthiest countries, per capita emissions are also much higher. For example, the level of per capita emissions in the United States is more than twice that of the average European's, 19 times higher than the average African's, and 23 times higher than the average Indian's.

By 2000, middle-income developing countries, which now include China, were responsible for roughly the same quantity of emissions as the developed countries, whereas in 1980 they produced only about half as much. In addition, the emissions from low-income countries are also growing fast. On a per capita basis, high-income countries, which include many fewer people, emit substantially more than the middle-income LDCs. On the other hand, emissions per unit of production are now lower in developed countries than in either middle- or low-income LDCs. Improvements in this type of environmental efficiency of production will have to be accelerated even more, however, to compensate for the increased emissions that result from economic growth. Despite the dramatic improvement in the developed-country emissions per dollar of GDP, total emissions still rose.[3]

Though developing countries still account for a relatively small proportion of industrial CO_2, they produce virtually all of the CO_2 in the second category, generally resulting from the burning of vegetation to clear new land. These emissions from "land use change" are calculated under the assumption that the CO_2 in vegetation is released into the atmosphere upon its removal. It is estimated that deforestation accounts for roughly 25% of all CO_2 emissions worldwide. Of potentially equal or greater significance is the fact that deforestation leads to the destruction of a vital source of atmospheric oxygen. Because trees consume carbon dioxide and release oxygen during the process of photosynthesis, the tropical rain forests represent an important mechanism through which the ecosystem regenerates itself. Clearing the rain forests will reduce the **absorptive capacity** of the environment for CO_2. Thus it is through changes in patterns of land use that the developing countries currently make their largest contribution to global concentrations of greenhouse gases. This fact has served to intensify pressures on LDC governments to limit the destruction of rain forests. In addition, accelerating extinctions pose a dangerous threat to **biodiversity**, with an estimated 12% of the world's bird species, 24% of mammal species, and 30% of fish species vulnerable or in immediate danger of extinction.[4] Although preserving forests and their fauna might be in everyone's long-term interests, in the short term a number of international and domestic economic factors make it difficult to do so.

One factor has been falling commodity prices and the need for foreign exchange. The bulk of the remaining rain forests are coincidentally located in a number of the most heavily indebted countries, whose export earnings have suffered greatly as a result of low commodity prices. To raise sufficient foreign exchange to meet debt-service requirements, these countries have been increasing commodity exports at a time when demand is slack and market values are low. Because the price elasticity of demand for LDC commodities is also generally quite low, attempts to expand international sales further depress commodity prices, confounding efforts to raise sufficient foreign exchange. Because timber exports are an important source of revenue for a number of highly indebted countries, falling terms of trade may actually increase the rate of extraction and force prices far below the true social value of standing forests.

Furthermore, falling commodity prices threaten the profitability of many export industries. As a result, LDC governments desperate for foreign exchange have frequently subsidized the production of exports. Occasionally these schemes have done tremendous damage to the environment while generating large losses for domestic governments, as is the case for many publicly subsidized cattle farms and timber concessions. It is unclear whether rising commodity prices in 2003 and 2004 augur a change in the long-term trend.

A second complicating factor has been widespread poverty and landlessness among farmers. Even though rain forest soils have only marginal cultivability, they represent the sole livelihood for many of the rural poor. Thus efforts to prohibit the clearing of rain forest land for agricultural use are likely to fail unless governments demonstrate a commitment to bring about land reform and create alternative rural economic opportunities.

By providing additional land, though marginal and only temporarily cultivable, the rain forests may stave off political confrontations that might otherwise precipitate reforms. A number of LDC governments have encouraged the cultivation of tropical forests through the transfer of land titles to the people clearing the property or by actively moving households from impoverished rural and urban areas through resettlement or transmigration programs. These policies may provide a short-run alternative to pursuing costly but more fundamental development reforms, expecially land reform. Though the latter are more desirable from a long-term perspective, officials experiencing acute revenue shortages and pressures to reduce government spending may be unwilling or unable to implement development-oriented programs. Resettlement is also politically easier because any successful long-term solution to the problems of landlessness and poverty generally requires some type of land reform, inevitably resisted by large landowners.

A third impediment to saving the forests is the developing world's dependence on traditional fuels. The vast majority of wood cut is used for home heating and cooking. Timber accounts for almost 90% of all fuel in sub-Saharan Africa and over two-thirds in South America and Asia. For the poorer, non-oil-exporting LDCs, traditional fuels are the predominant source of energy. Banning the use of timber for firewood would lead to an increase in expensive foreign imports of fossil fuels. A transition away from traditional fuels would increase foreign-exchange outflows and necessitate that low-priced alternative fuels be made readily available to small family farmers who depend on the forests for their daily energy needs.

Rain Forest Preservation as a Public Good: Who Should Pay?

Each of these problems must be addressed in order to halt permanent destruction of rain forests. Long-term solutions will involve increasing the accessibility of alternative fuels, managing sustainable timber schemes, and providing economic opportunities for impoverished peoples now resorting to clearing large tracts of fragile rain forest land. Each program will require careful planning, technical expertise, and sustained management. Like most investments designed to yield enduring rewards, initial outlays are likely to exceed short-term gains. Thus preservation of the remaining rain forests will, at least temporarily, intensify existing hardships, unless revenue shortfalls are met with external funds.

In our discussion of public goods in Chapter 10, we found that in the absence of government intervention, the free market is likely to provide a suboptimal level of resource preservation (see Figure 10.3). We can thus conclude that when foreign countries are allowed a free ride—that is, if they are allowed to benefit from rain forest preservation without contributing to it—deforestation will continue at an undesirable pace. To reduce the resulting inefficiencies, the model would suggest lowering the relative price per unit of protected forest for the LDC and increasing it for the outside beneficiaries. For the latter, this would simply entail the contribution of fees earmarked for the preservation of rain forests. For LDCs, there are a number of ways in which the price of forest conservation can be lowered.[5]

One would be improved efficiency of existing rain forest use. Much of the timber that is now burned to open land for cultivation could be harvested for financial gain. For example, it was estimated that in the 1990s Brazil lost some $2.5 billion annually in the burning of precious rain forest timber. Sustainable timber production for fuel or export can be achieved through the restriction of cutting cycles to 30-year intervals and the careful maintenance of new growth. It is generally impossible to regenerate a rain forest that has been clear-cut, so proper maintenance and supervision of logging are necessary. More careful oversight of timber concessions by LDC governments can prevent clear-cutting, reduce careless destruction of uncut trees, and increase the efficiency of revenue collection from concessions that are usually owned by domestic elites or large multinationals. A number of management projects of this sort, supported by multilateral development banks, are already under way. However, as yet less than 0.1% of tropical forests are sustainably managed.

Another boon to forest conservation would be development of markets for alternative rain forest products. Some of the costs of rain forest preservation can be offset by developing markets for sustainable forest products. Recent studies have indicated that the sale of products such as nuts, fruits, oils, sweeteners, resins, tannins, fibers, construction materials, and medicinal compounds may provide a more lucrative and sustainable stream of income from tropical forests. Because their extraction is labor-intensive, more jobs are created for local populations, in turn creating alternatives to slash-and-burn cultivation of rain forest land. In addition, there is a broader distribution of the benefits from natural resources. However, for such schemes to succeed, developed-country markets must be made accessible to developing-country producers. By opening their own markets to nontimber LDC exports and alternative rain forest products, developed countries can reduce the dependence of timber-rich, capital-poor countries on the destruction of their forests for quick earnings of foreign exchange.

Debt relief would also help. Because the shortage of foreign exchange is greatly exacerbated by external debt burdens, some form of debt relief will be necessary to reduce dependence on the exploitation of remaining forests. This is especially important in sub-Saharan Africa. Debt-for-nature swaps effectively convert foreign-denominated debt held by a foreign public or private agency into domestic debt that is used to finance the management of natural resources. This debt may be tied to the preservation of forests, and interest payments may be used to provide salaries and maintenance costs for conservation efforts. Though debt-for-nature swaps offer a promising approach to reducing rain forest destruction, there are many obstacles to their widespread use (see Chapter 10). Consequently, the area of land now protected by the schemes is still very small. International carbon sequestration payments are likely to play a critically important role in coming years along with biodiversity facilities.

Finally, forests could be saved through appropriate aid packages. Expanded aid from the rich countries for the support of programs to alleviate landlessness and poverty can help eliminate the socioeconomic causes of tropical deforestation. Timber rights can also be purchased by national and international agencies, and indigenous communities can be paid to monitor forest preservation, as proposed by Conservation International, an NGO.

Searching for Solutions: The 1992, 1997, and 2002 Summits

In June 1992, the second United Nations Conference on Environment and Development (UNCED)—the so-called **Earth Summit**—was held in Rio de Janeiro. (The first meeting had been held in Stockholm in 1972.) The Rio meeting brought together the leaders of 118 industrial and developing nations, along with hundreds of environmental NGOs and tens of thousands of concerned individuals. The task was to find ways to cope with the increasing dangers of permanent environmental damage resulting from the buildup of greenhouse gases (especially CO_2) leading to fears of global warming, the inexorable loss of biodiversity resulting in part from the destruction of tropical rain forests, and the concerns over the environmental consequences of rapid population and industrial growth in the developing world.

Although the vast majority of global environmental damage represents the cumulative and contemporary impact of Western industrialization, the focus of much of the Rio conference was on the developing world. With rapid population growth and major rural-to-urban population shifts under way, the developing world has the potential to greatly worsen current environmental degradation. The principal concern of the developed world (often unexpressed) was that successful economic growth in the heavily populated developing world could bring with it such negative environmental externalities to the **global commons** that everyone would ultimately suffer, rich and poor alike. Representatives of developing nations feared that they would be coerced into bearing the major burdens of adjustment. However, unlike the 1980s debt crisis, when LDCs had to bear almost all of the pain of IMF and World Bank stabilization and adjustment programs, in the case of the environment, developed-country lifestyles could be directly affected by LDC policy decisions. Such environmental interdependence allowed LDCs successfully to press their demands for more international financial and technical assistance to enable them to pursue environmentally sustainable development objectives. Although the major donor nation, the United States, made no specific additional aid commitments at the Rio conference, the European Union countries and Japan indicated a willingness to substantially increase funding. In addition, a developed-country donor group (including the United States) decided to create a new fund for the World Bank's International Development Agency (IDA) that would provide low-interest environmental loans to the world's least developed nations. Finally, the North agreed to double, and perhaps eventually triple, the $1.3 billion World Bank's Global Environment Facility (GEF), established in 1989 to finance LDC environmental projects.

The Rio summit also produced **Agenda 21**, a nonbinding 800-page blueprint to clean up the global environment and encourage environmentally sound development. Adopted by consensus, Agenda 21 emphasizes the following six areas of international activity:[6]

1. Allocating development assistance to programs focusing on poverty alleviation and environmental health such as providing sanitation and clean water, reducing indoor air pollution resulting from the burning of firewood, and meeting basic needs

2. Investing in research and extension services to reduce soil erosion and permit more environmentally sensitive agricultural practices

3. Allocating more resources to family planning and to expanding educational and job opportunities for women so that population growth can be reduced

4. Supporting LDC governments in their attempts to curtail or modify projects that harm the environment

5. Providing funds to protect natural habitats and biodiversity

6. Investing in research and development on noncarbon energy alternatives to respond to climate changes and reduce greenhouse gases

The Philippines' Agenda 21 plan is described in the case study in Chapter 10.

A follow-up to the Rio summit was held in Kyoto, Japan, in December 1997. The Kyoto summit focused on carbon dioxide emissions and the problem of global warming. A treaty was introduced that asked Western nations to reduce their greenhouse gases to pre-1990 levels by the year 2010. Developing countries did not agree to do anything, even though they will soon pass the West as sources of greenhouse gases. China, the second biggest polluter in the world, denounced the entire proceeding and would not sign the accord.

However, in November 2001, representatives of 180 countries agreed on methods to enforce the Kyoto accord. Essentially every country in the world except the United States participated in the agreement on ways to ensure compliance with the Kyoto treaty. The agreement calls on the industrial countries to reduce greenhouse gases, especially carbon dioxide from industry and cars. Each country must reduce emissions by an average of 5.2% below 1990 levels by 2012. International observers will monitor compliance, and penalties will be imposed on countries that fail to achieve their targets. The United States complained that, among other things, 1990 was a base year that was particularly unfair to its interests. Although some of the objections were broader, this complaint at least suggests that U.S. involvement may be achieved with additional negotiations at some point in the future. The treaty went formally into effect in 2004, when the threshold for ratification was achieved following Russia's signing on. The United States' failure to participate is an extremely serious problem for the future of sustainable development. For details, go to http://www.unfcc.int.

Analysts predict that global environmental concerns will continue to increase throughout the century. Even if the new treaty is enforced and the United States agrees to participate, total global emissions of carbon dioxide will still increase by some 1.5 billion tons per year by 2010. If the accord is not enforced, research suggests that global warming could become dangerous as early as 2050. Other environmental crises, such as rapid destruction of ocean ecosystems, are also looming.

With the focus shifting from simple economic growth to sustainable development and with worries mounting that the pattern and style of LDC development could lead to serious problems for the industrialized world, a new and more permanent form of global interdependence has emerged, in which LDC leverage on international economic and political decisions is greater than at any time since the OPEC oil price increases of the 1970s. It is hoped that the common interest of all nations in a cleaner and more livable world will generate a new spirit of cooperation between rich and poor countries. Developing countries must be allowed to pursue their primary objective of raising the levels of living of their rural and urban poor, while both rich and poor nations alike must make every effort to reduce the damage that each causes to the earth's common heritage of land, sea, and air.

A major follow-up conference stressing these themes was held in Johannesburg in 2002—details may be found at http://www.johannesburgsummit2002.org.

The Crisis in Sub-Saharan Africa

In recent years, international concern over extreme poverty has moved near the top of the world agenda for the first time since the 1970s—and this has focused attention on the plight of Africa. Although most of the developing world registered significant development progress after 1990, the sad exception is sub-Saharan Africa. There, the "lost decade of the 1990s" has been added to the preceding "lost decade of the 1980s," which had also afflicted most of Latin America and many other developing countries. By 2005, no clear sign of a turnaround had yet been seen. There have been two recent successes in Africa—Mauritus and Botswana (see the case study in Chapter 15), but they are rare exceptions.

At the heart of the African dilemma is an inexorable economic decline, a drop in per capita incomes, rapid increases in population, the loss of export revenues, the curtailment of foreign investment, the destruction of fragile ecosystems, war and civil strife, and the inability of many countries to feed their people and meet other basic human needs.[7] Between 1980 and 1990, per capita output fell by 42.5%, per capita consumption (a more significant measure of human well-being) fell by 40%, domestic investment declined by 29.7%, exports fell by 34.5%, per capita food production dropped by 12.2%, and the total external debt rose by 162% to a level as large as the region's total GNI![8]

After such a calamitous decade, many Africans hoped desperately for a turn-around; outside observers widely predicted that the 1990s would bring renewed development. While signs of renewal appeared for a time, and the experience was not as bad as that of the 1980s, hopes have dimmed. Between 1990 and 2000, GDP rose at a rate of 2.4% per year. But with population growth continuing at an extremely high average annual rate of 2.6%, output per person continued to fall, and with it personal incomes.

Africa's poverty rate rose to more than 46%, or 291 million people. In contrast, poverty has fallen in South Asia, once considered the most impoverished region.

From a global perspective, sub-Saharan Africa has fallen steadily behind the rest of the world. Its share of global GNI dropped from about 2% in 1960 to 1% in 2000, even though it has 11% of the world's population. In the 15 years between 1985 and 2000, its real GDP growth rate consistently lagged behind Asia and Latin America. Its share of global trade fell from 3.8% in 1970 to less than 1.5% in 2000. Steep drops in commodity prices cost the continent more than $80 billion in lost export earnings in 1985–1994 alone. Its share of LDC private direct investment dropped from 25% in 1970 to 4% in 2000.

It is in the social and human realms, however, where the toll of Africa's current crisis is most acutely felt. Severe cuts in health and educational expenditures in the 1980s—in part due to IMF and World Bank lending preconditions—resulted in sharp declines in school enrollment and disturbing increases in malnutrition and maternal and child mortality. For example, by 2003, there were over 200 million severely malnourished people in Africa. The under-age-5 mortality rate in 2002 was the highest in the world at 174 per 1,000. The saddest and most disturbing health phenomenon to hit Africa was the enormous impact of the spread in the 1990s of the **human immunodeficiency virus (HIV)**, which causes **acquired immunodeficiency syndrome** (**AIDS**), as described in Chapter 9.

The causes of the African dilemma are many and varied. Some were beyond its control (drought, depressed commodity prices, foreign capital withdrawal, diminished foreign aid); others can be ascribed to poor government policies (neglect of agriculture, inefficient state-owned enterprises, lack of concern with promoting export growth). Rapid population growth, the highest in the world, must be also considered. Whatever the causes, if the disasters of recent decades are not to be repeated, coordinated efforts by African governments and international assistance agencies will be required to reverse the decline. More emphasis must be placed on agricultural and rural development, with enhanced price and investment incentives for small farmers being accompanied by institutional and structural reforms designed to improve the marketing and distribution of agricultural produce. Concern with preventing further environmental deterioration and desertification must be increased. Inefficient SOEs and ossified public-sector bureaucratic procedures must be addressed, and managers must be made more accountable for resource allocation and investment decisions.[9] The draconian cuts in health and educational expenditures during the 1980s and 1990s are finally being reversed, but more financial resources (both public and private) must flow back to African nations. Observers such as Jeffrey Sachs of the Earth Institute at Columbia University have argued that the resources to be made available under the enhanced HIPC (highly indebted poor countries) World Bank–IMF initiative are far too small and have too many strings attached (see Chapter 14).

A difficult period lies ahead for sub-Saharan Africa. On the positive side, many African countries were beginning to stem the decline in the early years of this century, and some were beginning to show accelerating economic growth. However, famine affected southern Africa and countries such as Ethiopia. If development is going to succeed, Africa will be its severest test case. If it fails, not only will the nearly 700 million Africans south of the Sahara be its victims, but directly and indirectly, the wealthy nations of the industrialized world will have to bear a major moral responsibility for this failure, as well as share its health and environmental consequences.

Fortunately, OECD governments and international agencies have been reawakening in recent years to the moral and political urgency of action to end extreme poverty in Africa and elsewhere. Poverty eradication headed the agenda of the G-7 summit in Britain in 2005 as it did for the five-year review of the Millennium Development Goals. The test will be whether the wealthy countries are prepared to match their newly high-minded rhetoric with commensurate resources.[10]

Globalization and International Financial Reform

In recent years, a remarkable **globalization** of the world economy has taken place.[11] The increasing integration of national economies into global markets promises to alter dramatically the volume and character of international resource flows. Because the expansion of global trade is essentially constrained by the domestic and international banking sector, which provides financing for international transactions, the increasing size, competitiveness, and diffusion of international financial markets has the potential to draw low-income economies into the economic mainstream. For developing countries experiencing severe liquidity problems that constrain investment, limit the importation of inputs and replacement parts, and raise the level of risk associated with trade contracts, increased integration into expanding international financial markets could greatly improve prospects for economic flexibility and growth.

However, it is unclear how much low- and middle-income LDCs will benefit from the globalization of international markets. For a variety of reasons, the full participation of many poor nations in the global economy is yet to be realized.[12] At a time when national markets are opening up, it is ironic that some global financial markets remain restricted. In fact, despite the 1994 GATT agreement and creation of the WTO, protectionism against LDC products has greatly increased, and the real rate of interest paid by developing countries on borrowed capital is on occasion more than four times greater than that paid by their industrialized counterparts. The globalization of international financial markets thus reduces the transaction costs of trade for participants with access to international credit while increasing the relative disadvantage of those excluded from the benefits of financial globalization.

But even in cases where developing countries are directly involved in the physical, technological, and financial globalization process, the implications for long-term development are ambiguous. Money and information can now be instantly transmitted from one corner of the earth to another. Multinational corporations are creating **global factories** with both horizontal and vertical integration spread over many countries. And a small group of newly industrializing countries in East Asia, now expanded to include China, has captured the lion's share of LDC international flows of goods and services. The end of the Multi-fiber Agreement in 2005 was widely predicted to lead to further concentrations of manufactured exports from China.

The effects of such globalization are threefold. First, the power and influence of individual nation-states, particularly many of those in the developing world, is weakened. LDCs that are not linked in some way to the new dollar-, yen-, or euro-dominated regional trading blocs in North America, the Pacific Rim, or Europe, respectively, face particularly difficult times ahead. Second, there are increased risks of financial market instability (as evidenced by the Mexican crisis of 1995, the Asian crisis of 1997, and the crises in Turkey and Argentina in 2001), access to global markets may become more difficult for low-technology producers, and the effects of economic growth in the North may no longer automatically benefit the poorest nations of the South. Indeed, the nature of past North-South relationships may have hindered the performance of many LDCs in the international arena. Third, a striking manifestation of the growing inequality of nations in an era of rapid global transmission of information via satellite is the tremendous increase in international *illegal* migration from the poor South to the industrialized North. Just as capital has become more internationally mobile, so has labor. But unlike the movement of capital, the movement of unskilled Southern labor across Northern borders is not always a welcomed occurrence. In fact, some citizens of the industrialized world view this phenomenon as a threat to their economy, not to mention their culture and "way of life."[13] As a result, "human smuggling" has taken a terrible toll in lives lost and other suffering at the hands of corrupt profiteers.

If the twenty-first century is to hold greater promise for the many LDCs that have been unable to share in the fruits of global progress, effective management of new global challenges—in money and finance, in environmental matters, and in resource, labor, and technology flows—will require reforms to the international system. Among the changes often mentioned are the following:[14]

1. A reduction in the debt-service burdens of the LDCs least able to afford continued austerity measures, especially in sub-Saharan Africa.

2. The creation of new LDC-funding sources, such as a tax on international currency transactions like the so-called Tobin tax[15] to curb the speculative inflow and outflow of foreign capital—a central ingredient in the 1997 Asian currency crisis. Another suggested measure is to adopt something like the current successful policy of Chile requiring portfolio investors to deposit 30% of their investments in a one-year (or longer-term) interest-free account with no withdrawal privileges. This policy has spared Chile the "hot money" flows experienced by Asian and other Latin American nations.

3. Creation of a formal "national bankruptcy" procedure for over-indebted countries.

4. Reform of the two major existing institutions for global economic growth and stability, the IMF and the World Bank.

Regarding this last point, the IMF will need to exhibit greater flexibility in its conditionality requirements and focus more on reviving growth in debt-laden countries and less on imposing a fixed menu of stabilization measures. Developing countries need a greater voice in its voting structure and policymaking bodies.

The World Bank, like the IMF, adopted an inflexible program of structural adjustment loans in the 1980s that on balance may have done more harm than good to many poor countries. The Bank, which was established to borrow the savings of rich nations and lend them to poor countries to finance many of those projects (physical infrastructure, health and education facilities, etc.) that private investors would not undertake, has in some years actually *withdrawn* resources (in excess of $500 million in the early 1990s) from poor nations. Outflows have increased in recent years, but only modestly.

In its 2000 report, the International Financial Institutions Advisory Commission (IFIAC) of the U.S. Congress concluded that the IMF, World Bank, and the regional development banks needed thoroughgoing reform. The commission voted unanimously that the IMF, World Bank, and regional development banks "should write off in their entirety all claims against heavily indebted poor countries that implement an effective economic and social development strategy in conjunction with the World Bank and the regional development institutions." They proposed that the World Bank be transformed into a development agency, charged with making grants to low-income countries rather than loans. This would enable the World Bank to concentrate its knowledge on development activities rather than on loan repayment. These conclusions have been highly controversial. For example, it is argued that while middle-income countries generally have the resources to address absolute poverty, because of the nature of the political process this does not happen without outside funding in the form of World Bank loans. (For more details on the World Bank and the IFIAC proposals, see Appendix 14.1.)

After an almost messianic mission of preaching market-oriented stabilization and structural adjustment reforms, both the IMF and especially the World Bank have once again begun to focus on poverty alleviation and adopted greater flexibility in their programmatic activities. The challenge for the future is to increase their flow of resources from North to South and to adapt their lending to the real development needs of recipient nations. These reforms would help ensure that the developing world becomes integrated into global markets and that it benefits from expanding world trade.

Concluding Remarks

Our discussion in this final chapter has touched on some of the key economic and noneconomic manifestations of the growing globalization of trade and finance and the increasing interdependence of nations. We have seen that whereas three decades ago this interdependence was perceived primarily in terms of the dependence of poor nations on rich ones, today the situation is different. LDCs are now the fastest-growing export markets for developed countries. With rising concerns about unpredictable energy and commodity prices, as well as fears of global environmental damage, ethnic conflicts, emerging disease, and floods of illegal immigrants pouring across their borders, developed countries now understand that their future welfare depends increasingly on the economic performance and social achievements of the developing countries. Let there be no misunderstanding, however. Poor nations are now and will remain considerably more vulnerable to the economic events and policies of rich nations than vice versa. The special and tragic plight of sub-Saharan Africa bears witness to the particular dependence and vulnerability of the least developed countries.

The crucial question for the twenty-first century is whether this globalization of the international economy and the growing economic interdependence among all nations will lead to greater cooperation or more conflict. Some experts view the period ahead as one of great promise; others are less confident. Some even foresee major problems and disruptions with potentially tragic consequences.[16]

As a result of the oil and resource scarcities of the 1970s, the debt crisis of the 1980s, the globalization of trade and finance of the 1990s, and looming global environmental crises, industrialized countries must understand that the economic futures of *both* groups of nations are intimately linked. No longer can rich nations totally dominate the established international order without provoking harmful repercussions. Cooperation becomes essential. In the final analysis, therefore, the only feasible outcome of the movement toward globalization and international interdependence is one in which *everyone* wins or loses. In the interdependent world of the twenty-first century, global development can never again be a zero-sum game.

With each passing year, therefore, rich and poor nations alike share an increasingly common destiny. The world community must finally realize that a more equitable international economic order is not only possible but essential. Such a new order should be based on the fundamental principle that each nation's and each individual's development is intimately bound to the development of every other nation and every other individual. The future of all humankind is linked more closely today than ever before. All indications are that it will become even more so in the coming decades. Let us hope, therefore, that reason and good sense will prevail so that the developed and developing worlds can truly become part of One World—forged together by a common economic destiny and guided by the humane principles of peace, friendship, and mutual respect.

The Questions for Discussion and Further Reading sections for this chapter are available on this book's companion Web site at http://www.aw-bc.com/todaro_smith.

Concepts for Review

Absorptive capacity	Earth Summit	Global warming
Acquired immunodeficiency syndrome (AIDS)	Global commons	Greenhouse gases
	Global factories	Human immunodeficiency virus (HIV)
Agenda 21	Globalization	
Biodiversity		

Notes

1. *World Bank, World Development Indicators, 2001* and *2004* (Washington, D.C.: World Bank, 2001 and 2004).

2. William D. Nordhaus, "Climates and economic development: Climates past and climate change future," in *Proceedings of the World Bank Conference on Development Economics, 1993* (Washington, D.C.: World Bank, 1994), pp. 355–376. For an overview of evidence see National Research Council, *Climate Change Science: An Analysis of Some Key Questions* (Washington, D.C.: National Academy Press, 2001).

3. *World Development Indicators, 2001*, pp. 154–157.

4. *World Development Indicators, 2004*, p. 114.

5. For an analysis of the effects of changes in economic policies and parameters on deforestation, see Joachim von Amsberg, "Economic parameters of deforestation," *World Bank Economic Review* 12 (1998): 133–153.

6. World Bank, *World Development Report, 1992: Development and the Environment* (New York: Oxford University Press, 1992), box 9.5. For the full report plus analysis, see United Nations, *The Global Partnership for Environment and Development: A Guide to Agenda 21* (New York: United Nations, 1992), and International Institute for Environment and Development and World Resources Institute, *World Resources, 1994–1995* (New York: Basic Books,1994), ch.13.

7. International Institute for Environment and Development and the World Resources Institute, *World Resources, 1987* (New York: Basic Books, 1987), p. 221. See also Paul Collier and Jan W. Gunnings, "Explaining African economic performance," *Journal of Economic Literature* 37 (1999): 64–111; Jennifer Seymour Whitaker, *How Can Africa Survive?* (New York: Harper & Row, 1988); Paul Mosley, Turan Subasat, and John Weeks, "Assessing adjustment in Africa," *World Development* 23 (1995): 1459–1473; George B. N. Ayiettey, *Africa in Chaos* (New York: St. Martin's Press, 1998); and World Bank, *Can Africa Claim the 21st Century?* (Washington, D.C.: World Bank, 2000).

8. See United Nations Development Program and World Bank, *African Development Indicators* (New York and Washington, D.C.: United Nations Development Program and World Bank, 1992) and *World Development Indicators, 2001* and *2004*.

9. For an analysis of some of the problems of economic reform and privatization efforts in Africa from an institutional perspective, see Howard Stein, "Theories of institutions and economic reform in Africa," *World Development* 22 (December 1994): 1833–1849.

10. For the UN Millennium Project report on resources and policies needed to achieve the Millennium Development Goals with special emphasis on problems of Africa, released in January 2005, see http://unmp.forumone.com/. For a wide-ranging look at strategies for ending extreme proverty, see Stephen C. Smith, *Ending Global Proverty: A Guide to What Works* (New York: Palgrave Macmillan, 2005).

11. For an excellent survey of issues related to globalization, see United Nations Conference on Trade and Development, *Trade and Development Report, 1997: Globalization, Distribution, and Growth* (New York: United Nations, 1997).

12. For an analysis and data on the limited benefits of globalization for many LDCs, see ibid. and United Nations, *Human Development Report, 1997* (New York: United Nations, 1997), ch. 4.

13. A somber and striking scenario of millions of impoverished developing-world immigrants flooding across the borders of North America and Europe in the twenty-first century is portrayed by Matthew Connelly and Paul Kennedy in "Must it be the rest against the West?" *Atlantic*, December 1994, pp. 61–91. See also Hal Kane, "What's driving migration?" *World Watch*, January–February 1995, pp. 23–33.

14. See, for example, Manmohan Singh, "In a changing world: Challenges to the South" in *Change: Threat or Opportunity? Vol. 2: Economic Change*, ed. Üner Kirdar (New York: United Nations, 1992), ch. 11, and United Nations Development Program, *Human Development Report, 1994* (New York: Oxford University Press, 1994), pp. 80–89.

15. Named after the late Nobel laureate James Tobin, who first proposed such a tax. See United Nations Development Program, *Human Development Report, 1994*, p. 70.

16. For a particularly provocative analysis of the threat of global anarchy rather than global harmony, see Robert D. Kaplan, "The coming anarchy: How scarcity, overpopulation, tribalism, and disease are rapidly destroying the social fabric of our planet," *Atlantic*, February 1994, pp. 44–76.

Glossary

This glossary is designed to cover most of the major concepts and organizations discussed in the text. It includes all end-of-chapter "Concepts for Review" as well as general economic terms and concepts relevant to studying development economics. This should be especially helpful to noneconomics majors. Words that appear in *italics* in any definition are themselves defined elsewhere in the glossary.

Absolute advantage   If country A can produce more of a commodity with the same amount of real resources than country B (i.e., at a lower absolute *unit cost*), country A is, at most, said to have absolute advantage over country B. See also *comparative advantage*.

Absolute poverty   A situation where a population or section of a population is, at most, able to meet only its bare subsistence essentials of food, clothing, and shelter to maintain minimum *levels of living*. See also *international poverty line* and *subsistence economy*.

Absorptive capacity   The ability of a country to absorb foreign private or public financial assistance (to use the funds in a productive manner); also, the capacity of an ecosystem to assimilate potential pollutants—for example, the forests of the earth have a limited capacity to absorb additional CO_2 produced as a by-product of the burning of fossil fuels.

Accounting price   See *shadow price*.

Acquired immunodeficiency syndrome (AIDS)   Disease produced by a deadly virus that is spreading throughout the developing world and is transmitted predominantly through sexual contact. It is especially prevalent in Africa. See also *human immunodeficiency virus (HIV)*.

Adjustment assistance   Public financial assistance provided to workers and industries hurt by imports of lower-priced foreign *goods*. Such assistance allows them to "adjust" to a new occupation during a transitional period.

Age structure of the population   The age composition of a given population. For example, in *developing countries*, the age structure of the population is typified by a large portion of population under 15 years old, a slightly smaller proportion aged between 15 and 45 years, and a very small proportion above 45 years old. See *population pyramid*.

Agency costs   Costs of monitoring managers and other employees (called agents, but in a slightly different sense than its usual definition of independent economic actors) and of designing and implementing schemes to ensure compliance or provide incentives to follow the wishes of the employer.

Agenda 21   The primary document discussed at the United Nations Conference on Environment and Development in June 1992, which outlines the areas for international cooperation in promoting environmentally sustainable growth and development.

Agent   An economic actor, usually a firm, worker, or consumer, but possibly a government official, that chooses actions so as to maximize an objective.

Agglomeration economies   Cost advantages to producers and consumers from location in cities and towns, which take the forms of *urbanization economies* and *localization economies*.

Aggregate demand   A measure of the real purchasing power of the community. Commonly referred to as the total effective demand or total expenditure, it normally comprises private consumption (C), private and public investment (I), government expenditure (G), plus net exports ($X- M$).

Aggregate growth model   Formal economic model describing growth of the economy in one or at most a few sectors and variables. Examples include the *Harrod-Domar growth model* and the *Solow neoclassical growth model*.

Agrarian system   The pattern of land distribution, ownership, and management and also the social and institutional structure of the agrarian economy. Many Latin American and Asian agrarian systems are characterized by concentrations of large tracts of land owned by a few powerful landlords. *Rural development* in many LDCs may require extensive reforms of the existing agrarian system.

Agricultural extension services Services offered to farmers, usually by the government, in the form of transmitting information, new ideas, methods, and advice about, for instance, the use of fertilizers, control of pests and weeds, appropriate machinery, soil conservation methods, and simple accounting, in a bid to stimulate high farm yields.

Agricultural mechanization The extensive use of machinery in farm production activities, thereby reducing the amount of labor input necessary to produce a given level of output. See also *laborsaving technological progress.*

Agricultural sector The portion of the economy comprising agriculture, forestry, hunting, and fishing.

Aid weariness *Attitude* among some donor-country politicians and populations that foreign aid has been unsuccessful and that they are tired of giving it.

Allocative efficiency Producing the maximum output possible, given quantities of *inputs* and using cost-minimizing techniques of production.

Amortization Gradual payoff of a *loan* principal.

Andean Group A *customs union* formed in 1969 by Bolivia, Colombia, Ecuador, Peru, and Venezuela in an effort to promote *economic integration,* coordinate industrial development, regulate foreign investment, and maintain a common external *tariff* among the member countries.

Appropriate technology Technology that is appropriate for existing factor endowments. For example, a technology employing a higher proportion of labor relative to other factors in a labor-abundant economy is usually more appropriate than one that uses smaller labor proportions relative to other factors. See also *factor-price distortions* and *neoclassical price-incentive model.*

Asset ownership The ownership of land, *physical capital* (factories, buildings, machinery, etc.), *human capital,* and financial resources that generate income for owners. The distribution of asset ownership is a major determinant of the distribution of personal income in any nonsocialist society. See also *income distribution.*

Asymmetric information A situation in which one party to a potential transaction (often a buyer, seller, lender, or borrower) has more information than another party.

Attitude A state of mind or feeling of an individual, group, or society regarding issues such as material gain, hard work, saving for the future, sharing wealth, etc. See also *values.*

Autarky A *closed economy* that attempts to be completely self-reliant.

Average product Total output or product divided by total factor input (e.g., the average product of labor is equal to total output divided by the total amount of labor used to produce that output). See *marginal product.*

Balance of payments A summary statement of a nation's financial transactions with the outside world. See also *current account, capital account,* and *cash account.*

Balanced trade A situation in which the value of a country's exports and the value of its imports are equal.

Bads The opposite of *goods;* things such as garbage that one would pay to remove or eliminate rather than to acquire.

Barter transactions The trading of goods directly for other goods in economies not fully monetized.

Basic education The attainment of literacy, arithmetic competence, and elementary vocational skills.

Basic needs A term used by the *International Labor Organization* and others to describe the basic goods and services (food, shelter, clothing, sanitation, education, etc.) necessary for a minimum standard of living.

Basic transfer Net foreign-exchange inflow or outflow related to a country's international borrowing. The quantitative difference between the net capital inflow (gross inflow minus amortization on past debt) and interest payments on existing accumulated debt.

Big push A concerted, economywide, and probably public policy–led, effort to initiate or accelerate economic development across a broad spectrum of new industries and skills.

Bilateral assistance See *foreign aid.*

Biodiversity The variety of life forms within an ecosystem.

Biomass fuels Any combustible organic matter that may be used as fuel, such as firewood, dung, or agricultural residues.

Birthrate See *crude birthrate.*

Black market A situation in which there is illegal selling of goods at prices above a legal maximum set by the government. It occurs due to relative *scarcity* of the goods concerned and the existence of an excess demand for them at the established price. See also *rationing* and *exchange control.*

Bottlenecks Sectors in the economy where the development process leads to a more rapid expansion of demand than supply in the goods or factor markets.

Brady Plan A program, launched in March 1989, designed to reduce the size of outstanding LDC commercial debt through private debt forgiveness procured in exchange for *International Monetary Fund* and *World Bank* debt guarantees and greater

LDC adherence to the terms of *conditionality*. Named after former U.S. Treasury Secretary Nicholas Brady.

Brain drain The emigration of highly educated and skilled professional and technical manpower from the developing to the developed countries.

Buffer stocks Stocks of commodities held by countries or international organizations to moderate the commodities' price fluctuations.

Calorie requirement The calories needed to sustain the population at normal levels of activity and health, taking account of its age and sex distributions, average body weights, and physical environment.

Capability The freedoms that people have, given their personal features and their command over commodities. See the discussion of Amartya Sen's approach to defining development in Chapter 1.

Capital See *physical capital* and *human capital*.

Capital account The portion of a country's *balance of payments* that shows the volume of *private foreign investment* and public *grants* and *loans* that flow into and out of a country over a given period, usually one year. See also *current account* and *cash account*.

Capital accumulation Increasing a country's stock of real capital (net investment in fixed assets). To increase the production of capital goods necessitates a reduction in the production of consumer goods. Economic development depends to a large extent on the rate of capital accumulation.

Capital-augmenting technological progress *Technological progress* that raises the productivity of *capital* by *innovation* and *inventions*.

Capital flight Transfer of funds to a foreign country by a citizen or business.

Capital-intensive technique A process of production that uses a higher proportion of *capital* relative to other *factors of production* such as labor or land per unit output.

Capital-labor ratio The number of units of *capital* per unit of labor. In *traditional neoclassical growth theory*, lower capital-labor ratios in LDCs should mean higher returns to new investment and greater flows of capital from MDCs to LDCs. But see *new growth theory*.

Capital-output ratio A ratio that shows the units of capital required to produce a unit of output over a given period of time. See *Harrod-Domar growth model*.

Capital-saving technological progress *Technological progress* that results from some invention or *innovation* that facilitates the achievement of higher output levels using the same quantity of capital inputs.

Capital stock The total amount of physical goods existing at a particular time that have been produced for use in the production of other goods (including *services*).

Cartel An organization of producers agreeing to limit the output of their product in an effort to raise *prices* and *profits*.

Cash account The balancing portion of a country's *balance of payments*, showing how cash balances (*foreign reserves*) and short-term financial claims have changed in response to *current account* and *capital account* transactions.

Cash crops Crops produced entirely for the market (e.g., coffee, tea, cacao, cotton, rubber, pyrethrum, jute, wheat).

Casual employment Employment on an ad hoc basis without regular hours or a wage contract; most often found in the *informal sector*.

Center In *dependence* theory, the economic developed world.

Central American Common Market (CACM) An economic union formed in 1960 and disbanded in the 1970s. It consisted of five Central American nations: Costa Rica, El Salvador, Guatemala, Honduras, and Nicaragua.

Central bank Major financial institution responsible for issuing currency, managing foreign reserves, implementing monetary policy, and providing banking services to the government and *commercial banks*.

Ceteris paribus A Latin expression widely used in economics, meaning "all else being equal," indicating that all other variables are held constant.

Character of economic growth The distributive implications of the process of *economic growth;* for example, participation in the growth process or asset ownership. In other words, how *economic growth* is achieved and who benefits.

Clean technologies Technologies that by design produce less waste and use resources more efficiently.

Closed economy An economy in which there are no foreign trade transactions or any other form of economic contacts with the rest of the world. See also *autarky* and *inward-looking development policies*.

Collective self-reliance See *self-reliance*.

Collusion An agreement among sellers of a commodity (or commodities) to set a common price or share their commodity market.

Commercial bank A financial institution that provides a wide range of services, including accepting deposits and making *loans* for commercial purposes.

Commercial farming See *specialized farming*.

Commercial policy Policy encompassing instruments of trade protection employed by countries to foster industrial promotion, export diversification, employment creation, and other desired development-oriented strategies. They include *tariffs, quotas,* and *subsidies.*

Commodity terms of trade See *terms of trade.*

Common external tariff A tariff imposed by members of a *customs union, common market,* or *economic community* on imports from nonmembers.

Common market A form of *economic integration* in which there is free internal trade, a common *tariff,* and the free movement of labor and capital among partner states. The European Union is an example. See also *customs union* and *free-trade area.*

Common property resource A resource that is publicly owned and allocated under a system of unrestricted access.

Comparative advantage A country has a comparative advantage over another if in producing a commodity it can do so at a relatively lower *opportunity cost* in terms of the forgone alternative commodities that could be produced. Taking two countries, A and B, each producing two commodities, X and Y, country A is also said to have comparative advantage in the production of X if its *absolute advantage* margin is greater or its absolute disadvantage is less in X than in Y.

Complementarity When complementarities are present, an action taken by one film, worker, or organization increases the incentives for other agents to take similar actions. Complementarities often involve investments whose return depends on other investments being made by other agents.

Complementary investments Investments that complement and facilitate other productive factors— for example, *capital* with labor, education and training of unskilled workers, pesticides and fertilizer on farmland.

Complementary resources *Factors of production* that are necessarily used along with others to produce a given output or to accomplish a specific task; for example, worker-hours of farm labor are complementary to a hectare of land in the production of maize; machinery and equipment are complementary to labor in the construction of a road.

Comprador A local labor recruiter or purchasing agent employed by a foreign firm.

Comprador groups In *dependence* theory, local elites who act as fronts for foreign investors.

Comprehensive plan An *economic plan* that sets targets to cover all the major sectors of the national economy.

Concessional terms Terms for the extension of credit that are more favorable to the borrower than those available on the money markets.

Conditionality The requirement imposed by the *International Monetary Fund* that a borrowing country undertake fiscal, monetary, and international commercial reforms as a condition to receiving a *loan* for *balance of payments* difficulties.

Congestion The opposite of a *complementarity;* an action taken by one agent that decreases the incentives for other agents to take similar actions. For example, if most people travel on one highway between two cities, the incentive is present for travelers to try alternate routes.

Consumer surplus Excess utility over price derived by consumers because of negative sloping demand curve; measured as the triangular area under a demand curve above the price line.

Consumption possibility line In international *free-trade* theory, a locus of points showing the highest possible consumption combinations that can be attained as a result of trade. Graphically, the consumption possibility line is represented by the international price line at its tangency to the domestic *production possibility curve* of a country.

Coordination failure A state of affairs in which agents' inability to coordinate their behavior (choices) leads to an outcome (equilibrium) that leaves all agents worse off than in an alternative situation that is also an equilibrium.

Corruption The appropriation of public resources for private profit and other private purposes through the use and abuse of official power or influence.

Cost-benefit analysis A basic tool of economic analysis in which the actual and potential *private* and *social costs* of various economic decisions are weighed against actual and potential *private* and *social benefits.* Decisions or projects that yield the highest ratio of benefit to cost are usually thought to be most desirable. See also *project appraisal.*

Creditor nation A nation with a *balance of payments* surplus.

Crude birthrate The number of children born alive each year per 1,000 population (a crude birthrate of 20 per 1,000 is the same as a 2% increase). See also *total fertility rate* and *death rate.*

Curative medicine Medical care that focuses on curing rather than preventing disease; requires extensive availability of hospitals and clinics. See also *preventive medicine.*

Currency board A form of *central bank* that issues domestic currency for foreign exchange at fixed rates.

Currency substitution The use of foreign currency (e.g., U.S. dollars) as a medium of exchange in place of or along with the local currency (e.g., Mexican pesos).

Current account The portion of a *balance of payments* that portrays the market value of a country's "visible" (e.g., commodity trade) and "invisible" (e.g., shipping services) exports and imports with the rest of the world. See also *capital account* and *cash account.*

Current account balance The difference between (1) exports of *goods* and *services* plus inflows of unrequited official and private transfers and (2) imports of goods and services plus unrequited transfers to the rest of the world. Included in this figure are all interest payments on external public and publicly guaranteed debt.

Customs union A form of *economic integration* in which two or more nations agree to free all internal trade while levying a *common external tariff* on all nonmember countries. See also *common market* and *free-trade area.*

Death rate The yearly number of deaths per 1,000 population; an annual crude death rate of 15 per 1,000 would involve 1.5% of the population. See also *crude birthrate* and *infant mortality rate.*

Debt-for-equity swap A mechanism used by indebted LDCs to reduce the real value of external debt by exchanging equity in domestic companies (stocks) or fixed-interest obligations of the government (bonds) for private foreign debt at large discounts, for example, replacing $100 million of debt obligations with $50 million of equity claims against domestic real assets.

Debt-for-nature swap The exchange of foreign debt held by an organization for a larger quantity of domestic debt that is used to finance the preservation of a natural resource or environment in the debtor country.

Debtors' cartel A group of LDC debtors who join together to bargain as a group with creditors.

Debt renegotiation Changing the terms of existing *loans*, usually by extending repayment dates without increasing nominal interest rates.

Debt repudiation The 1980s MDC fear that LDCs would decide not to pay debt obligations.

Debt service The sum of interest payments and repayments of principal on external public and publicly guaranteed debt.

Debt-service ratio The ratio of interest and principal payments due in a year to export receipts for that year.

Decile A 10% portion of any numerical quantity; a population divided into deciles would be divided into 10 equal numeric groups. See also *quintile.*

Decreasing costs If *increasing returns* exist, a given proportionate change in output will require a smaller proportionate change in quantities of factor inputs, thus implying a fall in cost per unit of output. In short, a fall in average costs of production as output expands.

Deep intervention A government policy that can move the economy to a preferred equilibrium, or even to a higher permanent rate of growth, that can then be self-sustaining, so that the policy need no longer be enforced, because the better equilibrium will then prevail without further intervention.

Deficit Excess of expenditures over receipts. See *trade deficit.*

Deficit expenditure Amount by which government expenditure exceeds realized tax revenues. Deficit expenditure is normally financed by borrowed funds, and its major objective is to stimulate economic activity by increasing *aggregate demand.*

Deforestation The clearing of forested land. Deforestation is generally divided into two broad categories, tropical deforestation, which involves the clearing of dense rain forests in regions with high levels of precipitation, usually for agricultural purposes, and dry forest clearing, which occurs in areas with less precipitation, where most trees are cut for firewood.

Demand curve A graphical representation of the quantities of a commodity or resource that would be bought over a range of *prices* at a particular time, when all other prices and incomes are held constant. When demand curves of all consumers in the market are aggregated, a market demand curve is derived, showing the total amount of goods that consumers are willing to purchase at each price.

Demographic transition The phasing-out process of population growth rates from a virtually stagnant growth stage characterized by high *birthrates* and *death rates*, through a rapid-growth stage with high birthrates and low death rates, to a stable, low-growth stage in which both birth and death rates are low.

Demonstration effects The effects of transfers of foreign ways of life on nationals of a country. Such effects are mainly cultural and attitudinal, including consumption habits, modes of dressing, and approaches to education, leisure, and recreation.

Dependence A corollary of *dominance;* a situation in which the LDCs have to rely on developed-country domestic and international economic policy to stimulate their own *economic growth.* Dependence can also mean that the LDCs adopt developed-country education systems, technology, economic and political systems, attitudes, consumption patterns, dress, etc.

Dependency burden The proportion of the total population aged 0 to 15 and 65+, which is considered economically unproductive and therefore not counted in the labor force. In many LDCs, the population under the age of 15 accounts for almost half of the total population, thus placing a burden on the generally small productive labor force and on the government, which has to allocate *resources* for such things as education, public health, and housing for people who don't contribute to production.

Depreciation The decline over time in the value or price of one currency in terms of another as a result of market forces of supply and demand. See *devaluation* and *exchange rate.*

Derived demand Demand for a good that emerges indirectly from demand for another good. In education, demand for schooling derived from the ultimate demand for modern-sector jobs requiring a school certificate.

Desertification The transformation of a region into dry barren land with little or no capacity to sustain life without an artificial source of water. Desertification frequently involves the loss of topsoil, which leads to the permanent loss of cultivability.

Devaluation A lowering of the official *exchange rate* between one country's currency and all other currencies. See *depreciation.*

Developed world The now economically advanced capitalist countries of Western Europe, North America, Australia, New Zealand, and Japan. These were the first countries to experience sustained long-term *economic growth.*

Developing countries The present countries of Asia, Africa, the Middle East, Latin America, Eastern Europe, and the former Soviet Union, mainly characterized by low *levels of living*, high rates of *population growth*, low *income per capita*, and general economic and technological *dependence* on developed economies.

Development The process of improving the quality of all human lives. Three equally important aspects of development are (1) raising people's living levels—their incomes and consumption levels of food, medical services, education etc., through relevant *economic growth* processes; (2) creating conditions conducive to the growth of people's *self-esteem* through the establishment of social, political, and economic systems and *institutions* that promote human dignity and respect; and (3) increasing people's *freedom* by enlarging the range of their choice variables, as by increasing varieties of consumer goods and services.

Development banks Specialized public and private *financial intermediaries* providing medium- and long-term credit for development projects.

Development economics The study of how economies are transformed from stagnation to growth and from low-income to high-income status. See *development.*

Development plan The documentation by a government planning agency of the current national economic conditions, proposed public expenditures, likely developments in the *private sector*, a macro-economic projection of the economy, and a review of government policies. Many LDCs publish five-year development plans to announce their economic objectives to their citizens and others.

Diminishing returns The principle that if one *factor of production* is fixed and constant additions of other factors are combined with it, the marginal productivity of variable factors will eventually decline.

Direct taxes Taxes levied directly on individuals or businesses—for example, income taxes. See *indirect taxes.*

Disposable income The income that is available to households for spending and saving after personal income taxes have been deducted.

Diversified farming See *mixed farming.*

Division of labor Allocation of tasks among workers such that each one engages in tasks that he or she performs most efficiently. Division of labor promotes worker specialization and thereby raises overall *labor productivity*. It has its historical origins in Adam Smith's *Wealth of Nations.*

Dominance In international affairs, a situation in which the developed countries have much greater power than the less developed countries in decisions affecting important international economic issues, such as the prices of agricultural commodities and raw materials in world markets. See also *dependence.*

Doubling time Period that a given population takes to increase by its present size. Doubling time is approximated by dividing the numerical growth rate into 70—a population growing at 2% per year will double in size approximately every 35 years.

Dropout rate Proportion of school-aged children who do not complete a particular school cycle.

Dual exchange rate Foreign-exchange-rate system with a highly *overvalued* and legally fixed rate applied to capital and intermediate good imports and a second, illegal (or freely floating) rate for imported consumption goods.

Dualism The coexistence in one place of two situations or phenomena (one desirable and the other one not) that are mutually exclusive to different groups of society—for example, extreme poverty and affluence, modern and traditional economic sectors, growth and stagnation, university education among a few and mass illiteracy.

Earth Summit See *United Nations Conference on Environment and Development (UNCED).*

Economic community *Economic union* of countries seeking to coordinate fiscal and monetary policies as a step toward a common currency. This takes place in addition to maintaining a *common external tariff* and similar commercial policies and to removing restrictions on trade within the community.

Economic constraint A barrier to the attainment of a set target (e.g., *economic growth*) in a particular period of time. For example, *physical capital* has long been thought of as the major constraint on *economic growth* in LDCs.

Economic efficiency In production, utilizing factors of production in the least-cost combinations; in consumption, allocating expenditures to maximize consumer satisfaction (utility).

Economic good Any commodity or service that yields utility to an individual or community and must be paid for in money terms in a monetary economy or in kind in a nonmonetary economy.

Economic growth The steady process by which the productive capacity of the economy is increased over time to bring about rising levels of national output and income.

Economic infrastructure The underlying amount of physical and financial capital embodied in roads, railways, waterways, airways, and other forms of transportation and communication plus water supplies, financial institutions, electricity, and public services such as health and education. The level of infrastructural development in a country is a crucial factor determining the pace and diversity of economic *development*.

Economic integration The merging to various degrees of the economies and economic policies of two or more countries in a given region. See also *common market, customs union, free-trade area, trade creation,* and *trade diversion*.

Economic plan A written document containing government policy decisions on how *resources* shall be allocated among various uses so as to attain a targeted rate of *economic growth* over a certain period of time. See *economic planning* and *planning model*.

Economic planning A deliberate and conscious attempt by the state to formulate decisions on how the *factors of production* shall be allocated among different uses or industries, thereby determining how much of total *goods* and *services* shall be produced in one or more ensuing periods. See also *economic plan*.

Economic policy A statement of objectives and the methods of achieving these objectives (policy instruments) by government, political party, business concern, etc. Some examples of government economic objectives are maintaining *full employment*, achieving a high rate of *economic growth*, reducing *income inequalities* and regional development inequalities, and maintaining price stability. Policy instruments include fiscal policy, monetary and financial policy, and legislative controls (e.g., price and wage control, rent control).

Economic union The full integration of two or more economics into a single economic entity. See *economic integration*.

Economic variable A measure of economic activity such as income, consumption, or price that can take on different quantitative values. Variables are classified as either dependent or independent in accordance with the economic model being used. See *increasing returns* and *returns to scale*.

Economies of scale Economies of growth resulting from expansion of the scale of productive capacity of a firm or industry, leading to increases in its output and decreases in its cost of production per unit of output.

Educational certification The phenomenon by which particular jobs require specified levels of education. Applicants must produce certificates of completed schooling in the *formal educational system*.

Educational gender gap Male-female differences in school access and completion.

Effective rate of protection The degree of protection on *value added* as opposed to final f.o.b. price of imported product—usually higher than the *nominal rate of protection*.

Efficiency See *allocative efficiency, economic efficiency,* and *technical efficiency*.

Efficiency wage The notion that modern-sector urban employers pay a higher wage than the equilibrium wage rate in order to attract a higher-quality workforce or to obtain higher productivity on the job.

Elasticity of demand See *price elasticity of demand* and *income elasticity of demand*.

Elasticity of factor substitution A measure of the degree of substitutability between *factors of production* in any given production process when relative factor prices change.

Emerging-country stock markets Equity markets used to finance private corporations in newly industrializing countries such as Mexico, Malaysia, and South Korea.

Empowerment of women The idea that giving women power over their economic, social, and *reproductive choices* will raise their status, promote development, and reduce population growth.

Enclave economies LDC economies in which there are small pockets of economically developed regions (often due to the presence of colonial or foreign firms engaged in plantation and mining activities) with the rest of the larger outlying areas experiencing very little progress. See also *dualism*.

Endogenous growth theory *Economic growth* generated by factors within the production process (e.g., *economies of scale, increasing returns,* induced technological change) as opposed to outside (exogenous) factors such as increases in population. See *new growth theory.*

Enrollment ratios See *gross enrollment ratio* and *net enrollment ratio.*

Environmental accounting The incorporation of environmental benefits and costs into the quantitative analysis of economic activities.

Environmental capital The portion of a country's overall capital assets that directly relate to the environment—forests, soil quality, and rangeland.

Equalization (economic and social) The promotion of more equality in opportunities, status, income, wealth, and general level of living. See also *modernization ideals.*

Equilibrium price The price at which the quantity demanded of a good is exactly equal to the quantity supplied. It is often referred to as the price at which the market clears itself.

Equilibrium wage rate The wage rate that equates the demand for and supply of labor, that is, the wage at which all the people who want to work at that wage are able to find jobs and also at which employers are able to find all the workers they desire to employ. In other words, it is the wage rate that clears the labor market.

Euro A common European currency adopted by 12 countries of the European Union—Austria, Belgium, Finland, France, Germany, Greece, Ireland, Italy, Luxembourg, the Netherlands, Portugal, and Spain. The euro went into circulation on January 1, 2002; local currencies are no longer accepted.

Eurodollars Dollar deposits of European banks in American ones, or dollar deposits in European banks, which the European banks may use as reserves for dollar loans.

Exchange control A governmental policy designed to restrict the outflow of domestic currency and prevent a worsened *balance of payments* position by controlling the amount of *foreign exchange* that can be obtained or held by domestic citizens. Often results from *overvalued exchange rates.*

Exchange rate The rate at which *central banks* will exchange one country's currency for another (i.e., the official rate). See also *overvalued exchange rate* and *devaluation.*

Expected income In the *Todaro migration model*, the product of the urban wage rate and the probability of finding an urban job.

Export dependence A situation in which a country relies heavily on exports as the major source of finance needed for carrying out *development* activities. This is the situation of many LDCs, which must export primary products to earn valuable *foreign exchange.*

Export earnings instability Wide and unpredictable fluctuations in LDC commodity export earnings resulting from low *price* and *income elasticities of demand* leading to erratic movements in export prices.

Export incentives Public *subsidies*, tax rebates, and other kinds of financial and nonfinancial measures designed to promote a greater level of economic activity in export industries.

Export promotion Governmental efforts to expand the volume of a country's exports through *export incentives* and other means in order to generate more *foreign exchange* and improve the *current account* of its *balance of payments.*

Exports The value of all goods and nonfactor services sold to the rest of the world; they include merchandise, freight, insurance, travel, and other nonfactor services. The value of factor services (such as investment receipts and workers' remittances from abroad) is excluded from this measure. See also *merchandise exports and imports.*

External debt Total private and public foreign debt owed by a country.

Externality Any benefit or cost borne by an individual that is a direct consequence of another's behavior and for which there is no compensation. Externalities are internalized when adjustments are made such that each individual bears all the costs and benefits of his or her actions.

Factor endowment trade theory The neoclassical model of *free trade*, which postulates that countries will tend to specialize in the production of the commodities that make use of their abundant *factors of production* (land, labor, capital, etc.). They can then export the surplus in return for imports of the products produced by factors with which they are relatively less endowed. The basis for trade arises because of differences in relative factor prices and thus domestic price ratios as a result of differences in factor supplies. See also *comparative advantage.*

Factor mobility The unrestricted transference or free voluntary movement of *factors of production* among different uses and geographic locations.

Factor-price distortions Situations in which *factors of production* are paid prices that do not reflect their true *scarcity* values (i.e., their competitive market prices) because of institutional arrangements that tamper with the free working of market forces of supply and demand. In many LDCs, the prices paid for *capital* and *intermediate producer goods* are artificially low because of special capital depreciation allowances, tax rebates, investment *subsidies*, etc., while labor is paid a wage above its competitive market value partly because of trade union and political pressures. Factor-price distortions can lead to the use of inappropriate techniques of production. See also *neoclassical price-incentive model* and *appropriate technology.*

Factor-price equalization In *factor endowment trade theory*, the proposition that because countries trade at a common international price ratio, factor prices among trading partners will tend to be equalized given the assumption of identical technological possibilities for all commodities across countries. The prices of the more abundantly utilized *resources* will tend to rise, while those of the relatively scarce factors of production fall. Over time, international factor payments will tend toward equality; for example, real wage rates for labor will ultimately be the same in Britain and Botswana.

Factor share distribution of income See *functional distribution of income*.

Factors of production *Resources* or *inputs* required to produce a *good* or a *service*. Basic categories of factors of production are land, labor, and *capital*.

False-paradigm model The proposition that *developing countries* have failed to develop because their *development* strategies (usually given to them by Western economists) have been based on an incorrect model of development, one that, for example, overstressed *capital accumulation* without giving due consideration to needed social and institutional change.

Family farms Mostly small farm plots owned and operated by a single household.

Family-planning programs Public programs designed to help parents plan and regulate their family size in accordance with their ability to support a family. The program usually includes supplying contraceptives to the adult population, education on the use of birth control devices, mass-media propaganda on benefits derived from smaller families, and pre- and postnatal health care for mothers.

Fertility The yearly number of children born alive per 1,000 women within the childbearing age bracket (normally between the ages of 15 and 49 years). See also *crude birthrate* and *total fertility rate (TFR)*.

Final goods Commodities that are consumed to satisfy wants rather than passed on to further stages of production. Whenever a final good is not consumed but is used as an *input* instead, it becomes an *intermediate producer good*.

Financial intermediary Any financial institution, public or private, that serves to channel loanable funds from savers to borrowers. Examples include *commercial banks*, savings banks, *development banks*, and finance companies.

Financial liberalization Eliminating various forms of government intervention in financial markets, thereby allowing supply and demand to determine the level of interest rates, for example.

Financial repression The constraints on investment caused by the rationing of credit, usually to a few large borrowers, in financial markets where interest rates and hence the supply of savings are below market-determined levels.

Fixed exchange rate The exchange value of a national currency fixed in relation to another (usually the U.S. dollar), not free to fluctuate on the international money market.

Fixed inputs *Inputs* that do not vary as output varies. For example, a hectare of land is a fixed input on a small family farm because it can be used to produce different quantities of, say, maize output without its size changing. See also *variable inputs*.

Flexible exchange rate The exchange value of a national currency that is free to move up and down in response to shifts in demand and supply arising from international trade and finance.

Flexible wages Wages that adjust upward or downward depending on the direction of the forces of demand for and supply of labor—for example, if the demand for labor increases (decreases) or its supply decreases (increases), *ceteris paribus*, wages will increase (decrease).

Foreign aid The international transfer of public funds in the form of *loans* or *grants* either directly from one government to another (*bilateral assistance*) or indirectly through the vehicle of a multilateral assistance agency like the *World Bank*. See also *tied aid, private foreign investment*, and *nongovernmental organizations (NGOs)*.

Foreign direct investment (FDI) Overseas investments by private multinational corporations.

Foreign exchange Claims on a country by another held in the form of currency of that country. The foreign-exchange system enables one currency to be exchanged for (converted into) another, thus facilitating trade between countries. See also *exchange rate* and *foreign reserves*.

Foreign-exchange earnings The sum total of all foreign currency receipts less expenditures during a given fiscal year.

Foreign-exchange gap The shortfall that results when the planned merchandise *trade deficit* exceeds the value of capital inflows, causing output growth to be limited by inadequate *foreign exchange*. See *savings gap*.

Foreign reserves The total value (usually expressed in dollars) of all gold, currency, and *special drawing rights* held by a country as both a reserve and a fund from which international payments can be made.

Formal educational system The organized and accredited school system, with licensed teachers, standard curricula, regular academic years, and recognized certification. It encompasses primary, secondary, and tertiary educational institutions. See also *nonformal education*.

Foster-Greer-Thorbecke (FGT) index A class of measures of the level of *absolute poverty*, which include as special cases the headcount ratio and the normalized income shortfall, but in other cases, notably the P2 measure, satisfy all four axioms for desirable poverty measures, including distributional sensitivity.

Freedom   A situation in which a society has at its disposal a variety of alternatives from which to satisfy its wants. See also *development*.

Free market   See *market mechanism*.

Free-market analysis   Theoretical analysis of the properties of an economic system operating through an unfettered market mechanism; this approach typically argues that, given certain assumptions, an unregulated market performs better than one with government regulation.

Free-market exchange rate   Rate determined solely by international supply and demand for domestic currency expressed in terms of, say, U.S. dollars.

Free-rider problem   Situation in which people secure benefits that someone else pays for.

Free trade   Trade in which goods can be imported and exported without any barriers in the forms of *tariffs, quotas,* or other restrictions. Free trade has often been described as an engine of growth because it encourages countries to specialize in activities in which they have *comparative advantages,* thereby increasing their respective production efficiencies and hence their total output of *goods* and *services*.

Free-trade area   A form of *economic integration* in which free internal trade exists among member countries but each member is free to levy different external tariffs against nonmember nations. See also *customs union* and *common market*.

Full employment   A situation in which everyone who wants to work at the prevailing wage rate is able to get a job or, alternatively, a situation in which some job seekers cannot get employment at the going wage rate but open unemployment has been reduced to a desired level (such as 5%).

Functional distribution of income   The distribution of income to *factors of production* without regard to the ownership of the factors.

Functionings   What people do or can do with the commodities of given characteristics that they come to possess or control.

Gains from trade   The increase in output and consumption resulting from specialization in production and *free trade* with other economic units including persons, regions, or countries.

Gender gap   Any statistical gap between the measured characteristics of men and women in areas such as educational attainment, wage rates, or labor force participation.

General Agreement on Tariffs and Trade (GATT)   An international body set up in 1947 to probe into the ways and means of reducing tariffs on internationally traded *goods* and *services*. Between 1947 and 1962, GATT held seven conferences but met with only moderate success. Its major success was achieved in 1967 during the so-called Kennedy Round of talks when tariffs on primary commodities were drastically slashed and then in 1994 with the signing of the *Uruguay Round* agreement. Replaced in 1995 by the *World Trade Organization (WTO)*.

Gini coefficient   An aggregate numerical measure of *income inequality* ranging from 0 (perfect equality) to 1 (perfect inequality). It is measured graphically by dividing the area between the perfect equality line and the *Lorenz curve* by the total area lying to the right of the equality line in a Lorenz diagram. The higher the value of the coefficient, the higher the inequality of income distribution; the lower it is, the more equitable the distribution of income.

Global commons   International resources shared by all countries, such as oceans and air.

Global factory   A production facility whose various operations are distributed across a number of countries in order to take advantage of existing price differentials.

Globalization   The increasing integration of national economies into expanding international markets.

Global public goods   *Goods* (and *bads*) whose benefits (or costs) reach across national borders, generations, and population groups. Ozone depletion and greenhouse gas emissions are examples.

Global warming   Theory that world climate is slowly warming as a result of both MDC and LDC industrial and agricultural activities.

Goods   See *economic good* and *final goods*.

Government failure   Situation in which government intervention in an economy worsens outcomes.

Grant   An outright *transfer payment*, usually from one government to another (*foreign aid*); a gift of money or technical assistance that does not have to be repaid. See also *loan* and *tied aid*.

Greenhouse gases   Gases that trap heat within the earth's atmosphere and can thus contribute to *global warming*. See also *ozone depletion*.

Green revolution   The boost in grain production associated with the scientific discovery of new *hybrid seed* varieties of wheat, rice, and corn that have resulted in high farm yields in many LDCs.

Gross domestic investment   The outlays for additions to fixed assets of both the private and public sectors plus the net value of inventory changes. See also *investment*.

Gross domestic product (GDP) The total final output of *goods* and *services* produced by the country's economy, within the country's territory, by residents and nonresidents, regardless of its allocation between domestic and foreign claims. See also *gross national product (GNP)*.

Gross domestic savings The amount of *gross domestic investment* financed from domestic output. It is calculated as the difference between *gross domestic investment* and the deficit on *current account* of *goods* and nonfactor *services* (excluding net current transfers). It comprises both public and private savings. See also *savings*.

Gross enrollment ratio The ratio of the number of individuals enrolled in a given level of schooling (e.g. primary school) to the number of children in the age group that typically attends that level. Ratio can be greater than 100 if older children are attending the primary schools. See *net enrollment ratio*.

Gross national income (GNI) The total domestic and foreign output claimed by residents of a country. It comprises *gross domestic product (GDP)* plus factor incomes accruing to residents from abroad, less the income earned in the domestic economy accruing to persons abroad.

Group lending schemes A formal arrangement among a group of potential borrowers to borrow money from commercial or government banks as a single entity and then allocate funds and repay loans as a group, thereby lowering borrowing costs. See also *rotating savings and credit association (ROSCA)*.

Group of 7 The seven leading industrialized developed nations (the United States, Canada, Great Britain, France, Germany, Japan, and Italy), who meet annually to discuss global economic issues.

Growth poles Regions that are more economically and socially advanced than others around them, such as urban centers versus rural areas in LDCs. Large-scale economic activity tends to cluster around growth poles due to economies of agglomeration and the lower costs of locating an industry in an area where *economic infrastructure* has been built up.

Hard currency The currency of a major industrial country, such as the U.S. dollar, the German mark, or the Japanese yen, that is freely convertible into other "soft" currencies.

Harris-Todaro model An equilibrium version of the Todaro model, which predicts that expected incomes will be equated across rural and urban sectors when taking into account informal sector activities and outright unemployment.

Harrod-Domar growth model A functional economic relationship in which the growth rate of gross domestic product (g) depends directly on the national net savings rate (s) and inversely on the national *capital-output ratio* (k), that is, $g = s/k$. The model takes its name from a synthesis of analyses of the growth process by two economists, Sir Roy Harrod of Britain and E. V. Domar of the United States.

Headcount index The proportion of a country's population below the *poverty line*.

Hidden momentum of population growth A dynamic latent process of population increase that continues even after a fall in *birthrates* because of a large youthful population that widens the population's parent base. Fewer children per couple in the succeeding few generations will not mean a smaller or stable population size because at the same time there will be a much larger number of childbearing couples. Hence a given population will not stabilize until after two or three generations.

Highly indebted poor countries (HIPCs) The group of the world's poorest and most heavily indebted countries, as defined by the *World Bank* and IMF, which may be eligible for special debt relief under the HIPC Initiative.

Human capital Productive *investments* embodied in human persons. These include skills, abilities, ideals, and health resulting from expenditures on education, on-the-job training programs, and medical care. See also *physical capital*.

Human Development Index (HDI) An index measuring national socioeconomic development, based on measures of life expectancy at birth, educational attainment, literacy, and adjusted real per capita income.

Human immunodeficiency virus (HIV) The virus that causes *AIDS*.

Human Poverty Index (HPI) Index measuring deprivation in basic human development in a country. Variables used are the percentage of people expected to die before age 40, adult illiteracy rate, percentage of people without access to health services and safe water, and percentage of underweight children 5 years of age.

Human resources The quantity and quality of a nation's labor force.

Hybrid seeds Seeds produced by cross-breeding plants or crops of different species through scientific research. See also *green revolution*.

Idea gap The notion that one explanation for *underdevelopment* is that LDCs lack knowledge, information, skills, and other attributes of modern production methods in comparison to more developed countries. See *ingenuity gap* and *object gap*.

Imperfect competition A market situation or structure in which producers have some degree of control over the price of their product. Examples include *monopoly* and *oligopoly*. See also *perfect competition.*

Imperfect market A market where the theoretical assumptions of *perfect competition* are violated by the existence of, for example, a small number of buyers and sellers, barriers to entry, nonhomogeneity of products, and *incomplete information*. The three imperfect markets commonly analyzed in economic theory are *monopoly, oligopoly*, and monopolistic competition.

Import substitution A deliberate effort to replace major consumer imports by promoting the emergence and expansion of domestic industries such as textiles, shoes, and household appliances. Import substitution requires the imposition of protective *tariffs* and *quotas* to get the new industry started. See also *infant industry.*

Income distribution See *functional distribution of income* and *size distribution of income.*

Income effect The implicit change in real income resulting from the effects of a change in a commodity's price on the quantity demanded.

Income elasticity of demand The responsiveness of the quantity demanded of a commodity to changes in the consumer's income, measured by the proportionate change in quantity divided by the proportionate change in income.

Income gap The gap between the incomes accruing to the bottom (poor) and the top (rich) sectors of a population. The wider the gap, the greater the inequality in the *income distribution*. Also, the gap between *income per capita* levels in rich and poor nations. See *Gini coefficient.*

Income inequality The existence of disproportionate distribution of total *national income* among households whereby the share going to rich persons in a country is far greater than that going to poorer persons (a situation common to most LDCs). This is largely due to differences in the amount of income derived from ownership of property and to a lesser extent the result of differences in earned income. Inequality of personal incomes can be reduced by *progressive income taxes* and wealth taxes. See also *Gini coefficient* and *Lorenz curve.*

Income in kind A household's or firm's income in the form of *goods* or *services* instead of in the form of money. Payments in *barter transactions* and in *subsistence economies* are mainly made in kind.

Income per capita Total *gross national product* of a country divided by total population. Per capita income is often used as an economic indicator of *level of living* and *development*. It can, however, be a biased index because it takes no account of income distribution and the ownership of the assets that are employed to generate part of that income.

Income terms of trade A measure of the relative purchasing power of a country's exports arrived at by abstracting from relative export price movements. See *terms of trade.*

Incomplete information The notion that LDC markets do not function well because producers and consumers do not possess the requisite information to make efficient decisions. See *imperfect market.*

Increasing returns A disproportionate increase in output that results from a change in the scale of production. Some industries (e.g., utilities, transportation) are characterized by increasing returns over a wide range of output. This leads to *monopoly* situations. See also *economies of scale* and *returns to scale.*

Incremental capital-output ratio (ICOR) The amount of *capital* needed to raise output by one unit.

Indirect taxes Taxes levied on *goods* purchased by the consumer (and exported by the producer) for which the taxpayer's liability varies in proportion to the quantity of goods purchased or sold. Examples of indirect taxes are customs duties (*tariffs*), excise duties, sales taxes, and export duties. They are a major source of tax revenue for most LDCs as they are easier to administer and collect than *direct taxes* (e.g., income and property taxes).

Induced migration Process in which the creation of urban jobs raises *expected incomes* and induces more people to migrate from rural areas. See *Todaro migration model.*

Industrialization The process of building up a country's capacity to process raw materials and to manufacture *goods* for consumption or further production.

Industrialization strategy approach An outward-oriented school of thought in trade and development that emphasizes the importance of overcoming market failures through government policy to encourage technology transfer and exports of progressively more advanced products using greater skill and adding higher value; and the empirical study of specific *industrial policies* following this approach such as those used historically in South Korea.

Industrial policy Deliberate effort by governments to guide the market by coordinating and planning industrial activities.

Infant industry A newly established industry, usually set up behind the protection of a *tariff* barrier as a part of a policy of *import substitution*. Once the industry is no longer an infant, the protective tariffs are supposed to disappear, but often they do not.

Infant mortality rate Deaths among children between birth and 1 year of age per 1,000 live births.

Inferior good A *good* whose demand falls as consumer incomes rise. The *income elasticity of demand* of an inferior good is thus negative.

Inflation A period of above-normal general price increases as reflected, for example, in the consumer and wholesale price indexes. More generally, the phenomenon of rising prices.

Informal finance *Loans* not passed through the formal banking system—for example, family loans.

Informal sector The part of the urban economy of LDCs characterized by small competitive individual or family firms, petty retail trade and services, labor-intensive methods, free entry, and market-determined factor and product prices. It often provides a major source of urban employment and economic activity.

Infrastructure See *economic infrastructure*.

Ingenuity gap LDC deficiency compared with MDCs in the capacity to invent and innovate with new or existing technology. See also *idea gap* and *object gap*.

Innovation The application of inventions of new production processes and methods to production activities as well as the introduction of new products. Innovations may also include the introduction of new social and institutional methods of organization and management commensurate with modern ways of conducting economic activities. See *modernization ideals*.

Input-output model Formal model dividing the economy into sectors and tracing the flow of interindustry purchases (*inputs*) and sales (outputs).

Inputs *Goods* and *services*, such as raw materials and hours of labor, used in the process of production. See also *factors of production, physical resources*, and *human resources*.

Institutions Norms, rules of conduct, and generally accepted ways of doing things. Social institutions are well-defined, formal organizations of society that govern the way that society operates—for example, the class system, private versus communal ownership, or the educational system. Political institutions are the systems that govern the operations of the government of a particular society—formal power structures, political parties, and mechanisms for obtaining power. Economic institutions are formal and informal "rules of the economic game."

Integrated rural development The broad spectrum of rural development activities, including small-farmer agricultural progress, the provision of physical and social *infrastructure*, the development of rural nonfarm industries, and the capacity of the rural sector to sustain and accelerate the pace of these improvements over time.

Interdependence Interrelationship between *economic* and *noneconomic variables*. Also, in international affairs, the situation in which one nation's welfare depends to varying degrees on the decisions and policies of another nation. See also *dependence* and *dominance*.

Interest The payment (or price) for the use of borrowed funds. See also *interest rate* and *social rate of discount*.

Interest rate The annual amount that a borrower must pay a lender over and above the total amount borrowed, expressed as a percentage of the total amount of funds borrowed—for example, if a person borrowed 100 rupees for one year, at the end of which he or she had to repay 110 rupees, the interest rate would be 10% per annum.

Interindustry model See *input-output model*.

Interlocking factor markets Factor markets whose supply functions are interdependent, frequently because different *inputs* are provided by the same suppliers who exercise monopolistic or oligopolistic control over resources.

Intermediate producer goods Goods that are used as *inputs* into further levels of production, such as leather in shoe manufacture or iron ore in steel production. See also *final goods*.

Internalization The process whereby external environmental costs are borne by the producers or consumers who generate them, usually through the imposition of pollution or consumption taxes. See also *externality*.

Internal rate of return The discount rate that causes a project to have a net present value of zero, used to rank projects in comparison with market rates of *interest*.

International Bank for Reconstruction and Development (IBRD) See *World Bank*.

International commodity agreement Formal agreement by sellers of a common internationally traded commodity (e.g., coffee, sugar) to coordinate supply to maintain price stability.

International Development Association (IDA) An international body set up in 1960 to assist the *World Bank* in its efforts to promote the economic *development* of the underdeveloped countries by providing additional *capital* on a low-interest basis, especially to the poorest of the poor developing countries.

International Finance Corporation (IFC) An international financial institution set up in 1956 to supplement the efforts of the *World Bank* in providing development *capital* to private enterprises (mainly industrial) of the underdeveloped countries.

International Labor Organization (ILO) One of the functional organizations of the *United Nations*, based in Geneva, Switzerland, whose central task is to look into problems of world labor supply, its training, utilization, domestic and international distribution, etc. Its aim in this endeavor is to increase world output through maximum utilization of available *human resources* and thus improve *levels of living*.

International Monetary Fund (IMF) An autonomous international financial institution that originated in the Bretton Woods Conference of 1944. Its main purpose is to regulate the international monetary exchange system, which also stems from that conference but has since been modified. In particular, one of the central tasks of the IMF is to control fluctuations in *exchange rates* of world currencies in a bid to alleviate severe *balance of payments* problems.

International poverty line An international real income measure, usually expressed in constant dollars (e.g., $1 per day), used as a basis for estimating the proportion of the world's population that exists at bare levels of *subsistence*.

International reserve account See *cash account*.

International reserves A country's balance of gold, *hard currencies*, and *special drawing rights* used to settle international transactions.

Investment The part of *national income* or national expenditure devoted to the production of *capital goods* over a given period of time. Gross investment is the total expenditure on new capital goods, and net investment is the additional capital goods produced in excess of those that wear out and need to be replaced.

Invisible hand A concept originating in Adam Smith's famous book *The Wealth of Nations*, published in 1776, that holds that the unbridled pursuit of individual self-interest automatically contributes to the maximization of the social interest. See also *laissez-faire* and *perfect competition*.

Inward-looking development policies Policies that stress economic *self-reliance* on the part of LDCs, including the development of indigenous *appropriate technology*, the imposition of substantial protective *tariffs* and *nontariff trade barriers* to promote *import substitution*, and the general discouragement of *private foreign investment*. See also *autarky* and *outward-looking development policies*.

Keynesian model Model developed by Lord John Maynard Keynes in the early 1930s to explain the cause of economic depression and hence the unemployment of that period. The model states that unemployment is caused by insufficient *aggregate demand* and can be eliminated by, say, government expenditure that would raise aggregate demand and activate idle or underutilized resources and thus create jobs.

Kuznets curve A relationship between a country's *income per capita* and its equality of *income distribution* such that as per capita incomes increase, the distribution of income at first worsens and later improves from very low levels. Named after Nobel laureate Simon Kuznets, who first statistically identified this relationship for developed countries.

Labor-augmenting technological progress *Technological progress* that raises the productivity of an existing quantity of labor by general education, on-the-job training programs, etc. See also *laborsaving technological progress*.

Labor force All economically active persons, including the armed forces and the unemployed, but excluding housewives, students, and economically inactive groups.

Labor-intensive technique A method of production that uses proportionately more labor relative to other *factors of production*. See also *capital-intensive technique*.

Labor productivity The level of output per unit of labor *input*, usually measured as output per worker-hour or worker-year.

Laborsaving technological progress The achievement of higher output using an unchanged quantity of labor *inputs* as a result of some invention (e.g., the computer) or *innovation* (such as assembly-line production).

Labor turnover model Theory that the urban-rural wage gap is partly explained by the fact that urban modern-sector employers pay higher wages to reduce labor turnover rates and retain skilled workers. See *efficiency wage*.

Laissez-faire Free-enterprise market capitalism. See *perfect competition*.

Landlord The proprietor of a freehold interest in land with rights to lease out to tenants in return for some form of payment for the use of the land.

Land reform A deliberate attempt to reorganize and transform existing *agrarian systems* with the intention of improving the distribution of agricultural incomes and thus fostering *rural development*. Among its many forms, land reform may entail provision of secured tenure rights to the individual farmer, transfer of land ownership away from small classes of powerful landowners to tenants who actually till the land, appropriation of land estates for establishing small new settlement farms, or instituting land improvements and irrigation schemes.

Latifundio A very large landholding in the Latin American *agrarian system*, capable of providing employment for over 12 people, owned by a small number of *landlords*, and comprising a large proportion of total agricultural land. See also *medium-sized farms* and *minifundio*.

Least developed countries (LLDCs) The poorest LDCs.

Less developed countries (LDCs) See *developing countries*.

Levels of living The extent to which a person, family, or group of people can satisfy their material and spiritual wants. If they are able to afford only a minimum quantity of food, shelter, and clothing, their levels of living are said to be very low. If they enjoy a great variety of food, shelter, clothing, and other things, such as good health, education, and leisure, they are enjoying relatively high levels of living. See *development*.

Lewis two-sector model A theory of development advanced by W. Arthur Lewis in which *surplus labor* from the traditional agricultural sector is transferred to the modern industrial sector whose growth over time absorbs the surplus labor, promotes industrialization, and stimulates sustained development.

Life expectancy at birth The number of years newborn children would live if subject to the *mortality* risks prevailing for the cross section of population at the time of their birth. See also *crude birthrate*.

Linkage Connections between firms based on sales. A backward linkage is one in which a firm buys a good from another firm to use as an *input;* a forward linkage is one in which a firm sells to another firm. Such linkages are especially significant for industrialization strategy when one or more of the sectors involved have increasing *returns to scale* that a larger market takes advantage of.

Literacy The ability to read and write.

Literacy rate The percentage of the population age 15 and over able to read and write. Literacy rates are often used as one of the many social and economic indicators of the state of *development* of a country.

Loan A transfer of funds from one economic entity to another (government to government, individual to individual, bank to individual) that must be repaid with *interest* over a prescribed period of time. Hard loans are given at market rates of interest; soft loans are given at concessional or low rates of interest. See also *grant*.

Loan pushing Attempts by commercial banks to induce developing countries to accept more *loans* than they would prefer to. This can sometimes be accomplished by offering a take-it-or-leave-it package of both a loan amount and an *interest* rate. Such an offer may induce more borrowing than the country would prefer at that interest rate,

but the country still considers itself better off than with no borrowing.

Localization economies Agglomeration effects captured by particular sectors of the economy, such as finance or autos, as they grow within an area.

Lorenz curve A graph depicting the variance of the size *distribution of income* from perfect equality. See also *Gini coefficient*.

Low-income countries (LICs) Countries with a gross national income per capita of less than $765 in 2003.

Macroeconomic instability Situation in which a country has high *inflation* accompanied by rising budget and *trade deficits* and a rapidly expanding *money supply*.

Macroeconomics The branch of economics that considers the relationships among broad economic aggregates such as *national income*, total volumes of *saving, investment*, consumption expenditure, employment, and *money supply*. It is also concerned with determinants of the magnitudes of these aggregates and their rates of change over time. See also *Keynesian model*.

Macroeconomic stabilization Policies designed to eliminate *macroeconomic instability*.

Malnutrition A state of ill health resulting from an inadequate or improper diet, usually measured in terms of average daily protein consumption.

Malthusian population trap An inevitable population level envisaged by Thomas Malthus (1766–1834) at which population increase was bound to stop because after that level, life-sustaining *resources*, which increase at an arithmetic rate, would be insufficient to support human population, which increases at a geometric rate. Consequently, people would die of starvation, disease, wars, etc.

Managed float A fluctuating exchange rate but with central bank intervention to reduce erratic currency fluctuations.

Marginal cost The addition to total cost incurred by the producer as a result of varying output by one more unit.

Marginal net benefit The benefit derived from the last unit of a *good* minus its cost.

Marginal product The increase in total output resulting from the use of one additional unit of a variable *factor of production*. In the *Lewis two-sector model, surplus labor* is defined as workers whose marginal product is zero. See also *average product*.

Marginal utility The satisfaction derived by consuming one additional unit of a *good*. In neoclassical theory, a consumer's marginal utility is said to be maximized if his or her marginal utility per last unit of expenditure on that good is equal to the marginal utilities of all other goods consumed, divided by their respective prices.

Market economy A free private-enterprise economy governed by consumer sovereignty, a price *system*, and the forces of supply and demand.

Market failure A phenomenon that results from the existence of market imperfections (e.g., *monopoly* power, lack of *factor mobility*, significant *externalities*, lack of knowledge) that weaken the functioning of a free-market economy—it fails to realize its theoretical beneficial results. Market failure often provides the justification for government interference with the working of the *free market*.

Market-friendly approach The *World Bank* notion that successful *development* policy requires governments to create an environment in which markets can operate efficiently and to intervene selectively in the economy in areas where the market is inefficient (e.g., social and economic *infrastructure*, *investment* coordination, economic "safety net").

Market mechanism The system whereby *prices* of commodities or *services* freely rise or fall when the buyer's demand for them rises or falls or the seller's supply of them decreases or increases.

Market prices Prices established by demand and supply in a free-market economy.

Medium-size farm Multifamily farms in Latin America employing 4 to 12 workers. See also *minifundio* and *latifundio*.

Merchandise exports and imports All international changes in ownership of merchandise passing across the customs borders of the trading countries. Exports are valued f.o.b. (free on board). Imports are valued c.i.f. (cost, insurance, and freight).

Merchandise trade balance Balance on commodity exports and imports.

Microeconomics The branch of economics concerned with individual decision units—firms and households—and the way in which their decisions interact to determine relative prices of *goods* and *factors of production* and how much of these will be bought and sold. The market is the central concept in microeconomics. See also *price system* and *traditional economics*.

Microeconomic theory of fertility An extension of the theory of consumer behavior of individual couples. The central proposition of this theory is that family formation has costs and benefits and hence the size of families formed will depend on these costs and benefits. If the costs of family formation are high relative to its benefits, the rates at which couples will decide to bring forth children will decline, and vice versa. See also *opportunity cost of a woman's time*, *total fertility rate*, and *crude birthrate*.

Microfinance Financial services, particularly but not only credit, supplied in small allotments to people who might otherwise have no access to them, or at best only on very unfavorable terms.

Microfinance institution (MFI) A bank or NGO that provides *microfinance* services, particularly to the poor.

Middle-income countries (MICs) LDCs with per capita income above $765 and below $9,385 in 2003 according to *World Bank* measures.

Minifundio A landholding in the Latin American *agrarian system* considered too small to provide adequate employment for a single family. A *minifundio* is too small to provide the workers with *levels of living* much above the bare survival minimum. Holders of *minifundios* are often required to provide unpaid seasonal labor to *latifundios* and to seek outside low-paid employment to supplement their meager incomes. See also *latifundio* and *medium-sized farm*.

Mixed economic systems Economic systems that are a mixture of both capitalist and socialist economies. Most developing countries have mixed systems. Their essential feature is the coexistence of substantial private and public activity within a single economy.

Mixed farming The first step in the transition from *subsistence* to *specialized farming*. This evolutionary stage is characterized by the production of both staple crops and cash crops and, in addition, simple animal husbandry.

Model An analytical framework used to portray functional relationships among economic factors.

Monetary policy Activities of a *central bank* designed to influence financial variables such as *money supply* and *interest rates*.

Moneylender In Asia, a person who lends money at higher than market rates of *interest* to peasant farmers to meet their needs for seeds, fertilizers, and other *inputs*. Activities of moneylenders are often unscrupulous and can accentuate landlessness among the rural poor.

Money supply Sum total of currency in circulation plus *commercial bank* demand deposits and sometimes savings bank time deposits.

Monopolistic market control A situation in which the output of an industry is controlled by a single producer (or seller) or by a group of producers who make joint decisions.

Monopoly A market situation in which a product that does not have close substitutes is being produced and sold by a single seller. See also *perfect competition* and *oligopoly*.

More developed countries (MDCs) See *developed world*.

Mortality rate See *death rate*.

Multifiber Agreement (MFA) A set of nontariff bilateral *quotas* established by developed countries on imports of cotton, wool, and synthetic textiles and clothing from individual LDCs

Multilateral assistance agency See *foreign aid.*

Multinational corporation (MNC) An international or transnational corporation with headquarters in one country but branch offices in a wide range of both developed and developing countries. Examples include General Motors, Coca-Cola, Firestone, Philips, Volkswagen, British Petroleum, Exxon, and Sony.

Multiple equilibria A condition in which more than one equilibrium exists. These equilibria may be ranked, in the sense that one is preferred to another, but the unaided market will not move the economy to the preferred outcome.

National income See *gross national income (GNI).*

Natural increase The difference between the birthrate and the death rate of a given population.

Necessary condition A condition that must be present, although it need not be in itself sufficient, for an event to occur. For example, *capital* formation may be a necessary condition for sustained *economic growth* (before growth in output can occur, there must be tools to produce it). But for this growth to continue, social, institutional, and attitudinal changes may have to occur.

Necessity goods Life-sustaining items (food, shelter, protection, medical care).

Neoclassical counterrevolution The 1980s resurgence of neoclassical free-market orientation toward *development* problems and policies; counter to the interventionist *dependence* revolution of the 1970s.

Neoclassical economics See *traditional economics.*

Neoclassical growth model See *Solow neoclassical growth model.*

Neoclassical price-incentive model A model whose main proposition is that if *market prices* are to influence economic activities in the right direction, they must be adjusted to remove *factor-price distortions* by means of *subsidies*, taxes, or the like so that factor prices may reflect the true *opportunity cost* of the *resources* being used. See also *appropriate technology.*

Neocolonial dependence model A model whose main proposition is that *underdevelopment* exists in *developing countries* because of continuing exploitative economic, political, and cultural policies of former colonial rulers toward *less developed countries.*

Net enrollment ratio The ratio of the number of children actually attending school to the number of school-age children in the population. See *gross enrollment ratio.*

Net international migration Excess of persons migrating into a country over those who emigrate from that country. See *brain drain.*

Net present value The value of a future stream of net benefits discounted to the present by means of a competitive discount (*interest*) rate.

Network effects (or network externalities) A situation in which the value of a product or service depends positively on the number of other users. An example is e-mail.

Neutral technological progress Higher output levels achieved with same quantity or combination of all factor inputs.

New growth theory Also known as *endogenous growth* theory, an extension and modification of the *traditional neoclassical growth theory* designed to explain why long-run equilibrium growth can be positive and divergent among countries and why *capital* tends to flow from poor to rich countries despite the former's low *capital-labor ratios.* See also *endogenous growth.*

New institutionalism The recently revived notion that *institutions* matter significantly in economic *development.*

Newly industrializing countries (NICs) A small group of countries at a relatively advanced level of economic *development* with a substantial and dynamic industrial sector and with close links to the international trade, finance, and investment system (Argentina, Brazil, Greece, Mexico, Portugal, Singapore, South Korea, Spain, and Taiwan).

New political economy approach See *public-choice theory.*

New protectionism The various nontariff trade barriers erected by developed countries against the manufactured exports of developing nations, typically as *quotas* or "voluntary" export restrain by LDCs. See *Multifiber Agreement (MFA).*

Nominal rate of protection An ad valorem percentage *tariff* levied on imports. See *effective rate of protection.*

Noneconomic variables Elements of interest to economists in their work but not given a monetary value or expressed numerically because of their intangible nature. Sometimes noneconomic variables such as educational, health, cultural, political, and institutional factors are more important than the quantifiable economic variables in promoting *development.*

Nonformal education Any non-school-based program that provides basic skills and training to individuals. Examples include adult education, on-the-job training programs, and agricultural and other extension services. Compare *formal education system.*

Nongovernmental organizations (NGOs) Nonprofit organizations often involved in providing financial and *technical assistance* to LDCs. See *foreign aid*.

Nonrenewable resources Natural *resources* whose quantity is fixed and cannot be replaced. Examples include petroleum, iron ore, and coal. Compare *renewable resources*.

Nontariff trade barrier A barrier to *free trade* that takes a form other than a *tariff*, such as *quotas* or sanitary requirements for imported meats and dairy products.

Normal and superior goods *Goods* whose purchased quantities increase as the incomes of consumers increase. Such goods have a positive *income elasticity of demand*. Compare *inferior goods*.

Normative economics The notion that economics must concern itself with what "ought to be." Thus it is argued that economics and economic analysis always involve *value* judgments, whether explicit or implicit, on the part of the analyst or observer. See *positive economics*.

North-South trade models Trade and development models that focus on the unequal exchange between the North (MDCs) and the South (LDCs) and attempt to show theoretically why the South gains less from trade than the North.

Object gap The notion that LDCs suffer from a lack of material items, such as roads, buildings, and machinery, in comparison with developed countries. See *idea gap*.

Official development assistance (ODA) Net disbursements of *loans* or *grants* made on *concessional terms* by official agencies of member countries of the *Organization for Economic Cooperation and Development (OECD)*.

Official exchange rate Rate at which the *central bank* will buy and sell the domestic currency in terms of a foreign currency such as the U.S. dollar.

Oligopolistic market control A situation in which a small number of rival but not necessarily competing firms dominate an industry. All recognize the fact that they are interdependent and can maximize their individual advantages through explicit (*cartel*) or implicit (*collusion*) joint actions.

Oligopoly A market situation in which there are a few sellers and many buyers of similar but differentiated products. The *Organization of Petroleum Exporting Countries (OPEC)* is a good example of international oligopoly. See also *imperfect competition*.

Open economy An economy that encourages foreign trade and has extensive financial and nonfinancial contacts with the rest of the world in areas such as education, culture, and technology. See also *closed economy* and *outward-looking development policies*.

Opportunity cost In production, the real value of *resources* used in the most desirable alternative—for example, the opportunity cost of producing an extra unit of a manufactured *good* is the output of, say, food that must be forgone as a result of transferring resources from agricultural to manufacturing activities. In consumption, the amount of one commodity that must be forgone in order to consume more of another.

Opportunity cost of a woman's time Real or monetary wages or *profits* that a woman sacrifices by deciding to stay home and raise children instead of working for a wage or engaging in profit-making self-employment activities. The higher the opportunity cost of a woman's time involved in rearing children, the more unwilling she will be to have more children, at least in terms of the *microeconomic theory of fertility*.

Opportunity cost of education Lost income from paid employment during the time when an individual attends school.

O-ring model See *O-ring production function*.

O-ring production function A production function with strong complementarities among *inputs*, given by the products of the input qualities. It emphasizes the idea that in advanced economies, many tasks and activities must be done well in order for any of them to have adequate value.

Organization for Economic Cooperation and Development (OECD) An organization of 20 countries from the Western world, including all of those in Europe and North America. Its major objective is to assist the *economic growth* of its member nations by promoting cooperation and technical analysis of national and international economic trends.

Organization of Petroleum Exporting Countries (OPEC) An organization consisting of 13 major oil-exporting countries of the *developing countries* that acts as a *cartel* or *oligopoly* to promote their joint national interests. Members are Algeria, Ecuador, Gabon, Indonesia, Iran, Iraq, Kuwait, Libya, Nigeria, Qatar, Saudi Arabia, United Arab Emirates, and Venezuela.

Organized money market The formal banking system in which loanable funds are channeled through recognized and licensed *financial intermediaries*. See also *unorganized money market*.

Outward-looking development policies Policies that encourage *free trade*; the free movement of *capital*, workers, enterprises, and students; a welcome to *multinational corporations*; and an open system of communications. See also *open economy*.

Overvalued exchange rate An *official exchange rate* set at a level higher than its real or shadow value—

for example, 7 Kenyan shillings per dollar instead of, say, 10 shillings per dollar. Overvalued rates cheapen the real cost of imports while raising the real cost of exports. They often lead to a need for *exchange control.*

Ozone A highly reactive gas, O_3, that absorbs harmful ultraviolet rays in the upper atmosphere but is an important contributor to smog in the lower atmosphere.

Ozone depletion The loss of *ozone* resulting from atmospheric pollution especially from carbon monoxide pollution. See also *greenhouse gases.*

Paradigm Implicit assumptions from which theories evolve; a *model* or framework of analysis.

Parallel exchange rate See *dual exchange rate.*

Pareto improvement A situation in which one or more persons may be made better off without making anyone worse off. Alternatively, it is a situation in which all persons are made better off.

Pareto-optimal Describing a situation in which no one may be made better off without making someone else worse off.

Paris Club A group formed by representatives from industrialized creditor nations with substantial outstanding debt owed them by *developing countries.* Their mandate was to restructure the bilateral debt of highly indebted countries.

Partial plan A plan that covers only a part of the national economy (e.g., agriculture, industry, tourism).

Path dependency A condition in which the past condition of an individual or economy, measured by the level of one or more variables, affects future conditions.

Patrón In Latin America, a landlord to whom sharecroppers and other workers owe an economic and often political and social allegiance.

Patterns-of-development analysis See *structural-change theory.*

Pecuniary externality A positive or negative spillover effect on an agent's costs or revenues.

Per capita GNP See *income per capita.*

Perfect competition A market situation characterized by the existence of very many buyers and sellers of homogeneous *goods* or *services* with perfect knowledge and free entry so that no single buyer or seller can influence the price of the good or service. See also *laissez-faire* and *traditional economics.*

Periphery In *dependence* theory, the *developing countries.* Compare *center.*

Personal distribution of income See *size distribution of income.*

Physical capital Tangible *investment* goods (e.g., plant and equipment, machinery, buildings). See also *human capital.*

Physical resources The nonhuman *factors of production* (land and capital) used to produce *goods* and *services* to satisfy wants.

Planning model A mathematical model (e.g., an *input-output model* or macro planning model) designed to simulate quantitatively the major features of the economic structure of a particular country. Planning models provide the analytical and quantitative bases for most national and regional *development plans.*

Planning process The procedure for drawing up and carrying out a formal *economic plan.*

Policy instruments See *economic policy.*

Political economy The attempt to merge economic analysis with practical politics—to view economic activity in its political context. Much of classical economics was political economy, and today political economy is increasingly being recognized as necessary for any realistic examination of *development* problems.

Political will A determined effort by persons in political authority to achieve certain economic objectives, such as elimination of inequality, poverty, and unemployment through various reforms of social, economic, and institutional structures. Lack of political will is often said to be one of the main obstacles to *development* and one of the main reasons for the failure of many *development plans.*

Pollution tax A tax levied on the quantity of pollutants released into the physical environment.

Population density The number of inhabitants per unit area of land (e.g., per square kilometer).

Population-poverty cycle A theory to explain how poverty and high population growth become reinforcing.

Population pyramid A graphic depiction of the *age structure of the population,* with age cohorts plotted on the vertical axis and numbers of males and females in each cohort on the horizontal axis.

Portfolio investment Financial *investments* by private individuals, corporations, pension funds, and mutual funds in stocks, bonds, certificates of deposit, and notes issued by private companies and the public agencies of LDCs. See also *private foreign investment.*

Positive checks In Malthusian theory, the effects of war, disease, and famine in controlling excess population growth.

Positive economics The notion that economics should be concerned with what is, was, or will be, with answers to economic questions based on facts or empirical observation. See also *normative economics.*

Poverty See *absolute poverty.*

Poverty line See *international poverty line.*

Poverty-weighted index A welfare index in which income gains for lower-income groups are given greater weight than gains for upper-income groups.

Poverty trap A bad equilibrium for a family, community, or nation, involving a *vicious cycle* in which poverty and *underdevelopment* lead to more poverty and underdevelopment, often from one generation to the next.

Prebisch-Singer thesis The argument that the primary-product export orientation of LDCs results in a decline in their *terms of trade* and a loss of income.

Present value The discounted value at the present time of a sum of money to be received in the future.

Preventive checks In Malthusian theory, the effects of delayed marriage, sexual abstinence, and birth control in controlling excess population growth.

Preventive medicine Medical care that focuses on the prevention of sickness and disease through immunology and health education. See also *curative medicine*.

Price The monetary or real value of a *resource*, commodity, or *service*. The role of prices in a *market economy* is to ration or allocate resources in accordance with supply and demand; relative prices should reflect the relative *scarcity* of different resources, goods, or services.

Price band A fixed range of values between which prices are free to fluctuate but not allowed to rise above or fall below.

Price elasticity of demand The responsiveness of the quantity of a commodity demanded to a change in its price, expressed as the percentage change in quantity demanded divided by the percentage change in price.

Price elasticity of supply The responsiveness of the quantity of a commodity supplied to a change in its price, expressed as the percentage change in quantity supplied divided by the percentage change in price.

Price-incentive micro model See *neoclassical price-incentive model*.

Primary industrial sector The part of the economy that specializes in the production of agricultural products and the extraction of raw materials. Major industries in this sector include mining, agriculture, forestry, and fishing.

Primary products Products derived from all extractive occupations—farming, lumbering, fishing, mining, and quarrying; foodstuffs and raw materials.

Prisoner's dilemma A situation in which all parties would be better off cooperating than competing, but, given that cooperation has been initially achieved, each party would gain the most by cheating while others stick to the cooperative agreements.

Private benefits Gains that accrue to a single individual, such as *profits* received by an individual farm. See also *social benefits*.

Private benefits of education Benefits that accrue directly to a student and his or her family.

Private consumption The market value of all *goods* and *services* purchased or received as *income in kind* by households and nonprofit *institutions*; includes imputed rent for owner-occupied dwellings.

Private costs The direct monetary outlays or costs of an individual economic unit; the private costs of a firm are the direct outlays on *fixed* and *variable inputs* of production.

Private costs of education Direct and *opportunity costs* borne by a student and his or her family.

Private foreign investment The investment of private foreign funds in the economy of a developing nation, usually by *multinational corporations (MNCs)*. See also *foreign aid* and *portfolio investment*.

Private sector The part of an economy whose activities are under the control and direction of non-governmental economic units such as households or firms. Each economic unit owns its own *resources* and uses them mainly to maximize its own well-being.

Privatization Selling public assets (corporations) to individuals or private business interests. See *state-owned enterprises (SOEs)*.

Producer surplus Excess of total revenue over total costs (*profits*); also referred to as *scarcity rent*.

Product cycle In international trade, the progressive replacement of MDCs by LDCs in the production of manufactures of increasing complexity. For example, South Korea and Taiwan first exported textiles, then machinery, and now electronic equipment.

Product differentiation Attempt by producers to distinguish their product from similar ones by advertising or minor design changes.

Production function A technological or engineering relationship between the quantity of a *good* produced and the quantity of *inputs* required to produce it.

Production possibility curve A curve on a graph indicating alternative combinations of two commodities or categories of commodities (e.g., agricultural and manufactured goods) that can be produced when all the available *factors of production* are efficiently employed. Given available resources and technology, the curve sets the boundary between the attainable and the unobtainable. See also *opportunity cost* and *production function.*

Production technique   Method of combining *inputs* to produce the required output. A production technique is said to be appropriate ("best") if it produces a given output with the least cost (thus being economically efficient) or with the least possible quantity of real *resources* (technically efficient). A technique may be labor-intensive or capital-intensive.

Productive resources   See *physical resources* and *human resources.*

Productivity gap   The difference between per capita product of, say, the agricultural population (i.e., agricultural labor productivity) in LDCs versus developed countries. It has tended to be wide because of differences in the application of technological and biological improvements.

Profit   The difference between the market value of output and the market value of *inputs* employed to produce the output. Also, the difference between total revenue and total cost.

Profit maximization   Making the *profits* of a firm or a farm as large as possible. Producers often want to find the level of output that results in maximum profits, at least according to a fundamental assumption of *traditional economics.*

Progressive income tax   A tax whose rate increases with increasing personal incomes, such that the proportion of personal income paid in taxes by a rich person is higher than that paid by a poorer person. A progressive tax structure therefore tends to improve *income distribution.* Compare *regressive tax.*

Project appraisal   The quantitative analysis of the relative desirability (profitability) of investing a given sum of public or private funds in alternative projects—for example, building either a steel mill or a textile factory. *Cost-benefit analysis* is the main analytical tool of project appraisal.

Property rights   Legal titles given to landowners enabling them freely to buy and sell their plots, and other rights to use, gain income from, or sell property.

Public bad   An entity that imposes *costs* on individuals. Compare *public good.*

Public-choice theory   The theory that self-interest guides all individual behavior and that governments are inefficient and corrupt because people use government to pursue their own agendas. Free markets are perceived as more efficient and more just.

Public consumption   All current expenditures for purchases of *goods* and *services* by all levels of government; includes capital expenditures on national defense and security.

Public development assistance   See *foreign aid.*

Public good   An entity that provides benefits to all individuals simultaneously and whose enjoyment by one person is in no way diminished by that of another. Compare *public bad.*

Public sector   The portion of an economy whose activities (economic and noneconomic) are under the control and direction of the state. See also *private sector.*

Purchasing power equivalent   The real buying power of a given monetary income.

Purchasing power parity (PPP)   The purchasing power of a country's currency: the number of units of that currency required to purchase the same basket of *goods* and *services* that a U.S. dollar would buy in the United States.

Quintile   A 20% proportion of any numerical quantity. A population divided into quintiles would be divided into five groups of equal size. See also *decile.*

Quota   A physical limitation on the quantity of any item that can be imported into a country, such as so many automobiles per year. Also, a method for allocating limited school places by noncompetitive means—for example, by income or ethnicity.

Rate of population increase   Growth rate of a population including the natural increase plus any net effect of immigration and emigration.

Rationality   One of the behavioral foundations of the theory of *traditional economics*, holding that an economically rational person will always attempt to maximize satisfaction or *profits* or minimize *costs.* The notion of rationality includes the replacement of old traditional practices by modern methods of objective thinking and logical reasoning in production, distribution, and consumption. See also *profit maximization.*

Rationing   A system of distribution employed to restrict the quantities of *goods* and *services* that consumers or producers can purchase or be allocated freely. It arises because of excess demand and inflexible *prices.* Rationing can be done by coupons, points, or simply administrative decisions with regard to commodities, by academic credentialing with regard to job allocation, by industrial licenses with regard to capital good imports, etc. See also *black market.*

Recession   A period of slack general economic activity as reflected in rising unemployment and excess productive capacity in a broad spectrum of industries.

Redistribution policies Policies geared to reducing *income inequality* and expanding economic opportunities in order to promote *development*. Examples include *progressive income tax* policies, provision of *services* financed out of such taxation to benefit persons in the lower-income groups, *rural development* policies giving emphasis to raising *levels of living* for the rural poor through *land reform*, and other forms of asset and wealth redistribution.

Regional trading bloc An economic coalition among countries within a geographic region, usually characterized by liberalized internal trade and uniform restrictions on external trade, designed to promote regional economic integration and growth.

Regressive tax A tax structure in which the ratio of taxes to income tends to decrease as income increases. Relatively poor people will pay a larger proportion of their income in taxes than relatively rich people. A regressive tax therefore tends to worsen *income distribution*. See also *progressive tax*.

Renewable resources Natural *resources* that can be replaced so that the total supply is not fixed for all time. Examples include timber and other forest products. See also *nonrenewable resources*.

Rent In *macroeconomics*, the share of *national income* going to the owners of the productive *resource*, land (i.e., *landlords*). In everyday usage, the *price* paid for the use of property (e.g., buildings, housing). In *microeconomics*, economic rent is the payment to a *factor of production* over and above its highest *opportunity cost*.

Rent seeking Efforts by individuals and businesses in an LDC society to capture the economic *rent* arising from price distortions and physical controls caused by excessive government intervention, such as licenses, *quotas, interest rate* ceilings, and *exchange control*.

Replacement fertility The level of *fertility* at which childbearing women have just enough daughters to replace themselves in the population. This keeps the existing population size constant through an infinite number of succeeding generations. See also *total fertility rate* and *crude birthrate*.

Reproductive choice The argument that women should be able to determine on an equal status with their husbands and for themselves how many children they want and what methods to use to achieve their desired family size. See *empowerment of women*.

Research and development (R&D) Scientific investigation with a view toward improving the existing quality of human life, products, *profits, factors of production*, or knowledge. There are two categories of R&D: basic R&D (without a specific commercial objective) and applied R&D (with a commercial objective).

Reserves The sum of a country's holdings of gold, *special drawing rights*, and *foreign exchange* under the control of monetary authorities. Also known as gross international reserves.

Resource endowment A nation's supply of *factors of production*. Normally such endowments are supplied by nature (e.g., mineral deposits, raw materials, timber forests, labor). See also *factor endowment trade theory*.

Resources See *physical resources* and *human resources*. See also *fixed inputs* and *variable inputs*.

Restructuring Alteration of the terms and conditions of LDC debt repayment, usually by lowering *interest rates* or extending the repayment period.

Returns to scale How much output expands when all *inputs* are proportionally increased. See *economies of scale* and *increasing returns*.

Risk A situation in which the probability of obtaining some outcome of an event is not precisely known; that is, known probabilities cannot be precisely assigned to these outcomes, but their general level can be inferred. In everyday usage, a risky situation is one in which one of the outcomes involves some loss to the decision maker (e.g., changes of demand, weather, or tastes). See also *uncertainty*.

Romer endogenous growth model An *endogenous growth* model in which technological spillovers are present; the economywide capital stock positively affects output at the industry level, so there may be increasing *returns to scale* at the economywide level.

Rotating savings and credit association (ROSCA) A group formed by formal agreement among 40 to 50 individuals to pool their savings and allocate interest-free loans on a rotating basis to each member. See also *group lending schemes*.

Rural development See *integrated rural development*.

Rural-urban migration The movement of people from rural villages, towns, and farms to urban centers (cities) in search of jobs. See *Todaro migration model*.

Rural-urban migration model See *Todaro migration model*.

Savings The portion of *disposable income* not spent on consumption by households plus *profits* retained by firms. Savings are normally assumed to be positively related to the level of income (personal or national).

Savings gap The excess of funds that results when *capital* inflows plus domestic *savings* exceed domestic *investment* and the economy is at full capacity. See also *foreign exchange gap.*

Savings ratio *Savings* expressed as a proportion of *disposable income* over some period of time. It shows the fraction of *national income* saved over any period. *Savings ratio* is sometimes used synonymously with *average propensity to save*. See also *Harrod-Domar growth model.*

Scale-neutral Unaffected by size; applied to *technological progress* that can lead to the achievement of higher output levels irrespective of the size (scale) of a firm or farm, making it equally applicable to small- and large-scale production processes. An often cited example is the *hybrid seeds* of the *green revolution*, which can theoretically increase yields on both small and large farms (if *complementary resources* such as fertilizer, irrigation, and pesticides are available).

Scarcity In economics, a situation that arises when there is less of something (e.g., an *economic good*, *service*, or *resource*) than people would like to have if it were free. The quantity of goods and services are scarce relative to people's desire for them because the economy's resources used in their production are themselves scarce. Scarcity therefore gives rise to *price* and the need for efficient allocation of resources among alternative competing uses through, for example, the *free market* in capitalist economies or through a centralized command system in planned economies.

Scarcity rent The premium or additional *rent* charged for the use of a *resource* or *good* that is in fixed or limited supply. See *rent seeking.*

Scatter diagram A two-dimensional graph on which numerical values of statistically observed variables are plotted in pairs, one measured on the horizontal axis and the other on the vertical axis.

Secondary industrial sector The manufacturing portion of the economy, which uses raw materials and *intermediate producer goods* to produce *final goods* or other intermediate products. Industries such as motor assembly, textiles, and building and construction are part of this sector.

Self-esteem The feeling of worthiness that a society enjoys when its *social, political*, and *economic systems* and *institutions* promote human respect, dignity, integrity, self-determination, etc. See *development.*

Self-reliance Reliance on one's own capabilities, judgment, resources, and skills in a bid to enhance political, economic, social, cultural, attitudinal, and moral independence. Countries may also desire self-reliance in particular aspects such as food production, labor, and skills. Increasingly, the concept of *collective self-reliance* is being used in *developing-country* forums.

Self-sustaining growth *Economic growth* that continues over the long run based on *saving, investment*, and complementary private and public activities.

Services Economic activities other than industry and primary-goods production. Examples include banking, shipping, and tourism and legal, insurance, and financial activities. See also *tertiary industrial sector.*

Shadow price A price that reflects the true *opportunity cost* of a *resource.*

Sharecropper In the *agrarian systems* of LDCs, the tenant peasant farmer whose crop has to be shared with the *landlord*, who usually appropriates a large portion of total crop production.

Shifting cultivation A peasant agricultural practice in Africa in which land is tilled by a family or community for cropping until such time as it has been exhausted of fertility. Thereafter, the family or community moves to a new parcel of land, leaving the former one to regain fertility until eventually it can be cultivated again.

Size distribution of income The distribution of income according to size class of persons—for example, the share of total income accruing to, say, the poorest 40% of a population or the richest 10%, without regard to the sources of that income (whether it comes from wages, *interest, rent*, or *profits*). See also *functional distribution of income, Lorenz curve*, and *Gini coefficient.*

Social benefits Gains or benefits that accrue or are available to the society as a whole rather than solely to a private individual, such as the protection and security provided by the police or the armed forces, the external economies afforded by an effective health delivery system, and the widespread benefits of a literate population. See *private benefits.*

Social benefits of education Benefits of the schooling of individuals that accrue to the entire society, such as better government financing, improved teacher training, and a more literate workforce and citizenry.

Social capital The productive value of a set of social institutions and norms, including group trust, expected cooperative behaviors with predictable punishments for deviations, and a shared history of successful collective action, that raises expectations for participation in future cooperative behavior.

Social cost The cost of an economic decision, whether private or public, to society as a whole. Where there exist external diseconomies of production (e.g., pollution) or consumption (alcoholism), social costs will normally exceed private costs, and decisions based solely on private calculations will lead to misallocation of *resources.*

Social costs of education Costs borne by society from private education decisions, such as high educated unemployment.

Social indicators Noneconomic measures of *development*, such as *life expectancy at birth, infant mortality rate, literacy rate*, and physicians per 100,000 population.

Socialism See *command socialism* and *market socialism.*

Social profit The difference between *social benefits* and *social costs*, both direct and indirect.

Social rate of discount The rate at which a society discounts potential future *social benefits* to find out whether such benefits are worth their present *social cost*. The rate used in this discounting procedure is usually the social *opportunity cost* of the funds committed.

Social safety net A set of government programs such as food stamps, welfare payments, free health clinics, and unemployment insurance designed to provide the absolute poor with a minimal *level of living* below which they should not fall.

Social system The organizational and institutional structure of a society, including its *value*, attitudes, power structure, and traditions. Major social systems include political processes, religions, and ethnic divisions.

Soil erosion Loss of valuable topsoils resulting from deforestation and consequent flooding of productive farmland.

Solow neoclassical growth model Growth model in which there are *diminishing returns* to each *factor of production* but constant *returns to scale*. Exogenous technological change generates most long-term *economic growth.*

Solow residual The proportion of long-term *economic growth* not explained by growth in labor or *capital* and therefore assigned primarily to exogenous technological change.

Special drawing rights (SDRs) A form of international financial asset, often referred to as "paper gold," created by the *International Monetary Fund (IMF)* in 1970 and designed to supplement gold and dollars in settling international *balance of payments* accounts.

Specialization A situation in which *resources* are concentrated in the production of relatively few commodities. See also *comparative advantage* and *division of labor.*

Specialized farming The final and most advanced stage of the evolution of agricultural production in which farm output is produced wholly for the market. It is most prevalent in advanced industrial countries. High farm yields are ensured by a high degree of *capital* formation, *technological progress,* and scientific *research and development*. See also *subsistence farming.*

Stabilization policies A coordinated set of mostly restrictive fiscal and monetary policies aimed at reducing *inflation,* cutting budget deficits, and improving the *balance of payments*. See *conditionality* and *International Monetary Fund (IMF).*

Stages-of-growth model of development A theory of *development,* associated with the American economic historian Walt W. Rostow, according to which, in achieving development, a country passes through sequential stages.

Staple food A leading or main food consumed by a large portion of a country's population (e.g., maize meal in Kenya, Zambia, and Tanzania; rice in Southeast Asian countries; yams in West Africa; manioc in Brazil).

State-owned enterprises (SOEs) Public corporations and parastatal agencies (e.g., agricultural marketing boards) owned and operated by the government.

Structural adjustment loans *Loans* by the *World Bank* designed to foster structural adjustment in the LDCs by supporting measures to remove excessive governmental controls, getting factor and product *prices* to reflect *scarcity* values, and promoting market competition. See also *International Development Agency (IDA).*

Structural-change theory The hypothesis that *underdevelopment* is due to underutilization of *resources* arising from structural or institutional factors that have their origins in both domestic and international dualistic situations. *Development* therefore requires more than just accelerated *capital* formation as espoused in the *stages-of-growth* and *false-paradigm models of development.*

Structural transformation The process of transforming the basic industrial structure of an economy so that the contribution to *national income* by the manufacturing sector increasingly becomes higher than that by the agricultural sector. More generally, an alteration in the industrial composition of any economy. See also *primary, secondary,* and *tertiary industrial sectors.*

Subsidy A payment by the government to producers or distributors in an industry to prevent the decline of that industry (e.g., as a result of continuous unprofitable operations) or an increase in the *prices* of its products or simply to encourage it to hire more labor (as in the case of a *wage subsidy*). Examples are export subsidies to encourage the sale of exports; subsidies on some foodstuffs to keep down the cost of living, especially in urban areas; and farm subsidies to encourage expansion of farm production and achieve *self-reliance* in food production.

Subsistence economy An economy in which production is mainly for personal consumption and the standard of living yields no more than the basic necessities of life—food, shelter, and clothing. See also *subsistence farming*.

Subsistence farming Farming in which crop production, stock rearing, and other activities are conducted mainly for personal consumption, characterized by low productivity and high *risk* and *uncertainty*. See also *subsistence economy*.

Sufficient condition A condition that when present causes an event to occur—for example, being a low-income university student may be a sufficient condition to get a *loan* under a university education loan scheme. See also *necessary condition*.

Supply curve A positively sloped curve relating the quantity of a commodity supplied to its *price*.

Surplus An excess of revenues over expenditures. See *trade surplus*.

Surplus labor The excess supply of labor over and above the quantity demanded at the going free-market wage rate. In the *Lewis two-sector model* of economic *development*, surplus labor refers to the portion of the rural labor force whose *marginal productivity* is zero or negative. See also *under-employment*.

Sustainable development A pattern of *development* that permits future generations to live at least as well as the current generation.

Sustainable net national income (NNI*) An *environmental accounting* measure of the total annual income that can be consumed without diminishing the overall *capital* assets of a nation (including *environmental capital*).

Sustenance The basic *goods* and *services*, such as food, clothing, and shelter, that are necessary to sustain an average human being at the bare minimum *level of living*.

Synthetic substitutes Commodities that are artificially produced but can be substituted for the natural commodities (e.g., manufactured rubber, cotton, wool, camphor, and pyrethrum). Producers of raw materials, mainly LDCs, are becoming more and more vulnerable to competition from synthetics from industrialized countries as a result of the latter's more advanced state of scientific and technical progress.

Tariff A fixed percentage tax on the value of an imported commodity levied at the point of entry into the importing country.

Technical assistance *Foreign aid* (either bilateral or multilateral) that takes the form of the transfer of expert personnel, technicians, scientists, educators, economic advisers, and consultants rather than a simple transfer of funds.

Technological efficiency Producing the maximum output possible, given quantities of *inputs* and existing technology, without regard to effective market demand.

Technological externality A positive or negative spillover effect on a firm's production function through some means other than market exchange, such as productivity benefits of "learning by watching" how other firms produce *goods* or *services*. Compare *pecuniary externality*.

Technological progress Increased application of new scientific knowledge in form of inventions and *innovations* with regard to both *physical* and *human capital*. Such progress has been a major factor in stimulating the long-term *economic growth* of contemporary developed countries. See also *scale-neutral, labor-augmenting, laborsaving*, and *capital-augmenting technological progress*.

Tenant farmer One who farms on land held by a *landlord* and therefore lacks secure ownership rights and has to pay for the use of that land, for example, by surrendering part of his output to the owner. Examples are found in the Latin American and Asian *agrarian systems*. See also *sharecropper*.

Terms of trade The ratio of a country's average export *price* to its average import *price*; also known as the *commodity terms of trade*. A country's terms of trade are said to improve when this ratio increases and to worsen when it decreases, that is, when import prices rise at a relatively faster rate than export prices (the experience of most LDCs in recent decades). See *income terms of trade*.

Tertiary industrial sector The *services* and commerce portion of an economy. Examples of services include repair and maintenance of *capital goods*, haircuts, public administration, medical care, transport and communications, finance, and teaching. See also *primary* and *secondary industrial sectors*.

Tied aid *Foreign aid* in the form of bilateral *loans* or *grants* that require the recipient country to use the funds to purchase *goods* or *services* from the donor country.

Todaro migration model A theory that explains *rural-urban migration* as an economically rational process despite high urban unemployment. Migrants calculate urban *expected income* and move if this exceeds average rural income. See also *induced migration*.

Total factor productivity (TFP) Total monetary value of all units of output per unit of each and every *factor of production* in an economy. It is a measure of the average productivity of all factors employed in an economy.

Total fertility rate (TFR) The number of children that would be born to a woman if she were to live to the end of her childbearing years and bear children at each age in accordance with the prevailing age-specific fertility rates. See *fertility*.

Total net benefit   Sum of net benefits to all consumers and/or producers resulting from environmental policy interventions. In general, total benefits minus total costs.

Total poverty gap (TPG)   The sum of the difference between the *poverty line* and actual income levels of all people living below that line.

Trade creation   A situation in the theory of *customs unions* that occurs when, following the formation of the union, there is a shift in the geographic location of production from higher-cost to lower-cost member states. See also *trade diversion*.

Trade deficit   An excess of import expenditures over export receipts measured on the *current account*; also known as the merchandise trade deficit. See also *balance of payments* and *trade surplus*.

Trade diversion   Shift, upon formation of a *customs union*, of the locus of production of formerly imported goods from a lower-cost nonmember state to a higher-cost member nation. See also *trade creation*.

Trade liberalization   Removal of obstacles to free trade, such as *quotas, nominal* and *effective rates of protection*, and *exchange controls*.

Trade-off   The necessity of sacrificing (trading off) something in order to get more of something else—for example, sacrificing consumption now for consumption later by devoting some present *resources* to *investment*. See also *opportunity cost*.

Trade optimists   Theorists who believe in the benefits of *free trade, open economies*, and *outward-looking development policies*.

Trade pessimists   Theorists who argue that without tariff protection or quantitative restrictions on trade, LDCs inevitably gain little or nothing from an export-oriented, open-economy posture. See also *import substitution, Prebisch-Singer thesis*, and *infant industry*.

Trade surplus   An excess of export receipts over import payments. See also *trade deficit*.

Traditional economics   An approach to economics that emphasizes utility, profit maximization, and determination of equilibrium. The major focus is on the efficient allocation of scarce *resources* (see *economic efficiency*) through the *price system* and the forces of supply and demand. See also *microeconomics, macroeconomics, laissez-faire, invisible hand*, and *market economy*.

Traditional neoclassical growth theory   A theory based on growth models associated with Robert Solow and others in which long-run equilibrium growth is zero and *income per capita* tends to converge among different countries. It is an outgrowth

of the theory of *perfect competition* with constant *returns to scale*. Compare *new growth theory*.

Transaction costs   Costs of doing business related to gathering information, establishing reliable suppliers, formulating contracts, obtaining credit, etc.

Transfer payment   Any payment from one economic entity to another that takes the form of a gift, that is, any payment not for a service rendered that need not be repaid. Examples include unemployment insurance, food stamps, welfare payments, *subsidies*, and *grants*.

Transfer pricing   An accounting procedure usually designed to lower total taxes paid by *multinational corporations* in which intracorporate sales and purchases of *goods* and *services* are artificially invoiced so that *profits* accrue to the branch offices located in low-tax countries (tax havens) while offices in high-tax countries show little or no taxable profits.

Transition   See *economic transition*.

Transparency   Full disclosure by public and private banks of the quality and status of their loan and investment portfolios so that domestic and foreign investors can make informed decisions.

Trickle-down theory of development   The notion that *development* is purely an economic phenomenon in which rapid gains from the overall growth of *gross national product* and *income per capita* would automatically bring benefits (trickle down) to the masses in the form of jobs and other economic opportunities. The main preoccupation is therefore to get the growth job done while problems of *poverty*, unemployment, and *income distribution* are perceived to be of secondary importance.

Two-gap model   A theoretical *foreign aid* model comparing *savings* and *foreign-exchange* gaps to determine which is the binding constraint on *economic growth*.

Uncertainty   A situation in which the probability of obtaining a given outcome of an event is not known. There are thus a number of possible outcomes to which no objective probability can be attached. See also *risk*.

Underdevelopment   An economic situation in which there are persistent low *levels of living* in conjunction with *absolute poverty*, low *income per capita*, low rates of *economic growth*, low consumption levels, poor health services, high *death rates*, high birthrates, *dependence* on foreign economies, and limited *freedom* to choose among activities that satisfy human wants. See also *development*.

Underdevelopment trap   A *poverty trap* at the regional or national level, in which *underdevelopment* tends to perpetuate itself over time.

Underemployment A situation in which persons are working less than they would like to work, either daily, weekly, monthly, or seasonally. See also *surplus labor*.

Unit cost The average cost per unit of output of any *economic good* or *service*.

United Nations A global organization set up at the end of World War II with the basic aim of cultivating international cooperation and hence ensuring that any conflicts or misunderstanding between or among countries would be resolved by peaceful means. At present, the United Nations has a membership of more than 180 countries drawn from both the developed and less developed nations.

United Nations Conference on Environment and Development (UNCED) A conference held in Rio de Janeiro in June 1992, whose purpose was to enhance international cooperation in promoting sustainable environmental policy. Also known as the *Earth Summit*.

United Nations Conference on Trade and Development (UNCTAD) A body of the *United Nations* whose primary objective is to promote international trade and commerce with a principal focus on trade and *balance of payments* problems of developing nations. Its first secretary general was Raul Prebisch.

United Nations Development Program (UNDP) A body of the *United Nations* whose major function is to promote *development* in *developing countries*. Major development-oriented projects financed and carried out by the UNDP include the initiation of nutrition, health, and education programs and the building up of agricultural, industrial, and transport *infrastructure*.

United Nations Educational, Scientific and Cultural Organization (UNESCO) A major agency of the *United Nations* charged with promoting international understanding by spreading ideas of knowledge through the educational process, encouraging multiracial coexistence through reconciliation of cultural values of different societies, and sponsoring educational, cultural, and scientific exchange programs that make it possible for educators, artists, writers, and scientists from a wide variety of countries and cultures to meet and exchange ideas and knowledge.

United States Agency for International Development (USAID) A *bilateral assistance* agency of the U.S. government whose primary objective is to assist *developing countries* in their *development* efforts as part of U.S. foreign policy. The economic assistance given by USAID normally takes the form of educational *grants*, special-interest *loans*, and *technical assistance*. However, much of USAID's activity consists of noneconomic (mostly military) assistance to friendly LDC governments.

Unlimited supplies of labor Infinite elasticity of labor at a given wage as postulated in the *Lewis two-sector model*.

Unorganized money market The informal and often usurious credit system that exists in most *developing countries* (especially in rural areas) where low-income farms and firms with little collateral are forced to borrow from *moneylenders* and loan sharks at exorbitant rates of *interest*. Compare *organized money market*.

Urban bias The notion that most LDC governments favor the urban sector in their *development* policies, thereby creating a widening gap between the urban and rural economies. See *rural-urban migration*.

Urbanization The economic and demographic growth process of the urban centers.

Urbanization economies Agglomeration effects associated with the general growth of a concentrated geographic region.

Uruguay Round A round of the *General Agreement on Tariffs and Trade (GATT)* negotiations, started in Uruguay in 1986 and designed to promote international *free trade*. The resulting agreement was signed in April 1994 and took effect in 1995. See *World Trade Organization (WTO)*.

Value added Amount of product's final value added at each stage of production.

Values Principles, standards, or qualities considered worthwhile or desirable. A value judgment reflects personal or class beliefs. See also *normative economics*.

Variable inputs *Inputs* or *resources* whose required use in a *production function* will vary with changes in the level of output. For example, in the production of shoes, labor is usually a variable input because as more shoes are produced, more labor must be used. See also *fixed inputs*.

Vent-for-surplus theory of international trade A theory that states that the opening up of world markets to developing countries through international trade provides them with the opportunity to take advantage of formerly underutilized land and labor *resources* to produce larger *primary-product* outputs, the surplus of which can be exported to foreign markets. Such economies will usually be operating at a point somewhere inside their *production possibility curves* so that trade permits an outward shift of this production point.

Vicious cycle A self-reinforcing situation in which factors tend to perpetuate a certain undesirable phenomenon—for example, low incomes in poor countries lead to low consumption, which then leads to poor health and low *labor productivity* and eventually to the persistence of *poverty*.

Voluntary failure Inability of NGOs and the citizen sector more broadly to efficiently achieve social objectives in their areas of supposed comparative advantage, due for example to inability to raise adequate resources, orientation to the objectives of funders, or deflection from social to individual goals. (See Chapter 11, endnote 52.)

Wage-price spiral A *vicious cycle* in which higher consumer *prices* (e.g., as a result of *devaluation*) cause workers to demand higher wages, which in turn cause producers to raise prices and worsen inflationary forces.

Wage subsidy A government financial incentive to private employers to hire more workers, as through tax deductions for new job creation.

Where-to-meet dilemma A situation in which all parties would be better off cooperating than competing but lack information about how to do so. If cooperation can be achieved, unlike the *prisoner's dilemma,* there is no subsequent incentive to defect or cheat.

Workfare program A poverty program that requires program beneficiaries to work in exchange for benefits, such as a food-for-work program. The term *workfare* is used as a contrast with *welfare,* which provides benefits without work requirements.

World Bank An international financial institution owned by its 181 member countries and based in Washington, D.C. Its main objective is to provide *development* funds to *developing nations* in the form of *interest*-bearing *loans* and *technical assistance.* The World Bank operates with borrowed funds. See *International Development Association (IDA).*

World Health Organization (WHO) The key *United Nations* agency concerned with global health matters.

World Trade Organization (WTO) Geneva-based watchdog and enforcer of 1995 *Uruguay Round* agreement. Replaced the *General Agreement on Tariffs and Trade (GATT).*

Youth dependency ratio The proportion of young people under age 15 to the working population aged 16–64 in a country. See also *dependency burden.*

Name Index

Subject Index

The Developed and Developing World, 2005

○ Low-income countries
    ($765 or less)

◐ Lower-middle-income
    countries
    ($766–3,035)

◑ Upper-middle-income
    countries
    ($3,036–9,385)

● High-income countries
    ($9,386 or more)

● No data